Rick Steves'®

SPAIN

2014

CONTENTS

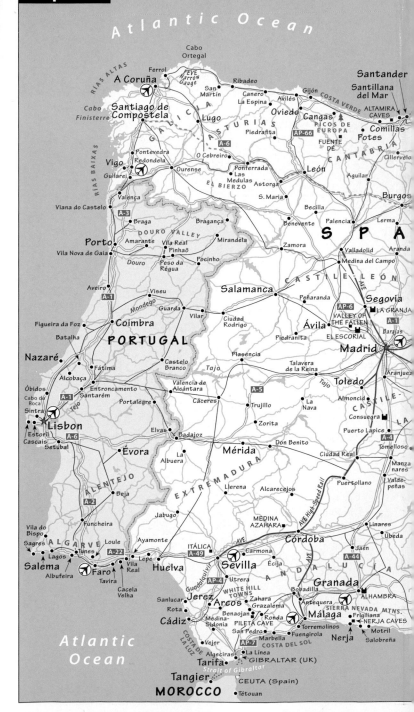

Spain

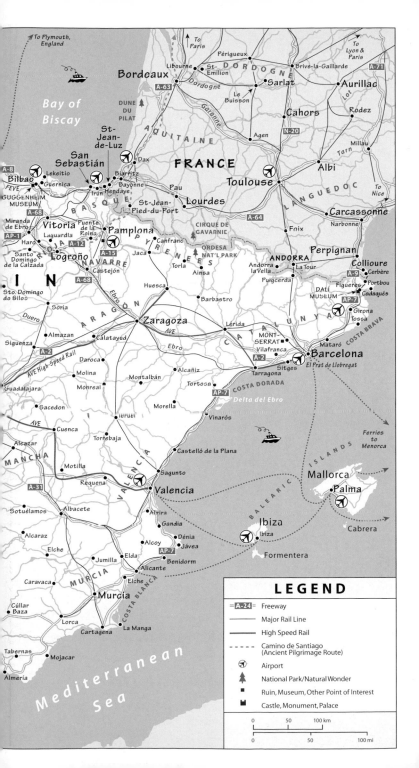

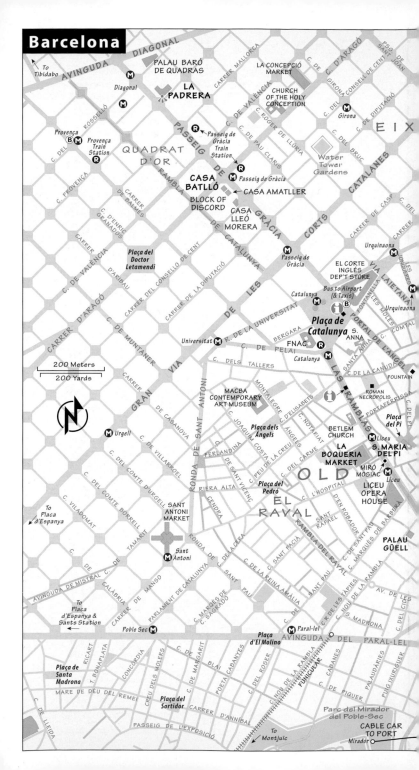

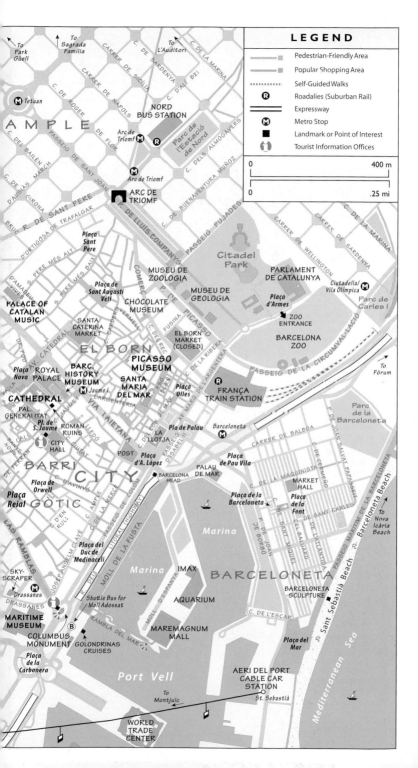

LEGEND

- Pedestrian-Friendly Area
- Popular Shopping Area
- Self-Guided Walks
- ® Roadalies (Suburban Rail)
- Expressway
- Ⓜ Metro Stop
- ■ Landmark or Point of Interest
- ⛎ Tourist Information Offices

0 ————— 400 m
0 ————— .25 mi

To Park Güell
To Sagrada Familia
To L'Auditori

C. DE LA MARINA
CARRER DE SARDENYA
C. DE SICÍLIA
C. DE DALÍ BEI
CARRER DE NÀPOLS
Ⓜ Tetuan
C. DE ROGER DE FLOR
PASSEIG DE SANT JOAN

A M P L E

NORD BUS STATION
Arc de Triomf Ⓜ ®
Parc de l'Estació de Nord
C. DELS ALMOGÀVERS

C. DEL BAILÉN
C. D'AUSIÀS MARCH
C. DE GIRONA
R. DE SANT PERE
Ⓜ Arc de Triomf

CARRER DE NÀPOLS
BRUC
R. D'ORTIGOSA DE TRAFALGAR
PASSEIG DE LLUÍS COMPANYS
C. D'ÀLÍ BEI
C. DE BUENAVENTURA MUÑOZ
PASSEIG DE PUJADES

■ **ARC DE TRIOMF**

CARRER DE LA MARINA
CARRER DE WELLINGTON
CARRER DE SARDENYA

Plaça Sant Pere

Citadel Park

Plaça de Sant Augustí Vell

CHOCOLATE MUSEUM

MUSEU DE ZOOLOGIA

MUSEU DE GEOLOGIA

PARLAMENT DE CATALUNYA

Plaça d'Armes

Ciutadella/ Vila Olímpica Ⓜ
Parc de Carles I

PALACE OF CATALAN MUSIC

SANTA CATERINA MARKET

EL BORN

EL BORN MARKET (CLOSED)

ZOO ENTRANCE

BARCELONA ZOO

PASSEIG DE LA CIRCUMVAL·LACIÓ

To Fòrum

Plaça Nova

ROYAL PALACE

BARC. HISTORY MUSEUM

PICASSO MUSEUM

SANTA MARIA DEL MAR

Ⓜ Jaume I

CATHEDRAL

PAL. GENERALITAT

Pl. de S. Jaume

ROMAN RUINS

⛎ **CITY HALL**

VIA LAIETANA

Plaça Olles

® **FRANÇA TRAIN STATION**

Parc de la Barceloneta

BARRI

POST

LA LLOTJA

Plaça d'A. López

C I T Y

G Ò T I C

Plaça de Orwell

Plaça Reial

Plaça del Duc de Medinaceli

LAS RAMBLAS

SKY-SCRAPER

Ⓜ Drassanes

MARITIME MUSEUM

COLUMBUS MONUMENT

GOLONDRINAS CRUISES

Plaça de la Carbonera

Shuttle Bus for Moll Adossat

ⓑ

BARCELONA HEAD

PALAU DE MAR

Plaça de Pau Vila

Barceloneta Ⓜ

CARRER DE BALBOA

Plaça de la Barceloneta

Plaça de la Font

MARKET HALL

BARCELONETA

BARCELONETA SCULPTURE

To Nova Icària Beach

Barceloneta Beach
Sant Sebastià Beach

Marina

IMAX

AQUARIUM

MAREMAGNUM MALL

MOLL D'ESPANYA

Plaça del Mar

Mediterranean Sea

Port Vell

AERI DEL PORT CABLE CAR STATION

To Montjuïc
St. Sebastià

WORLD TRADE CENTER

C. DE L'ESCAR

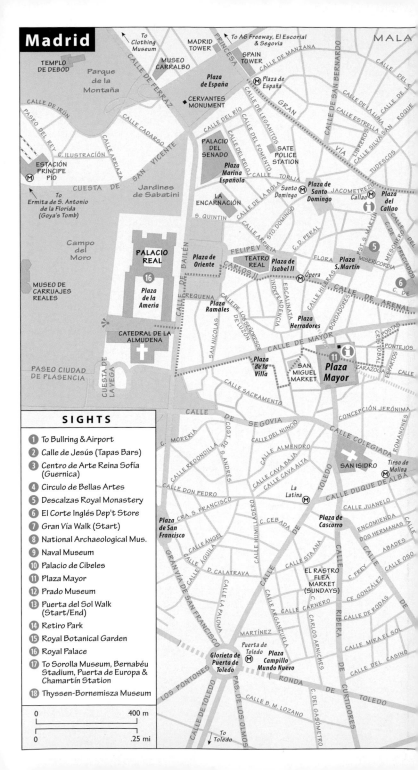

Madrid

MALA

To Clothing Museum

MADRID TOWER

To A6 Freeway, El Escorial & Segovia

SPAIN TOWER

TEMPLO DE DEBOD

Parque de la Montaña

MUSEO CARRALBO

Plaza de España

Plaza de España

CALLE DE MANZANA

CALLE DE SAN BERNARDO

CALLE DE FERRAZ

CALLE DE LEGANITOS

CERVANTES MONUMENT

GRAN VÍA

CALLE DE LA LUNA

CALLE DE LA

CALLE ESTRELLA

CALLE SILVA

SAN ROQUE

CALLE DEL RÍO

CALLE DE IRÚN

CALLE CADARSO

LIBREROS

TUDESCOS

PASEO DEL REY

C. ILUSTRACIÓN

CALLE DEL FOMENTO

SATE POLICE STATION

CALLE DE PRECIADOS

CALLE SAN VICENTE

PALACIO DEL SENADO

Plaza Marina Española

Plaza de Santo Domingo

Santo Domingo

Plaza del Callao

Callao

ESTACIÓN PRÍNCIPE PÍO

JACOMETREZO

CUESTA DE SAN VICENTE

Jardines de Sabatini

LA ENCARNACIÓN

CALLE DE LA BOLA TORIJA

S. QUINTIN

CALLE ARRIETA

C. D. PERAL

MESONERO ROMANOS

5

To Ermita de S. Antonio de la Florida (Goya's Tomb)

Campo del Moro

PALACIO REAL

16

Plaza de la Amería

Plaza de Oriente

TEATRO REAL

Plaza de Isabel II

Ópera

FELIPE V

FLORA

Plaza S. Martín

CALLE DE AREVAL

6

C. DE

MUSEO DE CARRUAJES REALES

CALLE DE BAILÉN

REQUENA

CALLE CARLOS III

ESCALINATA

INDEPENDENCIA

CALLE HILERAS

Plaza Ramales

BORDADORES

Plaza Herradores

CALLE DE SEÑORES DE LUZÓN

SAN NICOLAS

POSTAS

CRISTOBAL

PONTEJOS

ESPARTOS

CATEDRAL DE LA ALMUDENA

CALLE DE MAYOR

SAN MIGUEL MARKET

11

Plaza Mayor

ZARAGOZA

CALLE

PASEO CIUDAD DE PLASENCIA

CUESTA DE LA VEGA

Plaza de la Villa

CALLE SACRAMENTO

CONCEPCIÓN JERÓNIMA

CALLE DE SEGOVIA

ROMANONES

C. MORERÍA

C. COST. DS. ANDRÉS

CALLE DEL NUNCIO

CALLE ALMENDRO

CALLE COLEGIADA

SAN ISIDRO

Tirso de Molina

Tirso de Molina

SIGHTS

1 To Bullring & Airport
2 Calle de Jesús (Tapas Bars)
3 Centro de Arte Reina Sofía (Guernica)
4 Círculo de Bellas Artes
5 Descalzas Royal Monastery
6 El Corte Inglés Dep't Store
7 Gran Vía Walk (Start)
8 National Archaeological Mus.
9 Naval Museum
10 Palacio de Cibeles
11 Plaza Mayor
12 Prado Museum
13 Puerta del Sol Walk (Start/End)
14 Retiro Park
15 Royal Botanical Garden
16 Royal Palace
17 To Sorolla Museum, Bernabéu Stadium, Puerta de Europa & Chamartín Station
18 Thyssen-Bornemisza Museum

CALLE REDONDILLA

CALLE CAVA BAJA

CALLE CAVA ALTA

CALLE DUQUE DE ALBA

CALLE DON PEDRO

La Latina

La Latina

CALLE JUANELO

Plaza de San Francisco

CRA. S. FRANCISCO

C. CEBADA DE

Plaza de Cascorro

ENCOMIENDA

DOS HERMANAS

CALLE

CALLE ÁNGEL

CALLE AGUILA

CALLE HUMILLADERO

CALLE STA. ANA

ABADES

CALLE OSO

GRAN VÍA DE SAN FRANCISCO

D. CALATRAVA

CALLE ARGANZUELA

EL RASTRO FLEA MARKET (Sundays)

C. FREY

CALLE DE RODAS

GONZÁLEZ

CALLE CARNERO

RIBERA DE

CALLE LA PALOMA

CARLOS ARNICHES

CALLE MIRA EL SOL

MARTÍNEZ

Puerta de Toledo

Plaza Campillo Mundo Nuevo

CALLE DE CASINO

Glorieta de Puerta de Toledo

RONDA

DE

C. DEL GASÓMETRO

TOLEDO

LOS PONTONES

PASEO DE LOS OLMOS

CALLE P. M. LOZANO

CALLE DE CURTIDORES

To Toledo

| 0 | 400 m |
| 0 | .25 mi |

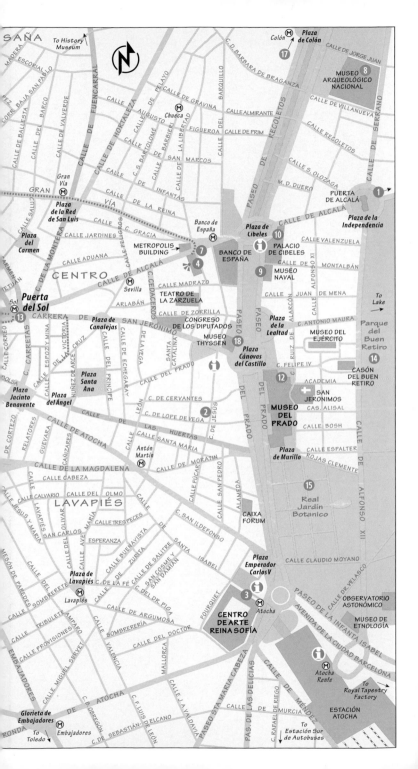

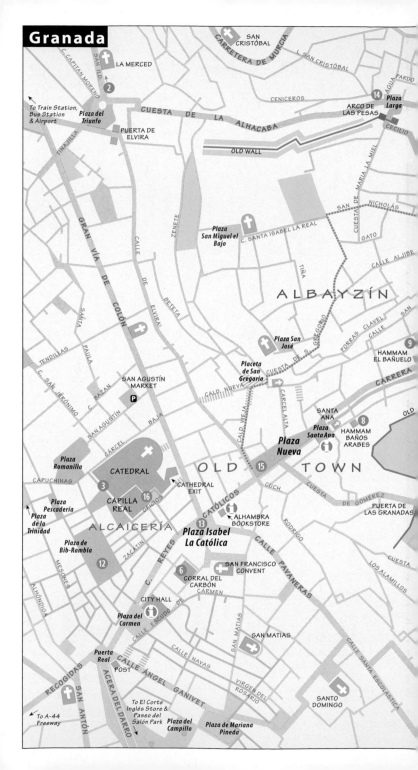

Granada

SAN CRISTÓBAL

CARRETERA DE MURCIA

L. SAN CRISTÓBAL

C. CAPITAN MORENO

SAN ILD.

LA MERCED

2

CENICEROS

14

Plaza Larga

ARCO DE LAS PESAS

To Train Station, Bus Station & Airport

Plaza del Triunfo

PUERTA DE ELVIRA

CUESTA DE LA ALHACABA

CECILIO

OLD WALL

AGUA

PARDO

TIMAJILLA

CALLE DE ELVIRA

ZENETE

Plaza San Miguel el Bajo

C. SANTA ISABEL LA REAL

SAN

CUESTA DE MARIA LA MIEL

NICHOLÁS

GATO

GRAN VÍA DE COLÓN

SANTA

PAULA

TENDILLAS

C. SAN JERÓNIMO

BETETA

TIÑA

CALLE ALJIBE

ALBAYZÍN

Plaza San José

PORRAS

CLAVEL

CALLE

SAN

9

HAMMAM EL BAÑUELO

C. BAZÁN

SAN AGUSTÍN MARKET

P

Placeta de San Gregorio

CUESTA DE S. GREGORIO

CALD. NUEVA

CARRERA

OLD

SAN AGUSTÍN

BAJA

CALD. VIEJA

CARCEL ALTA

SANTA ANA

Plaza Santa Ana

8

HAMMAM BAÑOS ARABES

GÁRCEL

Plaza Romanilla

CATEDRAL

3

Plaza Nueva

15

O L D   T O W N

CAPUCHINAS

Plaza Pescadería

Plaza de la Trinidad

ALCAICERÍA

CAPILLA REAL

16

DE DIOS

CATHEDRAL EXIT

CÚCH.

CUESTA

DE GOMEREZ

PUERTA DE LAS GRANADAS

CATÓLICOS

13

ALHAMBRA BOOKSTORE

Plaza de Bib-Rambla

12

ZACATÍN

REYES

Plaza Isabel La Católica

C.

6

CORRAL DEL CARBÓN

SAN FRANCISCO CONVENT

CARMEN

RODRIGO

CALLE PAVANERAS

CUESTA

LOS ALAMILLOS

MESONES

ALHÓNDIGA

CITY HALL

Plaza del Carmen

CALLE ESCUDO DE

SAN MATIAS

SAN MATIAS

SANTA ESCOLÁSTICA

Puerta Real

POST

RECOGIDAS

SAN ANTÓN

CALLE ÁNGEL GANIVET

ACERA DEL DARRO

CALLE NAVAS

VIRGEN DEL ROSARIO

SANTO DOMINGO

CALLE

To A-44 Freeway

To El Corte Inglés Store & Paseo del Salón Park

Plaza del Campillo

Plaza de Mariana Pineda

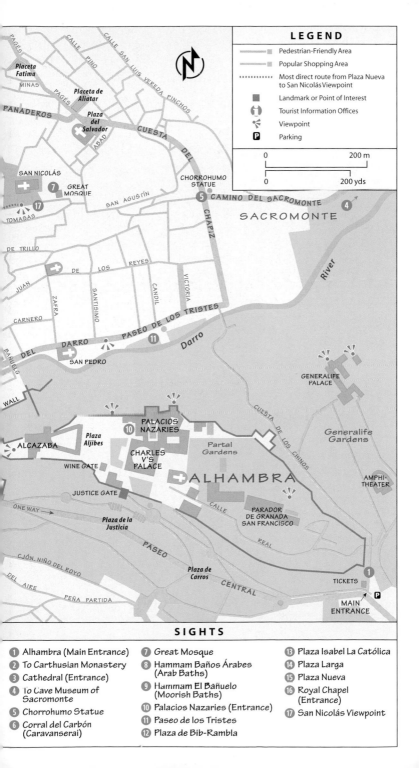

LEGEND

- Pedestrian-Friendly Area
- Popular Shopping Area
- Most direct route from Plaza Nueva to San Nicolás Viewpoint
- ■ Landmark or Point of Interest
- Tourist Information Offices
- Viewpoint
- P Parking

| 0 | 200 m |
| 0 | 200 yds |

SIGHTS

1. Alhambra (Main Entrance)
2. To Carthusian Monastery
3. Cathedral (Entrance)
4. To Cave Museum of Sacromonte
5. Chorrohumo Statue
6. Corral del Carbón (Caravanserai)
7. Great Mosque
8. Hammam Baños Árabes (Arab Baths)
9. Hammam El Bañuelo (Moorish Baths)
10. Palacios Nazaries (Entrance)
11. Paseo de los Tristes
12. Plaza de Bib-Rambla
13. Plaza Isabel La Católica
14. Plaza Larga
15. Plaza Nueva
16. Royal Chapel (Entrance)
17. San Nicolás Viewpoint

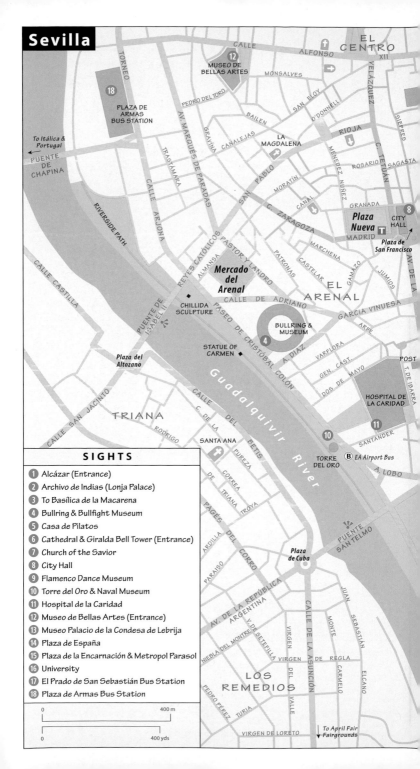

Sevilla

SIGHTS

1. Alcázar (Entrance)
2. Archivo de Indias (Lonja Palace)
3. To Basílica de la Macarena
4. Bullring & Bullfight Museum
5. Casa de Pilatos
6. Cathedral & Giralda Bell Tower (Entrance)
7. Church of the Savior
8. City Hall
9. Flamenco Dance Museum
10. Torre del Oro & Naval Museum
11. Hospital de la Caridad
12. Museo de Bellas Artes (Entrance)
13. Museo Palacio de la Condesa de Lebrija
14. Plaza de España
15. Plaza de la Encarnación & Metropol Parasol
16. University
17. El Prado de San Sebastián Bus Station
18. Plaza de Armas Bus Station

0 — 400 m
0 — 400 yds

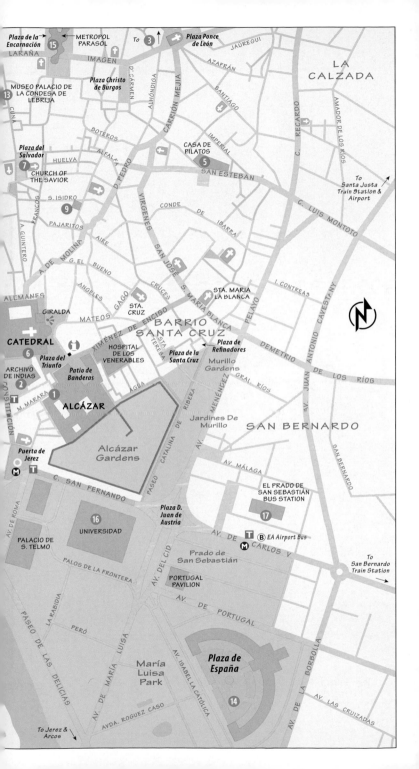

Plaza de la Encarnación
LARAÑA
METROPOL PARASOL
15
To 3
Plaza Ponce de León
JAÚREGUI
IMAGEN
AZAFRÁN
LA CALZADA
D. CARMEN
ALHÓNDIGA
CARRIÓN MEJIA
SANTIAGO
C. RECARDO
AMADOR DE LOS RÍOS
MUSEO PALACIO DE LA CONDESA DE LEBRIJA
13
Plaza Christo de Burgos
BOTEROS
IMPERIAL
CUNA
CASA DE PILATOS
5
Plaza del Salvador
7
HUELVA
ALFALFA
D. PEDRO
SAN ESTEBAN
CHURCH OF THE SAVIOR
To Santa Justa Train Station & Airport
A. GUINTERO
S. ISIDRO
9
VIRGENES
CONDE
DE
IBARRA
C. LUIS MONTOTO
FRANCOS
PAJARITOS
AIRE
SAN JOSÉ
A. DE MOLINA
G. EL BUENO
S. MARÍA BLANCA
I. CONTRERAS
ALEMANES
ANGELES
GAGO
CRUCES
STA. MARÍA LA BLANCA
GIRALDA
STA. CRUZ
PELAYO
CATEDRAL
MATEOS
XIMÉNEZ DE ENCISO
BARRIO SANTA CRUZ
Plaza de Refinadores
DEMETRIO
6
Plaza del Triunfo
HOSPITAL DE LOS VENERABLES
STA. TERESA
Plaza de la Santa Cruz
DE
LOS RÍOS
ARCHIVO DE INDIAS
2
Patio de Banderas
Murillo Gardens
GRAL. RIOS
JUAN ANTONIO CAVESTANY
1
ALCÁZAR
AGUA
PASEO CATALINA DE RIBERA
MENÉNDEZ
Jardines De Murillo
AV. DE
SAN BERNARDO
Puerta de Jerez
Alcázar Gardens
SAN BERNARDO
M
T
C. SAN FERNANDO
AV. MÁLAGA
Plaza D. Juan de Austria
EL PRADO DE SAN SEBASTIÁN BUS STATION
17
AV. DE ROMA
16
UNIVERSIDAD
AV. DEL CID
AV. DE CARLOS V
B EA Airport Bus
T
M
PALACIO DE S. TELMO
PALOS DE LA FRONTERA
Prado de San Sebastián
To San Bernardo Train Station
LA RABIDA
PERÓ
PORTUGAL PAVILION
AV. DE PORTUGAL
PASEO DE LAS DELICIAS
AV. DE MARÍA LUISA
María Luisa Park
AV. ISABELLA CATÓLICA
Plaza de España
AV. DE LA BORBOLLA
14
AV. LAS CRUIZADAS
To Jerez & Arcos
AVDA. ROGUEZ CASO

Spain

España

Like a grandpa bouncing a baby on his knee, Spain is a mix of old and new, modern and traditional. For the tourist, Spain means bullfights, massive cathedrals, world-class art, Muslim palaces, vibrant folk life, whitewashed villages, and bright sunshine. Yes, you'll find those things...but the country's special charm lies in its people and their unique lifestyle. Spain has a richness of history, of culture, and of people that has little to do with GDP stats. From the stirring *sardana* dance in Barcelona to the sizzling rat-a-tat-tat of flamenco in Sevilla, this country creates its own beat amid the heat.

Spain's diverse landscape and diverse history (a blend of Roman, Muslim, and Christian) have forged a country with a wide variety of regions, languages, and customs. If you fly over Spain you'll see that much of the country's center is a parched, red-orange desert. But Spain's topography resembles a giant upside-down bowl, with the high, flat, dry central plateau and a coastal lip. The north is mountainous and rainy; the south is hilly and hot. Ringing it all is 2,000 miles of coastline.

Spain's geography makes it less a centralized nation than a collection of distinct regions. In the central plain sits the urban island of Madrid, a region unto itself. Just south is Toledo, a medieval showpiece and melting-pot city with Christian,

Muslim, and Jewish roots. Farther south is Andalucía, a region formerly ruled by Muslims, now home to sleepy, sun-baked *pueblos blancos* (whitewashed hill towns). Spain's south coast, the Costa del Sol, is a palm-tree jungle of beach resorts, casinos, time-share condos, discos, and sunburned Brits on holiday. Along the Mediterranean coast (to the east), Spain has an almost Italian vibe, and Barcelona and Catalunya keep one eye cocked toward trends sailing in from the rest of Europe. Tourism is huge here. With 47 million inhabitants, Spain entertains 50 million visitors annually.

To the north is the Basque Country, which combines sparkling beaches, cutting-edge architecture, and proudly feisty locals. From here gregarious modern-day pilgrims follow the Camino de Santiago westward across the parched north of Spain into mellow and lush Galicia, where moss-covered churches and tree-strewn rolling hillsides beckon. Beyond its contiguous lands, Spain clings to the last of its far-flung holdings: a few Mediterranean islands (including Menorca, Mallorca, and Ibiza), Ceuta in Morocco, and the distant Canary Islands.

"Castilian"—what we call "Spanish"—is spoken throughout the country. But Catalans (around Barcelona) speak their own Romance language, Catalan. The Galicians speak Galego. And in the far north the Basques keep alive the ancient tongue of Euskara. A fringe group of separatist Basques (with their notorious and unpopular terrorist wing, ETA) has lobbied hard and sometimes violently for self-rule. But every region in Spain has its own dialect, customs, and (often half-hearted) separatist movement. Each region also hosts local festivals, whether parading Virgin Mary statues through the streets, running in front of a pack of furious bulls, or pelting each other with tomatoes. People think of themselves first and foremost as Basques, Catalans, Andalusians, Galicians, Leonese, and so on...and only second as Spaniards.

Spain is in Europe, but not *of* Europe—it has a unique identity and history, thanks largely to the Pyrenees Mountains that physically isolate it from the rest of the Continent. For

more than 700 years (711-1492), Spain's dominant culture was Muslim, not Christian. And after a brief Golden Age financed by New World gold (1500-1600), Spain retreated into three centuries of isolation (1600-1900). Spain's seclusion contributed to the creation of unusual customs—bullfights, flamenco dancing, and a national obsession with ham. Even as other countries opened up to one another in the 20th century, the fascist dictator Francisco Franco virtually sealed off Spain from the rest of Europe's democracies. But since Franco's death in 1975, Spaniards have almost swung to the opposite extreme, becoming wide open to new trends and technologies. (For more on Spanish history, see the Spain: Past & Present chapter.)

Spain Almanac

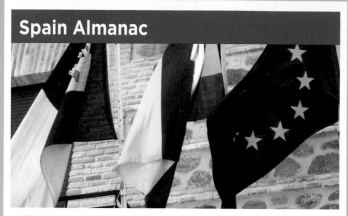

Official Name: It's officially the Reino de España (Kingdom of Spain), but locals just call it España.

Population: 47 million. Most speak the official national language of Castilian, but about 17 percent speak Catalan, 7 percent Galego (Galician), and 2 percent Euskara (Basque). The country is 94 percent Roman Catholic.

Latitude and Longitude: 40°N and 4°W (similar latitude to New York City).

Area: 195,000 square miles (about 18 percent bigger than California). This includes the Canary and Balearic islands, and small enclaves in Morocco. Spain's long-standing claim to Gibraltar remains a nagging dispute with Britain.

Geography: The interior of Spain is a high, flat plateau (the Meseta Central), with hot, dry summers and harsh winters. Surrounding the plateau are mountains (including the Pyrenees in the north) and 2,000 miles of coastline.

Agua Agua Everywhere: A leader in hydropower and irrigation, Spain, for its size, has more man-made lakes from dams (about 1,400) than any other country. Still, the average Spaniard uses one-third less energy than the average American. Spain's 1,800 rivers are mostly small, less than 50 miles long. The 600-mile Tajo River (a.k.a. Tagus in English, or Tejo in Portuguese) runs westward from Toledo through Portugal to the Atlantic. The Guadalquivir irrigates Andalucía and makes Sevilla an oceangoing port city.

Biggest Cities: Madrid (3.3 million; at more than 2,000 feet in altitude, it's Europe's second-highest capital), Barcelona (1.6

million), Valencia (810,000), and Sevilla (704,000). Spaniards are urban dwellers—only one in five lives outside a metropolitan area.

Economy: The Gross Domestic Product is $1.4 trillion; the GDP per capita is about $30,400. Major moneymakers include tourism, clothes, shoes, olives, wine, oranges, machine parts, and ships. Recently it had a 27 percent unemployment rate—about 5 million Spaniards were out of work.

Government: Guided symbolically by King Juan Carlos I, Spain is a parliamentary monarchy. The prime minister is chosen by election. Some of the 600-plus legislators (in two houses) are elected directly, some by regional parliaments. The country has 17 regional autonomous governments (e.g., Andalucía, Catalunya, Castile-La Mancha, Madrid), which in time will have full responsibility for health care, social programs, and education.

Flag: Spain's flag has three horizontal bands of red, yellow, and red. To the left of center is the coat of arms—a shield with a crown, framed by the Pillars of Hercules that symbolically flank the Straits of Gibraltar.

Soccer: The two perennial powerhouses in La Liga (The League) are Real Madrid and FC Barcelona. Spain is a three-time winner of the European championship, and in 2010, the Spanish national team won the World Cup, sparking a nationwide fiesta.

The Average José: The average Spaniard is 40 years old, will live to age 81, and resides in a home with one car and one TV. More than half of Spaniards use the Internet, and 1 in 10 owns a cat. The average Spaniard has a mobile phone, 1.5 kids, and sleeps 40 minutes less every night than the typical European.

Spaniards are proud and stoic. They can be hard to get to know—but once you've made that connection, you've

got a friend for life. The Spanish people have long had a reputation as being thrifty, straightforward, and unpretentious. Traditionally, their lives revolved around the Catholic Church and the family. Young adults tended to live at home until they got married—even into their late twenties or early thirties. Spaniards prided themselves on their nonmaterialistic values, owning just one car and one TV, and living in small urban apartments instead of giant suburban houses. The notorious "machismo" culture of domineering men ruled.

But Spain's old ways have changed. Although the vast majority of Spaniards are still nominally Catholic, the country is at the forefront of liberal reforms in abortion and gay marriage. Spain's extreme religiosity has been replaced by an extreme secularism. The old hierarchy of aristocrats, peasants, priests, and old ladies in black has become democratic and hang-loose. The allure of consumerism and status symbols has enticed many Spanish people to save (or borrow) for high-fashion clothes, second cars, and summer chalets, though the economic downturn has pushed materialistic dreams further out of reach. Still, throughout its recent economic boom and bust, Spain has remained affordable for visitors.

Even as the country plunges into the 21st century, some things never change. Daily lives focus on friends and family, as they always have. Many people (especially in rural areas) still follow the siesta schedule, which emphasizes a big midday meal with the family. Spaniards tend to have a small, quick breakfast, grab a late-morning sandwich to tide them over, then gather with friends and family for the siesta. From around 1:00 to 4:00 p.m., many businesses close as people go home to eat

lunch, socialize, and maybe grab a quick nap. The siesta is not so much a time to sleep as it is an opportunity for everyone to shut down their harried public life, and enjoy good food and the comfort of loved ones.

In the cool of the evening, Spain comes back to life. Whole families pour out of their apartments to stroll through the streets and greet their neighbors—a custom called the paseo. Even the biggest city feels like a rural village. People stop at bars for a drink or to watch a big soccer match on TV. They might order a bite to eat, enjoying appetizers called tapas Around 10:00 p.m. in the heat of summer, it's finally time for a light dinner. Afterward, even families with young children might continue their paseo or attend a concert. Spaniards are notorious night owls. Many clubs and restaurants don't even

open until after midnight. Dance clubs routinely stay open until the sun rises, and young people stumble out bleary-eyed and head for work. The antidote for late nights? The next day's siesta.

Spanish food is hearty and unrefined. Remember that Spain is not Mexico—you won't find tacos, Tabasco, or tequila. (Even things that sound Mexican can be very different—for example, a *tortilla* is an omelet.) Major meals feature meat (such as roast suckling pig) or seafood. Popular regional foods are gazpacho (cold tomato soup) and paella (seafood and meat cooked with saffron-flavored rice). Spaniards snack between meals on tapas. Most bars offer a variety of these appetizers served hot or cold. A few small plates of olives, chorizo (sausage), grilled shrimp, Russian salad, or deep-fried nuggets can add up to a multicourse meal.

The most treasured delicacy in Spain is *jamón*—cured ham that is sliced thin and served cold. Bars proudly hang ham hocks on their walls as part of the decor. Like connoisseurs of fine wine, Spaniards debate the merits of different breeds of pigs, what part of the pig they're eating, what the pig has eaten, and the quality of curing.

Drinking is part of the Spanish meal, and part of the social ritual. Spain produces large quantities of wine, especially their spicy red Rioja, made from the tempranillo grape.

For a country its size, Spain has produced an astonishing number of talented artists with distinctive styles—from El Greco's mystical religiosity to the sober realism of Diego Velázquez. (Madrid's Prado Museum is a veritable showcase of European Renaissance art, bought with the spoils from the New World.) Francisco Goya painted the Golden Age in decline. In the 20th century, Pablo Picasso shattered the two-dimensional picture plane, then pasted it back together by inventing Cubism. Later, he painted *Guernica,* an epic snapshot of the horrific Spanish Civil War. It's one of the most

powerful antiwar paintings ever created (now displayed in Madrid). Salvador Dalí created surreal juxtapositions of old and new, while his fellow Catalan Joan Miró picked up the Surrealist baton and ran with it. Spain carries on this rich tradition today, with a thriving contemporary arts scene.

In music, Spain continues its long tradition of great guitarists—classical, flamenco, and Gipsy Kings-style "new flamenco." In dance, you'll find the fiery flamenco (from Andalucía) and the stately do-si-do of the *sardana* (from Catalunya). Contemporary film includes works by director Pedro Almodóvar, who explores changing family and social roles as Spain moves from its conservative past to its wide-open future. And there's one contemporary Spaniard whose works will be known and appreciated for generations to come: Santiago Calatrava, an architect who designs buildings and bridges for the 21st century.

Whereas you can see some European countries by just passing through, Spain is a destination. Learn its history and accept it on its own terms. Gain (or just fake) an appreciation for cured ham, dry sherry, and bull's-tail stew, and the Spaniards will love you for it. If you go, go all the way. Immerse yourself in Spain.

INTRODUCTION

This book breaks Spain into its top destinations and will help you make the most of your trip—it offers a balanced, comfortable mix of exciting cities and cozy towns, topped off with an exotic dollop of Morocco. It covers the predictable biggies and stirs in a healthy dose of "Back Door" intimacy. Along with seeing a bullfight, the Prado, and flamenco, you'll greet pilgrims at Santiago de Compostela, visit a bull bar in Madrid, and buy cookies from cloistered nuns in a sun-parched Andalusian town. I've been selective, including only the most exciting sights and experiences. Rather than listing Spain's countless Costa del Sol beach resorts, I recommend my favorite: Nerja.

You'll get all the specifics and opinions necessary to wring the maximum value out of your limited time and money. If you plan a month or less in Spain, and you have a normal appetite for information, this book is all you need. If you're a travel-info fiend (like me), you'll find that this book sorts through all the superlatives and provides a handy rack upon which to hang your supplemental information.

Experiencing Spain's culture, people, and natural wonders economically and hassle-free has been my goal through three decades of traveling, tour-guiding, and writing. With this book I pass on to you the lessons I've learned, updated for 2014.

The best of Spain is, of course, only my opinion. But after spending half of my adult life researching and tour-guiding in Europe, I've developed a sixth sense for what travelers enjoy.

Map Legend

📷	Viewpoint	✈	Airport	)▬(	Tunnel
↟	Entrance	Ⓣ	Taxi Stand		Pedestrian Zone
🛈	Tourist Info	Ⓣ	Tram Stop		
WC	Restroom	Ⓑ	Bus Stop	-----	Railway
🏰	Castle	Ⓜ	Metro Stop	....	Ferry/Boat Route
🏛	Church	Ⓡ	Rodalies Rail Stop	⊢——⊣	Tram
✡	Synagogue	Ⓟ	Parking	◻◻◻◻	Stairs
▪	Statue/Point of Interest	)(	Mountain Pass	- - - -	Walk/Tour Route
		⬚	Park		
⊠	Elevator	◎	Fountain		Trail

Use this legend to help you navigate some of the maps in this book.

About This Book

Rick Steves' Spain 2014 is a tour guide in your pocket. This book is organized by destinations. Each is a mini-vacation on its own, filled with exciting sights, strollable neighborhoods, affordable places to stay, and memorable places to eat. In the following chapters, you'll find these sections:

Planning Your Time suggests a schedule for how to best use your limited time.

Orientation includes specifics on public transportation, helpful hints, local tour options, easy-to-read maps, and tourist information.

Sights describes the top attractions and includes their cost and hours.

Self-Guided Walks take you through interesting neighborhoods, with a personal tour guide in hand.

Sleeping describes my favorite hotels, from good-value deals to cushy splurges.

Eating serves up a range of options, from inexpensive eateries to fancy restaurants.

Connections outlines your options for traveling to destinations by plane, train, and bus. I've included route tips for drivers in car-friendly regions.

The **Spain: Past & Present** chapter gives you a quick overview of Spanish history, art, and architecture, and the tradition of bullfighting.

Key to This Book

Updates
This book is updated every year—but once you pin down Spain, it wiggles. For the latest, visit www.ricksteves.com/update, and for a valuable list of reports and experiences—good and bad—from fellow travelers, check www.ricksteves.com/feedback.

Abbreviations and Times
I use the following symbols and abbreviations in this book:

Sights are rated:

▲▲▲	Don't miss
▲▲	Try hard to see
▲	Worthwhile if you can make it
No rating	Worth knowing about

Tourist information offices are abbreviated as **TI,** and bathrooms are **WCs.** To categorize accommodations, I use a **Sleep Code** (described on page 21).

Like Europe, this book uses the **24-hour clock.** It's the same as ours through 12:00 noon, then keeps going: 13:00, 14:00, and so on. For anything over 12, subtract 12 and add p.m. (14:00 is 2:00 p.m.).

When giving **opening times,** I include both peak-season and off-season hours if they differ. So, if a museum is listed as "May-Oct daily 9:00-16:00," it should be open from 9 a.m. until 4 p.m. from the first day of May until the last day of October (but expect exceptions).

For **transit** or **tour departures,** I first list the frequency, then the duration. So, a train connection listed as "2/hour, 1.5 hours" departs twice each hour and the journey lasts an hour and a half.

The **appendix** is a traveler's tool kit, with telephone tips, useful phone numbers and websites, transportation basics (on trains, buses, car rentals, driving, and flights), recommended books and films, a festival list, a climate chart, a handy packing checklist, Spanish survival phrases, and a pronunciation guide for place names.

Browse through this book, choose your favorite destinations, and link them up. Then have a *maravilloso* trip! Traveling like a temporary local, you'll get the absolute most out of every mile, minute, and dollar. As you visit places I know and love, I'm happy you'll be meeting my favorite Spanish people.

Planning

This section will help you get started on planning your trip—with advice on trip costs, when to go, and what you should know before you take off.

Travel Smart

Your trip to Spain is like a complex play—it's easier to follow and really appreciate on a second viewing. While no one does the same trip twice to gain that advantage, reading this book in its entirety before your trip accomplishes much the same thing.

Design an itinerary that enables you to visit sights at the best possible times. Note holidays, specifics on sights, and days when sights are closed or most crowded (all covered in this book). To get between destinations smoothly, read the tips in this book's appendix on taking trains and buses, or renting a car and driving. A smart trip is a puzzle—a fun, doable, and worthwhile challenge.

When you're plotting your itinerary, strive for a mix of intense and relaxed stretches. To maximize rootedness, minimize one-night stands. It's worth taking a long drive after dinner (or a train ride with a dinner picnic) to get settled in a town for two nights. Every trip—and every traveler—needs slack time (laundry, picnics, people-watching, and so on). Pace yourself. Assume you will return.

Reread this book as you travel, and visit local tourist information offices (abbreviated as TI in this book). Upon arrival in a new town, lay the groundwork for a smooth departure; get the schedule for the train or bus that you'll take when you depart. Drivers can study the best route to their next destination.

Get online at Internet cafés or your hotel, and carry a mobile phone (or use a phone card) to make travel plans: You can find tourist information, learn the latest on sights (special events, tour schedule, etc.), book tickets and tours, make reservations, reconfirm hotels, research transportation connections, and keep in touch with your loved ones.

Enjoy the friendliness of the Spanish people. Connect with the culture. Set up your own quest for the best main square, paella, cloister, tapas bar, or whatever. Slow down and be open to unexpected experiences. Ask questions—most locals are eager to point you in their idea of the right direction. Keep a notepad in your pocket for noting directions, organizing your thoughts, and confirming prices. Wear your money belt, learn the currency, and figure out how to estimate prices in dollars. Those who expect to travel smart, do.

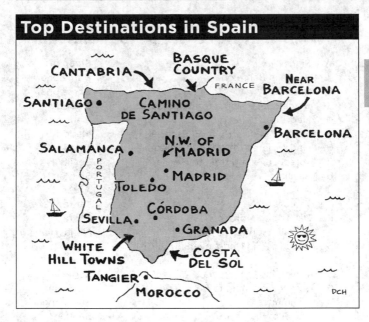

Top Destinations in Spain

CANTABRIA

BASQUE COUNTRY

FRANCE

NEAR BARCELONA

SANTIAGO

CAMINO DE SANTIAGO

BARCELONA

SALAMANCA

N.W. OF MADRID

PORTUGAL

TOLEDO

MADRID

SEVILLA

CÓRDOBA

GRANADA

WHITE HILL TOWNS

COSTA DEL SOL

TANGIER

MOROCCO

DCH

Trip Costs

Five components make up your trip costs: airfare, surface transportation, room and board, sightseeing and entertainment, and shopping and miscellany.

Airfare: A basic round-trip flight from the US to Barcelona or Madrid can cost, on average, about $1,000-1,800 total, depending on where you fly from and when (cheaper in winter). Consider saving time and money by flying into one city and out of another—for instance, into Barcelona and out of Santiago de Compostela.

Surface Transportation: For a three-week whirlwind trip to my recommended destinations, allow $700 per person for second-class trains and buses ($1,000 for first-class trains). For a three-week car rental, allow $300-500 per person (based on two people sharing) not including tolls, gas, and insurance. Leasing is worth considering for trips lasting three weeks or more. Car rentals and leases are cheapest if arranged from the US. Train passes normally must be purchased outside Europe but aren't necessarily your best option—you may save money by simply buying tickets as you go. Don't hesitate to consider flying, as budget airlines can be cheaper than taking the train (check www.skyscanner.com for intra-European flights). For more on public transportation and car rental, see "Transportation" in the appendix.

Room and Board: You can thrive in Spain in 2014 on $110 a day per person for room and board (more in big cities). This allows

Whirlwind Three-Week Tour of Spain

Day	Plan	Sleep in
1	Arrive in Barcelona	Barcelona
2	Barcelona	Barcelona
3	Barcelona, evening train to Madrid	Madrid
4	Madrid	Madrid
5	Madrid, or day trip to El Escorial	Madrid
6	Madrid, late afternoon to Toledo	Toledo
7	Toledo, evening train to Sevilla	Sevilla
8	Sevilla	Sevilla
9	Arcos	Arcos
10	Tarifa	Tarifa
11	Day trip to Morocco	Tarifa
12	Gibraltar, on to Nerja	Nerja
13	Beach day in Nerja, evening to Granada	Granada
14	Granada	Granada
15	Travel day to Segovia	Segovia
16	Segovia, evening to Salamanca	Salamanca
17	Salamanca	Salamanca
18	Travel to Santiago	Santiago
19	Santiago	Santiago
20	Travel to San Sebastián	San Sebastián
21	San Sebastián, side-trip to Bilbao	San Sebastián

This itinerary is designed for public transportation, but can be done by car with a few variations. Spain's long distances make it worth considering the option of flying for at least a portion of the trip. If you rent a car, it's best for Andalucía's hill towns (Arcos, Ronda, and more, in southern Spain), Camino de Santiago (east-west route in northern Spain), and Cantabria (chunk of north-central coast with beaches, mountains, and prehistoric cave replica), where sparse public transportation limits the efficiency of your sightseeing. To mix car and train transportation, consider getting a Spain Rail & Drive pass.

If you're a fan of Salvador Dalí's art, or if you want to make a pilgrimage to the holy site of Montserrat, allot an extra day in Barcelona for side-trips. If you want more Moorish sights, stay another day in Sevilla to make a quick trip to Córdoba (45 minutes on AVE high-speed train). If you're not interested in day-tripping to Tangier, Morocco, you could skip Tarifa and go to Ronda instead. To allow time to explore Gibraltar, add an extra day between Tarifa (or Ronda) and Nerja. If you're exploring the

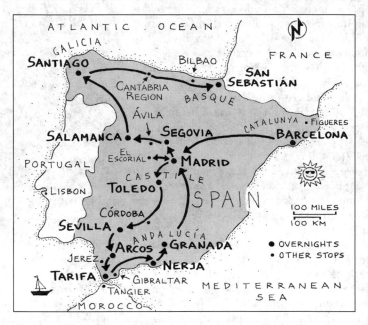

Camino de Santiago by car, consider reversing the above itinerary to start in San Sebastián, and figure on adding several days to a week to your trip.

The suggested itinerary assumes you'll fly into Barcelona and out of San Sebastián. If you're returning to Barcelona or Madrid from San Sebastián, it's roughly a six-hour train ride or a one-hour flight. Or you can take the TGV train from Figueres (north of Barcelona) to Paris (5.5 hours).

Shorter Itineraries: You can end the three-week route several days early by returning to Madrid from Salamanca and saving northern Spain for another trip. With the exception of the Basque Country, the north is less rewarding per mile and day.

Here's a two-week alternative, which could include a few car days in southern Spain near the end of your trip: Start in Barcelona (two days); train to Madrid (five days total, with two days in Madrid and three for side-trips to Toledo, El Escorial, and Segovia or Ávila); train to Granada (two days); bus to Nerja (one day, could rent car here); both Ronda and Arcos for drivers, or just Ronda by train (two days); to Sevilla (drop off car, two days); and then train to Madrid and fly home.

$10 for lunch, $25 for dinner, and $75 for lodging (based on two people splitting the cost of a $150 double room that includes breakfast). Students and tightwads can enjoy Spain for as little as $60 a day ($30 for a bed, $30 for meals and snacks).

Sightseeing and Entertainment: In big cities, figure about $17-20 per major sight (Madrid's Prado, Barcelona's Picasso Museum, Granada's Alhambra), $6 for minor ones (climbing church towers), and $35-50 for splurge experiences (flamenco, bullfights). An overall average of $25 a day works for most people. Don't skimp here. After all, this category is the driving force behind your trip—you came to sightsee, enjoy, and experience Spain.

Shopping and Miscellany: Figure $3 per coffee, beer, ice-cream cone, and postcard. Shopping can vary in cost from nearly nothing to a small fortune. Good budget travelers find that this category has little to do with assembling a trip full of lifelong and wonderful memories.

Sightseeing Priorities

Depending on the length of your trip, and taking geographic proximity into account, here are my recommended priorities:

3 days:	Madrid and Toledo
6 days, add:	Barcelona
10 days, add:	Sevilla, Granada
13 days, add:	Nerja, Ronda, Tangier (Morocco)
15 days, add:	Salamanca, Segovia
17 days, add:	Santiago de Compostela
21 days, add:	Basque Region (San Sebastián and Bilbao)
25 days, add:	Camino de Santiago (by car)

This includes nearly everything on the map on page 7.

When to Go

Spring and fall offer the best combination of good weather, light crowds, long days, and plenty of tourist and cultural activities.

July and August are the most crowded and expensive in the coastal areas, and less crowded but uncomfortably hot and dusty in the interior. Air-conditioning is essential. During these steamy months, lunch breaks can be long, especially in Andalucía.

Off-season, roughly November through March, expect shorter hours, more lunchtime breaks, and fewer activities. Confirm your sightseeing plans locally, especially when traveling off-season.

Though it can be brutally hot in the summer, winters can

be bitter cold, and spring and fall can be surprisingly crisp. For weather specifics, see the climate chart on page 959.

Know Before You Go

Your trip is more likely to go smoothly if you plan ahead. Check this list of things to arrange while you're still at home.

You need a **passport**—but no visa or shots—to travel in Spain. You may be denied entry into certain European countries if your passport is due to expire within three to six months of your ticketed date of return. Get it renewed if you'll be cutting it close. It can take up to six weeks to get or renew a passport (for more on passports, see www.travel.state.gov). Pack a photocopy of your passport in your luggage in case the original is lost or stolen.

Book rooms well in advance if you'll be traveling during peak season (July-Sept) or on any major holidays (see page 956).

Call your **debit- and credit-card companies** to let them know the countries you'll be visiting, to ask about fees, request your PIN code (it will be mailed to you), and more. See page 14 for details.

Do your homework if you want to buy **travel insurance.** Compare the cost of the insurance to the likelihood of your using it and your potential loss if something goes wrong. Also, check whether your existing insurance (health, homeowners, or renters) covers you and your possessions overseas. For more tips, see www.ricksteves.com/insurance.

If you're taking an **overnight train,** especially to international destinations, and you need a sleeping berth *(litera)*—and you must leave on a certain day—consider booking it in advance through a US agent (such as www.raileurope.com), even though it may cost more than buying it in Spain. All high-speed trains in Spain require a seat reservation, but it's usually possible to make arrangements in Spain just a few days ahead unless it's a holiday weekend. (For more on train travel, see the appendix.)

If you're planning on **renting a car** in Spain, bring your US driver's license and an International Driving Permit (see page 946).

Consider **making reservations for Granada's Alhambra** before leaving home. Although you can reserve tickets upon arrival in Spain (ideally before you reach Granada), tickets can be obtained up to three months in advance, and it's really worth booking as soon as you are confident of your dates (for more information, see page 596). You'll also need reservations if you want to visit the Salvador Dalí House near Cadaqués (see page 183), and it's smart to get them for the Altamira Caves in summer (see page 385).

If you plan to hire a **local guide,** reserve ahead by email. Popular guides can get booked up.

If you're bringing a **mobile device,** download any apps you might want to use on the road, such as translators, maps, and

Spain at a Glance

These attractions are listed (as in this book) roughly from north to south.

▲▲▲**Barcelona** The Catalan capital, with famous Ramblas people zone, atmospheric Gothic old town, and works by native sons Antoni Gaudí, Pablo Picasso, and Joan Miró.

▲**Near Barcelona** Top stops in Catalunya, including Salvador Dalí sights (Figueres and Cadaqués), pilgrimage to a rugged mountain retreat (Montserrat), and beach resort (Sitges).

▲▲**Basque Country** Feisty would-be breakaway region, anchored by the culinary capital of San Sebastián and the iconic modern Guggenheim Museum in Bilbao, with other attractions scattered through the countryside and across the border into France.

▲**Camino de Santiago** Centuries-old pilgrimage route running across the top of Spain from France to Santiago, with stops at big cities (Pamplona, Burgos, León) and charming villages (Puente de la Reina, O Cebreiro)...and plenty of pilgrim bonding.

▲**Santiago de Compostela** Moss-covered pilgrim capital, and the top town in green Galicia.

Cantabria The rustic northern coast of Spain, featuring world-class prehistoric art (Altamira Caves), Modernista architecture (Comillas), and high-mountain scenery (Picos de Europa).

▲**Salamanca** Spain's quintessential university town, with the country's finest main square.

▲▲▲**Madrid** The lively Spanish capital, boasting top-notch art treasures (Prado Museum collection, Picasso's *Guernica*), an

transit schedules. Check out **Rick Steves Audio Europe,** featuring hours of travel interviews and other audio content about Spain (via www.ricksteves.com/audioeurope, iTunes, Google Play, or the Rick Steves Audio Europe smartphone app; for details, see page 952).

Check the **Rick Steves guidebook updates** page for any recent changes to this book (www.ricksteves.com/update).

Because **airline carry-on restrictions** are always changing, visit the Transportation Security Administration's website (www.tsa.gov) for an up-to-date list of what you can bring on the plane with you...and what you must check.

unsurpassed tapas scene, and urban Spain at its best.

▲**Northwest of Madrid** Sights ranging from El Escorial (imposing Inquisition palace of Spanish royalty) and the Valley of the Fallen (a stern, underground Franco-era monument to the Spanish Civil War) to the pleasant towns of Segovia (with a towering Roman aqueduct) and Ávila (encircled by a medieval wall).

▲▲**Toledo** Hill-capping former capital, with a colorfully complex history, a magnificent cathedral, and works by hometown boy El Greco.

▲▲▲**Granada** Grand Moorish capital, home to the magnificent Alhambra palace and still-pungent North African culture.

▲▲▲**Sevilla** Soulful, flamenco-flavored cultural capital of southern Spain.

▲**Córdoba** Home to Spain's top surviving Moorish mosque, the Mezquita.

▲**Andalucía's White Hill Towns** Classic heartland of southern Spain, famous for its windswept landscape and idyllic towns, including Arcos de la Frontera, Ronda, and Grazalema.

Costa del Sol Spain's beach-resort zone, featuring a few charming towns (Nerja, Tarifa, and British-flavored Gibraltar) tucked between the concrete and traffic jams.

▲▲**Tangier, Morocco** Revitalized gateway to Africa, and an easy day trip from the Costa del Sol.

Practicalities

Emergency and Medical Help: In **Spain,** dial 091 for police help and 112 in any emergency (medical or otherwise). In **Morocco,** dial 190 for police.

If you get sick, do as the Spanish do and go to a pharmacist for advice. Or ask at your hotel for help—they'll know the nearest medical and emergency services.

Theft or Loss: To replace a passport, you'll need to go in person to an embassy or consulate office (see page 936). If your credit and debit cards disappear, cancel and replace them (see "Damage

Control for Lost Cards" on page 16). File a police report, either on the spot or within a day or two; you'll need it to submit an insurance claim for lost or stolen railpasses or travel gear, and it can help with replacing your passport or credit and debit cards. For more information, see www.ricksteves.com/help.

Thieves target tourists throughout Spain, especially in Barcelona, Madrid, Granada, and Sevilla. While hotel rooms are generally safe, thieves break into cars, snatch purses, and pick pockets. Thieves zipping by on motorbikes grab handbags from pedestrians or even from cars in traffic (by reaching through open car windows at stoplights). A fight or commotion is often created to enable pickpockets to work unnoticed. Someone in a small group pushing you as you enter or exit a subway car may have one hand in your pocket.

Be on guard, use a money belt, and treat any disturbance around you as a smoke screen for theft. Don't believe any "police officers" looking for counterfeit bills. When traveling by train, keep your luggage in sight and get a *litera* (berth in an attendant-monitored sleeping car) for safety on overnight trips. Drivers should read the tips on page 949.

Precautionary measures can minimize the effects of loss—back up your digital photos and other files frequently.

Time Zones: Spain, like most of continental Europe, is generally six/nine hours ahead of the East/West coasts of the US. The exceptions are the beginning and end of Daylight Saving Time: Europe "springs forward" the last Sunday in March (two weeks after most of North America), and "falls back" the last Sunday in October (one week before North America). Moroccan time is an hour earlier than Spain's, but can run up to two hours earlier with Daylight Saving Time (see page 879). For a handy online time converter, try www.timeanddate.com/worldclock.

Business Hours: For visitors, Spain is a land of strange and frustrating schedules. Many businesses respect the afternoon siesta. When it's 100 degrees in the shade, you'll understand why. The biggest museums stay open all day. Smaller ones often close for a siesta. Shops are generally open from 9:00 to 13:00 and from 16:00 to 20:00, longer in touristy places. Small shops are often open on Saturday only in the morning, and are closed all day Sunday. Banking hours are generally Monday through Friday from 9:00 to 14:00.

Saturdays are virtually weekdays, with earlier closing hours. Sundays have the same pros and cons as they do for travelers in the US: Sightseeing attractions are generally open, while shops and banks are closed, public transportation options are fewer (for example, no bus service to or from smaller towns), and there's no rush hour. Rowdy evenings are rare on Sundays.

Watt's Up? Europe's electrical system is 220 volts, instead of North America's 110 volts. Most newer electronics (such as laptops, battery chargers, and hair dryers) convert automatically, so you won't need a converter plug, but you will need an adapter plug with two round prongs, sold inexpensively at travel stores in the US. Avoid bringing older appliances that don't automatically convert voltage; instead, buy a cheap replacement in Europe.

Discounts: Discounts are not listed in this book. However, many sights offer discounts for youths (up to age 18), students (with proper identification cards, www.isic.org), families, seniors (loosely defined as retirees or those willing to call themselves seniors), and groups of 10 or more. Always ask. Some discounts are available only for citizens of the European Union (EU).

Online Translation Tip: You can use Google's Chrome browser (available free at www.google.com/chrome) to instantly translate websites. With one click, the page appears in (very rough) English translation. You can also paste the URL of the site into the translation window at www.google.com/translate.

Money

This section offers advice on how to pay for purchases on your trip (including getting cash from ATMs and paying with plastic), dealing with lost or stolen cards, VAT (sales tax) refunds, and tipping.

What to Bring

Bring both a credit card and a debit card. You'll use the debit card at cash machines (ATMs) to withdraw local cash for most purchases, and the credit card to pay for larger items. Some travelers carry a third card, in case one gets demagnetized or eaten by a temperamental machine.

For an emergency stash, bring several hundred dollars in hard cash in $20 bills. If you have to exchange the bills, go to a bank; avoid using currency-exchange booths because of their lousy rates and/or outrageous fees.

Cash

Cash is just as desirable in Europe as it is at home. Small European businesses (hotels, restaurants, shops, etc.) prefer that you pay your bills with cash. Some vendors will charge you extra for using a credit card, and some won't take credit cards at all. Cash is the best—and sometimes only—way to pay for bus fares, taxis, and local guides.

Throughout Europe, ATMs are the standard way for travelers to get cash. But stay away from "independent" ATMs such as Travelex, Euronet, and Forex, which charge huge commissions

Exchange Rate

1 euro (€) = about $1.30

To convert prices in euros to dollars, add about 30 percent: €20 = about $26, €50 = about $65. (Check www.oanda.com for the latest exchange rates.) Just like the dollar, one euro is broken down into 100 cents. Coins range from €0.01 to €2, and bills range from €5 to €500.

Gibraltar uses pounds (£) but also takes euros; you'll get a better exchange rate using pounds (£1 = about $1.60).

For Morocco, I list prices in dirhams (the official currency; 8 dirhams = about $1), although euros and dollars are usually accepted. I abbreviate dirhams as "dh" in this book, but the official abbreviation is MAD, to differentiate the currency from dirhams used by other countries.

and have terrible exchange rates.

To withdraw money from an ATM (called a *cajero automático* in Spain), you'll need a debit card (ideally with a Visa or MasterCard logo for maximum usability), plus a PIN code. Know your PIN code in numbers; there are only numbers—no letters—on European keypads. Although you can use a credit card for an ATM transaction, it only makes sense in an emergency, because it's considered a cash advance (borrowed at a high interest rate) rather than a withdrawal. Try to withdraw large sums of money to reduce the number of per-transaction bank fees you'll pay.

For increased security, shield the keypad when entering your PIN code, and don't use an ATM if anything on the front of the machine looks loose or damaged (a sign that someone may have attached a "skimming" device to capture account information). Some travelers make a point to monitor their accounts while traveling to detect any unauthorized transactions.

Pickpockets target tourists. To safeguard your cash, wear a money belt—a pouch with a strap that you buckle around your waist like a belt and tuck under your clothes. Keep your cash, credit cards, and passport secure in your money belt, and carry only a day's spending money in your front pocket.

Credit and Debit Cards

For purchases, Visa and MasterCard are more commonly accepted than American Express. Just like at home, credit or debit cards work easily at larger hotels, restaurants, and shops. I typically use my debit card to withdraw cash to pay for most purchases. I use my credit card only in a few specific situations: to book hotel reservations by phone, to make major purchases (such as car rentals, plane tickets, and long hotel stays), and to pay for things near the end of my trip (to avoid another visit to the ATM). While you could use a debit card to make most large purchases, using a credit card offers a greater degree of fraud protection (because debit cards draw funds directly from your account).

Ask Your Credit- or Debit-Card Company: Before your trip, contact the company that issued your debit or credit cards.

• Confirm that your **card will work overseas,** and alert them that you'll be using it in Europe; otherwise, they may deny transactions if they perceive unusual spending patterns.

• Ask for the specifics on transaction **fees.** When you use your credit or debit card—either for purchases or ATM withdrawals—you'll typically be charged additional "international transaction" fees of up to 3 percent (1 percent is normal) plus $5 per transaction. If your card's fees seem high, consider getting a different card just for your trip: Capital One (www.capitalone.com) and most credit unions have low-to-no international transaction fees.

• If you plan to withdraw cash from ATMs, confirm your daily **withdrawal limit,** and if necessary, ask your bank to adjust it. Some travelers prefer a high limit that allows them to take out more cash at each ATM stop (saving on bank fees), while others prefer to set a lower limit in case their card is stolen. Note that foreign banks also set maximum withdrawal amounts for their ATMs.

• Get your bank's emergency **phone number** in the US (but not its 800 number, which isn't accessible from overseas) to call collect if you have a problem.

• Ask for your credit card's **PIN** in case you need to make an emergency cash withdrawal or encounter Europe's "chip-and-PIN" system; the bank won't tell you your PIN over the phone, so allow time for it to be mailed to you.

Chip and PIN: While much of Europe is shifting to a "chip-and-PIN" security system for credit and debit cards, Spain still uses the old magnetic-swipe technology for most transactions. (European chip-and-PIN cards are embedded with an electronic security chip, and require the purchaser to punch in a PIN rather than sign a receipt.) If you happen to encounter chip-and-PIN, it will probably be at automated payment machines, such as those at train and subway stations, toll roads, parking garages, luggage lockers, and self-serve gas pumps. On the outside chance

INTRODUCTION

that a machine won't take your card, find a cashier who can make your card work (they can print a receipt for you to sign), or find a machine that takes cash. But don't panic. Most travelers who are carrying only magnetic-stripe cards never encounter any problems. You can always use an ATM to withdraw cash with your magnetic-stripe card, even in countries where people predominantly use chip-and-PIN cards.

Dynamic Currency Conversion: If merchants offer to convert your purchase price into dollars (called dynamic currency conversion, or DCC), refuse this "service." You'll pay even more in fees for the expensive convenience of seeing the amount in dollars.

Damage Control for Lost Cards

If you lose your credit, debit, or ATM card, you can stop people from using your card by reporting the loss immediately to the respective global customer-assistance centers. Call these 24-hour US numbers collect: Visa (tel. 303/967-1096, toll-free number in Spain is 900-991-124), MasterCard (tel. 636/722-7111), or American Express (tel. 336/393-1111). In Spain, to make a collect call to the US, dial 900-990-011. In Morocco, dial 002-110-011. Press zero or stay on the line for an English-speaking operator. European toll-free numbers (listed by country) can be found at the websites for Visa and MasterCard.

Providing the following information will allow for a quicker cancellation of your missing card: full card number, whether you are the primary or secondary cardholder, the cardholder's name exactly as printed on the card, billing address, home phone number, circumstances of the loss or theft, and identification verification (your birth date, your mother's maiden name, or your Social Security number—memorize this, don't carry a copy). If you are the secondary cardholder, you'll also need to provide the primary cardholder's identification-verification details. You can generally receive a temporary card within two or three business days in Europe (see www.ricksteves.com/help for more).

If you report your loss within two days, you typically won't be responsible for any unauthorized transactions on your account, although many banks charge a liability fee of $50.

Tipping

Tipping in Spain isn't as automatic and generous as it is in the US, but for special service, tips are appreciated, if not expected. As in the US, the proper amount depends on your resources, tipping philosophy, and the circumstances, but some general guidelines apply.

Restaurants: If you order a meal at a counter—as you often will when sampling tapas at a bar—there's no need to tip (though if you buy a few tapas, you can round up the bill a few small coins). At restaurants with table service, most Spaniards tip nothing or next to nothing; a service charge is generally included in the bill *(servicio incluido)*. If you like to tip for good service, give up to 5 percent extra. If service is not included *(servicio no incluido)*, you could tip up to 10 percent. At most places, you can leave the tip on the table. But if you're eating at an outdoor café, hand the tip to your server to avoid having it swiped by a passerby. Also, it's best to tip in cash even if you pay with your credit card. Otherwise the tip may never reach your server.

Taxis: To tip the cabbie, round up. Spanish people rarely give tips in taxis, unless it's to round up to the next full euro (if the fare is €4.85, they'll give €5). If the cabbie hauls your bags and zips you to the airport to help you catch your flight, you might want to toss in a little more. But if you feel like you're being driven in circles or otherwise ripped off, skip the tip.

Services: In general, if someone in the service industry does a super job for you, a small tip of a euro or two is appropriate...but not required. If you're not sure whether (or how much) to tip for a service, ask your hotelier or the TI.

Getting a VAT Refund

Wrapped into the purchase price of your Spanish souvenirs is a Value-Added Tax (VAT) of 21 percent (in Spain, it's called IVA— *Impuesto sobre el Valor Añadido*). You're entitled to get most of that tax back if you purchase more than €90.15 (about $117) worth of goods at a store that participates in the VAT-refund scheme. Typically, you must ring up the minimum at a single retailer— you can't add up your purchases from various shops to reach the required amount.

Getting your refund is usually straightforward and, if you buy a substantial amount of souvenirs, well worth the hassle. If you're lucky, the merchant will subtract the tax when you make your purchase. (This is more likely to occur if the store ships the goods to your home.) Otherwise, you'll need to:

Get the paperwork. Have the merchant completely fill out the necessary refund document. You'll have to present your passport. Get the paperwork done before you leave the store to ensure you'll have everything you need (including your original sales receipt).

Get your stamp at the border or airport. Process your VAT document at your last stop in the European Union (such as at the airport) with the customs agent who deals with VAT refunds. Arrive an additional hour early before you need to check in for your flight, to give you time to find the local customs office—and to stand in line. Keep your purchases readily available for viewing by the customs agent (ideally in your carry-on bag—don't make the mistake of checking the bag with your purchases before you've seen the agent). You're not supposed to use your purchased goods before you leave. If you show up at customs wearing your new flamenco outfit, officials might look the other way—or deny you a refund.

Collect your refund. You'll need to return your stamped document to the retailer or its representative. Many merchants work with a service, such as Global Blue or Premier Tax Free, that has offices at major airports, ports, or border crossings (either before or after security, probably strategically located near a duty-free shop). These services, which extract a 4 percent fee, can refund your money immediately in cash or credit your card (within two billing cycles). If the retailer handles VAT refunds directly, it's up to you to contact the merchant for your refund. You can mail the documents from home or, more quickly, from your point of departure (using an envelope you've prepared in advance or one that's been provided by the merchant). You'll then have to wait—it can take months.

Customs for American Shoppers

You are allowed to take home $800 worth of items per person duty-free, once every 30 days. You can also bring in duty-free a liter of alcohol. As for food, you can take home many processed and packaged foods: vacuum-packed cheeses, dried herbs, jams, baked goods, candy, chocolate, oil, vinegar, and honey. Fresh fruits and vegetables and most meats are not allowed. Any liquid-containing foods must be packed in checked luggage, a potential recipe for disaster. To check customs rules and duty rates, visit http://help.cbp.gov.

Sightseeing

Sightseeing can be hard work. Use these tips to make your visits to Spain's finest sights meaningful, fun, efficient, and painless.

Plan Ahead

Set up an itinerary that allows you to fit in all your must-see sights. For a one-stop look at opening hours, see the "At a Glance" sidebars for Barcelona, Madrid, Toledo, Granada, Sevilla, the Camino de Santiago, and the Basque Country. Most sights keep stable hours, but you can easily confirm the latest by checking with the TI or visiting museum websites.

Don't put off visiting a must-see sight—you never know when a place will close unexpectedly for a holiday, a strike, or restoration. Many museums are closed or have reduced hours at least a few days a year, especially on holidays such as Christmas, New Year's, and Labor Day (May 1). A list of holidays is on page 956; check museum websites for possible closures during your trip. In summer, some sights may stay open late. Off-season, many museums have shorter hours.

Going at the right time helps avoid crowds. This book offers tips on the best times to see specific sights. Try visiting popular sights very early or very late. Evening visits are usually peaceful with fewer crowds.

Several cities offer sightseeing passes that are worthwhile values for serious sightseers; do the math to see if they'll save you money.

Study up. To get the most out of the sight descriptions in this book, read them before you visit.

At Sights

Here's what you can typically expect:

Entering: Be warned that you may not be allowed to enter if you arrive 30 to 60 minutes before closing time. And guards start ushering people out well before the actual closing time, so don't save the best for last.

Some important sights have a security check, where you must open your bag or send it through a metal detector. Some sights require you to check daypacks and coats. (If you'd rather not check your daypack, try carrying it tucked under your arm like a purse as you enter.)

At churches—which generally offer interesting art (usually free) and a cool, welcome seat—a modest dress code (no bare shoulders or shorts) is encouraged through rarely enforced.

Photography: If the museum's photo policy isn't clearly posted, ask a guard. Generally, taking photos without a flash is usually allowed. Some sights ban photos altogether.

Temporary Exhibits: Museums may show special exhibits in addition to their permanent collection. Some exhibits are included in the entry price, while others come at an extra cost (which you may have to pay even if you don't want to see the exhibit).

Expect Changes: Artwork can be on tour, on loan, out sick, or shifted at the whim of the curator. To adapt, pick up a floor plan as you enter, and ask the museum staff if you can't find a particular item. Say the title or artist's name, or point to the photograph in this book, and ask, "*¿Dónde está?*" (dohn-day ay-stah; meaning, "Where is?").

Audioguides: Many sights rent audioguides, which generally offer dry-but-useful recorded descriptions in English (about €3-4). If you bring your own earbuds, you can enjoy better sound and avoid holding the device to your ear. To save money, bring a Y-jack and share one audioguide with your travel partner. Increasingly, sights are offering apps (often free) that you can download to your mobile device.

Services: Important sights may have an on-site café or cafeteria (usually a handy place to rejuvenate during a long visit). The WCs at sights are free and generally clean.

Before Leaving: At the gift shop, scan the postcard rack or thumb through a guidebook to be sure that you haven't overlooked something that you'd like to see.

Every sight or museum offers more than what is covered in this book. Use the information in this book as an introduction—not the final word.

Sleeping

I favor hotels and restaurants that are handy to your sightseeing activities. Rather than list hotels scattered throughout a city, I describe two or three favorite neighborhoods and recommend the best accommodations values in each, from bunk beds to fancy doubles with all the comforts.

A major feature of this book is its extensive and opinionated listing of good-value rooms. I like places that are clean, central, relatively quiet at night, reasonably priced, friendly, small enough to have a hands-on owner and stable staff, run with a respect for Spanish traditions, and not listed in other guidebooks. (In Spain, for me, six out of these eight criteria means it's a keeper.) I'm more impressed by a handy location and a fun-loving philosophy than flat-screen TVs and a pricey laundry service.

In Spain, high season *(temporada alta)* is from July to September; shoulder season *(temporada media)* is roughly April through June and October; and low season *(temporada baja)* runs from November through March. Book your accommodations well in advance if you'll be traveling during busy times (such as Semana Santa—Holy Week—in Spain, especially in the south). See page 956 for a list of major holidays and festivals in Spain; for tips on making reservations, see page 26.

Rates and Deals

I've described my recommended accommodations using a Sleep Code (see sidebar). Prices listed are for one-night stays in peak season, and assume you're booking directly (not through a TI or online hotel-booking engine). Booking services extract a commission from the hotel, which logically closes the door on special deals. Book direct. For virtually every hotel I list, I provide a website (which often has a built-in booking form) and an email address; you can expect an English response within a day (and often sooner).

Sleep Code

(€1 = about $1.30)

Price Rankings

To help you easily sort through my listings, I've divided the accommodations into three categories based on the price for a double room with bath during high season:

> **$$$**   **Higher Priced**
> **$$**   **Moderately Priced**
> **$**   **Lower Priced**

    I always rate hostels as **$,** whether or not they have double rooms, because they have the cheapest beds in town.

    Prices can change without notice; verify the hotel's current rates online or by email.

Abbreviations

To pack maximum information into minimum space, I use the following code to describe accommodations in this book. Prices listed are per room, not per person. When a price range is given for a type of room (such as double rooms listed for €100-150), it means the price fluctuates with the season, size of room, or length of stay; expect to pay the upper end for peak-season stays, especially in resort areas. Some hotels include the 10 percent IVA tax in the room price; others tack it onto your bill. Many hotels charge extra for breakfast, check the individual hotel listings for details.

    S = Single room (or price for one person in a double).

    D = Double or twin room. "Double beds" are often two twins sheeted together and are big enough for nonromantic couples.

    T = Triple (generally a double bed with a single).

    Q = Quad (usually two double beds; adding an extra child's bed to a T is usually cheaper).

    b = Private bathroom with toilet and shower or tub.

    s = Private shower or tub only (the toilet is down the hall).

    According to this code, a couple staying at a "Db-€140" hotel would pay a total of €140 (about $182) for a double room with a private bathroom. Unless otherwise noted, hotel staff speak basic English and credit cards are accepted. If the city adds a room tax on top of the national IVA tax, it generally isn't included in the rates I list.

    There's almost always Wi-Fi and/or a guest computer available, either free or for a fee.

Many hotels use "dynamic pricing," which means room rates change from day to day depending on demand. This makes it extremely difficult to predict what you will pay. For most hotels, I've tried to list just one price, which is what you'll most likely pay for a standard room during the busy season (ignoring the dramatically inflated rates hotels charge a few days each year). This rate is intended as a rough guideline, and may vary significantly based on demand—check the hotel's website, or email them, to find out specifics for the date of your visit. For other hotels, I list a range of prices. If the rate you're offered is at or near the bottom of my printed range, it's likely a good deal.

Given the economic downturn, hoteliers are often willing and eager to make a deal. I'd suggest emailing several hotels to ask for their best price. Comparison-shop and make your choice.

As you look over the listings, you'll notice that some accommodations promise special prices to Rick Steves readers. To get these rates, you must book directly with the hotel (that is, *not* through a booking site like TripAdvisor.com or Booking.com), mention this book when you reserve, and then show the book upon arrival. Rick Steves discounts apply to readers with ebooks as well as printed books. Because we trust hotels to honor this, please let me know if you don't receive a listed discount. Note, though, that discounts understandably may not apply to promotional rates.

In general, prices can soften if you do any of the following: offer to pay cash, stay at least three nights, or mention this book. You can also try asking for a cheaper room or a discount, or offer to skip breakfast.

Types of Accommodations

Hotels

Spain offers some of the best accommodations values in Western Europe. Most places are government-regulated, with posted prices. Don't judge economy hotels by their bleak and dirty entryways. Landlords, stuck with rent control, often stand firmly in the way of hardworking hoteliers who'd like to brighten up their buildings.

Rooms with private bathrooms are often bigger and renovated; cheaper rooms without bathrooms often will be dingier and/or on the top floor. All rooms have sinks with hot and cold water, and any room without a bathroom has access to one in the corridor.

Spain has stringent restrictions on smoking in public places. Smoking is not permitted in common areas, but hotels can designate 10 percent of their rooms for smokers.

Some hotels don't use central heat before November 1 and after April 1 (unless it's unusually cold); prepare for cool evenings if you travel in spring and fall. Summer can be extremely

Hotels in Spain: Know the Code

Spanish hotels come with a handy government-regulated classification system. Look for a blue-and-white plaque by the hotel door indicating the category:

Hotel (H)—The most comfortable and expensive accommodation option (rated with stars).

Hotel-Residencia (HR) and **Hostal-Residencia (HsR)**—Hotels without restaurants.

Parador—A government-run inn, often in a refurbished castle or palace. They can be expensive unless you qualify for a discounted rate.

Hostal (Hs)—Less expensive than a hotel, but still rated by stars. Don't confuse *hostales* with youth hostels.

Pensión (P), **Casa de Huéspedes (CH)**, and **Fonda (F)**—Cheaper, usually family-run places.

Albergue—Basic hostel.

Casa Particular—Private home renting budget rooms.

Casa Rural—Country house renting rooms, ranging from basic to fancy.

hot. Consider air-conditioning, fans, and noise (since you'll want your window open). Many rooms come with mini-refrigerators. Conveniently, expensive business-class hotels in big, nonresort cities often drop their prices in July and August, just when the air-conditioned comfort they offer is most important.

Be aware that some hotels have centrally controlled air-conditioning—the manager chooses the temperature (with an eye on his bottom line). In some hotel rooms, air-conditioning units are mounted high on the wall. These come with remote controls (sometimes require a deposit) that generally have similar symbols: fan icon (toggle through wind power); louver icon (choose steady air flow or waves); snowflake and sunshine icons (heat or cold); clock ("O" setting: run x hours before turning off; "I" setting: wait x hours to start); and the temperature control (20 degrees Celsius is comfortable).

If you're arriving early in the morning, your room probably won't be ready. You can drop your bag safely at the hotel and dive right into sightseeing.

Hotel elevators, while becoming more common, are often very small—pack light, or you may need to send your bags up separately.

Street noise in Spain is high (Spaniards are notorious night owls), and walls and doors tend to be very thin—earplugs are a necessity. Always ask to see your room first. If you suspect night noise will be a problem, request a quiet *(tranquilo)* room in the back or on an upper floor *(piso alto)*. In most cases, view rooms *(con vista)* come with street noise. You'll often sleep better and for less money in a room without a view.

Hoteliers can be a great help and source of advice. Most know their city well, and can assist you with everything from public transit and airport connections to finding a good restaurant, the nearest launderette, or an Internet café.

Even at the best places, mechanical breakdowns occur: Air-conditioning malfunctions, sinks leak, hot water turns cold, and toilets gurgle and smell. Report your concerns clearly and calmly at the front desk. For more complicated problems, don't expect instant results. Any legitimate place is legally required to have a complaint book *(libro de reclamaciones)*. A request for this book will generally prompt the hotelier to solve your problem to keep you from writing a complaint.

To guard against theft in your room, keep valuables out of sight. Some rooms come with a safe, and other hotels have safes at the front desk. I've never bothered using one.

Checkout can pose problems if surprise charges pop up on your bill. If you settle your bill the afternoon before you leave, you'll have time to discuss and address any points of contention (before 19:00, when the night shift usually arrives).

Above all, keep a positive attitude. Remember, you're on vacation. If your hotel is a disappointment, spend more time out enjoying the city you came to see.

Historic Inns: Spain has a system of luxurious government-sponsored, historic inns called *paradores*. These are often renovated castles, palaces, or monasteries, many with great views and stately atmospheres. While full of Old World character, they are usually run in a sterile, bureaucratic way and are generally pricier than hotels, but do offer discounts for travelers under 30 or over 60 (doubles $100-240; for details, bonus packages, and family deals, see www.parador.es). If you're not eligible for any deals, you'll get a better value by sleeping in what I call (and list in this book as) "poor man's *paradores*"—elegant, normal places that offer double the warmth and Old World intimacy for half the price.

Budget Hotels: *Hostales* and *pensiónes* are easy to find, inexpensive, and, when chosen properly, a fun part of the Spanish cultural experience. These places are often family-owned, and may or may not have amenities like private bathrooms and air-conditioning. Don't confuse a *hostal* with a hostel—a Spanish *hostal* is an inexpensive hotel, not a hostel with bunks in dorms.

Private Homes, *Casas Rurales,* and Hostels

Rooms in Private Homes: Especially in touristy areas, residents often open up a spare room to make a little money on the side. These rooms are usually as private as hotel rooms, often with separate entries. Especially in resort towns, the rooms might be in small apartment-type buildings. Ask for a *cama, habitación,* or *casa particular.* They're cheap ($15-30 per bed without breakfast) and usually a good experience.

Casas Rurales: Located mainly in rural areas throughout Spain, these accommodations can be furnished rooms, whole farmhouses, villas, or sprawling ranches. Some are simple, but others are luxurious, and they are mostly used by Spaniards, so you'll really be going local. Many are in the countryside, so you will need a car. For more information and reservations, try www.ecoturismorural.com or www.micasarural.com.

Hostels: You'll pay about €20-30 per bed to stay at a hostel *(albergue juvenil).* Travelers of any age are welcome if they don't mind dorm-style accommodations (usually in rooms of four to eight beds) and meeting other travelers. Cheap meals are sometimes offered, and most hostels offer kitchen facilities, guest computers, Wi-Fi, and self-service laundry. Nowadays, concerned about bedbugs, hostels are likely to provide all bedding, including sheets. Expect youth groups in spring, crowds in the summer, snoring, and variability in quality from one hostel to the next. Family and private rooms may be available on request.

Independent hostels tend to be easygoing, colorful, and informal (no membership required); www.hostelworld.com is the standard way backpackers search and book hostels these days, but also try www.hostelz.com, www.hostels.com, and www.hostelbookers.com.

Official hostels are part of Hostelling International (HI) and share an online booking site (www.hihostels.com). HI hostels typically require that you either have a membership card or pay extra per night.

Other Options

Whether you're in a city or the countryside, renting an apartment, house, or villa can be a fun and cost-effective way to delve into Europe. Websites such as HomeAway.com and its sister site VRBO.com let you correspond directly with European property owners or managers.

Airbnb.com makes it reasonably easy to find a place to sleep in someone's home. Beds range from air-mattress-in-living-room basic to plush-B&B-suite posh. If you want a place to sleep that's free, Couchsurfing.com is a vagabond's alternative to Airbnb. It lists millions of outgoing members, who host fellow "surfers" in their homes.

Making Hotel Reservations

Reserve your rooms several weeks in advance—or as soon as you've pinned down your travel dates—particularly if you'll be traveling during peak times. Note that some national holidays jam things up and merit your making reservations far in advance (see "Holidays and Festivals" on page 956).

Requesting a Reservation: It's usually easiest to book your room through the hotel's website. Many have a reservation-request form built right in. (For the best rates, be sure to use the hotel's official site and not a booking agency's site.) Simpler websites will generate an email to the hotelier with your request. If there's no reservation form, or for complicated requests, send an email (see below for a sample request). Most recommended hotels are accustomed to guests who speak only English.

The hotelier wants to know:
- the number and type of rooms you need
- the number of nights you'll stay
- your date of arrival
- your date of departure
- any special needs (such as bathroom in the room or down the hall, cheapest room, twin beds vs. double bed, crib, air-conditioning, quiet, view, ground floor or no stairs, and so on)

If you request a room by email, use the European style for writing dates: day/month/year. For example, for a two-night stay in July of 2014, ask for "1 double room for 2 nights, arrive 16/07/14, depart 18/07/14." Make sure you mention any discounts—for Rick Steves readers or otherwise—when you make the reservation.

Confirming a Reservation: When the hotel replies with its room availability and rates, just email back to confirm your reservation. Most places will request a credit-card number to hold your room. While you can email it (I do), it's safer to share that confidential info via a phone call, two emails (splitting your number between them), or the hotel's secure online reservation form. On the small chance that a hotel loses track of your reservation, bring along a hard copy of their confirmation.

Canceling a Reservation: If you must cancel your reservation, it's courteous—and smart—to do so with as much notice as possible, especially for smaller family-run places. Simply make a quick phone call or send an email. Request confirmation of your cancellation in case you are accidentally billed.

From: rick@ricksteves.com
Sent: Today
To: info@hotelcentral.com
Subject: Reservation request for 19-22 July

Dear Hotel Central,

I would like to reserve a double room for 2 people for
3 nights, arriving 19 July and departing 22 July. If possible,
I would like a quiet room with a bathroom inside the room.

Please let me know if you have a room available and
the price.

Thank you!
Rick Steves

Be warned that cancellation policies can be strict; read the fine print or ask about these before you book. For example, if you cancel on short notice, you could lose your deposit, or be billed for one night or even your entire stay. Internet deals may require prepayment, with no refunds for cancellations.

Reconfirming a Reservation: Call to reconfirm your room reservation a few days in advance. Smaller hotels and B&Bs appreciate knowing your estimated time of arrival. If you'll be arriving late (after 17:00), let them know.

Reserving Rooms as You Travel: You can make reservations as you travel, calling hotels a few days to a week before your arrival. If you'd rather travel without any reservations at all, you'll have greater success snaring rooms if you arrive at your destination early in the day. When you anticipate crowds (weekends are worst), call hotels at about 9:00 or 10:00 on the day you plan to arrive, when the receptionist knows who'll be checking out and which rooms will be available. If you encounter a language barrier, ask the fluent receptionist at your current hotel to call for you.

Phoning: For tips on how to call hotels overseas, see page 928.

Eating

Spanish cuisine is hearty and served in big, inexpensive portions. You can eat well in restaurants for about €15-20—or even more cheaply if you graze on tapas in bars.

The Spanish eating schedule—lunch from 13:00 to 16:00, dinner after 21:00—frustrates many visitors. Most Spaniards eat one major meal of the day—lunch *(comida/almuerzo)*—around 14:00, when stores close, schools let out, and people gather with their friends and family for the siesta. Because most Spaniards work until 19:30, supper *(cena)* is usually served at about 21:00 or 22:00. And, since few people want a heavy meal that late, many Spaniards build a light dinner out of appetizer portions called tapas.

Don't buck this system. Generally, no self-respecting *casa de comidas* ("house of eating"—when you see this label, you can bet it's a good, traditional eatery) serves meals at American hours. If you're looking for the "nontouristy restaurant," remember that a popular spot is often filled with tourists at 20:00; then at 22:00 the scene is entirely different—and more authentic.

Not only are mealtimes different—the portions are, too. It's unusual to find a restaurant with "starters" and "main dishes." Instead, most restaurants (like bars) serve their dishes in portions called *raciones,* or the smaller half-servings, *media-raciones.* (The smaller tapas, and even tinier *pinchos,* are more commonly served at bars than at sit-down restaurants; for details, see later.) Enjoy this as an opportunity to explore the regional cuisine. Ordering *media-raciones* may cost a bit more per ounce, but you'll broaden your tasting experience. Two people can fill up on four *media-raciones.*

No matter where you eat, you'll encounter the cured ham called *jamón;* for details, see "Sampling *Jamón*" sidebar. The cheapest meal is simply a *bocadillo de jamón* (sandwich of ham on a baguette), sold virtually everywhere.

The Spanish diet—heavy on *jamón,* deep-fried foods (usually fried in olive oil), more *jamón,* weird seafood, and *jamón* again—can be brutal on Americans more accustomed to salads, fruit, and grains. A few perfectly good vegetarian and lighter options exist, but you'll have to seek them out. The secret to getting your veggies at restaurants is to order two courses, because the first course generally has a green option. Resist the cheese-and-ham appetizers and instead choose first-course menu items such as creamed vegetable soup, *parrillada de verduras* (sautéed vegetables), or

Sampling *Jamón*

The staple of Spanish cuisine, *jamón* (hah-MOHN) is prosciutto-like ham that's dry-cured and aged. It's generally

sliced thin (right off the hock) and served raw and cold. *Jamón* can be eaten straight, served in a *bocadillo* (baguette sandwich), or mixed into a wide variety of dishes. Bars proudly hang ham hocks from the rafters as part of the decor. *Jamón* is more than a food. It's a way of life. Spaniards treasure memories of Grandpa thinly carving a *jamón,* supported in a *jamonero* (ham-hock holder), during Christmas, just as we savor the turkey carving at Thanksgiving.

Like connoisseurs of fine wine, Spaniards debate the merits of different breeds of pigs, the pig's diet, and the quality of the curing. The two major types of ham are *jamón serrano,* from white pigs whose meat is cured in the *sierras* (mountains) of Spain, and the higher-quality *jamón ibérico*, made with the back legs of black-hooved pigs (a.k.a. *pata negra*, "black foot"). Originating in Spain, these "Iberian" black pigs are said to be fatter and happier (slaughtered much later than other pigs), thereby producing particularly fine ham. Another indication of quality is *de bellota,* which means the pig was raised on acorns *(bellotas). Jamón ibérico de bellota* is, to Spanish connoisseurs, as good as it gets. (Ham labeled *Jamón ibérico de recebeo* or *de cebo* is still good, but comes from pigs that are partly or entirely grain-fed rather than acorn-fed.) Additionally, there are regional variations of *jamón* indicating high quality, some of them officially controlled by EU authorities.

To sample this delicacy without the high price tag you'll find in bars and restaurants, go to the local market. Ask for 100 grams of top-quality ham (*cien gramos de jamón ibérico extra;* about €70/kilo, so your portion will run about €7), and enjoy it as a picnic with red wine and a baguette. To round out the perfect picnic, also pick up 100 grams of *salchichón* (salami), 100 grams of *chorizo* (spicy sausage), 100 grams of characteristic *manchego* or *cabrales* cheese, and some olives and pickles.

ensalada mixta. (Spaniards rarely eat only a salad, so salads tend to be small and simple—just iceberg lettuce, tomatoes, and maybe olives and tuna.) Main courses such as meats or fish are usually served with only a garnish, not a side of vegetables. Fruit isn't normally served for breakfast or as a snack—it's a dessert. After-meal dessert menus usually have a fruit option.

Survival Tips: To get by in Spain, either adapt yourself to the Spanish schedule and cuisine, or scramble to get edible food in between. Have an early light lunch at a bar. Many Spaniards have a *bocadillo* (baguette sandwich) at about 11:00 to bridge the gap between their coffee-and-roll breakfast and lunch at 14:00 (hence the popularity of fast-food *bocadillo* chains such as Pans & Company). Besides *bocadillos,* bars often have slices of *tortilla española* (potato omelet) and fresh-squeezed orange juice.

Then, either have your main meal at a restaurant at 15:00, followed by a light tapas snack for dinner later; or reverse it, having a tapas meal in the afternoon, followed by a late restaurant dinner. Either way, tapas in bars are the key (see "Tapas Bars," later).

Breakfast

Hotel breakfasts are generally handy, optional, and pricey (about €6). Start your day instead with a Spanish flair at a corner bar or at a colorful café near the town market hall (and pay just €2-3). Ask for the *desayunos* (breakfast special, usually only available until noon), which can include coffee, a roll (or sandwich), and juice for one price—much cheaper than ordering them separately. Sandwiches can either be on white bread (called "sandwich") or on a baguette *(bocadillo).*

A basic and standard savory breakfast item is *tostada con aceite,* toasted bread with olive oil (sometimes with tomato as well). For something more substantial, look for a *tortilla española*—an inexpensive potato omelet cooked fresh each morning and served in slices. In Andalucía, get your morning protein with the *mollete con jamón y aceite,* a soft bread roll with Spanish ham and finger-licking good olive oil (sometimes comes with cheese, too).

Those with a sweet tooth will find various sweet rolls (*bollos* or *bollería*)—the familiar croissant, *palmera* (palm-shaped, like a French *palmier* or "elephant ear"), *caracola* ("snail"-shaped, similar to a cinnamon roll), *napolitana* (rolled pastry, filled with chocolate—like a French *pain au chocolat*—or *crema* like an éclair), *rosquilla* (donut), and *bamba de nata* (cream puff). If you like a donut and coffee in American greasy-spoon joints, you must try the Spanish equivalent: greasy cigar-shaped fritters called *churros* (or the thicker *porras*) that you dip in warm chocolate pudding or your *café con leche.*

Here are some key words for breakfast:

café solo	shot of espresso
café con leche	espresso with hot milk
cortado	espresso with a little milk
té or *infusión*	tea
zumo	juice
zumo de naranja (natural)	orange juice (freshly squeezed)
pan (de molde/de barra)	bread (sandwich bread/baguette)

tostada con aceite (y tomate)	toasted bread with olive oil (and tomato)
sandwich (tostado)	white bread sandwich (toasted)
bocadillo	baguette sandwich
...*con jamón/queso/mixto*	...with ham/cheese/both
...*mixto con huevo*	...with ham and cheese topped by an over-easy egg
tortilla española	potato omelet
bollos, bollería	sweet pastry
croissant (a la plancha)	croissant (grilled and slathered with butter)

Restaurants

When restaurant-hunting, choose a spot filled with locals, not the place with the big neon signs boasting, "We Speak English and Accept Credit Cards." Venturing even a block or two off the main drag leads to higher-quality food for less than half the price of the tourist-oriented places. Locals eat better at lower-rent locales.

Don't expect "My name is Carlos and I'll be your waiter tonight" cheery service. Service is often *serio*—it's not friendly or unfriendly...just white-shirt-and-bow-tie proficient.

Although not fancy, Spanish cuisine comes with an endless variety of regional specialties. Two famous Spanish dishes are paella and gazpacho. Paella features saffron-flavored rice as a background for whatever the chef wants to mix in—seafood, sausage, chicken, peppers, and so on. While paella is heavy for your evening meal, jump (like everyone else in the bar) at the opportunity to snare a small plate of paella when it appears hot out of the kitchen in a tapas bar. Avoid the paella shown in pretty pictures on a separate menu—it's from the microwave. Gazpacho, an Andalusian specialty, is a chilled soup of tomatoes, bread chunks, and

spices—refreshing on a hot day and commonly available in the summer (sometimes served in a glass). Spanish cooks love garlic and olive oil—many dishes are soaked in both.

For a budget meal in a restaurant, try a *plato combinado* (combination plate), which usually includes portions of one or two main dishes, a vegetable, and bread for a reasonable price; or the *menú del día* (menu of the day, also known as *menú turístico*), a substantial three- to four-course meal that usually comes with a carafe of house wine.

Spanish Regional Specialties

Asturias *(a la asturiana):* Squeezed between the Picos de Europa mountains and the North Atlantic, Asturias combines seafood with hearty mountain grub—including *fabas* (giant, white, fava-like beans); the powerful, white, Roquefort-like *cabrales* cheese; and *sidra* (hard cider), used both for drinking and for cooking.

Galicia *(a la gallega):* The green, rainy northwest of Spain is known for its octopus (*pulpo*, specifically *pulpo a la gallega,* chopped up and dusted with paprika) and its many pork dishes (such as *orejas,* fried pig's ears). Other specialties include *pimientos de Padrón* (deep-fried, small green peppers) and Ribeiro wine, served in little ceramic bowls (to disguise its lack of clarity).

Andalucía: This region's food makes ample use of onion, tomatoes, and peppers, which combine deliciously in *sofrito,* a base for many dishes. The most famous Andalusian dish is the zesty cold tomato soup, gazpacho. Córdoba specializes in *pisto* (a ratatouille-like vegetable stew) and *salmorejo* (a creamier variation on gazpacho, often with ham and egg). From the Moorish influence, you'll find the Arabic-flavored *pastela*—a savory phyllo pie with poultry, seasoned with cinnamon.

Castilla y León *(castellano/leonese):* This high, central plateau of Spain was the home of vast flocks of sheep in the Middle Ages. This influence—in the form of lamb and the famous *manchego* (from La Mancha) sheep's cheese—persists today. Other popular Castilian and Leonese meats are sausages, *cochinillo asado* (roast suckling pig: 21 days of mother's milk, into the oven, and onto your plate—oh, Babe), and *cecina* (beef that's cured like *jamón serrano*).

Catalunya: Like its culture and language, Catalan food is a fusion of Spanish and French. Every meal starts with *pan con tomate* (or *pan amb tomaquet* in Catalan): a baguette rubbed with crushed tomatoes, garlic, and olive oil. Favorite dishes include *fideuà,* a thin, flavor-infused noodle served with seafood, and *arròs negre,* black rice cooked in squid ink.

Basque Country: This is arguably the culinary capital of Spain, with inviting *pintxos* (tapas) bars that display a stunning array of help-yourself goodies (just grab what you like from the platters at the bar, and pay on the honor system). Top dishes include *txangurro* (spider crab), *antxoas* (tasty anchovies), *marmitako* (tuna stew), *ttoro* (seafood stew), and *txakolí* (fresh white wine, poured from high up). *Cazuelas* are hot meal-size servings (like *raciones* in Spanish).

Sometimes the distinction between a bar and a restaurant blurs. Formal restaurants have a standard à la carte menu. Most eateries have a bar with some tables in the back or outside. And though tourists are often hot on tapas, these places are likely to serve larger *raciones* rather than bite-size tapas or restaurant entrées. Typically, couples or small groups order a few *raciones* and share the plates family-style. This can be very economical if you don't over-order.

Whether you go to a restaurant or bar, you won't be bothered by indoor smoke. Smoking has been banned in closed public spaces.

Typical Desserts

In Spain, desserts are often an afterthought. Here are a few items you may see on Spanish menus:

arroz con leche	rice pudding
brazo de gitano	sponge cake filled with butter cream; literally "gypsy's arm"
flan de huevo	flan (crème caramel)
fruta de la estación	fruit in season
queso	cheese
helados (variados)	ice cream (various flavors)
torrijas	sweet fritters

Tapas Bars

You can eat well any time of day in tapas bars. Tapas are small portions of seafood, salads, meat-filled pastries, deep-fried tasties, and on and on.

Tapas typically cost about €1.50-2 apiece. Most bars push larger portions called *raciones* (dinner plate-sized) rather than smaller tapas (saucer-sized). Ask for the smaller tapas portions or a *media-ración* (listed as ½ *ración* on a menu)—though some bars simply don't serve anything smaller than a *ración*. There are happy exceptions: A small, free tapa may be included with your drink in some cities, including Madrid, León, Santiago de Compostela, Salamanca, Granada, and Nerja. Order your drink first to get the freebie; then order additional food as you like.

Eating and drinking at a bar is usually cheapest if you sit or stand at the counter *(barra)*. You may pay a little more to eat sitting at a table (*mesa* or *salón*) and still more for an outdoor table

INTRODUCTION

Tapas Menu Decoder

You can often just point to what you want on the menu, say *por favor,* and get your food, but these words will help.

Tapas Terms

pincho	bite-size portion
pinchito	tiny pincho
tapa	snack-size portion
½ *ración* (*media-ración*)	half portion
ración	full portion
surtido (*de*)	assortment (of)
frito	fried
a la plancha	grilled (on a flat-top griddle)
a la parrilla	barbecued
brocheta	shish kebab (on a stick)
¿Cuánto cuesta una tapa?	How much per tapa?

Sandwich Words

bocadillo	baguette sandwich, cheap and basic
canapé	tiny open-faced sandwich
flauta	sandwich made with flute-thin baguette
montadito	tapa "mounted" on bread
pulga, pulguita, pepito	a small, closed baguette sandwich
sandwich	American-style sandwich on square bread

Typical Tapas

aceitunas	olives
albóndigas	spiced meatballs with sauce
almejas (a la marinera)	clams (in paprika sauce)
almendras	almonds (usually fried)
anchoas	cured anchovies (salted or in oil)
atún	tuna
bacalao	cod

banderilla	skewer of spicy, pickled veggies
bombas	fried meat-and-potato ball
boquerones (en vinagre)	fresh anchovies (marinated in olive oil, vinegar, and garlic)
cabrillas	snails
calamares fritos	fried squid rings
callos	tripe stew
caracoles	tree snails (May-Sept)
cazón en adobo	salty marinated dogfish
champiñones	mushrooms
charcutería	cured meats
chorizo	spicy sausage
croquetas	croquettes—breaded and fried béchamel with fillings such as ham
empanadillas	pastries stuffed with meat or seafood
ensaladilla Rusa	potato salad with lots of mayo, peas, and carrots
espinacas (con garbanzos)	spinach (with garbanzo beans)
gambas	shrimp
a la plancha / al ajillo	grilled / with garlic
cáscara / peladas	shell / peeled
gazpacho	cold tomato soup
guiso	stew
jamón	cured ham (like prosciutto); for more on *jamón*, see page 29
judías (verdes)	(green) beans
lomo	pork tenderloin
mejillones	mussels
merluza	hake (whitefish)
morcilla	blood sausage
morros	pig snout
paella	saffron rice dish with seafood and meat
pan	bread

(continued on next page)

Tapas Menu Decoder
(continued from previous page)

patatas bravas	fried potatoes with spicy tomato sauce
pescaditos fritos	assortment of fried little fish
picos	little breadsticks
pimiento (relleno)	pepper (stuffed)
pimientos de Padrón	lightly fried small green peppers, only a few of which are jalapeño-hot
pinchos morunos	skewer of spicy lamb or pork
pisto	mixed sautéed vegetables
pollo (alioli)	chicken (with garlic and olive oil sauce)
pulpo	octopus
queso	cheese
queso manchego	classic Spanish sheep-milk cheese
rabas	squid tentacles
rabo de toro	bull's-tail stew (fatty and oh so tender)
revuelto (de setas)	scrambled eggs (with wild mushrooms)
salchichón	salami-like sausage
sardinas	sardines
sesos	lamb brains
tabla serrana	hearty plate of meat and cheese
tortilla española	potato omelet
tortilla de jamón / queso	potato omelet with ham / cheese
tortillitas de camarones	shrimp fritters (Andalucía)
variado fritos	mix of various fried fish

(terraza). Traditionally, tapas are served at the bar, and *raciones* (and *media-raciones*) are served at tables, where food is shared "family style."

Locate the price list (often posted in fine type on a wall somewhere) to know the menu options and price tiers. (It's bad form to order food at the bar, then take it to a table. If you're standing and a table opens up, it's OK to move as long as you signal to the waiter; anything else you order will be charged at the higher *mesa/ salón* price.) In the right place, a quiet snack and drink on a terrace on the town square is well worth the extra charge. But the cheapest seats sometimes get the best show. Sit at the bar and study your bartender—he's an artist.

These bars can be extremely crowded with locals, and non-Spanish speakers can find it hard to get in an order—or even find a place to sit. You'll have more room, and get better service, by showing up before the local crowd. Restaurants generally serve lunch from 13:00 to 16:00 and dinner from 20:00 until very late; try to be there by 13:30 for lunch, and 20:30-21:00 for dinner. (As Spaniards don't start lunch until about 14:00 and dinner until after 21:00, it's not too hard to avoid the crush.) For less competition at the bar, go on Monday and Tuesday.

I'll be blunt: The authentic tapas experience can be intimidating: elbowing up to a bar crowded with pushy Spaniards, squinting at a hand-scrawled monolingual chalkboard menu, and trying to communicate with the brusque bartender. Your bartender isn't a "waiter," in any sense. He's not there to patiently help you sort through your options—he wants to take your order, period. Hang back and observe before ordering. Read the posted or printed menu (likely in Spanish). Use the "Tapas Menu Decoder" starting on page 34 to sort through your options. You can also look around to see what appeals on other patrons' plates. Sometimes a few of the selections are displayed under glass at the counter. Handwritten signs that start out *"Hay"* mean "Today we have," as in *"Hay caracoles"* ("Today we have snails").

When you're ready to order, be assertive or you'll never be served. *Por favor* (please) grabs the guy's attention. Then quickly rattle off what you'd like (pointing to other people's food if necessary). Don't worry about paying until you're ready to leave (he's keeping track of your tab). To get the bill, ask: *"¿La cuenta?"*

In the Basque region, things are much more user-friendly but often even more crowded: Bars typically lay out an enticing array of platters piled with tapas. Just point to (or simply grab) what-

ever looks good. To find this type of bar elsewhere in Spain (most commonly in Barcelona), look for a place with *vasca* or *euskal* (both mean "Basque") in the name.

Chasing down a particular bar for tapas nearly defeats the purpose and spirit of tapas—they are impromptu. Just drop in at any lively place. I look for the noisy spots with piles of napkins and food debris on the floor (it's considered unsanitary to put trash back on the bar; go local and toss your napkins

Spanish Drinking Words

These words will help quench your thirst. *¡Salud!* (Cheers!)

Wine and Spirits

vino	wine
rojo / blanco	red / white
cava	sparkling wine (Spanish champagne)
un tinto / un blanco	small glass of house red / white wine
un crianza	glass of nicely aged, quality wine
un reserva / gran reserva	much higher-quality (and more expensive) wine
chato	small glass of house wine
tinto de verano	red wine with lemonade (similar to sangria)
seco / dulce	dry / sweet
mucho cuerpo	full-bodied
afrutado	fruity
vermú	vermouth
jerez	sherry (fortified wine from Jerez)
amontillado, fino, manzanilla	rich, dry sherries

on the floor, too), lots of customers, and the TV blaring. Popular television-viewing includes bullfights and soccer games, American sitcoms, and Spanish interpretations of soaps and silly game shows (you'll see Vanna Blanco).

Get a fun, inexpensive sampler plate. Ask for *una tabla de canapés variados* to get a plate of various little open-faced sandwiches. Or ask for a *surtido de* (an assortment of) *charcutería* (a mixed plate of meat) or *queso* (cheese). *Un surtido de jamón y queso* means a plate of different hams and cheeses. Order bread and two glasses of red wine on the right square, and you've got a romantic (and €10) dinner for two.

Spanish Drinks

Spain is one of the world's leading producers of grapes, and that means lots of excellent wine: both red *(tinto)* and white *(blanco)*. Major wine regions include Valdepeñas (both red and white

Beer

cerveza	beer
caña	small glass of draft beer
clara con limón / con casera	shandy—small beer with lemonade / with soda
doble, tubo	tall glass of beer
sidra	dry cider that's a bit more alcoholic than beer

Nonalcoholic

agua con / sin gas	water with / without bubbles
un vaso de agua (del grifo)	glass of tap water
una jarra de agua	pitcher of tap water
refresco	soft drink (common brands are Coca-Cola, Fanta—*limón* or *naranja*, and Schweppes—*limón* or *tónica*)
mosto	nonalcoholic grape juice, red or white, served wherever wine is served
una sin	nonalcoholic beer

wines made in Don Quixote country south of Toledo); Penedès (cabernet-style wines from near Barcelona); Rioja (spicy, lighter reds from the tempranillo grape, from the high plains of northern Spain); and Ribera del Duero (reds from northwest of Madrid). For a basic glass of red wine, you can order *un tinto*. But for quality wine, ask for *un crianza* (old), *un reserva* (older), or *un gran reserva* (oldest). The single most important tip for good, economical wine drinking is to ask for *un crianza*—for little or no extra money than a basic *tinto*, you'll get a quality, aged wine.

Sherry, a fortified wine from the Jerez region, is a shock to the taste buds if you're expecting a sweet dessert drink. Named for its city of origin, *jerez* ranges from dry *(fino)* to sweet *(dulce)*—

INTRODUCTION

> # How Was Your Trip?
>
> Were your travels fun, smooth, and meaningful? If you'd like to share your tips, concerns, and discoveries, please fill out the survey at www.ricksteves.com/feedback. I value your feedback. Thanks in advance—it helps a lot.

Spaniards drink the *fino* and export the *dulce*. *Cava* is Spain's answer to champagne. Sangria (a punch of red wine mixed with fruit slices) is refreshing and popular with tourists; Spaniards generally prefer *tinto de verano* (wine with lemonade).

Most places just have the standard local beer—a light lager—on tap. The brand is determined by regional pride, rather than quality. (For instance, Cruzcampo—which is very light so that hot, thirsty drinkers can consume more—is big in the south, whereas San Miguel is big in the north.) To get a small draft beer, ask for a *caña*. Nonalcoholic beer is quite popular and often on tap. If you say *"una sin,"* which means "one without," it's assumed you want a nonalcoholic beer. While *sin* comes with less than 1 percent alcohol, you can get totally alcohol-free brew by asking for *"zero punto zero"* (0.0). If you'd prefer a grape juice alternative to wine, ask for *mosto* (it comes in red or white).

Spain's bars often serve fresh-squeezed orange juice *(zumo de naranja natural).* For something completely different, try *horchata*, a sweet, milky beverage extracted from *chufa* tubers (a.k.a. tiger-nuts or earth almonds). If ordering mineral water in a restaurant, request a *botella grande de agua* (big bottle). They push the more profitable small bottles. For a glass of tap water, specify *un vaso de agua del grifo*. The waiter may counter with *"Embotellada?"*— "Bottled?"—hoping to sell you something. Be strong and insist on tap water *(del grifo)*, and you'll get it.

One challenge for tapas bar-hoppers is that you'll generally order a drink in each place. If you're visiting several different bars (as you should), this can add up. If you'd like to drink a lot without getting drunk, remember a few key terms: *caña* (small beer), *clara con limón* (small beer with lemonade) or *con casera* (with soda), *tinto de verano* (red wine with soda and often with a slice of lemon), and *una sin* (nonalcoholic beer, pronounced "seen").

Traveling as a Temporary Local

We travel all the way to Spain to enjoy differences—to become temporary locals. You'll experience frustrations. Certain truths that we find "God-given" or "self-evident," such as cold beer, ice in drinks, bottomless cups of coffee, and bigger being better, are suddenly not so true. One of the benefits of travel is the eye-opening realization that there are logical, civil, and even better alternatives. A willingness to go local ensures that you'll enjoy a full dose of Spanish hospitality.

Europeans generally like Americans. But if there is a negative aspect to the image the Spanish have of Americans, it's that we are loud, wasteful, ethnocentric, too informal (which can seem disrespectful), and a bit naive.

While Spaniards look bemusedly at some of our Yankee excesses—and worriedly at others—they nearly always afford us individual travelers all the warmth we deserve.

Judging from all the happy feedback I receive from travelers who have used this book, it's safe to assume you'll enjoy a great, affordable vacation—with the finesse of an independent, experienced traveler.

Thanks, and *buen viaje!*

Back Door Travel Philosophy
From *Rick Steves' Europe Through the Back Door*

Travel is intensified living—maximum thrills per minute and one of the last great sources of legal adventure. Travel is freedom. It's recess, and we need it.

Experiencing the real Europe requires catching it by surprise, going casual..."Through the Back Door."

Affording travel is a matter of priorities. (Make do with the old car.) You can eat and sleep—simply, safely, and enjoyably—anywhere in Europe for $120 a day plus transportation costs. In many ways, spending more money only builds a thicker wall between you and what you traveled so far to see. Europe is a cultural carnival, and time after time, you'll find that its best acts are free and the best seats are the cheap ones.

A tight budget forces you to travel close to the ground, meeting and communicating with the people. Never sacrifice sleep, nutrition, safety, or cleanliness to save money. Simply enjoy the local-style alternatives to expensive hotels and restaurants.

Connecting with people carbonates your experience. Extroverts have more fun. If your trip is low on magic moments, kick yourself and make things happen. If you don't enjoy a place, maybe you don't know enough about it. Seek the truth. Recognize tourist traps. Give a culture the benefit of your open mind. See things as different, but not better or worse. Any culture has plenty to share.

Of course, travel, like the world, is a series of hills and valleys. Be fanatically positive and militantly optimistic. If something's not to your liking, change your liking.

Travel can make you a happier American, as well as a citizen of the world. Our Earth is home to seven billion equally precious people. It's humbling to travel and find that other people don't have the "American Dream"—they have their own dreams. Europeans like us, but with all due respect, they wouldn't trade passports.

Thoughtful travel engages us with the world. In tough economic times, it reminds us what is truly important. By broadening perspectives, travel teaches new ways to measure quality of life.

Globetrotting destroys ethnocentricity, helping us understand and appreciate other cultures. Rather than fear the diversity on this planet, celebrate it. Among your most prized souvenirs will be the strands of different cultures you choose to knit into your own character. The world is a cultural yarn shop, and Back Door travelers are weaving the ultimate tapestry. Join in!

BARCELONA

Barcelona may be Spain's second city, but it's undoubtedly the first city of the proud and distinct region of Catalunya. Catalan flags wave side by side with the Spanish flag, and locals, while fluent in both languages, stubbornly insist on speaking Catalan first. This lively culture is on an unstoppable roll in Spain's most cosmopolitan and European corner.

Barcelona bubbles with life in its narrow Barri Gòtic alleys, along the pedestrian boulevard called the Ramblas, in the funky bohemian quarter of El Born, and throughout the chic, grid-planned new part of town called the Eixample. Its Old City is made for seeing on foot, full of winding lanes that emerge into secluded squares dotted with palm trees and ringed with cafés and boutiques. The waterfront bristles with life, overlooked by the park-like setting of Montjuïc. Everywhere you go, you'll find the city's architecture to be colorful, playful, and unique. Rows of symmetrical ironwork balconies are punctuated with fanciful details: bay windows, turrets, painted tiles, hanging lanterns, flower boxes, and carved reliefs.

Barcelona is full of history. You'll see Roman ruins, a medieval cathedral, twisty Gothic lanes, and traces of Columbus and the sea trade. As the Age of Exploration steered trade from the Mediterranean to the Atlantic, things got pretty quiet here (kept carefully under the thumb of Spanish rulers). But by the late 19th century, the city had boomed into an industrial powerhouse, and it was incubating a new artistic style—Modernism. Pablo Picasso lived in Barcelona as a teenager, right as he was on the verge of reinventing painting; his legacy is today's Picasso Museum. Catalan architects including Antoni Gaudí, Lluís Domènech

BARCELONA

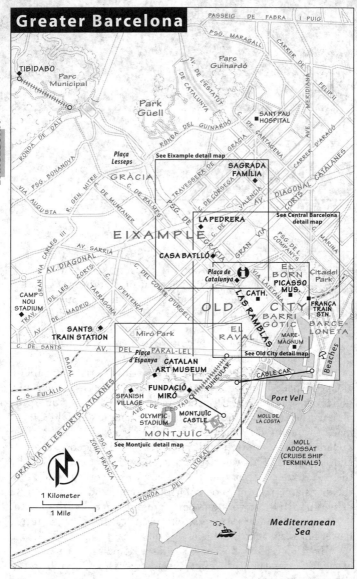

Greater Barcelona

PASSEIG DE FABRA I PUIG

PSG. MARAGALL

CARRER DE

FELIP II

MERIDIANA

TIBIDABO
Parc Municipal

AV. DE L'ESTATUT DE CATALUNYA

Parc Guinardó

Park Güell

CARRER D'ARAGO

CORTS CATALANES

RONDA DEL GUINARDÓ

C. DE CARTAGENA

SANT PAU HOSPITAL

Plaça Lessops

See Eixample detail map

SAGRADA FAMÍLIA

GRÀCIA

TRAVESSERA DE

C. DE CORSEGA

VALÈNCIA

DIAGONAL

AV.

RONDA DE DALT

VIA PSG. BONANOVA

VIA AUGUSTA

R. GEN. MITRE

C. DE BALMES

PSG. DE GRACIA

LA PEDRERA

See Central Barcelona detail map

EIXAMPLE

C. DE MUNTANER

CASA BATLLÓ

GRAN VIA

PSG. DE L. COMPANYS

MARINA

AV. SARRIA

Plaça de Catalunya

EL BORN

Citadel Park

GRAN VIA CARLES III

AV. DIAGONAL

C. DEL COMTE D'URGELL

PICASSO MUS.

CAMP NOU STADIUM

DE LES CORTS

C. D'ENTENCA

CATH.

FRANÇA TRAIN STN.

TARRAGONA

AV. DE MADRID

OLD CITY

LAS RAMBLAS

BARRI GÒTIC

BARCE-LONETA

SANTS TRAIN STATION

Miró Park

EL RAVAL

MARE-MAGNUM

C. DE SANTS

AV.

DEL PARAL-LEL

See Old City detail map

Beaches

C. S. EULÀLIA

Plaça d'Espanya

CATALAN ART MUSEUM

PUNICULAR

CABLE CAR

Port Vell

GRAN VIA DE LES CORTS CATALANES

SPANISH VILLAGE

FUNDACIÓ MIRÓ

AV. DE

MOLL DE LA COSTA

OLYMPIC STADIUM

MONTJUÏC CASTLE

MONTJUÏC

MOLL ADOSSAT (CRUISE SHIP TERMINALS)

PSG. DE LA ZONA FRANCA

See Montjuïc detail map

RONDA DEL LITORAL

1 Kilometer

1 Mile

Mediterranean Sea

i Montaner, and Josep Puig i Cadafalch forged the Modernista style and remade the city's skyline with curvy fantasy buildings—culminating in Gaudí's over-the-top Sagrada Família, a church still under construction. Salvador Dalí and Joan Miró join the long list of world-changing 20th-century artists with ties to this city. Meanwhile, world's fairs in 1888 and 1929 helped spruce up the city, and in 1992, Barcelona hosted the Summer Olympics—an event that once again re-energized this dynamic city and left it with a wealth of attractive public areas and great sights.

Today's Barcelona is as vibrant as ever. Locals still join hands and dance the everyone's-welcome *sardana* in front of the cathedral every weekend. Neighborhood festivals jam the events calendar. The cafés are filled by day, and people crowd the streets at night, pausing to fortify themselves with a perfectly composed bite of seafood and a drink at a tapas bar. Every hidden back lane provides shelter for an array of inviting shops. If you're in the mood to surrender to a city's charms, let it be in Barcelona.

Planning Your Time

Barcelona is easily worth two days, and no one would regret having a third day (or more). If you can spare only one full day for the city, it will be a scramble, but one you'll never forget.

When planning your time, be aware that many top sights are closed on Monday—making them especially crowded on Tuesday and Sunday (for a rundown of hours, see "At a Glance" on page 86). Some of Barcelona's major sights can have long lines; it's smart to make advance reservations (for tips, see page 55). If you're here on a weekend, dance the *sardana* (page 89).

Barcelona in 1 Day

For a relaxing day, stroll the Ramblas, see the Sagrada Família, add the Picasso Museum if you're a fan, and have dinner in the trendy El Born district.

To cram in much more, try the following ambitious but doable plan. You'll have to rush through the big sights (cathedral, Picasso Museum, Sagrada Família), having just enough time to visit each one but not to linger.

9:00   From Plaça de Catalunya (with its handy TI), follow my "Barri Gòtic Walk" and tour the cathedral.

11:00   Circle back to Plaça de Catalunya and follow my self-guided "Ramblas Ramble" to the harborfront.

12:30   Walk along the harborfront to El Born, grabbing a quick lunch and doing a little shopping.

14:00   Tour the Picasso Museum.

16:00   Take a taxi or the Metro to the Sagrada Família.

18:00   Taxi, bus, or walk to Passeig de Gràcia in the Eixample to see the exteriors of Gaudí's La Pedrera and the Block of Discord. Stroll back down toward Plaça de Catalunya.

19:00   If your energy is holding out, wander back into the Barri Gòtic at prime paseo time. Enjoy an early tapas dinner along the way, or a restaurant dinner later in the Old City.

Barcelona in 2, 3, or 4 Days

To better sample the city's ample charm, spread your visit over several days. With at least two days, divide and conquer the town geographically: Spend one day in the Old City (Ramblas, Barri Gòtic/cathedral area, Picasso Museum/El Born) and another on the Eixample and Gaudí sights (La Pedrera, Sagrada Família, Park Güell). Do Montjuïc on whichever day you're not exhausted (if any)—or, better yet, on a third day.

With extra time on any day, consider taking a hop-on, hop-off bus tour for a sightseeing overview (for instance, the Tourist Bus blue route links most Gaudí sights, and could work well on Day 2).

Day 1 (Old City)

9:00	Follow my "Barri Gòtic Walk" and tour the cathedral.
11:00	Head back to the Ramblas, then follow my "Ramblas Ramble" (touring Palau Güell if you're a Gaudí fan) down to the harborfront.
13:00	Grab lunch in El Born or the Barri Gòtic.
14:00	Tour the Palace of Catalan Music in El Born (advance reservation required).
15:00	Explore El Born, and tour the Picasso Museum.
Evening	Take your pick of activities: Assemble a tapas dinner by hopping from bar to bar in El Born, and take "A Short, Sweet Walk" (page 166) for dessert. (Other good neighborhoods for tapas are the classy Eixample or touristy Barri Gòtic.) Or wait to dine at a restaurant when locals do, around 21:00. Take in a performance of Spanish guitar, flamenco, or jazz, or a concert in a fancy setting (such as La Pedrera or the Palace of Catalan Music). Zip up to Montjuïc for the sunset and a drink (on the Catalan Art Museum's terrace), then head down to the illuminated Magic Fountains (Fri-Sat, plus Thu and Sun in summer).

Day 2 (Modernisme)

9:00	Spend the morning in the Eixample, and tour La Pedrera and/or Casa Batlló.
12:00	Grab an early lunch in the Eixample, then take a taxi or bus to the Sagrada Família.
14:00	Taxi or bus to Park Güell (for more Gaudí), or take a bus to Montjuïc and the 1929 World Expo Fairgrounds (if you're not going to Montjuïc on Day 3).
Evening	See options for Day 1, above.

Day 3 (Montjuïc)
Tour Montjuïc from top to bottom, stopping at sights of interest. The top priorities for most visitors are the Catalan Art Museum, CaixaForum, and Fundació Joan Miró. If the weather is good, see Montjuïc in the morning and spend the afternoon on the beach in Barceloneta. Find your favorite *chiringuito* (beach bar) for dinner.

Day 4 (Day Trip)
Several tempting day trips await nearby, including Montserrat, Sitges, and the Salvador Dalí sights at Figueres and Cadaqués (see the next chapter).

Connecting with the Rest of Spain
Located in the far northeast corner of Spain, Barcelona makes a good first or last stop for your trip. With the high-speed AVE train, Barcelona is three hours away from Madrid—faster and more comfortable than flying. Or you could sandwich Barcelona between flights. From the US, it's as easy to fly into Barcelona as it is to land in Madrid, Lisbon, or Paris. Those who plan on renting a car at some point during their trip can start here first, take the train or fly to Madrid, and sightsee Madrid and Toledo, all before picking up their car—cleverly saving on several days' worth of rental fees.

Orientation to Barcelona

Like Los Angeles, Barcelona is a basically flat city that sprawls out under the sun between the sea and the mountains. It's huge

(1.6 million people, with about 5 million people in greater Barcelona), but travelers need only focus on four areas: the Old City, the harbor/Barceloneta, the Eixample, and Montjuïc.

A large square, **Plaça de Catalunya,** sits at the center of Barcelona, dividing the older and newer parts of town. Below Plaça de Catalunya is the Old City, with the boulevard called the Ramblas running down to the harbor. Above Plaça de Catalunya is the modern residential area called the Eixample. The Montjuïc hill overlooks the harbor. Outside the Old City, Barcelona's sights are widely scattered, but with a map and a willingness to figure out the sleek Metro system (or a few euros for taxis), all is manageable.

Here are more details per neighborhood:

Old City (Ciutat Vella): This is the compact core of

BARCELONA

Barcelona Neighborhood Overview

Barcelona—ideal for strolling, shopping, and people-watching—where you'll probably spend most of your time. It's a labyrinth of narrow streets that once were confined by the medieval walls. The lively pedestrian drag called the **Ramblas**—one of Europe's most entertaining streets—runs through the heart of the Old City from Plaça de Catalunya down to the harbor. The Old City is divided into thirds by the Ramblas and another major thoroughfare, Via Laietana. Between the Ramblas and Via Laietana is the characteristic **Barri Gòtic** (BAH-ree GOH-teek, Gothic Quarter), with the cathedral as its navel. Locals call it simply "El Gòtic" for short. To the east of Via Laietana is the trendy **El Born** district (a.k.a. "La Ribera"), a shopping, dining, and nightlife mecca centered on the Picasso Museum and the Church of Santa Maria del Mar. To the west of the Ramblas is the **Raval** (rah-VAHL), enlivened by its university and modern-art museum. The Raval is of least interest to tourists (and, in fact, some parts of it are quite seedy and should be avoided).

Harborfront: The old harbor, **Port Vell,** gleams with landmark monuments and new developments. A pedestrian bridge links the Ramblas with the modern Maremagnum shopping/aquarium/entertainment complex. On the peninsula across the quaint sailboat harbor is **Barceloneta,** a traditional fishing neighborhood with gritty charm and some good seafood restaurants. Beyond Barceloneta, a gorgeous man-made **beach** several miles long leads east to the commercial and convention district called the **Fòrum.**

Daily Reminder

Sunday: Most sights are open, but the Boqueria and Santa Caterina markets are closed. Some sights close early today, including Fundació Joan Miró, Olympic and Sports Museum, and Camp Nou Stadium (all close at 14:30), along with the Catalan Art Museum and Chocolate Museum (both close at 15:00). Informal performances of the *sardana* national dance take place in front of the cathedral at noon (none in Aug). Some museums are free at certain times: Catalan Art Museum and Palau Güell (free on first Sun of month); Picasso Museum and Barcelona History Museum (free on first Sun of month plus other Sun from 15:00); and the Frederic Marès Museum (free every Sun from 15:00). The Magic Fountains come alive on summer evenings (May-Sept).

Monday: Many sights are closed, including the Picasso Museum, Catalan Art Museum, Palau Güell, Barcelona History Museum, *Santa Eulàlia* schooner (part of the Maritime Museum), Fundació Joan Miró, Frederic Marès Museum, Shoe Museum, and Olympic and Sports Museum. But most major Gaudí sights are open today, including the Sagrada Família, La Pedrera, Park Güell, and Casa Batlló.

Tuesday: All major sights are open.

Wednesday: All major sights are open. The CaixaForum may be open until 23:00 in July and August.

Thursday: All major sights are open. Fundació Joan Miró is open until 21:30 year-round, and the Magic Fountains spout on summer evenings (May-Sept).

Friday: All major sights are open. The Magic Fountains light up Montjuïc year-round.

Saturday: All major sights are open. Barcelonans dance the *sardana* most Saturdays at 18:00, and the Magic Fountains dance all year.

Late-Hours Sightseeing: Sights with **year-round** evening hours (19:30 or later) include the Picasso Museum, Park Güell, CaixaForum, Columbus Monument, Cathedral of Barcelona, CaixaForum, Las Arenas, Church of Santa Maria del Mar, and Maritime Museum (only temporary exhibits open while permanent exhibits undergo restoration, likely until the fall of 2014). Sights offering later hours only in **peak season** (roughly April-Sept) include the Sagrada Família, La Pedrera, Palau Güell, Fundació Joan Miró, Castle of Montjuïc, and Gaudí House Museum. The Tourist Bus runs until 20:00 every day in summer.

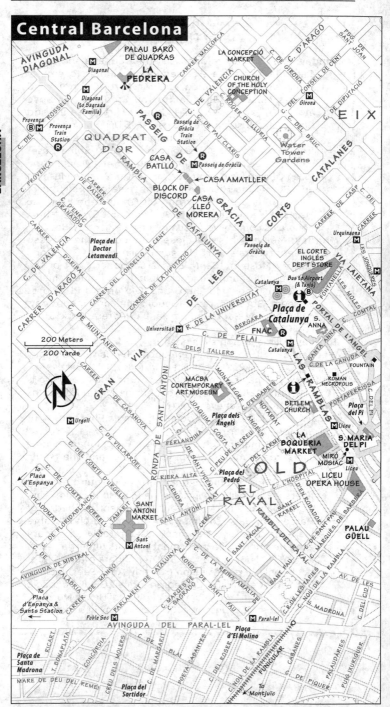

Central Barcelona

BARCELONA

BARCELONA

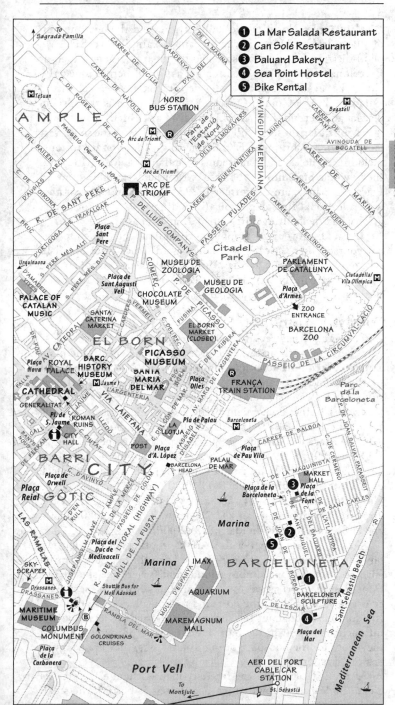

1. La Mar Salada Restaurant
2. Can Solé Restaurant
3. Baluard Bakery
4. Sea Point Hostel
5. Bike Rental

Eixample: North of the Old City, beyond the bustling hub of Plaça de Catalunya, is the elegant Eixample (eye-SHAM-plah) district, its grid plan softened by cut-off corners. Much of Barcelona's Modernista architecture is found here—especially along the swanky artery Passeig de Gràcia, an area called the **Quadrat d'Or** ("Golden Quarter"). To the north is the **Gràcia** district and beyond that, Antoni Gaudí's **Park Güell.**

Montjuïc: The large hill overlooking the city to the southwest is Montjuïc (mohn-jew-EEK), home to a variety of attractions, including some excellent museums (Catalan Art, Joan Miró) and the Olympic Stadium. At the base of Montjuïc, stretching toward Plaça d'Espanya, are the former **1929 World Expo Fairgrounds,** with additional fine attractions (including the CaixaForum art gallery and the bullring-turned-mall, Las Arenas).

Apart from your geographical orientation, you'll need to orient yourself linguistically to a language distinct from Spanish. Although Spanish ("Castilian"/*castellano*) is widely spoken, the native tongue in this region is Catalan—nearly as different from Spanish as Italian (see the sidebar on page 62).

Tourist Information

Barcelona's TI has several branches (central tel. 932-853-834, www.barcelonaturisme.cat). The primary one is beneath the main square, **Plaça de Catalunya** (daily 8:30-20:30, entrance along southeast side of square, across from El Corte Inglés department store—look for red sign and take stairs down, tel. 932-853-832).

Several other convenient branches include a kiosk near the top of the **Ramblas** (daily 8:30-20:30, at #115, mobile 618-783-479); on **Plaça de Sant Jaume,** just south of the cathedral (Mon-Fri 8:30-20:00, Sat 9:00-19:00, Sun 9:00-14:00, in the Barcelona City Hall at Ciutat 2); near the **cathedral,** in the Catalan College of Architects building (daily 9:00-19:00); inside the base of the **Columbus Monument** at the harbor (daily 8:30-19:30); at the **airport,** in both terminals 1 and 2B (both open daily 8:30-20:30); and at **Sants train station** (daily 8:00-20:00).

You'll also find smaller info kiosks in other touristy locales: on **Plaça d'Espanya,** in the park across from the **Sagrada Família** entrance, near the **Columbus Monument** (where the shuttle bus from the cruise port arrives), at the **Nord bus station,** at the various **cruise terminals** along the port, and two on **Plaça de Catalunya.** In addition, throughout the summer, young red-jacketed tourist-info helpers appear in the most touristy parts of town; although they work for the hop-on, hop-off Tourist Bus, they are happy to answer questions.

At any TI, pick up the free city map (although the free El Corte Inglés map provided by most hotels is better), the small

Metro map, the monthly *Barcelona Planning.com* guidebook (with basic tips on sightseeing, shopping, events, and restaurants), and the quarterly *See Barcelona* guide (with more in-depth practical information on museums and a neighborhood-by-neighborhood sightseeing rundown). The monthly *Time Out BCN Guide* offers a thorough but concise day-by-day list of events. And the monthly *Barcelona Metropolitan* magazine has timely and substantial coverage of local topics and events. All of these are free.

The TI is a handy place to buy tickets for the Tourist Bus (described later, under "Getting Around Barcelona") or for the TI-run walking tours (described later, under "Tours in Barcelona"). All of the TIs (except the kiosks) provide a room-booking service. They also sell tickets to FC Barcelona soccer games.

Modernisme Route: Inside the Plaça de Catalunya TI is the privately run **Ruta del Modernisme** desk, which gives out a handy route map showing all 116 Modernista buildings and offers a sightseeing discount package (€12 for a great guidebook and 20-50-percent discounts to many Modernista sights—worthwhile if going beyond the biggies I cover in depth; for €18 you'll also get a guidebook to Modernista bars and restaurants; www.rutadelmodernisme.com).

Regional Catalunya TI: The all-Catalunya TI can help with travel and sightseeing tips for the entire region, and even Madrid (Mon-Sat 10:00-19:00, Sun 10:00-14:00, on Plaça de Joan Carlos I, at the intersection of Passeig de Gràcia and Diagonal at Passeig de Gràcia 107, tel. 932-388-091, www.catalunya.com).

Sightseeing Passes: The **Articket BCN** ticket covers admission to six art museums and their temporary exhibits, letting you skip the ticket-buying lines. Sights include the recommended Picasso Museum, Catalan Art Museum, and Fundació Joan Miró (€30, valid for three months; sold at Plaça de Catalunya, Plaça de Sant Jaume, and Sants train station TIs and at participating museums; www.articketbcn.org). If you're planning to go to three or more of the museums, this ticket will save you money and time, especially at sights prone to long lines, such as the Picasso Museum. Just show your Articket BCN (to the ticket taker, at the info desk, or at the group entrance), and you'll get your entrance ticket pronto.

On the other hand, I'd skip the **Barcelona Card,** which covers public transportation (buses, Metro, Montjuïc funicular, and *golondrinas* harbor tour) and includes free admission to mostly minor sights and small discounts on many major sights (€37/2 days, €47/3 days, €56/4 days, €62/5 days, sold at TIs and El Corte Inglés department stores, discounted if you buy online at www.barcelonaturisme.com).

BARCELONA

Arrival in Barcelona

For more information on getting to or from Barcelona by train, plane, bus, or cruise ship, see "Barcelona Connections," at the end of this chapter.

By Train: Virtually all trains end up at Barcelona's **Sants train station,** west of the Old City (for details on getting downtown from Sants Station, see page 172). AVE trains from Madrid go only to Sants Station and the **Sagrera Station,** far to the northeast. But many other trains also pass through other stations en route, such as **França Station** (between the El Born and Barceloneta neighborhoods), or the downtown **Passeig de Gràcia** or **Plaça de Catalunya** stations (which are also Metro stops—and very close to most of my recommended hotels). Figure out which stations your train stops at (ask the conductor), and get off at the one most convenient to your hotel.

By Plane: Most international flights arrive at **El Prat de Llobregat Airport,** eight miles southwest of town. Some budget airlines, including Ryanair, fly into **Girona-Costa Brava Airport,** located 60 miles north of Barcelona near Girona. See page 174 for details on connecting either of these airports to central Barcelona.

By Car: Barcelona's parking fees are outrageously expensive (the lot behind La Boqueria market charges upwards of €25/day). You won't need a car in Barcelona, because the taxis and public transportation are so good.

Helpful Hints

Theft and Scam Alert: You're more likely to be pickpocketed here—especially on the Ramblas—than about anywhere else in Europe. Most crime is nonviolent, but muggings do occur. Leave valuables in your hotel and wear a money belt.

Street scams are easy to avoid if you recognize them. Most common is the too-friendly local who tries to engage you in conversation by asking for the time or whether you speak English. If a super-friendly man acts drunk and wants to dance because his soccer team just won, he's a pickpocket. Beware of thieves posing as lost tourists who ask for your help. Don't fall for any street-gambling shell games—you can be sure you'll lose if you play. Also beware of groups of women aggressively selling carnations, people offering to clean off a stain from your shirt, and people picking things up in front of you on escalators. If you stop for any commotion or show on the Ramblas, put your hands in your pockets before someone else does. Assume any scuffle is simply a distraction by a team of thieves. Don't be intimidated...just be smart.

Personal Safety: Some areas feel seedy and can be unsafe after dark; I'd avoid the southern part of the Barri Gòtic (basically the two or three blocks directly south and east of Plaça Reial—though the strip near the Carrer de la Mercè tapas bars is better), and I wouldn't venture too deep into the Raval (just west of the Ramblas). One block can separate a comfy tourist zone from the junkies and prostitutes.

Emergency Phone Numbers: General emergencies—112, police—092, ambulance—061 or 112.

Sight Reservations: Several of Barcelona's top sights can have long lines of up to an hour or more. To avoid needless waiting, you can buy tickets in advance by going online (or in some cases, calling). This is especially smart for the Picasso Museum (see page 94), Sagrada Família (see page 120), Casa Batlló (see page 116), and La Pedrera (see page 118). An Articket BCN (described on page 53) allows you to skip the lines at the Picasso Museum, but it doesn't cover any Gaudí sights. If you want to tour the Palace of Catalan Music, with its oh-wow Modernista interior, you'll need to reserve it in advance (see page 102).

Festivals: Major festivals include Festival Grèc, a summer arts festival (June-July, http://grec.bcn.cat); Montjuïc de Nit, featuring one day of music, cinema, art, theater, and dance (mid-July, www.bcn.cat/cultura/montjuicnit); and the Festes de Gràcia, an eight-day street party (mid-Aug, www.festa majordegracia.cat).

Language Barrier: In posted information throughout the city (such as museum descriptions), English plays third fiddle. You'll see Catalan first, Spanish *(castellano)* second, and English a distant third...or often not at all. Fortunately, many locals speak English.

Web Addresses: If a website doesn't work, try replacing the ".com" or ".es" with ".cat"—the web suffix for Catalunya. Many businesses are switching to this.

Internet Access: The free city network, **Barcelona WiFi,** has hundreds of hotspots around town; just look for the blue diamond-shaped sign with a big "W" (for details, see www .bcn.cat/barcelonawifi). **Navega Web** has lots of computers and cheap Internet access (€2/hour); it's conveniently located across from La Boqueria market, downstairs in the bright Centre Comercial New Park (daily 10:00-24:00, Ramblas 88-94, tel. 933-179-193).

Pharmacy: A 24-hour pharmacy is across from La Boqueria market at #98 on the Ramblas. Another is on the corner of Passeig de Gràcia and Provença, just opposite the entrance to La Pedrera.

Laundry: Several self-service launderettes are located around the Old City. The clean-as-a-whistle **LavaXpres** is centrally located near recommended Plaça de Catalunya and Ramblas hotels (self-service-€8/load, instructions in English, daily 8:00-22:00, Passatge d'Elisabets 3—see map on page 148, www.lavaxpres.com). **Wash 'n Dry,** just off the Ramblas, is in a seedier neighborhood just down the street past Palau Güell (self-service-€6.50/load, full service-€14.50/load, daily 9:00-23:00, Carrer Nou de la Rambla 19—see map on page 148, tel. 934-121-953).

Bike Rental: Biking is a joy in Citadel Park, the Eixample, and along the beach (suggested route described on page 107), but it's stressful in the city center, where pedestrians and cars rule. There are bike-rental places popping up in just about every part of the city; I've listed just a few. The handy **Un Cotxe Menys** ("One Car Less"), near the Church of Santa Maria del Mar (50 yards behind the flame memorial), rents bikes and gives out maps and suggested biking routes (€5/hour, €10/4 hours, €15/24 hours, daily 10:00-19:00, leave €150 or photo ID for deposit, Carrer de l'Esparteria 3—see map on page 148, tel. 932-682-105, www.bicicletabarcelona.com); they also lead bike tours (see "Tours in Barcelona," later).

To rent a bike on the Barceloneta beach, consider **Biciclot** (€5/hour, €10/3 hours, €17/24 hours, daily in summer 10:00-20:00, shorter hours off-season, on the sand 300 yards from Olympic Village towers at Passeig Maritime 33, tel. 932-219-778, www.bikinginbarcelona.net). Another beach option is **Barcelona Rent-A-Bike,** about four blocks from the Barceloneta Metro (€6/2 hours, €10/4 hours, €15/24 hours, includes helmet, daily 10:00-20:00, Passeig de Joan de Borbó 35, tel. 932-212-790, www.barcelonarentabike.com); they also have a location three blocks from Plaça de Catalunya (daily 9:30-20:00, inside the courtyard at Carrer dels Tallers 45—see map on page 148, tel. 933-171-970).

You'll see racks of government-subsidized "Bicing" **borrow-a-bikes** around town, but these are only for locals, not tourists.

Updates to this Book: For any changes to this book's coverage since it was published, see www.ricksteves.com/update.

Getting Around Barcelona

Barcelona's Metro and bus system is run by **TMB**—Transports Metropolitans de Barcelona (tel. 902-075-027, www.tmb.cat). It's worth asking for TMB's excellent Metro/bus map at the TI (not always available).

By Metro

The city's Metro, among Europe's best, connects just about every

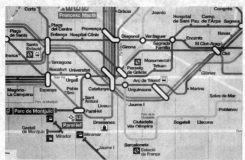

place you'll visit. A single-ride ticket *(bitlett senzill)* costs €2. The T10 Card is a great deal—€9.80 gives you 10 rides (cutting the per-ride cost more than in half). The card is sharable, even by companions traveling with you (insert the card in the machine per passenger). The back of your T10 card will show how many trips were taken, with the time and date of each ride. One "ride" covers you for 1.25 hours of unlimited use on all Metro and local bus lines, as well as local rides on the RENFE and Rodalies de Catalunya train lines (including rides to the airport and train station) and the suburban FGC trains. Transfers made within your 1.25-hour limit are not counted as a new ride, but you still must revalidate your T10 Card whenever you transfer.

Multiday passes are also available (€13.40/2 days, €19.20/3 days, €24.40/4 days, €29/5 days). Machines at the Metro entrance have English instructions and sell all types of tickets (most machines accept credit/debit cards as well as cash).

Whatever type of ticket you use, keep it until you have exited the subway. You don't need the ticket to go through the exit, but inspectors occasionally ask riders to show it.

Barcelona has several color-coded lines, but most useful for tourists is the **L3 (green)** line. Handy city-center stops on this line include (in order):

Sants Estació—Main train station

Espanya—Plaça d'Espanya, with access to the lower part of Montjuïc and trains to Montserrat

Paral·lel—Funicular to the top of Montjuïc

Drassanes—Bottom of the Ramblas, near Maritime Museum and Maremagnum mall

Liceu—Middle of the Ramblas, near the heart of the Barri Gòtic and cathedral

Plaça de Catalunya—Top of the Ramblas and main square with TI, airport bus, and lots of transportation connections

Passeig de Gràcia—Classy Eixample street at the Block of Discord; also connection to L2 (purple) line to Sagrada Família and L4 (yellow) line (described below)

Diagonal—Gaudí's La Pedrera

The **L4 (yellow)** line, which crosses the L3 (green) line at Passeig de Gràcia, is also useful. Helpful stops include **Joanic** (bus #116 to Park Güell), **Jaume I** (between the Barri Gòtic/cathedral

BARCELONA

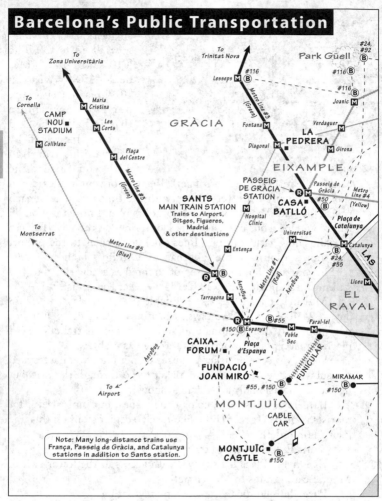

Barcelona's Public Transportation

To Zona Universitària
To Cornella
To Trinitat Nova
Park Güell
#24, #92
Lesseps
#116
#116
#116
Joanic
CAMP NOU STADIUM
Collblanc
Maria Cristina
Les Corts
GRÀCIA
Metro Line #5 (Green)
Fontana
Verdaguer
LA PEDRERA
Diagonal
Girona
Plaça del Centre
EIXAMPLE
PASSEIG DE GRÀCIA STATION
Passeig de Gràcia
Metro Line #4 (Yellow)
SANTS MAIN TRAIN STATION
Trains to Airport, Sitges, Figueres, Madrid & other destinations
CASA BATLLÓ
#50
Plaça de Catalunya
To Montserrat
Metro Line #5 (Blue)
Hospital Clinic
Universitat
Catalunya
#24, #55
Entença
Metro Line #1 (Red)
AeroBus
AeroBus
LAS
Liceu
Tarragona
EL RAVAL
#150
Espanya
#55
Paral·lel
Metro Line #3
CAIXA-FORUM
Plaça d'Espanya
Poble Sec
FUNICULAR
AeroBus
FUNDACIÓ JOAN MIRÓ
#55, #150
MIRAMAR
#150
To Airport
MONTJUÏC
CABLE CAR
Note: Many long-distance trains use França, Passeig de Gràcia, and Catalunya stations in addition to Sants station.
MONTJUÏC CASTLE
#150

and El Born/Picasso Museum), and **Barceloneta** (at the south end of El Born, near the harbor action).

Before riding the Metro, study a map (available at TIs and posted at entrances) to get familiar with the system. Look for your line number and color, and find the end stop for your direction of travel. Enter the Metro by inserting your ticket into the turnstile (with the arrow pointing in), then reclaim it. Then, follow signs for your line and direction. On board, most trains have handy lighted displays that indicate upcoming destinations. Because the lines cross one another multiple times, there can be several ways to make any one journey. (It's a good idea to keep a general map with you—especially if you're transferring.)

BARCELONA

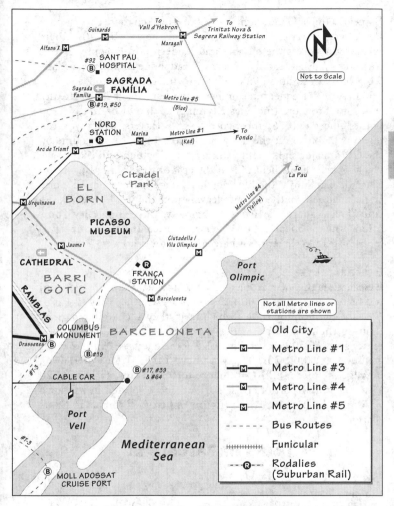

To Vall d'Hebron
To Trinitat Nova & Segrera Railway Station
Guinardó
Maragall
Alfans X
#92
SANT PAU HOSPITAL
SAGRADA FAMÍLIA
Sagrada Família
#19, #50
Metro Line #5 (Blue)
NORD STATION
Marina
Metro Line #1 (Red)
To Fondo
Arc de Triomf
Citadel Park
To La Pau
EL BORN
Urquinaona
Metro Line #4 (Yellow)
PICASSO MUSEUM
Jaume I
CATHEDRAL
Ciutadella / Vila Olimpica
BARRI GÒTIC
FRANÇA STATION
RAMBLAS
Barceloneta
Port Olimpic
COLUMBUS MONUMENT
BARCELONETA
Drassenes
#19
#17, #39 & #64
CABLE CAR
Port Vell
#1-3
Mediterranean Sea
MOLL ADOSSAT CRUISE PORT

Not to Scale

Not all Metro lines or stations are shown

Old City
Metro Line #1
Metro Line #3
Metro Line #4
Metro Line #5
Bus Routes
Funicular
Rodalies (Suburban Rail)

Watch your valuables. If I were a pickpocket, I'd set up shop along the made-for-tourists L3 (green) line.

By Bus

Given the excellent Metro service, it's unlikely you'll take a **local bus** (also €2, covered by T10 Card, insert ticket in machine behind driver), although I've noted places where the bus makes sense. In particular, buses are useful for reaching Park Güell or the beach, and for connecting the sights on Montjuïc.

The handy **hop-on, hop-off Tourist Bus** (Bus Turístic) offers three multi-stop circuits in colorful double-decker buses that go topless in sunny weather. The two-hour blue route covers north

Barcelona (most Gaudí sights); the two-hour red route covers south Barcelona (Barri Gòtic, Montjuïc); and the shorter, 40-minute green route covers the beaches and modern Fòrum complex (this route runs April-Oct only). All have headphone commentary (daily 9:00-20:00 in summer, 9:00-19:00 in winter, buses run every 5-25 minutes, most frequent in summer, www.barcelonabusturistic.cat). Ask for a brochure (includes city map) at the TI or at a pick-up point. One-day (€26) and two-day (€34) tickets, which you can buy on the bus or at the TI, offer 10 to 20 percent discounts on the city's major sights and walking tours, which will likely save you about the equivalent of half the cost of the Tourist Bus. From Plaça de Catalunya, the blue northern route leaves from El Corte Inglés; the red southern route leaves from the west—Ramblas—side of the square. A different company, **Barcelona City Tour,** offers a nearly identical service (same price and discounts, two loops instead of three, www.barcelonacitytour.cat).

By Taxi

Barcelona is one of Europe's best taxi towns. Taxis are plentiful (there are more than 11,000) and honest, whether they like it or not. The light on top shows which tariff they're charging; a green light on the roof indicates that a taxi is available. Cab rates are reasonable (€2.50 drop charge, €1/kilometer, these *"Tarif 2"* rates are in effect 8:00-20:00, pay higher *"Tarif 1"* rates off-hours, luggage-€1/piece, €2.10 surcharge to/from train station, €4.20 surcharge for airport or cruise port, other fees posted in window). Save time by hopping a cab (figure €10 from Ramblas to Sants Station).

Tours in Barcelona

On Foot

Walking Tours

The TI at Plaça de Sant Jaume offers great guided walks through the **Barri Gòtic** in English. You'll learn the medieval story of the city as you walk from Plaça de Sant Jaume through the cathedral neighborhood (€15, daily at 9:30, 2 hours, groups limited to 35, buy your ticket 15 minutes early at the TI desk—not from the guide, in summer stop by the office a day ahead to reserve, tel. 932-853-832, www.barcelonaturisme.cat).

The TI at Plaça de Catalunya offers a **Picasso** walk, taking you through the streets of his youth and early career and finishing in the Picasso Museum (€21, includes museum admission; Tue, Thu, and Sat at 15:00; 2 hours including museum visit). There are also **gourmet** walks (€21, Fri and Sat at 10:00, 2 hours), **Modernisme** walks (€15, Fri and Sat June-Sept at 18:00, 2 hours), and a **Maritime** tour that includes a *golondrinas* boat trip on the harbor (€19, Fri and Sat at 10:00, 2 hours). Other themes include literary Barcelona, the Spanish Civil War, and movie locations (drop by the office for a full list). These tours depart from the TI at Plaça de Catalunya (except the Maritime tour, which begins at the Columbus Monument); it's always smart to reserve in advance.

The Ruta del Modernisme desk inside the Plaça de Catalunya TI also does tours of specific **Modernista buildings** that are otherwise not open to the public (see page 53).

"Free" Walking Tours

Several companies offer "free" walks that rely on—and expect—tips to stay in business. Though led by young people who've basically memorized a clever script (rather than trained historians), these walks can be a fun, casual way to get your bearings.

I like **Runner Bean Tours,** run by Gorka, Ann-Marie, and a handful of local guides. They offer 2.5-hour, English-only walks covering the Old City and Gaudí (both tours depart from Plaça Reial at 11:00 daily year-round, plus daily at 16:30 in April-Oct, www.runnerbeantours.com, mobile 636-108-776). They also do night tours, family walks, and more. Groups can range from just a couple of people up to 30.

Discover Walks does similar tours, with three different two-hour itineraries: Gaudí (daily at 10:30, meet in front of Casa Batlló); Ramblas and Barri Gòtic (daily at 15:00, meet in front of Liceu Opera House on the Ramblas); and Picasso's Barcelona, covering the El Born neighborhood (daily at 17:00, meet at Plaça de l'Angel next to Jaume I Metro stop). This company distinguishes itself by using exclusively native-born guides—no expats (suggested tips: €5/person for a bad guide, €10 for a good one, €15 for a great one, www.discoverwalks.com, tel. 931-816-810).

Local Guides

The **Barcelona Guide Bureau** is a co-op with about 20 local guides who give personalized four-hour tours; **Joana Wilhelm** and **Carles Picazo** are excellent (€102/person for 2, €53/person for 4, per-person price continues to drop as group gets bigger, these prices include public-transportation costs, Via Laietana 54, tel. 932-682-422 or 933-107-778, www.bgb.es).

José Soler is a great and fun-to-be-with local guide who enjoys tailoring a walk through his hometown to your interests (€195/half-day per group, mobile 615-059-326, www.pepitotours .com, info@pepitotours.com). He can also take up to six people by car for a four-hour Barcelona Highlights tour (€395) and will meet you at the cruise port or airport.

Cristina Sanjuán of Live Barcelona is another good, professional guide who leads walking tours and can also arrange cruise excursions. It's best to reserve by email (€155/2 hours, €20/each

"You're Not in Spain, You're in Catalunya!"

This is a popular nationalistic refrain you might see on T-shirts or stickers around town. Catalunya is *not* the land of bullfighting and flamenco that many visitors envision when they think of Spain (best to wait until you're in Madrid or Sevilla for those).

The region of Catalunya—with Barcelona as its capital—has its own language, history, and culture, and the people have a proud, independent spirit. Historically, Catalunya ("Cataluña" in Spanish, sometimes spelled "Catalonia" in English) has often been at odds with the central Spanish government in Madrid. The Catalan language and culture were discouraged or even outlawed at various times in history, as Catalunya often chose the wrong side in wars and rebellions against the kings in Madrid. In the Spanish Civil War (1936-1939), Catalunya was one of the last pockets of democratic resistance against the military coup of the fascist dictator Francisco Franco, who punished the region with four decades of repression. During that time, the Catalan flag was banned—but locals vented their national spirit by flying their football team's flag instead.

Three of Barcelona's monuments are reminders of royal and Franco-era suppression. Citadel Park (Parc de la Ciutadella) was originally a much-despised military citadel, constructed in the 18th century to keep locals in line. The Castle of Montjuïc, built for similar reasons, has been the site of numerous political executions, including hundreds during the Franco era. The Sacred Heart Church atop Tibidabo, completed under Franco, was meant to atone for the sins of Barcelonans during the civil war—the main sin being opposition to Franco. Although rivalry between Barcelona and Madrid has calmed down in recent times, it rages any time the two cities' main football clubs meet.

To see real Catalan culture, look for the *sardana* dance or an exhibition of *castelleres* (both described on page 89). The main symbol of Catalunya is the dragon, which was slain by St. Jordi ("George" in English)—the local patron saint. You'll find dragons all over Barcelona, along with the Catalan flag—called the Senyera—with four horizontal red stripes on a gold field. Nineteenth-century Catalan Romantics embraced a vivid story about the origins of their flag: In the ninth century, Wilfred the Hairy—a Count of Barcelona and one of the founding fathers of Catalunya—was wounded in battle. A grateful neighboring king rewarded Wilfred's bravery with a copper shield and ran Wilfred's four bloody fingers across its surface, leaving four red stripes. While almost certainly false, this legend hints at the nostalgic mood in 19th-century Barcelona, when the Renaixença

(Catalan cultural revival) prodded historians to dig deeply into their medieval past to revive obscure historical figures and lend legitimacy to the resurgent Catalan nation.

The Catalan language is irrevocably tied to the history and spirit of the people here. After the end of the Franco era in the mid-1970s, the language made a huge comeback. Schools are now required by law to conduct all classes in Catalan; most school-age children learn Catalan first and Spanish second. While all Barcelonans still speak Spanish, nearly all understand Catalan, three-quarters speak Catalan, and half can write it.

Here are the essential Catalan phrases:

English	Catalan	Pronounced
Hello	*Hola*	OH-lah
Please	*Si us plau*	see oos plow
Thank you	*Gracies*	GRAH-see-es
Goodbye	*Adéu*	ah-DAY-oo
Long live Catalunya!	*¡Visca Catalunya!*	BEE-skah kah-tah-LOON-yah

When finding your way, these terms will come in handy:

exit	*sortida*	sor-TEE-dah
square	*plaça*	PLAS-sah
street	*carrer*	kah-REHR
boulevard	*passeig*	PAH-sage
avenue	*avinguda*	ah-veen-GOO-dah

Most place names in this chapter are listed in Catalan. Here's how to pronounce the city's major landmarks:

Plaça de Catalunya	PLAS-sah duh kah-tah-LOON-yah
Eixample	eye-SHAM-plah
Passeig de Gràcia	PAH-sage duh grass-EE-ah
Catedral	KAH-tah-dral
Barri Gòtic	BAH-ree GOH-teek
El Born	"el born"
Montjuïc	mohn-jew-EEK

additional hour; €195 extra for a car for up to 2 people, €220 extra for up to 6, can combine with airport transfer; tel. 936-327-259, mobile 609-205-844, www.livebarcelona.com, info@livebarcelona .com).

On Wheels
Guided Bus Tours

The **Barcelona Guide Bureau** offers several sightseeing tours leaving from Plaça de Catalunya. Departure times can change. Tours are designed to end at a major sight in case you'd like to spend more time there. The Gaudí tour visits Casa Batlló and Sagrada Família, as well as the facade of La Pedrera (€62, includes Sagrada Família and Casa Batllò admission, daily at 9:00, 3.5 hours). Other tours offered year-round include the Montjuïc tour (€33, includes Spanish Village admission, daily at 12:30, 2.5 hours); the All Barcelona Highlights tour (€59, includes Sagrada Família and Spanish Village admissions, daily at 10:00, also mid-April-Oct at 12:30, 5 hours); and the Montserrat tour (€47, Mon-Sat at 15:00, 4 hours), which offers a convenient way to get to this mountaintop monastery if you don't want to deal with public transportation (see Near Barcelona chapter). During the high season, there are additional Gaudí-focused tours, Ramblas walks, shopping tours, and a Fundació Joan Miró tour. You can get detailed information and book tickets at a TI, on their website (10 percent discount for 7-day advance purchase), or simply by showing up at their departure point on Plaça de Catalunya in front of the Deutsche Bank (next to the Hard Rock Café—look for the guides holding orange umbrellas; tel. 933-152-261, www.barcelonaguidebureau .com).

Catalunya Tourist Bus also runs excursions to nearby destinations, including some that are difficult to reach by public transportation. Trips include **Montserrat** (€61, 8 hours, includes Gaudí's unfinished Colònia Güell development) and **Salvador Dalí sights** in Figueres and Girona (€73, 11 hours). Both itineraries depart Tuesday through Sunday at 8:30 from Plaça de Catalunya in front of El Corte Inglés (live trilingual commentary in Catalan, Spanish, and English; €5 extra for a more in-depth English audioguide; book at TIs, by phone, or online—10 percent Web discount; tel. 932-853-832, www.catalunyabusturistic.com).

For information on **hop-on, hop-off bus tours,** see "Getting Around Barcelona," earlier.

Bike Tours

Several companies run bike tours around Barcelona.

Un Cotxe Menys ("One Car Less") organizes three-hour English-only bike tours daily at 11:00 year-round (April-mid-Sept also Fri-Mon at 16:30; also rents bikes—see "Helpful Hints," earlier). Your guide leads you from sight to sight, mostly on bike paths and through parks, with a stop-and-go commentary (€22 includes bike rental and drink, no reservations needed, tours meet just outside TI on Plaça Sant Jaume in Barri Gòtic—or, 10 minutes later, at their bike shop in El Born near the Church of Santa Maria del Mar; Carrer de l'Esparteria 3—see map on page 148, tel. 932-682-105, www.bicicletabarcelona.com).

Barcelona CicloTour runs a similar itinerary (€22, departs from Hard Rock Café on Plaça de Catalunya daily at 11:00, 16:30 tour daily mid-April-Oct and Sat-Sun in Nov; 19:30 night tour departs Fri-Sun June-Sept and Fri-Sat in Oct; tel. 933-171-970, www.barcelonaciclotour.com).

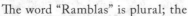

Weekend Tour Packages for Students

Andy Steves (my son) runs Weekend Student Adventures, offering active and experiential three-day weekend tours from €199, designed for American students studying abroad (www.wsaeurope .com for details on tours of Barcelona and other great cities).

Self-Guided Walks

These walks through the atmospheric Old City introduce you to places you may want to explore further. They're easy to follow, pass by some major sights, and provide background to this complex metropolis. The first begins at Barcelona's main square and leads you down the city's main drag: the Ramblas. The second walk guides you into the heart of the Barri Gòtic, the neighborhood around Barcelona's cathedral.

▲▲▲The Ramblas Ramble
From Plaça de Catalunya to the Waterfront

For more than a century, this walk down Barcelona's main boulevard has drawn locals and visitors alike. While its former elegance has been tackified somewhat by tourist shops and fast-food joints, this still has the best people-watching in town. Walk the Ramblas at least once to get the lay of the land, then venture farther afield. It's a one-hour, level stroll, with an easy return by Metro. The Ramblas is two different streets by day and by night; stroll it from top to bottom in the evening and again the next morning, grabbing breakfast on a stool in a market café.

The word "Ramblas" is plural; the

BARCELONA

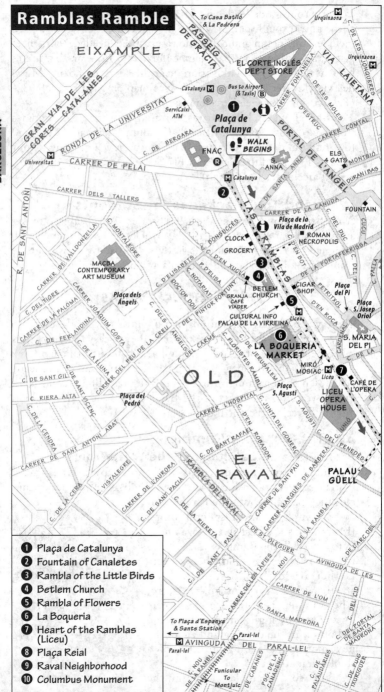

Ramblas Ramble

To Casa Batlló & La Pedrera

Urquinaona

EIXAMPLE

PASSEIG DE GRÀCIA

VIA LAIETANA

Urquinaona

GRAN VIA DE LES CORTS CATALANES

EL CORTE INGLÉS DEP'T STORE

Catalunya

Bus to Airport (& Taxis)

ServiCaixi ATM

CARRER FONTANELLA

CARRER DE LES MOLES

Plaça de Catalunya

RONDA DE LA UNIVERSITAT

C. DE BERGARA

PORTAL DE L'ÀNGEL

CARRER D'ESTRUC

CARRER COMTAL

Universitat

FNAC

WALK BEGINS

ELS GATS

MONTSIÓ

CARRER DE PELAI

S. ANNA

DURAN I BAS

Catalunya

CARRER DE SANTA ANNA

CARRER DELS TALLERS

CARRER DE LA CANUDA

FOUNTAIN

LAS RAMBLAS

Plaça de la Vila de Madrid

CARRER DE SANT ANTONI

R. DE VALLDONZELLA

C. MONTALEGRE

PONSUCCÉS

CLOCK

ROMAN NECROPOLIS

CEL DUC

CUCU

MACBA CONTEMPORARY ART MUSEUM

CARRER DE JOAQUIM COSTA

Plaça dels Àngels

C. D'ELISABETS

C. D'EN XUCLÀ

GROCERY

D'EN BOT

DE LA PORTAFERRISSA

PALLA

P. D'ELISA

C. NOTARIAT

DOCTOR DOU

DEL PINTOR FORTUNY

GRANJA CAFÉ VIADER

BETLEM CHURCH

CIGAR SHOP

Plaça del Pi

Plaça S. Josep Oriol

CARRER DE LA PALOMA

C. DEL TIGRE

CARRER DE FERLANDINA

ANGELS

DEL CARME

CULTURAL INFO PALAU DE LA VIRREINA

D'EN ROCA

Liceu

S. MARIA DEL PI

C. DE LA LLUNA

C. DE SANT GIL

CARRER DEL PEU DE LA CREU

O L D

LA BOQUERIA MARKET

CARDENAL

C. RIERA ALTA

C. DE SANT VICENÇ

C. DE JERUSALEM

C. FLORISTES RAMBLA

MIRÓ MOSIAC

Liceu

CAFÉ DE L'OPERA

C. DE LA CENDRA

Plaça del Pedró

CARRER DE SANT ANTONI ABAT

CARRER L'HOSPITAL

C. D'EN ROBADOR

Plaça S. Agustí

S. AGUSTÍ

C. DEL COMERÇ

LICEU OPERA HOUSE

C. DE SANT RAFAEL

C. JUNTA DEL COMERÇ

C. DEL PENEDÈS

C. VISTALEGRE

C. DE L'AURORA

RAMBLA DEL RAVAL

E L RAVAL

CARRER DE SANT PAU

CARRER MARQUÉS DE BARBERÀ

DE LA RAMBLA

PALAU GÜELL

C. DE LA RIERETA

C. DE SANT PACIÀ

CARRER DE SANT PAU

C. DE ST. OLEGUER

C. NOU

AVINGUDA DE LES

C. DEL CID

C. DE SANT PAU

C. DE LES TAPIES

CARRER DE L'OM

C. DEL PORTAL DE SANTA MADRONA

C. DE PUIG I XURIGUER

To Plaça d'Espanya & Sants Station

SANTA MADRONA

Paral·lel

Paral·lel

M AVINGUDA DEL PARAL·LEL

Funicular To Montjuïc

1. Plaça de Catalunya
2. Fountain of Canaletes
3. Rambla of the Little Birds
4. Betlem Church
5. Rambla of Flowers
6. La Boqueria
7. Heart of the Ramblas (Liceu)
8. Plaça Reial
9. Raval Neighborhood
10. Columbus Monument

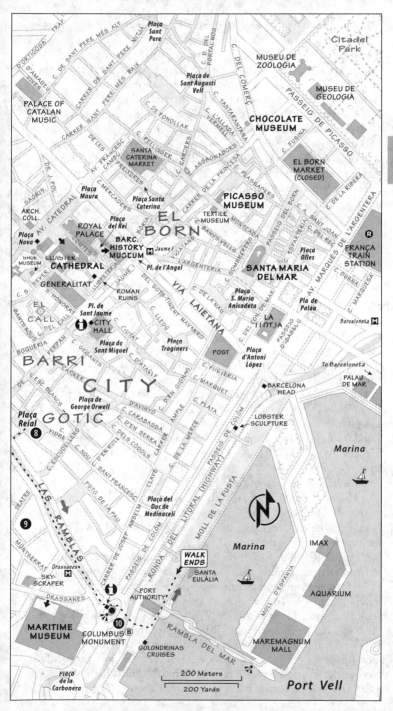

street is actually a succession of five separately named segments. But street signs and addresses treat it as a single long street—"La Rambla," singular. On this pedestrian-only Champs-Elysées, you'll raft the river of Barcelonese life, passing a grand opera house, elegant cafés, flower stands, retread prostitutes, brazen pickpockets, power-dressing con men, artists, street mimes, an outdoor pet market, great shopping, and people looking to charge more for a shoeshine than what you paid for the shoes.

• *Start your ramble on Plaça de Catalunya, at the top of the Ramblas.*

❶ **Plaça de Catalunya:** Dotted with fountains, statues, and pigeons, and ringed by grand Art Deco buildings, this plaza is Barcelona's center. The square's stern, straight lines are a reaction to the curves of Modernisme (which predominates in the Eixample district, just to the north). Plaça de Catalunya is the hub for the Metro, bus, airport shuttle, and Tourist Bus. It's where Barcelona congregates

to watch soccer matches on the big screen, to demonstrate, to celebrate, and to enjoy outdoor concerts and festivals. It's the center of the world for 10 million Catalan people.

Geographically, the 12-acre square links old Barcelona (the narrow streets to the south) with the new (the broad boulevards to the north). Four great thoroughfares radiate from here. The Ramblas is the popular pedestrian promenade. Passeig de Gràcia has fashionable shops and cafés (and noisy traffic). Rambla de Catalunya is equally fashionable but cozier and more pedestrian-friendly. Avinguda Portal de l'Angel (shopper-friendly and traffic-free) leads to the Barri Gòtic (note that my self-guided "Barri Gòtic Walk" begins from right here).

Historically, Plaça de Catalunya links the modern city with its past. In the 1850s, when Barcelona tore down its medieval walls to expand the city, this square on the edge of the walls was one of the first places to be developed.

At the Ramblas end of the square, the odd, inverted-staircase **monument** represents the shape of Catalunya and honors one of its former presidents, Francesc Macià i Llussà, who declared independence for the breakaway region in 1931. (It didn't quite stick.) Sculptor Josep Maria Subirachs, whose work you'll see at the Sagrada Família (see page 120), designed it.

The venerable Café Zürich, just across the street from the monument, is a popular downtown rendezvous spot for locals. Homesick Americans might prefer the nearby Hard Rock Café.

• *Cross the street and start heading down the Ramblas. To get oriented, pause 20 yards down, at the ornate lamppost with a fountain as its base (on the right, near #129).*

❷ **Fountain of Canaletes:** The black-and-gold fountain has been a local favorite for more than a century. When Barcelona tore down its medieval wall and transformed the Ramblas from a drainage ditch into an elegant promenade, this fountain was one of its early attractions. Legend says that a drink from the fountain ensures that you'll come back to Barcelona one day. Watch the tourists—eager to guarantee a return trip—struggle with the awkwardly high water pressure. It's still a popular let's-meet-at-the-fountain rendezvous spot and a gathering place for celebrations and demonstrations. Fans of the Barcelona soccer team rally here before a big match—some touch their hand to their lips, then "kiss" the fountain with their hand for good luck. It's also a good spot to fill up your water bottle.

• *Continue strolling.*

All along the Ramblas are **newsstands** (open 24 hours). Among their souvenirs, you'll see soccer paraphernalia, especially the scarlet-and-blue of FC Barcelona (known as "Barça"). The team is owned by its more than 170,000 "members"—fans who buy season tickets, which come with a share of ownership (the team's healthy payroll guarantees that they're always in contention). Their motto, "More than a club" *(Mes que un club)*, suggests that Barça represents not only athletic prowess but Catalan cultural identity. This comes to a head during a match nicknamed "El Clásico," in which they face their bitter rivals, Real Madrid (whom many Barça fans view as stand-ins for Castilian cultural chauvinism).

Walk 100 yards farther to #115 and the venerable **Royal Academy of Science and Arts building** (it's now home to a performing-arts theater). Look up: The clock high on the facade marks official Barcelona time—synchronize. Notice the **TI** kiosk right on the Ramblas—a handy stop for any questions. The **Carrefour** supermarket just behind it has cheap groceries (at #113, Mon-Sat 10:00-22:00, closed Sun).

• *You're now standing at the...*

❸ **Rambla of the Little Birds:** Traditionally, kids brought their parents here to buy pets, especially on Sundays. But animal-rights groups lobbied to cut back on the stalls because so many families were making impulse buys with no serious interest in taking care of these cute little critters—and many ended up being flushed. Today, only a couple of traditional pet stalls survive—and there's not a bird in sight. Now you'll find tourists oohing and aahing over little bunnies, hamsters, goldfish, and turtles—easier for Barcelona's apartment-dwellers to care for than dogs and cats.

• *At #122 (the big, modern Citadines Hotel on the left, just behind a pet kiosk), take a 100-yard detour through a passageway marked* Passatge de la Ramblas *to a recently discovered...*

Roman Necropolis: Look down and imagine a 2,000-year-old tomb-lined road. In Roman cities, tombs (outside the walls) typically lined the roads leading into town. Emperor Augustus spent a lot of time in modern-day Spain conquering new land, so the Romans were sure to incorporate Hispania into the empire's infrastructure. This road, Via Augusta, led into the Roman port of Barcino (today's highway to France still follows the route laid out by this Roman thoroughfare). Looking down at these ruins, you can see how Roman Barcino was about 10 feet lower than today's street level. For more on this city's Roman chapter, follow my "Barri Gòtic Walk," later.

• *Return to the Ramblas and continue 100 yards or so to the next street, Carrer de la Portaferrissa (across from the big church). Turn left a few steps and look right to see the* **decorative tile** *over a fountain still in use by locals. The scene shows the original city wall with the gate that once stood here and the action on what is today's Ramblas. Now cross the boulevard to the front of the big church.*

❹ **Betlem Church:** It's dedicated to Bethlehem, and for centuries locals have flocked here at Christmastime to see Nativity scenes. The church is 17th-century Baroque: Check out the sloping roofline, ball-topped pinnacles, corkscrew columns, and scrolls above the entrance. The Baroque and also Renaissance styles are relatively unusual in Barcelona because it missed out on several centuries of architectural devel-

opment. Barcelona enjoyed two heydays: during the medieval period (before the Renaissance) and during the turn of the 20th century (after Baroque). In between those periods, from about 1500 until 1850, the city's importance dropped—first, New World discoveries shifted lucrative trade to ports on the Atlantic, and then the Spanish crown kept unruly Catalunya on a short leash.

For a sweet treat, head around to the narrow lane on the far side of the church (running parallel to the Ramblas) to the recommended **Café Granja Viader,** which has specialized in baked and dairy delights since 1870. Step inside to see Viader family photos and early posters advertising Cacaolat—the local chocolate milk Barcelonans love. (For more sugary treats nearby, follow "A Short, Sweet Walk" on page 166.)

• *Continue down the boulevard, through the stretch called the...*

❺ **Rambla of Flowers:** This colorful block, lined with flower stands, is the Rambla of Flowers. Besides admiring the blossoms

on display, gardeners will covet the seeds sold here for varieties of radishes, greens, peppers, and beans seldom seen in the US—including the iconic green Padrón pepper of tapas fame (if you buy seeds, you're obligated to declare them at US customs when returning home). On the left, at #100, **Gimeno** sells cigars. Step inside and appreciate the dying art of cigar boxes. Go ahead, do something forbidden in America but perfectly legal here...buy a Cuban (little singles for €1). Tobacco shops sell stamps and phone cards, plus bongs and marijuana gear—the Spanish approach to pot is very casual. While people can't legally sell marijuana, they're allowed to grow it for personal use and consume it.

• *Continue to the Metro stop marked by the red* M. *At #91 (on the right) is the arcaded entrance to Barcelona's great covered market, La Boqueria. If this main entry is choked with visitors (as it often is), you can skirt around the sides by entering one block in either direction (look for the round arches that mark passages into the market colonnade).*

❻ **La Boqueria:** This lively market hall is an explosion of chicken legs, bags of live snails, stiff fish, delicious oranges, odd

odors, and sleeping dogs. The best day for a visit is Saturday, when the market is thriving. It's closed on Sundays, and locals avoid it on Mondays, when it's open but (they believe) vendors are selling items that aren't necessarily fresh—especially seafood, since fishermen stay home on Sundays.

Since as far back as 1200, Barcelonans have bought their animal parts here. The market was originally located by the walled city's entrance, as many medieval markets were (since it was more expensive to trade within the walls). It later expanded into the colonnaded courtyard of a now-gone monastery before being topped with a colorful arcade in 1850.

While tourists are drawn like moths to a flame to the area around the main entry (below the colorful stained-glass sign), locals know that the stalls up front pay the highest rent—and therefore have to inflate their prices and cater to out-of-towners. For example, the juices along the main drag just inside the entrance are tempting, but if you venture to the right a couple of alleys, the clientele gets more local and the prices drop dramatically.

Stop by the recommended **Pinotxo Bar**—it's just inside the market, under the sign—and snap a photo of Juan. Animated Juan and his family are always busy feeding shoppers. Getting Juan to crack a huge smile and a thumbs-up for your camera makes a great shot...and he loves it. The stools nearby are a fine perch for enjoying both your coffee and the people-watching.

The market and lanes nearby are busy with tempting little eateries (several are listed on page 162). Drop by a café for an *espresso con leche* or breakfast *tortilla española* (potato omelet). Once you get past the initial gauntlet, do some exploring. The small square on the north side of the market hosts a farmers' market in the mornings. Wander around—as local architect Antoni Gaudí used to—and gain inspiration.

• *Head back out to the street and continue down the Ramblas.*

It's clear that, as you walk the Ramblas, you're skirting along the west boundary of the old Barri Gòtic neighborhood. As you walk, glance to the left through a modern archway for a glimpse of the medieval church tower of **Santa Maria del Pi,** a popular venue for guitar concerts (see "Nightlife in Barcelona" on page 143). This also marks Plaça del Pi and a great shopping street, Carrer Petritxol, which runs parallel to the Ramblas.

Now look across to the other side of the Ramblas. At the corner, find the highly regarded **Escribà** bakery, with its fine Modernista facade and interior (look for the *Antigua Casa Figueras* sign arching over the doorway). Notice the beautiful mosaics of twining plants, the stained-glass peacock displaying his tail feathers, and the undulating woodwork. In the sidewalk in front of the door, a plaque dates the building to 1902 (plaques like this identify historic shops all over town).

• *After another block, you reach the Liceu Metro station, marking the...*

❼ **Heart of the Ramblas (Liceu):** At the Liceu Metro station's elevators, the Ramblas widens a bit into a small, lively square (Plaça de la Boqueria). Liceu marks the midpoint of the Ramblas, halfway between Plaça de Catalunya and the waterfront.

Underfoot in the center of the Ramblas, find the much-trod-upon red-white-yellow-and-blue **mosaic** by homegrown abstract artist Joan Miró. The mosaic's black arrow represents an anchor, a reminder of the city's attachment to the sea. Miró's simple, colorful designs are found all over the city, from murals to mobiles to the La Caixa bank logo. The best place in Barcelona to see his work is in the Fundació Joan Miró at Montjuïc (see page 134).

The surrounding buildings have playful ornamentation typical of the city. The **Chinese dragon** holding a lantern (at #82) decorates a former umbrella shop (notice the fun umbrella mosaics high up). While the dragon may seem purely decorative, it's actually an important symbol of Catalan pride for its connection to the local patron saint, St. Jordi (George).

Hungry? Swing around the back of the umbrella shop to the recommended **Taverna Basca Irati** tapas bar (a block up Carrer del Cardenal Casanyes). This is one of many user-friendly, Basque-style tapas bars in town; instead of ordering, you can just grab or point to what looks good on the display platters, then pay per piece.

Back on the Ramblas, a few steps down (on the right) is the **Liceu Opera House** (Gran Teatre del Liceu), which hosts world-class opera, dance, and theater (box office around the right side, open Mon-Fri 13:30-20:00). Opposite the opera house is Café de l'Opera (#74), an elegant stop for an expensive beverage. This bustling café, with Modernista decor and a historic atmosphere, boasts that it's been open since 1929, even during the civil war.

• *We've seen the best stretch of the Ramblas; to cut this walk short, you could catch the Metro back to Plaça de Catalunya. Otherwise, let's continue to the port. The wide, straight street that crosses the Ramblas in another 30 yards (Carrer de Ferran) leads left to Plaça de Sant Jaume, the government center.*

Head down the Ramblas another 50 yards (to #46), and turn left down an arcaded lane (Correr de Colom) to the square called...

❽ Plaça Reial: Dotted with palm trees, surrounded by an arcade, and ringed by yellow buildings with white Neoclassical trim, this elegant square has a colonial ambience. It comes complete with old-fashioned taverns, modern bars with patio seating, and a Sunday coin-and-stamp market (10:00-14:00). Completing the picture are Gaudí's first public works (the two colorful helmeted lampposts). While this used to be a seedy and dangerous part of town, recent gentrification efforts have given it new life, making it inviting and accessible. (The small streets stretching toward the water

from the square remain a bit sketchier.) It's a lively hangout by day or by night (for nightlife options, see page 144). Big spaces like this (as well as the site of La Boqueria market) often originated as monasteries. When these were dissolved in the 19th century, their fine colonnaded squares were incorporated into what were considered generally more useful public spaces.

Head back out to the Ramblas. Across the boulevard, a half-block detour down Carrer Nou de la Rambla brings you to **Palau Güell,** designed by Antoni Gaudí (on the left, at #3-5). Even from the outside, you get a sense of this innovative apartment, the first of Gaudí's Modernista buildings. As this is early Gaudí (built 1886-1890), it's darker and more Neo-Gothic than his more famous later work. The two parabolic-arch doorways and elaborate wrought-iron work signal his emerging nonrectangular style. Recently renovated, Palau Güell offers an informative look at a Gaudí interior (see listing on page 112). Pablo Picasso had a studio at #10 (though there's nothing to see there today).

• *Proceed along the Ramblas.*

❾ Raval Neighborhood (Barri Xines): The neighborhood on the right-hand side of this stretch of the Ramblas is El Raval. Its nickname was Barri Xines—the world's only Chinatown with nothing even remotely Chinese in or near it. Named for the prejudiced notion that Chinese immigrants went hand-in-hand with poverty, prostitution, and drug dealing, the neighborhood's actual inhabitants were poor Spanish, North African, and Roma (Gypsy) people. At night, the Barri Xines was frequented by prostitutes, many of them transvestites, who catered to sailors wandering up from the port. Today, it's becoming gentrified, but it's still a pretty rough neighborhood.

At about this part of the Ramblas, you may see the first of the drag's medley of surreal and goofy **human statues.** These performers—with creative and elaborate costumes—must audition and be registered by the city government; to avoid overcrowding, only 15 can work along the Ramblas at any one time. To enliven your Ramblas ramble, stroll with a pocket full of small change. As you wander along, drop coins into their cans (the money often kicks them into entertaining gear). Warning: Wherever people stop to gawk, pickpockets are at work.

You're also likely to see some good old-fashioned **shell games** in this part of town. Stand back and observe these nervous no-necks at work. They swish around their little boxes, making sure to show you the pea. Their shills play and win. Then, in hopes of making easy money, fools lose big time.

Near the bottom of the Ramblas, take note of the Drassanes Metro stop, which can take you back to Plaça de Catalunya when this walk is over. The skyscraper to the right of the Ramblas is the Edificio Colón. When it was built in 1970, the 28-story structure was Barcelona's first high-rise. Near the skyscraper is the Maritime Museum, housed in what were the city's giant medieval shipyards (permanent collection closed until the fall of 2014; see listing on page 105).

• *Up ahead is the...*

⑩ Columbus Monument: The 200-foot column commemorates Christopher Columbus' stop in Barcelona after his first

trip to America (see listing on page 106).

Continue ahead to the **waterfront.** Barcelona is one of Europe's top 10 ports, though this stretch of the harbor is a pleasant marina with sailboats.

Stand here and survey some of your sightseeing options: At your feet are the *golondrinas* harbor cruise boats (page 106). Across the harbor (though not really visible from here) is the spit of land called Barceloneta, home to some nice restaurants and sandy beaches (see page 107). To the right of the harbor rises the majestic, 570-foot bluff of Montjuïc, a park-like setting dotted with a number of sights and museums (see page 130).

The pedestrian bridge jutting into the harbor is a modern extension of the Ramblas called La Rambla del Mar ("Rambla of the Sea"). This popular wooden bridge—with waves like the sea—leads to Maremagnum, a shopping mall with a cinema, a huge aquarium, restaurants, and piles of people. Late at night, it's a rollicking youth hangout.

• *Your ramble is over. If it's a nice day, consider strolling the promenade and looping back around on La Rambla del Mar. Or maybe explore El Born. Or, if you're truly on vacation, walk through Barceloneta to the beach.*

If you'd like to get to other points in town, your best bet is to backtrack to the Drassanes Metro stop. Alternatively, you can catch buses #14 or #59 from along the top of the promenade to Plaça de Catalunya.

▲▲The Barri Gòtic
From Plaça de Catalunya to the Cathedral

Barcelona's Barri Gòtic, or Gothic Quarter, is a bustling world of shops, bars, and nightlife packed into narrow, winding lanes and undiscovered courtyards. This is Barcelona's birthplace—where the ancient Romans built a city, where medieval Christians built their cathedral, and where Barcelonans lived within a ring of protective walls until the 1850s, when the city expanded.

Today, this area—nicknamed simply "El Gòtic"—is Barcelona's most historic neighborhood. Concentrate on the area around the cathedral (since the section near the port is somewhat dull and seedy). The Barri Gòtic is a tangled-yet-inviting grab bag of grand squares, schoolyards, Art Nouveau storefronts, musty junk shops, classy antique shops (on Carrer de la Palla), street

BARCELONA

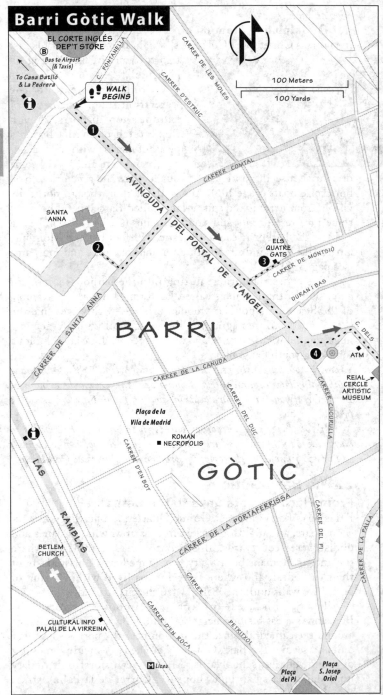

Barri Gòtic Walk

EL CORTE INGLÉS DEP'T STORE

Ⓑ Bus to Airport (& Taxis)

To Casa Batlló & La Pedrera

👣 WALK BEGINS

100 Meters

100 Yards

N

❶

CARRER DE LES MOLES

CARRER D'ESTRUC

C. FONTANELLA

CARRER COMTAL

AVINGUDA DEL PORTAL DE L'ANGEL

SANTA ANNA

❷

ELS QUATRE GATS

❸ CARRER DE MONTSIÓ

DURAN I BAS

CARRER DE SANTA ANNA

BARRI

C. DELS

❹ ATM

REIAL CERCLE ARTISTIC MUSEUM

CARRER DE LA CANUDA

CARRER CUCURULLA

Plaça de la Vila de Madrid

CARRER DEL DUC

ROMAN NECROPOLIS

CARRER D'EN BOT

GÒTIC

CARRER DEL PI

LAS RAMBLAS

BETLEM CHURCH

CARRER DE LA PORTAFERRISSA

CARRER DE LA PALLA

CARRER D'EN ROCA

CARRER

PETRITXOL

CULTURAL INFO PALAU DE LA VIRREINA

Ⓜ Liceu

Plaça del Pi

Plaça S. Josep Oriol

BARCELONA

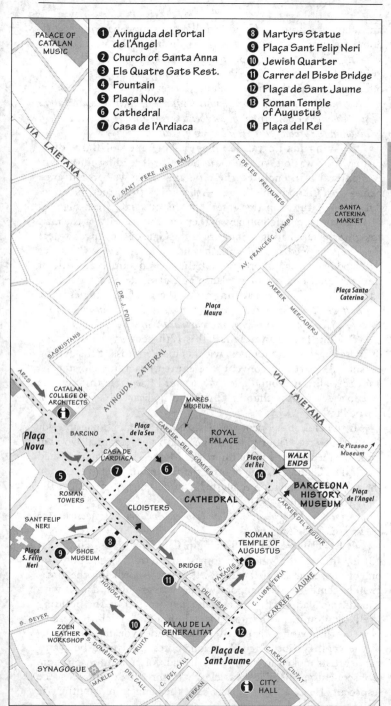

1. Avinguda del Portal de l'Àngel
2. Church of Santa Anna
3. Els Quatre Gats Rest.
4. Fountain
5. Plaça Nova
6. Cathedral
7. Casa de l'Ardiaca
8. Martyrs Statue
9. Plaça Sant Felip Neri
10. Jewish Quarter
11. Carrer del Bisbe Bridge
12. Plaça de Sant Jaume
13. Roman Temple of Augustus
14. Plaça del Rei

PALACE OF CATALAN MUSIC

VIA LAIETANA

C. SANT PERE MÉS BAIX

C. DE LES FREIXURES

SANTA CATERINA MARKET

AV. FRANCESC CAMBÓ

CARRER MERCADERS

Plaça Santa Caterina

C. DR. J. POU

Plaça Maura

VIA LAIETANA

SAGRISTANS

ARCS

CATALAN COLLEGE OF ARCHITECTS

AVINGUDA CATEDRAL

Plaça de la Seu

MARÈS MUSEUM

CARRER DELS COMTES

ROYAL PALACE

Plaça Nova

BARCINO

CASA DE L'ARDIACA

Plaça del Rei

WALK ENDS

To Picasso Museum

5

ROMAN TOWERS

7

6

CATHEDRAL

14

BARCELONA HISTORY MUSEUM

Plaça de l'Àngel

SANT FELIP NERI

CLOISTERS

CARRER DEL VEGUER

Plaça S. Felip Neri

9

SHOE MUSEUM

8

ROMAN TEMPLE OF AUGUSTUS

HONORAT

BRIDGE

11

13

C. PARADIS

C. LLIBRETERIA

CARRER JAUME I

S. SEVER

ZOEN LEATHER WORKSHOP

S. DOMÈNEC

10

FRUITA

C. DEL BISBE

PALAU DE LA GENERALITAT

12

CARRER CIUTAT

SYNAGOGUE

MARLET

DEL CALL

C. DEL CALL

FERRAN

Plaça de Sant Jaume

CITY HALL

musicians strumming Catalan folk songs, and balconies with domestic jungles behind wrought-iron bars. Go on a cultural scavenger hunt. Write a poem. Take artsy pictures. This self-guided walk gives you a structure, covering the major sights and offering a historical overview before you get lost.

• *Start on Barcelona's grand, main square, Plaça de Catalunya (described on page 68). From the southeast corner (near El Corte Inglés), head down the broad pedestrian boulevard called...*

❶ **Avinguda Portal de l'Angel:** For much of Barcelona's history, this was one of the main boulevards leading into town. A medieval wall enclosed the city, and there was an entrance here—the "Gate of the Angel"—that gives the street its name. An angel statue atop the gate kept the city safe from plagues and bid voyagers safe journey as they left the security of the city. Imagine the fascinating scene here at the Gate of the Angel, where Barcelona stopped and the wilds began.

Today's street is pretty globalized and sanitized, full of international chain stores. Pause at Carrer de Santa Anna to admire the Art Nouveau awning at (another) El Corte Inglés store.

• *A half-block detour to the right on Carrer de Santa Anna (at #32) leads to a pleasant, flower-fragrant courtyard with the...*

❷ **Church of Santa Anna:** This 12th-century gem was one of those *extra muro* churches, with its marker cross still standing outside. As part of a convent, the church has a fine cloister, an arcaded walkway around a leafy courtyard (viewable through the gate to the left of the church). Climb the modern stairs for views of the bell tower.

If the church is open, you'll see a bare Romanesque interior and Greek-cross floor plan, topped with an octagonal wooden roof. The recumbent-knight tomb is of Miguel de Boera, renowned admiral of Charles V. The door at the far end of the nave leads to the cloister (€2 donation requested, church hours vary but usually daily 11:00-19:00).

• *Backtrack to Avinguda Portal de l'Angel. At Carrer de Montsió (on the left), side-trip half a block to...*

❸ **Els Quatre Gats ("The Four Cats"):** This restaurant (at #3) is a historic monument, tourist attraction, nightspot, and one of my recommended eateries. It's famous for being the circa-1900 bohemian-artist hangout where Picasso nursed drinks with friends and had his first one-man show (in 1900). The building itself, by prominent architect Josep Puig i Cadafalch, represents Neo-Gothic Modernisme. Stepping inside, you feel the turn-of-the-century vibe. Rich Barcelona elites and would-be avant-garde artists looked to Paris, not Madrid, for cultural inspiration. Consequently, this place was clearly inspired by the Paris scene (especially Le Chat Noir cabaret/café, the hangout of Montmartre intellectuals). Like Le Chat Noir, Els Quatre Gats even published its own artsy magazine for a while. The story of the name? When the proprietor told his friends that he'd stay open 24 hours a day, they said, "No one will come. It'll just be you and four cats" (Catalan slang for "a few crazy people"). While you can have a snack, meal, or drink here, if you just want to look around, ask, *"Solo mirar, por favor?"*

• *Return to Avinguda Portal de l'Angel and continue down the street until you run into a building at a fork in the road, with a...*

❹ **Fountain:** The fountain's blue-and-yellow tilework depicts ladies carrying jugs of water. In the 17th century, this was the last watering stop for horses before leaving town. As recently as 1940, one in nine Barcelonans got their water from fountains like this. It's still used today.

• *Take the left fork, passing by the Reial Cercle Artistic Museum (temporary exhibits). Enter the large square called...*

❺ **Plaça Nova:** Two bold **Roman towers** flank the main street. These once guarded the entrance gate of the ancient Roman city of Barcino. The big stones that make up the base of the (reconstructed) towers are actually Roman. At the base, find the **modern bronze letters** spelling out "BARCINO." The city's name may have come from Barca, one of Hannibal's generals, who is said to have passed through during Hannibal's roundabout invasion of Italy. At Barcino's peak, the **Roman wall** (see the section stretching to the left of the towers) was 25 feet high and a mile around, with 74 towers. It enclosed an area of 30 acres—population 4,000.

One of the towers has a section of **Roman aqueduct** (a modern reconstruction). These bridges of stone carried fresh water from the distant hillsides into the walled city. Here the water supply split into two channels, one to feed Roman industry, the other for the general populace. The Roman aqueducts would be the best water system Barcelona would have until the 20th century.

Opposite the towers is the modern Catalan College of Architects building (TI inside) with a **frieze designed by Picasso** (1960). In Picasso's distinctive, simplified style, it shows branch-waving kings and children celebrating a local festival. Picasso spent his formative years (1895-1904, ages 14-23) in the Barri Gòtic. He had a studio a block east of here (where the big Caixa Catalunya building stands today). He drank with fellow bohemians at Els Quatre Gats (which we just passed) and frequented brothels a

Mapping Barcelona's History

Open up any city map and read some history into it. Find the Old City *(Ciutat Vella)*, the dense neighborhood of higgledy-piggledy streets between Plaça de Catalunya and the water, with the cathedral at the center. Around that stretches the waffle-shaped grid of modern boulevards built as the city expanded.

The city grew with its history. Find the original Roman town from the time of Christ. It's the knot of streets clustered around today's cathedral, enclosed by an oval-shaped ring of Roman walls.

When Rome fell (around A.D. 500), the Christian Visigoths made the cathedral the center of town, and the populace remained huddled inside the Roman walls. During the Dark Ages, the city was ruled briefly by Moors (714-801) and Franks (ninth century). When the Counts of Barcelona unified Catalunya (10th century), the city began expanding. They built churches outside the Roman walls (or *extra muro*), each a magnet gathering a small community. By 1250, they needed to build a larger wall to contain these new settlers. This medieval wall is the arc on your map that stretches from Plaça de Catalunya to the sea, embracing the whole Old Town.

By 1850, the growing city was bursting at the seams. The outer wall was torn down and replaced by a series of circular boulevards (named Rondas, meaning "to go around"). The city expanded northward in a regimented grid of modern boulevards. The small-street neighborhoods in this urban waffle show where a little town was consumed by the growing city. The popular Passeig de Gràcia was literally the "Road to Gràcia"—once a separate town, now a characteristic Barcelona neighborhood. In 1992, Barcelona hosted the Summer Olympics, which quickly accelerated modernization and expanded the city still more.

Today, the population sprawls beyond city maps, creating a greater metropolitan area of some five million people.

few blocks south of here on Carrer d'Avinyo ("Avignon"), which inspired his seminal Cubist painting *Les Demoiselles d'Avignon*. Picasso's Barri Gòtic was a hotbed of trendsetting art, propelling Picasso forward just before he moved to Paris and remade modern art.

• *Now head to the left and take in the mighty facade of the...*

❻ **Cathedral of Barcelona (Catedral de Barcelona):** This location has been the center of Christian worship since the fourth century, and this particular building dates (mainly) from the 14th century. The facade is a virtual catalog of Gothic motifs: a pointed arch over the entrance, robed statues, tracery in windows, gargoyles, and bell towers with winged angels. The style is French

Flamboyant (meaning "flame-like"), and the roofline sports the prickly spires meant to give the impressions of a church flickering with spiritual fires. The facade is typically Gothic...but not medieval. It's a Neo-Gothic work from the 19th century. The area in front of the cathedral is where they dance the *sardana* (see page 89). Standing in front of the Barcelona cathedral, if you look left, you can see the colorful swooping roof of the Santa Caterina Market (described on page 103).

The cathedral's interior—with its vast size, peaceful cloister, and many ornate chapels—is worth a visit. For specifics, see the listing on page 85.

• *The Frederic Marès Museum (see page 91 for details) is just to the left of the cathedral. But for now, return to the Roman towers. Pass between the towers up Carrer del Bisbe, and take an immediate left, up the ramp to the entrance of the...*

❼ **Casa de l'Ardiaca** *(Archivo):* It's free to enter this mansion, which was once the archdeacon's house and today functions as the city archives. The elaborately carved doorway is Renaissance. To the right of the doorway is a carved mail slot by 19th-century Modernist architect Lluís Domènech i Montaner. Enter through a small courtyard with a fountain. Notice how the century-old palm tree seems to be held captive by urban man. Next, step inside the lobby of the city archives, where there are often free temporary exhibits. At the left end of the lobby, step through the archway and look down into the stairwell—this is the back side of the ancient Roman wall. Back in the courtyard, head up to the balcony for closer views of the cathedral steeple and gargoyles.

• *Return to Carrer del Bisbe and turn left. After a few steps you reach a small square with a bronze statue ensemble.*

❽ **Martyrs Statue:** Five Barcelona patriots calmly receive their last rites before being garroted (strangled) for resisting Napoleon's 1809 invasion of Spain. They'd been outraged by French atrocities in Madrid (depicted in Goya's *Third of May* painting in the Prado Museum—see page 466). The plaque marking their mortal remains says these martyrs to independence gave their lives *"por Dios, por la Patria, y por el Rey"*—for God, country, and king.

The plaza offers interesting views of the cathedral's towers. The doorway here is the (not-always-open) "back door" entrance to the cathedral (at the cloister), letting you avoid the long lines at the cathedral's main entrance.

• *Exit the square down tiny Carrer de Montjuïc del Bisbe. This leads to the cute...*

❾ **Plaça Sant Felip Neri:** This shady square serves as the playground of an elementary school and is often bursting with youthful energy. The Church of Sant Felip Neri, which Gaudí attended, is still pocked with bomb damage from the civil war.

As a stronghold of democratic, anti-Franco forces, Barcelona saw a lot of fighting. The shrapnel that damaged this church was meant for the nearby Catalan government building (Palau de la Generalitat, which we'll see later on this walk).

The buildings here were paid for by the guilds that powered the local economy. On the corner where you entered the square is the former home of the shoemakers' guild; today it's the fun little **Shoe Museum** (described on page 91).

• *Exit the square down Carrer de Sant Felip Neri. At the T-intersection, you have a choice:*

You can turn left, returning to the square with the Martyrs Statue, then turn right, walking along Carrer del Bisbe to the bridge (described later).

Or if you're curious about the Jewish chapter of Barcelona's story, turn right at the T-intersection onto Carrer de Sant Sever, then immediately left on Carrer de Sant Domènec del Call (look for the blue El Call sign). You've entered the...

❿ Jewish Quarter (El Call): In Catalan, a Jewish quarter goes by the name El Call—literally "narrow passage," for the tight lanes where medieval Jews were forced to live, under the watchful eye of the nearby cathedral. At its peak, some 4,000 Jews were crammed into just a few alleys.

Walk down Carrer de Sant Domènec del Call. You'll pass (on the right) the **Zoen leather workshop and showroom** (at #15), where everything is made on the spot, followed by a charming square. At the next lane (Carrer de Marlet), turn right. On the right-hand side is the low-profile entrance to what (most likely) was Barcelona's **main synagogue** during the Middle Ages (€2.50 requested donation). The structure dates from the third century, but it was destroyed during a brutal pogrom in 1391. The city's remaining Jews were expelled in 1492, and artifacts of their culture—including this synagogue—were forgotten for centuries. In the 1980s, a historian tracked down the synagogue using old tax-collector records. Another clue that this was the main synagogue: In accordance with Jewish traditions, it stubbornly faces east (toward Jerusalem), putting it at an angle at odds with surrounding structures. The sparse interior includes access to two small subterranean rooms with Roman walls topped by a medieval Catalan vault. Look through the glass floor to see dyeing vats used for a later shop on this site (run by former Jews who had forcibly been converted to Christianity).

• *From the synagogue, start back the way you came but continue straight ahead, onto Carrer de la Fruita. At the T-intersection, turn left, then right, to find your way back to the Martyrs Statue. From here, turn right down Carrer del Bisbe to the...*

⓫ Carrer del Bisbe Bridge: This Bridge-of-Sighs-like structure connects the Catalan government building on the right with the Catalan president's residence (ceremonial, not actual). Though the bridge looks medieval, it was constructed in the 1920s by Joan Rubió, who also did the carved ornamentation on the buildings.

It's a photographer's dream. Check out the jutting angels on the bridge, the basket-carrying maidens on the president's house, the gargoyle-like faces on the government building. Zoom in even closer. Find monsters, skulls, goddesses, old men with beards, climbing vines, and coats of arms—a Gothic museum in stone.

• *Continue along Carrer del Bisbe to...*

⓬ Plaça de Sant Jaume (jow-mah): This stately central square of the Barri Gòtic, once the Roman forum, has been the seat of city government for 2,000 years. Today the two top governmental buildings in Catalunya face each other.

For more than six centuries, **Palau de la Generalitat** has housed the autonomous government of Catalunya. It always flies the Catalan flag (red and yellow stripes) next to the obligatory Spanish one. Above the doorway is Catalunya's patron saint— St. Jordi (George), slaying the dragon. From these balconies, the nation's leaders (and soccer heroes) greet the people on momentous days. The square is often the site of demonstrations, from a single aggrieved citizen with a megaphone to riotous thousands.

The **Barcelona City Hall** (Casa de la Ciutat) sports a statue of the king "Jaume el Conqueridor"—not to be confused with Sant Jaume, the plaza's namesake (free, open Sun 10:00-13:30). King Jaume I (1208-1276, also called "the Just") is credited with freeing Barcelona from French control, granting self-government, and setting it on a course to become a major city. He was the driving force behind construction of the Royal Palace (which we'll see shortly).

Locals treasure the independence these two government buildings represent. In the 20th century, Barcelona opposed the dictator Francisco Franco (who ruled from 1939 to 1975), and Franco retaliated. He abolished the regional government and (effectively) outlawed the Catalan language and customs. Two years after Franco's death, joyous citizens packed this square to celebrate the return of self-rule.

Look left and right down the main streets branching off the square. Carrer de Ferran (which leads to the Ramblas) is classic Barcelona—lined with ironwork streetlamps and balconies draped with plants.

In ancient Roman days, Plaça de Sant Jaume was the town's forum, or central square, located at the intersection of the two main streets—the *decumanus* (Carrer del Bisbe) and the *cardus* (Carrer de la Llibreteria). The forum's biggest building was a massive temple of Augustus, which we'll see next.

• *Facing the Generalitat, exit the square to the right, heading uphill on tiny Carrer del Paradís. Follow this street as it turns right. When it swings left, pause at #10, the entrance to the...*

❸ **Roman Temple of Augustus** (Temple Roma d'August): You're standing at the summit of Mont Tàber. A plaque on the wall says it all: "Mont Tàber, 16.9 meters"— elevation 55 feet. The Barri Gòtic's highest spot is also marked with a millstone inlaid in the pavement at the doorstep of #10. It was here, atop this lofty summit, that the ancient Romans founded the town of Barcino around 15 B.C. They built a *castrum* (fort) on the hilltop, protecting the harbor.

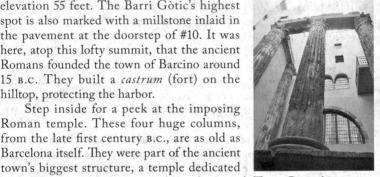

Step inside for a peek at the imposing Roman temple. These four huge columns, from the late first century B.C., are as old as Barcelona itself. They were part of the ancient town's biggest structure, a temple dedicated to the Emperor Augustus, worshipped as a god. These Corinthian columns (with deep fluting and topped with leafy capitals) were the back corner of a 120-foot-long temple that extended from here to the Fòrum (free, good English info, Mon 10:00-14:00, Tue-Sat 10:00-19:00, Sun 10:00-20:00).

• *Continue down Carrer del Paridís one block. When you bump into the back end of the cathedral, take a right, and go downhill a block (down Baixada de Santa Clara) until you emerge into a square called...*

❹ **Plaça del Rei:** The buildings that enclose this square once housed Spain's kings and queens. The central section (topped by a four-story addition) was the core of the Royal Palace. It has a vast hall on the ground floor that served as the throne room and reception room. From the 13th to the 15th century, the Royal Palace housed Catalunya's counts as well as resident Spanish kings. In 1493, a triumphant Christopher Columbus, accompanied by six New World natives (whom he called "Indians") and several pure-gold statues, entered the Royal Palace. King Ferdinand and Queen Isabel rose to welcome him home and honored him with the title "Admiral of the Oceans."

To the right is the palace's church, the Chapel of St. Agatha. It sits atop the foundations of the Roman wall.

To the left is the Viceroy's Palace (for the ruler's right-hand man), which also served as the archives of the Kingdom of Aragon.

After Catalunya became part of Spain in the 15th century, the Royal Palace became a small regional residence, and the Viceroy's Palace became the headquarters of the local Inquisition. Today the Viceroy's Palace is once again home to the archives. Step inside to see an impressive Renaissance courtyard, a staircase with coffered wood ceilings, and a temporary exhibit space. Among the archive's treasures (though it's rarely on display) is the 1491 Santa Fe Capitulations, a contract between Columbus and the monarchs about his upcoming voyage.

Ironically, Columbus and the Kingdom of Aragon played a role in Barcelona's decline as an independent kingdom. When Ferdinand of Aragon married Isabel of Castile, Catalunya got swallowed up in greater Spain. Columbus' discovery of new trade routes made Barcelona's port less important, and soon the royals moved elsewhere.

The Barcelona History Museum's entrance is just around the corner from Plaça del Rei (see listing on page 90). It gives visitors the only peek they'll get of the palace interior (and there's disappointingly little to see), but more important, provides a fine way to retrace all the history we've seen on this walk—from modern to medieval to the Roman foundations of Barcino.

• *Your walk is over. It's easy to get your bearings by backtracking to either Plaça de Sant Jaume or the cathedral. The Jaume I Metro stop is two blocks away (leave the square on Carrer del Veguer and turn left). Or simply wander and enjoy Barcelona at its Gothic best.*

Sights in Barcelona

In the Barri Gòtic, near the Cathedral

For an interesting route from Plaça de Catalunya to the cathedral neighborhood, see my self-guided walk of the Barri Gòtic (described earlier). And if you're in town on a weekend, don't miss the *sardana* dances (see sidebar).

▲Cathedral of Barcelona

Although Barcelona's most important church doesn't rank among Europe's finest cathedrals (frankly, it barely cracks the top 20), it's important, easy to visit, and—at certain times of the day—free.

Cost and Hours: Generally open to visitors Mon-Fri 8:00-19:30, Sat-Sun 8:00-20:00. Free to enter Mon-Sat before 12:45, Sun before 13:45, and daily after 17:15, but you must pay to enter the cathedral's three minor sights

Barcelona at a Glance

▲▲▲**Ramblas** Barcelona's colorful, gritty, tourist-filled pedestrian thoroughfare, with the thriving La Boqueria market. **Hours:** Always open (but market closed Sun). See page 65.

▲▲▲**Picasso Museum** Extensive collection offering insight into the brilliant Spanish artist's early years. **Hours:** Tue-Sun 10:00-20:00, closed Mon. See page 94.

▲▲▲**Sagrada Família** Gaudí's remarkable, unfinished church—a masterpiece in progress. **Hours:** Daily April-Sept 9:00-20:00, Oct-March 9:00-18:00. See page 120.

▲▲**Barri Gòtic** City's Gothic Quarter, with the cathedral, remnants of Barcelona's Roman past, and Picasso's old haunt. **Hours:** Always open. See page 75.

▲▲**Palace of Catalan Music** Best Modernista interior in Barcelona. **Hours:** 50-minute English tours daily every hour 10:00-15:00, plus frequent concerts. See page 102.

▲▲**La Pedrera** Barcelona's quintessential Modernista building and Gaudí creation. **Hours:** Daily March-Oct 9:00-20:00, Nov-Feb 9:00-18:30. See page 118.

▲▲**Park Güell** Colorful Gaudí-designed park overlooking the city. **Hours:** Daily 10:00-20:00. See page 128.

▲▲**Catalan Art Museum** World-class showcase of this region's art, including a substantial Romanesque collection. **Hours:** May-Sept Tue-Sat 10:00-20:00 (until 18:00 Oct-April), Sun 10:00-15:00, closed Mon. See page 136.

▲▲**CaixaForum** Modernista brick factory now occupied by cutting-edge cultural center featuring excellent temporary art exhibits. **Hours:** Mon-Fri 10:00-20:00, Sat-Sun 10:00-21:00, July-Aug open late on some days—likely Wed until 23:00. See page 138.

▲**Cathedral of Barcelona** Colossal Gothic cathedral ringed by distinctive chapels. **Hours:** Generally open to visitors Mon-Fri 8:00-19:30, Sat-Sun 8:00-20:00. See page 85.

▲*Sardana* **Dances** Patriotic dance in which proud Catalans join hands in a circle, often held outdoors. **Hours:** Every Sun at 12:00, usually also Sat at 18:00, no dances in Aug. See page 89.

▲**Barcelona History Museum** One-stop trip through town history, from Roman times to today. **Hours:** Tue-Sat 10:00-19:00, Sun 10:00-20:00, closed Mon. See page 90.

▲**Santa Caterina Market** Fine market hall built on the site of an old monastery and updated with a wavy Gaudí-inspired roof. **Hours:** Mon 7:30-14:00, Tue-Wed and Sat 7:30-15:30, Thu-Fri 7:30-20:30, closed Sun. See page 103.

▲**Church of Santa Maria del Mar** Catalan Gothic church in El Born, built by wealthy medieval shippers. **Hours:** Daily 8:00-13:30 & 17:00-19:30. See page 103.

▲**Maritime Museum** A sailor's delight, housed in an impressive medieval shipyard (but permanent collection likely closed until fall of 2014). **Hours:** Temporary exhibits daily 10:00-20:00. See page 105.

▲**Barcelona's Beach** Fun-filled, man-made stretch of sand reaching from the harbor to the Fòrum. **Hours:** Always open. See page 107.

▲**Palau Güell** Exquisitely curvy Gaudí interior and fantasy rooftop. **Hours:** April-Sept Tue-Sun 10:00 20:00, Oct-March Tue-Sun 10:00-17:30, closed Mon year-round. See page 112.

▲**Block of Discord** Noisy block of competing Modernista facades by Gaudí and his rivals. **Hours:** Always viewable. See page 113.

▲**Casa Batlló** Gaudí-designed home topped with fanciful dragon-inspired roof. **Hours:** Daily 9:00-20:00. See page 116.

▲**Fundació Joan Miró** World's best collection of works by Catalan modern artist Joan Miró. **Hours:** July-Sept Tue-Sat 10:00-20:00 (until 19:00 Oct-June), Thu until 21:30, Sun 10:00-14:30, closed Mon year-round. See page 134.

▲**1929 World Expo Fairgrounds** Expo site at the base of Montjuïc, featuring playful Magic Fountains, the impressive CaixaForum art gallery, cheesy Spanish Village, and a mall converted from a bullring. **Hours:** Grounds always open. See page 138.

▲**Magic Fountains** Lively fountains near Plaça d'Espanya. **Hours:** Generally May-Sept Thu-Sun 21:00-23:30, no shows Mon-Wed; Oct-April Fri-Sat 19:00-21:00, no shows Sun-Thu. See page 138.

BARCELONA

(museum-€2, terrace-€3, choir-€2.50). The church is officially "closed" for a few hours each afternoon (Mon-Sat 13:00-17:00, Sun 14:00-17:00), but you can still get in by paying for the interior sights. These sights have shorter hours than the church itself: museum daily 10:00-19:00; terrace Mon-Sat 9:00-18:00, closed Sun; choir Mon-Sat 9:00-19:00, closes in the afternoon on Sun. Tel. 933-151-554, www.catedralbcn.org.

Dress Code: The dress code is strictly enforced—no tank tops, shorts, or skirts above the knee.

Getting There: The huge, can't-miss-it cathedral is in the center of the Barri Gòtic, on Plaça de la Seu, Metro: Jaume I.

Getting In: The main, front door is open most of the time. While it can be crowded, the line generally moves fast. Sometimes you can also enter directly into the cloister around back (through door facing the Martyrs Statue on the small square along Carrer del Bisbe).

WCs: A tiny, semi-private WC is in the center of the cloister.

Visiting the Church: This has been Barcelona's holiest spot for 2,000 years. The Romans built their Temple of Jupiter here. In A.D. 343, the pagan temple was replaced with a Christian cathedral. That building was supplanted by a Romanesque-style church (11th century). The current Gothic structure was built in the 14th century (1298-1450), during the medieval glory days of the Catalan nation. The facade was humble, so in the 19th century the proud local bourgeoisie redid it in a more ornate, Neo-Gothic style. Construction was capped in 1913 with the central spire, 230 feet tall.

Inside, the nave is ringed with 28 **side chapels,** financed by local guilds eager to display their wealth—if not to ingratiate themselves to God. Besides being worship spaces, these serve as interior buttresses supporting the roof (which is why the exterior walls are smooth, without the normal Gothic buttresses outside). Barcelona—the city of 32 official public holidays—honors many of the homegrown saints found in these chapels.

In the middle of the nave, the 15th-century **choir** *(coro)* features ornately carved stalls. During the standing parts of the Mass, the chairs were folded up, but VIPs still had those little wooden ledges to lean on. Each was creatively carved and—since you couldn't sit on sacred things—the artists were free to enjoy some secular and naughty fun here.

Look behind the **high altar** (beneath the crucifix) to find the archbishop's chair, or cathedra. As a cathedral, this church is the archbishop's seat—hence its Catalan nickname of *La Seu*. To the left of the altar is the organ and the elevator up to the **terrace.**

The steps beneath the altar lead to the **crypt,** featuring the marble-and-alabaster sarcophagus (1327-1339) with the remains of

Circle Dances in Squares and Castles in the Air

From group circle dancing to human towers, Catalans have some interesting and unique traditions. A memorable

Barcelona experience is watching (or participating in) the patriotic *sardana* dances (worth ▲). Locals of all ages seem to spontaneously appear. For some it's a highly symbolic, politically charged action representing Catalan unity—but for most it's just a fun chance to kick up their heels. Participants gather in circles after putting their things in the center—symbolic of community and sharing (and the ever-present risk of theft).

All are welcome, even tourists cursed with two left feet. The dances are held in the square in front of the cathedral every Sunday at 12:00 and usually also on Saturdays at 18:00 (none in Aug); the event lasts between one and two hours.

Holding hands, dancers raise their arms—slow-motion, *Zorba the Greek*-style—as they hop and sway gracefully to the music. The band *(cobla)* consists of a long flute, tenor and soprano oboes, strange-looking brass instruments, and a tiny bongo-like drum *(tambori)*. The rest of Spain mocks this lazy circle dance, but considering what it takes for a culture to survive within another culture's country, it is a stirring display of local pride and patriotism. During 36 years of Franco dictatorship, the *sardana* was forbidden.

Another Catalan tradition is the *castell,* a tower erected solely of people. *Castells* pop up on special occasions, such as the Festes de Gràcia in August and the Mercè festival in September. Towers can be up to 10 humans high. Imagine balancing 50 or 60 feet in the air, with nothing but a pile of flesh and bone between you and the ground. The base is formed by burly supports called *baixos;* above them are the *manilles* ("handles"), which help haul up the people to the top. The *castell* is capped with a human steeple—usually a child—who extends four fingers into the air, representing the four red stripes of the Catalan flag. A scrum of spotters (called *pinyas*) cluster around the base in case anyone falls. *Castelleres* are judged both on how quickly they erect their human towers and how fast they can take them down. Besides festivals, you may also see people forming these towers in front of the cathedral on summer Saturdays around 19:00 (confirm locally before showing up).

One thing that these two traditions have in common is their communal nature. Perhaps it's no coincidence, as Catalunya is known for its community spirit, team building, and socialistic bent.

St. Eulàlia. The cathedral is dedicated
to this saint.

Exit out the right transept and
into the circa-1450 **cloister**—the
arcaded walkway surrounding a lush
courtyard. Ahhhh. It's a tropical
atmosphere of palm, orange, and
magnolia trees; a fish pond; trickling
fountains; and squawking geese. The
nearby fountain has a tiny statue of St.
Jordi slaying the dragon. During the
Corpus Christi festival (June), kids come here to watch a hollow
egg dance atop the fountain's spray. As you wander the cloister
(clockwise), check out the coats of arms as well as the tombs in the
pavement. These were rich merchants who paid good money to be
buried as close to the altar as possible. Notice the symbols of their
trades: scissors, shoes, bakers, and so on. The resident geese have
been here for at least 500 years. There are always 13, in memory of
Eulàlia's 13 years and 13 torments.

The little **museum,** at the far end of the cloister, has the six-
foot-tall 14th-century Great Monstrance, a ceremonial display case
for the communion wafer that's paraded through the streets during
the Corpus Christi festival. The next room, the Sala Capitular, has
several altarpieces, including a *pietá* (a.k.a. *Desplà*) by Bartolomé
Bermejo (1490).

▲Barcelona History Museum
(Museu d'Història de Barcelona: Plaça del Rei)

At this main branch of the city history museum (MUHBA for
short), you can walk through the history of Barcelona, with a focus
on the city's Roman roots.

Cost and Hours: €7; ticket includes English audioguide
and other MUHBA branches, including La Casa del Guarda in
Park Güell; free all day first Sun of month and other Sun from
15:00—but no audioguide during free times; open Tue-Sat 10:00-
19:00, Sun 10:00-20:00, closed Mon; last entry 30 minutes before
closing, Plaça del Rei, enter on Vageur street, Metro: Jaume I, tel.
932-562-122.

Visiting the Museum: Though the museum is housed in
part of the former Royal Palace complex, you'll see only a bit
of that grand space. Instead, the focus is on the exhibits in the
cellar. While posted information is only in Catalan and Spanish,
you'll find abundant English handouts, and the included English
audioguide provides informative, if dry, descriptions of the
exhibits.

Start by watching the nine-minute introductory video in
the small theater (at the end of the first floor); it plays alternately

in Catalan, Spanish, and English, but it's worth viewing in any language. Then take an elevator down 65 feet (and 2,000 years—see the date spin back while you descend) to stroll the streets of Roman Barcino—founded by Emperor Augustus around 10 B.C.

The history is so strong here, you can smell it. This was a working-class part of town. The archaeological route leads you through areas used for laundering clothes and dyeing garments, the remains of a factory that salted fish and produced garum (a fish-derived sauce used extensively in ancient Roman cooking), and winemaking facilities.

Next, you'll wander through bits of a seventh-century early Christian church and an exhibit in the 11th-century count's palace that shows you Barcelona through its glory days in the Middle Ages.

Finally, head upstairs (or ride the elevator to floor 0) to see a model of the city from the early 16th century. From here, you can also enter **Tinell Hall** (part of the Royal Palace), with its long, graceful, rounded vaults. Nearby, step into the 14th-century **Chapel of St. Agatha,** if it's hosting a temporary exhibit.

Frederic Marès Museum (Museu Frederic Marès)

This museum, with the eclectic collection of local sculptor and packrat Frederic Marès (1893-1991), sprawls around a peaceful courtyard through several old Barri Gòtic buildings. The biggest part of the collection, on the ground and first floors, consists of sculpture—from ancient works to beautiful, evocative Gothic pieces to items from the early 20th century. Even more interesting is the extensive "Collector's Cabinet," consisting of items Marès found representative of everyday life in the 19th century. Lovingly displayed on the second and third floors, the collection contains rooms upon rooms of scissors, keys, irons, fans, nutcrackers, stamps, pipes, snuff boxes, opera glasses, pocket watches, bicycles, toy soldiers, dolls, and other bric-a-brac. And in Marès' study are several sculptures by the artist himself. The tranquil courtyard café offers a pleasant break, even when the museum is closed (café open in summer only, until 22:00).

Cost and Hours: €4.20, free Sun from 15:00, 1.5-hour audioguide-€1; open Tue-Sat 10:00-19:00, Sun 11:00-20:00, closed Mon; Plaça de Sant Iu 5-6, Metro: Jaume I, tel. 932-563-500, www.museumares.bcn.cat.

Shoe Museum (Museu del Calçat)

Shoe lovers enjoy this small museum of footwear in glass display cases, watched over by an earnest attendant. You'll see shoes from the 1700s to today: fancy ladies' boots, Tibetan moccasins, big clown shoes, expeditionary boots that have been to Mount Everest, and shoes of minor celebrities such as the president of Catalunya. The huge shoes at the entry are designed to fit the foot

BARCELONA

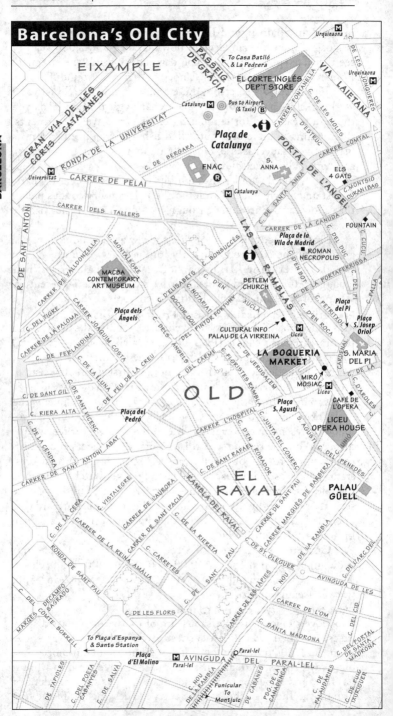

Barcelona's Old City

EIXAMPLE

PASSEIG DE GRACIA

To Casa Batlló & La Pedrera

EL CORTE INGLÉS DEP'T STORE

Urquinaona

Urquinaona

VIA LAIETANA

DE LES JOUQUERES

Catalunya

Bus to Airport (& Taxis)

Plaça de Catalunya

CARRER FONTANELLA

C. DE LES MOLES

C. D'ESTRUC

PORTAL DE L'ANGEL

CARRER COMTAL

GRAN VIA DE LES CORTS CATALANES

RONDA DE LA UNIVERSITAT

C. DE BERGARA

FNAC

S. ANNA

ELS 4 GATS

C. MONTSIÓ

Universitat

CARRER DE PELAI

Catalunya

C. DE SANTA ANNA

DURANIBAS

CARRER DELS TALLERS

CARRER DE LA CANUDA

C. DEL DUC

FOUNTAIN

R. DE SANT ANTONI

C. MONTALEGRE

BONSUCCÉS

Plaça de la Vila de Madrid

ROMAN NECROPOLIS

C. CUCURO

LAS RAMBLAS

MACBA CONTEMPORARY ART MUSEUM

CARRER DE VALLDONZELLA

C. D'ELISABETS

C. D'EN

C. D'EN BOT

C. DE LA PORTAFERRISSA

C. PALLA

CARRER DE LA PALOMA

C. DEL TIGRE

CARRER JOAQUIM COSTA

DOCTOR DOU

C. NOTARIAT

XUCLA

BETLEM CHURCH

C. PETRITXOL

Plaça del Pi

Plaça S. Josep Oriol

Plaça dels Àngels

DEL PINTOR FORTUNY

C. DE FERLANDINA

C. DELS

CULTURAL INFO PALAU DE LA VIRREINA

C. D'EN ROCA

Liceu

C. DE LA LLUNA

ÀNGELS

C. DEL CARME

C. DE JERUSALEM

LA BOQUERIA MARKET

S. MARIA DEL PI

C. C. D'AROLES

C. DE SANT GIL

C. DEL PEU DE LA CREU

FLORISTES RAMBLA

MIRÓ MOSIAC

Liceu

CAFÉ DE L'OPERA

C. DE SANT VICENÇ

C. RIERA ALTA

Plaça del Pedró

O L D

Plaça S. Agusti

LICEU OPERA HOUSE

C. DE LA CENDRA

CARRER L'HOSPITAL

C. D'EN ROBADOR

C. JUNTA DEL COMERÇ

C. AGUSTI

C. DEL PENEDÈS

CARRER DE SANT ANTONI ABAT

C. DE SANT RAFAEL

EL RAVAL

CARRER DE SANT PAU

PALAU GÜELL

C. DE LA CERA

C. VISTALEGRE

CARRER DE L'AURORA

RAMBLA DEL RAVAL

CARRER MARQUES DE BARBERA

RONDA DE SANT PAU

CARRER DE SANT PACIÀ

C. DE LA RIERETA

C. DE ST. OLEGUER

DE LA RAMBLA

C. DE L'ARC DEL

CARRER DE LA REINA AMALIA

C. CARRETES

PAU

C. NOU

AVINGUDA DE LES

MARQUES COMTE BORKELL

C. DEL DECAMPO SAGRADO

C. DE LES FLORS

CARRER DE LES TAPIES

CARRER DE L'OM

C. SANTA MADRONA

C. DEL CID

C. DE L'PARC DEL

To Plaça d'Espanya & Sants Station

Plaça d'El Molino

AVINGUDA

DEL PARAL-LEL

C. DE PORTAL DE SANTA MADRONA

C. DE TAPIOLES

C. DEL POETA CABANYES

C. DE SANÇ

Paral-lel

Paral-lel

C. NOU DE LA RAMBLA

Funicular To Montjuïc

PSG. DE LA CANAPBENEGA

DE CABANES

C. DE PUIG

TRIGUIER

C. DE PALAUDARINES

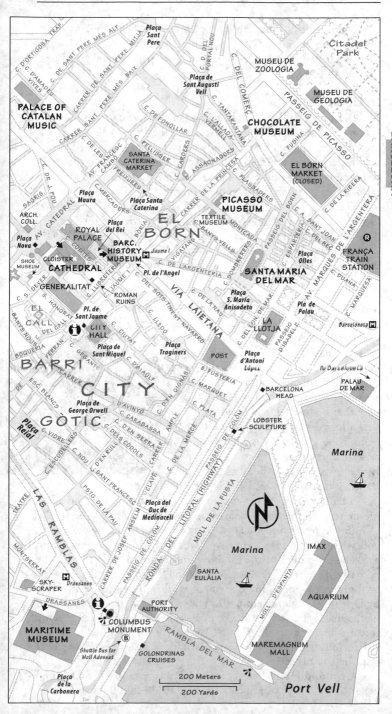

BARCELONA

of the Columbus Monument at the bottom of the Ramblas.

Cost and Hours: €2.50, Tue-Sun 11:00-14:00, closed Mon, on Plaça Sant Felip Neri, Metro: Jaume I, see page 82 for directions, tel. 933-014-533.

In El Born

The Old City's El Born neighborhood (also known as "La Ribera") is home to several great sights, including the Picasso Museum. But even without those, the neighborhood is a joy to explore. El Born's narrow lanes are crammed with artsy boutiques, inviting cafés and restaurants, funky one-off shops, rollicking nightlife, and a higher ratio of locals to tourists than most other city-center zones.

Getting There: It's just across Via Laietana from the Barri Gòtic's Plaça de l'Angel (Metro: Jaume I). Carrer de l'Argenteria ("Silversmiths Street") runs diagonally from Plaça de l'Angel straight down to the Church of Santa Maria del Mar. The Palace of Catalan Music is to the north, and the Picasso Museum is roughly in the center.

▲▲▲Picasso Museum (Museu Picasso)

Pablo Picasso may have made his career in Paris, but the years he spent in Barcelona—from ages 14 through 23—were among the most formative of his life. It was here that young Pablo mastered the realistic painting style of his artistic forebears—and it was also here that he first felt the freedom that allowed him to leave that all behind and give in to his creative, experimental urges. When he left Barcelona, Picasso headed for Paris...and revolutionized art forever.

The pieces in this excellent museum capture that priceless moment just before this bold young thinker changed the world. While you won't find Picasso's famous, later Cubist works here, you will enjoy a representative sweep of his early years, from art-school prodigy to the gloomy hues of his Blue Period to the revitalized cheer of his Rose Period. You'll also see works from his twilight years, including dozens of wild improvisations inspired by Diego Velázquez's seminal *Las Meninas,* as well as a roomful of works that reflect the childlike exuberance of an old man playing like a young kid on the French Riviera. It's undoubtedly the top collection of Picassos here in his native country and the best anywhere of his early years.

Cost and Hours: €14, free all day first Sun of month and other Sun from 15:00; open Tue-Sun 10:00-20:00, closed Mon,

BARCELONA

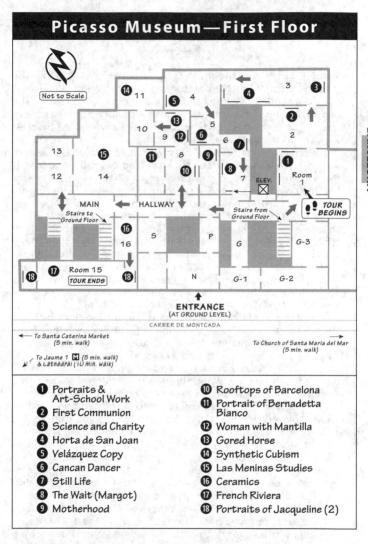

Picasso Museum—First Floor

Not to Scale

14 11

5 4 4 3 3

10 13 2 2

9 12 6 2

5 6

13 11 8 9 6 1

15 8 8 7 Room 1

12 14 10 ELEV.

MAIN HALLWAY Stairs from Ground Floor TOUR BEGINS

Stairs to Ground Floor

16 S P G G-3

16

18 17 Room 15 18 N G-1 G-2

TOUR ENDS

ENTRANCE
(AT GROUND LEVEL)

CARRER DE MONTCADA

← To Santa Caterina Market (5 min. walk)

To Church of Santa Maria del Mar (5 min. walk) →

To Jaume 1 Ⓜ (5 min. walk) & Cathedral (10 min. walk)

1. Portraits & Art-School Work
2. First Communion
3. Science and Charity
4. Horta de San Joan
5. Velázquez Copy
6. Cancan Dancer
7. Still Life
8. The Wait (Margot)
9. Motherhood
10. Rooftops of Barcelona
11. Portrait of Bernadetta Bianco
12. Woman with Mantilla
13. Gored Horse
14. Synthetic Cubism
15. Las Meninas Studies
16. Ceramics
17. French Riviera
18. Portraits of Jacqueline (2)

last entry 20 minutes before closing, Carrer de Montcada 15-23, ticket office at #21, Metro: Jaume I, tel. 932-563-000, www.museupicasso.bcn.cat.

Crowd-Beating Tips: There's almost always a line, sometimes with waits of more than an hour. The busiest times are mornings before 13:00, all day Tuesday, and during the free entry times on Sundays (see above). If you have an Articket BCN (see page 53), skip the line by going to the "Meeting Point" entrance (30 yards to the right of the main entrance). You can also skip the line by buying your ticket online at www.museupicasso.bcn.cat (no

Pablo Picasso
(1881-1973)

Pablo Picasso was the most famous and—OK, I'll say it—the greatest artist of the 20th century. Always exploring, he became the master of many styles (Cubism, Surrealism, Expressionism, and so on) and of many media (painting, sculpture, prints, ceramics, and assemblages). Still, he could make anything he touched look unmistakably like "a Picasso."

Born in Málaga, Spain, Picasso was the son of an art teacher. At a very young age, he quickly advanced beyond his teachers. Picasso's teenage works are stunningly realistic, with wise insight into the people he painted. As a youth in Barcelona, he fell in with a bohemian crowd that mixed wine, women, and art.

In 1900, at age 19, Picasso started making trips to Paris; at this time, he also rejected the surname his father had given him (Ruiz) in favor of his mother's. Four years later, he moved to the City of Light and absorbed the styles of many painters (especially Henri de Toulouse-Lautrec) while searching for his own artist's voice. His paintings of beggars and other social outcasts show the empathy of a man who was himself a poor, homesick foreigner. When his best friend, Spanish artist Carlos Casagemas, committed suicide, Picasso plunged into a **Blue Period** (1901-1904)—so called because the dominant color in these paintings matches the melancholy mood and subject matter (emaciated beggars, hard-eyed pimps, and so on).

In 1904, Picasso got a steady girlfriend (Fernande Olivier) and suddenly saw the world through rose-colored glasses—the **Rose Period.** He was further jolted out of his Blue Period by the "flat" look of the Fauves. Not satisfied with their take on 3-D, Picasso played with the "building blocks" of line and color to find new ways to reconstruct the real world on canvas.

At his studio in Montmartre, Picasso and his neighbor Georges Braque worked together, in poverty so dire they often didn't know where their next bottle of wine was coming from. And then, at the age of 25, Picasso reinvented painting. Fascinated by the primitive power of African and Iberian tribal masks, he sketched human faces with simple outlines and almond eyes. Intrigued by the body of his girlfriend, Fernande, he sketched it from every angle, then experimented with showing several different views on the same canvas. A hundred paintings and nine months later, Picasso gave birth to a monstrous canvas of five nude, fragmented prostitutes with mask-like faces—*Les Demoiselles d'Avignon* (1907).

This bold new style was called **Cubism.** With Cubism, Picasso shattered the Old World and put it back together in a new way. The subjects are somewhat recognizable (with the help of the titles), but they're built with geometric shards (let's call them "cubes")—like viewing the world through a kaleidoscope of brown and gray. Cubism gives us several different angles of the subject at once—say, a woman seen from the front and side angles simultaneously, resulting in two eyes on the same side of the nose. This involves showing the traditional three dimensions, plus Einstein's new fourth dimension—the time it takes to walk around the subject to see other angles.

In 1918, Picasso married his first wife, Olga Kokhlova, with whom he had a son. He then traveled to Rome and entered a **Classical Period** (the 1920s) of more realistic, full-bodied women and children, inspired by the three-dimensional sturdiness of ancient statues. While he flirted with abstraction, throughout his life, Picasso always kept a grip on "reality." His favorite subject was people. The anatomy might be jumbled, but it's all there.

Though he lived in France and Italy, Picasso remained a Spaniard at heart, incorporating Spanish motifs into his work. Unrepentantly macho, he loved bullfights, seeing them as a metaphor for the timeless human interaction between the genders. The horse—clad with blinders and pummeled by the bull—has nothing to do with the fight. To Picasso, the horse symbolizes the feminine, and the bull, the masculine. Spanish imagery—bulls, screaming horses, a Madonna—appears in Picasso's most famous work, *Guernica* (1937, on display in Madrid). The monumental canvas of a bombed village summed up the pain of Spain's brutal civil war (1936-1939) and foreshadowed the onslaught of World War II.

At war's end, Picasso left Paris, his wife, and all of his emotional baggage behind, finding fun in the sun in the **South of France.** Sun! Color! Water! Spacious skies! Freedom! Senior citizen Pablo Picasso was reborn, enjoying worldwide fame. He lives at first with the beautiful young painter Françoise Gilot, mother of two of his children, but soon replaces her with another young beauty, Jacqueline Roque, who becomes his second wife. Dressed in rolled-up white pants and a striped sailor's shirt, bursting with pent-up creativity, Picasso often cranked out more than a painting a day. Picasso's Riviera works set the tone for the rest of his life—sunny, lighthearted, childlike, experimenting in new media and using motifs of the sea, of Greek mythology (fauns, centaurs), and animals (birds, goats, and pregnant baboons). His simple drawing of doves became an international symbol of peace.

Picasso also made collages, built "statues" out of wood, wire, ceramics, papier-mâché, or whatever, and even turned everyday household objects into statues (like his famous bull's head made of a bicycle seat with handlebar horns). **"Multimedia"** works like these have become so standard today that we forget how revolutionary they were when Picasso invented them. His last works have the playfulness of someone much younger. As it is often said of Picasso, "When he was a child, he painted like a man. When he was old, he painted like a child."

additional booking fee). Stuck in line without a ticket? Figure that about 25 people are admitted every 10 minutes.

Getting There: From the Jaume I Metro stop, it's a quick five-minute walk. Just head down Carrer de la Princesa (across the busy Via Laietana from the Barri Gòtic), turning right on Carrer de Montcada.

Audioguide: The 1.5-hour audioguide costs €3 and offers ample detail about the collection.

Services: The ground floor, which is free to enter, has a required bag check, as well as a handy array of other services (bookshop, WC, and cafeteria).

Cuisine Art: The museum itself has a good **café** (€8 sandwiches and salads). Outside the museum, right along Carrer de Montcada in either direction, are two great recommended tapas bars (both closed Mon): With your back to the museum, a few steps to the left is **El Xampanyet,** while to the right (across Carrer de la Princesa and up a block) is **Bar del Pla.**

❷ Self-Guided Tour: The Picasso Museum's collection of paintings is presented more or less chronologically (though specific pieces may be out for restoration or on tour, and the rooms are sometimes rearranged). But with the help of thoughtful English descriptions for each stage (and guards who don't let you stray), it's easy to follow the evolution of Picasso's work. This tour is arranged by the stages of his life and art.

• *Begin in Rooms 1 and 2.*

Boy Wonder: Pablo's earliest art (in the first room) is realistic and earnest. His work quickly advances from childish pencil drawings (such as *Hercules,* 1890), through a series of technically skilled art-school works (copies of plaster feet and arms), to oil paintings of impressive technique. Even at a young age, his **portraits** of grizzled peasants demonstrate surprising psychological insight. Because his dedicated father—himself a curator and artist—kept everything his son ever did, Picasso must have the best-documented youth of any great painter.

• *In Room 2, you'll find more paintings relating to Pablo's...*

Developing Talent (Adolescence): During a summer trip to Málaga, Picasso dabbles in a series of fresh, Impressionistic-style landscapes (relatively rare in Spain at the time). As a 15-year-old, Pablo dutifully enters art-school competitions. His first big work, *First Communion,* features a prescribed religious subject, but Picasso makes it an excuse to paint his family. His sister Lola is the model for the communicant, and the features of the man beside her belong to Picasso's father. Notice Lola's exquisitely painted veil. This piece was heavily influenced by the academic style of local painters.

Picasso's relatives star in a number of portraits from this time.

If it's on view, find the **portrait of his mother** (this and other family portraits may be out on loan to the Picasso Museum in Málaga). The teenage Pablo is working on the fine details and gradients of white in her blouse and the expression in her cameo-like face. Notice the signature. Spaniards keep both parents' surnames, with the father's first, followed by the mother's: Pablo Ruiz Picasso.

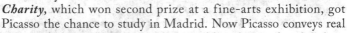

• *Continue into Room 3.*

Early Success: *Science and Charity,* which won second prize at a fine-arts exhibition, got Picasso the chance to study in Madrid. Now Picasso conveys real

feeling. The doctor (modeled on Pablo's father) represents science. The nun represents charity and religion. From her hopeless face and lifeless hand, it seems that Picasso believes nothing will save this woman from death. Pablo painted a little perspective trick: Walk back and forth across the room to see the

bed stretch and shrink. Three small studies for this painting (on the right) show how this was an exploratory work. The frontier: light.

Picasso travels to Madrid for further study. Stifled by the stuffy fine-arts school there, he hangs out instead in the Prado Museum and learns by copying the masters. (An example of his impressive mimicry is coming up later, in Room 4.) Having absorbed the wisdom of the ages, in 1898 Pablo visits **Horta de San Juan,** a rural Catalan village, and finds his artistic independence. (See the small landscapes and scenes of village life he did there.) Poor and without a love in his life, he returns to Barcelona.

• *Head to Room 4.*

Barcelona Freedom (1900): Art Nouveau is all the rage in Barcelona. Upsetting his dad, Pablo quits art school and falls in with the avant-garde crowd. These bohemians congregate daily at Els Quatre Gats ("The Four Cats," a popular restaurant to this day—see page 164).

Picasso even created the **menu cover** for this favorite hangout (it's sometimes on view here in Room 4). Further establishing his artistic freedom, he paints **portraits** of his new friends (including one of Jaume Sabartés, who later became his personal assistant and donated the works to establish this museum). Still a teenager, Pablo puts on his first one-man show at Els Quatre Gats in 1900.

Notice young Picasso's nearly perfect **copy** of a portrait of Philip IV by an earlier Spanish master, Diego Velázquez. Near the end of the museum, we'll see a much older Picasso—now confident with his boldly idiosyncratic style—riffing on another Velázquez painting.

• *The next few pieces are displayed in Rooms 5, 6, and 7.*

Paris (1900-1901): In 1900 Picasso makes his first trip to Paris, a city bursting with life, light, and love. Dropping the paternal surname Ruiz, Pablo establishes his commercial brand name: "Picasso." Here the explorer Picasso goes bohemian and befriends poets, prostitutes, and artists. He paints **cancan dancers** like Toulouse-Lautrec, **still lifes** like Paul Cézanne, brightly colored Fauvist works like Henri Matisse, and Impressionist **land-**

scapes like Claude Monet. In *The Wait (Margot)*, the subject—with her bold outline and strong gaze—pops out from the vivid, mosaic-like background.

• *Turn right into the hall, then—farther along—right again, to find Rooms 8 and 9.*

Blue Period (1901-1904): Picasso continues traveling to Paris. But the bleak weather, the suicide of his best friend, and his own poverty lead Picasso to abandon jewel-bright color for his Blue Period. He cranks out stacks of blue art just to stay housed and fed.

With blue backgrounds (the coldest color) and depressing subjects, this period was revolutionary in art history. Now the artist is painting not what he sees, but what he feels. Just off of Room 8, look for the touching portrait of a mother and child, *Motherhood* (this very fragile pastel is only displayed intermittently), which captures the period well. Painting misfits and street people, Picasso, like Velázquez and Toulouse-Lautrec, sees "the beauty in ugliness."

Back home in Barcelona, Picasso paints his hometown at night from **rooftops** (in the main part of Room 8). The painting is still blue, but here we see proto-Cubism...five years before the first real Cubist painting.

• *Just off of Room 8, we get a hint of Picasso's...*

Rose Period (1904-1907): Picasso is finally lifted out of his funk after meeting a new lady, Fernande Olivier. He moves out of the blue and into the happier Rose Period. For a fine example, see the portrait of a woman wearing a classic Spanish mantilla *(Portrait of Bernadetta Bianco)*. Its soft pink and reddish tones are the colors of flesh and sensuality.

• *Move into Rooms 9-11.*

Barcelona (1917): Picasso spent six months back in Barcelona in 1917 (his girlfriend, a Russian dancer with the Ballets Russes, had a gig in town). The paintings in these rooms demonstrate the artist's irrepressible versatility: He's already developed Cubism (with his friend Georges Braque; more on this below), but he also continues to play with other styles. In *Woman with Mantilla* (Room 9), we see a little Post-Impressionistic Pointillism in a portrait that is as elegant as a classical statue. Nearby, *Gored Horse* has all the anguish and power of his iconic *Guernica* (painted years later).

Pablo's role in the invention of the revolutionary Cubist style is well known—at least I hope so, since this museum has no true Cubist paintings. A Cubist work gives not only the basics of a subject—it shows every aspect of it simultaneously. The technique of "building" a subject with "cubes" of paint simmered in Picasso's artistic stew for years. In this museum, you'll see some so-called **Synthetic Cubist paintings**—a later variation that flattens the various angles, as opposed to the purer, original "Analytical Cubist" paintings, in which you can simultaneously see several 3-D facets of the subject.

• *Remember that this museum focuses on Picasso's early years. As a result, it has very little from the most famous and prolific "middle" part of his career—basically, from Picasso's invention of Cubism to his sunset years on the French Riviera. Skip ahead more than 30 years and into Rooms 12-14 (at the end of the main hallway on the right).*

Picasso and Velázquez (1957): This series of rooms relates to what many consider the greatest painting by anyone, ever: Diego Velázquez's *Las Meninas* (the original is displayed

in Madrid's Prado Museum). Heralded as the first completely realistic painting, *Las Meninas* became an obsession for Picasso centuries later.

Picasso, who had great respect for Velázquez, painted more than **50 interpretations** of this piece. These two Spanish geniuses were artistic equals. Picasso seems to enjoy a relationship with Velázquez. Like artistic soul mates, they spar and tease. He deconstructs Velázquez and then injects light, color, and perspective to horse around with the earlier masterpiece. In the big black-and-white canvas, the king and queen (reflected in the mirror in the back of the room) are hardly seen, while the self-portrait of the painter towers above everyone. The two women of the court on the right look like they're in a tomb—but they're wearing party shoes. Browse the various studies, a playground of color and perspective. See the fun Picasso had playing paddleball with Velázquez's tour de force—filtering Velázquez's realism through the kaleidoscope of Cubism.

• *Head back down the hall and turn right, through the* **ceramics** *area (Room 16), to find a flock of carefree white birds in Room 15.*

The French Riviera: The Spaniard spends the last 36 years of his life living simply in the south of France. Picasso said many times that "Paintings are like windows open to the world." We see his sunny Riviera world: With simple black outlines and Crayola colors, Picasso paints sun-splashed nature, peaceful doves, and the joys of the beach. He dabbles in the timeless art of ceramics, shaping bowls and vases into fun animals decorated with simple, playful designs. He's enjoying life. Portraits of his second (and much younger) wife, Jacqueline Roque, hang at each end of Room 15.

Picasso died with brush in hand, still growing. Sadly, since Picasso vowed never to set foot in a fascist, Franco-ruled Spain, the artist never returned to his homeland...and never saw this museum (his death came in 1973—two years before Franco's). However, to the end, Picasso continued exploring and loving life through his art.

Other Sights in El Born
▲▲Palace of Catalan Music (Palau de la Música Catalana)
This concert hall, built in just three years and finished in 1908, features an unexceptional exterior but boasts my favorite Modernista interior in town (by Lluís Domènech i Montaner). Its inviting arches lead you into the 2,138-seat hall (accessible only with a tour). A kaleidoscopic skylight features a choir singing around the sun, while playful carvings and mosaics celebrate music and Catalan culture. If you're interested in Modernisme, taking this tour (which starts with a relaxing 12-minute video) is one of the best experiences in town—and helps balance the hard-to-avoid

over-focus on Gaudí as "Mr. Modernisme."

Cost and Hours: €17, 50-minute tours in English run daily every hour 10:00-15:00, tour times may change based on performance schedule, about 6 blocks northeast of cathedral, Carrer Palau de la Música 4-6, Metro: Urquinaona, tel. 902-442-882, www.palaumusica.cat.

Advance Reservations Required: You must buy your ticket in advance to get a spot on an English guided tour (tickets available up to 4 months in advance—ideally buy yours at least 2 days before, though they're sometimes available the same day or day before—especially Oct-March). You can buy the ticket in person at the concert hall box office (less than a 10-minute walk from the cathedral or Picasso Museum, open daily 9:30-15:30); by phone with your credit card (no extra charge, tel. 902-475-485); or online at the concert hall website (€1 fee, www.palaumusica.cat).

Concerts: The other way to see the hall is by attending a concert (300 per year, €22-49 tickets, see website for details, box office tel. 902-442-882).

▲Santa Caterina Market

This eye-catching market hall was built on the ruins of an old monastery, then renovated in 2006 with a wildly colorful, swooping, Gaudí-inspired roof and shell built around its original white walls (a good exhibition at the far corner provides a view of the foundations and English explanations). The much-delayed construction took so long that locals began calling the site the "Hole of Shame." Come for the outlandish architecture, but stay for a chance to shop for a picnic without the tourist logjam of La Boqueria market on the Ramblas.

Cost and Hours: Free, Mon 7:30-14:00, Tue-Wed and Sat 7:30-15:30, Thu-Fri 7:30-20:30, closed Sun, Avinguda de Francesc Cambó 16, www.mercatsantacaterina.cat.

▲Church of Santa Maria del Mar

This so-called "Cathedral of the Sea" was built entirely with local funds and labor, in the heart of the wealthy merchant El Born

quarter. Proudly independent, the church features a purely Catalan Gothic interior that was forcibly uncluttered of its Baroque decor by civil war belligerents.

Cost and Hours: Free except from 13:30-16:30, when it costs €3; open daily 8:00-13:30 & 17:00-19:30; €5 guided rooftop tours in summer, English tours on the hour Mon-Fri 13:00-19:00, Sat-Sun at 11:00 and 12:00; Plaça Santa Maria, Metro: Jaume I, tel. 933-435-633, www.stamariadelmar.org.

Visiting the Church: Before entering, look at the figures on the front door. These represent the *bastaixos* who hauled the stone used to build the church all the way from Montjuïc quarries.

Step inside, to the largely unadorned Gothic space. It used to be more highly decorated with Baroque frills. But during the civil war (1936-1939), the Catholic Church sided with the conservative forces of Franco against the people. In retaliation, the working class took their anger out on this church, burning all of its wood furnishings and decor (carbon still blackens the ceiling).

Today the church remains stripped down—naked in all its Gothic glory. This is where shipwrights and merchants came to worship. The tree-like columns inspired Gaudí (their influence on the columns inside his Sagrada Família church is obvious). Sixteenth-century sailors left models of their ships at the foot of the altar for Mary's protection. Even today a classic old Catalan ship remains at Mary's feet. As within Barcelona's cathedral, here you can see the characteristic Catalan Gothic buttresses flying inward, defining the chapels that ring the nave. Brilliant stained glass—most notably the rose window over the main entry—floods the interior with soft light.

Nearby: Around the right side of the church is a poignant memorial to the "Catalan Alamo" of September 11, 1714, when the Spanish crown besieged and conquered Barcelona, slaughtering Catalan insurgents and kicking off more than two centuries of cultural suppression.

Passeig del Born

This long boulevard is the neighborhood center. Formerly a jousting square (as its Roman circus-esque shape indicates), it got its name, "El Born," from an old Catalan word for "tournament" (the name was eventually given to the entire neighborhood). These days, Passeig del Born is a popular springboard for exploring tapas bars, fun restaurants, and nightspots in the narrow streets all around. Wandering around here at night, you'll find piles of inviting and intriguing little restaurants (I've listed my favorites on page 167). At the far end of Passeig del Born is the vast-but-vacant, steel-frame, 19th-century El Born Market, which served as the city's main produce market hall until 1971, when it was relocated to the suburbs. Plans are under way to convert the market hall into a cultural center and museum.

You'll also find great shopping near this strip—be sure to venture up **Carrer dels Flassaders** (funky shops, to the left as you face the old market hall) and down **Carrer del Rec** (fashionable boutiques, to the right as you face the market). For more tips, see "Shopping in Barcelona," later.

Chocolate Museum (Museu de la Xocolata)

This museum, only a couple of blocks from the Picasso Museum (and near Citadel Park—see listing, later), is fun for chocolate lovers. Operated by the local confectioners' guild, it tells the story of chocolate from Aztecs to Europeans via the port of Barcelona, where it was first unloaded and processed. But the history lesson is just an excuse to show off a series of remarkably ornate candy sculptures. These works of edible art—which change every year but often include such Spanish themes as Don Quixote or bullfighting—begin as store-window displays for Easter or Christmas. Once the holiday passes, the confectioners bring the sculptures here to be enjoyed.

Cost and Hours: €4.30, Mon-Sat 10:00-19:00 (until 20:00 mid-June-mid-Sept), Sun 10:00-15:00, Carrer del Comerç 36, Metro: Jaume I, tel. 932-687-878, www.museuxocolata.cat.

On the Harborfront, at the Bottom of the Ramblas

▲Maritime Museum (Museu Marítim)

Barcelona's medieval shipyard, the best preserved in the entire Mediterranean, is home to an excellent museum. Its permanent

collection is closed for renovation (until the fall of 2014), but the museum is hosting a series of worthwhile temporary exhibits during the revamp.

The building's cavernous halls evoke the 14th-century days when Catalunya was a naval and shipbuilding power, cranking out 30 huge galleys a winter. As in the US today, military and commercial ventures mixed and mingled as Catalunya built its trading empire. When the permanent collection reopens, it'll cover the salty history of ships and navigation from the 13th to the 20th century. In the meantime, an impressively huge and richly decorated royal galley remains on display.

Cost and Hours: Museum price depends on exhibits but usually €5, daily 10:00-20:00, last entry 30 minutes before closing, nice café with seating inside or out on the museum courtyard (free to enter), Avinguda de la Drassanes, Metro: Drassanes, tel. 933-429-920, www.mmb.cat.

Nearby: Your ticket also includes entrance to the *Santa Eulàlia*, an early 20th-century schooner docked just a short walk from the Columbus Monument (€1 for entry without museum visit, April-Oct Tue-Fri and Sun 10:00-20:30, Sat 14:00-20:30, closes at 17:30 in Nov-March, closed Mon year-round). On

Saturday mornings, the schooner sets sail around the harbor for three hours—reserve well in advance; spots book up weeks in advance (Sat 10:00-13:00, adult-€12, children 6-14-€6, family rates available, tel. 933-429-920, reserves.mmaritim@diba.cat).

Columbus Monument (Monument a Colóm)

Located where the Ramblas hits the harbor, this 200-foot-tall monument was built for the 1888 world's fair and commemorates Columbus' visit to Barcelona following his first trip to America. A tight four-person elevator takes you to a glassed-in observation area at the top for congested but sweeping views—but the elevator is often closed; ask at any TI before making a special trip here to ride it. There is a small and usually uncrowded TI inside the base of the monument.

Cost and Hours: Monument—free and always open; elevator ride-€4, daily May-Oct 8:30-20:30, Nov-April 8:00-20:00.

Golondrinas Cruises

At the harbor near the Columbus Monument, tourist boats called *golondrinas* offer two different unguided trips. As Barcelona's skyline isn't all that striking from the water, these trips are pretty pointless unless you'd just like to go for a boat ride. The shorter version goes around the harbor in 35 minutes (€7, daily on the hour 11:30-19:00, every 30 minutes mid-June-mid-Sept, may not run Nov-April, tel. 934-423-106, www.lasgolondrinas.com). The longer 1.5-hour trip goes up the coast to the Fòrum complex and back (€14.80, can disembark at Fòrum in summer only, about 7/day, daily 11:30-19:30, shorter hours off-season).

Near the Waterfront, East of the Old City and Harbor

Citadel Park (Parc de la Ciutadella)

In 1888, Barcelona's biggest, greenest park, originally the site of a much-hated military citadel, was transformed for a Universal Exhibition (world's fair). The stately Triumphal Arch at the top of the park, celebrating the removal of the citadel, was built as the main entrance. Inside you'll find wide pathways, plenty of trees and grass, a zoo, and museums of geology and zoology. Barcelona, one of Europe's most densely populated cities, suffers from a lack of real green space. This park is a haven and is especially enjoyable on weekends, when it teems with happy families. Enjoy the ornamental fountain that the young Antoni Gaudí helped design, and consider a jaunt in a rental rowboat on the lake in the center of the park. Check out the tropical Umbracle greenhouse and the Hivernacle winter garden, which has a pleasant café-bar (Mon-Sat 10:00-14:00 & 17:00-20:30, Sun 10:30-14:00, shorter hours off-season.

Cost and Hours: Park—free, daily 10:00 until dusk, north of França train station, Metro: Arc de Triomf, Barceloneta, or Ciutadella-Vila Olímpica.

▲**Barcelona's Beach, from Barceloneta to the Fòrum**
Barcelona has created a summer tourist beach trade by building a huge stretch of beaches east from the town center. Before the

1992 Olympics, this area was an industrial wasteland nicknamed the "Catalan Manchester." Not anymore. The industrial zone was demolished and dumped into the sea, while sand was dredged out of the seabed to make the pristine beaches locals enjoy today. The scene is great for sunbathing and for an evening paseo before dinner. It's like a resort island—complete with lounge chairs, volleyball, showers, WCs, bike paths, and inviting beach bars called *chiringuitos*. Looking out to sea from the beach, you can't miss the W Hotel, shaped like a windblown sail, dominating a small peninsula—controversial among locals for displacing a popular nude beach.

Getting There: The Barceloneta Metro stop will leave you blocks from the sand. To get to the beaches without a hike, take the bus. From the Ramblas, bus #59 will get you as far as Barceloneta Park. To reach the more-distant beaches, catch bus #41 in Plaça de Catalunya, which skirts Citadel Park before heading toward the water.

Biking the Beach: For a break from the city, rent a bike (in El Born, Citadel Park, or Barceloneta—for details, see page 56) and take the following little ride: Explore Citadel Park, filled with families enjoying a day out (described earlier). Then roll through Barceloneta. This artificial peninsula was once the home of working-class sailors and shippers. From the Barceloneta beach, head north to the Olympic Village, where the former apartments for 13,000 visiting athletes now house permanent residents. The village's symbol, Frank Gehry's striking "fish," shines brightly in the sun. A bustling night scene keeps this stretch of harborfront busy until the wee hours. From here you'll come to a series of man-made crescent-shaped beaches, each with trendy bars and cafés. If you're careless or curious (down by Platja de la Mar Bella), you might find yourself pedaling past people working on an all-over tan. In the distance is the huge solar panel marking the site of the Fòrum shopping and convention center.

Modernisme and the Renaixença

Modernisme is Barcelona's unique contribution to the Europe-wide Art Nouveau movement. Meaning "a taste for what is modern"—things like streetcars, electric lights, and big-wheeled bicycles—this free-flowing organic style lasted from 1888 to 1906.

Broadly speaking, there were two kinds of Modernisme (Catalan Art Nouveau). Early Modernisme is a kind of Neo-Gothic, clearly inspired by medieval castles and towers—logically, since architects wanted to recall the days when Barcelona was at the peak. From that same starting point, Antoni Gaudí branched off on his own, adding the color and curves we most associate with Barcelona's Modernisme look.

The aim was to create objects that were both practical and decorative. To that end, Modernista architects experimented with new construction techniques. Their most important material was concrete, which they could use to make a hard stone building that curved and rippled like a wave before sprinkling it with brightly colored glass and tile. The structure was fully modern, but the decoration was a clip-art collage of nature images, exotic Moorish or Chinese themes, and fanciful Gothic crosses and knights to celebrate Catalunya's medieval glory days.

The Fòrum

The original 1860 vision for Barcelona's enlargement would have extended the boulevard called Diagonal right to the sea. Developers finally realized this goal nearly a century and a half later, with the opening of the Fòrum. Go here for a taste of today's Barcelona: nothing Gothic, nothing quaint, just big and modern—a mall and a convention center. The Fòrum also tries to be an inspiration for environmental engineering. Waste is burned to produce heat. The giant solar panel creates perfectly clean and sustainable energy.

In 2004, Barcelona hosted the "Forum of the Cultures," an attempt to create a world's fair that recognized not states, but people. Roma (Gypsies), Basques, Māoris, Native Americans, and Catalans all assembled here in a global celebration of cultural diversity, multiculturalism, peace, and sustainability. The bash for this planet's "nations without states" was a moderate success, with triennial follow-ups in Mexico in 2007; Chile in 2010; and Naples, Italy, in 2013 (next up: Amman, Jordan in 2016). Local government officials hoped the event—like the city's many other

It's iron-ic to think that Modernisme was a response to the Industrial Age—and that all those organic shapes were only made possible thanks to Eiffel Tower-like iron frames. As you wander through the Eixample looking at all those fanciful facades and colorful, leafy, flowing, blooming shapes in doorways, entrances, and ceilings, remember that many of these homes were built at the same time as the first skyscrapers in Chicago and New York City.

But Modernisme was not just an architectural style. It was also a way of life and the language of power for the new rich in the 1880s. If you were a wealthy Catalan textile magnate, it was the ultimate status symbol to live the Modernista lifestyle. It's no accident that Modernista mansions come with big bay windows and outlandish decoration: The people who paid for them wanted both to be seen—and to be recognized for their forward-thinking embrace of the new art.

Underpinning Modernisme was the Catalan cultural revival movement, called the Renaixença. As Europe was waking up to the modern age, downtrodden peoples across Europe—from the Basques to the Irish to the Hungarians to the Finns—were throwing off the cultural domination of other nations and celebrating what made their own culture unique. Here in Catalunya, the Renaixença encouraged everyday people to get excited about all things Catalan—from their language, patriotic dances, and inspirational art to their surprising style of architecture.

"expos"—would goose development...and it did. Barcelona now has a modern part of town.

Getting There: You can get out to the Fòrum by bike, bus, or taxi via the long and impressive beach. Or the Metro zips you there in just a few minutes from the center (Fòrum Station).

Modernista Sights

For many visitors, Modernista architecture is Barcelona's main draw. And one name tops them all: Antoni Gaudí (1852-1926). Barcelona is an architectural scrapbook of Gaudí's galloping gables and organic curves. A devoted Catalan and Catholic, he immersed himself in each project, often living on-site. At various times, he called Park Güell, La Pedrera, and the Sagrada Família home. For more on Gaudí and some of his contemporaries, see the sidebar above.

I've covered the main Gaudí attractions in the order you'd reach them from the harbor to the outskirts—starting along the Ramblas and in the Eixample before heading out to Sagrada Família and Park Güell (farther afield, but worth the trip). And for

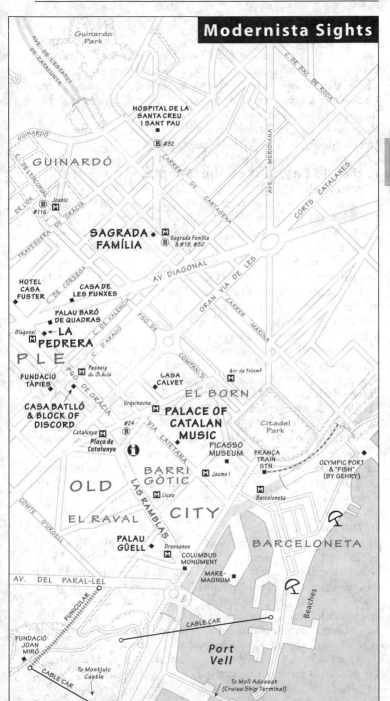

Modernista Sights

Guinardo Park

AVE. DE L'ESTATUT DE CATALUNYA

C. DE BAC DE RODA

GUINARDÓ

HOSPITAL DE LA SANTA CREU I SANT PAU
Ⓑ #92

C. DE L'ESCORIAL

GUINARDÓ

CARRER DE CARTAGENA

AVE. MERIDIANA

CORTS CATALANES

DE L'OR
Ⓑ #116
Ⓜ Joanic

TRAVESSERA DE GRÀCIA

SAGRADA FAMÍLIA Ⓜ Ⓑ Sagrada Família & #19, #50

C. DE CÒRSEGA

AV. DIAGONAL

GRAN VIA DE LES

HOTEL CASA FUSTER

CASA DE LES PUNXES

PALAU BARÓ DE QUADRAS

C. DE VALÈNCIA

PSG. DE

CARRER MARINA

Diagonal Ⓜ **LA PEDRERA**

D'ARAGÓ

PLE

PG. DE GRÀCIA

Ⓜ Passeig de Gràcia

COMPANYS

FUNDACIÓ TÀPIES

CASA CALVET

Arc de Triomf

EL BORN

Citadel Park

CASA BATLLÓ & BLOCK OF DISCORD

Urquinaona Ⓜ

PALACE OF CATALAN MUSIC

Catalunya Ⓜ

#24 Ⓑ

VIA LAIETANA

Plaça de Catalunya Ⓘ

PICASSO MUSEUM

FRANÇA TRAIN STN.

OLYMPIC PORT & "FISH" (BY GEHRY)

OLD

BARRI GÒTIC

Ⓜ Jaume I

COMTE D'URGELL

EL RAVAL

LAS RAMBLAS

Ⓜ Liceu

CITY

Ⓜ Barceloneta

BARCELONETA

Beaches

PALAU GÜELL Drassanes Ⓜ

COLUMBUS MONUMENT

MARE-MAGNUM

AV. DEL PARAL·LEL

FUNICULAR

CABLE CAR

Port Vell

FUNDACIÓ JOAN MIRÓ

CABLE CAR

To Montjuic Castle

To Moll Adossat (Cruise Ship Terminal)

those who want to visit both of the outlying sights in one trip, I've included tips on how to connect them.

Note that two other (non-Gaudí) Modernista works are covered in other sections: Lluís Domènech i Montaner's **Palace of Catalan Music** in El Born (see page 102), and Josep Puig i Cadafalch's **CaixaForum,** at the base of Montjuïc (page 138). For information on even more Modernista sights, you can visit the Plaça de Catalunya TI, where you'll find a special desk set aside just for Modernisme seekers (see page 52).

In the Old City, Just off the Ramblas
▲Palau Güell

Just as the Picasso Museum reveals a young genius on the verge of a breakthrough, this early Gaudí building (completed in 1890) shows the architect taking his first tentative steps toward what would become his trademark curvy style. Dark and masculine, with its castle-like rooms, Palau Güell (Catalans pronounce it "gway") was custom-built to house the Güell clan and gives an insight into Gaudí's artistic genius. The included 24-stop audioguide provides all the details. Despite the eye-catching roof (visible from the street if you crane your neck), I'd skip Palau Güell if you plan to see the more interesting La Pedrera (described later).

Cost and Hours: €12, includes audioguide, free first Sun of the month, open April-Sept Tue-Sun 10:00-20:00, Oct-March Tue-Sun 10:00-17:30, closed Mon year-round, last entry one hour before closing, a half-block off the Ramblas at Carrer Nou de la Rambla 3-5, Metro: Liceu or Drassanes, tel. 933-173-974, www.palauguell.cat.

Buying Tickets: As with any Gaudí sight, you may encounter lines. Since it's not possible to reserve tickets in advance, you'll have to buy them at the ticket window to the left of the entryway, then line up to the right. Each ticket has an entry time, so at busy times you may have to return later, even after buying your ticket.

In the Eixample

The Eixample ("Expansion") was built when a bulging Barcelona burst out of its medieval walls in the mid-19th century. With wide sidewalks, hardy shade trees, chic shops, and plenty of Art Nouveau fun, this carefully planned "new town," just north of the Old City, has a rigid grid plan cropped back at the corners to create space and lightness at each intersection. Conveniently, all of this new construction provided a generation of Modernista architects with a blank canvas for creating boldly experimental designs.

For the best Eixample example, ramble Rambla de Catalunya (unrelated to the more famous Ramblas) and pass along Passeig de Gràcia. While you could simply walk around and see what

Modernista masterpieces you stumble upon, most visitors make a beeline to Gaudí's La Pedrera (Metro: Diagonal) and the Block of Discord, where three Modernista greats jockey for your attention (Metro: Passeig de Gràcia). By the way, if you're tempted to snap photos from the middle of the street, be careful—Gaudí died after being struck by a streetcar.

▲Block of Discord

Three colorful Modernista facades compete for your attention along a single block: Casa Lleó Morera, Casa Amatller, and

Casa Batlló (the only one you can get inside, pictured at right). All were built by well-known architects at the end of the 19th century. Because the mansions look as though they are trying to outdo each other in creative twists, locals nicknamed the noisy block the "Block of Discord." You'll find the houses on Passeig de Gràcia (at the Metro stop of the same name), between Carrer del Consell de Cent and Carrer d'Aragó—three blocks above Plaça de Catalunya and four blocks below La Pedrera.

Casa Lleó Morera (#35): This paella-like mix of styles is the work of the architect Lluís Domènech i Montaner, who also designed the Palace of Catalan Music (you'll notice similarities). The lower floors have classical columns and a Greek-temple-like bay window. Farther up are Gothic balconies of rosettes and tracery, while the upper part has faux Moorish stucco work. The whole thing is ornamented with fantastic griffins, angels, and fish. Flanking the third-story windows are figures holding the exciting inventions of the day—the camera, lightbulb, and gramophone—designed to demonstrate just how modern the homeowners were in this age of Modern-isme. Unfortunately, the wonderful interior is closed to the public.

Casa Amatller (#41): Josep Puig i Cadafalch custom-designed this house for the Amatller family. The facade features a creative mix of three of Spain's historical traditions: Moorish-style pentagram-and-vine designs; Gothic-style tracery, gargoyles, and bay windows; and the step-gable roof from Spain's Habsburg connection to the Low Countries. Notice the many layers of the letter "A": The house itself (with its gable) forms an A, as does the decorative frieze over the bay window on the right side of the facade. Within that frieze, you'll see several more As sprouting from branches (*amatller* means "almond tree"). The reliefs above the smaller windows show off the hobbies of the Amatller clan: Find the cherubs holding the early box camera, the open book, and the amphora jug (which the family collected). Look through the second-floor bay

BARCELONA

Barcelona's Eixample

To Joanic

Plaça de la Virreina

C. DE L'OR
C. DE VERDI
CARRER DEL TORRENT DE L'OLLA
CARRER DE TORRIJOS
C. RAMÓN Y CAJAL
TRAVESSERA DE GRÀCIA
PASSEIG DE GRÀCIA
PASSEIG DE SANT JOAN
CARRER
PASSEIG

CARRER D'ASTÚRIES

To Fontana & Lesseps & Casa Vicens

C. DE MONTSENY
C. DE ROS D'OLANO

Plaça del Sol

CARRER DE LA BAILÉN

GRÀCIA

Plaça de Rius i Tallet

CARRER DE CÒRSEGA

CARRER DE GRÀCIA

MARKET

Gràcia

GRANADA DEL PENEDÈS

VIA AUGUSTA

C. DE GOYA
C. DE MOZART
C. DE MOZART

HOTEL CASA FUSTER

Gràcia

CASA DE LES PUNXES

CARRER DEL ROSSELLÓ

PALAU BARÓ DE QUADRAS

EIX

AVINGUDA DIAGONAL

RAMBLA DE CATALUNYA

Diagonal

LA PEDRERA

CARRER MALLORCA

CARRER DE PARIS

CARRER DE CÒRSEGA

Diagonal (to Sagrada Família)

PASSEIG DE GRÀCIA

Provença

CARRER DEL ROSSELLÓ

PROVENÇA TRAIN STATION

QUADRAT D'OR

PASSEIG DE GRÀCIA TRAIN STATION

CASA BATLLÓ

Passeig de Gràcia

CARRER DE PROVENÇA

CARRER DE BALMES

CARRER D'ENRIC GRANADOS

FUNDACIÓ TÀPIES

CASA AMATLLER

RAMBLA DE CATALUNYA

C. DE MUNTANER

CARRER D'ARIBAU

CARRER DE VALÈNCIA

BLOCK OF DISCORD

Plaça del Doctor Letamendi

CARRER DE CASANOVA

CARRER DEL CONSELL DE CENT

CARRER DE LA DIPUTACIÓ

N

200 Meters
200 Yards

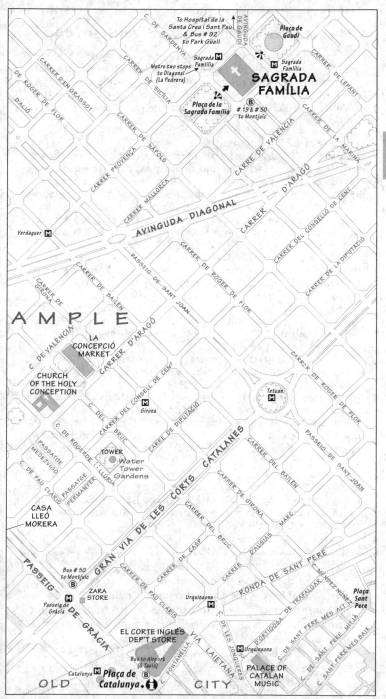

BARCELONA

Modernista Masters: Gaudí and Beyond

Yes, you'll hear plenty about Gaudí, but he's merely one of many great minds who contributed to the architectural revolution of Modernisme. Here's a rundown of the movement's stars. For a sense of the historical context that gave rise to these talented architects, see the "Modernisme and the Renaixença" sidebar, earlier.

The Stars of Modernisme

Antoni Gaudí (1852-1926), Barcelona's most famous Modernista artist, was descended from four generations of metalworkers—a lineage of which he was quite proud. He incorporated ironwork into his architecture and came up with novel approaches to architectural structure and space. Gaudí's work strongly influenced his younger Catalan contemporary, Salvador Dalí. Notice the similarities: While Dalí was creating unlikely and shocking juxtapositions of photorealistic images, Gaudí did the same in architecture—using the spine of a reptile for a bannister or a turtle shell design on windows. Entire trips (and lives) are dedicated to seeing the works of Gaudí, but on a brief visit in Barcelona, the ones most worth considering are his great unfinished church, the Sagrada Família; several mansions in the town center, including La Pedrera, Casa Batlló, and Palau Güell; and Park Güell, his ambitious and never-completed housing development (all described in this chapter).

While Gaudí gets 90 percent of the tourists' attention, two other great Modernista architects were just as important: Lluís Domènech i Montaner and Josep Puig i Cadafalch. Gaudí was a remarkable innovator, but these two were perhaps more purely representative of the Modernista style.

Lluís Domènech i Montaner (1850-1923), a professor and politician, was responsible for some major civic buildings, including his masterwork, the Palace of Catalan Music (described on page 102), and the Hospital de Sant Pau, a sprawling complex covering nine blocks (roughly between the Sagrada Família and Park Güell). Domènech i Montaner also designed Casa Lleó Morera on the Block of Discord (see page 113) and Casa Fuster (now a luxury hotel—see page 120), along with several works in the towns of Canet de Mar, Comillas, and others.

window to see the corkscrew column. If you want, you can pop inside for a closer look at the elaborate entrance hall.

For another dimension of Modernisme, peek into the ground-floor windows of the Bagues Joieria jewelry shop and notice the slinky pieces by Spanish Art Nouveau jeweler Masriera.

Casa Batlló (#43): The most famous facade on the block, rated ▲, is the green-blue, ceramic-speckled Casa Batlló, designed by Antoni Gaudí, with an interior that's open to the public. It has

Josep Puig i Cadafalch (1867-1956) was a city planner who oversaw the opening up of Via Laietana (through the middle of the Old City), the redevelopment of Montjuïc for the 1929 World Expo, and a redesign of the monastery at Santa Maria de Montserrat. Later he flourished as a Modernista architect in his own right, best known for manor houses such as Casa de les Punxes (Diagonal 416-420, not far from La Pedrera) and Casa Amatller on the Block of Discord (described on page 113). He designed the brick Casaramona factory complex, which was recently converted into the cutting-edge CaixaForum exhibition space (see page 138). Perhaps most importantly, Puig i Cadafalch designed Casa Martí, a home for the Modernista hangout bar Els Quatre Gats, which became a cradle of sorts for the whole movement (the bar still welcomes visitors—see page 164).

Supporting Cast

All architects worked with a team of people who, while not famous, made real contributions. For example, Gaudí's colleague **Josep Maria Jujol** (1879-1949) is primarily responsible for much of what Gaudí became known for—the broken-tile mosaic decorations (called *trencadís*) on Park Güell's benches and La Pedrera's chimneys.

Joan Martorell i Montells (1833-1906) was a professor, mentor, and employer of a young Antoni Gaudí. Although an accomplished architect in his own right (particularly in the Cantabrian town of Comillas—see page 389), perhaps Martorell's most important role was as a facilitator of his prized student: He introduced Gaudí to his primary patron, Eusebi Güell (described next), and oversaw the committee that hired Gaudí to build the Sagrada Família.

Each of these architects also had deep-pocketed patrons who financed their works. Gaudí's most important benefactor was **Eusebi Güell** (1846-1918), who used his $90 billion fortune to bankroll Gaudí and others, much as the Medici financed Michelangelo and Leonardo da Vinci. Güell's name still adorns two of Gaudí's most important works: Palau Güell and Park Güell (described on pages 112 and 128).

tibia-like pillars and skull-like balconies, inspired by the time-tested natural forms that Gaudí knew made the best structural supports. The tiled roof has a soft-ice-cream-cone turret topped with a cross. The humpback roofline suggests a cresting dragon's back. It's thought that Gaudí based the work on the popular legend of St. Jordi (George) slaying the dragon. But some see instead a Mardi Gras theme, with mask-like balconies, a colorful confetti-like facade, and the ridge of a harlequin's hat up top.

The inscrutable Gaudí preferred to leave his designs open to interpretation.

While the highlight is the roof, the interior of this Gaudí house is also interesting—and even more over-the-top than La Pedrera's (described later). Paid for with textile industry money, the house features a funky mushroom-shaped fireplace nook on the main floor, a blue-and-white-ceramic-slathered atrium, and an attic (with more parabolic arches). There's barely a straight line in the house. You can also get a close-up look at the dragon-inspired rooftop. Because preservation of the place is privately funded, the entrance fee is steep—but it includes a good (if long-winded) audioguide.

Cost and Hours: €20.35, daily 9:00-20:00, may close early for special events—closings posted in advance at entrance, tel. 932-160-306, www.casabatllo.cat. Purchase a ticket online to avoid lines—which are especially fierce in the morning. Your eticket isn't a timed reservation (it's good any time), but it will let you skip to the front of the queue.

▲▲La Pedrera (Casa Milà)

One of Gaudí's trademark works, this house—built between 1906 and 1912—is an icon of Modernisme. The wealthy industrialist Pere Milà i Camps commissioned it, and while some still call it "Casa Milà," most take one look at its jagged, rocky facade and opt for the more colorful nickname, La Pedrera—"The Quarry." While it's fun to ogle from the outside, it's also worth going inside, as it features the city's

purest Gaudí interior. And buying a ticket also gets you access to the delightful rooftop, with its forest of colorfully tiled chimneys (note that the roof may close when it rains).

Cost and Hours: €16.50, good audioguide-€4, daily March-Oct 9:00-20:00, Nov-Feb 9:00-18:30, last entry 30 minutes before closing, at the corner of Passeig de Gràcia and Provença (visitor entrance at Provença 261-265), Metro: Diagonal, info tel. 902-400-973, www.lapedrera.com.

Crowd-Beating Tips: As lines can be long (up to a 1.5-hour wait to get in), it's best to reserve ahead at www.lapedrera.com (tickets come with an assigned entry time and let you skip the line). If you come without a ticket, the best time to arrive is right when it opens.

Free Entrance to Atrium: For a peek at the interior without paying for a ticket, find the door directly on the corner, which leads to the main atrium. Upstairs on the first floor are temporary exhibits (generally free, open daily 10:00-20:00, may be closed between exhibitions).

Nighttime Visits: The building hosts guided after-hour visits dubbed "The Secret Pedrera." On this pricey visit, you'll tour the building with the lights turned down low (€30; English tour offered daily March-Oct at 21:15, but check changeable schedule and offerings online).

Concerts: On summer weekends, La Pedrera has an evening rooftop concert series, "Summer Nights at La Pedrera," featuring live jazz. In addition to the music, it gives you the chance to see the rooftop illuminated (€27, late June-early Sept Thu-Sat at 22:30, book advance tickets online or by phone, tel. 902 101 212, www .lapedrera.com).

Visiting the House: A visit to La Pedrera covers three sections: the apartment, the attic, and the rooftop. Enter and head upstairs to the apartment. If it's near closing time, continue up to see the attic and rooftop first to make sure you have enough time to enjoy Gaudí's works and the views.

The typical bourgeois **apartment** is decorated as it might have been when the building was first occupied by middle-class urbanites (a seven-minute video explains Barcelona society at the time). Notice Gaudí's clever use of the atrium to maximize daylight in all of the apartments.

The **attic** houses a sprawling multimedia exhibit tracing the history of the architect's career with models, photos, and videos of

his work. It's all displayed under distinctive parabola-shaped arches. While evocative of Gaudí's style in themselves, the arches are formed this way partly to support the multilevel roof above. This area was also used for ventilation, helping to keep things cool in summer and warm in winter. Tenants had storage spaces and did their laundry up here.

From the attic, a stairway leads to the undulating, jaw-dropping **rooftop,** where 30 chimneys and ventilation towers play volleyball with the clouds.

Back at the **ground level** of La Pedrera, poke into the dreamily painted original entrance courtyard.

More Modernista Sights in the Eixample

While the buildings listed earlier are the best Modernista facades in this area, fans of this era may want to seek out a few more examples:

Just around the corner from the Block of Discord, at Carrer d'Aragó 255, the **Fundació Antoni Tàpies,** dedicated to a 20th-century abstract artist from Barcelona, is housed in a Lluís Domènech i Montaner-designed building that sums up the Modernist credo. Constructed of modern brick, iron, and glass, it's decorated with playful motifs and is spacious, functional, and full of light inside. The actual museum collection is worthwhile only for Tàpies fans (€7, Tue-Sun 10:00-19:00, closed Mon, www .fundaciotapies.org).

The **Hotel Casa Fuster** is another fine Modernista building by Lluís Domènech i Montaner (directly across the boulevard called Diagonal from the top of Passeig de Gràcia, at the far end of the small park, Passeig de Gràcia 132).

Nearby are two works by Josep Puig i Cadafalch (a few blocks east from the top of Passeig de Gràcia on Diagonal). **Palau Baró de Quadras** (at #373, on the right) today houses Casa Àsia. Another block and a half down is the distinctively turreted Casa Terrades—better known as **Casa de les Punxes** ("House of Spikes," at #416, on the left).

▲▲▲Sagrada Família (Holy Family Church)

Architect Antoni Gaudí's most famous and awe-inspiring work is this unfinished, super-sized church. With its cake-in-the-rain facade and otherworldly spires, the church is not only an icon of Barcelona and its trademark Modernista style, but also a symbol of this period's greatest practitioner. As an architect, Gaudí's foundations were classics, nature, and religion. The church represents all three.

Gaudí labored on the Sagrada Família for 43 years, from 1883 until his death in 1926. Nearly a century after his death, people continue to toil to bring Gaudí's designs to life. There's something powerful about a community of committed people with a vision, working on a church that won't be finished in their lifetime—as was standard in the Gothic age. The progress of this remarkable building is a testament to the generations of architects, sculptors, stonecutters, fund-raisers, and donors who've been caught up in the audacity of Gaudí's astonishing vision. After paying the steep admission price (becoming a partner in this building project), you will actually feel good. If there's any building on earth I'd like to see, it's the Sagrada Família...finished.

Cost and Hours: Church-€13.50, tower elevators-€4.50 each, €17 combo-ticket also includes Gaudí House and Museum at Park Güell (see page 128), daily April-Sept 9:00-20:00, Oct-March 9:00-18:00, last entry 15 minutes before closing, Metro: Sagrada

Família, exit toward Plaça de la Sagrada Família, tel. 932-073-031, www.sagradafamilia.cat.

Getting There: The Sagrada Família Metro stop puts you right on the doorstep: Exit toward Plaça de la Sagrada Família. The ticket windows and entrance for individuals (not groups) are on the west side of the church (at the Passion Facade). Inviting parks flank the building, facing the two completed facades.

Crowd-Beating Tips: The ticket windows and entrance for individuals are on the west side of the church, at the Passion Facade. Though the line can seem long (often curving around the block), it generally moves quickly; you can ask for an estimate from the guards at the front of the line. Still, waits can be up to 45 minutes at peak times (most crowded in the morning). To minimize your wait, arrive right at 9:00 (when it opens) or after 16:00. To skip the line, buy advance tickets, take a tour, or hire a private guide.

Advance Tickets: To avoid the ticket-buying line, reserve an entry time and buy tickets in advance (€1.30 booking fee). The easiest option is to book online at www.sagradafamilia.cat, which allows you to print tickets at home or collect them from any ServiCaixi ATM terminal in Barcelona. You can also purchase tickets—even for same-day entry—directly from ServiCaixa ATMs. These special ATMs are found at some La Caixa bank branches in the city—including on Plaça de Catalunya and just across the street from the church (to the left as you face the ticket windows—but this machine gets hard use and is often out of order). Start the ATM transaction by selecting "Event Tickets/Entradas Espectáculos" at the top of the screen. (The initial instructions may be in Spanish, but English-only users can figure it out.)

With prepurchased tickets, head straight for the "online ticket office" window, to the right of the main ticket line, and show your ticket to the guard.

Tours: The 50-minute English tours (€4.50) run May-Oct daily at 11:00, 12:00, 13:00, and 15:00; Nov-April Mon-Fri at 11:00, 13:00, and 15:00, Sat-Sun at 11:00, 12:00, 13:00, and 15:00. Or rent the good 1.5-hour audioguide (€4.50). Good English information is posted throughout.

Tower Elevators: Two different elevators (€4.50 each, pay at main ticket office, each ticket comes with an entry time) take you partway up the towers for a great view of the city and a gargoyle's-eye perspective of the loopy church.

The easier option is the **Passion Facade elevator,** which takes you 215 feet up and down. If you want, you can climb higher, but expect the spiral stairs to be tight, hot, and congested.

The **Nativity Facade elevator** is more exciting and demanding. You'll get the opportunity to cross the dizzying bridge between the towers, but you'll need to take the stairs all the way down.

Construction Update: Since Gaudí's death in 1926, construction has moved forward in fits and starts, though much progress was made in recent decades, thanks to Barcelona's 1992 Olympics renaissance, the ensuing rediscovery of the genius of Gaudí, and advances in technology. In 2010, the main nave was finished enough to host a consecration Mass by the pope (as a Catholic church, it is used for services, though irregularly). As I stepped inside on my last visit, the brilliance of Gaudí's vision for the interior was apparent.

The main challenges today: Ensure that construction can withstand the vibrations caused by the speedy AVE trains rumbling underfoot, construct the tallest church spire ever built, and find a way to buy out the people who own the condos in front of the planned Glory Facade so that Gaudí's vision of a grand esplanade approaching the church can be realized. The goal, which seems overly optimistic but tantalizing nonetheless, is to finish the church by the 100th anniversary of Gaudí's death, in 2026.

◑ Self-Guided Tour: Start at the ticket entrance (at the Passion Facade) on the western side of the church. The view is best from the park across the street. Before heading to the ticket booth, take in the...

❶ Exterior: Stand and imagine how grand this church will be when completed. The four 330-foot spires topped with crosses are just a fraction of this mega-church. When finished, the church will have 18 spires. Four will stand at each of the three entrances. Rising above those will be four taller towers, dedicated to the four Evangelists. A tower dedicated to Mary will rise still higher—400 feet. And in the very center of the complex will stand the grand 560-foot Jesus tower, topped with a cross that will shine like a spiritual lighthouse, visible even from out at sea.

The Passion Facade that tourists enter today is only a side entrance to the church. The grand main entrance will be around to the right. That means that the nine-story apartment building will eventually have to be torn down to accommodate it. The three facades—Nativity, Passion, and Glory—will chronicle Christ's life from birth to death to resurrection. Inside and out, a goal of the church is to bring the lessons of the Bible to the world. Despite his boldly modern architectural vision, Gaudí was fundamentally traditional and deeply religious. He designed the Sagrada Família to be a bastion of solid Christian values in the midst of what was a humble workers' colony in a fast-changing city.

When Gaudí died, only one section (on the Nativity Facade) had been completed. The rest of the church has been inspired by Gaudí's long-range vision, but designed and executed by others. This artistic freedom was amplified in 1936, when civil war shelling burned many of Gaudí's blueprints. Supporters of the ongoing

BARCELONA

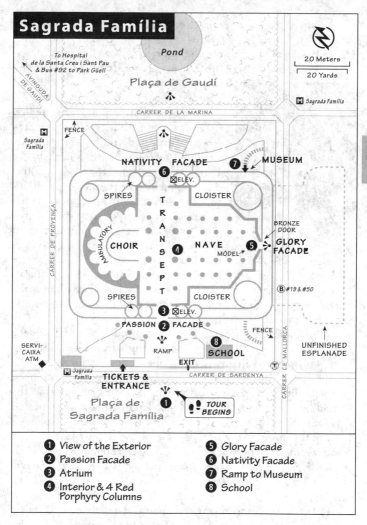

Sagrada Família

Pond

Plaça de Gaudí

20 Meters
20 Yards

To Hospital
de la Santa Creu i Sant Pau
& Bus #92 to Park Güell

AVINGUDA DE GAUDÍ

Ⓜ Sagrada Família

Ⓜ Sagrada Família

CARRER DE LA MARINA

FENCE

NATIVITY FACADE

Ⓜ Sagrada Família

❼ → MUSEUM

❻ ⊠ELEV.

SPIRES

CLOISTER

BRONZE DOOR

T R A N S E P T

CARRER DE PROVENÇA

AMBULATORY

CHOIR

NAVE

❹

MODEL

❺ GLORY FACADE

Ⓑ #19 & #50

SPIRES

CLOISTER

❸ ⊠ELEV.

CARRER DE MALLORCA

PASSION ❷ FACADE

RAMP

❽ SCHOOL

FENCE

UNFINISHED ESPLANADE

SERVI-CAIXA ATM

EXIT

Ⓜ Sagrada Família

CARRER DE SARDENYA

Ⓣ

TICKETS & ENTRANCE

Plaça de Sagrada Família

❶

TOUR BEGINS

❶ View of the Exterior
❷ Passion Facade
❸ Atrium
❹ Interior & 4 Red Porphyry Columns
❺ Glory Facade
❻ Nativity Facade
❼ Ramp to Museum
❽ School

work insist that Gaudí, who enjoyed saying, "My client [God] is not in a hurry," knew he wouldn't live to complete the church and recognized that later architects and artists would rely on their own muses for inspiration. Detractors maintain that the church's design is a uniquely, intensely personal one and that it's folly (if not disrespectful) for anyone to try to guess what Gaudí would have intended. Studying the various plans and models in the museum below the church, it's clear that Gaudí's plan evolved dramatically the longer he worked. Is it appropriate to keep implementing a century-old vision that can no longer be modified by its creator? Discuss.

• *Pass through the ticket entrance into the complex, approaching closer to the...*

❷ **Passion Facade:** Judge for yourself how well Gaudí's original vision has been carried out by later artists. The Passion Facade's

four spires were designed by Gaudí and completed (quite faithfully) in 1976. But the lower part was only inspired by Gaudí's designs. The stark sculptures were interpreted freely (and controversially) by Josep Maria Subirachs (b. 1927), who completed the work in 2005.

Subirachs tells the story of Christ's torture and execution. The various scenes—Last Supper, betrayal, whipping, and so on—zigzag up from bottom to top, culminating in Christ's crucifixion over the doorway. The style is severe and unadorned, quite different from Gaudí's signature playfulness. But the bone-like archways are closely based on Gaudí's original designs. And Gaudí had made it clear that this facade should be grim and terrifying.

The facade is full of symbolism. A stylized Alpha-and-Omega is over the door (which faces the setting sun). Jesus, hanging on the cross, has hair made of an open book, symbolizing the word of God. To the left of the door, there's a grid of numbers, always adding up to 33—Jesus' age at the time of his death. The distinct face of the man below and just left of Christ is a memorial to Gaudí. Now look high above: The two-ton figure suspended between the towers is the soul of Jesus, ascending to heaven.

• *Enter the church. As you pass through the* ❸ *Atrium, look down at the fine porphyry floor (with scenes of Jesus' entry into Jerusalem), and look right to see one of the elevators up to the towers. For now, continue into the...*

❹ **Interior:** Typical of even the most traditional Catalan and Spanish churches, the floor plan is in the shape of a Latin cross, 300 feet long and 200 feet wide. Ultimately, the church will encompass 48,000 square feet, accommodating 8,000 worshippers. The nave's roof is 150 feet high. The crisscross arches of the ceiling (the vaults) show off Gaudí's distinctive engineering. The church's roof and flooring were only completed in 2010—just in time for Pope Benedict XVI to arrive and consecrate the church.

Part of Gaudí's religious vision was a love for nature. He said, "Nothing is invented; it's written in nature." Like the trunks of trees, these **columns** (56 in all) blossom with life, complete with branches, leaves, and knot-like capitals. The columns are a variety of colors—brown clay, gray granite, dark-gray basalt. The taller columns are 72 feet tall; the shorter ones are exactly half that.

The angled columns form many **arches.** You'll see both parabolas (U-shaped) and hyperbolas (flatter, elliptical shapes). Gaudí's starting point was the Gothic pointed arch used in medieval churches. But he tweaked it after meticulous study of which arches are best at bearing weight.

Little **windows** let light filter in like the canopy of a rainforest, giving both privacy and an intimate connection with God. The clear glass is temporary and will gradually be replaced by stained glass. As more and more stained glass is installed, splashes of color will breathe even more life into this amazing space. Gaudí envisioned an awe-inspiring canopy with a symphony of colored light to encourage a contemplative mood.

High up at the back half of the church, the U-shaped **choir**—suspended above the nave—can seat 1,000. The singers will eventually be backed by four organs (there's one now).

Work your way up the grand nave, walking through this forest of massive columns. At the center of the church stand four **red porphyry columns,** each marked with an Evangelist's symbol and name in Catalan: angel (Mateu), lion (Marc), bull (Luc), and eagle (Joan). These columns support a ceiling vault that's 200 feet high—and eventually will also support the central steeple, the 560-foot Jesus tower with the shining cross. The steeple will be further supported by four underground pylons, each consisting of 8,000 tons of cement. It will be the tallest church steeple in the world, though still a few feet shorter than the city's highest point at the summit of Montjuïc hill, as Gaudí believed that a creation of man should not attempt to eclipse the creation of God.

Stroll behind the altar through the **ambulatory** to reach a small chapel set aside for prayer and meditation. Look through windows down at the **crypt** (which holds the tomb of Gaudí). Peering down into that surprisingly traditional space, imagine how the church was started as a fairly conventional, 19th-century Neo-Gothic building until Gaudí was given the responsibility to finish it.

• *Head to the far end of the church, to what will eventually be the main entrance. Just inside the door, find the **bronze model** of the eventual floor plan of the completed church. Facing the doors, look high up to see Subirachs' statue of one of Barcelona's patron saints, **Jordi**. Go through the doors to imagine what will someday be the...*

❺ **Glory Facade:** As you exit, study the fine **bronze door,** emblazoned with the Lord's Prayer in Catalan, surrounded by

"Give us this day our daily bread" in 50 languages. Once outside, you'll be face-to-face with...drab, doomed apartment blocks. In the 1950s, the mayor of Barcelona, figuring this day would never really come, sold the land destined for the church project. Now the city must buy back these buildings in order to complete Gaudí's vision: that of a grand esplanade leading to this main entry. Four towers will rise up. The facade's sculpture will represent how the soul passes through death, faces the Last Judgment, avoids the pitfalls of hell, and finds its way to eternal glory with God. Gaudí purposely left the facade's design open for later architects—stay tuned.

• *Re-enter the church, backtrack up the nave, and exit through the right transept. Once outside, back up as far as you can to take in the...*

❻ **Nativity Facade:** This is the only part of the church essentially finished in Gaudí's lifetime. The four spires decorated with his unmistakably nonlinear sculpture mark this facade as part of his original design. Mixing Gothic-style symbolism, images from nature, and Modernista asymmetry, the Nativity Facade is the best example of Gaudí's original vision, and it established the template for future architects.

The theme of this facade, which faces the rising sun, is Christ's birth. A statue above the doorway shows Mary, Joseph, and Baby Jesus in the manger, while curious cows peek in. It's the Holy Family—or "Sagrada Família"—to whom this church is dedicated. Flanking the doorway are the three Magi and adoring shepherds. Other statues show Jesus as a young carpenter and angels playing musical instruments. Higher up on the facade, in the arched niche, Jesus crowns Mary triumphantly.

The facade is all about birth and new life, from the dove-covered Tree of Life on top to the turtles at the base of the columns flanking the entrance. At the bottom of the Tree of Life is a white pelican. Because it was believed that this noble bird would kill itself to feed its young, it was often used in the Middle Ages as a symbol for the self-sacrifice of Jesus. The chameleon gargoyles at the outer corners of the facade (just above door level) represent the changeability of life. It's as playful as the Passion Facade is grim. Gaudí's plans were for this facade to be painted. Cleverly, this attractive facade was built and finished first to bring in financial support for the project.

The four **spires** are dedicated to Apostles, and they repeatedly bear the word "Sanctus," or holy. Their colorful ceramic caps symbolize the miters (formal hats) of bishops. The shorter spires (to the left) symbolize the Eucharist (communion), alternating between a chalice with grapes and a communion host with wheat.

To the left of the facade is one section of the **cloister.** Whereas most medieval churches have their cloisters attached to one side of the building, the Sagrada Família's cloister will wrap around the church, more than 400 yards long.

• *Notice the second* **elevator** *up to the towers. But for now, head down the ramp to the left of the façade, where you'll find WCs and the entrance to the...*

❼ **Museum:** Housed in what will someday be the church's crypt, the museum displays Gaudí's original **models and drawings,** and chronicles the progress of construction over the last 130 years. Wander among the plaster models used for the church's construction, including a model of the nave so big you walk beneath it. The models make clear the influence of nature. The columns seem light, with branches springing forth and capitals that look like palm trees. You'll notice that the models don't always match the finished product—these are ideas, not blueprints set in stone. The Passion Façade model (near the entrance) shows Gaudí's original vision, with which Subirachs tinkered very freely (see page 124).

Turn up the main hallway. On the left you can peek into a busy **workshop** still used for making the same kind of plaster models Gaudí used to envision the final product in 3-D. Farther along, a small hallway on the right leads to some original Gaudí architectural **sketches** in a dimly lit room and a worthwhile 20-minute **movie** (generally shown in English at :50 past each hour).

From the end of this hall, you have another opportunity to look down into the crypt and at **Gaudí's tomb.** Gaudí lived on the site for more than a decade and is buried in the Neo-Gothic 19th-century crypt. There's a move afoot to make Gaudí a saint. Perhaps someday his tomb will be a place of pilgrimage.

Back in the main hallway, on the right is the intriguing **"Hanging Model"** for Gaudí's unfinished Church of Colònia Güell (in a suburb of Barcelona), featuring a similar design to the Sagrada Família. The model illustrates how the architect used gravity to calculate the arches that support the church. Wires dangle like suspended chains, forming perfect hyperbolic arches. Attached to these are bags, representing the weight the arches must support. Flip these arches over, and they can bear the heavy weight of the roof. The mirror above the model shows how the right-side-up church is derived from this. Across the hall is a small exhibit commemorating **Pope Benedict XVI**'s 2010 consecration visit.

After passing some original sculptures from the Glory Façade (on the right) and continuing beneath a huge plaster model, turn right to find **three different visions** for this church. Notice how the arches evolved as Gaudí tinkered, from the original, pointy Neo-Gothic arches, to parabolic ones, to the hyperbolic ones he

BARCELONA

eventually settled on. Also in this hall are replicas of the **pulpit** and **confessional** that Gaudí, the micromanager, designed for his church. Before exiting at the far end of the hall, scan the photos (including one of the master himself) and timeline illustrating how construction work has progressed from Gaudí's day to now.

• *You'll exit near where you started, at the Passion Facade.*

❽ **School:** The small building outside the Passion Facade was a school Gaudí erected for the children of the workers building the church. Today it includes more exhibits about the design and engineering of the church, along with a classroom and a replica of Gaudí's desk as it was the day he died. Pause for a moment to pay homage to the man who made all this possible. Gaudí—a faithful Catholic whose medieval-style mysticism belied his Modernista architecture career—was certainly driven to greatness by his passion for God.

• *Our tour is over. From here, you have several options.*

Return to Central Barcelona: *You can either hop on the Metro or take one of two handy buses (both stop on Carrer de Mallorca, directly in front of the Glory Facade). Bus #19 takes you back to the* **Old City** *in 15 minutes, stopping near the cathedral and in the El Born district. Bus #50 goes from the Sagrada Família to the heart of the* **Eixample** *(corner of Gran Via de les Corts Catalanes and Passeig de Gràcia), then continues on to Plaça Espanya and up* **Montjuïc** *(but only as far as the cable-car station/funicular; see "Getting to Montjuïc" on page 131).*

Visit Park Güell: *Gaudí's colorful park (described next) sits nearly two (uphill) miles to the northwest. By far the easiest way to get there is to spring for a taxi (around €10-12). But if you prefer public transportation and don't mind a little walking, here's a scenic way to get there that also takes you past another, often overlooked Modernista masterpiece: With the Nativity Facade at your back, walk to the near-left corner of the park across the street. Then cross the street to reach the diagonal Avinguda de Gaudí (between the Repsol gas station and the KFC). Follow the funky lampposts four blocks gradually uphill (about 10 minutes) along Avinguda de Gaudí, a pleasantly shaded, café-lined pedestrian street. Soon you reach the striking Modernista-style* **Hospital de la Santa Creu i Sant Pau,** *designed by top architect Lluís Domènech i Montaner (for more on him, see page 116). Cross the street and go up one block (left) on Carrer de Sant Antoni Maria Claret to catch bus #92, which will take you to the side entrance of Park Güell.*

▲▲Park Güell

Gaudí fans enjoy the artist's magic in this colorful park, located on the outskirts of town. While it takes a bit of effort to get here, Park Güell (Catalans pronounce it "gway") offers a unique look at Gaudí's style in a natural rather than urban context. Designed as an upscale housing development for early-20th-century urbanites, the park's Monumental Zone is home to some of Barcelona's most famous symbols, including a whimsical staircase guarded by a dragon and a wavy bench with a view—all of it slathered with fragments of vivid tile. It also features a panoramic terrace supported by a forest of columns. Even without its Gaudí connection, Park Güell is simply a fine place to enjoy a break from a busy city, where green space is relatively rare.

Cost and Hours: Park—free, Monumental Zone—€8, €7 in advance, ticket reserves entry at specific time and date, best to buy tickets in advance; daily 10:00-20:00, tel. 932-130-488, www.parkguell.cat; Gaudí House and Museum—€5.50, €17 combo-ticket also includes Sagrada Família, daily April-Sept 10:00-20:00 (until 18:00 Oct-March); La Casa del Guarda—€2, included in Barcelona History Museum ticket (see page 90), daily April-Sept 10:00-20:00 (until 18:00 Oct-March), tel. 933-190-222.

Getting There: To reach Park Güell—about 2.5 miles north of Plaça de Catalunya—it's easiest to take a **taxi** from downtown (around €12). Otherwise, from Plaça de Catalunya public **bus** #24 goes to the park's side entrance; the blue Tourist Bus stops two blocks below the park's main entrance (at the intersection of Carrer Larrard and Travessera de Dalt). Or you can ride the Metro to Joanic, exit toward Carrer de l'Escorial, and find the bus stop in front of #20, where you can catch bus #116 to the park's main entrance. For ideas on linking Sagrada Família to Park Güell, see opposite page.

Visiting the Park: This tour assumes you're arriving at the front/main entrance and visiting the Monumental Zone. As you wander the park, imagine living here a century ago—if this gated

community had succeeded and was filled with Barcelona's wealthy.

Front Entrance: Entering the park, you walk by Gaudí's wrought-iron gas lamps (1900-1914). His dad was a blacksmith, and he always enjoyed this medium. Two gate houses made of gingerbread flank the entrance. One houses a good bookshop; the other is home to the Gaudí-built La Casa del Guarda (dull exhibit, totally skippable). The Gaudí House and Museum, described later, is better.

Stairway and Columns: Climb the grand stairway, past the famous ceramic dragon fountain. At the top, dip into the "Hall of 100 Columns," designed to house a produce market for the neighborhood's 60 mansions. The fun columns—each different, made from concrete and rebar, topped with colorful ceramic, and studded with broken bottles and bric-a-brac—add to the market's vitality.

As you continue up (on the left-hand staircase), look left, down the playful "pathway of columns" that supports a long arcade. Gaudí drew his inspiration from nature, and this arcade is like a surfer's perfect tube.

Terrace: Once up top, sit on a colorful bench—designed to fit your body ergonomically—and enjoy one of Barcelona's best views. Look for the Sagrada Família church in the distance. Gaudí was an engineer as well. He designed a water-catchment system by which rain hitting this plaza would flow into and through the columns from the market below, and power the park's fountains.

When considering the failure of Park Güell as a community development, also consider that it was an idea a hundred years ahead of its time. Back then, high-society ladies didn't want to live so far from the cultural action. Today, the surrounding neighborhoods are some of the wealthiest in town, and a gated community here would be a big hit.

Gaudí House and Museum: This pink house with a steeple, standing in the middle of the park (near the side entrance), was actually Gaudí's home for 20 years, until his father died (though Gaudí did not design the actual house). His humble artifacts are mostly gone, but the house is now a museum with some quirky Gaudí furniture and a chance to wander through a model home used to sell the others. Though small, it offers a good taste of what could have been.

Montjuïc

Montjuïc (mohn-jew-EEK, "Mount of the Jews"), overlooking Barcelona's hazy port, has always been a show-off. Ages ago it was capped by an impressive castle. When the Spanish enforced their rule, they built the imposing fortress that you'll see the shell of today. The hill has also played an integral role in the construction of Barcelona's great structures—significant parts of the historic city, the cathedral, the Sagrada Família, and much more were all built with stones quarried from Montjuïc.

Montjuïc has also been prominent during the last century. In 1929, it hosted an international fair, from which many of today's sights originated. And in 1992, the Summer Olympics directed the world's attention to this pincushion of attractions once again. While Montjuïc lacks any single knockout, must-see sight, it is home to a variety of very good ones, and most visitors should find one or two attractions here to suit their interests. For the majority of travelers, the most worthwhile sights are the Fundació Joan Miró, Catalan Art Museum, and CaixaForum.

Sightseeing Strategies: I've listed these sights by altitude, from highest to lowest—from the hill-topping castle down to the 1929 World Expo Fairgrounds at the base of Montjuïc (described in the next section). If you're visiting all of my listed sights, ride to the top by bus, funicular, or taxi, then visit them in this order so that most of your walking is downhill. However, if you want to visit only the Catalan Art Museum and/or CaixaForum, you can just take the Metro to Plaça d'Espanya and ride the escalators up (with some stair-climbing as well) to those sights.

Getting to Montjuïc: You have several choices. The simplest is to take a **taxi** directly to your destination (about €7-8 from downtown).

Buses can also take you up to Montjuïc. From Plaça de Catalunya, **bus #55** rides as far as Montjuïc's cable-car station/ funicular. If you want to get higher (to the castle), ride the Metro or bus #9 or #50 from Plaça de Catalunya to Plaça d'Espanya, then make the easy transfer to **bus #150** to ride all the way up the hill. Alternatively, the red Tourist Bus will get you to the Montjuïc sights.

Another option is by **funicular** (covered by Metro ticket, every 10 minutes, 7:30-22:00, from 9:00 on Sat-Sun). To reach it, take the Metro to the Paral-lel stop, then follow signs for *Parc Montjuïc* and the little funicular icon—you can enter the funicular without using another ticket. From the top of the funicular, turn left and walk gently downhill two minutes to the Miró museum, six minutes to the Olympic Stadium, or ten minutes to the Catalan Art Museum. If you're heading all the way up to the castle, you can catch a bus or cable car from the top of the funicular (see castle listing, later).

For a scenic (if slow) approach to Montjuïc, you could ride

the fun circa-1929 Aeri del Port **cable car** *(telefèric)* from the tip of the Barceloneta peninsula (across the harbor, near the beach) to the Miramar viewpoint park in Montjuïc. (Another station, right along the port near the Columbus Monument, is currently closed.) Since the cable car is expensive,

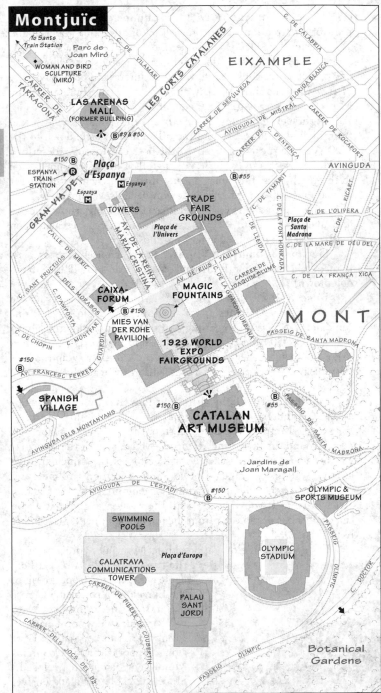

Montjuïc

BARCELONA

To Sants
Train Station

Parc de
Joan Miró

WOMAN AND BIRD
SCULPTURE
(MIRÓ)

CARRER DE TARRAGONA

LAS ARENAS MALL
(FORMER BULLRING)

B #9 & #50

EIXAMPLE

C. DE CALABRIA

C. DE VILAMARI

LES CORTS CATALANES

CARRER DE SEPULVEDA

FLORIDA BLANCA

AVINGUDA DE MISTRAL

C. DE D'ENTENÇA

CARREE C.

CARRER DE ROCAFORT

#150

Plaça
d'Espanya

ESPANYA
TRAIN STATION

R

M Espanya

Espanya
M

GRAN VIA DE

TOWERS

AV. DE LA REINA MARIA CRISTINA

Plaça de
l'Univers

B #55

TRADE
FAIR
GROUNDS

AVINGUDA

C. DE TAMARIT

C. DE LA FONT HONRADA

AV. DE RIUS I TAULET

CALLE DE MEXIC

C. SANT FRUCTUOS

C. DELS MORABOS

C. D'AMPOSTA

CAIXA-
FORUM

B #150

C. DE LLEIDA

C. DE L'OLIVERA

C. DE RICART

Plaça de
Santa
Madrona

C. DE LA MARE DE DÉU DEL

C. DE LA FRANÇA XICA

MAGIC
FOUNTAINS

CARRER DE JOAQUIM BLUME

C. DE LA GUARDIA URBANA

MONT

C. DE CHOPIN

C. MONTFAR

MIES VAN
DER ROHE
PAVILION

1929 WORLD
EXPO
FAIRGROUNDS

PASSEIG DE SANTA MADRONA

#150

B

AV. FRANCESC FERRER I GUARDIA

SPANISH
VILLAGE

#150 B

CATALAN
ART MUSEUM

B #55

PASSEIG DE SANTA MADRONA

AVINGUDA DELS MONTANYANS

Jardins de
Joan Maragall

AVINGUDA DE L'ESTADI

B #150

OLYMPIC &
SPORTS MUSEUM

SWIMMING
POOLS

Plaça d'Europa

CALATRAVA
COMMUNICATIONS
TOWER

PALAU
SANT
JORDI

OLYMPIC
STADIUM

PASSEIG OLIMPIC

C. DOCTOR

CARRER DE PIERRE DE COUBERTIN

CARRER DELS JOCS DEL 92

PASSEIG OLIMPIC

Botanical
Gardens

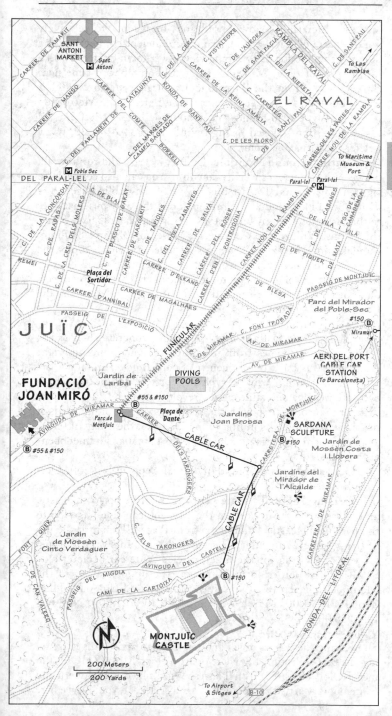

loads excruciatingly slowly, and goes between two relatively remote parts of town, it's really not an efficient connection. It's only worthwhile for its sweeping views over town or if you'd like to, say, cap off your Montjuïc day with some beach time near Barceloneta. From the Barceloneta cable-car station, catch a public bus (#17, #39, or #64) to reach the Barceloneta Metro stop (€11 one-way, €16.50 round-trip, 3/hour, daily 11:00-19:00, until 20:00 June-Sept, closed in high wind, tel. 934-414-820, www.telefericodebarcelona.com).

Getting Around Montjuïc: Up top, it's easy and fun to walk between the sights—especially downhill. You can also connect the sights using the red Tourist Bus or one of the public buses: **Bus #150** does a loop around the hilltop and is the only bus that goes to the castle; on the way up, it stops at or passes near CaixaForum, the Spanish Village, the Catalan Art Museum, Olympic Stadium, Fundació Joan Miró, the lower castle cable-car station/top of the funicular, and finally, the castle. On the downhill run, it loops by Miramar, the cable-car station for Barceloneta. **Bus #55** connects only the funicular/cable-car stations, Fundació Joan Miró, and the Catalan Art Museum.

Castle of Montjuïc

The castle, while just an empty brick-and-concrete shell today, offers great city views from its ramparts...and some poignant history. It was built by the central Spanish government in the 18th century with a Vauban-type star fortress design to keep an eye on Barcelona and stifle citizen revolt. When the 20th-century dictator Franco was in power, the castle was the site of hundreds of political executions. Its military function gone, these days it serves as a park, jogging destination, and host to a popular summer open-air cinema.

Cost and Hours: Free, daily April-Sept 9:00-21:00, Oct-March 9:00-19:00.

Getting There: To spare yourself the hike up to the castle and to see some great views of the city, you can ride bus #150 to the base of the castle, catching it from Plaça d'Espanya, the top of the Montjuïc funicular, or various other points on Montjuïc. Or you can spring for the much pricier **cable car** (Telefèric de Montjuïc), which departs from near the upper station of the Montjuïc funicular (€7.30 one-way, €10.30 round-trip, daily June-Sept 10:00-21:00, March-May and Oct 10:00-19:00, Nov-Feb 10:00-18:00).

▲Fundació Joan Miró

Showcasing the talents of yet another Catalan artist, this museum has the best collection anywhere of art by Joan Miró (ZHOO-ahn mee-ROH, 1893-1983). You'll also see works by other Modern and contemporary artists. If you don't like abstract art, you'll leave here

scratching your head. But those who love this place are not faking it...they understand the genius of Miró and the fun of abstract art.

Cost and Hours: €11, great audioguide-€4; July-Sept Tue-Sat 10:00-20:00 (until 19:00 Oct-June), Thu until 21:30, Sun 10:00-14:30; closed Mon year-round, 200 yards from top of funicular, Parc de Montjuïc, tel. 934-439-470, www.fundaciomiro-bcn.org. The museum has a cafeteria, a café, and a bookshop.

Visiting the Museum: The building itself, designed in 1975 by Josep Lluís Sert (a friend of Miró and a student of Le Corbusier), was purpose-built to show off the art of Miró and his contemporaries. Consider renting the wonderful audioguide, well worth the extra charge.

Barcelona-born Joan Miró divided his time between Paris and Catalunya (including Barcelona and his favorite village, Mont-roig del Camp). As you wander, ponder this: Miró believed that everything in the cosmos is linked—colors, sky, stars, love, time, music, dogs, men, women, dirt, and the void. He mixed simple symbols of these things creatively, as a poet uses words. It's as liberating for the visual artist to be abstract as it is for the poet: Both can use metaphors rather than being confined to concrete explanations. Miró would listen to music and paint. It's interactive, free interpretation. He said, "For me, simplicity is freedom."

Here are some tips to help you enjoy and appreciate Miró's art: First meditate on it, then read the title (for example, *The Smile of a Tear*), then meditate on it again. Repeat the process until you have an epiphany. There's no correct answer—it's pure poetry. Devotees of Miró say they fly with him and don't even need drugs. Psychoanalysts liken Miró's free-for-all canvases to Rorschach tests. Is that a cigar in that star's mouth?

COPA DEL MUNDO DE FUTBOL · ESPAÑA 82

Olympic and Sports Museum (Museu Olímpic i de l'Esport)
This museum rides the coattails of the stadium across the street (see next listing). You'll twist down a timeline-ramp that traces the history of the Olympic Games, interspersed with random exhibits about various sports. Downstairs you'll find exhibits designed to test your athleticism, a play-by-play rehash of the '92 Barcelona Olympiad, a commemoration of Juan Antonio Samaranch (the

influential Catalan president of the IOC for two decades), a sports media exhibit, and a schmaltzy movie collage. High-tech but hokey, the museum is worth the time and money only for those nostalgic for the '92 Games.

Cost and Hours: €5.10, April-Sept Tue-Sat 10:00-20:00 (until 18:00 Oct-March), Sun 10:00-14:30, closed Mon year-round, Avinguda de l'Estadi 60, tel. 932-925-379, www.museuolimpicbcn .cat.

Olympic Stadium (Estadi Olímpic)

Aside from the memories of the medals, Barcelona's Olympic Stadium, originally built for the 1929 World Expo, offers little to see today. But if the doors are open, you're welcome to step inside. History panels along the railings overlooking the playing field tell the stadium's dynamic story and show the place in happier times (filled with fans as Bon Jovi, the Rolling Stones, and Madonna pack the place). The stadium was restored for the 1992 Summer Olympics, which were particularly memorable for the USA's basketball Dream Team, and as the first Games after the breakups of Yugoslavia and the Soviet Union (whose athletes took the field as the "Unified Team").

Nearby: Hovering over the stadium is the futuristic **Montjuïc Communications Tower,** designed by prominent Spanish architect Santiago Calatrava and used to transmit Olympic highlights and lowlights around the world.

▲▲Catalan Art Museum (Museu Nacional d'Art de Catalunya)

The big vision for this wonderful museum is to showcase Catalan art from the 10th century through about the mid-20th century. Often called "the Prado of Romanesque art" (and "MNAC" for short), it holds Europe's best collection of Romanesque frescoes. It also offers a particularly good sweep of modern Catalan art—fitting, given Catalunya's astonishing contribution to the Modern. Art aficionados are sure to find  something in this diverse collection to tickle their fancy. It's all housed in the grand Palau Nacional, an emblematic building of the 1929 International Exhibition, with magnificent views over Barcelona.

Cost and Hours: €12, includes temporary exhibits, ticket valid for two days within one month, free Sat from 15:00 and first Sun of month; audioguide-€3.10; open May-Sept Tue-Sat 10:00-20:00 (until 18:00 Oct-April), Sun 10:00-15:00, closed Mon, last entry 30 minutes before closing; in massive National Palace building above Magic Fountains, near Plaça d'Espanya—take escalators up; tel.

936-220-376, www.mnac.cat.

Visiting the Museum: As you enter, pick up a map. The left wing is Romanesque, and the right wing is Gothic, exquisite Renaissance, and Baroque. Upstairs is more Baroque, plus modern art, photography, coins, and more.

The MNAC's rare, world-class collection of **Romanesque** (Romànic) art came mostly from remote Catalan village churches (most of the pieces were moved to the museum in the early 1920s to save them from scavenging art dealers). The Romanesque wing features a remarkable array of 11th- to 13th-century frescoes, painted wooden altar fronts, and ornate statuary. This classic Romanesque art—with flat 2-D scenes, each saint holding his symbol, and Jesus (easy to identify by the cross in his halo)—is impressively displayed on replicas of the original church ceilings and apses.

Across the way, in the **Gothic** wing, fresco murals give way to vivid 14th-century wood-panel paintings of Bible stories. A roomful of paintings (Room 26) by the Catalan master Jaume Huguet (1412-1492) deserves a look, particularly his *Consecration of St. Agustí Vell.*

For a break, glide under the huge **dome,** which once housed an ice-skating rink. This was the prime ceremony room and dance hall for the 1929 World Expo.

From the big ballroom, you can ride the glass elevator upstairs to the **Renaissance and Baroque** section, covering Spain's Golden Age (Zurbarán, heavy religious scenes, Spanish royals with their endearing underbites) and Romanticism (dewy-eyed Catalan landscapes). Down on the ground floor are minor works by major—if not necessarily Catalan—names (Velázquez, El Greco, Tintoretto, Rubens, and so on).

Another museum highlight is the **Modern** section, which takes you on an enjoyable walk from the late 1800s to about 1950. It's kind of a Catalan Musée d'Orsay, offering a big chronological clockwise circle covering Symbolism, Modernisme, *fin de siècle* fun, Art Deco, and more. Find the early 20th-century paintings by Catalan artists Santiago Rusiñol and Ramon Casas, both of whom had a profound impact on a young Picasso (and, through him, on all of modern art). Casas was also one of the financiers of Els Quatre Gats, the hangout of Modernista artists (see page 164); his fun Toulouse-Lautrec-esque works, including a whimsical self-portrait on a tandem bicycle, are crowd-pleasers. Crossing over to the "Modern 2" section, you'll find furniture (pieces that complement the empty spaces you likely saw in Gaudí's buildings—including a Gaudí wooden sofa), Impressionism, the shimmering landscapes of Joaquim Mir, and several distinctly Picasso portraits of women.

The museum also has a coin collection, seductive sofas

scattered about, the chic and pricey Oleum restaurant (with vast city views), and a comfy outdoor terrace café (serving snacks and more city views).

▲1929 World Expo Fairgrounds

With the World Expo in 1929, Montjuïc morphed into an extravagant center for fairs, museums, and festivals. Nearly everything you see here dates from 1929 (the exceptions are CaixaForum and the Las Arenas mall). The expo's theme was to demonstrate how electricity was about more than lightbulbs: Electricity powered the funicular, the glorious expo fountains, the many pavilion displays, and even the flame atop the fountain marking the center of Plaça d'Espanya (and celebrating the electric company that sponsored the show). If Barcelona is known for growing through big events, this certainly is a good example.

Standing at Plaça d'Espanya (or, better yet, on the rooftop terrace of the bullring mall—described later), look through the double-brick-tower gate, down the grand esplanade, and imagine it alive with fountains and lined by proud national pavilions showing off all that was modern in 1929. Today the site is home to the Fira de Barcelona convention center. The Neo-Baroque fountain provides a brilliant centerpiece for Plaça d'Espanya.

Getting There: The fairgrounds sprawl at the base of Montjuïc, from the Catalan Art Museum's doorstep to Plaça d'Espanya. The easiest option is to see these sights on your way down from Montjuïc. Otherwise, ride the Metro to Espanya, then use the series of stairs and escalators to climb up through the heart of the fairgrounds (eventually reaching the Catalan Art Museum).

▲Magic Fountains (Font Màgica)

Music, colored lights, and huge amounts of water make an artistic and coordinated splash in the evening at Plaça d'Espanya.

Cost and Hours: Free, 20-minute shows start on the half-hour; almost always May-Sept Thu-Sun 21:00-23:30, no shows Mon-Wed; Oct-April Fri-Sat 19:00-21:00, no shows Sun-Thu; these are first and last show times; from the Espanya Metro stop, walk toward the towering National Palace.

▲▲CaixaForum

The CaixaForum Social and Cultural Center (sponsored by the leading Catalan bank) is housed in one of Barcelona's most important Art Nouveau buildings. In 1911, Josep Puig i Cadafalch (a top architect often overshadowed by Gaudí) designed the Casaramona textile factory, which showed off Modernista design in an industrial rather than a residential context. It functioned as a factory for less than a decade, then later served a long stint as a police station under Franco. Beautifully refurbished in 2002, the facility reopened as a great center for bringing culture and art to the people of Barcelona for free.

Cost and Hours: Free, Mon-Fri 10:00-20:00, Sat-Sun 10:00-21:00, July-Aug open Wed until 23:00, Avinguda de Francesc Ferrer i Guàrdia 6-8, tel. 934-768-600, http://obrasocial.lacaixa .es—click on "Culture."

Visiting the Center: From the lobby, signs point to *Sala 2, 3, 4,* and *5;* each hosts different (and typically outstanding) temporary exhibitions. Ride the escalator to the first floor, which features a modest but interesting exhibit about the history and renovation of the building, including a model and photos. Then head into the appealing red-brick courtyard, from which you can access the various exhibition halls. (The sight features generally limited English descriptions.)

Take the stairs or elevator up to the Modernista Terrace, boasting a wavy floor, bristling with fanciful brick towers, and offering views over the complex and to Montjuïc. Enjoy the genius of Puig i Cadafalch's Modernista design, which provided state-of-the-art working conditions—natural light, good ventilation, and even two trademark towers filled with water (which could be broken to put out any factory fire). The various buildings (designed to be separate from each other to reduce the risk of fire) were built on terraces to level out the Montjuïc slope. Notice that there's no smokestack. This was one of the first electric-powered factories in town.

Mies van der Rohe Pavilion (Pabellón Mies van der Rohe)

Architecture pilgrims flock to the pavilion that Ludwig Mies van der Rohe designed for the German exhibits at the 1929 expo. Even though it was dismantled at the end of the fair, the building was heralded as a seminal example of modern architecture, and in the 1980s, the city of Barcelona reconstructed it on the original site. It's small and stripped-down—a strictly functional "Modernist" (i.e., decidedly not Modernista) structure. Inside are examples of the Barcelona Chair, a tubular steel and leather-cushioned chair that's an icon of 20th-century furniture design. This building—staring down the CaixaForum from across the street—is a reminder that even just a couple of decades later, architecture highbrows already considered the over-the-top flourishes of Modernisme passé and overdone, or even embarrassing; Gaudí, Puig i Cadafalch, and company would fall out of fashion until the late 20th century.

Cost and Hours: €5, daily 10:00-20:00, Avinguda de Francesc Ferrer i Guàrdia 7, tel. 934-234-016, www.miesbcn.com.

Spanish Village (Poble Espanyol)

This five-acre model village (a long hike up from the main World Expo esplanade; best to take bus #150 up) was built as part of the expo to show off the cultural and architectural diversity in Spain. Replicating traditional architecture from all over the country, the village was mostly a shell to contain gift shops—and today it still serves the same purpose. Craftspeople do their clichéd thing (mostly in the morning), and friendly shopkeepers offer plenty of tasty samples of traditional and local edibles. I think it's tacky and overpriced, but if you never expect to visit an authentic Spanish village (this place is popular with cruise groups), here's a pale substitute.

Cost and Hours: €11, €3.50 audioguide explains all the buildings, daily 10:00-20:00 or later, closes earlier off-season, www.poble-espanyol.com.

Las Arenas (Bullring Mall)

What do you do with a big bullfighting arena that's been sitting empty for decades? Make a mall. The grand Neo-Moorish Modernista *plaça de toros* functioned as an arena for bullfights from around 1900 to 1977, and then reopened in 2011 as a mall. It now hosts everything you'd expect in a modern shopping center: lots of brand-name shops, a food-circus basement, a 12-screen cinema complex, a rock-and-roll museum, and a roof terrace with stupendous views of Plaça d'Espanya and Montjuïc (reachable by external glass elevator for €1 or from inside for free).

The **terrace,** with some of the best free views in town, is ringed with eateries. From here you get a bird's-eye perspective of the fairgrounds. In the opposite direction, the park at your feet (called Parc de Joan Miró) includes the giant Miró sculpture *Woman and Bird (Dona i Ocell).* This was one of three works (along with the mosaic on the Ramblas—see page 72) that the city commissioned Miró to create in order to welcome visitors. Miró's sense of humor is evident—if the sculpture seems phallic, keep in mind that the Catalan word for "bird" is also slang for "penis."

Cost and Hours: Free, daily 10:00-22:00, restaurants serve until 24:00 and later, Gran Via de les Corts Catalanes 373-385, Metro: Espanya, www.arenasdebarcelona.com.

Away from the Center

Tibidabo

At the top of Barcelona's highest peak, you're offered the city's oldest amusement park (great for kids). "Tibidabo" comes from the Latin for "to thee I shall give," the words the devil used when he was tempting Christ. It's still an enticing offer: Besides the rollicking fun fair, Tibidabo is home to the Neo-Gothic Sacred Heart Church, and—if the weather and air quality are good—almost limitless views of the city and the Mediterranean.

Cost and Hours: €28.50, hours depend on season—generally Wed-Sun from 12:00 in July-Aug, weekends only off-season, tel. 932-117-942, www.tibidabo.cat.

Getting There: From the Plaça de Catalunya Metro station (under Café Zürich), take the L7 (brown) line to the Tibidabo stop (the blue Tourist Bus also goes to the Tibidabo stop). Then take Barcelona's only remaining tram—Tramvía Blau—from Plaça John F. Kennedy to Plaça Dr. Andreu (€4 one-way, buy tickets on board, 2-4/hour). From there, take the funicular to the top (€7.70, €4.10 if you're also paying park admission, tel. 906-427-017). A special "Tibibus" (#T2A) runs at 10:30 from Plaça de Catalunya to the park every day that it's open (€2.95, board in front of Caja Madrid bank).

Camp Nou Stadium

The home turf of FC Barcelona is a mecca for soccer fans. A tour takes you into the press room, by the box seats, through the trophy room, and past the warm-up bench, ending in a ground-level view of the field and, of course, a big shop to buy all of your official "Barça" gear. You'll also get to tour a museum tracing the highlights of Barça history, with lots of interactive touch screens and the six championship cups that the team won in a single season ("the sextuple," 2009-2010)—a feat, they say, that will never be repeated. For more on this team and its significance to Barcelona and Catalunya, see page 69.

Cost and Hours: €23 for Camp Nou Experience (includes tour and museum); mid-April-early Oct Mon-Sat 10:00-20:00 (until 18:30 rest of year), Sun 10:00-14:30; shorter hours on game days, Metro: Maria Cristina or Collblanc, tel. 902-189-900, www .fcbarcelona.cat.

Shopping in Barcelona

Barcelona is a fantastic shopping destination, whether you prefer high-end fashion, department stores stocked with everyday European fashions, artisan shops with a centuries-long tradition, or funky little boutiques.

Souvenir Ideas

In this very artistic city, consider picking up prints, books, posters, decorative items, or other keepsakes featuring works by your favorite **artist** (Picasso, Dalí, Miró, Gaudí, etc.). Gift shops at major museums can be entered gratis (such as the Picasso Museum and at Gaudí's La Pedrera) and are a bonanza for art and design lovers; model-ship builders will be fascinated by the offerings at the Maritime Museum shop.

Foodies might enjoy shopping for local **food items**—olive oil, wine, spices (such as saffron or sea salts), high-quality canned foods and preserves, dried beans, and so on. Remember, food items must be sealed to make it back through US customs (see page 18). Cooks can look for Euro-style gadgets at **kitchen-supply** stores.

In this design-oriented city, **home decor** shops are abundant and fun to browse, offering a variety of Euro housewares unavailable back home. For something more classic, look for glassware or other items with a dash of Modernista style.

Fashionistas can shop for **espadrilles** (*espadenya* in Catalan). These soft-canvas, rope-soled shoes originated as humble Catalan peasant footwear but have become trendy as a lightweight summer shoe. A few shops in Barcelona, such as La Manual Alpargatera (in the Barri Gòtic at 7 Carrer d'Avinyó), still make these the traditional way.

Sports fans love jerseys, scarves, and other gear associated with the wildly popular **Barça** soccer team.

Shopping Neighborhoods and Streets
Barri Gòtic
Stay off of the wide, touristy Carrer de la Portaferrissa between the cathedral and the Ramblas. For a far more colorful route that leads past many fun-to-browse shops, try this: Facing the Roman towers and big BARCINO letters (on Plaça Nova, near the cathedral), turn 90 degrees to the right and head up Carrer de la Palla. At the fork, you can either detour left, down Carrer dels Banys Nous, or head right, continuing along Carrer de la Palla. That street pops you out into the delightful Plaça de Sant Josep Oriol, facing the Church of Santa Maria del Pi (a popular venue for guitar concerts—described later). Jog around the right side of the church, through the cute little Plaça del Pi, and head up Carrer Petritxol. You'll wind up on Carrer de la Portaferrissa, one block from the Ramblas.

Other Barri Gòtic streets are loaded with fun shopping opportunities. On the other side of the Ramblas (two blocks below Plaça de Catalunya), stroll down skinny Carrer de Bonsuccés (it turns into Carrer d'Elisabets) and poke into the little boutiques along the way (such as the tiny, fashionable clothing store Passé Composé, at #12).

For department and chain stores, simply wander down **Avinguda Portal de l'Angel,** the street that connects Plaça de Catalunya with the cathedral, at the northern edge of the Barri Gòtic. In a few short blocks, you'll find the big El Corte Inglés department store, Zara (clothing), and a branch of practically every Spanish chain store.

El Born
For a slightly edgier and less touristy shopping experience, head to the El Born neighborhood. The main spines of El Born—Carrer de la Princesa, the perpendicular Carrer de Montcada, and the diagonal Carrer de l'Argenteria—are largely disappointing for shoppers. But if you lose yourself in the smaller back lanes between those arteries, you'll discover a world of artsy, funky little

boutiques. Stroll along Carrer dels Flassaders (which runs behind the Picasso Museum), Carrer dels Banys Vells (between Montcada and l'Argenteria), and Carrer del Rec (just south of Passeig del Born)—and all of the little lanes crossing each of these streets.

Eixample

This ritzy area is home to many of the city's top-end shops. In general, you'll find a lot of big international names along Passeig de Gràcia, the main boulevard that runs north from Plaça de Catalunya to the Gaudí sights—an area fittingly called the Golden Quarter (Quadrat d'Or). Appropriately enough, the "upper end" of Passeig de Gràcia has the fancier shops—Gucci, Louis Vuitton, Escada, Chanel, and so on—while the southern part of the street is relatively "low-end" (Zara, Mango). One block to the west, Rambla de Catalunya holds more local (but still expensive) options for fashion, home decor, jewelry, perfume, and so on. The streets that connect Rambla de Catalunya to Passeig de Gràcia also have some fine shops.

This neighborhood is also home to some fun kitchen stores: Try Gadgets & Cuina (Carrer d'Aragó 249) or Cooking (Carrer de Provença 246).

Nightlife in Barcelona

Like all of Spain, Barcelona is extremely lively after hours. People head out for dinner at 22:00, then bar-hop or simply wander the streets until well after midnight (*matinada* is the Catalan word for "the wee hours" or "dawn"). Some days, it seems more people are out and about at 2:00 in the morning (party time) than at 2:00 in the afternoon (siesta time). The most "local" thing you can do here after the sun sets is to explore neighborhood watering holes and find your favorite place for a cocktail. I've described several parts of town ideally suited to doing just that, along with options for evening sightseeing or catching a musical performance.

Information: The TI hands out a free, monthly, user-friendly *Time Out BCN Guide* (in English, with descriptions of each day's main events and websites for getting tickets). The TI's culture website (barcelonacultura.bcn.cat) is also helpful. The weekly *Guía del Ocio,* sold at newsstands for €1.20 (or free in some hotel lobbies), is a Spanish-language entertainment listing (with guidelines for English-speakers inside the back cover; also available online at www.guiadelocio.com).

Palau de la Virreina Cultura, an arts-and-culture information office, provides details on Barcelona cultural events—music, opera, and theater (daily 10:00-20:30, Ramblas 99—see map on page 66, tel. 933-161-000). A ticket desk is next door.

Getting Tickets: Most venues have links to booking engines on their websites. The majority of tickets for Barcelona events are booked through www.ticketmaster.es or www.telentrada.com. You can also get tickets through the box offices in the main El Corte Inglés department store or the giant FNAC electronics store (both on Plaça de Catalunya, extra booking fee), or at the ticket desk in Palau de la Virreina (listed above).

After-Hours Hangout Neighborhoods

Most Barcelonans' idea of "nightlife" is bar-hopping with a circle of friends while nibbling tapas and enjoying a variety of drinks. The streets are jammed with people. Here are some top areas.

El Born

Passeig del Born, a broad, park-like strip stretching from the Church of Santa Maria del Mar up to the old market hall, is lined with inviting bars and nightspots. The side streets also teem with options. Wander to find your favorite.

Right on Passeig del Born is **Miramelindo,** a local favorite—mellow yet convivial, with two floors of woody ambience and a minty aura from all those mojitos the bartenders are mashing up (Passeig del Born 15). **Palau Dalmases,** in the atmospheric courtyard of an old palace, slings cocktails when it's not hosting flamenco shows. **La Vinya del Senyor,** one of my recommended eateries, is a fine place for a good glass of wine out on the square in front of the Church of Santa Maria del Mar.

Plaça Reial (in the Barri Gòtic) and Nearby

This charmingly trendy square is buried deep in the Barri Gòtic just off the Ramblas. Once seedy, it now bustles with popular bars and restaurants offering inflated prices at inviting outdoor tables. While not a great place to eat (the only one worth seriously considering for a meal is the recommended **Les Quinze Nits**), this is a great place to sip a before- or after-dinner drink. **Ocaña Bar,** at #13, has a dilapidated-mod interior, a see-through industrial kitchen, and rickety-chic secondhand tables out on the square (€4-9 tapas, reasonable drinks, open nightly). Or there's always the student option: Buy a cheap €1 beer from a convenience store (you'll find several just off the square, including a few along Carrer dels Escudellers, just south of Plaça Reial), then grab a free spot on the square, either at one of the few fixed chairs, perched along the rim of the fountain, or simply leaning up against a palm tree.

Wandering the streets near the square leads to other nightlife options. **Carrer de Escudellers** is a significantly rougher scene, with a few trendy options mixed in with several sketchy dives. Much closer to the harbor, **Carrer de la Mercè,** described on page 165 under "Eating in Barcelona," is a mix of salty sailors' pubs and more youthful bars. The next street up, **Carrer Ample,** has a similar scene.

The Beach at Barceloneta

A broad beach stretches for miles from the former fishermen's quarter at Barceloneta to the Fòrum. Every 100 yards or so is a *chiringuito*—a shack selling drinks and light snacks. Originally these sold seafood, but now they keep locals and tourists well-lubricated. It's a very fun, lively scene on a balmy summer evening and a nice way to escape the claustrophobic confines of the city to enjoy some sea air and the day's final sun rays.

Barceloneta itself has a broad promenade facing the harbor, lined with interchangeable seafood restaurants. But the best beach experience is beyond the tip of Barceloneta. From here, a double-decker boardwalk runs the length of the beach, with a cool walkway up above and a series of fine seafood restaurants with romantic candlelit beachfront seating tucked down below.

Gràcia

A bit farther flung, and more local-feeling because of it, the Gràcia neighborhood sits between the Eixample and Park Güell. Known for its design schools and international art house cinema, the Cines Verdi (www.cines-verdi.com/barcelona), it's the unpretentious but intellectual corner of town. Though it lacks the twisty-Gothic-lanes ambience of the Old City, Gràcia feels more like a small town (which it was, before it was swallowed up by an expanding Barcelona). It's popular with students (both local and international) and can be a bit rowdy. For the highest concentration of fun, check out Carrer de Verdi, Plaça de la Virreina, Carrer de Torrijos, and Plaça del Sol. The district is even more vibrant in August, when it hosts the Festes de Gràcia, with street music everywhere.

The Eixample

Barcelona's upscale uptown isn't quite as lively or funky as some other neighborhoods, but a few streets have some fine watering holes. Walk along the inviting, park-like Rambla de Catalunya, or a couple of blocks over, along Carrer d'Enric Granados and Carrer d'Aribau (near the epicenter of the Eixample's gay community).

Music

Serious Concerts

Several seriously classy venues host high-end performances. The **Palace of Catalan Music** (Palau de la Música Catalana), with one of the finest Modernista interiors in town (see listing on page 102), offers a full slate of performances, ranging from symphonic to Catalan folk songs to chamber music to flamenco (€22-49 tickets, box office open daily 9:30-21:00, Carrer Palau de la Música 4-6, Metro: Urquinaona, box office tel. 902-442-882, www.palaumusica.cat).

The **Liceu Opera House** (Gran Teatre del Liceu), right on the heart of the Ramblas, is a pre-Modernista, sumptuous venue for opera, dance, children's theater, and concerts (tickets from €12, La

Rambla 51-59, box office just around the corner at Carrer Sant Pau 1, Metro: Liceu, box office tel. 934-859-913, www.liceubarcelona.cat).

Some of Barcelona's top sights—including **La Pedrera, CaixaForum,** and **Fundació Joan Miró** (all described earlier)— also host good-quality concerts; for details, check their websites.

Touristy Performances of Spanish Clichés

Two famously Spanish types of music—flamenco and Spanish guitar—have little to do with Barcelona or Catalunya, but are performed to keep visitors happy. If you're headed for other parts of Spain where these musical forms are more typical (such as Andalucía for flamenco), you may as well wait until you can experience the real deal. But if this is your best chance to see these types of performances, here are some options.

Flamenco: Tarantos, on Plaça Reial in the heart of the Barri Gòtic, puts on cheap, brief (30 minutes), riveting flamenco performances several times nightly. While flamenco is foreign to Catalunya (locals say that it's like going to see country music in Boston), this is a fun and easy way to enjoy it. Performances are in a touristy little bar/theater with about 50 seats and reliably good-quality performers (€8, nightly at 20:30, 21:30, and 22:30; Plaça Reial 17, tel. 933-191-789, www.masimas.com/en/tarantos). It's right on Plaça Reial, so it's easy to drop by and get tickets.

Other options include the pricey **Tablao Cordobés** on the Ramblas (€42 includes a drink, €77 includes mediocre buffet dinner and better seats, 2-3 performances/day, La Rambla 35, tel. 933-175-711, www.tablaocordobes.com) and **Palau Dalmases** in the heart of the El Born district (€20 includes a drink, daily at 19:30 and 21:30, in atmospheric old palace courtyard, Carrer de Montcada 20, tel. 933-100-673, www.palaudalmases.com).

For flamenco in a concert-hall setting, try one of the Palace of Catalan Music's regular performances (see listing earlier, under "Serious Concerts").

Spanish Guitar: "Masters of Guitar" concerts are offered nearly nightly at 21:00 in the Barri Gòtic's Church of Santa Maria del Pi (€21 at the door, €3 less if you buy at least 3 hours ahead— look for ticket-sellers in front of church and scattered around town, Plaça del Pi 7; sometimes in Sant Jaume Church instead, Carrer de Ferran 28; tel. 647-514-513, www.maestrosdelaguitarra.com). The same company also does occasional concerts in the Palace of Catalan Music (€28-32).

Sleeping in Barcelona

Book ahead. Barcelona is Spain's most expensive city. Still, it has reasonably priced rooms. Cheap places are more crowded in summer; fancier business-class hotels fill up in winter and offer

Sleep Code

(€1 = about $1.30, country code: 34)
S = Single, **D** = Double/Twin, **T** = Triple, **Q** = Quad, **b** = bathroom, **s** = shower only. Unless otherwise noted, credit cards are accepted and English is spoken. Some hotels include the 10 percent IVA tax in the room price; others tack it onto your bill. Additionally, the city levies a tourist tax (ranges from €0.65-2.25/person per night). Hotel breakfasts can range from simple spreads (either included or cheap) to pricey buffets.

To help you easily sort through these listings, I've divided the accommodations into three categories based on the price for a standard double room with bath (during high season):

$$$ Higher Priced—Most rooms €150 or more.
$$ Moderately Priced—Most rooms between €100-150.
$ Lower Priced—Most rooms €100 or less.

Prices can change without notice; verify the hotel's current rates online or by email. For the best prices, always book direct.

discounts on weekends and in summer. When considering relative hotel values, in summer and on weekends you can often get modern comfort in business-class hotels for about the same price (€100) as you'll pay for ramshackle charm (and only a few minutes' walk from the Old City action). Most TI branches (including those at Plaça de Catalunya, Plaça de Sant Jaume, and the airport) offer a room-finding service, though it's cheaper to go direct.

While many of my recommendations are on pedestrian streets, night noise can be a problem (especially in cheap places, which have single-pane windows). For a quiet night, ask for "*tranquilo*" rather than "*con vista*."

Business-Class Comfort near Plaça de Catalunya

These hotels have sliding-glass doors leading to shiny reception areas, air-conditioning, and modern bedrooms. Most are on big streets within two blocks of Barcelona's exuberant central square, where the Old City meets the Eixample. As business-class hotels, they have hard-to-pin-down prices that fluctuate with demand. I've listed the average rate you'll pay. But in summer and on weekends, supply often far exceeds the demand, and many of these places cut prices to around €100—always check websites for a deal. Most of these are located between two Metro stops: Catalunya and Universitat; if arriving by Aerobus, note that the bus also stops

BARCELONA

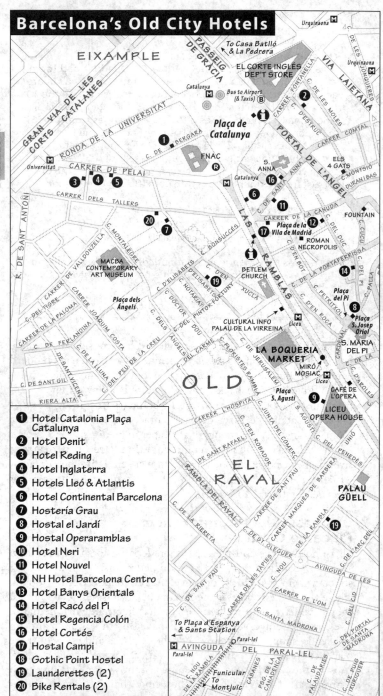

Barcelona's Old City Hotels

1. Hotel Catalonia Plaça Catalunya
2. Hotel Denit
3. Hotel Reding
4. Hotel Inglaterra
5. Hotels Lleó & Atlantis
6. Hotel Continental Barcelona
7. Hostería Grau
8. Hostal el Jardí
9. Hostal Operaramblas
10. Hotel Neri
11. Hotel Nouvel
12. NH Hotel Barcelona Centro
13. Hotel Banys Orientals
14. Hotel Racó del Pi
15. Hotel Regencia Colón
16. Hotel Cortés
17. Hostal Campi
18. Gothic Point Hostel
19. Launderettes (2)
20. Bike Rentals (2)

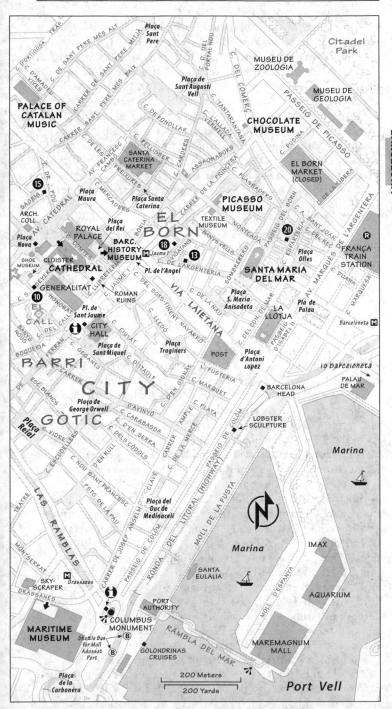

at both places. The last three hotels listed here face a busy street; request a quieter room in back.

$$$ Hotel Catalonia Plaça Catalunya has four stars, an elegant old entryway with a modern reception area, splashy public spaces, slick marble and hardwood floors, 140 comfortable but simple rooms, and a garden courtyard with a pool a world away from the big-city noise. It's a bit pricey for the quality of the rooms—you're paying for the posh lobby (Db-€200 but can swing much higher or lower with demand, extra bed-€38, breakfast-€19, air-con, elevator, guest computer, free Wi-Fi, a half-block off Plaça de Catalunya at Carrer de Bergara 11, Metro: Catalunya, tel. 933-015-151, www.hoteles-catalonia.com, catalunya@hoteles -catalonia.es).

$$ Hotel Denit is a small, stylish, 36-room hotel on a pedestrian street two blocks off Plaça de Catalunya. It's chic, minimalist, and fun: Guidebook tips decorate the halls, and the rooms are sized like T-shirts ("small" Sb-€79-109, "medium" Db-€99-119, "large" Db-€119-144, "XL" Db-€149-164, includes breakfast, air-con, elevator, guest computer, free Wi-Fi, Carrer d'Estruc 24-26, Metro: Catalunya, tel. 935-454-000, www.denit .com, info@denit.com).

$$ Hotel Reding, on a quiet street a 10-minute walk west of the Ramblas and Plaça de Catalunya action, is a slick and sleek place renting 44 mod rooms at a reasonable price (Db-€125—this rate includes breakfast with this book in 2014 but only if you book directly with the hotel—otherwise pay €14 for breakfast, prices go up during trade fairs, extra bed-€38, air-con, elevator, guest computer, free Wi-Fi, Carrer de Gravina 5-7, Metro: Universitat, tel. 934-121-097, www.hotelreding.com, recepcion@hotelreding.com).

$$ Hotel Inglaterra is owned by the same people as Hotel Denit (listed above) but on the other side of Plaça de Catalunya. It has 60 rooms, a more traditional style, a rooftop terrace, and swimming pool (Sb-€119, Db-€125, €30 more for bigger "deluxe" rooms, breakfast included if you book through their website— otherwise it's €15, air-con, elevator, guest computer, free Wi-Fi, Carrer de Pelai 14, Metro: Universitat, tel. 935-051-100, www .hotel-inglaterra.com, reservas@hotel-inglaterra.com).

$$ Hotel Lleó (YEH-oh) is well-run, with 92 big, bright, and comfortable rooms; a great breakfast room; and a generous lounge (Db-€140-170 but flexes way up with demand, can be cheaper in summer, extra bed-about €30, breakfast-€13, air-con, elevator, guest computer, free Wi-Fi, small rooftop pool, Carrer de Pelai 22, midway between Metros: Universitat and Catalunya, tel. 933-181-312, www.hotel-lleo.com, info@hotel-lleo.com).

$$ Hotel Atlantis is solid, with 50 big, nondescript, modern rooms and fair prices for the location (Sb-€92, Db-€120, Tb-€138, check for deals on website, air-con, elevator, guest computer, free Wi-Fi, Carrer de Pelai 20, midway between Metros: Universitat and Catalunya, tel. 933-189-012, www.hotelatlantis-bcn.com, inf@hotelatlantis-bcn.com).

Affordable Hotels with "Personality" on or near the Ramblas

These places are generally family-run, with ad-lib furnishings, more character, and lower prices.

$$ Hotel Continental Barcelona, in a building overlooking the top of the Ramblas, offers classic, tiny view-balcony opportunities if you don't mind the noise. Its 39 comfortable but faded rooms come with clashing carpets and wallpaper, and perhaps one too many clever ideas. Choose between your own little Ramblas-view balcony (where you can eat your breakfast) or a quieter back room. J. M.'s (José María's) free breakfast and all-day snack-and-drink bar are a plus (Sb-€98, Db-€108, twin Db-€118, Db with Ramblas balcony-€128, extra bed-€40/adult or €20/child, 5 percent discount off these rates with this book in 2014 when you book directly with the hotel, includes breakfast, air-con, elevator, quiet terrace, guest computer, free Wi-Fi, Ramblas 138, Metro: Catalunya, tel. 933-012-570, www.hotelcontinental.com, barcelona @hotelcontinental.com).

$$ Hostería Grau is homey, family-run, and newly renovated in an eco-conscious style. Its 24 cheery rooms are a few blocks off the Ramblas in the colorful university district—but double-glazed windows keep it quiet (Db-€110-115, "superior" Db-€120-130, Tb-€135-145, Qb-€160-180, prices can jump during fairs and big events, 5 percent discount off these rates when you book directly with the hotel, breakfast extra, strict cancellation policy, air-con, elevator, some rooms with terrace, guest computer, free Wi-Fi, 200 yards up Carrer dels Tallers from the Ramblas at Ramelleres 27, Metro: Catalunya, tel. 933-018-135, www.hostalgrau.com, reservas@hostalgrau.com, Monica).

$ Hostal el Jardí offers 40 clean, remodeled rooms on a breezy square in the Barri Gòtic. Many of the tight, plain, comfy rooms come with petite balconies (for an extra charge) and enjoy an almost Parisian ambience. It's a good deal only if you value the quaint-square-with-Barri-Gòtic ambience—you're definitely paying for the location. Book well in advance, as this family-run place has an avid following (small basic interior Db-€75, nicer interior Db-€90, outer Db with balcony or twin with window-€95, large outer Db with balcony or square-view terrace-€110, no charge for extra bed, breakfast-€6, air-con, elevator, some stairs, free Wi-Fi, halfway between Ramblas and cathedral at Plaça Sant Josep Oriol 1, Metro: Liceu, tel. 933-015-900, www.eljardi-barcelona.com, reservations@eljardi-barcelona.com).

$ Hostal Operaramblas, with 68 plain rooms 20 yards off the Ramblas, is clean, institutional, modern, and a great value. The street can feel a bit seedy at night, but it's safe, and the hotel is very secure (Sb-€46, Db-€66, book through website and use code "operaramblas" for 10 percent discount, no breakfast but coffee and snack machines in lobby, air-con only in summer, elevator, pay guest computer, free Wi-Fi, Carrer de Sant Pau 20, Metro: Liceu, tel. 933-188-201, www.operaramblas.com, info@operaramblas.com).

Places in the Old City

These accommodations are buried in Barcelona's Old City, mostly in the Barri Gòtic. The Catalunya, Liceu, and Jaume I Metro stops flank this tight tangle of lanes; I've noted which stop(s) are best for each.

$$$ Hotel Neri is posh, pretentious, and sophisticated, with 22 rooms spliced into the ancient stones of the Barri Gòtic, overlooking an overlooked square (Plaça Sant Felip Neri) a block from the cathedral. It has big flat-screen TVs, pricey modern art on the bedroom walls, dressed-up people in its gourmet restaurant, and stuffy service (Db-€260-300, suites-€320-400, generally cheaper on weekdays, breakfast-€22, air-con, elevator, free Wi-Fi, rooftop tanning deck, Carrer de Sant Sever 5, Metro: Liceu or Jaume I, tel. 933-040-655, www.hotelneri.com, info@hotelneri.com).

$$$ Hotel Nouvel, in an elegant, Victorian-style building on a handy pedestrian street, is less business-oriented and offers more character than the others listed here. It boasts royal lounges and 78 comfy rooms (Sb-€132, Db-€205, online deals can be much much cheaper, extra bed-€35, includes breakfast, €20 deposit for TV remote, air-con, elevator, guest computer, pay Wi-Fi, Carrer de Santa Anna 20, Metro: Catalunya, tel. 933-018-274, www.hotel nouvel.com, info@hotelnouvel.com).

$$$ NH Hotel Barcelona Centro, with 156 rooms and tasteful chain-hotel predictability, is professional yet friendly, buried in the Barri Gòtic just three blocks off the Ramblas (Db-€160, but rates fluctuate with demand, bigger "superior" rooms on a corner with windows on 2 sides-€25 extra, breakfast-€16, air-con, elevator, pay guest computer, free Wi-Fi, Carrer del Duc 15, Metro: Catalunya or Liceu, tel. 932-703-410, www.nh-hotels.com, barcelona centro@nh-hotels.com).

$$ Hotel Banys Orientals, a modern, boutique-type place, has a people-to-people ethic and refreshingly straight prices. Its 43 restful rooms are located in the El Born district on a pedestrianized street between the cathedral and Church of Santa Maria del Mar (Sb-€87, Db-€105, breakfast-€10, air-con, guest computer, free Wi-Fi, Carrer de l'Argenteria 37, 50 yards from Metro:

Jaume I, tel. 932-688-460, www.hotelbanysorientals.com, reservas @hotelbanysorientals.com). They also run the adjacent, recommended El Senyor Parellada restaurant.

$$ Hotel Racó del Pi, part of the H10 hotel chain, is a quality, professional place with generous public spaces and 37 modern, bright, quiet rooms. It's located on a wonderful pedestrian street immersed in the Barri Gòtic (Db-often around €130-145, can be as low as €100, cheaper if you book "nonrefundable" room online, breakfast-€10, air-con, guest computer, free Wi-Fi, around the corner from Plaça del Pi at Carrer del Pi 7, 3-minute walk from Metro: Liceu, tel. 933-426-190, www.h10hotels.com, h10.raco .delpi@h10.es).

$$ Hotel Regencia Colón, in a handy location one block in front of the cathedral, offers 50 slightly older but solid, classy, and well-priced rooms (Db-€120-140 but can go higher or lower with demand—check the website for the best rates, extra bed-€37, breakfast-€13, air-con, elevator, free Wi-Fi, Carrer dels Sagristans 13-17, Metro: Jaume I, tel. 933-189-858, www.hotelregenciacolon .com, info@hotelregenciacolon.com).

$ Hotel Cortés has 44 rooms on a traffic-free shopping street just off Avinguda Portal de l'Angel (between Plaça de Catalunya and the cathedral). It's a bit sterile and scruffy, but well-priced and wonderfully located. Back rooms overlook an old *extra muro* cloister, while front rooms face the busy pedestrian drag (Sb-€70, Db-€100, includes breakfast, air-con, elevator, free Wi-Fi, Carrer de Santa Anna 25, Metro: Catalunya, tel. 933-179-112, www.hotel cortes.com, reservas@hotelcortes.com).

$ Hostal Campi is big, subdued, and ramshackle, but offers simple class. This easygoing old-school spot rents 24 rooms a few doors off the top of the Ramblas (S-€35, D-€60, Ds-€62, Db-€69, T-€78, Tb-€92, no breakfast, lots of stairs with no elevator, guest computer, free Wi-Fi in sitting room and some rooms, Carrer de la Canuda 4, Metro: Catalunya, tel. 933-013-545, www.hostalcampi .com, reservas@hostalcampi.com, Margarita and Nando).

In the Eixample

For an uptown, boulevard-like neighborhood, sleep in the Eixample, a 10-minute walk from the Ramblas action (see map on page 154). Most of these places use the Passeig de Gràcia or Catalunya Metro stops. Because these stations are so huge—especially Passeig de Gràcia, which sprawls underground for a few blocks—study the maps posted in the station to establish which exit you want before surfacing.

$$ Hotel Granvía, filling a palatial 1870s mansion, offers a large, peaceful sun patio and 58 spacious rooms (Sb-€75-185, Db-€90-150, superior Db-€105-225, family room-€120-245,

BARCELONA

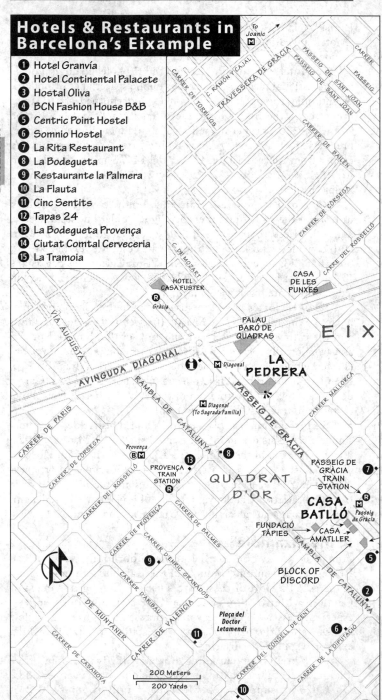

Hotels & Restaurants in Barcelona's Eixample

1 Hotel Granvía
2 Hotel Continental Palacete
3 Hostal Oliva
4 BCN Fashion House B&B
5 Centric Point Hostel
6 Somnio Hostel
7 La Rita Restaurant
8 La Bodegueta
9 Restaurante la Palmera
10 La Flauta
11 Cinc Sentits
12 Tapas 24
13 La Bodegueta Provença
14 Ciutat Comtal Cerveceria
15 La Tramoia

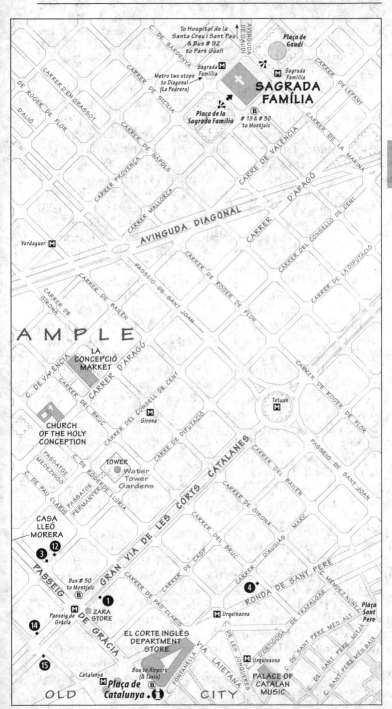

BARCELONA

mention Rick Steves to get best available rate, breakfast-€14, air-con, elevator, free Wi-Fi, Gran Via de les Corts Catalanes 642, Metro: Passeig de Gràcia, tel. 933-181-900, www.hotelgranvia.com, hgranvia@nnhotels.com).

$$ Hotel Continental Palacete, with 19 small rooms, fills a 100-year-old chandeliered mansion. With flowery wallpaper and ornately gilded stucco, it's gaudy in the city of Gaudí, but it's also friendly, quiet, and well-located. Guests have unlimited access to the outdoor terrace and the "cruise-inspired" fruit, veggie, and drink buffet (Sb-€108, Db-€145, €35-45 more for bigger and brighter view rooms, 5 percent discount with this book in 2014 when you book directly with the hotel, extra bed-€55/adult or €40/child, includes breakfast, air-con, guest computer, free Wi-Fi, 2 blocks north of Plaça de Catalunya at corner of Rambla de Catalunya and Carrer de la Diputació, 30 Rambla de Catalunya, Metro: Passeig de Gràcia, tel. 934-457-657, www.hotelcontinental.com, palacete@hotelcontinental.com).

$ Hostal Oliva, run with care by Oliva herself, is a spartan, old-school place with 15 basic, bright, high-ceilinged rooms and no breakfast or public spaces. It's on the fourth floor of a classic old Eixample building in a perfect location, just a couple of blocks above Plaça de Catalunya (S-€41, D-€71, Db-€91, elevator, free Wi-Fi, corner of Passeig de Gràcia and Carrer de la Diputació, Passeig de Gràcia 32, Metro: Passeig de Gràcia, tel. 934-880-162, www.hostaloliva.com, hostaloliva@lasguias.com).

$ BCN Fashion House B&B is a meditative place with 10 rooms, a peaceful lounge, and a leafy backyard terrace on the first floor of a nondescript old building (S-€36-56, D-€56-83, bigger "veranda" D-€73-93, Db-€90-125, 2-night minimum stay, breakfast-€6, Wi-Fi, between Carrer d'Ausiàs Marc and Ronda de Sant Pere at Carrer del Bruc 13, just steps from Metro: Urquinaona, mobile 637-904-044, www.bcnfashionhouse.com, info@bcnfashionhouse.com).

Hostels

Equity Point Hostels: Barcelona has a terrific chain of well-run and centrally located hostels (tel. 932-312-045, www.equity-point.com), providing €25-32 dorm beds (prices lower off-season) in 4- to 14-bed coed rooms with €2 sheets and towels, guest computers, free Wi-Fi, included breakfast, lockers (B.Y.O. lock, or buy one there), and plenty of opportunities to meet other backpackers. They're open 24 hours but aren't party hostels, so they enforce quiet after 23:00. There are three locations to choose from: the Eixample, Barri Gòtic, or near the beach. **$ Centric Point Hostel** is a huge place renting 400 cheap beds at what must be the best address in Barcelona (bar, kitchen, Passeig de Gràcia 33—see map

on page 154, Metro: Passeig de Gràcia, tel. 932-151-796, www
.centricpointhostel.com). **$ Gothic Point Hostel** rents 130 beds
a block from the Picasso Museum (roof terrace, Carrer Vigatans
5—see map on page 148, Metro: Jaume I, reception tel. 932-687-
808, www.gothicpoint.com). **$ Sea Point Hostel** has 70 beds on
the beach nearby (Plaça del Mar 4—see map on page 50, Metro:
Barceloneta, reception tel. 932-247-075, www.seapointhostel.com).

$ Somnio Hostel, an innovative smaller place run by a pair
of American expats, has 26 beds in 10 rooms. Choose between
dorms and private rooms (bunk in 6-bed dorm-€30, S-€50, D-€87,
Db-€95; prices include sheets, towels, and lockers; air-con, guest
computer, free Wi-Fi, Carrer de la Diputació 251, second floor,
Metro: Passeig de Gràcia, tel. 932-725-308, www.somniohostels
.com, info@somniohostels.com). They have a second location that's
five blocks farther out.

Apartments

$$ Cross-Pollinate is a reputable online booking agency repre-
senting B&Bs and apartments in a handful of European cities,
including Barcelona. Choose a place online and submit a reser-
vation; if the place is available, you'll be charged a small deposit
and emailed the location and check-in details. Policies vary from
owner to owner, but in most cases you'll pay the balance on arrival
in cash. Barcelona listings range from a B&B double room near
Sagrada Família for €70 per night to a three-bedroom Eixample
apartment sleeping eight for €295 per night. Minimum stays
vary from one to three nights (US tel. 800-270-1190, www.cross
-pollinate.com, info@cross-pollinate.com).

$$ Tournights Barcelona, run by American Frederick, rents
55 renovated apartments with kitchens. Most are near the beach in
the lively Barceloneta neighborhood; others are in the Barri Gòtic
or Eixample (2 people-€105 April-Oct, €85 Nov-March; prices
vary with size—see photos and videos on website, €50 cleaning
fee, 3-night minimum stay, discount for 7-night stay, 20 percent
deposit required to reserve online, pay balance in cash when you
arrive, no breakfast, arrange meeting to check in when you reserve,
mobile 620-585-594, www.tournights.com, info@tournights.com).

Eating in Barcelona

Barcelona, the capital of Catalan cuisine—starring seafood—
offers a tremendous variety of colorful eateries, ranging from basic
and filling to chic and trendy. Most of my listings are lively spots
with a busy tapas scene at the bar, along with restaurant tables for
raciones. A regional specialty is *pa amb tomàquet* (pah ahm too-
MAH-kaht), toasted bread rubbed with a mix of crushed tomato

and olive oil.

I've listed mostly practical, characteristic, colorful, and affordable restaurants. My recommendations are grouped by neighborhood—along the Ramblas, in the Barri Gòtic, in El Born (best for foodies), in the Eixample, and in Barceloneta. I also include some budget options scattered throughout the city and a suggested route for finding Catalan sweets. Note that many restaurants close in August (or July), when the owners take a vacation.

Restaurants generally serve lunch from 13:00 to 16:00 and dinner from 20:00 or even later (Spaniards don't start dinner until about 22:00). It's deadly to your Barcelona experience to eat too early—if a place feels touristy, come back later and it may be a thriving local favorite.

Throughout the city, you'll see signs both for Spanish *tapas* and Catalan *tapes* (same pronunciation and meaning). Note: Unlike in many Spanish cities, most Barcelona tapas bars do *not* provide a free, small tapa with the purchase of a drink; if you want food, order it separately. For more on tapas, see page 33.

Catalans seem to have an affinity for Basque culture, so you'll find a lot of **Basque-style tapas places** here (look for *basca* or *euskal taberna; euskal* means "Basque"). Enticing buffets of bite-size tapas invite you to simply take what you want. These places are particularly user-friendly, since you don't have to look at a menu or wait to be served—just grab what looks good, order a drink, and save your toothpicks (they'll count them up at the end to tally your bill). I've listed several such places (including Taverna Basca Irati, Xaloc, and Sagardi Euskal Taberna), though Barcelona has many other similar options.

Along the Ramblas

Within a few steps of the Ramblas, you'll find handy lunch places, an inviting market hall, and some good vegetarian options. For locations, see the map on page 160.

Lunching Simply Yet Memorably near the Ramblas

Although these places are enjoyable for a lunch break during your Ramblas sightseeing, many are also open for dinner.

Taverna Basca Irati serves 40 kinds of hot and cold Basque *pintxos* for €1.95 each. These are small open-faced sandwiches—like sushi on bread. Muscle in through the hungry local crowd, get an empty plate from the waiter, and then help yourself. Every

Budget Meals Around Town

Sandwiches: Bright, clean, and inexpensive sandwich shops proudly hold the cultural line against the fast-food invasion

that has hamburgerized the rest of Europe. Catalan sandwiches are made to order with crunchy French bread. Rather than butter, locals prefer *tomàquet* (a spread of crushed tomatoes). You'll see two big local chains (Bocatta and Pans & Company) everywhere, but these serve mass-produced McBaguettes ordered from a multilingual menu. I've had better luck with hole-in-the-wall sandwich shops—virtually as numerous as the chains—where you can see exactly what you're getting.

International Options: Try **Mucci's Pizza** for good, fresh €2 pizza slices and empanadas (two locations just off the Ramblas, at Bonsuccés 10 and Tallers 75, www.muccis.com). **Wok to Walk** makes tasty food on the run, serving up noodles and rice in takeaway containers with your choice of meat and/ or veggies and finished with a savory sauce (€6-9, 3 locations—by the main door of the Boqueria Market, two steps from the Liceu Opera House, and near Plaça de Sant Jaume, www.woktowalk.com). **Kebab** places are another good, super-cheap standby; you'll see them all over town, offering a quick and tasty meal for about €3-4.

few minutes, waiters circulate with platters of new, still-warm munchies. Grab one as they pass by...it's addictive (you'll be charged by the number of toothpicks left on your plate when you're done). Wash it down with €3-4 glasses of Rioja (full-bodied red wine), Txakolí (sprightly Basque white wine) or *sidra* (apple wine) poured from on high to add oxygen and bring out the flavor (daily 11:00-24:00, a block off the Ramblas, behind arcade at Carrer del Cardenal Casanyes 17, Metro: Liceu, tel. 933-023-084).

Restaurant Elisabets is a rough little neighborhood eatery packed with antique radios. It's popular with locals for its €12 "home-cooked" three-course lunch special; even cheaper *menú rapid* options are also available (13:00-16:00 only). Stop by for lunch, survey what those around you are enjoying, and order what looks best. Apparently, locals put up with the service for the tasty food (Mon-Sat 7:30-23:00, closed Sun and Aug, €3 tapas all day, 2 blocks west of Ramblas on far corner of Plaça del Bonsuccés at Carrer d'Elisabets 2, Metro: Catalunya, tel. 933-175-826, run by Pilar).

BARCELONA

Barcelona's Old City Restaurants

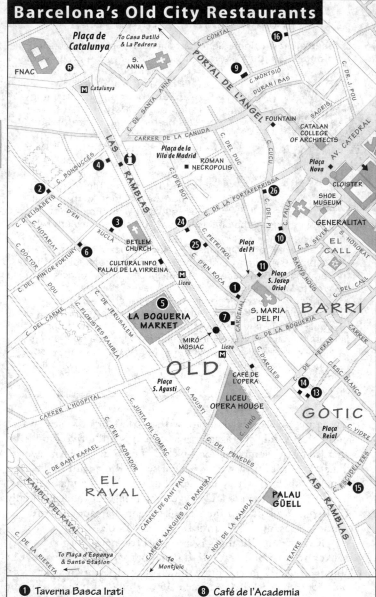

Plaça de Catalunya

To Casa Batlló & La Pedrera

FNAC ®

S. ANNA

C. COMTAL

16

PORTAL DE L'ANGEL

9 C. MONTSIÓ

DURAN I BAS

C. DR. J. POU

M *Catalunya*

C. DE SANTA ANNA

LAS RAMBLAS

FOUNTAIN

SAGRIS

CATALAN COLLEGE OF ARCHITECTS

CARRER DE LA CANUDA

Plaça de la Vila de Madrid

C. BONSUCCÉS

4 ℹ

2

C. D'ELISABETS

C. D'EN

C. DEL DUC

ROMAN NECROPOLIS

C. DEL PI

C. CUCU

AV. CATEDRAL

Plaça Nova

CLOISTER

SHOE MUSEUM

3

C. NOTARIAT

XUCLA

BETLEM CHURCH

C. D'EN BOT

C. DE LA PORTAFERRISSA

26

C. PALLA

GENERALITAT

C. DOCTOR

6

CULTURAL INFO PALAU DE LA VIRREINA

24

C. PETRIXOL

25

Plaça del Pi

10

EL CALL

C. S. SEVER

C. S. HONORAT

C. DEL PINTOR FORTUNY

M *Liceu*

C. D'EN ROCA

11

Plaça S. Josep Oriol

BANYS NOUS

C. DEL CARME

C. DE JERUSALEM

5 LA BOQUERIA MARKET

1

S. MARIA DEL PI

CARDENAL

C. DEL CALL

BARRI

C. DOU

C. DE FLORISTES RAMBLA

7

MIRÓ MOSAIC

Liceu M

C. DE LA BOQUERIA

CARRER

OLD

Plaça S. Agustí

S. AGUSTI

CAFÉ DE L'OPERA

C. D'AROLES

C. DE FERRAN

C. ESC BLANCS

CARRER HOSPITAL

C. JUNTA DEL COMERC

C. D'EN ROBADOR

C. DE SANT RAFAEL

LICEU OPERA HOUSE

C. UNIO

C. DE

14

13

GÒTIC

Plaça Reial

C. VIDRE

EL RAVAL

RAMBLA DEL RAVAL

CARRER DE SANT PAU

CARRER MARQUÈS DE BARBERÀ

C. DEL PENEDÈS

PALAU GÜELL

C. ESCUDELLERS

LAS RAMBLAS

15

C. DE LA RIERETA

To Plaça d'Espanya & Sants Station

C. NOU DE LA RAMBLA

TEATRE

To Montjuïc

1	Taverna Basca Irati	**8**	Café de l'Academia
2	Restaurant Elisabets	**9**	Els Quatre Gats
3	Café Granja Viader	**10**	Xaloc
4	Carrefour Market	**11**	Bar del Pi
5	La Boqueria Market Eateries	**12**	Restaurant Agut
6	Biocenter Veggie Rest.	**13**	Les Quinze Nits
7	Juicy Jones	**14**	La Crema Canela

BARCELONA

Café **Granja Viader** is a quaint time capsule, family-run since 1870. They boast about being the first dairy business to bottle and distribute milk in Spain. This feminine-feeling place—specializing in baked and dairy treats, toasted sandwiches, and light meals—is ideal for a traditional breakfast. Or indulge your sweet tooth: Try a glass of *orxata* (or *horchata*—*chufa*-nut milk, summer only), *llet mallorquina* (Majorca-style milk with cinnamon, lemon, and sugar), *crema catalana* (crème brûlée, their specialty), or *suis* ("Swiss"—hot chocolate with a snowcap of whipped cream). *Mel y mató* is fresh cheese with honey...very Catalan (Mon-Sat 9:00-13:15 & 17:00-21:15, closed Sun, a block off the Ramblas behind Betlem Church at Xuclà 4, Metro: Liceu, tel. 933-183-486).

Cafeteria: For a quick, affordable lunch with a view, the ninth-floor cafeteria at **El Corte Inglés** can't be beat (€10 salads and sandwiches, also café with €1.50 coffee and sit-down restaurant with €20 fixed-price meals, Mon-Sat 10:00-22:00, closed Sun, Plaça de Catalunya, Metro: Catalunya, tel. 933-063-800).

Picnics: Shoestring tourists buy groceries at **El Corte Inglés** (described above, supermarket in basement), **Carrefour** (Mon-Sat 10:00-22:00, closed Sun, Ramblas 113, Metro: Liceu), and **La Boqueria** market (closed Sun, described next).

In and near La Boqueria Market

Try eating at La Boqueria market at least once (#91 on the Ramblas). Like all farmers' markets in Europe, this place is ringed by colorful, good-value eateries. Lots of stalls sell fun takeaway food—especially fruit salads and fresh-squeezed juices—ideal for picnickers. There are several good bars around the market busy with shoppers munching at the counter (breakfast, tapas all day, coffee). The market, and most of the eateries listed here (unless noted), are open Monday through Saturday from 8:00 until 20:00 (though things get very quiet after about 16:00) and are closed on Sunday (nearest Metro: Liceu). For a more complete

description of the market itself, see page 71 of my "Ramblas Ramble."

Pinotxo Bar is just to the right as you enter the market. It's a great spot for coffee, breakfast (spinach *tortillas*, or whatever's cooking with toast), or tapas. Fun-loving Juan and his family are La Boqueria fixtures. Grab a stool across the way to sip your drink with people-watching views. Be careful—this place can get expensive.

Kiosko Universal is popular for its great prices on wonderful fish dishes. As you enter the market from the Ramblas, it's all the way to the left. If you see people waiting, ask who's last in line *("¿El último?")*. You'll eat immersed in the spirit of the market (€7-14 dishes of the day with different fresh-fish options, €7 mixed veggies, €10 mushroom stir-fries, always packed but better before 12:30, tel. 933-178-286).

Restaurant la Gardunya, at the back of the market, offers tasty meat and seafood meals made with fresh ingredients bought directly from the market (€13.50 fixed-price lunch includes wine and bread, €16.50 three-course dinner specials include wine, €10-20 à la carte dishes, kitchen serves Mon-Sat 13:00-16:00 & 20:00-24:00 but open from 7:00, closed Sun, mod seating indoors or outside watching the market action, Carrer Jerusalem 18, tel. 933-024-323).

Vegetarian Eateries near Plaça de Catalunya and the Ramblas

Biocenter, a Catalan soup-and-salad restaurant busy with local vegetarians, takes its cooking very seriously and feels a bit more like a real restaurant than most (€8-10 weekday lunch specials include soup or salad and plate of the day, €15 dinner specials, otherwise €7-9 salads and €11-13 main dishes, Mon-Sat 13:00-23:00, Sun 13:00-16:00, 2 blocks off the Ramblas at Carrer del Pintor Fortuny 25, Metro: Liceu, tel. 933-014-583).

Juicy Jones is a tutti-frutti vegan/vegetarian eatery with colorful graffiti decor, a hip veggie menu (served downstairs), groovy laid-back staff, and a stunning array of fresh-squeezed juices served at the bar. Pop in for a quick €2.50 "juice of the day." For lunch you can get the Indian-inspired €6 *thali* plate, the €6.25 plate of the day, or an €8.50 meal including one of the two plates plus soup or salad and dessert (daily 9:00-23:30, also tapas and salads, Carrer del Cardenal Casanyes 7, Metro: Liceu, tel. 933-024-330). There's another location on the other side of the Ramblas (Carrer Hospital 74).

In the Barri Gòtic

These eateries populate Barcelona's atmospheric Gothic Quarter, near the cathedral. Choose between a sit-down meal at a restaurant or a string of tapas bars. For locations, see the map on page 160.

Restaurants in the Barri Gòtic

Café de l'Academia is a delightful place on a pretty square tucked away in the heart of the Barri Gòtic—but patronized mainly by the neighbors. They serve refined cuisine with Catalan roots using what's fresh from the market. The candlelit, air-conditioned interior is rustic yet elegant, with soft jazz, flowers, and modern art. And if you want to eat outdoors on a convivial, mellow square... this is the place. Reservations can be smart (€10-13 first courses, €12-16 second courses, fixed-price lunch for €10 at the bar or €14 at a table, Mon-Fri 13:30-16:00 & 20:30-23:30, closed Sat-Sun, near the City Hall square, off Carrer de Jaume I up Carrer de la Dagueria at Carrer dels Lledó 1, Metro: Jaume I, tel. 933-198-253).

Els Quatre Gats ("The Four Cats") was once the haunt of the Modernista greats—including a teenaged Picasso, who first publicly displayed his art here, and architect Josep Puig i Cadafalch, who designed the building. Inspired by Paris' famous Le Chat Noir café/cabaret, Els Quatre Gats celebrated all that was modern at the turn of the 20th century (for more on the illustrious history of the place, see page 78 in the "Barri Gòtic Walk"). You can snack or drink at the bar, or go into the back for a sit-down meal. While touristy (less so later), the food and service are good, and the prices aren't as high as you might guess (€17 three-course lunch special Mon-Fri 13:00-16:00, €12-22 plates, daily 10:00-24:00, just steps off Avinguda Portal de l'Angel at Carrer de Montsió 3, Metro: Catalunya, tel. 933-024-140).

Xaloc is *the* place in the old center for nicely presented gourmet tapas. It's a classy, woody, modern dining room with a fun energy, good service, and reasonable prices. The walls are covered with *Ibérica* hamhocks and wine bottles. They focus on homestyle Catalan classics and serve only one quality of ham—and it's tops. A gazpacho, plank of ham, *pa amb tomàquet,* and nice glass of wine make a terrific light meal (€2-6 tapas, €5-12 main dishes, open daily 11:00-23:00, kitchen serves 13:00-17:00 & 19:00-23:00, a block toward the cathedral from Plaça de Sant Josep Oriol at Carrer de la Palla 13, Metro: Catalunya, tel. 933-011-990).

Bar del Pi is a simple, hardworking bar serving good salads, sandwiches, and tapas. It has just a handful of tables on the most inviting little square in the Barri Gòtic (Tue-Sun 9:00-23:00, closed Mon, on Plaça de Sant Josep Oriol 1, Metro: Liceu, tel. 933-022-123).

Restaurant Agut, around since 1924, features a comfortable, wood-paneled dining room that's modern and sophisticated, but still retains a slight bohemian air. The pictures lining the walls are by Catalan artists who are said to have exchanged their canvases for a meal. The menu includes very tasty traditional Catalan food, with some seasonal specialties (€13 three-course weekday lunch special, €10-14 starters, €13-25 main dishes, Tue-Sat 13:30-16:00 & 21:00-23:30, Sun 13:30-16:00 only, closed Mon, just up from Carrer de la Mercè and the harbor at Carrer d'En Gignàs 16, Metro: Jaume I, tel. 933-151-709).

Andilana Restaurants: A local chain called Andilana has several bright, modern eateries that are wildly popular for their artfully presented Spanish and Mediterranean cuisine, crisp ambience, and unbeatable prices (www.grupandilana.com). Because of their three-course €10 lunches and €16-21 dinners (both with wine), all are crowded with locals and in-the-know tourists (à la carte: €7-9 starters, €8-11 main dishes; the first three are near Metro: Liceu). Warning: These places are notoriously busy—arrive 30 minutes before opening, or be prepared to wait. **Les Quinze Nits** has great seating right on atmospheric Plaça Reial (daily 12:30-23:30, at #6—you'll see the line, tel. 933-173-075). Two others are within a block: **La Crema Canela,** a few steps above Plaça Reial, feels cozier than the others and is the only one that takes reservations (Mon-Thu 13:00-23:00, Fri-Sun until 23:30, Passage de Madoz 6, tel. 933-182-744). **La Fonda** is a block below Plaça Reial (daily 13:00-23:30, Carrer dels Escudellers 10, tel. 933-017-515). Another location, **La Dolça Herminia,** is near the Palace of Catalan Music in El Born (daily 13:00-15:45 & 20:30-23:30, 2 blocks toward Ramblas from Palace of Catalan Music at Carrer de les Magdalenes 27, Metro: Jaume I, tel. 933-170-676); another restaurant in the chain, **La Rita,** is described later, under "Restaurants in the Eixample."

Tapas on Carrer de la Mercè In the Barri Gòtic

This area lets you experience a rare, unvarnished bit of old Barcelona with great *tascas*—colorful local tapas bars. Get small plates (for

maximum sampling) by asking for "tapas," not the bigger *"raciones."* Glasses of *vino tinto* go for about €1. And though trendy uptown restaurants are safer, better-lit, and come with English menus and less grease, these places will stain your journal. The neighborhood's dark, the regulars are rough-edged, and you'll get a glimpse of a crusty Barcelona from before the affluence hit. Nowadays many new, mod restaurants are popping up in the city, but don't be seduced— you came here for something different. Try *pimientos de Padrón*— Russian roulette with little green peppers that are lightly fried in oil and salted...only a few are jalapeño-spicy. At the cider bars, it's traditional to order *queso de cabrales* (a very moldy blue cheese) and spicy chorizo (sausage), ideally prepared *al diablo* ("devil-style")— soaked in wine, then flambéed at your table. Several places serve *leche de pantera* (panther milk)—liquor mixed with milk.

From the bottom of the Ramblas (near the Columbus Monument, Metro: Drassanes), hike east along Carrer de Josep

A Short, Sweet Walk

Let me propose this three-stop dessert (or, since these places close well before the traditional Barcelona dinnertime, a late-afternoon snack). Start with a chunk of *torró* or a glass of *orxata*, then munch some *churros con chocolate*, and end with a visit to a fine *xocolateria*—all within a three-minute walk of one another in the Barri Gòtic just off the Ramblas (Metro: Liceu). Start at the corner of Carrer de la Portaferrissa midway down the Ramblas. For the best atmosphere, begin your walk at about 18:00 (note that the last place is closed on Sun). For locations, see the map on page 160.

Torró at Casa Colomina: Walk down Carrer de la Portaferrissa to #8 (on the right). Casa Colomina, founded in 1908, specializes in homemade *torró* (or *turrón* in Spanish)—a variation of nougat made with almond, honey, and sugar, brought to Spain by the Moors 1,200 years ago. Three different kinds are sold in €8-12 slabs: *blando, duro,* and *yema*—soft, hard, and yolk (€2 prewrapped chunks on the counter). In the summer, the shop also sells ice cream and the refreshing *orxata* (or *horchata,* a drink made from *chufa* nuts—a.k.a. earth almonds or tiger nuts). Order a glass and ask to see and eat a *chufa* nut (Mon-Sat 10:00-20:30, Sun 12:30-20:30, tel. 933-122-511).

Churros con Chocolate at Granja La Pallaresa: Continue down Carrer de la Portaferrissa, taking a right at Carrer Petritxol to this fun-loving *xocolateria*. Elegant, older ladies gather here for the Spanish equivalent of tea time—dipping their greasy *churros* into pudding-thick cups of hot chocolate (€4.50 for five *churros con chocolate*). Or, for a more local treat, try an *ensaïmada* (a Mallorca-style croissant with powdered sugar) or the *crema catalana*, like a crème brûlée (Mon-Fri 9:00-13:00 & 16:00-21:00, Sat-Sun 9:00-13:00 & 17:00-21:00, Carrer Petritxol 11, tel. 933-022-036).

Homemade Chocolate at Fargas: For your last stop, head for the ornate Fargas chocolate shop. Continue down Carrer Petritxol to the square, hook left through the two-part square, and then left up Carrer del Pi to the corner of Carrer de la Portaferrissa. Since the 19th century, gentlemen with walking canes have dropped by here for their chocolate fix. Founded in 1827, this is one of the oldest and most traditional chocolate shops in Barcelona. If they're not too busy, ask to see the old chocolate mill *("¿Puedo ver el molino?")* to the right of the counter. (It's still used, but nowadays it's powered by a machine rather than a donkey in the basement.) They sell even tiny quantities (one little morsel) by the weight, so don't be shy. A delicious chunk of the crumbly semisweet house specialty costs €0.50 (glass bowl on the counter). The tempting bonbons in the window cost about €1-2 each (Mon-Sat 9:30-13:30 & 16:00-20:00, closed Sun).

Anselm Clavé. When you reach Plaça de la Mercè, follow the small street (Carrer de la Mercè) that runs along the right side of the square's church. For a montage of edible memories, wander the next three or four blocks and consider these spots, stopping wherever looks most inviting. Most of these places close down around 23:00. If you want more refined bar-hopping possibilities, skip over to Carrer Ample and Carrer d'En Gignàs, the streets parallel to Carrer de la Mercè inland.

BARCELONA

Bar Celta (marked *la pulpería,* at #16) has a bit less character than the others, but eases you into the scene with fried fish, octopus, and *patatas bravas,* all with Galician Ribeiro wine. Farther down at the corner (#28), **La Plata** keeps things wonderfully simple, serving extremely cheap plates of sardines (€2.50), little salads, and small glasses of keg wine (less than €1). **Tasca el Corral** (#17) serves mountain favorites from northern Spain by the half-*ración* (see their list), such as *queso de cabrales* and chorizo *al diablo* with *sidra* (hard cider sold by the bottle–€6). **Sidrería Tasca La Socarrena** (#21) offers hard cider from Asturias in €6.50 bottles with *queso de cabrales* and chorizo. At the end of Carrer de la Mercè, **Cerveceria Vendimia** slings tasty clams and mussels (hearty *raciones* for €4-6 a plate—they don't do smaller portions, so order sparingly). Sit at the bar and point to what looks good. Their *pulpo* (octopus) is more expensive and is the house specialty.

In El Born, near the Picasso Museum

El Born (a.k.a. La Ribera), the hottest neighborhood in town, sparkles with eclectic and trendy as well as subdued and classy little restaurants hidden in the small lanes surrounding the Church of Santa Maria del Mar. While I've listed a few well-established tapas bars that are great for light meals, to really dine, simply wander around for 15 minutes and pick the place that tickles your gastronomic fancy. I think those who say they know what's best in this area are kidding themselves—it's changing too fast, and the choices are too personal. One thing's for sure: There are a lot of talented and hardworking restaurateurs with plenty to offer. Consider starting off your evening with a glass of fine wine at one of the *enotecas* on the square facing the Church of Santa Maria del Mar (such as La Vinya del Senyor). Sit back and admire the pure Catalan Gothic architecture. Most of my listings are either on Carrer de l'Argenteria (stretching from the church to the cathedral area) or on or near Carrer de Montcada (near the Picasso Museum). Many restaurants and shops in this area are, like the Picasso Museum, closed on Mondays. For locations, see the map on page 160.

Bar del Pla is a local favorite—near the Picasso Museum but far enough away from the tourist crowds. This classic diner/bar, overlooking a tiny crossroads next to Barcelona's oldest church, serves traditional Catalan dishes, *raciones,* and tapas. Prices are the same at the bar or at a table, but eating at the bar puts you in the middle of a great scene (€4-11 tapas, Tue-Sun 12:00-24:00, closed Mon; with your back to the Picasso Museum, head right 2 blocks, past Carrer de la Princesa, to Carrer de Montcada 2; Metro: Jaume I, tel. 932-683-003).

La Vinya del Senyor is recommendable for its location—with wonderful tables on the square facing the Church of Santa Maria del Mar in the middle of a charming and lively pedestrian zone. Their wine list is extensive—7 cl gives you a few sips, while 14 cl is a standard serving. They also have good cheeses, hams, and tapas (Tue-Sun 12:00-24:00, closed Mon, Plaça de Santa Maria 5, Metro: Jaume I or Barceloneta, tel. 933-103-379).

El Senyor Parellada, filling a former cloister, is an elegant restaurant with a smart, tourist-friendly waitstaff. It serves a fun menu of Mediterranean and Catalan cuisine with a modern twist, all in a classy chandeliers-and-white-tablecloths setting (€10-18 plates, open daily 13:00-15:45 & 20:30-23:30, Carrer de l'Argenteria 37, 100 yards from Metro: Jaume I, tel. 933-105-094).

Sagardi Euskal Taberna offers a wonderful array of Basque goodies—tempting *pintxos* and *montaditos* (miniature sandwiches) at €1.95 each—along its huge bar. Ask for a plate and graze (just take whatever looks good). You can sit on the square with your plunder for 20 percent extra. Wash it down with Txakolí, a Basque white wine poured from the spout of a huge wooden barrel into a glass as you watch. When you're done, they'll count your toothpicks to tally your bill (daily 12:00-24:00, Carrer de l'Argenteria 62-64, Metro: Jaume I, tel. 933-199-993).

Sagardi, hiding behind its thriving tapas bar (described above), is a mod, rustic, and minimalist woody restaurant committed to serving Basque T-bone steaks and grilled specialties with only the best ingredients. A big open kitchen with sizzling grills contributes to the ambience. Reservations are smart (€12-24 first courses, €20-28 second courses, plan on €50 for dinner, daily 13:00-16:00 & 20:00-24:00, Carrer de l'Argenteria 62, Metro: Jaume I, tel. 933-199-993, www.sagardi.com).

Taller de Tapas ("Tapas Workshop") is an upscale, trendier tapas bar and restaurant that dishes up well-presented, sophisticated morsels and light meals in a medieval-stone-yet-mod setting. Pay 15 percent more to sit on the square. Elegant, but a bit stuffy, it's favored by local office workers who aren't into the Old World Gothic stuff. Four plates will fill a hungry diner for about €20 (daily 8:30-24:00, Carrer de l'Argenteria 51, Metro: Jaume I, tel. 932-688-559, www.tallerdetapas.com).

El Xampanyet ("The Little Champagne Bar"), a colorful

family-run bar with a fun-loving staff (Juan Carlos, his mom, and the man who may be his father), specializes in tapas and anchovies. Don't be put off by the seafood from a tin: Catalans like it this way. A *sortido* (assorted plate) of *carne* (meat) or *pescado* (fish) with *pa amb tomàquet* makes for a fun meal. It's filled with tourists during the sightseeing day, but this is a local favorite after dark. The scene is great but—especially during busy times—it's tough without Spanish skills. When I asked about the price, Juan Carlos said, "Who cares? The ATM is just across the street." Plan on spending €25 for a meal with wine (same price at bar or table, Tue-Sat 12:00-15:30 & 19:00-23:00, Sun 12:00-16:00 only, closed Mon, a half-block beyond the Picasso Museum at Carrer de Montcada 22, Metro: Jaume I, tel. 933-197-003).

In the Eixample

The people-packed boulevards of the Eixample (Passeig de Gràcia and Rambla de Catalunya) are lined with appetizing eateries featuring breezy outdoor seating. Choose between a real restaurant or an upscale tapas bar. For locations, see the map on page 154.

Restaurants in the Eixample

La Rita is a fresh and dressy little restaurant serving Catalan cuisine near the Block of Discord. Their lunches (three courses with wine for €10, daily 13:00-15:45) and dinners (€10 plates, €21 fixed-price dinners, daily 20:30-23:30) are a great value. Like most of its sister Andilana restaurants—described on page 164—it takes no reservations and its prices attract a loyal following, so arrive just before the doors open...or wait (near corner of Carrer de Pau Claris and Carrer d'Aragó at d'Aragó 279, a block from Metro: Passeig de Gràcia, tel. 934-872-376).

La Bodegueta is an atmospheric below-street-level bodega serving hearty wines, homemade vermouth, *anchoas* (anchovies), tapas, and *flautas*—sandwiches made with flute-thin baguettes. On a nice day, it's great to eat outside, sitting in the median of the boulevard under shady trees. Its daily €12 lunch special of three courses with wine is served 13:00-16:00. A long block from Gaudí's La Pedrera, this makes a fine sightseeing break (Mon-Sat 7:00-24:00, Sun 18:30-24:00, at intersection with Carrer de Provença, Rambla de Catalunya 100, Metro: Provença, tel. 932-154-894).

Restaurante la Palmera serves a mix of Catalan, Mediterranean, and French cuisine in an elegant room with bottle-lined walls. This untouristy place offers great food, service, and value—for me, a very special meal in Barcelona. They have three zones: the classic main room, a more forgettable adjacent room, and a few outdoor tables. I like the classic room. Reservations are smart (€12-16 plates, creative €20 six-plate *degustation* lunch—also available during dinner Mon-Thu, open Mon-Sat 13:00-15:45 & 20:30-23:15, closed Sun, Carrer d'Enric Granados 57, at the corner with Carrer Mallorca, Metro: Provença, tel. 934-532-338, www.lapalmera.cat).

La Flauta fills two floors with enthusiastic eaters (I prefer the ground floor). It's fresh and modern, with a fun, no-stress menu featuring €5 small plates, creative €5 *flauta* sandwiches, and a €12.50 three-course lunch deal including a drink. Consider the list of tapas del día. Good €2.60 wines by the glass are listed on the blackboard. This is a place to order high on the menu for a satisfying, moderately priced meal (Mon-Sat 7:00-24:00, closed Sun, upbeat and helpful staff recommends the fried vegetables, no reservations, just off Carrer de la Diputació at Carrer d'Aribau 23, Metro: Universitat, tel. 933-237-038).

Cinc Sentits ("Five Senses"), with only about 30 seats, is my gourmet recommendation. At this chic, minimalist, but slightly snooty place, all the attention goes to the fine service and beautifully presented dishes. The €59 *essència menú* and the €79 *sensacions menú* are unforgettable extravaganzas. Expect *menús* only—no à la carte. It's run by Catalans who lived in Canada (so there's absolutely no language barrier) and serve avant-garde cuisine inspired by Catalan traditions and ingredients. Reservations are essential (Tue-Sat 13:30-15:00 & 20:30-22:00, closed Sun-Mon, near Carrer d'Aragó at Carrer d'Aribau 58, between Metros: Universitat and Provença, tel. 933-239-490, www.cincsentits.com, maître d' Amelia).

Tapas Bars in the Eixample

Many trendy and touristic tapas bars in the Eixample offer a cheery welcome and slam out the appetizers. These four are particularly handy to Plaça de Catalunya and the Passeig de Gràcia artery (for all of them, the closest Metro stops are Catalunya and Passeig de Gràcia).

Tapas 24 makes eating fun. This local favorite, with a few street tables, fills a spot a few steps below street level with happy energy, funky decor (white counters and mirrors), and absolutely excellent tapas. The menu has all the typical standbys and quirky inventions (such as the McFoie burger), plus daily specials. Service is friendly, and the owner, Carles Abellan, is one of Barcelona's hot chefs. This is a chance to eat his food at reasonable prices, which are the same whether you dine at the bar, a table, or outside. Figure about €45 for lunch for two with wine (€4-12 tapas, €12-15 plates, Mon-Sat 9:00-24:00, closed Sun, just off Passeig de Gràcia at Carrer de la Diputació 269, tel. 934-880-977).

La Bodegueta Provença is a lively tapas bar/café with a multigenerational clientele and a pleasant buzz. Sit at a stool at the marble counter or grab a table, indoors or out. If you and your partner are hungry, order the half-kilo grilled steak piled high with Padrón peppers—wow! (€5-8.50 tapas, Mon-Sat 7:00-24:00, Sun 13:00-24:00, Carrer de Provença 233, tel. 932-151-725).

Ciutat Comtal Cerveceria brags that it serves the best *montaditos* (€2-4 little open-faced sandwiches) and beers in Barcelona. It's an Eixample favorite, with an elegant bar and tables plus good seating out on the Rambla de Catalunya for all that people-watching action. It's packed 21:00-23:00, when you'll likely need to put your name on a list and wait. While it has no restaurant-type menu, the list of tapas and *montaditos* is easy, fun, and comes with a great variety (including daily specials). This place is a cut above your normal tapas bar, but with reasonable prices (most tapas around €4-10, daily 8:00-24:00, facing the intersection of Gran Via de les Corts Catalanes and Rambla de Catalunya at Rambla de Catalunya 18, tel. 933-181-997).

La Tramoia, at the opposite corner from Ciutat Comtal Cerveceria, serves piles of €1.75 *montaditos* and tapas at its ground-floor bar and at nice tables inside and out. If Ciutat Comtal Cerveceria is jammed, you're more likely to find a seat here. The brasserie-style restaurant upstairs bustles with happy local eaters enjoying grilled meats (€9-20 plates), but I'd stay downstairs for the €4-9 tapas (daily 12:00-24:00 for tapas, 13:00-16:00 & 17:30-24:00 for meals, also facing the intersection of Gran Via de les Corts Catalanes and Rambla de Catalunya at Rambla de Catalunya 15, tel. 934-123-634).

In Barceloneta

The nearest Metro stop to this former sailors' quarter is Barceloneta. For locations, see the map on page 50.

Along the Waterfront: Barceloneta's harborfront (Passeig de Joan de Borbó), facing the city, is lined with multiple, interchangeable seafood restaurants and cafés. Locals love to come here for celebrity-spotting. One of many eateries along here is **La Mar Salada,** a traditional seafood restaurant with a slight modern twist. Their à la carte menu includes seafood-and-rice dishes, fresh fish, and homemade desserts. A nice meal will run you about €35-40 per person (€16 fixed-price weekday meal, Mon and Wed-Fri 13:00-16:00 & 20:00-23:00, Sat-Sun 13:00-23:00, closed Tue, indoor and outdoor seating, Passeig de Joan de Borbó 59, tel. 932-212-127).

In the Heart of Barceloneta: **Can Solé,** serving seafood since 1903, is a splurge. Hiding on a nondescript urban lane, this venerable restaurant draws a celebrity crowd, judging by the autographed pictures of the famous and not-so-famous that line the walls. But the place is homey, with sky-blue walls and café curtains, and the charming owner couldn't be more gracious (Tue-Sat 13:30-16:00 & 20:30-23:00, Sun 13:30-16:00 only, closed Mon, Carrer de Sant Carles 4, one block off the harborfront promenade, tel. 932-215-012, www.restaurantcansole.com).

Bakery: **Baluard,** one of Barcelona's most highly regarded artisan bakeries, faces one side of the big market hall in the center of Barceloneta. Line up with the locals to get a loaf of heavenly bread, a pastry, or a slice of pizza (Mon-Sat 8:00-21:00, closed Sun, Carrer del Baluard 38, tel. 932-211-208).

Barcelona Connections

By Train
Sants Station

Barcelona's main train station is vast and sprawling, but manageable. In the large lobby area under the upper tracks, you'll find a TI, ATMs, a world of handy shops and eateries, car-rental kiosks, and, in the side concourse, a classy, quiet Sala Club lounge for travelers with first-class reservations (TV, free drinks, study tables, and coffee bar). Sants is the only Barcelona station with luggage storage (small bag-€3.60/day, big bag-€5.20/day, requires  security check, daily 5:30-23:00, follow signs to *consigna,* at far end of hallway from tracks 13-14).

In the vast main hall is a very long wall of ticket windows. Figure out which one you need before you wait in line (all are labeled in English). Generally, windows 1-7 (on the left) are for local commuter and *media distancia* trains, such as to Sitges; windows 8-21 handle advance tickets for long-distance *(larga distancia)* trains beyond Catalunya; the information windows are 22-26—go here first if you're not sure which window you want; and windows 27-31 sell tickets for long-distance trains leaving today. The information booths by windows 1 and 21 can help you find the right line and can provide some train schedules. Scattered nearby are two types of train-ticket vending machines: The red-

and-gray machines sell tickets for local and *media distancia* trains within Catalunya; the purple machines are for national RENFE trains, but these don't sell tickets—you can only use them to print out prereserved tickets (if you have a confirmation code).

Getting Downtown: To reach the center of Barcelona, take a train or the Metro. To ride the subway, follow signs for the Metro (red *M*), and hop on the L3 (green) or L5 (blue) line, both of which link to a number of useful points in town. To zip downtown even faster (just five minutes), you can take any Rodalies de Catalunya suburban train from track 8 (R1, R3, or R4) to Plaça de Catalunya (departs at least every 10 minutes). Purchase tickets for the trains or Metro at touch-screen machines near the tracks (where you can also buy the cost-saving T10 Card, explained on page 57).

Train Connections

Unless otherwise noted, these trains all depart from Sants Station; however, remember that some trains also stop at other stations more convenient to the downtown tourist zone: França Station, Passeig de Gràcia, or Plaça de Catalunya. Figure out if your train stops at these stations (and board there) to save yourself the trip to Sants.

If departing from the downtown Passeig de Gràcia Station, where three Metro lines converge with the rail line, you might find the underground tunnels confusing. You can't access the RENFE station directly from some of the entrances. Use the northern entrances to this station (rather than the southern "Consell de Cent" entrance, which is closest to Plaça de Catalunya). Train info: tel. 902-320-320, www.renfe.com.

From Barcelona by Train to Madrid: The AVE train has shaved hours off the journey to Madrid, making it faster than flying (when you consider that you're zipping from downtown to downtown). The train departs at least hourly (nonstop service 2.5 hours; with a few stops, 3 hours). Regular reserved AVE tickets can be prepurchased (often with a discount) at www.renfe.com and picked up at the station. If you have a railpass, you'll pay only a reservation fee of €23 for first class, which includes a meal (€10 second class, buy at any train station in Spain). Passholders can't reserve online through RENFE but can make the reservation at www.raileurope.com for delivery before leaving the US ($17 in second class, $40 in first class). There's also a slow overnight train to Madrid's Chamartín station (9 hours).

From Barcelona by Train to: Sitges (departs from both Passeig de Gràcia and Sants, 4/hour, 40 minutes), **Montserrat** (departs from Plaça d'Espanya—*not* from Sants, hourly, 1 hour, includes cable car or rack train to monastery—see details on page 191), **Figueres** (hourly, 2-2.25 hours), **Sevilla** (11/day, 5.5-6 hours;

also 1 night train, 13 hours), **Granada** (1/day, 9.5 hours via AVE and Altaria, transfer in Madrid; also 1 night train daily, 10.5 hours), **Salamanca** (8/day, 6-7.5 hours, change in Madrid from Atocha Station to Chamartín Station via Metro or *cercanías* train; also 1/day with a change in Valladolid, 8.5 hours), **San Sebastián** (2/day, 6 hours), **Málaga** (2/day direct on AVE, 5.75 hours; more with transfer), **Lisbon** (no direct trains, head to Madrid and then catch night train to Lisbon, 17 hours—or fly).

From Barcelona by Train to France: Direct high-speed trains should connect Barcelona to Paris, Lyon, and Toulouse by the end of 2013 (likely connection to **Paris,** 2/day, 6 hours, more connections possible with multiple changes). If the project is delayed, you may need to transfer at the **Figueres-Vilafant** station. For slower but more frequent connections to France, you can also change in **Cerbère** (2/day from Barcelona, 2-4 hours). Connections include **Nice** (2/day, 10 hours, change in Figueres-Vilafant and Valence; slower and cheaper connections possible with multiple changes including Cerbère), **Avignon** (2/day, 5.75 hours, change in Figueres-Vilafant and Nîmes), **Paris** (1 night train, 13.5 hours, change in Cerbère, may not run Fri-Sun in off-season).

By Bus

Most buses depart from the Nord bus station at Metro: Arc de Triomf, but confirm when researching schedules (www.barcelonanord.com). Destinations served by Alsa buses (tel. 902-422-242, www.alsa.es) include **Madrid** (nearly hourly, 8 hours) and **Salamanca** (2/day, 11 hours). Sarfa buses (tel. 902-302-025, www.sarfa.com) serve many **coastal resorts,** including **Cadaqués** (2-3/day, 3 hours). The Mon-Bus rides from downtown Barcelona and the airport to **Sitges** (4/day, 55 minutes from Barcelona, 45 minutes from airport, www.monbus.cat). One bus departs daily for the **Montserrat** monastery, leaving from Carrer de Viriat near Sants train station (see page 172).

By Plane

El Prat de Llobregat Airport

Barcelona's primary airport is eight miles southwest of town. It has two large terminals: 1 and 2. Air France, Air Europa, American, British Airways, Delta, Iberia, Lufthansa, United, US Airways, Vueling, and others use the newer terminal 1. EasyJet and minor airlines use terminal 2 (which is divided into sections A, B, and C). The terminals are linked by shuttle buses.

Terminal 1 and the bigger sections of terminal 2 (A and B) each have a post office, a pharmacy, a left-luggage office, plenty of good cafeterias in the gate areas, and ATMs (use the bank-affiliated ATMs in the arrivals hall). TIs are located in terminals

1 and 2B (airport code: BCN, info tel. 913-211-000, www.aena
-aeropuertos.es).

Getting Downtown: To reach central Barcelona cheaply and
quickly, take either the bus or train (about 30 minutes on either).
The **Aerobus** (#A1 and #A2, corresponding with terminals 1 and
2) stops immediately outside the arrivals lobby of both terminals
(and in each section of terminal 2). In about 30 minutes, it
takes you to downtown, where it makes several stops, including
Plaça d'Espanya and Plaça de Catalunya—near many of my
recommended hotels (departs every 5 minutes, from airport 6:00-
1:00 in the morning, from downtown 5:30-24:15, €5.90 one-way,
€10.30 round-trip, buy ticket from machine or from driver, tel.
934-156-020, www.aerobusbcn.com).

The RENFE **train** (on the "R2 Sud" Rodalies line) leaves
from terminal 2 and involves more walking. Head down the long
orange-roofed overpass between sections A and B to reach the
station (2/hour at about :08 and :38 past the hour, 20 minutes
to Sants Station, 25 minutes to Passeig de Gràcia Station—near
Plaça de Catalunya and many recommended hotels, 30 minutes
to França Station; €3.80 or covered by T10 Card—described on
page 57—which you can purchase at automated machines at the
airport train station). Long-term plans call for the RENFE train
and eventually the AVE to be extended to terminal 1, and for the
Metro's L9 (orange) line to be extended to both terminals 1 and 2.
Stay tuned.

A **taxi** between the airport and downtown costs about €36—
about €30 on the meter plus a €4.20 airport supplement and fee of
€1 per bag. For good service, add a 10 percent tip.

Girona-Costa Brava Airport

Some budget airlines, including Ryanair, use this airport, located
60 miles north of Barcelona near Girona (airport code: GRO,
tel. 972-186-600, www.aena-aeropuertos.es). Ryanair runs a **bus**,
operated by Sagalés, to the Barcelona Nord bus station (€16,
departs airport about 20-25 minutes after each arriving flight, 1.25
hours, tel. 902-361-550, www.sagales.com). You can also take a
Sagalés bus (hourly, 25 minutes, €2.50) or a taxi (€25) to the town
of Girona, then catch a train to Barcelona (at least hourly, 1.25
hours, €15-20). A taxi between the Girona airport and Barcelona
costs at least €120.

By Cruise Ship

Cruise ships arrive in Barcelona at three different ports (all just
southwest of the Old City, beneath Montjuïc). If your trip includes
cruising beyond Barcelona, consider my guidebook, *Rick Steves'*
Mediterranean Cruise Ports.

Most American cruise lines put in at **Moll Adossat/Muelle Adosado,** a long two miles from the bottom of the Ramblas. This port has four modern, airport-like terminals (lettered A through D); most have a café, shops, and TI kiosk; some have Internet access and other services. Two other terminals are far less commonly used: the **World Trade Center,** just off the southern end of the Ramblas, and **Moll de la Costa,** tucked just beneath Montjuïc (ride the free, private shuttle bus to World Trade Center; from there, it's a short walk or taxi ride to the Columbus Monument).

Getting Downtown: From any of the cruise terminals, it's easy to reach the Ramblas. **Taxis** meet each arriving ship and are waiting as you exit any of the terminal buildings. The short trip into town (i.e., to the bottom of the Ramblas) runs about €15 (the €4.20 cruise-port surcharge is legit). During high season, a ride into town can take longer and cost €10 more. For a one-way journey to other parts of town, expect to pay these fares: to the Picasso Museum or Plaça de Catalunya—€15; to the Sagrada Família—€20; and to the airport—€35-40.

You can also take a **shuttle bus** from Moll Adossat/Muelle Adosado to the Columbus Monument (at the bottom of the Ramblas), then walk or hop on public transportation to various sights. The #T3 shuttle bus (also called Portbús) departs from the parking lot in front of the terminal—follow *Public Bus* signs (€3.50 round-trip, €2.50 one-way, buses leave every 20-30 minutes, timed to cruise ship arrival, tel. 932-986-000). Pay careful attention to where they drop you off; you'll catch the return bus here later (across the street, heading back toward the port, look for blue-and-white sign).

NEAR BARCELONA

Figueres • Cadaqués • Sitges • Montserrat

Four fine sights are day-trip temptations from Barcelona. Fans of Surrealism can combine a fantasy in Dalí-land by stopping at the Dalí Theater-Museum in Figueres (about two hours from Barcelona) and spending a day or two in the classy but sleepy port-town getaway of Cadaqués (pictured above, an hour from Figueres; note that the Salvador Dalí House in Cadaqués requires reservations to visit). For the consummate day at the beach, head 45 minutes south to the charming and free-spirited resort town of Sitges. Pilgrims with hiking boots head 1.5 hours into the mountains for the most sacred spot in Catalunya: Montserrat.

Figueres

The town of Figueres (feeg-YEHR-ehs)—conveniently connected by train to Barcelona—is of sightseeing interest only for its Salvador Dalí Theater-Museum. In fact, the entire town seems Dalí-dominated. But don't be surprised if you also find French shoppers bargain-hunting. Some of the cheapest shops in Spain—called *ventas*—are here to lure French visitors.

Getting to Figueres

Figueres is an easy day trip from Barcelona, or a handy stopover en route to France. It's cheap and convenient to take a regional train to Figueres Station—they depart from Barcelona's Sants Station or from the RENFE station at Metro: Passeig de Gràcia (hourly, 2-2.25 hours; €14.20 *media distancia* trains are 20 minutes faster

than €10.60 *regional* trains). High-speed trains between Barcelona and France stop instead at the recently opened Figueres-Vilafant Station, on the other side of town. But even if you're visiting Figueres on your way to Paris, it's best to take the slower, regional train to Figueres Station in the morning, visit the museum, then go back to the same station to take a regional train to Cerbère, and from there catch the night train to Paris. For bus connections to Cadaqués, see page 183.

Arrival in Figueres: From Figueres Station, simply follow *Museu Dalí* signs (and the crowds) for the 15-minute walk to the museum.

Sights in Figueres

▲▲▲Dalí Theater-Museum (Teatre-Museu Dalí)

This is *the* essential Dalí sight—and, if you like Dalí, one of Europe's most enjoyable museums, period. Inaugurated in 1974, the museum is a work of art in itself. Ever the entertainer and promoter, Dalí personally conceptualized, designed, decorated,

and painted it to showcase his life's work. The museum fills a former theater and is the artist's mausoleum (his tomb is in the crypt below center stage). It's also a kind of mausoleum to Dalí's creative spirit.

Dalí had his first public art showing at age 14 here in this building when it was a theater, and he was baptized in the church just across the street. The place was sentimental to him. After the theater was destroyed in the Spanish Civil War, Dalí struck a deal with the mayor: Dalí would rebuild the theater as a museum to his works, Figueres would be put on the sightseeing map...and the money's been flowing in ever since.

Even the building's exterior—painted pink, studded with golden loaves of bread, and topped with monumental eggs and a geodesic dome—exudes Dalí's outrageous public persona.

Cost and Hours: €12; July-Sept daily 9:00-20:00; March-June and Oct Tue-Sun 9:30-18:00, closed Mon; Nov-Feb Tue-Sun 10:30-18:00, closed Mon; last entry 45 minutes before closing, tel. 972-677-500, www.salvador-dali.org. No flash photography. The free bag check has your belongings waiting for you at the exit.

Coin-Op Tip: Much of Dalí's art is movable and coin-operated—bring a few €0.20 and €1 coins.

◉ Self-Guided Tour: The museum has two parts: the theater-mausoleum and the "Dalí's Jewels" exhibit in an adjacent building. There's no logical order for a visit (that would be un-Surrealistic), and the museum can be mobbed at times. Naturally, there's no audioguide. Dalí said there are two kinds of visitors: those who don't need a description, and those who aren't worth a description. At the risk of offending Dalí, I've written this loose commentary to attach some meaning to your visit.

Stepping through or around the courtyard, go into the **theater** (with its audience of statues) and face the stage—and Dalí's unmarked crypt. You know how you can never get a cab when it's raining? Pop a coin into Dalí's personal 1941 Cadillac, and it rains inside the car. Look above, atop the tire tower: That's the boat Dalí enjoyed with his soul mate, Gala—his emotional life preserver, who kept him from going overboard. When she died, so did he (for his last seven years). Blue tears made of condoms drip below the boat.

Up on the **stage,** squint at the big digital Abraham Lincoln, and president #16 comes into focus. Approach the painting to find that Abe's facial cheeks are Gala's butt cheeks. Under the

Salvador Dalí
(1904-1989)

When Salvador Dalí was asked, "Are you on drugs?" he replied, "I am the drug...take me."

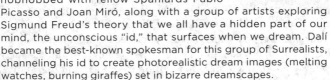

Labeled by various critics as sick, greedy, paranoid, arrogant, and a clown, Dalí produced some of the most thought-provoking and trailblazing art of the 20th century. His erotic, violent, disjointed imagery continues to disturb and intrigue today.

Born in Figueres to a well-off family, Dalí showed talent early. He was expelled from Madrid's prestigious art school—twice—but formed longtime friendships with playwright Federico García Lorca and filmmaker Luis Buñuel.

After a breakthrough art exhibit in Barcelona in 1925, Dalí moved to Paris. He hobnobbed with fellow Spaniards Pablo Picasso and Joan Miró, along with a group of artists exploring Sigmund Freud's theory that we all have a hidden part of our mind, the unconscious "id," that surfaces when we dream. Dalí became the best-known spokesman for this group of Surrealists, channeling his id to create photorealistic dream images (melting watches, burning giraffes) set in bizarre dreamscapes.

His life changed forever in 1929, when he met an older, married Russian woman named Gala who would become his wife, muse, model, manager, and emotional compass. Dalí's popularity spread to the US, where he (and Gala) weathered the WWII years.

painting, a door leads to the **Treasures Room,** with the greatest collection of original Dalí oil paintings in the museum. (Many of the artworks on the walls are prints.) You'll see Cubist visions of Cadaqués and dreamy portraits of Gala. Crutches—a recurring Dalí theme—represent Gala, who kept him supported whenever a meltdown threatened.

The famous **Homage to Mae West room** is a tribute to the

sultry seductress. Dalí loved her attitude. Saying things like, "Why marry and make one man unhappy, when you can stay single and make so many so happy?" Mae West was to conventional morality what Dalí was to conventional art. Climb to the

In his prime, Dalí's work became less Surrealist and more classical, influenced by past masters of painted realism (Velázquez, Raphael, Ingres) and by his own study of history, science, and religion. He produced large-scale paintings of historical events (e.g., Columbus discovering America, the Last Supper) that were collages of realistic scenes floating in a surrealistic landscape, peppered with thought-provoking symbols.

Dalí—an extremely capable technician—mastered many media, including film. *An Andalusian Dog* (*Un Chien Andalou*, 1929, with Luis Buñuel) was a cutting-edge montage of disturbing, eyeball-slicing images. He designed Alfred Hitchcock's big-eye backdrop for the dream sequence of *Spellbound* (1945). He made jewels for the rich and clothes for Coco Chanel, wrote a novel and an autobiography, and pioneered what would come to be called "installations." He also helped develop "performance art" by showing up at an opening in a diver's suit or by playing the role he projected to the media—a super-confident, waxed-mustached artistic genius.

In later years, Dalí's over-the-top public image contrasted with his ever-growing illness, depression, and isolation. He endured the scandal of a dealer overselling "limited editions" of his work. When Gala died in 1982, Dalí retreated to his hometown, living his last days in the Torre Galatea of the Theater-Museum complex, where he died of heart failure.

Dalí's legacy as an artist includes his self-marketing persona, his exceptional ability to draw, his provocative pairing of symbols, and his sheer creative drive.

NEAR BARCELONA

vantage point where the sofa lips, fireplace nostrils, painting eyes, and drapery hair come together to make the face of Mae West.

Dalí's art can be playful, but also disturbing. He was passionate about the dark side of things, but with Gala for balance, he managed never to go off the deep end. Unlike Pablo Casals (the Catalan cellist) and Pablo Picasso (another local artist), Dalí didn't go into exile under Franco's dictatorship. Pragmatically, he accepted both Franco and the Church, and was supported by the dictator. Apart from the occasional *sardana* dance (see sidebar on page 89), you won't find a hint of politics in Dalí's art.

Wander around. You can spend hours here, wondering, is it real or not real? Am I crazy, or is it you? Beethoven is painted with squid ink applied by a shoe on a stormy night. Jesus is made with candle smoke and an eraser. It's fun to see the Dalí-ization of art classics. Dalí, like so many modern artists, was inspired by the masters—especially Velázquez.

The former theater's **smoking lounge** is a highlight, displaying portraits of Gala and Dalí (with a big eye, big ear, and a dark side) bookending a Roman candle of creativity. The fascinating ceiling painting shows the feet of Gala and Dalí as they bridge earth and the heavens. Dalí's drawers are wide open and empty, indicating that he gave everything to his art.

Leaving the theater, keep your ticket and pop into the adjacent **"Dalí's Jewels"** exhibit. It shows sketches and paintings of jewelry Dalí designed, and the actual pieces jewelers made from those surreal visions: a mouth full of pearly whites, a golden finger corset, a fountain of diamonds, and the breathing heart. Explore the ambiguous perception worked into the big painting titled *Apotheosis of the Dollar.*

Cadaqués

Since the late 1800s, Cadaqués (kah-dah-KEHS) has served as a haven for intellectuals and artists alike. The fishing village's craggy coastline, sun-drenched colors, and laid-back lifestyle inspired Fauvists such as Henri Matisse and Surrealists such as René Magritte, Marcel Duchamp, and Federico García Lorca. Even Picasso, drawn to this enchanting coastal haunt, painted some of his Cubist works here.

Salvador Dalí, raised in nearby Figueres, brought international fame to this sleepy Catalan port in the 1920s. As a kid Dalí spent summers here in the family cabin, where he was inspired by the rocky landscape that would later be the backdrop for many Surrealist canvases. In 1929, he met his future wife, Gala, in Cadaqués. Together they converted a fisherman's home in nearby Port Lligat into their semi-permanent residence, dividing their time between New York, Paris, and Cadaqués. And it was here that Dalí did his best work.

In spite of its fame, Cadaqués is mellow and feels off the beaten path. If you want a peaceful beach-town escape near Barcelona, this is a good place. From the moment you descend into the town, taking in whitewashed buildings and deep blue waters, you'll be struck by the port's tranquility and beauty. Join the locals playing chess or cards at the cavernous Casino Coffee House (harborfront, with games and Internet access). Have a glass of *vino tinto* or *cremat* (a traditional rum-and-coffee drink served flambé-style) at one of the seaside cafés. Savor the lapping waves, brilliant sun, and gentle breeze. And, for sightseeing, the reason to come to Cadaqués is the Salvador Dalí House, a 20-minute walk from the town center at Port Lligat.

Getting to Cadaqués

Reaching Cadaqués is very tough without a car. There are no trains and only a few buses a day.

By Car: It's a twisty drive from Figueres (figure 45-60 minutes). In Cadaqués, drivers should park in the big lot just above the city—don't try to park near the harborfront. To reach the Salvador Dalí House, follow signs near Cadaqués to Port Lligat (easy parking).

By Bus: Sarfa buses serve Cadaqués from **Figueres** (3/day, 1 hour, €6) and from **Barcelona** (2/day, 2.75 hours, €24). Bus info: Barcelona toll tel. 902-302-025, Cadaqués tel. 972-258-713, Figueres tel. 972-674-298, www.sarfa.com.

Tourist Information

The TI is at Carrer Cotxe 2 (July-Sept Mon-Sat 9:00-21:00, Sun 10:00-13:00 & 17:00-20:00, shorter hours off-season plus closed for lunch, tel. 972-258-315, www.visitcadaques.org).

Sights near Cadaqués

In Port Lligat
▲▲▲**Salvador Dalí House (Casa Museu Salvador Dalí)**
Once Dalí's home, this house gives fans a chance to explore his labyrinthine compound. This is the best artist's house I've toured

in Europe. It shows how a home can really reflect the creative spirit of an artistic genius and his muse. The ambience, both inside and out, is perfect for a Surrealist hanging out with his creative playmate. The bay is ringed by sleepy islands. Fishing boats are jumbled on the beach. After the fishermen painted their boats, Dalí asked them to clean their brushes on his door—creating an abstract work of art he adored (which you'll see as you line up to get your ticket).

The interior is left almost precisely as it was in 1982, when Gala died and Dalí moved out. See Dalí's studio (the clever easel cranks up and down to allow the artist to paint while seated, as he did eight hours a day); the bohemian-yet-divine living room (complete with a mirror to reflect the sunrise onto their bed each morning); the phallic-shaped swimming pool, which was the scene of orgiastic parties; and the painter's study (with his favorite mustaches all lined up). Like Dalí's art, his home is offbeat, provocative, and fun.

Cost and Hours: €11; mid-June–mid-Sept daily 9:30-21:00;

mid-Feb-mid-June and mid-Sept-early Jan Tue-Sun 10:30-18:00, closed Mon; closed early Jan-mid-Feb. Last tour departs 50 minutes before closing. No bags of any kind are allowed in the house; the baggage check is free.

Reservations: You must reserve in advance—call, use the website, or send email with specifics on the day and time you want to visit (tel. 972-251-015, www.salvador-dali.org, pllgrups @fundaciodali.org). In summer, book a week in advance. You must arrive 30 minutes early to pick up your ticket, or they'll sell it.

Visiting the House: Only 8-10 people are allowed in (no large groups) every 10 minutes. Once inside, there are five sections, each with a guard who gives you a brief explanation in English, and then turns you loose for a few minutes. The entire visit takes 50 minutes. Before your tour, enjoy the 15-minute video that plays in the waiting lounge (with walls covered in Dalí media coverage) just across the lane from the house.

Getting There: Parking is free nearby. There are no buses or taxis. The house is a 20-minute, one-mile walk over the hill from Cadaqués to Port Lligat. (The path, which cuts across the isthmus, is much shorter than the road.)

Sleeping in Cadaqués

$$ Hotel Llané Petit, with 32 spacious rooms (half with view balconies), is a small resort-like hotel with its own little beach, a 10-minute walk south of the town center (Db-€124 mid-July-Aug, €94 in shoulder season, €74 in winter, seaview rooms-about €30 more, breakfast-€12, air-con, elevator, Dr. Bartomeus 37, tel.

Sleep Code

(€1 = about $1.30, country code: 34)
S = Single, **D** = Double/Twin, **T** = Triple, **Q** = Quad, **b** = bathroom, **s** = shower only. Unless otherwise noted, credit cards are accepted and English is spoken. Some hotels include the 10 percent IVA tax in the room price; others tack it onto your bill.

To help you easily sort through these listings, I've divided the accommodations into two categories based on the price for a standard double room with bath (during high season):

$$ Higher Priced—Most rooms €95 or more.
$ Lower Priced—Most rooms less than €95.

Prices can change without notice; verify the hotel's current rates online or by email. For the best prices, always book direct.

972-251-020, www.llanepetit.com, info@llanepetit.com). Reserve direct with this book for a free breakfast (not valid on weekends in high season and long weekends in shoulder season).

$ Hotel Nou Estrelles is a big, concrete exercise in efficient, economic comfort. Facing the bus stop a few blocks in from the waterfront, this family-run hotel offers 15 rooms at a great value (Db-€85-90 in high season, €60-74 in shoulder season, €55 in winter, extra bed-€10-15, breakfast-€7, air-con, elevator, Carrer Sant Vicens, tel. 972-259-100, www.hotelnouestrelles.com, reservas @hotelnouestrelles.com, Emma).

$ Hostal Marina is a cheap, low-energy place, with 27 rooms and a great location a block from the harborfront main square (high season: D-€55, Db-€90; low season: D-€40, Db-€50-60; balcony rooms-€10 extra, no breakfast, no elevator, Riera 3, tel. 972-159-091).

Eating in Cadaqués

There are plenty of eateries along the beach. A lane called Carrer Miguel Rosset (across from Hotel La Residencia) also has several places worth considering. At **Casa Anita,** you'll sit with others around a big table and enjoy house specialties such as *calamares a la plancha* (grilled squid) and homemade *helado* (ice cream). Finish your meal with a glass of sweet Muscatel (Calle Miquel Rosset 16, tel. 972-258-471, Joan and family).

Sitges

Sitges (SEE-juhz) is one of Catalunya's most popular resort towns. Because the town beautifully mingles sea and light, it's long

been an artists' colony. Here you can still feel the soul of the Modernistas...in the architecture, the museums, the salty sea breeze, and the relaxed rhythm of life.

Today's Sitges is a world-renowned vacation destination among the gay community. Despite its jet-set status, the Old Town has managed to retain its charm. With a much slower pulse than Barcelona, Sitges is an enjoyable break from the big city.

If you visit during one of Sitges' two big **festivals** (St.

Bartholomew on Aug 24 and St. Tecla on Sept 23), you may see teams of *castellers* competing to build human pyramids.

Getting to Sitges

Southbound **trains** depart Barcelona from the Sants and Passeig de Gràcia stations (take Rodalies train on the dark-green line R2 toward Sant Vincenç de Calders, 4/hour, 40 minutes).

The Mon-Bus Company runs an easy and direct **bus** route from downtown Barcelona (with stops near the university and Plaça d'Espanya) that stops at Barcelona's airport en route to Sitges (4/day, 55 minutes from Barcelona, 45 minutes from airport, www.monbus.cat).

Orientation to Sitges

Tourist Information

The TI is a couple of blocks northwest of the train station (mid-June–mid-Sept Mon-Sat 10:00-20:00, mid-Sept–mid-June Mon-Sat 10:00-14:00 & 16:00-18:30, Sun 10:00-14:00 year-round, Sínia Morera 1, tel. 938-944-251, www.sitgestur.cat). Pick up the good map (with info on sights on the back) and brochures for any museums that interest you. The TI can also help you find a room.

Arrival in Sitges

From the train station, exit straight ahead (past a TI kiosk—open in summer) and walk down Carrer Francesc Gumà. When it dead-ends, continue right onto Carrer de Jesús, which takes you to the town's tiny main square, Plaça del Cap de la Villa. (Keep an eye out for directional signs.) From here, turn right down Carrer Major ("Main Street"), which leads you past the old market hall (now an art gallery) and the town hall, to a beautiful terrace next to the main church (pictured at right). Poke into the Old Town or take the grand staircase down to the beach promenade.

Sights in Sitges

Sitges basically has two attractions: its tight-and-tiny Old Town (with a few good museums) and its long, luxurious beaches.

Old Town

Take time to explore the Old Town's narrow streets. They're crammed with cafés, boutiques, and all the resort staples.

The focal point, on the waterfront, is the 17th-century

Baroque-style **Sant Bartomeu i Santa Tecla Church.** The terrace in front of the church will help you get the lay of the land.

As an art town, Sitges has seen its share of creative people—some of whom have left their mark in the form of appealing museums. Walking along the water behind the church, you'll find two of the town's three museums, which unfortunately will likely be closed for the next couple of years. When open, the **Museu Maricel** displays the eclectic artwork of a local collector, including some Modernista works, pieces by local Sitges artists, and a collection of maritime-themed works. The **Museu Cau Ferrat** bills itself as a "temple of art," as collected by local intellectual Santiago Rusiñol. In addition to paintings and drawings, there's ironwork, glass, and ceramics. Also on this square, you'll see **Palau Maricel**—a sumptuous old mansion that's sometimes open to the public for concerts in the summer (ask at TI). The third museum, which will remain open during the closure of the first two, is the **Museu Romàntic.** Offering a look at 19th-century bourgeois lifestyles in an elegant mansion, it's a few blocks up (one block west of main square: Head out of the square on the main pedestrian street, then take the first right turn, to Sant Gaudenci 1). Inside, amidst gilded hallways, you'll find a collection of more than 400 antique dolls (€3.50; July-Sept Tue-Sat 9:30-14:00 & 16:00-19:00, Sun 10:00-15:00; Oct-June Tue-Sat 9:30-14:00 & 15:30-18:30, Sun 10:00-15:00; closed Mon year-round; tel. 938-942-969).

Beaches

Nine beaches, separated by breakwaters, extend about a mile southward from town. Stroll down the seaside promenade, which stretches from the town to the end of the beaches. Anyone can enjoy the sun, sea, and sand; or you can rent a beach chair to relax like a pro. The crowds thin out about halfway down, and the last three beaches are more intimate and cove-like. Along the way, restaurants and *chiringuitos* (beach bars) serve tapas, paella, and drinks.

If you walk all the way to the end, you can continue inland to enjoy the nicely landscaped **Terramar Gardens** (Jardins de Terramar; free, daily mid-June-mid-Sept 10:30-20:30, mid-Sept-mid-June 9:00-19:00).

Sleeping in Sitges

Because it's an in-demand resort town, hotel values are not much better here than in Barcelona (especially in summer). But if you prefer a swanky beach town to a big city, consider these options. Note that this is a party town, so expect some noise after hours (request a quiet room). I've listed peak-season prices (roughly mid-July-mid-Sept); these drop substantially off-season. The first one is

NEAR BARCELONA

on the beach, whereas the other two are old villas with colorful tile floors a few blocks into town.

$$ Hotel Celimar, with 25 small but modern rooms, occupies a classic Modernista building facing the beach (Db-€130-150, €20 extra for sea view, average price off-season-€90, check website for latest prices, air-con, elevator, free Wi-Fi, Paseo de la Ribera 20, tel. 938-110-170, www.hotelcelimar.com, info@hotelcelimar.com).

$$ Hotel Romàntic is family-run, old-fashioned-elegant, and quirky. Its 78 rooms (including some in the annex, Hotel de la Renaixença) are nothing special, but the whole place feels classic and classy—especially the plush lounge and bar (S-€75, Sb-€85, D-€105, Db-€115, €10 extra for balcony, includes breakfast, no air-con or elevator, free Wi-Fi, Sant Isidre 33, tel. 938-948-375, www.hotelromantic.com, romantic@hotelromantic.com).

$$ El Xalet (as in "Chalet") is of a similar vintage, with a little less style and lower prices. They have 11 rooms in the main hotel and another 12 in their annex, Hotel Noucentista, up the street—both in fine old Modernista buildings (Db-€100, €25 extra for suite, includes breakfast, air-con, free Wi-Fi, Carrer Illa de Cuba 35, tel. 938-110-070, www.elxalet.com, info@elxalet.com).

Montserrat

Montserrat—the "serrated mountain"—rockets dramatically up from the valley floor northwest of Barcelona. With its unique rock formations, a dramatic mountaintop monastery (also called Montserrat), and spiritual connection with the Catalan people and their struggles, it's a popular day trip. This has been Catalunya's most important pilgrimage site for a thousand years. Hymns explain how the  mountain was carved by little angels with golden saws. Geologists blame nature at work.

Once upon a time, there was no mountain. A river flowed here, laying down silt that hardened into sedimentary layers of hard rock. Ten million years ago, the continents shifted, and the land around the rock massif sank, exposing this series of peaks that reach upward to 4,000 feet. Over time, erosion pocked the face with caves and cut vertical grooves near the top, creating the famous serrated look.

The monastery is nestled in the jagged peaks at 2,400 feet,

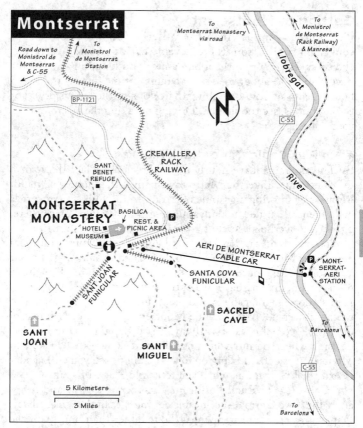

but it seems higher because of the way the rocky massif rises out of nowhere. The air is certainly fresher than in Barcelona. In a quick day trip, you can view the mountain from its base, ride a funicular up to the top of the world, tour the basilica and museum, touch a Black Virgin's orb, hike down to a sacred cave, and listen to Gregorian chants by the world's oldest boys' choir.

Montserrat's monastery is Benedictine, and its 30 monks carry on its spiritual tradition. Since 1025, the slogan *"ora et labora"* ("prayer and work") has pretty much summed up life for a monk here.

The Benedictines welcome visitors—both pilgrims and tourists—and offer this travel tip: Please remember that the most important part of your Montserrat visit is not enjoying the architecture, but rather discovering the religious, cultural, historical, social, and environmental values that together symbolically express the life of the Catalan people.

Getting to Montserrat

Barcelona is connected to the valley below Montserrat by a convenient train; from there, a cable car or rack railway (your choice) takes you up to the mountaintop. Both options are similar in cost and take about the same amount of time (hourly trains, 1.5 hours each way from downtown Barcelona to the monastery). For ticket options, see the sidebar. Driving or taking the bus round out your options.

Train Plus Cable Car or Rack Railway

By Train: Trains leave hourly from Barcelona's Plaça d'Espanya to Montserrat. Take the Metro to Espanya, then follow signs for Montserrat showing a graphic of a train to the FGC (Ferrocarrils de la Generalitat de Catalunya) underground station. Once there, check the overhead screens to find the track for train line R5 (direction: Manresa, departures at :36 past each hour; additional departures Mon-Fri at 11:56, 13:56, 14:56, and 15:56).

You'll ride about an hour on the train. As you reach the base of the mountain, you have two options: Get out at the Montserrat-Aeri station for the cable car, or continue another few minutes to the next station—Monistrol de Montserrat (or simply "Monistrol de M.")—for the rack railway. (You'll have to make this decision when you buy your ticket in Barcelona—see "Tickets to Montserrat" sidebar.) Hang on to your train ticket; you will need it to exit the FGC station when you return to Plaça d'Espanya.

Cable Car or Rack Train? For the sake of scenery and fun, I enjoy the little German-built cable car more than the rack railway. Departures are more frequent (4/hour rather than hourly on the railway), but because the cable car is small, you might have to wait for a while to get on. If you are afraid of heights, take the rack train. Paying the extra €5 to ride both isn't worthwhile.

By Cable Car, at the Montserrat-Aeri Station: Departing the train, follow signs to the cable-car station (covered by your train or combo-ticket; 4/hour, 5-minute trip, daily March-Oct 9:40-14:00 & 14:35-19:00, Nov-Feb 10:10-14:00 & 14:35-17:45—note the lunch break, www .aeridemontserrat.com). Because the cable car is smaller than the train, don't linger or you may have to wait for the next car. On the way back down, cable cars depart from the monastery every 15 minutes; make sure to give yourself enough time to catch the Barcelona-bound trains leaving at :48 past the hour (don't cut it too close, in case the cable car runs late).

Tickets to Montserrat

Various combo-tickets cover your journey to Montserrat, as well as some of the sights you'll visit there. All begin with the train from Barcelona's Plaça d'Espanya, and include either the cable car or rack railway—you'll have to specify one or the other when you buy the ticket (same price for either option). You can't go one way and come back the other, unless you pay extra (about €5) for the leg that's not included in your ticket.

The basic option is to buy a **train ticket** to Montserrat (€17.85 round-trip, includes the cable car or rack railway to monastery, Eurailpass not valid, tel. 932-051-515, www.fgc .es). Note that if you buy this ticket in Barcelona, then decide at Montserrat that you want to use the funiculars to go higher up the mountain or to the Sacred Cave, you can buy a €9.50 ticket covering both funiculars at the TI or at either funicular.

If you plan to do some sightseeing once at Montserrat, it makes sense to spend a little more on one of two combo-tickets from the train company: The €26.60 **Trans Montserrat** ticket includes your round-trip Metro ride in Barcelona to and from the train station, the train trip, the cable car or rack railway, unlimited trips on the two funiculars at Montserrat, and entry to the disappointing audiovisual presentation. The €42.65 **Tot Montserrat** ticket includes all of this, plus the good Museum of Montserrat and a self-service lunch (served daily 12:00-16:00). Both tickets are well-explained in the Barcelona TI's online shop (http://bcnshop.barcelonaturisme.com; look for them under the "Near Barcelona" tab).

If you plan to do it all, you'll save at least €5 with either of these combo-tickets. But during the off-season, ask the TI if one of the funiculars or the cable car is closed for maintenance; if so, the combo-ticket may not be worth it.

You can buy any of these tickets from the automated machines at Barcelona's Plaça d'Espanya Station (tourist officials are standing by in the morning to help you figure it out). To use your included round-trip Metro ride to get *to* the station, buy the ticket in advance at the Plaça de Catalunya TI in Barcelona.

By Rack Railway (Cremallera), at the Monistrol de Montserrat Station: From this station you can catch the Cremallera rack railway up to the monastery (covered by your train or combo-ticket; cheaper off-season, hourly, 20-minute trip, www .cremallerademontserrat.com). On the return trip, this train departs the monastery at :15 past the hour, allowing you to catch the Barcelona-bound train leaving Monistrol de Montserrat at :44 past the hour. The last convenient connection back to Barcelona leaves the monastery at 19:15 (Sat-Sun at 20:15). Confirm the schedule when you arrive, as specific times tend to change year to year. Note that there is one intermediate stop on this line (Monistrol-Vila, at a large parking garage), but—going in either direction—you want to stay on until the end of the line.

By Car or Bus

By Car: Once drivers get out of Barcelona (Road A-2, then C-55), it's a short 30-minute drive to the base of the mountain, then a 10-minute series of switchbacks to the actual site (where you can find parking for €5/day). It may be easier to park your car down below and ride the cable car or rack railway up; there is plenty of free parking at the Monistrol-Vila rack-railway station (cable car—€6.60 one-way, €10 round-trip; rack railway—€6 one-way, €9.50 round-trip, €12.90 version also includes Museum of Montserrat).

By Bus: One **bus** per day connects downtown Barcelona directly to the monastery at Montserrat (departs from Carrer de Viriat near Barcelona's Sants Station daily at 9:15, returns from the monastery to Barcelona at 18:00 June-Sept or at 17:00 Oct-May, €6 each way, 1.25- to 1.5-hour trip depending on traffic, operated by Autocares Julià, www.autocaresjulia.es). You can also take a four-hour **bus tour** offered by the Barcelona Guide Bureau (€47, leaves Mon-Sat at 15:00 from Plaça Catalunya; see page 64). However, since the other options are scenic, fun, and relatively easy, the only reason to take a bus is to avoid transfers.

Orientation to Montserrat

When you arrive at the base of the mountain, look up the rock face to find the cable-car line, the monastery near the top, and the tiny building midway up (marking the Sacred Cave).

However you make your way up to the Montserrat monastery, it's easy to get oriented once you arrive at the top. Everything is within a few minutes' walk of your entry point. All of the transit options—including the rack railway and cable car—converge at the big train station. Above those are both funicular stations: one up to the ridgetop, the other down to the Sacred Cave trail. Across the street is the TI, and above that (either straight up the stairs, or up the ramp around the left side) is the main square. To the right of the station, a long road leads along the cliff to the parking lot; a humble farmers' market along here sells *mel y mató*, a characteristic Catalan cheese with honey.

Crowd-Beating Tips: Arrive early or late, as tour groups mob the place midday. Crowds are less likely on weekdays and worst on Sundays.

The History of Montserrat

The first hermit monks built huts at Montserrat around A.D. 900. By 1025, a monastery was founded. The Montserrat Escolania, or Choir School, soon followed, and is considered to be the oldest music school in Europe (they still perform—see "Choir Concert" on page 197).

Legend has it that in medieval times, some shepherd children saw lights and heard songs coming from the mountain. They traced the sounds to a cave (now called the Sacred Cave, or Santa Cova), where they found the Black Virgin statue (La Moreneta), making the monastery a pilgrim magnet.

In 1811 Napoleon's invading French troops destroyed Montserrat's buildings, though the Black Virgin, hidden away by monks, survived. Then, in the 1830s, the Spanish royalty—tired of dealing with pesky religious orders—dissolved the monasteries and convents.

But in the 1850s, the monks returned as part of Catalunya's (and Europe's) renewed Romantic appreciation for all things medieval and nationalistic. (Montserrat's revival coincided with other traditions born out of rejuvenated Catalan pride: the much-loved FC Barcelona soccer team; Barcelona's Palace of Catalan Music; and even the birth of local sparkling wine, *cava*.) Montserrat's basilica and monastery were reconstructed and became, once more, the strongly beating spiritual and cultural heart of the Catalan people.

Then came Francisco Franco, the dictatorial leader who wanted a monolithic Spain. To him Montserrat represented Catalan rebelliousness. During Franco's long rule, from 1939 to 1975, the *sardana* dance was still illegally performed here (but with a different name), and literature was published in the outlawed Catalan language. In 1970, 300 intellectuals demonstrating for more respect for human rights in Spain were locked up in the monastery for several days by Franco's police.

But now Franco is history. The 1990s brought another phase of rebuilding (after a forest fire and rain damage), and the Montserrat community is thriving once again, unafraid to display its pride for the Catalan people, culture, and faith.

Tourist Information

The square below the basilica houses a helpful TI, right across from the rack railway station (daily from 9:00, closes just after last train heads down—roughly 18:45, or 20:15 on weekdays in July-Aug, tel. 938-777-701, www.montserratvisita.com). Pick up the free map and get your questions answered. A good audioguide, available only at the TI, describes the general site and basilica (€6 includes book;

€14 includes entrance to museum, bland audiovisual presentation, and book). If you're a hiker, ask for the handout outlining hiking options here. Trails offer spectacular views (on clear days) to the Mediterranean and even (on clearer days) to the Pyrenees.

The audiovisual center (upstairs from the TI) provides some cultural and historical perspective—and an entrance to their big gift shop. The lame interactive exhibition—nowhere near as exciting as the mountains and basilica outside—includes computer touch screens and a short 20-minute video in English. Learn about the mountain's history, and get a glimpse into the daily lives of the monastery's resident monks (€5, covered by Trans Montserrat and Tot Montserrat combo-tickets, same hours as TI).

Self-Guided Spin Tour

From the main square in front of the basilica complex, face the main facade and take this spin tour. Like a good pilgrim, face Mary, the high-up centerpiece of the facade. Below her to the left is St. Benedict, the sixth-century monk who established the rules that came to govern Montserrat's monastery. St. George, the symbol of Catalunya, is on the right (amid victims of Spain's civil war).

Five arches line the base of the facade. The one on the far right leads pilgrims to the high point of any visit, the Black Virgin (a.k.a. La Moreneta). The center arch leads into the basilica's courtyard, and the arch second from left directs you to a small votive chapel filled with articles representing prayer requests or thanks.

Now look left of the basilica, where delicate arches mark the 15th-century monks' cloister. The monks have planted four trees here, hoping to harvest only their symbolism (palm = martyrdom, cypress = eternal life, olive = peace, and laurel = victory). Next to the trees are a public library and a peaceful reading room. The big archway is the private entrance to the monastery. Still turning to your left, then comes the modern hotel and, below that, the glass-fronted museum. Other buildings provide cells for pilgrims. The Sant Joan funicular lifts hikers up to the trailhead (you can see the tiny building at the top). From there you can take a number of fine hikes (described later). Another funicular station descends to the Sacred Cave. And, finally, five arches separate statues of founders of the great religious orders. Step over to the arches for a commanding view (on a clear day) of the Llobregat River, meandering all the way to the Mediterranean.

Sights in Montserrat

Basilica

Although there's been a church here since the 11th century, the present structure was built in the 1850s, and the facade only dates from 1968. The decor is Neo-Romanesque, so popular with the Romantic artists of the late 19th century. The basilica itself is ringed with interesting chapels, but the focus is on the Black Virgin (La Moreneta) sitting high above the main altar.

Cost and Hours: Free, La Moreneta viewable Mon-Sat 8:00-10:30 & 12:00-18:30, Sun 19:30-20:15; church itself has longer hours and daily services (Mass at 11:00 at the main altar; at 12:00 and 19:30 in side chapels; vespers at 18:45); www.abadiamontserrat.net.

Visiting the Basilica: Montserrat's top attraction is **La Moreneta,** the small wood statue of the Black Virgin, discovered in the Sacred Cave in the 12th century. Legend says she was carved by St. Luke (the gospel writer and supposed artist), brought to Spain by St. Peter, hidden away in the cave during the Moorish invasions, and miraculously discovered by shepherd children. (Carbon dating says she's 800 years old.) While George is the patron saint of Catalunya, La Moreneta is its patroness, having been crowned as such by the pope in 1881. "Moreneta" is usually translated as "black" in English, but the Spanish name actually means "tanned." The statue was originally lighter, but darkened over the centuries from candle smoke, humidity, and the natural aging of its original varnish. Pilgrims shuffle down a long, ornate passage leading alongside the church for their few moments alone with the Virgin (Keep an eye on the time if you want to see the statue; there are no visits Mon-Sat 10:30-12:00, or before 19:30 on Sun).

Join the line of pilgrims (along the right side of the church).

Though Mary is behind a protective glass case, the royal orb she cradles in her hands is exposed. Pilgrims touch Mary's orb with one hand and hold their other hand up to show that they accept Jesus. Newlyweds in particular seek Mary's blessing.

If you're not ushered right to the exit, immediately after La Moreneta, turn right into the delightful Neo-Romanesque prayer **chapel,** where worshippers sit behind the Virgin and continue to pray. The ceiling, painted in the Modernista style in 1898 by Joan Llimona, shows Jesus and Mary high in heaven. The trail connecting Catalunya with heaven seems to lead through these serrated mountains. The lower figures symbolize Catalan history and culture.

You'll leave by walking along the **Ave Maria Path** (along the outside of the church), which thoughtfully integrates nature and the basilica. Thousands of colorful votive candles are all busy helping the devout with their prayers. Before you leave the inner courtyard and head out into the main square, pop in to the humble little room with the many votive offerings. This is where people leave personal belongings (wedding dresses, baby's baptism outfits, wax replicas of body parts in need of healing, and so on) as part of a prayer request or as a thanks for divine intercession.

Museum of Montserrat

This bright, shiny, and cool collection of paintings and artifacts was mostly donated by devout Catalan Catholics. While it's nothing really earth-shaking, you'll enjoy an air-conditioned wander past lots of antiquities and fine artwork. Head upstairs first to see some lesser-known works by the likes of Picasso, El Greco, Caravaggio, Monet, Renoir, Pissarro, Degas, John Singer Sargent, and some local Modernista artists. One gallery shows how artists have depicted the Black Virgin of Montserrat over the centuries in many different styles. There's even a small Egyptian section, with a sarcophagus and mummy. Down on the main floor, you'll see ecclesiastical gear, a good icon collection, and more paintings, including—at the very end—a Dalí painting, some Picasso sketches and prints, and a Miró.

Cost and Hours: €7, covered by Tot Montserrat combo-ticket, daily July-Aug 10:00-18:45, Sept-June 10:00-17:45, tel. 938-777-745.

Sant Joan Funicular and Hikes

This funicular climbs 820 feet above the monastery in five minutes. At the top of the funicular, you are at the starting point of a 20-minute walk that takes you to the Sant Joan Chapel (follow sign for *Ermita de St. Joan*). Other hikes also begin at the trailhead by the funicular (get details from TI before you ascend; basic map with suggested hikes posted by upper funicular station). For a quick and easy chance to get out into nature and away from the crowds, simply ride up and follow the most popular hike, a 45-minute mostly downhill loop through mountain scenery back to the monastery. To take this route, go left from the funicular station; the trail—marked *Monestir de Montserrat*—will first go up to a rocky crest before heading downhill.

Cost and Hours: Funicular—€5.35 one-way, €8.45 round-trip, covered by Trans Montserrat and Tot Montserrat combo-tickets, goes every 20 minutes, more often with demand.

Sacred Cave (Santa Cova)

The Moreneta was originally discovered in the Sacred Cave (or Sacred Grotto), a 40-minute hike down from the monastery (then another 50 minutes back up). The path (c. 1900) was designed by devoted and patriotic Modernista architects, including Gaudí and Josep Puig i Cadafalch. It's lined with Modernista statues depicting scenes corresponding to the Mysteries of the Rosary. While the original Black Virgin statue is now in the basilica, a replica sits in the cave. A three-minute funicular ride cuts 20 minutes off the hike. If you're here late in the afternoon, check the schedule before you head into the Sacred Cave to make sure you don't miss the final ride back down the mountain. Missing the last funicular could mean catching a train back to Barcelona later than you had planned.

Cost and Hours: Funicular—€2.15 one-way, €3.30 round-trip, covered by Trans Montserrat and Tot Montserrat combo-tickets, goes every 20 minutes, more often with demand.

Choir Concert

Montserrat's Escolania, or Choir School, has been training voices for centuries. Fifty young boys, who live and study in the monastery itself, make up the choir, which performs daily except Saturday. The boys sing for only 10 minutes, the basilica is jam-packed, and it's likely you'll see almost nothing. Also note that if you attend the evening performance, you'll miss the last train or cable-car ride down the mountain.

Cost and Hours: Free, Mon-Fri at 13:00, Sun at 12:00, and Sun-Thu at 18:45, choir on vacation late June-late Aug.

Sleeping in Montserrat

An overnight here gets you monastic peace and a total break from the modern crowds. There are ample rustic cells for pilgrim visitors, but tourists might prefer this place:

$$ Hotel Abat Cisneros, a three-star hotel with 82 rooms and all the comforts, is low-key and appropriate for a sanctuary (Sb-€44-67, Db-€77-116, price depends on season, includes breakfast, half- and full-board available, elevator, guest computer, free Wi-Fi, tel. 938-777-701, www.montserratvisita.com, reserves @larsa-montserrat.com).

Eating in Montserrat

Montserrat is designed to feed hordes of pilgrims and tourists. You'll find a cafeteria along the main street (across from the train station) and a grocery store and bar with simple sandwiches where the road curves on its way up to the hotel. In the other direction, follow the covered walkway below the basilica to reach the Mirador dels Apòstols, with a bar, cafeteria, restaurant, and picnic area. The Hotel Abat Cisneros also has a restaurant. The best option is to pack a picnic from Barcelona, especially if you plan to hike.

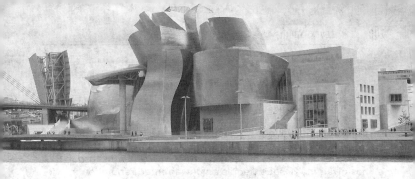

BASQUE COUNTRY

Euskal Herria

Straddling two nations on the Atlantic Coast—stretching about 100 miles from Bilbao, Spain, north to Bayonne, France—lies the ancient, free-spirited land of the Basques. The Basque Country is famous for its sunny beaches and scintillating modern architecture...and for its feisty, industrious natives. It's also simply beautiful: Bright white chalet-style homes with deep-red and green shutters scatter across lush, rolling hills; the Pyrenees Mountains soar high above the Atlantic; and surfers and sardines share the waves.

Insulated from mainstream Europe for much of their history, the plucky Basques have wanted to be left alone for more than 7,000 years. An easily crossed border separates the French *Pays Basque* from the Spanish *País Vasco,* allowing you to sample both sides from a single base (in Spain, I prefer fun-loving San Sebastián; in France, I hang my beret in cozy St-Jean-de-Luz).

Much unites the Spanish and French Basque regions: They share a cuisine, Union Jack-style flag (green, red, and white), and common language (Euskara), spoken by about a half-million people. (Virtually everyone also speaks Spanish and/or French.) And both have been integrated by their respective nations, sometimes forcibly. The French Revolution quelled French Basque ideas of independence; 130 years later, Spain's fascist dictator, Generalísimo Francisco Franco, attempted to tame his own separatist-minded Basques.

But over the past few generations, things have started looking up. The long-suppressed Euskara language is enjoying a resurgence. And, as the European Union celebrates ethnic regions rather than nations, the Spanish and French Basques are feeling

Who Are the Basques?

To call the Basques "mysterious" is an understatement. Before most European nations had ever set sail, Basque whalers competed with the Vikings for control of the sea. During the Industrial Revolution and lean Franco years, Basque steel kept the Spanish economy alive. In the last few decades, the separatist group ETA has given the Basque people an unwarranted reputation for violence. And through it all, the Basques have spoken a unique language that to outsiders sounds like gibberish or a secret code.

So just who are the Basques? Even for Basques, that's a difficult question. According to traditional stereotypes, Basques are thought of as having long noses, heavy eyebrows, floppy ears, stout bodies, and a penchant for wearing berets. But widespread Spanish and French immigration has made it difficult to know who actually has Basque ethnic roots. (In fact, some of the Basques' greatest patriots have had no Basque blood.) And so today, anyone who speaks the Basque language, Euskara, is considered a "Basque."

Euskara, related to no other surviving tongue, has been used since Neolithic times—making it, very likely, the oldest European language that's still spoken. With its seemingly impossible-to-pronounce words filled with k's, tx's, and z's (restrooms are *komunak: gizonak* for men and *emakumeak* for women), Euskara makes speaking Spanish suddenly seem easy. (Some tips: *tx* is pronounced "ch" and *tz* is pronounced "ts." Other key words: *kalea* is "street," and *ostatua* is a cheap hotel.) Kept alive as a symbol of Basque cultural identity, Euskara typically is learned proudly as a second or third language. Many locals can switch effortlessly from Euskara to Spanish or French.

The Basque economy has historically been shaped by three factors: the sea, agriculture, and iron deposits.

Basque sailors were some of the first and finest in Europe, as they built ever-better boats to venture farther and farther into the Atlantic in search of whales. By the year 1000, Basque sailors were chasing whales a thousand miles from home, in the Norwegian fjords. Despite lack of physical evidence, many historians surmise that the Basques must have sailed to Newfoundland long before Christopher Columbus landed in the Caribbean.

When the "Spanish" era of exploration began, Basques continued to play a key role, as sailors and shipbuilders. Columbus' *Santa María* was likely Basque-built, and his crew included many Basques. History books teach that Ferdinand Magellan was the first to circumnavigate the globe, with the footnote that he was killed partway around. Who took over the helm for the rest of the journey, completing the circle? It was his Basque captain, Juan Sebastián de Elcano. And a pair of well-traveled Catholic priests, known for their far-reaching missionary trips that led to founding the Jesuit order, were also Basques: St. Ignatius of Loyola and St. Francis Xavier.

Later, the Industrial Age swept Europe, gaining a foothold in Iberia when the Basques began using their rich iron deposits to make steel. Pioneering Basque industrialists set the tempo as they dragged Spain into the modern world. Cities such as Bilbao were heavily industrialized, sparking an influx of workers from around Spain (which gradually diluted Basque blood in the Basque Country).

The independence-minded Basques are notorious for their stubbornness. In truth, as a culturally and linguistically unique island surrounded by bigger and stronger nations, the Basques have learned to compromise. Historically Basques have remained on good terms with outsiders, so long as their traditional laws, the *Fueros,* were respected. Though outdated, the *Fueros* continue to symbolize a self-governance that the Basques hold dear. It is only when foreign law has been placed above the *Fueros*—as many of today's Basques feel Spanish law is—that the people become agitated.

In recent years, much of the news of the Basques—especially in Spain—was made by the terrorist organization ETA, whose goal has been to establish an independent Basque state. (ETA stands for the Euskara phrase "Euskadi Ta Askatasuna," or "Basque Country and Freedom.") ETA has been blamed for more than 800 deaths since 1968, but in late 2011, the group declared an end to its campaign of violence (but not its call for independence). While many people in the Basque Country would like a greater degree of autonomy from Madrid, only a tiny minority of the population supports ETA, and the vast majority rejects violence.

This is only a first glimpse into the important, quirky, and fascinating Basque people. To better understand the Basques, there's no better book than Mark Kurlansky's *The Basque History of the World*—essential pre-trip reading for historians. And various museums in this region also illuminate Basque culture and history, including the Museum of San Telmo in San Sebastián (see page 213), the Assembly House and Basque Country Museum in Guernica (page 235), and the Museum of Basque Culture in Bayonne (page 269).

BASQUE COUNTRY

more united. This heavily industrialized region is enjoying a striking 21st-century renaissance. In Spain, the dazzling architecture
of the Guggenheim Bilbao modern-art museum and the glittering
resort of San Sebastián are drawing enthusiastic crowds. And in
France, long-ignored cities such as Bayonne and the surfing mecca
of Biarritz are being revitalized. At the same time, traditional
small towns—like Spain's Lekeitio and Hondarribia, and France's
St-Jean-de-Luz and nearby mountain villages—are also thriving,
making the entire region colorful, fun, welcoming...and unmistakably Basque.

Planning Your Time

One day is enough for a quick sample of the Basque Country,
but two or three days lets you breathe deep and hold it in. Where
you go depends on your interests: Spain or France? Cities (such
as Bilbao and Bayonne) or resorts (such as San Sebastián and
St-Jean-de-Luz)?

If you want to slow down and focus on Spain, spend one day
relaxing in San Sebastián and the second side-tripping to Bilbao
(and Guernica, if you have a car).

Better yet, take this easy opportunity to dip into France. Sleep in one country, then side-trip into the other, devoting one day to Spain (San Sebastián and maybe Bilbao), and a second day to France (St-Jean-de-Luz and Bayonne).

Wherever you go, your Basque sightseeing should be a fun blend of urban, rural, cultural, and culinary activities.

Getting Around the Basque Country

The tourist's Basque Country—from Bilbao to Bayonne—stays close to the coastline. Fortunately, everything is connected by good roads and public transportation.

By Bus and Train: From San Sebastián, the bus is the best way to reach Bilbao (and from there, Guernica). To go between San Sebastián and France, a train—with a transfer in Hendaye—is your best bet. Once in France, the three main towns (St-Jean-de-Luz, Bayonne, and Biarritz) are connected by bus and by train. Even if you rent a car, I'd do these three towns by public transit. Specific connections are explained in each section.

Note that a few out-of-the-way areas—Spain's Bay of Biscay and France's Basque villages of the interior—are impractical by

Basque Country at a Glance

▲▲**San Sebastián (Spain)** Relaxing upscale city with beach-front promenade wrapped around chic shopping neighborhood and tasty tapas bars.

▲▲**Bilbao (Spain)** Revitalized regional capital with architectural gem—Guggenheim Bilbao—and atmospheric Old Town.

▲▲**St-Jean-de-Luz (France)** Sleepy seaside retreat in the French *Pays Basque* that serves as home base for countryside exploration.

▲**Guernica (Spain)** Village at the heart of Basque culture that was devastated by bombs during the Spanish Civil War—later immortalized by Picasso masterpiece.

▲**Bayonne (France)** Urban French scene with a Basque twist, home to impressive cultural museum, scenic ramparts, and lots of ham.

Biarritz (France) Beach resort known for its mix of international glitz and surfer dudes.

public transportation...but worth the trouble by car.

By Car: San Sebastián, Bilbao, St-Jean-de-Luz, and Bayonne are connected by a convenient expressway, called A-8 in Spain and A-63 in France (rough timings: Bilbao to San Sebastián, 1.25 hours; San Sebastián to St-Jean-de-Luz, 45 minutes; St-Jean-de-Luz to Bayonne, 30 minutes).

Language Warning: For the headers throughout this chapter, I've listed place names using the Spanish or French spelling first and the Euskara spelling second. In the text, I use the spelling that prevails locally. While most people refer to towns by their Spanish or French names, many road signs list places in Euskara. (In Spain, signs are usually posted in both Euskara and Spanish, either on the same sign or with dual signage on opposite sides of the street. In less separatist-minded France, signs are often only in French.) The Spanish or French version is sometimes scratched out by locals, so you might have to navigate by Euskara names.

Also note that in terms of linguistic priority (e.g., museum information), Euskara comes first, Spanish and French tie for second, and English a distant fourth...and it often doesn't make the cut.

Cuisine Scene in the Basque Country

Mixing influences from the mountains, sea, Spain, and France, Basque food is reason enough to visit the region. The local cuisine—dominated by seafood, tomatoes, and red peppers—offers some spicy dishes, unusual in most of Europe. And though you'll find similar specialties throughout the Basque lands, Spain is still Spain and France is still France. Here are some dishes you're most likely to find in each area.

Spanish Basque Cuisine: Hopping from bar to bar sampling *pintxos*—the local term for tapas—is a highlight of any trip (for details, see the sidebar on page 225). Local brews include *sidra* (hard apple cider) and *txakolí* (cha-koh-LEE, a light, sparkling white wine—often theatrically poured from high above the glass for aeration). You'll want to sample the famous *pil-pil*, made from emulsifying the skin of *bacalao* (dried, salted cod) into a mayonnaise-like substance with chili and garlic. Another tasty dish is *kokotxas*, usually made from hake *(merluza)* fish cheeks, prepared like *pil-pil*, and cooked slowly over a low heat so the natural gelatin is released, turning it into a wonderful sauce—*¡qué bueno!* Look also for white asparagus from Navarra. Wine-wise, I prefer the reds and rosés from Navarra. Finish your dinner with *cuajada*, a yogurt-like, creamy milk dessert that's sometimes served with honey and nuts. Another specialty, found throughout Spain, is *membrillo*, a sweet and *muy* dense quince jelly. Try it with cheese for a light dessert, or look for it at breakfast.

French Basque Cuisine: The red peppers (called *piments d'Espelette*) hanging from homes in small villages give foods a distinctive flavor and often end up in *piperade,* a dish that combines peppers, tomatoes, garlic, ham, and eggs. Peppers are also dried and used as condiments. Look for them with the terrific Basque dish *axoa* (a veal or lamb stew on mashed potatoes). Look also for anything "Basque-style" *(basquaise)*—cooked with tomato, eggplant, red pepper, and garlic. Don't leave without trying *ttoro* (tchoo-roh), a seafood stew that is the Basque Country's answer to bouillabaisse and cioppino. *Marmitako* is a hearty tuna stew. Local cheeses come from Pyrenean sheep's milk *(pur brebis),* and the local ham *(jambon de Bayonne)* is famous throughout France. After dinner try a shot of *izarra* (herbal-flavored brandy). To satisfy your sweet tooth, look for *gâteau basque,* a local tart filled with pastry cream or cherries from Bayonne. Hard apple cider is a tasty and local beverage. The regional wine Irouléguy comes in red, white, and rosé, and is the only wine produced in the French part of Basque Country (locals like to say that it's made from the smallest vineyard in France but the biggest in the Northern Basque Country).

Spanish Basque Country (El País Vasco)

Four of the seven Basque territories lie within Spain. Many consider Spanish Basque culture to be feistier and more colorful than the relatively assimilated French Basques—you'll hear more Euskara spoken here than in France.

For nearly 40 years, beginning in 1939, the figure of Generalísimo Franco loomed large over the Spanish Basques. Franco depended upon Basque industry to keep the floundering Spanish economy afloat. But even as he exploited the Basques economically, he so effectively blunted Basque culture that the language was primarily Spanish by default. Franco kicked off his regime by offering up the historic Basque town of Guernica as target practice to Hitler's air force. The notorious result—the wholesale slaughter of innocent civilians—was immortalized by Pablo Picasso's mural *Guernica*.

But Franco is long gone, and today's Basques are looking to the future. The iron deposits have been depleted, prompting the Basques to re-imagine their rusting cities for the 21st century. True to form, they're rising to the challenge. Perhaps the best example is Bilbao, whose iconic Guggenheim Museum—built on the former site of an industrial wasteland—is the centerpiece of a bold new skyline.

San Sebastián is the heart of the tourist's *País Vasco*, with its sparkling, picturesque beach framed by looming green mountains and a charming Old Town with gourmet *pintxos* (tapas) spilling out of every bar. On-the-rise Bilbao is worth a look for its landmark Guggenheim and its atmospheric Old Town. For small-town fun, drop by the fishing village of Lekeitio (near Bilbao). And for history, Guernica has some intriguing museums.

This chapter focuses on Basque destinations on or near the ocean. Some inland Basque towns and cities—most notably Pamplona—are covered in the Camino de Santiago chapter.

San Sebastián / Donostia

Shimmering above the breathtaking Concha Bay, elegant and prosperous San Sebastián (Donostia in Euskara, which locals lovingly shorten to Donosti) has a favored location with golden beaches, capped by twin peaks at either end, and with a cute little island in the center. A delightful beachfront promenade runs

the length of the bay, with an intriguing Old Town at one end and a smart shopping district in the center. It has 186,000 residents and almost that many tourists in high season (July-Sept). With a romantic setting, a soaring statue of Christ gazing over the city, and a late-night lively Old Town, San Sebastián has a mini Rio de Janeiro aura. Though the actual "sightseeing" isn't much, the scenic city itself provides a pleasant introduction to Spain's Basque Country. And as a culinary capital of Spain—with many local restaurants getting international attention—competition is tight to dish up some of the top tapas anywhere.

In 1845, Queen Isabel II's doctor recommended she treat her skin problems by bathing here in the sea. (For modesty's sake, she would go inside a giant cabana that could be wheeled into the surf—allowing her to swim far from prying eyes, never having to set foot on the beach.) Her visit mobilized Spain's aristocracy, and soon the city was on the map as a seaside resort. By the turn of the 20th century, San Sebastián was the toast of the belle époque, and a leading resort for Europe's beautiful people. Before World War I, Queen María Cristina summered here and held court in her Miramar Palace overlooking the crescent beach (the turreted, red-brick building partway around the bay). Hotels, casinos, and theaters flourished. Even Franco enjoyed 35 summers in a place he was sure to call San Sebastián, not Donostia.

Planning Your Time

San Sebastián's sights can be exhausted in a few hours, but it's a great place to be on vacation for a full, lazy day (or longer). Stroll the two-mile-long promenade with the locals and scout the place you'll grab to work on a tan. The promenade leads to a funicular that lifts you to the Monte Igueldo viewpoint. After exploring the Old Town and port, walk up to the hill of Monte Urgull. If you have more time, enjoy the delightful aquarium. Museum-goers find it worthwhile to visit the Museum of San Telmo, the largest of its kind on Basque culture. A key ingredient of any visit to San Sebastián is enjoying tapas in the Old Town bars.

Orientation to San Sebastián

The San Sebastián that we're interested in surrounds Concha Bay (Bahía de la Concha). It can be divided into three areas: Playa de la Concha (best beaches), the shopping district (called Centro), and the skinny streets of the grid-planned Old Town (called Parte Vieja, to the north of the shopping district). Centro, just east of Playa de la Concha, has beautiful turn-of-the-20th-century architecture, but no real sights. A busy drag called Alameda del Boulevard (or just "Boulevard") stands where the city

wall once ran, and separates the Centro from the Old Town.

It's all bookended by mini-mountains: Monte Urgull to the north and east, and Monte Igueldo to the south and west. The river (Río Urumea) divides central San Sebastián from the district called Gros, with a lively night scene and surfing beach.

Tourist Information

San Sebastián's TI, conveniently located right on the Boulevard, has information on city and regional sights, bike rentals (see "Helpful Hints," later), and bus and train schedules. Pick up the free map and various pamphlets with English descriptions of three self-guided walking tours—the Old Town/Monte Urgull walk is best. The TI also offers guided walking tours—see page 211 (July-Sept Mon-Sat 9:00-20:00, Sun 10:00-19:00; Oct-June Mon-Thu 9:00-13:30 & 15:30-19:00, Fri-Sat 10:00-19:00, Sun 10:00-14:00; Boulevard 8, tel. 943-481-166, www.sansebastianturismo .com).

Arrival in San Sebastián

By Train: The town has two train stations (neither has luggage storage, but you can leave bags at Navi.net Internet café downtown—see "Helpful Hints," later).

If you're coming on a regional train from Hendaye/Hendaia on the French border, get off at the **Amara EuskoTren Station** (five stops before the end of the line, which is called Lasarte-Oria). It's a level 15-minute walk to the center: Exit the station and walk across the long plaza, then veer right and walk eight blocks down Calle Easo (toward the statue of Christ hovering on the hill) to the beach. The Old Town will be ahead on your right, with Playa de la Concha to your left. To speed things up, catch bus #21, #26, or #28 along Calle Easo and take it to the Boulevard stop, near the TI at the bottom of the Old Town.

If you're arriving by train from elsewhere in Spain (or from France after transferring in Irún), you'll get off at the main **RENFE station.** It's just across the river from the Centro shopping district. There are no convenient buses from the station—to get to the Old Town and most recommended hotels, catch a taxi (they wait out front, €6 to downtown). Or just walk (about 10-15 minutes)—beyond the tree-lined plaza, cross the fancy dragon-decorated María Cristina Bridge, turn right onto the busy avenue called Paseo de los Fueros, and follow the Urumea River until the last bridge. The modern, blocky Kursaal Conference Center across the river serves as an easy landmark.

By Bus: A few buses—such as those from Hondarribia and the airport—can let you off at pretty Plaza de Gipuzkoa (first stop after crossing the river, in Centro shopping area, one block from the Boulevard, TI, and Old Town). But most buses—including those from Bilbao—take you instead to San Sebastián's makeshift "bus station" (dubbed Amara) at a big roundabout called Plaza Pío XII. It's basically a parking lot with a few bus shelters and a TI kiosk (open July-Aug only). At the end of the lot nearest the big roundabout, you'll see directional signs pointing you toward the town center (about a 30-minute walk). To save time and energy, catch local bus #21, #26, or #28 from the bus stop at the start of Avenida de Sancho el Sabio and get off at the Boulevard stop, near the TI at the start of the Old Town.

By Plane: San Sebastián Airport (airport code: EAS) is beautifully situated along the harbor in the nearby town of Hondarribia, 12 miles east of the city, just across the bay from France (tel. 902-404-704, www.aena.es). An easy regional bus (#E21) connects the airport to San Sebastián's Plaza de Gipuzkoa, just a block south of the Boulevard and TI (€2, about hourly Mon-Sat 6:00-20:15, Sun 9:40-20:55, 35 minutes, www.ekialdebus.net). Buses #E25 and #E27 also connect the airport to San Sebastián, but #E21 is much faster. A taxi into town costs about €35.

If you arrive at **Bilbao Airport,** go out front and take the Pesa bus directly to San Sebastián (€16.50, pay driver, runs hourly 7:45-23:45, 1 hour, drops off at Amara bus station; buy ticket *to* the airport at Pesa office in San Sebastián at Avenida de Sancho el Sabio 33; www.pesa.net).

By Car: Take the Amara freeway exit, follow *centro ciudad* signs into the city center, and park in a pay lot (many are well-signed—the Kursaal underground lot is the most central). If you're picking up or returning a rental car, you'll find **Europcar** at the RENFE train station (tel. 943-322-304). Less centrally located are **Hertz** (Centro Comercial Garbera, Travesía de Garbera 1, bus #16 connects with downtown, tel. 943-392-223) and **Avis** (a taxi ride away at Hotel Barceló Costa Vasca, Pío Baroja 15, tel. 943-461-556).

Helpful Hints

Internet Access: A half-dozen Internet cafés are well-advertised throughout the Old Town, most offering fast access for about

€2/hour; try **Navi.net** (Mon-Fri 9:30-22:00, Sat-Sun 10:00-22:00, closed for lunch in winter, Calle Narrica 12). These days, government-subsidized Wi-Fi access is available just about everywhere (including at most hotels).

Bookstore: Elkar, an advocate of Basque culture and literature, has two branches on the same street in the Old Town. Both have a collection of Basque literature, and one has a wide selection of guidebooks, maps, and books in English (Mon-Sat 10:00-14:00 & 16:00-20:00, Sun 11:00-14:00 & 16:30-20:30, Calle Fermín Calbetón 21 and 30, tel. 943-420-080).

Baggage Storage: There's no baggage storage at the train or bus stations. **Navi.net** Internet café, listed above, has space for about 80 bags (first-come, first-served; €0.50/hour, €5/overnight, €10/24 hours).

Laundry: Wash & Dry is in the Gros neighborhood, across the river (self-service €14/load, daily 8:00-22:00; drop-off service €22/load, Mon-Fri 9:30-13:00 & 16:00-20:00; Iparragirre 6, tel. 943-293-150).

Bike Rental: The city has some great bike lanes and is a good place to enjoy on two wheels. (But pedestrians need to be careful—never stand in bike lanes at intersections.) Like many cities in Europe, San Sebastián has an automated bike-sharing program. Rent directly from the **TI**—there are over 10 stands spread around the city. Bikes must be returned to any stand within four hours, but you can pick up another one after 30 minutes. The program is in flux, so expect changes to prices and hours (€8/day, €15/3 days, €20 cash-only deposit; rental office hours Mon-Sat 10:00-13:00 & 15:30-18:00, Sun 10:30-13:00, longer in summer; tel. 943-481-166). The TI also offers an English-language **bike tour** of the city in the summer (€14, July-Aug at 11:00 and 17:00, 1.5 hours, includes bike).

For longer-term bike rentals, try **Bici Rent Donosti** (also rents scooters in summer, Avenida de Zurriola 22, three blocks across river from TI, mobile 639-016-013) or **Sanse Bikes** (near the town hall at Boulevard 25, tel. 943-045-229).

Marijuana: While Spain is famously liberal about marijuana laws, the Basque Country is even more so. Walking around San Sebastián, you'll see "grow shops" sporting the famous green leaf (shopkeepers are helpful if you have questions). The sale of marijuana is still illegal, but the consumption of marijuana is decriminalized and people are allowed to grow enough for their personal use at home. With the town's mesmerizing aquarium and delightfully lit bars filled with enticing munchies, it just makes sense here.

Getting Around San Sebastián

By Bus: Along the Boulevard at the bottom edge of the Old Town, you'll find a line of public buses ready to take you anywhere in town; give any driver your destination, and he or she will tell you the number of the bus to catch (€1.60, pay driver).

Some handy bus routes: #21, #26, and #28 connect the Amara bus station and Amara EuskoTren Station to the TI (get off at the Boulevard stop); #16 begins at the Boulevard/TI stop, goes along Playa de la Concha and through residential areas, and eventually arrives at the base of the Monte Igueldo funicular. The TI has a bus-route map (or see www.dbus.es).

By Taxi: Taxis start at €6, which covers most rides in the center. You can't hail a taxi on the street—you must call one (tel. 943-404-040 or 943-464-646) or find a taxi stand (most convenient along the Boulevard).

By Metro: A new subway system—called Metro Donostialdea—is currently under construction in San Sebastián; it will connect the main areas of the city and eventually extend to the airport. Officials are also upgrading San Sebastián's EuskoTren line as part of this transit system. It'll eventually be renamed, but for now, locals continue to call it by its nickname—Topo ("Mole")—because it goes underground part of the time.

Tours in San Sebastián

Walking Tours

The TI runs English-language walking tours. Options include Essential San Sebastián (€10, 2 hours), Flavors of San Sebastián (€18, 2 hours, includes three *pintxos* and three drinks), Romantic San Sebastián (through the elegant Centro district, €10, 2 hours), and—during the September film festival—San Sebastián: A Film City (€14, 2 hours, includes one *pintxo* and one drink). Schedules vary—ask at the TI, call 943-217-717, or check www .sansebastianreservas.com for info and reservations.

Local Guides

Itsaso Petrikorena is good (mobile 647-973-231, betitsaso@yahoo .es). **Gabriella Ranelli,** an American who's lived in San Sebastián for over 20 years, specializes in culinary tours. She can take you on a sightseeing spin around the Old Town, along with a walk through the market and best *pintxo* bars (€185/half-day, €395/day, higher depending on destinations, transportation included for up to four people, mobile 609-467-381, www.tenedortours .com, info@tenedortours.com). Gabriella also organizes cooking classes—where you shop at the market, then join a local chef to cook up some tasty *pintxos* of your own (€135/person for a small group)—as well as wine-tastings (start at €55/person).

BASQUE COUNTRY

Gastronomic Tours

San Sebastián Food offers travelers the opportunity to enter one of San Sebastián's exclusive "private eating clubs" (described on page 213) and even participate in preparing a gourmet meal. Prices start around €175 per person (4-person minimum), including ingredients and wine. They also organize €90 pintxo tours that have you hopping from bar to bar (includes food and wine) and €85 Iberian ham-cutting courses with sherry tasting (Calle Aldamar 30, mobile 634-759-503, www.sansebastianfood.com, info@sansebastianfood.com).

Tours on Wheels

Two tour options on wheels (following a similar route around the bay) are available, but most travelers won't find them necessary in this walkable city: the **"txu-txu"** tourist train (€5, daily July-mid-Sept 10:30-21:00, mid-Sept-June 11:00-18:30, closed Jan-Feb and Mon off-season, 40-minute round-trip, tel. 943-422-973), and the **Donosti Tours** hop-on, hop-off bus tour along the bay and around the city (€12, full loop takes about one hour, ticket good for 24 hours, leaves from Victoria Eugenia theater on the Boulevard, tel. 943-441-828, www.busturistikoa.com, Raquel).

Basque Excursions

Based in San Sebastián, **Agustin Ciriza** leads walking tours of his hometown and minibus tours for up to eight people through the Spanish and French Basque Country, with destinations including Bilbao, Hondarribia, Biarritz, the Biscay Coast, Bayonne, and Pamplona (even during the running of the bulls). He also offers guided kayaking expeditions, pilgrimages, mountain treks, surf lessons, surfing trips, wine tours to the Rioja region, and wine tastings, food tours, and cooking classes in town. Prices start at €75 per person for a half-day excursion (minimum two people, mobile 686-117-395, www.gorilla-trip.com, agus@gorilla-trip.com).

Sights in San Sebastián

▲▲Old Town (Parte Vieja)

Huddled in the shadow of its once-protective Monte Urgull, the Old Town is where San Sebastián was born about 1,000 years ago. Because the town burned down in 1813 (as Spain, Portugal, and England fought the French to get Napoleon's brother off the Spanish throne), the architecture you see is generally Neoclassical and uniform. Still, the grid plan of streets hides heavy Baroque and Gothic churches, surprise plazas, and fun little shops, including venerable pastry stores, rugged produce markets, Basque-independence souvenir shops, and seafood-to-go delis. The highlight of the Old Town is its array of incredibly lively tapas bars—though here these snacks are called *pintxos* (PEEN-chohs; see "Eating in San Sebastián" on page 224). To see the fishing industry in action, wander out to the port (described later).

Although the struggle for Basque independence is currently in a relatively calm stage, with most people opposing violent ETA tactics, there are still underlying tensions between Spain and the Basque people. In the middle of the Old Town, **Calle Juan de Bilbao** is the political-action street. Here you'll find people more sympathetic to the struggle (whereas for others, it's a street to avoid). Speaking Basque is encouraged.

Flagpoles mark **"private eating clubs"** throughout the Old Town (otherwise unmarked). Basque society is matrilineal and very female-oriented. A husband brings home his paycheck and hands it directly to his wife, who controls the house's purse strings (and everything else). Basque men felt they needed a place where they could congregate and play "king of the castle," so they formed these clubs where members could reserve a table and cook for their friends. The clubs used to be exclusively male; women are now allowed as invited guests...but never in the kitchen, which remains the men's domain.

▲Plaza de la Constitución

The Old Town's main square is where bullfights used to be held. Notice the seat numbering on the balconies: Even if you owned an

apartment here, the city retained rights to the balconies, which it could sell as box seats. (Residents could peek over the paying customers' shoulders.) Above the clock, notice the seal of San Sebastián: a merchant ship with sails billowing in the wind. The city was granted trading rights by the crown—a reminder of the Basque Country's importance in Spanish seafaring. Inviting café tables spill into the square from all corners.

Museum of San Telmo (San Telmo Museoa)

A recent addition to this fascinating museum innovatively wrapped a modern facade around a 16th-century Dominican convent and its peaceful cloister. It's now the largest museum of Basque culture in the country. Exhibits of archaeological and ethnographic artifacts demonstrate the traditional folkways of Basque life and vividly tell the history of the region. An art historical painting collection features a few gems (El Greco, Rubens, Tintoretto), while 19th- and 20th-century paintings by Basque artists offer an interesting peek into the spirit, faces, and natural beauty of these fiercely independent people.

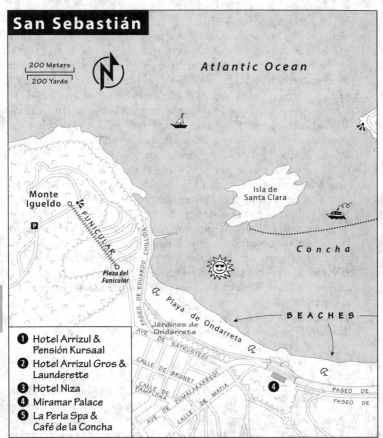

San Sebastián

Atlantic Ocean

200 Meters
200 Yards

Monte Igueldo

FUNICULAR

Plaza del Funicular

Isla de Santa Clara

Concha

PASEO DE EDUARDO CHILLIDA

Playa de Ondarreta

Jardines de Ondarreta

AVE. DE SATRUSTEGI

CALLE DE BRUNET

CALLE DE PAMPLONA

AVE. DE ZUMALAKABEGI

CALLE DE MATIA

BEACHES

PASEO DE

PASEO DE

1 Hotel Arrizul & Pensión Kursaal
2 Hotel Arrizul Gros & Launderette
3 Hotel Niza
4 Miramar Palace
5 La Perla Spa & Café de la Concha

Cost and Hours: €5, free on Tue, open Tue-Sun 10:00-20:00, closed Mon, Plaza Zuloaga 1, tel. 943-481-580, www.santelmomuseoa.com.

▲Bretxa Public Market (Mercado de la Bretxa)

Wandering through the public market is a fun way to get in touch with San Sebastián and Basque culture. Although the sandstone market building facing the Boulevard and the large, former Pescadería building have both been converted into a modern shopping complex, the farmers' produce market thrives here (lined up along the left side of the mall), as does the fish and meat market (underground).

Hours: Mon-Fri 8:00-14:00 & 17:00-20:00, Sat 8:00-14:00, closed Sun, Bretxa Plaza.

Visiting the Market: To get to the modern fish and meat market, walk past the produce vendors (look under the eaves of the building to see what the farmers are selling), and find a big glass

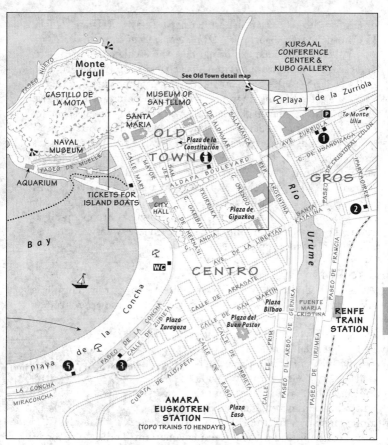

cube in the square, where an escalator takes you down into the market.

At the bottom of the escalator, notice the **fish stall** on the left (marked *J. Ma. Mujika*). In the case, you'll see different cuts of *bacalao* (cod). Entire books have been written about the importance of cod to the evolution of seafaring in Europe. The fish could be preserved in salt to feed sailors on ever-longer trips into the North Atlantic, allowing them to venture beyond the continental shelf (into deeper waters where they couldn't catch fresh fish). Cod was also popular among Catholic landlubbers on Fridays. Today cod remains a Basque staple. People still buy the salted version, which must be soaked for 48 hours (and the water changed three times) to become edible. If you're in a rush, you can buy de-salted cod... but at a cost in flavor. Stroll behind this stall to explore the fresh fish market—often with the catch of the day set up in cute little scenes. Few fish stands are open on Monday, because boats don't go out on Sunday; even fishermen need a day off. There's a free **WC** in the market—just ask *"¿Dónde está el servicio, por favor?"*

When you're done exploring, take the escalator up, turn left, and cross the street to the **Aitor Lasa** cheese shop (Mon-Fri 8:30-14:00 & 17:15-20:00, Sat 8:30-14:30, closed Sun, Aldamar 12, tel. 943-430-354). Pass the fragrant piles of mushrooms at the entrance and head back to the display case, showing off the Basque specialty of *idiazábal*—raw sheep's milk cheese. Notice the wide variety, which depends on the specific region it came from, whether it's smoked or cured, and for how long it's been cured *(curación)*. If you're planning a picnic, this is a very local (and expensive) ingredient. To try the cheese that won first prize a few years back in the Ordizia International Cheese Competition, ask for *"El queso con el premio de Ordizia, por favor."* The owners are evangelical about the magic of combining the local cheese with walnuts and *casero* (homemade) apple jam.

The Port

At the west end of the Old Town, protected by Monte Urgull, is the port. Take the passage through the wall at the appropriately named Calle Puerto, and jog right along the level, portside promenade, Paseo del Muelle. You'll pass fishing boats unloading the catch of the day (with hungry locals looking on), salty sailors' pubs, and fishermen mending nets. Also along this strip are the skippable  Naval Museum and the entertaining aquarium. Trails to the top of Monte Urgull are just above this scene, near Santa María Church (or climb the stairs next to the aquarium).

Cruises

Small boats cruise from the Old Town's port to the island in the bay (Isla Santa Clara), where you can hike the trails and have lunch at the lone café, or pack a picnic before setting sail. **Motoras de la Isla** offers two different options: the direct red *(roja)* route to the island (€3.80 round-trip, small ferry departs May-Sept only, every half-hour, 10:00-20:00) and the blue *(azul)* route, which cruises the bay for 25 minutes in a glass-bottom boat before dropping passengers off (€6 round-trip, hourly, 11:00-19:30; tel. 943-000-045, www.motorasdelaisla.com). The *Ciudad San Sebastián* catamaran gives 40-minute tours of the bay from Monte Igueldo to Zurriola Beach (€9, tel. 943-287-932, www.ciudadsansebastian.com).

Naval Museum (Museo Naval)

This museum's two floors of exhibits describe the seafaring city's history, revealing the intimate link between the Basque culture and the sea.

Cost and Hours: €1.20, free on Thu, borrow English description at entry, Tue-Sat 10:00-13:30 & 16:00-19:30, Sun 11:00-14:00, closed Mon, Paseo del Muelle 24, tel. 943-430-051.

▲▲Aquarium

San Sebastián's aquarium is surprisingly good. Exhibits are thoughtfully described in English and include a history of the sea, a collection of naval vessels, and models showing various drift-netting techniques. You'll see a petting tank filled with nervous fish; a huge whale skeleton; a trippy, illuminated, slowly tumbling tank of jellyfish; and a mesmerizing 45-foot-long tunnel that lets you look up into a wet world of floppy rays, menacing sharks, and local fish. The local section ends with a tank of shark fetuses safely incubating away from hungry predators. Local kids see the tropical wing and holler, "Nemo!"

Cost and Hours: €13, €7 for kids under 13; July-Aug daily 10:00-21:00; Easter-June and Sept Mon-Fri 10:00-20:00, Sat-Sun 10:00-21:00; Oct-Easter Mon-Fri 10:00-19:00, Sat-Sun 10:00-20:00; last entry one hour before closing, at the end of Paseo del Muelle, tel. 943-440-099, www.aquariumss.com.

▲Monte Urgull

The once-mighty castle (Castillo de la Mota) atop the hill deterred most attackers, allowing the city to prosper in the Middle Ages. The free museum within the castle, featuring San Sebastián history, is mildly interesting. Seek out the crumbling memorial to British soldiers who gave their lives to defend the city from Napoleon. The best views from the hill are not from the statue of Christ, but from the ramparts on the left side (as you face the hill), just above the port's aquarium. **Café El Polvorín,** nestled in the park, is a free-spirited place with salads, sandwiches, and good sangria.

A walkway allows you to stroll the mountain's entire perimeter near sea level. This route is continuous from Hotel Parma to the aquarium, and offers an enjoyable after-dinner wander. You can also walk a bit higher up over the port (along the white railing)—called the *paseo de las curas,* or "priest's path," where the clergy could stroll unburdened by the rabble in the streets below. These paths are technically open only from sunrise to sunset (daily May-Sept 8:00-21:00, Oct-April 8:00-19:00), but you can often access them later.

The Beach and Beyond

▲▲La Concha Beach and Promenade

The shell-shaped Playa de la Concha, the pride of San Sebastián, has one of Europe's loveliest stretches of sand. Lined with a two-mile-long promenade, it allows even backpackers to feel

aristocratic. Although it's pretty empty off-season, sunbathers pack its shores in summer. But year-round it's surprisingly devoid of eateries and money-grubbing businesses. There are free showers, and *cabinas* provide lockers, showers, and shade for a fee. For a century, the lovingly painted wrought-iron balustrade that stretches the length of the promenade has been a symbol of the city; it shows up on everything from jewelry to headboards. It's shaded by tamarisk trees, with branches carefully pruned into knotty bulbs each winter that burst into leafy shade-giving canopies in the summer—another symbol of the city. **Café de la Concha** serves reasonably priced, mediocre food, but you can't beat the location of its terrace overlooking the beach (€15 weekday lunch special, tel. 943-473-600).

The **Miramar palace and park,** which divides the crescent beach in the middle, was where Queen María Cristina held court when she summered here. Her royal changing rooms are used today as inviting cafés, restaurants, and a fancy spa. You can walk in the park, although the palace, used as a music school, is closed to the public.

La Perla Spa

The spa overlooking the beach attracts a less royal crowd today and appeals mostly to visitors interested in sampling "the curative properties of the sea." You can enjoy its Talasso Fitness Circuit, featuring a hydrotherapy pool, a relaxation pool, a panoramic Jacuzzi, cold-water pools, a seawater steam sauna, a dry sauna, and a relaxation area.

Cost and Hours: €27 for 2-hour fitness circuit, €32 for 3-hour circuit, daily 8:00-22:00, €3 caps and €1 rental towels, bring a swimsuit or buy one for €33, on the beach at the center of the crescent, Paseo de la Concha, tel. 943-458-856, www.la-perla.net.

Monte Igueldo

For commanding city views (if you ignore the tacky amusements on top), ride the funicular up Monte Igueldo, a mirror image of Monte Urgull. The views over San Sebastián, along the coast, and into the distant green mountains are sensational day or night. The entrance to the funicular is on the road behind the tennis

club on the far western end of Playa de Ondarreta, which extends from Playa de la Concha to the west.

Cost and Hours: Funicular—€3 round-trip; changeable hours but roughly April-Sept Mon-Tue and Thu-Sun 10:00-22:00, closed Wed; Oct-March Mon-Tue and Thu-Fri 11:00-18:00, Sat-Sun 11:00-20:00, closed Wed. If you drive to the top, you'll pay €1.90 to enter. Bus #16 takes you from the Old Town to the base of the funicular in about 10 minutes.

Peine del Viento

Besides the gorgeous view from the top of Monte Igueldo, another classic San Sebastián scene is at this group of three statues by native son Eduardo Chillida (1924-2002). From the base of the Monte Igueldo funicular, walk around the tennis court complex to the edge of the beach. Curly steel prongs "comb the wind" (as the sculptures' name means) among crashing waves. Chillida lived and died on Monte Igueldo, so these sculptures are now considered a memorial to one of Spain's most internationally recognized modern sculptors.

In Gros

Gros and Zurriola Beach

The district of Gros, just east across the river from the Old Town, offers a distinct Californian vibe. Literally a dump a few years ago (gross indeed), today it has a surfing scene on Zurriola Beach (popular with students and German tourists) and a futuristic conference center (described next). Long-term plans call for a new promenade that will arc over the water and under Monte Ulía.

▲Kursaal Conference Center and Kubo Gallery

These two Lego-like boxes (just east and across the river from the Old Town, in Gros) mark the spot of what was once a grand casino, torn down by Franco to discourage gambling. Many locals wanted to rebuild it as it once was, in a similar style to the turn-of-the-20th-century buildings in the Centro, but—in an effort to keep up with the postmodern trends in Bilbao—city leaders opted instead for Rafael Moneo's striking contemporary design. The complex is supposed to resemble the angular rocks that make up the town's breakwater. The Kursaal houses a theater, conference facilities, some gift shops and travel agencies, a restaurant, and the Kubo Gallery. The gallery, located in a small cube farthest from the river, offers temporary exhibits by international artists and promotes contemporary Basque artists. Each exhibit is complemented by a 10-minute video that plays continuously in the gallery theater.

Cost and Hours: Free, Kubo Gallery open Tue-Sun 11:30-13:30 & 17:00-21:00, closed Mon, tel. 943-012-400, www.sala-kubo-aretoa.com.

Sleeping in San Sebastián

Rates in San Sebastián fluctuate with the season. When you see a range of prices in these listings, the top end is for summer (roughly July-Sept), and the low end is for the shoulder season (May-June and Oct); outside of these times, you'll pay even less. Since breakfast is often not included, I've recommended some good options elsewhere in town (see "Eating in San Sebastián," later).

In or near the Old Town

$$$ **Hotel Parma** is a business-class place with 27 fine rooms and family-run attention to detail and service. It stands stately on the edge of the Old Town, away from the bar-scene noise, and overlooks the river and a surfing beach (Sb-€69-102, windowless interior Db-€101-154, view Db-€122-169, breakfast-€11, air-con, modern lounge, free Wi-Fi, Paseo de Salamanca 10, tel. 943-428-893, www.hotelparma.com, hotelparma@hotelparma.com; Iñaki, Pino, Maria Eugenia, and Eider).

$$ **Pensión Edorta** ("Edward"), deep in the Old Town, elegantly mixes wood, brick, and color into nine modern, stylish rooms (D-€40-70, Db-€60-90, extra bed-€20-25, slightly more in Aug, elevator, free Wi-Fi, Calle Puerto 15, tel. 943-423-773, www.pensionedorta.com, info@pensionedorta.com, Javier).

$$ **Pensión Amaiur** is a flowery place with long, narrow halls and 12 great-value rooms within the Old Town. Kind Virginia gives the justifiably popular *pensión* a homey warmth. Some rooms face a *frontón* (*pelota* court), while a couple have private balconies facing the street. Completely renovated in 2013, there are common rooms on each floor to prepare meals—a great spot to hang out and sharing travel tips. Bring earplugs to block out noise from the tapas-going crowd, or ask for an interior room (S-€40-45, quiet interior D-€60-70, Db-€76-90, T-€76-90, Tb-€90-120, kitchen facilities, pay guest computer, free Wi-Fi, next to Santa María Church at Calle 31 de Agosto 44, tel. 943-429-654, www.pensionamaiur.com, amaiur@telefonica.net).

Across the River, in Gros

The pleasant Gros district—San Sebastián's "uptown"—is marked by the super-modern, blocky Kursaal conference center. The nearby Zurriola Beach is popular with surfers. These hotels are less than a five-minute walk from the Old Town. For locations, see the map on page 214.

$$$ **Hotel Arrizul** is bright and fresh, with mod, minimalist decor in each of its 12 rooms (Sb-€55-105, Db-€90-145, Db suite-€110-180, extra bed-€35, breakfast-€7, air-con, elevator, free Wi-Fi, nearby underground parking-€20, Peña y Goñi 1, tel.

Sleep Code

(€1 = about $1.30, country code: 34)

S = Single, **D** = Double/Twin, **T** = Triple, **Q** = Quad, **b** = bathroom, **s** = shower only. Unless otherwise noted, credit cards are accepted and English is spoken, but breakfast is generally not included. This code applies to this chapter's listings in both Spain and France. The word *ostatua* (which you'll see throughout the Basque Country) means "pension." Some Spanish hotels include the 10 percent IVA tax in the room price; others tack it onto your bill.

To help you sort easily through these listings, I've divided the accommodations into three categories based on the price for a standard double room with bath in peak season:

$$$ Higher Priced—Most rooms €90 or more.
  $$ Moderately Priced—Most rooms between €60-90.
   $ Lower Priced—Most rooms €60 or less.

Prices can change without notice; verify the hotel's current rates online or by email. For the best prices, always book direct.

943-322-804, www.arrizul.com, info@arrizulhotel.com). Its sister hotel, **Hotel Arrizul Gros,** is only five blocks away and has 17 rooms with similar decor (slightly lower rates, includes small breakfast) plus 15 spacious apartment rentals (apartments: 2 people-€145-199, 4 people-€185-249, 5 people-€215-279; Iparraguirre 3, same contact info as main Hotel Arrizul).

$$ Pensión Kursaal has 21 basic but colorful and modern rooms in a historic building with white and beige decor (Db-€50-91, family room-€84-141, elevator, pay guest computer, free Wi-Fi, parking-€12, Peña y Goñi 2, tel. 943-292-666, www.pensionesconencanto.com, kursaal@pensionesconencanto.com).

On the Beach

$$$ Hotel Niza, set in the middle of Playa de la Concha, is often booked well in advance. Half of its 40 rooms (some with balconies) overlook the bay. From its chandeliered and plush lounge, a classic elevator takes you to comfortable pastel rooms with wedding-cake molding (tiny interior Sb-€55-68, Db-€132-157, view rooms cost the same—request one when you reserve... but no promises, extra bed-€22, only streetside rooms have air-con, fans on request, great buffet breakfast-€11, free guest computer and Wi-Fi, parking-€15/day—must reserve in advance, Zubieta 56, see map on page 214 for location, tel. 943-426-663, www.hotelniza.com, niza@hotelniza.com). The breakfast room

San Sebastián's Old Town

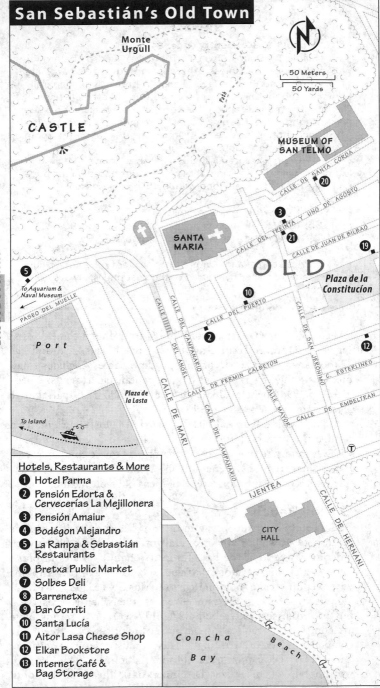

Monte Urgull

CASTLE

MUSEUM OF SAN TELMO

CALLE DE SANTA CORDA

20

3

21

CALLE DEL TREINTA Y UNO DE AGOSTO

CALLE DE JUAN DE BILBAO

19

SANTA MARIA

O L D

Plaza de la Constitución

5

To Aquarium & Naval Museum

PASEO DEL MUELLE

10

CALLE DEL PUERTO

CALLE DEL CAMPANARIO

CALLE DEL ANGEL

CALLE DE SAN JERONIMO

CALLE DE MARI

2

C. ESTERLINES

12

Port

Plaza de la Lasta

CALLE DE FERMIN CALBETON

CALLE MAYOR

CALLE DE EMBELTRAN

To Island

CALLE DEL CAMPANARIO

T

IJENTEA

CITY HALL

CALLE DE HERNANI

Concha Bay

Beach

Hotels, Restaurants & More

1 Hotel Parma
2 Pensión Edorta & Cervecerías La Mejillonera
3 Pensión Amaiur
4 Bodégon Alejandro
5 La Rampa & Sebastián Restaurants
6 Bretxa Public Market
7 Solbes Deli
8 Barrenetxe
9 Bar Gorriti
10 Santa Lucía
11 Aitor Lasa Cheese Shop
12 Elkar Bookstore
13 Internet Café & Bag Storage

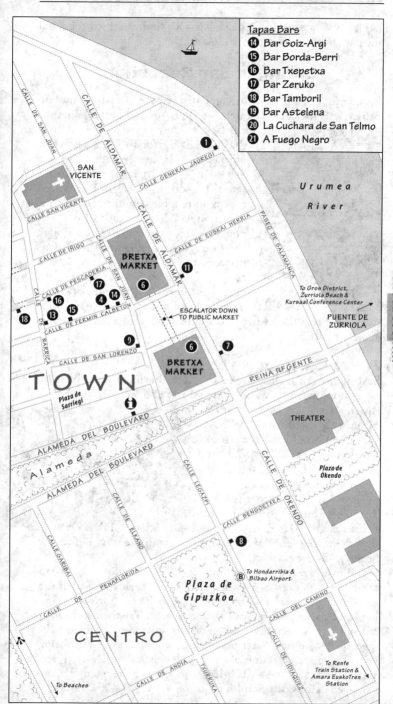

Tapas Bars
14 Bar Goiz-Argi
15 Bar Borda-Berri
16 Bar Txepetxa
17 Bar Zeruko
18 Bar Tamboril
19 Bar Astelena
20 La Cuchara de San Telmo
21 A Fuego Negro

has a sea view and doubles as a bar with light snacks throughout the day (Bar Narru, daily 7:30-24:00).

Eating in San Sebastián

Basque food is regarded as some of the best in Spain, and San Sebastián is the culinary capital of the Basque Country. What the

city lacks in museums and sights, it more than makes up for in food. (For tips on Basque cuisine, see page 205.) San Sebastián is proud of its many Michelin-rated fine-dining establishments, but they require a big commitment of time and money. Most casual visitors will prefer to hop from pub to pub through the Old Town, following the crowds between Basque-font signs. I've listed a couple of solid traditional restaurants, but for the best value and memories, I'd order top-end dishes with top-end wine

in top-end bars. Some places close for siesta in the late afternoon and early evening.

Pintxo Bar-Hopping

San Sebastián's Old Town provides the ideal backdrop for tapas-hopping; just wander the streets and sidle up to the bar

in the liveliest spot. Calle Fermín Calbetón has the best concentration of bars; the streets San Jerónimo and 31 de Agosto are also good. I've listed these top-notch places in order as you progress deeper into the Old Town—though you have to backtrack after Bar Zeruko. Note

that there are plenty of other options along the way. Before you begin, study the sidebar.

Bar Goiz-Argi ("Morning Light"), every local's top recommendation, serves its tiny dishes with pride and attitude. Advertising *pintxos calientes*, they cook each treat for you, allowing you a montage of petite gourmet snacks. Try their *tartaleta de txangurro* (spider-crab spread on bread), spicy *morcilla* (blood sausage made with rice), or their signature *brocheta de gambas* (shrimp kebab). A good selection of open wine bottles are clearly priced and displayed on the shelf (great prices, no chairs, congregate at bar, open daily, Calle Fermín Calbetón 4, tel. 943-425-204).

Do the *Txikiteo:* A Tapas Cheat Sheet

Txikiteo (chih-kee-TAY-oh) is the Basque word for hopping from bar to bar, enjoying small sandwiches and tiny snacks (*pintxos,* PEEN-chohs) and glasses of wine. Local competition drives small bars to lay out the most appealing array of *pintxos*. The selection is amazing, but the key to eating well here is going for the *pintxos calientes*—the hot tapas advertised on blackboards and cooked to order. Tapas are best, freshest, and accompanied by the most vibrant crowd from 12:00 to 14:00 and from 20:00 to 22:30. Watch what's being served—the locals know each bar's specialty. No matter how much you like a place, just order one dish; you want to be mobile.

Later in the evening, bars get more crowded and challenging for tourists. To get service amid the din, speak loudly and directly (little sweet voices get ignored), with no extra words. Expect to share everything. Double-dipping is encouraged. It's rude to put a dirty napkin on the table; it belongs on the floor.

Basque tapas bars distinguish themselves by laying out big platters of help-yourself goodies. This user-friendly system lets you point to—or simply take—what looks good, rather than navigating a menu. If you can't get the bartender's attention to serve you a particular *pintxo,* don't be shy—just grab it and a napkin, and munch away. You pay when you leave; just keep a mental note of the tapas you've eaten. There's a code of honor. Everyone is part of the extended Basque family.

If you want a meal instead of *pintxos,* some bars—even ones that look only like bars from the street—have attached dining rooms, usually in the back.

For a full list of Spanish tapas terms (which work here in Basque Country, too), see page 34. Here are a few terms unique to Basque bars:

pintxos: tapas (small plates)

antxoas: anchovies (not the cured, heavily salted kind you always hated)

txampis (chahm-pees): mushrooms

txangurro (chan-GOO-roh): spider crab, a delicacy, often mixed with onions, tomatoes, and wine, served hot or made into a spread to put on bread

marmitako: tuna stew

ttoro: seafood stew

cazuelas: hot meal-size servings (like *raciones* in Spanish)

txakoli (chah-koh-LEE): fresh white wine, poured from high to aerate it and to add sparkle. Good with seafood, and therefore fits the local cuisine well.

zurito (thoo-REE-toh): small beer

Zenbat da?: "How much?" (to ask for the bill)

BASQUE COUNTRY

Bar Borda-Berri (loosely, "Mountain Hut"), a couple doors down, features a more low-key ambience and top-quality €3 *pintxos*. There are only a few items at the bar; check out the chalkboard menu for today's options, order, and they'll cook it fresh. The specialty here is melt-in-your-mouth beef cheeks *(carrillera de tenera)* in a red-wine sauce, risotto with wild mushrooms, and foie gras (grilled goose liver) with apple jelly, which is even better paired with a glass of their best red wine (closed Mon, Calle Fermín Calbetón 12, tel. 943-430-342).

Bar Txepetxa is *the* place for anchovies. A plastic circle displaying a variety of *antxoas* tapas makes choosing your anchovy treat easy. These fish are fresh—not cured and salted like those most Americans hate (€2.50/*pintxo*, Tue lunch only, closed Sun-Mon, Calle Pescadería 5, tel. 943-422-227).

Bar Zeruko offers fun for molecular gastronomy fans in a bright, modern setting. The selections are seasonal, but look for *hoguera*, a piece of cod served over a smoking mini-hearth with a side of "liquid" salad. Award-winning chef Joxean Calvo continually surprises his patrons (€5 *pintxos*, Tue-Sat 11:00-16:00 & 19:00-24:00, Sun 19:00-24:00, closed Mon, Calle Pescadería 10, tel. 943-423-451, www.barzeruko.com).

Bar Tamboril is a traditional spot right on the main square favored for its seafood, mushrooms *(txampis tamboril)*, and anchovy tempura along with its good prices. Their list of hot *pintxos* (grab the little English menu on the bar) makes you want to break the one-tapa-per-stop rule (Calle Pescadería 2, tel. 943-423-507).

Bar Astelena, across the square from Tamboril, serves a delicious blend of traditional and modern plates, all thoughtfully presented. Try any of the specials, particularly the *solomillo a lo pobre* (small sirloin fillet with mini-fries and a fried egg). Other standouts include *rabo de buey* (oxtail) and capellini-wrapped prawns. There's no English menu, but the staff is happy to help translate (€3-4 *pintxos*, Calle de Iñigo 1, tel. 943-425-245).

La Cuchara de San Telmo, with cooks taught by a big-name Basque chef, Alex Mondiel, is a cramped place that devotes as much space to its thriving kitchen as its bar. It has nothing precooked and set on the bar—order your mini-gourmet plates with a spirit of adventure from the constantly changing blackboard. Their foie gras with apple jelly is rightfully famous (€3 *pintxos*, closed Mon, tucked away on a lonely alley called Santa Corda behind Museum of San Telmo at 31 de Agosto #28, tel. 943-435-446).

A Fuego Negro is cool and upscale compared with the others, with a hip, slicker vibe and a blackboard menu of *pintxos* and drinks (there's an English translation sheet). They have a knack for mixing gourmet pretentiousness with whimsy here: Try their *arroz, tomate, y un huevo* (risotto with tomato and egg); *bakailu* (cod); and *regaliz* (licorice ice cream) trio for a unique taste-bud experience (€3.60). Enjoy their serious and extensive wine selection (closed Mon, 31 de Agosto #31, tel. 650-135-373). An inviting little section in the back makes this a sit-down dining opportunity.

Cervecerías La Mejillonera is famous among students for its big, cheap beers, *patatas bravas,* and mussels ("*tigres*" is the spicy favorite). A long, skinny stainless-steel bar and lots of photos make ordering easy—this is the only place in town where you pay when served. Throw your mussels shells on the floor like the locals (Calle Puerto 15, tel. 943-428-465).

Restaurants

Bodégon Alejandro is a good spot for modern Basque cuisine in a traditional cellar setting (three-course fixed-price lunch-€20, Tue-Sun 13:00-15:30 & 20:30-22:30 except closed Sun night, closed Mon, in Old Town on Calle Fermín Calbetón 4, tel. 943-427-158).

Seafood Along the Port: For seafood with a salty sailor's view, check out the half-dozen hardworking, local-feeling restaurants that line the harbor on the way to the aquarium. **La Rampa** is an upscale eatery, specializing in crab *(txangurro)* and lobster dishes and seafood *parillada* (€30-50 for dinner, closed Tue evenings, also closed Wed and Sun in winter, Paseo Muelle/Kaiko Pasealekua 26-27, tel. 943-421-652, www.restaurantelarampa.com). Also along here, locals like **Sebastián** (more traditional, closed Tue).

Picnics and Takeout

A picnic on the beach or atop Monte Urgull is a tempting option. You can assemble a bang-up spread at the **Bretxa Public Market** at Plaza de Sarriegi (described earlier).

Solbes, just across the street from the Bretxa Public Market, has a reputation as *the* gourmet deli store in the Old Town. There's a remarkable wine selection in the back cellar, plus high-quality cured meats and cheeses out front. Be sure to price fruits and veggies on the scale yourself to avoid confusion at checkout (Mon-Sat 9:00-20:30, closed Sun, Calle Aldamar 4, tel. 943-427-818).

Upscale **Barrenetxe** has an amazing array of breads, prepared foods, and some of the best desserts in town. In business since 1699, their somewhat formal service is justified. There's also coffee served in a new bar section (daily 8:00-20:00, Plaza de Guipúzcoa 9, tel. 943-424-482).

Breakfast

If your hotel doesn't provide breakfast—or even if it does—consider one of these places. The first is a traditional stand-up bar; the second is a greasy spoon.

Bar Gorriti, delightfully local, is packed with market workers

BASQUE COUNTRY

and shoppers starting their day. You'll stand at the bar and choose a hot-off-the-grill *francesca jamón* omelet (fluffy mini-omelet sandwich topped with a slice of ham) and other goodies (€2 each). This and a good cup of coffee makes for a very Basque breakfast. By the time you get there for breakfast, many market workers will be taking their mid-morning break (daily, breakfast served 7:00-10:00, facing the side of the big white market building at San Juan 3, tel. 943-428-353).

Santa Lucía, a 1950s-style diner, is ideal for a cheap Old Town breakfast or *churros* break (*churros* are like deep-fried doughnut sticks that can be dipped in pudding-like hot chocolate). Photos of two dozen different breakfasts decorate the walls, and plates of fresh *churros* keep patrons happy. Grease is liberally applied to the grill...from a squeeze bottle (daily 8:30-21:30, Calle Puerto 6, tel. 943-425-019).

San Sebastián Connections

By Train

San Sebastián has two train stations: RENFE and Amara EuskoTren (described under "Arrival in San Sebastián" on page 208). The station you use depends on your destination.

RENFE Station: This station handles long-distance destinations within Spain (most of which require reservations). Connections include **Irún** (8/day, 25 minutes), **Hendaye,** France (4/day, 30 minutes; better connections on EuskoTren, described below), **Madrid** (4/day, 5.25-7.25 hours), **Burgos** (6/day, 3 hours), **León** (2/day, 5 hours), **Pamplona** (2/day, 1.75 hours), **Salamanca** (5/day, 6 hours), **Barcelona** (2/day, 6 hours), and **Santiago de Compostela** (1/day direct, 10.5 hours).

Amara EuskoTren Station: If you're going into France, take the regional Topo train (which leaves from the Amara EuskoTren Station) over the French border into **Hendaye** (usually 4/hour Mon-Fri, 2/hour Sat-Sun, 35 minutes). From Hendaye, connect to France's SNCF network (www.sncf.com), where connections include **Paris** (6/day direct, 5.5-6 hours; 12-hour night train, weekends only off-season, reservations required). Unfortunately, San Sebastián's EuskoTren Station doesn't have information on Paris-bound trains from Hendaye. EuskoTren tickets to Hendaye must be used within two hours of purchase (or else they expire).

Also leaving from San Sebastián's Amara EuskoTren Station are slow regional trains to destinations in Spain's Basque region, including **Bilbao** (hourly, 2.5 hours—the bus is faster, EuskoTren info: tel. 902-543-210, www.euskotren.es). Although the train ride from San Sebastián to Bilbao takes twice as long as the bus, it passes through more interesting countryside. The Basque Country shows off its trademark green and gray: lush green vegetation and gray clouds. It's an odd mix of heavy industrial factories, small homegrown veggie gardens, streams, and every kind of livestock you can imagine.

By Bus

San Sebastián's "bus station," called Amara (for the neighborhood), is a congregation of bus parking spots next to the big Hotel Amara Plaza, at the Plaza Pío XII (on the river, four blocks south of EuskoTren Station; take bus #21, #26, or #28 from Boulevard). Some schedules are posted at various stops, but confirm departure times. You must buy your tickets in advance at the bus companies, with offices on either side of the block north of the station area (toward downtown, along Avenida de Sancho el Sabio and Paseo de Vízcaya). Bus tickets are not available from the driver. The Pesa office, which serves St-Jean-de-Luz and Bilbao, is located at Avenida de Sancho el Sabio 33 (tel. 902-101-210, www.pesa.net). The Alsa office—which serves Madrid, Burgos, and León—is just beyond Pesa at Sancho el Sabio 31 (tel. 902-422-242, www.alsa.es). Conda—which serves Pamplona and Bayonne—shares an office with Alsa (tel. 943-461-064, www.conda.es). The Vibasa office—which serves Burgos, Pamplona, and Barcelona—is on the other side of the block along the river, at Calle Vizcaya 15 (closed 13:30-15:00, tel. 902-101-363, www.vibasa.com).

From San Sebastián, buses go to **Bilbao** (2/hour, hourly on weekends, 6:30-22:00, 1.25 hours, get ticket from Pesa office, departs from Amara; morning buses fill with tourists, commuters, and students, so consider buying your ticket the day before; once in Bilbao, buses leave you at Termibús stop with easy tram connections to the Guggenheim modern-art museum); **Bilbao Airport** (a Pesa bus leaves directly from Plaza Pío XII, hourly, 1.25 hours, get tickets from Pesa office), **Pamplona** (8-10/day, 1 hour, Conda office), **León** (1/day, 6 hours, Alsa office), **Madrid** (8/day, 6 hours direct, otherwise 7 hours; a few departures direct to Madrid's Barajas Airport, 5.25 hours; Alsa office), **Burgos** (7/day, 2-3.25 hours, Alsa or Vibasa office), and **Barcelona** (2/day and 1 at night, 7 hours, Vibasa office).

To visit **Hondarribia** (described next), you can catch bus #E21 or #E23 much closer to the center at Plaza de Gipuzkoa (1 block south of TI; about 3/hour, 35 minutes, #E21 goes to airport en route to Hondarribia).

Buses to French Basque Country: A bus goes from San Sebastián's Amara bus station to **St-Jean-de-Luz** (Mon-Sat only, 2/day at 9:00 and 14:30, none on Sun, 1 hour, return trips at 12:45

and 19:15, only 1/week off-season, get ticket from Pesa office), then continues directly to **Biarritz** (1.25 hours from San Sebastián) and **Bayonne** (1.5 hours from San Sebastián).

Fuenterrabía / Hondarribia

For a taste of small-town *País Vasco,* dip into this enchanting, seldom-visited town. It's more commonly known by its Euskara

name, Hondarribia, than the Spanish version, Fuenterrabía. Much smaller and easier to manage than San Sebastián, and also closer to France (across the picturesque Bay of Txingudi from Hendaye), Hondarribia allows travelers a stress-free opportunity to enjoy Basque culture. While it's easy to think of this as a border town (between France and Spain), culturally it's in the middle of the Basque Country.

The town comes in two parts: the lower port town and the historic, balcony-lined streets of the hilly and walled upper town. The upper town, which feels quite manicured, is a delightful place to poke around if you have time. The main square is fronted by Charles V's austere, oddly squat castle (now a parador inn—see next page). You can follow the TI's self-guided tour of the Old Town (English brochure available) or just lose yourself within the walls to discover hidden plazas and former royal residences. In the modern lower town, straight shopping streets serve a local clientele, and a pleasant walkway takes strollers along the beach.

Tourist Information: There are two TIs. One is located on the main square, Plaza de Armas, across from the parador; the other is at Minatera 9, near the port (both July-Sept daily 10:30-13:30 & 15:30-20:00; Oct-June Tue-Sat 10:00-13:30 & 15:30-18:30, Sun 10:00-14:00, closed Mon; tel. 943-645-458, www .bidasoaturismo.com).

Arrival in Hondarribia: For some beach time, drivers can use the metered parking by the port (marked with blue lines, prepay for parking at machine). If you're here during the week off-season, the giant lot on the beach is free. Drivers who only want to explore the Old Town should follow signs to *Casco Viejo* and park at the free, tree-lined lot immediately across from the gate in the city wall; look for its giant coat-of-arms (Alameda de Daniel Vázquez Díaz). Buses into town stop near the main square.

Sleeping in Hondarribia: Accommodations are pricey here, but it's a nice small-town alternative to San Sebastián. **$$$ Parador El Emperador,** with 34 rooms housed in a former imperial fortress, is the town's splurge. Tourists are allowed to have sangria in the *muy* cool bar, though the terraces are for guests only (Sb-€188, Db-€248, Db with view-€270, includes breakfast, elevator, free Wi-Fi, Plaza de Armas 14, tel. 943-645-500, www.parador.es, hondarribia@parador.es). **$$ Hotel San Nikolas,** facing the parador from across the square, offers a more affordable alternative, with 17 nicely appointed rooms (many with views) above a local café (Sb-€41-61, Db-€66-83, Db with sea view-€83-99, higher price is for mid-July-mid-Sept, can be even cheaper Mon-Thu off-season, elevator, free Wi-Fi, Plaza de Armas 6, tel. 943-644-278, www.hotelsannikolas.es, info@hotelsannikolas.es).

Hondarribia Connections: From Hondarribia, buses go to **San Sebastián**'s Plaza de Gipuzkoa (about 3/hour, 35 minutes on express buses #E23 or #E21, departs near main square—#E21 also stops at airport; or twice as long on local public buses #E26 and night bus #E77) and to **Irún** near the French border (2/hour, 20 minutes, buses #E25 and night bus #E77). A **boat** goes to **Hendaye** (4/hour in summer, 2/hour off-season, 10 minutes, runs about 11:00-19:00 or until dark).

Route Tips for Drivers: Leaving San Sebastián passing Zurriola Beach in Gros, first follow signs to *Irún/Frantxia;* signs for *Hondarribia* appear after about 20 minutes. If continuing on to St-Jean-de-Luz, signs to *Baiona* lead back to the main highway and the French border. Have coins ready to chuck into the automatic toll booth.

The Bay of Biscay

Between the two Spanish Basque cities of San Sebastián and Bilbao is a beautiful countryside of rolling green hills and a scenic, jagged coastline that looks almost Celtic. Aside from a scenic joyride, this area merits a visit for the cute fishing and resort town of Lekeitio.

Route Tips for Drivers

San Sebastián and Bilbao are connected in about an hour and a quarter by the A-8 expressway (€9.50 toll). While speedy and scenic, this route is nothing compared to some of the free, but slower, back roads with lots of twists and turns that connect the two towns.

If side-tripping from San Sebastián to Bilbao, you can drive directly there on A-8 in the morning. But coming home to San Sebastián, consider this more scenic route: Take A-8 until the turnoff for Guernica (look for *Amorebieta/Gernika-Lumo* sign), then head up into the hills on BI-635. After visiting Guernica, follow signs along the very twisty BI-2238 road to Lekeitio (about 40 minutes). Leave Lekeitio on the road just above the beach; after crossing the bridge, take the left fork and follow BI-3438 to Markina/Ondarroa (with a striking modern bridge and nice views back into the steep town; follow *portua* signs for free 30-minute parking at the port). Continue to Mutriku and Deba as you hug the coastline east toward San Sebastián. There's a good photo-op pullout as you climb along the coast just after Deba. Soon after, you'll have two opportunities to get on the A-8 (blue signs) for a quicker approach to San Sebastián; but if you've enjoyed the scenery so far, stick with the coastal road (white signs, N-634) through Zumaia and Getaria, rejoining the expressway at the high-class resort town of Zarautz.

Lequeitio/Lekeitio

More commonly known by its Euskara name, Lekeitio (leh-KAY-tee-oh)—rather than the Spanish version, Lequeitio—this small

fishing port has an idyllic harbor and a fine beach. It's just over an hour by bus from Bilbao and an easy stop for drivers, and is protected from the Bay of Biscay by a sand spit that leads to the lush and rugged little San Nicolás Island. Hake boats fly their Basque flags, and proud Basque locals black out the Spanish translations on street signs.

Lekeitio is a teeming resort during July and August (when its population of 7,000 triples as big-city Basque folks move into their vacation condos). Isolated from the modern rat race by its location down a long, windy little road, it's a backwater fishing village the rest of the year.

Sights here are humble, though the 15th-century St. Mary's Parish Church is a good example of Basque Gothic, with an impressive altarpiece (Mon-Sat 8:00-12:00 & 17:00-19:30, Sun 9:00-12:30). The town's back lanes are reminiscent of old days when

fishing was the only industry. Fisherwomen sell their husbands' catches each morning from about 10:30 along the port. The golden crescent beach is as inviting as the sandbar, which—at low tide—challenges you to join the seagulls out on San Nicolás Island.

The best beach in the area for surfers and sun lovers is Playas Laga (follow signs off the road from Bilbao to Lekeitio). Relatively uncrowded, it's popular with body-boarders.

Getting There: Buses connect Lekeitio with **Bilbao** (hourly, 1.25 hours; same bus stops at **Guernica**, 40 minutes) and **San Sebastián** (4/day Mon-Fri, 2/day Sat-Sun, 1.25 hours). But this destination is most logical for those with a car. Drivers can park most easily in the lot near the bus station. Exit the station left, walk along the road, then take the first right (down the steep, cobbled street) to reach the harbor. There is no luggage storage in town.

Tourist Information: The TI faces the fish market next to the harbor (July-Aug daily 10:00-14:00 & 16:00-20:00; Sept-June Tue-Sat 10:30-13:30 & 16:00-19:00, Sun 10:00-14:00, closed Mon; tel. 946-844-017, www.lekeitio.com).

Sleeping in Lekeitio: **$$ Emperatriz Zita Hotel** is the obvious best bet for your beach-town break. It's named for Empress Zita (who lived here in exile after her Habsburg family lost World War I and was booted from Vienna). Zita's mansion burned down, but this 1930s rebuild still has a belle époque aristocratic charm, solid classy furniture in 42 spacious rooms, real hardwood floors, and an elegant spa in the basement. Located on the beach a few steps from the harbor, with handy free parking and a view restaurant, it's a fine value (Sb-€60-77, Db-€70-101, Db suite-€103-134, views—ask for *vistas del mar*—are worth it, prices can be higher July-Aug and Sat all year, extra bed-€25, breakfast-€10, elevator, free Wi-Fi, Santa Elena Etorbidea, tel. 946-842-655, www.aisiahoteles.com, lekeitio@aisiahoteles.com). The hotel also has a thermal seawater pool, a Jacuzzi, and a full-service spa (all available at reasonable prices).

Eating in Lekeitio: Although it's sleepy off-season, the harbor promenade is made-to-order in summer for a slow meal or a tapas crawl. **Restaurante Kaia** offers a mostly seafood menu, with a €15 fixed-priced lunch (Tue-Sat lunch and dinner, Sun dinner only, closed Mon, on the harbor at Txatxo Kaia 5, tel. 946-840-284).

Guernica / Gernika

The workaday market town of Guernica (GEHR-nee-kah) is near and dear to Basques and pacifists alike. This is the site of the Gernikako Arbola—the oak tree of Gernika, which marked the assembly point where the regional Basque leaders, the Lords of Bizkaia, met through the ages to assert their people's freedom. Long the symbolic heart of Basque separatism, it was also a natural target for Franco (and Hitler) in the Spanish Civil War—resulting in an infamous bombing raid that left the town in ruins (see "The Bombing of Guernica" sidebar), as immortalized by Picasso in his epic work *Guernica*.

Today's Guernica, rebuilt after being bombed flat in 1937 and nothing special at first glance, holds some of the Basque Country's more compelling museums. And Basque bigwigs have reclaimed the town as a meeting point—they still elect their figurehead leader on that same ancient site under the oak tree.

Orientation to Guernica

Guernica is small (about 17,000 inhabitants) and compact, focused on its large market hall (Monday market 9:00-14:00).

Tourist Information: The TI is in the town center (daily 10:00-14:00 & 16:00-18:00, longer hours in summer, Artekalea 8, tel. 946-255-892, www.gernika-lumo.net). Pick up the free, good town map. If you'll be visiting both the Peace Museum and the Basque Country Museum, buy the €6 combo-ticket here.

Arrival in Guernica: Drivers will find a handy parking lot near the train tracks at the end of town. Buses drop off passengers along the main road skirting the town center. No matter where you enter, the TI is well-signed (look for yellow *i* signs)—head there first to get your bearings.

Sights in Guernica

I've arranged Guernica's sights in the order of a handy sightseeing loop from the TI.

• *Exit the TI to the left, cross the street, and walk up the left side of the square, where you'll find the...*

▲Gernika Peace Museum

Because of the brutality of the Guernica bombing, and the powerful Picasso painting that documented the atrocities of war, the name "Guernica" has become synonymous with pacifism. This thoughtfully presented exhibit has taken a great tragedy of 20th-century history and turned it into a compelling cry for peace in our time. Borrow the English translations at the entry, request an English showing of the movie upstairs, and head up through the two-floor exhibit. The first floor begins by considering different ways of defining "peace." You'll then enter an apartment and hear a local woman, Begoña, describe her typical Guernica life in the 1930s...until the bombs dropped (a mirror effect shows you the devastating aftermath). You'll exit through the rubble into an exhibit about the town's history, with a special emphasis on the bombing. Finally, a 10-minute movie shows grainy footage of the destruction, and ends with a collage of peaceful reconciliations in recent history—in Ireland, South Africa, Guatemala, Australia, and Berlin. On the second floor, Picasso's famous painting is superimposed on three transparent panels to highlight different themes. The exhibit concludes with a survey of the recent history of conflicts in the Basque Country.

Cost and Hours: €5; Tue-Sat 10:00-19:00, Sun 10:00-14:00, closed Mon; Foru Plaza 1, tel. 946-270-213, www.peacemuseum guernica.org.

• *Continue uphill to the big church. At the road above the church, you can turn right and walk a block and a half to find an underwhelming tile replica of* **Picasso's Guernica** *(left-hand side of the street). Or you can head left to find the next two attractions.*

▲Basque Country Museum (Euskal Herria Museoa)

This well-presented exhibit offers a good overview of Basque culture and history. Start in the ground-floor theater (Room 4) and see the overview video (request English). Follow the suggested route and climb chronologically up through Basque history, with the necessary help of an included audioguide. You'll find exhibits about traditional Basque architecture and landscape, lots of antique maps, and a region-by-region rundown of the Basque Country's seven territories. One interesting map shows Basque emigration over the centuries—including to the US. The top floor is the most engaging, highlighting Basque culture: sports, dances, cuisine, myths and legends, music, and language, plus a wraparound movie featuring images of a proud people living the Basque lifestyle.

Cost and Hours: €3, free on Sat, includes audioguide—except on Sat, open Tue-Sat 10:00-14:00 & 16:00-19:00, Sun 10:30-14:30, closed Mon, Allendesalazar 5, tel. 946-255-451.

The Bombing of Guernica

During the civil war, Guernica was the site of one of history's most reviled wartime acts.

Monday, April 26, 1937, was market day, when the town was filled with farmers and peasants from the countryside selling their wares. At about 16:40 in the afternoon, a German warplane appeared ominously on the horizon, and proceeded to bomb bridges and roads surrounding the town. Soon after, more planes arrived. Three hours of relentless saturation bombing followed, as the German and Italian air forces pummeled the city with incendiary firebombs. People running through the streets or along the green hillsides were strafed with machine-gun fire. As the sun fell low in the sky and the planes finally left, hundreds—or possibly thousands—had been killed, and many more wounded. (Because Guernica was filled with refugees from other besieged towns, nobody is sure how many perished.)

Hearing word of the attack in Paris, Pablo Picasso—who had been commissioned to paint a mural for the 1937 world's fair—was devastated at the news of what had gone on in Guernica. Inspired, he painted what many consider the greatest antiwar work of art, ever. (For more on this great painting, now displayed in Madrid, see page 472.)

Why did the bombings happen? Reportedly, Adolf Hitler wanted an opportunity to try out his new saturation-bombing attack strategy. Spanish dictator Francisco Franco, who was fed up with the independence-minded Basques, offered up their historic capital as a candidate for the experiment.

There's no doubt that Guernica, a gateway to Bilbao, was strategically located. And yet, a small munitions factory that supplied anti-Franco forces with pistols oddly wasn't hit by the bombing. Historians believe most of the targets here were far from strategic. Why attack so mercilessly, during the daytime, on market day, when innocent casualties would be maximized? Like the famous silent scream of Picasso's *Guernica* mother, this question haunts pacifists everywhere to this day.

▲▲Gernika Assembly House and Oak Tree

In the Middle Ages, the meeting point for the Basque general assembly was under the old oak tree on the gentle hillside above Guernica. The tradition continues today, as the tree stands at the center of a modest but interesting complex celebrating Basque culture and self-government.

Cost and Hours: Free, daily 10:00-14:00 & 16:00-18:00, June-Sept until 19:00, on Allendesalazar, tel. 946-251-138.

➋ Self-Guided Tour: As you enter the grounds past the guard hut, on the right you'll see an **old tree trunk** in the small colonnade dating from the 1700s. Basque traditions have lived much, much longer than a single tree's life span. When one dies, it's replaced with a new one. This is the oldest surviving trunk.

The exhibit has four parts: a stained-glass window room, the oak-tree courtyard, the assembly chamber, and a basement theater (request the 10-minute video in English that extols the virtues and beauties of the Basque Country).

Inside the main building, request a copy of the English-language brochure that describes in detail the importance of this

site. First find the impressive **stained-glass window room.** The computer video here gives a good six-minute overview of the exhibit (plays in English when you click). The gorgeous stained-glass ceiling is rife with Basque symbolism. The elderly leader stands under the oak holding a book with the

"Old Law" *(Lege Zarra),* which are the laws by which the Basques lived for centuries. Below him are groups representing the three traditional career groups of this industrious people: sailors and fishermen; miners and steelworkers; and farmers. Behind them all is a classic Basque landscape: On the left is the sea, and on the right are rolling green hills dotted with red-and-white homes. Small, square panels around the large window represent all the important towns in the region, with Guernica's oak tree easy to pinpoint.

Out back, a Greek-style tribune surrounds the fateful **oak tree.** This little fella is from 2005, planted here when the earlier one "finished out its life cycle" after standing here for nearly a century and a half. This tree is a descendant of that one, and possibly of all the trees here since ancient times. This location is where Basque leaders have met in solidarity across the centuries.

In the Middle Ages, after Basque lands became part of Castile, Castilian kings came here to pledge respect to the old Basque laws. When Basque independence came under fire in the 19th century, patriots rallied by singing a song about this tree ("Ancient and holy symbol / Let thy fruit fall worldwide / While we gaze in adoration / Upon thee, our blessed tree"). After the 1937 bombing, in which this tree's predecessor was miraculously unscathed, hundreds of survivors sought refuge under its branches. Today, although official representatives in the Spanish government are elected at the polls, the Basques choose their figurehead leader, the Lehendakari ("First One"), in this same spot.

Step back inside and enter the **assembly chamber**—like a mini-parliament for the region of Bizkaia ("Vízcaya" in Spanish, "Biscay" in English; one of the seven Basque territories). Notice the holy water and the altar—a sign that there's no separation of church and state in Basque politics. The large paintings above the doors show the swearing of allegiance to the Old Law. Portraits of 26 former Lords of Bizkaia maintain a watchful eye over the current assembly's decisions.

Guernica Connections

Guernica is well-connected to **Bilbao** (2 trains/hour, 50 minutes, arrive at Bilbao's Atxuri Station; also 4 buses/hour, 40 minutes) and to **Lekeitio** (hourly buses, 40 minutes). Connections are sparser on weekends. The easiest way to connect to San Sebastián is via Bilbao, though you can also get there on the slow "Topo" EuskoTren train (transfer in Lemoa, about 3-4 hours).

Bilbao / Bilbo

In recent years, Bilbao (bil-BOW, rhymes with "cow") has seen a transformation like no other Spanish city. Entire sectors of the industrial city's long-depressed port have been cleared away to allow construction of a new convention center and the stunning Guggenheim Museum.

Bilbao retains less and less of its grim industrial past...and looks toward an exciting new future. But some of the grime hangs on. The city mingles beautiful but crumbling old buildings; eyesore high-rise apartment blocks; brand-new super-modern additions to the skyline (such as the Guggenheim and its neighbor, the 40-story Iberdrola Tower); and, scattered in the lush green hillsides all around the horizon, typical whitewashed Basque homes with red roofs. Bilbao enjoys a vitality and well-worn charm befitting its status as a regional capital of culture and industry.

Planning Your Time
For most visitors, the Guggenheim is the main draw (and many could spend the entire day there). But with a little more time, it's also worth hopping on a tram to explore the atmospheric Old Town (Casco Viejo). With extra time, take the Mount Artxanda funicular for a breathtaking overview of the entire area. Don't bother coming to Bilbao on Monday, when virtually all its museums—including the almighty Guggenheim—are closed (except in July-Aug).

Orientation to Bilbao

When you're in the center, Bilbao feels smaller than its population of 350,000. The city, nestled amidst green hillsides, hugs the Bilbao

River as it curves through town. The Guggenheim is more or less centrally located near the top of that curve; the bus station is to the west; the Old Town (Casco Viejo) and train stations are to the east; and a super-convenient and fun-to-ride green tram called the EuskoTran ties it all together.

Tourist Information

Bilbao's handiest TI is next to the **Guggenheim** (look for the *i* sign on top of a pole). Pick up a city map and the bimonthly *Bilbao Guide.* If you're interested in something beyond the Guggenheim, ask about walking tours in English (€4.50, Sat-Sun year-round, more often in summer) and grab the Bilbao museums brochure, describing museums dedicated to everything from bullfighting and seafaring to sports and Holy Week processionals (July-Aug daily 10:00-19:00; Sept-June Mon-Fri 10:00-19:00, Sat 11:00-19:00, Sun 11:00-15:00; tel. 944 795 760, www.bilbao.net). Convenient TI branches are open at the **airport** (daily), at the **Plaza del Ensanche** near the Zubizuri Bridge (Mon-Fri only), and at Arriaga Theater at **Plaza de Arriaga,** near the Old Town (daily, but the Arriaga TI will likely close sometime in 2014).

Arrival in Bilbao

Most travelers—whether arriving by train, bus, or car—will want to go straight to the Guggenheim. Thanks to a perfectly planned tram system (EuskoTran), this couldn't be easier. From any point of entry, simply buy a €1.40 single-ride ticket at a user-friendly green machine (€3.85 for an all-day pass), hop on a green-and-gray tram, enjoy the Muzak, and head for the Guggenheim stop (there's only one line, trams come every 10-15 minutes, tel. 902-543-210, www.euskotren.es—choose "Tranvía Bilbao"). When you buy your ticket, validate it immediately at the machine (follow the red arrow), since you can't do it once on board. If you get lost, ask: "*¿Dónde está el Guggenheim?*"

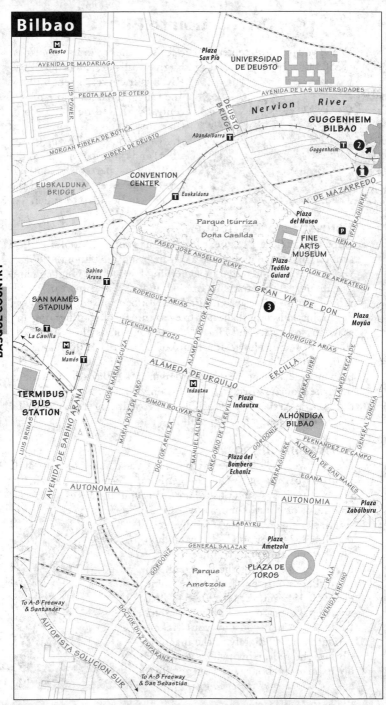

Bilbao

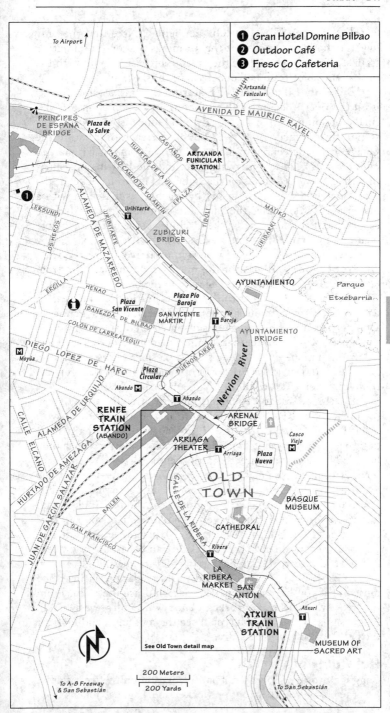

❶ Gran Hotel Domine Bilbao
❷ Outdoor Café
❸ Fresc Co Cafeteria

To Airport

PRINCIPES
DE ESPAÑA
BRIDGE

AVENIDA DE MAURICE RAVEL

Artxanda
Funicular

Plaza de
la Salve

PASEO CAMPO DE VOLANTÍN

HUERTAS DE LA VILLA

CÁSTAÑOS

ARTXANDA
FUNICULAR
STATION

EPALZA

TÍBOLI

MATIKO

ALAMEDA DE MAZARREDO

URIBITARTE

Uribitarte

ZUBIZURI
BRIDGE

URIBARRI

LERSUNDI

LOS HEROS

ERCILLA

HENAO

IBAÑEZDA DE BILBAO

COLÓN DE LARREATEGUI

DIEGO LÓPEZ DE HARO

Moyúa

ALAMEDA DE URQUIJO

CALLE ELCANO

HURTADO DE AMEZAGA

JUAN DE GARCÍA SALAZAR

BAILÉN

SAN FRANCISCO

Plaza
San Vicente

SAN VICENTE
MÁRTIR

Plaza Pío
Baroja

AYUNTAMIENTO

Parque
Etxebarria

Pío
Baroja

AYUNTAMIENTO
BRIDGE

Nervión River

BUENOS AIRES

Plaza
Circular

Abando

Abando

RENFE
TRAIN
STATION
(ABANDO)

ARRIAGA
THEATER

Arriaga

ARENAL
BRIDGE

Casco
Viejo

Plaza
Nueva

OLD
TOWN

BASQUE
MUSEUM

CATHEDRAL

CALLE DE LA RIBERA

Ribera

LA
RIBERA
MARKET

SAN
ANTÓN

Atxuri

ATXURI
TRAIN
STATION

MUSEUM OF
SACRED ART

See Old Town detail map

N

200 Meters

200 Yards

To A-8 Freeway
& San Sebastián

To San Sebastián

(DOHN-day ay-STAH el "Guggenheim"). Note that the only luggage storage in town is at the Termibús Station (not at either train station). Don't confuse the green tram (Eusko*Tran*) with the slow, scenic, blue train to San Sebastián (Eusko*Tren*).

By Train: Bilbao's **RENFE station** (serving most of Spain) is on the river in central Bilbao. The train station is on top of a small shopping mall (a Europcar rental office is near the train-station ticket office, tel. 944-239-390). To reach the tram to the Guggenheim, descend into the stores. Leave from the exit marked *Hurtado de Amézaga,* and go right to find the BBK bank. Enter, find the *Automatikoa* door on the right, and buy your ticket at the green machine marked *Abando* (the machine is mixed in with a bunch of ATMs). Leave the bank and continue right around the corner. Validate your ticket at the machines at the tram stop before boarding the tram (direction: La Casilla).

Trains coming from San Sebastián arrive at the riverside **Atxuri Station,** southeast of the museum. From here the tram (direction: La Casilla) follows the river to the Guggenheim stop.

By Bus: Buses stop at the **Termibús Station** on the western edge of downtown, about a mile southwest of the Guggenheim. Don't expect a real building—it's just a covered parking lot with small portables. The tram (San Mamés Station) is on the road just below the station—look for the steel *CTB* sign or follow the *Tran* signs. Buy and validate a ticket at the machine, and hop on the tram (direction: Atxuri) to the Guggenheim or Old Town.

By Plane: Bilbao's compact, modern, user-friendly airport (airport code: BIO) is about six miles north of downtown. Everything branches off the light-and-air-filled main hall, designed by prominent architect Santiago Calatrava. A handy bus (#3247) takes you directly to the center (€1.35, pay driver, 2/hour, 20-minute trip, makes three stops downtown—the first one is closest to the Guggenheim—before ending at the Termibús Station). To find the bus, turn right out of the terminal. A taxi into town costs about €25. To get to San Sebastián, you can take a direct bus from Bilbao Airport (€16.50, pay driver, runs hourly, 1.25 hours, drops off at Plaza Pío XII in San Sebastián, www.pesa.net). A taxi directly to San Sebastián will run you €150.

By Car: A big underground parking garage is near the museum; if you have a car, park it here and use the tram. From the freeway, take the exit marked *Centro* (with bull's-eye symbol), follow signs to *Guggenheim* (you'll see the museum), and look for the big *P* that marks the garage.

Helpful Hints

Baggage Storage: The Termibús Bus Station on the west side of the city is your best option (lockers: €1/bag, use tokens from nearby machine; desk: €2/bag, Mon-Fri 7:00-22:00, Sat-Sun 8:00-21:00, Gurtubay 1, tel. 944-395-077).

Laundry: The self-service **Lavandería Autoservicio Adei** is handy for visitors staying in the Old Town (€7/load, daily 8:00-22:00, Ribera 9, mobile 665-710-082).

Tours in Bilbao

Walking Tours

Bilbao Walking Tours offers 1.5-hour tours Saturdays and Sundays (more often in summer): an Old Town tour (starts at the Arriaga TI at 10:00—but confirm where tour begins as this location may close in 2014), and a modern-city tour showing the city's history since the 19th century (starts at the Guggenheim TI at 12:00). Tours are in Spanish and English, and you must call ahead to reserve (€4.50, tel. 944 795 760, www.bilbao.net /bilbaoturismo, informacion@bilbaoturismo.bilbao.net).

Tram Tour

Riding the EuskoTran round-trip between the Atxuri and Euskalduna stops is a great way to see the city's oldest and newest neighborhoods, especially on rainy days. For more on this tram, see "Arrival in Bilbao," earlier.

Bus Tour

The TI runs a decent hop-on, hop-off bus tour around the city. The hour-long trip picks up on the hour outside the Guggenheim TI, and has stops in the Old Town and across the river (€14, ticket good for 24 hours, buy at TI or from driver at any stop, July-Aug daily 11:00-18:00, shorter hours rest of year, no buses Jan-March or Tue in shoulder season, tel. 696-429-848, www.busturistikoa .com).

Boat Tour

For a different view of the city, try the **Bilboats** one-hour tour along the river, offering plenty of architectural Kodak moments. The tour begins near Ayuntamiento Bridge (€12, daily in spring and summer at 13:00, 16:00, 17:30, and 19:00, fewer departures off-season; reserve ahead, as trips are canceled if less than 10 people buy tickets; tram stop: Pío Baroja, Metro stop: Abando; Plaza de Pío Baroja, tel. 946-424-157, www.bilboats.com). For hardcore sailors, a two-hour version goes all the way into the Bay of Biscay on weekends (€17, leaves at 10:30).

Local Guide

Knowledgeable Bilbao resident **Iratxe Muñoz** offers tours of the city, including the Guggenheim and the Basque region (rates vary, mobile 607-778-072, www.apite.eu/iratxemunoz, iratxe.m @apite.eu).

BASQUE COUNTRY

Sights in Bilbao

▲▲▲Guggenheim Bilbao

Although the collection of art in this museum is no better than those in Europe's other great modern-art museums, the building itself—designed by Frank Gehry and opened in 1997—is reason enough for many travelers to happily splice Bilbao into their itineraries. Even if you're not turned on by contemporary art, the Guggenheim is a must-see experience. Its 20 galleries, on three floors, are full of surprises, and it's well worth the entry fee just to appreciate the museum's structural design, which is a masterpiece in itself.

Cost and Hours: €13, includes excellent audioguide; July-Aug daily 10:00-20:00; Sept-June Tue-Sun 10:00-20:00, closed Mon; same-day re-entry allowed—get wristband on your way out; café, no photos inside galleries, tram stop: Guggenheim, Metro stop: Moyúa, Avenida Abandoibarra 2, tel. 944-359-080, www.guggenheim-bilbao.es.

Tours: Free, one-hour guided tours in Spanish generally run 2/day, at 12:30 and 17:00. Show up at least 30 minutes early to put your name on the list at the tour desk (to the left as you enter). Guided tours in English are available only by advance reservation and with a fee (€95 for up to 20 people).

Background: Frank Gehry's groundbreaking triumph offers a fascinating look at 21st-century architecture. Using cutting-edge technologies, unusual materials, and daring forms, he created a piece of sculpture that smoothly integrates with its environment and serves as the perfect stage for some of today's best art. Clad in limestone and titanium, the building connects the city with its river. Gehry meshed many visions. To him, the building's multiple forms jostle like a loose crate of bottles. The building is inspired by a silvery fish...and also evokes wind-filled sails heading out to sea. Gehry keeps returning to his fish motif, reminding visitors that, as a boy, he was inspired by carp...even taking them into the bathtub with him.

➋ Self-Guided Tour: The audioguide will lead you room-by-room through the collection, but this information will get you started.

Guarding the main entrance is artist Jeff Koons' 42-foot-tall **West Highland Terrier.** Its 60,000 plants and flowers, which blossom in concert, grow through steel mesh. A joyful structure, it brings viewers back to their childhood—perhaps evoking

BASQUE COUNTRY

humankind's relationship to God—or maybe it's just another notorious Koons hoax. One thing is clear: It answers to "Puppy." Although the sculpture was originally intended to be temporary, the people of Bilbao fell in love with *Puppy*—so they bought it.

Descend to the **main entrance.** After buying your ticket, be sure to pick up the free exhibit audioguide. At the information desk, pick up the small English brochure explaining the architecture and museum layout, and the seasonal *Guggenheim Bilbao* magazine that details the art currently on display.

After presenting your ticket, enter the **atrium.** This acts as the heart of the building, pumping visitors from various rooms on three levels out and back, always returning to this central area before moving on to the next. The architect invites you to caress the sensual curves of the walls. There are virtually no straight lines (except the floor). Notice the sheets of glass that make up the elevator shaft—overlapping each other like a fish's scales. Each glass and limestone panel is unique, designed by a computer and shaped by a robot...as will likely be standard in constructing the great buildings of the future.

From the atrium, step out onto the riverside **terrace.** The "water garden" lets the river symbolically lap at the base of the building. This pool is home to four unusual sculptures (the first two appear occasionally throughout the day): a five-part "fire fountain" (notice the squares in the pool to the right); a "fog sculpture" that billows up from below; another piece by Jeff Koons, *Tulips*, which is a colorful, chrome bouquet of inflated flowers; and the most recent addition, *Tall Tree and the Eye* by British artist Anish Kapoor. Composed of 73 reflective spheres arranged vertically, the sculpture endlessly reflects both the Guggenheim and the river.

Still out on the terrace, notice the museum's commitment to public spaces: On the right a grand **staircase** leads under a big green bridge to a tower; the effect wraps the bridge into the museum's grand scheme. The 30-foot-tall **spider,** called *Maman* ("Mommy"), is French artist Louise Bourgeois' depiction of her mother: She spins a beautiful and delicate web of life...which is used to entrap her victims. (It makes a little more sense if you understand that the artist's mother was a weaver. Or maybe not.)

Gehry designed the vast **ground floor** mainly to house often-huge modern-art installations. Computer-controlled lighting adjusts for different exhibits. Surfaces are clean and bare, so you can focus on the art. While most of the collection comes and goes, Richard Serra's huge *Matter of Time* sculpture in the largest gallery (#104) is permanent. Who would want to move those massive metal coils? The intent is to have visitors walk among these metal walls—the "art" is experiencing this journey.

Because this museum is part of the Guggenheim "family"

of museums, the **collection** perpetually rotates among the sister Guggenheim galleries in New York, Venice, and Berlin. The best approach to your visit is simply to immerse yourself in a modern-art happening, rather than to count on seeing a particular piece or a specific artist's works.

You can't fully enjoy the museum's architecture without taking a circular stroll up and down each side of the river along the handsome promenade and over the two modern **pedestrian bridges.** (After you tour the museum, you can borrow a free "outdoor audioguide" to learn more—ID required—but it doesn't say much or take you across the river.) The building's skin—shiny and metallic, with a scale-like texture—is made of thin titanium, carefully created to give just the desired color and reflective quality. The external appearance tells you what's inside: The blocky limestone parts contain square-shaped galleries, and the titanium sections hold nonlinear spaces.

As you look out over the rest of the city, think of this: Gehry designed his building to reflect what he saw here in Bilbao. Now other architects are, in turn, creating new buildings that complement his. It's an appealing synergy for this old city.

Leaving the Museum: To get to the Old Town from the Guggenheim, take the tram that leaves from the river level beside the museum, just past the kid-pleasing fountain (ride it in direction: Atxuri). Hop off at the Arriaga stop, near the dripping-Baroque riverfront theater of the same name. From here, cross the street to enter the heart of the Old Town.

Near the Guggenheim
Fine Arts Museum (Museo de Bellas Artes)
Often overshadowed by the Guggenheim, the Fine Arts Museum contains a thoughtfully laid out collection arranged chronologically from the 12th century to the present. Find minor works by many Spanish artists such as Goya, El Greco, Picasso, Murillo, Zurbarán, Sorolla, Chillida, Tàpies, and Barceló—along with a handful of local painters. Other international artists in the collection include Gauguin, Klee, Bacon, Cassatt, and more. The museum is at the edge of the lovely Doña Casilda Iturrizar Park, perfect for a stroll after your visit.

Cost and Hours: €6, Tue-Sun 10:00-20:00, closed Mon, last entry 15 minutes before closing, a short walk from the Guggenheim at Museo Plaza 2, Metro stop: Moyúa, tel. 944-396-060, www.museobilbao.com.

Alhóndiga Bilbao
Bilbao's new culture and leisure center, designed by French architect Philippe Starck, is worth a quick visit or a lazy afternoon. Not one of the 43 interior columns is alike—the designs are meant

to represent the entirety of materials and styles from antiquity to today. The center houses a cinema, auditorium, exhibition spaces, and restaurant. Most impressive is its glass-bottomed rooftop pool—from the atrium below, visitors can gaze up at backstrokers in the water above.

Cost and Hours: Entry to the Alhóndiga itself is free; a €10 day pass gives you access to the pool and sundeck. Mon-Fri 7:00-23:00, Sat 8:30-24:00, Sun 8:30-23:00, 10-minute walk from the Guggenheim at Plaza Arriquibar 4, tel. 944-014-014, www .alhondigabilbao.com.

Funicular de Artxanda

Opened in 1915, this funicular still provides *bilbainos* with a green escape from their somewhat grimy city. The three-minute ride offers sweeping views of the city on the way to the top of Mount Artxanda, where there's a park, restaurants, and a sports complex. Bring a picnic on a sunny afternoon, and take a moment to ponder the giant thumbprint sculpture dedicated to Basque soldiers who fought against Franco during the civil war.

Cost and Hours: €1, leaves every 15 minutes, Mon-Sat 7:15-22:00, Sun 8:15-22:00, until 23:00 on summer weekends, cross the Zubizuri Bridge and walk two blocks along Calle Mújica y Burton to the cable-car station, Plaza del Funicular, tel. 944-454-966.

Old Town (Casco Viejo)

Bilbao's Old Town, with tall, narrow lanes lined with thriving shops and tapas bars, is worth a stroll. Because the weather is wetter here than in many other parts of Spain (hence the green hillsides), the little balconies that climb the outside walls of buildings are glassed in, creating cozy little breakfast nooks.

Whether you want to or not, you'll eventually wind up at Old Bilbao's centerpiece, the **Santiago Cathedral,** a 14th-century Gothic church with a tranquil interior that has been scrubbed clean inside and out (free, €1 to dip into cloister, Mon-Fri 10:00-13:00 & 17:00-19:30, closed Sat-Sun, tel. 944-153-627).

Various museums (including those dedicated to diocesan art and the Holy Week processions) are in or near the Old Town, but on a quick visit only one is worth considering...

Basque Museum (Euskal Museoa)

It's fitting that Bilbao, a leading city of Spain's Basque region, would have a museum dedicated to its unique culture. Unfortunately, the almost complete lack of English leaves the exhibits shrouded in mystery—much like the Basques themselves. Around a ground-floor cloister, you'll see old stone monuments. The first floor delves into the Basque cultural heritage, displaying ceramics, guns, looms, and other tools. Special emphasis is given to nautical artifacts from this seafaring people, Basque settlers in the American West, and the pastoral lifestyles of rural Basques. The top floor is dedicated to archaeology, with exhibits about old tools and settlements.

Cost and Hours: €3, Tue-Sat 11:00-17:00, Sun 11:00-14:00, closed Mon, Miguel de Unamuno Plaza 4, tel. 944-155-423, www .euskal-museoa.org/es.

La Ribera Market

With a new, three-star Michelin restaurant, Bilbao seems poised to give San Sebastián a run for its money as culinary capital of the Basque Country. As part of an urban renewal plan, the 1929 La Ribera city market has recently reopened to an enthusiastic public. Stroll the stalls for the freshest fish (look for the busiest sellers), shop for produce, and admire a series of Art Deco stained-glass panels on the top floor. The city's coat-of-arms, with two wolves, can be found in the largest panels. There's been a market here since Bilbao was founded in 1300.

Cost and Hours: Free entry, Mon-Fri 8:00-14:00 & 17:00-19:00, Sat 8:00-14:30, closed Sun, tel. 946-023-791, www .mercadodelaribera.net.

Sleeping in Bilbao

(€1 = about $1.30, country code: 34)
Bilbao merits an overnight stay. Even those who are interested only in the Guggenheim find that there's much more to see in this historic yet quickly changing city.

Near the Guggenheim Museum

$$$ Gran Hotel Domine Bilbao is *the* place for well-heeled modern-art fans looking for a splurge close to the museum. It's right across the street from the main entrance to the Guggenheim and Jeff Koons' *Puppy*. The hotel is gathered around an atrium with a giant "stone tree" and other artsy flourishes, and its decor (by a prominent Spanish designer) was clearly inspired by Gehry's masterpiece. The 145 plush rooms are distinctly black, white, steel, and very postmodern (standard Db-€130-200, museum-view "executive" rooms for €50 more, rates vary widely with events and demand, breakfast-€26, air-con, elevator, free guest computer and Wi-Fi, great museum-view breakfast terrace, free gym with wet and dry saunas, Alameda Mazarredo 61, tel. 944-253-300, www.gran hoteldominebilbao.com, recepcion.domine@hoteles-silken.com).

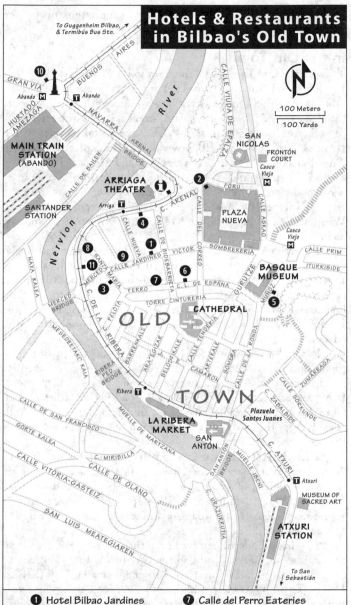

Hotels & Restaurants in Bilbao's Old Town

To Guggenheim Bilbao, & Termibús Bus Stn.

GRAN VIA

Abando 🅼

🅃 Abando

HURTADO AMEZAGA

BUENOS AIRES

NAVARRA

ARENAL BRIDGE

River

CALLE VIUDA DE EPALZA

100 Meters

100 Yards

MAIN TRAIN STATION (ABANDO)

CALLE DE BAILEN

SANTANDER STATION

ARRIAGA THEATER

Arriga 🅃

Nervión

CALLE NUEVA

C. ARENAL

CALLE DEL CORREO

SAN NICOLAS

FRONTÓN COURT

Casco Viejo 🅼

FORU

PLAZA NUEVA

CALLE ASKAO

Casco Viejo 🅼

CALLE PRIM

ITURRIBIDE

BASQUE COUNTRY

VICTOR

CALLE DE BIDEBARRIETA

SOMBRERERIA

BASQUE MUSEUM

SANTA MARIA

Calle Jardines

MERCED

C. DE LA S. RIBERA

MERCED BRIDGE

MESEDEETAKC KAIA

C. PELOTA

PERRO

TORRE CINTURERIA

OLD

C.L. DE ESPAÑA

GURUTZE

CATHEDRAL

NAXA KALEA

RIBERA PED. BRIDGE

BARRENKALE

ARETEGAR

BELOSTIKALE

CALLE TENDERIA

ARTEKALE

CAMARON

SOMERA

CALLE DE LA RONDA

MUÑOZ

ZUMARRAGA

CALLE DE SAN FRANCISCO

GORTE KALEA

CALLE VITORIA-GASTEIZ

C. MIRIBILLA

CALLE DE OLANO

Ribera 🅃

MUELLE DE MARTZANA

TOWN

LA RIBERA MARKET

SAN ANTÓN

SANTON BRIDGE

Plazuela Santos Juanes

C. SORKUNDE

C. ZABALBIDE

C. ATXURI

MUELLE IBENI

🅃 Atxuri

MUSEUM OF SACRED ART

SAN LUIS MEATEGIAREN

C. URAZURRUTIA

ATXURI STATION

To San Sebastián

1 Hotel Bilbao Jardines
2 Tryp Arenal
3 Iturrienea Ostatua & Kasko Restaurant
4 Hotel Arriaga
5 La Estrella Ostatu
6 Pensión Ladero

7 Calle del Perro Eateries
8 Calle Santa María Eateries
9 Calle Jardines Eateries
10 La Granja Restaurant
11 Launderette

If arriving by tram, take the main museum steps up by the fountains to reach the hotel.

In the Old Town

To reach the Old Town, take the tram to the Arriaga stop.

$$ Hotel Bilbao Jardines is a fresh new place buried in the Old Town with 32 modern but basic rooms with squeaky floors (Sb-€58, Db-€75, less off-season, breakfast-€5, quieter rooms in back, air-con, elevator, free Wi-Fi, free rental bicycles, Calle Jardines 9, tel. 944-794-210, www.hotelbilbaojardines.com, info @hotelbilbaojardines.com, Marta, Felix, and Monica).

$$ Tryp Arenal is a chain hotel with simple, business-class rooms and helpful staff in a great location across from the Arriaga Theater (Db-€60-80, breakfast-€8, air-con, elevator, free Wi-Fi, Calle Los Fueros 2, tel. 944-153-100, www.melia.com, tryp .arenal@melia.com).

$ Iturrienea Ostatua, next door to the recommended Kasko restaurant on a pedestrian street in the Old Town, is a tidy, B&B-style accommodation renting 21 rooms packed with brick, stone, and antiques (Sb-€50, Db-€60, twin Db-€66, Tb-€80, breakfast-€6, free Wi-Fi, near the river at Santa María 14, tel. 944-161-500, www.iturrieneaostatua.com, info@iturrieneaostatua.com, friendly Igone).

$ Hotel Arriaga offers 21 traditional but well-maintained rooms and a spirited reception (Sb-€45, Db-€54, extra bed-€16, some rooms overlook a busy street—request a quiet back room, free guest computer and Wi-Fi, lounge, parking-€8, Ribera 3, tel. 944-790-001, www.hotelarriaga.es, info@hotelarriaga.es, Jon). As you cross the bridge from the station, it's just behind the big theater of the same name.

$ La Estrella Ostatu is a family-run establishment with 26 simple but neat rooms up a twisty staircase near the Basque Museum (Sb-€35, Db-€60 in summer, cheaper off-season, break-fast-€3-4, María Muñoz 6, tel. 944-164-066, www.la-estrella -ostatu.com, laestrellabilbao@yahoo.es, just enough English spoken, Jesus and Begoña).

$ Pensión Ladero, renting 12 ramshackle but clean and cheap rooms, is a fine budget option in the Old Town. They don't accept reservations, so call upon arrival to check availability (S-€22, D-€32, T-€50, Q-€60, up 4 flights of stairs; some rooms up a very tight spiral staircase—watch your head—share one bathroom, while remaining rooms use the other three bathrooms on the main floor; cash only, Lotería 1, tel. 944-150-932, www.pensionladero .es, Margarita). You'll find the *pensión* just before the cathedral at the center of the Old Town.

Eating in Bilbao

Near the Guggenheim Museum

The easiest choice is the good **cafeteria** in the museum itself (upper level, separate entry above museum entry; Tue-Sun 9:30-20:00, closed Mon, €25 lunch deal offered 13:00-15:15, reservations smart, tel. 944-239-333).

The circular structure outside the museum by the playgrounds and fountains is a pleasant **outdoor café** serving €2.50 tapas (point at the ones you like on the bar). If the tables are full, you can take your food to one of the stone benches nearby. In the evenings, they sometimes have live music.

The streets in front of the museum have a handful of both sit-down and carry-out eateries (cafés, pizzerias, sandwich shops) to choose from. National chain **Fresc Co** is a healthy and cheap option for lunch or dinner, with an all-you-can-eat salad buffet including some hot dishes, dessert, and coffee for less than €10 (daily 12:30-24:00, 10-minute walk from the Guggenheim, 3 blocks west of Plaza Moyúa at Gran Vía 55).

In the Old Town

Bilbao has developed a thriving restaurant and tapas-bar scene in recent years. For pointers on Basque food, see page 205. You'll find plenty of options on the lanes near the cathedral. Most restaurants around the Old Town advertise a fixed-price lunch for around €12; some close for siesta between 16:00 and 20:00.

The street called **Calle del Perro** is tops for the tasty little tapas called *pintxos* (PEEN-chohs). **Xukela Bar** is my favorite, with its inviting atmosphere, good wines, and an addictive array of €1.60 tapas spread along its bar (tables only for clients eating hot dishes, Calle del Perro 2, tel. 944-159-772). Calle del Perro is also good for sit-down restaurants. Browse the menus and interiors and choose your favorite. Well-regarded options include three places virtually next door to each other: **Egiluz** (€11 meals served in small restaurant up steep spiral staircase in the back); **Río-Oja** (€8 specialties, focus on shareable traditional dishes called *cazuelitas*); and **Rotterdam** (€10-15 plates, also has *cazuelitas;* try the *chipirones en su tinta*—squids in their own ink, served with a glass of house red for €11).

The street called **Calle Santa María** caters to a younger crowd, with softer lighting and a livelier atmosphere, and has three bars worth considering: Gatz, Santa María, and Kasko. **Kasko** is the most upscale option, with stuffy service, a pianist, and an interesting fixed-price dinner (starter, main course, dessert, and good wine served 20:30-23:00 for €27 Sun-Thu and €32 Fri-Sat, Santa Maria 16, tel. 944-160-311, www.restaurantekasko.com).

Eateries also abound on **Jardines** street, including the popular **Berton** (meals and *pintxos*, at #11, closed Mon, tel. 944-167-035). **Gorbea** brings a splash of modernity into the Old Town, with younger but professional wait staff serving generous portions of modern cuisine and traditional Basque classics (at #3, tel. 944-795-482, www.restaurantegorbea.net). **La Deliciosa** is just that, with a whopping eight choices for each course (at #1, tel. 944-150-944).

Near the RENFE Train Station

There's not much on the main facade to distinguish it, but stepping through **La Granja**'s revolving doors is like entering a time machine. Founded in 1926, the interior seems more like a dusty gentlemen's club than a restaurant. The food is simply presented with oh-so-correct waiters and classic white tablecloths. It's a good spot to fuel up on coffee before hopping on the tram to the Guggenheim (€13.50 fixed-price lunch, daily, at Plaza Circular 3 but look for rear entrance on Calle Ledesma, tel. 944-230-813).

Bilbao Connections

From Bilbao by Bus to: San Sebastián (2/hour, hourly on weekends, 6:30-22:00, 1.25 hours, arrives at San Sebastián's Amara Station), **Guernica** (4/hour, fewer on weekends, 40 minutes), **Lekeitio** (hourly, 1.25 hours), **Pamplona** (5-6/day, 2 hours), **Burgos** (8/day, fewer on weekends, 2-3 hours), **Santander** (hourly, 1.5 hours, transfer there to bus to **Santillana del Mar** or **Comillas**—see Cantabria chapter). These buses depart from Bilbao's Termibús Station (www.termibus.es).

By RENFE Train to: Madrid (4/day, 5 hours), **Barcelona** (2/day, 6.5 hours), **Burgos** (3/day, 2.5-3 hours), **Salamanca** (3/day, 6 hours), **León** (1/day, 5 hours). Remember, these trains leave from the RENFE station, across the river from the Old Town (tram stop: Abando). A planned new train line (coming in 2017) will connect Bilbao to other cities in a snap (30 minutes to San Sebastián, 2.25 hours to Madrid, 5.5 hours to Paris)—but it's still slow trains for now.

By EuskoTren to: San Sebastián (hourly, long and scenic 2.5-hour trip to San Sebastián's Amara EuskoTren Station, €9.15 round-trip ticket saves €1.50, EuskoTren info: tel. 902-543-210, www.euskotren.es), **Guernica** (2/hour, 50 minutes, take Bilbao-Bermeo line, direction: Bermeo). These trains depart from Bilbao's Atxuri Station, just beyond the Old Town past the Ribera Market.

French Basque Country (Le Pays Basque)

Compared to their Spanish cousins across the border, the French Basques seem French first and Basque second. You'll see less Euskara writing here than in Spain, but these destinations have their own special spice, mingling Basque and French influences with beautiful rolling countryside and gorgeous beaches.

Just 45 minutes apart by car, San Sebastián and St-Jean-de-Luz bridge the Spanish and French Basque regions. Between them you'll find the functional towns of Irún (Spain) and Hendaye (France), and the delightful hill town of Hondarribia, which is worth a visit if you have time to spare (see page 230).

My favorite home base here is the central, comfy, and manageable resort village of St-Jean-de-Luz. It's a stone's throw to Bayonne (with its "big-city" bustle and good Basque museum) and the snazzy beach town of Biarritz. A drive inland rewards you with a panoply of adorable French Basque villages. And St-Jean-de-Luz is a relaxing place to "come home" to, with its mellow ambience, fine strolling atmosphere, and good restaurants.

BASQUE COUNTRY

St-Jean-de-Luz / Donibane Lohizune

St-Jean-de-Luz (san zhahn-duh-looz) sits cradled between its small port and gentle bay. The days when whaling, cod fishing, and pirating made it wealthy are long gone, but don't expect a cute Basque backwater. Tourism has become the economic mainstay, and it shows. Pastry shops serve Basque specialties, and store windows proudly display berets (a Basque symbol). Ice-cream lickers stroll traffic-free streets, while soft, sandy beaches tempt travelers to toss their itineraries into the bay. The knobby little mountain La Rhune towers above the festive scene. Locals joke that if it's clear enough to see La Rhune's peak, it's going to rain, but if you can't see it, it's raining already.

The town has little of sightseeing importance, but it's a good base for exploring the Basque Country and a convenient beach and port town that provides the most enjoyable dose of Basque culture in France. The town fills with French tourists in July and August—especially the first two weeks of August, when it's practically impossible to find a room without a reservation made long in advance...or even walk down the main street.

Orientation to St-Jean-de-Luz

St-Jean-de-Luz's old city lies between the train tracks, the Nivelle River, and the Atlantic. The main traffic-free street, Rue Gambetta, channels walkers through the center, halfway between the train tracks and the ocean. The small town of Ciboure, across the river, holds nothing of interest.

The only sight worth entering in St-Jean-de-Luz is the church where Louis XIV and Marie-Thérèse tied the royal knot (Eglise St. Jean-Baptiste, described later). St-Jean-de-Luz is best appreciated along its pedestrian streets, lively squares, and golden, sandy beaches. With nice views and walking trails, the park at the far eastern end of the beachfront promenade at Pointe Ste. Barbe makes a good walking destination.

Tourist Information

The helpful TI is next to the big market hall, along the busy Boulevard Victor Hugo (July-Aug Mon-Sat 9:00-19:30, Sun 10:00-13:00 & 15:00-19:00; Sept-June Mon-Sat 9:00-12:30 & 14:00-19:00, Sun 10:00-13:00—except Jan-March, when it's closed Sun; 20 Boulevard Victor Hugo, tel. 05 59 26 03 16, town info: www.saint-jean-de-luz.com, regional info: www.terreetcote basques.com).

Arrival in St-Jean-de-Luz

By Train or Bus: From the train station, the pedestrian underpass leads to the bus station. From there, it's easy to get to the TI and the center of Old Town (just a few blocks away—see map).

By Car: Follow signs for *Centre-Ville*, then *Gare* and *Office de Tourisme*. The Old Town is not car-friendly. Its one-way lanes cut back and forth across pedestrian streets—your best bet may be paying to park in the big underground garage behind the TI (€1.20/hour, €11/day). For other parking options, ask your hotelier or the TI.

By Plane: The nearest airport is Biarritz-Anglet-Bayonne Airport, 10 miles to the northeast near Biarritz. The tiny airport is easy to navigate, with a useful TI desk (airport code: BIQ, airport tel. 05 59 43 83 83, www.biarritz.aeroport.fr). To reach St-Jean-de-Luz, you can take a public bus (€3, 7/day, 30 minutes, tel. 05 59 26 06 99, www.transports-atcrb.com) or a 20-minute taxi ride (about €30).

Helpful Hints

Market Days: Tuesday and Friday mornings (and summer Saturdays), the farmers' stands spill through the streets from

It Happened at Hendaye

If taking the train between the Spanish and French Basque regions, you'll change trains at the nondescript little Hendaye Station. While it seems innocent enough, this was the site of a fateful meeting between two of Europe's most notorious 20th-century dictators.

In the days before World War II, Adolf Hitler and Francisco Franco maintained a diplomatic relationship. But after the fall of France, they decided to meet secretly in Hendaye to size each other up. On October 23, 1940, Hitler traveled through Nazi-occupied France, then waited impatiently on the platform for Franco's delayed train. The over-eager Franco hoped the Führer would invite him to join in a military alliance with Germany (and ultimately share in the expected war spoils).

According to reports of the meeting, Franco was greedy, boastful, and misguided, leading Hitler to dismiss him as a buffoon. Franco later spun the situation by claiming that he had cleverly avoided being pulled into World War II. In fact, his own incompetence is what saved Spain. Had Franco made a better impression on Hitler here at Hendaye, it's possible that Spain would have entered the war, which could have changed the course of Spanish, German, and European history.

BASQUE COUNTRY

Les Halles covered market on Boulevard Victor Hugo, and seem to give everyone a rustic whiff of "life is good."

Supermarkets: There are three **Petit Casino** groceries. One is across from the market hall next to the TI, and another is on Boulevard Victor Hugo near the recommended Hôtel Le Petit Trianon (Mon-Tue and Thu-Sat 8:30-13:00 & 15:30-19:30, Sun 9:00-13:00 & 16:30-19:30, closed Wed). Yet another, at the east end of Rue Gambetta, is smaller (open Wed but closed Sun).

Internet Access: The **TI** has free Wi-Fi. if you need a computer, your best bet is **Internet World,** run by friendly Irish expats Margaret and Peter (July-Aug Mon-Sat 10:00-21:00, closed Sun; Sept-June daily 10:00-13:00 & 15:00-18:00; 7 Rue Tourasse, tel. 05 59 26 86 92).

Laundry: Laverie Automatique du Port is at 4 Boulevard Thiers (self-service €5.20/load, daily 7:00-21:00, change machine; full-service available Tue-Fri 9:30-12:30 & 14:30-18:00; mobile 06 80 06 48 36).

Car Rental: Avis, at the train station, is handiest (Mon-Fri 8:00-18:00, Sat 9:00-18:00, closed Sun, tel. 05 59 26 79 66).

Dipping into France

If you're heading from Spain to France, you don't have to worry about currency changes—both countries use the euro—or lengthy border stops (although police might ask to see your passport on trains going into Spain). Here are a few other practicalities:

Phones: France's telephone country code is 33. Spanish phone cards and stamps will not work in France. If you have a mobile phone with a Spanish SIM card, it should work here—but at a higher rate per minute (although texting is cheap).

Hours: France typically does not enjoy the same "siesta" as Spain, so shops don't close for a mid-afternoon break. The French eat lunch and dinner closer to the European mainstream time (around 12:00-13:30 & 19:00-21:00)—much earlier than Spaniards do.

Hotel Tips: The French have a simple hotel-rating system based on amenities, indicated in this chapter by asterisks. One star is modest, two has most of the comforts, and three is generally a two-star place with a fancier lobby and more elaborately designed rooms. Four or five stars offer more luxury than you'll probably have time to appreciate.

Restaurant Tips: In France, if you ask for the *menu* (muh-noo), you won't get a list of dishes; you'll get a fixed-price meal. *Menus*, which include three or four courses, are generally a good value if you're hungry: You'll get your choice of soup, appetizer, or salad; your choice from three or four main-course options with vegetables; plus a cheese course and/or a choice of desserts. Service is included (*service compris* or *prix net*), but wine and other drinks generally are extra.

Tours in St-Jean-de-Luz

Tourist Train

A little tourist train does a 30-minute trip around town (€5.50, departs every 45 minutes from the port, runs April-Oct 10:30-19:00, no train Nov-March, mobile 06 85 70 72 85). It's only worth the money if you need to rest your feet.

Bus Excursions

Le Basque Bondissant runs popular day-trip excursions, including a handy jaunt to the Guggenheim Bilbao (€35 round-trip, includes €13 museum admission, Wed only, departs 9:30 from green bus terminal across the street from train station, returns 19:30). Other itineraries include Ainhoa, Espelette, St-Jean-Pied-de-Port, Loyola and the Cantabrian coast, San Sebastián, and a trip to the *ventas* (discount stores in the foothills of the Pyrenees). You can get information and buy tickets at the TI, or visit the Le Basque Bondissant office in the bus station (Mon-Fri 8:45-12:00 & 13:30-17:30 except closed Wed afternoon, closed Sat-Sun, tel. 05 59 26 30

French Survival Phrases: Although some French Basques speak Euskara, most speak French in everyday life. You'll find these phrases useful:

Good day.	*Bonjour.*	bohn-zhoor
Mrs. / Ma'am	*Madame*	mah-dahm
Mr. / Sir	*Monsieur*	muhs-yuh
Please?	*S'il vous plaît?*	see voo play
Thank you.	*Merci.*	mehr-see
You're welcome.	*De rien.*	duh ree-an
Excuse me.	*Pardon.*	par-dohn
Yes. / No.	*Oui. / Non.*	wee / nohn
Okay.	*D'accord.*	dah-kor
Cheers!	*Santé!*	sahn-tay
Goodbye.	*Au revoir.*	oh ruh-vwahr
women / men	*dames / hommes*	dahm / ohm
one / two / three	*un / deux / trois*	uhn / duh / trwah
Do you speak English?	*Parlez-vous anglais?*	par-lay voo ahn-glay

BASQUE COUNTRY

74, www.basque-bondissant.com). Advance reservations are recommended in winter, when trips are canceled if not enough people sign up.

Boat Trips

Le Passeur, at the port, offers mini-Atlantic cruises and fishing excursions (May-Sept, no guides; cruises-€10/45 minutes, €17/1.75 hours; fishing trips-€35; tickets sold on boat, mobile 06 09 73 61 81).

Self-Guided Walk

Welcome to St-Jean-de-Luz

To get a feel for the town, take this hour-long self-guided stroll. You'll start at the port and make your way to the historic church.

Port: Begin at the little working port (at Place des Corsaires, just beyond the parking lot). Pleasure craft are in the next port over, in Ciboure. Whereas fishing boats used to catch lots of whales and anchovies, now they take in sardines and tuna—and take out tourists on joyrides. Anchovies, once a big part of the

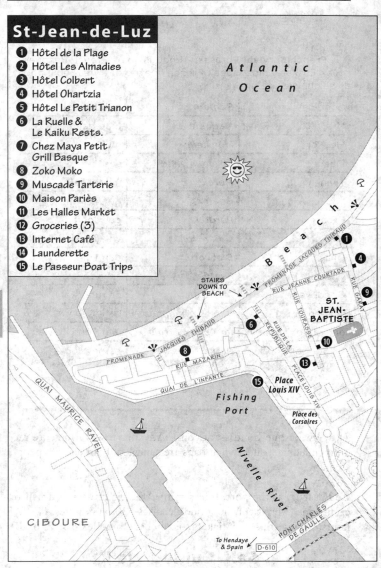

St-Jean-de-Luz

1. Hôtel de la Plage
2. Hôtel Les Almadies
3. Hôtel Colbert
4. Hôtel Ohartzia
5. Hôtel Le Petit Trianon
6. La Ruelle & Le Kaiku Rests.
7. Chez Maya Petit Grill Basque
8. Zoko Moko
9. Muscade Tarterie
10. Maison Pariès
11. Les Halles Market
12. Groceries (3)
13. Internet Café
14. Launderette
15. Le Passeur Boat Trips

BASQUE COUNTRY

fishing business, were overfished nearly into extinction, so they've been protected by the EU for the last few years (though now some limited fishing is permitted).

St-Jean-de-Luz feels cute and nonthreatening now, but in the 17th century it was home to the Basque Corsairs. With the French government's blessing, these pirates who worked the sea—and enriched the town—moored here.

• *After you walk the length of the port, on your right is the tree-lined...*

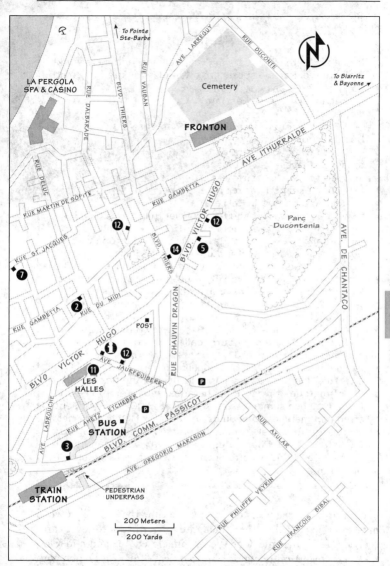

Place Louis XIV: The town's main square, named for the king who was married here, is a hub of action that serves as the town's communal living room. During the summer, the bandstand features traditional Basque folk music and dancing at 21:00 (almost nightly July-Aug, otherwise Sun and Wed). Facing the square is the City Hall (Herriko Etchea) and the **House of Louis XIV** (he lived here for 40 festive days in 1660). A visit to this house is worthwhile only if you like period furniture, though it's only

Pelota

In keeping with their seafaring, shipbuilding, and metalworking heritage, Basque sports are often feats of strength: Who can lift the heaviest stone? Who can row the fastest and farthest?

But the most important Basque sport of all is *pelota*—similar to what you might know as jai alai. Players in white pants and red scarves or shirts use a long, hook-shaped wicker basket (called a *txistera* in Euskara) to whip a ball (smaller and far bouncier than a baseball) back and forth off walls at more than 150 miles per hour. This men's-only game can be played with a wall at one or both ends of the court. Most matches are not professional, but betting on them is common. It can also be played without a racket—this handball version is used as a starter game for kids. Children use a bouncy rubber ball, while adults use a ball with a wooden center that's rather rough on the hands and needs a lot of strength to keep moving.

It seems that every small Basque town has two things: a church and a *pelota* court (called *frontón*). While some *frontóns* are simple and in poor repair, others are freshly painted as a gleaming sign of local pride.

The TI in St-Jean-de-Luz sells tickets and has a schedule of matches throughout the area; you're more likely to find a match in summer (almost daily at 21:00 July-mid-Sept, afternoon matches sometimes on Sat-Sun). Matches are held throughout the year (except for winter) in the villages (ask for details at TI). The professional *cesta punta* matches on Tuesdays and Fridays often come with Basque folkloric halftime shows.

open for part of the year; the rest of the time the privately owned mansion is occupied by the same family that's had it for over three centuries (€5, June-mid-Oct Wed-Mon, closed Tue and mid-Oct-July, visits by 40-minute guided tour only, 2-4/day, in French with English handouts, tel. 05 59 26 27 58, www.maison-louis-xiv.fr).

The king's visit is memorialized by a small black equestrian statue at the entrance of the City Hall (a miniature of the huge statue that marks the center of the Versailles courtyard). The plane trees, with truncated branches looking like fists, are cut back in the winter so that in the summer they'll come back with thick, shady foliage.

• *Opposite the port on the far side of the square is...*

Rue de la République: This historic lane leads from Place

Louis XIV to the beach. Once the home of fishermen, today it's lined with mostly edible temptations. Facing the square, **Maison Adam** still uses the family recipe to bake the macaroons Louis XIV enjoyed during his visit (at #6; look for the gigantic display of plastic red peppers, and then go next door for their sweets). You can buy one (€1), or sample a less historic but just as tasty *gâteau basque,* a baked tart with a cream or cherry filling.

Don't eat your dessert just yet, though, because farther down Rue de la République you'll find **Pierre Oteiza,** stacked with rustic Basque cheeses and meats from mountain villages (with a few samples generally out for the tasting, and handy €3.50 paper cones of salami or cheese slices—perfect for munching during this walk; closed 13:00-14:00).

You'll likely eat on this lane tonight. The recommended **Le Kaiku,** the town's top restaurant, fills the oldest building in St-Jean-de-Luz (with its characteristic stone lookout tower), dating from the 1500s. This was the only building on the street to survive a vicious 1558 Spanish attack. Each end of the street is flanked by a cannon, which may be from Basque pirate ships. At the upper end of the street, notice the photo of fisherwomen with baskets on their heads, who would literally run to Bayonne to sell their fresh fish.

• *Continue to the...*

Beach: A high embankment protects the town from storm waters, but generally the Grande Plage—which is lovingly groomed daily—is the peaceful haunt of sun-seekers, soccer players, and happy children. Walk the elevated promenade (to the right). Various tableaux tell history in French. Storms (including a particularly disastrous one in 1749) routinely knocked down buildings. Repeated flooding around 1800 drove the population down by two-thirds. Finally, in 1854, Napoleon III—who had visited here and appreciated the town—began building the three breakwaters you see today. Decades were spent piling 8,000 fifty-ton blocks, and by 1895 the town was protected. To develop their tourist trade, they built a casino and a fine hotel, and even organized a special getaway train from Paris. During those days there were as many visitors as residents (3,000).

• *Stroll through the seaside shopping mall fronting the late-Art-Deco-style La Pergola, which houses a casino and the Hélianthal spa center (entrance around back) and overlooks the beach. Anyone in a white robe strolling the beach is from the spa. Beyond La Pergola is the pink, Neo-Romantic Grand Hôtel (c. 1900), with an inviting terrace for an expensive coffee break (€7 cappuccino). From here circle back into town along Boulevard Thiers until you reach the bustling...*

Rue Gambetta: Turn right at the green cross and circle back to your starting point, following the town's lively pedestrian shopping street. You'll notice many stores selling the renowned *linge Basque*—cotton linens such as tablecloths, napkins, and dishcloths, in the characteristic Basque red, white, and green. There are as many candy shops as there are tourists. Keep an eye open for a local branch of the British auction house Christie's, which specializes in high-end real estate. Video screens in the window advertise French castles for a mere €2 million, while local vacation homes go for considerably less.

• *Just before Place Louis XIV, you'll see the town's main church.*

Eglise St. Jean-Baptiste: The marriage of Louis XIV and Marie-Thérèse put St-Jean-de-Luz on the map, and this church is where it all took place. The ultimate in political marriages, the knot tied between Louis XIV and Marie-Thérèse in 1660 also cinched a reconciliation deal between Europe's two most powerful countries. The king of Spain, Philip IV—who lived in El Escorial palace—gave his daughter in marriage to the king of France, who lived in Versailles. This marriage united Europe's two largest palaces, which helped end a hundred years of hostility and forged an alliance that enabled both to focus attention on other matters (like England). Little St-Jean-de-Luz was selected for its 15 minutes of fame because it was roughly halfway between Madrid and Paris, and virtually on the France-Spain border. The wedding cleared out both Versailles and El Escorial palaces, as anyone who was anyone attended this glamorous event.

The church, centered on the pedestrian street Rue Gambetta, seems modest enough from the exterior...but step inside (Mon-Sat 8:00-12:00 & 14:00-18:30, Sun 8:00-12:00 & 15:00-19:30). The local expertise was in shipbuilding, so the ceiling resembles the hull of a ship turned upside down. The dark wood balconies running along the nave segregated the men from the women and children (men went  upstairs until the 1960s, as they still do in nearby villages) and were typical of Basque churches. The number of levels depended on the importance of the church, and this church, with three levels, is the largest Basque church in France.

The three-foot-long paddle-wheel ship hanging in the center was a gift from Napoleon III's wife, Eugènie. It's a model of an ill-fated ship that had almost sunk just offshore when she was on it. The 1670 Baroque altar feels Franco-Spanish and features 20 French saints. Locals of this proud and rich town call it the finest in the Basque Country. The box seats across from the pulpit were reserved for leading citizens who were expected to be seen in church and set a good example. Today the mayor and city council members sit here on festival Sundays. The place has great acoustics, and the 17th-century organ is still used for concerts (around €10, mostly in summer, get schedule at TI or online at www .orgueluz.c.la, tickets available at door and possibly in advance at the TI).

As you leave the church, turn left to find the bricked-up doorway—the church's original entrance. According to a quaint but untrue legend, it was sealed after the royal marriage (shown on the wall to the right in a photo of a painting) to symbolize a permanent closing of the door on troubles between France and Spain.

Sleeping in St-Jean-de-Luz

(€1 = about $1.30, country code: 33, * = French hotel rating system, 0-5 stars)

Hotels are a good value here. The higher prices are for peak season (generally July-Sept). In winter, some prices drop below those I've listed. Most hoteliers speak English, and breakfast is not included. Those wanting to eat and sleep for less will do slightly better just over the border, in San Sebastián.

$$$ Hôtel de la Plage* has the best location, right on the ocean. Its 22 rooms, 16 with ocean views, have a lively yellow-and-blue modern nautical decor (Db-€89-119, ocean view Db-€119-169, family rooms for up to 5-€30 per extra person, breakfast-€11 but free for kids, air-con, elevator, free Wi-Fi, garage-€15, 33 Rue Garat, tel. 05 59 51 03 44, www.hoteldelaplage.com, reservation@hotel delaplage.com, run by friendly Pierre, Laurent, and Frederic).

$$$ Hôtel Les Almadies,* on the main pedestrian street, is a bright boutique hotel with seven flawless rooms, comfy public spaces with clever modern touches, a pleasant breakfast room and lounge, an inviting sun deck, and a caring owner (Db-€100-135, higher prices are for rooms with tubs, buffet breakfast-€12, free Wi-Fi, parking-€10, 58 Rue Gambetta, tel. 05 59 85 34 48, www .hotel-les-almadies.com, hotel.lesalmadies@wanadoo.fr, Monsieur and Madame Hargous will charm you with their Franglish).

$$$ Hôtel Colbert,* a Best Western, has 34 modern, tastefully appointed rooms across the street from the train station (Sb-€80-133, Db-€96-162, extra bed-€15, family room-€241-339, breakfast-€14, air-con, elevator, free Wi-Fi, private parking-€20, 3 Boulevard du Commandant Passicot, tel. 05 59 26 31 99, www .hotelcolbertsaintjeandeluz.com, contact@hotelcolbertsaintjean deluz.com).

$$ Hôtel Ohartzia* ("Souvenir"), one block off the beach, is comfortable, clean, and peaceful, with the most charming facade I've seen. It comes with 17 simple but well-cared-for rooms, generous and homey public spaces, and a delightful garden. Recently renovated, four rooms are 21st-century modern, and two have small, interior terraces. Higher prices are for the four rooms with tubs (mid-July-Sept Db-€85-91, March-mid-July Db-€75-79, Oct-Feb Db-€69-74, extra bed-€15, breakfast-€8, free Wi-Fi, 28 Rue Garat, tel. 05 59 26 00 06, www.hotel-ohartzia.com, hotel .ohartzia@wanadoo.fr). Their front desk is technically open only 8:00-21:00, but owners Madame and Monsieur Audibert (who speak little English) live in the building; their son Benoît speaks English well.

$$ Hôtel Le Petit Trianon,** on a major street a couple of blocks above the Old Town's charm, is simple and traditional, with 25 tidy rooms and an accommodating staff (July-Sept Db-€88, Tb-€115, Qb-€150; April-June and Oct-mid-Nov Db-€73, Tb-€95, Qb-€120; even less off-season, air-con in most rooms, breakfast-€8, free Wi-Fi, limited parking-€10, 56 Boulevard Victor Hugo, tel. 05 59 26 11 90, www.hotel-lepetittrianon.com, lepetittrianon@wanadoo.fr). To get a room over the quieter courtyard, ask for *côté cour* (koh-tay koor).

Eating in St-Jean-de-Luz

St-Jean-de-Luz restaurants are known for offering good-value, high-quality cuisine. You can find a wide variety of eateries in the old center. For forgettable food with unforgettable views, choose from several places overlooking the beach. Most places serve from 12:15 to 14:00, and from 19:15 on. Remember, in France *menu* means a fixed-price, multicourse meal.

The traffic-free Rue de la République, which runs from Place Louis XIV to the ocean promenade, is lined with hardworking restaurants (two of which are recommended below). Places are empty at 19:30, but packed at 20:30. Making a reservation, especially on weekends or in summer, is wise. Consider a fun night of bar-hopping for dinner in San Sebastián instead (an hour away in Spain, described on page 224).

La Ruelle serves good, traditionally Basque cuisine—mostly seafood—in a convivial dining room packed with tables, happy eaters, and kitschy Basque decor. André and his playful staff obviously enjoy their work, which gives this popular spot a relaxed and fun ambience. They offer a free sangria to diners with this book. Portions are huge; their €20 *ttoro* (seafood stew) easily feeds two—splitting is OK if you order two starters (€20-25 *menus*, closed Tue-Wed Oct-May, 19 Rue de la République, tel. 05 59 26 37 80).

Le Kaiku is *the* gastronomic experience in St-Jean-de-Luz. They serve modern, creatively presented cuisine, and specialize in wild seafood (rather than farmed). This dressy place is the most romantic in town, but manages not to be stuffy (€25 lunch *menus,* €30 dinner *menus,* closed Tue-Wed except July-Aug, 17 Rue de la République, tel. 05 59 26 13 20, www.kaiku.fr, Serge and Julie). For the best experience, talk with Serge about what you like best and your price limits (about €55 will get you a three-course meal *à la carte* without wine).

Chez Maya Petit Grill Basque serves hearty traditional Basque cuisine. Their €18 *ttoro* was a highlight of my day. They have €21 and €30 *menus,* but à la carte is more interesting. If you stick around in warm weather, you'll see the clever overhead fan system kick into action (closed for lunch Mon and Thu and all day Wed, 2 Rue St. Jacques, tel. 05 59 26 80 76).

Zoko Moko offers Mediterranean nouvelle cuisine, with artistic creations on big plates. Get an *amuse-bouche* (an appetizer chosen by the chef) and a *mignardise* (a fun bite-sized dessert) with each main plate ordered (€25 lunchtime *plats,* €43 evening *menu,* closed Mon, Rue Mazarin 6, tel. 05 59 08 01 23, www.zoko-moko .com, owner Charles).

Fast and Cheap: Consider the takeaway crêpe stands on Rue Gambetta. For a sit-down salad or a tart—either sweet or savory— consider **Muscade Tarterie** (€8-13 per slice; closed Mon; 20 Rue Garat, tel. 05 59 26 96 73).

Sweets: **Maison Pariès** is a favorite for its traditional sweets. Locals like their fine chocolates, *tartes,* macaroons, fudge (*kanougas),* and *touron* (like marzipan, but firmer), which comes in a multitude of flavors—brought by Jews who stopped here just over the border in 1492 after being expelled from Spain. The delectable chocolate version of the *gâteau basque* is also worth a try (9 Rue Gambetta, tel. 05 59 26 01 46).

St-Jean-de-Luz Connections

The train station in St-Jean-de-Luz is called St-Jean-de-Luz-Ciboure. Its handy departure board displays lights next to any trains leaving that day. Buses leave from the green building across the street. There is reduced bus and rail service on Sundays and off-season.

From St-Jean-de-Luz by Train to: Bayonne (hourly, 25 minutes), **St-Jean-Pied-de-Port** (5/day, 6/day in summer, 2 hours with transfer in Bayonne), **Paris** (5/day direct via high-speed TGV, 5.5 hours; more with transfer in Bordeaux, 6 hours), **Bordeaux** (7/day, 2.5 hours), **Sarlat** (1/day, 2/day on weekends, 6-8 hours, transfer in Bordeaux), **Carcassonne** (1/day, 5 hours, transfers likely in Bayonne and Toulouse).

By Train to San Sebastián: First, take the 10-minute train to the French border town of Hendaye (Gare SNCF stop, about 10/day). Or get to Hendaye by bus (3/day, 35 minutes); check the schedule to see which leaves first.

Leave the Hendaye SNCF train station to the right, and look for the small building on the same side of the street, where you'll catch the commuter EuskoTren into San Sebastián (usually 4/hour Mon-Fri, 2/hour Sat-Sun, runs 7:00-22:33, 35 minutes). Locals call this line the Topo ("Mole"), since part of it runs underground— although officially, it's part of the new Metro Donostialdea system for San Sebastián.

By Bus: Buses leave from the bus station directly in front of the train station (cross the road by using the pedestrian underpass). All tickets are bought on the bus. A Spanish Pesa bus runs to **San Sebastián** (Mon-Sat only, 2/day direct—likely at 12:45 and 19:15, none on Sun, 1 hour, only 1/week off-season, info in Spain tel. 902-101-210, www.pesa.net). Local ATCRB bus #816 connects St-Jean-de-Luz either to **Bayonne** or **Biarritz** almost hourly. Confusingly, this one bus can run two different routes (one to Bayonne, the other to Biarritz Centre, 45 minutes to either one)— check the destination carefully. Bus #24 connects St-Jean-de-Luz to **Sare** (Mon-Fri 6/day, Sat 2/day, none Sun, 30 minutes, tel. 09 70 80 90 74, www.transports-atcrb.com).

By Excursion: If you're without a car, consider using **Le Basque Bondissant**'s day-trip excursions to visit otherwise difficult-to-reach destinations, such as the Guggenheim Bilbao (see "Tours in St-Jean-de-Luz," earlier).

By Taxi to San Sebastián: This will cost you about €75 for up to four people, but it's convenient (tel. 05 59 26 10 11 or mobile 06 25 76 97 69).

Route Tips for Drivers

A one-day side-trip to both Bayonne and Biarritz is easy from St-Jean-de-Luz. These three towns form a sort of triangle (depending on traffic, each one is less than a 30-minute drive from the other). Hop on the autoroute to Bayonne, sightsee there, then take D-810 into Biarritz. Leaving Biarritz, continue along the coastal D-810. In Bidart, watch (on the right) for the town's proud *frontón* (*pelota* court) and stop for a photo of the quaint town hall. Consider peeling off to go into the village center of Guéthary, with another *frontón* and a massive town hall. If you're up for a walk on the beach, cross the little bridge in Guéthary, park by the train station, and hike down to the walkway along the surfing beach (lined with cafés and eateries). When you're ready to move on, you're a very short drive from St-Jean-de-Luz.

Bayonne / Baiona

To feel the urban pulse of French Basque Country, visit Bayonne—modestly but honestly nicknamed "your anchor in the Basque

Country" by its tourist board. With frequent, fast train and bus connections with St-Jean-de-Luz, Bayonne makes an easy half-day side-trip.

Come here to browse through Bayonne's atmospheric and well-worn-yet-lively Old Town, and to admire its impressive Museum of Basque Culture. Known for establishing Europe's first whaling industry and for inventing the bayonet, Bayonne is more famous today for its ham *(jambon de Bayonne)* and chocolate.

Get lost in Bayonne's Old Town. In pretty Grand Bayonne, tall, slender buildings, decorated in Basque fashion with green-and-red shutters, climb above cobbled streets. Be sure to stroll the streets around the cathedral and along the banks of the smaller Nive River, where you'll find the market (Les Halles).

Orientation to Bayonne

Bayonne's two rivers, the grand Adour and the petite Nive, divide the city into three parts: St-Esprit, with the train station; and the more interesting Grand Bayonne and Petit Bayonne, which together make up the Old Town.

Tourist Information

The TI is in a modern parking lot a block off the mighty Adour River, on the northeastern edge of Grand Bayonne. They have very little in English other than a map and a town brochure (July-Aug Mon-Sat 9:00-19:00, Sun 10:00-18:00; March-June and Sept-Oct Mon-Fri 9:00-18:30, Sat 10:00-18:00, closed Sun; shorter hours in off-season; Place des Basques, tel. 08 20 42 64 64, www.bayonne-tourisme.com). There's a pay WC in the rear.

Arrival in Bayonne

By Train: The TI and Grand Bayonne are a 15-minute walk from the train station: Walk straight out of the station, cross the parking lot and traffic circle, and then cross the imposing bridge (Pont St. Esprit). Once past the big Adour River, continue across a smaller bridge (Pont Mayou), which spans the smaller Nive River. Stop on Pont Mayou to orient yourself: You just left Petit Bayonne

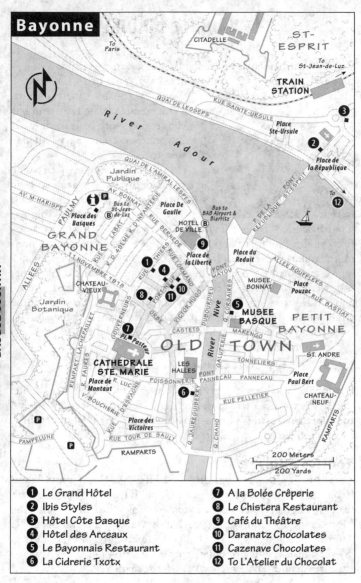

Bayonne

1. Le Grand Hôtel
2. Ibis Styles
3. Hôtel Côte Basque
4. Hôtel des Arceaux
5. Le Bayonnais Restaurant
6. La Cidrerie Txotx
7. A la Bolée Crêperie
8. Le Chistera Restaurant
9. Café du Théâtre
10. Daranatz Chocolates
11. Cazenave Chocolates
12. To L'Atelier du Chocolat

BASQUE COUNTRY

(left side of Nive River); ahead of you is Grand Bayonne (spires of cathedral straight ahead, TI a few blocks to the right). The Museum of Basque Culture is in Petit Bayonne, facing the next bridge up the Nive River.

By Car or Bus: The handiest parking is also where buses arrive in Bayonne: next to the TI at the modern parking lot on the edge of Grand Bayonne. To reach the town center from here, walk past the war memorial and through the break in the ramparts. Follow the walkway until you reach a fancy gate that leads through a tunnel. After the tunnel, turn right at the next street; the cathedral should immediately come into view. Continue behind the cathedral and walk down, down, down any of the atmospheric streets to find Les Halles (the market) and the Nive River.

To reach this parking lot, **drivers** take the *Bayonne Sud* exit from the autoroute, then follow green *Bayonne Centre* signs, then white *Centre-Ville* signs (with an *i* for tourist information). You'll see the lot on your right. Payment machines only accept coins for a maximum of two hours. In high season, when this lot can be full, use one of the lots just outside the center (follow signs to *Glain* or *Porte d'Espagne* as you arrive in town), then catch the little orange *navette* (shuttle bus) to get into the center (free, find route maps posted at stops in town, every 7 minutes, Mon-Sat 7:30-19:30, closed Sun).

Helpful Hints

Loaner Bikes: Although Bayonne's sights are easily reached on foot (except the chocolate workshop), pedaling about by bike is simple and relaxing. The TI lends a limited number of orange bikes for free to adults during office hours (must leave passport or driver's license and a €150 deposit, same hours and contact information as TI, www.cyclocom.fr).

Laundry: Laverie is just blocks from the cathedral (self-service €4/wash, daily 8:00-20:00, 6 Rue d'Espagne, tel. 05 59 59 54 03).

Sights in Bayonne

▲Museum of Basque Culture (Musée Basque)

This museum (in Petit Bayonne, facing the Nive River at Pont Marengo) explains French Basque culture from cradle to grave—in French, Euskara, and Spanish. The only English you'll read is "do not touch" (unless you buy their informative €5 English booklet). Artifacts and videos take you into traditional Basque villages and sit you in the front row of time-honored festivals, letting you envision this otherwise hard-to-experience culture.

Cost and Hours: €6.50, free first Sun of month; open July-Sept daily 10:00-18:30, Thu until 20:30; Oct-June Tue-Sun 10:00-18:30, closed Mon; last entry one hour before closing, 37 Quai des Corsaires, tel. 05 59 59 08 98, www.musee-basque.com.

Visiting the Museum: On the ground floor, you'll begin with a display of carts and tools used in rural life, then continue past some 16th-century gravestones. Look for the *laiak*—distinctive forked hoes used to work the ground. At the end of this section you'll watch a grainy film on Basque rural lifestyles.

The next floor up begins by explaining that the house *(etxea)* is the building block of Basque society. More than just a building, it's a social institution—Basques are named for their house, not vice versa. You'll see models and paintings of Basque houses, then domestic items, a giant door, kitchen equipment, and furniture (including a combination bench-table, next to the fireplace). After an exhibit on Basque clothing, you'll move into the nautical life, with models, paintings, and actual boats. The little door leads to a large model of the port of Bayonne in 1805, back when it was a strategic walled city.

Upstairs you'll learn that the religious life of the Basques was strongly influenced by the Camino de Santiago pilgrim trail, which passes through their territory. One somber room explains Basque funeral traditions. The section on social life includes a video of Basque dances (typically accompanied by flute and drums). These are improvised, but according to a clearly outlined structure—not unlike a square dance.

The prominence given to the sport of *pelota* (see sidebar on page 260) indicates its importance to these people. One dimly lit room shows off several types of *txistera* baskets (*chistera* in French), gloves, and balls used for the game; videos show you how these items are made. The museum wraps up with a brief lesson on the region's history from the 16th to the 20th centuries, including exhibits on the large Jewish population here (who had fled from a hostile Spain) and the renaissance of Basque culture in the 19th century.

Cathédrale Ste. Marie

Bankrolled by the whaling community, this cathedral sits dead-center in Grand Bayonne and is worth a peek. Find the unique keystones on the ceiling along the nave, then circle behind the church to find the peaceful and polished 13th-century cloisters.

Cost and Hours: Cathedral—free, Mon-Sat 10:00-11:45 & 15:00-17:45, Sun 15:30-18:00; cloisters—free, daily 9:00-12:30 & 14:00-17:00, until 18:00 mid-May-mid-Sept.

Sweets Shops

With no more whales to catch, Bayonne turned to producing mouthwatering chocolates and marzipan; look for shops on the arcaded Rue du Port Neuf (running between the cathedral and the Adour River). **Daranatz** is Bayonne's best chocolate shop, with bars of chocolate blended with all kinds of flavors—one with a general mix of spices (lots of cardamom), one with just cinnamon, and another with *piments d'Espelette* (15 Arceaux Port Neuf, tel. 05 59 59 03 55, www.chocolat-bayonne-daranatz.fr). **Cazenave,** founded in 1854, is a fancy *chocolaterie* with a small café in the back. Try their foamy hot chocolate with fresh whipped cream on the side, served with buttered toast for €9 (Tue-Sat 9:00-12:00 & 14:00-19:00, closed Sun-Mon, 19 Arceaux Port Neuf, tel. 05 59 59 03 16, www.chocolats-cazenave.fr).

Chocolate Workshop
L'Atelier du Chocolat is a chocolate factory and boutique in an industrial part of town. You'll see a detailed exhibit on the history and making of chocolate, some workers making luscious goodies (9:30-11:00 only), and a video. The generous chocolate tasting at the end is worth the ticket price for chocoholics.

Cost and Hours: €5.80, Mon-Sat 9:30-12:30 & 14:00-18:00, closed Sun, last entry 1.5 hours before closing, 7 Allée de Gibéléou, tel. 05 59 55 70 23, www.atelierduchocolat.fr.

Getting There: Take city bus #A2 from the TI or the Mairie stop across from the town hall (buy €1 ticket on board), get off at the Jean-Jaurès stop, walk under the railway bridge past the roundabout, and follow signs.

Ramparts
The ramparts around Grand Bayonne are open for walking and great for picnicking (access from park at far end of TI parking lot). However, the ramparts do not allow access to either of Bayonne's castles—both are closed to the public.

Sleeping in Bayonne

(€1 = about $1.30, country code: 33, * = French hotel rating system, 0-5 stars)

$$$ Le Grand Hôtel*** is the best of the limited options in Bayonne—it's well-located in Grand Bayonne, with all the comforts and a pleasant staff. While renovating their old building, the owners took care to maintain the original, classic decor (Sb-€75-160, Db-€81-166, breakfast-€13, elevator, free Wi-Fi, parking-€13, 21 Rue Thiers, tel. 05 59 59 62 00, www .bw-legrandhotel.com, infos@bw-legrandhotel.com, Caroline).

$$$ Ibis Styles Bayonne Gare Centre*** sits next to the Pont Saint Esprit near the train station. Some of its 45 white, bright rooms overlook the river (Sb-€86-116, Db-€96-135, Tb-€99-145, includes breakfast, elevator, parking-€8, 1 Place de la République, tel. 05 59 55 08 08, www.ibis.com, h8716@accor.com).

$$ Hôtel Côte Basque** is conveniently located by the train station in the Saint Esprit neighborhood, just across the river from the Old Town. It's on a busy street, but the small-but-comfortable rooms have double-paned windows to cut the noise

(Sb-€61-66, Db-€64-69, Tb-€71-76, breakfast-€10, elevator, free Wi-Fi, 2 Rue Maubec, tel. 05 59 55 10 21, www.hotel-cotebasque .fr, hotelcotebasque@orange.fr).

$$ Hôtel des Arceaux** is a family-run B&B-style establishment with 16 rooms on a small pedestrian street in Grand Bayonne. It's just around the corner from the cathedral (Db-€66-76, breakfast-€7, free Wi-Fi, 26 Rue Port Neuf, tel. 05 59 59 15 53, www.hotel-arceaux.com, hotel.arceaux@wanadoo.fr).

Eating in Bayonne

The Grand Bayonne riverside has several tapas restaurants, a couple of easy *bistrots,* and a pizza place. The Petit Bayonne riverside has some *bistrots* and a few more proper sit-down restaurants. The pedestrian streets surrounding the cathedral in Grand Bayonne offer casual dining spots serving crêpes, *tartines,* quiches, and salads. Most places have outdoor tables in nice weather.

Le Bayonnais, next door to the Museum of Basque Culture, serves traditional Basque specialties à la carte. Sit in the blue-tiled interior or out along the river (€18 weekday lunch and dinner *menu* on weekdays, closed Sun-Mon, Quai des Corsaires 38, tel. 05 59 25 61 19).

La Cidrerie Txotx (pronounced "choch") has a Spanish-bodega ambience under a chorus line of hams. You can also sit outside, along the river, just past the market hall (€8-10 Basque tapas or €12-19 *plats,* daily, 49 Quai Jauréguiberry, tel. 05 59 59 16 80).

A la Bolée serves up inexpensive sweet and savory crêpes in a cozy atmosphere along the side of the cathedral (daily, 10 Place Pasteur, tel. 05 59 59 18 75).

Le Chistera, run by a family that's spent time in the US, proudly serves traditional Basque dishes made with market-fresh ingredients. Try the *poulet* with Basque sauce or one of their soups, and polish off your meal with homemade *gâteau basque* (€16 lunch *menu,* €25-30 dinners, Tue-Wed 12:00-14:00, Thu-Sun 12:00-14:00 & 19:30-21:00, closed Mon, 42 Rue Port Neuf, tel. 05 59 59 25 93, www.lechistera.com).

Café du Théâtre has pleasant outdoor tables by the river. Try it for a simple early breakfast (Place de la Liberté, tel. 05 59 59 09 31).

Picnic Supplies: If the weather's good, consider gathering a picnic from the shops along the pedestrian streets, at Les Halles market (only open in the mornings), in the Casino minimart (Mon-Sat 8:00-13:00 & 15:30-20:00, closed Sun, 38 Rue Port Neuf), or at the Monoprix (Mon-Sat 8:30-20:30, closed Sun, 8 Rue Orbe). Don't forget the chocolate, then head for the park around the ramparts below the *Jardin Botanique* (benches galore).

Bayonne Connections

Chronoplus buses run throughout the area regularly. Most lines run two to three times an hour from about 7:00 to 20:00, but are noticeably less frequent on Saturdays and even sparser on Sundays. Buy a €1 ticket on the bus; if you plan to ride twice or more in one day, buy the 24-hour ticket for €2 (tel. 05 59 52 59 52, www .chronoplus.eu).

From Bayonne by Bus to: BAB (Biarritz-Anglet-Bayonne) Airport (2-3/hour, 15 minutes, line #C is best option), **Biarritz** (2-3/hour, fewer on Sun, 30 minutes, Chronoplus lines #A1 and #A2), and **St-Jean-de-Luz** (almost hourly, 45 minutes, ATCRB line #816, €3). Pick up BAB and Biarritz buses by the Mairie/ Théâter stop on the riverside; catch the St-Jean-de-Luz bus from Place des Basques by the TI. Buses to the inland Basque villages of Espelette and Ainhoa are impractical.

By Train to: St-Jean-Pied-du-Port (5/day, 6/day in summer, 1.25 hours).

By Taxi to: Biarritz (20 minutes, about €30) and **St-Jean-de-Luz** (30 minutes, about €50—or more if traffic is heavy, tel. 05 59 59 48 48).

Biarritz / Biarritz

A glitzy resort town steeped in the belle époque, Biarritz (bee-ah-ritz) is where the French Basques put on the ritz. In the 19th century, this simple whaling harbor became, almost overnight,

a high-class aristocrat-magnet dubbed the "beach of kings." Although St-Jean-de-Luz and Bayonne are more fully French and more fully Basque, the made-for-international-tourists, jet-set scene of Biarritz is not without its charms. Perched over a popular surfing beach, anchored by grand hotels and casinos, hemmed in by jagged and picturesque rocky islets at either end, and watched over by a lighthouse on a distant promontory, Biarritz is a striking beach resort. However, for sightseers with limited time, it's likely more trouble than it's worth.

Orientation to Biarritz

Biarritz feels much bigger than its population of 30,000. The town sprawls, but virtually everything we're interested in lines up along the waterfront: the beach, the promenade, the hotel and shopping zone, and the TI.

Tourist Information

The TI is in a little pink castle two blocks up from the beach (just above the beach and casino, hiding behind the City Hall—look for *hôtel de ville* signs). Pick up the free map and get details on any sightseeing that interests you (July-Aug daily 9:00-19:00; Sept-June Mon-Fri 9:00-18:00, Sat-Sun 10:00-17:00; Square d'Ixelles, tel. 05 59 22 37 00, www.biarritz.fr).

Arrival in Biarritz

By Car: Drivers follow signs for *Centre-Ville*, then carefully track signs for specific parking garages. The most central garages are called *Grande Plage, Casino, Bellevue,* and *St. Eugénie* (closest to the water). Signs in front of each tell you whether it's full *(complet)*, in which case move on to the next one.

By Bus: Buses stop at "Biarritz Centre," a parking lot next to the TI (buses to/from Bayonne stop along the side of the lot; buses to/from St-Jean-de-Luz stop at the end of the lot). If you're taking a bus, be aware that some stop at the outskirts of town—only take one to "Centre."

Don't bother taking the **train** to or from Biarritz, as the station is about two miles from the tourist area (but if you must, bus #A1 connects the train station to the city center hourly, €1, buy ticket from driver).

There is no baggage storage in Biarritz.

Sights in Biarritz

There's little of sightseeing value in Biarritz. The TI can fill you in on the town's four museums (Marine Museum—described later; Chocolate Planet and Museum—intriguing, but a long walk from the center; Oriental Art Museum—large, diverse collection of art from across Asia; and Biarritz Historical Museum—really?).

Your time is best spent strolling along the various levels that climb up from the sea. (Resist the urge to check out the pebble beach for now.) From the TI, you can do a loop: First head west on the lively **pedestrian streets** that occupy the plateau above the water, which are lined with restaurants, cafés, and high-class, resorty window-shopping. (Place Georges Clemenceau is the grassy "main square" of this area.) Biarritz is picnic-friendly, with *beaucoup* benches facing the waves. Consider stocking up before continuing this walk.

Work your way past the Église Sainte Eugénie out to the point with the **Marine Museum** (Musée de la Mer). The most convenient of Biarritz's attractions, this pricey Art Deco museum/aquarium wins the "best rainy-day option" award, with a tank of seals and a chance to get face-to-teeth with live sharks (€13.50, daily 9:30-20:00, July-Aug until 24:00, last entry one hour before closing, tel. 05 59 22 75 40, www.museedelamer.com).

Whether or not you're visiting the museum, it's worth hiking

down to the entrance, then wandering out on the walkways that connect the big offshore rocks. These lead to the so-called **Virgin Rock** (Rocher de la Vierge), topped by a statue of Mary. Spot any surfers?

From here stick along the water as you head back toward the TI. After a bit of up and down over the rocks, don't miss the trail down to **Fishermen's Wharf** (Port des Pêcheurs), a little pocket of salty authenticity that clings like barnacles to the cliff below the hotels. The remnants of an aborted construction project from the town's glory days, this little fishing settlement of humble houses and rugged jetties seems to faintly echo the Basque culture that thrived here before the glitz hit. Many of the houses have been taken over by the tourist trade (gift shops and restaurants).

Continuing along the water (and briefly back up to street level), make your way back to the town's centerpiece, the **big beach** (Grande Plage). Dominating this inviting stretch of sand is the Art Deco casino, and the TI is just above that. If you haven't yet taken the time on your vacation to splash, wade, or stroll on the beach...now's your chance.

Biarritz Connections

From Biarritz by Bus to: St-Jean-de-Luz (nearly hourly, fewer on Sundays, 45 minutes, ATCRB line #816) and **Bayonne** (2-3/hour, fewer on Sundays, 30 minutes, Chronoplus lines #A1 and #A2).

Villages in the French Basque Country

Traditional villages among the green hills, with buildings colored like the Basque flag, offer the best glimpse of Basque culture. Cheese, hard cider, and *pelota* players are the primary products

BASQUE COUNTRY

of these villages, which attract few foreigners but many French summer visitors. Most of these villages have welcomed pilgrims bound for Santiago de Compostela since the Middle Ages. Today's hikers trek between local villages or head into the Pyrenees. The most appealing villages lie in the foothills of the Pyrenees, spared from beach-scene development.

Use St-Jean-de-Luz as your base to visit the Basque sights described below. For information on another French Basque village a bit farther away—St-Jean-Pied-de-Port (Donibane Garazi), the starting point of the Camino de Santiago pilgrim trail—see page 286. You can reach some of these places by public transportation, but the hassle outweighs the rewards.

Do a circuit of these towns in the order they're listed here (and, with time, also add St-Jean-Pied-de-Port at the end). Assuming you're driving, I've included route instructions as well.

• *Only 15 minutes from St-Jean-de-Luz, follow signs for* Ascain, *then* Sare. *On the twisty-turny road toward Sare, you'll pass the station for the train up to...*

La Rhune/Larrun

Between the villages of Ascain and Sare, near the border with Spain, a small cogwheel train takes tourists to the top of La Rhune, the region's highest peak (2,969 feet). You'll putt-putt up the hillside for 35 minutes in a wooden, open-air train car to reach panoramic views of land and sea (adults-€15 round-trip, kids-€8, all pay €2-3 more in summer, runs March-mid-Nov daily, closed mid-Nov-Feb, departures weather-dependent—the trip is worthless if it's not clear, goes every 35 minutes when busiest July-Aug, tel. 05 59 54 20 26, www.rhune.com). For those traveling without a car, **Le Basque Bondissant** runs a shuttle for peak-season tourists from St-Jean-de-Luz (€17, kids-€10, train ticket included, see page 256).

• *Continue along the same road, and look out for pull-offs with room for a couple of cars, typically placed at the most scenic spots. Stop to smell the grass before the next stop...*

Sare/Sara

Sare, which sits at the base of the towering mountain La Rhune, is among the most picturesque villages—and the most touristed. It's easily reached from St-Jean-de-Luz by bus or car. The small TI is on the main square (Mon-Fri 9:30-12:30 & 13:30-18:00, Sat 9:30-12:30, closed Sun year-round and Sat Nov-March, tel. 05 59 54 20 14, www.sare.fr). Nearby is a cluster of hotels and the town church (which has an impressive interior, with arches over the gold-slathered altar and Basque-style balconies lining the nave). Reforms in the 18th century prohibited burials at or near Catholic churches, but Basque-style tombstones still surround the main church. At the far end of the square is the town's humble *frontón* (*pelota* court).

• *Leaving Sare, first follow signs for* toutes directions, *then* St-Pée, *and watch for the turnoff to...*

Ainhoa/Ainhoa

Ainhoa is a colorful, tidy, picturesque one-street town that sees

fewer tourists (which is a good thing). Its chunks of old walls and gates mingle with red-and-white half-timbered buildings. The 14th-century church—with a beautiful golden *retable* (screen behind the altar)—and the *frontón* share center stage. Parking is plentiful; resist the urge to turn off at the *frontón*—it's better to continue on for parking near the TI.

Ainhoa is also a popular starting point for hikes into the hills. For a spectacular village-and-valleys view, drive five minutes (or walk 90 sweaty minutes) up the steep dirt road to the Chapelle de Notre-Dame d'Aranazau ("d'Aubepine" in French). Start in the central parking lot directly across the main street from the church, then head straight uphill into the clouds. Follow signs for *oratoire,* then count the giant white crosses leading the way to the top. The chapel is occasionally closed, and cloudy days don't offer spectacular views, but the ethereal experience is worth the steep detour for drivers.

• *As you leave Ainhoa, you'll have to backtrack the way you came in to find the road to...*

Espelette/Ezpeleta

Espelette won't let you forget that it's the capital of the region's AOC red peppers *(piments d'Espelette),* with strands of them dangling like good-luck charms from many houses and storefronts. After strolling the charming, cobbled center, head to the well-restored château and medieval tower of former local barons, which now houses the town hall, exhibition space, and the **TI** (Mon-Fri 8:30-12:30 & 14:00-18:00, Sat 9:30-12:30, closed Sun, tel. 05 59 93 95 02, www.espelette.fr). Or wander downhill

toward the pink *frontón,* following the *église* signs past houses constructed in the 1700s and a captivating stream, to find the town church. Climb up into the church balconies for some fancy views.

Sleeping and Eating: For a good regional meal, consider the **$$ Hôtel Euzkadi**** restaurant, with a *muy* Spanish ambience (€18-36 *menus,* daily 12:30-14:00 & 19:30-21:00, July-Aug closed Mon, Sept-June closed Mon-Tue, 285 Karrika Nagusia, tel. 05 59 93 91 88). The hotel has 27 rooms with modern touches and a swimming pool (Db-€78-84, air-con, elevator, free Wi-Fi, www.hotel-restaurant-euzkadi.com).

• *From Espelette, if you have time, you can follow signs to* Cambo les Bains, *then* **St-Jean-Pied-de-Port** *(40 minutes, covered in the next chapter).*

THE CAMINO DE SANTIAGO

*St-Jean-Pied-de-Port • Pamplona
• Burgos • León • O Cebreiro • Lugo*

The Camino de Santiago—the "Way of St. James"—is Europe's ultimate pilgrimage route. Since the Middle Ages, humble pilgrims have trod hundreds of miles across the north of Spain to pay homage to the remains of St. James in his namesake city, Santiago de Compostela. After several lonely centuries, the route has been rediscovered, and more and more pilgrims are traveling—by foot, bike, and horse—along this ancient pathway.

While dedicating a month of your life to walk the Camino is admirable, you might not have that kind of time. But with a car (or public transportation), any traveler can use the Camino as a sightseeing spine—a string of worthwhile cities, towns, and countryside sights—and an opportunity to periodically "play pilgrim."

There were many ancient pilgrimage routes across Europe to Santiago de Compostela, but the most popular one across Spain—and the route described here—has always been the so-called "French Road" (Camino Francés), which covers nearly 500 miles across northern Spain from the French border to Santiago.

The route begins in the French foothills of the Pyrenees, in the Basque village of St-Jean-Pied-de-Port. Twist up and over rugged Roncesvalles Pass into Spain, and on to Pamplona—the delightful, Basque-flavored capital of Navarre, famous for its Running of the Bulls. From here head west through the fertile hills of Navarre to the vineyards of La Rioja, then across the endless wheat fields and rough, arid plains of northern Castile to Burgos and León, with their beautiful dueling Gothic cathedrals—one a riot of architectural styles, the other gracefully simple but packed with stained glass.

La Historia del Camino

The first person to undertake the Camino de Santiago was... Santiago himself. After the death of Christ, the apostles scattered to the corners of the earth to spread the Word of God. Supposedly, St. James went on a missionary trip from the Holy Land all the way to the northwest corner of Spain, which, at that point, really was the end of the Western world. (For more on St. James, see the sidebar on page 362.)

According to legend, St. James' remains were discovered in 813 in the town that would soon bear his name. This put Santiago de Compostela on the map, as one of three places—along with Rome and Jerusalem—where remains of apostles are known to be buried. In 951 Godescalco, the Bishop of Le Puy in France, walked to Santiago de Compostela to pay homage to the relics. As other pilgrims followed his example, the Camino de Santiago informally emerged. Then, in the 12th century, Pope Callistus II decreed that any person who walked to Santiago in a Holy Year, confessed their sins, and took communion at the cathedral would be forgiven. This opportunity for a cheap indulgence made the Camino de Santiago one of the most important pilgrimages in the world.

It's probably no coincidence that St. James' remains were "discovered" and promoted just as the Reconquista was in full swing. The pope's decree helped to consolidate the Christians' hold over lands retaken from the Moors. Pilgrims were ideal candidates to repopulate and defend northern Spain. Many of those who made the journey to Santiago stuck around somewhere along the route (often because of privileges granted them by local rulers who needed help rebuilding). It became a self-sustaining little circle: Pilgrims came along the Camino, saw great sights, and decided to stay...to build even greater sights for the next pilgrims to enjoy.

The Christian monarchy designated an old Roman commercial road from France across northern Iberia as the "official" route, and soon churches, monasteries, hostels, hospitals, blacksmiths, and other pilgrims' services began to pop up. Religious-military orders such as the Knights of Santiago and the Knights Templar protected the route from bandits and fought alongside Christian armies against the Moorish resurgence, allowing the evolving Catholic state to gather strength in the safe haven created by the Camino.

In the Middle Ages, pilgrims came to Santiago from all over Europe—mostly from France, but also from Portugal, Italy, Britain, the Netherlands, Germany, Scandinavia, and Eastern Europe. Many prominent figures embarked on the journey, including St. Francis of Assisi, Dutch painter Jan van Eyck, and the Wife of Bath in Chaucer's *Canterbury Tales*.

This steady flow of pilgrims from around Europe resulted in a rich exchange of knowledge, art, and architecture. Even today you'll find magnificent cathedrals along the Camino in cities such as Burgos and León, which incorporated and improved on the latest in cathedral design from France at that time.

By 1130 the trek was so popular that it prompted a French monk named Aimery Picaud to pen (likely with the help of some ghostwriters) a chronicle of his journey, including tips on where to eat, where to stay, the best way to get from place to place, and how to pack light and use a money belt. This *Codex Calixtinus* (Latin for "Camino Through the Back Door") was the world's first guidebook—the great-great-granddaddy of the one you're holding right now.

In the age of Columbus, the Renaissance, and the Reformation, interest in the Camino dropped way off. When the Moors were finally defeated in 1492, the significance of Reconquista icon St. James fell by the wayside. The discovery of the New World in the same year led both the Church and the monarchy to turn their attention across the Atlantic, and the pilgrimage began to wane. That was followed by a century of religious wars pitting Catholics against Protestants, which also distracted potential pilgrims. Feeling threatened by the pirate Francis Drake (not considered "sir" in Spain), the church hid the remains of St. James so thoroughly that they were actually lost for generations. Meanwhile, the rise of humanism during the Renaissance diminished the mystique of the pilgrimage. For the next centuries, and as recently as a few decades ago, only a few hardy souls still followed the route.

Then, in the late 1960s, a handful of parish priests along the Camino began working to recover the route, establishing associations of "friends of the Camino" that would eventually agree on a path and mark it. They received help from none other than Generalísimo Francisco Franco, who decided that Catholicism and nationalism went hand-in-hand. By reviving the Camino, he reasoned, Spain was assured to relive its most glorious days. In 1982, and again in 1989, Pope John Paul II visited Santiago de Compostela, reminding the world of the town's historic significance. In 1987 the European Union designated the Camino as Europe's first Cultural Itinerary. And after the success of the 1992 Expo in Sevilla, the Galician government decided to pour funds into reviving the tradition for the Holy Year in 1993. They made Santiago a high-profile destination and shelled out big pesetas for concerts by stars including the Rolling Stones, Bruce Springsteen, and Julio Iglesias (whose father was born in Galicia).

The plan worked, and now—aided by European Union funding—the route has enjoyed a huge renaissance of interest, with 100,000 pilgrims each year trekking to Santiago. Shirley MacLaine has made the journey (her book *The Camino: A Journey of the Spirit* is popular among pilgrims). Even Hollywood has joined the trek with the 2010 movie *The Way*, starring Martin Sheen as a grieving father making his way along the Camino after his estranged son dies during an attempt at the pilgrimage. Cyclists and horse riders are now joining hikers on the journey, and these days it's "in" to follow the seashells to Santiago.

Camino de Santiago Overview

As the path crosses into Galicia near the time-passed stony mountain village of O Cebreiro, the terrain changes, becoming lush and green. This last leg of the journey, in Galicia, is the most popular: Pilgrims pass simple farms, stone churches, moss-covered homes with slate roofs, apple orchards, flocks of sheep, dense forests of oak, sweet chestnut, and eucalyptus...and plenty of other pilgrims. Just before Santiago, the ancient walled Roman city of Lugo is a worthwhile detour for car travelers.

Whether undertaken for spiritual edification or sightseeing pleasure, the Camino de Santiago ties together some of Spain's most appealing landscape, history, architecture, and people.

Getting Around the Camino de Santiago

By Car: This chapter is geared for car pilgrims who want to trace the Camino and linger at the highlights. Italicized directions marked by a bullet point are designed for drivers (with specific route tips, road numbers, and directional signs). To supplement these instructions, it's essential to get a good road map (most TIs can give you a free map covering just their province, or you can buy a better one by Michelin or Mapa Total for about €6). Driving the full Camino nonstop would take about 12 hours. Assuming you're taking the most direct (expressway/*autovía*) route, figure these estimated times for specific legs of the Camino by car (these times don't take into account stops or detours, such as the Rioja Wine Loop):

- St-Jean-Pied-de-Port to Pamplona—1.5 hours
- Pamplona to Burgos—2.25-3 hours (depending on route)
- Burgos to León—2 hours

Best Stages for a Short Walk

The Camino de Santiago is divided into 34 stages of about 12-15 miles apiece (approximately one day's walk). Even if you're doing most of the Camino by car, consider taking an extra day or two to walk one of these recommended stages (to get back to your car, catch a bus—TIs have schedules—or, where buses aren't an option, take a taxi). These stages are scattered throughout the Camino, and are listed from east to west.

Roncesvalles to Zubiri (21.5 km/13.5 miles)—This is the first stage in Spain, after the arduous trek over the Pyrenees. It's mostly (though not entirely) downhill, through rolling hills and meadows, amidst sheep and charming villages.

Puente la Reina to Estella (19 km/12 miles)—Here the Camino becomes a bit more level and arid. This leg begins in an appealing pilgrim town, then passes through gentle farm fields and along a three-and-a-half-mile stretch of Roman road (from Cirauqui to Lorca).

Pieros to Villafranca del Bierzo (7.5 km/5 miles)—For this stretch, the Camino ascends through the hilly El Bierzo region, en route to Galicia. The last bit of this leg takes you through vineyards and vegetable patches into Villafranca, entering town at the Romanesque church of Santiago.

Ambasmestas to O Cebreiro (13.2 km/8.2 miles)—If you're not intimidated by a steep uphill hike, this leg is a gorgeous introduction to Galicia—culminating at a perfect little hilltop village.

Sarria to Portomarin (21.5 km/13.5 miles)—Because it's about 100 kilometers (62 miles) from Santiago (the minimum to qualify for a *compostela* certificate), Sarria is a popular starting point for short-haul pilgrims. From here you can make it to Santiago in less than a week. The terrain: pretty Galicia.

- León to Astorga—1 hour
- Astorga to O Cebreiro—1.5 hours
- O Cebreiro to Lugo—1 hour
- Lugo to Santiago—1.75 hours

Many freeways are marked *Autovía Camino de Santiago* to keep you on track. But be warned that *Camino de Santiago* directional signs in small towns can be misleading, since they're sometimes intended for foot pilgrims, not drivers. Navigate by town names and road numbers instead.

By Public Transportation: Most of the Camino route can be done by bus and/or train. However, it can be difficult, or even impossible, to reach some of the out-of-the-way stops between the

The Camino de Santiago at a Glance

These attractions are listed in the order you'll reach them as you traverse the Camino de Santiago.

▲**St-Jean-Pied-de-Port** Tranquil French mountain village clustered along a babbling stream—the perfect springboard for the Camino. See page 286.

Roncesvalles Middle-of-nowhere spot where Camino walkers catch their collective breath after the exhausting first leg over the Pyrenees. See page 291.

▲▲**Pamplona** Thriving Basque town (a.k.a. Iruña) with atmospheric narrow lanes, fine churches, and world-famous Running of the Bulls. See page 292.

▲**Puente la Reina** Classic Camino pilgrim town with a perfectly picturesque bridge. See page 308.

Irache Monastery Legendary "wine fountain" lifting pilgrims' spirits in the middle of nowhere. See page 309.

▲**La Rioja** A detour from the Camino (near the skippable city of Logroño) into pastoral wine country, worthwhile for oenophiles and those intrigued by charming wine towns (Laguardia) and contemporary architecture (with wineries by Gehry and Calatrava). See page 312.

big cities (such as O Cebreiro). Where feasible, I've listed train and bus connections for each of the main stops. Trains cover all the major cities, and Alsa buses also link the main stops (www.alsa.es).

The Old-Fashioned Way: If you're walking or biking the entire Camino, don't rely exclusively on my coverage in this chapter (which describes the major towns and cities, but ignores so much more). Equip yourself with a good day-by-day guidebook with details on each leg, and get good advice about what to pack. For starters, see the sidebar on page 324.

Planning Your Time

Drivers begin in Basque Country (San Sebastián in Spain or St-Jean-de-Luz in France), where you can pick up your rental

Santo Domingo de la Calzada Dusty village with fun legends and pilgrim amenities. See page 312.

▲**Burgos** Sprawling but walkable city centered on its glorious Gothic cathedral, with loads of quirky touches. See page 313.

▲▲**León** Bustling city with grand Gothic cathedral (crammed with Spain's best stained glass), fresco-slathered Romanesque chapel (in the San Isidro Museum), and lively tapas-bar scene. See page 327.

▲**Astorga** Pleasant town graced with Antoni Gaudí's visit-worthy Bishop's Palace. See page 340.

Villafranca del Bierzo Sleepy pilgrim town perched on rugged hills at the edge of Galicia. See page 342.

▲▲**O Cebreiro** Quintessential Galician mountain village, with stone *palloza* hobbit houses, a pre-Romanesque church, and oodles of pilgrim ambience. See page 343.

▲**Lugo** Atmospheric Galician city just off the Camino, lassoed by stout, mossy walls. See page 346.

▲▲**Santiago de Compostela** Destination of all those pilgrims, with an invigorating cityscape and a dramatic cathedral that's not a letdown, even after a 500-mile walk. See the next chapter.

car. If you're in a hurry or don't plan to visit France, you can skip St-Jean-Pied-de-Port and connect easily to Pamplona from Spain's Basque Country.

Day 1: Drive through the French Basque villages (see previous chapter) to St-Jean-Pied-de-Port, then over Roncesvalles Pass to Pamplona. Sleep in Pamplona.

Day 2: Explore Pamplona, then drive westward to Burgos (stopping en route at Puente la Reina, and detouring for the Rioja Wine Loop if you have time and a healthy interest in wine). Sleep in Burgos.

Day 3: Sightsee Burgos this morning, then drive to León and dip into the cathedral there. Sleep in León—or, if you're tired of big cities, continue an hour farther to sleep in Astorga.

Day 4: Continue westward to Galicia, stopping at O Cebreiro and Lugo before arriving at Santiago de Compostela.

Orientation to the Camino

The term "Camino de Santiago," as mentioned earlier, actually refers to many different routes across Europe. All (like this chapter) travel from east to west. For our description of the popular "French Road" (Camino Francés), we'll begin in the French Basque town of St-Jean-Pied-de-Port, cross over the Pyrenees at Roncesvalles, then pass through three northern Spanish cities (Pamplona, Burgos, León), before climbing into green Galicia, ending at Santiago de Compostela.

Tourist Information: Pilgrims will find no shortage of helpful resources along the way. In addition to TIs in each town (listed in this chapter), you'll also find "Pilgrim Friend" associations and other offices (often attached to an *albergue* or *refugio*) that offer kind advice to the weary traveler.

Holy Year: The Compostela Holy Year *(Año Xacobeo)* occurs when the Feast of St. James (July 25) falls on a Sunday (next in 2021); during a Holy Year, traffic on the trails doubles, and the pilgrim atmosphere is even more festive.

Tours: Iberian Adventures runs guided and self-guided walking tours in English for individuals and small groups along the Camino de Santiago and in the Rioja wine region. Company owner Jeremy Dack highlights each area's natural environment, history, culture, cuisine, and wine, and emphasizes environmental awareness and respect for local customs (tel. 965-840-568, mobile 620-939-116, www.iberianadventures.com, info @iberianadventures.com). Jeremy also leads hiking tours of Spain's major mountain ranges.

St-Jean-Pied-de-Port

Just five miles from the Spanish border, the walled town of St-Jean-Pied-de-Port (san-zhahn-pee-ay-duh-por) is the most popular village in all the French Basque countryside (you may also see it labeled as Donibane Garazi, its Basque name). Traditionally, St-Jean-Pied-de-Port has been the final stopover in France for Santiago-bound pilgrims, who gather here to cross the Pyrenees together and continue their march through Spain. The scallop shell of "St. Jacques" (French for  "James") is etched on walls throughout the town.

About half the visitors to this town are pilgrims; the rest are mostly French tourists. Gift shops sell a strange combination of pilgrim gear (such as quick-drying shirts and shorts) and Basque souvenirs. This place is packed in the summer (so come early or late).

Orientation to St-Jean-Pied-de-Port

Tourist Information: The TI, on the main road along the outside of the walled Old Town, can give you a town map (Mon-Sat 9:00-12:00 & 14:00-18:00, closed Sun, tel. 05 59 37 03 57). For Camino information, you'll do better at the Pilgrim Friends Office (described below). Ask the TI about weekly *pelota vasca* games (usually Mon at 16:00 or 17:00 at the trinquet court on Place du Trinquet).

Arrival in St-Jean-Pied-de-Port: Parking is ample and well-signed from the main road. If arriving by **train,** exit the station to the left, then follow the busy road at the traffic circle toward the city wall.

Sights in St-Jean-Pied-de-Port

There's little in the way of sightseeing here, other than pilgrim-spotting. But St-Jean-Pied-de-Port feels like the perfect "Welcome to the Camino" springboard for the upcoming journey. Many modern pilgrims begin their Camino in this traditional spot because of its easy train connection to Bayonne, and because—as its name implies ("St. John at the Foot of the Pass")—it offers a very challenging but rewarding first leg: up, over, and into Spain.

Enter the Old Town on restaurant row, Rue d'Uhart, then

turn left onto Rue d'Espagne. The **Notre-Dame Gate,** which was once a drawbridge, is straight ahead. Cross the old bridge over the Nive River (the same one that winds up in Bayonne) and head up the main walking drag, **Rue de la Citadelle.** With its rosy-pink buildings and ancient dates above its doorways, this lane simply feels old. Notice lots of signs for *chambres* (rooms) and *refuges*—humble, hostel-like pilgrim bunkhouses.

Partway up, on the left at #39, look for the **Pilgrim Friends Office** (Les Amis du Chemin de Saint-Jacques, daily 7:30-11:45 & 13:00-18:45 & 19:45-22:00, tel. 05 59 37 05 09). This is where pilgrims check in before their long journey to Santiago; about 46,000 pilgrims started out here in 2012 (compared with just

Camino de Santiago: Eastern Half

4,000 about a decade ago).

Where do they all come from? In 2012, about 9,000 French pilgrims set out here. The second largest group hailed from Spain (7,300), with Italy and Germany following. The US came in fifth, with almost 3,000 pilgrims. For €2, a pilgrim can buy the official credential *(credenciel* in French, *credencial* in Spanish)* that she'll get stamped at each stop between here and Santiago to prove she walked the whole way and thereby earn her *compostela* certificate. Pilgrims also receive a warm welcome, lots of advice (like a handy chart breaking down the walk into 34 stages, with valuable distance and elevation information), and help finding a bunk (the well-traveled staff swears that no pilgrim ever goes without a bed in St-Jean-Pied-de-Port).

A few more steps up, on the left, you'll pass the skippable €3 Bishop's Prison (Prison des Evêques). Continue on up to the **citadel,** dating from the mid-17th century—when this was a highly strategic location, keeping an eye on the easiest road over the Pyrenees between Spain and France. Although not open to the public (as it houses a school), the grounds around this stout fortress offer sweeping views over the French Basque countryside.

Sleeping in St-Jean-Pied-de-Port

Lots of humble pilgrim lodgings line the main drag, Rue de la Citadelle. If you're looking for a bit more comfort, consider these options.

Sleep Code

(€1 = about $1.30, France country code: 33, Spain country code: 34)
S = Single, **D** = Double/Twin, **T** = Triple, **Q** = Quad, **b** = bathroom, **s** = shower only, * = French hotel rating system (0-5 stars). Unless otherwise noted, credit cards are accepted and English is spoken, but breakfast is not included. Some hotels include the 10 percent IVA tax in the room price; others tack it onto your bill.

To help you easily sort through these listings, I've divided the accommodations into three categories based on the price for a standard double room with bath during high season:

$$$ Higher Priced—Most rooms €95 or more.
 $$ Moderately Priced—Most rooms between €55-95.
  $ Lower Priced—Most rooms €55 or less.

Prices can change without notice; verify the hotel's current rates online or by email. For the best prices, always book direct.

CAMINO DE SANTIAGO

$$ Hotel Ramuntcho** is the only real hotel option in the Old Town, located partway up Rue de la Citadelle. Its 16 rooms above a restaurant are straightforward but modern (Db-€67-81, breakfast-€9, free Wi-Fi, 1 Rue de France, tel. 05 59 37 03 91, http://hotel-ramuntcho.com, hotel.ramuntcho@wanadoo.fr).

$$ Itzalpea, a café and tea house, rents five rooms along the main road just outside the Old Town (Sb-€55-58, Db-€65-78 depending on size, includes breakfast, closed Sat off-season, air-con, 5 Place du Trinquet, tel. 05 59 37 03 66, www.maisondhotes-itzalpea.com, itzalpea@wanadoo.fr).

$ Chambres Chez l'Habitant has five old-fashioned, pilgrim-perfect rooms along the main drag. Welcoming Maria and Jean Pierre speak limited English, but their daughter can help translate (€20-25 per person in D, Db, Q, or Qb, includes breakfast, 15 Rue de la Citadelle, tel. 05 59 37 05 83, www.chambres-camino.com).

Eating in St-Jean-Pied-de-Port

Tourists, pilgrims, and locals alike find plenty of places to eat along Rue de la Citadelle (heading up to the citadel), Rue du Trinquet (the main traffic street into town), and Rue d'Uhart. Consider **Café Navarre** (1 Place Juan de Huarte, tel. 05 59 37 01 67) or **Cafe Ttipia** (2 Place Charles Floquet, tel. 05 59 37 11 96).

Picnics: If you're lucky enough to land here on a Monday morning, shop at the weekly market. Farmers, cheesemakers, and winemakers bring their products in from the countryside.

St-Jean-Pied-de-Port Connections

A scenic train conveniently links St-Jean-Pied-de-Port to **Bayonne** (5/day, 6/day in summer, 1.25 hours) and from there to **St-Jean-de-Luz** (about 25 minutes beyond Bayonne, www.sncf.fr). It's about a 1.25-hour drive from St-Jean-de-Luz. A single bus departure from St-Jean-Pied-de-Port serves **Pamplona** (daily, leaves at 16:00, 1.75 hours, run by the Spanish line Alsa or its sister company Conda, www.alsa.es).

From St-Jean-Pied-de-Port to Pamplona

The first stretch of the Camino, crossing the Pyrenees from France into Spain, is among the most dramatic. There's little in the way of civilization, but it's a memorable start for the journey.

• *From St-Jean-Pied-de-Port, look for green signs to* Pamplona*, then follow road signs to* Arnéguy *on road D-933. (But be warned that the road signs for* Camino de Santiago *take a much more roundabout high mountain, one-lane road instead of the direct road to the border.)*

Crossing the Pyrenees: Roncesvalles (Roncevaux/Orreaga)

As you go over the stone bridge in the village of **Arnéguy,** you're also passing from France to Spain. For centuries this bridge was the site of a delicate dance between nervous smugglers and customs police. Today you'll barely notice you've crossed a border, except for the gigantic *ventas*—large duty-free malls catering to a mainly Spanish clientele. Along the drive, keep a watchful eye out for stone pillars with crosses—old trail markers for pilgrims.

The road meanders through a valley before twisting up to the pass called **Puerto de Ibañeta** (also known as the Roncesvalles Pass). This scrubby high-mountain pass is one of the Basque Country's most historic spots. The most accessible gateway through the Pyrenees between France and Spain, this pass has been the site of several epic battles. According to a popular medieval legend, Charlemagne's nephew Roland was killed fighting here. Vengeful Basque tribes, seeking retribution for Charlemagne's sacking of Pamplona, followed the army as it began its return to France—and felled the mighty Roland along this very road. Several centuries later, Napoleon used the same road to invade Spain.

Coming down from the pass, you reach **Roncesvalles/**

Orreaga ("Valley of Pines"), which gave this area its name. This jumble of buildings surrounding a monastery is sort of a pilgrim depot, where travelers can pause to catch their collective breath after clearing the first arduous leg of the Camino. The big building on the right is  a simple *refugio*, filled with bunk beds. In the afternoon, you might see pilgrims washing their clothes at the spigots in front, then hanging them to dry amidst the cows and knobby trees out back. The big church (on the left) has a tourable cloister and museum (€4.30 for both, cloister only—€2.70, includes audioguide, guided tours but no fixed times or guarantee of English). As you leave town, you pass the first sign for Santiago de Compostela...790 kilometers (490 miles) straight ahead.

From here to Pamplona, the Camino passes through some pretty rolling hills and meadows, and several appealing villages. The first after Roncesvalles, called **Auritz/Burguete,** was supposedly Hemingway's favorite place to fish for trout when he needed to recover from a Pamplona bender.

Zubiri marks the halfway point between the pass and Pamplona, with two powerful reminders of the old Basque Country: a Guardia Civil bunker built to withstand separatist bomb attacks, and a giant magnetite quarry mined for steel production.

• *Around that next bend is the first big city on the Camino: Pamplona.*

Pamplona

Proud Pamplona, with stout old walls standing guard in the Pyrenees foothills, is the capital of the province of Navarre ("Navarra" in Spanish). At its peak in the Middle Ages, Navarre was a grand kingdom that controlled parts of today's Spain and France. (The current king of Spain, Juan Carlos, is a descendant of the French line of Navarre royalty.) After the French and Spanish parts split, Pamplona remained the capital of Spanish Navarre.

Today Pamplona—called "Iruña" in the Basque language—feels at once affluent (with the sleek new infrastructure of a town on the rise), claustrophobic (with its warren of narrow lanes), and fascinating (with its odd traditions, rich history, and ties to Hemingway). Culturally, the city is a lively hodgepodge of Basque and *Navarro*. Locals like to distinguish between *Vascos* (people of Basque citizenship—not them) and *Vascones* (people who identify culturally as Basques—as do many *Navarros*). Pamplona is also an important seat for a controversial wing of the Catholic Church, Opus Dei, founded in Spain in 1928 by the Catholic priest Josemaría Escrivá. He established the private Pamplona-based University of Navarra, and Opus Dei also runs a hospital and several schools in the city.

Of course, Pamplona is best known as the host of one of Spain's (and Europe's) most famous festivals: the Running of the Bulls (held in conjunction with the Fiesta de San Fermín, July 6-14). For latecomers, San Fermín Txikito ("Little San Fermín") offers a less touristy alternative in late September. But there's more to this town than bulls—and, in fact, visiting at other times is preferable to the crowds and 24/7 party atmosphere that seize Pamplona during the festival. Contrary to the chaotic or even backward image that its famous festival might suggest, you're likely to find Pamplona welcoming, sane, and enjoyable.

Orientation to Pamplona

Pamplona has about 200,000 people. Most everything of interest is in the tight, twisting lanes of the Old Town (Casco Antiguo), centered on the main square, Plaza del Castillo. The newer Ensanche ("Expansion") neighborhood just to the south—with a sensible grid plan—holds several good hotels and the bus station.

Tourist Information

Pamplona's well-organized TI is located near the Running of the Bulls Monument. Pick up the handy map/guide and get your questions answered (likely Mon-Sat 10:00-17:00, Sun 10:00-14:00, free Wi-Fi, Avenida Roncesvalles 4, tel. 848-420-420, www.turismodepamplona.es). The TI sells colorful posters of San Fermín festivities from the 1900s for €0.60. Between mid-March and mid-September you'll also find a TI kiosk in front of City Hall (Mon-Sat 10:30-14:00 & 16:30-20:00, no midday closure in summer, Sun 10:30-14:00, closed during Fiesta de San Fermín).

Local Guide: Francisco Glaría is a top-notch guide—and simply a delight to be with—who enjoys leading visitors through Pamplona (€140/half-day up to 4 hours, mobile 629-661-604, www.novotur.com, francisco@novotur.com).

No Bull—There's Another Fiesta: The last weekend in September, Pamplona celebrates **San Fermín Txikito** ("Little San Fermín"), a bull-free and practically tourist-free festival centered around the church of San Fermín de Aldapa (located behind the Mercado Santo Domingo on Calle Aldapa). Used only for Mass the rest of the year (and housing little of interest except a small

Pamplona

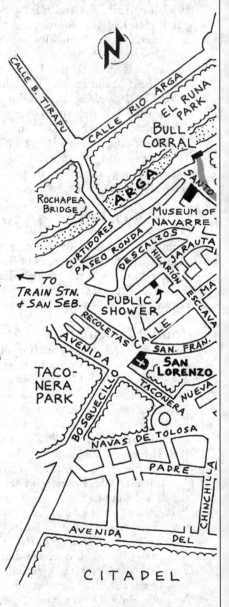

RUNNING OF THE BULLS ROUTE

P PARKING

⚵ VIEW

1 Gran Hotel La Perla
2 Palacio Guendulain
3 Hostal Navarra
4 Hotel Europa
5 Hotel Yoldi
6 Hotel Castillo de Javier
7 Pensión Arrieta
8 Bar Cervecería La Estafeta & Bodegon Sarria
9 Gaucho Bar
10 Café Roch
11 La Mandarra de la Ramos & San Nicolás Eateries
12 La Mejillonera
13 Café Iruña
14 San Ignacio Restaurante
15 Ultramarinos Beatriz Shop
16 Kukuxumusu T-Shirt Shop
17 Hemingway Bust
18 Navarre Gov't Building
19 Museum of the Running of the Bulls

200 YARDS
200 METERS

DCH

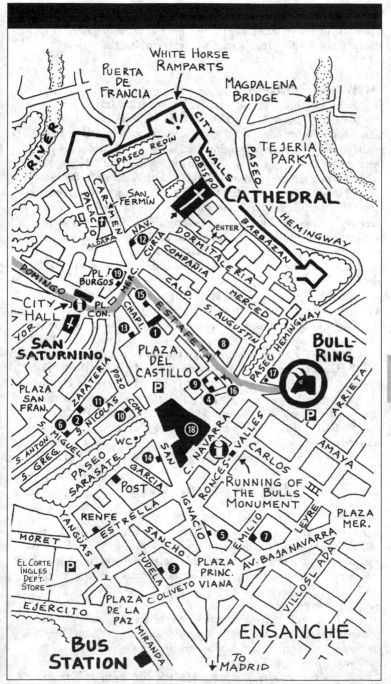

statue of the saint), each fall this church opens its doors to become the heart of a celebration involving concerts, brass-band and food competitions, and parades of giant mannequins throughout the city.

Arrival in Pamplona

You can store bags at the bus station, but not at the train station.

By Bus: The sleek, user-friendly bus station is underground along the western edge of the Ensanche area, about a 10-minute walk from the Old Town sightseeing zone. The station has pay Internet terminals and a multilingual information desk that makes trip planning a breeze (Mon-Fri 10:00-14:00 & 15:00-19:00, Sat-Sun 10:00-13:00 & 16:00-19:00). On arrival, go up the escalators, cross the street, turn left, and walk a half-block, where you can turn right down the busy Conde Oliveto street. Along this street, you're near several of my recommended accommodations—or you can walk two blocks to the big traffic circle called Plaza Príncipe de Viana. From here, turn left up Avenida de San Ignacio to reach the Old Town.

By Train: The RENFE station is farther from the center, across the river to the northwest. It's easiest to hop on public bus #9 (€1.30, every 15 minutes), which drops you at the big Plaza Príncipe de Viana traffic circle south of the Old Town (described above)—look for a square with a fountain in the center.

By Car: Everything is well-marked: Simply follow the bull's-eyes to the center of town, where individual hotels are clearly signposted. There's also handy parking right at Plaza del Castillo and Plaza de Toros (close to several recommended hotels).

By Plane: The Pamplona Airport is located about four miles outside the city (airport code: PNA, tel. 902-404-704, www.aena.es). A taxi from the airport to the city center costs around €12.

Self-Guided Walk

The Walking of the Tourists

Even if you're not in town for the famous San Fermín festival, you can still get a good flavor of the town by following in the foot- and hoof-steps of its participants. This walk takes you through the town center along the same route of the famous Running of the Bulls.

• *Begin by the river, at the...*

Bull Corral: During the San Fermín festival, the bulls are released from here at 8:00 each morning. They first run up Cuesta de Santo Domingo; signs labeled *El Encierro* mark their route. Follow them.

A few blocks ahead on the left, the **Museum of Navarre**

(Museo de Navarra) has four floors of artifacts and paintings celebrating the art of Navarre, from prehistoric to modern (€2, free Sat afternoons and all day Sun, open Tue-Sat 9:30-14:00 & 17:00-19:00, Sun 11:00-14:00, closed Mon, Santo Domingo 47, tel. 848-426-492, www.cfnavarra.es/cultura/museo). Formerly a 16th-century hospital, the building retains its Neoclassical entrance. Art is displayed chronologically: prehistoric tools and pottery and Roman mosaics on the first floor, Gothic and Renaissance artifacts along with castle frescoes on the second floor, Baroque and 19th- and 20th-century works (including Goya's painting *Retrato de Marques de San Adrian*) on the third floor, and 20th- and 21st-century paintings by local artists on the top floor. The ground floor hosts rotating exhibitions, often of modern art. Spacious and well-arranged, the museum can be toured within an hour—consider circling back here after our walk.

Check out the adjoining church (on the left as you exit, show museum ticket), with its impressive golden Baroque-Rococo altarpiece depicting the Annunciation.

• *Continue along Cuesta de Santo Domingo.*

Embedded in the wall on your right, look for the small shrine containing an image of San Fermín. Farther up on your left is the food **market of Santo Domingo,** a handy spot to buy picnic supplies, including fine local cheeses (supermarket upstairs, market stalls downstairs, Mon-Sat 8:00-14:00, closed Sun).

• *Ahead in the square is...*

City Hall (Ayuntamiento): When Pamplona was just starting out, many Camino pilgrims who had been "just pass-

ing through" decided to stick around. They helped to build the city you're enjoying today, but tended to cling to their own regional groups, which squabbled periodically. So in 1423, the King of Navarre (Charles III) tore down the internal walls and built a City Hall here to unite the community. This version (late Baroque, from the 18th century) is highly symbolic: Hercules demonstrates the city's strength, while the horn-blower trumpets Pamplona's greatness.

The festival of San Fermín begins and ends on the balcony of this building (with the flags). Look in the direction you just came (also the route of the bulls), and find the line of metal squares in the pavement—used to secure barricades for the run. There are four rows, creating two barriers on each side. The inner space is for press and emergency medical care; spectators line up along the outer barrier. This first stretch is uphill, allowing the bulls to use

The Symbols of Santiago

The pilgrim route leading to Santiago de Compostela—and the city itself—are rife with symbolism. Here are a few of the key items you'll see along the way.

- **St. James:** The Camino's namesake is also its single biggest symbol. St. James can be depicted three ways: as a pilgrim, as an apostle, and as a Crusader (slaughtering Moors). For more, see the sidebar on page 362.
- **The Scallop Shell (*Vieira*):** Figuratively, the various routes from Europe to Santiago come together like the lines of a scallop shell. And literally, scallops are abundant on the Galician coast. Though medieval pilgrims only carried shells with them on the return home—to prove they'd been here, and to scoop water from wells—

today's pilgrims also carry them on the way *to* Santiago. The yellow sideways shell that looks like a starburst marks the route for bikers.
- **The Gourd:** Gourds were used by pilgrims to drink water and wine.
- **The Yellow Arrow:** These arrows direct pilgrims at every intersection from France to Santiago.
- **The Red Cross:** This long, skinny cross with curly ends at the top and sides, and ending in a sword blade at the bottom, represents the Knights of Santiago. This 12th-century Christian military order had a dual mission: to battle Muslim invaders while providing hospice and protection to pilgrims along the Camino de Santiago.
- **The Tomb and Star:** St. James' tomb (usually depicted as a simple coffin or box), and the stars that led to its discovery, appear throughout the city of Santiago, either together or separately.

their strong hind legs to pick up serious momentum.

• *Follow the route of the bulls two blocks down Mercaderes street (next to Alexander Jewelry). Turn right onto...*

La Estafeta Street: At this turn, the bulls—who are now going downhill—begin to lose their balance, often sliding into the barricade. At the **Museum of the Running of the Bulls** (El Museo del Encierro), you can learn all about this unique Pamplona tradition, get your picture taken with an actual (stuffed) bull, and view a simulation of the event (€8, Mon-Fri 11:00-14:00 & 16:00-19:00, Sat-Sun 11:00-20:00, shorter hours off-season, closed Sun afternoon in winter, last entry 30 minutes before closing, between

Plaza del Ayuntamiento and Calle Estafeta at Calle Mercaderes 17, tel. 948-225-413, www.sanferminencierro.com). Note that if you want to side-trip to the cathedral—described later, under "Sights in Pamplona"—it's dead ahead, three blocks up the skinny lane called "Curia" from this corner.

Once the bulls regain their footing, they charge up the middle of La Estafeta. Notice how narrow the street is: No room for barricades...no escape for the daredevils trying to outrun the bulls.

On days that the bulls aren't running, La Estafeta is one of the most appealing streets in Pamplona. It's home to some of the best tapas bars in town (see "Eating in Pamplona," later). Because the Old Town was walled right up until 1923, space in here was at a premium—making houses tall and streets narrow.

Partway down the first block on the right, look for the hole-in-the-wall **Ultramarinos Beatriz** shop (at #22)—most locals just call it "Beatriz"—makers of the best treats in Pamplona (Mon-Fri 9:00-14:00 & 16:30-20:00, Sat 9:00-14:00, closed Sun, tel. 948-220-618). Anything with chocolate is good, but the mini-croissants are sensational. They come in three types: *garrotes de chocolate*, filled with milk chocolate; *cabello de angel*, filled with sweet pumpkin fibers; and *manzana*, apple (€3 for a box of six, also sold by weight). So simple...but oh so good.

Halfway down the street, notice the alley on the right leading to the main square (we'll circle back to the square later). Farther down, near the very end of La Estafeta (on the right, at #76), look for the shop called **Kukuxumusu**—Basque for "the kiss of a flea." These whimsical, locally designed cartoon T-shirts are a local favorite. The giant digital clock outside the shop counts down to the next Running of the Bulls.

• *La Estafeta eventually leads you right to Pamplona's...*

Bullring: At the end of the run, the bulls charge down the ramp and through the red door. The bullring is used only nine days each summer (during the festival). The original arena from 1923 was expanded in the 1960s (see the extension at the top), doubling its capacity and halving its architectural charm. Bullfights start at 18:00, and tickets are expensive. But the price plummets if you buy tickets from scalpers after the first or second bull. The audience at most bullfights is silent, but Pamplona's spectators are notorious for their raucous behavior. They're known to intentionally spill things on tourists just to get a reaction...respond with a laugh and a positive attitude, and you'll earn their respect—and you'll probably have the time of your life.

Look for the big bust of **Ernest Hemingway,** celebrated by Pamplona as if he were a native son. Hemingway came here for the first time during the 1923 Running of the Bulls. Inspired by the spectacle and the gore, he later wrote about the event in his classic

CAMINO DE SANTIAGO

The Running of the Bulls: Fiesta de San Fermín

"A San Fermín pedimos, por ser nuestro patrón, nos guíe en el encierro, dándonos su bendición."

"We ask San Fermín, because he is our Patron, to guide us through the Running of the Bulls, giving us his blessing."

Song sung before the run

For nine days each July, a million visitors pack into Pamplona to watch a gang of reckless, sangria-fueled adventurers thrust themselves into the path of an oncoming herd of furious bulls. Locals call it *El Encierro* (literally, "the enclosing"—as in, taking the beasts to be enclosed in the bullring)...but everyone else knows it as the "Running of the Bulls."

The festival begins at City Hall at noon on July 6, with various events filling the next nine days and nights. Originally celebrated as the feast of San Fermín—who is still honored by a religious procession through town on July 7—it has since evolved into a full slate of live music, fireworks, general revelry, and an excuse for debauchery. After dark the town erupts into a rollicking party scene. To beat the heat, participants chug refreshing sangria or *kalimotxo* (*calimocho* in Spanish)—half red wine, half cola. The town can't accommodate the crowds, so some visitors day-trip in from elsewhere (such as San Sebastián), and many young tourists simply pass out in city parks overnight (public showers are on Calle Hilarión Eslava in the Old Town).

The Running of the Bulls takes place each morning of the festival and is broadcast nationwide on live TV. The bulls' pho- tos appear in the local paper beforehand, allowing runners to size up their opponents. If you're here to watch, stake your claim at a vantage point along the outer barrier by 6:30 or 7:00 in the morning. Don't try to stand along the inner barrier—reserved for press and medical personnel—or you'll be evicted when the action begins.

Before the run starts, runners sing a song to San Fermín (see lyrics above) three times to ask for divine guidance. Soon the bulls will be released from their pen near Cuesta de Santo Domingo. From here they'll stampede a half-mile through the town center...with thrill-seekers called *mozos* (and female *mozas*) running in front of the herd, trying to avoid a hoof or horn in the rear end.

Mozos traditionally wear white with strips of red tied around their necks and waists, and carry a newspaper to cover the bull's eyes when they're ready to jump out of the way. Two legends explain the red-and-white uniform: One says it's to honor San Fermín, a saint (white) who was martyred (red); the other says that the runners dress like butchers, who began this tradition. (The bulls are color-blind, so they don't care.)

At 8:00, six bulls are set loose. The beginning of the run is marked by two firecrackers—one for the first bull to leave the pen, and another for the last bull. The animals charge down the street, while the *mozos* try to run in front of them for as long as possible before diving out of the way. The bulls are kept on course by fencing off side-streets (with openings just big enough for *mozos* to escape). Shop windows and doors are boarded up.

A bull becomes most dangerous when separated from the herd. For this reason, a few steer—who are calmer, slower, have bigger horns, and wear a bell—are released with the bulls, and a few more trot behind them to absorb angry stragglers and clear the streets. (There's no greater embarrassment in this *muy macho* culture than to think you've run with a bull...only to realize later that you actually ran with a steer.)

The bulls' destination: the bullring...where they'll be ceremonially slaughtered as the day's entertainment. (For more on bullfighting, see page 924.)

If you're considering running with the bulls, it's essential to equip yourself with specific safety information not contained in this book. Locals suggest a few guidelines: First, understand that these are very dangerous animals, and running with them is entirely at your own risk. Be as sober as possible, and wear good shoes to protect your feet from broken glass and from being stepped on by bulls and people. (Runners wearing sandals might be ejected by police.) You're not allowed to carry a backpack, as its motion could distract the bulls. If you fall, wait for the animals to pass before standing up—it's better to be trampled by six bulls than to be gored by one. Ideally, try to get an experienced *mozo* to guide you on your first run.

Cruel as this all seems to the bulls—who scramble for footing on the uneven cobblestones as they rush toward their doom in the bullring—the human participants don't come away unscathed. Each year, dozens of people are gored, trampled, or otherwise injured. Over the last century, 15 runners have been killed at the event. But far more people have died from overconsumption of alcohol.

The festival ends at midnight on July 14, when the townspeople congregate in front of the City Hall, light candles, and sing their sad song, *"Pobre de Mí"*: "Poor me, the Fiesta de San Fermín has ended."

CAMINO DE SANTIAGO

The Sun Also Rises. He said that he enjoyed seeing two wild animals running together: one on two legs, and the other on four. This literary giant put Pamplona and its humble, obscure bullfighting festival on the world map; visitors come from far and wide even today, searching for adventure in Hemingway's Pamplona. He came to his last Running of the Bulls in 1959 and reportedly regretted the attention his writing had brought to what had been a simple local festival. But the people of Pamplona appreciate "Papa" as one of their own. At the beginning of the annual festival, young people tie a red neckerchief around this statue so Hemingway can be properly outfitted for the occasion.

• *Walk 20 yards, keeping the bullring on your left, then cross the busy street and walk a block into the pedestrian zone to the life-size...*

Running of the Bulls Monument (Monumento al Encierro): This statue (from 2007, pictured on page 300) shows six bulls, two steer, and ten runners in action. Find the self-portrait of the sculptor (bald, lying down, and about to be gored). The statue has quickly become a local favorite, but is not without controversy: There are 10 *mozos* but no *mozas*—where are the female runners?

• *From here you can turn right and walk two blocks up the street to the main square...*

Plaza del Castillo: While not as grand as Spain's top squares, there's something particularly cozy and livable about Pamplona's.

It's dominated by the Navarre government building (sort of like a state capitol). Several Hemingway sights surround this square. The recommended Gran Hotel La Perla, in the corner, was his favorite place to stay. It recently underwent a head-to-toe five-star renovation, but Hemingway's room was kept exactly as he liked it, right down to the furniture he used while writing...and two balconies overlooking the bull action on Estafeta street. He also was known to frequent Bar Txoko at the top of the square (as well as pretty much every other bar in town) and the venerable Café Iruña at the bottom of the square. The recommended Café Iruña actually has a separate "Hemingway Corner" room, with a life-size statue of "Papa" to pose with.

• *You've survived the run. Now enjoy the rest of Pamplona's sights.*

Sights in Pamplona

▲Cathedral (Catedral)

The Camino de Santiago is lined with great cathedrals—but Pamplona's is an architectural also-ran. However, after an expensive makeover, it looks like new and holds an interesting museum with a thoughtful message for pilgrims and tourists alike.

Cost and Hours: €5; May-Nov Tue-Sat 10:30-19:00, Sun 10:30-14:00, closed Mon; Dec-April Tue-Sat 10:30-17:00, Sun 10:30-14:00, closed Mon; last entry one hour before closing, tel. 948-212-594.

◐ Self-Guided Tour: The cathedral—a Gothic core wrapped in a Neoclassical shell—is shiny and clean from the outside, but the interior is dark and mysterious. Follow signs for *entrada* at the left side of the main entrance, buy your ticket, and go inside.

In the back-left corner chapel, dedicated to San Juan Bautista, find the Renaissance **crucifix**—shockingly realistic for a no-name artist of the time (compare it with the more typical one in the next chapel). The accuracy of Christ's musculature leads some to speculate that the artist had a model. (When you drive a nail through a foot, toes splay as you see here...but this is rarely seen on other crucifixes of the time.) It's said that if the dangling lock of hair touches Jesus' chest, the world will end.

The prominent **tomb** dominating the middle of the nave holds Charles III (the king of Navarre who united the disparate groups of Pamplona) and his wife. The blue fleur-de-lis pattern is a reminder that the kings of Navarre once controlled a large swath of France. Notice that Charles' face is realistic, indicating that it was sculpted while he was still alive, whereas his wife's face is idealized—done after she died. Around the base of the tomb, monks from various orders mourn the couple's death.

In the **choir,** look for the statue nicknamed "Mary of the Adopted Child." The Baby Jesus was stolen from this statue in the 16th century and replaced with a different version...which looks nothing like his mother. (The mother, dating from the 13th century, is the only treasure surviving from the previous church that stood on this spot.)

Leave the cathedral and head to the **museum,** in the former cloister and attached buildings. The exhibits document the origins of Western thought and religion without focusing on one particular civilization or geographic area. Pass the spiral staircase into a room that chronicles the stages of cathedral construction. Next, wander through the Gothic cloister to the Archaeology Hall and the main exhibit.

Ramparts View: Exit the cathedral to the left, walking to the tree-lined square. Continue to the small viewpoint overlooking the White Horse Ramparts. This is your best chance to see part of Pamplona's imposing **city walls**—designed to defend against potential invaders from the Pyrenees, still 80 percent intact, and now an inviting parkland. Belly up to the overlook, with views across the city's suburban sprawl. Beyond those hills on the horizon to the left are San Sebastián and the Bay of Biscay. Camino pilgrims enter town through the Puerta de Francia gate below and on the left. This area is popular with people who are in town for the Running of the Bulls but didn't make hotel reservations. Sadly, it's not unusual for people to fall asleep on top of the wall...then roll off to their deaths.

Other Churches

As a prominent town on a pilgrim route, Pamplona has its share of other interesting churches. These two are worth a quick visit. They're both on the Camino trail through town; to reach them, simply head west along Calle Mayor from the City Hall Square (near where the self-guided walk begins).

Church of San Saturnino

The most important pilgrim church in Pamplona, this is an architectural combination: a 15th-century Gothic body with an 18th-century Baroque altar. Duck inside: This is where pilgrims can get their credential stamped (someone's usually on duty in the pews). At the end across from where you enter, you'll see an altar with the Holy Virgin of the Camino. As you continue your journey, you'll notice that most churches along the Camino are dedicated to Mary. According to legend, when St. James himself came on a missionary trip through northern Spain, he suffered a crisis of faith around Zaragoza (not far from here). But, inspired by the Virgin, he managed to complete his journey to Galicia. Pilgrims following in his footsteps find similar inspiration from Mary today.

Cost and Hours: Free, Mon-Sat 9:00-12:30 & 18:00-20:00, Sun 10:15-13:30 & 18:00-20:00.

Church of San Lorenzo

San Fermín is a big name in town, and you'll find him in a giant side-chapel of this church, overlooking the ring road at the edge of the Old Town. Enter the church and turn right down the transept to find the statue of **San Fermín**, dressed in red and wearing a gold miter (tall hat). Pamplona was founded by the Roman Emperor Pompey (hence the name) in the first century B.C. Later, a Roman general here became the first in the empire to allow Christians to worship openly. The general's son—Fermín—even preached the word himself...until he was martyred. Fermín has been the patron saint here ever since. Just below the statue's Adam's apple, squint to see a reliquary holding Fermín's actual finger. The statue—gussied up in an even more over-

the-top miter and staff—is paraded around on Fermín's feast day, July 7, which was the origin of today's bull festival. This chapel is the most popular place in town for weddings.

Cost and Hours: Free, Mon-Sat 8:00-12:30 & 17:30-20:30, Sun 8:30-13:45 & 17:30-20:00.

Sleeping in Pamplona

(€1 = about $1.30, country code: 34)

Because Pamplona is a business-oriented town, prices go up during the week; on weekends (Fri-Sun), you can usually score a discount. When I've listed a range, you can assume the high prices are for weekdays (Mon-Thu). All prices go way, way up for the San Fermín festival, when you must book as far in advance as possible.

$$$ Gran Hotel La Perla is the town's undisputed top splurge. Hemingway's favorite hotel, sitting right on the main square, has recently undergone a top-to-bottom five-star renovation. Its 44 rooms offer luxury at Pamplona's best address (standard Db-€140-270, bigger and fancier rooms-€375-550, rates can drop dramatically—check for deals online, breakfast-€20, air-con, elevator, free guest computer and Wi-Fi, restaurant, Plaza del Castillo 1, tel. 948-223-000, www.granhotellaperla.com, informacion@granhotellaperla.com). Well-heeled lit lovers can drop €550 for a night in the Hemingway room, still furnished as it was when "Papa" stayed there (with a brand-new bathroom grafted on the front).

$$$ At Palacio Guendulain, pander to your inner aristocrat at a hotel owned by the Count of Guendulain. Currently living in Madrid, he had his mansion in Pamplona converted into a luxurious 25-room hotel decorated with family crests, antiques, and Spanish Old Masters. A collection of carriages in the courtyard, ultra-modern bathrooms, and a gym under construction over the family chapel create a curious juxtaposition of old and new (Db *"clasica"*-€130-165, Db *"deluxe"*-€165-200, Db suite-€370-400, extra bed-€53, rates can drop off-season, breakfast-€17, air-con, elevator, guest computer and Wi-Fi, restaurant open to non-guests, Zapateria 53, tel. 948-225-522, www.palacioguendulain.com).

$$ Hostal Navarra is the best value in Pamplona, with 14 modern, well-maintained, clean rooms. Near the bus station, but an easy walk from the Old Town, it's well-run by Miguel, who speaks English (Sb-€45-50, Db-€55-66, breakfast-€7, free Wi-Fi, reception closes at 23:00—notify if you'll be arriving later, 10 percent discount if you mention this book and reserve direct through 2014 except in July-Aug, Calle Tudela 9, tel. 948-225-164, www.hostalnavarra.com, info@hostalnavarra.com).

$$ Hotel Europa, a few blocks off the square, offers 21 rooms with reasonable prices for its high class and ideal location (Sb-€69-78, Db-€75-92, breakfast-€9.50, air-con, elevator, free Wi-Fi, Calle Espoz y Mina 11, tel. 948-221-800, www.hoteleuropapamplona .com, europa@hreuropa.com). The ground-floor restaurant is a well-regarded splurge among locals.

$$ Hotel Yoldi is a comfortable business-style hotel in a 19th-century building. Well-located just off Plaza del Príncipe de Viana, its 50 modern rooms are handy for travelers arriving by bus from the train station (Sb-€55-65, Db-€70-75, elevator, free Wi-Fi, café, Avenida de San Ignacio 11, tel. 948-224-800, www .hotelyoldi.com, yoldi@hotelyoldi.com).

$$ Hotel Castillo de Javier, right on the bustling San Nicolás bar street (request a quieter back room), rents 19 small, simple rooms (Sb-€45, Db-€63, breakfast-€4.30, air-con, elevator, free Wi-Fi, Calle San Nicolás 50-52, tel. 948-203-040, www .hotelcastillodejavier.com, info@hotelcastillodejavier.com). This is a step up from the several cheap *hostales* that line the same street.

$ Pensión Arrieta is an old-fashioned budget option renting 13 basic rooms in in the new part of town. Carmen and Máximo don't speak English, but their daughter Maika does (D-€40, Db-€50, Calle de Emilio Arrieta 27, tel. 948-228-459, www .pensionarrieta.net, pensionarrieta@pensionarrieta.net).

Eating in Pamplona

All of these eateries are within a couple minutes' walk of one another, and the tapas bars make a wonderful little pub crawl.

Tapas Crawl

On Calle de la Estafeta: The best concentration of trendy tapas bars is on and near the skinny drag called La Estafeta. My favorites here are **Bar Cervecería La Estafeta** (try the *gulas*—baby eels—stuffed in a red pepper, daily, at #54, tel. 948-222-157) and **Bodegon Sarria** (great bull photos, English menu, dining room to enjoy Navarre dishes, at #52, tel. 948-227-713).

Gaucho Bar is a proud little prizewinning place serving gourmet tapas cooked to order for €2.50-3 each. You could sit down and enjoy three tapas, and have an excellent meal (daily, just a few steps off the main square at Calle Espoz y Mina 7, tel. 948-225-073, no English).

Café Roch is a time-warp with a line of delightful tapas (€1.60 each). Their most popular are the stuffed pepper and the fried Roquefort (find the tobacco shop at #35 on Plaza del Castillo—it's a block away on the left at Calle de las Comedias 6, tel. 948-222-390).

On Calle San Nicolás: The narrow and slightly seedy Calle San Nicolás has more than its share of hole-in-the-wall tapas joints, with an older, more traditional clientele, and greasier, more straightforward tapas. **La Mandarra de la Ramos** ("Ramos' Apron"), at #9, is a pork lover's paradise, where cured legs dangle enticingly over your head. Ham it up with a couple of *tostadas de jamón,* best washed down with a glass of the local *vino tinto* (daily, just around the corner from Café Roch, tel. 948-212-654).

Near the Cathedral: **La Mejillonera** satisfies seafood lovers with its simple, homey atmosphere. Order a *caña* (small draft beer) and a *media* (half-portion) *de calamares bravos.* These deep-fried mini-calamari are the perfect vehicle for picking up all that mayo and hot sauce (daily, Calle Navarrería 12, tel. 948-229-184).

Restaurants

Café Iruña, which clings to its venerable past and its connection to Hemingway (who loved the place), serves up drinks out on the main square and food in the delightful old 1888 interior. While the food is mediocre, the ambience is great. Find the little "Hemingway's Corner" (El Rincón de Hemingway) side-eatery in back, where the bearded one is still hanging out at the bar. Enjoy black-and-white photos of Ernesto, young and old, in  Pamplona (€13.50 fixed-price meal for lunch and dinner, pricier €22 Sat dinner deal, open daily, Plaza del Castillo 44, tel. 948-222-064, www.cafeiruna.com).

San Ignacio Restaurante is a good choice for a real restaurant, with a classy upstairs dining room serving local fare (€5-19 starters, €11-22 main dishes, fixed-price meal-€22 on weekdays or €29 on weekends, open daily for lunch 13:00-15:30, Thu-Sat also dinner from 21:00, facing the back of the Navarre government building at Avenida San Ignacio 4, tel. 948-221-874, www .restaurantesanignacio.com).

Pamplona Connections

Note that the bus station is closer to the Old Town than the train station, and that most connections are faster by bus anyway.

From Pamplona by Bus to: Burgos (3/day with change in Vitoria, 3-4 hours), **San Sebastián** (8-10/day, 1 hour), **Bilbao** (5-6/day, 2 hours), **Madrid** (7/day, 5 hours), **Madrid Barajas Airport** (6/day, 5-6 hours; this bus may serve other airports in the future—

CAMINO DE SANTIAGO

see www.alsa.es; buy ticket online or from the driver). For bus schedules, see www.autobusesdenavarra.com, tel. 948-203-566.

By Train to: Burgos (2/day, 2-3.5 hours, better option than bus—fast train leaves at midday), **San Sebastián** (2/day, 1.75 hours), **León** (2/day, 4-5.5 hours), **Madrid** (4/day direct, 3 hours).

From Pamplona to Burgos

The stretch of the Camino between Pamplona and Burgos is particularly appealing, with several tempting stopovers. As you finish your descent from the rugged Pyrenees, you enter the flatter, more cultivated landscape that typifies the long middle stretch of the Camino (basically from here to Galicia). The two best stops along here are the small town of Puente la Reina (with an iconic old bridge and fun pilgrim vibes) and a potential detour for wine lovers through La Rioja wine country.

• *Begin by taking the A-12 expressway west from Pamplona (toward* Logroño). *Consider stopping in Puente la Reina, as it's a very easy detour—the exit* (Puente la Reina norte) *is well-marked from the expressway. Approaching town, watch for the first bell tower; parking is on the left.*

Puente la Reina / Gares

The Camino de Santiago's two French routes converge in this cozy sun-baked village, just one walking stage (about 12 miles) west of Pamplona. Named for a graceful 11th-century stone bridge at its center, the village retains a pilgrims' vibe. All the sights here fall on a straight axis: church, main street, and bridge with built-in TI (open Easter-mid-Oct Mon-Fri 10:00-17:00, Sat 10:00-14:00, Sun 11:00-14:00; mid-Oct-Easter Tue-Sat 10:00-14:00 & 16:00-19:00, Sun 11:00-14:00, closed Mon; Calle Mayor 105, tel. 948-341-301). Parking the car and wandering around here gives "car hikers" a whiff of Camino magic.

As you enter the town, watch (on the left) for the **Church of the Crucifixion** (Iglesia del Crucifijo), with a stork's nest on the steeple. The Knights of St. John, who came to protect pilgrims from the Moors, founded this church in the 12th century. Inside you'll find a distinctive Y-shaped crucifix that shows a Christ who's dead, yet still in pain (by a German craftsman—a reminder of the rich influx of pan-European culture the Camino enjoyed). It was likely carried by German pilgrims all the way across Europe to this spot. Across the street is a pilgrims' *refugio* run by a contemporary religious order—Padres Reparadores—offering bunks and credential stamps to Camino walkers (daily 10:00-20:00, closes at 18:00 in winter). The TI can also give pilgrims that coveted stamp.

The straight, wide **Calle Mayor** connects the church and *refugio* with the bridge. Classic Camino towns feature main drags like this one. They were born as a collection of services flanking the path. Pilgrims needed to eat, sleep, pray, and deal with health problems. The more stone a house showed off (rather than brick), the wealthier the owner. You'll see modern flooring being stripped away to reveal now-trendy river-pebble cobbles inside.

The main street leads directly to the most interesting sight in town (and its namesake), the **"Bridge of the Queen"** (which you

can also see on the right as you drive across the modern bridge near the end of town). With a graceful six-arch Romanesque design that peaks in the middle, the bridge represents a lifespan: You can't quite see where you're going until you get there. The extra holes were designed to let high water through, so that water pressure wouldn't push the stone construction over—clever 11th-century engineering. Pilgrims enjoy congregating on the riverbank under the arches of this bridge (ramp on right side)—a great place to stop and stretch your legs. Ponder this scene: the bridge, pilgrims, the flowing river, happy birdsong...it's timeless.

• *From here, hop immediately back on the A-12 expressway (toward* Estella*) to speed along. As you pass by Estella/Lizarra (home to the imposing Romanesque Palace of the Kings of Navarre), you'll begin to notice that you're entering wine country with scrubby vegetation, red soil, and hill towns dotting the landscape. Take exit 44, direction:* Ayegui, *and follow signs to* Irache Monastery.

Even if you're still on the expressway, it's worth another quick detour (again well-signed, just beyond Estella) to the fun...

Irache Monastery and Wine Fountain (Monasterio de Irache)

This monastery, immersed in vineyards, has a unique custom of offering free wine to pilgrims. From the parking lot near the monastery, consider briefly wandering through the large, barren church and odd, double-decker cloister (get your credential stamped inside). Then go inside the Museo del Vino to purchase a €1 cup (if you didn't bring

La Rioja Wine Loop

Serious wine lovers enjoy detouring off the Camino at **Logroño**
to visit the wine village
of Laguardia, tour some
unique wineries, and sam-
ple Rioja wine.

For many lovers
of Spanish wines, it just
doesn't get better than
Rioja (ree-OH-hah, with a
guttural *h*). Rioja wine is
a D.O.C. product, meaning that it can only be produced in the
Rioja region. Protected from the elements by the Cantabrian
Mountains to the north (which you'll see from Laguardia), vineyards have thrived in the valley of the Ebro River since Roman
times. Rioja wines, which can be red, white, or rosé, grow in a
variety of soil types dominated by red clay and limestone. The
reds, made primarily from the tempranillo grape (Spain's "noble
grape"), are medium- to full-bodied in the Bordeaux style and
characterized by aging in oak barrels—infusing them with over-
tones of vanilla. You'll see four types of Rioja wines, depending on how long they've been aged (from shortest to longest,
and cheapest to most expensive): simply Rioja (or sometimes
cosecha, "harvest"), *crianza*, *reserva*, and *gran reserva*.

Be warned that the Rioja region is not well set up for
impromptu visitors. All wine-tasting experiences prefer reservations, and most require them. If you're serious about your Rioja,
set up here for a day or two, pick your designated driver, do some
homework (www.laguardia-alava.com is helpful), and reserve at
the wineries of your choice. Although Laguardia is connected by
bus to Pamplona (via Logroño), most of the experience here lies
in the countryside—workable only by car.

• *From Logroño follow A-124 northwest to Laguardia. Adventurous drivers should consider taking a small detour from A-124:
Get off at A-4202 (toward Lapuebla de Labarca), then head north
to Laguardia on A-3216. Your reward is pulling off and examining
grapes that are planted up to the roadside. In Laguardia, follow
signs to a pay parking garage or continue to the Navaridas lot for
free parking outside the town wall.*

Laguardia is the scenic center of the Rioja wine-tasting
country. This walled town—literally "The Guard," for its position
watching out for potential invaders coming in from the mountains—is perched on a promontory with fine views of the surrounding region. There's not much in the way of sightseeing, but
poke around a bit. Under your feet are more than 200 wine cel-
lars *(bodegas)* where Rioja quietly ages. Only two in town are
open for visitors: **El Fabulista** (€7 for two tastes and a one-hour
guided visit, Plaza San Juan, tel. 945-621-192, www.bodegael
fabulista.com, Alonso) and **Carlos San Pedro** (€4 for one taste,
Calle Páganos 44, tel. 605-033-043); for both, you can try just

dropping in (each offers four to five scheduled visits per day), but it's better to call ahead. Laguardia's **TI** can give you information on wine-tastings in town and nearby, but—once again—they'll warn you that most wineries require reservations (TI open Mon-Fri 10:00-14:00 & 16:00-19:00, Sat 10:00-14:00 & 17:00-19:00, Sun 10:45-14:00, Calle Mayor 52, tel. 945-600-845, www .laguardia-alava.com).

The countryside around Laguardia is blanketed with vineyards. For those just passing through, three wine-related attractions are worth considering. All are within a few minutes' drive of Laguardia. Note that Ysios and Marqués de Riscal are architectural gems worth dropping by to see even if you couldn't care less about the wine.

Villa Lucía is a sort of wine museum about La Rioja's favorite product, as well as its traditional architecture. Call ahead if you want to join a tour (various programs for €6.50-11, Tue-Sun 9:00-14:00 & 16:30-20:00, closed Mon, on the right as you reach the edge of town, tel. 945-600-032, www.villa-lucia.com).

Ysios is a modern winery with an undulating silver roof

 designed by the bold and prolific Spanish architect Santiago Calatrava. Wine lovers enjoy the one-hour tours of the cellar, in which countless casks age under the wavy ceiling (€12, includes one taste; daily at 11:00 and 13:00; call first to ensure a space, tel. 902-239-773, www .bodegasysios.com). But even from the outside, it's a worthwhile photo op for anyone (just a three-minute drive behind Laguardia, toward the mountains—behind the town, look for *Ysios* signs; you'll see the building from far off).

• *From the Laguardia area, follow signs south to Elciego (on A-3210, pull off into town and walk up to the church for a great photo op), then head to...*

Marqués de Riscal, in the village of Elciego, was one of the pioneer winemakers of the Rioja wine industry. Its new winery features a distinctive hotel designed by Frank Gehry (of Bilbao Guggenheim fame). The wine cellar is tourable (€10, includes two tastes, sometimes 1/day in English, closed Mon, call first, tel. 945-180-888, www.marquesderiscal.com). The hotel (Db-€400-1,000), with its colorful, wavy design, seems out of place in this otherwise humble village.

• *If you're ready to move along, you can head south from Elciego toward Cenicero. In Cenicero, you can rejoin the AP-68 expressway, or continue down (following signs for Nájera) to highway N-120 (turn off at A-12, which is also confusingly called N-120; avoid signs to N-120a) to rejoin the Camino road into Burgos.*

your own). Walk down following signs for *fuente de vino* to find a faucet that dispenses free wine (daily 8:00-20:00; also one for water). The Spanish poem on the sign explains, "To drink without abusing, we invite you happily; but to be able to take it along, you must pay for the wine." In other words, pilgrims are allowed to drink as much wine as they like...provided they don't take any with them. If you do want to bring some along, you're in luck: The wine for sale inside the Museo del Vino is of much better quality and costs half as much as comparable wines elsewhere in Spain (€2-3 for an average red, €9 for the really good stuff). At the faucet, note the webcam—text friends to look for you at www.irache.com. Hi, Mom!

• *Continuing south, you can choose your route: To save time, zip on the A-12 expressway right to Logroño. But for a scenic and only slightly slower meander through some cute villages (El Busto, Sansol) and larger towns (Los Arcos and Viana, with its ornate cathedral), take the expressway only as far as Los Arcos, then follow N-111 (sometimes written as N-1110) from there. Either way, you'll end up at...*

Logroño and La Rioja

Just before the skippable big city of Logroño, you'll cross the Ebro River. Today, as in centuries past, this river marks the end of the Basque territory (and Navarre) and the beginning of the rest of Spain. With more than 150,000 residents, Logroño is the largest city of La Rioja. Renowned for its robust wines, the Rioja region has historically served as a buffer between the Basques and the powerful forces to the south and east (the Moors or the Castilian Spaniards).

• *Again, choose your route from here. If you have time and a healthy interest in wine (and vineyard scenery), detour off the Camino by heading north on A-124 to the village of Laguardia, rejoining the expressway—and the Camino—later (see "La Rioja Wine Loop" sidebar). Otherwise, stick with the expressway to Santo Domingo de la Calzada.*

Note that west of Logroño, the expressway does a big jog to the north (AP-68, then AP-1). You'll save miles (though not necessarily time) and stick closer to the Camino if instead you take the N-120 highway from here to Burgos. Along the way is...

Santo Domingo de la Calzada

This Rioja town, a larger version of Puente la Reina, has a fine cathedral, oodles of historic buildings, tranquil squares, and all the trappings of a pilgrim zone (seashells in the pavement, *refugios*, vending machines, and launderettes). You'll see images of a rooster and a hen everywhere in town, thanks to a colorful

local legend: A chaste pilgrim refused to be seduced by the amorous daughter of an innkeeper. For revenge she hid a silver cup in his bed and accused him of theft. The judge, eager to hang the lad, proclaimed that the pilgrim was as dead as the roasted rooster and hen the judge was about to eat. The charred birds suddenly stood up and began to crow and cluck, saving the pilgrim from certain death.

• *Soon after Santo Domingo de la Calzada, you pass into the region of...*

Castile and León (Castilla y León)

Welcome to Spain's largest "state" (about the size of Indiana). If you've always wanted to see the famous plains of Spain...this is it. This vast, arid high-altitude Meseta Central ("Inner Plateau") stretches to hilly, rainy Galicia in the northwest and all the way past Madrid to the south coast. Those walking the entire Camino find this flat, dry stretch to be either the best part (getting away from it all with a pensive stroll) or the worst part (boring and potentially blistering-hot).

• *The next big city on the Camino is just around the bend: Burgos.*

Burgos

Burgos (BOOR-gohs) is a pedestrian-friendly city lined up along its pretty river. Apart from its epic history and urban bustle, Burgos has one major claim to touristic fame: its glorious Gothic-style cathedral, packed to the gills with centuries' worth of elaborate decorations.

Like so many towns in the north of Spain, the burg of Burgos was founded during the Reconquista to hold on to land that had been won back from the Moors. Its position on the Camino de Santiago, and the flourishing trade in wool (sent to the Low Countries to become Flemish tapestries), helped it to thrive. Beginning in 1230, it became the capital of the kingdom of Castile for half a millennium (having usurped the title from León). The

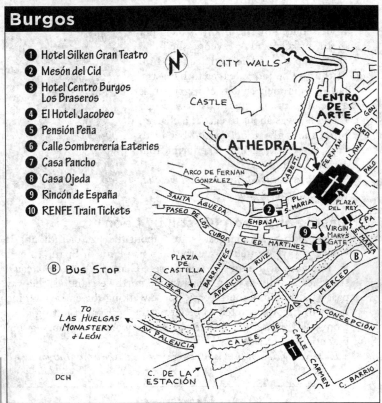

Burgos

1 Hotel Silken Gran Teatro
2 Mesón del Cid
3 Hotel Centro Burgos Los Braseros
4 El Hotel Jacobeo
5 Pensión Peña
6 Calle Sombrerería Eateries
7 Casa Pancho
8 Casa Ojeda
9 Rincón de España
10 RENFE Train Tickets

CITY WALLS

CASTLE

CENTRO DE ARTE

CATHEDRAL

ARCO DE FERNAN GONZÁLEZ

SANTA ÁGUEDA

PASEO DE LOS CUBOS

EMBAJA.

C. EP. MARTINEZ

PL. S. MARIA

PLAZA DEL REY

VIRGIN MARY'S GATE

B BUS STOP

PLAZA DE CASTILLA

LA ISLA

BARRANTES

APARICIO Y RUIZ

TO LAS HUELGAS MONASTERY + LEÓN

AV. PALENCIA

CALLE DE

CALLE DE LA MERCED

CONCEPCIÓN

B

DCH

C. DE LA ESTACIÓN

CALLE CARMEN

C. BARRIO

CAMINO DE SANTIAGO

town's favorite son is the great 11th-century Spanish hero El Cid (locals say "el theeth"), who valiantly fought against the Moors. The 20th century saw the town decline, even as it briefly became the capital of Franco's forces during the Spanish Civil War (1936-1939). Later the dictator industrialized Burgos to even out the playing field (Catalunya and the Basque Country—on the political and geographical fringes of Spain—had previously been the centers of industry).

Today the outskirts of Burgos still feel workaday, but the Old Town gleams with a hint of elegance. The city constantly tries to improve itself—new public sculpture decorates nearly every plaza, greeting strollers on their evening paseo. Old architecture blends with the new (for example, find the public library at the end of Calle San Juan). Wealthy, well-dressed locals fill Burgos' churches on weekends for weddings, christenings, and first communions. Stately plane trees line up along the riverside promenade. And watching over everything is that grand cathedral.

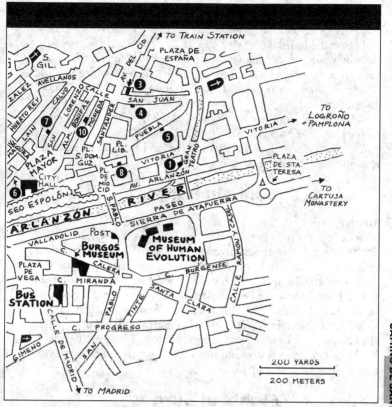

Orientation to Burgos

With about 180,000 inhabitants, Burgos is bisected by the Arlanzón River. The Old Town is centered on the huge cathedral. The city center is mostly pedestrianized and very manageable.

Tourist Information

Burgos' TI is on the square along the side of the cathedral (just across from the side entrance). Pick up the free map and information brochure (July-Aug daily 10:00-20:00; Sept-June Mon-Fri 10:00-14:00 & 16:00-19:00, Sat-Sun 9:30-20:00; Plaza Alonso Martínez, tel. 947-288-874, www.aytoburgos.es).

Arrival in Burgos

By Bus: The bus station is just across the river from the cathedral. Exit the station to the left, then turn right at the busy street and cross the bridge (you'll see the large arch and spires).

By Train: Burgos' Rosa de Lima Station is a long 40-minute walk from town, and the bus service into town isn't much of a help to tourists (bus #25, direction: Plaza de España, then a 10-minute walk to cathedral, 2/hour Mon-Fri, 1/hour Sat-Sun). Unless you're poor or a pilgrim, catch a taxi for €8. The bus stop and taxi stand are both at the station's main entrance. The RENFE office at Calle Moneda 21 sells train tickets (Mon-Fri 9:30-13:30 & 17:00-20:00, closed Sat-Sun).

By Car: Burgos is easy and well-signed. Simply follow signs to the city center *(centro ciudad)*, then look for a pay garage when you see the cathedral spires. Plaza Mayor and Plaza de España are the most central garage locations.

Tours in Burgos

Tourist Train
This little train runs both by day and by night (day-€4.20, night-€5.20, departs from the cathedral, buy tickets from shop on Plaza del Rey Fernando, tel. 947-101-888). The shorter 45-minute day tour is only really worth taking if you want to get a good shot of the cathedral from the best viewpoint in town—the Mirador, up by the ruins of the castle (2/hour; July-Sept daily 11:00-21:00; Oct-March Mon-Fri 15:00-18:00, Sat-Sun 11:00-18:00). I prefer the one-hour night tour for an enjoyable view of Burgos after dark, when its monuments are illuminated (departure times vary with the sunset, check at shop or TI).

Sights in Burgos

▲▲Cathedral (Catedral)
Burgos is rightfully famous for its showpiece Gothic cathedral. With its soaring, frilly spires and an interior that's been augmented across the centuries, Burgos' cathedral is an impressive sight. Unfortunately, the church's cultural and spiritual significance is badly presented; what precious English information it provides is stilted and boring. Use this self-guided tour to make the place meaningful.

Cost and Hours: €7, or €3.50 for pilgrims, includes audioguide, daily mid-March-Oct 9:30-19:30, Nov-mid-March 10:00-19:00, last entry one hour before closing, free lockers, tel. 947-204-712, www.catedraldeburgos.es.

○ Self-Guided Tour: Begin by facing the **main facade** of the grand church, which was built over the course of a century. You can read the building's history in its architecture: It was started in the 13th century by French architects, who used a simple, graceful style similar to Paris' famous Notre-Dame (mentally erase the tops of the spires and you'll recognize that famous cathedral). In the 14th century, German cathedral-builders took over, adding the flamboyant fringe to the tops of the towers (similar to the cathedral in Köln, Germany).

The entrance on this side is open only for worshippers, who have access to two chapels at the back of the cathedral (where hourly Mass takes place). Tourists head around the right side of the church to buy tickets and enter. As you walk there, you'll realize that this "front door" facade is only one small part of the vast complex—more spires and frills lie beyond.

Buy your ticket and enter through the side door. After you show your ticket and pick up the audioguide, you'll turn left and do a clockwise spin around the church, stopping at many of the 18 **chapels.** These chapels were added over many centuries, in different styles, and were decorated in creative ways by a wide range of benefactors. (To aid with navigation for certain stops, I've listed the numbers that are posted for audioguide users.) The first few chapels are just a warm-up: The Chapel of St. John of Sahagún (#6) features Baroque relic altars and some frescoes (unusual in this church), while the Chapel of the Presentation (#8) features a painting by an Italian Renaissance master, Il Piombo.

At the back of the church, the barriers separate the worship area from the tourist zone. But look high up, just to the right of the rose window, to see the church mascot: The **"Fly-Catcher" clock** (El Papamoscas), which rings out every quarter-hour. Above the clock is a whimsical statue of its German maker, whose mouth opens and closes when the bell rings at the top of each hour. (The tourists who congregate here and crane their necks to gape up at the show seem to be imitating the clockmaker.)

Continue to the chapel dedicated to **St. Anne** (Santa Ana, #12). Here you'll find a spectacular Gothic altar, showing the family tree of Jesus springing out of a reclining Jesse. (The sculptor included his self-portrait as one of the evangelists—find the

bespectacled guy, the second from left in the bottom row.) Facing the altar is a Flemish tapestry and some original 15th-century vestments.

You've now circled back around to the transept. On your left are the sumptuous **Golden Stairs** (#13, designed by a Flemish Renaissance master who had studied under Michelangelo) and an ornate,

CAMINO DE SANTIAGO

silver processional stand. On the right you can enter the choir area. Step into the very center of the choir—also the very center of the cathedral—and place yourself directly under the sumptuous Plateresque-style dome, then look up and spin. Look back down again to see the **tomb of El Cid** (Rodericus Didaci Campidoctor) and his wife (#15). El Cid's well-traveled remains were interred in Valencia, then in various points in Burgos, before being brought here in the early 20th century.

Take a look at the **main altar,** with a fine statue of Mary slathered in silver. Also poke around the carved wooden **choir**—much like the choir in Toledo's cathedral—with a giant 16th-century songbook for Gregorian chants and two organs (used only for special occasions).

Directly behind the main altar, enter the cathedral's best chapel, the **Chapel of the High Constable** (#22). Because it has

its own altar, two side naves, and a choir and organ (in the back), it's been called "the cathedral within the cathedral." A high constable is a knight who won a crown in battle for his king or queen—the highest of VIPs in the Middle Ages. And yet, this chapel shows the influence not of a powerful man, but of a powerful woman. It was commissioned by the high constable's wife (who's entombed with him at the center of the chapel). She wanted the chapel decorations to demonstrate equality of the sexes (a

bold statement in the late 15th century). Notice that most of the decorations on "his" side (left) are male-oriented, including the two brutes holding the coat of arms, and the figures on the side altar. But "her" decorations (right) are more feminine—damsels holding the coat of arms, and mostly women decorating the side altar. The yin and yang of the sexes is even suggested by the black-and-white flooring. Also notice a pair of grand paintings here (unrelated to the sexual politics): on "his" side a beautiful Flemish depiction of a woman in a red dress (likely from the school of Hans Memling); and on "her" side Mary Magdalene, by a favorite pupil of Leonardo da Vinci (who probably put his own touches on the work as well).

Continuing around, you'll walk past the beautifully carved main sacristy (#23), then enter the **upper cloister** (#24). The tour route takes you counterclockwise around this cloister, to a few more chapels and museum exhibits: The Corpus Christi Chapel (#26) features stairs up to the library (closed to the public) and access to the chapter house (#27), where the monks would meet. The next chapel (Santa Catalina's Chapel, #28) displays a remarkable copy of a 10th-century Bible. In the same case is a copy of El Cid's pre-nup. (To protect his assets, he found a clever legal loophole to transfer ownership of all he had to his wife.) Around the top of this room are dozens of paintings depicting centuries' worth of bishops.

Continuing to the **Chapel of St. John the Baptist and St. James** (#29), you find the cathedral's museum collection, including ecclesiastical items (such as some exquisitely detailed crosses and chalices), an emotive statue of Christ being whipped, and an altar depicting St. James the Moor-Slayer (see page 362).

Finally you'll head downstairs to the **lower cloister** (#33). At the foot of the stairs is a schmaltzy portrait of El Cid, and beyond

that, a series of three chambers lead off to the right. In the first is a model of the original Romanesque church (with the current Gothic footprint around it for comparison), Romanesque capitals from cathedral columns, and a sarcophagus. The second chamber emphasizes the Gothic aspects of the cathedral and contains a large model of the entire cathedral complex. Farther down the cloister, Renaissance exhibits include a restored heraldic stained-glass window and a carved nativity scene. The third chamber on the right is a mini-cinema showing a 15-minute film documenting the history of the cathedral and its recent restorations (Spanish only, 2/hour).

Backtrack to El Cid, and then continue around the cloister to see glass cases displaying several original statues and carvings retrieved during the restoration work (and replaced with copies). The patio often houses contemporary art exhibitions (open May-Sept only). Exit through the ticket office, which also contains the gift shop and the lockers. Go in peace—and if you're carrying a pilgrim's credential, stamp it yourself here. You've earned it.

Other Sights

On a short visit, the cathedral is the main sight. But if you have the time, a few other attractions might be worth a look.

Museum of Human Evolution (Museo de la Evolución Humana)

This museum was inspired by discoveries of Pleistocene-era remains in the nearby Atapuerca Mountains, about nine miles east of Burgos. The Atapuerca find constitutes one of the most important settlements of the first Europeans. Housed in a new glass building by the river, the museum displays these remains. Flanking the museum are a research center and a large conference center. In front of the museum is a sculpture of a naked man walking hand in hand with a child, surrounded by various metal tubes symbolizing their evolution...a surprising topic for a city with such a conservative religious history.

Cost and Hours: €6, free on Wed afternoon, open Tue-Fri 10:00-14:30 & 16:30-20:00, Sat 10:00-20:00, Sun 10:00-15:00, closed Mon, Paseo Sierra de Atapuerca, tel. 902-024-246, www .museoevolucionhumana.com.

Other Museums

On the hill behind the cathedral, **Centro de Arte** is a contemporary art museum with temporary exhibits (free, Tue-Fri 12:00-14:00 & 17:30-20:00 except Fri until 21:00, Sat 11:30-14:30 & 17:30-21:00, Sun 11:30-14:30, closed Mon, tel. 947-256-550, www.cabdeburgos .com). Just across the river, near the bus station, the **Museo de Burgos** celebrates the cultural heritage of Burgos province. Its five floors of painting and sculpture and two floors of archaeological exhibits ring the gorgeous courtyard of a fine old 1540 convent. The somewhat-hard-to-appreciate museum features La Tizona, the famous sword of El Cid (€1.20; July-Sept Tue-Sat 10:00-14:00 & 17:00-20:00, Sun 10:00-14:00, closed Mon; Oct-June Tue-Sat 10:00-14:00 & 16:00-19:00, Sun 10:00-14:00, closed Mon; Calle Miranda 13, tel. 947-265-875, www.museodeburgos.com).

Plaza Mayor and Promenade

Burgos' main square, a long block from the cathedral, is urban-feeling and strangely uninviting, with long marble benches. The

stone building with two clock towers is the town hall; if you walk under here you'll emerge at the city's delightful riverside promenade. Lined with knobby plane trees and outdoor cafés, it has an almost Provençal ambience. Going left along the promenade takes you to **Plaza del Mío Cid,** with an equestrian statue celebrating Burgos' favorite son, "My El Cid." Going right along the promenade leads you to the impressive **Arco de Santa María** (Virgin Mary's Gate), one of six surviving entrances of this stout-walled city's original 12 gates. Built in the 13th century and decorated in 16th-century Renaissance style, the gate's interior recently opened to the public. Although there isn't much to see inside—temporary art exhibits and old pharmacy artifacts—it's free (Tue-Sat 11:00-13:50 & 17:00-21:00, Sun 11:00-13:50, closed Mon). After climbing through, go outside to look up at the gate, and in a deep, strong voice, declare: "Burgos." Passing through this gate takes you directly to the cathedral.

▲Huelgas Monastery (Monasterio de las Huelgas)

In addition to its grand cathedral, Burgos has a pair of impressive monasteries. The Cistercian monastery of Huelgas is the easiest

to reach (though still a bit of a walk from the cathedral). Entrance is by one-hour tour only, and English tours are very rare. Inside you'll see a "pantheon" of royal tombs, a Gothic cloister with Mudejar details, a chapter house with 13th-century stained glass, and a Romanesque cloister.

The highlight is a statue of St. James with an arm that could be moved to symbolically "knight" the king by placing a sword on his shoulders (since only a "saint"—or statue of a saint—was worthy of knighting royalty). Finally you'll tour a museum of rare surviving clothes from common people (not just religious vestments) from the 13th and 14th centuries.

Cost and Hours: €7, free all day Wed and Thu afternoons, open Tue-Sat 10:00-13:00 & 16:00-17:30, Sun 10:30-14:00, closed Mon, required tours depart about every 20 minutes, try asking your guide for some English info, tel. 947-201-630, www.monasteriodelashuelgas.org.

Getting There: It's about a 20-minute walk west of the city center, or you can take bus #5, #7, or #35 (catch the bus across the bridge from the cathedral).

Cartuja Monastery (Cartuja de Miraflores)

Unless you adore monasteries, seeing both Huelgas and Cartuja is probably redundant—and Cartuja is farther out of town. However, the Cartuja Monastery is a nice destination for a pleasant three-mile walk. (Bring a picnic.) To get there, cross the river by Plaza del Mío Cid and turn left, following the river until you reach the monastery. Or take a taxi there (€8) and walk back.

Cost and Hours: Free but donations gladly accepted, Mon-Sat 10:15-15:00 & 16:00-18:00, Sun 11:00-15:00 & 16:00-18:00, tel. 947-268-799, www.cartuja.org.

Near Burgos

Atapuerca

Nine miles out of Burgos sit the Sierra de Atapuerca Mountains, home to the site where archaeologists have discovered human remains dating back over a million years. Scholars are drooling over the find, which offers significant new insights into the lives of prehistoric humans—well-explained by the Museum of Human

Evolution in Burgos (described earlier). To visit Atapuerca, travel by car or taxi from Burgos to the village of Ibeas de Juarros, where a shuttle bus will transfer you to the site (advance reservations essential, get details at TI or the Museum of Human Evolution, tel. 902-024-246, www.atapuerca.org, reservas@museo evolucionhumana.com).

Santo Domingo de Silos

This unassuming village—about 40 miles (an hour's drive) south of Burgos—has a fine Benedictine monastery that's become a quirky footnote in popular music. The monastery's monks are famous for their melodic Gregorian chants, which were recorded and released as the hugely popular album *Chant* in 1994. (It went on to sell six million copies.) Although the monks don't perform concerts, some of their daily services—which are free and open to the public—include chanting. The lengthy vespers *(visperas)* service is entirely chanted (daily at 19:00, 2.5 hours); there's also some chanting at the shorter Eucharist service (Mon-Sat at 9:00, Sun at 11:00). You can also tour the cloister and museum (€3.50, open to the public Tue-Sat 10:00-13:00 & 16:30-18:00, Sun 12:00-13:00 & 16:00-18:00, closed Mon). Call to confirm before making the trip (tel. 947-390-049, www.abadiadesilos.es).

Sleeping in Burgos

(€1 = about $1.30, country code: 34)

When I've listed a price range, it fluctuates with demand; the top rates are for summer (June-Sept).

$$$ Hotel Silken Gran Teatro is comfortable, modern, and well-located beside the river (connected by a footbridge to the Museum of Human Evolution complex). Prices for its 117 rooms vary wildly depending on season and view—book well in advance for a good deal (Sb-€68-70, Db-€68-175, extra bed-€32, breakfast-€14, air-con, elevator, free Wi-Fi, café, restaurant, free gym, no public lounge, parking-€15/day, Avenida de Arlanzón 8, tel. 947-253-900, www.hotelgranteatro.com, reservas.granteatro @hoteles-silken.com).

$$ Mesón del Cid enjoys Burgos' best location, gazing across a quiet square at the cathedral's front facade (full-frontal cathedral views are worth the extra €15). The 55 rooms in two buildings come with classy tile floors and old-fashioned furniture (Sb-€60-75, Db-€75-90, breakfast-€11, air-con, elevator, free guest computer and Wi-Fi, Plaza de Santa María 8, tel. 947-208-715, www.mesondelcid.es, mesondelcid@mesondelcid.es).

$$ Hotel Centro Burgos Los Braseros, set back a little from the street, offers modern class for reasonable prices. Its lobby and 59 rooms are slick and stylish (Sb-€50-56, Db-€60-66, much higher on holidays, includes breakfast, air-con, elevator, request quiet room, free Wi-Fi, restaurant, café, Avenida del Cid 2, tel. 947-252-958, www.hotelcentroburgos.com, reservas@hotelcentroburgos .com).

$$ El Hotel Jacobeo is a cheaper option, with 14 modern rooms along a lively pedestrian street (Sb-€35-40, Db-€45-72, skimpy breakfast-€4.50, free Wi-Fi, all rooms face the back—so it's quiet, Calle de San Juan 24, tel. 947-260-102, www.hoteljacobeo .com, hoteljacobeo@hoteljacobeo.com).

$ Pensión Peña is Burgos' best budget option. Lively Loli, who speaks no English, rents eight simple but bright and well-maintained rooms (sharing three bathrooms) on the second floor of an old apartment building with a new elevator. Loli takes no advance reservations, but you can call in the morning to see if she has a room (D-€25-29, La Puebla 18, tel. 947-206-323, mobile 639-067-089).

Eating in Burgos

On Calle Sombrerería: Several good eateries are on this street. **Bar Gaona Jardin,** at #29 (tel. 947-206-191), has a leafy interior and cooks up nice, hot tapas. **Estrella de Galicia,** with a modern, bright ambience, offers a preview of the cuisine you'll enjoy in Santiago—Galician food, wine, and beer (€11 meal offered weekdays, €5-7 *raciones,* €10-15 main dishes, daily, alongside church at Calle de la Paloma 35, tel. 947-276-902). Across the street, **Cervecería Morito** offers a more chaotic local ambience—one tight room with tables and a bar, or pay a little more to eat at the terrace across the road (€3-4 sandwiches, €5-7 *raciones,* handy photo menu, daily, Calle Sombrerería 27, tel. 947-267-555). At the end of the street, **Pecaditos** is a local favorite for its tasty tapas and bargain prices (€1 tapas, daily, Calle Sombrerería 3, tel. 947-267-633).

Elsewhere in Burgos: **Casa Pancho** is a long, inviting bar where hardworking José, Angel, and Begoña churn out fresh-cooked tapas. Two or three tapas off of their *Carta de los Pinchos* can make a good meal (the menu's photos of dishes are described in English). Their specialty is *cojonuda* (quail egg, blood sausage, and green pepper on bread—all for €1). You're welcome to take a table for about 10 percent extra—still a great value. To sample a good Spanish wine with your tapas, try a glass of the strong local red, Ribera del Duero, or a white Albariño from Galicia—each about €2.50 (daily, Calle San Lorenzo 13, tel. 947-203-405). A couple more good tapas bars are within steps of here.

Casa Ojeda is a venerable institution that's a reliable choice for a real restaurant meal. Specializing in Burgos cuisine, they offer seating at the bar downstairs (tapas, €6 half-*raciones,* €13

Walking the Way

The Camino by car? Purists cringe at the thought—arguably, it contradicts the whole point of the Camino to do it in a rush. If you have a month of your life to devote to the trek, consider following the Camino the intended and traditional way.

As walking the Camino is in vogue, there's no shortage of good Camino guidebooks and maps. Try *Walking the Camino de Santiago* by Bethan Davies and Ben Cole, *A Pilgrim's Guide to the Camino de Santiago* by John Brierly, or *Buen Camino* by Jim and Eleanor Clem. For a more philosophical take, check out *Following the Milky Way* by Elyn Aviva and *On Pilgrimage* by Jennifer Lash. The Spanish national tourism office has posted good online resources at http://bit.ly/d1mjax.

Get a good book. Read and study it. Pack carefully. Solicit advice from people who've done it. Then enjoy the journey.

The procedure for walking the Camino has remained the same throughout history. The gear includes a cloak; a pointy, floppy hat; a walking stick; and a gourd (for drinking from wells). The route of the Camino is marked with yellow arrows or scallop shells at every intersection. (For more on the significance of these items, and others, see sidebar on page 298.)

Early in the journey, pilgrims buy their "credential" *(credencial)*—a sort of passport, which they get stamped and dated at churches and lodgings along the way. (They can also show it to stay at cheap *refugios* and to get a reduced pilgrim's rate at many museums and churches en route.) At the end, they present their stamped credential in Santiago and receive a special certificate called a *compostela*. Only those who meet the two

principal criteria qualify: You must do the pilgrimage for "spiritual" reasons; and you must walk at least the last 100 kilometers (about 62 miles, roughly from Sarria) or ride your bike or horse the last 200 kilometers (124 miles) into Santiago.

Doing the entire French Road from the border to Santiago takes about four to six weeks on foot (averaging 12-15 miles per day, with an occasional rest day—32 days is a typical Camino). Bikers can do it in about two weeks. Many of the trails, originally dirt paths, are now being paved. The journey itself is a type of hut-hopping: At regular intervals along the route (about every 5-10 miles), pilgrims can get a bunk for the night at humble little hostels called *albergues* (ahl-BEHR-gehs), *refugios* (reh-FOO-hee-ohs), or *hospitales* (oh-spee-TAH-lehs). Some of these are run by the government (€5-10 per bunk, closer to €3 in Galicia, even if they're "free" a donation is requested; no reservations taken—first-come, first-served, with priority given to credential-holding pilgrims arriving on foot). Others are privately run (typically a bit more expensive—€10-20—and sometimes take reservations). A wide variety of other accommodations are available for those who prefer more comfort, ranging from simple *hostales* to grand hotels and *paradores* (I've listed my favorites in this chapter).

What began as a religious trek to atone for one's sins has evolved into a journey undertaken by anyone—spiritual or secular—who just wants some time to think. Although some pilgrims do the trip for "fun," those who take it seriously caution that it's one of the most wrenching things you can do. After a few weeks on the Camino, many pilgrims begin to develop a telltale limp...you'll notice it getting more pronounced as you move west. (There's a reason old pilgrim hostels are sometimes called "hospitals.")

But there are worse things than blisters and sore muscles. The Camino can take a psychological toll on pilgrims. Trudging step after step across endless plains toward an ever-receding horizon, you're forced to introspection. Religious or not, you can't help but come to terms with your regrets, demons, "sins," or anything else that's on your conscience.

This process of self-reflection is symbolized by picking up a small stone somewhere early on the Camino, then depositing it at the Iron Cross near the end of the trek—releasing yourself from whatever's been weighing you down. The absolution of sins that awaited medieval pilgrims isn't so different from the "find myself" motives of today's iPhone-toting tourists. Whether you're pardoned by the Church, or simply unburdened of what's been nagging you, it's liberating all the same.

A wonderful pilgrim camaraderie percolates along the length of the Camino, as a United Nations of vagabonds—young and old—swap stories and tips. Driving, on foot, or on bike, you'll keep crossing paths with the same pilgrims again and again... the guy who checked in before you at the hotel last night is at the cathedral with you the next morning. Along the way, the standard greeting (like a Jacobean "Happy Travels") is *"Buen Camino!"*

No matter how you get to Santiago, you'll share in the jubilation pilgrims have felt through the ages when—four miles out of town—the spires of the cathedral come into view.

CAMINO DE SANTIAGO

combo-plate) or in the upstairs dining room (pricier meals served 21:00-24:00: €10 starters, €16-40 main dishes). Relax and enjoy the subdued, rapidly aging ambience (closed Sun evening, Calle Vitoria 5, tel. 947-209-052, www.restauranteojeda.com).

Rincón de España has a great location on Plaza del Rey, close to the cathedral. It's popular with locals for its regional dishes, including *cochinillo* (roast suckling pig) and *cordero* (roast lamb) cooked in a wood-fired oven. The restaurant's two indoor rooms often are full with wedding parties on weekends, and its outdoor terrace sports views of the cathedral spires. Brothers Javi and Fernando (who speaks English) are sommeliers and have a good local wine list. Try their *morcilla* (blood sausage, a local specialty) and, for dessert, the traditional *leche frita*—fried milk (€14.50 fixed-price meal available for lunch and dinner, €7.50-20 main dishes, daily 12:30-15:45 & 19:30-23:30, closed Mon-Tue afternoons in Oct-April, Calle Nuño Rastura 11, tel. 947-205-955, www.rincondeespana.com).

Burgos Connections

From Burgos by Bus to: Pamplona (3/day, 3-4 hours, transfer in Vitoria), **León** (4-5/day, 2-3.25 hours, Alsa), **Bilbao** (8/day, fewer on weekends, 2-3 hours, Alsa), **Santiago de Compostela** (1/day, 8.5 hours, Alsa), **San Sebastián** (7/day, 3-3.5 hours), **Salamanca** (2-3/day, 3.5-4 hours, Alsa), **Madrid** (hourly, 7/day go directly to T4 at Barajas airport, 3 hours, Alsa). Keep in mind that Sunday connections are very sparse. If traveling by Alsa, find the user-friendly ticket machine at the bus station.

By Train to: Pamplona (2/day, 2-3.5 hours, better option than bus), **León** (6/day, 2 hours), **Bilbao** (3/day, 2.5-3 hours), **San Sebastián** (6/day, 3hours), **Salamanca** (7/day, 2.5-3.5 hours, transfer in Valladolid or Palencia), **Madrid** (8/day, 2.5-4.5 hours).

From Burgos to León

While there are some worthwhile stops between Burgos and León, this is a good place to put some serious miles under your belt: Follow signs for the A-231 expressway and zip between the cities in less than two hours. Sticking with the true Camino—a confusing spaghetti of roads without a single, straight highway to keep you on track—takes you through a poorer, very humble countryside with few sights. Some travelers enjoy dipping into towns along here such as **Castrojeriz, Frómista,** and **Carrión de los Condes**—or the slightly larger town of **Sahagún,** with its impressive monastery and massive bell tower—but on a tight itinerary, your time is better spent in Burgos or our next stop, León.

León

With a delightfully compact Old Town (surrounded by ugly sprawl), León (lay-OWN) has an enjoyable small-town atmosphere. But most importantly, it has a pair of sights that serve as a textbook for medieval European art styles: Romanesque (the San Isidoro Monastery, with astonishingly well-preserved frescoes) and Gothic (the cathedral, with the best stained glass outside of France).

León means "lion" in Spanish—but in this case, the name derives from Rome's seventh legion, which was stationed here. Founded as a Roman camp at the confluence of two rivers in A.D. 68, León gradually grew prosperous because of the gold trade that passed through here (mined in the Las Médulas hillsides to the west). Later, as the Moors were pushed ever southward, the capital of the Reconquista moved from Oviedo to here in 910, and for three centuries León was the capital of a vast kingdom (until it was supplanted by Burgos). Today's León has relatively little industry, but is the capital of one of Spain's biggest provinces, making it an administrative and business center. It's also a major university town, with some 15,000 students who imbue it with an enjoyable vitality.

Orientation to León

The big city of León, with 133,000 people (200,000 in the metro area), sits along the Bernesga River. On a short visit tourists can ignore everything outside the rectangular Old Town, which is set a few blocks up from the river.

Tourist Information

León's TI is on the square facing the cathedral (July-mid-Sept Mon-Sat 9:30-14:00 & 17:00-20:00, Sun 9:30-17:00; mid-Sept-June Mon-Sat 9:30-14:00 & 16:00-19:00, Sun 9:30-17:00; Plaza de la Regla 2, tel. 987-237-082).

Local Guide: Blanca Lobete is an excellent, energetic teacher who shares León's architectural gems with travelers (€91/3 hours, mobile 669-276-335, guiaslegio@hotmail.com).

CAMINO DE SANTIAGO

Arrival in León

By Train or Bus: The train and bus stations are along the river, about a 15-minute walk from the town center. To reach the Old Town from the stations, cross the big bridge, continue in the same direction through a roundabout, and walk straight up Avenida Ordoño II. You'll hit the turreted Gaudí building, marking the start of the Old Town. From here the San Isidoro Museum is to the left, and the cathedral is straight ahead (up Calle Ancha).

By Car: Compared to the other cities in this chapter, León is not well-signed. Do your best to follow directions to the city center *(centro ciudad);* once there, you can park in a very convenient underground parking garage at Plaza Santo Domingo (€16/day), right at the start of the Old Town (and within a three-minute walk of all my recommended accommodations). Nearby Plaza Mayor also has a parking garage.

Self-Guided Walk

Welcome to León

León's two most worthwhile sights complement each other perfectly: the remarkable Romanesque frescoes at San Isidoro, and the gorgeous stained glass of the cathedral. To connect these major sights, follow this walk through León's city center. (If you're rushed, head straight for the cathedral.)

• *Start at...*

Plaza San Marcelo: The old **City Hall** (Casa Consistorial) sports a variety of flags, from national to provincial. Next to the column in the plaza's small park (at the north end of the square), you'll find a **relief map** depicting León's development during three major periods. León began as a Roman military camp nearly 2,000 years ago—we'll see some Roman defensive walls later in this walk. After the Moorish occupation of the Iberian Peninsula, the city fell into decline, but later re-emerged as the capital of a Christian kingdom. Medieval walls enlarged the city, and as evidenced by the modern street plan, León continues to prosper to this day.

• *From the park, turn left one short block, then turn right to skirt around the edge of the Plaza Santo Domingo roundabout. Walk up Calle Ramón y Cajal (keeping the church tower in sight), then head up the stairs at the Roman wall to...*

Plaza San Isidoro: On this square, you'll find the 11th-century **San Isidoro Church** and its excellent **museum**. Look for the plaque on Calle El Cid (the big street immediately across from the church) dedicated to León's favorite son, Guzmán el Bueno. This hero of the Reconquista was born in this mansion (for more on Guzmán, see page 859). The church is free, so go into the side entrance and take a peek. If you want to visit the museum—with its gorgeous Romanesque frescoes (described later)—turn right as you exit the church.

• *After your visit, with your back to the church's main entrance, cross the square and turn right on the narrow side street. At the next street, turn left and head for an ugly modern building with stone panels. Take the street on the left side of that building, Calle Ruíz de Salazar. As you walk, it's hard to miss the turreted medieval-looking building in the distance. Follow this street directly to...*

Casa de Botines: This is one of few works by Antoni Gaudí outside of Catalunya (another is the Bishop's Palace in Astorga, described later in this chapter). Now the Casa de Botines is a bank and generally not open to visitors unless there's a special exhibition. Gaudí preferred to use local materials, such as the slate roof (typical in León province). The rough stone exterior is intended to hang on to falling snow to create an atmospheric effect. Over the door is St. George, the patron saint of Gaudí's native Catalunya. Notice the architect himself on the bench across the square, appreciating his work.

• *At the end of the square, you reach an important thoroughfare. Turn left onto...*

Calle Ancha: This "Wide Street" cuts through the heart of the Old Town. It was widened in the mid-19th century to create an appropriate pathway to the cathedral and is lined with grand mansions of local wealthy people who wanted to live close to God. It's only been pedestrianized for the last decade, creating a much-enjoyed people zone.

As you walk up Calle Ancha toward the cathedral, the neighborhood to the left is called **Barrio del Cid** (for a supposed former resident). The area to the right is known as the **Barrio Húmedo,** or "Wet Quarter," for all the bars that speckle its streets (see "Eating in León," later). Deep in the Barrio Húmedo is the appealing main square, **Plaza Mayor** (which transforms into a market every Wed and Sat morning), overshadowed by the **cathedral** a few blocks away.

• *The end of Calle Ancha is also the end of your walk—at León's monumental cathedral (described next).*

Sights in León

▲▲Cathedral (Catedral)

León's 13th-century Gothic cathedral is filled with some of the finest stained glass in all of Europe. While its windows are being restored, you have a rare chance to see their gorgeous colors up close and personal.

Cost and Hours: Cathedral-€5 (includes audioguide), cloister and museum-€3, window restoration exhibit-€3; May-Sept Mon-Fri 9:30-13:30 & 16:00-20:00, Sat 9:30-12:00 & 14:00-18:00, Sun 9:30-11:00 & 14:00-20:00; Oct-April Mon-Sat 9:30-13:30 & 16:00-19:00, Sun 9:30-14:00; last entry 30 minutes before closing, window restoration exhibit hours often shorter, tel. 987-875-767, www.catedraldeleon.org.

❷ **Self-Guided Tour:** Take a look at the facade.

Exterior: If you've just seen Burgos' cathedral, León's—while impressive—might seem a let-down. But reserve judgment until you get inside. León's cathedral was actually built in response to the one in Burgos, to keep León on the map after Burgos wrested capital status from León in 1230. But, whereas Burgos' was built over two centuries, this cathedral took only about 50 years to complete. The  focus was on creating a simple, purely Gothic cathedral to showcase its grand stained-glass windows. The three porticos (doorways with pointed arches) are textbook Gothic. Notice the gap between the two towers and the main facade, which allows even more light to reach those windows. This also gives the cathedral a feeling of lightness. The one exception to the pure-Gothic construction: Notice the tower on the right is a bit taller—it was capped in the 15th century with a frilly spire to keep up with what was going on in Burgos.

Now approach the **main door,** above which is a carving of the Last Judgment. Above Mary, St. Michael weighs souls to determine who is going to party with the musicians of heaven (left; his scale bar is missing) or burn with the cauldrons and demons of hell (right). If you look carefully you'll see that all of those kicking back in heaven are members of the clergy or royalty. This subtle message made the Camino de Santiago even more appealing to pilgrims: If you weren't a priest or an aristocrat, completing the

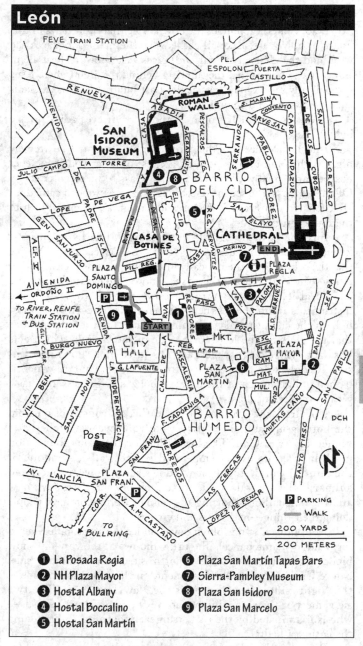

León

FEVE Train Station

PL. ESPOLON — Puerta Castillo

ROMAN WALLS

San Isidoro Museum

BARRIO DEL CID

CATHEDRAL

END

Casa de Botines

PLAZA SANTO DOMINGO

PLAZA REGLA

To River, RENFE Train Station & Bus Station

START

CITY HALL

MKT.

PLAZA MAYOR

PLAZA SAN MARTÍN

BARRIO HÚMEDO

Post

PLAZA SAN FRAN.

TO BULLRING

P Parking
Walk

200 YARDS
200 METERS

CAMINO DE SANTIAGO

① La Posada Regia
② NH Plaza Mayor
③ Hostal Albany
④ Hostal Boccalino
⑤ Hostal San Martín
⑥ Plaza San Martín Tapas Bars
⑦ Sierra-Pambley Museum
⑧ Plaza San Isidoro
⑨ Plaza San Marcelo

Camino was your only ticket to eternal bliss.

Before entering, ponder the crucial role that **light** plays in this house of holy glass. Like all cathedrals, the main door faces the west, and the altar (at the far end) faces east—toward Jerusalem. But that also means that the sun rises behind the altar (where Jesus symbolically resides) and sets at the Last Judgment. This theme is continued again and again inside.

Speaking of which, go on in and let your eyes adjust to the light.

Interior: Notice how the purely Gothic structure—extremely high, with columns and pointed arches to direct your gaze ever heavenward—really allows the stained glass to take center stage. Of all this glass (the second-most glass in any European cathedral, after Chartres in France), 70 percent is original, from the 13th to the 16th centuries.

Imagine how the light in here changes, like living inside a kaleidoscope, as the sun moves across the sky each day. Notice that the colors differ thematically in various parts of the cathedral. Above the main door, the rose window (dedicated, like the cathedral itself, to the Virgin Mary, with 12 angels playing instruments around her) is the most colorful, as it receives the most light at the end of the day. Turning to face the front altar, notice that the glass on the left (north) side of the church, which gets less light, symbolizes darkness and obscurity—blue dominates this side. The glass on the right (south) side of the church, which is bathed in light much of the day, symbolizes brightness and has a greater variety of colors.

Now trace the layers of Gothic **cathedral construction** from the bottom up, as the building (like your eyes) stretches ever higher, closer to God. The lowest level is the stone foundation (with pointed archways embedded in the walls), symbolic of the mineral world. The first windows show flowers, trees, and animals—the natural world. At the top of each nature window are three medallions showing the human world: common people doing their thing—both vices and virtues.

Above this first row of windows, notice the stone gallery (used for window maintenance). The **tall windows** at the very top show biblical characters. On the left (north) side—the "darkness" side, before Christ—is the Old Testament; on the right (south) side—the "light" side, after Christ—is the New Testament. The two sides meet at the rose window (above the main altar) of Jesus—who is illuminated by the rising sun each morning, enlightening the entire cathedral.

Peek into the carved wooden **choir** at the center of the nave (closed to visitors). The curved wooden part over the top of the chair is a "sounding board" *(tornavóz)*, helping voices to carry.

The giant glass door replaced a solid wooden one in the early 20th century—opening up the church even more to God's light.

Head for the **transept.** Unfortunately, this part of the cathedral almost didn't survive a well-intended but botched Baroque-era reconstruction. A heavy dome placed over the transept proved too heavy for the four graceful main pillars, causing a significant chunk of the church to collapse. The transept's blue (north) rose window, featuring Christ, survives from the 13th century, while the red (south) one, with Mary, is from the 19th century.

Circling back behind the altar, you'll find a chapel with the **"White Virgin"** on the right, the original 13th-century statue (whose face was painted white) from the front facade of the church. Note the differences between the 16th-century stained glass above the Virgin (with one large, multipaneled scene) and the 13th- and 14th-century glass in the flanking chapels (with one scene per panel—and even tinier bits of glass).

Cloister and Museum: For a close-up look at all the decorative bits missing from the cathedral's interior, visit the cloister and museum (entrance at left side of main facade). Confusingly, it's divided into two different parts; the staff will open the door to each section, and then lock you in—supposedly to preserve temperature and humidity conditions. Don't worry. When finished with the first part, return to the door and wait patiently. Security cameras show them you need to be released. You'll let yourself out of the second section.

The **cloister** offers a good view of the flying buttresses that made the stained glass structurally possible. By removing the weight from the walls and transferring it to these buttresses, medieval engineers could build higher and make larger and larger windows.

In the **museum** are a series of rooms displaying some giant discarded Baroque elements (such as turret-tops) that were added to the facade in the 16th century, and later removed because they cluttered up the architectural harmony. One of the more interesting pieces is a Visigothic antiphonary—the most complete surviving liturgical book of chants from Spain's early-Christian days. How the chants sound remains a mystery since it wasn't written in a specific key, and modern musicians cannot transcribe any of it. Other items include a Mudejar armoire from the 13th century, studies of the cathedral's stained glass, textiles, and some modern-day artwork.

Window Restoration: The cathedral's 737 stained glass panels are undergoing a painstaking restoration. Each window is being carefully removed from its old lead frame, dry-cleaned (with minimal use of liquid solvents), and reset. The windows can be admired from the cathedral floor, but close-up views can only be seen as part of a separate exhibit (entrance on the left side of the cathedral, Spanish-only tours every hour but occasionally more frequent, English brochures provided). A lighted display shows which panels have been restored, which are being worked on, and which are remaining.

Restoring the 20,450 square feet of glass includes preventative steps. A solid, clear pane of glass is set in the original's place, so that the freshly cleaned stained glass can sit inside, protected from the elements. A mesh metal panel is also installed on the exterior for an added layer of protection. Historians are creating an extensive photographic record of the process—which is of vital importance since the last restoration from the 19th century misplaced some panels.

Near the Cathedral
Sierra-Pambley Museum

This nondescript house facing the cathedral contains the well-preserved living quarters of a 19th-century businessman and some fascinating reminders of early education in Spain. Those interested in 19th- and 20th-century decorative arts must pay to tour the rooms, but the education exhibit is free.

At the age of 60, Francisco Blanco y Sierra Pambley created a foundation to educate students; classes were to be free of religious or political dogma. Several schools were founded, and the students thrived in this environment, supported by the latest technological innovations. You'll see a Kodak movie projector and a typewriter used to instruct girls—as this was one of the very few places in Spain where girls could receive any kind of formal education.

Unfortunately, Sierra Pambley was ahead of his time. When the Second Republic gained control of Spain in 1931, the foundation's humanist views came under suspicion. In 1936, all funds and property were confiscated; one director was even executed by a firing squad. The schools eventually came under the jurisdiction of the Catholic Church. After the death of Franco, the foundation was reinstituted, and its remaining funds returned to the organization.

Cost and Hours: Apartment-€3, education exhibit-free, Tue-Sat 11:00-14:00 & 17:00-20:00, closed Mon, no English descriptions, Calle Sierra Pambley 2, tel. 987-229-369, www.sierrapambley.org/museo.

▲▲San Isidoro Museum (Museo de San Isidoro)

San Isidoro is an 11th-century Romanesque church that's been gradually added on to over the centuries. The church itself is free and always open to worshippers, but the attached museum is the real attraction. Inside you'll see a library, a cloister, a chapter house, and a "pantheon" of royal tombs featuring some of the most exquisite Romanesque frescoes in Spain.

Cost and Hours: €5; July-Aug Mon-Sat 9:00-20:00, Sun 9:00-14:00; Sept-June Mon-Sat 10:00-13:30 & 16:00-18:30, Sun 10:00-13:30; Plaza San Isidoro 4, tel. 987-876-161, www .sanisidorodeleon.net.

⊙ Self-Guided Tour: Buy your ticket and go directly into the **Royal Pantheon** (Pantéon Real). This area, now enclosed in the middle of the complex, was once the portico in front of the west door of the church. In 2002, historians discovered the tombs of 23 medieval kings and queens (which are now held in the stone tombs), 12 *infantes* (children of the monarch), and 9 counts. But who's buried here pales in comparison to the beautiful, vivid frescoes on the vaulting above them. Created in the late 11th and early 12th centuries, these frescoes have never been repainted—they're incredibly well-preserved. While most Romanesque frescoes have been moved to museums, this is a rare opportunity to see some in situ (where the artist originally intended).

Follow along as the frescoes trace the life of Christ (counterclockwise, starting on the wall in the front right corner). In the scene of the Annunciation, you'll notice a sense of motion (Mary's billowing clothes) that's unusual for typically stiff and un-lifelike Romanesque art. Above that, on the ceiling in the corner, an angel appears to shepherds dressed in traditional 11th-century Leonese clothing. There's even a Leonese mastiff dog, lapping at his master's milk (while he's distracted by the angel).

In the next ceiling section (closer to the entry), Roman soldiers carry out the gruesome slaughter of the innocents. Then it's time for the Last Supper (center of the ceiling). As you take in the bold colors, notice that only 11 of the Apostles have halos...all but Judas (under the table). At the corner, find the black rooster *(gallus),* a symbol of Jesus, who harkened the dawn of a new day for God's people. But in the next section we see the rooster used as a different symbol—as Peter denies Christ three times before the cock crows. Also see Jesus' arrest, Simon helping Jesus carry the cross, and Pontius Pilate washing his hands of the whole business. Finally (on wall, left of main altar) we see Jesus nailed to the cross.

The final panel, in the middle of the room, is the most artistically and thematically impressive: Jesus returning triumphant to judge the living and the dead. He's depicted here as Pantocrator ("all-powerful"). Over his shoulders are the symbols for alpha and omega, and he's surrounded by the four evangelists, depicted—

according to the prophecy of Ezekiel—as animals: angel, bull, eagle, and lion. The most interesting detail is the calendar running along the archway near Jesus' right hand. The 12 medallions—one for each month (labeled in Latin)—are symbolized by people's activities during that month. In January, the man closes one door (or year) while he opens the next. He proceeds to warm himself by the fire (February), prune (March), plant his crops (April), harvest (July), forage (September), slaughter the fattened pig (October), and bless his bread by the fire at Christmas (December). The message: Jesus is present for this entire cycle of life.

There's more to the museum. Continue counterclockwise into the **cloister,** with its spectacular ceiling tracery. You'll find a small room with a giant 12th-century rooster weathervane that used to top the nearby tower (now replaced by a replica)—a symbol of the city.

You can also climb the tight spiral staircase (near where you came in) to the evocative old **library** (an interesting mix of Gothic design and Renaissance decoration). Marvel at the size of all those Gregorian chant books as well as a giant Mozarabic Bible from 960—you can page through a facsimile in the gift shop. The **chapter house** displays a glittering assortment of Romanesque reliquary chests and Asian silk embroidery, an amazing luxury for medieval kings.

Sleeping in León

(€1 = about $1.30, country code: 34)
All of these listings are inside the Old Town. If there's a range, you can assume that the high end is for summer. Hotels often make last-minute or off-season deals.

$$$ La Posada Regia is a smart little hotel with 36 rooms in two buildings just off the main walking street. The old-fashioned, pleasant decor is a combination of wood beams and patches of stone (Sb-€40-80, Db-€50-139, Regidores 9-11, tel. 987-213-173, www.regialeon.com, posada@regialeon.com).

$$$ NH Plaza Mayor is the Old Town splurge, with 51 rooms right on Plaza Mayor (some with views for no extra charge—request one). Part of a classy chain, this place offers modern four-star comfort at reasonable prices (Sb-€70-100, Db-€75-120, deals often as low as Sb/Db-€65, breakfast-€15, air-con, elevator, free Wi-Fi, Plaza Mayor 15, tel. 987-344-357, www.nh-hotels.com, nhplazamayor@nh-hotels.com).

$$ Hostal Albany offers 19 very mod rooms at a good price, just a few steps off the main walking street and cathedral square (Sb-€40-51, Db-€57-68, prices drop Jan-Feb, breakfast-€3, air-con, elevator, free Wi-Fi, Calle La Paloma 13, tel. 987-264-600, www.albanyleon.com, info@albanyleon.com).

$$ Hostal Boccalino, spacious and practical, rents 35 good rooms at a good price on a stately square facing the monastery (Sb-€35-45, Db-€55-65, Tb-€90, elevator, free Wi-Fi and drinks from cooler, Plaza de San Isidoro 9, tel. 987-223-060, www .hostalboccalino.com, boccalino_3@hotmail.com). They also have 10 comparable rooms above their restaurant in a nearby building (similar prices, same reception, no elevator).

$ Hostal San Martín is a good budget option. Popular with pilgrims, it has 11 rooms; some quiet ones overlook a small square in the Old Town (S-€23, Sb-€31, D-€31, Db-€43, Tb-€55, request quiet room in back, no elevator, free Wi-Fi, cozy lounge; Plaza Torres de Omaña 1—located up the stairs on the right as you enter, second floor; tel. 987-875-187, www.sanmartinhostales.com, sanmartinhostal@hotmail.com).

Eating in León

León is one of few Spanish cities whose bars still honor the old tradition of giving a free (if modest) tapa to anyone buying a drink. Your best bet for finding eats in León is to stroll the **Barrio Húmedo** area, south of Calle Ancha. This zone is packed with restaurants and bars offering good food and ambience.

Plaza San Martín Pub Crawl: In the "Wet Quarter," locals head for Plaza San Martín to eat and drink. Survey the many little bars on or near the square, noting how locals know each bar's specialty and generally stick to that dish when ordering. Consider these joints: **La Bicha** is a dirty little hole-in-the-wall where Paco works hard maintaining his reputation for making León's best *morcilla* (blood sausage with rice, spreadable and served without the skin) and for being a colorful local character. He'll fry up a plateful and serve it with some buttered toast and a nice *crianza* wine (plate big enough for four, €6, tel. 987-256-518). **El Llar** is famous for its potatoes (free with a drink). Of the two sauces, I'd get the cheese (tapas in bar, restaurant upstairs serves €5-10 starters and €12-15 main dishes, tel. 987-254-287). **Bar Rebote** serves six different croquettes—one free with each drink (tel. 987-213-510). If you're still hungry, head down Calle Mulhacín to find **La Competencia** (Calle de Mulhacín 8, tel. 987-849-477). Fight your way in for free pizza slices (downstairs) and potatoes with ham (upstairs). **Mesón el Tizón** fills one tight room with a bar in front and seating in back—order hot *raciones* from its chalkboard menu (Calle de las Carnicerías 1, tel. 987-256-049).

Camino de Santiago: Western Half

CAMINO DE SANTIAGO

León Connections

From León by Bus to: Astorga (hourly, 50 minutes) **Burgos** (7/day, 2-3.25 hours), **Santiago de Compostela** (1/day, 6 hours), **Madrid** (10/day, 4 hours). All buses are run by Alsa (tel. 902-422-242, www.alsa.es).

By Train to: Burgos (4/day, 2 hours), **San Sebastián** (2/day, 5 hours), **Pamplona** (2/day, 4-5.5 hours), **Santiago de Compostela** (3/day, 5 hours), **Madrid** (8/day, 3-4.5 hours).

From León to Galicia

This section, arguably the most diverse stretch of the Camino, begins in the flatness of the Meseta Central around León. Then, around Astorga, the landscape gradually becomes more varied and lush, as the Camino approaches the mountainous El Bierzo region (the northwest fringe of Castile and León). Before you know it, you're in the very Celtic-feeling terrain of Galicia.

• *Begin by making your way west, to Astorga. You can stay on the N-120 highway, or pay a €5 toll to zip there more quickly on the AP-71 expressway.*

Astorga

Astorga (ah-STOR-gah) sits at the intersection of two ancient roads: the Camino and a north-south trade route from Sevilla to the north coast. When León was a humble Roman camp, "Asturica" was the provincial capital. But today the fortunes are reversed, as welcoming, laid-back, sleepy Astorga (with about 12,000 people)—just big enough to have some interesting sightseeing and good hotels and restaurants—is a nice small-town alternative to the big city of León. The main attraction here is the memorable Bishop's Palace by Antoni Gaudí.

Tourist Information: Astorga's TI shares a square with the Bishop's Palace and cathedral (daily in summer 10:30-14:00 & 16:00-19:00, shorter hours and closed Mon off-season, Plaza Eduardo de Castro 5, tel. 987-618-222).

Arrival in Astorga: The **bus** station is just outside the Old Town, behind the Bishop's Palace. **Drivers** follow signs for *centro ciudad* and *centro urbano*, drive through the middle of town, and park in front of the TI and cathedral (to park in a blue-painted spot, prepay at the meter and put the ticket on your dashboard). Or park below the cathedral outside the Roman wall for free.

Sights: The striking **Bishop's Palace** (Palacio Episcopal), rated ▲, is a fanciful Gothic-style castle, similar to Gaudí's Casa de Botines in León. Inside you'll  see Gaudí's genius in the bishop's fine rooms, decorated with frescoes. The palace hosts a museum that describes the Camino and the history of Astorga, and provides a safe place for some of the region's fine medieval church art. You'll see a 17th-century statue of Pilgrim James, a few historical Camino documents, ecclesiastical gear, and a gallery of contemporary Spanish art from the surrounding region. Not as good as it should be, with little posted information (and none in English), the museum is worthwhile mostly for a chance to see a medieval-inspired Gaudí interior (€3, €5 combo-ticket with cathedral museum—see below; April-Sept Tue-Sat 10:00-14:00 & 16:00-20:00, Sun 10:00-14:00; off-season Tue-Sat 11:00-14:00 & 16:00-18:00, Sun 11:00-14:00; closed Mon year-round; last entry 30 minutes before closing; tel. 987-616-882).

Next to (and upstaged by) the palace is Astorga's light-filled Gothic **cathedral,** with a marvelously carved choir and a chapel to St. James that is popular with pilgrims. It's free to enter in the morning (9:00-10:30), but after 10:30 you can get in only by paying for the attached museum, which shows off a treasury collection of paintings, altarpieces, and vestments (€3, €5 combo-ticket with Bishop's Palace, same hours as the palace).

Rounding out Astorga's attractions are a chocolate museum and a Roman museum.

Sleeping in Astorga: If you prefer to sleep in a small town, Astorga is a good alternative to the big city of León (though values here are no better than in the city).

$$ Hotel Gaudí has 35 woody rooms over a restaurant across from the cathedral; some have views of the Bishop's Palace (Sb-€40-50; Db-€50-70; breakfast-€9, extra bed-€15-20, air-con in most rooms, elevator, free Wi-Fi, Plaza Eduardo de Castro 6, tel. 987-615-654, www.gaudihotel.es, reservas@gaudihotel.es).

$$ Astur Hotel Plaza, which feels more business-class, has 37 rooms right on the main square. Choose between a room overlooking the square—with a clock tower that clangs every 15 minutes—or a quieter back room (Sb-€50-63, Db-€70-105, breakfast-€8, air-con, Wi-Fi, Plaza de España 2-3, tel. 987-617-665, www.hotelasturplaza.es, info@hotelasturplaza.es).

$$ Ciudad de Astorga Hotel has 33 business-class rooms with contemporary decor, a pleasant patio, and a spa with garden terrace. It's about three blocks from the cathedral (Sb-€45-76, Db-€60-106, bigger Db-€70-116, breakfast-€9, air-con, free Wi-Fi, Calle de los Sitios 7, tel. 987-603-001, www.hotelciudaddeastorga.com, reservas@hotelciudaddeastorga.com).

Eating in Astorga: **Restaurante Las Termas,** a couple of blocks from the cathedral right along the Camino, is well-regarded for its food—especially the traditional stew, *cocido maragato* (€10-16 main dishes, open for lunch only—13:00-16:00, closed Mon, Calle Santiago 1, tel. 987-602-212). **Hotel Gaudí,** listed earlier, has an atmospheric bar with tapas and *raciones,* and a restaurant with €13-16 fixed-price meals and €10-20 main dishes (open daily).

Connections: Astorga is well-connected by bus to **León** (hourly, 50 minutes), **Ponferrada** (hourly, 1 hour), **Villafranca del Bierzo** (6/day, 2 hours), and **Lugo** (7/day, 2.75 hours).

• *After Astorga, you can either zip up to Galicia on the A-6 expressway (toward* Ponferrada*), or stick with the Camino a bit farther south on much slower regional roads (LE-142). These two routes converge again at the small city of Ponferrada. Soon after, A-6 climbs up into the hills and to the town of Villafranca del Bierzo (described later).*

If you're sticking with the Camino, you'll be near the...

Iron Cross (Cruz de Ferro)

Near the top of Mount Irago is an iron cross atop a tall wooden pole, set in a huge pile of stones built up over the years by pilgrims unloading their "sins" brought from home (or picked up en route). It's a major landmark for Camino pilgrims, but difficult to reach

CAMINO DE SANTIAGO

for drivers (figure an hour's hike off the main road). From the cross it's a 30-minute walk to the nearly ruined stone village of Foncebadón.

Villafranca del Bierzo

Villafranca is the capital of the westernmost part of León, El Bierzo, which is trying to build a good reputation for its wine and culinary specialties. Dubbed "Little Compostela" for its array of historical buildings, this town is set in an attractive hilly terrain strewn with grapevines, cherry trees, and vegetable patches. Though hardly thrilling, Villafranca del Bierzo is worth a quick stop for its pilgrim  ambience (**TI** open Tue-Sun 10:00-14:00 & 16:00-20:00, until 19:00 off-season, closed Mon year-round, Avenida Díaz Ovelar 10, tel. 987-540-028, www.villafrancadelbierzo.org). There's plenty of free parking near the TI, just past the large church on the right when entering town.

Church of St. James' Gate of Forgiveness

To play pilgrim, hike from the main square up to the town's stout 14th-century castle (not open to the public). Then follow signs for *Iglesia Románica,* the Romanesque 12th-century Church of St. James (Santiago). The church has a "gate of forgiveness" (*puerta del pardón,* on the side facing the town). Thanks to a 16th-century papal ruling, if a pilgrim had come this far, fell ill, and couldn't continue over the rugged terrain to Santiago, he or she was pardoned anyway. (Handy loophole.)

Villafranca *Albergue*

Next to the church is a funky pilgrims' dorm with oodles of pilgrims bonding. It was built on the site of a medieval clinic that cared for those who needed to take advantage of the *puerta del perdón* (at the time, the clinic here was the only source of medical aid for 300 miles). Today this 80-bed *albergue* provides €8-10 bunks to 10,000 pilgrims a year. They even have a separate room for snorers. If you'd like to learn about the system (or buy a scallop shell), stop in. It's run by Jesús, whose father began helping pilgrims here in the 1930s. Jesús welcomes curious non-pilgrims, albeit with the motto "The tourist demands, the pilgrim thanks" (tel. 987-540-260).

Sleeping and Eating: **\$\$ Hotel La Puerta del Perdón** is just the place for fancy pilgrims or anyone needing a comfortable and economical place to sleep and eat in Villafranca. It's got seven rooms and is warmly run by Herminio. Their fine little restaurant is open to the public for lunch, but only to hotel guests for dinner

(Db-€55-70, includes breakfast, facing the castle on the uphill side a block below the Church of St. James at Plaza de Prim 4, tel. 987-540-614, www.lapuertadelperdon.com, info@lapuertadelperdon.com).

• *Just after Villafranca del Bierzo on the A-6 expressway, you cross into the final region on the Camino: Galicia.*

Galicia

In its final stretch, the Camino leaves the broad expanse of the Meseta Central and climbs steeply into Galicia (gah-LEE-thcc-ah). Green and hilly, Galicia shatters visitors' preconceptions about Spain. There's something vaguely Irish about Galicia—and it's not just the mossy stonework and green, rolling hills. The region actually shares a strain of Celtic heritage with its cousins across the Cantabrian Sea. People here are friendly, and if you listen hard enough, you might just hear the sound of bagpipes.

• *Shortly after entering Galicia, take the freeway exit and follow signs to* Pedrafita do Cebreiro. *From Pedrafita, a well-maintained mountain road (LU-633) twists its way up to the classic Galician pilgrim village of O Cebreiro. The road has plenty of pull-offs for photo ops. The town itself is not well-marked; turn off at* Conxunto Histórico-Artístico *for parking.*

O Cebreiro

An impossibly quaint hobbit hamlet perched on a ridge high above nothing, O Cebreiro (oh theh-BRAY-roh) whispers, "Welcome

to Galicia." This rustic village evokes an uncomplicated, almost prehistoric past, when people lived very close to nature, in stone igloos with thatched roofs. With sweeping views across the verdant but harsh Galician landscape, O Cebreiro is constantly pummeled by some of the fiercest weather in Spain. And it's all within a five-minute drive of the freeway.

Wander around. Enjoy the remoteness. O Cebreiro smells like wood fires, manure, and pilgrim B.O. Get a snack or drink at a bar, or browse through a gift shop. A few townspeople (who jabber at each other in Galego—see page 351—and cock their heads quizzically when asked about newfangled inventions like email) share the town with weary pilgrims on an adrenaline high after finally reaching Galicia. The local dogs, who've known each other their whole lives, still bark at each other territorially from across the street, completely ignoring the backpackers who regularly trudge through town.

Sights in O Cebreiro

▲Pallozas

From Celtic times 1,500 years ago, right up until the 1960s, the villagers of O Cebreiro lived in humble round stone huts with peaked thatched roofs, called *pallozas*. One of the nine surviving *pallozas* has been turned into a loosely run museum, where an attendant is paid by the government to welcome visitors and answer questions.

Cost and Hours: Free, Wed-Sun 11:00-14:00 & 15:00-18:00, closed Mon-Tue. If a door of a round hut is open, poke inside.

Visiting the Huts: Here visitors can learn about the lifestyle of the people who lived in *pallozas* until not so long ago. Upon entering a *palloza*, you'll find the only "private" room in the house, belonging to the parents. Beyond that is a living area around a humble fire. (Notice there's no chimney—smoke seeps out through the thatch.) Ponder the ancient furniture. Surrounding the fire are clever benches (which were also used, by the kids, as very hard beds) with pull-down counters so they could double as a table at mealtime. The big beam with the chain could be swung over the fire for cooking. Looking up, you'll see the remains of a wooden ceiling that prevented sparks from igniting the thatch. The giant black-metal spirals suspended from the ceiling were used to smoke chorizo sausage—very efficient. Attached to this living area is a miniature "barn." Animals lived on the lower level, while people slept on the upper level (which has been removed, but you can still see on the wall where the floor was once supported)—kept warm by all that livestock body heat. About a dozen people (and their animals) lived in one small hut. But thanks to the ideal insulation provided by the thatch, and the warmth from the fire and animals, it was toasty even through the difficult winter.

▲Royal St. Mary's Church (Santa María la Real)

All roads lead to the village church. Founded in the year 836—not long after the remains of St. James were found in Santiago—this pre-Romanesque building is supposedly the oldest church on the entire French Road of the Camino. The interior is surprisingly spacious, but very simple. Notice the sunken floor: The build-

ing is actually embedded into the ground for added protection against winter storms. The desk inside stamps pilgrims' credentials and sells votive candles. (I don't think there's anything wrong with giving your guidebook an O Cebreiro stamp—I did.) The baptistery, in a tiny side room near the entrance, is separate from the main part of the church, as dictated by ancient tradition. It has a giant and very rough font used for immersion baptisms. In the chapel to the right of the main altar is a much-revered 12th-century golden chalice and reliquary, which holds items relating to a popular local miracle: A peasant from a nearby village braved a fierce winter snowstorm to come to this church for the Eucharist. The priest scoffed at his devotion, only to find that the host and wine had physically turned into the body and blood of Christ, staining the linens beneath them, which are now in the silver box.

Cost and Hours: Free, daily 9:00-21:00.

Sleeping and Eating in O Cebreiro

(€1 = about $1.30, country code: 34)

The only businesses in town are a half-dozen very humble pub-restaurants, which feed pilgrims and other visitors hearty Galician cuisine in a communal atmosphere. You'll see signs offering a stick-to-your-ribs €10 "pilgrim menu." Many of these places also rent a few rooms upstairs. With inclement weather, doors are often closed—don't be shy; just walk right in. Be warned that these rooms are very rustic, English can be tricky, and reservations are only by phone. Try **$$ Hospedería San Giraldo de Aurillac** (Db-€60, 17 rooms in 3 buildings, tel. 982-367-125); **$ Casa Carolo** (D-€35, Db-€48, tel. 982-367-168); or **$ Mesón Antón** (D/Db-€40, tel. 982-151-336). The *albergue,* which is open only to pilgrims, is perched on a hill at the edge of town and charges €3 per bed.

O Cebreiro Connections

By Car

From O Cebreiro you've got another route decision to make.

To stick with the Camino, you'll continue on LU-633, along twisty roads, toward Santiago. Along the way you'll pass through some interesting larger towns. **Samos** has a gigantic monastery and perfectly manicured cloister garden. **Sarria** is forgettable, but it's just over 100 kilometers (62 miles) from Santiago, making it a popular place to begin a truncated pilgrimage (since you need to walk at least that far to earn your *compostela* certificate). **Portomarín** is a relatively new town, built only after the River Miño was flooded to create a reservoir in the 1950s. The stout and blocky late-Romanesque Church of San Juan was moved to a new site, stone by stone—and if you look closely enough you can see how the stones were numbered to keep track of where they fit.

I prefer the faster expressway route (backtrack to A-6, which you'll take north, following signs for A Coruña), which offers the opportunity to dip into the appealing walled city of Lugo.

Lugo

While not technically on the French Road of the Camino de Santiago, the midsized city of Lugo (pop. 98,000) warrants a detour for car travelers. Boasting what are arguably the best-preserved Roman walls in Spain—a mile and a third long, completely encircling the town, draped with moss, and receding into the misty horizon— Lugo offers an ideal place for an evocative stroll. Lugo feels like a poor man's Santiago, with a patina of poverty and atmospherically crumbling buildings. Evocative chimneys thrust up through rickety old slate roofs. And yet there's something proud and welcoming about the town. Aside from the walls, Lugo has a cathedral and gregarious Galician charm, making it a fine place to spend some time.

Orientation to Lugo

Tourist Information: The TI is a few steps up a pedestrian street off the main square, Plaza Maior—look for the yellow signs (Mon-Fri 9:30-14:00 & 16:30-19:00, Sat 11:00-13:30, closed Sun; Praza do Campo 11, tel. 982-251-658, www.lugoturismo.com).

Arrival in Lugo: The **bus** station is just outside the town walls; once inside the Old Town, the main square and TI are a block away. The **train** station is two blocks east of the town walls. **Drivers** follow signs to *centro ciudad* and *centro urbano*. Once you enter the town walls, parking garages are signed for *Plaza de Santo Domingo* or *Anxel Fole*—both are centrally located.

Sights in Lugo

The town's **Roman walls** *(murallas Romanas)* are free and always open, providing a kind of circular park where locals and visitors can stroll at rooftop level. You can access the walls at various points around town (you'll find stairs near most of the gates where traffic enters the Old Town), and it takes about 45 minutes to walk the entire way around. With less time the most interesting stretch is along the west side of town: Walk up the ramp behind the cathedral and turn right, watching behind you for tingly views of the walls and cathedral spires.

Lugo's **cathedral** is vast, dark, and dusty, with an unexpected Rococo altarpiece glittering with silver (free, daily 8:25-20:45, €2 to enter cloister). While it's a lovely cathedral, it pales in comparison to Santiago's.

Lugo also has a provincial museum and a Roman museum.

Sleeping in Lugo

(€1 = about $1.30, country code: 34)

Sleeping in Lugo is worth considering to break the long journey to Santiago from Cantabria or León. Budget *hostales* cluster just southeast of the town walls (near the bus station). The following two hotels are the only ones inside the Old Town. They may be willing to deal—ask for their best price.

$$$ Pazo Orban e Sangro is the town splurge, renting 12 rooms with hardwood floors, flat-screen TVs, slippery rates, and luxurious furnishings. It's just inside the town walls near the cathedral (Db-€60-120, breakfast-€10, air-con, elevator, free Wi-Fi, Travesía do Miño, tel. 982-240-217, www.pazodeorban.es, info@pazodeorban.es).

$$ Hotel Méndez Núñez, right in the heart of the Old Town, has a classy old lobby, a medieval-feeling lounge, and 70 rooms with worn furniture but new bathrooms (Sb-€40-50, Db-€50-90, breakfast-€7, air-con, elevator, free guest computer and Wi-Fi, Calle Reina 1, tel. 982-230-711, www.hotelmendeznunez.com, hotel@hotelmendeznunez.com).

Lugo Connections

Lugo is connected by bus to **Santiago de Compostela** (6/day, 2.5 hours, Alsa), **Astorga** (8/day, 2.5-3 hours, Alsa), and **León** (9/day, 3.5-5 hours, Alsa).

• *After Lugo, the end is in sight. You have one final route decision to make: The fastest way (about 1.5 hours to Santiago) is to stick with the A-6 expressway north to A Coruña, then pay €5 to take the AP-9 tollway back south to Santiago. But if you'd like to rejoin the Camino for the last stretch—following in the footsteps (or tire treads) of a millennium of pilgrims—follow signs from Lugo toward* Ourense *(on N-540/N-640, about 20-30 minutes longer than expressway option). In Guntín, split off on N-547 and head for Santiago de Compostela.*

However you arrive, see the next chapter and enjoy one of Europe's great pilgrim cities.

Buen Camino!

SANTIAGO
DE COMPOSTELA

The best destination in the northwestern province of Galicia, Santiago de Compostela rivals Granada as the most magical city in Spain. While Granada reminds visitors of Spain's Moorish past, Santiago de Compostela has long had a powerful and mysterious draw on travelers: More than a thousand years' worth of Christian pilgrims have trod the desolate trail across the north of Spain just to peer up at the façade of its glorious cathedral.

But there's more to this city than pilgrims and the remains of St. James. Contrary to what you've heard, the rain in Spain does *not* fall mainly on the plain—it falls in Galicia. This "Atlantic Northwest" of Spain is like the Pacific Northwest of the United States, with hilly, lush terrain that enjoys far more precipitation than the interior, plus dramatic coastal scenery, delicious seafood, fine local wines, and an easygoing ambience. The Spanish interior might be arid, but the northwest requires rain gear. Even the tourists here have a grungy vibe: Packs of happy hippie pilgrims seek to find themselves while hiking the ancient Camino de Santiago from France (described in the previous chapter).

You'll see few signs of the country's financial problems in Santiago, where many locals work to serve the constant flow of tourists. As a pilgrim mecca, the city's accommodations, eateries, and sights are geared toward low-budget travelers. Santiago's top sight—the cathedral—is free to enter, along with many of its other attractions.

Santiago has a generally festive atmosphere, as travelers from every corner of the globe celebrate the end of a long journey. It's a sturdy city that, in its day, was one of Europe's most important religious centers, built of granite and later turned mossy green by the notorious weather.

Planning Your Time

Santiago's biggest downside is its location: Except by air, it's a very long trip from any other notable stop in Spain. But if you decide to visit, you—like a millennium's worth of pilgrims before you—will find it's worth the trek. You can get a good feel for Santiago in a day, but a second day relaxing on the squares makes the long trip here more worthwhile.

The city has one real sight: the cathedral, with its fine museum and the surrounding squares. The rest of your visit is for munching seafood, pilgrim-watching, and browsing the stony streets. The highlight of a visit just may be hanging out on the cathedral square at about 10:00 to welcome pilgrims completing their long journey.

Orientation to Santiago

Santiago is built on hilly terrain, with lots of ups and downs. The tourist's Santiago is small: You can walk across the historical center, or Zona Monumental, in about 15 minutes. There you'll find the city's centerpiece—the awe-inspiring cathedral—as well as several other churches, a maze of pretty squares, a smattering of small museums, a bustling restaurant scene, and all of my recommended hotels.

The historical center is circled by a busy street that marks the former location of the town wall (easy to see on a map). Outside of that is the commercial city center—a modern, urban district called Céntrico. A 10-minute walk through Céntrico takes you to the train station.

Tourist Information

The TI for both **city and regional information** is at Rúa do Vilar 30-32 (June-Sept daily 9:00-21:00; Oct-May Mon-Sat 9:00-19:00, Sun 9:00-14:00 & 16:00-19:00, tel. 981-555-129, www.santiagoturismo.com). It runs walking tours and rents audioguides (see "Tours in Santiago," later). Ask the TI what's going on when you're in town.

Conveniently next door and sharing the same address is the Turismo do Porto e Norte de Portugal, which offers information about destinations just across the border in **Portugal,** plus tips on how to get there (Mon-Fri 10:00-14:00 & 15:00-19:00, Sat 11:00-14:00 & 17:00-19:00, closed Sun, tel. 981-526-559, www.portoenorte.pt).

The Galego Language

Like Catalunya and the Basque Country, Galicia has its own distinctive language. Galego (called "*Gallego*" in Spanish, and sometimes called "Galician" in English) is a cross between Spanish and Portuguese. Historically, Galego was closer to Portuguese. But Queen Isabel imported the Spanish language to the region in the 15th century, and ever since, the language has gradually come to sound more and more like Spanish. In an attempt at national unity, dictator Francisco Franco banned Galego in the mid-20th century (along with Catalan and the Basque language, Euskara). During these trying times, Galicians spoke Spanish in public—and Galego at home. Since the end of the Franco era, Galego has reemerged as a proud part of this region's cultural heritage. Street signs and sight names are posted in Galego, and I've followed suit in this chapter.

If you don't speak Spanish, you'll hardly notice a difference. Most apparent is the change in articles: *el* and *la* become *o* and *a*—so the big Galician city La Coruña is known as "A Coruña" around here. You'll also see a lot more x's, which are pronounced "sh" (such as "Xacobeo," shah-koh-BAY-oh, the local word for St. James' pilgrimage route). The Spanish greeting *buenos días* becomes *bos días* in Galego. The familiar *plaza* becomes *praza*. And if you want to impress a local, change your *gracias* to *grazas* (GRA-thas)—a Galego thank you.

Arrival in Santiago de Compostela

There's luggage storage at the bus station, but not at the train station.

By Train: Santiago's train station is on the southern edge of the modern Céntrico district. You'll find ATMs, a cafeteria, car-rental offices, and a helpful train information office. To reach the center of town, leave the station and walk up the grand granite staircase, jog right, cross the busy Avenida de Lugo, and walk uphill for 10 minutes on Rúa do Hórreo to Praza de Galicia, a few steps from the historical center. A taxi from the station to your hotel will cost you about €7.

By Bus: From the bus station, northeast of the cathedral, it's about a 15-minute, mostly downhill walk to the center. Exit the station straight ahead on Rúa de Ánxel Casal and go to the Praza da Paz roundabout (with a large statue of St. James as a pilgrim). Turn left here onto Rúa da Pastoriza; follow it as it changes its name to Basquiños and Santa Clara before becoming Rúa da de San Roque, which will bring you into town. I'd rather hop on local bus #5 (€1) and take it to the market or to Praza de Galicia (to reach the historical center from here, walk uphill to cross busy Rúa da Senra—the Alameda park will be on your left). Taxis, visible from the bus stop, whisk you to the center for about €6.

By Plane: Santiago's small airport (airport code: SCQ) is about six miles from the city center. A bus connects the airport to the bus station, train station, then to Praza de Galicia at the south end of the historical center (€3, catch bus at exit by car rentals, 2/hour, 6:15-24:35, 35 minutes, may have to place big bags underneath the bus, www.empresafreire.com). A taxi into town costs €20.

By Car: There are only two freeway off-ramps to the city. The north exit (#67) is best for the airport and the old center. For car rental return at the train station, take SC-20 south and follow *estación ferrocarril* signs. If continuing your journey, note that parking is "*aparcadoiro*" in Galego. Xoán XXIII is the parking lot closest to the cathedral.

Helpful Hints

Closed Days: Many museums (except church-related ones) are closed on Monday. The colorful produce market is closed on Sunday, slow on Monday, and busiest on Thursday and Saturday mornings.

Church Hours: The cathedral and other major churches in Santiago are open 9:00-21:00 without a siesta, while minor ones have limited visiting hours. Special Masses for pilgrims are held daily at noon in the cathedral. The big Masses on Sunday are at 10:00 and noon.

Festivals: Late July is the main party time in Santiago, when the city hosts a world music festival and impromptu concerts all over town, along with fireworks on July 24 and 31. During this time, the royal family (or their representative) attends Mass in Santiago, staying at the parador in a suite overlooking the square (described under "Sleeping in Santiago," later). Crowds and prices increase in Holy Years (when the Feast of St. James—July 25—falls on a Sunday, next in 2021). The second-most important musical event in town—with several days of free concerts—occurs around Ascension (May 29 in 2014). In late May, an international film festival called *Curtocircuito* offers showings at various venues throughout the city (tel. 948-542-303, www.curtocircuito.org).

Internet Access: Most hotels offer Wi-Fi for guests. Many cafés in town offer free Wi-Fi to customers (look for window signs), as does the bus station.

Laundry: Axiña, a self-service *lavandería,* is a 15-minute walk from the historical center (self-service-€6/load, €7 for full service, Mon-Fri 8:30-13:00 & 16:00-20:30, Sat 8:30-13:30, closed Sun, Rúa de Ramón Cabanillas 1, tel. 981-591-323).

Shopping: Jet, the black gemstone (called *azabache* in Spanish) similar to onyx, is believed to keep away evil spirits—and to bring in tourist euros. Along with jet, the silver trade has long been important in Santiago...and continues to be a popular item for tourists. Although the Galicians are a superstitious people and have beliefs about good and bad witches, the made-in-Taiwan witches you see in souvenir shops around the city are a recent innovation. Maybe the best souvenir is a simple seashell, like the ones pilgrims carry with them along the Camino.

Best Views: There are beautiful views back toward the cathedral from the Alameda park. From the cathedral, follow Rúa do Franco to the end. Swing right into the park and continue up Paseo de Santa Susana to the viewpoint (mirador) along Paseo da Ferradura. You can enjoy another excellent view from the very top of the park (clearly marked on TI maps).

Tours in Santiago

The city TI offers a two-hour English-language **walking tour** that covers the cathedral and the surrounding plazas (€12, April-Sept Thu-Sat at 16:00, Sun at 12:00, details at TI). Ask about the TI's other tours, including gastronomy tours, nighttime tours, and more. Or you can rent an **audioguide,** and follow the suggested three-hour route (€12/24-hour rental). Either tour is better than taking the silly **tourist train,** which only does a circuit around the outskirts of the old city (€6, 45 minutes, meet in front of the cathedral on Praza do Obradoiro).

It's easy to visit the cathedral and nearby sights on your own with the information in this book, but if you have the extra cash, you could hire a **local guide** (3.5 hours, €90 Mon-Fri, €100 Sat-Sun). Patricia Furelos (mobile 630-781-795, patriciafurelos @yahoo.es) and Manuel Ruzo (mobile 639-888-064, manuel@art naturagalicia.com) are equally good, or contact the Association of Professional Guides of Galicia (tel. 981-569-890, guiasgalicia @ctv.es).

SANTIAGO DE COMPOSTELA

Santiago de Compostela

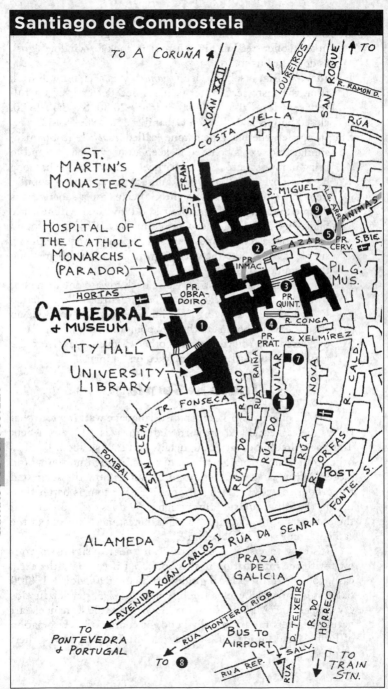

SANTIAGO DE COMPOSTELA

BUS STATION

GALICIAN CONTEMPORARY ART MUSEUM

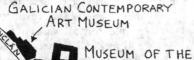

MUSEUM OF THE GALICIAN PEOPLE

VALLE INCLÁN

DAS RODAS

CASAS

SAN PEDRO

TO AIRPORT, CITY OF CULTURE OF GALICIA, ARZUA, LEÓN & PARIS

PORTA DO CAMIÑO

DA CERCA

ITO

RUA DAS AMEAS

⑥
MARKET

UNIV.

TROMPAS

RÚA DA VIRXE DA CERCA

ANT.

① Praza do Obradoiro
② Praza da Inmaculada
③ Praza da Quintana
④ Praza das Praterías
⑤ Praza de Cervantes
⑥ Praza de Abastos
⑦ Office for Pilgrims
⑧ To Launderette
⑨ Folk Music Clubhouse

CAMINO DE SANTIAGO

100 YARDS
100 METERS

SANTIAGO DE COMPOSTELA

DCH

Sights in Santiago

▲▲Cathedral

Santiago's cathedral isn't the biggest in Spain, nor is it the most impressive. Yet it's certainly the most mystical, exerting a spiri-

tual magnetism that attracts people from all walks of life and from all corners of the globe. (To more fully appreciate the pilgrim experience, read the first part of the previous Camino de Santiago chapter before visiting the cathedral.)

Exploring one of the most important churches in Christendom, you'll do some time travel, putting yourself in the well-worn shoes of the millions of pilgrims who have trekked many miles to this powerful place.

Cost and Hours: Free, daily 9:00-21:00; if a service is going on, the front entrance is likely closed—but you can enter around either side about 100 yards to the left or the right; www .catedraldesantiago.es.

Backpacks: If you're not allowed to bring backpacks into the church, you'll find free baggage storage next to the Office for Pilgrims on Rúa do Vilar (see map).

❷ Self-Guided Tour: Begin facing the cathedral's main facade, in the big square called...

Praza do Obradoiro

Find the pavement stone with the scallop shell right in the middle of this square. For more than a thousand years, this spot has been

where millions of tired pilgrims have taken a deep breath and thought to themselves: "I made it!" To maximize your chance of seeing pilgrims, be here at about 10:00—the last stop on the Camino de Santiago is two miles away, and pilgrims try to get to the cathedral in time for

the 12:00 Mass. It's great fun to chat with pilgrims who've just completed their journey. They seem to be very centered and content with the experience, and tuned in to the important things in life... like taking time to talk with others. You'll likely see pilgrims who met along the way arrive separately, ecstatically reunite, then leave together, having found each other at the grand finale. Every time I

visit, I find myself taking photos for people and agreeing to email copies to them. Even if you're shy, it's a fun and easy way to meet pilgrims by offering to capture their personal triumphs.

• *Before heading into the cathedral, take a spin around the square (start facing the cathedral).*

To your left is the **Hospital of the Catholic Monarchs** (Hostal dos Reis Católicos). Isabel and Ferdinand came to Santiago in 1501 to give thanks for successfully forcing the Moors out of Granada. When they arrived, they found many sick pilgrims at the square. (Numerous pilgrims came to Santiago to ask for help in over-coming an illness, and the long walk here often only made their condition worse.) Isabel and Ferdinand decided to build this hospital to give pilgrims a place to recover on arrival (you'll see their coats of arms flanking the intricately carved entryway). It was  free and remained a working hospital until 1952—many locals were born there—when it was converted into a fancy parador and restaurant (see "Sleeping in Santiago" and "Eating in Santiago," later). The modern white windows set against the old granite facade might seem jarring—but this contrast is very common in Galicia, maximizing the brightness that accompanies any sunny spells in this notoriously rainy region.

Another 90 degrees to the left is the Neoclassical **City Hall** (Concello). Notice the equestrian statue up top. That's St. James, riding in from heaven to help the Spaniards defeat the Moors. All over town, Santiago's namesake and symbol—a Christian evangelist on a horse, killing Muslims with his sword—is out doing his bloody thing. See any police on the square? There's a reason for their presence. In its medieval day, Santiago's cathedral was one of the top three pilgrimage sites in the Christian world (after Jerusalem and Rome). It remains important today, and with St. James taking such joy in butchering Muslims, it is considered a high-profile target for Islamic fundamentalists.

Completing the square (90 more degrees to the left) is the original **University** building (its rectory faces the square, the tower behind with the flags marks the original building, which is now the library). Santiago has Spain's third-oldest university, with more than 30,000 students (medicine and law are especially popular).

You'll likely see Spanish school groups on the square, field-tripping from all over the country. Teachers love to use this spot for an architecture lesson, since it features four different architectural styles (starting with the cathedral and spinning left): 18th-century Baroque; 16th-century Plateresque; 18th-century Neoclassical; and medieval Romanesque (the door of the rectory).

• *Now take a look at the...*

Cathedral Facade

Twelve hundred years ago, a monk followed a field of stars (probably the Milky Way) to the little Galician village of San Fiz de Solovio and discovered what appeared to be the long-lost tomb of St. James. On July 25, 813, the local bishop declared that St. James' remains had been found. They set to building a church here and named the place Santiago (St. James) de Compostela (*campo de estrellas*, or "field of stars," for the celestial bodies that guided the monk).

Originally a simple chapel, the cathedral you see today has gradually been added on to over the last 12 centuries. By the 11th century, the church was overwhelmed by the crowds. Construction of a larger cathedral began in 1075, and the work took 150 years. (The granite workers who built it set up shop on this very square—still called Praza do Obradoiro, literally, "Workers' Square.") Much of the design is attributed to a palace artist named Maestro Mateo, whom you'll meet a little later.

The exterior of the cathedral you see today is *not* the one that medieval pilgrims saw (though the interior is much the same). In the mid-18th century, Santiago's bishop—all fired up from a trip to Baroque-slathered Rome and wanting to improve the original, now-deteriorating facade—decided to spruce up the building with a new Baroque exterior. He also replaced the simple stonework in the interior with gaudy gold.

Study the facade. Atop the middle steeple is St. James (dressed like the pilgrim he was). Beneath him is his tomb, marked by a star—one of the many symbols you'll see all over the place (to decipher the symbols, see sidebar on page 298). On either side of the tomb are Theodorus and Athanasius, James' disciples who brought his body to Santiago. On the side pillars are, to the left, James' father, Zebedee; and to the right, his mother, Salomé.

Don't you wish you had a miniature replica of this beautiful facade to carry around with you? Actually, you probably do. Check your pocket for a copper-colored euro coin worth €0.01, €0.02, or €0.05. There it is! Of all the churches in

Spain, they chose this one as their representative in euro-land. It's even more important when you consider the significance of the images depicted on Spain's other euro coinage: a portrait of the author of *Don Quixote*, Miguel de Cervantes, Spain's greatest contributor to world literature; and the current king, Juan Carlos I. Sevilla and Toledo may have bigger cathedrals, but Santiago has the symbolism to propel its church into this powerful triumvirate.

The cathedral also houses a museum with three parts; as you face this facade, the door to the main museum is to the right, the entry to the crypt is dead ahead (under the staircase), and the door on the left leads to an empty palace and the cathedral rooftop (see Gelmírez Palace listing, later).

• *Now, head up the stairs and enter the cathedral. Once inside go to the rear of the nave and look up at the...*

Portico of Glory

The portico is currently being restored (due to wrap up sometime in 2014). Be sure to watch the free video that shows the portico in all its glory. The video runs in the crypt (go outside and downstairs to crypt, then make free reservation for viewing time); after a live intro, usually in Spanish, the video is presented in several languages.

Whether you view the portico in its place or in the video, imagine taking a step back in time. Remember, it used to be the main facade of the cathedral, sculpted in about 1180 by Maestro Mateo. Pretend you're a medieval pilgrim, and you've just walked 500 miles from the Frankish lands to reach this cathedral. You're here to request the help of St. James in recovering from an illness or to give thanks for a success. Maybe you've come to honor the wish of a dying relative or to be forgiven for your sins. Whatever the reason, you came here on foot.

You can't read, but you can tell from the carved images that this magnificent door represents the Glory of God. Old Testament prophets on the left announce Christ's coming. New Testament apostles on the right spread his message. Jesus reigns directly above, approachable to the humble Christian pilgrim via St. James with his staff.

Theologically, pilgrims are coming not for St. James, but to get to Christ via St. James. Look for Jesus, front and center, surrounded by Matthew, Mark, Luke, and John. Beside them are angels carrying tools for the Crucifixion—the cross, the crown of thorns, the spear, and a jug of vinegar. Arching above them are 24 musicians playing celestial music—each one with a different medieval instrument. Below St. James is a column with the Tree of Jesse—showing the genealogy of Jesus with Mary near the top and, above her, the Holy Trinity: Father, Son, and a dove representing the Holy Spirit.

As a pilgrim, you would walk to the column in the middle of the entryway (now ringed by a railing to keep crowds from gathering here). Squint down the nave to the end, and you'll see the stone statue of St. James that marks his tomb. Trembling with excitement at the culmination of your long journey, you'd place your hand into the well-worn finger holes on the column (see five grooves at about chest level) and bow your head, giving thanks to St. James for having granted you safe passage. Then you'd go around to the other side of the post and, at knee level, see Maestro Mateo, who carved this fine facade. What a smart guy! People used to kneel and tap their heads against his three times to help improve their intelligence (a ritual among university scholars here)—until a metal barrier was erected. (Grades have dropped recently.) Such a high-profile self-portrait of an artist in the 12th century was unprecedented. In Santiago he was something like the Leonardo of his day.

• *Now wander down the...*

Nave

Look up to take in the barrel vault and the heavy, dark Romanesque design of the church. (The original freestanding church had about 80 glorious alabaster windows. They were mostly bricked up when a complex of buildings was built around the church.) Up near the top, notice the gallery. This is where sweaty, smelly pilgrims slept. Check out the most modern addition to the side naves: TV monitors. Now when crowds fill the cathedral for Mass, everyone has a good view of the service.

• *Continue up the nave until you reach the high altar, where you'll see a thick rope hanging from a pulley system high in the dome, which is sometimes attached to the...*

Botafumeiro

This huge silver-plated incense burner (120 pounds and about the size of a small child) is suspended from the ceiling during special Masses, occurring about 13 times a year (ask at TI if one is scheduled during your visit, or check www.catedraldesantiago.es), or when a pilgrim pays about €300 to see it in action. During Holy Years, it swings nearly daily at the end of each pilgrims' Mass at 12:00. Supposedly the custom of swinging this giant incense dispenser began in order to counteract the stench of the pilgrims. After communion, eight men

(called *tiraboleiros*) pull on the rope, and this huge contraption swings in a wide arc up and down the transept, spewing sweet-smelling smoke. If you're here to see it, the most impressive view is from either side of the main altar. From this position, the *botafumeiro* seems to whiz directly over your head. When not in use, the *botafumeiro* and a replica are kept on display in the cathedral library (see "Cathedral Museum," later).

• *Stand in the center of the nave, in front of the...*

Altar

The big gold altar has all three representations of St. James in one place (see sidebar on page 364): Up top, on a white horse, is James

the *Matamoros*—Moor-Slayer; below that (just under the canopy) is pilgrim James; and below that is the original stone Apostle James by Maestro Mateo—still pointing down to his tomb after all these centuries.

The dome over the altar was added in the 16th century to bring some light into this dark Romanesque church.

On the columns up and down the nave and transept, notice the symbols carved into the granite. These are the markings of the masons who made the columns—to keep track of how many they'd be paid for.

• *Following the pilgrims' route, go down the ambulatory on the left side of the altar—passing where the* botafumeiro *rope is moored to the pillar—and walk down the little stairway (see the green light, on your right) to the level of the earlier, 10th-century church and the...*

Tomb of St. James

There he is, in the little silver chest, marked by a star—Santiago. Pilgrims kneel in front of the tomb and make their request or say their thanks.

• *Continue through the little passage, up the stairs, turn left, and wander around the ambulatory, noticing the various chapels (built by noblemen who wanted to be buried close to St. James). At the very back of the church (behind the altar) is the greenish...*

Holy Door

This special door is open only during Holy Years, when pilgrims use it to access the tomb and statue of the apostle. The current door, sculpted by a local artist for the 2004 Holy Year, shows six scenes from the life of St. James: the conversion moment when Jesus invited those Galilean fishermen to become "fishers of men";

St. James

Santiago is Spanish for "St. James." James and his brother John, sons of Zebedee and Salomé, were well-off fishermen on the Sea of Galilee. One fateful day, a charismatic visionary came and said to them, "Come with me, and I will make you fishers of men." They threw down their nets and became apostles.

Along with Peter, James and John were supposedly Jesus' favorites—he called them the "sons of thunder." After Jesus' death, the apostles spread out and brought his message to other lands. St. James spent a decade as a missionary bringing Christianity to the farthest reaches of the known world—which, back then, was northwest Spain. The legend goes that as soon as he returned home to the Holy Land, in A.D. 44, James was beheaded by Herod Agrippa. Before his body and head could be thrown to the lions—as was the custom in those days—they were rescued by two of his disciples, Theodorus and Athanasius.

These two brought his body back to Spain in a small boat and entombed it in the hills of Galicia—hiding it carefully so it would not be found by the Roman authorities. There it lay hidden for almost eight centuries. In 813, a monk—supposedly directed by the stars—discovered the tomb, and the local bishop proudly exclaimed that St. James was in Galicia. Santiago de Compostela was born.

But is this the *real* story? Historians figure the "discovery" of the remains of St. James in Spain provided a necessary way to rally Europe against the Moors, who had invaded Spain and were threatening to continue into Europe. The "marketing" of St. James was further bolstered by his miraculous appearance, on horseback and wielding a sword, to fight for the Christian army in the pivotal battle of Clavijo during the Reconquista. With St. James *Matamoros* ("the Moor-Slayer") in Iberia, all of Europe was inspired to rise up and push the Muslims back into Africa...which they finally did in 1492. James eventually became Spain's patron saint, and for centuries, Spanish armies rode into battle with the cry, "*Santiago y cierra, España!*" ("For St. James! Spaniards strike!").

Sure, the whole thing was likely a propaganda hoax to get a local populace to support a war. But yesterday's and today's pilgrims may not care whether the body of St. James actually lies in this church. The pilgrimage to Santiago is a spiritual quest powered through the ages by faith.

Jesus with the 12 apostles (James is identified by his scallop shell); James doing his "fishing" in Spain; his return to Jerusalem in A.D. 44 to be beheaded; the ship taking his body back to Spain; and the discovery of James' body in 813. At the bottom, the little snail is the symbol of the pilgrim...slow and steady, with everything on its back.

Hug St. James

There's one more pilgrim ritual to complete. Near the exit from the tomb, find a little door—perhaps with a line of pilgrims (10 yards away, by another green light, closed 13:30-16:00 and after 20:00). Climb the stairs under the huge babies, and find Maestro Mateo's stone statue of St. James—gilded and caked with precious gems. Embrace him from behind and enjoy a saint's-eye view of the cathedral...under the vigilant eye of a cathedral watchman, there to ensure you're not overcome by the unholy temptation to pry loose a jewel.

• *Congratulations, pilgrim! You have completed the Camino de Santiago. Now go in peace.*

Other Sights at the Cathedral

The Cathedral Museum (enter through door on the right, as you face main facade) and crypt (under the main staircase in front) share one ticket; the Gelmírez Palace (door on the left) and rooftop are covered by a separate ticket.

▲▲Cathedral Museum (Museo da Catedral)

The cathedral's museum shows off some interesting pieces from the fine treasury collection and artifacts from the cathedral's history.

Cost and Hours: €6, €4 for pilgrims; daily 10:00-20:00; last entry one hour before closing, toll tel. 902-557-812, ticket office in crypt under main stairs into cathedral, www.catedralde santiago.es.

➋ Self-Guided Tour: The museum is laid out chronologically from bottom to top. There's virtually no English inside, so pick up the included English audioguide from the ticket office as you go in.

Crypt: Wander into the crypt and see some serious medieval engineering. Because the church was built on a too-small hill, the crypt was made to support the part of the nave that hung over the hillside. The Romanesque vaulting and carved decoration is more Maestro Mateo mastery. A video in Spanish shows the continuing restoration of the Portico of Glory (see page 359).

Ground Floor: Here you'll find the remaining pieces of Maestro Mateo's original stone choir (stone seats for priests; these seats filled the center of the nave in the 12th century), pieced together as part of a new replica. Nearby, look for a miniature

The Three Santiagos

You'll see three different depictions of St. James in the cathedral and throughout the city:

1. Apostle James: James dressed in typical apostle robes, often indiscernible from the other apostles (sometimes with a pilgrim's stick or shell).

2. Pilgrim James: James wearing some or all of the traditional garb of the Camino de Santiago pilgrim: brown cloak, floppy hat, walking stick, shell, gourd, and sandals. Among pilgrims, he's the one carrying a book.

3. Crusader James, the Moor-Slayer (Matamoros): Centuries after his death, the Spaniards called on St. James for aid in various battles against the Moors. According to legend, St. James appeared from the heavens on a white horse and massacred the Muslim foes. Locals don't particularly care for this depiction, especially these days, when they worry it might provoke attacks by fringe Islamic fundamentalist elements, which is probably why the cathedral chapel dedicated to this version of James conveniently has floral displays that cover the slain Moors.

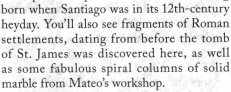

model of the choir. Notice the expressive faces Mateo carved into the granite. Working in the Romanesque style, he was well ahead of his time artistically. Consider the cultural value of a place in Europe where people from all corners came together, shared, and then dispersed.

In some ways, the concept of Europe as a civilization was being born when Santiago was in its 12th-century heyday. You'll also see fragments of Roman settlements, dating from before the tomb of St. James was discovered here, as well as some fabulous spiral columns of solid marble from Mateo's workshop.

First Floor: The four statues of a pregnant Mary illustrate a theme that's unusual in most of Europe, but common in Galicia and neighboring Portugal in the 15th century.

The final room on this floor is dedicated to various portrayals of St. James (see sidebar), with several incarnations of him as Matamoros (the Moor-Slayer). Notice the wooden door showing the rescue of James' body by his disciples and its transfer to Galicia.

Second Floor: Enter the cloister, where a series of tombs holding the remains of cathedral priests line the floor. Pass by the ornate chapel and enter the courtyard to see a fountain (which once stood in front of the cathedral and was used by pilgrims to cleanse themselves) and the original church bells (replaced with new models in 1989). As you walk left (clockwise) around the cloister, the second door leads to the Royal Chapel, with a beautiful-smelling cedar altar that houses dozens and dozens of relics. The centerpiece (eye level) holds the remains (likely the skull) of St. James the Lesser (the *other* Apostle James). Look up to find St. James riding heroically out of the woodwork to rally all of Europe to reconquer the Iberian Peninsula. This altarpiece was restored after a fire around 1900.

• *Cross the hall to the...*

Treasury: An altar dedicated to the King Ferdinand III takes center stage. The fancy solid-gold monstrance is used for carrying the communion host around the cathedral on Corpus Christi (the wafer sits in the little round window in the middle). Other bits of religious finery await your inspection.

• *Return to the cloister and back through the door you entered to the...*

Library/Archive: This is where they store old books, a funky rack for reading those huge tomes ("turn pages" by spinning the rack) and the *botafumeiro* (gigantic incense burner). There's always a replica here offering a close-up look.

• *Leave the library and go up one more floor to enjoy views from a fine balcony overlooking Praza do Obradoiro.*

Third Floor: Take a look inside the dark room to the right of the stairs. Here you'll find the painstakingly restored *gallardete* (long, triangular standard) flown from the Spanish captain's ship during the 1571 Battle of Lepanto. *Don Quixote* author Miguel de Cervantes was wounded in this battle—and likely saw this very flag—as Spain fought to victory over the Turks, gaining control of the Mediterranean.

You'll then walk through several rooms of restored tapestries. The first room is from designs by Rubens. The two middle rooms show idealistic 18th-century peasant life—wives helping their men to be less moronic (but there's still a man peeing in the corner). Don't miss the intimate 18th-century Madonna and Child statue in the glass case. The nursing *Virgen de la Leche* looks out at us as she feeds her son. The last room has a series of 12 tapestries, designed by Goya, with exacting details of life around 1790.

Gelmírez Palace (Pazo de Xelmírez)

The medieval home and traditional residence of the archbishop houses temporary exhibits that change every six months but offers little else of interest. You can access the palace (covered by your museum ticket) through the doorway to the left of Portico de Glory (Tue-Sat 10:00-11:00 & 16:00-20:00, Sun 10:00-14:00, closed Mon, tel. 981-552-985, www.catedraldesantiago.es).

Cathedral Squares

There is a square on each side of the cathedral. You've already visited Praza do Obradoiro, in the front. Here are the other three, working clockwise (to reach the first one, go up the passage—which street musicians appreciate for its acoustics—to the left as you're facing the main cathedral facade).

Praza da Inmaculada

This was the way most medieval pilgrims using the French Road actually approached the cathedral. Across the square is **St. Martin's Monastery** (Mosteiro de San Martiño Pinario), one of two monasteries that sprang up around the church to care for pilgrims. Today it houses a museum of ecclesiastical artifacts and special exhibits.

Walk to the corner of the square with the arcade, and go to the post with the sign for *Rúa da Acibechería* (next to the garbage can, under the streetlight). If you look to the roof of the cathedral, between the big dome and the tall tower, you can make out a small white cross. This is where the clothes of medieval pilgrims were burned when they finally arrived at Santiago. This ritual was created for hygienic reasons in an age of frightful diseases...and filthy pilgrims.

• *Continue along the arcade and around the corner, and you'll enter...*

Praza da Quintana

The door of the cathedral facing this square is the Holy Door, only opened during Holy Years. There's St. James, flanked by the

disciples who brought his body back to Galicia. Below them are more biblical characters, perhaps the 12 apostles and 12 prophets. Tip: Old Testament prophets hold scrolls. New Testament apostles hold books.

Across the square from the cathedral stands the imposing **St. Pelayo Monastery** (Mosteiro San Paio). The windows of its cells (now used by Benedictine sisters—notice the bars and privacy screens) face the cathedral. The church at the north end of this monastery is worth a peek. It has a frilly Baroque altar and a statue with a typical Galician theme: a pregnant Mary (to the left as you face main altar). The nuns sing at the evening vespers following the 19:30 Mass (Mon-Fri; 30 minutes earlier Sat-Sun). Just off this sanctuary is the entrance to the monastery's **Sacred Art Museum** (Museo de Arte Sacra), with a small but interesting collection (€1.50, Tue-Sun 11:00-13:30 & 16:00-18:30, closed Mon). The nuns of St. Pelayo make Galicia's famous *tarta de Santiago*—almond cake with a cross of Santiago in powdered sugar dusted on top. To buy one, exit the church to the right, head up the stairs, and walk around behind the monastery to find the entrance on Rúa de San Paio de Antealtares. Once inside, go to the small window on the left (generally open Mon-Sat 9:00-14:00 & 15:30-19:00; they only sell entire cakes—a big one for €10.50 and a very big one for €18; ring bell and remember that patience is a virtue).

• *Continue around to the...*

Praza das Praterías

This "Silversmiths' Square" is where Santiago's silver workers used to have their shops (and some still do). Overlooking the square is a tall **tower.** Imagine the fortified, typically Romanesque cathedral complex before the decorative Baroque frills were added; it looked more like a hulking fortress for fending off invading enemies from Normans to Moors to English pirates.

The **fountain** features a woman sitting on St. James' tomb, holding aloft a star—a typical city symbol. The mansion facing the cathedral is actually a collection of buildings with a thin-yet-effective Galician Baroque facade built to give the square architectural harmony. Its centerpiece even copies the fountain's star.

Beyond the fountain, a few steps down Rúa do Vilar (on the left), is the **Office for Pilgrims.** This is where pilgrims stop to pick up their *compostela*, the certificate that documents their successful *camino*. (The adjacent gift shop displays a copy of one in its window as an advertisement for pilgrims to get their *compostela* laminated.) While tourists aren't really welcome in here, you can pop your head into the hallway, where there's often a pile of hiking sticks abandoned by happy pilgrims who've finished their trek. Upstairs is a RENFE train ticket information desk—but it does not sell tickets (daily 9:00-21:00).

More Sights in Santiago

▲▲Market (Mercado de Abastos)

This wonderful market, housed in Old World stone buildings, offers a good opportunity to do some serious people-watching (Mon-Sat 8:00-14:00, closed Sun). It's busiest and best on Thursday and Saturday, when villagers from the countryside come to sell things. (Monday's the least interesting day, since the fishermen don't go out on Sunday.)

Percebes = Barnacles

Local gooseneck barnacles, called *percebes,* are a delicacy. *Percebes* only grow on rocks that see a lot of dangerous waves. It takes specialists—

a team of two gatherers—to harvest them: one with a rope tied to his waist, the other spotting him from above. Because of the danger, *percebes* are really expensive. You'll see them stacked in the windows of seafood bars where you'll pay about €7 for 100 grams ($40/lb). Check the price carefully when you order, as there are varieties that can cost many times that much. Two beers and a small 100-gram plate to split with your travel partner make for a wonderful snack. Just twist, rip, and bite: It's a bit like munching the necks off butter clams. I ask for toasted bread on the side.

For the freshest *percebes* at half the price—and twice the experience—buy them at the market, then let **Marisco-Mania** boil them for you right there in their market café. They'll boil up any seafood you buy in the market (it takes just a few minutes; minimum portion a half-kilo or about one pound), charging €3 per person for table service, plus 10 percent of your market bill; you must bring the receipt for whatever they're cooking up for you (Tue-Sat 8:00-18:00, closed Mon, aisle 5 in the market, tel. 981-575-720, mobile 619-351-278).

The market was built in the 1920s (to consolidate Santiago's many small markets) in a style perfectly compatible with the medieval wonder that surrounds it. Today it offers an opportunity to get up close and personal with some still-twitching seafood. Keep an eye out for the specialties you'll want to try later—octopus, shrimp, crabs, lobsters, and expensive-as-gold *percebes* (barnacles; see sidebar). You'll also see large loaves of country bread,

chicken the color it should be, and the local *chorizo* (spicy sausage).

Grelos are a local type of turnip greens with a thick stalk and long, narrow leaves—grown only here, and often used in the *caldo galego* soup. The little green *pimientos de padrón* (in season June-Oct) look like jalapeños, but lack the kick...sometimes.

In the cheese cases you'll see what look like huge yellow Hershey's Kisses...or breasts—in fact, this creamy cheese is called *tetilla* ("small breast" in Galego). According to local legend, artists at the cathedral sculpted a very curvaceous woman and the locals loved it. The bishop made them redo the statue with less sexy lines, so the locals got even by making their cheese look like breasts. Through the centuries since, Santiago has been full of tasty reminders of a woman's physical beauty. A smoked version of the cheese, called *San Simón da Costa,* can be found as well.

▲Museum of Pilgrimages (Museo das Peregrinacións)

This museum examines various aspects of the pilgrimage phenomenon. You'll see a map of pilgrimage sites around the world, and then learn more about the pilgrimage that brings people to Santiago. There are models of earlier versions of the cathedral, explanations of the differing depictions of St. James throughout history (apostle, pilgrim, and Crusader), and coverage of the various routes to Santiago and stories of some prominent pilgrims. This well-presented place lends historical context to all of those backpackers you see in the streets. Although exhibits themselves are not described in English, the thorough info sheets available throughout the museum are well worth reading.

Cost and Hours: Free, Tue-Fri 10:00-20:00, Sat 10:30-13:30 & 17:00-20:00, Sun 10:30-13:30, closed Mon, Praza das Praterías, tel. 981-581-558, www.mdperegrinacions.com.

Museum of the Galician People (Museo do Pobo Galego)

This museum gives insights into rural Galician life. As you tour this collection, remember that if you side-trip a few miles into the

countryside, you'll find traditional lifestyles thriving even today. Beautifully displayed around an 18th-century cloister, the museum springs from a unique triple staircase, which provided privacy to various hierarchies of the monks who lived here, depending on which stairway you climbed. The collection shows off boat-building and fishing techniques, farming implements and simple horse-drawn carts, tools of trade and handicrafts (including carpentry, pottery, looms, and baskets), traditional costumes, and a collection of musical instruments, with an emphasis on the bagpipes *(gaitas).* If the farm tools seem old-fashioned, there's a reason: Old inheritance laws mean that plots have gotten increasingly smaller, so modern farming machinery is impractical—keeping traditional equipment alive. There's virtually no English.

SANTIAGO DE COMPOSTELA

Cost and Hours: €3, free on Sun, open Tue-Sat 10:30-14:00 & 16:00-19:30, Sun 11:00-14:00, closed Mon, at northeast edge of historical center in monastery of San Domingos de Bonaval, just beyond Porta do Camiño, tel. 981-583-620, www.museodopobo.es.

Nearby: Behind the museum is a plush and peaceful **park**—once crowded with tombstones. Next door, in a striking modern building, is the **Galician Contemporary Art Museum** (Centro Galego de Arte Contemporánea), with continually rotating exhibits—mostly by local artists (free, Tue-Sun 11:00-20:00, closed Mon, tel. 981-546-619).

City of Culture of Galicia (Cidade da Cultura de Galicia)

This super-modern cultural complex, built on a hillside near Santiago de Compostela, was intended to put Santiago on the map as a 21st-century city (similar to Bilbao's Guggenheim). Instead, its costs have exceeded its expectations. Inaugurated in 2011 as the Archives and Library of Galicia, it offers exhibits and tours.

Cost and Hours: Free, daily 8:30-14:30 & 16:00-20:00, tours at 11:30 and 17:30, tel. 881-997-565, www.cidadedacultura.org.

Entertainment in Santiago

Street Music

You'll likely hear bagpipes *(gaitas)* being played in the streets of Santiago. Nobody knows for certain how this unlikely instrument caught on in Galicia, but supposedly the tradition has been passed down since the Celts lived here. (Bagpipes seem to be unique to Celts like the Scottish and Irish, but nearly all European ethnic groups have had bagpipes in their past. If anything, the Celts just endured their sound more willingly.) Some singers use bagpipes, too, including Milladoiro (a group popular with middle-aged Galicians) and Carlos Nuñez (trendy with younger people). Caped university students, called *tunas,* can be seen singing traditional songs (without bagpipes) around town every night during the summer.

Galician Folk-Music Concerts

Whereas summertime is lively with folk-music concerts (ask for details at the TI), the rest of the year is not. One good bet is to drop by a practice session of the troupe called Cantigas e Agarimos (meets Wed and Fri at 21:30 for an hour, maybe at Rúa da Algalia de Arriba 11 or possibly playing at a nearby location—confirm schedule at TI, tel. 981-581-257). Since 1921, this group has shared the traditional Galician culture with visitors in performances throughout the year.

Sleeping in Santiago

To cater to all those pilgrims, Santiago has a glut of cheap, basic accommodations. There aren't many affordable big hotels in town for tour groups, so they tend to stay along the Rías Baixas (fjord-like estuaries) about an hour to the south, where beds are cheap. That means many of Santiago's visitors are day-trippers, arriving at about 10:30 and leaving in the afternoon. After dark, it's just you, the locals, the pilgrims, and St. James. High season is roughly Easter through September; most places charge more during this time. The trickiest dates to book are Easter Sunday weekend and the Feast of St. James (July 24-25), so if you plan to be in town around these times, reserve your rooms well ahead. When I list a range of prices, it represents low season to high season. Any single prices listed are an average (midseason). The *hostales* speak enough English to make a reservation by phone (though sometimes not much more).

$$$ Altaïr Hotel, owned by the Liñares family (see Costa Vella listing, later), is located in a renovated three-story residence. Its 11 spacious rooms and mod decor can best be described as "rustic minimalist." Exposed stone walls and open beams mixed with a sleek design provide a unique yet surprisingly affordable experience (Sb-€75-87, Db-€95-120, superior Db-€120-140, extra bed-€20, tasty €8.50 breakfast—free with this book in 2014 when you book directly with the hotel by email, free Wi-Fi, affordable

SANTIAGO DE COMPOSTELA

Sleep Code

(€1 = about $1.30, country code: 34)
S = Single, **D** = Double/Twin, **T** = Triple, **Q** = Quad, **b** = bathroom, **s** = shower only. Unless otherwise noted, credit cards are accepted, English is spoken, and breakfast generally costs extra. Some hotels include the 10 percent IVA tax in the room price; others tack it onto your bill.

To help you easily sort through these listings, I've divided the accommodations into three categories based on the price for a standard double room with bath:

$$$ Higher Priced—Most rooms €95 or more.
$$ Moderately Priced—Most rooms between €55-95.
$ Lower Priced—Most rooms €55 or less.

Prices can change without notice; verify the hotel's current rates online or by email. For the best prices, always book direct.

Santiago Hotels & Restaurants

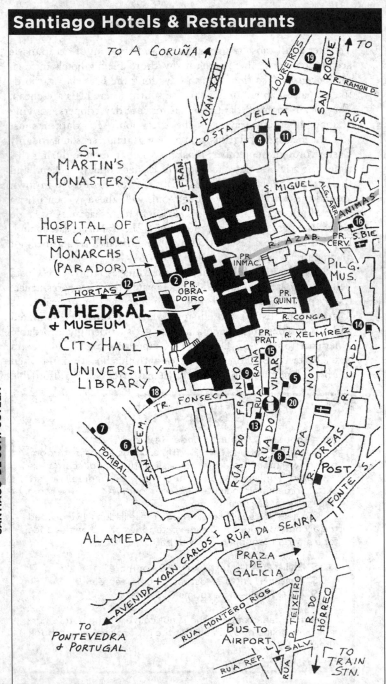

TO A CORUÑA

TO

XOAN XXII

COSTA VELLA

LOUREIROS

SAN ROQUE

R. RAMON D.

RÚA

ST. MARTIN'S MONASTERY

S. FRAN.

S.

S. MIGUEL

ALG. ARRANIMAS

HOSPITAL OF THE CATHOLIC MONARCHS (PARADOR)

PR. INMAC.

R. AZAB.

PR. CERV.

S.BIE

PILG. MUS.

HORTAS

PR. OBRADOIRO

PR. QUINT.

CATHEDRAL & MUSEUM

R. CONGA

R. XELMÍREZ

CITY HALL

PR. PRAT.

R. CALD.

UNIVERSITY LIBRARY

TR. FONSECA

RAIZA

RÚA DO VILAR

NOVA

RÚA DO FRANCO

R. ORFAS

POST

FONTE S.

POMBAL

SAN CLEM.

RÚA DA SENRA

ALAMEDA

PRAZA DE GALICIA

AVENIDA XOÁN CARLOS I

RÚA MONTERO RIOS

BUS TO AIRPORT

R. D. TEIXEIRO

R. DO HÓRREO

TO PONTEVEDRA & PORTUGAL

RÚA REP.

RÚA SALV.

TO TRAIN STN.

SANTIAGO DE COMPOSTELA

1 4 11 19 16 12 2 9 15 5 20 14 18 13 8 7 6

BUS STATION

GALICIAN CONTEMPORARY
ART MUSEUM

VALLE INCLÁN

DAS RODAS

MUSEUM OF THE
GALICIAN
PEOPLE

CASAS

SAN PEDRO

TO
AIRPORT,
CITY OF CULTURE OF GALICIA,
ARZUA, LEÓN & PARIS

PORTA DO
CAMIÑO

ITO

DA CERCA

RUA DAS AMEAS

MARKET

UNIV.

RUA DA VIRXE

TROMPAS

ANT.

1. Altaïr Hotel
2. Hostal dos Reis Católicos,
   Dos Reis & Enxebre Rest.
3. Hotel Virxe da Cerca
4. Hotel Residencia Costa Vella
   & Café Costa Vella
5. Hotel Airas Nunes
6. Hotel San Clemente
7. Hotel Pombal
8. Hostal Suso
9. Hospedaje Ramos
10. Hostal Residencia Giadás
11. Pensión Girasol
12. Casa Marcelo Restaurante
13. O Gato Negro
14. A Curtidoría Restaurante
15. O Beiro Vinoteca
16. Restaurante Casa Manolo
17. O Dezaseis Restaurante
18. Cotolay Bar Restaurante
19. La Bodeguilla de San Roque
20. Café Casino

━━━ CAMINO DE SANTIAGO

100 YARDS

100 METERS

DCH

SANTIAGO DE COMPOSTELA

laundry service for guests, Rúa dos Loureiros 12, tel. 981-554-712, www.altairhotel.net, info@altairhotel.net).

$$$ Hostal dos Reis Católicos (Hospital of the Catholic Monarchs) was founded by the Catholic Monarchs at the beginning of the 16th century to care for pilgrims arriving from the Camino. It was converted into an upscale parador in 1952 and inaugurated by Franco (when royal family members are in town, they stay in his former suite overlooking the square). This grand building has 137 rooms surrounding a series of four courtyards packed with Santiago history. It has the best address in Santiago... and prices to match (standard Db-€284, includes great breakfast, Db price can fall to €150—check website or call for deals, parking-€18.50/day, Praza do Obradoiro 1, tel. 981-582-200, www.paradores-spain.com/spain/pscompostela.html, santiago@parador.es). Ask Enrique, who has worked here for 40 years, to print out the history of the parador in English.

Still remembering its roots, the parador follows Ferdinand and Isabel's edict to watch over pilgrims by offering three free meals to the first 10 who arrive each day (usually around 8:00). Pilgrims dine in a special room next to the staff quarters. They were originally allowed to eat in the main dining room, but guests started complaining about the stink. At first, special cloaks were given to pilgrims to try to mask the odor, but when that failed, they were moved to their own eating quarters.

$$$ Hotel Virxe da Cerca is on the edge of the historical center, across the busy street from the market. Its standard rooms are in a modern building, but some of its "superior" and all of its "special" historic rooms—with classy old stone and hardwoods—are in a restored 18th-century Jesuit residence. While the modern rooms feel particularly impersonal, all 42 rooms surround a lush garden oasis (standard Db-€75-130, superior Db-€20 extra, breakfast-€11, beautiful glassed-in breakfast room overlooks garden, elevator, guest computer, free Wi-Fi, Rúa da Virxe da Cerca 27, tel. 981-569-350, www.pousadasdecompostela.com, vdacerca@pousadasdecompostela.com).

$$ Hotel Residencia Costa Vella is my favorite spot in Santiago, with 14 comfortable rooms combining classic charm and modern comforts. The glassed-in breakfast room and lounge terrace overlook a peaceful garden, with lovely views of a nearby church and monastery and into the countryside beyond. They deserve a feature in *Better Stones and Tiles* magazine (Sb-€54-60, standard Db-€70-81, Db with balcony-€85-97, breakfast-€6, free Wi-Fi, affordable laundry service for guests, parking-€10/day, Rúa da Porta da Pena 17, tel. 981-569-530, www.costavella.com, hotelcostavella@costavella.com, friendly José, Roberto, and wonderful staff).

$$ Hotel Airas Nunes, Hotel San Clemente, and **Hotel Pombal** are all affiliated with Hotel Virxe da Cerca. They're uniformly good, stress-free, and professional-feeling, all located in restored old buildings with classy touches. All three hotels charge €6 for breakfast and €20 for extra beds, and share the same contact info (tel. 981-569-350, www.pousadasdecompostela.com, info@pousadasdecompostela.com). Hotel Airas Nunes is deep in the old center a few blocks in front of the cathedral (10 rooms, Db-€60-85, Rúa do Vilar 17, reception tel. 981-554-706). Hotel San Clemente is just outside the historical center (Db-€65-80, Rúa de San Clemente 28, reception tel. 981-569-260). Hotel Pombal is a slight step up from the other two in terms of quality and price. Situated in the Alameda park, many of its rooms offer great views of the cathedral (Db-€80-95, €10 more for views, Rúa do Pombal 12, reception tel. 981-569-350).

$ Hostal Suso, run by the four Quintela brothers, is a great value, offering 14 inexpensive, recently renovated rooms around an airy atrium over a fun little bar, which rustles up a good €4.50 *tortilla de gambas* (shrimp omelet). It's located in the heart of Santiago (Sb-€20-25, Db-€40-49, breakfast at bar-€3.50-5, Rúa do Vilar 65, tel. 981-586-611, www.hostalsuso.com, hostalsuso @gmail.com).

$ Hospedaje Ramos rents 10 big, tasteful, clean rooms right in the center. It has lots of stairs, which is a blessing since they take you farther away from the night noise (Sb-€26, Db-€39, no credit cards, no breakfast, Rúa da Raiña 18, tel. 981-581-859, Louisa speaks a few words of English).

$ Hostal Residencia Giadás, tucked away just beyond the market, faces a tidy little square as if it owns it. The eight rooms, some with slanted floors, are simple but charming (Sb-€35, Db-€55, Tb-€74, elevator, next to Porta do Camiño at Praza do Matadoiro 2, tel. 981-587-071, www.hostalgiadas.com, info @hostalgiadas.com, Giadás family).

$ Pensión Girasol rents 12 decent rooms above a cheery cafeteria for a good price in a great neighborhood (S-€25, Sb-€35-40, D-€35-45, Db-€48-55, Porta da Pena 4, tel. 981-566-287, www .hgirasol.com, girasol@hgirasol.com).

Eating in Santiago

Strolling through the streets of Santiago is like visiting a well-stocked aquarium: Windows proudly display every form of edible sea life, including giant toothy fish, scallops and clams of every shape and size, monstrous shrimp, gooseneck barnacles (*percebes;* see sidebar, earlier), and—most importantly—octopus. The fertile fjords of the Galician coast are just 20 miles away, and the region's many fishing villages keep the capital city swimming in seafood. As the seafood is so fresh, the focus here is on purity rather than sauces. The seafood is served simply—generally just steamed or grilled, and seasoned only with a little olive oil, onions, peppers, and paprika.

Tasting octopus *(pulpo)* is obligatory in Galicia. It's most often prepared *a la gallega* (also called *pulpo a feira*): After the octopus is beaten to tenderize it, then boiled in a copper pot, its tentacles are snipped into bite-size pieces with scissors. It's topped with virgin olive oil, coarse sea salt, and a mixture of sweet and spicy paprika, then served on a round wooden plate. Eat it with toothpicks, never a fork. It's usually accompanied by large hunks of country bread to sop up the olive oil, and washed down by local red *mencia* or white *ribeiro* wine, often served in little saucer-like ceramic cups *(cunca)*.

Not a fan of seafood? You can slurp the *caldo galego*, a traditional broth that originally came from the leftover stock used to prepare an elaborate Sunday feast (cabbage or *grelos*, potatoes, and so on—not too exciting, but providing comfort on a rainy day). Starting in July, look for *pimientos de Padrón*—miniature green peppers sautéed in olive oil with a heavy dose of rock salt.

Restaurants generally serve lunch from 13:00 to 16:00 and dinner from 20:00 until very late (Spaniards don't start dinner until about 21:00). It's frustrating to try to eat before the locals do. If you find a restaurant serving before 13:00 or 21:00, you'll be all alone with a few sorry-looking tourists. Early-bird eaters should know that ordering a drink at any bar will generally get you a free tapa—Santiago is one of the few places in Spain that still honors this tradition.

For a quick meal on the go, grab a traditional meat pie, or *empanada*, which comes *de carne* (with pork), *de bonito* or *de atún* (tuna), *de bacalao* (salted cod), *de zamburiñas* (tiny scallops), *de berberechos* (cockles)—and these days, even *de pulpo* (octopus).

And for dessert: Locals enjoy *queixo con mel* (cheese with honey) at the end of a meal. In the tourist zones, bakeries push samples of *tarta de Santiago*, the local almond cake. (Historically, the cake was cooked by sisters in Santiago's convents.) The Galician version of firewater, *orujo*, is a popular after-dinner drink, thought to aid digestion. A somewhat lighter and tastier option is *licor de hierbas*, a distilled, Mountain Dew-colored blend of *orujo* flavored with local herbs.

Gourmet Dining, Modern Cuisine

Casa Marcelo, Santiago's elite gourmet option, earned a Michelin star for its international cuisine. If you want to dine elegantly and have the money, this dressy 11-table restaurant is the place. For €60 (plus wine), you get a fixed-price meal featuring the chef's seasonal specials. Recent innovations include a soufflé-like version of the *tarta de Santiago*. The kitchen is in plain view, so you'll get caught up in the excitement of cooking (open for dinner Tue-Sat, also open for lunch on Sat, closed Sun-Mon, reservations required— usually days in advance, down the steep lane below the cathedral, at Rúa das Hortas 1, tel. 981-558-580).

Restaurant Row in the Old Center: Rúa do Franco

Since hungry pilgrims first filled the city in the Middle Ages, Rúa do Franco (named not for the dictator but for the first French pilgrims) has been lined with eateries and bars. Today this street, which leads away from the cathedral, remains lively with foreign visitors—both tourists and pilgrims. There are plenty of seafood places, a few time-warp dives, and several lively bars with little €1.50 *montaditos* (sandwiches) for the grabbing. I'd stroll it once to see what appeals, and then go back to eat. **O Gato Negro,** a no-frills seafood tapas bar stuck in the past and filled with loyal locals, is worth seeking out. It's one of the last places to serve *ribeiro* wine in a ceramic cup (Tue-Sat 12:30-15:00 & 19:00-late, Sun 12:30-15:00, closed Mon, near Rúa do Franco on side street Rúa da Raiña—look for black cat sign outside).

Memorable Eating in the Old Center

A Curtidoría Restaurante ("The Tannery") is a modern, spacious, and romantic place in the old town, rare for its open feeling. While the food is nothing exceptional, the setting is enjoyable and it's a solid value for a midday meal (€13 lunch special menu, paella and fish, €20-33 per plate, Rúa da Conga 2, tel. 981-554-342).

O Beiro Vinoteca, designed to show off the fine wines of Galicia and Spain, serves by the glass from a huge menu and complements its wine with simple, appropriate *raciones*. Run by Pepe Beiro, it's much classier than your average tapas bar. The tasting action is on the ground floor with cozy seating in the back, while tables for dining are upstairs. If you drop in for just a glass of wine, you'll get a free tapa (sometimes closed Mon, half a block from cathedral at Rúa da Raiña 3, tel. 981-581-370).

Hostal dos Reis Católicos, the fancy old hospital sharing the square with the cathedral, has two fine restaurants downstairs. The main restaurant, **Dos Reis,** fills a former stable with a dramatic stone vault. It offers international dishes—often with live piano and nearly dead guests. A typical parador restaurant, it comes with stiff tuxedoed service, white tablecloths, and not a hint of fun (daily, tel. 981-582-200). Surprisingly, a few steps away is a wonderful alternative—**Enxebre** has a livelier easygoing-tavern vibe, good traditional Galician food, and reasonable prices (€5-14 dishes, daily, tel. 981-050-527).

Restaurante Casa Manolo serves only one thing: a €9 fixed-price meal consisting of two generous courses, water, bread, and a packaged dessert. It's popular with students on a tight budget who want a classy meal out. This smart little family-run eatery combines sleek contemporary design, decent Galician and Spanish food, and excellent prices. The service is rushed (a good thing if you're in a hurry), but the value is unbeatable (arrive when they open or plan on waiting; Mon-Sat lunch 13:00-16:00, dinner 20:00-23:30, Sun lunch only, at the bottom of Praza de Cervantes, tel. 981-582-950).

Budget Values Away from the Tourist Center

O Dezaseis ("The Sixteen") is every local's favorite (and mine, too). As soon as you walk down into its sprawling, high-energy vaulted dining room, you know this is the best place in town. In-the-know locals are dining under stone walls, heavy beams, and modern art while enjoying friendly service. You can choose from meat and fish plates (€12-14), but simply ordering one *ración* per person (€4-11) and splitting their hearty mixed salad for some veggies make a fine and inexpensive meal. They do octopus just right here and have nice wines at good prices (Mon-Sat 14:00-16:00 & 20:30-midnight, closed Sun, reservations smart, Rúa de San Pedro 16, tel. 981-564-880).

Cotolay Bar Restaurante and two adjacent bar-restaurants are a hit with locals for drinks with free tapas. They are good budget bets for a meal of *raciones* without the tourists (€5-15 *raciones*, Mon-Sat 11:00-late, closed Sun, Rúa de San Clemente, tel. 981-573-014).

La Bodeguilla de San Roque offers a good selection of *raciones* and wines in a relaxed family atmosphere. If the upstairs restaurant is full, have a drink at the bar to pass the time (€5-8 *raciones*, Rúa da San Roque 13, tel. 981-564-379).

Cafés

Café Costa Vella, in the breakfast room and garden of the highly recommended Hotel Residencia Costa Vella, is a little Eden tucked just beyond the tourist zone. The café welcomes non-guests for coffee and a relaxing break in a poetic time-warp garden with leafy views (great €3.50 toasted sandwiches, plus a wide array of drinks, daily 8:00-23:00, Rúa da Porta da Pena 17, tel. 981-569-530).

Café Casino, a former private club, is a tired taste of turn-of-the-20th-century elegance with occasional live piano music. Local tour guides recommend this café to their timid British groups, who wouldn't touch an octopus with a 10-foot pole. While they have sandwiches and salads, I would just consider this an elegant coffee or tea stop (Rúa do Vilar 35, tel. 981-577-503).

Santiago Connections

From Santiago de Compostela by Train to: Madrid (4/day, 5.5-9.5 hours, overnight train departs at 22:33, arrives at Madrid Chamartín at 8:00), **Salamanca** (1/day, 6.75 hours, transfer in Medina del Campo), **León** (2/day, 4.5-5 hours), **Bilbao** (2/day, no direct service, 12 hours), **San Sebastián** (1/day, 10.5 hours), **Santander** (2/day, 9 hours, transfer in Palencia), **Lugo** (10/day, 3-4 hours, requires transfer in A Coruña—bus is better), **Porto,** Portugal (2/day via Vigo, 3 hours). Train info: toll tel. 902-320-320, www.renfe.com.

By Bus to: Lugo (7/day, 2-3 hours), **Madrid** (5/day, 8 hours, includes night bus 21:30-6:30; arrives at Estación Sur, then 1 hour later at Madrid's Barajas Airport Terminal 4), **Salamanca** (3/day, 6-7.5 hours), **Astorga** (5/day, 4-5.5 hours), **León** (1/day, 6 hours), **Burgos** (1/day, 9 hours, also 1 night bus, 7 hours), **Bilbao** (3/day continue to **San Sebastián,** includes 1 night bus, 9.5 hours to Bilbao, 1.5 hours more to San Sebastián), **Porto,** Portugal (1/day, 4 hours, stops at Porto's airport before arriving to city center). Bus info: tel. 981-542-416. All long-distance destinations are served by the Alsa bus company (toll tel. 902-422-242, www.alsa.es).

CANTABRIA

Santillana del Mar • Altamira Caves
• Comillas • Picos de Europa

If you're connecting the Basque Country and Galicia (Santiago de Compostela) along the coast, you'll go through the provinces of Cantabria and Asturias. Both are interesting, but Cantabria (kahn-TAH-bree-ah) has a few villages and sights that are especially worth a visit. The quaint town of Santillana del Mar makes a fine home base for visiting the prehistoric Altamira Caves. Comillas is a pleasant beach town with a surprising abundance of Modernista architecture.

The dramatic peaks of the Picos de Europa and their rolling foothills define this region, giving it a more rugged feel than the "Northern Riviera" ambience of the Basque region. A drive through the Cantabrian countryside is rewarded with endless glimpses of charming stone homes. Though it's largely undiscovered by Americans, Cantabria is heavily touristed by Europeans in July and August, when it can get very crowded.

Planning Your Time

Cantabria doesn't rank high on the list of sightseeing priorities in Spain (unless you're a die-hard fan of either prehistoric art or Barcelona-style Modernista architecture). Don't go out of your way to get here. However, if you're passing through, there are some charming diversions along the way. A night or two in this region breaks up the long drive from Bilbao to Santiago (figure over seven hours straight through).

Assuming you're coming from San Sebastián and can spare two nights, this is a good plan:

Day 1: Leave San Sebastián early for the Guggenheim in Bilbao (trip takes about an hour by expressway, longer along the

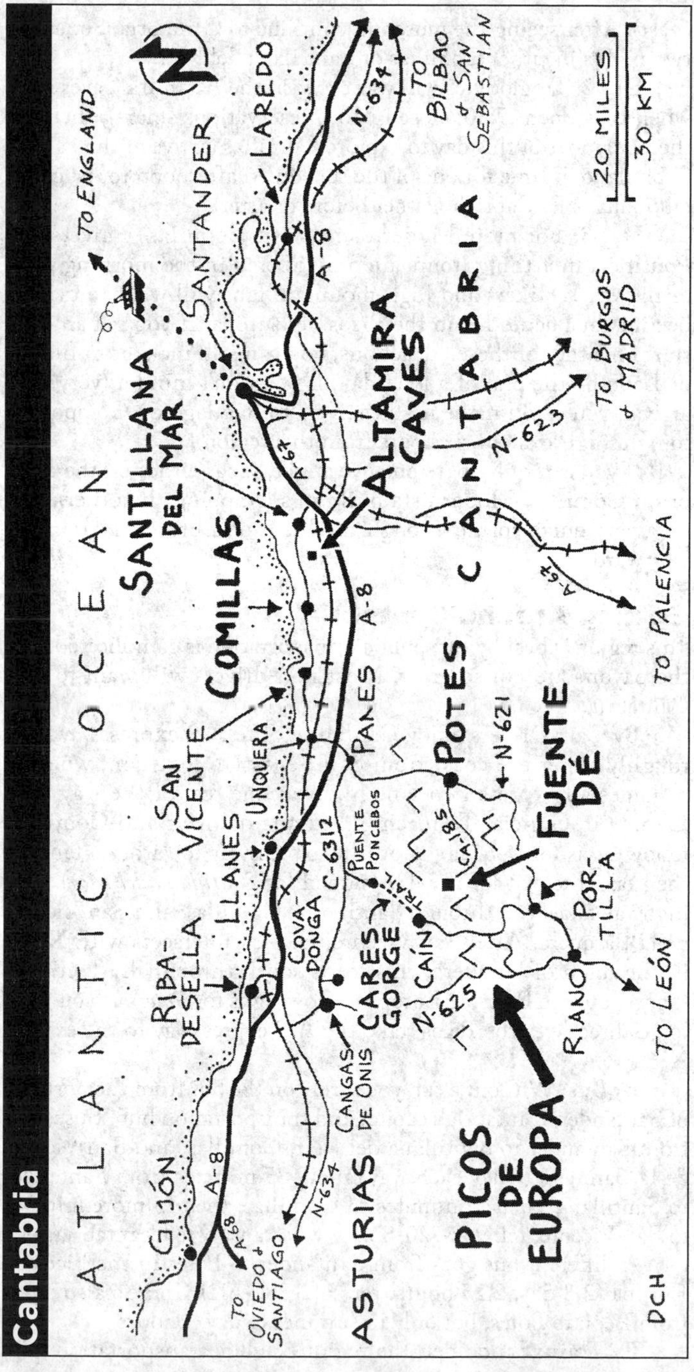

Cantabria

ATLANTIC OCEAN

TO ENGLAND

SANTANDER

LAREDO

N-634

TO BILBAO + SAN SEBASTIAN

A-8

20 MILES
30 KM

SANTILLANA DEL MAR

ALTAMIRA CAVES

C A N T A B R I A

A-67

N-623

TO BURGOS + MADRID

COMILLAS

A-8

A-67

TO PALENCIA

SAN VICENTE

UNQUERA

PANES

POTES

N-621

FUENTE DÉ

LLANES

C-6312

PUENTE PONCEBOS

CA-185

TRAIL

POR-TILLA

RIBA-DESELLA

COVA-DONGA

CARES GORGE

CAÍN

N-625

RIAÑO

TO LEÓN

GIJÓN

A-8

CANGAS DE ONIS

N-634

A-68

TO OVIEDO + SANTIAGO

ASTURIAS

PICOS DE EUROPA

DCH

CANTABRIA

coast). After seeing the museum, continue to Cantabria. Set up for two nights in either Comillas or Santillana del Mar.

Day 2: Troglodytes will want to visit the Altamira Caves right when they open (9:30, closed Mon, reservations smart), then use the remainder of this day to explore Comillas (arrive at the Palacio Sobrellano in time for one of the scheduled afternoon tours; check out Gaudí's El Capricho either before or after).

Day 3: For more Modernisme, visit Comillas' Universidad Pontifícia first thing (tours are only offered in the morning most of the year). Hikers and high-mountain fans will want to make a beeline for Fuente Dé in the Picos de Europa. If you get an early start on either of these attractions, you can still make it to Burgos or León by the end of a long day; if you don't mind a (very) late arrival, you could make it all the way to Santiago de Compostela tonight (figure about six hours from this region).

If you can only spare one overnight, focus either on the caves or on Comillas' Modernista buildings (skipping the other), and do a very quick sprint through the Picos de Europa on your way westward.

Getting Around Cantabria

This region is best by car; public transportation is complicated, and the payoffs are not so great. Most non-drivers will want to skip Cantabria.

By Car: Drivers enjoy Cantabria. The A-8 expressway runs roughly along the coast from San Sebastián to Gijón, where it becomes an express two-lane highway the rest of the way to A Coruña in Galicia. To reach Santillana del Mar and Comillas, follow signs for *A-67* (a jog off the expressway toward Santander), then take the exit for CA-131 (signed for *Santillana del Mar*). This highway takes you through Santillana, Comillas, and San Vicente de la Barquera. After San Vicente, CA-131 intersects with N-621 in the town of Unquera; this leads south through La Hermida Gorge into the Picos de Europa (follow signs for *Potes*). If you want to go directly to the Picos, take the A-8 expressway to the exit for N-621.

By Bus: Without a car, you'll rely on the bus from the port city of Santander, Cantabria's capital and transportation hub. Buses run from Santander to Santillana del Mar, Comillas, and San Vicente de la Barquera (7/day each way, about 35 minutes from Santander to Santillana, then 15 minutes to Comillas, then 15 more minutes to San Vicente, tel. 942-720-822, www.transportedecantabria.es).

A different bus goes from Santander to Potes in the Picos de Europa (2-3/day, 2.25 hours, tel. 942-880-611). There's also a bus from León to Potes, but only in summer (1/day, 3 hours).

By Train: Santander, the region's public transportation hub, is connected by train with **Madrid** (1/day, 5.25 hours, Atocha Station), and **Santiago de Compostela** (2/day, 9 hours, transfer in Palencia). A scenic train line called the FEVE runs from Bilbao to Santander (3/day, 3 hours) and on to Ovideo, but it's not particularly helpful for visiting the destinations in this chapter.

Santillana del Mar

Every guidebook imparts the same two tidbits about Santillana del Mar: One is that it's known as the "town of three lies," as it's

neither holy *(santi)*, nor flat *(llana)*, nor on the ocean *(del Mar)*. The other is that the existentialist philosopher Jean-Paul Sartre once called it the "prettiest village in Spain."

The town is worth the fuss—it's what Spaniards would call *preciosa*. Santillana is a proud little stone village, with charming time-warp qualities that have (barely) survived the stampede of multinational tour groups here to visit the nearby Altamira Caves. In this traditionally agricultural area, locals kept livestock in their yards until tourists complained about the smell and authorities banned farm animals in the city center.

Santillana consists of three cobbled streets and a collection of squares, climbing up over mild hills from where the village meets the main road. While Santillana has several sights that cater to the tourist throngs (including a much-promoted zoo), the only sight that makes a visit worthwhile—aside from the town itself—is the cave paintings of Altamira in the nearby countryside.

Tourist Information: The modern TI is right at the entrance to the town (daily July-mid-Sept 9:00-21:00, off-season 9:30-13:30 & 16:00-19:00, Jesús Otero 20, tel. 942-818-251). Only residents (and guests of hotels that offer parking) are allowed to drive in the center; instead, leave your car in one of the two big parking lots (pay in-season, free off-season)—one by the TI, and the other just to the south, at Plaza del Rey.

Sleeping in Santillana

Santillana makes a good home base for visiting the region and the caves. My listings are right in town; the first three places are on Santillana's main square, Plaza Ramón Pelayo. The fourth

Sleep Code

(€1 = about $1.30, country code: 34)
S = Single, **D** = Double/Twin, **T** = Triple, **Q** = Quad, **b** = bathroom, **s** = shower only. Unless otherwise noted, English is spoken and credit cards are accepted. Prices vary with season (highest July-Aug and Holy Week). I've listed shoulder- and peak-season rates. Some hotels include the 10 percent IVA tax in the room price; others tack it onto your bill.

To help you sort easily through these listings, I've divided the accommodations into three categories based on the price for a standard double room with bath:

$$$ **Higher Priced**—Most rooms €110 or more.
 $$ **Moderately Priced**—Most rooms between €70-110.
  $ **Lower Priced**—Most rooms €70 or less.

Prices can change without notice; verify the hotel's current rates online or by email. For the best prices, always book direct.

is farther up, just around the corner (to the right) from the big Collegiate Church.

$$$ *Paradores:* Two swanky, arrogant *paradores* hold court on the main square—**Parador de Santillana** (Sb-€100-129, Db-€161-244 depending on amenities, look for deals online, breakfast-€17, Plaza Ramón Pelayo 11, tel. 942-818-000, www.parador.es, santillana@parador.es) and **Parador de Santillana Gil Blas** (Sb-€148, Db-€185-240 depending on amenities, breakfast-€18, same address, tel. 942-028-028, www.parador.es, santillanagb @parador.es).

$$ Hotel Altamira offers 32 well-priced rooms in an atmospheric 16th-century palace on the main square (Sb-€50-64, standard Db-€65-95, big Db with sitting room a worthwhile splurge at €84-102, 20 percent more in Aug and Holy Week, cheaper Nov-March, extra bed-€24-33, free Wi-Fi, breakfast-€9, Calle Cantón 1, tel. 942-818-025, www.hotelaltamira.com, info@hotelaltamira .com).

$ Hospedaje Octavio is a charming budget option with 11 comfortable, wood-beamed rooms (Db-€25-40 depending on season, cheaper for bathroom on the hall, Plaza Las Arenas 4, tel. 942-818-199, www.hospedajeoctavio.com, pensioncasaoctavio @gmail.com, Octavio and Milagros don't speak English, but their sons do).

CANTABRIA

Altamira Caves

Not far from Santillana del Mar, the Altamira Caves contain some of the best examples of prehistoric art anywhere. In 1879, the young daughter of a local archaeologist discovered several 14,000-year-old paintings in a limestone cave. By the 1960s and 1970s, it became a tremendously popular tourist destination. The number of visitors became too much for the delicate paintings, and the cave was closed in 1979. A replica cave and museum opened in 2001 near the original site, allowing visitors to experience these pieces of prehistoric artwork in something approximating their original setting. The Spanish cultural ministry hopes to someday reopen the original cave on a restricted basis, but those plans are on hold for the time being. Although you can't visit the original cave, prehistoric-art fans will still find Altamira worth the trip.

Note that if all you're really interested in is the art itself, another replica of the paintings can be seen at Madrid's National Archaeological Museum. However, these aren't nearly as well done and won't be on display until the museum reopens after renovation, possibly in 2014.

Getting to the Altamira Caves

The caves are on a ridge in the countryside a little over a mile southwest of Santillana del Mar. There's no public transportation to the site. To get from Santillana del Mar to the caves, it's either a 30-minute walk or a cheap taxi ride (mobile 608-483-441). Bolder travelers hitch a bus ride with a friendly tour group.

Orientation to the Altamira Caves

Cost and Hours: €3, free Sat after 14:00 and all day Sun; open May-Oct Tue-Sat 9:30-20:00, may be open even later some nights in summer, Sun 9:30-15:00; Nov-April Tue-Sat 9:30-18:00, Sun 9:30-15:00; closed Mon year-round; last tour departs 30 minutes before closing; tel. 942-818-005, http://museodealtamira.mcu.es.

Reservations: Only 240 people are allowed to enter the replica cave each hour (20 people/tour, tours leave about every 5 minutes—or, at slower times, when enough people gather). This means that in the busy summer season, spaces fill up fast, and groups or individuals with reservations get priority. In July and August and on free Sundays, they recommend getting to the museum when it opens (9:30) to claim your tour appointment. Better yet, during busy times, consider making an advance reservation for the replica cave (no extra charge) through the bank Santander Centro Hispano. There are three ways to do this: Drop by any Santander bank branch; reserve by phone (toll tel. 902-242-424, wait through recording and ask for English speaker); or book online (in Spanish only, no online reservations possible for free Sunday visits, https://secure.santander.com/ventaentradas/Altamira). Request a specific date and time (one-hour window) for your visit. Take your ticket or confirmation number to the information counter at the caves, where you can schedule a guided tour.

Visiting the Caves: You'll buy your ticket at a separate *taquilla* office outside museum complex, and be given a laminated card with the time of your replica cave *(Neocueva)* entry. Once inside, your visit has two parts: First, there's a fine **museum** (to the right of the information desk) with good English descriptions, featuring models and reproductions of the cave dwellers who made these drawings (and their clothes, tools, and remains). Videos and illuminated pictures help bring these people to life; scenes of how early tools were made are particularly fascinating. The exhibit finishes with an account of the cave's discovery and its eventual acceptance by the scientific community (who were initially skeptical that "primitive" people were capable of such sophisticated art). Second, you'll take a 30-minute guided tour of the highly detailed **replica cave.**

Unfortunately, English-speakers don't get much respect at Altamira: Posted information in English is measly, and the guided tours are only in Spanish. Follow along with my self-guided tour.

Self-Guided Tour

You'll begin the tour by watching a four-minute film about the various inhabitants of the cave, the discovery of the paintings in 1879, and the era of over-visitation. Then you'll enter the first part of the replica cave. Guides eagerly point out information panels translated into English, but those are only marginally helpful. Here's the gist:

In the Cave

The painstaking replica in the *Neocueva* ("Neo-cave") was achieved with special computers so that the cave art can still be enjoyed without endangering the actual paintings. The Neo-cave, made of 80 percent stone, also simulates the original cave's temperature, sounds, and humidity.

About 14,000 years ago, hunters, gatherers, and fishermen lived in these caves. They huddled around a fire, protected from the elements. They liked the location because of its proximity to the ocean and a river.

Excavation Site

This area displays tools used by modern scientists to dig up relics from various periods. We're talking about the Upper Paleolithic era—the time of Cro-Magnon cave people, with big hands and high foreheads. The Upper Paleolithic is divided into three periods, and this cave was inhabited, on two separate occasions, during two of those periods: the Solutrean (about 18,500 years ago) and the Magdalenian (14,000 years ago). You'll see that there are three layers to the excavation: On the bottom are artifacts from Solutrean cavemen (hunting tools and chips of flint); above that is mostly clay, with the remains of a cave bear you'll see in a few minutes; and the top layer holds hearths and tools from the Magdalenian period.

As you continue on to the next stop, you'll pass the bones of a cave bear that once lived in Altamira. Look for his paw prints nearby.

Artists' Workshop

See the tools used by the prehistoric artists, as well as a video showing how the paintings were created. The most dramatic paintings—all the red buffaloes—were made with reddish ochre dissolved in water, outlined in black charcoal. Marrow-burning stone lamps provided light. Many of the images were engraved into the surface of the cave (using flint) before being painted. The reproductions in the Neo-cave were done using the same techniques.

Art!

Finally we reach the paintings themselves. This part of the cave has various names, including the "Great Hall," the "Great Ceiling," the "Polychrome Room," or even "the Sistine Chapel of Prehistoric Art." The ledge with the lights shows the floor level of the original cave. This didn't give the cavemen much room to paint, making their creations even more remarkable. Among the fauna depicted in this room are 16 bison, a couple of running boars, some horses, and a giant deer—plus a few handprints and several mysterious symbols.

Unfortunately, the posted English information ends here. These are some of the things to look for:

Bumps and Cracks: The artists incorporated the ceiling's many topographical features into their creations (see the bison with the large, swollen back, or the one with the big head).

Overlap: Some paintings actually overlap onto each other.

CANTABRIA

These were painted during two different eras. (The most impressive batch—including all those bison—is thought to be by the same artist.)

Detail: While a few paintings are incomplete, others are finished. Check out the bison with the highly detailed hooves and beard.

The "Old Horse": The horse with its rear end against the wall is probably among the oldest in the cave.

The "Great Deer": The biggest painting of all (over seven feet across) is the deer with the little black bison under his chin. Notice it's not quite in proportion; due to the tight quarters, the artist couldn't take a step back to survey his work.

Symbols: The strange, hieroglyphic-like symbols scattered around the cave, called tectiforms, are difficult to interpret. Scientists have found very similar symbols in caves that were far apart and wondered if they were some sort of primitive written language (for example, an outline of a horse with a particular symbol might explain how to set traps for hunting).

Behavior: The artists captured not only the form, but also the behavior of the animals they depicted. Notice the lowing bison, the curled-up bison, the bison turning its head, and the running boars (with the extra legs).

What's amazing about these paintings is simply that they were made by Cro-Magnon cave people. And yet the artists had an incredible grasp of delicate composition, depicting these animals with such true-to-life simplicity. Some of them are mere outlines, a couple of curvy lines—masterful abstraction that could make Picasso jealous.

So why did they make these paintings? Nobody knows for sure. General agreement is that it wasn't simply for decoration and that the paintings must have served some religious or shamanistic purpose.

Final Cave

The most impressive paintings were discovered in a single room (whose replica you just visited). However, beyond that room, the cave extended another several hundred feet, though that area was not reproduced. As you leave the replica cave, you'll see a few more replicas—mostly carvings—that came from other parts of the original cave. Most of them are those mysterious symbols, but at the very end, you'll also see three masks carved into the rock.

Walk upstairs to exit the museum. There's an exhibit comparing Altamira to other prehistoric sites.

Before leaving, the truly inquisitive can take a peek at the original cave entrance: After exiting the museum, enter the park area on your right. Follow the path to two modern temporary exhibit buildings. In the distance—below the house—is the wrought-iron gate that protects the original cave. That's as close as you can get.

Comillas

Just 15 minutes beyond Santillana del Mar, perched on a hill overlooking the Atlantic, you'll find quirky Comillas. Comillas

presides over a sandy beach, but feels more like a hill town, with twisty lanes clambering up away from the sea. Comillas is not as undeniably charming as Santillana—it would do well to go traffic-free, as its neighbor has—but it makes for a better home base if you prefer beach access, fascinating architecture, and a more lived-in feel to touristy quaintness.

Tourist Information: The western-most square, Plaza Joaquín de Piélagos, is where you'll find the TI (unpredictable hours; posted as July-Aug daily 9:00-21:00;

May June and Sept daily 9:00 14:00 & 16:00 18:00; Oct-April Mon-Sat 9:00-14:00 & 16:00-18:00, Sun 9:00-14:00; Calle Aldea 6, tel. 942-722-591).

Sights in Comillas

Comillas enjoys a surprising abundance of striking Modernista architecture. (For more on this unique, Barcelona-born take on Art Nouveau, see page 108.) There are three biggies: El Capricho and Palacio del Sobrellano line up along a ridge at the west end of town (just beyond the town center and parking lot, over the big park), while Universidad Pontificia faces them from a parallel ridge.

El Capricho
This villa, commissioned in 1883 by Máximo Díaz de Quijano (brother-in-law of the First Marquis of Comillas), was designed by the great Catalan architect Antoni Gaudí. While officially called Villa Quijano, the nickname "El Capricho"—which roughly means "The Whim"—stuck. It housed an expensive restaurant from 1985 until 2009, when it was opened to the public. As one of Gaudí's very first creations—built at the same time as Casa Vicens in Barcelona—the house attracts architecture fans from around the world. El Capricho's sunflower-dappled exterior alludes to

Comillas' Catalunya Connections

Comillas might be just another coastal Cantabrian village if it weren't for the efforts of its most famous son, Antonio López y López (1817-1883). His father died when he was a child, and his widowed mother had a hard time making ends meet—so López took any job he could find in order to earn a few pesetas. Eventually he saved enough money to travel to Cuba at the age of 14, and discovered that the New World was a land of opportunity.

López used the contacts he made abroad to build a lucrative business shipping flour and other foodstuffs to Cuba, then one of Spain's most important colonies. The business expanded over time to become the Compañía Transatlántica Española (a.k.a. the Spanish Line), one of the most successful maritime companies in Spanish history. (More recently, it has come to light that some of the López fortune came from the slave trade.)

López, his wife, and their four children were constantly on the move between the Old World and the New. An 1853 cholera epidemic in Cuba forced their return to Spain, and again, fortune smiled on López. His eldest daughter married the extraordinarily wealthy Barcelona businessman Eusebi Güell in 1871. As Güell's father had also amassed a large fortune in Cuba through maritime interests, it was a perfect match, allowing López to continue to move up in Catalunya's high society.

During this time, Spain was clinging to the last remaining fragments of its former worldwide empire, and King Alfonso XII struggled with constant budget problems. He asked the successful López for funds and ships to transport troops to Cuba in order to stifle a rebellion. In return, Alfonso XII granted López the titles Marquis of Comillas and Grandeza de España (a rank second only to the king's own immediate family).

Inspired by his son-in-law Güell's fondness for Modernisme in Barcelona, the new Marquis began to display his wealth in Comillas. Architect Joan Martorell i Montells built the Palacio de Sobrellano, wrapping the López family in Art Nouveau luxury, as well as the adjacent chapel and (across town) a sprawling seminary complex, the Universidad Pontificia. Next door to the Palacio, forms on the tower of Gaudí's El Capricho mimic the architect's first Barcelona creation, Casa Vicens. Yet another Modernista great, Lluís Domènech i Montaner, also received commissions for several local works, and many famous Catalan sculptors decorated the town... making Comillas the only place outside of Catalunya with so many works by Barcelona's finest architects.

Gaudí's plan for the building: His "sunflower design" attempted to maximize exposure to light by arranging rooms so that they would get sun during the part of the day that they were most used. Some of the restaurant modifications are still in place upstairs. An excellent video with English subtitles explains local history and how Gaudí became involved in a project so far from his hometown of Barcelona.

Cost and Hours: €5, daily 10:30-20:00, last entry 30 minutes before closing, tel. 942-720-365, www.elcaprichodegaudi.com

Getting There: Although El Capricho is next to the Palacio de Sobrellano (described next), there's no direct access between them. Enter from the back, via a driveway on Paseo Estrada (CA-135, the road into town).

Palacio de Sobrellano

Designed by Gaudí's mentor Joan Martorell i Montells, this building hints at early Barcelona-style Modernisme. Guided tours (Spanish only, no English translations available) are the only way to visit the spectacular home, but it's worth an hour to see how the other half lived. The Marquis amassed an impressive collection of artifacts, some of which are still on display.

Cost and Hours: €3, grounds open at 9:30, one-hour guided visits leave on the half-hour Tue-Sun 10:30-13:30 & 15:30-18:30, closed Mon, tel. 942-720-339, www.culturadecantabria.com /sobrellano.asp.

Visiting the Palace: The tour begins with an introduction to Antonio López y López, the First Marquis of Comillas, who put this town on the world architecture map (see sidebar; his descendant, the Fourth Marquis of Comillas, recently sold this palace to the provincial government, which opened the building to tourists). Then you'll pass through the billiards room to the dining room, with its fantastic fireplace intact. The throne room contains an abundance of stained glass and paintings commemorating four important family moments: the opening of the Universidad Pontificia (described next); the inauguration of the church next door, Capilla-Panteón; a naval review during a visit by King Alfonso XII (who spent a summer here in Comillas); and the sailing from Barcelona of a López-funded vessel—full of soldiers—to squash a Cuban rebellion.

Nearby: The pointy-spired Art Nouveau church called **Capilla-Panteón,** between the palace and El Capricho, was also designed by Martorell. It contains the first furniture ever designed by Antoni Gaudí (€3, same hours as Palacio de Sobrellano, ask for details at the palace).

Universidad Pontificia

This huge building, peering back at the town from a parallel ridge, was also designed by Joan Martorell i Montells. Workers laid the

CANTABRIA

foundation stone in 1883, a few months after the death of the First Marquis of Comillas. While originally built as a Jesuit seminary, today the building is used by the Fundación Comillas to teach Spanish and Hispanic culture. Although the obligatory guided tour is in Spanish only, English handouts translate the majority of the visit.

Cost and Hours: €3.50, guided visits at the top of each hour, daily 10:00-13:00, June-Sept also 17:00-20:00, mobile 630-256-767, www.fundacioncomillas.es.

Visiting the Building: Martorell's brick-and-ceramic gate prepares visitors for what lies ahead after their uphill hike: *IHS* (the first three letters of Jesus's name in Greek, frequently used by Jesuits), pages' robes inscribed with *1892* (the year the seminary opened), and *Leon XIII* (the pope at the time of construction). Tilework endlessly hails Mary.

Huff up to the top of the hill to buy your tickets. Tours begin at the seminary's former main entrance: the heavy, bronze Door of Virtues (Puerta de las Virtudes). Richly decorated by another leading early-20th-century Catalan architect, Lluís Domènech i Montaner, the door depicts young women as the seven heavenly virtues standing over the seven deadly sins.

Push through the door to reach a sumptuous Art Nouveau interior, with walls covered in *esgrafiado* (a technique where designs are pressed into wet plaster, then painted when dry). Carved wooden ceilings drip above female figures representing traits such as Tenderness, Patience, and Obedience. Don't miss the cat and mice carved into the base of the staircase. Fellow architects at the time thought the staircase would collapse, unable to support itself, so Montaner whimsically incorporated a favorite children's story into the design: Mice invent a plan to know when a dangerous cat is coming close—place a bell around his neck. But no mouse wants to risk his life by getting close enough to place the bell. The fable teaches a moral lesson about great plans that cannot be executed. Montaner proved all naysayers wrong by being the only brave mouse...and the staircase still stands proudly today.

Circling the staircase, stained glass windows depict the coat-of-arms of the Marquis of Comillas, and wooden panels above show beasts from the flood—amazingly carved *in situ*. The tour continues to a modern meeting room decorated by colorful biblical scenes painted on cloth (painstakingly restored by craftsmen from the Prado Museum in Madrid). The last stop on your tour is one of two interior patios with brickwork wells. You'll see the seminary church, covered with the same *Ave María* tiles as the entrance gate. While the church interior isn't open to the public (it's the last part of the complex awaiting restoration), tour guides allow you ample time to wander to the church's main facade and ponder the seaside views.

More Modernisme

The beachside road below, lined with a few hotels, is worth a stroll, especially to get a glimpse of a guardian angel. Domènich i Montaner converted old church ruins into an interesting cemetery with one spectacular tomb: His vault for the **Piélago family** depicts an angel riding the surf atop a giant wave.

On the opposite hill, look for an Art Nouveau statue, donated by the town, portraying the **First Marquis of Comillas.** López proudly stands atop a column, carried by one of his ships.

The town center, a two-minute walk inland, is just as pleasant—with an odd jumble of squares surrounding the big Parochial Church. A final bit of Modernisme is the Domènich i Montaner **lamppost/fountain** (near the TI), which commemorates Comillas as the first town in Spain to have electricity.

Near Comillas

As you continue west from Comillas on CA-131, the road follows the coast, soon crossing a wide bay over a long, dramatic bridge to **San Vicente de la Barquera.** This salty seaside resort overlooks a boat-filled harbor, with glimpses of the dramatic Picos de Europa in the distance.

Sleeping in Comillas

($1 = about €1.30, country code: 34)

Both of these listings are in the town center, south of the big Parochial Church, near the long, skinny restaurant-lined Plaza de Primo de Rivera (also known as "El Corro"). The first hotel is the big red building a block off the south end of the square; the other is a few blocks above the square, on the street uphill from Bar Los Castaños.

$$ Hotel Marina de Campíos offers 20 modern, colorful rooms, each named for a different opera (standard Db-€75-110, "junior" Db-€95-130, "senior" Db-€125-150, higher prices are for mid-July-Aug, includes breakfast, closed on weekdays mid-Sept-June and completely closed mid-Dec-mid-Jan, elevator, Calle General Piélagos 14, tel. 942-722-754, www.marinadecampios .com, reservas@marinadecampios.com).

$ Pasaje San Jorge, with 11 cozy and comfortable rooms in a hundred-year-old house, hovers just beyond the town center. Gemma offers plenty of good sightseeing advice (Db-€65-75, higher prices are for July-Aug, cheaper off-season, includes breakfast, Calle Carlos Díaz de la Campa 16, tel. 942-720-915, www.pasajesanjorge.com, pasajesanjorge@pasajesanjorge.com).

CANTABRIA

Picos de Europa

The Picos de Europa—comprising one of Spain's most popular national parks—are a relatively small stretch of cut-glass mountain peaks (the steepest in Spain, some taller than 8,500 feet) just 15 miles inland from the ocean. These dramatic mountains are home to goats, brown bears, eagles, vultures, wallcreepers (rare birds), and happy hikers. Outdoorsy types could spend days exploring this dramatic patch of Spain, which is packed with visitors in the summer. We'll focus on the two most important excursions: taking the Fuente Dé funicular up to a mountaintop, and hiking the yawning chasm of the Cares Gorge.

Orientation to the Picos de Europa

The Picos de Europa are a patch of mountains covering an area of about 25 miles by 25 miles. They're located where three of Spain's regions converge: Cantabria, Asturias, and León. (Frustratingly, each region's tourist office pretends that the parts of the park in the other regions don't exist—so it's very hard to get information, say, about Asturias' Cares Gorge when you're in Potes, Cantabria.) In addition to three regions, the park contains three different limestone massifs—large masses of rock—separated by rivers.

As you venture into the Picos de Europa, pick up a good map; the green 1:80,000-scale map is handy, featuring roads, trails, and topographical features. Serious hikers will want a guidebook (I like the Sunflower guide, published by a British company—www.sunflowerbooks.co.uk). These resources, along with a wide variety of other maps and books, are available locally.

I'll focus on the Cantabrian part of the Picos, which contains the region's most accessible and enjoyable bits: the scenic drive through La Hermida Gorge, the charming mountain town of Potes, and the sky-high views from the top of the Fuente Dé cable car. This part of the Picos is doable as a long day trip from Santillana del Mar or Comillas (but is easier if you stay in Potes). The next best activity is the Cares Gorge hike—deeper in the park and requiring another full day.

Planning Your Time
If you're really serious about tackling the region, and want to do both Fuente Dé and the Cares Gorge, this is the most sensible plan:

Day 1: Drive from Comillas/Santillana del Mar to Potes and do the Fuente Dé cable car and hike (sleep in Potes).

Day 2: Day-trip to the Cares Gorge hike via Caín (sleep in Potes).

Day 3: Move on to your next destination.

Getting Around the Picos de Europa
The Picos de Europa are best with a car. If you don't have wheels, skip it, because bus connections are sparse, time-consuming, and frustrating (see "Getting Around Cantabria" on page 382).

The A-8 expressway squeezes between the Picos and the north coast of Spain; roads branch into and around the Picos, but beware: Many of them traverse high-mountain passes—often on bad roads—and can take longer to drive through than you expect. *Puerto* means "pass" (slow going) and *desfiladero* means "gorge" (quicker but often still twisty).

Assuming you're most interested in Potes and Fuente Dé, you'll focus on the eastern part of the park, approaching from the A-8 expressway (or from Santillana del Mar and Comillas). You'll go through Unquera and catch N-621 into the park (follow signs for *Potes*). Wind your way through La Hermida Gorge (Desfiladero de la Hermida) and stop for a photo en route to Potes (about one hour, depending on traffic). The road crisscrosses back and forth between both banks of the Río Deva for spectacular scenery. Count on 30 more minutes to arrive at Fuente Dé.

The Cares Gorge, officially in Asturias, can be approached from either the south (the village of Caín, deep in the mountains beyond Potes) or the north (Puente Poncebos, with easier access)—but be aware that there's no direct road between the gorge and Potes.

Sights in the Picos de Europa

I've arranged these sights as you'll come to them if you approach from the northeast (that is, from the expressway, Santillana del Mar, or Comillas).

Potes
This quaint mountain village, at the intersection of four valleys, is the hub of Cantabria's Picos de Europa tourist facilities. It's got an impressive old convent and a picturesque stone bridge spanning the

Río Deva. It's a good place to buy maps and books, mainly geared toward UK tourists who arrive by ferry in Santander. Free parking can be found all around the church. Check in at the **TI** with any travel questions (unpredictable hours, but generally July-Sept daily 10:00-14:00 & 16:00-19:00; less off-season—often closed Sun and Mon afternoons and all day Tue; Plaza de las Serna, tel. 942-732-188).

Sleeping in Potes: **$ Casa Cayo** has 17 cozy rooms and a fine restaurant that overlooks the river (Sb-€35, Db-€50, Tb-€60, closed Christmas-Feb, Calle Cántabra 6, tel. 942-730-150, www.casacayo.com, informacion@casacayo.com).

▲▲Fuente Dé Cable Car (Teleférico Fuente Dé)

Perhaps the single most thrilling activity in Picos de Europa is to take the cable car at Fuente Dé. The longest single-span cable car in Europe zips you up 2,600 feet in just four ear-popping minutes (but in summer, you may have to wait more than two hours to take it). Once at the top (altitude 6,000 feet), you're rewarded with a breathtaking panorama of the Picos de Europa. The huge, pointy Matterhorn-like peak on your right is Peña Remoña (7,350 feet). The cable-car station on top has WCs, a cafeteria (commanding views, miserable food), and a gift shop (limited hiking guides—equip yourself before you ascend).

Cost and Hours: €16 round-trip, €9.70 one-way (if you're hiking down—explained later), runs every 30 minutes (or more frequently with demand); daily July-mid-Sept 9:00-20:00, mid-Sept-Dec and Feb-June 10:00-18:00—or until 19:00 on June weekends, closed Jan unless weather is unseasonably good. Every 100 hours, the cable car must be closed briefly for maintenance—so it's a good idea to check ahead before making the drive. Note that this is a very popular destination in summer, and you may have to wait in long lines both to ascend and to descend (up to 2.5 hours in early Aug, 1 hour in late July; quieter in June, early July, and Sept—if you're concerned, call ahead to find out how long the wait is before you make the 14-mile drive from Potes).

Information: Cable car tel. 942-736-610. The local government website provides links to the *teleférico* for the most accurate information on cable car hours (www.cantur.com). The Picos de Europa National Park runs a helpful information kiosk in the parking lot during peak season (July-Aug), with handouts and advice on hikes (including the one described above). Even better, stop at the bigger National Park office on the way to Fuente Dé from Potes; about a mile after you leave Potes, look on the right for the green *Picos de Europa* signs (daily 9:00-18:00, in summer may be open until 20:00, tel. 942-730-555).

Getting There: By car, the road dead-ends at Fuente Dé (to return to Potes, you'll have to backtrack). If you're relying on public transportation, you can take the bus from Potes to Fuente Dé (2/day)—but it runs only in summer.

Hiking Back Down: Once you're up there, those with enough time and strong knees should consider hiking back down. From the cable-car station at the top, follow the yellow-and-white signs to *Espinama*, always bearing to the right. You'll hike gradually uphill (gain about 300 feet), then down (3,500 feet) the back side of the mountain, with totally different views than the cable-car ride up: green, rolling hills instead of sharp, white peaks. Once in Espinama, you'll continue down along the main road back to the parking lot at the base of the cable car (signs to *Fuente Dé*). Figure about four hours total (nine miles) at a brisk pace from the top back to the bottom. Note that the trails are covered by snow into April and sometimes even May; ask at the ranger station near Potes about conditions before you hike (see "Information," earlier).

▲Cares Gorge (Garganta del Cares)

This impressive gorge hike—surrounded on both sides by sheer cliff walls, with a long-distance drop running parallel to (and sometimes under) the trail—is ideal for hardy hikers. The trail was built in the 1940s to maintain the hydroelectric canal that runs through the mountains, but today it has become a very popular summer-hiking destination. The trail follows the Río Cares seven miles between the towns of Caín (in the south) and Camarmeña (near Puente Poncebos, in the north). Along the way, you'll cross harrowing bridges and take trails burrowed into the rock face. Because it's deeper in the mountains and requires a good six hours (13 miles round-trip, with some ups and downs), it's best left to those who are really up for a hike and not simply passing through the Picos. Visitors who just want a glimpse will hike only partway in before heading back.

Getting There: To reach Caín from Potes, you'll drive on rough, twisty roads (N-621) over the stunning Puerto de San Gloria pass (5,250 feet, watched over by a sweet bronze deer), into a green, moss-covered gorge. Just past the village of Portilla de la Reina, turn right (following signs for *Santa Marina de Valdeón*) to reach Caín. Note that this is a very long day trip from Potes, and almost brutal if home-basing in Comillas or Santillana del Mar.

The approach to the gorge from the north (Puente Poncebos) is easier, but won't take you near Potes and Fuente Dé. You can reach Puente Poncebos via AS-114 to Las Arenas, then follow the Cares River on AS-264 to Puente Poncebos.

CANTABRIA

SALAMANCA

This sunny sandstone city boasts Spain's grandest plaza, its oldest university, and a fascinating history, all swaddled in a strolling, college-town ambience. Salamanca—a youthful and untouristy Toledo—is a series of monuments and clusters of cloisters. The many students help keep prices down. Take a paseo with the local crowd down Calle de Rúa Mayor and through Plaza Mayor. The young people congregate until late in the night, chanting and cheering, talking and singing. When I asked a local woman why young men all alone on Plaza Mayor suddenly break into song, she said, "Doesn't it happen where you live?"

Planning Your Time

Salamanca, with its art, university, and atmospheric Plaza Mayor, is worth a day and a night, but it is stuck out in the boonies. It's feasible as a side-trip from Madrid (it's 2.5 hours one-way from Madrid by car, bus, or train), even with a stop in Ávila on the way. If you're bound

for Santiago de Compostela or Portugal, Salamanca is a natural stop.

Orientation to Salamanca

Tourist Information

The main TI is on **Plaza Mayor** (summer Mon-Fri 9:00-14:00 & 16:30-20:00, Sat 10:00-20:00, Sun 10:00-14:00; winter Mon-Sat until 18:30, Sun until 14:00; Plaza Mayor 19, tel. 923-218-342). Pick up the free map, city brochure, and current list of museum hours. Summertime-only TIs spring up at the train and bus stations.

The TI website (www.salamanca.es) is a good source of practical information, including a printable city-center map *(Plano de la ciudad)*, a downloadable city guide, and directions on how to arrive from various points in Spain. You can also check the regional TI website (www.turismocastillayleon.com) to find out about events and festivals in and around Salamanca.

Tours: The Plaza Mayor TI rents a decent MP3 **audioguide** of the city (€12/24 hours, €20 deposit, includes map). A two-hour **guided walking tour,** in English, leaves from the Plaza Mayor TI and includes entry to the cathedrals and a few other free sights (€20/person, 10-person minimum, runs April-June only Mon-Fri at 14:00).

Sightseeing Pass: The **Salamanca Card,** sold at the TI and participating sights, covers entry to the main monuments and museums and includes the city audioguide (€19/24 hours, €23/48 hours, www.salamancacard.com). Some of my recommended hotels offer extras such as free breakfast or late check-out with the Salamanca Card.

Arrival in Salamanca

From either Salamanca's train or bus station to Plaza Mayor, it's a 25-minute walk, an easy bus ride (€1.05, pay driver), or a €7 taxi trip. The train station has no lockers; day-trippers can store bags at the bus station *(consignas;* €2, at bay level facing main building on your left).

By Train: Salamanca has two train stations: the main train station and (a bit closer to the town center) Salamanca Alamedilla Station. To walk from the main train station into the center of town, exit left and walk down to the ring road, cross it at Plaza de España, then angle slightly left up Calle Azafranal. Alternatively, exit the front of the main station, cross the street, and take bus #1, which lets you off just past the Plaza del Mercado (the market), next to Plaza Mayor.

Some trains continue on to Salamanca Alamedilla Station, which is closer to town—if you arrive here, walk down Avenida Alamedilla past a park to Plaza de España, then to Calle Azafranal. Note that you cannot depart from or buy tickets at Salamanca Alamedilla Station.

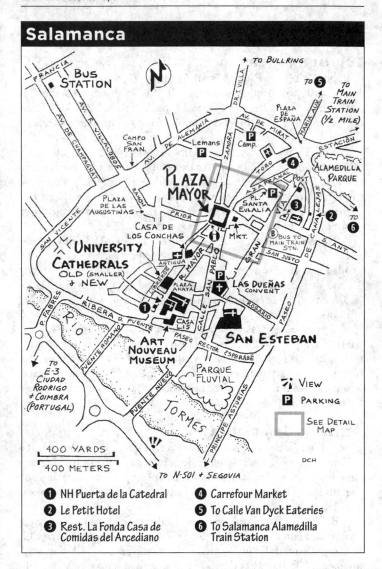

Salamanca

- 1 NH Puerta de la Catedral
- 2 Le Petit Hotel
- 3 Rest. La Fonda Casa de Comidas del Arcediano
- 4 Carrefour Market
- 5 To Calle Van Dyck Eateries
- 6 To Salamanca Alamedilla Train Station

By Bus: To walk into the center from the bus station, exit right and walk down Avenida Filiberto Villalobos; take a left on the ring road and the first right on Ramón y Cajal, head through Plaza de las Augustinas, and continue on Calle Prior to reach Plaza Mayor. Or take bus #4 (exit station right, catch bus on same side of the street as the station) to the city center; the closest stop is on Gran Vía, about two blocks east of Plaza Mayor (ask the driver or a fellow passenger, "¿Para Plaza Mayor?").

By Car: Drivers will find a handy underground parking lot at Plaza Santa Eulalia (€13/day, open 24 hours daily). Two other convenient lots are Parking Plaza del Campillo and Parking Le Mans (€14/day). You can also try one of the hotels with valet parking for comparable fees.

Helpful Hints

Book Ahead for September: During this month, Salamanca's Feria, patron saint celebration, and bullfighting events fill up hotels and increase room prices.

Internet Access: Navega Internet Center has several computers and a call center; it also sells phone cards (Mon and Wed-Sat 11:00-14:15 & 17:00-23:00, Tue 18:00-23:00, closed Sun, between Plaza del Mercado and Gran Vía at Obispo Jarrín 14, tel. 923-215-447).

Travel Agency: Viajes Salamanca books flights, trains, and some buses, including buses to Coimbra, Portugal (Plaza Mayor 24, tel. 923-211-414).

Local Guide: Ines Criado Velasco, a good English-speaking guide, is happy to tailor a town walk to your interests (€80/2 hours—a special rate for readers of this book in 2014, €95/3 hours, prices increase on holidays, €150/day for groups of 1-30, mobile 609-557-528, inescriado@yahoo.es).

Tourist Tram: The small tram you might see waiting at the New Cathedral does 20-minute loops through town with Spanish narration (€4, departs every 30 minutes from cathedral, daily 11:00-14:00 & 16:00-19:00, no lunch break July-Aug, mobile 649-625-703).

Sights in Salamanca

▲▲Plaza Mayor

Built from 1729 to 1755, this ultimate Spanish plaza is a good place to nurse a cup of coffee (try the venerable Art Nouveau-style Café Novelty) and watch the world go by.

The town hall, with the clock, grandly overlooks the square. The Arco del Toro (built into the eastern wall) leads to the covered market. While most European squares honor a king or saint, this golden-toned square—ringed by famous Castilians—is for all the people. The square niches above the colonnade surrounding the plaza depict writers (Miguel de Cervantes), heroes and conquistadors (Christopher Columbus and Hernán Cortés), as well as numerous kings and dictators (Francisco Franco).

Plaza Mayor has long been Salamanca's community living room. The most important place in town, it seems to be continually hosting some kind of party. Imagine the excitement of the days (until 1893) when bullfights were held in the square. Now old-timers gather here each day, remembering an earlier time when the girls would promenade clockwise around the colonnade while the boys cruised counterclockwise, looking for the perfect *queso* (cheese), as they'd call a cute dish. Perhaps the best time of all for people-watching is Sunday after Mass (13:00-15:00), when the grandmothers gather here in their Sunday best.

▲▲Cathedrals, Old and New

These cool-on-a-hot-day cathedrals share buttresses, and both are richly ornamented. The Old Cathedral is 12th-century Romanesque while the "New" Cathedral, built from 1513 to 1733, is a spacious, towering mix of Gothic, Renaissance, and Baroque.

Cost and Hours: New Cathedral— free, daily April-Sept 9:00-20:00, sometimes closed 14:00-16:00, Oct-March 9:00-13:00 & 16:00-18:00; Old Cathedral—€4.75, free entry if you attend Mass (though you'll still have to pay to enter the cloister), daily April-Sept 10:00-19:30, sometimes closed 13:30-16:00, Oct-March 10:00-12:30 & 16:00-17:30; tower—€3.75 but free Tue 10:00-12:00, daily March-Dec 10:00-20:00, Jan-Feb 10:00-18:00, last entry 45 minutes before closing. Cathedral tel. 923-217-476, tower tel. 619-081-843, www.catedral salamanca.org.

Visiting the Cathedrals: To get to the old, you have to walk through the new.

New Cathedral: Before entering the New Cathedral, check out its ornate front door (west portal on Rúa Mayor). The **facade** is decorated Plateresque, with masonry so intricate it looks like silverwork *(plata)*. It's Spain's version of Flamboyant Gothic. At the side door (around the corner to the left as you face the main entrance), look for the astronaut added by a capricious restorer in 1993. This caused an outrage in town, but now locals shrug their shoulders and say, "He's the person closest to God." I'll give you a chance to find him on your own. Otherwise, look at the end of this listing for help.

Inside, fancy stone trim is everywhere, and the dome decoration is particularly wonderful. Occasionally the music is live, not recorded. The *coro,* or choir, blocks up half of the church (normal for Spanish Gothic), but its wood carving is sumptuous; look up to see the recently restored, elaborate organ.

• *Head into the Old Cathedral (the entrance is near the rear of the New Cathedral). A free English leaflet is available.*

Old Cathedral: Sit in a front pew to study the altarpiece's 53 scenes from the lives of Mary and Jesus (by the Italian Florentino, 1445) surrounding a precious 12th-century statue of the Virgin of the Valley. High above, notice the dramatic Last Judgment fresco of Jesus sending condemned souls into the literal jaws of hell.

Enter the **cloister** (off the right transept) and explore the chapels, notable for their unusual tombs, ornate altarpieces, and ceilings with leering faces. If you speak Spanish, press the button on the wall at the entrance of each chapel to hear a description. In the Capilla de Santa Barbara (second on the left as you enter), you can sit as students once did for their tests. During these final exams, a stern circle of professors formed around the student at the tomb of the Salamanca bishop, who founded the University of Salamanca around 1230. (The university originated with a group of teacher-priests who met in this room.)

As you continue through the cloister, you'll see the chapterhouse *(salas capitulares),* contained in three rooms on your left, with a gallery of 15th-century Castilian paintings. Next is the Capilla de Santa Catalina, which was used as the university's library until 1610. The room is lined with tombs and paintings from the 15th to 17th centuries. See if you can find the original chapterhouse weather vane—it's shaped like a rooster. The Capilla de Anaya, farthest from the cloister entrance, has a gorgeously carved 16th-century alabaster tomb (look for the dog and lion making peace—or negotiating who gets to eat the worried-looking rabbit—at the foot of the tomb) and a wooden 16th-century Mudejar organ. (Mudejar is the Romanesque-Islamic Moorish design style made in Spain after the Christian conquest.)

For a fantastic view of the upper floors and terraces of both cathedrals, and a look at the inside passages with small exhibits about the cathedrals' history and architecture, visit the **tower** (marked *Jerónimos*). It was sealed after Lisbon's 1755 earthquake to create structural support and reopened in 2002. (To climb the tower, exit the cathedral to the left to find a separate entrance around the corner.)

Finally, go find that astronaut: He's just a little guy, about the size of a Ken-does-Mars doll, entwined in the stone trim to the left of the door, roughly 10 feet up. If you like that, check out the dragon (an arm's length below). Historians debate whether he's eating an ice-cream cone or singing karaoke.

▲▲University

The University of Salamanca, the oldest in Spain (est. 1230), was one of Europe's leading centers of learning for 400 years. Columbus came here for travel tips. Today, though no longer so prestigious, it's laden with history and popular with Americans, who enjoy its excellent summer program. The old lecture halls around the cloister, where many of Spain's Golden Age heroes studied, are open to the public.

Cost and Hours: Lecture halls—€10, audioguide-€2; Mon-Sat Oct-March 10:00-18:00, April-June 10:00-19:00, July-Sept 10:00-14:00 & 17:00-20:00; Sun 10:00-13:00 year-round; last entry 30 minutes before closing. Museum—Free, Tue-Sat 9:30-13:30 & 16:00-18:30, Sun 10:00-14:00, closed Mon, no photos allowed. Tel. 923-294-400, ext. 1150.

Visiting the University: Enter the university from Calle Libreros. The ornately decorated grand **entrance** is a great example of Spain's Plateresque style. The people studying the facade aren't art fans. They're trying to find a tiny frog on a skull that students looked to for good luck.

But forget the frog. Follow the **facade**'s symbolic meaning. It was made in three sections by Charles V. The bottom celebrates the Catholic Monarchs. Ferdinand and Isabel saw that the university had no buildings befitting its prestige, and they granted the money for this building. The Greek script says something like, "From the monarchs, this university. From the university, this tribute as a thanks."

The immodest middle section celebrates the grandson of Ferdinand and Isabel, Charles V. He appears with his queen, as well as the Habsburg double-headed eagle and the complex coat of arms of the mighty Habsburg Empire. Since this is a Renaissance structure, it features Greek and Roman figures in the shells. And, as a statement of educational independence from medieval Church control, the top shows the pope flanked by Hercules and Venus.

Pay the admission fee to enter the university's old **lecture halls.** Pick up a free English-language leaflet, and follow it by going left (clockwise) around the courtyard. The lecture halls are well-described with informative panels in English, as well as several videos.

In the **Hall of Fray Luis de León,** the narrow wooden-beam tables and benches—whittled down by centuries of studious doodling—are originals. Professors spoke from the Church-threatening *cátedra* (pulpit). It was here that freethinking brother

SALAMANCA

Luis de León returned, after the Inquisition jailed and tortured him for five years; he had challenged the Church's control of the word of God by translating part of the Bible into Castilian. He started his first post-imprisonment lecture with, "As we were saying..." Such courageous men of truth believed the forces of the Inquisition were not even worth acknowledging.

The altarpiece in the **chapel** on the opposite side of the courtyard depicts professors swearing to Mary's virginity. (How did they know?) Climb upstairs for a peek into the oldest **library** in Spain. Outside the library, look into the courtyard at the American sequoia, brought here 150 years ago and standing all alone. Notice also the big nests in the bell tower. Storks stop here from February through August on their annual journey from Morocco to northern Europe. There are hundreds of these stork nests in Salamanca.

As you leave the university, you'll see the statue of Fray Luis de León. Behind him, to your left, is the entrance to a peaceful courtyard. Within the courtyard is the **Museum of the University,** notable for Fernando Gallego's fanciful 15th-century *Sky of Salamanca.*

Can't forget about the frog? It's on the right pillar of the facade, nearly halfway up, on the leftmost of three skulls.

▲Art Nouveau Museum (Museo Art Nouveau y Art Deco)
Located in the Casa Lis, this museum—with its beautifully displayed collection of stained glass, vases, furniture, jewelry, cancan statuettes, and toy dolls—is a refreshing change of pace. Nowhere else in Spain will you enjoy an Art Nouveau collection in a building from the same era. Find the stunning sculptures of Josephine Baker and Carmen Miranda, along with lots of pieces by René Lalique. The museum is a donation of a private collection. The English brochure contains a translation of the Spanish text posted in each room of the collection. After your visit, sit with a reasonably priced coffee and contemplate the stained-glass facade from the interior of the museum's beautiful Art Nouveau café.

Cost and Hours: €4 but free Thu 11:00-14:00; April-mid-Oct Tue-Fri 11:00-14:00 & 17:00-21:00, Sat-Sun 11:00-21:00; mid-Oct-March Tue-Fri 11:00-14:00 & 16:00-19:00, Sat-Sun 11:00-20:00; closed Mon year-round; strictly no photos—required camera check at ticket counter, between the cathedrals and the river at Calle Gibraltar 14, tel. 923-121-425, www.museocasalis.org.

Church of San Esteban
Dedicated to St. Stephen (Esteban) the martyr, this complex contains a recently restored cloister, tombs, museum, sacristy, and church.

Cost and Hours: €3, daily 10:00-14:00 & 16:00-20:00, until 19:00 in winter, museum closed Sun-Tue, last entry 45 minutes before closing, tel. 923-215-000.

Visiting the Church: The visitors' entrance is to the right of the church entrance (which is closed except during services).

Before you enter, notice the Plateresque **facade** and its bas-relief of the stoning of St. Stephen. The crucifixion above is by Italian Renaissance artist Benvenuto Cellini. As you enter the building, look at the large poster explaining the facade's many characters.

After buying your ticket, walk around the cloister to the opposite corner, where signs indicate ways to the church *(iglesia)*, sacristy *(sacristía)*, choir *(coro)*, and museum *(museo)*. Head to the church first. Once inside, follow the free English pamphlet.

The nave is overwhelmed by a 100-foot, 4,000-piece wood **altarpiece** by José Benito Churriguera (1665-1725) that replaced the original Gothic one in 1693. You'll see St. Dominic on the left, St. Francis on the right, and a grand monstrance holding the Communion wafers in the middle, all below a painting of St. Stephen being stoned. This is a textbook example of the intricately detailed Churrigueresque style that influenced many South American mission buildings. Quietly ponder the dusty, gold-plated cottage cheese, as tourists shake their heads and say "too much" in their mother tongue.

Upstairs, step into the balcony **choir loft** for a fine overview of the nave. The staircase itself is architecturally unique, built without any interior support; the staircase is still standing, but you'll notice that when you walk, you definitely lean inward. The big spinnable book holder in the middle of the room held giant music books—large enough for all to chant from in an age when there weren't enough books for everyone.

Also upstairs is the **museum,** with temperature-controlled glass cases that preserve illustrated 14th- to 16th-century Bibles and choir books. Notice also how the curved ivory Filipino saints all look like they're carved out of an elephant's tusk. And don't miss the fascinating "chocolate box reliquaries" on the wall in the back on the right from 1580. Survey whose bones are collected between all the inlaid ivory and precious woods.

Convento de las Dueñas

Located next door to the Church of San Esteban, the much simpler *convento* is a joy. It consists of a double-decker cloister with a small museum of religious art. Check out the stone meanies exuberantly decorating the capitals on the cloister's upper deck. No English information is displayed, but an English booklet is available for €1.50. The nuns sell sweets daily except Sunday (€4.50 for a small box of their specialty, *amarguillos*—almonds, egg whites, and sugar; no assortments possible even though their display box raises hopes).

Cost and Hours: €2, variable hours but generally Mon-Sat in summer 11:00-12:45 & 16:30-18:45, in winter until 17:30, closed Sun year-round, tel. 923-215-442.

Roman Bridge

Historians enjoy the low-slung Roman Bridge (Puente Romano), much of it original, spanning the Río Tormes. The *ibérico* (ancient pre-Roman) faceless bull blindly guards the entrance to the bridge; you'll find this symbol of Salamanca on every city coat of arms in town.

▲*Tuna* Music

Traditionally, Salamanca's poorer students earned money to fund their education by singing in the streets. This 15th- to 18th-

century tradition survives today, as musical groups of students (representing the various faculties)—dressed in the traditional black capes and leggings—sing and strum mandolins and guitars. They serenade the public in the bars on and around Plaza Mayor. The name *tuna*, which has nothing to do with fish, refers to a vagabond student lifestyle and later was applied to the music these students sing. They're out only on summer weeknights (singing for tips from 22:00 until after midnight), because they make more serious money performing for weddings on weekends.

Sleeping in Salamanca

Salamanca, a student town, has plenty of good eating and sleeping values. Most of my listings are on or within a three-minute walk of Plaza Mayor (NH Puerta de la Catedral and Le Petit Hotel are a little farther—for locations, see map on page 400). Directions are given from Plaza Mayor, assuming you are facing the building with the clock (e.g., 3 o'clock is 90 degrees to your right as you face the clock). The city is noisy on the weekends, so if you're a light sleeper, ask for an interior room.

$$$ NH Puerta de la Catedral is a fancy business-class hotel on a quiet pedestrian street around the corner from the cathedral entrance. It's worth the extra euros for a room with a great view of the cathedral (Db-€90, extra bed-€45, €22 more for view/terrace rooms, higher rates on weekends and holidays, breakfast-€15, air-con, elevator, free Wi-Fi in lobby, parking-€19/day, Plaza de Juan XXIII 5, tel. 923-280-829, www.nh-hotels.com, nhpuertadelacatedral@nh-hotels.com).

Sleep Code

(€1 = about $1.30, country code: 34)
S = Single, **D** = Double/Twin, **T** = Triple, **Q** = Quad, **b** = bathroom, **s** = shower only. Unless otherwise noted, credit cards are accepted, English is spoken, and breakfast is not included. Some hotels include the 10 percent IVA tax in the room price; others tack it onto your bill.

To help you easily sort through these listings, I've divided the accommodations into three categories, based on the price for a standard double room with bath during high season:

$$$ Higher Priced—Most rooms €70 or more.
 $$ Moderately Priced—Most rooms between €45-70.
  $ Lower Priced—Most rooms €45 or less.

Prices can change without notice; verify the hotel's current rates online or by email. For the best prices, always book direct.

$$$ Hotel Torre del Clavero has little character, but its 26 rooms are clean and contemporary. It's conveniently located between Plaza Mayor and the Church of San Esteban, across the street from the Clavero tower. Its private garage is a plus for drivers (Db-€84, higher rates on holidays, extra bed-€20, breakfast-€3.50, cable Internet in rooms, guest computer, parking-€11/day; from Casa de las Conchas on Calle de Rúa Mayor, go three blocks south on Calle de Jesús to Calle del Consuelo 21, or from Gran Vía turn onto Calle de las Varillas then left onto Calle del Consuelo; tel. 923-280-410, www.hoteltorredelclavero.com, info @hoteltorredelclavero.com).

$$$ Hotel Room Mate Vega, across the street from the covered market, has wannabe-hip business-class rooms in a good location (Sb-€45-65, Db-€50-90, Tb-€110, more on weekends and holidays, breakfast-€7, air-con, elevator, guest computer, free Wi-Fi, parking-€12/day; 2 blocks off Plaza Mayor—across from covered market, exit Plaza Mayor at 3 o'clock, Plaza del Mercado 16; tel. 923-272-250, www.room-matehotels.com, vega@room -matehotels.com).

$$$ Petit Palace Las Torres is a chain hotel with 53 modern, spacious rooms (several with see-through bathroom doors) and all the amenities. It's nothing special...except that it's located right on Plaza Mayor (weekday Sb/Db-€50, weekend Sb/Db-€80-90, plaza-view room-€30 extra, 30 percent more during Sept religious festival, breakfast-€7, air-con, elevator, guest computer, free Wi-Fi, a few free loaner bikes, pay parking at nearby Lemans lot,

Central Salamanca

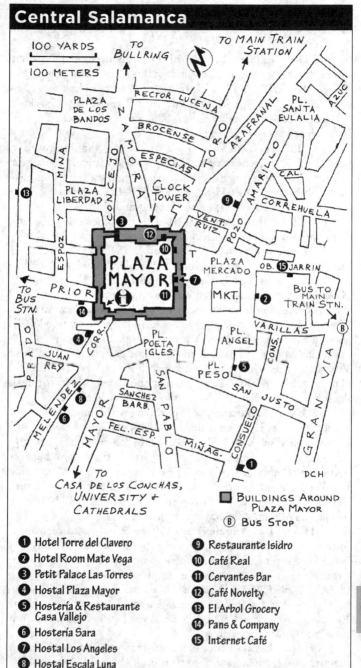

1 Hotel Torre del Clavero
2 Hotel Room Mate Vega
3 Petit Palace Las Torres
4 Hostal Plaza Mayor
5 Hostería & Restaurante Casa Vallejo
6 Hostería Sara
7 Hostal Los Angeles
8 Hostal Escala Luna

9 Restaurante Isidro
10 Café Real
11 Cervantes Bar
12 Café Novelty
13 El Arbol Grocery
14 Pans & Company
15 Internet Café

SALAMANCA

exit Plaza Mayor at 11 o'clock to find hotel entry just off square at Calle Concejo 4, tel. 923-212-100, www.hthotels.com, tor @hthotels.com).

$$ Hostal Plaza Mayor, with 19 nicely decorated but small rooms, has a good location a block southwest of Plaza Mayor (Sb-€30-39, Db-€50-65, Tb-€75-97, air-con, most rooms served by elevator, free Wi-Fi, parking-€15/day, exit Plaza Mayor at 7 o'clock, Plaza del Corrillo 20, tel. 923-262-020, www.hostalplazamayor.es, hostalplazamayor@hotmail.com).

$$ Hostería Casa Vallejo is a welcoming, family-run place, with 12 rustic and renovated rooms a block away from Plaza Mayor. The attached, recommended tapas bar/restaurant serves up tasty deals (Sb-€30-38, Db-€45-80, extra person-€12, breakfast-€3, air-con, elevator, free Wi-Fi, closed second and third weeks of July, San Juan de la Cruz 3, tel. 923-280-421, www.hosteriacasavallejo .com, info@hosteriacasavallejo.com, Amparo).

$$ Le Petit Hotel, while away from the characteristic core, faces a peaceful park and a church, two blocks east of Gran Vía. It rents 23 spotless and homey yet modern rooms. The rooms with views of the church are brightest, and the fourth-floor rooms are the most recently updated—request *vista de iglesia* and *cuarta planta* (Sb-€36, Db-€49, Tb-€59, Qb-€69, air-con, elevator, free Wi-Fi; about 6 blocks east of Plaza Mayor at Ronda Sancti Spiritus 39— exit Plaza Mayor at 3 o'clock and continue east, turn left on Gran Vía, right on Sancti Spiritus at Banco Simeon, and left after the church; tel. 923-600-773, www.lepetithotel.net; kind Hortensia doesn't speak English, but her son Juan Carlos does).

$$ Hostería Sara offers tidy rooms with simple decor and handy kitchenettes. Ask for the upper floors for quieter rooms with double-paned windows (Sb-€48-53, Db-€53-60, Tb-€70-80; €5 more for rooms with kitchenettes that have a fridge, two burners, and a sink; rates drop about €10 off-season, air-con, elevator, free Wi-Fi; 2 blocks off Plaza Mayor—exit the square at about 7 o'clock, toward cathedral at Meléndez 11; tel. 923-281-140, www .hostalsara.org, info@hostalsara.org).

$ Hostal Los Angeles rents 19 simple but cared-for rooms, four of which overlook the square. Stand on the balcony and inhale the essence of Spain. View rooms are popular and more expensive—when you reserve, request *"Con vista, por favor"* (S-€15-22, Sb-€20-35, D-€23-35, Db-€28-55, T-€45-55, Tb-€45-65, Q-€55-65, rates drop on weekdays and off-season, Plaza Mayor 10, about 3 o'clock, tel. 923-218-166, www.pensionlosangeles.com, info@pensionlosangeles.com, Karel).

$ Hostal Escala Luna is recently renovated, with 22 clean, bright, quiet, cheap, and cozy rooms (Sb-€24, Db-€30-40, Tb-€45-55, Qb-€60-75, higher rates are for weekends, first night charged when you reserve, 48-hour notice required for refund, breakfast-€3, free Wi-Fi, laundry service-about €12/load; 2 blocks off Plaza Mayor—exit the square at about 7 o'clock, toward cathedral at Meléndez 13, first floor; tel. 923-218-749, www .hostalescalalunasalamanca.com, info@escalaluna.com).

Eating in Salamanca

Local specialties include *serrano* ham, which is in just about everything (see sidebar on page 29), roast suckling pig (called *tostón* around here), and *sopa de ajo,* the local garlic soup. *Patatas meneadas* (potatoes with Spanish paprika and bacon) is a simple but tasty local tapa. If you always wanted seconds at Communion, buy a bag of the local specialty called *obleas*—flat wafers similar to giant Communion hosts.

Plenty of good, inexpensive restaurants are located between Plaza Mayor and Gran Vía, and as you leave Plaza Mayor toward Calle de Rúa Mayor. You'll also find lots of tapas places along and around Calle de Rúa Mayor, but they are often overrun with students. Restaurants generally serve lunch from 13:30 to 16:00 and dinner from about 20:30 until very late (remember, Spaniards don't start dinner until about 21:00). Tapas bars and cafés may be open all day, though they serve simpler food off hours.

Drinks ordered at a bar usually come with a free *pincho,* a taste of one of the larger portions of tapas. Sometimes you can even choose between several options. For the price of three drinks, you can make a light meal of *pinchos* while standing or sitting at the bar. Try the recommended Cervantes Bar or one of the places outside the old town.

Sit-Down Meals

Restaurante Casa Vallejo, open since 1941, is known for its grilled meats, traditional dishes, and good wine. You'll spend about €35-40 for a satisfying meal (Tue-Sat 13:30-16:00 & 20:30-23:00, Sun 13:30-16:00, closed Mon, restaurant is inside the recommended Hostería Casa Vallejo at San Juan de la Cruz 3, tel. 923-280-421).

La Fonda Casa de Comidas del Arcediano is a dark, woody place with solid, traditional cuisine that caters to longtime residents. You'll happily spend about €25 for dinner (daily 13:30-16:00 & 21:00-24:00, reserve on weekends, 15 yards down the arcade from corner of Gran Vía and Cuesta de Sancti Spiritus at La Reja 2—see map on page 400, tel. 923-215-712).

Restaurante Isidro is a thriving Salamancan (and guidebook) favorite—a straightforward, hardworking eatery where Alberto offers a good assortment of fish and specialty meat dishes with quick and friendly service (€11 fixed-price meal, €25 à la carte dinners, big portions, good roasts, Tue-Sat 13:00-16:00 & 20:00-24:00, Sun 13:00-16:00, closed Mon, Pozo Amarillo 19, about a block north of covered market near Plaza Mayor, tel. 923-262-848).

Casual Eateries on Plaza Mayor and Rúa Mayor

Here you can enjoy a meal sitting on the finest square in Spain and savor some of Europe's best people-watching. The bars, with little tables spilling onto the square, serve *raciones* and €2 glasses of wine. A *ración de la casa* (house specialty of hams, sausages, and cheese), a *ración* of *patatas bravas* (chunks of potatoes with a slightly spicy tomato sauce), and two glasses of wine make up a nice dinner for two for about €25—one of the best eating values in all of Europe. For dessert, stroll with an ice-cream cone from Café Novelty.

Café Real serves tapas-style bar snacks (daily 7:30-24:00, tel. 923-210-556).

Cervantes Bar is more of a restaurant, with a wide selection of meals, €10 salads, and sandwiches. They also have an indoor section with tables that overlook Plaza Mayor from one floor up; it's a popular student hangout. Don't forget to ask for your *pincho*, a snack that comes with your drink, if you're standing at the bar (daily 8:00-late, tel. 923-217-213).

Café Novelty is Plaza Mayor's Art Nouveau café. Dating from 1905, it's the oldest cafe in Salamanca—and has some customers who look like they've been there since it opened. It's filled with character and literary memories. The metal sculpture depicts a famous local writer, Torrente Ballester. Their ice cream sweetens a stroll around the plaza (daily 8:00-24:00, tel. 923-214-956).

Picnic Food

The covered *mercado* (market) on Plaza Mercado has fresh fruits and veggies (Mon 8:00-14:30 & 16:00-19:00, Tue-Sat 8:00-14:30 but may be open later on Tue in summer, closed Sun, on east side of Plaza Mayor).

Supermarkets: A small **El Arbol** grocery, two blocks west of Plaza Mayor at Iscar Peyra 13, has just the basics (Mon-Sat 9:30-21:30, closed Sun). For variety, the big **Carrefour Market** supermarket is your best bet, but it's a six-block walk north of Plaza Mayor on Calle del Toro (Mon-Sat 10:00-22:00, closed Sun, across from Plaza San Juan de Sahagún and its church—see map page 400).

Sandwiches: The **Pans & Company** sandwich chain is always fast and affordable, with a branch on Calle Prior across from Burger King (daily 10:30-24:00).

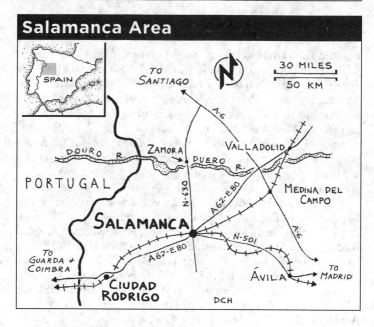

Off the Beaten Path

Locals and students head just a bit outside the old town to hit the tapa/*pincho* scene along a main artery called **Calle Van Dyck**. It's about a 20-minute walk or a short taxi ride from the edge of the old town, but it's worth the effort as there are several cheap and tasty options. You'll spend, on average, €2.50 for a *caña* (small beer), which comes with a small tapa. To get there on foot, go to the end of Calle del Toro, cross the main drag (Avenida de Mirat), and go up Calle Maria Auxiliadora; after crossing the wide Avenida de Portugal, take the third left onto Calle Van Dyck (see map on page 400).

Start at the neighborhood classic, which has been around for more than 40 years—**Cafe Bar Chinitas** at #18—where Victorio, Manoli, and their son Javi serve up a delicious selection of 45 tapas (closed Mon, also closed Sun June-July and all of Aug, tel. 923-229-471). Or try the Galician seafood eatery **Casa Chicho,** farther down the street at #34 (closed Sun night and all day Mon-Tue, tel. 923-123-775). There are many other options on the streets around Van Dyck; try **Bahía de Salamanca** for Andalusian-style seafood, especially the *fritura variada* (fried fish mix) or the *boquerones rellenos* (stuffed anchovies; closed Wed, Avenida de Portugal 76).

Salamanca Connections

From Salamanca by Train to: Madrid (7/day, 2.75 hours, Chamartín Station), **Ávila** (8/day, 1-1.5 hour), **Barcelona** (8/day, 6-7.5 hours, change in Madrid from Chamartín Station to Atocha Station via Metro or *cercanías* train; also possible 1/day with change in Valladolid, 8.5 hours), **Santiago** (1/day, 6.75 hours, transfer in Medina del Campo), **Burgos** (7/day, 2.5-3.5 hours, transfer in Valladolid or Palencia), **Lisbon,** Portugal (1/day, 6.5 hours, departs Salamanca Station at about 1:00 in the morning, no kidding; catch a taxi to the train station, ask your hotel to arrange taxi in advance). Train info: toll tel. 902-320-320, www.renfe.com.

By Bus to: Madrid (hourly express, 2.5-3 hours, arrives at Madrid's Estación Sur, Avanza bus), **Segovia** (4/day, 2.75 hours, Auto-Res bus), **Ávila** (4-5/day, 1.5-2 hours, Auto-Res bus), **Ciudad Rodrigo** (nearly hourly, 1 hour, El Pilar bus), **Santiago** (3/day plus 1 night bus, 6-7.5 hours, Alsa bus), **Barcelona** (2/day with transfer in Valladolid or Palencia, 11 hours, Alsa bus), **Burgos** (2-3/day, 3.5-4 hours, Alsa bus), **Coimbra,** Portugal (1/day, departs at 11:45, 5 hours; same bus continues to **Lisbon** in about 10 hours total, Alsa bus). Bus info: Alsa (tel. 902-422-242, www.alsa.es), Avanza and Auto-Res (tel. 902-020-052, www.avanzabus.com), El Pilar (tel. 923-222-608, www.elpilar-arribesbus.com); also try www.movelia.es for multiple company listings.

Ciudad Rodrigo

Ciudad Rodrigo is worth a visit only if you're driving from Salamanca to Coimbra, Portugal (although buses connect Salamanca and Ciudad Rodrigo with surprising efficiency in about an hour).

This rough-and-tumble old town of 16,000 people caps a hill overlooking the Río Agueda. Spend an hour wandering among the Renaissance mansions that line its streets and exploring its cathedral and Plaza Mayor. Have lunch or a snack at **El Sanatorio** (Plaza Mayor 14, tel. 923-461-054). The tapas are cheap, the crowd is local, and the walls are a Ciudad Rodrigo scrapbook, including some bullfighting that makes the Three Stooges look demure.

Ciudad Rodrigo's **cathedral**—pockmarked with scars from Napoleonic cannon balls—has some entertaining carvings in the choir and some pretty racy work in its cloisters. Who says, "When you've seen one Gothic church, you've seen 'em all"?

The **TI** is two blocks from Ciudad Rodrigo's Plaza Mayor, just inside the old wall near the cathedral (Mon-Fri 9:00-14:00 &

17:00-19:00, Sat-Sun 10:00-14:00 & 17:00-20:00, Plaza Ameyuelas 5, tel. 923-460-561). They can recommend a good hotel, such as **$$$ Hotel Conde Rodrigo** (Sb-€78, Db-€90, rates can drop almost 50 percent off-season, extra bed-€18, 34 rooms, air-con, elevator, free Wi-Fi, Plaza San Salvador 9, tel. 923-461-404, www .conderodrigo.com, info@conderodrigo.com).

MADRID

Today's Madrid is upbeat and vibrant. You'll feel it. Even the living-statue street performers have a twinkle in their eyes.

Madrid is the hub of Spain. This modern capital—Europe's second-highest, at more than 2,000 feet—has a population of 3.3 million, with about 6 million living in greater Madrid.

Like its people, the city is relatively young. In medieval times, it was just another village, wedged between the powerful kingdoms of Castile and Aragon. When newlyweds Ferdinand and Isabel united those kingdoms (in 1469), Madrid—sitting at the center of Spain—became the focal point of a budding nation. By 1561, Spain ruled the world's most powerful empire, and King Philip II moved his capital from tiny Toledo to spacious Madrid. Successive kings transformed the city into a European capital. By 1900, Madrid had 500,000 people, concentrated within a small area. In the mid-20th century, the city exploded with migrants from the countryside, creating today's modern sprawl. Fortunately for tourists, there's still an intact, easy-to-navigate historic core.

Madrid is working hard to make itself more livable. Massive urban-improvement projects such as pedestrianized streets, parks, commuter lines, and Metro stations are popping up everywhere. The investment is making once-shady neighborhoods safe and turning ramshackle zones into trendy ones. These days the broken concrete and traffic chaos of the not-so-distant past are gone. Even with austerity measures related to Spain's ongoing economic crisis, funding for the upkeep of this great city has been maintained. Madrid feels orderly and welcoming.

Tourists are the real winners. Dive headlong into the grandeur and intimate charm of Madrid. Feel the vibe in Puerta del Sol, the

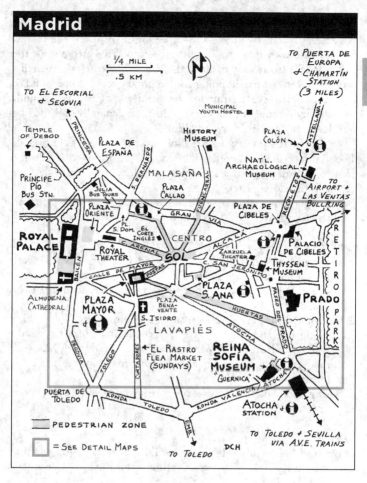

pulsing heart of modern Madrid and of Spain itself. The lavish Royal Palace, with its gilded rooms and frescoed ceilings, rivals Versailles. The Prado has Europe's top collection of paintings, and nearby hangs Picasso's chilling masterpiece, *Guernica*. Retiro Park invites you to take a shady siesta and hopscotch through a mosaic of lovers, families, skateboarders, pets walking their masters, and expert bench-sitters. Save time for Madrid's elegant shops and people-friendly pedestrian zones. On Sundays, cheer for the bull at a bullfight or bargain like mad at a mega-size flea market. Swelter through the hot, hot summers or bundle up for the cold, dry winters. Save some energy for after dark, when Madrileños pack the streets for an evening paseo that can continue past midnight. Lively Madrid has enough street-singing, bar-hopping, and people-watching vitality to give any visitor a boost of youth.

Planning Your Time

Madrid is worth two days and three nights on even the fastest trip. Divide your time among the city's top three attractions: the Royal Palace (worth a half-day), the Prado Museum (also worth a half-day), and the bar-hopping contemporary scene. On a Sunday, consider allotting extra time for the flea market (year-round) and/or a bullfight (some Sun in March-mid-Oct; generally daily during San Isidro festival in May-early June).

Note that some sights are closed on Monday, including El Escorial (see next chapter); sights open on Monday include the Prado (open daily), Royal Palace (open daily), and Centro de Arte Reina Sofía (closed Tue).

For good day-trip possibilities from Madrid, see the next two chapters (Northwest of Madrid and Toledo).

Day 1

Morning: Take a brisk 20-minute good-morning-Madrid walk from Puerta del Sol to the Prado (taking the pedestrianized Calle de las Huertas). Spend the rest of the morning at the Prado.

Afternoon: Enjoy an afternoon siesta in Retiro Park. Then tackle modern art at the Centro de Arte Reina Sofía (Picasso's *Guernica*). Ride bus #27 from the Prado out through Madrid's modern section to Puerta de Europa for a dose of the non-touristy, no-nonsense big city.

Evening: End your day with a progressive tapas dinner at a series of characteristic bars.

Day 2

Morning: Follow my self-guided walk, which loops to and from Puerta del Sol, with a tour through the Royal Palace in the middle.

Afternoon: Your afternoon is free for other sights, shopping, or a side-trip to the palace at El Escorial (closed Mon). Be out at the magic hour—before sunset—when beautifully lit people fill Madrid.

Evening: Take in a flamenco or zarzuela performance.

Orientation to Madrid

Puerta del Sol marks the center of Madrid. No major sight is more than a 20-minute walk or a €6 taxi ride from this central square. Get out your map and frame off Madrid's historic core: To the west of Puerta del Sol is the Royal Palace. To the east, you'll find the Prado Museum, along with the Reina Sofía museum. North of Puerta del Sol is Gran Vía, a broad east-west boulevard bubbling

MADRID

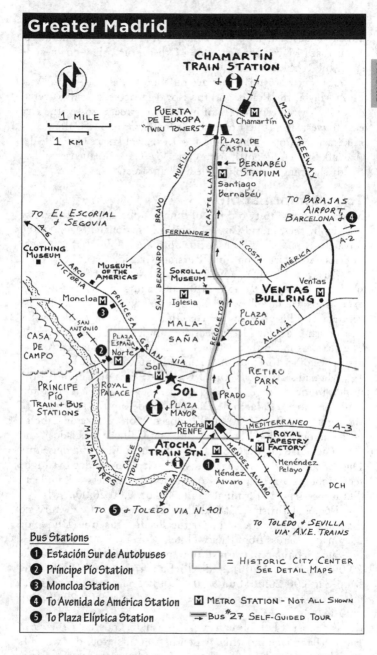

Greater Madrid

CHAMARTÍN TRAIN STATION

PUERTA DE EUROPA "TWIN TOWERS"

Chamartín

M-30 FREEWAY

PLAZA DE CASTILLA

Bernabéu Stadium

Santiago Bernabéu

MURILLO

BRAVO

CASTELLANO

1 MILE

1 KM

TO EL ESCORIAL & SEGOVIA

A-6

Clothing Museum

VICTORIA

ARCO

PRINCESA

SAN BERNARDO

FERNANDEZ

J. COSTA

AMÉRICA

TO BARAJAS AIRPORT BARCELONA

A-2

Museum of the Americas

Sorolla Museum

Iglesia

RECOLETOS

Ventas

VENTAS BULLRING

Moncloa

SAN ANTONIO

MALA-SAÑA

PLAZA COLÓN

ALCALÁ

CASA DE CAMPO

PLAZA ESPAÑA

Norte

GRAN VÍA

VÍA

Sol

RETIRO PARK

Príncipe Pío Train + Bus Stations

Royal Palace

★ SOL

PLAZA MAYOR

PRADO

Atocha RENFE

MEDITERRANEO

A-3

MANZANARES

CALLE TOLEDO

ATOCHA TRAIN STN.

Méndez Álvaro

MÉNDEZ ALVARO

Royal Tapestry Factory

Menéndez Pelayo

CABEZA

DCH

TO TOLEDO VIA N-401

TO TOLEDO & SEVILLA VIA A.V.E. TRAINS

Bus Stations

1 Estación Sur de Autobuses
2 Príncipe Pío Station
3 Moncloa Station
4 To Avenida de América Station
5 To Plaza Elíptica Station

☐ = HISTORIC CITY CENTER
SEE DETAIL MAPS

M METRO STATION - NOT ALL SHOWN

➔ BUS #27 SELF-GUIDED TOUR

with shops and cinemas. Between Gran Vía and Puerta del Sol is a lively pedestrian shopping zone. And southwest of Puerta del Sol is Plaza Mayor, the center of a 17th-century, slow-down-and-smell-the-cobbles district.

This entire historic core around Puerta del Sol—Gran Vía, Plaza Mayor, the Prado, and the Royal Palace—is easily covered on foot. A wonderful chain of pedestrian streets crosses the city east to west, from the Prado to Plaza Mayor (along Calle de las Huertas) and from Puerta del Sol to the Royal Palace (on Calle del Arenal). Stretching north from Gran Vía, Calle de Fuencarral is a trendy shopping and strolling pedestrian street.

Tourist Information

Madrid is home to two types of tourist information offices: city TIs run by the Madrid City Council, and regional TIs run by the privately owned Turismo Madrid. Both are helpful, but you'll get more biased information from Turismo Madrid.

City-run TIs share a website (www.esmadrid.com), a central phone number (tel. 914-544-410), and hours (daily 9:30-20:30); exceptions are noted in the listings below. The best and most central city TI is on **Plaza Mayor.** They offer several guided walks in English each day (described later, under "Tours in Madrid"). They can also help direct travelers to the nearby foreign tourist assistance office (SATE; see "Helpful Hints" for details).

Madrid's other city-run TIs are at **Plaza de Colón** (in the underground passage accessed from Paseo de la Castellana and Calle de Goya), **Palacio de Cibeles** (inside, up the stairs and to the right, Tue-Sun 10:00-20:00, closed Mon), **Plaza de Cibeles** (at Paseo del Prado), **Plaza de Calloa** (at Calle de Preciados), and **Paseo del Arte** (on Calle Santa Isabel, near Reina Sofía museum). During the busy summer months, the city council deploys high-tech mobile TIs to major sites around town. Travelers will find city TIs at the **airport** (Terminals 2 and 4, daily 9:00-20:00).

Regional Turismo Madrid TIs share a website (www.turismo madrid.es) and are located near the **Prado Museum** (Duque de Medinaceli, across from Palace Hotel, Mon-Fri 8:00-15:00, closed Sat-Sun), **Chamartín train station** (near track 20, Mon-Sat 8:00-20:00, Sun 9:00-14:00), and **Atocha train station** (AVE side, Mon-Sat 8:00-20:00, Sun 9:00-20:00). There are also regional TIs at the **airport** (Terminals 1 and 4, Mon-Sat 9:00-20:00, Sun 9:00-14:00).

At most TIs, you can pick up a map and the *Es Madrid* English-language monthly, which lists events around town. TIs occasionally distribute the *Guía del Ocio* (described later) for free; just ask. You'll also find a free, well-designed *Public Transport* map that includes detailed transportation routes throughout the city center. Get this and use it.

Sightseeing Pass: Very energetic travelers can save a little money and some valuable sightseeing time by buying the **Madrid Card.** It covers more than 50 sights (including the Royal Palace, Prado, Thyssen-Bornemisza, and Reina Sofía) and lets you skip lines—a definite plus in high season, especially at the palace and the Prado. Additionally, the pass covers the Bernabéu Stadium tour, all the Essential Madrid tours, and it's good for a 10 percent discount at El Corte Inglés. The three-day card is the best bargain (€64; other options include €44/24 hours and €54/48 hours, online discounts available, www.madridcard.com). You can pay extra to add the hop-on, hop-off bus tour (saves a maximum of €2) or public transport (only worthwhile if you ride multiple times a day).

Entertainment Guides: For arts and culture listings, the TI's printed material is not very good. Pick up the Spanish-language weekly entertainment guide *Guía del Ocio* (€1, sold at newsstands, sometimes free at TI) or check their complete website: www .guiadelocio.com. It lists daily live music *("Conciertos")*, museums (under *"Arte"*—with the latest times, prices, and special exhibits), restaurants (an exhaustive listing), TV schedules, and movies ("V.O." means original version, *"V.O. en inglés sub"* means a movie is played in English with Spanish subtitles rather than dubbed).

Helpful Website: While not officially part of the TI, www .madridman.com is run with passion by American Scott Martin and offers tips on sightseeing, hotels, restaurants, and more.

Arrival in Madrid

For more information on arriving at or departing from Madrid's airport, train stations, and bus stations, see "Madrid Connections," at the end of this chapter.

By Train

Madrid's two train stations, Chamartín and Atocha, are both on Metro lines with easy access to downtown Madrid. Chamartín handles most international trains and the AVE (AH-vay) train to and from Segovia. Atocha generally covers southern Spain, as well as the AVE trains to and from Barcelona, Córdoba, Sevilla, and Toledo. For details on both stations, see page 509.

Traveling Between Chamartín and Atocha Stations: You can take the Metro (line 1, 30-40 minutes, €1.50; see "Getting Around Madrid" on page 426), but the *cercanías* trains are faster (6/hour, 13 minutes, Atocha-Sol-Chamartín lines C3 and C4 are the most convenient, €1.50, free with railpass or any regular train ticket to Madrid—show it at ticket window in the middle of the turnstiles, depart from Atocha's track 6 and generally Chamartín's track 1, 3, 8, or 9—but check the *Salidas Inmediatas* board to be sure).

By Bus

Madrid has several bus stations, each one handy to a Metro station: Príncipe Pío (for Segovia, Metro: Príncipe Pío); Estación Sur de Autobuses (for Ávila, Salamanca, and Granada; Metro: Méndez Álvaro); Plaza Elíptica (for Toledo, Metro: Plaza Elíptica); Moncloa (for El Escorial, Metro: Moncloa); and Avenida de América (for Pamplona and Burgos, Metro: Avenida de América). If you take a taxi from the station to your hotel, you'll pay an extra €5.50 supplement. For more on bus connections, see page 512.

By Plane

Both international and domestic flights arrive at Madrid's Barajas Airport. Options for getting into town include public bus, *cercanías* train, Metro, taxi, and minibus shuttle. For details, see page 513.

Helpful Hints

Theft Alert: Be wary of pickpockets—anywhere, anytime. Areas of particular risk are Puerta del Sol (the central square), El Rastro (the flea market), Gran Vía (the paseo zone: Plaza del Callao to Plaza de España), the Ópera Metro station (or anywhere on the Metro), bus #27, the airport, and any crowded street. Be alert to the people around you: Someone wearing a heavy jacket in the summer is likely a pickpocket. Lately, teenagers dress like Americans and work the areas around the three big art museums; being under 18, they can't be charged in any meaningful way by the police. Assume any fight or commotion is a scam to distract people about to become victims of a pickpocket. Wear your money belt. For help if you get ripped off, see the next listing.

Tourist Emergency Aid: SATE is an assistance service for tourists who might need, for any reason, to visit a police station or lodge a complaint. Help ranges from canceling stolen credit cards to assistance in reporting a crime (central police station, daily 9:00-24:00, near Plaza de Santo Domingo at Calle Leganitos 19). They can help you get to the police station and will even act as an interpreter if you have trouble communicating with the police. Or you can call in your report to the SATE line (24-hour tel. 902-102-112, English spoken once you get connected to a person), then go to the police station (where they'll likely speak only Spanish) to sign your statement.

You may see a police station in the Sol Metro station; this office handles only Metro theft.

Prostitution: Diverse by European standards, Madrid is spilling over with immigrants from South America, North Africa, and Eastern Europe. Many young women come here, fall on hard times, and end up on the streets. While it's illegal to make money from someone else selling sex (i.e., pimping), prostitutes over 18 can solicit legally (€30, FYI). Calle de la Montera (leading from Puerta del Sol to Plaza Red de San Luis) is lined with what looks like a bunch of high-school girls skipping out of school for a cigarette break. Again, don't stray north of Gran Vía around Calle de la Luna and Plaza Santa María Soledad—while the streets may look inviting, this area is a meat-eating flower.

One-Stop Shopping: The dominant department store is **El Corte Inglés,** which takes up several huge buildings in the commercial pedestrian zone just off Puerta del Sol (Mon-Sat 10:00-22:00, Sun 11:00-21:00, navigate with the help of the info desk near the door of the main building—the tallest building with the biggest sign, a block off Puerta del Sol, Preciados 3, tel. 913-798-000). They give out good, free Madrid maps. In the main building, you'll find two handy travel agencies (see listing later), a post office, souvenirs, a modern cafeteria (seventh floor), and a supermarket with a fancy "Club del Gourmet" section (with edible souvenirs) in the basement. Across the street is its Librería branch—a huge bookstore with English-language guidebooks. The second building fronting Puerta del Sol contains six floors of music, computers, home electronics, and SIM cards for mobile phones (passport required, second floor), with a box office on the top floor selling tickets to whatever's on in town. Locals figure you'll find anything you need at El Corte Inglés. Salespeople wear flag pins indicating which languages they can speak. If doing any serious shopping here, look into their discounts (10 percent for tourists) and VAT refund policy (21 percent but with a minimum purchase requirement; see page 17 for details).

Free Sights: The Prado is free every evening (Mon-Sat 18:00-20:00, Sun 17:00-19:00), the Reina Sofía museum has free hours every night but Tuesday, when it's closed (Mon and Wed-Sat 19:00-21:00, Sun 15:00-19:00), the Thyssen-Bornemisza is free on Monday afternoons (12:00-16:00), and the Museum of the Americas is free on Sunday. These Madrid sights are always free: Hermitage of San Antonio de la Florida, Bullfighting Museum, Caja Madrid, and the Temple of Debod.

Internet Access: Most hotels offer Wi-Fi and a guest computer in the lobby for those without a mobile device. Any *locutorio* call center should have a few computers and is generally the cheapest Internet option in the neighborhood. Near the Puerta del Sol, **Workcenter** has plenty of terminals and is a

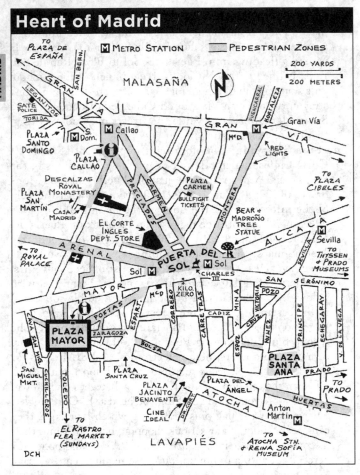

Heart of Madrid

productive place to kill time if you're waiting for the tapas-crawl action to heat up (Mon-Fri 8:00-21:00, Sat-Sun 10:00-14:30 & 17:00-20:30, Calle Sevilla 4—see map on page 503, tel. 913-601-395).

Bookstores: For books in English, try **FNAC Callao** (Calle Preciados 28, tel. 902-100-632), **Casa del Libro** (English on ground floor, Gran Vía 29, tel. 902-026-402), and **El Corte Inglés** (guidebooks and some fiction, in its Librería branch kitty-corner from main store, fronting Puerta del Sol—see "One-Stop Shopping," earlier).

Laundry: Ask your hotelier if they have laundry service. Or try **Higiensec,** which offers self-service laundry (€7/load to wash, a few euros more to dry) as well as drop-off laundry service and dry cleaning (Mon-Sat 9:00-21:00, closed Sun, between Calle

Daily Reminder

Sunday: Some flamenco places are closed today. The Museum of the Americas, National Archaeological Museum, and Clothing Museum close at 15:00. The Prado Museum, Centro de Arte Reina Sofía, and the Thyssen-Bornemisza Museum close at 19:00. The Prado Museum is free after 17:00, the Centro de Arte Reina Sofía is free after 15:00, and the Museum of the Americas is free all day. The flea market at El Rastro runs until 15:00.

Monday: These sights are closed today: Naval Museum, Museum of the Americas, National Archaeological Museum, Clothing Museum, Hermitage of San Antonio de la Florida, and El Escorial (next chapter). The Thyssen-Bornemisza Museum closes at 16:00. The Thyssen-Bornemisza Museum is free from 12:00-16:00, the Prado Museum is free after 18:00, and the Reina Sofía is free after 19:00.

Tuesday: The Reina Sofía is closed today. The Naval Museum and Clothing Museum close at 19:00. The Prado Museum is free after 18:00.

Wednesday: All major sights are open, but the Naval Museum and Clothing Museum close at 19:00. The Prado Museum is free after 18:00, and the Reina Sofía is free after 19:00.

Thursday: All major sights are open, but the Naval Museum and Clothing Museum close at 19:00. The Prado Museum is free after 18:00, and the Reina Sofía is free after 19:00.

Friday: All major sights are open, but the Naval Museum and Clothing Museum close at 19:00. The Centro de Arte Reina Sofía is open until 21:00. The Prado Museum is free after 18:00, and the Reina Sofía is free after 19:00.

Saturday: All major sights are open today, but the Naval Museum and Clothing Museum close at 19:00. Midday, enjoy the scene at Retiro Park. The Prado Museum is free after 18:00, and the Reina Sofía is free after 19:00.

Late-Hours Sightseeing: Sights with evening hours (20:30 or later) include the Centro de Arte Reina Sofía (Mon and Wed-Sat until 21:00), the Thyssen-Bornemisza Museum (Tue-Sat until 22:00 in summer), and the Clothing Museum (Thu until 22:30 in summer).

del Arenal and Calle Mayor at Plaza de Herradores 8—see map on page 491, tel. 915-428-492). **LavaMatic,** near Plaza Santa Ana and my suggested tapas crawl, offers self-service laundry (€6.50/load to wash and dry). Arrive early as they tend to be busy mid-afternoon (Mon-Fri 8:00-22:00, Sat-Sun 8:00-21:00, Calle de la Cruz 35—see map on page 491).

Travel Agencies: The grand department store **El Corte Inglés** has two travel agencies (air and rail tickets, but not reservations

MADRID

for railpass holders, €2 fee, on first and seventh floors, for hours and contact info see "One-Stop Shopping," earlier). These are a fast and easy place to buy AVE and other train tickets.

Updates to This Book: For news about changes to this book's coverage since it was published, see www.ricksteves.com /update.

Getting Around Madrid

If you want to use Madrid's excellent public transit, pick up the fine *Public Transport* map/flier (free, available at TIs or at Metro info booths in most stations—near the entrance turnstiles). The metropolitan Madrid transit website (www.ctm-madrid.es) covers all public transportation options (Metro, bus, and suburban rail).

By Metro: The city's broad streets can be hot and exhausting. A subway trip of even a stop or two saves time and energy. Madrid's Metro is simple, speedy, and cheap. It costs €1.50 for a ride within zone A, which covers most of the city, but not trains out to the airport. The 10-ride, €12 Metrobus ticket can be shared by several travelers and works on both the Metro and buses. Buy tickets in the Metro (from easy-to-use machines or ticket booths), at newspaper stands, or at Estanco tobacco shops. Insert your ticket in the turnstile, then retrieve it and pass through. The Metro stops running at 1:30 in the morning and resumes operation at 6:00. At all times, be alert to thieves, who thrive in crowded stations.

Study your Metro map—the simplified map on the opposite page can get you started. The lines are color-coded and numbered; use end-of-the-line station names to choose your direction of travel. Once in the Metro station, signs direct you to the train line and direction (e.g., Linea 1, *Valdecarros*). To transfer, follow signs in the station leading to connecting lines. Once you reach your final stop, look for the green *salida* signs pointing to the exits. Use the helpful neighborhood maps to choose the right *salida,* and save yourself lots of walking. Metro info: www.metromadrid.es.

By Bus: City buses, though not as easy as the Metro, can be useful (€1.50 tickets sold on bus, €12 for a 10-ride Metrobus ticket, bus maps at TI or info booth on Puerta del Sol, poster-size maps usually posted at bus stops, buses run 6:00-24:00, much less frequent *Buho* buses run all night). Bus info: www.emtmadrid.es.

By Taxi: Madrid's 15,000 taxis are reasonably priced and easy to hail. A green light on the roof indicates that a taxi is available.

Madrid Metro

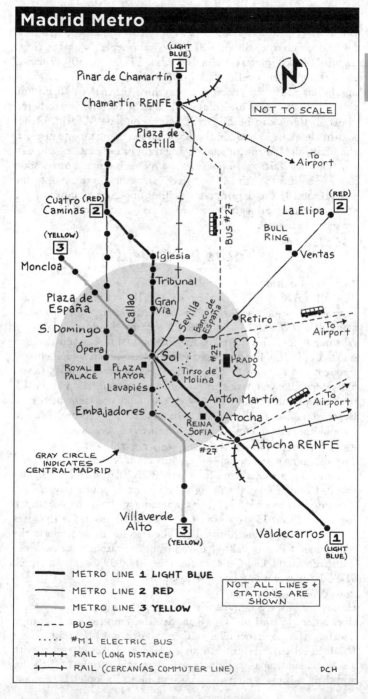

(LIGHT BLUE) **1**

Pinar de Chamartín

Chamartín RENFE

NOT TO SCALE

Plaza de Castilla

To Airport

Cuatro (RED) **2** Caminas

La Elipa (RED) **2**

BULL RING

(YELLOW) **3**

Moncloa

Iglesia

BUS #27

Ventas

Tribunal

Plaza de España

Callao

Gran Vía

Sevilla

Banco de España

Retiro

To Airport

S. Domingo

Ópera

Sol

#27

PRADO

ROYAL PALACE

PLAZA MAYOR

Tirso de Molina

Lavapiés

Antón Martín

To Airport

Embajadores

REINA SOFÍA

Atocha

GRAY CIRCLE INDICATES CENTRAL MADRID

#27

Atocha RENFE

Villaverde Alto

3 (YELLOW)

Valdecarros **1** (LIGHT BLUE)

—— METRO LINE **1** LIGHT BLUE

— METRO LINE **2** RED

—— METRO LINE **3** YELLOW

- - - BUS

····· #M1 ELECTRIC BUS

++++ RAIL (LONG DISTANCE)

+ + RAIL (CERCANÍAS COMMUTER LINE)

NOT ALL LINES + STATIONS ARE SHOWN

DCH

Foursomes travel as cheaply by taxi as by Metro. For example, a ride from the Royal Palace to the Prado costs about €6. After the €2.10 drop charge, the per-kilometer rate depends on the time: *Tarifa 1* (€1/kilometer) is charged Mon-Fri 6:00-21:00; *Tarifa 2* (€1.17/kilometer) is valid after 21:00 and on Saturdays, Sundays, and holidays. If your cabbie uses anything other than *Tarifa 1* on weekdays (shown as an isolated "1" on the meter), you're being cheated. Rates can be higher if you go outside Madrid. Other legitimate charges include the €5.50 supplement for the airport, the €5.50 supplement for leaving any train or bus station, and €20 per hour for waiting. Make sure the meter is turned on as soon as you get into the cab so the driver can't tack anything onto the official rate. If the driver starts adding up "extras," look for the sticker detailing all legitimate surcharges (which should be on the passenger window).

Tours in Madrid

Essential Madrid
The Plaza Mayor TI organizes a daily schedule of cheap, interesting guided walks. Tours depart from this TI most days at 12:00, 16:00, and 18:00 (€5.90, 20 percent discount for booking all three tours, 1.5-2 hours, in English only). Check their detailed booklet or online for specifics and departure times, which change frequently (www.esmadrid.com). Groups can be very small, so you almost feel like you have a private guide. Buy your ticket at the TI, over the phone at 902-221-424, or online at www.entradas.com (search for "Essential Madrid"). Tours can fill up in high season, so booking at least a few hours in advance is a good idea.

"Bus Turístico Madrid" Hop-On, Hop-Off Tours
Two different hop-on, hop-off circuits cover the city: historic and modern. Buy a ticket from the driver (€21/1 day, €25/2 days), and you can hop from sight to sight and route to route as you like, listening to a recorded English commentary along the way. Each route has about 15 stops and takes about 1.5 hours, with buses departing every 10 or 20 minutes. The two routes intersect at the south side of Puerta del Sol and in front of Starbucks across from the Prado (daily 9:30-24:00 in summer, 10:00-19:00 in winter, tel. 917-791-888, www.autobusturisticomadrid.com).

Tour Companies
Carlos Galvin, a Spaniard who led tours for my groups for more than a decade, and his wife from Seattle, Jennifer, run **Letango Tours,** offering itineraries within Madrid and beyond. Their "Madrid Discoveries" tour, mixing a market walk and history with a culinary-and-tapas introduction, gets you close to the Madrileños and their culture (3 hours, €225/group, up to 5 people). Carlos and

Jennifer also offer customized tours (whether city, regional, or country-wide) and bookings anywhere in Spain (mobile 655-818-740 and 661-752-458, www.letangospaintours.com, tours@letango .com).

Madrid Audio Walks, run by Nygil Murrell, offers both live-guided walks and tours (including a €15 walk through historic Madrid, a €25 or €50 wine-tasting, and a €55 or €80 tapas tour) and downloadable audio tours for self-guided walks ($8). Nygil's blog is loaded with insightful and beautifully photographed stories of Madrid life from an American expat's perspective (mobile 620-883-900, www.madridaudiowalks.com, nmurrell@madridaudio walks.com).

Madrid Museum Tours, led by Hernán Amaya Satt and his expert team, organizes more than 40 itineraries, including five different Prado tours, a gossip-filled "secrets of Madrid" walk, and activities around the city and beyond (€158/3 hours, mobile 680-450-231, www.madridmuseumtours.com, info@madridmuseum tours.com). Rick Steves readers get a 20 percent discount on all weekday tours (prices go up about 20 percent on weekends and holidays; transportation and admission costs not included).

Local Guides
Frederico, Cristina, and their team are licensed guides who lead city walks through Madrid. They specialize in family tours of Madrid (prices per group: €155/2 hours, €195/4 hours, €235/6 hours) and to nearby towns (with public or private transit, tel. 913-102-974, mobile 649-936-222, www.spainfred.com, spainfred@gmail .com).

Stephen Drake-Jones, a British expat, leads walks of historic old Madrid almost daily (12:00 and 20:00). A historian with a passion for the Duke of Wellington (the general who stopped Napoleon), Stephen founded Madrid's Wellington Society and has been its chairman for over 30 years. For €65, you become a member and get a 3.5-hour tour with three stops for drinks and tapas (€10 more for fine wines). On his themed tours, eccentric Stephen sorts out Madrid's Habsburg and Bourbon history, plus the Spanish Civil War and Hemingway's Madrid. He likes wine, a lot—if that's a problem, skip the tour (for details on his other tours, see www.wellsoc.org; mobile 609-143-203, chairman@well soc.org).

Other good licensed local guides include: **Inés Muñiz Martin** (a third-generation Madrileña, €110-180/2-5 hours, 25 percent more on weekends and holidays, mobile 629-147-370, www .immguidedtours.com, info@immguidedtours.com), and **Susana Jarabo** (with a master's in art history, €200/4 hours; extra rental charge to tour by bike, scooter, or Segway; mobile 667-027-722, susanjarabo@yahoo.es).

Big-Bus City Sightseeing Tours

Julià Travel leads standard guided bus tours departing from Plaza de España 7 (office open Mon-Fri 8:00-19:00, Sat-Sun 8:00-15:00, tel. 915-599-605). Their city offerings include a 2.5-hour Madrid tour with a live guide in two or three languages (€23, one stop for a drink at Hard Rock Café, one shopping stop, no museum visits, daily at 9:00 and 15:00, no reservation required—just show up 15 minutes before departure). Julià Travel also runs day trips to El Escorial and the Valley of the Fallen (€57, 5 hours, Tue-Sun at 8:45, none Mon) and Toledo (€47/5 hours, daily at 8:45 and 15:00; €63/8 hours, daily at 9:00). Combination tours include Madrid and Toledo (€61, half-day in Toledo plus 3-hour Madrid tour, daily at 8:45) and Toledo plus El Escorial/Valley of the Fallen (€92, full day, Tue-Sun at 9:00, none Mon). Note that just the eight-hour Toledo-only tour includes the cathedral, while the half-day Toledo and combo-tours skip this town's one must-see sight...but not the long shopping stops (the shops give kickbacks to the guides). See their website for other tours and services (www.juliatravel.com).

Self-Guided Tours by Bus or Minibus

A ride on public **bus #27** from the Prado Museum up Paseo del Prado and the **Paseo de la Castellana** to the Puerta de Europa and back gives visitors a glimpse of the modern side of Madrid (see page 481), while a ride on electric **minibus #M1** takes you through the characteristic, gritty old center (see page 482).

Self-Guided Walk

Puerta del Sol to Royal Palace Loop

Madrid's historic center is pedestrian-friendly and filled with spacious squares, a trendy market, bulls' heads in a bar, and a cookie-dispensing convent. Allow about two hours for this mile-long triangular walk. You'll start and finish on Madrid's central square, Puerta del Sol (Metro: Sol).

• *Head to the middle of the square, by the equestrian statue of King Charles III, and survey the scene.*

▲▲Puerta del Sol

The bustling Puerta del Sol is Madrid's—and Spain's—center. It's a hub for the Metro, *cercanías* (local) trains, revelers, protestors, and pickpockets. In recent years it has undergone a facelift to become a mostly pedestrianized, wide-open space. Nearly traffic-free, it's a popular site for political

demonstrations. Don't be surprised if you come across a large, peaceful protest here.

The equestrian statue in the middle of the square honors **King Charles III** (1716-1788) whose enlightened urban policies earned him the affectionate nickname "the best mayor of Madrid." He decorated the city squares with beautiful fountains, got those meddlesome Jesuits out of city government, established the public school system, mandated underground sewers, opened his private Retiro park to the general public, built the Prado, made the Royal Palace the wonder of Europe, and generally cleaned up Madrid. (For more on Charles, see page 450.)

Head to the uphill end of the square and find the **statue of a bear** pawing a tree—a symbol of Madrid since medieval times. Bears used to live in the royal hunting grounds outside the city. And the *madroño* trees produce a berry that makes the traditional *madroño* liqueur. Near the statue, locate the Metro entrance and the glass-fish entrance to the *cercanías* trains.

Charles III faces a red-and-white building with a bell tower. This was Madrid's first post office, founded by Charles III in the 1760s. Today it's the **county governor's office** (Residencia de la Comunidad de Madrid), home to the president who governs greater Madrid. The building is notorious for having once been dictator Francisco Franco's police headquarters. An amazing number of those detained and interrogated by the Franco police tried to "escape" by jumping out its windows to their deaths. Notice the hats of the civil guardsmen at the entry. It's said the hats have square backs, cleverly designed so that the men can lean against the wall while enjoying a cigarette.

Appreciate the **harmonious architecture** of the buildings that circle the square—yellow-cream, four stories, balconies of iron, shuttered windows, and balustrades along the rooflines (with TV antennas on top).

Crowds fill the square on New Year's Eve as the rest of Spain watches the Times Square-style action on TV. The bell atop the governor's office chimes 12 times, while Madrileños eat one grape for each ring to bring good luck through each of the next 12 months.

• *Cross the square, walking to the governor's office.*

Look at the curb directly in front of the entrance to the governor's office. The marker is **"kilometer zero,"** the symbolic center of Spain (with its six main highways indicated). Standing on the zero marker with your back to the governor's office, get oriented visually: At twelve o'clock (straight ahead), notice how the pedestrian commercial zone (with the huge El Corte Inglés department store) is thriving. At one o'clock starts the seedier Calle de la Montera, a street with shady characters and prostitutes

MADRID

Puerta del Sol to Royal Palace Loop

that leads to the trendy, pedestrianized Calle de Fuencarral. At three o'clock, the biggest Apple Store in Europe is set to open in late 2013; the Prado is about a mile farther to your right. At ten o'clock, you'll see the pedestrianized Calle del Arenal Street (which leads to the Royal Palace) dumping into this square...just where you will end this walk.

Near the entrance to the governor's office are **two plaques** tied to important dates, expressing thanks from the regional government to its citizens for assisting in times of dire need. To the left of the entry, a plaque on the wall honors those who helped during the terrorist bombings of March 11, 2004 (we have our 9/11—Spain commemorates its 3/11). A similar plaque on the right marks the spot where the war against Napoleon started in 1808. When Napoleon invaded Spain and tried to appoint his brother (rather than the Spanish heir) as king of Spain, an angry crowd gathered outside this building. The French soldiers attacked and simply massacred the mob. Painter Francisco de Goya, who worked just up the street, observed the event and captured the tragedy in

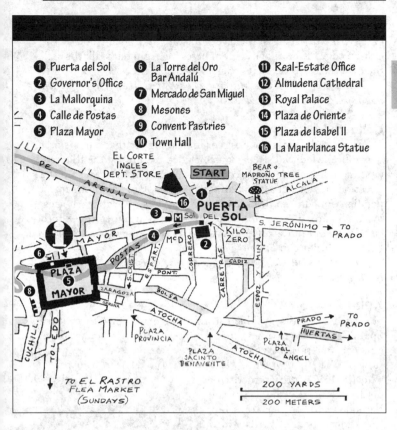

1. Puerta del Sol
2. Governor's Office
3. La Mallorquina
4. Calle de Postas
5. Plaza Mayor
6. La Torre del Oro Bar Andalú
7. Mercado de San Miguel
8. Mesones
9. Convent Pastries
10. Town Hall
11. Real-Estate Office
12. Almudena Cathedral
13. Royal Palace
14. Plaza de Oriente
15. Plaza de Isabel II
16. La Mariblanca Statue

his paintings *Second of May, 1808* and *Third of May, 1808*, now in the Prado.

On the corner of Calle Mayor and Puerta del Sol (downhill end of Puerta del Sol, across from McDonald's) is the busy *confitería* **La Mallorquina**, *"fundada en 1.894"* (daily 9:00-21:00, closed mid-July-Aug). Go inside for a tempting peek at racks with goodies hot out of the oven. Enjoy observing the churning energy at the bar lined with Madrileños popping in for a fast coffee and a sweet treat. The shop is famous for its cream-filled *Napolitana* pastry (€1.20). Or sample Madrid's answer to doughnuts, *rosquillas* (*tontas* means "silly"—plain, and *listas* means "all dressed up and ready to go"—with icing, about €0.50 each). The room upstairs is more genteel, with nice views of the square. Buy a pastry. (Even if you don't finish it, there's always a beggar outside who'd love to.)

From inside the shop, look back toward the entrance and notice the tile above the door with the 18th-century view of Puerta del Sol. Compare this with today's view out the door. This was before the square was widened, when a church stood at its top end.

Puerta del Sol ("Gate of the Sun") is named for a long-gone gate, with the rising sun carved onto it, that once stood at the eastern edge of the old city. From here, we begin our walk through the historic town that dates back to medieval times.

• *Head west on busy Calle Mayor, just past McDonald's, and veer left up the pedestrian alley called...*

Calle de Postas

The street sign shows the post coach heading for that famous first post office. Medieval street signs included pictures so the illiterate (and monolingual tourists) could "read" them. Fifty yards up the street on the left, at Calle San Cristóbal, is Pans & Company, a popular Catalan sandwich chain offering lots of healthy choices. While Spaniards consider American fast food unhealthy—both culturally and physically—they love it. McDonald's and Burger King are thriving in Spain.

• *Continue up Calle de Postas, and take a slight right on Calle de la Sal through the arcade, where you emerge into...*

▲Plaza Mayor

This square is a vast, cobbled, traffic-free chunk of 17th-century Spain. In medieval times, this was the city's main square. The

equestrian statue (wearing a ruffled collar) honors Philip III, who (in 1619) transformed the medieval marketplace into a Baroque plaza. The square is 140 yards long and 102 yards wide, enclosed by three-story buildings with symmetrical windows, balconies, slate roofs, and steepled towers. Each side of the square is uniform, as if a grand palace were turned inside-out. This distinct "look," pioneered by architect Juan de Herrera (who finished El Escorial), is found all over Madrid.

This site served as the city's 17th-century open-air theater. Upon this stage, much Spanish history has been played out: bullfights, fires, royal pageantry, and events of the gruesome Inquisition. Worn-down reliefs on the seatbacks under the lampposts tell the story. During the Inquisition, many were tried here—suspected heretics, Protestants, Jews, tour guides without a local license, and Muslims whose "conversion" to Christianity was dubious. The guilty were paraded around the square before their executions, wearing billboards listing their many sins (bleachers were built for bigger audiences, while the wealthy rented balconies). The heretics were burned, and later, criminals were slowly strangled as they held a crucifix, hearing the reassuring words of a priest as this life was squeezed out of them with a garrote.

The square's buildings are mainly private apartments. Want one? Costs run from €400,000 for a tiny attic studio to €2 million and up for a 2,500-square-foot flat. The square is painted a democratic shade of burgundy—the result of a citywide vote. Since the end of decades of dictatorship in 1975, there's been a passion for voting here. Three different colors were painted as samples on the walls of this square, and the city voted for its favorite.

A stamp-and-coin market bustles at Plaza Mayor on Sundays (10:00-14:00). The Casa Yustas shop at #30 (in the northeast corner) has been making hats here since 1894.

The building to Philip's left, on the north side beneath the twin towers, was once home to the baker's guild and now houses the TI. It's wonderfully air-conditioned and offers cheap daily walking tours. Consider reserving a spot now (for details, see "Tours in Madrid," earlier).

Day or night, Plaza Mayor is a colorful place to enjoy an affordable cup of coffee or overpriced food. Throughout Spain, lesser *plazas mayores* provide peaceful pools in the whitewater river of Spanish life.

• *For some interesting, if gruesome, bullfighting lore, drop by...*

La Torre del Oro Bar Andalú

This bar is a good place to finish off your Plaza Mayor visit (north side of the square at #26, a few doors to the left of the TI). The bar has *Andalú* (Andalusian) ambience and an entertaining staff. Step inside, stand at the bar, and order a drink—a *caña* (small draft beer) shouldn't cost more than €2. Warning: They may push expensive tapas on tourists. The price list posted outside the door makes your costs perfectly clear: "*barra*" indicates the price at the bar; "*terraza*" is the price at an outdoor table.

The interior is a temple to bullfighting, festooned with gory decor. Notice the breathtaking action captured in the many photographs. Look under the stuffed head of Barbero the bull. At eye level you'll see a *puntilla*, the knife used to put poor Barbero out of his misery at the arena. The plaque explains: weight, birth date, owner, date of death, which matador killed him, and the location. Just to the left of Barbero, there's a photo of longtime dictator Franco with the famous bullfighter Manuel Benítez Pérez—better known as El Cordobés, the Elvis of bullfighters and a working-class hero. At the top of the stairs to the WC, find the photo of El Cordobés and Robert Kennedy—looking like brothers. Under them is a shot of Che Guevara enjoying a bullfight.

At the end of the bar, in a glass case, is the "suit of lights" the great El Cordobés wore in an ill-fated 1967 fight, in which the bull gored him. El Cordobés survived; the bull didn't. Find the photo of Franco with El Cordobés at the far end, to the left of Segador the bull. Under the bull (to the left, over the counter) is a photo of El Cordobés' illegitimate son kissing a bull. Disowned by El Cordobés senior, yet still using his dad's famous name after a court battle, the junior El Cordobés is one of this generation's top fighters.

Back in the case with the "suit of lights," notice the photo of a matador (not El Cordobés) horrifyingly hooked by a bull's horn. For a series of photos showing this episode (and the same matador healed afterwards), look to the left of Barbero back by the door.

Consider taking a break at one of Torre del Oro's sidewalk tables (or at any café/bar terrace facing Madrid's grandest square). Cafetería Margerit (nearby) occupies the sunniest corner of the square and is a good place to enjoy a coffee with the view. The scene is easily worth the extra euro you'll pay for the drink.

• *Leave Plaza Mayor on Calle de Ciudad Rodrigo (at the northwest corner of the square), passing a series of solid turn-of-the-20th-century storefronts and sandwich joints, such as Casa Rúa, famous for their cheap* bocadillos de calamares—*fried squid rings on a roll. Emerging from the arcade, turn left and head downhill toward the covered market hall.*

Mercado de San Miguel

To wash down those *calamares* in a more refined setting, pop into the Mercado de San Miguel (daily 10:00-24:00, later on weekends). This historic iron-and-glass structure from 1916 stands on the site of an even earlier marketplace. Renovated in the 21st century, it now hosts some 30 high-end vendors of fresh produce, gourmet foods, wines by the glass, tapas, and full meals. Locals and tourists alike pause here for its food, natural-light ambience, and social scene.

Alongside the market, look down the street called Cava de San Miguel. If you like singing and sangria, come back after 22:00 and visit one of the *mesones* that line the street. These cave-like bars, stretching far back from the street, get packed with Madrileños out on dates who—emboldened by sangria and the setting—are prone to suddenly breaking out in song. It's a lowbrow, electric-keyboard, karaoke-type ambience, best on Friday and Saturday nights. The odd shape of these bars isn't a contrivance for the sake of atmosphere—Plaza Mayor was built on a slope, and these underground vaults are part of a structural system that braces the leveled plaza.

• *From the front of the market, continue west a few steps, then turn left, heading downhill on Calle del Conde de Miranda. At the first corner, turn right and cross the small plaza to the brick church in the far corner.*

Church and Convent of Corpus Christi

The proud coats of arms over the main entry announce the rich family that built this Hieronymite church and convent in 1607. In 17th-century Spain, the most prestigious thing a noble family could do was build and maintain a convent. To harvest all the goodwill created in your community, you'd want your family's insignia right there for all to see. (You can see the donating couple, like a 17th-century Bill and Melinda, kneeling before the communion wafer in the central panel over the entrance.) Inside is a quiet oasis with a Last Supper altarpiece.

Now for a unique shopping experience. A half-block uphill from the church entrance is its associated convent—it's the big brown door on the left, at Calle del Codo 3 (Mon-Sat 9:30-13:00 & 16:00 18:30, closed Sun). The sign reads: *Venta de Dulces* (Sweets for Sale). To buy goodies from the cloistered nuns, buzz the *monjas* button, then wait patiently for the sister to respond over the intercom. Say *"dulces"* (DOOL-thays), and she'll let you in. When the lock buzzes, push open the door and follow the sign to the *torno*, the lazy Susan that lets the sisters sell their baked goods without being seen. Scan the menu, announce your choice to the sequestered sister, place your money on the *torno*, and your goodies (and change) will appear. Of the many choices listed, *galletas* (shortbread cookies) are the least expensive (a *medio*-kilo costs about €8). Or try the *pastas de almendra* (almond cookies).

• *Continue uphill on Calle del Codo (where those in need of bits of armor shopped—see the street sign) and turn left, heading toward the Plaza de la Villa (pictured here). Before entering the square, notice an* **old door** *to the left of the* Real Sociedad Económica *sign, made of wood lined with metal. This is considered the oldest door in town*  *on Madrid's oldest building—inhabited since 1480. It's set in a Moorish keyhole arch. Look up at what was a prison tower. Now continue into the square called Plaza de la Villa, dominated by Madrid's...*

Town Hall

The impressive structure features Madrid's distinctive architectural style—symmetrical square towers, topped with steeples and a slate roof. The building still functions as Madrid's ceremonial Town Hall, though the city council and hands-on duties have moved elsewhere. Over the doorway, the three coats of arms sport many symbols of Madrid's rulers: Habsburg crowns, castles of Castile, and (the shield on the left) the city symbol—the berry-eating bear. This square was the ruling center of medieval Madrid, a tiny remnant of the 14th-century town. Even before then, when Madrid was an Arab-Moorish community, this was the only square in town.

Imagine how Philip II took this city by surprise in 1651 when he decided to move the capital of Europe's largest empire (even bigger than ancient Rome at the time) from Toledo to humble Madrid. To better administer their empire, the Habsburgs went on a building spree. But because their empire was drained of its riches by prolonged religious wars, they built Madrid with cheap brick instead of elegant granite.

The statue in the garden is of Philip II's admiral, Don Alvaro de Bazán—mastermind of the Christian victory over the Turkish Ottomans at the naval battle of Lepanto in 1571. This pivotal battle, fought off the coast of Greece, slowed the Ottoman threat to Christian Europe. However, mere months after Bazán's death in 1588, his "invincible" Spanish Armada was destroyed by England...and Spain's empire began its slow fade.

• *From here, busy Calle Mayor leads downhill toward the Royal Palace.*

Sights Along Calle Mayor

Two blocks down Calle Mayor (at #75, on the left, next to a venerable bakery), a real-estate office *(inmobiliaria)* advertises apartments and condos. Places for rent *(alquilar)*, priced by the month, are in the hundreds or low thousands of euros. Those for sale *(venta)* have six-digit prices. To roughly convert square meters to square feet, multiply by 10.

A few steps farther down, on a tiny square, a **statue** memorializes a 1906 assassination attempt. The target was Spain's King Alfonso XIII and his bride, Victoria Eugenie, as they paraded by on their wedding day. While the crowd was throwing flowers, an anarchist (what terrorists used to be called) threw a bouquet lashed to a bomb from a balcony at #84 (across the street). He missed the royal newlyweds, but killed 23 people. Gory photos of the event hang inside the recommended Casa Ciriaco restaurant, which now occupies #84 (photos to the right of the entrance). The king and queen went on to live to a ripe old age, producing many grandchildren, including today's King Juan Carlos.

• *Continue down Calle Mayor one more block to a busy street, Calle de Bailén. Take in the big, domed...*

Almudena Cathedral
(Catedral de Nuestra Señora de la Almudena)

Madrid's massive, gray-and-white cathedral (110 yards long and 80 yards high) opened in 1993, 100 years after workers started building it. This is the side entrance for tourists (€1 donation requested). The main entrance (selling €6 museum-and-cupola tickets) is a block north, facing the Royal Palace. If you go inside, you'll see a refreshingly modern and colorful ceiling, a glittering 5,000-pipe organ, and a grand 15th-century painted altarpiece—striking in the otherwise Neo-Gothic interior. The highlight is the 12th-century coffin (empty, painted leather on wood, in a chapel behind the altar) of Madrid's patron saint, Isidro. A humble farmer, the exceptionally devout Isidro was said to have been helped by angels who did the plowing for him while he prayed. Forty years after he died, this coffin was opened, and his body was found to have been miraculously preserved. This convinced the pope to canonize Isidro as the patron saint of Madrid and of farmers, with May 15 as his feast day.

Turn right on Calle de Bailén to reach the main entrance. The doors feature reliefs of the cathedral's 1993 consecration, including one with Pope John Paul II, King Juan Carlos, and Queen Sofía.

• *From the cathedral's front steps, face the imposing...*

Royal Palace

Since the ninth century, this spot has been Madrid's center of power: from Moorish castle to Christian fortress to Renaissance palace to the current structure, built in the 18th century. With its expansive courtyard surrounded by imposing Baroque architecture, it represents the wealth of Spain before its decline. Its 2,800 rooms, totaling nearly 1.5 million square feet, make it Europe's largest palace.

• *You could visit the palace now, using my self-guided tour (see page 446). Or, to follow the rest of this walk back to Puerta del Sol, continue one long block north up Calle de Bailén (walking alongside the palace) to where the street opens up into...*

Plaza de Oriente

As its name suggests, this square faces east. The grand yet people-friendly plaza is typical of today's Europe, where energetic governments are converting car-congested wastelands into public spaces like this. A recent mayor of Madrid earned the nickname "The Mole" for all the digging he did. Where's the traffic? Under your feet.

Spain's Royal Families: From Habsburg to Bourbon

Spain as we know it was born when four long-established medieval kingdoms were joined by the 1469 marriage of Isabel, ruler
of Castile and León, and Ferdinand, ruler of Aragon and Navarre.
The so-called "Catholic Monarchs" (Reyes Católicos) wasted no
time in driving the Islamic Moors out of Spain (the Reconquista).
By 1492, Isabel and Ferdinand conquered a fifth kingdom,
Granada, establishing more or less the same borders that Spain
has today.

This was an age when "foreign policy" was conducted, in
part, by marrying royal children into other royal families. Among
the dynastic marriages of their children, Isabel and Ferdinand
arranged for their third child, Juana "the Mad," to marry the
crown prince of Austria, Philip "the Fair." This was a huge coup
for the Spanish royal family. A member of the Habsburg dynasty,
Philip was heir to the Holy Roman Empire, which then encom-
passed much of today's Austria, Czech Republic, Hungary,
Transylvania, the Low Countries, southern Italy, and more. And
when Juana's brothers died, making her ruler of the kingdoms
of Spain, it paved the way for her son, Charles, to inherit the
kingdoms of his four grandparents—creating a vast realm and
famously making him the most powerful man in Europe. He ruled
as both Charles I (a.k.a. Carlos I) of Spain (1516) and Charles V of
the Holy Roman Empire (1519).

He was followed by Philip II, Philip III, Philip IV, and finally
Charles II. Over this period, Spain rested on its Golden Age lau-
rels, eventually squandering much of its wealth and losing some
of its holdings. Arguably the most inbred of an already very
inbred dynasty (his parents were uncle and niece), Charles II was
weak, sickly, and unable to have children, ending the 200-year
Habsburg dynasty in Spain with his death in 1700.

Charles II willed the Spanish crown to the Bourbons of
France, and his grandnephew Philip of Anjou, whose grand-

Notice the quiet. You're surrounded by more than three
million people, yet you can hear the birds, bells, and fountain. The
park is decorated with statues of Visigothic kings who ruled from
the third to seventh century. Romans allowed them to administer
their province of Hispania on the condition that they'd provide
food and weapons to the empire. The Visigoths inherited real
power after Rome fell, but lost it to invading Moors in 711. The
fine bronze equestrian statue of Philip IV (honoring the king who
built the Royal Palace) was a striking technical feat in its day, as
the horse stood up on its hind legs (possible only with the help
of Galileo's clever calculations and by using the tail for more
support). The king faces Madrid's opera house, the 1,700-seat

daddy was the "Sun King" Louis XIV of France, took the throne. But the rest of Europe feared allowing the already powerful Louis XIV to add Spain (and its vast New World holdings) to his empire. Austria, the Germanic States, Holland, and England backed a different choice (Archduke Charles of Austria). So began the War of Spanish Succession (1700-1714), involving all of Europe. The French eventually prevailed, but with the signing of the Treaty of Utrecht (1713), Philip had to give up any claim to the throne of France. This let him keep the Spanish crown but ensured that his heirs—the future Spanish Bourbon dynasty—couldn't become too powerful by merging with the French Bourbons.

In 1714, the French-speaking Philip became the first king of the Bourbon dynasty in Spain (with the name Philip V). He breathed much-needed new life into the monarchy, which had grown ineffectual and corrupt under the inbred Habsburgs. When the old wooden Habsburg royal palace burned on Christmas Eve of 1734, Philip (who was born at Versailles) built a new and spectacular late-Baroque-style palace as a bold symbol of his new dynasty. This is the palace that wows visitors to Madrid today. Construction was finished in 1764, and Philip V's son Charles III was the palace's first occupant. Charles III's decorations are what you'll see if you visit the palace's interior.

The Bourbon palace remained the home of Spain's kings from 1764 until 1931, when democratic elections led to the Second Spanish Republic and forced King Alfonso XIII into exile. After Francisco Franco took power in 1939, he sidelined the royals by making himself ruler-for-life. But later he handpicked as his successor Alfonso XIII's grandson, the Bourbon Prince Juan Carlos, whom Franco believed would continue his hardline policies. When Franco died in 1975, Juan Carlos surprised everyone by voluntarily turning the real power back over to Spain's parliament. Today Spain is a constitutional monarchy with a figurehead Bourbon king—Juan Carlos I—still at the helm.

Royal Theater (Teatro Real), rebuilt in 1997. To your left, in the distance, the once-impressive **Madrid Tower** skyscraper (460 feet tall, built of concrete in 1957) marks Plaza de España (and the end of my "Gran Vía Tour"—see page 476).

• *Walk along the Royal Theater, on the right side, to the...*

Plaza de Isabel II

This square is marked by a statue of Isabel II, who ruled Spain in the 19th century. Although she's immortalized here, Isabel had a rocky reign, marked by uprisings and political intrigue. A revolution in 1868 forced her to abdicate, and she lived out her life in exile.

MADRID

Madrid at a Glance

▲▲▲**Royal Palace** Spain's sumptuous, lavishly furnished national palace. **Hours:** Daily April-Sept 10:00-20:00, Oct-March 10:00-18:00. See page 445.

▲▲▲**Prado Museum** One of the world's great museums, loaded with masterpieces by Diego Velázquez, Francisco de Goya, El Greco, Hieronymus Bosch, Albrecht Dürer, and more. **Hours:** Mon-Sat 10:00-20:00, Sun 10:00-19:00. See page 456.

▲▲▲**Centro de Arte Reina Sofía** Modern-art museum featuring Picasso's epic masterpiece *Guernica*. **Hours:** Mon and Wed-Sat 10:00-21:00, Sun 10:00-19:00, closed Tue. See page 469.

▲▲**Puerta del Sol** Madrid's lively central square. **Hours:** Always bustling. See page 430.

▲▲**Thyssen-Bornemisza Museum** A great complement to the Prado, with lesser-known yet still impressive works and an especially good Impressionist collection. **Hours:** Mon 12:00-16:00, Tue-Sun 10:00-19:00, until 22:00 Tue-Sat in summer. See page 468.

▲▲**Bullfight** Spain's controversial pastime. **Hours:** Scattered Sundays and holidays March-mid-Oct, plus almost daily in May-early June. See page 483.

▲▲**Flamenco** Captivating music and dance performances, at various venues throughout the city. **Hours:** Shows every night, some places closed on Sun. See page 487.

▲**Plaza Mayor** Historic cobbled square. **Hours:** Always open. See page 434.

▲**Retiro Park** Festive green escape from the city, with rental

Evidence of Moorish walls turn up in this neighborhood and elsewhere in Madrid. Check out the tactile model in this square: The position of the old Moorish fortress and walls is outlined, with the modern city faintly depicted underneath. Feel it. Notice also the grooved sidewalk you're standing on—designed for the white canes of people who can't see. These grooved sidewalks are all over southern Europe, and no one has ever seen anyone using them. (I'm all for heroic measures in the name of accessibility, but if anyone does the pro-rated cost, it would be cheaper to provide private sedan chairs.)

rowboats and great people-watching. **Hours:** Closes at dusk. See page 475.

▲**Royal Botanical Garden** A relaxing museum of plants, with specimens from around the world. **Hours:** Daily 10:00-21:00, until 18:00 in winter. See page 475.

▲**Naval Museum** Seafaring history of a country famous for its Armada. **Hours:** Tue-Sun 10:00-19:00, closed Mon and Aug. See page 475.

▲**Museum of the Americas** Pre-Columbian and colonial artifacts from the New World. **Hours:** Tue-Sat 9:30-20:30, until 18:30 in off-season, Sun 10:00-15:00, closed Mon. See page 479.

▲**National Archaeological Museum** Traces the history of Iberia through artifacts. Reopening after major renovation in late 2013. **Hours:** Likely Tue-Sat 9:30-20:00, Sun 9:30-15:00, closed Mon. See page 479.

▲**Clothing Museum** A clothes look at the 18th to 21st century. **Hours:** Tue-Sat 9:30-19:00, Sun 10:00-15:00, Thu until 22:30 in summer, closed Mon. See page 480.

▲**Hermitage of San Antonio de la Florida** Church with Goya's tomb, plus frescoes by the artist. **Hours:** Tue-Sun 9:30-20:00, closed Mon. See page 480.

▲**El Rastro** Europe's biggest flea market, filled with bargains and pickpockets. **Hours:** Sun 9:00-15:00, best before 11:00. See page 485.

▲**Zarzuela** Madrid's delightful light opera. **Hours:** Evenings. See page 486.

• *From here, follow Calle del Arenal, walking gradually uphill. You're heading straight to Puerta del Sol.*

Calle del Arenal

As depicted on the tiled street signs, this was the "street of sand"—where sand was stockpiled during construction. Each cross street is named for a medieval craft that, historically, was plied along that lane (for example, "Calle de Bordadores" means "Street of the Embroiderers"). Wander slowly uphill. As you stroll, imagine this street as a traffic inferno—which it was until the city pedestrianized it a decade ago. Notice also how orderly the side streets are. Where a mess of cars once lodged chaotically on the sidewalks, smart bollards *(bolardos)* now keep vehicles off the walkways. The fancier facades (such as the former International Hotel at #19) are in the "eclectic" style (Spanish for Historicism— meaning a new interest in old styles) of the late 19th century.

The brick **St. Ginés Church** (on the right) means temptation to most locals. It marks the turn to the best *chocolatería* in town. From the uphill corner of the church, look to the end of the lane where—like a high-calorie red-light zone—a neon sign spells out *Chocolatería San Ginés*...every local's favorite place for hot chocolate and *churros* (always open). Also notice the charming bookshop clinging like a barnacle to the wall of the church. It's been selling books on this spot since 1650.

Next door is the **Joy Eslava disco,** a former theater famous for operettas in the Gilbert-and-Sullivan days and now a popular club. In Spain, when you're 18 you can do it all (buy tobacco, drink, drive, serve in the military). This place is an alcohol-free disco for the younger kids until midnight, when it becomes a thriving adult space, with the theater floor and balconies all teeming with clubbers. Their slogan: "Go big or go home."

Next, at #11, **Fútbol House** carries team regalia, postcards of today's stars, official mouthguards, and so on for soccer fans. Many Europeans come to Madrid primarily to see its 80,000-seat Bernabéu soccer stadium. The Starbucks on the next corner (opposite) is popular with young locals for its inviting ambience and American-style muffins, even though the coffee is too tame for many Spaniards.

Kitty-corner from there (at #7) is **Ferpal,** an old-school deli with an inviting bar and easy takeout options. Wallpapered with ham hocks, it's famous for selling the finest Spanish cheeses, hams, and other tasty treats. Spanish saffron is half what you'd pay for it back in the US. While they sell quality sandwiches, cheap and ready-made, it's fun to buy some bread and—after a little tasting—choose a ham or cheese for a memorable picnic or snack. If you're lucky, you may get to taste a tiny bit of Spain's best ham (Ibérico de Bellota). Close your eyes and let the taste fly you to a land of very happy acorn-fed pigs.

Across the street, in a little mall (at #8), a lovable mouse cherished by Spanish children is celebrated with a six-inch-tall bronze statue in the lobby. Upstairs is the fanciful **Casita Museo de Ratón Pérez** (€2.50, daily 11:00-14:00 & 17:00-20:00, Spanish only) with a fun window display. A steady stream of adoring children and their parents pour through here to learn about the wondrous mouse who is Spain's tooth fairy.

On the other side of the street (#3, opposite Burger King) is

Pronovias, a famous Spanish wedding-dress shop that attracts brides-to-be from across Europe. Computer terminals inside let young women virtual-shop for the dress of their dreams.

• *You're just a few steps from where you started this walk, at Puerta del Sol. Back in the square, you're met by a statue popularly known as La Mariblanca. This mythological Spanish Venus—with Madrid's coat of arms at her feet—stands tall amid all the modernity, as if protecting the people of this great city.*

Sights in Madrid

▲▲▲Royal Palace (Palacio Real)

This is Europe's third-greatest palace, after Versailles and Vienna's Schönbrunn. It has arguably the most sumptuous original interior, packed with tourists and royal antiques.

The palace is the product of many kings over several centuries. Philip II (1527-1598) made a wooden fortress on this  site his governing center when he established Madrid as Spain's capital. When that palace burned down, the current structure was built by King Philip V (1683-1746). Philip V wanted to make it his own private Versailles, to match his French upbringing: He was born in Versailles—the grandson of Louis XIV—and ordered his tapas in French. His son, Charles III (whose statue graces Puerta del Sol), added interior decor in the Italian style, since he'd spent his formative years in Italy. These civilized Bourbon kings were trying to raise Spain to the cultural level of the rest of Europe. They hired foreign artists to oversee construction and established local Spanish porcelain and tapestry factories to copy works done in Paris or Brussels. Over the years, the palace was expanded and enriched, as each Spanish king tried to outdo his predecessor.

Today's palace is ridiculously super-sized—with 2,800 rooms, tons of luxurious tapestries, a king's ransom of chandeliers, frescoes by Tiepolo, priceless porcelain, and bronze decor covered in gold leaf. While these days the royal family lives in a mansion a few miles away, this place still functions as the ceremonial palace, used for formal state receptions, royal weddings, and tourists' daydreams.

Cost and Hours: €10 without a tour, €17 with a one-hour tour (explained later); daily April-Sept 10:00-20:00, Oct-March 10:00-18:00, last entry one hour before closing; tel. 914-548-800, www.patrimonionacional.es. The palace can close for royal functions—

call ahead to check.

Crowd-Beating Tips: The palace is most crowded on Wednesdays and Thursdays, when it's free for locals. On any day, arrive early or go late to avoid lines and crowds. Madrid Card holders get to skip the line: Enter around the right side at the group entry point, a block down, along Calle de Bailén.

Getting There: From Puerta del Sol, walk 15 minutes down the pedestrianized Calle del Arenal. Metro: Ópera.

Tours: You can wander on your own or join a €7 **tour.** Check the time of the next English-language tour and decide as you buy your ticket; the tours are dry, depart sporadically, and aren't worth a long wait. The museum **guidebook** demonstrates a passion for meaningless data. The excellent €4 **audioguide** is much more interesting.

Services: Free lockers and a WC are just past the ticket booth. Upstairs you'll find a refreshing air-conditioned cafeteria (with salad bar) and a more serious bookstore with good books on Spanish history.

Photography: Not allowed.

❷ Self-Guided Tour

You'll follow a simple, 24-room, one-way circuit on a single floor. The short English descriptions posted in each room complement what I describe below.

• *Buy your ticket, pass through the bookstore, stand in the middle of the vast open-air courtyard, and face the palace entrance.*

The Palace Exterior: The palace sports the French-Italian Baroque architecture so popular in the 18th century—heavy columns, classical-looking statues, a balustrade roofline, and false-front entrance. The entire building is made of gray-and-white local stone (very little wood) to prevent the kind of fire that leveled the previous palace. Imagine the place in its heyday, with a courtyard full of soldiers on parade, or a lantern-lit scene of horse carriages arriving for a ball.

• *Enter the palace and show your ticket.*

The Palace Lobby: In the old days, horse-drawn carriages would drop you off here. Today, stretch limos do the same thing for gala events. (If you're taking a guided palace tour, this is where you wait to begin.) The modern black bust in the corner is of the current, very popular constitutional monarch—King Juan Carlos I. He's a "people's king," credited with bringing democracy to Spain after 36 years under dictator Franco.

The Grand Stairs: Gazing up the imposing staircase, you can see that Spain's kings wanted to make a big first impression. Whenever high-end dignitaries arrive, fancy carpets are rolled down the stairs (notice the little metal bar-holding hooks). Begin

MADRID

Tiepolo's Frescoes

In 1762, King Charles III invited Europe's most celebrated palace painter, Giambattista Tiepolo (1696-1770), to decorate three rooms in the newly built palace. Sixty-six-year-old

Tiepolo made the trip from Italy with his two well-known sons as assistants. They spent four years atop scaffolding decorating in the fresco technique, troweling plaster on the ceiling and quickly painting it before it dried.

Tiepolo's translucent ceilings seem to open up to a cloud-filled heaven, where Spanish royals cavort with Greek gods and pudgy cherubs. Tiepolo used every trick to "fool the eye" (trompe l'oeil), creating dizzying skyscapes of figures tumbling at every angle. He mixes 2-D painting with 3-D stucco figures that spill over the picture frame. His colorful, curvaceous ceilings blend seamlessly with the flamboyant furniture of the room below. Tiepolo's Royal Palace frescoes are often cited as the final flowering of Baroque and Rococo art.

your ascent, up steps that are intentionally shallow, making your climb slow and regal. Overhead, the white-and-blue ceiling fresco gradually opens up to your view. It shows the Spanish king, sitting on clouds, surrounded by female Virtues.

At the first landing, the blue-and-red coat of arms represents Juan Carlos. While dictator Franco chose him to be his successor, J. C. knew Spain was ripe for democracy. Rather than become "Juan the Brief" (as some were nicknaming him), he returned real power to the parliament. You'll see his (figure) head on the back of the Spanish €1 and €2 coins.

Continue up to the top of the stairs. Before entering the first room, look to the right of the door to find a white marble bust of J. C.'s great-great-g-g-g-great-grandfather Philip V, who began the Bourbon dynasty in Spain in 1700 and had this palace built.

Guard Room: The palace guards used to hang out in this relatively simple room. Notice the two fake doors, added to give the room symmetry. The old clocks—still in working order—are part of a collection of hundreds amassed as a hobby by Spain's royal family. Throughout the palace, the themes chosen for the ceiling frescoes relate to the function of the room they decorate. In this room, the ceiling fresco is the first we'll see in a series by the great Venetian painter Giambattista Tiepolo (see sidebar). It depicts the legendary hero Aeneas (in red, with the narrow face of Charles III) standing in the clouds of heaven, gazing up at his mother Venus (with the face of Charles' own mother).

Notice the carpets in this room. Although much of what you see in the palace dates from the 18th century, the carpet on the left (folded over to show the stitching) is new, from 1991. It was produced by Madrid's royal tapestry factory, the same works that made the older original carpet (displayed next to the modern one). Though recently produced, the new carpet was woven the traditional way—by hand. The fine inlaid stone table in this room is important to Spaniards because it was here, in 1985, that the king signed the treaty finalizing Spain's entry into the European Union.

Hall of Columns: Originally a ballroom and dining room, today this space is used for formal ceremonies and intimate concerts. This is where Spain formally joined the European Union in 1985 (the fancy table used to be in here) and honored its national soccer team after their 2010 World Cup victory. The tapestries (like most you'll see in the palace) are 17th-century Belgian, from designs by Raphael.

The central theme in the ceiling fresco (by Jaquinto, following Tiepolo's style) is Apollo driving the chariot of the sun, while Bacchus enjoys wine, women, and song with a convivial gang. This is a reminder that the mark of a good king is to drive the chariot of state as smartly as Apollo, while providing an environment where the people can enjoy life to the fullest.

Throne Room: This room, where the Spanish monarchs preside, is one of the palace's most glorious. And it holds many of the oldest and most precious things in the palace: silver-and-crystal chandeliers (from Venice's Murano Island), elaborate lions, and black bronze statues from the fortress that stood here before the 1734 fire. The 12 mirrors, impressively large in their day, each represent a different month.

The throne stands under a gilded canopy, on a raised platform, guarded by four lions (symbols of power found throughout the palace). The coat of arms above the throne shows the complexity of the Bourbon empire across Europe—which, in the 18th century, included Tirol, Sicily, Burgundy, the Netherlands, and more. Though the room was decorated under Charles III (late 18th century), the throne itself dates only from 1977. In Spain, a new throne is built for each king or queen, complete with a gilded portrait on the back. The room's chairs also indicate the current monarchs—"JC I" and "Sofía."

Today, this room is where the king's guests salute Juan Carlos before they move on to dinner. He receives them relatively informally...standing at floor level, rather than seated up on the throne.

The ceiling fresco (1764) is the last great work by Tiepolo (see sidebar), who died in Madrid in 1770. His vast painting (88 × 32 feet) celebrates the vast Spanish empire—upon which the sun also never set. The Greek gods look down from the clouds, overseeing Spain's empire, whose territories are represented by the people ringing the edges of the ceiling. Find the Native American (hint: follow the rainbow to the macho red-caped conquistador who motions to someone he conquered). From the near end of the room (where tourists stand), look up to admire Tiepolo's skill at making a pillar seem to shoot straight up into the sky. The pillar's pedestal has an inscription celebrating Tiepolo's boss, Charles III ("Carole Magna"). Notice how the painting spills over the gilded wood frame, where 3-D statues recline alongside 2-D painted figures. All of the throne room's decorations—the fresco, gold garlands, mythological statues, wall medallions—unite in a multimedia extravaganza.

• *The next several rooms were the living quarters of King Charles III (r. 1759-1788). First comes his **lounge** (with red walls), where the king would enjoy the company of a similarly great ruler—the Roman emperor Trajan—depicted "triumphing" on the ceiling. The heroics of Trajan, one of two Roman emperors born in Spain, naturally made the king feel good. Next, you enter the blue-walled...*

Antechamber: This was Charles III's dining room. The four paintings—all originals by Francisco de Goya—are of Charles III's son and successor, King Charles IV (looking a bit like a dim-witted George Washington), and his wife, María Luisa (who wore the pants in the palace). María Luisa was famously hands-on, tough, and business-like, while Charles IV was pretty wimpy as far as kings go. To meet the

demand for his work, Goya made copies of these portraits, which you'll see in the Prado.

The 12-foot-tall clock—showing Cronus, god of time, in porcelain, bronze, and mahogany—sits on a music box. Reminding us of how time flies, Cronus is shown both as a child and as an

Charles III
(1716-1788)

Of the many monarchs who've enlarged or redecorated the Royal Palace, it was Charles III who set the tone for its Baroque-Rococo interior. Charles' mother was Italian, and he spent his formative years in Italy. When he became Spain's king, he brought along sophisticated Italian artists to decorate his new home—the painter Tiepolo, the architect Sabatini, and the decorator Gasparini. They created some of the most elaborate, jaw-dropping rooms tourists see in the palace today.

Charles was an enlightened ruler who tried to reform Spain along democratic principles. He failed. After his death, Spain dwindled into repressive irrelevance. But over the centuries, each of his successors labored to top Charles in ostentatious decoration, making Madrid's Royal Palace his greatest legacy.

old man. The palace's clocks are wound—and reset—once a week (they grow progressively less accurate as the week goes on). The gilded decor you see throughout the palace is bronze with gold leaf. Velázquez's famous painting, *Las Meninas* (which you'll marvel at in the Prado), originally hung in this room.

Gasparini Room: (Gasp!) The entire room is designed, top to bottom, as a single gold-green-pink ensemble: from the frescoed ceiling, to the painted stucco figures, silk-embroidered walls, chandelier, furniture, and multicolored marble floor. Each marble was quarried in, and therefore represents, a different region of Spain. Birds overhead spread their wings, vines sprout, and fruit bulges from the surface. With curlicues everywhere (including their reflection in the mirrors), the room dazzles the eye and mind. It's a triumph of the Rococo style, with exotic motifs such as the Chinese people sculpted into the corners of the ceiling. (These figures, like many in the palace, were formed from stucco, or wet plaster.) The fabric gracing the walls was recently restored. Sixty people spent three years replacing the rotten silk fabric and then embroidering back on the silver, silk, and gold threads.

Note the micro-mosaic table—a typical royal or aristocratic souvenir from any visit to Rome in the mid-1800s. The chandelier, the biggest in the palace, is mesmerizing, especially with its glittering canopy of crystal reflecting in the wall mirrors.

The room was the king's dressing room. For a divine monarch, dressing was a public affair. The court bigwigs would assemble here as the king, standing on a platform—notice the height of the mirrors—would pull on his leotards and toy with his wig.

• *In the next room, the silk wallpaper is from modern times—the intertwined "J. C. S." indicates King Juan Carlos and Queen Sofía. Pass through the silk room to reach...*

Charles III Bedroom: Charles III died here in his bed in 1788. His grandson, Ferdinand VII, redid the room to honor the great man. The room's blue color scheme recalls the blue-clad monks of Charles' religious order. A portrait of Charles (in blue) hangs on the wall. The ceiling fresco shows Charles establishing his order, with its various (female) Virtues. At the base of the ceiling (near the harp player) find the baby in his mother's arms—that would be Ferdy himself, the long-sought male heir, preparing to continue Charles' dynasty.

The chandelier is in the shape of the fleur-de-lis (the symbol of the Bourbon family) capped with a Spanish crown. As you exit the room, notice the thick walls between rooms. These hid service corridors for servants, who scurried about mostly unseen.

Porcelain Room: This tiny but lavish room is paneled with green-white-gold porcelain garlands, vines, babies, and mythological figures. The entire ensemble was disassembled for safety during the civil war. (Find the little screws in the greenery that hides the seams between panels.) Notice the clock in the center with Atlas supporting the world on his shoulders.

Yellow Lounge: This was a study for Charles III. The properly cut crystal of the chandelier shows all the colors of the rainbow. Stand under it, look up, and sway slowly to see the colors glitter. This is not a particularly precious room. But its decor pops because the lights are generally left on. Imagine the entire palace as brilliant as this when fully lit. As you leave the room, look back at the chandelier to notice its design of a temple with a fountain inside.

• *Next comes the. . .*

Gala Dining Hall: Up to 12 times a year, the king entertains as many as 144 guests at this bowling lane-size table, which can be extended to the length of the room. The parquet floor was the preferred dancing surface when balls were held in this fabulous room. Note the vases from China, the tapestries, and the ceiling fresco depicting Christopher Columbus kneeling before Ferdinand and Isabel, presenting exotic souvenirs and his new, red-skinned friends. Imagine this hall in action when a foreign dignitary dines here. The king and queen preside from the center of the room. Find their chairs (slightly higher than the rest). The tables are set with fine crystal and cutlery (which we'll see a couple of rooms later). And the whole place glitters as the 15 chandeliers (and their 900 bulbs) are fired up.

• *Pass through the next room of coins and medals, known as the **Cinema Room** because the royal family once enjoyed Sunday afternoons at the movies here. The royal string ensemble played here to entertain during formal dinners. From here, move into the...*

Silver Room: Some of this 19th-century silver tableware—knives and forks, bowls, salt and pepper shakers, and the big tureen—is used in the Gala Dining Hall on special occasions. If you look carefully, you can see quirky royal necessities, including a baby's silver rattle and fancy candle-snuffers.

• *Head straight ahead to the...*

Crockery and Crystal Rooms: Philip V's collection of china is the oldest and rarest of the various pieces on display; it came from China before that country was opened to the West. Since Chinese crockery was in such demand, any self-respecting European royal family had to have its own porcelain works (such as France's Sèvres or Germany's Meissen) to produce high-quality knockoffs (and cutesy Hummel-like figurines). The porcelain technique itself was kept a royal secret. As you leave, check out Isabel II's excellent 19th-century crystal ware.

• *Exit to the hallway and notice the interior courtyard you've been circling one room at a time.*

Courtyard: You can see how the royal family lived in the spacious middle floor while staff was upstairs. The kitchens, garage, and storerooms were on the ground level. The current prince recently married a commoner (for love) and celebrated their wedding party in this courtyard, which was decorated as if another palace room. Spain's royals take their roles and responsibilities seriously, making a point to be approachable and empathizing with their subjects—and they are very popular (despite the antics of the younger generation and the elderly but frisky king).

• *Between statues of the giants of Spanish royal history (Isabel and Ferdinand), you'll enter the...*

Royal Chapel: This chapel is used for private concerts and funerals. The royal coffin sits here before making the sad trip to El Escorial to join the rest of Spain's past royalty (see next chapter). The glass case contains the entire body of St. Felix, given to the Spanish king by the pope in the 19th century. Note the "crying room" in the back for royal babies. While the royals rarely worship here (they prefer the cathedral adjacent to the palace), the thrones are here just in case.

• *Pass through the **Queen's Boudoir**—where royal ladies hung out—and into the...*

Stradivarius Room: The current queen likes classical music. When you perform for her, do it with these precious 350-year-old violins. Of all the instruments made by Antonius Stradivarius (1644-1737), only 300 survive. This is the world's best collection and the only matching quartet set: two violins, a viola, and a cello. Charles III, a cultured man, fiddled around with these. Today, a single Stradivarius instrument might sell for $15 million.

Billiards and Smoking Rooms: The billiards room (with its English men's-club paneling) and the adjacent smoking room were for men only. The porcelain and silk decoration of the trippy smoking room—showing Chinese workers, peacocks, and turtles—imitates a Chinese opium den, which, in its day, was furnished only with pillows.

Stucco Study: Small and intimate, the room has delicate Wedgwood-china-style decor featuring slender columns, vines, garlands, and birds. This Neoclassical mode became the rage in Europe after 1748, when the ancient Roman city of Pompeii was excavated. Next to the adjoining man-caves, the stucco study served as the hangout and gossip headquarters for ladies of the court.

Fine Woods Room: The same man who created the fabulous Gasparini Room gave us this fine room of French inlaid wood.

• *Exit the palace down the same grand stairway you climbed 24 rooms ago. Cross the big courtyard, heading to the far-right corner to the...*

Armory: Here you'll find weapons and armor belonging to many great Spanish historical figures. While some of it was actually for fighting, remember that the great royal pastimes included hunting and tournaments, and armor was largely for sport or ceremony. Much of this armor dates from Habsburg times, before this palace was built (it came here from the earlier fortress or from El Escorial). Circle the big room clockwise.

In the three glass cases on the left, you'll see the oldest pieces in the collection. In the central case (case III), the shield, sword, belt, and dagger belonged to Boabdil, the last Moorish king, who surrendered Granada in 1492. In case IV, the armor and swords are Ferdinand's, the husband of Isabel, and Boabdil's contemporary.

The center of the room is filled with knights in armor on horseback—mostly suited up for tournament play. Many of the pieces belonged to the two great kings who ruled Spain at its 16th-century peak, Charles I and his son Philip II.

The long wall on the left displays the personal armor wardrobe of Charles I (a.k.a. the Holy Roman emperor Charles V). At the far end, you'll meet Charles on horseback. The mannequin of the king wears the same armor and assumes the same pose as in Titian's famous painting of him (in the Prado).

The opposite wall showcases the armor and weapons of Philip II, the king who watched Spain start its long slide downward. Philip, who impoverished Spain with his wars against the

Protestants, anticipated that debt collectors would ransack his estate after his death and specifically protected his impressive collection of armor by founding this armory.

The tapestry above the armor once warmed the walls of the otherwise stark palace that predated this one. Tapestries traveled ahead of royals to decorate their living space. They made many palaces "fit for a king" back when the only way to effectively govern was to be on the road a lot.

Downstairs is more armor, a mixed collection mostly from the 17th century. You'll find early guns and Asian armor. The pint-size armor you may see wasn't for children to fight in. It's training armor for noble youngsters, who as adults would be expected to ride, fight, and play gracefully in these clunky getups. Before you leave, notice the life-saving breastplates dimpled with bullet dents (to right of exit door).

• *Climb the steps from the armory exit to the viewpoint.*

View of the Gardens: Looking down from this high bluff, it's clear why rulers have built on this strategically located spot (great for protecting the historic capital, Toledo) since the ninth century. The vast palace backyard, once the king's hunting ground, is now a city park, dotted with fountains.

• *Walk to the center of the huge square and face the palace. Notice how the palace of the king faces the palace of the bishop (the cathedral). Facing the palace, the weapons are on your left, and the royal pharmacy is on your right. It's all here: church, state, guns, and drugs.*

Royal Pharmacy: Wander through six rooms stacked with jars and jugs of herbal cures, past exotic beakers, and under portraits of royal doctors. See the kitchen where they cooked up all the goodies. The pharmacy is still in operation, after 400 years. Good English descriptions explain 18th- and 19th-century medicine.

• *Whew. After all those rooms, frescoes, chandeliers, knickknacks, kings, and history, consider a final stop in the palace's upstairs café for a well-deserved rest.*

Madrid's Museum Neighborhood

Three great museums, all within a 10-minute walk of one another, cluster in east Madrid. The Prado is Europe's top collection of paintings. The Thyssen-Bornemisza sweeps through European art from old masters to moderns. And the Centro de Arte Reina Sofía has a choice selection of modern art, starring Picasso's famous *Guernica*.

Combo-Ticket: If visiting all three museums, you can save a few euros by buying the **Paseo del Arte** combo-ticket (€21.60, sold at all three museums, good for a year). Note that the Prado is free to enter every evening, the Reina Sofía has free hours every

MADRID

Madrid's Museum Neighborhood

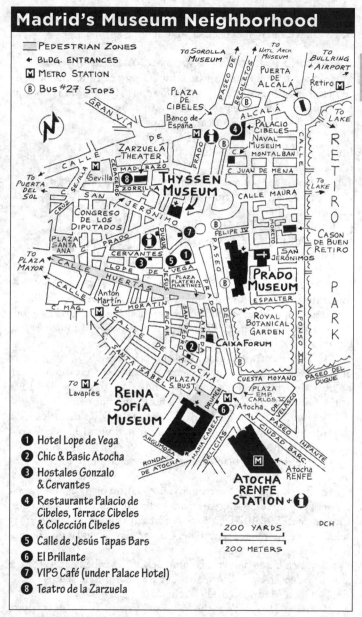

PEDESTRIAN ZONES
← BLDG. ENTRANCES
Ⓜ METRO STATION
Ⓑ BUS #27 STOPS

1 Hotel Lope de Vega
2 Chic & Basic Atocha
3 Hostales Gonzalo & Cervantes
4 Restaurante Palacio de Cibeles, Terrace Cibeles & Colección Cibeles
5 Calle de Jesús Tapas Bars
6 El Brillante
7 VIPS Café (under Palace Hotel)
8 Teatro de la Zarzuela

200 YARDS
200 METERS

DCH

night but Tuesday—when it's closed, and the Thyssen-Bornemisza is free on Monday (see specifics in following listings).

▲▲▲Prado Museum (Museo Nacional del Prado)

With more than 3,000 canvases, including entire rooms of masterpieces by superstar painters, the Prado (PRAH-doh) is my vote for the greatest collection anywhere of paintings by the European masters. The Prado is *the* place to enjoy the great Spanish painter Francisco de Goya, and it's also the home of Diego Velázquez's *Las Meninas,* considered by many to be the world's finest painting, period. In addition to Spanish works, you'll find paintings by Italian and Flemish masters, including Hieronymus Bosch's fantastical *Garden of Earthly Delights* altarpiece.

Cost and Hours: €14, additional (obligatory) charge for temporary exhibits, free Mon-Sat 18:00-20:00 and Sun 17:00-19:00, under age 18 always free; open Mon-Sat 10:00-20:00, Sun 10:00-19:00, last entry 30 minutes before closing.

Crowd-Beating Tips: Lunchtime (13:00-16:00), when there are fewer groups, and weekdays are generally less crowded. It can be busy on free evenings and weekends. The ticket-buying lines at the Goya entrance can be long. Those who book in advance (by phone or online) or have a Madrid Card can pick up their tickets at the adjacent group entrance, skipping the main line. Here are your time-saving options:

1. Use the ticket machines at the Goya entrance (credit cards only).

2. Book an entry time in advance online or by phone (www.museodelprado.es, use credit card and print out ticket with entry time; or call 902-107-077, give credit card number, chose entry time, and get a reference number). Same-day advance purchase is possible if space is available.

3. Buy a Paseo del Arte combo-ticket (described earlier) at the less-crowded Thyssen-Bornemisza or Reina Sofía museums.

4. Get a Madrid Card beforehand (see page 421).

Getting There: It's at the Paseo del Prado. The nearest Metro stops are Banco de España (line 2) and Atocha (line 1), each a five-minute walk from the museum. It's a 15-minute walk from Puerta del Sol.

Getting In: While there are several entrances, you must buy tickets at the Goya (north) entrance. (Even at free-entry times, you

MADRID

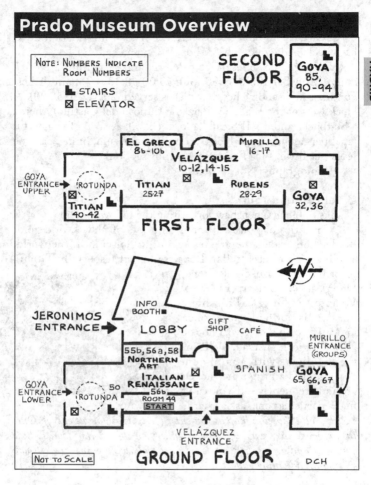

Prado Museum Overview

NOTE: NUMBERS INDICATE ROOM NUMBERS

◣ STAIRS
☒ ELEVATOR

SECOND FLOOR

GOYA 85, 90-94

EL GRECO 8b-10b

MURILLO 16-17

VELÁZQUEZ 10-12, 14-15

GOYA ENTRANCE UPPER →

ROTUNDA

TITIAN 25-27

RUBENS 28-29

TITIAN 40-42

GOYA 32, 36

FIRST FLOOR

—N—

JERONIMOS ENTRANCE →

INFO BOOTH

LOBBY

GIFT SHOP

CAFÉ

MURILLO ENTRANCE (GROUPS)

55b, 56a, 58 NORTHERN ART

ITALIAN RENAISSANCE 56b ROOM 49 START

SPANISH

GOYA 65, 66, 67

GOYA ENTRANCE LOWER →

ROTUNDA

50

VELÁZQUEZ ENTRANCE

NOT TO SCALE

GROUND FLOOR

DCH

need to pick up a gratis ticket at the Goya ticket window.) Once you have your ticket, you can enter at either the Goya, Jerónimos, or Velázquez entrances. The Murillo entrance is generally reserved for student groups.

Information: Tel. 913-302-800, www.museodelprado.es.

Audioguide: The €3.50 audioguide is a helpful supplement to my self-guided tour. Given the ever-changing locations of paintings (making my tour tough to follow), the audioguide is a good investment, allowing you to wander and dial up commentary on 250 masterpieces. And, if you're on a tight budget, remember that two can listen cheek-to-cheek, sharing one device. It comes with a standard jack (bring your own earbuds, and a splitter).

Cloakroom: Your bags will be scanned as you enter. Larger bags must be checked (free). No drinks, food, backpacks, or large umbrellas are allowed inside.

Services: The Jerónimos entrance has an information desk, bag check, audioguides, bookshop, WCs, and café.

Eating: The self-service cafeteria and restaurant are open daily (Mon-Sat 10:00-19:30, Sun 10:00-18:30, €9 main dishes, €6 salads and sandwiches, hot dishes served only 12:30-16:00). A block west of the Prado (at Plaza de Canova del Castillo), there's a Starbucks and a VIPS café (a local chain). A strip of wonderful tapas bars are just a few blocks east of the museum, lining Calle de Jésus (see listings in "Eating in Madrid" section).

Photography: Not allowed.

◒ Self-Guided Tour

Thanks to Gene Openshaw for writing the following tour.

Centuries of powerful kings (and lots of New World gold) funded the Prado, the greatest painting museum in the world. You'll see first-class Italian Renaissance art (especially Titian), Northern art (Bosch, Rubens, Dürer), and Spanish art (El Greco, Velázquez, Goya). This huge museum is not laid out chronologically, so this tour will not be chronological. Instead, we'll hit the highlights with a minimum of walking. Paintings are moved around frequently—if you can't find a particular one, ask a guard.

• *Pick up the museum map as you enter (free, available at entry). Once inside, make your way to the main gallery on the ground floor. Follow your map and signs to* sala 49. *Look for the following paintings in Room 49 and the adjoining galleries.*

Italian Renaissance

During its Golden Age (the 1500s), Spain may have been Europe's richest country, but Italy was still the most cultured. Spain's kings loved how Italian Renaissance artists captured a three-dimensional world on a two-dimensional canvas, bringing Bible scenes to life and celebrating real people and their emotions.

Raphael (1483-1520) was the undisputed master of realism. When he painted *The Cardinal* (*El Cardenal*, c. 1510), he showed the sly Vatican functionary with a day's growth of beard and an air of superiority, locking eyes with the viewer. The cardinal's slightly turned torso is as big as a statue. Nearby are Raphael's *Holy Family* and other paintings.

Fra Angelico's *The Annunciation* (*La Anunciación*, c. 1426) is in nearby Room 56b. It's half medieval piety, half Renaissance real-

ism. In the crude Garden of Eden scene (on the left), a scrawny, sinful First Couple hovers unrealistically above the foliage, awaiting eviction. The angel's Annunciation to Mary (right side) is more Renaissance, both with its upbeat message (that Jesus will be born to redeem sinners like Adam and Eve) and in the budding photorealism, set beneath 3-D arches. (Still, aren't the receding bars of the porch's ceiling a bit off? Painting three dimensions wasn't that easy.)

Nearby (likely in Room 56b), the tiny *Death of the Virgin (El Transito de la Virgen)*, by **Andrea Mantegna** (c. 1431-1506), shows his mastery of Renaissance perspective. The apostles crowd into the room to mourn the last moments of the Virgin Mary's life. The receding floor tiles and open window in the back create the subconscious effect of Mary's soul finding its way out into the serene distance.

• *Find examples of Northern European art, including Dürer, in Room 55b.*

Northern Art

Albrecht Dürer's *Self-Portrait (Autorretrato)*, from 1498, is possibly the first time an artist depicted himself. The artist, age 26, is German, but he's all dolled up in a fancy Italian hat and permed hair. He'd recently returned from Italy and wanted to impress his countrymen with his sophistication. Dürer (1471-1528) wasn't simply vain. He'd grown accustomed, as an artist in Renaissance Italy, to being treated like a prince. Note Dürer's signature, the pyramid-shaped "A. D." (D inside the A), on the windowsill.

Dürer's 1507 panel paintings of Adam and Eve are the first full-size nudes in Northern European art. Like Greek statues, they pose in their separate niches, with three-dimensional, anatomically correct bodies. This was a bold humanist proclamation that the body is good, man is good, and the things of the world are good.

• *Return to Room 49, and enter the adjoining Room 57b. Keep going until you find Room 58.*

Roger van der Weyden (c. 1399-1464)'s *Descent from the Cross*

(El Descendimiento) is a masterpiece. The Flemish painter reveals the psychological drama of this biblical event by placing the characters of real people in a contemporary (1435) scene. The Flemish were masters of detail, as you can see in the cloth, jewels, faces, and even tears. These effects are all enhanced by the artist's choice of oil paint, a relatively new and vibrant medium especially suited to conveying textural realism and intense color. The creative composition suggests that, in losing her son, Mary suffered along with Jesus. Note the realism, especially in the mournful faces, and the gorgeous arc of Mary Magdalene's pose (far right). As the Netherlands was then a part of the Spanish empire, this painting ended up in Madrid.

• *Continue to Room 56a.*

Hieronymus Bosch (c. 1450-1516), in his cryptic triptych *The Garden of Earthly Delights* (*El Jardín de las Delicias,* c. 1505), relates the message that the pleasures of life are fleeting, and we'd better avoid them or we'll wind up in hell.

This is a triptych—a three-paneled altarpiece, with a central image and two hinged outer panels. When the panels are closed, another image is revealed on their back side. All four images work together to teach a religious message. First notice the back side of this otherwise colorful work. It's a black-and-white scene depicting Creation on Day Three—before God added animals and humans to the mix. So, imagine the altarpiece closed. All is mellow. Then open it up, bring on the people, and splash into the colorful *Garden of Earthly Delights*.

On the left is Paradise, showing naked Adam and Eve before original sin. Everything is in its place, with animals behaving

virtuously. Innocent Adam and Eve get married, with God himself performing the ceremony.

The central panel is a riot of hedonistic men and women on a perpetual spring break. Men on horseback ride round and round, searching for but never reaching the elusive Fountain of Youth. Others frolic in earth's "Garden," oblivious to where they came from (left) and where they may end up (exit...right).

Now, go to Hell (right panel). It's a burning Dante's Inferno-inspired wasteland where genetic-mutant demons torture sinners. Everyone gets their just desserts, like the glutton who is eaten and re-eaten eternally, the musician strung up on his own harp, and the gamblers with their table forever overturned. In the center, hell is literally frozen over. A creature with a broken eggshell body hosting a tavern, tree-trunk legs, and a hat featuring a bagpipe (symbolic of hedonism) stares out—it's the face of Bosch himself.

If you like this Bosch, you'll enjoy the others in this gallery. The table in the center features his *Seven Deadly Sins (Los Pecados Capitales,* late 15th century). Each of the four corners has a theme: death, judgment, paradise, and hell. The fascinating wheel, with Christ in the center, names the sins in Latin (lust, envy, gluttony, and so on), and illustrates each with a vivid scene that works as a slice of 15th-century Dutch life.

Another triptych, *The Hay Wagon (El Carro de Heno,* c. 1516), hangs nearby. Like *The Garden of Earthly Delights*, and with the same vivid imagery, it teaches morality in what must have been a very effective and frightening way back when Bosch painted it.

Nearby, **Pieter Bruegel** the Elder's (c. 1525-1569) work chronicles the 16th century's violent Catholic-Protestant wars in *The Triumph of Death (El Triunfo de la Muerte).* The painting is one big, chaotic battle, featuring skeletons attacking helpless mortals. Bruegel's message is simple and morbid: No one can escape death.

• *But you can escape this room. Continue through the next few galleries (55a and 55) and into the red lobby. Find the elevators on the left, and go up to level 1. Exiting the elevator, turn left into Room 11. This is one of several rooms with work by Velázquez—including* Las Meninas, *around the corner in the large, lozenge-shaped Room 12.*

Spanish Masters

Diego Velázquez (vel-LAHTH-keth, 1599-1660) was the photojournalist of court painters, capturing the Spanish king and his court in formal portraits that take on aspects of a candid snapshot. Room 12 is filled with the portraits Velázquez was called on to produce. Kings and princes prance like Roman emperors. Get up close and notice that his remarkably detailed costumes

are nothing but a few messy splotches of paint—the proto-Impressionism Velázquez helped pioneer.

The room's centerpiece, and perhaps the most important painting in the museum, is Velázquez's **Maids of Honor** *(Las Meninas,* c. 1656). It's a peek at nannies caring for Princess

Margarita and, at the same time, a behind-the-scenes look at Velázquez at work. One hot summer day in 1656, Velázquez (at left, with paintbrush and Dalí moustache) stands at his easel and stares out at the people he's painting—the king and queen. They would have been standing about where we are, and we see only their reflection in the mirror at the back of the room. Their daughter (blonde hair, in center) watches her parents being painted, joined by her servants *(meninas)*, dwarves, and the family dog. At that very moment, a man happens to pass by the doorway at back and pauses to look in. Why's he there? Probably just to give the painting more depth.

This frozen moment is lit by the window on the right, splitting the room into bright and shaded planes that recede into the distance. The main characters look right at us, making us part of the scene, seemingly able to walk around, behind, and among the characters. Notice the exquisitely painted mastiff.

If you stand in the center of the room, the 3-D effect is most striking. This is art come to life.

• *Facing this painting, leave to the left and go two rooms to reach Room 10.*

Look around this gallery and see how Velázquez enjoyed capturing light—and capturing the moment. *The Drinkers (Los Borrachos,* c. 1628) is a cell-phone snapshot in a blue-collar bar, with a couple of peasants mugging for a photo-op with a Greek god—Bacchus, the god of wine. This was an early work, before Velázquez got his court-painter gig. A personal homage to the hardworking farmers enjoying the fruit of their labor, it shows how Velázquez had a heart for real people and believed they deserved portraits, too. Notice the almost-sacramental presence of the ultrarealistic bowl of wine in the  center, as Bacchus, with the honest gut, crowns a fellow hedonist.

• *Backtrack through the big gallery with* Las Meninas *to Room 14.*

Velázquez's boss, King Philip IV, had an affair, got caught, and repented by commissioning *Christ Crucified (Cristo Crucificado,* c. 1632). Christ hangs his head, humbly accepting his punishment. Philip would have been left to stare at the slowly dripping blood, contemplating how long Christ had to suffer to atone for Philip's sins. This is an interesting death scene. There's no anguish, no tension, no torture. Light seems to emanate from Jesus as if nothing else matters. The crown of thorns and cloth wrapped around his waist are particularly vivid. Above it all, a sign reads in three languages: "Jesus of Nazareth, King of the Jews."

MADRID

• *The nearby rooms (16 and 17) are filled with Murillo paintings. In the first room are several immaculately conceived virgins.*

Bartolomé Murillo (1618-1683) put a human face on the abstract Catholic doctrine that Mary was conceived and born free of original sin. In *Immaculate Conception* (*La Inmaculada Concepción de El Escorial*, c. 1665), his "immaculate" virgin floats in a cloud of Ivory Soap cleanliness, radiating youth and wholesome goodness. She wears the usual colors of the Virgin Mary—white for purity and blue for divinity. (Murillo and his style are described on page 675.) Sweet and escapist, Murillo's work was a hit, and it must have been very comforting to the wretched people of post-plague Sevilla (his hometown was hit hard in 1647-1652).

• *Return to the main hallway (Rooms 28 and 29) for lots of fleshy excitement, courtesy of Peter Paul Rubens.*

Northern Baroque

A native of Flanders, **Peter Paul Rubens** (1577-1640) painted Baroque-style art meant to play on the emotions, titillate the senses, and carry you away. His paintings surge with Baroque energy and ripple with waves of figures. Surveying his big, boisterous canvases, you'll notice his trademarks: sex, violence, action, emotion, bright colors, and ample bodies, with the wind machine set on full. Gods are melodramatic, and nymphs flee half-human predators. Rubens painted the most beautiful women of his day—well-fed, no tan lines, squirt-gun breasts, and very sexy.

Rubens' *The Three Graces* (*Las Tres Gracias*, c. 1635) celebrates cellulite. The ample, glowing bodies intertwine as the women exchange meaningful glances. The Grace at the left is Rubens' young second wife, Hélène Fourment, who shows up regularly in his paintings.

• *From the main hall with the Rubens, look to the near end of the hall, where Goya's royal portraits hang. We'll end up there. But first, head the other way to Titian and El Greco. Titians line the big hall, and the El Grecos are in Rooms 8b, 9b, and 10b.*

Spanish Mystic

El Greco (1541-1614) was born in Greece (his name is Spanish for "The Greek"), trained in Venice, then settled in Toledo—60 miles from Madrid. His paintings are like Byzantine icons drenched in Venetian color and fused in the fires of Spanish mysticism. (For more on El Greco, see page 573 and visit Toledo.) The El Greco paintings displayed here rotate, but they all glow with his unique style.

In *Christ Carrying the Cross* (*Cristo Abrazado a la Cruz,* c. 1602), Jesus accepts his fate, trudging toward death with blood running down his neck. He hugs the cross and directs his gaze along the crossbar. His upturned eyes (sparkling with a streak of white paint) lock onto his next stop—heaven.

The Adoration of the Shepherds (*La Adoración de los Pastores,* c. 1614), originally painted for El Greco's own burial chapel in Toledo, has the artist's typical two-tiered composition—heaven above, earth below. The long, skinny shepherds are stretched unnaturally in between, flickering like flames toward heaven.

The Nobleman with His Hand on His Chest (*El Caballero de la Mano al Pecho,* c. 1580) shows an elegant and somewhat arrogant man whose hand has the middle fingers touching—El Greco's trademark way of expressing elegance (or was it the 16th-century symbol for "Live long and prosper"?). The signature is on the right in faint Greek letters—"Doménikos Theotokópoulos," El Greco's real name.

• *Return to the main gallery. In the center, under the dome (and opposite* Las Meninas*), Charles I sits royally on horseback.*

Venetian Painter to the Court

Spain's Golden Age kings Charles I (a.k.a. Charles V) and Philip II were both staunch Catholics, but that didn't stop them from amassing this sometimes surprisingly racy collection. Both kings sat for portraits by the Venetian master **Titian** (c. 1485-1576).

In *Emperor Charles V on Horseback* (*El Emperador Carlos V en la Batalla de Mühlberg,* 1548), the king rears on his horse, raises his lance, and rides out to crush an army of Lutherans. Charles, having inherited many kingdoms and baronies through his family connections, was the world's most powerful man in the 1500s. (You can see the suit of armor depicted in the painting in the

Royal Palace.)

In contrast (just to the right), Charles I's son, *Philip II* (*Felipe II*, c. 1551), looks pale, suspicious, and lonely—a scholarly and complex figure. He built the austere, monastic palace at El Escorial, but also indulged himself with Titian's bevy of Renaissance Playmates—a sampling of which is here in the Prado.

These are the faces of the Counter-Reformation. While father and son ruled very differently, both had underbites, a product of royal inbreeding (which Titian painted...but very delicately). For more Titians, stroll the grand gallery (Rooms 25 and 26).

• *Now walk to the far end of the main gallery and enter the round Room 32, where you'll see royal portraits by Goya. The museum's exciting Goya collection is on three levels at this end of the building: classic Goya (royal portraits and* La Maja), *on this floor; early cartoons, upstairs; and his dark and political work, downstairs.*

Painter of Kings and Demons

Follow the complex **Francisco de Goya** (1746-1828) through the stages of his life—from dutiful court painter, to political rebel and scandal-maker, to the disillusioned genius of his "black paintings."

In the group portrait *The Family of Charles IV* (*La Familia de Carlos IV,* 1800), the royals are all decked out in their Sunday

best. Goya himself stands at his easel to the far left, painting the court (a tribute to Velázquez in *Las Meninas*) and revealing the shallowness beneath the fancy trappings. Charles, with his ridiculous hairpiece and goofy smile, was a vacuous, henpecked husband. His toothless yet domineering queen upstages him, arrogantly stretching her swanlike neck. The other adults, with their bland faces, are bug-eyed with stupidity.

Surrounding you in this same room are other portraits of the king and queen. Also notice the sketch paintings, quick studies done with the subjects posing for Goya. He used these for reference to complete his larger, more finished canvases.

• *To the right, in Room 36, is Goya's most scandalous work.*

Rumors flew that Goya was fooling around with the vivacious Duchess of Alba, who may have been the model for two similar paintings, **Nude Maja** (*La Maja Desnuda,* c. 1800) and **Clothed Maja** (*La Maja Vestida,* c. 1808). A *maja* was a trendy, working-class girl. Whether

she's a duchess or a *maja,* Goya painted a naked lady—an actual person rather than some mythic Venus. And that was enough to risk incurring the wrath of the Inquisition. The nude stretches in a Titian-esque pose to display her charms, the pale body with realistic pubic hair highlighted by cool green sheets. (Notice the artist's skillful rendering of the transparent fabric on the pillow.) According to a believable legend, the two paintings were displayed in a double frame, with the *Clothed Maja* sliding over the front to hide the *Nude Maja* from Inquisitive minds.

• *Find the nearby staircase and elevator, and head up to level 2 for more Goya.*

These rooms display Goya's **designs for tapestries** (known as "cartoons") for nobles' palaces. As you stroll around, the scenes

make it clear that, while revolution was brewing in America and France, Spain's lords and ladies were playing, blissfully ignorant of the changing times. Dressed in their "Goya-style" attire, they're picnicking, dancing, flying kites, playing paddleball

and Blind Man's Bluff, or just relaxing in the sun—as in the well-known *The Parasol* (*El Quitasol,* Room 85).

• *For more Goya, take the stairs or elevator down to level 0. Find Room 66, which leads into Goya's final paintings, with a darker edge. Room 65 takes you to powerful military scenes.*

Goya became a political liberal, a champion of democracy. He was crushed when France's hero of the French Revolution, Napoleon, morphed into a tyrant and invaded Spain. In the ***Second of May, 1808*** (*El 2 de Mayo de 1808,* 1814), Madrid's citizens rise up to protest the occupation in Puerta del Sol, and the French send in their dreaded Egyptian mercenaries. They plow through the dense

tangle of Madrileños, who have nowhere to run. The next day, the ***Third of May, 1808*** (*El 3 de Mayo de 1808,* 1814), the French rounded up ringleaders and executed them. The colorless firing squad—a faceless machine of death—mows them down, and

they fall in bloody, tangled heaps. Goya throws a harsh prison-yard floodlight on the main victim, who spreads his arms Christ-like to ask, "Why?"

Politically, Goya was split—he was a Spaniard, but he knew France was leading Europe into the modern age. His art, while political, has no Spanish or French flags. It's a universal comment on the horror of war. Many consider Goya the last classical and first modern painter...the first painter with a social conscience.

• *About face to the "black paintings" in Rooms 66 and 67.*

Depressed and deaf from syphilis, Goya retired to his small home and smeared its walls with his **"black paintings"**— dark in color and in mood. During this period in his life, Goya would paint his nightmares...literally. The style is considered Romantic—emphasizing emotion over beauty—but it foreshadows 20th-century Surrealism with its bizarre imagery, expressionistic and thick brushstrokes, and cynical outlook.

Stepping into Room 67, you are surrounded by art from Goya's dark period. These paintings are the actual murals from the walls of his house, transferred onto canvas. Imagine this in your living room. Goya painted what he felt with a radical technique unburdened by reality—a century before his time. And he painted without being paid for it—perhaps the first great paintings done not for hire or for sale. We know frustratingly little about these works because Goya wrote nothing about them.

Dark forces convened continually in Goya's dining room, where *The Witches' Sabbath* (*El Aquelarre,* c. 1823) hung. The witches, who look like skeletons, swirl in a frenzy around a dark, Satanic goat in monk's clothing who presides over the obscene rituals. The black goat represents the Devil and stokes the frenzy of his wild-eyed subjects. Amid this adoration and lust, a noble lady (far right) folds her hands primly in her lap ("I thought this was a Tupperware party!"). Or, perhaps it's a pep rally for her execution, maybe inspired by the chaos that accompanied Plaza Mayor executions. Nobody knows for sure.

In *Duel with Cudgels* (*Duelo a Garrotazos,* c. 1823), two giants stand face-to-face, buried up to their knees, and flail at each other with clubs. It's a standoff between superpowers in the never-ending cycle of war—a vision of a tough time when people on the streets would kill for a piece of bread.

In *Saturn Devouring One of His Sons* (*Saturno Devorando a un Hijo,* c. 1823), the king of the Roman gods—fearful that his progeny would overthrow him—eats one of his offspring. Saturn, also known as Cronus (Time), may symbolize how time devours us all. Either way, the painting brings new meaning to the term "child's portion."

Dog Semi-Submerged (*Perro Semihundido,* c. 1823) is, according to some, the hinge between classical art and modern art. The dog, so full of feeling and sadness, is being swallowed by quicksand...much as, to Goya, the modern age was overtaking a more classical era. And look closely at the dog. It also can be seen as a turning point for Goya. Perhaps he's bottomed out—he's been overwhelmed by depression, but his spirit has survived. With the portrait of this dog, color is returning.

• *Step back into Room 66, and look on the right.*

The last painting we have by Goya is *The Milkmaid of Bordeaux* (*La Lechera de Burdeos*, c. 1826). Somehow, Goya pulled out of his depression and moved to France, where he lived until his death at 82. While painting as an old man, color returned to his palette. His social commentary, his passion for painting what he felt (more than what he was hired to do), and, as you see here, the freedom of his brushstrokes explain why many consider Francesco de Goya to be the first modern artist.

• *There's lots more to the Prado, but there's also lots more to Madrid. The choice is yours.*

▲▲Thyssen-Bornemisza Museum (Museo del Arte Thyssen-Bornemisza)

Locals call this stunning museum simply the Thyssen (TEE-sun). It displays the impressive collection that Baron Thyssen (a wealthy German married to a former Miss Spain) sold to Spain for $350 million. The museum offers a unique chance to enjoy the sweep of all art history—including a good sampling of the "isms" of the 20th century—in one collection. It's basically minor works by major artists and major works by minor artists. (Major works by major artists are in the Prado.) But art lovers appreciate how the good baron's art complements the Prado's collection by filling in where the Prado is weak—such as Impressionism, which is the Thyssen's forte.

Cost and Hours: €9 (up to €8 more for optional special exhibits), under age 12 free, audioguide-€4; Mon 12:00-16:00, Tue-Sun 10:00-19:00, Tue-Sat until 22:00 in summer, last entry 30 minutes before closing.

Getting There: It's kitty-corner from the Prado at Paseo del Prado 8 in Palacio de Villahermosa (Metro: Banco de España).

Information: Tel. 902-760-511, www.museothyssen.org.

Services: Free baggage storage, cafeteria and restaurant, shop/bookstore.

Visiting the Museum: After purchasing your ticket, continue down the wide main hall past larger-than-life paintings of King Juan Carlos and Queen Sofía, and then paintings of the baron (who died in 2002) and his art-collecting baroness, Carmen. At the info desk, pick up two museum maps (one for numbered rooms, another for lettered rooms). Each of the three floors is divided into two separate areas: the permanent collection (blue-numbered rooms) and additions from the baroness since the

1980s (red-lettered rooms). Most visitors stick to the permanent collection.

Ascend to the top floor and work your way down, taking a delightful walk through art history. Visit the rooms on each floor in numerical order, from Primitive Italian (Room 1) to Surrealism and Pop Art (Room 48).

Temporary exhibits at the Thyssen often parallel those at the free **Caja Madrid** exhibit hall, across from the Descalzas Royal Monastery on Plaza San Martín, a short walk from Puerta del Sol (see page 478).

Leaving the Museum: If you're heading to the Reina Sofía and you're tired, hail a cab at the gate to zip straight there, or take bus #27, which stops in the square with the Neptune fountain, in front of the Starbucks (ride to the end of Paseo del Prado, get off at the McDonald's, and cross the street, going away from the Botanical Gardens, to Plaza Sánchez Bustillo and the museum).

▲▲▲Centro de Arte Reina Sofía

Home to Picasso's *Guernica,* the Reina Sofía is one of Europe's most enjoyable modern art museums. Its exceptional collection

of 20th-century art is housed in what was Madrid's first public hospital. The focus is on 20th-century Spanish artists—Picasso, Dalí, Miró, Gris, and Tàpies—but you'll also find plenty of works by Kandinsky, Braque, and many other giants of modern art.

The current curator, who has a passion for cinema, has paired paintings with films from the same decade, which play continuously in nearby rooms. This provides a fascinating insight into the social context that inspired the art of Spain's tumultuous 20th century. Those with an appetite for modern and contemporary art can spend several delightful hours in this museum.

Cost and Hours: €8 (includes most temporary exhibits), €3 entry if you're under 18 or over 65, free Mon and Wed-Sat 19:00-21:00, Sun 15:00-19:00 (free times are often crowded, and you must pick up a ticket); open Mon and Wed-Sat 10:00-21:00, Sun 10:00-19:00 (fourth floor not accessible Sun after 15:00), closed Tue.

Getting There: It's a block from the Atocha Metro stop, on Plaza Sánchez Bustillo (at Calle de Santa Isabel 52). In the Metro station, follow signs for the Reina Sofía exit. Emerging from the Metro, walk straight ahead a half-block and look for an opening between the group of buildings. You'll see the tall, exterior glass elevators that flank the museum's main entrance.

Information: Tel. 917-741-000, www.museoreinasofia.es.

Audioguide: The hardworking audioguide is €4.

Services: Bag storage is free. The *librería* just outside the Nouvel wing has a larger selection of Picasso and Surrealist reproductions than the main gift shop at the entrance. The museum's café (a long block around the left from the main entrance) is a standout for its tasty cuisine. And the square immediately in front of the museum is ringed by fine places (like the recommended El Brillante) for a simple meal or drink.

Photography: Photos are not allowed in the room containing *Guernica* or in the surrounding rooms. Otherwise, photos without flash are OK.

❷ Self-Guided Tour

Pick up a free map and use the good information sheets to supplement this tour.

The permanent collection is divided into three groups: art from 1900 to 1945 (second floor), art from 1945 to 1968 (fourth floor), and art from 1962 to 1982 (adjoining Nouvel wing, which also has space for bigger installations). Temporary exhibits are on the first and third floors.

While the collection is roughly chronological, it's displayed thematically. The second-floor grand hallway leads around a courtyard connecting a series of rooms, each clearly labeled with a theme. For a good first visit, ride the fancy glass elevator to level 2 and tour that floor clockwise (Goya, Surrealism, Cubism, Picasso's *Guernica*), and then finish with post-WWII art on level 4.

• *Begin in Room 201, with examples of...*

Proto-Modern Goya

The installations at many museums leave you scratching your head in frustration. But the wonderful curator of the Reina Sofía insightfully begins your look at modern art with Goya engravings. That's because Goya is a proto-modernist—the first painter with a social conscience, the first to show inner feelings, and the first to deal with social reality. He painted because he had something to say, not just to get a paycheck.

• *Browse through the next rooms, whose underlying theme is the conflict between tradition (the powerful Church) and progress (social modernization). Find your way to Room 205 and...*

Surrealism and Salvador Dalí

In 1914 a generation marched enthusiastically into combat, believing the Great War would be the "war to end all wars." Many artists embraced this fight, volunteered to serve, and died for the cause. But when it was over, it was clear: World War I brought no lasting change. Frustrated, many survivors turned their backs on society.

In the postwar years, a class of artists abandoned the outer world and looked inside (with inspiration from Freud). They painted mindscapes rather than landscapes. They had learned that reality is deeper than what you first "see." These were the Surrealists. To "see" their art, you need to vary your position: your physical perspective and your mental perspective. See it happy, sad, before coffee, after coffee.

In the Dalí room, you'll see the artist's distinct, Surrealist, melting-object style. Dalí places familiar items in a stark landscape, creating an eerie effect. Figures morph into misplaced faces and body parts. Background and foreground play mind games—is it an animal (seen one way) or a man's face? A waterfall or a pair of legs? It's a wide shot...no, it's a close-up. Look long at paintings like Dalí's *Endless Enigma* (1938) and *The Invisible Man* (c. 1933); they take different viewers to different places.

The Great Masturbator (1929) is psychologically exhausting, depicting in its Surrealism a lonely, highly sexual genius in love with his muse, Gala (while she was still married to a French poet). This is the first famous Surrealist painting.

During this productive period, Dalí was working on the classic Surrealist film *Un Chien Andalou* (*The Andalusian Dog*, 1928) with his collaborator Luis Buñuel (the film plays in the gallery). Both men were members of the Generation of '27, a group of nonconformist Spanish bohemians whose creative interests had a huge influence on art and literature in their era.

• *Skirt around the courtyard to find Room 210 and...*

Cubism

Cubism was born in the first decade of the 20th century. You could make a good case that the changes in society in the year 1900 were more profound than those we lived through in 2000. Trains and cars brought speed to life. Electricity brought light. Einstein introduced us to abstract ideas. Photography captured reality. And art broke away. At the turn of the century there were two ways to express art: line (Picasso) and color (Matisse)—but it was still in two dimensions. With Cubism, three dimensions are shown in two. Imagine walking around a statue to take in all the angles, and then attempting to put it on a 2-D plane. With Cubism, everyone sees things differently. To appreciate it, take your time and free your imagination.

Room 210 shows the birth of Cubism—a movement in which Spaniards were very much at the forefront (with works by Picasso, Braque, Léger, and Gris). To literally see a 2-D picture plane leap to life, watch the Lumière brothers' early film *Danse Serpentine* (c. 1898).

• *In Room 206, you come to what is likely the reason for your visit...*

Picasso's *Guernica*

Perhaps the single most impressive piece of art in Spain is Pablo Picasso's *Guernica* (1937). The monumental canvas—one of Europe's must-see sights—is not only a piece of art but a piece of history, capturing the horror of modern war in a modern style.

While it's become a timeless classic representing all war, it was born in response to a specific conflict—the civil war (1936-1939), which pitted the democratically elected Second Republican government against the fascist general Francisco Franco. Franco won and ended up ruling Spain with an iron fist for the next 36 years. At the time Franco cemented his power, *Guernica* was touring internationally as part of a fund-raiser for the Republican cause. With Spain's political situation deteriorating and World War II looming, Picasso in 1939 named New York's Museum of Modern Art as the depository for the work. It was only after Franco's death, in 1975, that *Guernica* ended its decades of exile. In 1981 the painting finally arrived in Spain (where it had never before been), and it now stands as Spain's national piece of art.

Guernica—The Bombing: On April 26, 1937, Guernica—a Basque market town in northern Spain and an important Republican center—was the target of the world's first saturation-bombing raid on civilians. Franco gave permission to his fascist confederate Hitler to use the town as a guinea pig to try out Germany's new air force. The raid leveled the town, causing destruction that was unheard of at the time (though by 1944 it would be commonplace). For more on the town of Guernica and the bombing, see page 236.

News of the bombing reached Picasso in Paris, where coincidentally he was just beginning work on a painting commission awarded by the Republican government. Picasso scrapped his earlier plans and immediately set to work sketching scenes of the destruction as he imagined it. In a matter of weeks he put these bomb-shattered shards together into a large mural (286 square feet). For the first time, the world could see the destructive force of the rising fascist movement—a prelude to World War II.

Guernica—**The Painting:** The bombs are falling, shattering the quiet village. A woman looks up at the sky (far right), horses scream (center), and a man falls from a horse and dies, while a wounded woman drags herself through the streets. She tries to escape, but her leg is too thick, dragging her down, like trying to run from something in a nightmare. On the left, a bull—a symbol of Spain—ponders it all, watching over a mother and her dead baby...a modern *pietà*. A woman in the center sticks her head out to see what's going on. The whole scene is lit from above by the stark light of a bare bulb. Picasso's painting threw a light on the brutality of Hitler and Franco, and suddenly the whole world was watching.

Picasso's abstract, Cubist style reinforces the message. It's as if he'd picked up the shattered shards and pasted them onto a canvas. The black-and-white tones are as gritty as the black-and-white newspaper photos that reported the bombing. The drab colors create a depressing, almost nauseating mood.

Picasso chose images with universal symbolism, making the work a commentary on all wars. Picasso himself said that the central horse, with the spear in its back, symbolizes humanity succumbing to brute force. The fallen rider's arm is severed and his sword is broken, more symbols of defeat. The bull, normally a proud symbol of strength and independence, is impotent and frightened. Between the bull and the horse, the faint dove of peace can do nothing but cry.

The bombing of Guernica—like the entire civil war—was an exercise in brutality. As one side captured a town, it might systematically round up every man, old and young—including priests—line them up, and shoot them in revenge for atrocities by the other side.

Thousands of people attended the Paris exhibition, and *Guernica* caused an immediate sensation. They could see the horror of modern war technology, the vain struggle of the Spanish Republicans, and the cold indifference of the fascist war machine. Picasso vowed never to return to Spain while Franco ruled (the dictator outlived him).

With each passing year, the canvas seemed more and more prophetic—honoring not just the hundreds or thousands who died in Guernica, but also the estimated 500,000 victims of Spain's bitter civil war and the 55 million worldwide who perished in World War II. Picasso put a human face on what we now call "collateral damage."

• *After seeing* Guernica, *view the additional exhibits that put the painting in its social context.*

Other Picasso Exhibits

On the back wall on the *Guernica* room is a line of **photos** showing the evolution of the painting, from Picasso's first concept to the final mural. The photos were taken in his Paris studio by Dora Maar, Picasso's mistress-du-jour (and whose portrait by Picasso hangs nearby). Notice how his work evolved from the defiant fist in early versions to a broken sword with a flower.

The room behind *Guernica* contains **studies** Picasso did for the painting. These studies are filled with motifs that turn up in the final canvas—iron-nail tears, weeping women, and screaming horses. Picasso returned to these images in his work for the rest of his life. He believed that everyone struggles internally with aspects of the horse and bull: rationality and brutality, humanity and animalism. The Minotaur—half-man and half-bull—powerfully captures Picasso's poet/rapist vision of man. Having lived through the brutality of the age—World War I, the Spanish Civil War, and World War II—his outlook is understandable.

In one corner of this room, you'll also find a **model of the Spanish Pavilion** at the 1937 Paris exposition where *Guernica* was first displayed (look inside to see Picasso's work). Picasso originally toyed with painting an allegory on the theme of the artist's studio for the expo. But the bombing of Guernica jolted him into the realization that Spain was a country torn by war. Thanks to *Guernica*, the pavilion became a vessel for propaganda and a fund-raising tool against Franco.

In nearby Room 206.03, you'll see posters and political cartoons that are pro-communist and anti-Franco. Made the same year as *Guernica*, these touch on timeless themes related to rich elites, industrialists, the Church, and the military industrial complex versus the common man.

The remaining rooms display pieces from contemporary artists reacting to the conflict of the time, whether through explicit commentary—as in Horacio Ferrer's *Madrid 1937: Black Airplanes* (Room 206.04)—or through new, innovative styles inspired by the changing political and social culture.

• *Head up to level 4, where the permanent collection continues.*

Post-WWII Art

After World War II, the center of the art world moved from Paris to New York City. Spain was ruled by a dictatorship, and the avant-garde could not be so *avant*. The organizing theme in this part of the museum is "Art in a Divided World." On this floor, especially, you'll want to take full advantage of the English information sheets in each room and the narration provided by your audioguide.

You'll see Kandinsky as a bridge into abstract art and the

Abstract Expressionism of Jackson Pollock and company. Room 419 is especially interesting, with late works by Picasso and Miró (from the 1960s and 1970s). On this floor, you can see photographs and watch films documenting Spain's slow recovery from its devastating civil war. The physical and psychological damage of the war weighed on Spain for decades afterward.

• *End your visit in the...*

Nouvel Wing
The newest wing of the museum features art from the 1960s through the 1980s, with a thematic focus on the complexity and plurality of modern times. While these galleries have fewer household names, the pieces displayed demonstrate the many aesthetic directions of more recent modern art.

Near the Prado
▲Retiro Park (Parque del Buen Retiro)
Once the private domain of royalty, this majestic park has been a favorite of Madrid's commoners since Charles III decided to share it with his subjects in the late 18th century. Siesta in this 300-acre green-and-breezy escape from the city. At midday on Saturday and Sunday, the area around the lake becomes a street carnival, with jugglers, puppeteers, and lots of local color. These peaceful gardens offer great picnicking and people-watching (closes at dusk). From the Retiro Metro stop, walk to the big lake (El Estanque), where you can rent a rowboat. Past the lake, a grand boulevard of statues leads to the Prado.

▲Royal Botanical Garden (Real Jardín Botánico)
After your Prado visit, you can take a lush and fragrant break in this sculpted park. Wander among trees from around the world, originally gathered by—who else?—the enlightened King Charles III. This garden was established when the Prado's building housed the natural science museum. A flier in English explains that this is actually more than a park—it's a museum of plants.

Cost and Hours: €3, daily 10:00-21:00, until 18:00 in winter, last entry 30 minutes before closing, entrance is opposite the Prado's Murillo/south entry, Plaza de Murillo 2.

▲Naval Museum (Museo Naval)
This museum tells the story of Spain's navy, from the Armada to today, in a plush and fascinating-to-boat-lovers exhibit. Given Spain's importance in maritime history, there's quite a story to tell. Because this is a military facility, you'll need to show your passport to get in. A good English brochure is available.

Cost and Hours: Free, Tue-Sun 10:00-19:00, closed Mon and Aug, a block north of the Prado, across boulevard from Thyssen-Bornemisza Museum, Paseo del Prado 5, tel. 915-238-789.

CaixaForum

Across the street from the Prado and Royal Botanical Garden, this impressive exhibit hall has sleek architecture and an outdoor hanging garden—a bushy wall festooned with greens designed by a French landscape artist. The forum, funded by La Caixa Bank, features world-class art exhibits—generally 20th-century art, well-described in English and changing three times a year. Ride the elevator to the top, where you'll find a chic café with €13 weekday lunch specials and sperm-like lamps swarming down from the ceiling; from here, explore your way down.

Cost and Hours: €4, daily 10:00-20:00, Paseo del Prado 36, tel. 913-307-300.

Palacio de Cibeles

This former post-office headquarters was recently converted to a cultural center—featuring mostly empty exhibition halls, an auditorium, and public hang-out spaces—and renamed the Cibeles CentroCentro of Culture and Citizenship. (Say that five times fast!) The temporary exhibits can be skipped. The real attraction lies in the gorgeous 360-degree rooftop views from the eighth-floor observation deck. Visit the recommended sixth-floor Restaurante Palacio de Cibeles and bar for similar views from its two terraces.

Cost and Hours: €2 elevator ride to observation deck, visiting the Palacio itself is free—take advantage of its air-conditioning and free Wi-Fi; building open Tue-Sun 10:00-20:00, terrace visits possible every half hour 10:30-13:30 & 16:00-19:00, closed Mon, Plaza de Cibeles 1, tel. 914-800-008, www.centrocentro.org.

Elsewhere in Madrid

▲Gran Vía Tour

For a walk down Spain's version of Fifth Avenue, stroll the Gran Vía. Built primarily between 1900 and the 1950s, this boulevard affords a fun view of early-20th-century architecture and a chance to be on the street with workaday Madrileños. I've broken the walk into five sections, each of which was the ultimate in its day.

❶ Circulo de Bellas Artes: Begin at this 1920s skyscraper offering the best rooftop view around (Calle de Alcalá #42, Metro: Banco de España, a venerable café operates on its ground floor). Ride the elevator to the seventh-floor roof terrace (€3, daily 11:00-15:00 & 16:00-21:00), and stand under a black, Art Deco statue of Minerva, perhaps put here to associate Madrid with this mythological protectress of culture and high thinking. Walk the perimeter of the rooftop from the far left for a clockwise tour.

Looking to the left, you'll see the gold-fringed dome of the landmark Metropolis building (inspired by Hotel Negresco in Nice), once the headquarters of an insurance company. It stands

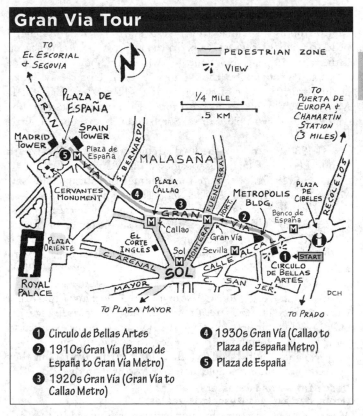

Gran Via Tour

TO EL ESCORIAL & SEGOVIA

N

☰ PEDESTRIAN ZONE
⌐ VIEW

PLAZA DE ESPAÑA

SPAIN TOWER

MADRID TOWER

¼ MILE
.5 KM

TO PUERTA DE EUROPA & CHAMARTÍN STATION (3 MILES)

❺ Plaza de España

MALASAÑA

CERVANTES MONUMENT

S. BERNARDO

PLAZA CALLAO

❹ ❸

GRAN VÍA

METROPOLIS BLDG.

PLAZA DE CIBELES

Banco de España

❷

RECOLETOS

PLAZA ORIENTE

EL CORTE INGLÉS

Callao

MONTERA

FUENCARRAL

HORT.

Gran Vía

Sevilla

ALCALÁ

START ❶

CIRCULO DE BELLAS ARTES

ℹ️

ROYAL PALACE

C. ARENAL

SOL

MAYOR

CALLE SAN JER.

DCH

TO PLAZA MAYOR

TO PRADO

❶ Circulo de Bellas Artes

❷ 1910s Gran Vía (Banco de España to Gran Vía Metro)

❸ 1920s Gran Vía (Gran Vía to Callao Metro)

❹ 1930s Gran Vía (Callao to Plaza de España Metro)

❺ Plaza de España

at the start of the Gran Vía and its cancan of proud facades celebrating the good times in pre-civil war Spain. On the horizon, the Guadarrama Mountains hide Segovia. Farther to the right, in the distance, skyscrapers mark the city's north gate, Puerta de Europa (with its striking slanted twin towers). The big traffic circle and fountain below are part of Plaza de Cibeles, with its ornate and bombastic cultural center and observation deck (Palacio de Cibeles; described earlier). Behind that is the vast Retiro Park. Farther to the right, the big low-slung building surrounded by green is the Prado Museum. And, finally, at the far right (and hard to see), is the old town.

Descend the elevator and cross the busy boulevard immediately in front of Circulo de Belles Artes to reach the start of Gran Vía.

❷ **1910s Gran Vía:** This first stretch, from the Banco de España Metro stop to the Gran Vía Metro stop, was built in the 1910s. While the people-watching and window-shopping can be enthralling, be sure to look up and enjoy the beautiful facades, too.

❸ **1920s Gran Vía:** The second stretch, from the Gran Vía Metro stop to the Callao Metro stop, starts where two recently pedestrianized streets meet up. To the right, Calle de Fuencarral is the trendiest pedestrian zone in town, with famous brand-name shops and a young vibe (the 14-story 1920s Telefónica skyscraper at the corner was one of the city's first). To the left, Calle de la Montera is notorious for its prostitutes. The action pulses from the McDonald's down a block or so. Some find it an eye-opening little detour.

❹ **1930s Gran Vía:** The final stretch, from the Callao Metro stop to Plaza de España, is considered the "American Gran Vía," built in the 1930s to emulate the buildings of Chicago and New York City. You'll even see the Nebraska Cafeteria restaurant—a reminder that American food was trendy long before the advent of fast-food chains. This section is the Spanish version of Broadway, with all the big theaters and plays.

❺ **Plaza de España:** End your walk at Plaza de España (with a Metro station of the same name). Once the Rockefeller Plaza of Madrid, these days it's pretty tired. While statues of the epic Spanish characters Don Quixote and Sancho Panza (part of a Cervantes monument) are ignored in the park, two Franco-era buildings do their best to scrape the sky above. Franco wanted to show he could keep up with America, so he had the Spain Tower (shorter) and Madrid Tower (taller) built in the 1950s. But they succeed in reminding people more of Moscow than the USA.

Descalzas Royal Monastery (Monasterio de las Descalzas Reales)

Madrid's most visit-worthy monastery was founded in the 16th century by Philip II's sister, Joan of Habsburg (known to Spaniards as Juana and to Austrians as Joanna). She's buried here. The monastery's chapels are decorated with fine art, Rubens-designed tapestries, and the heirlooms of the wealthy women who joined the order (the nuns were required to give a dowry). Because this is still a working Franciscan monastery, tourists can enter only when the nuns vacate the cloister, and the number of daily visitors is limited. The scheduled tours often sell out—come in the morning to buy your ticket, even if you want an afternoon tour.

Cost and Hours: €7, visits guided in Spanish or English depending on demand, Tue-Sat 10:00-14:00 & 16:00-18:30, Sun 10:00-14:30, closed Mon, last entry one hour before closing, Plaza de las Descalzas Reales 1, near the Ópera Metro stop and just a short walk from Puerta del Sol, tel. 914-548-800.

Nearby: Across the street from the monastery, the **Caja Madrid** exhibit hall showcases temporary exhibits that parallel those at the Thyssen-Bornemisza Museum (free to enter, free guided visits available—must reserve online, Tue-Sun 10:00-

20:00, closed Mon and between exhibits, Plaza San Martín, tel. 902-245-810, www.fundacioncajamadrid.es).

▲Museum of the Americas (Museo de América)

Thousands of pre-Columbian and colonial artworks and artifacts make up the bulk of this worthwhile museum, though it offers few English explanations. Covering the cultures of the Americas (North and South), its exhibits focus on language, religion, and art, and provide a new perspective on the cultures of our own hemisphere. Highlights include one of only four surviving Mayan codices (ancient books) and a section about the voyages of the Spanish explorers, with their fantastical imaginings of mythical creatures awaiting them in the New World.

Cost and Hours: €3, free on Sun; open Tue-Sat 9:30-20:30, Nov-April until 18:30, Sun 10:00-15:00, closed Mon; northwest of the city center at Avenida de los Reyes Católicos 6, Metro: Moncloa, tel. 915-492-641, http://museodeamerica.mcu.es.

Getting There: The museum is a 15-minute walk from the Moncloa Metro stop: Take the Calle de Isaac Peral exit, cross Plaza de Moncloa, and veer right to Calle de Fernández de los Ríos. Follow that street (toward the shiny Faro de Moncloa tower), and turn left on Avenida de los Reyes Católicos. Head around the base of the tower, which stands at the museum's entrance.

▲National Archaeological Museum (Museo Arqueológico Nacional)

A major renovation of this museum is scheduled to be finished sometime in late 2013. Until then, only about 300 of its most noteworthy pieces are on display. If you're here after all of its rooms have reopened, you'll follow a chronological walk through the story of Iberia. With a rich collection of artifacts, the museum shows off the wonders of each age: Celtic pre-Roman, Roman, a fine and rare Visigothic section, Moorish, Romanesque, and beyond. You may also find underwhelming replica artwork from northern Spain's Altamira Caves (big on bison), giving you a faded peek at the skill of the cave artists who created the originals 14,000 years ago. (For more on the real Altamira Caves, see the Cantabria chapter.)

Cost and Hours: Free, ask about audioguide, likely Tue-Sat 9:30-20:00, Sun 9:30-15:00, closed Mon, north of the Prado at Calle Serrano 13, Metro: Serrano or Colón, tel. 915-777-912, http://man.mcu.es.

Sorolla Museum (Museo Sorolla)

Painter Joaquín Sorolla (1863-1923) is known for his portraits, landscapes, and use of light. It's a relaxing experience to stroll through the rooms of his former house and studio, especially to see the lazy beach scenes of his hometown, Valencia. The museum is best experienced when daylight streams through the house, which is how the artist intended for people to view his work. Take a break after your visit to reflect in the small garden in front of his house.

Cost and Hours: €3, free on Sun; open Tue-Sat 9:30-20:00, Sun 10:00-15:00, closed Mon; north of city center at General Martínez Campos 37, Metro: Iglesia, tel. 913-101-584, http://museo sorolla.mcu.es.

History Museum (Museo de Historia)

This museum covers the history of Madrid in old paintings and interesting models. The entrance features a fine Baroque door by architect Pedro de Ribera, with a depiction of St. James the Moor-Slayer (see page 362). The museum has been undergoing major renovations and is re-opening section by section. All rooms should be open by early 2014, but confirm with the TI or call before you make the trip.

Cost and Hours: Free, Tue-Fri 9:30-20:00, Sat-Sun 9:30-14:00, closed Mon, Calle de Fuencarral 78, Metro: Tribunal or Bilbao, tel. 917-011-863.

▲Clothing Museum (Museo del Traje)

This museum shows the history of clothing from the 18th century until today. In a cool and air-conditioned chronological sweep, the museum's one floor of exhibits includes regional ethnic costumes, a look at how bullfighting and the French influenced styles, accessories through the ages, and Spanish flappers. The only downside of this marvelous, modern museum is that it's a long way from anything else of interest.

Cost and Hours: €3, free Sat 14:30-19:00 and all day Sun; open Tue-Sat 9:30-19:00, until 22:30 Thu in summer, Sun 10:00-15:00, closed Mon, last entry 30 minutes before closing; northwest of city center at Avenida de Juan Herrera 2; Metro: Moncloa and a longish walk, bus #46, or taxi; tel. 915-497-150, http://museo deltraje.mcu.es.

▲Hermitage of San Antonio de la Florida (Ermita de San Antonio de la Florida)

In this simple little Neoclassical chapel from the 1790s, Francisco de Goya's tomb stares up at a splendid cupola filled with his own proto-Impressionist frescoes. He used the same unique technique that he employed for his "black paintings" (described earlier, in the Prado Museum listing). Use the mirrors to enjoy the drama and energy he infused into this marvelously restored masterpiece.

Cost and Hours: Free, Tue-Sun 9:30-20:00, closed Mon, Glorieta de San Antonio de la Florida 5; Metro: Príncipe Pío, then eight-minute walk down Paseo de San Antonio de la Florida; tel. 915-420-722, www.madrid.es/ermita.

Royal Tapestry Factory (Real Fábrica de Tapices)

Have a look at traditional tapestry-making. You can actually order a tailor-made tapestry (starting at $10,000).

Cost and Hours: €4, by tour only, tours depart on the half-hour—some in English; open Mon-Fri 10:00-14:00, closed Sat-Sun and Aug, last entry at 13:30; south of Retiro Park at Calle Fuenterrabia 2, Metro: Menendez Pelayo, take Gutenberg exit, tel. 914-340-550, www.realfabricadetapices.com.

Temple of Debod (Templo de Debod)

In 1968, Egypt gave Spain its own ancient temple. It was a gift of the Egyptian government, which was grateful for the Spanish dictator Franco's help in rescuing monuments that had been threatened by the rising Nile waters above the Aswan Dam. Consequently, Madrid is the only place I can think of in Europe where you can actually wander through an intact original Egyptian temple—complete with fine carved reliefs from 200 B.C. Set in a romantic park that locals love for its great city views (especially at sunset), the temple—as well as its art—is well-described. The much-touted but uninspiring "grand Madrid view" only causes me to wonder why anyone would build a city here.

Cost and Hours: Free; April-Sept Tue-Fri 10:00-14:00 & 18:00-20:00, Sat-Sun 10:00-14:00, closed Mon; Oct-March Tue-Fri 9:45-13:45 & 16:15-18:15, Sat-Sun 9:30-20:00, closed Mon; last entry 15 minutes before closing; in Parque de Montaña, north of the Royal Palace, www.madrid.es (search for "Templo de Debod").

Experiences in Madrid

▲▲Self-Guided Bus Tour: Paseo de la Castellana

Tourists risk leaving Madrid without ever seeing the modern "Manhattan" side of town. But it's easy to do. From the Prado Museum, bus #27 makes the trip straight north along Paseo del Prado and then Paseo de la Castellana, through the no-nonsense skyscraper part of this city of more than three million. The line ends at the leaning towers of Puerta de Europa (Gate of Europe). This trip is simple and cheap (€1.50, buses run every 10 minutes, sit on the right if possible, beware of pickpockets). You just joyride for 30 minutes to the last stop (longer if it's rush hour), get out when everyone else does, ogle the skyscrapers, and catch the Metro for a 20-minute ride back to the city's center. At twilight, when fountains and facades are floodlit, the ride is particularly enjoyable.

Historic District: Bus #27 rumbles from Atocha Station past the Royal Botanical Garden (opposite McDonald's) and the Velázquez entrance to the Prado (if you're starting from here, catch the bus from the museum side to head north).

Look out for these landmarks: the Prado Museum (right); a square with a fountain of Neptune (left); an obelisk and war memorial to those who have died for Spain (right, with the stock market behind it); the Naval Museum (right); Plaza de Cibeles (with the fancy City Hall, the Bank of Spain, and other huge buildings); and then the National Library (right).

Modern District: The roundabout with a statue of Columbus marks the end of the historic town and the beginning of the modern city. At this point the boulevard changes its name. It used to be named for Franco; now it's named for the people he no longer rules—*la Castellana* (Castilians). Next comes the American Embassy (hard to see behind its fortified wall, right) and some circa 1940s buildings that once housed Franco's ministries (left, typical fascist architecture). Continuing up the boulevard, look left to see the Picasso Tower, resembling one of New York's former World Trade Center towers (designed by the same architect), the huge Bernabéu soccer stadium (right, home of Real Madrid, Europe's most successful soccer team, described later), and the Ministry of Defense (left).

Your trip ends at Plaza de Castilla, where you can't miss the avant-garde Puerta de Europa, consisting of the twin "Torres Kios," office towers that lean at a 15-degree angle (one has the big green bear logo of the Bank of Madrid). In the distance, you can see four of the tallest buildings in Spain. The plaza sports a futuristic golden obelisk by contemporary Spanish architect Santiago Calatrava.

It's the end of the line for the bus—and for you. You can return directly to Puerta del Sol on the Metro, or cross the street and ride bus #27 along the same route back to the Prado Museum or Atocha Station.

▲Electric Minibus Joyride and the Lavapiés District

For a relaxing ride through the characteristic old center of Madrid, hop the little electric **minibus #M1** (€1.50, 5/hour, 20-minute trip, Mon-Sat 8:00-20:00, none on Sun). These are designed especially for the difficult-to-access streets in the historic heart of the city, and they're handy for seniors who could use a lift (offer your seat if there's a senior standing). Catch the minibus at the Sevilla Metro stop and simply ride it to the end (Metro: Embajadores). Enjoy this gritty slice of workaday Madrid—both people and architecture—as you roll slowly through Plaza Santa Ana, down a bit of the pedestrianized Calle de las Huertas, past gentrified Plaza Tirso de Molina (its junkies now replaced by a family-friendly flower market), and through Plaza de Lavapiés and a barrio of African and Bangladeshi immigrants. Jump out along the way to explore Lavapiés on foot (see description on next page), or stay on until you get to Embajadores. From there, you can catch the next #M1 minibus back to the Sevilla Metro stop (it returns along a different route) or descend into the subway system.

In the Lavapiés neighborhood, the multiethnic tapestry of Madrid enjoys seedy-yet-fun-loving life on the streets.

Neighborhoods like this typically experience the same familiar evolution: Initially they're so cheap that only immigrants, the downtrodden, and counter-culture types live there. The diversity and color they bring attracts those with more money. Businesses erupt to cater to those bohemian/trendy tastes. Rents go up. Those who gave the area its colorful energy in the first place can no longer afford to live there. They move out...and here comes Starbucks.

For now, Lavapiés is still edgy, yet comfortable enough for most. To help rejuvenate the area, the city built the big Centro Dramático Nacional theater just downhill from Lavapiés' main square.

The district has almost no tourists. (Some think it's too scary.) Old ladies with their tired bodies and busy fans hang out on their tiny balconies as they have for 40 years, watching the scene. Shady types lurk on side streets (don't venture off the main drag, don't show your wallet or money, and don't linger late on Plaza de Lavapiés).

If you're walking, start from Plaza de Antón Martín (Metro: Antón Martín) or Plaza Santa Ana. Find your way to Calle del Ave María (on its way to becoming Calle del Ave Allah) and on to Plaza de Lavapiés (Metro: Lavapiés), where elderly Madrileños hang out with the swarthy drunks; a mosaic of cultures treat this square as a communal living room. Then head up Calle de Lavapiés to the recently remodeled Plaza Tirso de Molina (Metro stop). This square was once plagued by druggies. Now home to flower kiosks and a playground, it's homey and inviting. This is a good example of Madrid's vision for reinvigorating its public spaces.

For food, you'll find plenty of tapas bars plus gritty Indian (almost all run by Bangladeshis) and Moroccan eateries. On Calle del Ave María, Bar Melos is a thriving dive jammed with a hungry and nubile crowd. It's famous for its giant patty melts called *zapatillas de lacón y queso* (because they're the size and shape of a *zapatilla,* or slipper; €11, feeds at least two, closed Sun-Mon, Calle del Ave María 44). Nuevo Café Barbieri, one of a dying breed of mirrored cafés with a circa-1940 ambience, offers classical music in the afternoon and jazz in the evening (closed Sun-Mon, Calle del Ave María 45). The Indian places line Calle de Lavapiés.

▲▲Bullfight
Madrid's Plaza de Toros hosts Spain's top bullfights on some Sundays and holidays from March through mid-October, and nearly every day during the San Isidro festival (May-early June—often sold out long in advance). Fights start between 17:00 and 21:00 (early in spring and fall, late in summer). The bullring is at the Ventas Metro stop (a 25-minute Metro ride from Puerta del Sol, tel. 913-562-200, www.las-ventas.com). For info on the background and "art" of bullfighting, see page 924.

Getting Tickets: Bullfight tickets range from €5 to €150. There are no bad seats at Plaza de Toros; paying more gets you in the shade and/or closer to the gore. (The action often intention- ally occurs in the shade to reward the expensive-ticket holders.) To be close to the bullring, choose areas 8, 9, or 10; for shade: 1, 2, 9, or 10; for shade/sun: 3 or 8; for the sun and cheapest seats: 4, 5, 6, or 7. Note these key words: *corrida*— a real fight with professionals;

novillada—rookie matadors, younger bulls, and cheaper tickets. Getting tickets through your hotel or a booking office is conve- nient, but they add 20 percent or more and don't sell the cheap seats. There are two booking offices; call both before you buy: at Plaza del Carmen 1 (Mon-Sat 9:30-13:00 & 16:30-19:00, Sun 9:30-14:00, tel. 915-319-131, or buy online at www.bullfighttickets madrid.com; run by José and his English-speaking son, also José, who also sells soccer tickets) and at Calle Victoria 3 (Mon-Fri 10:00-14:00 & 17:00-19:00, Sat-Sun 10:00-13:00, tel. 915-211-213).

To save money, you can stand in the ticket line at the bullring. Except for important bullfights—or during the San Isidro festival—there are generally plenty of seats available. About a thousand tickets are held back to be sold in the five days leading up to and on the day of a fight. Scalpers hang out before the popular fights at the Calle Victoria booking office. Beware: Those buying scalped tickets are breaking the law and can lose the ticket with no recourse.

For a dose of the experience, you can buy a cheap ticket and just stay to see a couple of bullfights. Each fight takes about 20 minutes, and the event consists of six bulls over two hours. Or, to keep your distance but get a sense of the ritual and gore, tour the bull bar on Plaza Mayor (described on page 435).

Bullfighting Museum (Museo Taurino): This museum, located at the back of the bullring, is not as good as the ones in Sevilla or Ronda (free, Mon-Fri 9:30-14:30, Sun 10:00-13:00, closed Sat year-round, closes early on fight days and all day Sun in off-season, tel. 917-251-857).

"Football" and Bernabéu Stadium

Madrid, like most of Europe, is enthusiastic about soccer (which they call *fútbol*). The Real ("Royal") Madrid team plays to a spirited crowd Saturdays and Sundays from September through May (tickets from €50—sold at bullfight box offices listed earlier). One of the most popular sightseeing activities among European visitors to Madrid is touring the 80,000-seat stadium. The €19 unguided visit includes the box seats, dressing rooms, technical zone, playing field, trophy room, and a big panoramic stadium view (Mon-Sat 10:00-19:00, Sun 10:30-18:30, shorter hours on game days, Metro: Santiago Bernabéu, tel. 913-984-300, www .realmadrid.com). Even if you can't catch a game, you'll see plenty of Real Madrid's all-white jerseys and paraphernalia around town.

Shopping in Madrid

Shoppers focus on the colorful pedestrian area between and around Gran Vía and Puerta del Sol. The giant Spanish department store El Corte Inglés, a block off Puerta del Sol, is a handy place to pick up just about anything you need (Mon-Sat 10:00-22:00, Sun 11:00-21:00, see page 423). The fanciest big-name shops (Gucci, Prada, and the like) tempt strollers along Calle de Fuencarral or Calle Serrano.

El Rastro: Europe's biggest flea market, rated ▲, is a field day for shoppers, people-watchers, and pickpockets (Sun only, 9:00-15:00). It's best before 11:00, though bargain shoppers like to go around 14:00, when vendors are more willing to strike end-of-day deals. Thousands of stalls titillate more than a million browsers with mostly new junk. Locals have lamented the tackiness of El Rastro lately—on the main drag, you'll find cheap underwear and bootleg CDs, but no real treasures.

For an interesting market day (Sun only), start at Plaza Mayor, where Europe's biggest stamp and coin market thrives. Enjoy this genteel delight as you watch old-timers paging lovingly through each other's albums, looking for win-win trades. When you're done, head south or take the Metro to Tirso de Molina. Walk downhill, wandering off on the side streets to browse antiques, old furniture, and garage-sale-style sellers who often simply throw everything out on a sheet. A typical Madrileño's Sunday could involve a meander through the Rastro streets with several stops for *cañas* (small beers) at the gritty bars along the way, then a walk to the Cava Baja area for more beer and tapas (see page 501). El Rastro offers a fascinating chance to see gangs of young thieves overwhelming and ripping off naive tourists with no police anywhere in sight. Seriously: Don't even bring a wallet. The pickpocket action is brutal, and tourists are targeted.

Fans: Casa de Diego sells *abanicos* (fans), *mantones* (typical Spanish shawls), *castañuelas* (castanets), *peinetas* (hair combs), and umbrellas. Even if you're not in the market, it's fun to watch the women flip open their final fan choices before buying (Mon-Sat 9:30-20:00, closed Sun, Puerta del Sol 12, tel. 915-226-643).

Classical Guitars: Guitar lovers know that the world's finest classical guitars are made in Spain. Several of the top workshops, within an easy walk of Puerta del Sol, offer inviting little showrooms with a peek at their craft and an opportunity to strum the final product. Consider the workshops of José Romero (Calle de Espoz y Mina 30, tel. 915-214-218) and José Ramirez (Calle de la Paz 8, tel. 915-314-229). Union Musical is a popular guitar shop off Puerta del Sol (Carrera de San Jerónimo 26, tel. 914-293-877). If you're looking to buy, be prepared to spend €1,000.

Nightlife in Madrid

Those into clubbing may have to wait until after midnight for the most popular places to even open, much less start hopping. Spain has a reputation for partying very late and not stopping until offices open in the morning. (Spaniards, who are often awake into the wee hours of the morning, have a special word for this time of day: *la madrugada*.) If you're out early in the morning, it's actually hard to tell who is finishing their day and who's just starting it. Even if you're not a party animal after midnight, make a point to be out with the happy masses, luxuriating in the cool evening air between 22:00 and midnight. The scene is absolutely unforgettable.

▲▲▲Paseo
Just walking the streets of Madrid seems to be the way the Madrileños spend their evenings. Even past midnight on a hot summer night, entire families with little kids are strolling, enjoying tiny beers and tapas in a series of bars, licking ice cream, and greeting their neighbors. Good areas to wander include along Gran Vía (from about Plaza de Callao to Plaza de España), perhaps following my "Gran Vía Tour" suggested earlier; from Puerta del Sol to Plaza Mayor and down Calle del Arenal until you hit Plaza de Isabel II; the pedestrianized Calle de las Huertas from Plaza Mayor to the Prado; and, to window shop with the young and trendy, from Gran Vía up Calle de Fuencarral (keep going until you hit traffic).

▲Zarzuela
For a delightful look at Spanish light opera that even English speakers can enjoy, try zarzuela. Guitar-strumming Napoleons in red capes; buxom women with masks, fans, and castanets; Spanish-speaking pharaohs; melodramatic spotlights; and aficionados clapping and singing along from the cheap seats, where the acoustics are best—this is zarzuela...the people's opera. Originating in Madrid, zarzuela is known for its satiric humor

and surprisingly good music. Performances occur at Teatro de la Zarzuela, which alternates between zarzuela, ballet, and opera throughout the year. The TI's monthly guide has a special zarzuela section.

Getting Tickets: Prices range from €16-40, 50 percent off for Wed shows and anytime for those over 65, Teatro de la Zarzuela box office open Mon-Fri 12:00-18:00 and Sat-Sun 15:00-18:00 for advance tickets or until showtime for same-day tickets, near the Prado at Jovellanos 4—see map on page 455, Metro: Sevilla or Banco de España, tel. 915-245-400, http://teatrodelazarzuela.mcu .es. To purchase tickets online, go to the theater section of www .ticketmaster.es; you can either pick them up at the box office or print them up at one of the ServiCaixa ATMs around town (there's one at Gran Vía 36, Metro: Callao).

▲▲Flamenco

Although Sevilla is the capital of flamenco, Madrid has a few easy and affordable options. And on summer evenings, Madrid puts on live flamenco events in the Royal Palace gardens (ask TI for details). Among the listings below, Casa Patas is grumpy, while Carboneras is friendlier—but Casa Patas has better-quality artists and a riveting seriousness. Considering that prices at Las Carboneras essentially match those at Casa Patas, the "House of Feet" is the better value.

Taberna Casa Patas attracts big-name flamenco artists. You'll quickly understand why this intimate venue (30 tables, 120 seats) is named "House of Feet." Since this is for locals as well as tour groups, the flamenco is contemporary and may be jazzier than your notion—it depends on who's performing (€32 includes cover and first drink, Mon-Thu at 22:30, Fri-Sat at 21:00 and 24:00, closed Sun, 1.25-1.5 hours, reservations smart, no flash cameras, Cañizares 10—see map on page 503, tel. 913-690-496, www .casapatas.com). Its restaurant is a logical spot for dinner before the show (€30 dinners, Mon-Sat from 20:00). Or, since it's three blocks south of the recommended Plaza Santa Ana tapas bars, this could be your pre- or post-tapas-crawl entertainment.

Las Carboneras, more downscale, is an easygoing, folksy little place a few steps from Plaza Mayor with a nightly hour-long flamenco show (€33 includes entry and a drink, €58 gets you a table up front with dinner and unlimited cheap drinks if you reserve ahead, manager Enrique promises a €5/person discount if you book direct and show this book in 2014, Mon-Thu at 20:30 and 22:30, Fri-Sat at 20:30 and 23:00, closed Sun, reservations recommended, Plaza del Conde de Miranda 1—see map on page 497, tel. 915-428-677, www.tablaolascarboneras.com). Dinner is served one hour before showtime.

Las Tablas Flamenco offers a less expensive nightly show respecting the traditional art of flamenco. You'll sit in a plain room with a mix of tourists and cool, young Madrileños in a modern, nondescript office block just over the freeway from Plaza de España (€27 with drink, reasonable drink prices, shows daily 22:00, additional early show Thu-Sun 20:00, 1.25-hour show, corner of Calle de Ferraz and Cuesta de San Vicente at Plaza España 9—see map on page 499, tel. 915-420-520, www.lastablasmadrid.com).

More Flamenco: Regardless of what your hotel receptionist may want to sell you, other flamenco places—such as Arco de Cuchilleros (Calle de los Cuchilleros 7), Café de Chinitas (Calle Torija 7, just off Plaza Mayor), Corral de la Morería (Calle de Morería 17), and Torres Bermejas (off Gran Vía)—are filled with tourists and pushy waiters.

Mesones

These long, skinny, cave-like bars, famous for customers drinking and singing late into the night, line the lane called Cava de San Miguel, just west of Plaza Mayor (see map on page 497). If you were to toss lowbrow barflies, Spanish karaoke, electric keyboards, crass tourists, cheap sangria, and greasy calamari into a late-night blender and turn it on, this is what you'd get. It's generally lively only on Friday and Saturday.

Late-Night and Jazz Bars

If you're just picking up speed at midnight and looking for a place filled with old tiles and a Gen-X crowd, power into **Bar Viva Madrid** (daily 13:00-3:00 in the morning, downhill from Plaza Santa Ana at Calle Manuel Fernández y González 7—see map on page 503, tel. 914-293-640). The same street has other late-night bars filled with music. Or hike on over to **Chocolatería San Ginés** (described on page 509) for a dessert of *churros con chocolate*.

For live jazz, **Café Central** is the old town favorite. Since 1982 it's been known as the place where rising stars get their start (€14, nightly at 21:00, cheap drinks, great scene, Plaza del Ángel 10—see map on page 503, tel. 913-694-143, www.cafecentralmadrid.com).

Movies

During the dictatorial days of Franco, movies were always dubbed in Spanish, making them easier to censor. (One famously awkward example: Franco's censors were scandalized by a film depicting a man and a woman having an implied affair, so they edited the voiceover to make the characters brother and sister. But the onscreen chemistry was still sexually charged—so they wound up turning a questionable relationship into an incestuous one.) As a result, movies in Spain remain about the most often dubbed in Europe. To see a movie with its original soundtrack, look for "V.O." (meaning "original version"). Cine Ideal, with nine screens, is a good place for the latest films in V.O. (€9, €7.30 on Mon, assigned seats during most days and showings, good to get tickets early on weekends, 5-minute walk south of Puerta del Sol at Calle del Dr. Cortezo 6—see map on page 424, tel. 913-692-518 for info, www.yelmocines.es). For extensive listings, see the *Guía del Ocio* entertainment guide (described on page 421) or a local newspaper.

Sleeping in Madrid

Madrid has plenty of centrally located budget hotels and *pensiones*. Most of the accommodations I've listed are within a few minutes' walk of Puerta del Sol.

You should be able to find a sleepable double for €60, a good double for €90, and a modern, air-conditioned double with all the comforts for €120. Prices vary throughout the year at bigger hotels, but remain about the same for the smaller hotels and *hostales*. It's almost always easy to find a place. Anticipate full hotels only during May (the San Isidro festival, celebrating Madrid's patron saint with bullfights and zarzuelas—especially around his feast day on May 15) and September (when conventions can clog the city). During the hot months of July and August, prices can be soft—ask for a discount.

With all of Madrid's street noise, I'd request the highest floor possible. Also, twin-bedded rooms are generally a bit larger than double-bedded rooms for the same price. Remember, you may find good deals by emailing several hotels (including business-class hotels) to ask for their best price. And during slow times, drop-ins

---

Sleep Code

(€1 = about $1.30, country code: 34)
S = Single, **D** = Double/Twin, **T** = Triple, **Q** = Quad, **b** = bathroom, **s** = shower only. Unless otherwise noted, credit cards are accepted, English is spoken, and breakfast is *not* included. Some hotels include the 10 percent IVA tax in the room price; others tack it onto your bill.

To help you easily sort through these listings, I've divided the accommodations into three categories, based on the price for a standard double room with bath during high season:

$$$ Higher Priced—Most rooms €120 or more.
  $$ Moderately Priced—Most rooms between €70-120.
    $ Lower Priced—Most rooms €70 or less.

Prices can change without notice; verify the hotel's current rates online or by email. For the best prices, always book direct.

can often score a room in business-class hotels for just a few euros more than the budget hotels (which don't have prices that fluctuate as wildly with demand).

Smoking bans have changed the atmosphere in hotel reception areas and hallways, but things aren't completely smoke-free, as hotels are still allowed to designate up to 10 percent of their rooms for smokers.

Mid-Range and Fancier Places

These mostly business-class hotels are good values (especially Hotel Europa) for those willing to spend a little more. Their formal prices may be inflated, but most offer weekend and summer discounts when it's slow. Drivers pay about €24 a day in garages.

Near Puerta del Sol and Gran Vía

These hotels are located in and around the pedestrian zone north and west of Puerta del Sol. For most of these, use Metro: Sol (except Hotel Ópera—Metro: Ópera; and Hotel Preciados—Metro: Callao).

$$$ Hotel Liabeny rents 220 plush, spacious, business-class rooms offering all the comforts (Sb-€108, Db-€127, Tb-€165, 10 percent cheaper mid-July-Aug and Fri-Sat, prices vary widely according to demand, breakfast-€16.50, air-con, free Wi-Fi, sauna, gym, off Plaza del Carmen at Salud 3, tel. 915-319-000, www .liabeny.es, info@liabeny.es).

$$$ Hotel Preciados, a four-star business hotel, has 95 welcoming, sleek, and modern rooms as well as elegant lounges. It's well-located and reasonably priced for the luxury it provides (Db-€125-160, prices often soft, checking Web specials in advance or dropping in will likely enable you to snag a room for around €100, breakfast-€15, free mini-bar, free Wi-Fi, parking-€18/day, just off Plaza de Santo Domingo at Calle Preciados 37, tel. 914-544-400, www.preciadoshotel.com, preciadoshotel@preciadoshotel.com).

$$$ Hotel Francisco I is a big, quiet, and well-run place with 60 rooms, nicely situated midway between the Royal Theater and Puerta del Sol (Sb-€105, Db-€140, Tb-€180, includes breakfast, prices fluctuate—book a month or more in advance to save 30 percent, no air-con, showers only—no tubs, free Wi-Fi, Calle del Arenal 15, tel. 915-480-204, www.hotelfrancisco.com, info @hotelfrancisco.com).

$$$ Hotel Carlos V is a Best Western with 67 high-ceilinged and somewhat worn-out rooms, elegant breakfast (not included), and a pleasant lounge (Sb-€80-120, standard Db-€100-173, Tb-€115-200, rates depend on demand and season, breakfast-€9, air-con, non-smoking floors, elevator, free Wi-Fi, Maestro

MADRID

Madrid's Center—
Hotels & Restaurants

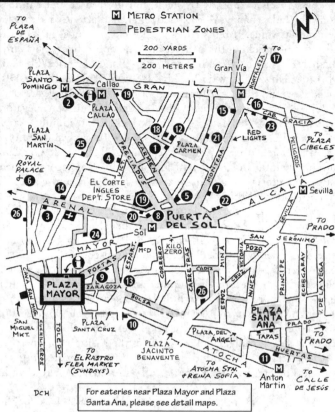

Ⓜ Metro Station

Pedestrian Zones

① Hotel Liabeny
② Hotel Preciados
③ Hotel Francisco I
④ Hotel Carlos V
⑤ Hotel Europa & Cafetería
⑥ To Hotel Ópera
⑦ Ateneo Hotel
⑧ Hotel Moderno
⑨ Petit Palace Posada del Peine
⑩ Hotel Plaza Mayor
⑪ Chic & Basic Colors
⑫ Hostales Acapulco & Triana; Pensión Arcos
⑬ Hostal Santa Cruz

⑭ Hostales Mayrit & Ivor
⑮ Hotel Praktik Metropol; Hostales Residencia Luis XV & Jerez
⑯ Hostal Aliste
⑰ To Madrid Municipal Youth Hostel
⑱ Restaurante Puerto Rico
⑲ El Corte Inglés Cafeterias (2)
⑳ Casa Labra Taberna Restaurante
㉑ Artemisia II Veggie Rest.
㉒ Rodilla; Pans & Co.
㉓ Fresc Co Buffet
㉔ Chocolatería San Ginés
㉕ Chocolaterías Valor
㉖ Launderette (2)

MADRID

Victoria 5, tel. 915-314-100, www.hotelcarlosv.com, recepcion @hotelcarlosv.com).

$$ Hotel Europa, with sleek marble, red carpet runners along the halls, happy Muzak charm, and an attentive staff, is a tremendous value. It rents 100 squeaky-clean rooms, many with balconies overlooking the pedestrian zone or an inner courtyard. The hotel has an honest ethos and offers a straight price (Sb-€80, Db-€100, Db with view-€120, Tb-€143, Qb-€170, Quint/b-€190, breakfast extra, these are maximum prices for Rick Steves readers in 2014—sometimes cheaper with Web specials, air-con, elevator, gym with sauna, roof-top solarium, free guest computer and Wi-Fi, Calle del Carmen 4, tel. 915-212-900, www.hoteleuropa .eu, info@hoteleuropa.eu, run by Antonio and Fernando Garaban and their helpful and jovial staff, Javi and Jim). The recommended Europa cafeteria-restaurant next door is a lively and convivial scene—fun for breakfast.

$$ Hotel Ópera, a serious and contemporary hotel with 79 classy rooms, is located just off Plaza Isabel II, a four-block walk from Puerta del Sol toward the Royal Palace (Db-€85-110 but prices spike wildly with demand, 10 percent discount if you reserve direct with this year's book, includes breakfast, air-con, elevator, sauna and gym, free guest computer and Wi-Fi, ask for a higher floor—there are nine—to avoid street noise, Cuesta de Santo Domingo 2, see map on page 499, Metro: Ópera, tel. 915-412-800, www.hotelopera.com, reservas@hotelopera.com). Hotel Ópera's cafeteria is deservedly popular. Consider their "singing dinners"—great operetta music with a delightful dinner—offered nightly (around €60, reservations smart, call 915-426-382 or reserve at hotel).

$$ Ateneo Hotel, just steps off Puerta del Sol, lacks public spaces and character, but its 38 rooms are close to business-class (Db-€75-90, occasionally less or more, 5 percent discount if you book direct with this year's book, air-con, elevator, guest computer and free Wi-Fi, Calle de la Montera 22, tel. 915-212-012, www .hotelateneo.es, info@hotelateneo.es).

$$ Hotel Moderno, renting 97 rooms in a quiet, professional, and friendly atmosphere, has a comfy second-floor lounge and is just steps off Puerta del Sol (Db-€90-120, extra person-€25, breakfast-€10, air-con, Wi-Fi, Calle del Arenal 2, tel. 915-310- 900, www.hotel-moderno.com, info@hotel-moderno.com).

Near Plaza Mayor
Both of these are a block off Plaza Mayor.

$$$ Petit Palace Posada del Peine feels like part of a big, modern chain (which it is), but fills its well-located old building with fresh, efficient character. Behind the ornate and sparkling

Old World facade is a comfortable and modern business-class hotel with 67 rooms (Db-€100-160 depending on demand, breakfast-€9, air-con, free use of laptops in all rooms, free Wi-Fi, Calle Postas 17, tel. 915-238-151, www.hthoteles.com, posada@hthoteles.com).

$$ Hotel Plaza Mayor, with 34 solidly outfitted rooms, is tastefully decorated and beautifully situated a block off Plaza Mayor (Sb-€50-70, Db-€60-80, superior Db-€90-100, Tb-€90-110, air-con, elevator, free Wi-Fi, Calle Atocha 2, tel. 913-600-606, fax 913-600-610, www.h-plazamayor.com, info@h-plazamayor .com). Director Leo offers a free breakfast to travelers who book direct (by email, phone, or fax—not through the website), pay the rates listed above, and show this year's book.

Near the Prado

$$ Hotel Lope de Vega offers good business-class hotel value near the Prado. It is a "cultural-themed" hotel inspired by the 17th-century writer Lope de Vega. With 59 rooms, it feels cozy and friendly for a formal hotel (Sb-€97, Db-€117, extra person-€25, rates can vary wildly based on demand, one child under 12 sleeps free, air-con, elevator, guest computer and Wi-Fi, limited parking-€25/day—request ahead, Calle Lope de Vega 49—see map on page 455, tel. 913-600-011, www.hotellopedevega.com, lopedevega@hotellopedevega.com).

Moderate Chain-Hotel Option

$$ Chic & Basic is not chic, but this chain offers a clean, fresh, contemporary option in three central Madrid locations with similar prices and a shared website (Sb-€65-85, Db-€75-120, www .chicandbasic.com, reservas@chicandbasic.com). Chic & Basic Colors could be noisy at night and has more of a hostel vibe, but it's near plenty of cafés and restaurants on a pedestrian street between Puerta del Sol and the Prado (Calle Huertas 14, tel. 914 296 935). Chic & Basic Mayerling is not picturesque, but it's well-situated between Puerta del Sol and the Plaza Mayor/Cava Baja tapas area (Calle del Conde de Romanones 6, tel. 914-201-580). Chic & Basic Atocha is right around the corner from the museums and Atocha Station (Calle Atocha 113, tel. 913-692-895).

Cheap Sleeps

Near Plaza del Carmen

These three are all in the same building at Calle de la Salud 13, north of Puerta del Sol. The building overlooks Plaza del Carmen—a little square with a sleepy, almost Parisian ambience.

$ Hostal Acapulco rents 16 bright rooms with air-conditioning and all the big hotel gear. The neighborhood is quiet enough that it's smart to request a room with a balcony

(Sb-€49-54, Db-€59-64, Tb-€77-80, show this book for a 5 percent discount at check-in, elevator, free guest computer and Wi-Fi, fourth floor, limited parking available—ask when you reserve, tel. 915-311-945, www.hostalacapulco.com, hostal_acapulco@yahoo.es, Ana, Marco, and Javier).

$ Hostal Triana, also a good deal, is bigger—with 40 rooms—and offers a little less charm for a little less money (Sb-€39, Db-€53, Tb-€69, rooms facing the square have air-con and cost €3 extra, other rooms have fans, elevator, free Wi-Fi, first floor, tel. 915-326-812, www.hostaltriana.com, triana@hostaltriana.com, Victor González).

$ Pensión Arcos is tiny, granny-run, and old-fashioned—it's been in the Hernández family since 1936. You can reserve by phone (in Spanish), and you must pay in cash—but its five rooms are clean, extra quiet, and served by an elevator. You also have access to a tiny roof terrace and a nice little lounge. For cheap beds in a great locale, assuming you can communicate, this place is unbeatable (D-€36, Db-€40, air-con, free Wi-Fi, closed Aug, fifth floor, tel. 915-324-994, Anuncia and Sabino).

Near Puerta del Sol

$ Hostal Santa Cruz, simple and well-located, has 16 rooms at a good price (Sb-€40, Db-€55, Tb-€75, air-con, elevator, free Wi-Fi, Plaza de Santa Cruz 6, second floor, tel. 915-222-441, www.hostalsantacruz.com, info@hostalsantacruz.com).

$ Hostal Mayrit and **Hostal Ivor** rent 28 rooms with thoughtful touches on pedestrianized Calle del Arenal (Sb-€45-55, Db-€55-65, air-con, elevator, near Metro: Ópera at Calle del Arenal 24, reception on third floor, tel. 915-480-403, www.hostalivor.com, reservas@hostalivor.com).

At the Top of Calle de la Montera

These places are a few minutes' walk from Puerta del Sol and a stone's throw from Gran Vía at the top of Calle de la Montera, which some dislike because of the young prostitutes who hang out here. They're legal, and the zone is otherwise safe and comfortable.

$$ Hotel Praktik Metropol sports plaid-and-striped hipster decor in its 70 fresh, modern rooms. Many rooms are tiny and on the building's interior—it's worth paying extra for the bigger superior double. Ask for a corner room (interior Sb-€55-89, standard interior Db-€65-99, superior exterior Db-€75-109, higher rates Thu-Sat, breakfast-€4, air-con, elevator, free Wi-Fi, Calle de Montera 47, reception on second floor, tel. 915-212-935, www.hotelpraktikmetropol.com, reservas@hotelpraktikmetropol.com).

$ Hostal Aliste rents 11 decent rooms in a dreary-yet-secure building at a great price (Sb-€29, Db-€39, extra bed-€15, these prices for Rick Steves readers in 2014 who book direct and show this book at check-in, air-con-€5, elevator, free guest computer and Wi-Fi, Caballero de Gracia 6, third floor, tel. 915-215-979, www.hostalaliste.net, info@hostalaliste.net, Rachel and Eduardo).

$ Hostal Residencia Luis XV is a big, plain, well-run, and clean place offering a good value. It's on a quiet eighth floor—there's an elevator (Sb-€45, Db-€59, Tb-€75, air-con, elevator, free Wi-Fi, Calle de la Montera 47, tel. 915-221-021, www.hrluisxv.net, reservas@hrluisxv.net). They also run the 36-room **Hostal Jerez**—similar in every way—on the sixth floor (tel. 915-327-565, www.hrjerez.net, reservas@hrjerez.net). Both properties are completely non-smoking.

Near the Prado

Two fine budget *hostales* are at Cervantes 34 (Metro: Antón Martín—but not handy to Metro; see map on page 455). Both are homey, with inviting lounge areas; neither serves breakfast.

$ Hostal Gonzalo has 15 spotless, comfortable rooms on the third floor and is well-run by friendly and helpful Javier. It's deservedly in all the guidebooks, so reserve in advance (Sb-€45, Db-€60, Tb-€75, air-con, elevator, free Wi-Fi, tel. 914-292-714, www.hostalgonzalo.com, hostal@hostalgonzalo.com).

Downstairs, the nearly as polished **$ Hostal Cervantes** also has 15 rooms (Sb-€40, Db-€50-55, Tb-€60-65, cheaper when slow and for longer stays, some rooms with air-con, free guest computer and Wi-Fi, tel. 914-298-365, www.hostal-cervantes.com, correo @hostal-cervantes.com, Fabio).

Youth Hostel

$ Madrid Municipal Youth Hostel (Albergue Juvenil Madrid) is fairly new and decidedly big, with 132 beds. A Metro ride north of downtown, it has four to six beds per room with lockers, modern bathrooms, and lots of extras, such as a laundry room, billiards, and movies (dorm bed-about €19, includes sheets and breakfast, coed rooms, towels-€3, free guest computer, 24-hour reception; Metro: Tribunal, then walk 2 minutes down Calle de Barceló to Calle de Mejia Lequerica 21; tel. 915-939-688, www.ajmadrid.es, info@ajmadrid.es).

Apartment Rentals

Tournights Spain, run by American Frederick, rents 20 roomy apartments with fully furnished kitchens in various locations throughout the heart of Madrid. Some are near Puerta del Sol, and others are within easy walking distance of the Prado and Reína Sofia (2 people-€80-120, 4 people-€100-180, prices vary with season and size—see website, €50 cleaning fee, 3-night minimum stay, discount for 7-night stay, 20 percent deposit required to reserve online, air-con, free Wi-Fi, mobile 620-585-594, www .tournights.com, info@tournights.com).

Eating in Madrid

In Spain, only Barcelona rivals Madrid for taste-bud thrills. You have three dining choices: a memorable, atmospheric sit-down meal in a well-chosen restaurant; a forgettable, basic sit-down meal; or a meal of tapas at a bar or two...or four. Unless otherwise noted, restaurants start serving lunch at 13:00 or 13:30 and dinner around 20:30. Depending on what time you show up, the same place may seem forlorn, touristy, or thriving with local eaters. Many restaurants close in August. Madrid has famously good tap water, and waiters willingly serve it free—just ask for *agua del grifo*. Restaurants and bars in Spain are smoke-free.

I've broken my recommended choices into groups: serious dining establishments; tapas places; lunch spots near the big sights; and simple, quick, and economical venues.

Fine Dining

D'Fabula, as its name indicates, offers a fairy tale of a menu and an elegant, peaceful setting. Its award-winning young chef, Ana Roldan, lovingly concocts weird and experimental tapas. Sit at the bar (to get help ordering) and go into orbit with inverted *patatas bravas,* delightful croquettes, "Planet Mars" (needs instruction), and so on. Prices are the same at the bar, in the dining room, and on the wonderful terrace (€3-4 tapas, €15-25 plates, daily from 20:00, just below Mercado de San Miguel but out of the rat race at Plaza Conde de Barajas 3, tel. 913-664-962).

Restaurante Casa Paco is a Madrid tradition. Check out its old walls plastered with autographed photos of Spanish celebrities who have enjoyed their signature dish—ox grilled over a coal fire. Though popular with tourists, the place is authentic, confident, and uncompromising. It's a worthwhile splurge if you want to dine out well and carnivorously (€15-25 plates, ox sold by weight, 200 grams—which is almost half a pound—is a hearty steak, Plaza de la Puerta Cerrada 11, tel. 913-663-166, www.casapaco1933.com).

Sobrino del Botín is a hit with many Americans because "Hemingway ate here." It's grotesquely touristy, pricey, and the last place "Papa" would go now...but still, people love it and go for the roast suckling pig, their specialty. I'd eat upstairs for a still-traditional, but airier style over the darker downstairs (€40-50 meals, daily 13:00-16:00 & 20:00-24:00, a block downhill from Plaza Mayor at Cuchilleros 17, tel. 913-664-217).

Casa Lucio is a favorite splurge for traditional specialties

Eating near Plaza Mayor

TO ROYAL PALACE

TO PUERTA DEL SOL & M →

CALLE MAYOR

POSTAS

ZARAGOZA

PLAZA MAYOR

TO PLAZA S ANA

C. CODO

CAVA S. MIGUEL

SAN MIGUEL MARKET

PLAZA CONDE BARAJAS

C. CUCHIL.

IMPERIAL

GERONA

LECHUGA

PALACIO SANTA CRUZ

SAN JUSTA

PLAZA PUERTA CERRADA

C. CONCEPCIÓN

C. SEGOVIA

C. NUNCIO

BAJA

C. GRAFAL

CALLE TOLEDO

C. COLEGIATA

TO M Tirso de Molina

C. ALMENDRO

CAVA

SAN ISIDRO

CALLE

DCH

200 YARDS
200 METERS

M La Latina

M METRO STATION
PEDESTRIAN ZONES

1 D'Fabula Restaurante
2 Restaurante Casa Paco
3 Sobrino del Botín
4 Casa Lucio
5 El Madroño
6 Txakolina Pintxoteca Madrileña
7 Taberna Huevos de Los Lucio

8 Taberna Tempranillo
9 Giangrossi Helado Artesanal Ice Cream
10 Casa Rúa
11 La Torre del Oro Bar Andalú
12 Las Carboneras (Flamenco)
13 Mesones ("Cave Bars")

among power-dressing Madrileños. The king and queen of Spain eat in this formal place, but it's accessible to commoners. This is a good restaurant for a special night out and a full-blown meal, but you pay extra for this place's fame (€50 for dinner, daily 20:30-24:00 plus Sun-Fri 13:00-16:00, closed Aug, Calle Cava Baja 35; unless you're the king or queen, reserve several days in advance—and don't even bother on weekends; tel. 913-653-252, www.casalucio.es).

Restaurante Palacio de Cibeles is on the sixth floor of the Palacio de Cibeles and features an outdoor terrace with spectacular views. The elegant restaurant of highly respected Toledo-based chef Adolfo features an extensive wine list and a fresh, creative Spanish menu that changes frequently based on season and availability (€50-60 for dinner, daily 13:00-16:00 & 20:00-24:00). The neighboring **Terrace Cibeles** serves drinks and light bites late into the night (daily 13:00-24:00), and the first-floor **Colección Cibeles,** though lacking views, serves an excellent €19 tapas *menu* with five small plates and two glasses of wine (daily 10:00-24:00, Plaza de Cibeles 1, central tel. 915-231-454).

El Caldero ("The Pot") is a romantic spot and *the* place for paella and other rice dishes. A classy, in-the-know crowd appreciates its subdued elegance and crisp service. The house specialty, *arroz caldero* (a variation on paella), is served with panache from a cauldron hanging from a tripod. Most of the formal rice dishes come in pots for two, including the €30-per-couple paella (€36 with seafood, closed for dinner Sun-Mon, Calle de las Huertas 15—see map on page 503, tel. 914-295-044). Wash it all down with the house sangria.

Casa Ciriaco is a tired but classic old place, popular with Madrileños who appreciate good traditional cooking—like stews—served with no affectation (€35 meals, €20 soup and steak specials, closed Wed and Aug, Calle Mayor 84, tel. 915-480-620). It was from this building in 1906 that an anarchist bombed King Alfonso XIII and his bride on their wedding day; the royal couple survived, but many others were killed (for details, see page 438). Photos of the carnage are inside the front door.

La Bola Taberna, touristy but friendly and tastefully elegant, specializes in *cocido Madrileño*—Madrid stew. The stew consists of various meats, carrots, and garbanzo beans in earthen jugs. This is a winter dish, prepared here for the tourists all year. The stew is served as two courses: First enjoy the broth as a soup, then dig into the meat and veggies (€19 stew, about €35/person for full meal, cash only, closed Sun, midway between Royal Palace and Gran Vía at Calle Bola 5, tel. 915-476-930).

Treating Tapas Bars as a Restaurant: Of the many recommended *tabernas* and tapas bars along Calle Cava Baja and Calle

MADRID

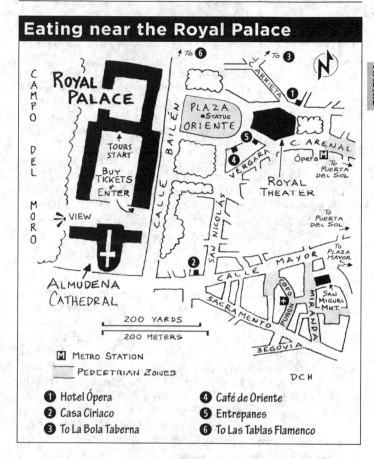

Eating near the Royal Palace

CAMPO DEL MORO

ROYAL PALACE

↑ To ⑥   ↑ To ❸

CARRIETA

❶

PLAZA
■STATUE
ORIENTE

C. ARENAL

CALLE BAILÉN

TOURS
START

BUY
TICKETS
&
ENTER

⑤
④
VERGARA

Ópera Ⓜ
To
PUERTA
DEL SOL

ROYAL
THEATER

VIEW

SAN NICOLÁS

To
PUERTA
DEL SOL

ALMUDENA
CATHEDRAL

❷

CALLE MAYOR

To
PLAZA
MAYOR

SACRAMENTO

CODO
PUÑON

3
P L A Z A

SAN
MIGUEL
MKT.

SEGOVIA

DCH

200 YARDS
200 METERS

Ⓜ METRO STATION

PEDESTRIAN ZONES

❶ Hotel Ópera
❷ Casa Ciriaco
❸ To La Bola Taberna

④ Café de Oriente
⑤ Entrepanes
⑥ To Las Tablas Flamenco

de Jesús (see listings later), several have tables and menus that lend themselves to fine dining. If you don't mind the commotion of the nearby bar action, you can order high on the menu in these places and, I'd say, eat better and more economically than in the more formal restaurants listed earlier.

Tapas-Hopping from Bar to Bar

For maximum fun, people, and atmosphere, go mobile for dinner: Do the *tapeo*, a local tradition of going from one bar to the next, munching, drinking, and socializing. If done properly, a pub crawl can be a highlight of your trip. Before embarking upon this culinary adventure, study and use the tapas tips on page 33. Your ability to speak a little Spanish will get you a much better (and less expensive) experience. While tiny tapas plates are standard in Andalucía, these days most of Madrid's bars offer bigger plates for around €6 (vegetables) to €15 (fish). Called *raciones*, these are ideal for a small group to share. The real action begins late (around 21:00). But for beginners, an earlier start, with less commotion, can be easier.

In Madrid, any proper bar gives a **free tapa** to anyone ordering a drink. But if you order any food with your drink, you won't get the free dish. If you care (and you should), always order the drink alone first and expect a tapa. If you don't get one, ask, *"Tapa?"* as if expecting the little bonus. Once you get it, order additional food as you like.

There are tapas bars almost everywhere, but three areas in the city center are particularly rewarding for a bar-crawl meal. Calle de Jesús (near the Prado) is the easiest, with several wonderful and diverse places in a two-block row. Trendy Calle Cava Baja has fancier offerings and feels most energetic, and the area between Puerta del Sol and Plaza Santa Ana is most central.

The Great Tapas Row on Calle de Jesús

This two-block stretch of tapas bars offers an amazing variety of fun places. Each has its own personality, and many have small and inviting sections with tables. Make the circuit and eyeball each place to see which appeals—you'll see that there's no reason to spend all your time and appetite at your first stop. Calle de Jesús stretches between Calle de Cervantes and Calle de las Huertas, behind the Palace Hotel (across the boulevard from the Prado). In the middle is the Plaza de Jesús, so named because this is the location of the Basilica of Jesús de Medinaceli (home to a relic that attracts huge crowds of pilgrims on special days). Start near the church at the first recommended bar, Cervecería Cervantes. I haven't given the nitty-gritty specifics for these places as they are mostly open every day for long hours.

Cervecería Cervantes serves hearty *raciones*, specializes in octopus, and has both a fine bar and good restaurant seating (intersection of Plaza de Jesús and Calle de Cervantes, tel. 914-296-093).

Taberna de la Daniela has a lovely dining area if you want to settle in for awhile. It's popular for its speciality *cocido madrileño*, a rich chickpea-based soup (Plaza de Jesús 7, tel. 913-896-238).

La Dolores, with a rustic little dining area, has been a hit since 1908 and is still extremely popular. Its canapés (€2.50 little sandwiches) are listed on the wall (Plaza de Jesús 4, tel. 914-292-243).

Cervezas La Fabrica packs in seafood lovers at the bar; there's a quieter back room for those preferring a table. Prices are the same in both spots (Calle de Jesús 2, tel. 913-690-671).

Cervecería Los Gatos is a kaleidoscope of Spanish culture, with chandeliers swinging above wine barrels in the bar area and characteristic tables below (Calle de Jesús 2, tel. 914-293-067).

La Anchoíta is named "the little anchovy" for its top-notch *anchoas* (cured anchovies) and *boquerones* (uncured anchovies). When these tasty little tidbits share a slice of bread, it's a "matrimonial." The three taps serve regular beer, "sin" (nonalcoholic) beer, and *vermut* (vermouth) from a tap shaped like a shrimp. If drinking white wine, get it in a frozen glass—ask for *"vaso helado"* (Calle de Jesús 4, tel. 913-601-674).

El Olivar seems humble, but serves particularly tasty *raciones*—especially their *pimientos de Padrón*—little green peppers (Calle de Jesús 6, tel. 914-294-724).

Cervecería El Diario, while a tavern dating from 1879, feels the most formulaic. They're known for their *calamares* (intersection of Calle de las Huertas and Calle de Jesús, tel. 914-292-800).

Taberna Maceira may be your favorite of the bunch. A bit farther down the strip, it's a Galician place with a wonderfully woody and rustic energy. It's a restaurant (not a bar) specializing in octopus, cod fish, *pimientos de Padrón* (green peppers), and *caldo Gallego* (white bean soup)—all classic Galician specialties of northwest Spain. Every day, the sign reads, *no hay Coca-Cola*—"no Coke" (Calle de Jesús 7, tel. 914-291-584).

An American diner named Peggy Sue's and an Irish bar mark the end of Calle de Jesús.

Tapas on Calle Cava Baja

Just a few minutes' walk south of Plaza Mayor, Calle Cava Baja fills each evening with mostly young, professional Madrileños prowling for chic tapas and social fun. Come at night only and treat the entire street as a destination. I've listed a few standards, but excellent new eateries are always opening up. For a good, authentic Madrid dinner experience, take time to survey the many options along this street and then choose your favorites. Remember, it's easier and touristy early, jammed with locals later. (If you want a formal dining experience on this street, survey the lot and pick one you like with tables in the back, or see the places recommended under "Fine Dining," earlier.) These tapas bars, listed in the order you'll reach them as you walk from Plaza Mayor up Calle Cava Baja, are worth special consideration (see map on page 497):

El Madroño ("The Berry Tree," a symbol of Madrid) is more of a cowboy bar, a block to the right (with your back to Plaza Mayor) off the top of Calle Cava Baja. Preserving a bit of old Madrid, a tile copy of Velázquez's famous *Drinkers* grins from its facade. Inside, look above the stairs for photos of 1902 Madrid. Study the coats of arms of Madrid through the centuries as you try a *vermut* (vermouth) on tap and a €4 sandwich. Or ask to try the *licor de madroño;* a small glass *(chupito)* costs €2. Indoor seating is bright and colorful; the sidewalk tables come with great people-watching. Munch *raciones* at the bar or front tables to be in the fun scene, or have a quieter sit-down meal at the tables in the back (closed Mon, Plaza de la Puerta Cerrada 7, tel. 913-645-629).

Txakolina Pintxoteca Madrileña is a thriving bar serving Basque-style *pinchos* (fancy sandwiches—*pintxo* in Basque) to a young crowd (€3/*pincho*, Calle Cava Baja 26, tel. 913-664-877).

Taberna Los Huevos de Lucio, owned by the same family as the reputable Casa Lucio (described earlier, under "Fine Dining"), is a jam-packed bar serving good tapas, salads, *huevos estrellados* (scrambled eggs with fried potatoes), and wine. If you'd like to make it a sit-down meal, head to the tables in the back. Their basement is much less atmospheric (Calle Cava Baja 30, tel. 913-662-984).

Taberna Tempranillo, ideal for hungry wine lovers, offers fancy tapas and fine wine by the glass (see listing on the board). While there are a few tables, the bar is just right for hanging out. With a phrase book in hand or a spirit of adventure, use their fascinating menu to assemble your dream meal. When I order high on their menu, I'm generally very happy. This place is typically packed and full of commotion—the crowds can be overwhelming. Arrive by 20:00 or plan to wait (closed Aug, Calle Cava Baja 38, tel. 913-641-532).

Ice Cream Finale: **Giangrossi Helado Artesanal** serves Argentinean-style ice cream, considered to be some of Madrid's best. With a plush white leather lounge and lots of great flavors, this hipster ice cream shop offers a sweet way to finish your dining experience in this area (they also serve cocktails). Enjoy a couple of free tastes before you choose (at the end of Calle Cava Baja at #40, 50 yards from La Latina Metro stop, tel. 913-660-272).

Central Pub-Crawl Tapas Route

The little streets between Puerta del Sol, San Jerónimo, and Plaza Santa Ana hold tasty surprises. Here I've described a five-stop tapa crawl. These places are good, but don't be afraid to make some discoveries of your own.

• *Start at the intersection of Carrera de San Jerónimo and Calle Victoria.*

The atmospheric **Museo del Jamón** (Museum of Ham), festooned with ham hocks, is a fun place to see—unless you're a pig (or a vegetarian). Its frenetic, cheap, stand-up bar (with famously rude service) is an assembly line of fast-and-simple *bocadillos* and *raciones*. If you order anything,

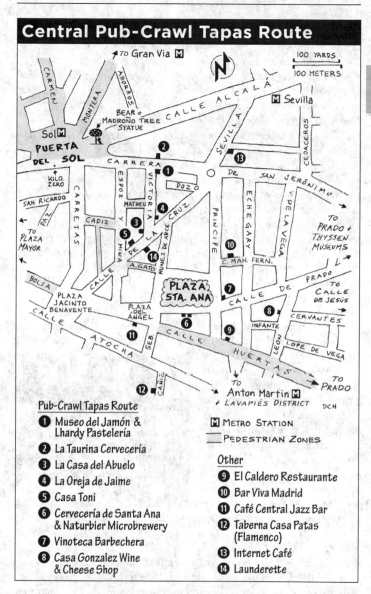

Central Pub-Crawl Tapas Route

To Gran Via M

N

100 YARDS
100 METERS

CARMEN

AHORROS

MONTERA

CALLE ALCALÁ

M Sevilla

SEVILLA

CEDACEROS

BEAR +
MADROÑO TREE
STATUE

Sol M

PUERTA
DEL SOL

R

2

1

13

CARRERA

DE SAN JERÓNIMO

KILO
ZERO

ESPOZ

VICTORIA

POZO

MATHEU

DE

Y

SAN RICARDO

CADIZ

4

PRINCIPE

ECHEGARAY

V DE LA VEGA

TO
PRADO +
THYSSEN
MUSEUMS

CARRETAS

3

5

MINA

ARCE

CRUZ

NÚÑEZ DE

10

TO
PLAZA
MAYOR

CALLE

14

A. GATO

C. MAN. FERN.

DE PRADO

TO
CALLE
DE JESÚS

BOLSA

PLAZA
JACINTO
BENAVENTE

PLAZA
DEL
ÁNGEL

PLAZA
STA.
ANA

7

CALLE

DE

CERVANTES

CALLE

11

6

8

INFANTE

LOPE DE VEGA

ATOCHA

SEB.

CALLE

9

HUERTAS

LEON

TO
PRADO

12

CANIZ

TO
Anton Martin M
+ LAVAPIÉS DISTRICT

DCH

Pub-Crawl Tapas Route

1. Museo del Jamón & Lhardy Pastelería
2. La Taurina Cervecería
3. La Casa del Abuelo
4. La Oreja de Jaime
5. Casa Toni
6. Cervecería de Santa Ana & Naturbier Microbrewery
7. Vinoteca Barbechera
8. Casa Gonzalez Wine & Cheese Shop

M METRO STATION

PEDESTRIAN ZONES

Other

9. El Caldero Restaurante
10. Bar Viva Madrid
11. Café Central Jazz Bar
12. Taberna Casa Patas (Flamenco)
13. Internet Café
14. Launderette

get only a cheap sandwich, because the staff is not honest. Take advantage of the easy photo-illustrated menus that show various dishes and their prices. The best ham is the pricey *jamón ibérico*—from pigs who led stress-free lives in acorn-strewn valleys. Point clearly to what you want, and be very specific to avoid being served a pricier meal than you intended. For instance, if you're on a budget, don't let them sell you the *jamón ibérico*, which costs

€14; a plate of low-end *jamón blanco* costs just €2.50. For a small sandwich, ask for a *chiquito* (€1.50, or €4 for *ibérico;* daily 9:00-24:00, sit-down restaurant upstairs, air-con).

• *Across the street is the touristy and over-priced bull bar,* **La Taurina.** *(I wouldn't eat here, but you're welcome to ponder the graphic photos that celebrate the gory art of bullfighting.) And next door take a detour from your pub crawl with something better for grandmothers.*

Lhardy Pastelería offers a genteel taste of Old World charm in this district of rowdy pubs. This place has been a fixture since 1839 for Madrileños wanting to duck in for a cup of soup or a light snack. Step right in, and pretend you're an aristocrat back between the wars. Serve yourself. You'll pay as you leave (on the honor system). Help yourself to the silver water dispenser (free), a line of elegant bottles (each a different Iberian fortified wine: sherry, port, and so on, €2.50/glass), a revolving case of meaty little pastries (€1 each), and a fancy soup dispenser (chicken broth consommé-€2.50, or €3 with a splash of sherry...local style—bottles in the corner, help yourself; Mon-Sat 9:00-15:00 & 17:00-22:00, Sun 10:00-15:00, Carrera de San Jerónimo 8).

• *Next, forage up Calle Victoria.*

La Casa del Abuelo is where seafood lovers savor sizzling plates of tasty little *gambas* (shrimp) and *langostinos* (prawns), with bread to sop up the delight-ful juices. As drinks are cheap and dishes are small and pricey, you might just want to share a *ración* or sample some wine. Try *gambas a la plan-cha* (grilled shrimp, €9.10) or *gambas al ajillo* (ah-HEE-yoh, shrimp cooked in oil and gar-lic, €9.90) and a €2.10 glass of sweet red house wine. They

serve gazpacho May through September (daily 12:00-24:00, Calle Victoria 12).

• *Head around the corner onto Calle de la Cruz.*

At **La Oreja de Jaime,** the specialty is sautéed pigs' ears (*oreja,* €5). While pig ears are a Madrid dish (fun to try, hard to swallow), this place is Galician—they serve *pimientos de Padrón* (sautéed miniature green peppers—quite possibly the tastiest plate of the entire crawl, €4.50) and the distinctive *ribeiro* (ree-BAY-roh) wine, served Galician-style, in characteristic little ceramic bowls to disguise its lack of clarity (Calle de la Cruz 12, tel. 647-293-693).

• *For a finale, continue up Calle de la Cruz.*

Memorable little **Casa Toni** is my favorite stop on this crawl. Run by Toni, it has a helpful English menu and several fun, classic dishes to try: *patatas bravas* (fried potatoes in a spicy sauce, €4.20), *berenjena* (deep-fried slices of eggplant, €5), *champiñones* (sautéed mushrooms, €5.70), and gazpacho—the cold tomato-and-garlic soup (€2.50) that is generally served only during the hot season, but available here year-round just for you (closed July, Calle de la Cruz 14, tel. 915-322-580).

More Options: If you're hungry for more, and want a trendy, up-to-date, pricier tapas experience, head for Plaza Santa Ana, with lively bars spilling out onto the square. Survey the entire scene. Consider **Cervecería de Santa Ana** (tasty tapas with two zones: rowdy, circa-1900 beer hall and classier sit-down) or **Naturbier,** a local microbrewery. **Vinoteca Barbechera,** at the downhill end of the square, has an inviting menu of tapas and fine wines by the glass (indoor and outdoor seating). **Casa Gonzalez,** a venerable gourmet cheese and wine shop with a circa-1930s interior, offers a genteel opportunity to enjoy a plate of first-class cheese and a fine glass of wine with friendly service and a fun setting recalling the happy days of the Republic of Spain—after the monarchy but before Franco. Their €20 assortment of five Spanish cheeses— more than enough for two—is a cheese lover's treat (nice wines by the glass, Mon-Sat 9:30-24:00, Sun 11:00-18:00, three blocks past Plaza Santa Ana at Calle de León 12, tel. 914-295-618, Francisco).

Lunch near the Big Sights

The big three sights (Royal Palace, Prado Museum, and Reina Sofía) are consuming enough that you'll likely be hungry when you leave. Each has a fine cafeteria inside. But there are also plenty of good eateries nearby, seemingly made-to-order for travelers needing a bite.

After visiting the Royal Palace, I'd find a place near the Royal Theater or on Calle del Arenal. Café de Oriente and Entrepanes (each described below) are great options. The Prado and Reina Sofía are near my favorite strip of tapas bars—nine great places in a two-block stretch of Calle de Jesús that are fast, fun, economical, and full of locals (described earlier). For something right at Reina Sofía, choose Brillante (described later) or one of the many good eateries ringing the square facing the museum's entry. And across the boulevard from the Prado you'll find a VIPS (described later) and a Starbucks.

Near the Royal Palace: **Café de Oriente** serves a great three-course lunch special for €12 (served Mon-Fri 13:00-16:00 only) in fin-de-siècle elegance immediately across the park from the Royal Palace. While its lunch special is reasonable, the restaurant and terrace menus are pricey (Plaza de Oriente 2, tel. 915-413-974, www.cafedeoriente.es).

Entrepanes is a clever chain offering cheap salads, tapas, and little sandwiches that you order using a form. Check what you like, pay at counter, wait for your name to be called, and sit where you like—including outside with fine view of street scene as pedestrians stroll by the opera (every item-€1.50-€4, daily 12:00-24:00, Calle de Carlos III 3, tel. 915-482-893).

Near Reina Sofía: **El Brillante** is a classic dive right on Plaza Sánchez Bustillo, the square in front of the Centro de Arte Reina Sofía. It offers pricey tapas and baguette sandwiches, but everyone comes for the fried squid sandwiches (evidenced by the older *señoras* with mouthfuls of *calamares*). Sit at the simple bar or at an outdoor table (long hours daily, two entrances—one on Plaza Sánchez Bustillo, the other at Plaza del Emperador Carlos V 8, tel. 915-286-966).

Near the Prado: **VIPS** is a bright, popular chain restaurant, handy for a cheap and filling salad. Engulfed in a shop selling books and candy, this is a high-energy, no-charm eatery (daily 9:00-24:00, across the boulevard from northern end of Prado, under Palace Hotel). Next door is Spain's first Starbucks, opened in 2001.

Eating Cheaply
On or near Plaza Mayor

Madrileños enjoy a bite to eat on Plaza Mayor (without its high costs) by grabbing food to go from a nearby bar and just planting themselves somewhere on the square to eat (squid sandwiches are popular). But for many tourists, dinner at a sidewalk café right on Plaza Mayor is worth the premium price (consider Cervecería Pulpito, southwest corner of the square at #10). See map on page 497 for locations of places recommended below.

Squid Sandwiches: Plaza Mayor is famous for its *bocadillos de calamares*. For a tasty €2.65 squid-ring sandwich, line up at **Casa Rúa** at Plaza Mayor's northwest corner, a few steps up Calle Ciudad Rodrigo (daily 11:00-23:00). Hanging up behind the bar is a photo-advertisement of Plaza Mayor from the 1950s, when the square contained a park.

Bullfighting Bar: The walls of **La Torre del Oro Bar Andalú** are lined with grisly bullfight photos (read the gory description on page 924). This place is good for drinks, but you pay a premium for the tapas and food...the cost of munching amidst all that bullephenalia while enjoying their excellent Plaza Mayor outdoor seating (daily 8:00-15:00 & 18:00-24:00, closed in Jan).

Breakfast in Madrid

Most hotels don't include breakfast (and many don't even serve it), so you may be out on the streets first thing looking for a place to eat. Non-touristy cafés only offer a hot drink and a pastry, with perhaps a potato omelet and sandwiches (toasted cheese, ham, or both). Touristy places will have a *desayuno* menu with various ham-and-eggs deals. Try *churros* once (see the listings for my favorite places); if you're not in the mood for heavy chocolate in the morning, go local and dip your *churros* in a *café con leche*. Starbucks, a temptation for many due to its familiarity, is often nearby. Get advice from your hotel staff for their favorite breakfast place. My typical breakfast, found at any corner bar: *café con leche*, *tortilla española* (a slice of potato omelet), and *jugo de naranja natural* (fresh-squeezed orange juice).

Mercado de San Miguel: This early-20th-century market sparkles after a recent renovation and bustles with a trendy food circus of eateries (daily 10:00-24:00, later on weekends). While it's expensive and touristy, it's also fun and accessible. You can stroll while you munch, hang out at bars, or take a break at one of the market's food-court-style tables.

Near Puerta del Sol

Restaurante Puerto Rico, a simple no-nonsense place, serves good meals for great prices to smart Madrileños in a long, congested hall (€10 three-course fixed-price meal, long hours daily, Chinchilla 2, between Puerta del Sol and Gran Vía, tel. 915-219-834).

Restaurante-Cafeteria Europa is a fun, high-energy scene with a mile-long bar, old-school waiters, great people-watching, local cuisine, and a fine €11 fixed-price lunch (offered daily 13:00-16:00, inside only). The menu lists three price levels: bar (inexpensive), table (generally pricey), or terrace (sky-high but with good people-watching). Your best value is to stick to the lunch menu if you're sitting inside, or order off the plastic *barra* menu if you sit at the bar—the €3 ham-and-egg toast or the homemade *churros* make a nice breakfast (daily 7:00-24:00, next to Hotel Europa, 50 yards off Puerta del Sol at Calle del Carmen 4, tel. 915-212-900).

El Corte Inglés' top-floor cafeterias (in both of its buildings) are fresh, modern, and popular, though not particularly cheap. One is just off Puerta del Sol at the intersection of Calle de Preciados and Calle de Tetuán, but the better one is near Plaza Callao: Its snazzy Gourmet Experience houses a specialty grocery mart and 10 different mini-restaurants with cuisines ranging from Mexican to Chinese. The lunch hour is busy, though it's worth the wait for its great views of Gran Vía and Plaza de España. Take a seat at any of the indoor tables, or out on the open terrace (Mon-Sat 10:00-24:00, Sun 11:00-24:00, shorter hours at Puerta del Sol location).

Casa Labra Taberna Restaurante is famous as the birthplace of the Spanish Socialist Party in 1879...and as a spot for great cod. Packed with Madrileños, it manages to be both dainty and rustic. It's a wonderful scene with three distinct sections: the stand-up bar (cheapest, with two lines: one for munchies, the other for drinks), a peaceful little sit-down area in back (a little more expensive but still cheap; €6 salads), and a fancy restaurant (€20 fixed-price lunch). Their tasty little €1.25 *tajada de bacalao* cod dishes put them on the map. The waiters are fun to joke around with (daily 11:00-15:30 & 18:00-23:00, a block off Puerta del Sol at Calle Tetuán 12, tel. 915-310-081).

Vegetarian: **Artemisia II** is a hit with vegetarians who like good, healthy food without the typical hippie ambience that comes with most veggie places (great €12 three-course fixed-price lunch Mon-Fri only, open daily 13:30-16:00 & 21:00-24:00, 2 blocks north of Puerta del Sol at Tres Cruces 4, a few steps off Plaza del Carmen, tel. 915-218-721).

Fast-Food Chains, Buffets, and Picnics

Fast-Food Sandwich Joints: For an easy, light, and cheap meal, look for the Spanish answers to Subway: **Rodilla** and **Pans & Company** (open daily 9:00-23:00). You'll see them on Puerta del Sol and nearly every square, offering all the ambience of a McDonald's and a good selection of fresh sandwiches and prepackaged salads.

Buffet Places: Many central eateries advertise cheap buffets. With plenty of drinks, desserts, and the chance to eat at nearly any hour, places like **Fresc Co** (Calle de Caballero de Gracia 8) tempt mostly students and tourists with great prices and the thrill of being free to go back for more.

Picnic: The department store **El Corte Inglés** has well-stocked meat and cheese counters in its lower-level grocery store (Mon-Sat 10:00-22:00, Sun 11:00-21:00).

Churros con Chocolate

Those not watching their cholesterol will want to try the deep-fried doughy treats called *churros* (or the thicker *porras*), best enjoyed by dipping them in pudding-like hot chocolate. Though many *chocolaterías* offer the dunkable fritters, *churros* are most delicious when consumed fresh out of the greasy cauldron at a place that actually fries them. Two of my favorites are near Puerta del Sol (see the map on page 491 for locations).

Chocolatería San Ginés is a classy institution, much beloved by Madrileños for its *churros con chocolate* (€3.70). Dunk your *churros* into the warm chocolate pudding, as locals have done here for more than 100 years. Though quiet before midnight, it's packed with the disco crowd in the wee hours; the popular dance club Joy Eslava is next door (open 24 hours a day; from Puerta del Sol, take Calle del Arenal 2 blocks west, turn left on bookstore-lined Pasadizo de San Ginés, and you'll see the café at #5; tel. 913-656-546).

Chocolaterías Valor is a modern chain that does *churros* with pride and gusto. A few minutes' walk from nearly all my hotel recommendations, it's a fine place for breakfast. With a website like www.amigosdelchocolate.com, you know where their heart is (€4 *churros con chocolate,* daily 8:00-22:30, Fri-Sat until 24:00, a half-block below Plaza Callao and Gran Vía at Postigo de San Martín 7, tel. 915-229-288).

Madrid Connections

By Train
Madrid has two main train stations: Chamartín and Atocha. Both stations offer long-distance trains (*largo recorridos*) as well as smaller local trains (*regionales* and *cercanías*) to nearby destinations. You can **buy tickets** at the stations, at travel agencies, or online. (For all the details, see the appendix.) While travel agencies add a small fee, they can be a good place to buy tickets, especially during the high season or holidays, when the station's ticket counters have long lines. Convenient locations include the El Corte Inglés travel agency at Atocha (Mon-Fri 8:00-22:00, Sat-Sun 10:00-18:00, on ground floor of AVE side at the far end) and the El Corte Inglés department store at Puerta del Sol (see "Travel Agencies" on page 425).

Chamartín Station
The TI is near track 20. The impressively large information, tickets, and customer-service office is at track 11. You can relax in the Sala VIP Club if you have a first-class railpass and first-class seat or sleeper reservations (between tracks 13 and 14, cooler of free drinks). Luggage storage *(consignas)* is across the street, opposite track 17. The station's Metro stop is also called Chamartín (not "Pinar de Chamartín"). For train connections from here, see later.

Atocha Station
The station is split in two: an AVE side (mostly long-distance trains) and a *cercanías* side (mostly local trains to the suburbs—known as *cercanías*—and the Metro for connecting into downtown). These two parts are connected by a corridor of shops. Each side of the

station has separate schedules and customer-service offices. The TI, which is in the AVE side, offers tourist info, but no train info (Mon-Sat 8:00-20:00, Sun 9:00-14:00, tel. 915-284-630). To get to Atocha, use the "Atocha RENFE" Metro stop (not "Atocha").

Ticket Offices: The *cercanías* side has two offices—a small one for local trains and a big one for major trains (such as AVE). The AVE side has a pleasant, airy office that sells tickets for AVE and other long-distance trains (there are two lines: "Tickets in Advance" or "Selling Out Today"/"Departures Today"). A ticket counter will sometimes open up to sell tickets for trains departing soon—if you need to make a last-minute purchase, look for your destination and departure time, and get in line at that counter. If the line at one office is long, check the other offices. To secure your place in line, grab a number from a machine, usually located in the middle of the office by a sign with an image of a ticket. Ticket machines outside and around the office require a chip-and-PIN credit card.

AVE Side: Located in the towering old-station building, this half of the station boasts a lush, tropical garden filling its grand hall. It has the AVE trains, other fast trains (Grandes Líneas), a pharmacy (daily 8:00-22:00, facing garden), and the wicker-elegant Samarkanda—both an affordable cafeteria (daily 13:00-20:00) and a pricey restaurant (daily from 21:00, tel. 915-309-746). Luggage storage *(consigna)* is below Samarkanda  (daily 6:00-22:20). In the departure lounge on the upper floor, TV monitors announce track numbers. (A few trains, such as those for Toledo, Alicante, and Valencia, depart from the lower floor.) For information, try the *Información* counter (daily 6:30-22:30), next to Centro Servicios AVE (which handles only AVE changes and problems). The *Atención al Cliente* office deals with problems on Grandes Líneas (daily 6:30-23:30). Also on the AVE side is the Club AVE/Sala VIP, a lounge reserved solely for AVE business-class travelers and for first-class ticket-holders or Eurailers with a first-class reservation (upstairs, past the security check on right; free drinks, newspapers, showers, and info service).

***Cercanías* Side:** This is where you'll find the local *cercanías* trains, *regionales* trains, some eastbound faster trains, and the "Atocha RENFE" Metro stop. The *Atención al Cliente* office in the *cercanías* section has information only on trains to destinations near Madrid. During busy times, some AVE trains will pull in on this side—clearly marked signs lead you to the Metro, taxi stand, or back to the AVE side.

Terrorism Memorial: The terrorist bombings of March 11, 2004, took place in Atocha and on local lines going into and out of the station. Security is understandably tight here. A moving memorial is in the *cercanías* part of the station near the Atocha RENFE Metro stop. Walk inside and under the cylinder to read the thousands of condolence messages in many languages (daily 11:00-14:00 & 17:00-19:00). The 36-foot-tall cylindrical glass memorial towers are visible from outside on the street.

AVE Trains

Spain's AVE bullet train opens up some good itinerary options. You can get from Madrid's Atocha Station to **Barcelona** in about three hours, with trains running almost hourly. The AVE train is generally faster and easier than flying, but not necessarily cheaper. Basic second-class tickets are €120 one-way for most departures; first-class tickets are €210. Advance purchase discounts (40-60 days ahead) are available through the national rail company (RENFE), but sell out quickly. Save by not traveling on holidays.

The AVE is also handy for visiting **Sevilla** (and, on the way, **Córdoba**). The basic Madrid-Sevilla second-class AVE fare is €85, depending upon departure time; first-class AVE costs €130 and comes with a meal. Consider this exciting day trip: 7:00-depart Madrid, 8:45-12:40-in Córdoba, 13:30-20:45-in Sevilla, 23:15-back in Madrid.

Other AVE destinations include **Toledo, Segovia,** and **Valencia.** Prices vary with times, class, date of purchase—RENFE has recently started discounting unsold AVE tickets as departure dates near. Eurail Pass holders pay a seat reservation fee (for example, Madrid to Sevilla is €10.35 second-class, but only at RENFE ticket windows—discount not available at ticket machines). Reserve each AVE segment ahead (tel. 902-320-320 for Atocha AVE info). For the latest, pick up the AVE brochure at the station, or check www.renfe.com.

Train Connections

Below I've listed both non-AVE and (where available) AVE trains to help you compare your options. General train info: tel. 902-320-320; international journeys: tel. 902-243-402; www.renfe.com.

From Madrid by Train to: Toledo (AVE or cheaper Avant: nearly hourly, 30 minutes, from Atocha), **El Escorial** (2/hour, but bus is better—see page 518), **Segovia** (AVE: 8/day, 30 minutes plus 20-minute shuttle bus into Segovia center, from Chamartín, take train going toward Valladolid; slower *cercanías* trains: 9/day, 2 hours, from both Chamartín and Atocha), **Ávila** (nearly hourly until 22:30, 1.5-2 hours, more frequent departures from Chamartín than Atocha), **Salamanca** (7/day, 2.75 hours, from

Chamartín), **Valencia** (AVE: nearly hourly, 1.75 hours, from Atocha; in Valencia, AVE passengers arrive at Joaquín Sorolla station), **Santiago de Compostela** (4/day, 5.5-9.5 hours, includes night train, from Chamartín), **Barcelona** (AVE: at least hourly, 2.5-3 hours from Atocha; plus 1 night train from Chamartín, 9 hours), **San Sebastián** (4/day, 5.25-7.25 hours, from Chamartín), **Bilbao** (4/day, 5 hours, from Chamartín), **Pamplona** (4/day direct, 3 hours, from Atocha), **Burgos** (8/day, 2.5-4.5 hours, from Chamartín), **León** (8/day, 3-4.5 hours, from Chamartín), **Granada** (2/day, 4.5 hours, from Atocha), **Sevilla** (AVE: hourly, 2.5 hours, departures from 16:00-19:00 can sell out far in advance, from Atocha), **Córdoba** (AVE: 2-3/hour, 1.75 hours; Altaria trains: 4/day, 2 hours; all from Atocha), **Málaga** (AVE: 12/day, 2.5-3 hours, from Atocha), **Algeciras** (2/day, 5.5 hours, from Atocha), **Lisbon** (1/night, 9.5 hours, from Chamartín).

By Bus

Madrid has several major bus stations with good Metro connections. Multiple bus companies operate from these stations, including Alsa (tel. 902-422-242, www.alsa.es), Avanza and Auto-Res (tel. 902-020-052, www.avanzabus.com), and La Sepulvedana (tel. 901-119-699, www.lasepulvedana.es). If you take a taxi from any bus station, you'll be charged a legitimate €5.50 supplement (not levied for trips to the station).

Plaza Elíptica Station: Served by Alsa. Buses to **Toledo** leave from here (2/hour, 1-1.5 hours, *directo* faster than *ruta*, Metro: Plaza Elíptica).

Estación Sur de Autobuses (South Station): Served by Alsa, Socibus, and Avanza. From here, buses go to **Ávila** (9/day, 6/day on weekends, 1.5 hours, Avanza), **Salamanca** (hourly express, 2.5-3 hours, Avanza), **León** (10/day, 3.5-4.5 hours, Alsa), **Santiago de Compostela** (5/day, 8 hours, includes 24:30-9:00 night bus, Alsa), **Granada** (nearly hourly, 5-5.75 hours, Alsa), and **Lisbon** (2/day, 9 hours, €41.50 one-way, Avanza). The station sits squarely on top of the Méndez Álvaro Metro (has TI, tel. 914-684-200, www.estacionautobusesmadrid.com).

Príncipe Pío Station: Príncipe Pío is the old North train station, which has now morphed into a trendy mall and a bus hub for local lines including **Segovia** (2/hour departing on half-hour from platforms 6 or 7, 1.25-1.5 hours, runs from around 6:30-21:30, service starts later on Sun). From Metro: Príncipe Pío, follow signs to *terminal de autobuses* or follow pictures of a bus. Buy a ticket from the Sepulvedana window (platform 4). Reservations are rarely necessary.

Moncloa Station: This station, in the Moncloa Metro station, serves **El Escorial** (4/hour, 45-55 minutes; for details, see page

518). To reach the **Valley of the Fallen,** it's best to connect via El Escorial (see page 526 for details).

Avenida de América Station: Served by Alsa. Located at the Avenida de América Metro, buses go to **Burgos** (hourly, 3 hours) and **Pamplona** (7/day, 5 hours).

By Plane
Madrid's Barajas Airport

Ten miles east of downtown, Madrid's modern airport has four terminals. Terminals 1, 2, and 3 are connected by long indoor walkways (about an 8-minute walk apart) and serve airlines including Delta, United, US Airways, and Air Canada. The newer Terminal 4 serves airlines including Iberia, Vueling, Ryanair, British, and American, and also has a separate satellite terminal called T4S. To transfer between Terminals 1-3 and Terminal 4, you can take a 10-minute shuttle bus (free, leaves every 10 minutes from departures level), or take the Metro (stops at Terminals 2 and 4). Make sure to allow enough time if you need to travel between terminals (and then for the long walk within Terminal 4 to the gates). For more information about navigating this massive airport, go to www.aena-aeropuertos.es (airport code: MAD).

International flights typically use Terminals 1 and 4. At the Terminal 1 arrivals area, you'll find a helpful, though privately run, English-speaking Turismo Madrid **TI** (marked *Oficina de Información Turística,* Mon-Sat 8:00-20:00, Sun 9:00-14:00, tel. 913-058-656), **ATMs,** a **flight info office** (marked simply *Information* in airport lobby, open daily 24 hours, tel. 902-353-570), a **post-office** window, a **pharmacy,** lots of **phones** (buy a phone card from the nearby machine), a few scattered **Internet** terminals (small fee), **eateries,** a **RENFE office** (where you can get train info and buy long-distance train tickets, daily 8:00-21:00, tel. 902-320-320), and on-the-spot **car-rental agencies.** The super-modern Terminal 4 offers essentially the same services. **Luggage storage** *(consigna)* is in Terminal 2, near the Metro exit. Some buses leave from the airport to far-flung destinations, such as Pamplona (see www.alsa.es; buy ticket online or from the driver).

Consider flying between Madrid and other cities in Spain (see "Cheap Flights" in the appendix). Domestic airline Vueling (www .vueling.com) is popular for its discounts (e.g., Madrid-Barcelona flight as cheap as €30 if booked in advance).

Getting Between the Airport and Downtown

By Public Bus: The yellow **Exprés Aeropuerto** runs between the airport (all terminals) and Atocha Station (€5, pay driver in cash, departing from arrivals level every 15-20 minutes, ride takes about 40 minutes, runs 24 hours a day; from 23:30 to 6:00, the bus only goes to Plaza de Cibeles, not all the way to Atocha). From Atocha, you can take a taxi or the Metro to your hotel. The bus back to the airport leaves Atocha from near the taxi stand on the *cercanías* side (from 23:30-6:00, it departs downtown from Plaza de Cibeles).

Bus #200 (from all terminals) is less handy than the express bus because it leaves you farther from downtown (at the Metro stop at Avenida de América, northeast of the historical center). This bus departs from the arrivals level about every 10 minutes and takes about 20 minutes to reach Avenida de América (runs 6:00-24:00, buy €1 ticket from driver; or get a shareable 10-ride Metrobus ticket at a tobacco shop).

By Cercanías Train: From Terminal 4, passengers can ride a *cercanías* (local) train to Atocha Station (€2.40, 2/hour, 25 minutes) or Chamartín Station (€2.40, 2/hour, 12 minutes). The bus is still a convenient choice for arriving or departing from the other airport terminals.

By Metro: Considering the ease of riding the Exprés Aeropuerto bus in from the airport, I'd rather bus than Metro. The subway involves two transfers to reach the city; it's not difficult, but usually involves climbing some stairs (€2; or add a €1 supplement to your 10-ride Metrobus ticket). The airport's futuristic "Aeropuerto T-1, T-2, T-3" Metro stop (notice the ATMs, subway info booth, and huge lighted map of Madrid) is in Terminal 2. Access the Metro at the check-in level; to reach the Metro from Terminal 1's arrivals level, stand with your back to the baggage claim, then go to your far right, up the stairs, and follow red-and-blue Metro diamond signs to the station (8-minute walk). The Terminal 4 stop is the end of the line. To get to Puerta del Sol, take line 8 for 12 minutes to Nuevos Ministerios, then continue on line 10 to Tribunal, then line 1 to Puerta del Sol (30 minutes more total); or exit at Nuevos Ministerios and take a €5 taxi or bus #150 straight to Puerta del Sol.

By Minibus Shuttle: The AeroCity shuttle bus provides door-to-door transport in a seven-seat minibus with up to three hotel stops en route. It's promoted by hotels, but if you want door-to-door service, simply taking a taxi generally offers a better value.

By Taxi: With cheap and easy alternatives available, there's not much reason to take a taxi unless you have lots of luggage or just want to go straight to your hotel. If you do take a taxi between the airport and downtown, allow about €30 during the day *(Tarifa 1)* or €35-40 at night and on Saturdays, Sundays, and holidays *(Tarifa 2)*. For Terminal 4, add about €10. Insist on the meter. The €5.50 airport supplement is legal. There is no charge for luggage. Plan on getting stalled in traffic.

By Car

Avoid driving in Madrid. If you're planning to rent a car, do it when you depart the city.

Renting a Car: It's cheapest to make car-rental arrangements before you leave home. In Madrid, consider **Europcar** (central reservations tel. 902-105-030, San Leonardo 8 office tel. 915-418-892, Chamartín Station tel. 912-035-070, airport tel. 902-105-055), **Hertz** (central reservations tel. 902-402-405, Plaza de España 18 tel. 915-425-805, Chamartín Station tel. 917-330-400, airport tel. 913-228-331), **Avis** (central reservations tel. 933-443-700, Gran Vía 60 tel. 915-484-204, airport tel. 902-200-162), and **Enterprise Atesa** (central reservations tel. 902-100-101). Ask about free delivery to your hotel. At the airport, most rental cars are returned at Terminal 1.

Route Tips for Drivers: To leave Madrid from Gran Vía, simply follow signs for *A-6* (direction *Villalba* or *A Coruña*) for Segovia, El Escorial, or the Valley of the Fallen (see next chapter for details).

MADRID

NORTHWEST OF MADRID

El Escorial • Valley of the Fallen • Segovia • Ávila

Before slipping out of Madrid, consider several fine side-trips northwest of Spain's capital city, all conveniently reached by car, bus, or train.

Spain's lavish, brutal, and complicated history is revealed throughout Old Castile. This region, where the Spanish language originated, is named for its many castles—battle scars from the long-fought Reconquista.

An hour from Madrid, tour the imposing and fascinating palace at El Escorial, headquarters of the Spanish Inquisition. Nearby, at the awe-inspiring Valley of the Fallen, pay tribute to the countless victims of Spain's bloody civil war.

Segovia, with its remarkable Roman aqueduct (pictured at top of page) and romantic castle, is another worthwhile side-trip. At Ávila you can walk the perfectly preserved medieval walls.

Planning Your Time

You can see El Escorial and the Valley of the Fallen in less than a day, but don't go on a Monday, when both sights are closed. By car, see them en route to Segovia; by bus, make them a day trip from Madrid.

Segovia, worth a half-day of sightseeing, is easy to reach from Madrid. If you have time, spend the night—the city is a joy in the evenings. Ávila, while charming, merits only a

Northwest of Madrid

quick stop (if you're driving and in the area) to marvel at its medieval walls and, perhaps, check out St. Teresa's finger (1.5 hours from Madrid, also a logical stop on the way to/from Salamanca by train).

In total, these sights are worth two days if you're in Spain for less than a month. If you're a history buff in Spain for just a week, squeeze in a quick side-trip from Madrid to El Escorial and the Valley of the Fallen.

El Escorial

The Monasterio de San Lorenzo de El Escorial is a symbol of power rather than elegance. This 16th-century palace, 30 miles northwest of Madrid, gives us a better feel for the Counter-Reformation and the Inquisition than any other building.

Getting to El Escorial

Most people visit El Escorial from Madrid. By public transportation, the bus is most convenient (since it gets you closer to the palace than the train). Remember that it makes sense to combine El Escorial with a visit to the nearby Valley of the Fallen.

By Bus: Buses leave from the Moncloa bus station, which is in the basement of Madrid's Moncloa Metro station (4/hour, fewer on weekends, 45-55 minutes, €4.20 one-way, buy ticket from driver; in Madrid take bus #664 or slower #661 from Moncloa's platform 11, Herranz Bus, tel. 918-969-028). The bus drops you downtown in San Lorenzo de El Escorial, a pleasant 10-minute stroll from the palace (see map): Exit the bus station from the back ramp that leads over the parked buses (noting that return buses to Madrid leave from platform 3 below this ramp), turn left, and follow the cobbled pedestrian lane, Calle San Juan. This street veers to the right and becomes Calle Juan de Leyva. In a few short blocks, it dead-ends at Duque de Medinaceli, where you'll turn left and see the palace. Stairs lead past several decent eateries, through a delightful square, past the TI (Tue-Sat 10:00-14:00 & 15:00-18:00, Sun 10:00-14:00, closed Mon; tel. 918-905-313), and directly to the tourist entry of the immense palace/monastery.

By Train: Local trains (*cercanías* line C-8A) run at least twice an hour from Madrid's Atocha and Chamartín stations to El Escorial. From the station, walk 20 minutes uphill through Casita del Príncipe park, straight up from the station. Or you can take a shuttle bus from the station (2/hour, usually timed with arrival of trains, €1) or a taxi (€5) to the San Lorenzo de El Escorial town center and the palace.

By Car: It's quite simple. Taxi to your car-rental office in Madrid (or ask if they'll deliver the car to your hotel). Pick up the car by 8:30 and ask for directions to highway A-6. From Gran Vía in central Madrid, follow signs to *A-6* (direction *Villalba* or *A Coruña*). The freeway leads directly out of town. Stay on A-6

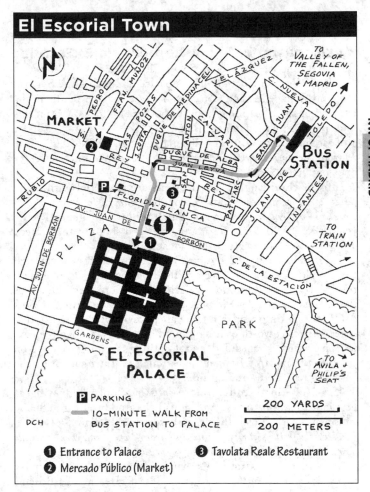

El Escorial Town

- ① Entrance to Palace
- ② Mercado Público (Market)
- ③ Tavolata Reale Restaurant

P PARKING
10-MINUTE WALK FROM BUS STATION TO PALACE

200 YARDS
200 METERS

past the first El Escorial exit. At kilometer 37 you'll see the cross marking the Valley of the Fallen ahead on the left. Exit 47 takes you to both the Valley of the Fallen (after a half-mile, a granite gate on right marks Valle de los Caídos turnoff) and El Escorial (follow *San Lorenzo del Escorial* signs).

The nearby **Silla de Felipe** (Philip's Seat) is a rocky viewpoint where the king would come to admire his palace as it was being built. From El Escorial, follow directions to Ávila, then M-505 to Valdemorillo; look for a sign on your right after about a mile.

When you leave El Escorial for Madrid, Toledo, or Segovia, follow signs to *A-6 Guadarrama*. After about six miles you pass the Valley of the Fallen and hit the freeway.

Sights in El Escorial

▲▲▲Monasterio de San Lorenzo de El Escorial

Built at a time when Catholic Spain felt threatened by Protestant "heretics," the construction of this palace dominated the Spanish economy for a generation (1562-1584). Because of this bully in the national budget, Spain has almost nothing else to show from this most powerful period of her history.

Cost and Hours: €10, April-Sept Tue-Sun 10:00-20:00, Oct-March Tue-Sun 10:00-18:00, closed Mon year-round, last entry one hour before closing.

Information: English descriptions are scattered within the palace. For more information, get the *Guide: Monastery of San Lorenzo El Real de El Escorial*, which follows the general route you'll take (€8.90, available at any of several shops in the palace). Tel. 918-905-904, www.patrimonionacional.es.

Tours: For an extra €7, a guided 1.5-hour **tour** takes you through the complex and covers other buildings on the grounds, including the Palace of the Bourbons (Palacio de los Borbones), House of the Infants (Casita del Infante), and House of the Prince (Casita del Príncipe). Unfortunately, there are so few tours in English that it generally isn't worth waiting around for one. Ask when the next tour in English is scheduled, and if nothing's running soon, go on your own: You can follow my self-guided tour, which covers the basics, or rent the €4 **audioguide.**

❂ Self-Guided Tour: The *monasterio* looks confusing at first, but the *visita* arrows and signs help guide you through one continuous path. This is the general order you'll follow.

• *Pass through the security scanner, buy your ticket, and then continue down the hall past the* consigna *baggage check (sala 1) to the...*

Museum of Tapestries: This chamber is hung with 16th-century tapestries, including fascinating copies of Hieronymus Bosch's most famous and preachy paintings (which Philip II fancied). Don't miss El Greco's towering painting of the *Martyrdom of St. Maurice*. This was the artist's first commission after arriving in Spain from Venice. It was too subtle and complex for the king, so El Greco moved on to Toledo to find work.

• *Continue downstairs to the fascinating...*

Museum of Architecture (Museo de Arquitectura): It has long, parallel corridors of fine models of the palace and some of the actual machinery and tools used to construct it. Huge stone-pinching winches, fat ropes, and rusty mortar spades help convey the immensity of this 21-year project involving 1,500 workers. At the big model, you can see how the complex is shaped like a grill. San Lorenzo—St. Lawrence, a Christian Spaniard martyred by pagan Romans (A.D. 258)—was burned to death on a grill.

El Escorial—Ground Floor

TO TRAIN STN.

ROYAL LIVING QUARTERS

50 YARDS
50 METERS

G A R D E N S

MUSEUM OF PAINTINGS (DOWNSTAIRS)

WALKING GALLERY

ROYAL PANTHEON (STAIRS LEAD DOWN TO CRYPT)

MUSEUM OF ARCHITECTURE (DOWNSTAIRS)

ALTAR

(DOME)

BASILICA

PANTHEON OF ROYAL CHILDREN

HALL OF THE BATTLES (UPPER FLOOR)

CLOISTER

CHAPTER ROOMS

TO TOWN, T.I. & BUS STN.

CELLINI'S CHRIST

SHOP

WC

ENTRANCE → START TICKETS

OLD CHURCH

PATIO OF THE KINGS

MONASTERY (CLOSED TO PUBLIC)

COLLEGE (CLOSED TO PUBLIC)

LIBRARY (UPPER FLOOR)

FINISH

G A R D E N S

DCH

P L A Z A

Throughout the palace, you'll see this symbol associated with the saint. The grill's "handle" was the palace, or residence of the royal family. The monastery and school gathered around the huge basilica.

• *Next linger in the...*

Museum of Paintings: Consider the 15th- to 17th-century Flemish, Spanish, and Italian works. Contemplate Rogier van der Weyden's *Calvary,* with mourning Mary and St. John at the feet of the crucified Christ. (It's interesting to compare it with Van der Weyden's similar *Descent from the Cross,* which hangs in the Prado in Madrid. For an in-the-moment comparison, check out artist Michiel Coxcie's copy on the nearby wall.)

• *Pass through the peaceful and empty Courtyard of the Fountainheads (Patio de Mascarones), and go upstairs to the...*

Hall of Battles (Sala de Batallas): Its paintings celebrate Spain's great military victories—including the Battle of San Quentin over France (1557) on St. Lawrence's feast day, which inspired the construction of El Escorial. The sprawling series, painted in 1590, helped teach the new king all the elements of warfare. Stroll the length for a primer on army skills.

• *Head downstairs, following signs to* Palacio de los Austrias, *then follow a corridor lined with various family trees (some scrawny, others lush and fecund). The hall leads into the...*

Royal Living Quarters (the building's grill handle): Immediately inside the first door, find the small portrait of Philip II flanked by two large paintings of his daughters. The palace was like Philip: austere. Notice the simple floors, plain white walls, and bare-bones chandelier. This was the bedroom of one of his daughters. The sheet warmer beside her bed was often necessary during the winter. Bend down to see the view from her bed...of the high altar in the basilica next door. The entire complex of palace and monastery buildings was built around that altar.

In the next room, the **Guard's room,** notice the reclinable sedan chair that Philip II, thick with gout, was carried in (for seven days) on his last trip from Madrid to El Escorial. He wanted to be here when he died.

The **Audience Chamber** is now a portrait gallery filled with Habsburg royals painted by popular local artists. The portraits of unattractive people that line the walls provide an instructive peek at the consequences of mixing blue blood with more of the same blue blood (inbreeding among royals was a common problem throughout Europe in those days).

The Spanish emperor Charles V (1500-1558) is over the fireplace mantel. Charles, Philip II's dad, was the most powerful man in Europe, having inherited not only the Spanish crown, but also Germany, Austria, the Low Countries (Belgium and the Netherlands), and much of Italy. When he announced his abdication in 1555, his son Philip II inherited much of this territory...plus the responsibility of managing it. Philip's draining wars with France, Portugal, Holland, and England—including the disastrous defeat of Spain's navy, the Spanish Armada, by England's Queen Elizabeth I (1588)—knocked Spain from its peak of power and began centuries of decline.

The guy with the good-looking legs next to Charles was his illegitimate son, Don Juan de Austria—famous for his handsome looks, thanks to a little fresh blood. Other royal offspring weren't so lucky: When one king married his niece, the result was Charles II (1665-1700, opposite Charles V). His severe underbite (an inbred royal family trait) was the least of his problems. An epileptic before that disease was understood, poor "Charles the Mad" would be the last of the Spanish Habsburgs. He died without an heir in 1700, ushering in the continent-wide War of the Spanish Succession and the dismantling of Spain's empire.

In the **Walking Gallery,** the royals got their exercise privately, with no risk of darkening their high-class skins with a tan. Study the 16th-century maps along the walls. The slate strip on the floor is a sundial from 1755. It lined up with a (now plugged) hole in

History of El Escorial

The giant, gloomy building made of gray-black stone looks more like a prison than a palace. About 650 feet long and 500 feet wide, it has 2,600 windows, 1,200 doors, more than 100 miles of passages, and 1,600 overwhelmed tourists.

Four hundred years ago, the enigmatic, introverted, and extremely Catholic King Philip II (1527-1598) ruled his bulky empire and directed the Inquisition from here. To Philip, the building embodied the wonders of Catholic learning, spirituality, and arts. To 16th-century followers of Martin Luther, it epitomized the evil of closed-minded Catholicism. To architects, the building—built on the cusp between styles—exudes both Counter-Reformation grandeur and understated Renaissance simplicity. Today it's a time capsule of Spain's "Golden Age," packed with history, art, and Inquisition ghosts. (And at an elevation of nearly 3,500 feet, it can be friggin' cold.)

The building was conceived by Philip II to serve several purposes: as a grand mausoleum for Spain's royal family, starting with his father, Charles V (called Carlos I in Spain); as a monastery to pray (a lot) for the royal souls; as a small palace to use as a Camp David of sorts for Spain's royalty; and as a school to embrace humanism in a way that promoted the Catholic faith.

Spanish architect Juan Bautista de Toledo, who had studied in Italy, was called by Philip II to carry out the El Escorial project, but he died before it was finished. His successor, Juan de Herrera, made extensive changes to Toledo's original design and completed the palace in 1584.

the wall so that at noon a tiny beam hit the middle of the three lines. Palace clocks were set by this. Where the ray crossed the strip indicated the date and sign of the zodiac.

As you enter the **King's Antechamber,** look back to study the fine inlaid-wood door (a gift from the German emperor that celebrates the exciting humanism of the age).

Philip II's bedroom is austere, like his daughter's. Look at the king's humble bed...barely queen-size. He too could view Mass at the basilica's high altar without leaving his bed. The red box next to his pillow holds the royal bedpan. But don't laugh—the king's looking down from the wall to your left. At age 71, Philip II, the gout-ridden king of a dying empire, died in this bed (1598).

• *From here his body was taken to our next stop, the...*

Royal Pantheon (Panteón Real): This is the gilded resting place of 26 kings and queens...four centuries' worth of Spanish monarchy. All the kings are included—but the only queens here are the ones who became mothers of kings.

A post-mortem filing system is at work in the Pantheon. From the entrance, kings are on the left, queens on the right. (The only exception is Isabel II, since she was a ruling queen and her husband was a consort.) The first and greatest, Charles V and his Queen Isabel, flank the altar on the top shelf. Her son, Philip II, rests below Charles and opposite (only) one of Philip's four wives, and so on. There is a waiting process, too. Before a royal corpse can rest in this room, it needs to decompose for at least 25 years. The bones of the current king Juan Carlos' grandmother, Victoria Eugenia (who died in 1964), were transferred into the crypt in late 2011. The two empty niches are already booked: Juan Carlos' father, Don Juan (who died in 1993), is on the waiting list...controversially. Technically, he was never crowned king of Spain—Generalísimo Francisco Franco took control of Spain before Don Juan could ascend to the throne, and he was passed over for the job when Franco reinstituted the monarchy. Juan Carlos' mother is the most recent guest in the rotting room. So where does that leave Juan Carlos and Sofía? This hotel is *todo completo*.

The next rooms are filled with the tombs of lesser royals: Each bears that person's name (in Latin), relationship to the king, and slogan or epitaph. From here, it's on to the wedding-cake **Pantheon of Royal Children** (Panteón de los Infantes), which holds the remains of various royal children who died before the age of seven (and their first Communion).

• *Head past the tiny gift shop and continue upstairs to the...*

Chapter Rooms (Salas Capitulares): These rooms are where the monks met to do church business; they're also lined with big-name paintings by José Ribera, El Greco, Titian, and Velázquez. (More great paintings are in the monastery's Museum

of Painting.) Continue to the final room to see some atypical Bosch paintings and the intricate, portable altar of Charles V.

• *Next find the...*

Cloister: The cloister glows with bright, restored paintings by Pellegrino Tibaldi. Off the cloister is the **Old Church** (Iglesia Vieja), which they used from 1571 to 1586, while finishing the basilica. During that time the bodies of several kings, including Charles V, were interred here. Among the many paintings, look for the powerful *Martyrdom of St. Lawrence* by Tiziano (Titian) above the main altar.

• *Follow the signs to the...*

Basilica: Find the flame-engulfed grill in the center of the altar wall that features San Lorenzo (the same St. Lawrence from the painting) meeting his famous death—and taking "turn the other cheek" to new extremes. Lorenzo was so cool, he reportedly told his Roman executioners, "You can turn me over now—I'm done on this side." With your back to the altar, go to the right corner for the artistic highlight of the basilica: Benvenuto Cellini's marble sculpture, *The Crucifixion.* Jesus' features are supposedly modeled after the Shroud of Turin. Cellini carved this from Carrara marble for his own tomb in 1562 (according to the letters under Christ's feet).

• *Cross the courtyard to enter the immense...*

Library *(biblioteca):* It's clear that education was a priority for

the Spanish royalty. Savor this room. The ceiling (by Tibaldi, depicting various disciplines labeled in Latin, the lingua franca of the multinational Habsburg Empire) is a burst of color. At the far end of the room, the armillary sphere—an elaborate model of the solar system—looks like a giant gyroscope, revolving unmistakably around the Earth, with a misshapen, under-explored North America. As you leave, look back above the wooden door. The plaque warns *"Excomunión..."* —you'll be excommunicated if you take a book without checking it out properly. Who needs late fees when you hold the keys to hell?

Eating in El Escorial

The **Mercado Público,** a four-minute walk from the palace, is the place to shop for a picnic (Mon-Wed and Fri 9:30-13:30 & 17:00-20:00, Thu and Sat 9:30-14:00, closed Sun, Calle del Rey 9).

On the **Plaza de las Ánimas,** just two blocks north of the palace complex, you can find a handful of nondescript but decent restaurants serving fixed-price lunches (best on weekdays). **Tavolata Reale** dishes out pizza and offers a change of pace from Spanish fare (Tue-Sat 12:00-17:00 & 20:00-24:00, Sun 12:00-17:00, closed Mon, inside a mini-shopping gallery off Plaza Jacinto Benavente at Plaza de las Ánimas 3, tel. 918-905-599).

NW OF MADRID

Valley of the Fallen

Six miles from El Escorial, high in the Guadarrama Mountains, is the Valley of the Fallen (Valle de los Caídos). A 500-foot-tall

granite cross marks this immense and powerful underground monument to the victims of Spain's 20th-century nightmare—the Spanish Civil War (1936-1939).

Cost and Hours: €9, ask about audioguide; April-Sept Tue-Sun 10:00-19:00, Oct-March Tue-Sun 10:00-18:00, closed Mon year-round, last entry one hour before closing, basilica closes 30 minutes before site closes.

Information: Tel. 918-905-611, www.patrimonionacional.es.

Funicular: The funicular is closed while the base of the cross is under construction, with no reopening date yet set. When it's running, the funicular costs about €1.50 one-way (prices and hours likely to change; €2.50 round-trip, pay fare at machine; April-Sept Tue-Sun 11:00-18:30, 3/hour; Oct-March Tue-Sun 11:00-16:30, 2/hour; closed Mon year-round; last ticket sold 30 minutes before closing).

Mass: You can enter the basilica during Mass, but you can't sightsee or linger afterward. One-hour services run Tue-Sat at 11:00 and Sun at 11:00, 13:00, and 17:30. During services, the entire front of the basilica (altar and tombs) is closed. Mass is usually accompanied by the resident boys' choir, the "White Voices" (Spain's answer to the Vienna Boys' Choir).

Getting There: Most visitors side-trip to the Valley of the Fallen from the nearby El Escorial. If you don't have your own wheels, the easiest way to get between these two sights is to negotiate a deal with a **taxi** (to take you from El Escorial to Valley of the Fallen, wait for you 30-60 minutes, and then bring you back to El Escorial, about €45 total). Or, ask about bus service between El Escorial and the Valley of the Fallen (1/day Tue-Sun at 15:15, bus returns to El Escorial at 17:30, 15 minutes, discounted bus fare may be available with site admission). Drivers can find tips under "Getting to El Escorial—By Car" on page 518.

Visiting the Monument: Approaching by car or bus, you enter the sprawling park through a granite gate. The best views of the cross are from the bridge (but note that it's illegal for drivers to stop anywhere along this road). To the right, tiny chapels along the ridge mark the Stations of the Cross, where pilgrims stop on

The Spanish Civil War
(1936-1939)

Thirty-three months of warfare killed roughly 500,000 Spaniards. Unlike America's Civil War, which split the US north and south, Spain's war was between classes and ideologies, dividing every city and village, and many families. It was especially cruel, with atrocities and reprisals on both sides.

The war began as a military coup to overthrow the democratically elected Republic, a government that the army and other conservative powers considered too liberal and disorganized. The rebel forces, called the Nationalists (Nacionalistas), consisted of the army, monarchy, Catholic Church, big business, and rural estates, with aid from Germany, Italy, and Portugal. Trying to preserve the liberal government were the Republicans (Republicanos), also called Loyalists: the government, urban areas, secularists, small business, and labor unions, with aid from the United States (minimal help) and the "International Brigades" of communists, socialists, and labor organizers.

In the summer of 1936, the army rebelled and took control of its own garrisons, rejecting the Republic and pledging allegiance to Generalísimo Francisco Franco (1892-1975). These Nationalists launched a three-year military offensive to take Spain region by region, town by town. The government ("Republicans") cobbled together an army of volunteers, local militias, and international fighters. The war pitted conservative Catholic priests against socialist factory workers, rich businessmen against radical students, sunburned farmers loyal to the old king against upwardly mobile small businessmen. People suffered. You'll notice that many elderly Spaniards are very short—a product of growing up during these hungry and very difficult civil war years.

Spain's civil war attracted international attention. Adolf Hitler and Benito Mussolini sent troops and supplies to their fellow fascist Franco. It was Hitler's Luftwaffe that helped Franco bomb the town of Guernica (April of 1937), an event famously captured on canvas by Pablo Picasso (for more on the bombing, see sidebar on page 236; to read about the painting, see page 472). On the Republican side, hundreds of Americans (including Ernest Hemingway) steamed over to Spain, some to fight for democracy as part of the "Abraham Lincoln Brigade."

By 1938, only Barcelona and Madrid held out. But they were no match for Franco's army. On April 1, 1939, Madrid fell and the war ended, beginning 36 years of iron-fisted rule by Franco.

their hike to this memorial.

In 1940 prison workers dug 220,000 tons of granite out of the hill beneath the cross to form an underground basilica, then used the stones to erect the cross (built like a chimney, from the inside). Since it's built directly over the dome of the subterranean basilica, a seismologist keeps a careful eye on things.

The stairs that lead to the imposing monument are grouped in sets of tens, meant to symbolize the Ten Commandments (including "Thou shalt not kill"—hmm). The emotional *pietà* draped over the basilica's entrance is huge—you could sit in the palm of Christ's hand. The statue was sculpted by Juan de Ávalos, the same artist who created the dramatic figures of the four Evangelists at the base of the cross. It must have had a powerful impact on mothers who came here to remember their fallen sons.

Basilica: A solemn silence and a stony chill fill the basilica. At 300 yards long, it was built to be longer than St. Peter's...but the Vatican had the final say when it blessed only 262 of those yards. Many Spaniards pass under the huge, foreboding angels of fascism to visit the grave of General Franco—an unusual place of pilgrimage, to say the least.

After walking through the two long vestibules, stop at the iron gates of the actual basilica. The line of torch-like lamps adds to the shrine ambience. Franco's prisoners, the enemies of the right, dug this memorial out of solid rock from 1940 to 1950. (Though it looks like bare rock still shows on the ceiling, it's just a clever design.) The sides of the monument are lined with copies of 16th-century Brussels tapestries of the Apocalypse, and side chapels contain alabaster copies of Spain's most famous statues of the Virgin Mary.

Interred behind the high altar and side chapels (marked "RIP, 1936-1939, died for God and country") are the remains of approximately 50,000 people, both Franco's Nationalists and the anti-Franco Republicans, who lost their lives in the war. Regrettably, the urns are not visible, so it is Franco who takes center stage. His grave, strewn with flowers, lies behind the high altar. In front of the altar is the grave of José Antonio Primo de Rivera (1903-1936), the founder of Spanish fascism, who was killed by Republicans during the civil war. Between these fascists' graves, the statue of a crucified Christ is lashed to a timber Franco himself is said to have felled. The seeping stones seem to weep for the victims. Today, families of the buried Republicans remain upset that their kin are lying with Franco and his Nationalists.

As you leave, stare into the eyes of those angels with swords and two right wings and think about all the "heroes" who keep dying "for God and country," at the request of the latter. The expansive view from the monument's terrace includes the peaceful, forested valley and sometimes snow-streaked mountains.

Visiting the Cross: For an even better view of the area, consider taking the funicular (if it's running) to the base of the cross. The funicular ride includes a short commentary in English, plus there's a restaurant and public WC at the top. You can hike back down in 25 minutes. If you have a car, you can drive up past the monastery and hike from the start of the trail marked *Sendero a la Cruz*.

Sleeping and Eating: Near the parking lot and bus stop at Valley of the Fallen are a small snack bar and some picnic tables. Basic overnight lodging is available at the **$$ Hospedería de la Santa Cruz,** a 100-room monastery behind the cross (Sb-€40-48, Db-€34-55, includes meals and a pass to enter and leave the park after hours, tel. 918-905-511, www.valledeloscaidos.es/hospederia, info@hospederiasantacruz.com, no English spoken). A meditative night here is good mostly for monks.

Segovia

Fifty miles from Madrid, this town of 55,000 boasts a thrilling Roman aqueduct, a grand cathedral, and a historic castle. Since the city is more than 3,000 feet above sea level and just northwest of a mountain range, it is exposed to cool northern breezes, and people come here from Madrid for a break from the summer heat.

Day-Tripping from Madrid: Considering the easy train and bus connections (30 minutes one-way by AVE train, 1.5 hours by bus), Segovia makes a fine day trip from Madrid. The disadvantages of this plan are that you spend the coolest hours of the day (early and late) en route, you miss the charming evening scene in Segovia, and you'll pay more for a hotel in Madrid than in Segovia. If you have time, spend the night. But even if you just stay the day, Segovia still offers a rewarding and convenient break from the big-city intensity of Madrid.

Orientation to Segovia

Segovia is a medieval "ship" ready for your inspection. Start at the stern—the aqueduct—and stroll up Calle de Cervantes and Calle Juan Bravo to the prickly Gothic masts of the cathedral. Explore the tangle of narrow streets around playful Plaza Mayor and then descend to the Alcázar at the bow.

Tourist Information

Segovia has four TIs. The TI on Plaza Mayor covers both Segovia and the surrounding region (at #10, daily July-mid-Sept 9:00-20:00, mid-Sept-June Mon-Sat 9:30-14:00 & 16:00-19:00, Sun 9:30-17:00, tel. 921-460-334, www.turismocastillayleon.com). The TI at Plaza del Azoguejo, at the base of the aqueduct, specializes in Segovia and has friendly staff, WCs (€0.20), and a gift shop (daily 10:00-12:00 & 17:00-19:00, Sat until 20:00, see wooden model of Segovia, tel. 921-466-720, www.turismodesegovia.com). Smaller TIs are at the bus station (behind a window, daily 10:00-14:00 & 15:30-17:00, tel. 921-436-569) and the AVE train station (Mon-Fri 8:15-15:15, Sat-Sun 10:00-14:15 & 16:00-17:45, tel. 921-447-262).

Arrival in Segovia

If day-tripping from Madrid, check the return schedule when you arrive here (or get one at the Segovia TI). You'll find luggage storage near the exit from the bus station (€3/day, tokens sold daily 9:00-14:00 & 16:00-19:00, gives you access to locker until end of day). There's no luggage storage at the train station.

By Bus: It's a 10-minute walk from the bus station to the town center: Exit left out of the station, continue straight across the street, and follow Avenida Fernández Ladreda, passing San Millán church on the left, then San Clemente church on the right, before coming to the aqueduct.

By Train: From the AVE train station (called Guiomar), ride bus #11 for 20 minutes to the base of the aqueduct. To reach the center from the less-convenient cercanías train station, you can catch bus #6 or #8, take a taxi, or walk 30 minutes (start at Paseo del Conde de Sepulvedana—which becomes Paseo Ezequiel González, head to the bus station, then turn right and head down Avenida Fernández Ladreda to the aqueduct).

By Car: For driving directions and parking tips, see "Route Tips for Drivers" on page 543.

Helpful Hints

Shopping: If you buy handicrafts such as tablecloths from street vendors, make sure the item you want is the one you actually get; some unscrupulous vendors substitute inferior goods at the last minute. A flea market is held on Plaza Mayor on Thursdays (roughly 8:00-15:00).

Local Guide: Elvira Valderrama Rascon, a hardworking young woman, is a good English-speaking guide (€115/3 hours, mobile 636-227-949, elvisvalrras@yahoo.es).

Sightseeing Bus: Bus Turístico is a weak version of a hop-on, hop-off bus, but it does give you a chance to take great panoramic photos of Segovia's boat-like shape, with the mountains as a backdrop. Pick it up at the aqueduct, and stay on for the full loop—it's not really worth using it as a means of getting around town (€5.90, buy ticket on bus or at aqueduct TI; July-mid-Sept departs hourly 10:00-23:00, otherwise at 11:00, 12:00, 13:00, 16:00, and 17:00; tel. 921-466-721, www.urbanosdesegovia.com).

Free Churches: Segovia has plenty of little Romanesque churches that are free to enter shortly before or after Mass (see TI for a list of times), and many have architecturally interesting exteriors that are worth a look. On your way to the main sights, keep your eyes peeled for these hidden treasures: Coming from the bus station on Avenida Fernández Ladreda toward the center of town, you can see the San Millán church; on Plazas San Martín and San Esteban are two churches sharing their squares' names (though you can't go inside San Esteban); and on the way to the Alcázar on Plaza de la Merced is the San Andrés church.

Self-Guided Walk

Welcome to Historic Segovia

This 15-minute walk goes uphill from the Roman aqueduct to the city's main square along the pedestrian-only street. It's most enjoyable just before dinner, when it's cool and filled with strolling Segovians.

Start at Segovia's emblematic Roman aqueduct (described later, under "Sights in Segovia"). Walk about 100 yards up Calle de Cervantes, which becomes Calle Juan Bravo, until you reach the **"house of a thousand beaks"** (Casa de los Picos) on your

right. This building's original Moorish design is still easy to see, despite the wall just past the door that blocks your view from the street. This wall, the architectural equivalent of a veil, hid this home's fine courtyard—Moors didn't flaunt their wealth. You can step inside to see art students at

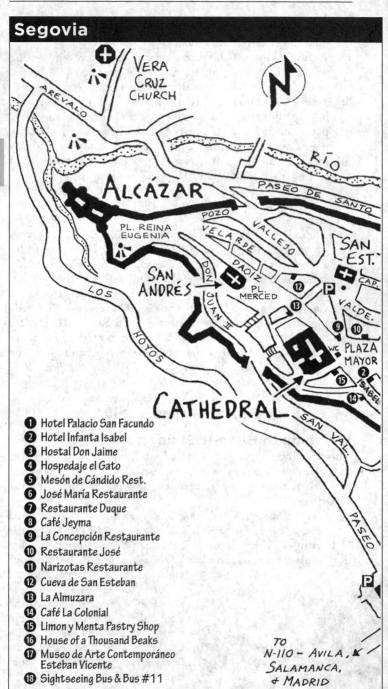

Segovia

VERA CRUZ CHURCH

AREVALO

RÍO

PASEO DE SANTO

ALCÁZAR

PL. REINA EUGENIA

POZO

VELARDE

VALLEJO

SAN EST.

CAP.

LOS

SAN ANDRÉS

DON JUAN II

DAOIZ

PL. MERCED

⑫

⑬

P

VALDE.

⑨

⑩

HOYOS

WC

PLAZA MAYOR

②

⑮

⑭

ISABEL

CATHEDRAL

SAN VAL.

PASEO

P

1 Hotel Palacio San Facundo
2 Hotel Infanta Isabel
3 Hostal Don Jaime
4 Hospedaje el Gato
5 Mesón de Cándido Rest.
6 José María Restaurante
7 Restaurante Duque
8 Café Jeyma
9 La Concepción Restaurante
10 Restaurante José
11 Narizotas Restaurante
12 Cueva de San Esteban
13 La Almuzara
14 Café La Colonial
15 Limon y Menta Pastry Shop
16 House of a Thousand Beaks
17 Museo de Arte Contemporáneo Esteban Vicente
18 Sightseeing Bus & Bus #11

TO N-110 – AVILA, SALAMANCA, & MADRID

work and perhaps an exhibit on display, but it's most interesting from the exterior. Notice its truncated tower, one of many fortified towers that marked the homes of feuding local noble families. In medieval Spain, clashing loyalties led to mini-civil wars. In the 15th century, as Ferdinand and Isabel centralized authority in Spain, nobles were required to lop their towers. You'll see the once-tall, now-stubby towers of 15th-century noble mansions all over Segovia. Another example of a similar once-fortified, now-softened house with a cropped tower is about 50 yards farther down the street, on the left, on tiny Plaza del Platero Oquendo.

Continue uphill until you come to the complicated **Plaza de San Martín,** a commotion of history surrounding a striking statue of Juan Bravo. When Charles V, a Habsburg who didn't even speak Spanish, took power, he imposed his rule over Castile. This threatened the local nobles, who, inspired and led by Juan Bravo, revolted in 1521. Although Juan Bravo lost the battle—and his head—he's still a symbol of Castilian pride. This statue was erected in 1921 on the 400th anniversary of his death.

In front of the Juan Bravo statue stands the bold and bulky **House of Siglo XV.** Its fortified *Isabelino* style was typical of 15th-century Segovian houses. Later, in a more peaceful age, the boldness of these houses was softened with the decorative stucco work—Arabic-style floral and geometrical patterns—that you see today (for example, in the big house across the street). The 14th-century Tower of Lozoya, behind the statue, is another example of the lopped-off towers.

On the same square, the 12th-century Church of St. Martín is Segovian Romanesque in style (a mix of Christian Romanesque and Moorish styles).

If you continue up the street another 100 yards, you'll see the **Corpus Christi Convent** on the left. For a donation, you can pop in to see the Franciscan church, which was once a synagogue, which was once a mosque. While sweet and peaceful, with lots of art featuring St. Francis, the church is skippable.

Keep going until you reach Segovia's inviting **Plaza Mayor**—once the scene of executions, religious theater, and bullfights with spectators jamming the balconies. The bullfights ended in the 19th century. When Segovians complained, they were given a more gentle form of entertainment—bands in the music kiosk. Today the very best entertainment here is simply enjoying a light meal, snack, or drink in your choice of the many restaurants and cafés lining the square. The Renaissance church opposite the City Hall and behind the TI was built to replace the church where Isabel was proclaimed Queen of Castile in 1474. The symbol of Segovia is the aqueduct where you started—find it in the seals on the Theater Juan Bravo and atop the City Hall. Finally, treat yourself to the town's specialty pastry, *ponche segoviano* (marzipan cake), at the recommended Limón y Menta, the bakery on the corner where you entered Plaza Mayor.

Sights in Segovia

▲Roman Aqueduct

Segovia was a Roman military base and needed water. Emperor Trajan's engineers built a nine-mile aqueduct to channel water

from the Río Frío to the city, culminating at the Roman castle (which is the Alcázar today). The famous and exposed section of the 2,000-year-old *acueducto romano* is 2,500 feet long and 100 feet high, has 118 arches, was made from 20,000 granite blocks without any mortar, and can still carry a stream of water. It actually functioned until the late 19th century. On Plaza del Azogüejo, a grand stairway leads from the base of the aqueduct to the top—offering close-up looks at the imposing work.

▲Cathedral

Segovia's cathedral, built in Renaissance times (1525-1768, the third on this site), was Spain's last major Gothic building. Embellished to the hilt with pinnacles and flying buttresses, the exterior is a great example of the final, overripe stage of Gothic, called Flamboyant. Yet the Renaissance arrived before it was finished—as evidenced by the fact that the cathedral is crowned by a dome, not a spire.

Cost and Hours: €3, free Sun 9:30-13:15 (cathedral access only— no cloisters), open daily April-Oct 9:30-18:30, Nov-March 9:30-17:00, last entry 30 minutes before closing, tel. 921-462-205.

Visiting the Cathedral: The spacious and elegantly simple interior provides a delightful contrast to the frilly exterior. The **choir** features finely carved wooden stalls from the previous church (1400s). The *cátedra* (bishop's chair) is in the center rear of the choir.

The many side chapels are mostly 16th-century, and come with big locking gates—a reminder that they were the private sacred domain of the rich families and guilds who "owned" them. They could enjoy private Masses here with their names actually spoken in the blessings and a fine burial spot close to the altar.

Find the **Capilla La Concepción** (a chapel in the rear that looks like a mini-art gallery). Its many 17th-century paintings hang behind a mahogany wood gate imported from colonial America. The painting, *Tree of Life*, by Ignacio Ries (left of the altar), shows hedonistic mortals dancing atop the Tree of Life. As a skeletal Grim Reaper prepares to receive them into hell (by literally chop-

ping down the tree...timberrrr), Jesus rings a bell imploring them to wake up before it's too late. The center statue is Mary of the Apocalypse (as described in Revelations, standing on a devil and half-moon, which looks like bull's horns). Mary's pregnant, and the devil licks his evil chops, waiting to devour the baby Messiah.

Opposite from where you entered, a fine door (which leads into the cloister) is crowned by a painted Flamboyant Gothic *pietà* in its tympanum (the statue of Jesus with a skirt, on the left, is a reminder of how prudishness from the past looks silly in the present).

The **cloisters** hold a nice little one-room museum containing French tapestries, paintings, and silver reliquaries. In the first room on the right, a glass case displays keys to the 17th-century private-chapel gates. Next, the gilded chapter room is draped with precious Flemish tapestries. Notice the gilded wagon. The Holy Communion wafer is placed in the top of this temple-like cart and paraded through town each year during the Corpus Christi festival. From the cloister courtyard, you can see the Renaissance dome rising above the otherwise Gothic rooftop.

▲Alcázar

In the Middle Ages, this fortified palace was one of the favorite residences of the monarchs of Castile, a key fortress for controlling the region. The Alcázar grew through the ages, and its function changed many times: After its stint as a palace, it was a prison for 200 years, and then a Royal Artillery School. It burned in 1862. Since the fire, it's basically been a museum.

Cost and Hours: Palace-€4.50, daily April-Sept 10:00-19:00, Oct-March 10:00-18:00; tower-€2, same hours except closed third Tue of month. Buy your tickets at Real Laboratorio de Chimia, facing the palace on your left. At the entrance, pass your ticket through the turnstiles on the right for the palace, or the turnstiles on the left for the tower.

Information: Pick up a free English leaflet as you enter. Tel. 921-460-759, www.alcazardesegovia.com.

Audioguide: The 45-minute, €3 audioguide describes each room.

Visiting the Alcázar: You'll enjoy a one-way route through 11 rooms, including a fine view terrace. Visit the tower afterward; its 152 steps up a tight spiral staircase reward you with the only 360-degree city view in town. What you see today in the Alcázar is rebuilt—a Disney-esque exaggeration of the original. Still, its fine Moorish decor and historic furnishings are fascinating. The sumptuous ceilings are accurately restored in Mudejar style, and the throne-room ceiling is the artistic highlight of the palace.

Look for a big mural of Queen Isabel the Catholic being proclaimed Queen of Castile and León in Segovia's main square in 1474. The **Hall of the Monarchs** is lined with the busts of the 52 rulers of Castile and León who presided during the long and ultimately successful Reconquista (711-1492): from Pelayo (the first), clockwise to Juana VII (the last). There were only seven queens during the period (the numbered ones). In this current age of Islamic extremists decapitating Christians, study the painting of St. James the Moor-Slayer—with Muslim heads literally rolling at his feet (poignantly...in the chapel). James is the patron saint of Spain. His name was the rallying cry in the centuries-long Christian crusade to push the Muslim Moors back into Africa.

Stepping onto the **terrace** (the site of the original Roman military camp, circa A.D. 100) with its vast views, marvel at the natural fortification provided by this promontory cut by the confluence of two rivers. The terrace is closed in the winter and sometimes on windy days. The Alcázar marks the end (and physical low point) of the gradual downhill course of the nine-mile-long Roman aqueduct. Can you find the mountain nicknamed *Mujer Muerta* ("dead woman")?

In the **armory** (just after the terrace), find the king's 16th-century ornately carved ivory crossbow, with the hunting scene shown in the adjacent painting. The final rooms are the Museum of Artillery, recalling the period (1764-1862) when this was the Royal Artillery School. It shows the evolution of explosive weaponry, with old photos and prints of the Alcázar.

Church of Santos Justo y Pastor

This simple yet stately old church has fascinating 12th- and 13th-century frescoes filled with Gothic symbolism, plus a stork's nest atop its tower. From the base of the aqueduct, it's a short climb uphill into the newer part of town. Kind old Rafael, the volunteer caretaker, welcomes you.

Cost and Hours: Free, Mon-Sat 10:30-13:45 & 16:00-19:00; closed Sun and when Rafael needs to run an errand; located a couple of blocks from Plaza del Azoguejo, tel. 921-422-413.

Museo de Arte Contemporáneo Esteban Vicente

A collection of local artist Esteban Vicente's abstract art is housed in two rooms of the remodeled remains of Henry IV's 1455 palace. Wilder than Rothko but more restrained than Pollock, Vicente's vibrant work influenced post-WWII American art. The temporary exhibits can be more interesting than the permanent collection.

Cost and Hours: €3, free on Thu; open Thu-Fri 11:00-14:00 & 16:00-19:00, Sat 11:00-20:00, Sun 11:00-15:00, closed Mon-Wed; tel. 921-426-010, www.museoestebanvicente.es.

Near Segovia

Vera Cruz Church

This 12-sided, 13th-century Romanesque church, built by the Knights Templar, once housed a piece of the "true cross." You can enjoy a postcard view of the city from the church, and more views follow as you continue around Segovia on the small road below the castle, labeled *ruta turística panorámica*.

Cost and Hours: €2, free Tue afternoon; open Tue-Sun 10:30-13:30 & 16:00-19:00, until 18:00 in winter, closed Mon and Nov; outside town beyond the castle, a 25-minute walk from main square; tel. 921-431-475.

▲La Granja de San Ildefonso Palace

This "little Versailles," six miles south of Segovia, is much smaller and happier than nearby El Escorial. The palace and gardens were built by the homesick French-born King Philip V, grandson of Louis XIV. Today it's restored to its original 18th-century splendor, with its royal collection of tapestries, clocks, and crystal (actually made at the palace's royal crystal factory). Plumbers and gardeners imported from France and Italy made Philip a garden that rivaled Versailles'. The fanciful fountains feature mythological stories (explained in the palace audioguide). The Bourbon Philip chose to be buried here rather than with his Habsburg predecessors at El

Escorial. His tomb is in the adjacent church, included with your ticket.

Cost and Hours: Palace—€9, ticket valid 48 hours, audioguide-€4; April-Sept Tue-Sun 10:00-20:00, Oct-March Tue-Sun 10:00-18:00, closed Mon year-round; last entry one hour before closing; park—free, daily 10:00-20:00, until 19:00 in winter; tel. 921-470-019, www.patrimonionacional.es.

Getting There: La Sepulvedana buses make the 25-minute trip from Segovia (catch at the bus station) to San Ildefonso-La Granja (about 2/hour 7:30-21:30, fewer on weekends, tel. 902-119-699, www.lasepulvedana.es)

Sleeping in Segovia

The best places are on or near the central Plaza Mayor. This is where the city action is—the best bars, most tourist-friendly and *típico* eateries, and the TI. During busy times—on weekends and in July and August—arrive early or call ahead.

In the Old Center, near Plaza Mayor

$$$ Hotel Palacio San Facundo, on a quiet square a few blocks off Plaza Mayor, is luxuriously modern in its amenities but has preserved its Old World charm. This palace-turned-monastery has 29 uniquely decorated rooms surrounding a sky-lit central patio (Sb/Db-€100-170, superior Db-€160-220, Tb-€150-255, rates fluctuate significantly with season and demand, check online for

---

Sleep Code

(€1 = about $1.30, country code: 34)

S = Single, **D** = Double/Twin, **T** = Triple, **Q** = Quad, **b** = bathroom, **s** = shower only. Unless otherwise noted, you can assume credit cards are accepted and English is spoken. Breakfast is generally *not* included. Some hotels include the 10 percent IVA tax in the room price; others tack it onto your bill.

To help you easily sort through these listings, I've divided the accommodations into three categories, based on the price for a standard double room with bath during high season:

$$$ Higher Priced—Most rooms €80 or more.
 $$ Moderately Priced—Most rooms between €40-80.
  $ Lower Priced—Most rooms €40 or less.

Prices can change without notice; verify the hotel's current rates online or by email. For the best prices, always book direct.

best prices, includes breakfast, elevator, parking-€18/day, air-con, free Wi-Fi, tel. 921-463-061, Plaza San Facundo 4, www.hotelpalaciosanfacundo.com, info@hotelpalaciosanfacundo.com, José Luis). From Plaza Mayor, take Cronista Lecea; it's a four-minute walk directly to Plaza San Facundo.

$$$ Hotel Infanta Isabel, right on Plaza Mayor, is the ritziest hotel in the old town, with 38 elegant rooms, some with plaza views (Sb-€67-77, Db-€97-125 depending on room size, Sb and Db-€60 in winter, breakfast on the square-€9, elevator, valet parking-€12/day, tel. 921-461-300, www.hotelinfantaisabel.com, admin@hotelinfantaisabel.com).

Outside the Old Town, near the Aqueduct

$$ Hostal Don Jaime, opposite the Church of San Justo, is a friendly family-run place with 38 basic, worn, yet well-maintained rooms. Seven more rooms are in an annex across the street (S-€25, D-€32, Db-€50, Tb-€60, Qb-€70, show this book and get a free breakfast in 2014—otherwise €3.50, parking-€8/day; Ochoa Ondategui 8—from TI at Plaza del Azogüejo, cross under the aqueduct, go right, angle left, then snake uphill for 2 blocks; tel. 921-444-787, hostaldonjaime@hotmail.com).

$ Hospedaje el Gato, a family-run place on a quiet non-descript square just outside the old town, has 10 modern, comfortable rooms (Sb-€35 Sun-Thu, Sb-€50 Fri-Sat, Db-€50, Tb-€65, air-con, bar serves breakfast and good tapas, parking-€10/day, uphill from Hostal Don Jaime and aqueduct at Plaza del Salvador 10, tel. 921-423-244, mobile 678-405-079, fax 921-438-047, hbarelgato@yahoo.es but prefer phone or fax reservations).

Eating in Segovia

Look for Segovia's culinary claim to fame, roast suckling pig (*cochinillo asado:* 21 days of mother's milk, into the oven, and onto your plate—oh, Babe). It's worth a splurge here, or in Toledo or Salamanca.

For lighter fare, try *sopa castellana*—soup mixed with eggs, ham, garlic, and bread—or warm yourself up with the *judiones de La Granja,* a popular soup made with flat white beans from the region.

Ponche segoviano, a dessert made with an almond-and-honey *mazapán* base, is heavenly after an earthy dinner or with a coffee in the afternoon (at the recommended Limón y Menta).

Places to Eat Roast Suckling Pig

Mesón de Cándido, one of the top restaurants in Castile, is famous for its memorable dinners. Even though it's filled with tourists, it's a grand experience. Take time to wander around and survey the photos of celebs—from King Juan Carlos to Antonio Banderas and Melanie Griffith—who've suckled here. Try to get a table in a room with an aqueduct view (€35 fixed-price *cochinillo* meal includes starter, dessert, and wine; €22 *cochinillo* and wine only; daily 13:00-16:30 & 20:00-23:30, Plaza del Azogüejo 5, air-con, under aqueduct, call for reservations or make them online, tel. 921-428-103, www.mesondecandido.es, candido@mesonde candido.es). Three gracious generations of the Cándido family still run the show.

José María is *the* place to pig out in the old town, a block off Plaza Mayor. And though it doesn't have the history or fanfare of Cándido, Segovians claim this high-energy place serves the best roast suckling pig in town. It thrives with a hungry mix of tourists and locals (€40 à la carte dinner, €25 *cochinillo,* daily 13:00-16:00 & 20:00-23:30, air-con, Cronista Lecea 11, call for reservations or make them online, tel. 921-466-017, www.rtejosemaria.com, reservas@rtejosemaria.es).

Restaurante Duque claims to be the oldest eatery in Segovia, open since 1895. The venerable institution is currently run by fourth-generation Marisa, who is spearheading a modern menu of tapas alongside the rustic, traditional dishes of her ancestors. You'll find boisterous young people bellied up to the bar, while both locals and tourists enjoy the comfortable dining room (€32-39 three-course *cochinillo* dinners, daily 12:30-23:30, sometimes closes in afternoon, a few blocks down from Plaza Mayor across from "house of a thousand beaks" at Calle Cervantes 12, tel. 921-462-486).

Mostly Pig-Free Places in the Old Center

Plaza Mayor, the main square, provides a great backdrop for a light lunch, dinner, or drink. Prices at the cafés are generally reasonable, and many offer a good selection of tapas and *raciones.* Grab a table at the place of your choice and savor the scene. **Café Jeyma** has a fine setting and cathedral view. **La Concepción Restaurante** is also good (€35 meals, closer to the cathedral). For a filling lunch on the plaza, try **Restaurante José,** which has a three-course fixed-price meal (€14, start with the delicate *bacalao pimientos*—red peppers stuffed with salt cod; includes wine, bread, and excellent cathedral views).

Narizotas serves more imaginative and non-Castilian alternatives to the gamey traditions. Dine outside on a delightful square or inside with modern art under medieval timbers. For a wonderful dining experience, try their chef's choice mystery samplers, either the "Right Hand" (€41, about 10 courses) or the "Left Hand" (€37, about six courses); both include wine, water, dessert, and coffee. They offer a less elaborate three-course €13 fixed-priced meal, and their à la carte menu is also a treat (daily 13:00-16:00 & 20:30-24:00, midway down Calle Juan Bravo at Plaza de Medina del Campo 1, tel. 921-462-679, www .narizotas.net).

Cueva de San Esteban serves traditional home cooking with a stress-free photo menu at the door, hearty, big-enough-to-split plates, and—of course—*cochinillo* (daily 11:00-24:00, full meals served 13:00-16:00, 2 blocks past Plaza Mayor on a quiet back street, Calle Valdelaguila 15, tel. 921-460-982).

La Almuzara is a garden of veggie and organic delights: whole-wheat pizzas, tofu, seitan, and even a few dishes with meat (€10 plates, Tue 20:00-24:00, Wed-Sun 12:00-16:00 & 20:00-24:00, closed Mon, between cathedral and Alcázar at Marques del Arco 3, tel. 921-460-622).

Breakfast: In the morning, I like to eat on Plaza Mayor (many choices) while enjoying the cool air and the people scene. Or, 100 yards down the main drag toward the aqueduct, **Café La Colonial** serves good breakfasts (with seating on a tiny square or inside, Plaza del Corpus).

Nightlife: Inexpensive bars and eateries line Calle de Infanta Isabel, just off Plaza Mayor. For nightlife, the bars on Plaza Mayor, Calle de Infanta Isabel, and Calle de Isabel la Católica are packed. There are a number of late-night dance clubs along the aqueduct.

Dessert: **Limón y Menta** offers a good, rich *ponche segoviano* (marzipan) cake by the slice for €3—or try the lighter honey-and-almond *crocantinos* (daily 9:00-21:00 but hours can vary, seating inside, Calle de Isabel la Católica 2, tel. 921-462-141).

Market: An outdoor produce market thrives on Plaza Mayor on Thursday (roughly 8:00-15:00). Nearby, a few stalls are open daily except Sunday on Calle del Cronista Ildefonso Rodríguez.

Segovia Connections

From Segovia to Madrid: You have three options: bus, fast train, or slow train. Even though the 30-minute AVE train takes less than half as long as the bus, you'll spend more time getting to the AVE stations in Segovia and Madrid than to the bus stations, so the total time spent in transit is about the same. *Cercanías* commuter trains also run to Madrid, but take two hours and don't save you much money.

Buses run from Segovia to Madrid's Príncipe Pío Metro station; many stop first at Madrid's Moncloa Metro station, where you can get off if convenient to your hotel (2/hour, departing on the half-hour, 1.25-1.5 hours; Mon-Fri first departure at 6:00, Sat at 7:30, Sun at 8:30; last return at 21:30; tel. 902-119-699, www .lasepulvedana.es). Consider busing from Segovia to Ávila for a visit, then continuing to Salamanca by bus or train.

If you're riding the bus from Madrid to Segovia, about 30 minutes after leaving Madrid you'll see—breaking the horizon on the left—the dramatic concrete cross of the Valley of the Fallen. Its grand facade marks the entry to the mammoth underground memorial (described earlier in this chapter).

The **AVE train** goes between Segovia's Guiomar station and Madrid's Chamartín station (8/day, 30 minutes). To get to Guiomar station, take city bus #11 from the base of the aqueduct (20 minutes, buses usually timed to match arrivals). You can also take the *cercanías* **commuter train** to Madrid, though this option is slower (9/day, 2 hours, leaves from Segovia's inconvenient *cercanías* station, arrives in Madrid at both Chamartín and Atocha stations). To reach the sleepy, dead-end *cercanías* station, walk 20 minutes past the bus station along Paseo de Ezequiel González (which turns into Paseo del Conde de Sepulvedana); catch bus #6 (leaves from the bus station) or #8 (leaves from the aqueduct); or take a taxi. Train info: Tel. 902-320-320.

From Segovia by Bus to: La Granja Palace (about 2/ hour 7:30-21:30, fewer on weekends, 25 minutes), **Ávila** (5/day weekdays, 2/day weekends, 1 hour), **Salamanca** (2/day, more with transfer in Labajos, 2.75 hours, Auto-Res bus, tel. 902-020-052, www.avanzabus.com).

Route Tips for Drivers

From Madrid to Segovia: Leave Madrid on A-6. Exit 39 gets you to Segovia via a slow, winding route over the scenic mountain. Exit at 60 (after a long toll tunnel—about €3 depending on time of day), or get there quicker by staying on the toll road all the way to Segovia (add roughly €2 weekdays or €3 on weekends). At the Segovia aqueduct, follow *casco histórico* signs to the old town (on the side where the aqueduct adjoins the crenellated fortress walls).

Parking in Segovia: Free parking is available in the Alcázar's lot, but you must move your car out by 19:00 (or by 18:00 Oct-March), when the gates close. Or try the lot northwest of the bus station by the statue of Cándido, along the street called Paseo de Ezequiel González. Outside the old city, there's an Acueducto Parking underground garage kitty-corner from the bus station. Although it can be a hard slog up the hill to the Alcázar on a hot day, it beats trying to maneuver uphill through tight bends. There's also the huge and convenient Padre Claret garage near the aqueduct (€1.55/hour).

The city center has lots of parking spaces, but they're not free. If you want to park in the old town, be legal or risk an expensive ticket. Buy a ticket from the nearby machine to park in areas marked by blue stripes, and place the ticket on your dashboard (€1.80/hour, pay meter every 2 hours 9:00-14:00 & 16:30-20:00; free parking 20:00-9:00, Sat afternoon, and all day Sun).

Segovia to Salamanca (100 miles): Leave Segovia by driving around the town's circular road, which offers good views from below the Alcázar. Then follow signs for *Ávila* (road N-110). Notice the fine Segovia view from the three crosses at the crest of the first hill. The Salamanca road leads around the famous Ávila walls to the right. The best wall view is from the signposted *Cuatro Postes,* a mile northwest of town. Salamanca (N-501) is clearly marked, about an hour's drive away.

About 20 miles before Salamanca, you might want to stop at the huge bull on the left side of the road. There's a little dirt lane leading right up to it. As you get closer, it becomes more and more obvious it isn't alive. Bad boys climb it for a goofy photo. For a great photo op of Salamanca, complete with river reflection, stop at the edge of the city (at the light before the first bridge). The only safe parking in Salamanca is in a garage; try the underground lot at Plaza Santa Eulalia, Plaza del Campillo, or Lemans (closer to recommended Petit Palace Las Torres). See the Salamanca chapter for more information.

Ávila

Yet another popular side-trip from Madrid, Ávila is famous for its perfectly preserved medieval walls, as the birthplace of St. Teresa, and for its yummy *yema* treats. For more than 300 years, Ávila was on the battlefront between the Muslims and Christians, changing hands several times. Today perfectly peaceful Ávila has a charming old town. With several fine churches and monasteries, it makes for an enjoyable quick stop between Segovia and Salamanca (each about an hour away by car).

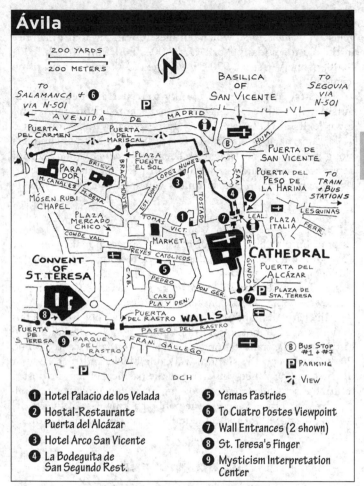

Ávila

200 YARDS
200 METERS

TO
SALAMANCA & ⑥
VIA N-501

BASILICA
OF
SAN VICENTE

TO
SEGOVIA
VIA
N-501

AVENIDA DE MADRID

PUERTA
DEL CARMEN

PUERTA
DEL
MARISCAL

PUERTA DE
SAN VICENTE

PARADOR

BRIEVA

PLAZA
FUENTE
EL SOL

LOPEZ NUÑEZ

PUERTA DEL
PESO DE
LA HARINA

TO
TRAIN
& BUS
STATIONS

M. CANALES

H. BENA

BRACAMONTE

EST. DOM

DEL TOSTADO

③

SAN

④ ②

LESQUINAS

MÓSEN RUBI
CHAPEL

PLAZA
MERCADO
CHICO

TOMAS

VICT.

①

⑦

LEAL.

PLAZA
ITALIA

FERR.

CONDE VAL.

MARKET

REYES CATÓLICOS

⑤

CATHEDRAL

CONVENT
OF
ST. TERESA

N.A.B.

PEDRO

CARD.
PLA Y DEN.

DON GER.

SE GUNDO

PUERTA DEL
ALCÁZAR

PLAZA DE
STA. TERESA

⑦

⑧

PUERTA
DEL RASTRO

WALLS

PUERTA
DE
S. TERESA

⑨

PARQUE
DEL
RASTRO

PASEO DEL RASTRO

FRAN. GALLEGO

DCH

Ⓑ BUS STOP
#1 & #7
Ⓟ PARKING
🔭 VIEW

① Hotel Palacio de los Velada
② Hostal-Restaurante
   Puerta del Alcázar
③ Hotel Arco San Vicente
④ La Bodeguita de
   San Segundo Rest.
⑤ Yemas Pastries
⑥ To Cuatro Postes Viewpoint
⑦ Wall Entrances (2 shown)
⑧ St. Teresa's Finger
⑨ Mysticism Interpretation
   Center

Orientation to Ávila

On a quick stop, everything in Ávila that matters is within a few
blocks of the cathedral (which actually forms part of the east end
of the city wall).

Tourist Information

The TI has good, free maps and information (Mon-Sat 9:30-14:00
& 16:00-19:00, Sun 9:30-17:00, on Calle San Segundo, just outside
the wall gate near the cathedral, tel. 920-211-387). Another TI,
with a friendlier staff, is located outside the wall, opposite the
Basilica of San Vicente. They sell handy €.50 maps and €1 mini-
guidebooks in English, which provide details on the palaces and

churches. If you want to see more than the highlights, consider the general *Descubre Ávila*, which outlines 10 walking-tour itineraries in the old town (daily April-Oct 9:00-20:00, Nov-March 9:00-18:00, public WCs, tel. 920-354-000 ext. 370, www.avilaturismo .com/en).

Sightseeing Train: A clunky tourist train departs from outside the wall by Puerta de San Vicente, choo-choos into town, exits at the westernmost gate, loops by the Monasterio de la Encarnación (where St. Teresa lived), and then shudders along back to the north wall. Check the *próxima salida* sign for departure times, which are usually hourly (€4 day pass, daily 9:00-18:00, narration in Spanish unless you specify English, mobile 630-945-021).

Arrival in Ávila

Approaching by bus, train, or car, you'll need to make your way through the nondescript modern part of town to find the walled old town.

By Bus or Train: There are lockers at Ávila's bus station (use the newer-looking locks), but not at the train station.

The cathedral and wall are 15 minutes by foot from the bus station, and 20 minutes from the train station. City buses #4 and #1 run from the train station to the Basilica of San Vicente (to find the bus stop, exit the station, walk one block, and turn right at the first street). When you arrive at the basilica, check the posted return bus schedule to ensure you can make your train connection.

By Car: Drivers can use the public parking east of Puerta del Alcázar, just south of the cathedral, or at Parking Dornier (€1.25/hour).

Sights in Ávila

▲The Wall

Built from around 1100 on even more ancient remains, Ávila's fortified wall is the oldest, most complete, and best-preserved in Spain. It has four gates and three entrances, allowing visitors the chance to walk almost three-quarters of the wall: One entrance is just off Plaza de Santa Teresa (Puerta del Alcázar). The best one, which leads to a longer walk, starts from inside the TI on Calle San Segundo, by the gate closest  to the cathedral (Puerta del Peso de la Harina) and takes you to the third and fourth gates: Puerta del Carmen (exit only) and Puerta

Puente Adaja (on the end farthest from the cathedral—look for the door marked *subida a la muralla*).

An interesting paseo scene takes place along the wall each night—make your way along the southern wall (Paseo del Rastro) to Plaza de Santa Teresa for spectacular vistas across the plains.

Cost and Hours: €5, includes audioguide in English; July-Aug daily 10:00-20:00; April-June and Sept-Oct Tue-Sun 10:00-20:00, closed Mon; Nov-March Tue-Sun 10:00-18:00, closed Mon; last entry 45 minutes before closing.

Viewing the Wall: The best views of the wall itself are actually from street level. If you're wandering the city and see arched gates leading out of the old center, pop out to the other side and take in the impressive wall from the ground. Drivers can see the especially impressive north side as they circle to the right from Puerta de San Vicente to catch the highway to Salamanca.

Viewing Ávila from Cuatro Postes

The best overall view of the walled town of Ávila is about a mile away on the Salamanca road (N-501), at a clearly marked turnout for the Cuatro Postes (four posts). You can reach the Cuatro Postes by catching city bus #7 (€1) at the stop in front of the Basilica of San Vicente—it goes through the old town, then out to the Cuatro Postes viewpoint, back to San Vicente, and on to the RENFE train station. Bus #7 doesn't run on weekends; ask at the TI for walking directions (about 30 minutes each way), or take bus #1 to the stop nearest the Hermitage of San Segundo and walk five minutes to the viewpoint.

Cathedral

While it started as Romanesque, Ávila's cathedral, finished in the 16th century, is considered the first Gothic cathedral in Spain. Its position—with its granite apse actually part of the fortified wall—underlines the "medieval alliance between cross and sword." You can tour the cathedral, its sacristy, cloister, and museum—which includes an El Greco painting.

Cost and Hours: €4, audioguide in English-€2; Mon-Fri 10:00-18:00, Sat 10:00-19:00, Sun 12:00-15:00; generally closes one hour earlier off-season; last entry 45 minutes before closing; Plaza de la Catedral.

Convent of St. Teresa

Built in the 17th century on the spot where the saint was born, this convent is a big hit with pilgrims (10-minute walk from cathedral). St. Teresa (1515-1582)—reforming nun, mystic, and writer—bought a house in Ávila and converted it into a convent with more stringent rules than the one she belonged to. She faced opposition in her hometown from rival nuns and those convinced her visions of heaven were the work of the devil. However, with her mentor and fellow mystic St. John of the Cross, she established convents of

Discalced (shoeless) Carmelites throughout Spain, and her visions and writings led her to sainthood (she was canonized in 1622).

A lavishly gilded side chapel marks the actual place of her birth (left of main altar, door may be closed). A separate room of relics (outside, facing the church on your right, Sala de Reliquias) houses a shop that shows off Teresa's finger, complete with a fancy emerald ring, along with one of her sandals and the bones of St. John of the Cross. A museum dedicated to the saint is in the crypt at the side entrance and is worth a visit for devotees.

Cost and Hours: Convent—free, daily 9:30-13:30 & 15:30-19:30, until 19:00 in winter, no photos of finger allowed; museum—€2, April-Oct Tue-Sun 10:00-14:00 & 16:00-20:00, Nov-March Tue-Sun 10:00-13:30 & 15:30-17:30, closed Mon year-round, last entry 30 minutes before closing.

Mysticism Interpretation Center (Centro de Interpretación del Misticismo)

If St. Teresa were alive today, she'd love this place, which explores modern mysticism from a Catholic perspective. Pick up the English handout that explains the art and texts, then take the elevator down on a "journey to the inner realms of the Self."

Cost and Hours: €2.50, Tue-Sun 10:00-13:30 & 16:00-17:30, closed Mon, last entry 30 minutes before closing, tel. 920-212-154, www.avilamistica.es.

Yemas

These pastries, made by local nuns, are more or less soft-boiled egg yolks that have been cooled and sugared (*yema* means yolk). They're sold all over town. The shop **Las Delicias del Convento** is actually a retail outlet for the cooks of the convent (€3.60 for a small box, Tue-Fri 10:30-14:00 & 17:00-20:00, Sat 10:30-14:30 & 16:30-20:30, Sun 10:30-18:00, closed Mon, hours and closed day vary by season, a block from TI at Calle de los Reyes Católicos 12, tel. 920-220-293).

Sleeping in Ávila

Ávila is cold in fall, winter, and early spring, so you'll likely need to turn up the heat in these hotels.

$$$ Hotel Palacio de los Velada is antique and classy and faces the cathedral. Located in a five-centuries-old palace, it has 144 elegant rooms surrounding a huge and inviting arcaded courtyard (Sb-€150, Db-€190, third person-€30 extra on weekends, lower rates Mon-Thu and for 2-night weekend stays, higher on holidays, rates fluctuate wildly—check website for latest, air-con, elevator, Plaza de la Catedral 10, tel. 920-255-100, www.veladahoteles.com, reserves.avila@veladahoteles.com).

$$ Hostal Puerta del Alcázar has 27 basic yet spacious rooms right next to the Puerta del Peso de la Harina just outside the wall (Sb-€33-43, Db-€45-55, Tb-€77, Qb-€99, includes breakfast, air-con, free Wi-Fi, San Segundo 38, tel. 920-211-074, www.puertadelalcazar.com, info@puertadelalcazar.com). It's home to a recommended restaurant.

$$ Hotel Arco San Vicente has a friendly staff and a great location two blocks from the cathedral and one block from the Basilica of San Vicente, with its handy stop for buses to the train station or the Cuatro Postes viewpoint (Sb-€35-40, Db-€45-65, breakfast-€6, air-con on second floor, elevator, free Wi-Fi, limited parking-€10/day, Calle López Núñez 6, tel. 920-222-498, www.arcosanvicente.com, info@arcosanvicente.com).

Eating in Ávila

Ávila specialties include *chuletón,* a thick steak, and *judías del Barco de Ávila,* big white beans often cooked in a meaty stew. Around Plaza del Mercado Chico, the main square of the old center, are several good spots to try the stew or to have a reasonable fixed-price lunch (many of which include the *judías*).

La Bodeguita de San Segundo is good for a light lunch. Owned by a locally famous wine connoisseur, it serves fine wine by the glass with tapas such as smoked-cod salad and wild-mushroom scrambled eggs (daily 11:00-24:00, sometimes closes in afternoon, €2 bread charge, along the outside of wall near cathedral at San Segundo 19, tel. 920-228-634).

Hostal-Restaurante Puerta del Alcázar, filled with more locals than hotel guests, serves elaborate salads, fixed-price meals (€13-21 Mon-Fri, €16-21 Sat-Sun), and more. You can sit indoors or, even better, outdoors with cathedral views (Mon-Sat 13:00-16:00 & 21:00-23:30, Sun 13:00-16:00, San Segundo 38, tel. 920-211-074).

Picnics: The town's market house is a good spot to pick up fruit and water (Mon-Thu 9:00-14:00 & 17:00-20:00, Fri 9:00-20:00, Sat 9:00-14:00, closed Sun, between Plaza del Mercado Chico and the cathedral). On Friday mornings, there's a farmers' market on Plaza del Mercado Chico.

Café: For a pleasant break from sightseeing, pop in to the courtyard of the recommended **Hotel Palacio de los Velada** for a drink (€3 coffee and hot chocolate).

Ávila Connections

The bus terminal is closed on Sundays, but you can purchase tickets when boarding the bus.

From Ávila to: Segovia (5 buses/day weekdays, 2 on weekends, 1 hour), **Madrid** (nearly hourly until 21:10, 1.5-2 hours, more frequent connections with Chamartín Station than Atocha; 9 buses/day, 6 on weekends, 1.5 hours; Estación Sur, tel. 914-684-200), **Salamanca** (8 trains/day, 1-1.5 hours; 4-5 buses/day, 1.5 hours). Train info: Toll tel. 902-320-320, www.renfe.com. Bus info: Tel. 902-020-052, www.avanzabus.com.

TOLEDO

An hour south of Madrid by car, Toledo teems with tourists, souvenirs, and great art by day, and delicious dinners, echoes of El Greco, and medieval magic by night. Incredibly well-preserved and full of cultural wonder, the entire city has been declared a national monument.

Spain's former capital crowds 2,500 years of tangled history—Roman, Jewish, Visigothic, Moorish, and Christian—onto a high, rocky perch protected on three sides by the Tajo River. To keep the city's historic appearance intact, the Spanish government has forbidden any modern exteriors. The rich mix of Jewish, Moorish, and Christian heritages makes it one of Europe's cultural highlights.

Today, Toledo thrives as a provincial capital and a busy tourist attraction. The last decade has been an eventful one for Toledo. A high-speed AVE train connection has made Toledo a quick, 30-minute ride from Madrid. While locals worried that this link would turn their town into a bedroom community for wealthy Madrileños, the high real-estate prices minimized the impact.

Another civic boost was a new convention center—the Palacio de Congresos Miradero. It was designed by Rafael Moneo—architect of the Los Angeles Cathedral, the Kursaal Conference Center in San Sebastián, and, in Madrid, the renovated Atocha Station and the Prado Museum's extension. While the center itself is of little interest to tourists, its huge underground parking garage and escalator into town make arrival by car much more efficient. The long-term vision is to make the old city center essentially traffic-free (except for residents' cars, public transit, and service vehicles).

This stony wonderland remains the historic, artistic, and spiritual center of Spain. Despite tremendous tourist crowds, Toledo sits enthroned on its history, much as it was when Europe's most powerful king, Charles V (called Carlos I in Spain), and its most famous resident artist, El Greco, called it home. And because 2014 marks the 400th anniversary of El Greco's death, the town's sights have been beautifully renovated and are ready for prime time.

Planning Your Time

To properly see Toledo's sights—including its museums (great El Greco) and cathedral (best in Spain)—and to experience its medieval atmosphere (wonderful after dark), you'll need two nights and a day.

Get an early start and stay out late. If going by train, keep in mind that the early and late trains tend to sell out to commuters and day-trippers. Plan carefully for lunchtime closures and take a rest break during Toledo's notorious midday heat in summer. Tourists day-tripping from Madrid can pack the city during midday, while those spending the night enjoy an entirely different (and better) Toledo experience.

Orientation to Toledo

Toledo sits atop a circular hill, with the cathedral roughly dead-center. Lassoed into a tight tangle of streets by the sharp bend of the Tajo River (called the "Tejo" in Portugal, where it hits the Atlantic at Lisbon), Toledo has Spain's most confusing medieval street plan. But it's a small town within its walls, with only 10,000 inhabitants (84,000 live in greater Toledo, including its modern suburbs). The major sights are well-signposted, and most locals will politely point you in the right direction if you ask. (You are, after all, the town's bread and butter.)

The top sights stretch from the main square, Plaza de Zocodover (zoh-koh-doh-VEHR), southwest along Calle Comercio (a.k.a. Calle Ancha, "Wide Street") to the cathedral, and beyond that to Santo Tomé and more. The visitor's city lies basically along this small but central street, and most tourists never stray from this axis. Make a point to get lost. The town is compact. When it's time to return to someplace familiar, pull out the map or ask, *"¿Para Plaza de Zocodover?"* From the far end of town, handy bus #12 circles back to Plaza de Zocodover (see "Bus #12 Self-Guided Tour" on page 577).

While the city is very hilly (in Toledo, they say everything's uphill—it certainly feels that way), nothing is more than a short hike away.

Tourist Information

Toledo has four TIs. There's one at the **train station** (daily 9:00-15:00, tel. 925-239-121); one at **Bisagra Gate,** in a freestanding building in the park just outside the gate (Mon-Fri 9:00-18:00, Sat 9:00-19:00, Sun 9:00-15:00, longer hours in summer, tel. 925-220-843); another on **Plaza del Ayuntamiento** near the cathedral (daily 10:00-16:00, longer hours in summer, WC, tel. 925-254-030); and a kiosk on **Plaza de Zocodover** (daily 10:00-19:00). At any TI, you can pick up the town map, a copy of the *Toledo Tourist and Cultural Guide,* and the *Traveller's Gazette* (a bilingual newspaper with event listings). The TIs share a website: www.toledo-turismo.com.

Sightseeing Pass: Toledo's museum pass, the **Pulsera Turística,** covers entry to six monuments and churches for €8 (Santo Tomé, Sinagoga de Santa María la Blanca, San Juan de los Reyes Monasterio, Mezquita del Cristo de la Luz, Church of El Salvador, and Church of San Ildefonso/Jesuitas; sold at participating sights). Without the pass, entry to each is about €2.50 (if you saw everything, you'd pay about half-price). But the pass doesn't cover the city's top three sights—and few people are interested in visiting the last two churches it covers.

Arrival in Toledo

"Arriving" in Toledo means getting uphill to Plaza de Zocodover. As the bus and train stations are outside the town center and parking can be a challenge, this involves a hike, a taxi, or a city bus ride.

By Train: Toledo's early-20th-century train station is Neo-Moorish and a national monument itself for its architecture and art, which celebrate the three cultures that coexisted here.

Remember that early and late trains can sell out; reserve ahead. If you haven't yet bought a ticket for your departure from Toledo (even if it's for the next day), get it before you leave the Toledo station and choose a specific time rather than leave it open-ended. (If you prefer more flexibility, take the bus instead—see "By Bus" later.)

From the train station to Plaza de Zocodover, it's a €6 **taxi** ride, a 25-minute hike, or an easy ride on various buses. You can take **city bus** #5, #61, or #62; leaving the station, you'll see the bus stop 30 yards to the right (€1.40, pay on bus, confirm by asking,

TOLEDO

Toledo

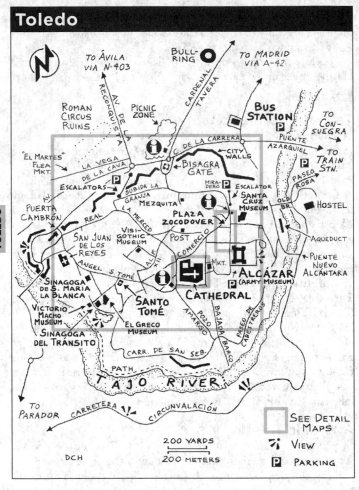

"*¿Para Plaza de Zocodover?*"). The **Tourist Bus** (described on page 557), which circles the city, also picks up outside the station, and stops briefly at the famous El Greco viewpoint before heading up to Plaza de Zocodover (€5; €8 for hop-on, hop-off version). Another option going directly to Plaza de Zocodover, the red **Centro Directo bus** (€2), is scheduled to meet arriving trains.

To **walk** into town, turn right as you leave the station, cross the bridge with the mighty Alcázar (now the Army Museum) on your left, pass the bus station (on your right), go straight through the roundabout, continue uphill to Bisagra Gate, and head into the old town to Plaza de Zocodover. A new escalator project will make this walk much easier—someday. Construction was put on hold in 2012, and it's uncertain when it will be finished.

Toledo's History

Perched strategically in the center of Iberia, for centuries Toledo was a Roman transportation hub with a thriving

Jewish population. After Rome fell, the city became a Visigothic capital (A.D. 554). In 711 the Moors (Muslims) made it a regional center. In 1085 the city was reconquered by Christians, but many Moors remained in Toledo, tolerated and respected as scholars and craftsmen.

Whereas Jews were commonly persecuted elsewhere in Europe, Toledo's Jewish community—educated, wealthy, and cosmopolitan—thrived from the city's earliest times. Jews of Spanish origin are called Sephardic Jews. The American expression "Holy Toledo" likely originated from the Sephardic Jews who eventually immigrated to America. To them, Toledo was the holiest Jewish city in Europe...Holy Toledo!

During its medieval heyday (c. 1350), Toledo was a city of the humanities, where God was known by many names. In this haven of cultural diversity, people of different faiths lived together in harmony.

Toledo remained Spain's political capital until 1561, when Philip II moved to more-spacious Madrid. Historians fail to agree on the reason for the move; some say that Madrid was the logical place for a capital in the geographic center of newly formed *España*, while others say that Philip wanted to separate politics from religion. (Toledo remained Spain's religious capital.) Whatever the reason, when the king moved out, Toledo was mothballed, only to be rediscovered by 19th-century Romantic travelers. They wrote of it as a mystical place, which it remains today.

TOLEDO

By Bus: At the bus station, buses park downstairs. Luggage lockers and a small bus-information office—where you can buy locker tokens—are upstairs opposite the cafeteria. Before leaving the station, confirm your departure time (around 2/hour to Madrid). Unlike the faster trains, buses don't tend to get booked up. You can put off buying a return ticket for the bus until just minutes before you leave Toledo. Specify you'd like a *directo* bus, because the *ruta* trip takes longer (1 hour versus 1.5 hours). However, if you miss the *directo* bus (or if it's sold out), the *ruta* option offers a peek of off-the-beaten-path Madrid suburbia; you'll arrive at the same time as taking the next *directo* bus. From the bus station, Plaza de Zocodover is a 15-minute hike, a €5 taxi ride, or a short bus ride (catch #5 or #12 downstairs; €1.40, pay on bus).

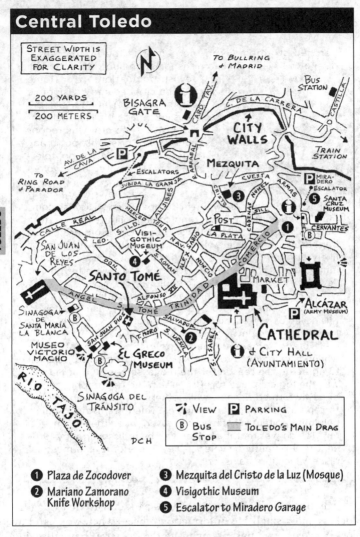

Central Toledo

STREET WIDTH IS
EXAGGERATED
FOR CLARITY

200 YARDS
200 METERS

TO BULLRING
+ MADRID

BISAGRA
GATE

C. DE LA CARRERA

BUS
STATION

CITY
WALLS

TO
RING ROAD
& PARADOR

AV. DE LA
CAVA

ESCALATORS

SUBIDA LA GRANJA

MEZQUITA

CUESTA

TRAIN
STATION

MIRA-
DERO
ESCALATOR

SANTA
CRUZ
MUSEUM

CALLE REAL

MERCED TEND.

ALJIBES

S. ILD.

VISI-
GOTHIC
MUSEUM

POST

LA PLATA

CADENAS

NUNCIO

SILL

COMERCIO

CERVANTES

SAN JUAN
DE LOS
REYES

S. LEO.

DON.

S. ROMAN

NAV.

ALEX.

SABIO

SANTO TOMÉ

ANGEL

S.

ALFONSO XII

TRINIDAD

MARKET

ALCÁZAR
(ARMY MUSEUM)

SINAGOGA
DE
SANTA MARÍA
LA BLANCA

SAN JUAN DIOS

TOMÉ

S.

T. MORO

S. URSULA

SALVADOR

S. ISABEL

CATHEDRAL

MUSEO
VICTORIO
MACHO

EL GRECO
MUSEUM

& CITY HALL
(AYUNTAMIENTO)

RIO TAJO

SINAGOGA DEL
TRÁNSITO

DCH

View	P Parking
B Bus Stop	Toledo's Main Drag

❶ Plaza de Zocodover
❷ Mariano Zamorano Knife Workshop
❸ Mezquita del Cristo de la Luz (Mosque)
❹ Visigothic Museum
❺ Escalator to Miradero Garage

By Car: If you're arriving by car, enjoy a scenic big-picture orientation by following the *Ronda de Toledo* signs on a big circular drive around the city. You'll view the city from many angles along the Circunvalación road across the Tajo Gorge. Stop at a viewpoint or drive to Parador de Toledo, just south of town, for the view (from the balcony) that El Greco made famous in his portrait of Toledo. The best time for this trip is the magic hour before sunset, when the top viewpoints are busy with tired old folks and frisky young lovers.

There are two big, free parking lots (one between the river and the bus station, the other between the river and the train station). If you're willing to pay, the most convenient place to park is in the big Miradero Garage at the convention center (€16/day; drive through Bisagra Gate, go uphill half a mile, look for sign on the left directing you to *Plaza del Miradero*). There is also parking farther into town at the Alcázar Garage (just past the Alcázar—€1.60/hour, €16.20/day). Many hotels offer discounted parking rates at nearby garages; ask when making your reservation.

A car is useless within Toledo's city walls, where the narrow, twisting streets are no fun to navigate. Ideally, see the old town outside of car-rental time. Pick up or drop off your car on the outskirts of town; **Avis** is at the train station (closed Sun, handy early and late drop options, tel. 925-215-794).

By Escalator into Town: A series of escalators runs outdoors past Bisagra Gate, giving you a free ride up, up, up into town (until 22:00). You'll end up near San Ildefonso—far from Plaza de Zocodover—but it's fun for the novelty. The other escalator, stretching from the Alcántara Bridge to the Miradero Garage and then farther up nearly to Plaza de Zocodover, is most helpful for people using the garage.

Helpful Hints

Internet Access: You'll find **Internet Locutorio** shops throughout Toledo (open long hours).

Taxis: There are three taxi stands in the old center: Plaza de Zocodover, Bisagra Gate, and Santo Tomé. Taxis routinely give visitors scenic circles around town with photo stops for around €15.

Local Guidebook: Consider the readable *Toledo: Its Art and Its History* (€5-6 big version, €4 small version, same text and photos in both, sold all over town). It explains all of the sights (which generally provide no on-site information) and gives you a photo to point at and say, "*¿Dónde está...?*"

Tours in Toledo

▲Tourist Bus

Toledo City Tour offers three tourist bus options that are great for day-trippers. For direct transportation to the city center, meet the bus at the train station, ride along the river to the famous lookout point, where you can get off for a five-minute photo stop, then continue around the city and up to Plaza de Zocodover, where you can get off and visit Toledo. Pay a little more, and you get a hop-on, hop-off version that allows you to stop at the photo viewpoint, Bisagra Gate, and the San Martín medieval bridge (€5 bus ride, €8 for hop-on, hop-off option, pay at stand in train station;

departures timed to train arrivals—first bus leaves train station at 9:50, then almost hourly until 18:00, March-Sept until 21:00; bus ride includes recorded English commentary on headphones; tel. 925-950-000, www.toledocitytour.es, infotoledo@toledocity tour.es).

Tourist Train

For a pleasant city overview, hop on the cheesy red TrainVision Tourist Tram. Crass as it feels, you get a 45-minute putt-putt through Toledo and around the Tajo River Gorge. It's a fine way for non-drivers to enjoy views of the city from across the Tajo Gorge (€5.20, buy ticket from the kiosk on the Plaza de Zocodover, leaves Plaza de Zocodover daily 1-2/hour from 10:00-18:30, later in summer, recorded English/Spanish commentary, tel. 625-301-890, www.toledotrainvision.com). There are no photo stops, but it goes slowly—for the best views of Toledo across the gorge, sit on the right side, not behind the driver.

Public Buses

For the cheapest tour, use public transportation. Take the "Bus #12 Self-Guided Tour" through town (see page 577). Or, for a "gorge-ous" loop trip, try bus #71, which leaves from opposite the entrance of the Alcázar (hourly 7:45-21:45) and offers the same classic view across the gorge as the tourist train; its route circles around to El Greco's famous viewpoint, where you can hop off and snap some photos, then wait at the same stop for the next bus to take you back.

Local Guides

Two good guides enjoy sharing their hometown in English: **Juan José Espadas** (a.k.a. Juanjo, who gracefully brings meaning to the complex mix of Toledo's history, art, and culture; tel. 667-780-475, juanjo@guiadetoledo.es) and **Almudena Cencerrado** (tel. 610-765-067, almuzen@hotmail.com). For a three-hour tour, they each charge €150.

Sights in Toledo

▲▲▲Cathedral

Holy Toledo! Spain's leading Catholic city has a magnificent cathedral. Shoehorned into the old center, its exterior is hard to appreciate. (As is so typical of religious sites in hard-fought Iberia, it was built after the Reconquista on the spot where a mosque once stood.) But the interior

Toledo at a Glance

▲▲▲**Cathedral** One of Europe's best, with a marvelously vast interior and great art. **Hours:** Mon-Sat 10:00-18:30, Sun 14:00-18:30. See page 558.

▲▲**Santa Cruz Museum** Renaissance building housing wonderful artwork, including 15 El Grecos. **Hours:** Mon-Sat 10:00-19:00, Sun 10:00-14:30. See page 566.

▲▲**Army Museum** Covers all things military—with the glaring exception of Spain's controversial civil war—and located in the imposing fortress, the Alcázar. **Hours:** Thu-Tue 11:00-17:00, closed Wed. See page 568.

▲**Santo Tomé** Simple chapel with El Greco's masterpiece, *The Burial of the Count of Orgaz*. **Hours:** Daily 10:00-17:45, until 18:45 April-mid-Oct. See page 571.

▲**El Greco Museum** Small collection of paintings, including the *View and Plan of Toledo*, El Greco's panoramic map of the city. **Hours:** Tue-Sat 9:30-18:30, until 20:00 in high season, Sun 10:00-15:00, closed Mon. See page 572.

▲**Museo Victorio Macho** Collection of 20th-century Toledo sculptor's works, with expansive river-gorge view. **Hours:** Mon-Sat 10:00-19:00, Sun 10:00-15:00. See page 574.

▲**San Juan de los Reyes Monasterio** Church/monastery intended as final resting place of Isabel and Ferdinand. **Hours:** Daily 10:00-18:45, until 18:00 in winter. See page 575.

Visigothic Museum Romanesque church housing the only Visigothic artifacts in town. **Hours:** Tue-Sat 10:00-14:00 & 16:00-18:30, Sun 10:00-14:00, closed Mon. See page 570.

Sinagoga del Tránsito Museum of Toledo's Jewish past. **Hours:** Tue-Sat 9:30-20:00—until 18:00 in winter, Sun 10:00-15:00, closed Mon. See page 572.

Sinagoga de Santa María la Blanca Synagogue that harmoniously combines Toledo's three religious influences: Jewish, Christian, and Moorish. **Hours:** Daily April-Sept 10:00-18:45, Oct-March 10:00-17:45. See page 575.

TOLEDO

is so lofty, rich, and vast that it'll have you wandering around like a Pez dispenser stuck open, whispering "Wow." The sacristy (under renovation until early 2014) has a collection of paintings that would put any museum on the map.

Cost and Hours: €8 includes audioguide, €11 also includes trip up bell tower at assigned times, tickets sold in shop opposite church entrance on Calle Cardenal; Mon-Sat 10:00-18:30, Sun 14:00-18:30, open earlier for prayer only, last entry 30 minutes before closing; photos allowed without flash, tel. 925-222-241. A WC is in the ticket center.

❍ Self-Guided Tour: Wander among the pillars, thick and sturdy as a redwood forest. Sit under one and imagine a time when the lightbulbs were candles and the tourists were pilgrims—when every window provided spiritual as well as physical light. The cathedral is primarily Gothic. But since it took more than 250 years to build (1226-1495)—with continuous embellishments after that (every archbishop wanted to leave his imprint)—it's a mix of styles, including Gothic, Renaissance, Baroque, and Neoclassical. Enjoy the elaborate wrought-iron work, lavish wood carvings, and window after colorful window of 500-year-old stained glass. Circling the interior are ornate chapels, purchased by the town's most noble families, and the sacristy, with its world-class collection of El Grecos and works by other famous painters.

This confusing collage of great Spanish art deserves a close look. Hire a private guide, discreetly freeload on a tour (they come by every few minutes during peak season), rent the audioguide, or follow this quick tour.

• *First, walk to the high altar.*

High Altar: Climb two steps and grip the iron grille as you marvel at one of the most stunning altars in Spain. Real gold on wood, by Flemish, French, and local artists, it's one of the country's best pieces of Gothic art. Study the wall of scenes from the life of Christ, frame by frame. All of the images seem to celebrate the colorful Assumption of Mary in the center, with Mary escorted by six upwardly mobile  angels. The crucified Christ on top is nine feet tall—taller than the lower statues—to keep this towering altar approachable. Don't miss the finely worked gold-plated iron grille itself—considered to be the best from the 16th century in Spain.

• *About-face to the...*

Choir: Facing the high altar, the choir is famous for its fine and richly symbolic carving. It all seems to lead to the archbishop's

Toledo's Cathedral

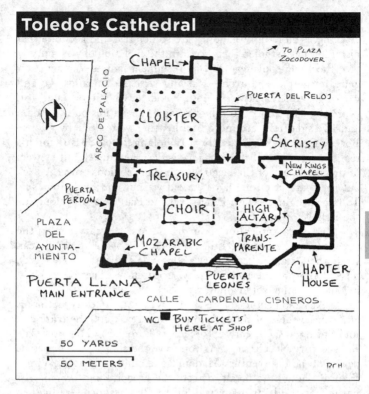

To Plaza Zocodover

Chapel→

ARCO DE PALACIO

Puerta del Reloj

CLOISTER

SACRISTY

New Kings Chapel

←TREASURY

Puerta Perdón→

CHOIR

HIGH ALTAR

PLAZA DEL AYUNTA- MIENTO

←MOZARABIC CHAPEL

TRANS- PARENTE

CHAPTER HOUSE

PUERTA LLANA→ MAIN ENTRANCE

PUERTA LEONES

CALLE   CARDENAL   CISNEROS

WC■ BUY TICKETS HERE AT SHOP

50 YARDS

50 METERS

DCH

TOLEDO

throne in the rear center. First, look carefully at the fine alabaster relief in the center (about where the bishop would rest his head on his throne): It shows a seventh-century Visigothic miracle, when Mary came down to give the local bishop the holy robe, legitimizing Toledo as the spiritual capital (and therefore political capital) of Spain.

Because of its primacy in Iberia, Toledo was the first city in the crosshairs of the Reconquista Christian forces. They recaptured the city in 1085 (over 400 years before they retook Granada). The fall of Toledo marked the beginning of the end of the Muslim domination of Iberia. A local saying goes, "A carpet frays from the edges, but the carpet of Al-Andalus (Muslim Spain) frayed from the very center" (meaning Toledo).

The lower wooden stalls are decorated with scenes showing the steady one-city-at-a-time finale of the Christian Reconquista, when Muslims were slowly pushed back into Africa. Set in the last decade of the Reconquista, these images celebrate the retaking of the towns around Granada: Each idealized castle has the reconquered town's name on it, culminating in the final victory at Granada in 1492 (these two reliefs flank the archbishop's throne). Although the castles are romanticized, the carvings of the clothing, armor, and weaponry are so detailed and accurate that historians have studied them to learn the evolution of weaponry.

The upper stalls feature Old Testament figures—an alabaster genealogy of the church—starting with Adam and Eve and working counterclockwise to Joseph and "S. M. Virgo Mater" (St. Mary the Virgin Mother). Notice how the statues on the Adam and Eve side (left) are more lifelike; they were done by Alonso Berruguete, nicknamed "the Michelangelo of Spain" for his realistic figures. All this imagery is designed to remind viewers of the legitimacy of the bishop's claims to religious power. Check out the seat backs, made of carved walnut and featuring New Testament figures—with Peter (key) and Paul (sword)—alongside the archbishop himself.

And, as is typical of choir decoration, the carvings on the misericords (the tiny seats that allowed tired worshippers to lean while they "stand") represent various sins and feature the frisky, folksy, sexy, profane art of the day. Apparently, since you sat on it, it could never be sacred anyway.

Take a moment to absorb the marvelous complexity, harmony, and cohesiveness of the art around you. Look up. There are two fine pipe organs: one early 18th-century Baroque and the other late 18th-century Neoclassical. As you leave the choir, note the serene beauty of the 13th-century Madonna and child at the front (Virgin Blanca), thought to be a gift from the French king to Spain. Its naturalism and intimacy was proto-Renaissance—radical in its day.

The iron grille of the choir is notable for the dedication of the man who built it. Domingo de Céspedes, a Toledo ironworker, accepted the commission to build the grille for 6,000 ducats. The project, which took from 1541 to 1548, was far more costly than he anticipated. The medieval Church didn't accept cost overruns, so to finish it he sold everything he owned and went into debt. He died a poor—but honorable—man. (That's a charming story, but the artistic iron gate before the high altar—described earlier—is the true treasure.)

• *Face the altar, and go around it to your right to the...*

Chapter House (Sala Capitular): Under its lavish ceiling, a fresco celebrates the humanism of the Italian Renaissance. There's a Deposition (taking crucified Jesus off the cross), a *pietà*, and a Resurrection on the front wall; they face a fascinating Last Judgment, where the seven sins are actually spelled out in the gang going to hell: arrogance (the guy striking a pose), avarice (holding his bag of coins), lust (the easy woman with the lovely hair and fiery crotch), anger (shouting at lust), gluttony (the fat guy), envy, and laziness. Think about how instructive this was in 1600.

Below the fresco, a pictorial review of 1,900 years of Toledo archbishops circles the room. The upper row of portraits dates from the 16th century. Except for the last two, these were not painted from life (the same face seems to be recycled over and over). The lower portraits were added one at a time from 1515 on and are of more historic than artistic interest. Imagine sitting down to church business surrounded by all this tradition and theology.

The current cardinal—whose portrait will someday grace the next empty panel—is the top religious official in Spain. He's conservative on issues unpopular with Spain's young: divorce, abortion, and contraception. When he speaks, it makes news all over Spain.

As you leave, notice the iron-pumping cupids carved into the pear-tree panels lining the walls.

• *Go behind the high altar to find the...*

Transparente: The Transparente is a unique feature of the cathedral. In the 1700s, a hole was cut into the ceiling to let a sunbeam brighten Mass. The open-ing faces east, and each morning the rising sun reminds all that God is light. Melding this big hole with the Gothic church presented a challenge: The result was a Baroque master-piece. Gape up at this riot of angels doing flip-flops, babies breathing thin air, bottoms of feet, and gilded sunbursts. Carved out of marble from Italy, it's bursting with motion and full of energy. Appreciate those tough little cherubs who are support-ing the whole thing—they've been waiting for help for about 300 years now.

Step back to study the altar, which looks chaotic, but is actually structured thoughtfully: The good news of salvation springs from Baby Jesus, up past the archangels (including one in the middle who knows how to hold a big fish correctly) to the Last Supper high above, and beyond into the light-filled dome. I like it, as did (I guess) the two long-dead cardinals whose faded red hats hang from the edge of the hole. (A perk that only a cardinal enjoys is to choose a burial place in the cathedral, and hang his hat over that spot until the hat rots.)

• *Before entering the sacristy (to your right), peek into the...*

Chapel of the New Kings (Capilla de Reyes Nuevos): In the 16th century, Emperor Charles V moved the tombs of eight kings who reigned before Ferdinand and Isabel to this spot.

• *Leaving this chapel, the next door on your right takes you into the...*

Sacristy: The cathedral's sacristy is a mini-Prado, with 18 El Grecos and masterpieces by Francisco de Goya, Titian, Peter Paul Rubens, Diego Velázquez, Caravaggio, and Giovanni Bellini. First, notice the fine perspective work on the ceiling. It was painted by Neapolitan artist Lucca Giordano around 1690. (You can see the artist himself—with his circa-1690 spectacles—painted onto the door high above on the left; look for it at the base of the ceiling.) Then walk to the end of the room for the most important painting in the collection, El Greco's *The Spoliation* (a.k.a. *Christ Being Stripped of His Garments*).

Spain's original great painter was Greek, and this is his first masterpiece after arriving in Toledo. El Greco's painting from 1579 hangs exactly where he intended it to—in the room where priests prepared themselves for Mass. It shows Jesus surrounded by a sinister mob and suffering the humiliation of being stripped in public before his execution.

The scarlet robe is about to be yanked off, and the women (lower left) avert their eyes, turning to watch a carpenter at work (lower right) who bores the holes for nailing Jesus to the cross. While the carpenter bears down, Jesus—the other carpenter—looks up to heaven. The contrast between the motley crowd gambling for his clothes and Jesus' noble face underscores the quiet dignity with which he endures this ignoble treatment. Jesus' delicate white hand stands out from the flaming red tunic with an odd gesture that's common in El Greco's paintings. Some say this was the way Christians of the day swore they were true believers, not merely Christians-in-name-only, such as former Muslims or Jews who converted to survive.

On the right is a religious painting by Goya, the *Betrayal of Christ,* which shows Judas preparing to kiss Jesus, thus identifying him to the Roman soldiers. Farther to the right is a scene rarely painted: a touching El Greco portrait called *St. Joseph and the Christ Child.* Joseph is walking with Jesus, just as El Greco enjoyed walking around the Toledo countryside with his sons. Notice Joseph's gentle expression—and the Toledo views in the background.

Opposite, in a glass case on the other wall, is a small-but-lifelike 17th-century carving of St. Francis by Pedro de Mena. It's just to the right of the Goya. Before you leave the sacristy, enjoy the many other El Grecos located here.

• *As you step out of the sacristy, look high up to your right at the oldest stained glass in the church (from the 14th century). Then, passing a chapel reserved for worship, you come to...*

The Cloister: The cloister is worth a stroll for its finely carved colonnade. Opposite the entry, take a peaceful detour to a funerary chapel. The ceiling over the marble tomb of a bishop is a fresco by a student of Giotto (a 14th-century Italian Renaissance master).

Treasury: The *tesoro* is tiny, but radiant with riches. The highlight is the 10-foot-high, 430-pound monstrance—the tower designed to hold the Holy Communion wafer (the host) during the festival of Corpus Christi ("body of Christ") as it's paraded through the city. Built in 1517 by Enrique de Arfe, it's made of 5,000 individual pieces held together by 12,500 screws. There are diamonds, emeralds, rubies, and 400 pounds of gold-plated silver. The inner part (which is a century older) is 35 pounds of solid gold. Yeow. The base is a later addition from the Baroque period.

To the right of the monstrance is a beautiful red-coral cross given by the Philippines. To the right of the cross is a facsimile of a 700-year-old Bible hand-copied and beautifully illustrated by French monks; it was a gift from St. Louis, the 13th-century king of France. Imagine looking on these lavish illustrations with medieval eyes—an exquisite experience. (The precious and fragile lambskin original is preserved out of public view.) The finely painted small crucifix on the opposite side in the corner (with the mirror behind it) is by the great Gothic Florentine painter Fra Angelico. It depicts Jesus alive on the back and dead on the front, and was a gift from Mussolini to Franco. Underneath, near the floor, you'll find Franco's rather plain sword. Hmmm. To the right of Fra Angelico's crucifix, find the gift (humble amid all this splendor) from Toledo's sister city: Toledo, Ohio.

Mozarabic Chapel: Before 10:00, the cathedral is open only for prayer (from north entrance). If you're here to worship at the 9:00 Mass (daily except Sunday), you can peek into the otherwise-locked **Mozarabic Chapel** (Capilla Mozárabe). This Visigothic Mass (in Latin) is the oldest surviving Christian ritual in Western Europe. You're welcome to partake in this stirring example of peaceful coexistence of faiths. Toledo's proud Mozarabic community of 1,500 people traces its roots to Visigothic times.

Central Toledo

In addition to the cathedral, the city's historic core contains these sights:

Plaza de Zocodover

The main square is Toledo's center and your gateway to the old town. The word "Zocodover" derives from the Arabic for "livestock market."

Because Toledo is the state capital of Castile-La Mancha, the regional government administration building overlooks Plaza de Zocodover. Look for the three flags: one for Europe, one for Spain, and one for Castile-La Mancha. And speaking of universal symbols—find the low-key McDonald's. A source of controversy, it was finally allowed...with only one small golden arch.

The square is a big local hangout and city hub. Once the scene of Inquisition judgments and bullfights, today it's a lot more peaceful. Old people arrive in the morning, and young people come in the evening. The goofy white tourist train leaves from here, as well as the Tourist Bus, Centro Directo bus, and city buses #5, #61, and #62, which lumber to the train station. Just uphill, near the taxi stand, is the stop for bus #12, which travels around the old town to Santo Tomé (and works as a good self-guided tour—described on page 571) and for bus #71, which heads out to the panoramic viewpoint made famous by El Greco.

▲▲Santa Cruz Museum (Museo de Santa Cruz)

This stately Renaissance building features 15 El Grecos. Formerly an orphanage and hospital, the building was funded by money left by the humanist and diplomat Cardinal Mendoza when he died in 1495. The cardinal, confirmed as Chancellor of Castile by Queen Isabel, was so influential that he was called "the third royal." In 2014, as Toledo celebrates the 400th anniversary of El Greco's death, the Santa Cruz Museum will host an exciting gathering of paintings by Toledo's hometown master.

Cost and Hours: Free, Mon-Sat 10:00-19:00, Sun 10:00-14:30; from Plaza de Zocodover, go through arch to Calle Miguel de Cervantes 3; tel. 925-221-036, www.patrimoniohistoricoclm.es/museo-de-santa-cruz. A WC is in the far corner of the lower cloister.

❍ Self-Guided Tour: Your visit has three parts—the cloister, rooms of tiles and ceramics (above the cloister), and the main building. Unfortunately, there is no printed English information and no audioguide available for this wonderful sight. On your visit, you'll enter from the upper cloister and tour four wings—including one with the collection of El Grecos. While you're welcome to browse through the ground floor of the main building (which is used for temporary exhibits), everything of importance is on the upper level.

• *First, look at the museum building itself.*

Renaissance Building: The building's facade still wears bullet scars from the Spanish Civil War. The exterior, cloister arches, and stairway leading to the upper cloister are fine examples of the Plateresque style. This ornate strain of Spanish Renaissance is named for the fancy work of silversmiths of the 16th century. During this time (c. 1500-1550), the royal court moved from Toledo to Madrid—when Madrid was a village and Toledo was a world power. (You'll see no Plateresque work in Madrid.) Note the Renaissance-era mathematics, ideal proportions, round arches, square squares, and classic columns.

• *From the main entrance, go to the right to stroll through the peaceful* **cloister***, then climb the stairs to the upper cloister and turn right to reach the...*

Tiles and Ceramics Exhibit: This beautiful private collection, which the Carranza family has loaned to the museum for the last 20 years, dates from the end of the Reconquista (1492). Each piece is categorized by the Spanish region where it was made. In spite of the lack of English explanations, this may be the only place in Spain where you can compare regional differences in tile work and pottery.

Stop at the second window (you can open it) for a fine view of the Alcázar fortress. During the civil war, there was a frantic battle between leftist forces holed up in this building and Franco's fascists in the Alcázar. Finger the metal bars, still riddled with 1936 bullet holes.

After leaving the ceramics collection, survey the courtyard from the top floor. This is a large-scale version of the typical Toledo home: two floors—winter quarters on top, summer on bottom—surrounding an inner courtyard. The courtyard pavement slopes in order to feed the family's well.

• *From the upper level of the cloister, near the top of the stairs, find the entry to the upper floor of the main building, which holds the...*

Permanent Collection: The museum, echoing the footprint of the building it fills, has the shape of a Greek cross. Its eclectic collection is divided among the four wings.

First Wing: Entering the first arm of the cross, you'll see a selection of prehistoric pieces, some Roman items, and a marble well bearing an Arabic inscription. Note the grooves in the sides made by generations of Muslims pulling their buckets up by rope. This well was once located in the courtyard of an 11th-century mosque, which stood where the cathedral does today.

Center of Building, Under Dome: As 1500 was a time of transition, the fine ceiling is an impressive mix of two styles: indigenous Moorish and typically ornate Spanish Renaissance. The intricate Moorish-style ceiling survives with its original 15th-century timbers. The Mendoza coat of arms commemorates the man who paid for this building. Imagine it in its day, when it was a fancy orphanage.

Second and Third Wings: Continue left to the medieval

Toledo's Muslim Legacy

You can see the Moorish influence in these sights:
- Mezquita del Cristo de la Luz, the last of the town's mosques
- Sinagoga del Tránsito's Mudejar plasterwork
- Sinagoga de Santa María la Blanca's mosque-like horseshoe arches and pinecone capitals
- Puerta del Sol (Gate of the Sun) and other surviving gates (with horseshoe arches) along the medieval wall
- The city's labyrinthine, medina-like streets

section in the second wing, where you'll find the lavish but faded *Astrolabe Tapestry* (c. 1480, Belgian). It shows a new view of the cosmos at the dawn of the Renaissance and the Age of Discovery: God (far left) oversees all, as Atlas (with the help of two women and a crank handle) spins the universe, containing the circular Earth. The wisdom gang (far right) heralds the wonders of the coming era. Rather than a map of Earth, this is a chart showing the cosmic order of things as the constellations spin around the stationary North Star (center).

The third wing has a forgettable collection of church paintings (generally skipped because of what's in the last wing).

Fourth Wing: The museum's 15 El Greco paintings fill this last wing. A highlight, at the far end of this hall, is the impressive *Assumption of Mary,* a spiritual poem on canvas. This altarpiece, finished one year before El Greco's death in 1614, is the culmination of his unique style, combining all of his techniques to express an otherworldly event.

Study the *Assumption* (which some believe is misnamed, and actually shows the Immaculate Conception—the plaque describing the work entitles it *Inmaculada Concepción*). Bound to earth, the city of Toledo sleeps, but a vision is taking place overhead. An angel in a billowing robe, as if doing the breaststroke with his wings, flies up, supporting Mary, the mother of Christ. She floats up through warped space, to be serenaded by angels and wrapped in the radiant light of the Holy Spirit. Mary flickers and ripples, charged from within by her spiritual ecstasy, caught up in a vision that takes her breath away. No painter before or since has captured the supernatural world better than El Greco. (For more on El Greco, see page 573.)

▲▲Army Museum (Museo del Ejército)

This new museum features endless rooms of Spanish military collections of armor, uniforms, cannons, guns, paintings, and models. It tells the military history of Spain from 1492 to the

20th century. The displays are wonderfully explained in English, and the audioguide is excellent. If you like military history, allow at least three hours for this, one of Europe's top military museums.

The museum has one major flaw: its lack of coverage of the country's civil war (1936-1939). The civil war is still considered too hot a topic to address substantially in Spain, even though an exhibit on this major 20th-century event would be fascinating and teach valuable lessons.

Cost and Hours: €5, €8 ticket includes excellent 2-hour audioguide, free on Sun; open Thu-Tue 11:00-17:00, closed Wed, hours subject to change—best to call ahead; last entry 30 minutes before closing, tel. 925-238-800, www.museo.ejercito.es.

Visiting the Museum: The museum is located in the Alcázar, the huge former imperial residence that dominates Toledo's skyline. It's built on the site of Roman, Visigothic, Moorish, and early Renaissance fortresses, the ruins of which (displayed just past the turnstile) are a poignant reminder of the city's strategic importance through the centuries.

Today's structure (originally built in the 16th century, then destroyed in the civil war and rebuilt) became a kind of right-wing Alamo. During the civil war, Franco's Nationalists (and hundreds of hostages) were besieged by Loyalist troops for two months in 1936. Finally, after many fierce but futile Republican attacks that destroyed much of the Alcázar, Franco sent in an army that took Toledo. The place was rebuilt and glorified under Franco.

It's a confusing floor plan, but if you start at the top floor and follow the "historical round" arrows, you'll enjoy a roughly chronological sweep. Since so much of this country's history is military, this museum tells much of the story of Spain.

Look for special theme rooms (e.g., the use of photography in the army, and the evolution of Spain's flag). The main courtyard—Italian-inspired Renaissance in style—comes with a proud statue of Charles V, the ultimate military king and Europe's most powerful 16th-century leader. While in the courtyard, consider the restoration of this massive-yet-elegant fortress.

The 20th-century section comes with some fascinating videos, but almost passes over the civil war. As the museum was preparing to open, a partisan controversy broke out on how to handle the conflict. So the curators decided to dodge that bullet by essentially skipping *the* major event of 20th-century Spanish history.

Mezquita del Cristo de la Luz

Of Muslim Toledo's 10 mosques, this barren little building (dating from about 1000) is the best survivor. Looking up, you'll notice the Moorish fascination with geometry—each dome is a unique design. The lovely keyhole arch faces Mecca. In 1187, after the Reconquista, the mosque was changed to a church, the Christian apse (with its crude Romanesque art) was added, and the former mosque got its current name. The small garden with its fountains is a reminder of the Quranic image of heaven.

Cost and Hours: €2.50, Mon-Fri 10:00-14:00 & 15:30-18:40, until 17:45 in winter, Sat-Sun 10:00-17:45, Cuesta de las Carmelitas Descalzas 10, tel. 925-254-191.

Visigothic Museum in the Church of San Román
(Museo de los Concilios y de la Cultura Visigoda)

This 13th-century Mudejar church (with its rare, strangely modernist 13th-century Romanesque frescoes) provides an exquisite space for a small but interesting collection of Visigothic artifacts. The Visigoths were the Christian barbarian tribe who ruled Spain between the fall of Rome and the rise of the Moors. The only things Visigothic about the actual building are the few capitals topping its columns, recycled from a seventh-century Visigothic church. Though the elaborate crowns are copies (the originals are in Madrid), other glass cases show off metal and stone artifacts from the age when Toledo was the capital of the Visigoths. The items, while featuring almost no human figures, are rich in symbolism. Their portability fits that society's nomadic heritage. Archaeologists have found almost no Visigothic artifacts within Toledo's fortified hill location. They lived in humble settlements along the river—apparently needing no defense system...until the Moors swept through in 711, ending two centuries of Visigothic rule in Iberia. Climb the steep stairs for a view of Toledo's rooftops from the church tower.

Cost and Hours: Free, Tue-Sat 10:00-14:00 & 16:00-18:30, Sun 10:00-14:00, closed Mon, no English information, Plaza San Román, tel. 925-227-872.

Southwest Toledo

These sights cluster at the southwest end of town. For efficient sightseeing, visit them in this order, then zip back home on bus #12 (listed at the end of this section).

▲Santo Tomé

A simple chapel on the Plaza del Conde holds El Greco's most beloved painting. *The Burial of the Count of Orgaz* couples heaven and earth in a way only The Greek could. It feels so right to see a painting in the same church where the artist placed it 400 years ago. It originally filled the space immediately to the right of where it is now, but as the popularity of this masterpiece was disturbing the main church, it was moved. Church officials even created a special entryway for viewing it.

Cost and Hours: €2.50, daily 10:00-17:45, until 18:45 April-mid-Oct, tel. 925-256-098. This sight often has a line; try going early or late to avoid tour groups.

Visiting Santo Tomé: Take this slow. Stay a while—let it perform. The year is 1323. Count Don Gonzalo Ruiz has died. You're at his burial right here in this chapel. The good count was so holy, even saints Augustine and Stephen have come down from heaven to lower his body into the grave. (The painting's subtitle is "Such is the reward for those who serve God and his saints.")

More than 250 years later, in 1586, a local priest (depicted on the far right, reading the Bible) hired El Greco to make a painting of the burial to hang over the count's tomb. The funeral is attended by Toledo's most distinguished citizens. (El Greco used local nobles as models.) The painting is divided in two by a serene line of noble faces—heaven above and earth below. Above the faces, the count's soul, symbolized by a little baby, rises up through a mystical birth canal to be reborn in heaven, where he's greeted by Jesus, Mary, and all the saints. A spiritual wind blows through as colors change and shapes stretch. This is Counter-Reformation propaganda—notice Jesus pointing to St. Peter, the symbol of the pope in Rome, who controls the keys to the pearly gates. Each face is a detailed portrait. It's clear that these portraits inspired the next great Spanish painter, Velázquez, a century later. El Greco himself (eyeballing you, seventh figure in from the left) is the only one not involved in the burial. The boy in the foreground—pointing to the two saints as if to say, "One's from the first century, the other's from the fourth...it's a miracle!"—is El Greco's son. On the handkerchief in the boy's pocket is El Greco's signature, written in Greek.

Don Gonzalo Ruiz's actual granite tombstone is at your feet. The count's two wishes upon his death were to be buried here and for his village to make an annual charity donation to feed Toledo's poor. Finally, more than two centuries later, the people of Orgaz said, "Enough!" and stopped the payments. The last of the money was spent to pay El Greco for this painting.

▲El Greco Museum (Museo del Greco)

This small museum, built near the site of El Greco's house, gives a look at the genius of his art and the Toledo in his day. Its small collection of paintings is accompanied by interactive touch screens and videos.

A comfy little theater shows a fine 10-minute video on both the life of the artist and the story of this museum. You then proceed through halls that show the evolution of El Greco's art. While there aren't many great El Grecos here, you'll see a hall lined with his *Twelve Apostles*, *San Bernardino of Siena* (in a chapel), and the highlight of the museum—the *View and Plan of Toledo*. El Greco's panoramic map shows the city in 1614. Study the actual map and list of sights. It was commissioned to promote the city (suddenly a former capital) after the king moved to Madrid.

Cost and Hours: €3, €5 combo-ticket with Sinagoga del Tránsito, free Sat afternoon from 14:00 and all day Sun, audioguide-€2; open Tue-Sat 9:30-18:30, until 20:00 in high season, Sun 10:00-15:00, closed Mon; next to Sinagoga del Tránsito on Calle Samuel Leví, tel. 925-223-665.

Sinagoga del Tránsito (Museo Sefardí)

Built in 1361, this is the best surviving slice of Toledo's Jewish past. Serving as Spain's national Jewish museum, it displays Jewish artifacts, including costumes, menorahs, and books. Your visit comes with three parts: the nave, a ground floor exhibition space with a history of Spain's Jews, and the women's gallery upstairs, which shows lifestyles and holy rituals among Sephardic Jews. While English sheets in each room explain the collection, to get the most out of the exhibits, rent the audioguide.

Cost and Hours: €3, €5 combo-ticket with El Greco Museum, free Sat afternoon from 14:00 and all day Sun, audioguide-€2; open Tue-Sat 9:30-20:00, until 18:00 in winter, Sun 10:00-15:00, closed Mon; last entry 15 minutes before closing, near El Greco Museum on Calle de los Reyes Católicos, tel. 925-223-665.

Visiting the Synagogue: This 14th-century synagogue was built at the peak of Toledo's enlightened tolerance—constructed for Jews with Christian approval by Muslim craftsmen. Nowhere else in the city does Toledo's three-culture legacy shine brighter than at this place of worship. But in 1391, just a few decades after it was built, the Church and the Spanish kings began a violent campaign to unite Spain as a Christian nation, forcing Jews and Muslims to convert or leave. In 1492 Ferdinand and Isabel exiled Spain's remaining Jews. It's estimated that in the 15th century, while some of Spain's Jews were killed, many others survived by

El Greco
(1541-1614)

Born on Crete and trained in Venice, Doménikos Theotokópoulos (tongue-tied friends just called him "The Greek") came to Spain to get a job decorating El Escorial. He failed there, but succeeded in Toledo, where he spent the last 37 years of his life. He mixed all three regional influences into his palette. From his Greek homeland, he absorbed the solemn, abstract style of icons. In Italy, he learned the bold use of color, elongated figures, twisting poses, and dramatic style of the later Renaissance. These elements were then fused in the fires of fanatic Spanish-Catholic devotion.

Not bound by the realism so important to his fellow artists, El Greco painted dramatic visions of striking colors and figures—bodies unnatural and lengthened as though stretched between heaven and earth. He painted souls, not faces. His work is on display at nearly every sight in Toledo. Thoroughly modern in his disregard for realism, he didn't impress the austere Philip II. But his art still seems as fresh as contemporary art does today. El Greco was essentially forgotten through the 18th and most of the 19th centuries. Then, with the Romantic movement (and the discovery of Toledo by Romantic-era travelers, artists, and poets), the paintings of El Greco became the hits they are today.

converting to Christianity. A third left the country.

Surveying the synagogue from the back, its interior decor looks more Muslim than Jewish. After Christians reconquered the city in 1085, many Moorish workmen stayed on, beautifying the city with their unique style called Mudejar. The synagogue's intricate, geometrical carving in stucco—nearly all original from 1360—features leaves, vines, and flowers; there are no human shapes, which are forbidden by the Torah—like the Quran—as being "graven images." In the frieze (running along the upper wall, just below the ceiling), the Arabic-looking script is actually Hebrew, quoting psalms (respected by all "people of the book"—Muslims, Jews, and Christians alike). The balcony was the traditional separate worship area for women.

Move up to the front. Stand close to the holy wall and study the exquisite workmanship (with reminders of all three religions: the coat of arms of the Christian king, Hebrew script, and Muslim decor). Look down. The small rectangular patch of the original floor only survived because the Christian altar table sat there. In the side room and upstairs, scale models of the development of the Jewish quarter and video displays give a picture of Jewish life in medieval Toledo.

▲Museo Victorio Macho

Overlooking the gorge and Tajo River, this small, attractive museum—once the home and workshop of the early-20th-century sculptor Victorio Macho—offers a delightful collection of his bold Art Deco-inspired work. Even if you skip the museum, enjoy the terrace view from its gate.

Cost and Hours: €3, Mon-Sat 10:00-19:00, Sun 10:00-15:00, between the two *sinagogas* at Plaza de Victorio Macho 2, tel. 925-284-225.

Visiting the Museum: The house itself is a cool oasis of calm in the city. Your visit comes in four stages: ticket room with theater, courtyard with view, crypt, and museum.

The small theater in the ticket room shows a good nine-minute video about the history of Toledo (nothing about Macho, but it's well worth the time—request the English-language version). Macho was Spain's first great modern sculptor. When his left-wing Republican (say that three times) politics made it dangerous for him to stay in Franco's Spain, he fled to the USSR, then Mexico and Peru, where he met his wife, Zoila. They later returned to Toledo, where they lived and worked until he died in 1966. Zoila eventually gave the house and Macho's art to the city.

Enjoy the peaceful and expansive view from the terrace. From here it's clear how the Tajo River served as a formidable moat protecting the city. Imagine trying to attack. The 14th-century bridge (on the right) connected the town with the region's *cigarrales*—mansions of wealthy families, whose orchards of figs and apricots dot the hillside even today. To the left (in the river), look for the stubs of 15th-century watermills; directly below is a riverside trail that's delightful for a stroll or jog.

The door marked *Crypta* leads to *My Brother Marcelo*—the touching tomb Macho made for his brother. Eventually he featured his entire family in his art.

A dozen steps above the terrace, you'll find a single room marked *Museo* filled with Macho's art. A *pietà* is carved expressively in granite. Next to the *pietà*, several self-portrait sketches show the artist's genius. The bronze statue is a self-portrait at age 17. In the next section, exquisite pencil-on-paper studies illustrate how a sculptor must understand the body (in this case, Zoila's body). The sketch of Zoila from behind is entitled *Guitar* (Spaniards traditionally think of a woman's body as a guitar). Other statues show the strength of the peoples' spirit as leftist Republicans stood up to Franco's fascist forces, and Spain endured its 20th-century bloodbath. The highlight is *La Madre* (from 1935), Macho's life-size sculpture of his mother sitting in a chair. It illustrates the sadness and simple wisdom of Spanish mothers who witnessed so much suffering. Upon a granite backdrop, her white marble hands and face speak volumes.

Sinagoga de Santa María la Blanca

This synagogue-turned-church has Moorish horseshoe arches and wall carvings. It's a vivid reminder of the religious cultures that

shared (and then didn't share) this city. While it looks like a mosque, it never was one. Built as a Jewish synagogue by Muslim workers around 1200, it became a church in 1492 when Toledo's Jews were required to convert or leave—hence the mix-and-match name. After being used as horse stables by Napoleonic troops, it was further ruined in the 19th century. Today, it's an evocative space, beautiful in its simplicity.

Cost and Hours: €2.50, daily April-Sept 10:00-18:45, Oct-March 10:00-17:45, Calle de los Reyes Católicos 4, tel. 925-227-257. Note the thirst-quenching bottled-water machine in the courtyard.

▲San Juan de los Reyes Monasterio

"St. John of the Monarchs" is a grand Franciscan monastery, impressive church, and delightful "Isabeline" cloistered court-yard. The style is late Gothic, contemporaneous with Portugal's Manueline (c. 1500) and Flamboyant Gothic elsewhere in Europe. It was the intended burial site of the Catholic Monarchs, Isabel and Ferdinand. But after the Moors were expelled in 1492 from Granada, their royal bodies were planted there to show Spain's commitment to maintaining a Moor-free peninsula.

Cost and Hours: €2.50, daily 10:00-18:45, until 18:00 in winter, last entry 30 minutes before closing, San Juan de los Reyes 2, tel. 925-223-802. After buying your ticket, look up. A skinny monk welcomes you (and reminds us of our mortality).

Visiting the Sight: The **facade** is famously festooned with 500-year-old chains. Moors used these to shackle Christians in Granada until 1492. It's said that the freed Christians brought these chains to the church, making them a symbol of their Catholic faith and a sign of victory.

Even without the royal tombs that would have dominated the space, the glorious **chapel** gives you a sense of Spain when it was Europe's superpower. The monastery was built to celebrate the 1476 Battle of Toro, which made Isabel the queen of Castile.

TOLEDO

Since her husband, Ferdinand, was king of Aragon, this effectively created the Spain we know today. (You could say 1476 is to Spain what 1776 is to the US.) Now united, Spain was able to quickly finish the Reconquista, ridding Iberia of its Moors within the next decade and a half.

Sitting in the chapel, you're surrounded by propaganda proclaiming Spain's greatness. The coat of arms is repeated obsessively. The eagle with the halo disk represents St. John, protector of the royal family. The yoke and arrows are the symbols of Ferdinand and Isabel. The lions remind people of the power of the kingdoms joined together under Ferdinand and Isabel. The coat of arms is complex because of Iberia's many kingdoms (e.g., a lion for Lyon, and a castle for Castile).

As you leave, look up over the door to see the Franciscan coat of arms—with the five wounds of the crucifixion (the stigmata—which St. Francis earned through his great faith) flanked by angels with dramatic wings.

Enjoy a walk around the **cloister.** Notice details of the fine carvings. Everything had meaning in the 15th century. In the corner

(opposite the entry), just above eye level, find a monkey—an insulting symbol of Franciscans—on a toilet reading the Bible upside-down. Perhaps a stone carver snuck in a not-too-subtle comment on Franciscan pseudo-intellectualism, with their big libraries and small brains.

Napoleon's troops are mostly to blame for the destruction of the church, a result of Napoleon's view that monastic power in Europe was a menace. While Napoleon's biggest error was to invade Russia, his second dumbest move was to alienate the Catholic faithful by destroying monasteries such as this one. This strategic mistake eroded popular support from people who might have seen Napoleon as a welcome alternative to the tyranny of kings and the Church.

If you're tired, skip going upstairs—if not, you can take a simple walk around the top level of the courtyard under a finely renovated Moorish-style ceiling.

▲Bus #12 Self-Guided Tour (A Sweat-Free Return Trip from Santo Tomé to Plaza de Zocodover)

When you're finished with the sights at the Santo Tomé end of town, you can hike all the way back (not fun)—or simply catch bus #12 from Plaza del Conde in front of Santo Tomé (fun!). Santo Tomé is the end of the line, so buses wait to depart from here twice hourly (at :25 and :55, until 21:55, pay driver €1.40), heading to Plaza de Zocodover. Closer to the synagogues and monastery, you can also catch the same bus at Plaza del Barrio Nuevo. The bus offers tired sightseers a quick, interesting 15-minute look at the town walls. Here's what you'll see on your way from Santo Tomé:

Leaving Santo Tomé, you'll first ride through Toledo's Jewish section. On the right, you'll pass the El Greco Museum, Sinagoga del Tránsito, and Sinagoga de Santa María la Blanca, followed by—on your left—the ornate Flamboyant Gothic facade of San Juan de los Reyes Monasterio. After squeezing through the 16th-century city gate, the bus follows along the outside of the mighty 10th-century wall. (Toledo was never conquered by force... only by siege.)

Just past the big escalator (which brings people from parking lots up into the city) and the Hotel Cardinal, the wall gets fancier,

as demonstrated by the little old Bisagra Gate. Soon after, you see the big new Bisagra Gate, the main entry into the old town. While the city walls date from the 10th century, this gate was built as an arch of triumph in the 16th century. The massive coat of arms of Emperor Charles V, with the double eagle, reminded people that he ruled a unified Habsburg empire (successor of ancient Rome), and they were entering the capital of an empire that, in the 1500s, included most of Western Europe and much of America. (We'll enter the town through this gate in a couple minutes after a stop at the bus station.)

Just outside the big gate is a well-maintained and shaded park—a picnic-perfect spot and one of Toledo's few green areas. After a detour to the bus station basement to pick up people coming from Madrid, you swing back around Bisagra Gate. As an example of how things have changed in the last generation, as recently as 1960, all traffic into the city at this point had to pass through this gate's tiny original entrance.

As you climb back into the old town, you'll pass the fine,

14th-century Moorish Puerta del Sol (Gate of the Sun) on your right. Then comes the modern Palacio de Congresos Miradero convention center on your left, which is artfully incorporated into the more historic cityscape. Within moments you pull into the main square, Plaza de Zocodover. You can do this tour in reverse by riding bus #12 from Plaza de Zocodover to Plaza del Conde (departing at :25 and :55, same price and hours).

Shopping in Toledo

Toledo probably sells more souvenirs than any city in Spain. This is *the* place to buy medieval-looking swords, armor, maces, three-legged stools, lethal-looking letter-openers, and other nouveau antiques. It's also Spain's damascene center, where, for centuries, craftspeople have inlaid black steel with gold, silver, and copper wire. Spain's top bullfighters wouldn't have their swords made anywhere else.

Knives: At the workshop of English-speaking **Mariano Zamorano,** you can see swords and knives being made. His family has been putting its seal on handcrafted knives since 1890. Judging by what's left of Mariano's hand, his knives are among the sharpest (Mon-Fri 10:00-14:00 & 16:00-19:00, Sat-Sun 10:00-14:00—although you may not see work done on weekends, 10 percent discount with this book, behind Ayuntamiento/City Hall at Calle Ciudad 19, tel. 925-222-634, www.marianozamorano.com).

Damascene: You can find artisans all over town pounding gold and silver threads into a steel base to create shiny inlaid plates, decorative wares, and jewelry. The damascene is a real tourist racket, but it's fun to pop into a shop and see the intricate handwork in action.

Nun-Baked Sweet Treats: Signs posted on convent doors all over town invite you in to buy *Dulces Artesanos* (sweets) including *mazapán*. Try the Santa Rita Convent—go in the main door to the left, press the buzzer, and a nun will appear in five minutes or so behind a turnstile window to take your order (small box—€6, Mon-Sat 9:00-13:00 & 15:00-16:15, until 18:00 on Sat, closed Sun, Calle Santa Ursula 3).

El Martes: Toledo's colorful outdoor market is a lively scene on Tuesdays at Paseo de Merchan, better known to locals as "La Vega" (9:00-14:00, outside Bisagra Gate near TI).

Sleeping in Toledo

Madrid day-trippers darken the sunlit cobbles, but few stay to see Toledo's medieval moonrise. Spend the night. Hotels often have a two-tiered price system, with prices 20 percent higher on Friday and Saturday. Spring and fall are high season; November through March and July and August are less busy. Similar to other places in Spain, Toledo's big and small hotels are making deals to confront the hard economic times. Fish around for deals and discounts. Most places have an arrangement with parking lots in town that can save you a few euros; ask when you reserve.

Near Plaza de Zocodover

$$ Hotel Toledo Imperial sits efficiently above Plaza de Zocodover, and rents 29 business-class rooms that are a solid value (Db-€50 Sun-Thu, Db-€85-100 Fri-Sat, higher rates with increased demand, includes breakfast, air-con, free Wi-Fi, Calle Horno de los Bizcochos 5, tel. 925-280-034, www.hoteltoledoimperial.com, reservas@hoteltoledoimperial.com).

$ Hotel Las Conchas, a three-star hotel with 33 rooms, gleams with marble. It's so sleek and slick it almost feels more like a hospital than a hotel (Sb-€30, Db-€50-60, book directly by email and ask for their best Rick Steves price, skimpy breakfast-€8, air-con, Wi-Fi, near the Alcázar at Juan Labrador 8, tel. 925-210-760, www.lasconchas.com, lasconchas@githoteles.es, Javier and Yuki).

Sleep Code

(€1 = about $1.30, country code: 34)

S = Single, **D** = Double/Twin, **T** = Triple, **Q** = Quad, **b** = bathroom, **s** = shower only. Unless otherwise noted, credit cards are accepted and rooms have air-conditioning. Some hotels include the 10 percent IVA tax in the room price; others tack it onto your bill.

To help you easily sort through these listings, I've divided the accommodations into three categories, based on the price for a standard double room with bath during high season:

$$$ Higher Priced—Most rooms €100 or more.
$$ Moderately Priced—Most rooms between €60-100.
$ Lower Priced—Most rooms €60 or less.

Prices can change without notice; verify the hotel's current rates online or by email. For the best prices, always book direct.

Near Plaza de Zocodover

1. Hotel Toledo Imperial
2. Hotel Las Conchas
3. Hostal Centro
4. Hostal Alcázar
5. El Trébol Restaurant
6. Restaurante Ludeña
7. Supermarket Coviran
8. Santo Tomé Mazapán Shop
9. Tourist Train
10. Convention Center & Escalator to Miradero Garage

$ Hostal Centro rents 28 spacious rooms with sparse, well-worn furniture and a ramshackle feel. It's wonderfully central, with a third of its rooms overlooking the main square. Request a quiet room on the back side to minimize night noise (Sb-€35, Db-€50, Tb-€65, book direct for a 10 percent discount with this book on weekdays, inviting Astroturf roof terrace with lounge chairs, 50 yards off Plaza de Zocodover—take the first right off Calle Comercio to Calle Nueva 13, tel. 925-257-091, www.hostalcentrotoledo.com, hostalcentro@telefonica.net, warmly run by Asun and David).

$ Hostal Alcázar, with 12 simple and spacious rooms and no public spaces, is quiet, modern, and a good value (Sb-€30, Db-€45-50, Tb-€60-65, Qb-€75-80, no breakfast, air-con, elevator, Juan Labrador 10, tel. 925-222-620, www.hostalalcazar.es, hostalalcazar@movistar.es, César).

Near Bisagra Gate

$$$ Hacienda del Cardenal, a 17th-century cardinal's palace built into Toledo's wall, is quiet and elegant, with a cool garden, a less-than-helpful staff, and a stuffy restaurant. This poor man's parador, at the dusty old gate of Toledo, is closest to the station, but below all the old-town action (Sb-€56-71, Db-€71-163, Fri-Sat-€20-40 more, 20 percent cheaper mid-Dec-mid-March, breakfast-€9, free Wi-Fi, enter through town wall 100 yards below Bisagra Gate, Paseo de Recaredo 24, tel. 925-224-900, www .haciendadelcardenal.com, hotel@haciendadelcardenal.com).

$$ Hospedería de los Reyes has 15 colorful and thoughtfully appointed rooms in an attractive, quiet, yellow building 100 yards downhill from Bisagra Gate, outside the wall. They also offer six apartments a block away, with kitchens and living rooms (Sb-€40-50, Db-€55-75, apartments-€65-90, breakfast-€4-6, air-con, free Wi-Fi, street parking nearby, Calle Perala 37, tel. 925-283-667, www.hospaderiadelosreyes.com, hospederiadelosreyes @hospederiadelosreyes.com, Alicia and Carolina).

$$ Hotel Abad sits at the bottom of the old town's hill just a block inside the Bisagra Gate and offers 22 clean, rustic rooms with stone walls, wooden rafters, and contemporary furnishings (Db-€64-120, higher rates for Fri-Sat, extra bed-€20, breakfast-€8, air-con, elevator, free Wi-Fi, Real del Arrabal 1, tel. 925-283-500, www.hotelabadtoledo.com, reservas@hotelabad.com).

$ Hostal Puerta de Bisagra is in a sprawling old building that is fresh and modern inside. Located just across from Bisagra Gate, it's convenient for arrivals, but a long hike uphill to the action (hop on any bus). Its 38 comfortable rooms are rented at some of the best prices in town (Sb-€40-50, Db-€50-60, lower rates Sun-Thu; breakfast-€6, air-con, free Wi-Fi, Calle del Potro 5, tel. 925-285-277, www.puertabisagra.com, hostal@puertabisagra.com).

$ Hotel Sol, with 15 nicely decorated pastel rooms, is a good value. It's on a quiet, ugly side street between Bisagra Gate and Plaza de Zocodover (Sb-€44, Db-€59, Tb-€72, 10 percent discount with this book, breakfast-€4, air-con, free Wi-Fi, private parking-€10/day; leave the busy main drag at Hotel Imperial and head 50 yards down the lane to Azacanes 8; tel. 925-213-650, www .hotelyhostalsol.com, info@hotelyhostalsol.com, José Carlos). Their 11-room **$ Hostal Sol** annex across the street is just as comfortable, smoke-free, and a bit cheaper (Sb-€36, Db-€49, Tb-€59, Qb-€72, 10 percent discount with this book, breakfast-€4, free Wi-Fi).

Deep in Toledo

$$ La Posada de Manolo rents 14 thoughtfully furnished rooms across from the downhill corner of the cathedral. Manolo Junior opened this fine *hostal* according to his father's vision: a comfortable place with each of its three floors themed differently—Moorish, Jewish, and Christian. They are deservedly listed in several US and European guidebooks, so they tend to fill up (Sb-€42, Db-€72, big Db-€84, includes buffet breakfast, 10 percent discount with this book when you reserve direct, air-con, no elevator, free Wi-Fi, two nice view terraces, Calle Sixto Ramón Parro 8, tel. 925-282-250, www.laposadademanolo.com, toledo@laposadademanolo.com).

Toledo Hotels & Restaurants

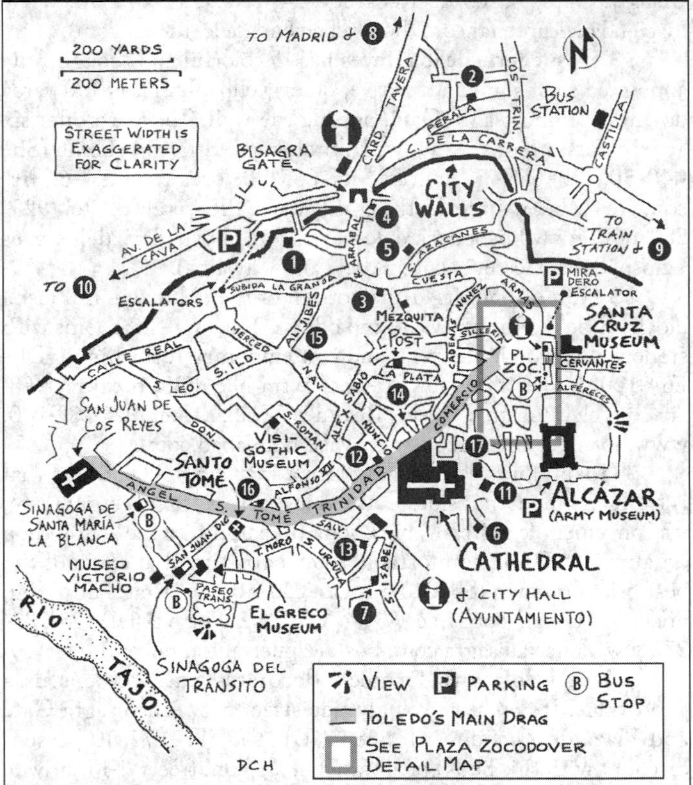

TO MADRID & 8
200 YARDS
200 METERS
STREET WIDTH IS EXAGGERATED FOR CLARITY
BISAGRA GATE
CARD. TAVERA
PERALA
LOS TRIN.
BUS STATION
CASTILLA
C. DE LA CARRERA
CITY WALLS
AV. DE LA CAVA
TO TRAIN STATION & 9
TO 10
ESCALATORS
SUBIDA LA GRANJA
ARRABAL
AZACANES
CUESTA
MIRA-DERO
ESCALATOR
ARMAS
MEZQUITA
NUÑEZ
SANTA CRUZ MUSEUM
ALJIBES
MERCED
POST
CADENAS
SILLERÍA
PL. ZOC.
CERVANTES
CALLE REAL
S. ILD.
NAV.
SABIO
LA PLATA
ALFÉRECES
S. LEO
SAN JUAN DE LOS REYES
DON
ALF. X
NUNCIO
S. ROMAN
VISI-GOTHIC MUSEUM
COMERCIO
SANTO TOMÉ
ALFONSO XII
TRINIDAD
ALCÁZAR (ARMY MUSEUM)
ANGEL
S. TOMÉ
SINAGOGA DE SANTA MARÍA LA BLANCA
SALV.
T. MORO
S. URSULA
S. ISABEL
CATHEDRAL
MUSEO VICTORIO MACHO
SAN JUAN DIO
PASEO TRANS.
EL GRECO MUSEUM
& CITY HALL (AYUNTAMIENTO)
RIO TAJO
SINAGOGA DEL TRÁNSITO
DCH
VIEW
PARKING
BUS STOP
TOLEDO'S MAIN DRAG
SEE PLAZA ZOCODOVER DETAIL MAP

1. Hacienda del Cardenal
2. Hospedería de los Reyes
3. Hotel Abad
4. Hostal Puerta de Bisagra
5. Hotel Sol
6. La Posada de Manolo & Madre Tierra Restaurante Vegetariano
7. Hotel Eurico & Hotel Santa Isabel
8. To Hotel María Cristina & Hostal Madrid
9. To Albergue Juvenil San Servando (Hostel)
10. To Parador de Toledo
11. Los Cuatro Tiempos Rest.
12. Colección Catedral
13. El Botero Taberna
14. Pizzeria Pastucci
15. Taberna La For de la Esquina
16. Restaurante Placido
17. Mercado Municipal (Market)

$$ Hotel Eurico, fresh and new, cleverly fits 23 sleek rooms into a medieval building buried deep in the old town. The staff is friendly, and the hotel offers a good value (Sb-€55-60, Db-€60-90, Tb-€70-120, breakfast-€5-8, air-con, Calle Santa Isabel 3, tel. 925-284-178, www.hoteleurico.com, reservas@hoteleurico.com).

$ Hotel Santa Isabel, in a 15th-century building two blocks from the cathedral, has 41 clean, modern, and comfortable rooms and squeaky tile hallways (Sb-€35-42, small old Db-€45-55, big new Db-€55-65, Db with view-€70-80, higher rates for Fri-Sat, extra bed-€10, 5 percent discount with this book, breakfast-€5, one floor allows smoking, air-con, elevator, free Wi-Fi, scenic roof terrace, parking-€10/day, buried deep in old town—take a taxi instead of the bus, drivers enter from Calle Pozo Amargo, Calle Santa Isabel 24, tel. 925-253-120, www.hotelsantaisabel.net, info@hotelsantaisabel.net).

Outside of Town, near the Bullring

These places are on a modern street next to the bullring (Plaza de Toros, bullfights only on holidays), just beyond Bisagra Gate. In this area, parking is free on the street. The bus station is a five-minute walk away, and city buses lumber by, all going directly to Plaza de Zocodover. There are many other similarly nondescript, comfy, and cheap places in this neighborhood.

$$ Hotel María Cristina, a sprawling 74-room hotel, has all the comforts under a thin layer of prefab tradition. Rates vary greatly—ask them for any special pricing or check website (Sb-€50-68, Db-€50-105, Tb-€148, suites-€100-170, breakfast-€9, air-con, elevator, restaurant, parking-€12/day, Marqués de Mendigorría 1, tel. 925-213-202, www.hotelesmayoral.com, informacion@hotelmariacristina.com).

$ Hostal Madrid has two locations on the same street with 29 rooms and a café next door (Sb-€28, Db-€40, Tb-€54, breakfast-€3, air-con, parking-€8/day, Marqués de Mendigorría 7 and 14, reception at #7, tel. 925-221-114, www.hostal-madrid.net, info@hostal-madrid.net).

Hostel

$ Albergue Juvenil San Servando youth hostel is lavish but fairly cheap, with 96 beds and small rooms for two or four people (€17/bed plus €12 obligatory *alberguista* membership, extra €3.50/day for the first six days of membership, swimming pool, views, cafeteria, good management, located in 10th-century Arab castle of San Servando, 10-minute walk from train station, 15-minute hike from town center, over Puente Viejo outside town, tel. 925-224-554, reservations tel. 925-221-676, alberguesclm@jccm.es, no English spoken).

Outside of Town with the Grand Toledo View

$$$ Parador de Toledo, with 79 rooms, is one of Spain's best-known inns. Its guests enjoy the same Toledo view that El Greco made famous from across the Tajo Gorge (Sb-€120-128, Db-€150-180, Db with view-€145-200, extra bed-€61, higher rates for March-Oct, call or check online for deals, breakfast-€18, €34 fixed-price meals sans drinks in their fine restaurant overlooking Toledo, 2 windy miles from town at Cerro del Emperador—it may come up as Carretera de Cobisa on GPS systems, tel. 925-221-850, www.parador.es, toledo@parador.es).

Eating in Toledo

Dining in Traditional Elegance

A day full of El Greco and the romance of Toledo after dark puts me in the mood for game and other traditional cuisine. Typical Toledo dishes include partridge *(perdiz)*, venison *(venado)*, wild boar *(jabalí)*, roast suckling pig *(cochinillo asado)*, or baby lamb *(cordero*—similarly roasted after a few weeks of mother's milk). After dinner, find a *mazapán* place for dessert. Restaurants generally serve lunch from 13:00 to 16:00 and dinner from 20:00 until very late (Spaniards don't start dinner until about 21:00).

Los Cuatro Tiempos Restaurante ("The Four Seasons") specializes in local game and roasts, proficiently served in a tasteful and elegant setting. They offer spacious dining with an extensive and inviting Spanish wine list. It's a good choice for a quiet, romantic dinner, and a good value for a midday meal (€16 weekday and €19 weekend three-course lunches, €30 à la carte dinners, Mon-Sat 13:00-16:00 & 20:30-23:00, Sun 13:00-16:00 only, at downhill corner of cathedral, Sixto Ramón Parro 5, tel. 925-223-782, www.restauranteloscuatrotiempos.com).

Colección Catedral is the wine bar of the highly respected local chef Adolfo, who runs a famous gourmet restaurant nearby plus several eateries in Madrid. His hope is to introduce the younger generation to the culture of fine food and wine. The bar offers up a somewhat pricey but always top-notch list of gourmet plates (€7-15 each) and fine local wines (€2-6 per glass—don't economize here), as well as a €13 three-course meal without wine and an excellent €18  fixed-price selection of tapas and wines. I like to sit next to the kitchen to be near the creative action. If the Starship *Enterprise* had a Spanish wine-and-tapas bar on its holodeck, this would be it. Wine is sold to take home or drink there for €3-8 more than the shop price (daily 12:00-24:00, across from cathedral at Calle Nuncio Viejo 1, tel. 925-224-244, Michael Angel takes good care of diners).

El Botero Taberna is a delightful little hideaway. The barman downstairs, who looks like a young Pavarotti, serves mojitos, fine wine, and exquisite tapas. Upstairs, there's an intimate, seven-table restaurant with romantic, white-tablecloth ambience and modern Mediterranean dishes (€29-€48 fixed-price meals, €15 starters, €20 main courses, dinner only, closed Sun, a block below cathedral at Calle de la Ciudad 5, tel. 925-229-088).

Simple Restaurants with Character

These places are listed in geographical order from Plaza Zocodover to Santo Tomé. Plaza de Zocodover is busy with eateries serving edible food at affordable prices, and its people-watching scene is great. But my recommended eateries are just a bit off the main drag on side streets. It's worth a few extra minutes—and the navigating challenge—to find places where you'll be eating with locals as well as tourists.

To dine with younger Spaniards, drop into **El Trébol,** tucked peacefully away just a short block off Plaza de Zocodover. Their €10 mixed grill can feed two. Locals enjoy their *pulgas* (€2.50 sandwiches). The seating inside is basic, but the outdoor tables are nice (daily 9:00-24:00, Calle de Santa Fe 1, tel. 925-281-297).

Restaurante Ludeña is a classic eatery with a bar, a well-worn dining room in back, and four tables on a sunny courtyard. It's very central; locals duck in here to pretend there's no tourism in Toledo (Plaza de la Magdalena 10, tel. 925-223-384).

Madre Tierra Restaurante Vegetariano is Toledo's answer to a vegetarian's prayer. Bright, spacious, classy, air-conditioned, and tuned in to the healthy eater's needs, its appetizing dishes are based on both international and traditional Spanish cuisine (€7-12 main courses, €12 fixed-price weekday meal, good tea selection, great veggie pizzas, closed Mon night and all day Tue, 20 yards below La Posada de Manolo just before reaching Plaza de San Justo, Bajada de le Tripería 2, tel. 925-223-571).

Pizzeria Pastucci, while nondescript, is a local favorite for pizza and pasta (big €14 pizza feeds two, daily 12:00-16:00 & 20:00-24:00, near cathedral at Calle de la Sinagoga 10, tel. 925-257-742).

Taberna La For de la Esquina is a local bar with a simple basement dining room and wonderful seating on a leafy square under a towering Jesuit church facade. Rustic and part of a fun neighborhood scene, this place is best when you want to eat outside on a square (€10 lunch specials, basic *raciones,* open daily, Plaza

Juan de Mariana 2, tel. 925-253-801).

Restaurante Placido, run by high-energy Anna and Grandma Sagradio, serves traditional family-style cuisine on a leafy terrace or in a wonderful Franciscan monastery courtyard (€15 and €22 fun fixed-price meals; open daily for lunch and dinner, about a block uphill from Santo Tomé at Calle Santo Tomé 2, tel. 925-222-603).

Picnics: Picnics are best assembled at the city market, **Mercado Municipal,** on Plaza Mayor (on the Alcázar side of cathedral, with a supermarket inside open Mon-Sat 9:00-15:00 & 17:00-20:00 and stalls open mostly in the mornings until 14:00, closed Sun). **Supermarket Coviran,** on Plaza de la Magdalena, has groceries at good prices (Mon-Sat 9:50-15:00 & 16:00-22:00, shorter hours on Sun, just below Plaza de Zocodover). For a picnic with people-watching on an atmospheric square, consider Plaza de Zocodover or Plaza del Ayuntamiento.

And for Dessert: *Mazapán*

Toledo's famous almond-fruity-sweet *mazapán* is sold all over town. As you wander, keep a lookout for convents advertising their version, *Dulces Artesanos.* The big *mazapán* producer is **Santo Tomé** (several outlets, including a handy one on Plaza de Zocodover, daily 9:00-22:00). Browse their tempting window displays. They sell *mazapán* goodies individually (two for about €1.50, *sin relleno*—without filling—is for purists, *de piñon* has pine nuts, *imperiales* is with almonds, others have fruit fillings). Boxes are good for gifts, but sampling is much cheaper when buying just a few pieces. Their *Toledana* is a nutty, crumbly, not-too-sweet cookie with a subtle thread of squash filling (€1.30 each).

For a sweet and romantic evening moment, pick up a few pastries and head down to the cathedral. Sit on the Plaza del Ayuntamiento's benches (or stretch out on the stone wall to the right of the TI). The fountain is on your right, Spain's best-looking City Hall is behind you, and there before you is her top cathedral—built back when Toledo was Spain's capital—shining brightly against the black night sky.

Toledo Connections

From Toledo to Madrid

While the AVE bullet train makes the trip to Madrid in half the time, buses depart twice as frequently. Three or four people traveling together can share a taxi economically. Whichever way you travel, Madrid and Toledo are very easily connected.

By Bus: 2/hour, 1-1.5 hours, *directo* is faster than *ruta,* bus drops you at Madrid's Plaza Elíptica Metro stop, Alsa bus company, tel. 902-422-242, www.alsa.es; you can almost always just drop in and buy a ticket minutes before departure.

By Train: Nearly hourly, 30 minutes by AVE or Avant to Madrid's Atocha Station, tel. 902-240-202, www.renfe.com; early and late trains can sell out—reserve ahead.

By Taxi: While it may seem extravagant, if you have limited time, lots of luggage, and a small group, simply taking a taxi from your Toledo hotel to your Madrid hotel is breathtakingly efficient (€80, one hour door-to-door, tel. 925-255-050 or 925-227-070). You can ask several cabbies for their best "off the meter" rate. A taxi to the Madrid airport costs €90 (find one who will go "off the meter") and takes an hour.

From Toledo to Other Points

To get to Granada, Sevilla, and elsewhere in Spain from Toledo, assume you'll have to transfer in Madrid. See "Madrid Connections" at the end of that chapter for information on reaching various destinations.

Route Tips for Drivers

Granada to Toledo (250 miles, 3.5 hours): The Granada-Toledo drive is long, hot, and boring. Start early to minimize the heat and make the best time you can. Follow signs for *Madrid/Jaén/A-44* into what some call "the Spanish Nebraska"—La Mancha (see next section). After Puerto Lapice, you'll see the Toledo exit.

Toledo to Madrid (40 miles, 1 hour): It's a speedy *autovía* north, past one last billboard to Madrid (on A-42). The highways converge into M-30, which encircles Madrid. Follow it to the left (*Nor* or *Oeste*) and take the Plaza de España exit to get back to Gran Vía. If you're airport-bound, keep heading into Madrid until you see the airplane symbol (N-II).

To drive to Atocha Station in Madrid, take the exit off M-30 for Plaza de Legazpi, then take Delicias (second on your right off the square). Parking for rental-car return is on the north side of the train station.

La Mancha

La Mancha, which is worth a visit if you're driving between Toledo and Granada, shows a side of Spain that you'll see nowhere else—vast and flat. Named for the Arabic word for "parched earth," it makes you feel small—lost in rough seas of olive-green polka dots. Random buildings look like houses and hotels hurled off some heavenly Monopoly board.

This is the setting of Miguel de Cervantes' *Don Quixote,* published in the early 17th century, after England sank the Armada and the Spanish Empire began its decline. Cervantes' star character fights doggedly for good, for justice, and against the fall of Spain and its traditional old-regime ideals. Ignoring reality, Don Quixote is a hero fighting a hopeless battle. Stark La Mancha is the perfect stage.

The epitome of *Don Quixote* country, the town of **Consuegra** (TI tel. 925-475-731, www.aytoconsuegra.es) must be the La Mancha Cervantes had in mind. Drive up to the ruined

12th-century castle and joust with a windmill. It's hot and buggy here, but the powerful view overlooking the village, with its sun-bleached light-red roofs, modern concrete reality, and harsh, windy silence, makes for a profound picnic (a one-hour drive south of Toledo). The castle belonged to the Knights of St. John (12th and 13th centuries) and is associated with their trip to Jerusalem during the Crusades. Originally built from the ruins of a nearby Roman circus, it has been recently restored (€4, includes windmill and archaeological museum in town). Sorry, the windmills are post-Cervantes, only 200 to 300 years old—but you can go inside the Molino de Bolero to see how it works (€1.50, included with €4 castle entry, daily 10:00-13:30 & 16:30-18:30—except opens at 10:30 Sat-Sun, shorter hours in winter).

The next castle north (above Almonacid, 8 miles from Toledo) is free. Follow the ruined lane past the ruined church up to the ruined castle. The jovial locals hike up with kids and kites.

GRANADA

For a time, Granada was the grandest city in Spain. But after the tumult that came with the change from Moorish to Christian rule, it lost its power and settled into a long slumber. Today, Granada seems to specialize in evocative history and good living. Settle down in the old center and explore monuments of the Moorish civilization and its conquest. Taste the treats of a North African-flavored culture that survives here today.

Compared to other Spanish cities its size, Granada is delightfully cosmopolitan—it's worked hard to accept a range of cultures, and you'll see far more ethnic restaurants here than elsewhere in Andalucía. Its large student population (70,000 students, including more than 10,000 from abroad) also lends it a youthful zest. The Grenadine people are serious about hospitality, and have earned a reputation among travelers for being particularly friendly and eager to help you enjoy their historic city.

Granada's magnificent Alhambra fortress was the last stronghold of the Moorish kingdom in Spain. The city's exotically tangled Moorish quarter, the Albayzín, invites exploration. From its viewpoints, romantics can enjoy the sunset and evening views of the grand, floodlit Alhambra.

An old Spanish saying goes, "Give him a coin, woman, for there is nothing worse in this life than to be blind in Granada." This city has much to see, yet it reveals itself in unpredictable ways; it takes a poet to sort through and assemble the jumbled shards of Granada. Peer through the intricate lattice of a Moorish window. Hear water burbling unseen among the labyrinthine hedges of the Generalife Gardens. Listen to a flute trilling deep in the swirl of alleys around the cathedral. Don't be blind in Granada—open all your senses.

Planning Your Time

Granada is worth two days and two nights, but you could conceivably hit its highlights in one very busy day. No matter what, reserve in advance for the Alhambra—at least several days, or, better, several weeks ahead (see "Getting Tickets for the Alhambra's Palacios Nazaries," on page 596).

If you only have one full day here, you could fit in the top sights by following this intense plan: In the morning, stroll the Pescadería market streets and follow my self-guided walk of the old town (or catch the 10:30 Cicerone walking tour), including a visit to the cathedral and its Royal Chapel. After a quick lunch, do the Alhambra in the afternoon (reservation essential). Hike the hippie lane into the Albayzín Moorish quarter (or catch minibus #31) to the San Nicolás viewpoint for the magic hour before sunset, then find the right place for a suitably late dinner. This is an extremely ambitious one-day plan; if you can spread it over two days, you'll be able to slow down and smell the incense (or make the most of one and a half days—e.g., if you're arriving in the early afternoon, do the self-guided walk before dinner).

When you're ready to move on, consider heading to nearby Nerja, the Costa del Sol's best beach town (2 hours by car or bus). You can also get to White Hill Towns such as Ronda (2.5 hours by train). Sevilla is an easy 3-hour train ride away. The Madrid-Granada train service is somewhat slow (4.5 hours), but passes through beautiful countryside.

Orientation to Granada

Modern Granada sprawls (300,000 people), but its sights are all within a 20-minute walk of Plaza Nueva, where dogs wag their tails to the rhythm of modern hippies and street musicians. Most of my recommended hotels are within a few blocks of Plaza Nueva. Make this the hub of your Granada visit.

Plaza Nueva was a main square back when kings called Granada home. This historic center is in the Darro River Valley, which separates two hills (the river now flows under the square). On one hill is the great Moorish palace, the Alhambra, and on the other is the best-preserved Moorish quarter in Spain, the Albayzín. To the southwest are the

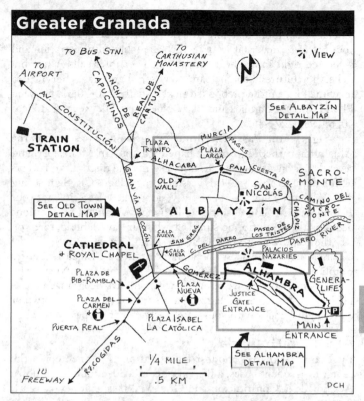

Greater Granada

[Map labels:]
TO BUS STN.
TO CARTHUSIAN MONASTERY
VIEW
TO AIRPORT
AV. CONSTITUCIÓN
ANCHA DE CAPUCHINOS
REAL DE CARTUJA
SEE ALBAYZÍN DETAIL MAP
TRAIN STATION
GRAN VÍA DE COLÓN
PLAZA TRIUNFO
PLAZA LARGA
MURCIA
PAGES
ALHACABA
PAN.
CUESTA DEL
SACRO-MONTE
OLD WALL
SAN NICOLÁS
CAMINO DEL SACROMONTE
SEE OLD TOWN DETAIL MAP
A L B A Y Z Í N
CHAPIZ
CALD. NUEVA
SAN GREG.
PASEO DE LOS TRISTES
DARRO RIVER
CATHEDRAL + ROYAL CHAPEL
CALD. VIEJA
C. DEL DARRO
PALACIOS NAZARIES
PLAZA DE BIB-RAMBLA
GOMEREZ
A L H A M B R A
GENERA-LIFE
PLAZA DEL CARMEN
PLAZA NUEVA
JUSTICE GATE ENTRANCE
PUERTA REAL
PLAZA ISABEL LA CATÓLICA
MAIN ENTRANCE
RECOGIDAS
¼ MILE
.5 KM
SEE ALHAMBRA DETAIL MAP
TO FREEWAY
DCH

GRANADA

cathedral, Royal Chapel, and Alcaicería (Moorish market), where the city's two main drags—Gran Vía de Colón (often just called "Gran Vía" by locals) and Calle Reyes Católicos—lead away into the modern city.

Tourist Information

The TI is tucked away just above Plaza Nueva on Santa Ana (Mon-Fri 9:00-19:30, Sat-Sun 9:30-15:00, above the church, tel. 958-575-202). Get a free city map and the *Pocket Guía* magazine in easy Spanish, and verify your Alhambra plans. To save yourself a trip to the train or bus stations, get schedule information here; the TI posts all departures on its walls. This TI covers not only Granada, but also Andalucía (pick up good, free maps for wherever else you're going in the region). A municipal TI, which covers only Granada, is inside City Hall on Plaza del Carmen, a short walk from the cathedral; they also sell the Bono Turístico city pass described later (Mon-Sat 10:00-19:00, Sun 10:00-14:00, tel. 958-248-280).

Alhambra Info: While any TI has information on the town's top sight, the very helpful info desk just inside the door of the official Alhambra bookstore (Tienda Librería de la Alhambra) is your best resource, as it's run by the Alhambra administration and is located right in the heart of town. The counter sells Alhambra tickets for future dates (no same-day sales) and has a ServiCaixa machine for printing prebooked tickets (daily 9:30-20:30, between Plaza Isabel La Católica and Plaza Nueva at Calle Reyes Católicos 40, tel. 958-227-846).

Sightseeing Pass: The **Bono Turístico** city pass covers the Alhambra, cathedral, Royal Chapel, Carthusian Monastery, and several trips on city buses, plus minor sights and discounts on others (€33/3 days, €37/5 days—this version also includes CitySightseeing bus). When you buy your pass, the vendor schedules a time for your Alhambra visit. (Because Bono Turístico Alhambra reservations occasionally book up, be sure that slots are available before you buy the pass.) Passes are sold at the TI in City Hall on Plaza del Carmen, at the Caja Granada Bank branch in Plaza Isabel La Católica, and at the "This is Granada" kiosk on Plaza Nueva; you can also book in advance online (www.bonoturisticogranada.com). Fancier hotels provide one free pass per room for stays of two or more nights; check with your hotel before buying a pass yourself.

Arrival in Granada

By Train: Granada's modest train station is connected to the center by frequent buses, a €7 taxi ride, or a 30-minute walk down Avenida de la Constitución and Gran Vía. If your itinerary is set, reserve your outbound train upon arrival. The train station does not have luggage storage, but you can store your bags at the nearby Granada iLocker (€3.50-5/day, price depends on bag size, daily 8:30-20:30, Avenida Andaluces 14, just across the parking lot in front of station, look for green door on your left).

Taxis wait out front, and it's a three-minute walk to reach the bus stop: Exiting the train station, walk straight ahead up the tree-lined Avenida Andaluces. At the first major intersection, turn right onto Avenida de la Constitución, and within a block you'll see a series of bus stops with routes marked on the signposts. Most of these buses stop at the cathedral (Gran Vía Catedral), which is four stops from the train station and the nearest stop to Plaza Nueva. Check the easy-to-read routes for the "Gran Vía Catedral" stop (your options include buses #1, #3, #4, #5, #6, #7, #8, #9, and others). An electronic board shows how long the wait is for each bus. When you board, buy a €1.20 ticket from the driver. For Plaza Nueva and most of my recommended hotels, get off at the cathedral (ask, "*¿Catedral?*"—kah-tay-DRAHL); cross the busy Gran Vía and walk three short blocks to Plaza Nueva.

By Bus: Located on the city outskirts, Granada's bus

station *(estación de autobuses)* has a good and cheap cafeteria, ATMs, luggage lockers (€3.50), coin-op Internet terminal, and a privately run tourist agency masquerading as a TI—all of these are downstairs, where you exit the buses. Upstairs is the main arrivals hall with ticket windows, ticket machines, and a helpful information counter in the main hall that hands out printed schedules for each route. All buses are operated by Alsa (tel. 902-422-242, www.alsa.es).

To get from the bus station to the city center, either take a 10-minute taxi ride (€8) or bus #3 or #33 (€1.20, pay driver). It's about a 20-minute bus ride; nearing the center, the bus goes up Gran Vía. For Plaza Nueva, get off at the "Gran Vía Catedral" stop near the cathedral (cathedral not visible from bus; ask, "*¿Catedral?*"—kah-tay-DRAHL), a half-block before the grand square called Plaza Isabel La Católica. From here, it's a short three-block walk to Plaza Nueva and most of my recommended hotels.

By Car: With all the one-way streets, GPS can be frustrating for tourists driving into Granada. And driving in Granada's historic center is restricted to buses, taxis, and tourists with hotel reservations. Signs are posted to this effect, and entrances are strictly controlled. Hidden cameras snap a photo of your license plate as soon as you enter the restricted zone. If you have a reservation, simply drive past the sign, check in, and make sure your hotel registers you with the local traffic police (this is routine for them, but if they don't do it within 48 hours, you'll be stuck with a steep ticket). Hotels provide parking or have a deal with a central-zone garage (such as Parking San Agustín, just off Gran Vía del Colón, €25/day).

If you're driving and don't have a hotel reservation in the center, find a place to park outside the prohibited zone. The Alhambra, above the old town, has a huge lot where you can park for €19 per 24 hours (and walk, catch the minibus, or taxi into the center). There are also garages just outside the restricted zone: the Triunfo garage to the east (€20/day, Avenida de la Constitución 5) or the Neptune garage (Centro Comercial Neptuno) to the south (€15/day, Calle Neptuno). To reach the city center from either parking garage, catch bus #6 nearby and get off at the "Gran Vía Catedral" stop (every 10-20 minutes, €1.20, pay driver).

If, upon arrival in Granada, you're driving directly to the Alhambra, you can easily avoid the historic center (see "Getting There" on page 608).

GRANADA

By Plane: Granada's sleepy airport, which serves only a dozen or so planes a day, is about 10 miles west of the city center (airport code: GRX, tel. 958-245-223—press "2" for English, www.aena -aeropuertos.es). To get between the airport and downtown, you can take a taxi (€30) or, much cheaper, the airport bus, timed to leave directly outside the terminal when flights arrive and depart (€3, 12/day, 40 minutes). If you're leaving from the town center, use the bus stop at Gran Vía del Colón, nearly across from the cathedral.

Helpful Hints

Theft Alert: In general, be on guard for pickpockets, especially late at night in the Albayzín. Your biggest threat is being conned while enjoying drinks and music in Sacromonte. Down-and-out women, usually hanging out near the cathedral and Alcaicería, will accost you with sprigs of rosemary, then demand a tip—just ignore them (for more advice on dealing with this, see "Rosemary Scam" on page 659).

Festivals and Concerts: From late June to early July, the **International Festival of Music and Dance** offers classical music, ballet, flamenco, and zarzuela (light opera) nightly in the Alhambra and other historic venues at reasonable prices. The ticket office is located in the Corral del Carbón (open mid-April-Oct). Beginning in February, you can also book tickets online at www.granadafestival.org. This festival is one of the most respected and popular in Spain, and tickets for major performers typically sell out months in advance. During the festival, flamenco is free every night at midnight; ask the ticket office or TI for the venue.

From fall through spring, the **City of Granada Orchestra** offers popular concerts—mostly on weekends— that generally sell out quickly (€6-23, late Sept-mid-May only, Auditorio Manuel de Falla, ticket office in Corral del Carbón, Mon-Sat 12:00-14:00 & 17:00-19:00, closed Sun, tel. 958-221-144, www.orquestaciudadgranada.es).

Internet Access: Almost all Granada hotels have Wi-Fi for their guests, and some have computers for use as well. Many Internet points are scattered throughout Granada, often part of *locutorios* (call centers).

Laundry: Tintorería-Lavandería Duquesa, a few blocks west of the cathedral area, offers a pricey service to wash, dry, and fold your clothes (€10/small load, same-day service possible if you bring it in the morning, no self-service, Mon-Fri 9:30-14:00 & 17:00-21:00, Sat 9:30-14:00, closed Sun, near the San Jerónimo Monastery at Duquesa 24, tel. 958-280-685).

Post Office: It's on Puerta Real (daily 8:30-20:30, tel. 958-221-138).

Travel Agencies: All travel agencies book flights, and many also sell long-distance bus and train tickets. Mega-chain **El Corte Inglés** sells plane, train, and bus tickets (Mon-Sat 10:00-22:00, closed Sun, Acera del Darro, floor 2, tel. 958-282-612).

Getting Around Granada

With cheap taxis, frisky minibuses, good city buses, and nearly all points of interest an easy walk from Plaza Nueva, you'll get around Granada easily.

Tickets for minibuses and city buses cost €1.20 per ride (buy from driver). Credibus magnetic cards save you money if you'll be riding often—or, since they're shareable, if you're part of a group (€5/7 trips, €10/16 trips, plus refundable €2 fee for each card issued). You can buy these from the driver as well. To get a €5 card, ask for "*un bono de cinco euros.*" For a €10 card, request "*un bono de diez euros.*" These are valid on minibuses and city buses (no fee for connecting bus if you transfer within 45 minutes).

By Minibus: Handy little made-for-tourists red minibuses, which cover the city center, depart every few minutes from Plaza Nueva, Plaza Isabel La Católica, and the cathedral (Gran Vía stops) until late in the evening (some bus stops marked on map on page 599). Here are several handy minibus routes to look for:

Bus #30 is the best for a trip up to the Alhambra, departing every 10-15 minutes from the "Gran Vía Catedral" stop, with Alhambra stops at the Generalife, Charles V's Palace, and Justice Gate (in that order).

Bus #31 departs from Plaza Nueva and winds around the Albayzín quarter (departs about every 15 minutes; see page 633).

Bus #35 follows the same route as #31, but also makes a side-trip into Sacromonte. It runs less frequently (every 30-40 minutes).

By City Bus: These are handy if you're visiting the Carthusian Monastery (bus #8) or going to the bus station (#3 or #33) or train station (#1 or #3-#9).

Tours in Granada

Walking Tours

Cicerone, run by María, offers informative 2.5-hour city tours. Their excellent guides describe the fitful and fascinating changes the city underwent as it morphed from a Moorish capital to a Christian one 500 years ago. While the tour doesn't enter any actual sights, it weaves together bits of the Moorish heritage that survive around the cathedral and the Albayzín. Tours start on Plaza de Bib-Rambla and finish on Plaza Nueva. Groups are small; reservations are encouraged (though not required). Visits are generally only in English, but may be in both English and

Getting Tickets for the Alhambra's Palacios Nazaries

The popular Palacio Nazaries is often sold out during the day. (The Generalife Gardens and Alcazaba fort don't sell out.) If you're not prepared, you could become one of the untold number of tourists who show up in Granada...and never see its main sight. You have three main options to ensure that you get into the Palacio during your stay. The easiest is the Bono Turístico city pass, which lets you choose virtually any entry time, even the same day (get details on page 592). You can also visit the Palacio at night, when it's rarely sold out (see page 611; if you do this, you can also get a daytime ticket for the rest of the complex, which never sells out). Or you can make a reservation.

Reserving in Advance: Getting a reservation is easy, provided you do it well in advance. You reserve a specific entry time (€1.30 surcharge) and pick up your tickets in Spain. Reserve as soon as you're ready to commit to a time, as much as three months before your visit. For most of the year, book at least two weeks in advance—more for Holy Week, weekends, and major holidays. Off-season (July-Aug and winter), you can generally book a few days in advance, or even walk right in—but it's not worth the risk. When you reserve, get the "General Daytime Visit" ticket (described on page 605). For advice on timing your visit, see the sidebar on page 610.

Here are your reservation options:

• When you book your hotel room, ask if your hotelier can reserve Alhambra tickets; if so, request a time slot.

• Order online at www.alhambra-tickets.es. Select the "General Daytime Visit" ticket, then choose your date and time period—morning (De 8:30h a 14h) or afternoon (De 14h a 20h)—then the exact half-hour time window for entry. Agotado means "sold out." Unless you're traveling with a child under 12 (Niños menos 12a), ignore the "special offers" options and simply hit "Continue."

• By phone, an English-speaking operator walks you through the process. Within Spain, dial 958-926-031 or 902-888-001. From the US, dial 011-34-958-926-031. The line is open Mon-Fri

Spanish on slow days (€15, show this book to save €3, kids under 14 free, daily March-Oct at 10:30, Nov-Feb at 11:00; to book a tour, visit the kiosk labeled *Meeting Point* on Plaza de Bib-Rambla—staffed by cheerful Rocio, or call 958-561-810 or mobile 607-691-676; www.ciceronegranada.com, reservas@ciceronegranada.com). They also offer tours of the Alhambra that include an entry time to Palacios Nazaries—handy if you have trouble getting a reservation on your own (€50, includes Alhambra ticket, ideally reserve at least 3-4 days ahead).

8:00-21:00 Spanish time, closed Sat-Sun. (While you wait for an operator, a recording tells you in Spanish the date of the next available tickets.)

Picking Up Tickets: Your reservation still needs to be converted to a printed ticket, which you pick up in Spain. To confirm your purchase, bring the same credit card you used to reserve. (To be 100 percent sure, also bring your credit card's PIN number and your passport.)

Save time by retrieving your tickets before you reach the crowded Alhambra. You can print tickets at one of Spain's many yellow, ATM like ServiCaixa terminals (such as the one across from the cathedral at Gran Vía 16). Or go to the official Alhambra bookstore in town (a half-block from Plaza Nueva at Calle Reyes Católicos 40) and get your ticket from their ServiCaixa machine or at the information desk. Picking up your ticket in advance lets you use the Justice Gate shortcut, avoiding the mob at the main entrance (described on page 612).

You can also pick up tickets at the Alhambra's main entrance, but it can be crowded. At the entrance, follow "Bookings collection with credit card" signs to the windows marked *Retirada de Reservas*, or use their less-crowded ServiCaixa machines (beyond the bookstore and café). Allow up to an hour to wait in line to pick up tickets and walk from there to the Palacio.

If You're in Granada Without a Palace Reservation: You can generally buy a ticket good for entry later the same day if you're in line at the main entrance by 7:30 (they open at 8:00). On a slow day, you can sometimes get in right away. The entrance's ServiCaixa ticket machines (for credit cards; these are just beyond the bookstore and café) are faster than the cash-only window labeled *Venta Directa*.

Otherwise, you can try one of the following: Take a guided tour, which admits you without reservations (see "Tours," pages 595 and 612); try for a last-minute reservation online, by phone, through your hotel, or at the Alhambra bookstore (the store sells tickets for future dates, but not same-day tickets); buy a Bono Turístico pass; or visit at night.

GRANADA

Local Guides

Margarita Ortiz de Landazuri (tel. 958-221-406, www.alhambra tours.com, info@alhambratours.com) and **Miguel Ángel** (mobile 617-565-711, miguelangelalhambratours@gmail.com) are both good, English-speaking, licensed guides with lots of experience and a passion for teaching. Guide rates are standard (€130/2.5 hours, €260/day).

Hop-On, Hop-Off Bus Tour

CitySightseeing operates a route with 11 stops around the city. But Granada doesn't lend itself to this type of tour, and the bus concentrates on far-flung areas that are far less interesting than the easy-to-walk city center (€18/48 hours, 1.5-hour loop, 2 buses/hour, 9:30-20:00 in summer, 9:30-18:00 in winter, only stops at the Carthusian Monastery in the afternoon, tel. 958-535-028, www.granadatour.com).

This is Granada Audio Tour
You can rent an MP3 player preloaded with four different walking-tour itineraries around the city, including the Alhambra. Two people get the system for up to two days for €15 (rent from "This is Granada" kiosk on Plaza Nueva, includes map, tel. 958-210-239).

Olive Oil Tour
This company helps you explore Granada's countryside and taste some local olive oil. Choose between a three-hour tour that departs in the morning or afternoon (€38) or a six-hour tour that includes lunch (€58). Tours are in English, and a driver will pick you up at your hotel (tel. 958-559-643, mobile 651-147-504, www.oliveoiltour.com, reservas@oliveoiltour.com).

Gayle's Granada Tapas Tours
Gayle Mackie takes small groups off the beaten path to a series of four characteristic tapas bars, providing food tips, light banter, and fascinating insights into Granada along the way. For a movable feast (and what amounts to a filling meal) with good wine and beer, join their "classic walk" (2.5 hours, €35/person, €5 discount with this book, tours for 2-6 people, daily at 13:30 or 20:00, other tapa tour variations include family and group options, mobile 619-444-984, www.granadatapastours.com).

Self-Guided Walk

▲▲Granada's Old Town
This short walk covers all the essential sights beyond the Alhambra. Along the way, we'll see vivid evidence of the dramatic Moorish-to-Christian transition brought about by the Reconquista, the long and ultimately successful battle to retake Spain from the Moors and re-establish Christian rule.

• *Start at Corral del Carbón, near Plaza del Carmen.*

❶ Corral del Carbón: A caravanserai (of Silk Road fame) was a protected place for merchants to rest their camels, spend the night, get a bite to eat, and spin yarns. This, the only surviving caravanserai of Granada's original 14, was just a block away from the silk market (Alcaicería; the next stop on this walk). Stepping through the caravanserai's grand

Granada's Old Town Walk

🅿 PARKING
🅣 TAXI STAND
➔ ENTRY POINT TO SIGHTS

TO TRAIN & BUS STATIONS

100 YARDS
100 METERS

ALBAYZÍN MOORISH QUARTER

MERCADO SAN AGUSTIN

GRAN VÍA DE COLÓN

CALLE VÁL.

TO SAN NICOLÁS VIEWPOINT & PLAZA LARGA

CATHEDRAL & ROYAL CHAPEL

PL. PESC.

CALD. NUEVA

S. GREGORIO

CETTI.

ELVIRA

CALD. VIEJA

CÁRCEL ALT.

AIRE

TO SACRO-MONTE

CATH EXIT

ALMIR.

ABER.

DARRO

PLAZA NUEVA

PL. S. ANA

PLAZA DE BIB-RAMBLA

OFICIOS

ERMITA

ZACATÍN

S. ANA

CUCH.

CUESTA GOMEREZ

HAMMAM BAÑOS ARABES

PLAZA ISABEL LA CATÓLICA

ANIMAS

CALLE REYES CATÓLICOS

PAVANERAS

PANERA

TO ALHAMBRA

PLAZA DEL CARMEN

START

CITY HALL

SIN MATIAS

PUERTA REAL

GRANADA

Walk
1. Corral del Carbón
2. Alcaicería
3. Plaza de Bib-Rambla
4. Cathedral
5. Royal Chapel Square
6. Plaza Isabel La Católica
7. Plaza Nueva
8. To Paseo de los Tristes & Hammam El Bañuelo

Other
9. Alhambra Bookstore, Info & Servi-Caixa Machine (Alhambra Tickets)
10. ServiCaixa Machine
11. Gran Vía Cathedral Bus Stop (to Alhambra; from Train & Bus Stations)
12. Gran Vía del Colón Bus Stop (to Train & Bus Stations; Airport)
13. Plaza Nueva Bus Stop (to Albayzín & Sacromonte)

Moorish door, you find a square with 14th-century Moorish brickwork surrounding a water fountain. This plain-yet-elegant structure evokes the times when traders would gather here with exotic goods and swap tales from across the Muslim world.

It's a common mistake to think of the Muslim Moors as somehow not Spanish. They lived here for seven centuries and were really just as "indigenous" as the Romans, Goths, and Celts. While the Moors were Muslim, they were no more connected to Arabia than they were to France.

After the Reconquista, this space was used as a coal storage facility (hence "del Carbón"). These days it houses two offices where you can buy tickets for musical events.

• *From the caravanserai, exit straight ahead and walk down Puente del Carbón to the big street named Calle Reyes Católicos (for the "Catholic Monarchs" Ferdinand and Isabel, who finally conquered the Moors). The street covers a river that once ran openly here, with a series of bridges (like the "Coal Bridge," Puente del Carbón) lacing together the two parts of town. Today, the modern commercial center is to your left. Continue one block farther to the yellow gate marked* Alcaicería. *The pedestrian street you're crossing, Zacatin, was the main drag, which ran parallel to the river before it was covered in the 19th century. Today it's a favorite paseo destination, busy each evening with strollers. Pass through the Alcaicería gate and walk 20 yards into the old market to the first intersection.*

❷ **Alcaicería:** Originally a Moorish silk market with 200 shops, the Alcaicería (al-kai-thay-REE-ah) was filled with precious salt, silver, spices, and silk. It had 10 armed gates and its own guards. Silk was huge in Moorish times, and silkworm-friendly mulberry trees flourished in the countryside. It was such an important product that the sultans controlled and guarded it by constructing this fine, fortified market. After the Reconquista, the Christians realized this market was good for business and didn't mess with it. Later, the more zealous Philip II had it shut down. A terrible fire in 1850 destroyed what was left. Today's Alcaicería was rebuilt in the late 1800s as a tourist souk (marketplace) to complement the romantic image of Granada popularized by the writings of Washington Irving.

Explore the mesh of tiny shopping lanes: overpriced trinkets, popcorn machines popping, men selling balloons, leather goods spread out on streets, kids playing soccer, barking dogs, dogged shoe-shine boys, and the whirring grind of bicycle-powered knife sharpeners. You'll invariably meet obnoxious and persistent women pushing their green sprigs on innocents in order to extort money. Be strong.

• *Turn left down Ermita lane. After 50 yards, leave the market via another fortified gate and enter a big square. The Neptune fountain marks the center of the...*

❸ **Plaza de Bib-Rambla:** This exuberant square, just two blocks behind the cathedral (from the fountain you can see its blocky spire peeking above the big orange building) was once the center of Moorish Granada. While Moorish rule of Spain lasted

700 years, the last couple of those centuries were a period of decline as Muslim culture split under weak leadership and Christian forces grew more determined. The last remnants of the Moorish kingdom united and ruled from Granada. As Muslims fled south from reconquered lands, Granada was flooded with refugees. By 1400, Granada had an estimated 100,000 people—huge for medieval Europe. This was the main square, the focal point of market and festivals, but it was much smaller then than now, pushed in by the jam-packed city.

Under Christian rule, Moors and Jews were initially tolerated (as they were considered good for business), and this area became the Moorish ghetto. Then, with the Inquisition (under Philip II, c. 1550), ideology trumped pragmatism, and Jews and Muslims were evicted or forced to convert. The elegant square you see today was built, and built big. In-your-face Catholic processions started here. To assert Christian rule, all the trappings of Christian power were layered upon what had been the trappings of Moorish power. Between here and the cathedral were the Christian University (the big orange building) and the adjacent archbishop's palace.

Today Plaza de Bib-Rambla is good for coffee or a meal amid the color and fragrance of flower stalls and the burbling of its Neptune-topped fountain. It remains a multigenerational hangout, where it seems everyone is enjoying a peaceful retirement. A block away (Neptune would get there if he could just turn 180 degrees and walk 100 yards), the Pescadería square is a smaller, similarly lively version of Bib-Rambla.

• *Leave the square by walking toward the cathedral, heading down the lane between the big orange building and Bar Manolo. In a block, you come to a small square fronting a very big church.*

❹ **Cathedral:** Wow, the cathedral facade just screams triumph. That's partly because its design is based on a triumphal arch, built over a destroyed mosque. Five hundred yards away, there was once open space outside the city wall with good soil for a foundation. But the Christian conquerors said, "No way." Instead, they destroyed the mosque and built their cathedral right here on difficult, sandy soil. This was the place where the people of Granada traditionally

GRANADA

worshipped—and now they would worship as Christians.

The church—started in the early 1500s and not finished until the late 1700s—has a Gothic foundation and was built mostly in the Renaissance style, with its last altars done in Neoclassical style. Hometown artist Alonso Cano (1601-1667) finished the building, at the king's request, in Baroque. Accentuating the power of the Roman Catholic Church, the emphasis here is on Mary rather than Christ. The facade declares *Ave Maria*. (This was Counter-Reformation time, and the Church was threatened by Protestant Christians. Mary was also more palatable to Muslim converts, as she is revered in the Quran.)

• *To tour the cathedral now, you can enter here (the interior is described in the self-guided cathedral tour on page 628). You'll exit on the far side, near the Royal Chapel Square (next on this walk).*

To skip the cathedral interior for now and continue with this walk, circle around the cathedral to the right, keeping the church to your left, until you reach the small square facing the Royal Chapel.

❺ Royal Chapel Square: This square was once ringed by important Moorish buildings. A hammam (public bath), a madrassa (school), a caravanserai (Day's Inn), the silk market, and the leading mosque were all right here. With Christian rule, the madrassa (the faux-gray-stone building with the walls painted in 3-D Baroque style) became Granada's first City Hall. The royal coffins were moved from the Alhambra's parador here to the Royal Chapel in 1521. (See the self-guided tour of the Royal Chapel on page 625.)

• *Continue up the cobbled, stepped lane to the big street, Gran Vía de Colón. With the arrival of cars and the modern age, the people of Granada wanted a Parisian-style boulevard. In the early 20th century, they mercilessly cut through the old town and created Gran Vía and its French-style buildings—in the process destroying everything in its path, including many historic convents.*

From here you could catch minibus #30 to the Alhambra, or go left two blocks, cross the street, and walk up Calle Cárcel Baja into the Albayzín. But for now let's continue our orientation tour. Cross the busy street, turn right, and walk down Gran Vía to the big square ahead. Face the statue above the fountain from across the busy intersection.

❻ Plaza Isabel La Católica: Granada's two grand boulevards, Gran Vía and Calle Reyes Católicos, meet a block off Plaza Nueva at Plaza Isabel La Católica. Above the fountain, a beautiful statue shows Columbus unfurling a long contract with Isabel. It lists the terms of

GRANADA

Columbus' *mcccclxxxxii* voyage: "For as much as you, Columbus, are going by our command to discover and subdue some Islands and Continents in the ocean...." The two reliefs show the big events in Granada of 1492: Isabel and Ferdinand accepting Columbus' proposal and a stirring battle scene (which never happened) at the walls of the Alhambra.

Isabel was driven by her desire to spread Catholicism. Spain, needing an alternate trade route to the Orient's spices after the Ottoman Empire cut off the traditional overland routes, was driven by trade. And Columbus was driven by his desire for money. As a reward for adding territory to Spain's Catholic empire, Isabel promised Columbus the ranks of Admiral of the Oceans and Governor of the New World. To sweeten the pot, she tossed in one-eighth of all the riches he brought home. Isabel died thinking that Columbus had found India or China. Columbus died poor and disillusioned.

Calle Reyes Católicos leads from this square downhill to the busy intersection with Puerta Real. From there, Acera del Darro takes you through modern Granada to the river via the huge El Corte Inglés department store and lots of modern commerce. This area erupts with locals out strolling each night. For the best Granada paseo, wander the streets here around 19:00.

• *Follow Calle Reyes Católicos a couple of blocks uphill to the left, where you'll find another square.*

❼ **Plaza Nueva:** Long a leading square in Granada, Plaza Nueva is dominated by the Palace of Justice (grand Baroque facade with green Andalusian flag). The fountain is capped by a stylized pomegranate—the symbol of the city, always open and fertile. The main action here is the comings and goings of the busy little shuttle buses serving the Albayzín. The local hippie community, nicknamed the *pies negros* (black feet) for obvious reasons, hangs out here and on Calle de Elvira. They squat—with their dogs and guitars—in abandoned caves above those the Gypsies occupy in Sacromonte. Many are the children of rich Spanish families from the north, hell-bent on disappointing their high-achieving parents.

• *Our tour continues with a stroll up Paseo de los Tristes. Leave Plaza Nueva opposite where you entered (via the street to the left of the church) and walk up the Darro River Valley. This is particularly enjoyable in the cool of the evening. If you're tired, note that minibus #31 runs from Plaza Nueva into and through the Albayzín quarter.*

❽ **Paseo de los Tristes:** This "Walk of the Sad Ones" was once the route of funeral processions to the cemetery at the edge of town. Leaving Plaza Nueva, pass the Church of Santa Ana on your right. This was originally a mosque—the church tower replaced a minaret. Notice the ceramic brickwork. This is Mudejar art by Moorish craftsmen, whose techniques were later employed by Christians. Inside you'll see a fine Alhambra-style cedar ceiling.

Follow Carrera del Darro high above the River Darro, which flows along the base of the Alhambra (look down by the river for a glimpse of feral cats). Six miles upstream, part of the Darro is diverted to provide water for the Alhambra's many fountains—a remarkable feat of Moorish engineering that allowed the grand fortress complex to be resistant to siege.

After passing two small, picturesque bridges, you'll see the broken nub of a once-grand 11th-century bridge over the river, leading to the Alhambra. Notice two slits in the column: One held an iron portcullis to keep bad guys from entering the town via the river. The second held a solid door that was lowered to build up water, then released to flush out the riverbed and keep it clean.

• *Across from the remains of the bridge is the brick facade of an evocative Moorish bath, the Hammam El Bañuelo.*

Hammam El Bañuelo (Moorish Baths): In Moorish times, hammams were a big part of the community (working-class homes didn't have bathrooms). Baths were strictly segregated (as they are today) and functioned as more than a place to wash: Business was done here, and it was a social meeting point. In Christian times it was assumed that conspiracies brewed in these baths—therefore, only a few of them survive. This place gives you the chance to explore the stark but evocative ruins of an 11th-century Moorish public bath (free, unreliably Tue-Sat 10:00-14:30, April-Sept opens at 9:00, closed Sun-Mon year-round, English descriptions posted throughout, photos OK, Carrera del Darro 31, tel. 958-027-800).

Entering the baths, you pass the house of the keeper and the foyer, then visit the cold room, the warm room (where services like massage were offered), and finally the hot, or steam, room. Beyond that, you can see the oven that generated the heat, which flowed under the hypocaust-style floor tiles (the ones closest to the oven were the hottest). The romantic little holes in the ceiling once had stained-glass louvers that attendants opened and closed with sticks to regulate the heat and steaminess. Whereas Romans soaked in their pools, Muslims just doused. Rather than being totally immersed, people scooped and splashed water over themselves. Imagine attendants stoking the fires under the metal boiler...while people in towels and wooden slippers (to protect their feet from the heated floors) enjoyed all the spa services you can imagine as beams of light slashed through the mist.

This was a great social mixer. As all were naked, class distinctions disappeared—elites learned the latest from commoners. Mothers found matches for their kids. A popular Muslim phrase sums up the attraction of the baths: "This is where anyone would spend their last coin."

• *Continuing straight ahead, on your right is the Church of San Pedro, the parish church of Sacromonte's Gypsy community (across from the Mudejar Art Museum). Within its rich interior is an ornate oxcart used to carry the host on the annual pilgrimage to Rocio, a town near the Portuguese border. Just past this, on your left, is Santa Catalina de Zafra, a convent of cloistered nuns (they worship behind a screen that divides the church's rich interior in half).*

This walk ends at Paseo de los Tristes—with its restaurant tables spilling out under the floodlit Alhambra. From here, the road arcs up into Sacromonte. If you've worked up a hunger, you can backtrack a few blocks to Calle de Gloria where the Convento de San Bernardo sells cookies and monastic wine. Look for the Venta de Dulces *sign; goods are sold from behind a lazy Susan.*

Sights in Granada

▲▲▲The Alhambra

This last and greatest Moorish palace is one of Europe's top sights. Attracting up to 8,000 visitors a day, it's the reason most tourists

come to Granada. Nowhere else does the splendor of Moorish civilization shine so beautifully.

The last Moorish stronghold in Europe is, with all due respect, really a symbol of retreat. For centuries, Granada was merely a regional capital. Gradually the Christian Reconquista moved south, taking Córdoba (1237) and Sevilla (1248). The Nazarids, one of the many diverse ethnic groups of Spanish Muslims, held together the last Moorish kingdom, which they ruled from Granada until 1492. As you tour their grand palace, remember that while Europe slumbered through the Dark Ages, Moorish magnificence blossomed—ornate stucco, plaster "stalactites," colors galore, scalloped windows framing Granada views, exuberant gardens, and water, water everywhere. Water—so rare and precious in most of the Islamic world—was the purest symbol of life to the Moors. The Alhambra is decorated with water: standing still, cascading, masking secret conversations, and drip-dropping playfully.

Cost: Various tickets cover the sights of the Alhambra. The one you want is the €13 **"General Daytime Visit"** (*visita diurna*

Granada at a Glance

▲▲▲**The Alhambra** The last and greatest Moorish palace, high-lighting the splendor of that civilization in the 13th and 14th centuries. Reservations are a must if you plan to visit during the day. **Hours:** The entire complex is open daily mid-March-mid-Oct 8:30-20:00, off-season 8:30-18:00. Palacios Nazaries and Generalife Gardens are open for nighttime visits mid-March-mid-Oct Tue-Sat 22:00-23:30, closed Sun-Mon; off-season Fri-Sat 20:00-21:30, closed Sun-Thu. See page 605.

▲▲**Royal Chapel** Lavish 16th-century Plateresque Gothic chapel with the tombs of Queen Isabel and King Ferdinand. **Hours:** March-Oct daily 10:15-13:30 & 16:00-19:30 except opens at 11:00 on Sun; Nov-Feb daily 10:15-13:30 & 15:30-18:30 except opens at 11:00 on Sun. See page 624.

▲▲**San Nicolás Viewpoint** Breathtaking vista over the Alhambra and the Albayzín. **Hours:** Always open; best at sunset. See page 633.

▲**Cathedral** The second-largest cathedral in Spain, unusual for its bright Renaissance interior. **Hours:** April-Oct Mon-Sat 10:30-13:15 & 16:00-20:00, Sun 16:00-20:00; Nov-March until 19:00. See page 628.

▲**The Albayzín** Spain's best old Moorish quarter. **Hours:** Always open, but use caution after dark. See page 630.

Cave Museum of Sacromonte A center with caves and displays on Roma cave-building, crafts, food, and music. **Hours:** Mid-March-mid-Oct daily 10:00-20:00, until 18:00 off-season. See page 636.

GRANADA

general) ticket, which covers the Alcazaba fort, Palacios Nazaries, and Generalife Gardens. This ticket is the only one that allows you to see Palacios Nazaries during the day. Note that same-day tickets are virtually never available—reservations are essential. (For reservation details, see sidebar on page 596.)

If you make the mistake of showing up without a reservation, get in line and look for the electric sign indicating just what's still available that day. Other, less-ideal tickets are available for people who've waited too long to get the General Daytime Visit ticket:

• Daytime ticket for just the Alcazaba and Generalife Gardens—€7

• Nighttime ticket for just Palacios Nazaries—€8

• Nighttime ticket for just Generalife Gardens—€5

Alcaicería Tiny shopping lanes filled with tacky tourist shops. **Hours:** Always open, with shops open long hours. See page 600.

Corral del Carbón Granada's only surviving caravanserai (inn for traveling merchants), with impressive Moorish door. **Hours:** Always viewable. See page 598.

Paseo de los Tristes A prime strolling strip above the Darro River lined with eateries and peppered with Moorish history. **Hours:** Always open; best in the evenings. See page 603.

Hammam El Bañuelo 11th-century ruins of Moorish baths. **Hours:** Unreliably Tue-Sat 10:00-14:30, April-Sept opens at 9:00, closed Sun-Mon year-round. See page 604.

Great Mosque of Granada Islamic house of worship featuring a minaret with a live call to prayer, an information center for the Muslim perspective on Granada history, and a courtyard with commanding views. **Hours:** Daily 11:00-14:00 & 18:00-21:00, shorter hours in winter. See page 634.

Hammam Baños Árabes Tranquil spot for soaks and massages in Arab baths. **Hours:** Daily 10:00-24:00. See page 630.

***Zambra* Dance** Touristy flamenco-like dance performance in Sacromonte district. **Hours:** Shows generally daily at 22:00. See page 637.

Carthusian Monastery Lavish Baroque monastery on the outskirts of town. **Hours:** Daily April-Oct 10:00-13:00 & 16:00-20:00, Nov-March 10:00-13:00 & 15:00-18:00. See page 638.

• "Circular Azul" ticket, which allows a nighttime visit of the Palacio Nazaries, then (the next morning) the Alcazaba and Generalife Gardens—€15

The Alhambra grounds are free to visit, as is Charles V's Palace (and the Alhambra Museum inside it).

Hours: The whole Alhambra complex is open daily mid-March-mid-Oct 8:30-20:00, off-season 8:30-18:00 (ticket office opens at 8:00, last entry one hour before closing, toll tel. 902-441-221, www.alhambra-patronato.es).

Palacios Nazaries and Generalife Gardens are also open most **evenings** (see "The Alhambra by Moonlight" on page 611) mid-March-mid-Oct Tue-Sat 22:00-23:30 (ticket office open 21:30-22:30), closed Sun-Mon; and off-season Fri-Sat 20:00-21:30

The Alhambra

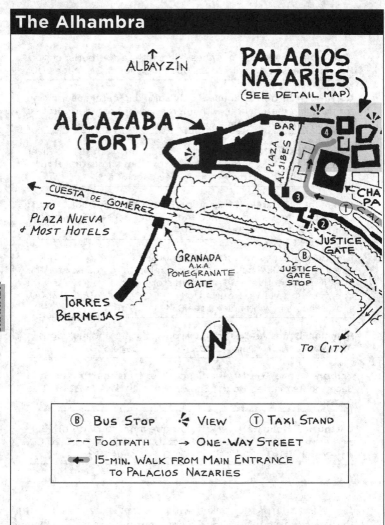

↑ ALBAYZÍN

PALACIOS NAZARIES
(SEE DETAIL MAP)

ALCAZABA (FORT)

BAR •

PLAZA ALJIBES

④

CUESTA DE GOMÉREZ

TO PLAZA NUEVA & MOST HOTELS

③

②

CHA PA

Ⓣ

JUSTICE GATE

GRANADA A.K.A. POMEGRANATE GATE

Ⓑ

JUSTICE GATE STOP

TORRES BERMEJAS

TO CITY

Ⓑ BUS STOP ⚡ VIEW Ⓣ TAXI STAND

--- FOOTPATH → ONE-WAY STREET

⬅ 15-MIN. WALK FROM MAIN ENTRANCE TO PALACIOS NAZARIES

GRANADA

(ticket office open 19:30-20:30), closed Sun-Thu.

Getting There: You have four options for getting to the Alhambra.

On Foot: From Plaza Nueva, hike 20-25 minutes up the street called Cuesta de Gomérez. Keep going straight—you'll see the Alhambra high on your left. (Along the way, after about 10 minutes, look for the Justice Gate shortcut, described later.) The ticket pavilion is on the far side of the Alhambra, near the Generalife Gardens.

By Bus: From the "Gran Vía Catedral" bus stop near the

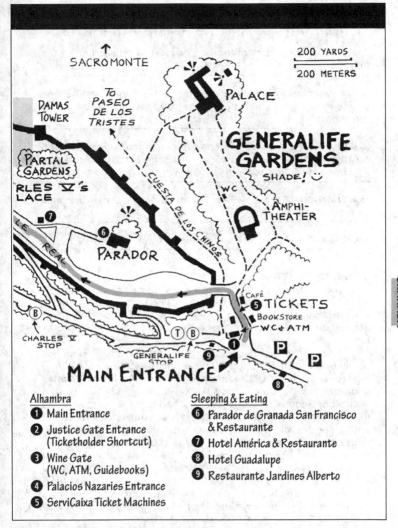

GRANADA

Alhambra
1. Main Entrance
2. Justice Gate Entrance (Ticketholder Shortcut)
3. Wine Gate (WC, ATM, Guidebooks)
4. Palacios Nazaries Entrance
5. ServiCaixa Ticket Machines

Sleeping & Eating
6. Parador de Granada San Francisco & Restaurante
7. Hotel América & Restaurante
8. Hotel Guadalupe
9. Restaurante Jardines Alberto

cathedral, catch a red #30 minibus, marked *Alhambra* (€1.20, runs every 10-15 minutes). There are three Alhambra stops (all shown on the map above): Justice Gate (best if you have a printed ticket—described later), Charles V, and Generalife (main ticket office and the gardens).

By Taxi: It's a €5 ride from the taxi stand on Plaza Nueva.

By Car: If you're coming from outside the city by car, you can drive to the Alhambra without passing through Granada's historic center. From the freeway, take the exit marked *Ronda Sur-Alhambra*. Signs will lead you to the Alhambra parking lot, conveniently

Planning Your Time at the Alhambra

The Alhambra consists of four sights clustered together atop a hill:

▲▲▲**Palacios Nazaries**—Exquisite Moorish palace, the one must-see sight. To see it during the day, advance reservations are a must.

▲▲**Charles V's Palace**—Christian Renaissance palace plopped on top of the Alhambra after the Reconquista, with the fine Alhambra Museum (free entry).

▲▲**Generalife Gardens**—Fancy, manicured gardens with small summer palace.

Alcazaba—Empty old fort with tower and views.

When to Go

Daytime tickets for Palacios Nazaries come stamped with a 30-minute time slot. Time your visit around that appointment, as your reservation is only good if you enter the palace within that 30-minute window. (Once inside the palace, you can linger as long as you like.)

How best to see the rest of the Alhambra complex depends on whether your Palacios Nazaries reservation is for a time before or after 14:00. If your entry time for Palacios Nazaries is before 14:00, you can visit the other Alhambra sights (the Alcazaba, Generalife Gardens, and Charles V's Palace) anytime in the morning, see Palacios Nazaries at your appointed time, and leave the Alhambra by 14:00 (although you can get away with staying longer in the fort, gardens, or Palacios Nazaries, you won't be allowed to *enter* any of these sites after 14:00). If your ticket is stamped for 14:00 or later, you cannot enter the Alhambra sights any earlier than 14:00. For instance, if you have a reservation to visit Palacios Nazaries at 16:30, you can enter the Alhambra sights any time after 14:00 and see the fort and Generalife Gardens before Palacios Nazaries.

Because of the time restriction on afternoon visits, morning tickets sell out the quickest. But for most travelers, an afternoon is ample time to see the site—the light is perfect, and there are fewer tour groups.

If you're picking up your tickets at the main entrance (at the top end), or just want to start with the gardens, be aware that you're a 15-minute walk away from Palacios Nazaries at the other end. Be sure to arrive at the Alhambra with enough time to make it to the palace before your allotted half-hour entry time slot ends. The ticket-checkers at Palacios Nazaries are strict.

Your Route

To minimize walking, see Charles V's Palace and the Alcazaba fort before your visit to Palacios Nazaries. When you finish touring the palace, you'll leave through the Partal Gardens, a pleasant 15-to-20-minute walk from the Generalife Gardens. Depending on the time, you can visit the Generalife Gardens before or after seeing Palacios Nazaries. If you have any time to kill before your palace appointment, do it luxuriously on the breezy view

terrace of the parador bar (actually within the Alhambra walls; for other options see "Eating," page 645). Drinks, WCs, and guidebooks are available at the Wine Gate, near the entrance of Palacios Nazaries, but not inside the palace.

The Alhambra by Moonlight

If you prefer doing things after dark, you can avoid the reservation hassle. Late-night visits to the Alhambra are easy (sepa-

rate nighttime tickets are sold for Palacio Nazaries and the Generalife Gardens; see "Cost," page 605)—just buy your ticket upon arrival, as night-visit tickets hardly ever sell out. Keep in mind that two separate tickets (Alcazaba and Generalife Gardens by day, Palacios Nazaries by night) cost the same as the Circular Azul ticket, and offer more flexibility, as you're not locked into the Circular Azul's next-morning stipulation.

You can't see the Alcazaba fort at night, but, hey, Palacios Nazaries provides 80 percent of the Alhambra's thrills anyway. Although a few small sections of both the palace and the gardens are closed at night, you'll see most of what the daytime visitors see. While some find the Alhambra disappointing at night, others find it even more magical (less crowded and beautifully lit); either way, it's better than not seeing it at all (for exact times see "Hours," page 607).

located near the entrance of the Alhambra (€2/hour). Overnight parking here is perfectly permissible (€19/24 hours, guarded at night). When you leave, be careful to go out the same way you came in, avoiding the driving ban in Granada's historic center.

Justice Gate Shortcut Entrance: If you already have your printed ticket in hand (i.e., you picked it up from a ServiCaixa machine in town), you can take a shortcut to the core of the complex by entering through the Justice Gate, downhill from the main entrance (if you're walking, this saves about 15 minutes of uphill climbing; you can also get off the minibus here). But if you want to go to the Generalife Gardens first, or don't yet have a ticket in hand, use the upper, main entrance.

Tours: Various companies run tours for about €44-50 that include transportation to the Alhambra and a guided tour of Palacios Nazaries (for example, GranaVisión has a tour for €44, tel. 958-535-872, www.granavision.com; Cicerone, listed on page 595, also has tours for €50).

Audioguides: The €6.50 "complete" audioguide brings the palace to life, with a quality description of 50 stops throughout the complex. The €4 "garden" audioguide covers just 15 stops, mostly outside the buildings (rent it at the entrance or at Charles V's Palace, leave €40 cash deposit or your ID—you'll need to return the audioguide where you picked it up). Audioguides are not available for night visits.

Guidebooks: Consider getting a guidebook in town and reading it the night before to understand the layout and history of this remarkable sight before entering. Official Alhambra bookstores (including the one in town, and those up at the grounds) push the €18 *Official Guide*, a well-produced, scholarly tome loaded with history, photos, maps, and practical information—but it weighs a ton. Other bookstores sell additional options. Of these, I enjoy the slick and colorful *Alhambra and Generalife in Focus* (€9); the thinner *The Alhambra and the Generalife* has less information and mostly photos (€8).

Photography: Photos with flash are allowed everywhere except in the Alhambra Museum.

Eating: Within the Alhambra walls, your food options are somewhat limited. Choose between the restaurant at the **parador** (*cafetería:* €9-13 sandwiches, €12-20 light meals; restaurant—get a table on the terrace: €10-15 starters, €18-27 main dishes, €34 fixed-price meal); the courtyard of the **Hotel América** (with pricey €15-20 meals but affordable €6 sandwiches and a great peaceful ambience, Sun-Fri 12:30-16:30, closed Sat); a small **bar-café kiosk** in front of the Alcazaba fort (€3 basic sandwiches and other snacks); and **vending machines** (at the WC) next to the Wine Gate, near Charles V's Palace. You're welcome to bring in a **picnic**

as long as you eat it in a public area.

For better-value (but touristy) options, head outside to the area around the parking lot and ticket booth at the top of the complex, where there's a strip of handy eateries. **Restaurante Jardines Alberto,** across from the breezy Restaurante La Mimbre, has a nice courtyard and offers a good value (€5 sandwiches, €8-12 salads, €12-22 main dishes, €14-17 fixed-price lunch, daily 9:00-23:00, until 20:00 off-season, Paseo de la Sabica 1, enter through street-level gift shop).

Nearby: If you're going to the Albayzín afterward, walk back into town along the **Cuesta de los Chinos.** (It starts near the ticket booth, by Restaurante La Mimbre and the minibus stop.) You'll walk on a desolate lane downhill along a stream, beneath the Alhambra ramparts, and past the sultan's cobbled horse lane leading up to Generalife Gardens. In 10 minutes you're back in town at Paseo de los Tristes, where you can stroll to Plaza Nueva or continue walking into the Albayzín district. Walking downhill on this trail from the Alhambra, you can't get lost.

⊖ Self-Guided Tour

I've listed these sights in the order you're likely to visit them. The first three sights cluster at the bottom/far end of the complex, while the Generalife Gardens are about a 15-minute walk away, at the top (main entrance). If you have a long time to wait for your Palacios Nazaries appointment, you could do the gardens first, then head down to the other three; otherwise it makes sense to start on the lower end of the hill and finish with the gardens.

▲▲Charles V's Palace and the Alhambra Museum

While it's only natural for a conquering king to build his own palace over his foe's palace, the Christian king Charles V (called

Carlos I in Spain) respected the splendid Moorish palace. And so, to make his mark, he built a modern Renaissance palace for official functions and used the existing Palacios Nazaries as a royal residence. With a unique circle-within-a-square design by Pedro Machuca, a pupil of Michelangelo, this is Spain's most impressive Renaissance building. Stand in the circular courtyard surrounded by mottled marble columns, then climb the stairs. Perhaps Charles' palace was designed to have a dome, but it was never finished—his son, Philip II, abandoned it to build his own, much more massive palace outside Madrid, El Escorial (the final and most austere example of

GRANADA

Spanish Renaissance architecture). Even without the dome, acoustics are perfect in the center—stand in the middle and sing your best aria. The palace doubles as one of the venues for the popular International Festival of Music and Dance.

The **Alhambra Museum** (Museo de la Alhambra, on the ground floor of Charles V's Palace), worth ▲, shows off some of the Alhambra's best surviving Moorish art. The museum's beautifully displayed and well-described artifacts—including tiles, pottery, pieces of fountains, and a beautiful carved-wood door—help humanize the Alhambra (free, Tue-Sun 8:30-14:00, closed Mon). The **Fine Arts Museum** (Museo de Bellas Artes, upstairs) is of little interest to most.

• *From the front of Charles V's Palace (as you face the Alcazaba fort), the entrance to Palacios Nazaries is to the right (look for the line snaking along the outside edge of the garden), while the Alcazaba is across a moat straight ahead (to get there, bear left through the keyhole-shaped Wine Gate—described in the sidebar on page 622—then hook right and walk up to the open area in front of the fort).*

Alcazaba

This fort—the original "red castle" ("Alhambra")—is the oldest and most ruined part of the complex, offering exercise and fine city views. What you see is from the mid-13th century, but there was probably a fort here in Roman times. Once upon a time, this tower defended a medina (town) of 2,000 Muslims living within the Alhambra walls. It's a huge, sprawling complex—wind your way through passages and court-

yards, over uneven terrain, to reach the biggest tower at the tip of the complex. Then climb stairs steeply up to the very top. From there (looking north), find Plaza Nueva and the San Nicolás viewpoint (in the Albayzín). To the south are the Sierra Nevada Mountains. Is anybody skiing today? Notice the tower's four flags: the blue of the European Union, the green and white of Andalucía, the red and yellow of Spain, and the red and green of Granada.

Speaking of flags, imagine that day in 1492 when the Christian cross and the flags of Aragon and Castile were raised on this tower, and (according to a probably fanciful legend) the fleeing Moorish king Boabdil (Abu Abdullah, in Arabic) looked back and wept. His mom chewed him out, saying, "You weep like a woman for what you couldn't defend like a man." With this defeat, more than seven centuries of Muslim rule in Spain came to an end. Much later, Napoleon stationed his troops at the Alhambra, contributing substantially to its ruin when he left.

• *If you're going from the Alcazaba to Palacios Nazaries, you'll have to backtrack through the Wine Gate, then look for the people lined up along the gardens in front of Charles V's Palace.*

▲▲▲Palacios Nazaries

During the 30-minute entry time slot stamped on your ticket, enter the jewel of the Alhambra: the Moorish royal palace. Once you're

in, you can relax—you're no longer under any time constraints. You'll walk through three basic sections: royal offices, ceremonial rooms, and private quarters. Built mostly in the 14th century, this palace offers your best possible look at the refined, elegant Moorish civilization of Al-Andalus (the Arabic word for the Moorish-controlled Iberian Peninsula).

You'll visit rooms decorated from top to bottom with carved wood ceilings, stucco "stalactites," ceramic tiles, molded-plaster walls, and filigree windows. Open-air courtyards feature fountains with bubbling water, which give the palace a desert-oasis feel. A garden enlivened by lush vegetation and peaceful pools is the Quran's symbol of heaven. The palace is well-preserved, but the trick to fully appreciating it is to imagine it furnished and filled with Moorish life...sultans with hookah pipes lounging on pillows upon Persian carpets, heavy curtains on the windows, and ivory-studded wooden furniture. The whole place was painted with bright colors, many suggested by the Quran—red (blood), blue (heaven), green (oasis), and gold (wealth). Throughout the palace, walls, ceilings, vases, carpets, and tiles were covered with decorative patterns, mostly poems and verses of praise from the Quran written in calligraphy and from local poets. Much of what is known about the Alhambra is known simply from reading the inscriptions that decorate its walls.

As you wander, keep the palace themes in mind: water, a near absence of figural images (forbidden by the Quran), "stalactite" ceilings—and few signs telling you where you are. As tempting as it might be to touch the stucco, don't—it is very susceptible to the oils from your hand. Use the map on the following page to locate the essential stops listed below.

• *Begin by walking through a few administrative rooms (the* mexuar*) with a stunning Mecca-oriented prayer room (the oratorio, with a niche on the right facing Mecca) and a small courtyard with a round fountain, until you hit the big rectangular courtyard with a fish pond lined by a myrtle-bush hedge.*

The Alhambra's Palacios Nazaries

CHARLES V APTS. &
WASH. IRVING ROOM

GRAND HALL
OF THE
AMBASSADORS →

VIEW OF
ALBAYZÍN

SHIP ROOM

PATIO
OF
LINDA-
RAJA

HALL
OF TWO
SISTERS

PARTAL
GARDENS

MEXUAR →

COURT-
YARD
OF THE
MYRTLES

TO GENERALIFE
GARDENS +
EXIT

WC

WALL

ENTER

COURTYARD
OF THE
LIONS

PARTAL
GARDENS

FIRST
TICKET
CHECKPOINT

ALHAMBRA MUSEUM

HALL OF
THE KINGS

SECRETS
ROOM

CHARLES
V's
PALACE

HALL OF THE
ABENCERRAJES

50 YARDS

50 METERS

DCH

VIEW

WALKING TOUR

1 Courtyard of the Myrtles
2 Ship Room
3 Grand Hall of the Ambassadors
4 Courtyard of the Lions
5 Hall of the Abencerrajes

6 Hall of the Kings (closed for restoration)
7 Hall of Two Sisters
8 Washington Irving Room
9 Hallway with a View
10 Partal Gardens

❶ Courtyard of the Myrtles (Patio de Arrayanes)

The standard palace design included a central courtyard like this. Moors loved their patios—with a garden and water, under the sky. In accordance with medi-eval Moorish mores, women rarely went out, so they stayed in touch with nature in court-yards like the Courtyard of the Myrtles—named for the two fra-grant myrtle hedges that added to the courtyard's charm. Notice the wooden screens (erected by

jealous husbands) that allowed the cloistered women to look out without being clearly seen. The upstairs was likely for winter use, and the cooler ground level was probably used in summer.

• *Head left from the entry through gigantic wooden doors into the long narrow antechamber to the throne room, called the...*

❷ Ship Room (Sala de la Barca)

It's understandable that many think the Ship Room is named for the upside-down-hull shape of its fine cedar ceiling. But the name is actually derived from the Arab word *baraka,* meaning "divine blessing and luck" (which was corrupted to *barca,* the Spanish word for "ship" or "boat"). As you passed through this room, blessings and luck are exactly what you'd need—because in the next room, you'd be face-to-face with the sultan.

• *Oh, it's your turn. Enter the ornate throne room.*

❸ Grand Hall of the Ambassadors (Gran Salón de los Embajadores)

The palace's largest room, the Gran Salón de los Embajadores (also known as the Salón de Comares), functioned as the throne room.

It was here that the sultan, seated on a throne opposite the entrance, received foreign emissaries. Ogle the room—a perfect cube—from top to bottom. The star-studded, domed wooden ceiling (made from 8,017 inlaid pieces like a giant jigsaw puzzle) suggests the complexity of Allah's infinite universe. Wooden "stalactites" form the cornice, running around the entire base of the ceiling. The stucco walls, even without their original paint and gilding, are still glorious. The filigree windows once held stained glass and had heavy drapes to block out the heat. Some precious 16th-century tiles survive in the center of the floor.

A visitor here would have stepped from the glaring Courtyard of the Myrtles into this dim, cool, incense-filled world, to meet the silhouetted sultan. Imagine the alcoves functioning busily as work stations, and the light at sunrise or sunset, rich and warm, filling the room.

Let your eyes trace the finely carved Arabic script. Muslims avoided making images of living creatures—that was God's work. But they could carve decorative religious messages. One phrase—"only Allah is victorious"—is repeated 9,000 times throughout the palace. Find the character for "Allah"—it looks like a cursive W with a nose on its left side. The swoopy toboggan blades underneath are a kind of artistic punctuation used to set off one phrase.

In 1492, two historic events likely took place in this room. Culminating a 700-year-long battle, the Reconquista was completed here as the last Moorish king, Boabdil, signed the terms of his surrender before eventually leaving for Africa.

And it was here that Columbus made one of his final pitches

GRANADA

Islamic Art

Rather than making paintings and statues, Islamic artists expressed themselves with beautiful but functional objects. Ceramics (most of them blue and white, or green and white), carpets, glazed tile panels, stucco-work ceilings, and glass tableware are covered with complex patterns. The intricate interweaving, repetition, and unending lines suggest the complex, infinite nature of God, known to Muslims as Allah.

You'll see only a few pictures of humans or animals, since Islamic doctrine is wary of any "graven images" or idols forbidden by God. However, secular art by Muslims for their homes and palaces was not bound by this restriction; you'll get an occasional glimpse of realistic art featuring men and women enjoying a garden paradise, a symbol of the Muslim heaven.

Look for floral patterns (twining vines, flowers, and arabesques) and geometric designs (stars and diamonds). The decorative motifs (Arabic script, patterns, flowers, shells, and so on) that repeat countless times throughout the palace were made by pressing wet plaster into molds. The most common pattern is calligraphy—elaborate lettering of an inscription in Arabic, the language of the Quran. A quote from the Quran on a vase or lamp combines the power of the message with the beauty of the calligraphy.

to Isabel and Ferdinand to finance a sea voyage to the Orient. Imagine the scene: The king, the queen, and the greatest minds from the University of Salamanca gathered here while Columbus produced maps and pie charts to make his case that he could sail west to reach the East. Ferdinand and the professors laughed and called Columbus mad—not because they thought the world was flat (most educated people knew otherwise), but because they thought Columbus had underestimated the size of the globe, and thus the length and cost of the journey.

But Isabel said, *"Sí, señor."* Columbus fell to his knees (promising to pack light, wear a money belt, and use the most current guidebook available).

Opposite the Ship Room entrance, photographers pause for a picture-perfect view of the tower reflected in the Courtyard of the Myrtles pool. This was the original palace entrance (before Charles V's Palace was built).

• *Continue deeper into the palace, to a courtyard where, 600 years ago, only the royal family and their servants could enter. It's the much-photographed...*

❹ Courtyard of the Lions (Patio de los Leones)

This delightful courtyard is named for the famous fountain ringed with 12 lions, marble originals from the 14th century. Why did

the architect choose 12? Since the fountain was a gift from a Jewish leader celebrating good relations with the sultan (Granada had a big Jewish community), the lions probably represent the 12 tribes of Israel. (Conquering Christians disassembled the fountain to see how it worked, rendering it nonfunctional until its 2012 restoration.) From the center, four streams went out—figuratively to the corners of the earth and literally to various more private apartments of the royal family. Notice how the court, with its 124 columns, resembles the cloister of a Catholic monastery. The craftsmanship is first-class. For example, the lead fittings between the precut sections of the columns allow things to flex during an earthquake, preventing destruction during shakes.

Six hundred years ago, the Muslim Moors could read the Quranic poetry that ornaments this court, and they could understand the symbolism of this lush, enclosed garden, considered the embodiment of paradise or truth. ("How beautiful is this garden / where the flowers of Earth rival the stars of Heaven. / What can compare with this alabaster fountain, gushing crystal-clear water? / Nothing except the fullest moon, pouring light from an unclouded sky.") Imagine—they appreciated this part of the palace even more than we do today.

• *On the right, off the courtyard, the only original door still in the palace leads into a square room called the...*

❺ Hall of the Abencerrajes (Sala de los Abencerrajes)

This was the sultan's living room, with an exquisite ceiling based on the eight-sided Muslim star. The room has a sad history. The father of Boabdil took a new wife and wanted to disinherit the children of his first marriage—one of whom was Boabdil. In order to deny power to Boabdil and his siblings, the sultan killed nearly all of the pre-Boabdil

Abencerraje family members. He thought this would pave the way for the son of his new wife to be the next sultan. He stacked 36 Abencerraje heads in the pool, under the sumptuous honeycombed stucco ceiling in this hall. But his scheme failed, and Boabdil ultimately assumed the throne. Bloody power struggles like this were the norm here in the Alhambra.

• *At the end of the court opposite where you entered is the...*

❻ Hall of the Kings (Sala de los Reyes)

This hall will most likely be closed for several years during restoration. If it were open, you'd see paintings on the goat-leather ceiling depicting scenes of the sultan and his family. The center room's group portrait shows the first 10 of the Alhambra's 22 sultans. The scene is a fantasy, since these people lived over a span of many generations. The two end rooms display scenes of princely pastimes, such as hunting and shooting skeet. In a palace otherwise devoid of figures, these offer a rare look at royal life in the palace.

• *Backtrack around the fountain. As you exit, you'll pass doors leading right and left to a 14th-century WC plumbed by running water and stairs up to the harem. Next is the...*

❼ Hall of Two Sisters (Sala de Dos Hermanas)

The Sala de Dos Hermanas—nicknamed for the giant twin slabs of white marble on the floor flanking the fountain—has another oh-wow stucco ceiling lit from below by clerestory window. This is a typical royal bedroom, with alcoves for private use and a fountain. Running water helped cool and humidify the room but also added elegance and extravagance, as running water was a luxury most could only dream of.

The room features geometric patterns and stylized Arabic script quoting verses from the Quran. If the inlaid color tiles look "Escher-esque," you've got it backward: Escher is Alhambra-esque. M. C. Escher was inspired by these very patterns on his visit. Study the patterns—they remind us of the Moorish expertise in math. The sitting room (farthest from the entry) has low windows, because Moorish people sat on the floor. Some rare stained glass survives in the ceiling. From here the sultana enjoyed a grand view of the medieval city (before the 16th-century wing was added, which blocks the view today).

• *That's about it for the palace. From here, we enter the later, 16th-century Christian section, and wander past the domed roofs of the old baths down a hallway to a pair of rooms decorated with a mahogany ceiling. Marked with a large plaque is the...*

❽ Washington Irving Room

Washington Irving wrote *Tales of the Alhambra* in this room. While living in Spain in 1829, Irving stayed in the Alhambra. It was a romantic time, when the palace was home to Gypsies and donkeys. His "tales" kindled interest in the Alhambra, causing it to become recognized as a national treasure. A plaque on the wall thanks Irving, who later served as the US ambassador to Spain (1842-1846). Here's a quote from Irving's *The Alhambra by Moonlight:* "On such heavenly nights I would sit for hours at my window inhaling the sweetness of the garden, and musing on the checkered fortunes of those whose history was dimly shadowed out in the elegant memorials around."

• *As you leave, stop at the open-air...*

❾ Hallway with a View

Here you'll enjoy the best-in-the-palace view of the labyrin-

thine Albayzín—the old Moorish town on the opposite hillside. Find the famous San Nicolás viewpoint (below where the white San Nicolás church tower breaks the horizon). Creeping into the mountains on the right are the Gypsy neighborhoods of Sacromonte. Still circling old Granada is the Moorish wall (built in the 1400s to protect the city's population, swollen by Muslim refugees

driven south by the Reconquista). For more on Albayzín sights, see page 630.

The Patio de Lindaraja (with its maze-like hedge pattern garden) marks the end of the palace visit. Before exiting, you can detour right into the adjacent "Secrets Room"—stark brick rooms of the former bath with fun acoustics. Whisper into a corner, and your friend—with an ear to the wall—can hear you in the opposite corner. Try talking in the exact center.

• *Step outside into our last stop...*

❿ The Partal Gardens (El Partal)

The Partal Gardens are built upon the ruins of the Partal Palace. Imagine a palace like the one you just toured, built around this reflecting pond. A fragment of it still stands—once the living quarters—on the cooler north side. The Alhambra was the site of seven different palaces in 150 years. You have toured parts of just two or three.

• *Leaving the palace, climb a few stairs, continue through the gardens, and follow signs directing you left to the Generalife Gardens or right to*

GRANADA

The Alhambra Grounds

As you wander the grounds, remember that the Alhambra was once a city of a thousand people fortified by a 1.5-mile rampart and 30 towers. The zone within the walls was the **medina,** a town with a general urban scene. As you stroll from the ticket booth down the garden-like Calle Real de la Alhambra to the palace, you're walking through the ruins of the medina (destroyed by the French in 1812). This path traces the wall, with its towers on your left. In the distance, notice the snow-

capped Sierra Nevada peaks—the highest mountains in Iberia. The Palacios Nazaries, Alcazaba fort, and Generalife Gardens all have entry fees and turnstiles. But the medina—with Charles V's Palace, a church, a line of shops showing off traditional wood-working techniques, and the fancy Alhambra parador—is wide open to anyone.

It's especially fun to snoop around the historic **Parador de Granada San Francisco,** which—as a national monument—is legally required to be open to the public. Once a Moorish palace within the Alhambra, it was later converted into a Franciscan monastery, with a historic claim to fame: Its church is where the Catholic Monarchs (Ferdinand and Isabel) chose to be

the Alcazaba (and the rest of the Alhambra grounds). If you're interested in poking around the Alhambra grounds, exit and do it now before entering the Generalife (because you can't easily backtrack into the Alhambra grounds after leaving the gardens).

When you're ready to go from the Partal Gardens to the Generalife Gardens, it's a delightful 15-minute stroll through lesser (but still pleasant) gardens, along a row of fortified towers—just follow signs for Generalife. Just before reaching Generalife, you'll cross over a bridge and look down on the dusty lane called Cuesta de los Chinos (a handy shortcut for returning to downtown later).

▲▲Generalife Gardens

If you have a long wait before your entry to Palacios Nazaries, tour these gardens first, then the Alcazaba fort and Charles V's Palace.

The sultan's vegetable and fruit orchards and summer garden retreat, called the Generalife (heh-neh-raw-LEE-fay), was outside the protection of the Alhambra wall—and, today, a short hike uphill past the ticket office. The thousand or so residents of the Alhambra enjoyed the fresh fruit and veggies grown here. But buried. For a peek, step in through the arch leading to a small garden area and reception. Enter to see the burial place, located in the open-air ruins of the church (just before the reception desk and the "guests-only-beyond-this-point" sign; the history is described in English). The slab on the ground near the altar—a surviving bit from the mosque that was here before the church—marks the place where the greatest king and queen of Spain were buried until 1521 (when they were moved to the Royal Chapel—described later). The next room is a delightful former cloister. Now a hotel, the parador has a restaurant and terrace café—with lush views of the Generalife—open to non-guests.

The medina's main road dead-ended at the **Wine Gate** (Puerta del Vino), which protected the fortress. When you pass through the Wine Gate, you enter a courtyard that was originally a moat, then a reservoir (in Christian times). The well—now encased in a bar-kiosk—is still a place for cold drinks. If you're done with your Alhambra visit, you can exit down to the city from the Wine Gate via the Justice Gate, immediately below.

most importantly, this little palace provided the sultan with a cool and quiet summer escape.

Follow the simple one-way path through the sprawling gardens (planted only in the 1930s—in Moorish times, there were no cypress topiaries here).

The sleek, modern theater has been renovated and continues to be an important concert venue for Granada. Its cypress-lined stage sees most activity during the International Festival of Music and Dance (described on page 594). Many of the world's greatest artists have performed here, including Arthur Rubenstein, Rudolf Nureyev, and Margot Fonteyn.

Head for the top of the theater, then walk through the manicured hedge gardens, along delightful ponds and fountains, to the palace.

At the small palace, pass through the dismounting room

(imagine dismounting onto the helpful stone ledge, and letting your horse drink from the trough here). Show your ticket and enter the most accurately re-created Arabian garden in Andalucía.

Here in the retreat of the Moorish kings, this garden is the closest thing on earth to the Quran's description of heaven. It was planted more than 600 years ago—that's remarkable longevity for a European garden. While there were originally only eight water jets, most of the details in today's garden closely match those lovingly described in old poems. The flowers, herbs, aromas, and water are exquisite...even for a sultan. Up the Darro River, the royal aqueduct diverted a life-giving stream of water into the Alhambra. It was channeled through this extra-long decorative fountain to irrigate the bigger garden outside, then along an aqueduct into the Alhambra for its thirsty residents. And though the splashing fountains are a delight, they are a 19th-century addition. The Moors liked a peaceful pond instead.

At the end of the pond, you enter the sultan's tiny three-room summer retreat.

From the end, climb 10 steps into the Christian Renaissance gardens (c. 1600). The ancient tree rising over the pond inspired Washington Irving, who wrote that this must be the "only surviving witness to the wonders of that age of Al-Andalus."

Climbing up and going through the turnstile, you enter the Romantic 19th-century garden. From here you have two options. If you're exhausted, just head to the right and follow *salida* signs toward the gardens' exit (next to the Alhambra's main entrance). But if you want a little more exercise (and views), turn left at the sign for *continuacion visita*, and take the half-mile loop up and around to see the staircase called Escalera del Agua, whose banisters double as little water canals. From the top, you'll have a chance to enter the "Romantic Viewpoint"—climb up the stairs for a top-floor view over the gardens (pleasant enough, but less impressive than other views at the Alhambra). Then hike back down through the garden and follow *salida* signs, through the long oleander trellis tunnel, to the exit. Remember: The most direct and scenic return to town is on the easily overlooked **Cuesta de los Chinos** pathway (described on page 613), which begins near the ticket booth.

Your visit to the Alhambra is complete, and you've earned your reward. "Surely Allah will make those who believe and do good deeds enter gardens beneath which rivers flow; they shall be adorned therein with bracelets of gold and pearls, and their garments therein shall be of silk" (Quran 22.23).

▲▲Royal Chapel (Capilla Real)

Without a doubt Granada's top Christian sight, this lavish chapel in the old town holds the dreams—and bodies—of Queen Isabel and King Ferdinand. The "Catholic Monarchs" were all about the Reconquista. Their marriage united the Aragon and Castile kingdoms, allowing an acceleration of the Christian and Spanish push south. In its last 10 years, the Reconquista snowballed. This last Moorish capital—symbolic of their victory—was their chosen burial place. While smaller and less architecturally striking than the cathedral (described later), the chapel is far more historically significant.

Cost and Hours: €4; March-Oct daily 10:15-13:30 & 16:00-19:30 except opens at 11:00 on Sun; Nov-Feb daily 10:15-13:30 & 15:30-18:30 except opens at 11:00 on Sun; no photos, entrance on Calle Oficios, just off Gran Vía del Colón—go through iron gate, tel. 958-227-848.

◆ Self-Guided Tour: In the lobby, before you show your ticket and enter the chapel, notice the **painting of Boabdil** (on the black horse) giving the key of Granada to the conquering King Ferdinand. Boabdil wanted to fall to his knees, but the Spanish king, who had great respect for his Moorish foe, embraced him instead. They fought a long and noble war (for instance, respectfully returning the bodies of dead soldiers). Ferdinand is in red, and Isabel is behind him wearing a crown. The painting is flanked high on the wall by portraits of Ferdinand and Isabel. Two small exhibits celebrate the 500th anniversaries of the death of Isabel in 2004 (with eight portraits) and of Philip the Fair (her son-in-law, a playboy who earned his nickname for his seductively good looks).

Isabel decided to make Granada the capital of Spain (and burial place for Spanish royalty) for three reasons: 1) With the conquest of this city, Christianity had finally overcome Islam in Europe; 2) her marriage with Ferdinand, followed by the conquest of Granada, had marked the beginning of a united Spain; and 3) in Granada, she agreed to sponsor Columbus.

Show your ticket and step into the **chapel.** It's Plateresque Gothic—light and lacy silver-filigree style, named for and inspired by the fine silverwork of the Moors. The chapel's interior was originally austere, with fancy touches added later by Ferdinand and Isabel's grandson Charles V. Five hundred years ago, this must have been the most splendid space imaginable. Because of its speedy completion (1506-1521), the Gothic architecture is unusually harmonious.

King Charles V thought it wasn't dazzling enough to honor his grandparents' importance, so he funded decorative touches like the screen and the Rogier van der Weyden painting *The Deposition* (left of the altar, one of five original versions he painted). Immediately to the right of that altar, with the hardest-working altar boys in Christendom holding up gilded Corinthian columns, is a chapel with a relic (an arm) of John the Baptist.

GRANADA

In the center of the chapel (in front of the main altar), the **four royal tombs** are Renaissance-style. Carved in Italy in 1521 out of Carrara marble, they were sent by ship to Spain. The faces—based on death masks—are considered accurate. If you're looking at the altar, **Ferdinand** and **Isabel** are on the right. (Isabel fans attribute the bigger dent she puts in the pillow to her larger brain.) Isabel's contemporaries described

the queen as being of medium height, with auburn hair and blue eyes, and possessing a serious, modest, and gentle personality. (Compare Ferdinand and Isabel's tomb statues with the painted and gilded wood statues of them kneeling in prayer, flanking the altarpiece.)

Philip the Fair and **Juana the Mad** (who succeeded Ferdinand and Isabel) lie on the left. Philip was so "Fair" that it drove the insanely jealous Juana "Mad." Philip died young, and for two years Juana kept his casket at her bedside, kissing his embalmed body good night. Philip and Juana's son, Charles V, was a key figure in European history, as his coronation merged the Holy Roman Empire (Philip the Fair's Habsburg domain) with Juana's Spanish empire. Europe's top king, Charles V ruled a vast empire stretching from Holland to Sicily, from Bohemia to Bolivia (1519-1556, see listing for his palace within the Alhambra on page 613).

When Philip II, the son of Charles V, decided to build El Escorial (his palace outside Madrid) and establish Madrid as the single capital of a single Spain, Granada lost power and importance. More importantly, Spain began to decline. After the reign of Charles V, Spain squandered her vast wealth trying to maintain this impossibly huge empire. The country's rulers did it not only for material riches, but to defend the romantic, quixotic dream of a Catholic empire—ruled by one divinely ordained Catholic monarch—against an irrepressible tide of nationalism and Protestantism that was sweeping across the vast Habsburg holdings in Central and Eastern Europe. Spain's relatively poor modern history can be blamed, in part, on its people's stubborn unwillingness to accept the end of this old-regime notion. Even Franco borrowed symbols from the Catholic Monarchs to legitimize his dictatorship and keep the 500-year-old legacy alive. Today's Spaniards reflect that the momentous marriage that created their country also sucked them into centuries of European squabbling, eventually leaving Spain impoverished.

Look at the intricate carving on the Renaissance tombs. It's a humanistic statement, with these healthy, organic, realistic figures rising out of the Gothic age.

From the feet of the marble tombs, step downstairs to see the actual **coffins.** They are plain. Ferdinand and Isabel were originally buried in the Franciscan monastery (in what is today the parador, up at the Alhambra). You're standing in front of the two people who created Spain. The fifth coffin (on right, marked *Principe Miguel*) belongs to a young Prince Michael, who would have been king of a united Spain and Portugal. (A sad—but too long—story...)

The **high altar** is one of the finest Renaissance works in Spain. It's dedicated to two Johns: the Baptist and the Evangelist. In the center you can see the Baptist and the Evangelist chatting as if over tapas—an appropriately humanistic scene. Scenes from the Baptist's life are on the left: John beheaded after Salomé's fine dancing, and (below) John baptizing Jesus. Scenes from the Evangelist's life are on the right: John's martyrdom (a failed attempt to boil him alive in oil), and, below, John on Patmos (where he may have written the last book of the Bible, Revelation). John is talking to the eagle that, according to tradition, flew him to heaven. A colorful series of reliefs at the bottom level recalls the Christian conquest of the Moors (left to right): Ferdinand, Boabdil with army and key to Alhambra, Moors expelled from Alhambra (right of altar table), conversion of Muslims by tonsured monks, and Ferdinand again.

A finely carved Plateresque arch, with the gilded royal initials *F* and *Y*, leads to a small glass pyramid in the **treasury.** This

holds Queen Isabel's silver crown ringed with pomegranates (symbolizing Granada), her scepter, and King Ferdinand's sword. Do a counterclockwise spin around the room to see it all, starting to the right of the entry arch. There you'll see the devout Isabel's prayer book, in which she followed the Mass. The book and its sturdy box date from 1496. According to legend, the fancy box on the other side of the door is supposedly the one that Isabel filled with jewels and gave to bankers as collateral for the cash to pay Columbus. In the corner (and also behind glass) is the ornate silver-and-gold cross that Cardinal Mendoza, staunch supporter of Queen Isabel, carried into the Alhambra on that historic day in 1492—and used as the centerpiece for the first Christian Mass in the conquered fortress. Next, the big silver-and-gold silk tapestry is the altar banner for the mobile campaign chapel of Ferdinand and Isabel, who always traveled with their army. In the case to its left, you'll see the

GRANADA

original Christian army flags raised over the Alhambra in 1492.

The next zone of this grand hall holds the first great art collection ever established by a woman. Queen Isabel amassed more than 200 important paintings. After Napoleon's visit, only 31 remained. Even so, this is an exquisite collection, all on wood, featuring works by Sandro Botticelli, Pietro Perugino, the Flemish master Hans Memling, and some less-famous Spanish masters.

Finally, at the end of the room, the two carved sculptures of Ferdinand and Isabel were the originals from the high altar. Charles V considered these primitive (I disagree) and replaced them with the ones you saw earlier.

To reach the cathedral (described next), exit the chapel behind Isabel, and walk around the block either way.

▲Cathedral

One of only two Renaissance churches in Spain (the other is in Córdoba), Granada's cathedral is the second-largest church in Spain after Sevilla's. While it was started as a Gothic church, it was built using Renaissance elements, and then decorated in Baroque style.

Cost and Hours: €4, audioguide-€2; April-Oct Mon-Sat 10:30-13:15 & 16:00-20:00, Sun 16:00-20:00; Nov-March until 19:00; last entrance 15 minutes before closing, tel. 958-222-959.

⊘ **Self-Guided Tour:** Enter the church from Plaza de las Pasiegas. Stand in the back of the nave for an overview.

From the back, survey the church. It's huge. It was designed to be the national church when Granada was the capital of a newly reconquered-from-the-Muslims Spain. High above the main altar are square niches originally intended for the burial of Charles V and his family. But King Philip II changed focus and abandoned Granada for El Escorial, so the niches are now plugged with paintings, including seven from the life of Mary by hometown great Alonso Cano.

The cathedral's cool, spacious, bright interior is mostly Baroque—a refreshing break from the dark Gothic of so many Spanish churches. In a move that was modern back in the 18th century, the walls of the choir (the big, heavy wooden box that dominates the center of most Spanish churches) were taken out so that people could be involved in the worship. (Back when a choir clogged the middle of the church, regular people only heard the Mass.) At about the same time, a bishop ordered the interior painted with lime (for hygienic reasons, during a time of disease).

The people liked it, and it stayed white.

Notice that the two rear chapels (on right and left) are Neoclassical in style—a reminder that the church took 300 years to finish.

As you explore, remember that the abundance of Marys is all part of the Counter-Reformation. Most of the side chapels are decorated in Baroque style. On the outer wall, directly to the right of the high altar, is a politically incorrect version of St. James the Moor-Slayer, with his sword raised high and an armored Moor trampled under his horse's hooves.

Now, walk to the front for a closer look at the altar. You pass a fine organ with horizontal trumpet pipes, unique to Spain.

Standing before the altar, notice the abundance of gold leaf. It's from the local Dorro River, which originally attracted Romans here for its gold. As this is a seat of the local bishop, there's a fine wooden bishop's throne on the right.

Between the fine Corinthian columns flanking the altar are paintings with a strong parenting theme: In the round tondo frames are Adam and Eve, from whom came mankind. Around them are the four evangelists, who—with the New Testament—brought the Good News of salvation to believers (not Jews or Muslims). Completing the big parenting picture are Ferdinand and Isabel, who brought Catholicism to the land. Their complex coat of arms celebrates how their marriage united kingdoms to essentially create the European country with the oldest border. When Reconquista forces finally won Granada in 1492, the puzzle was complete.

To your right is the ornate carved stone Gothic door to the Royal Chapel (described earlier), with a 15th-century facade that predates the cathedral. The chapel holds the most important historic relics in town—the tombs of the Catholic Monarchs. And, because the chapel and cathedral are run by two different religious orders, this door is always closed and there are separate admission fees for each.

Strolling behind the altar, look for the giant music sheets: They're mostly 16th-century Gregorian chants. Notice the sliding C clef. Rather than a fixed G or F clef, the monks knew that this clef—which could be located wherever worked best on the staff—marked middle C, and they chanted to notes relative to that. Go ahead—try singing a few verses of the Latin.

The cathedral's little museum is tucked away back near the cathedral's entrance, filling the ground floor of the big bell tower. In it, it's worth seeking out a beautiful bust of San Pablo (Paul, with a flowing beard)—a self-portrait by Cano.

The sacristy (near the exit and the St. James altarpiece, in the right corner) is worth a look. It's lush and wide-open; its gilded ceilings, mirrors, and wooden cabinets give it a light, airy feel. Two grandfather clocks made in London (one with Asian motifs) ensured that everyone got dressed on time. The highlight of this room: Cano's small, delicate painted wood statue of the *Immaculate Conception*.

Immediately in front of the cathedral is the stop for minibus #30 to the Alhambra. And four blocks away (if you head left up the busy street, then turn right) is the Albayzín.

Near Plaza Nueva
Hammam Baños Árabes (Arab Baths)

For an intimate and subdued experience, consider some serious relaxation at the Arab Baths, where you can enjoy the three different-temperature pools and a steam room. A maximum of 35 people are allowed in the baths at one time.

Cost and Hours: If you just want a 90-minute soak in the baths, the cost is €24; it costs more to add a 15-minute massage: a regular massage is €36, a traditional scrubbing massage is €43, and to have both costs €55. Open daily 10:00-24:00, appointments scheduled every even-numbered hour, coed with mandatory swimsuits, quiet atmosphere encouraged, free lockers and towels available, no loaner swimsuits but you can buy one for €12, just off Plaza Nueva—follow signs a few doors down from the TI to Santa Ana 16, 50 percent paid reservation required, tel. 958-229-978, www.hammamalandalus.com.

▲The Albayzín

Explore Spain's best old Moorish quarter, with countless color-ful corners, flowery patios, and shady lanes. While the city center of Granada—which is pleasant enough—feels more or less like many other Spanish cities, the Albayzín is unique. You can't say you've really seen Granada until you've at least strolled a few of its twisty lanes. Climb high to the San Nicolás church for the best view of the Alhambra.  Then wander through the mysterious back streets. (I've listed these sights roughly in order from the San Nicolás viewpoint.)

Getting to the Albayzín: City **minibus** #31 threads its way around the Albayzín from Plaza Nueva (see "Albayzín Circular Bus Tour," next), getting you scenically and sweatlessly to the San Nicolás viewpoint. You can also **taxi** to the San Nicolás church and explore from there. (Consider having your cabbie take you

GRANADA

Albayzín Neighborhood

NOTE: NOT TO SCALE
20 MIN. UPHILL WALK FROM PLAZA NUEVA TO SAN NICOLÁS

STREET WIDTH IS EXAGGERATED FOR CLARITY

VIEW

1. Hotel Santa Isabel la Real
2. El Numero 8 "Casa de Rafa" (Apts.)
3. Makuto Guesthouse
4. Plaza S. Miguel el Bajo Eateries
5. Casa Torcuato
6. Restaurante El Ladrillo
7. Rests. Estrellas de S. Nicolás & El Huerto de Juan Ranas; Great Mosque of Granada
8. Bar Kiki
9. Carmen Mirador de Aixa & Carmen de las Tomasas Rests.
10. Carmen de Aben Humeya Rest.
11. Placeta de San Gregorio Bars
12. Paseo de los Tristes Bars
13. Carmen de la Media Luna (Landmark)
14. Hammam El Bañuelo (Moorish Baths)
15. Hammam Baños Árabes (Arab Baths)
16. To Cave Museum of Sacromonte, Roma Caves & Zambra Dance Clubs

GRANADA

Safety in the Albayzín

With tough economic times, young ruffians are hanging out in the dark back lanes of the labyrinthine Albayzín quarter. While this charming Moorish district is certainly safe by day, it can be edgy after dark. Most of the area is fine to wander, though many streets are poorly lit, and the maze of lanes can make it easy to get lost and wind up somewhere you don't want to be. Some nervous travelers choose to avoid the neighborhood entirely after dark, but I recommend venturing into the Albayzín to enjoy its restaurants, ideal sunset views, and charming ambience. Just be sure to exer-  cise normal precautions: Leave your valu- ables at your hotel, stick to better-lit streets, and take a minibus or taxi home if you're unsure of your route. Violent crime is rare, but pickpocketing is common. Keep a very close eye on your stuff. Some visitors mistakenly think that the danger in this historic "Moorish" district is from Arabs, but the real crooks can be Northern and Eastern European hippies loitering in the squares.

Locals say the biggest hazard when walking in the Albayzín are the many deposits left by its four-legged inhabit- ants (and not cleaned up by their poorly trained owners). If you bury your nose in a guidebook while you walk, you'll likely wind up burying your shoe in something else.

on a detour to the Sacromonte enclave of cave-dwelling Gypsies, described later.)

It's a steep but fascinating 20-minute **walk** up: Leave the west end of Plaza Nueva on Calle de Elvira. After about 50 yards, at the pharmacy and newsstand, bear right on Calle Calderería Vieja. Follow this stepped street past Moroccan eateries and pastry shops, vendors of imported North African goods, halal butchers, and *teterías* (Moorish tea rooms). The lane bears right, then passes to the left of the church (becoming Cuesta de San Gregorio), and slants, winds, and zigzags uphill. Cuesta de San Gregorio eventually curves left and is regularly signposted. When you reach the Moorish-style house, La Media Luna (with the tall trees and keyhole-style doorway), stop for a photo and a breather, then follow the wall, continuing uphill. At the next intersection (with the black cats), turn right on Aljibe del Gato. Farther on, this street takes a 90-degree turn to the right; at this point, turn left onto Calle Atarasana Vieja. It's confusing, but keep going up, up, up. At the crest (and the dead-end), turn right on Camino Nuevo de San Nicolás, then walk 200 yards to the street that curves up left (look for a bus-stop sign—this is where the minibus would have dropped you off). Continue up the curve, and soon you'll see feet hanging from the plaza wall. Steps lead up to the church's viewpoint. Whew! You made it!

Albayzín Circular Bus Tour

The handy Albayzín minibus #31 makes a 20-minute loop through the quarter, departing from Plaza Nueva about every 15 minutes (pay driver €1.20). While good for a lift to the top of the Albayzín (buzz when you want to get off), I'd stay on for an entire circle and return to the Albayzín later for dinner—either on foot or by bus again. (Note: The less frequent minibus #35, departing every 30-40 minutes, does nearly the same trip with a side-trip up into Sacromonte.)

Here's the route: The minibus leaves Plaza Nueva and heads down the city's main drag, Gran Vía del Colón, turning right at the Gardens of the Triumph, which celebrate the Immaculate Conception of the Virgin Mary (notice her statue atop a column). Just above the gardens is the old Royal Hospital—built in the 16th century for Granada's poor by the Catholic kings. (After the Reconquista, they hoped to win the favor of the city's conquered residents.) Then the bus ascends, giving you a commanding view of Granada on the right. Turning downhill, the bus plunges into the thick of the Albayzín, with stops below the San Nicolás church (famous viewpoint, and the jumping-off point for my "Exploring the Albayzín" stroll, described later; the driver generally calls out this stop for tourists) and at Plaza San Miguel el Bajo (cute square with recommended eateries and another viewpoint). From here, you can ride back through the Gran Vía to Plaza Nueva.

▲▲San Nicolás Viewpoint (Mirador de San Nicolás)

For one of Europe's most romantic viewpoints, be here at sunset, when the Alhambra glows red and the Albayzín widows share

the benches with local lovers, hippies, and tourists (free, always open). In 1997, President Clinton made a point to bring his family here—a favorite spot from a trip he made as a student. But this was hardly an original idea; generations of visitors have been drawn here. For an affordable (€3-6) drink with the same million-euro view, step into the El Huerto de Juan Ranas Bar (just below and to the left, at Calle de Atarazana 8). Enjoy the Roma (Gypsy) musicians who perform here for tips. Order a drink, tip them, settle in, and consider it a concert.

Great Mosque of Granada

Granada's Muslim population is on the rebound, and now numbers 8 percent of the city's residents. A striking and inviting mosque is just next to the San Nicolás viewpoint (to your left as you face the Alhambra). Local Muslims write, "The Great Mosque of Granada signals, after a hiatus of 500 years, the restoration of a missing link with a rich and fecund Islamic contribution to all spheres of human enterprise and activity." Built in 2003 (with  money from the local community and Islamic Arab nations), it has a peaceful view courtyard and a minaret that comes with a live call to prayer five times a day (printed schedule inside). It's stirring to see the muezzin holler "God is Great" from the minaret without amplification (locals didn't want it amplified). Visitors are welcome in the courtyard, which offers Alhambra views without the hedonistic ambience of the more famous San Nicolás viewpoint.

Cost and Hours: Free, daily 11:00-14:00 & 18:00-21:00, shorter hours in winter, tel. 958-202-526, www.mezquitadegranada.com.

Background: While tourists come to Granada to learn about the expulsion of the Moors in 1492, local Muslims are frustrated by what a flier at the mosque calls the "errors, nonsense, and lies local guides perpetuate without knowledge nor shame which flocks of passive tourists accept without questioning." The flier tries to set the record straight, from the Muslim perspective: Muslims were as indigenous as any other group. After living here for seven centuries, the Muslims of Granada and Andalucía were as Iberian as the modern Spaniards of today. Islam is not a religion of immigrants; Islam is not a culture of the Orient and Arabs. "Muslim" and "Arab" are not interchangeable terms. The Muslims of Al-Andalus were not hedonistic. The Reconquista did not "liberate" Spain. Harems were not just full of sexy women. (For more on the Muslim perspective, visit the info desk at the mosque.)

To Muslims, the city is a symbol of the "holocaust" of the Reconquista, when 135,000 of their people were brutally expelled and many more suffered "forced conversion" in the 16th century. Today there are about 1 million Muslims in Spain (and about 5 million in France).

Exploring the Albayzín

From the San Nicolás viewpoint and the Great Mosque, you're at the edge of a hilltop neighborhood even the people of Granada recognize as a world apart. Each of the district's 20 churches sits on a spot once occupied by a mosque. When the Reconquista arrived in Granada, the Christians attempted to coexist with the Muslims. But after seven years, this idealistic attempt ended in failure, and the Christians forced the Muslims to convert. In 1567, Muslims were expelled, leading to 200 years of economic depression for the city. Eventually, large walled noble manor houses with private gardens were built here in the depopulated Albayzín. These survive today in the form of the characteristic *carmen* restaurants so popular with visitors.

From the San Nicolás viewpoint, turn your back to the Alhambra and walk north (passing the church on your right and the Biblioteca Municipal on your left). A lane leads past a white stone arch (on your right)—now a chapel built into the old Moorish wall. You're walking past the scant remains of the pre-Alhambra fortress of Granada. At the end of the lane, step down to the right through the 11th-century "New Gate" (Puerta Nueva—older than the Alhambra) and into **Plaza Larga.** In medieval times, this tiny square (called "long," because back then it was) served as the local marketplace. It still is a busy market each morning. Casa Pasteles, at the near end of the square, serves good coffee and cakes.

Leave Plaza Larga on **Calle Agua de Albayzín** (as you face Casa Pasteles, it's to your right). The street, named for the public baths that used to line it, shows evidence of the Moorish plumbing system: gutters. Back when Europe's streets were filled with muck, Granada actually had Roman Empire-style gutters with drains leading to clay and lead pipes.

You're in the heart of the Albayzín. Explore. Poke into an old church. They're plain by design to go easy on the Muslim converts, who weren't used to being surrounded by images as they worshipped. You'll see lots of real Muslim culture living in the streets, including many recent Spanish converts. When you are finished exploring, find your way back to the San Nicolás viewpoint, where you can catch minibus #31 or #35 (just below the viewpoint) back into town. Or it's a pleasant downhill walk, following San Gregorio back to Plaza Nueva.

Sacromonte

The Sacromonte district is home to Granada's thriving Roma community. Marking the entrance to Sacromonte is a statue of Chorrohumo (literally, "exudes smoke," and a play on the slang word for "thief": *chorro*). He was a Roma from Granada, popular in the 1950s for guiding people around the city.

While the neighboring Albayzín is a sprawling zone blanketing a hilltop, Sacromonte is much smaller—very compact and very steep. Most houses are burrowed into the wall of a cliff.

Sacromonte has one main street: Camino del Sacromonte, which is lined with caves primed for tourists and restaurants ready to fight over the bill. (Don't come here expecting to get a deal on anything.) Intriguing lanes run above and below this main drag—a steep hike above Camino del Sacromonte is the cliff-hanging, parallel secondary street, Vereda de Enmedio, which is less touristy, with an authentically residential vibe.

Cave Museum of Sacromonte (Museo Cuevas del Sacromonte)

This hilltop complex, also known as the Center for the Interpretation of Sacromonte (Centro de Interpretación del

Sacromonte), is a kind of open-air folk museum about Granada's unique Roma cave-dwelling tradition (though it doesn't have much on the people themselves). The exhibits, with good English descriptions, are spread through a series of whitewashed caves along a ridge, with spectacular views to the Alhambra. As you stroll from cave to cave, you'll learn about the local geology (rocks, flora, and fauna); crafts (basket-weaving, pottery-making, metalworking, and weaving); and lifestyles (including a look into a typical home and kitchen). There's also an exhibit about other cave-dwelling cultures from around the "troglodyte world," and one about Sacromonte's vital role in the development of Granada's local brand of flamenco. As you wander, imagine this in the 1950s, when it was still a bustling community of Roma cave-dwellers. Today, hippies squat in abandoned caves higher up.

Cost and Hours: €5, mid-March-mid-Oct daily 10:00-20:00, until 18:00 in winter, Barranco de los Negros, tel. 958-215-120, www.sacromontegranada.com.

Getting There: You can ride minibus #35 from Plaza Nueva (ask driver, "¿Museo Cuevas?," departs only every 30-40 minutes) or a taxi. You'll get off at the "Sacromonte 2" bus stop, next to the Venta El Gallo restaurant, at the bottom of the hill along the main road. From there, it's a very steep 10-minute hike past cave dwellings up to the top of the hill—follow the signs. If you don't want to wait for minibus #35, you can ride #31 to near the entrance of Sacromonte, and walk from there—giving you a good look at the whole area.

Performances: In summer (July-Aug), the center also features flamenco shows and classical guitar concerts in its wonderfully scenic setting (prices and schedules vary—see website above for details).

Granada's Roma (Gypsies)

Both the English word "Gypsy" and its Spanish counterpart, *gitano,* come from the word "Egypt"—where Europeans once believed these nomadic people had originated. Today the preferred term is "Roma," since "Gypsy" has acquired negative connotations (though for clarity's sake, I've used both terms throughout this book).

After migrating from India in the 14th century, the Roma people settled mostly in the Muslim-occupied lands in southern Europe (such as the Balkan Peninsula, then controlled by the Ottoman Turks). Under medieval Muslims, the Roma enjoyed relative tolerance. They were traditionally good with crafts and animals.

The first Roma arrived in Granada in the 15th century—and they've remained tight-knit ever since. Today 50,000 Roma call Granada home, many of them in the district called Sacromonte. In most of Spain, Roma are more assimilated into the general population, but Sacromonte is a large, distinct Roma community. (After the difficult Spanish Civil War era, they were joined by many farmers who, like the Roma, appreciated Sacromonte's affordable, practical cave dwellings—warm in the winter and cool in the summer.)

Spaniards, who generally consider themselves to be tolerant and not racist, claim that in maintaining such a tight community, the Roma segregate themselves. The Roma call Spaniards *payos* ("whites"). Recent mixing of Roma and *payos* has given birth to the term *gallipavo* (rooster-duck), although who's who depends upon whom you ask.

Are Roma thieves? Sure, some of them are. But others are honest citizens, trying to make their way in the world just like anyone else. Because of the high incidence of theft, it's wise to be cautious when dealing with a Roma person—but it's also important to keep an open mind.

Zambra Dance

A long flamenco tradition exists in Granada, and the Roma of Sacromonte are credited with developing this city's unique flavor of this Andalusian art form. Sacromonte is a good place to see *zambra*, a flamenco variation with a more Oriental feel in which the singer also dances. A half-dozen cave-bars offering *zambra* in the evenings line Sacromonte's main drag. Hotels are happy to book you a seat and arrange the included transfer. Two well-established venues are **Zambra Cueva de la Rocío** (€30, includes a drink and bus ride from and back to hotel, €25 without transport, daily show at 22:00, 1 hour, Camino del Sacromonte 70, tel. 958-227-129) and **María la Canastera** (€26, includes drink and bus from hotel, €20 without transport, daily show at 22:00, 1 hour,

Camino del Sacromonte 89, tel. 958-121-183, www.granadainfo .com/canastera). The biggest operation here is the restaurant **Venta El Gallo,** which has performances of more straightforward flamenco (not specifically *zambra*, €30 with bus from hotel, €25 without transport, daily shows at 21:15 and 22:45, Barranco los Negros 5, tel. 958-228-476). Or consider the summer performances at the **Cave Museum** (explained earlier). A final option for the more adventurous: Just go and explore late at night on your own (with no wallet and €30 in your pocket).

Enjoying the Paseo without the Tourists

While the old town is great for strolling, it's also fun to leave the aura of the Alhambra and just be in workaday Granada with everyday locals. A five-minute walk from Plaza Nueva gets you into a delightful and untouristy urban slice of Andalucía. Carrera de la Virgen is the town's mini-Ramblas. (From the old center, walk south down Calle Reyes Católicos to Puerta Real de España, and take a left.) It leads gracefully down to the Paseo del Salón riverbank park, great for making the local scene. Carrera de la Virgen also happens to pass the huge and practical El Corte Inglés department store (Mon-Sat 10:00-22:00, closed Sun).

Near Granada
Carthusian Monastery (La Cartuja)

A church with an interior that looks as if it squirted out of a can of whipped cream, La Cartuja is nicknamed the "Christian Alhambra" for its elaborate white Baroque stucco work. In the rooms just off the cloister, notice the gruesome paintings of martyrs placidly meeting their grisly fates.

Cost and Hours: €4, daily April-Oct 10:00-13:00 & 16:00-20:00, Nov-March 10:00-13:00 & 15:00-18:00, catch bus #8 from Gran Vía del Colón, tel. 958-161-932. The monastery is a mile north of town on the way to Madrid; drivers take the *Méndez Núñez* exit from the A-44 expressway and follow signs.

Sleeping in Granada

In July and August, when Granada's streets are littered with sunstroke victims, rooms are plentiful and prices soft. In the crowded months of April, May, September, and October, prices can spike up 20 percent. (If you see a price range below, it indicates low- to high-season rates—though I've excluded Holy Week and other inflated prices.) Except for the hotels in the Albayzín and near the Alhambra, most of my listings are within a 5-to-10-minute walk of Plaza Nueva (see map on page 641).

If you're traveling by car, you're free to drive into the prohibited

Sleep Code

(€1 = about $1.30, country code: 34)
S = Single, **D** = Double/Twin, **T** = Triple, **Q** = Quad, **b** = bathroom, **s** = shower only. Unless otherwise noted, credit cards are accepted and English is spoken. Some hotels include the 10 percent IVA tax in the room price; others tack it onto your bill. Breakfast is not included unless specified.

To help you easily sort through these listings, I've divided the accommodations into three categories based on the price for a standard double room with bath during high season:

$$$ Higher Priced—Most rooms €110 or more.
  $$ Moderately Priced—Most rooms between €60-110.
    $ Lower Priced—Most rooms €60 or less.

Prices can change without notice; verify the hotel's current rates online or by email. For the best prices, always book direct.

GRANADA

center zone, but be sure your hotel registers you immediately with the traffic police (see "Arrival in Granada" on page 592).

On or near Plaza Nueva

Each of these (except the hostel) is big, professional, plenty comfortable, and perfectly located. Prices vary with demand.

$$$ Hotel Casa 1800 Granada, with 25 rooms around a beautiful, airy old courtyard in the lower part of the Albayzín (just steps above the Paseo de los Tristes), sets the bar for affordable class. It's tidy and well-run, and offers special extras, such as a complimentary tea and coffee bar each afternoon (standard Db-€155, pricier "superior" and "deluxe" rooms available but not much different, big buffet breakfast-€9.50, air-con, elevator, free Wi-Fi, Benalúa 11, tel. 958-210-700, www.hotelcasa1800granada.com, info@hotel casa1800granada.com).

$$$ Hotel Maciá Plaza, right on the colorful Plaza Nueva, has 44 smallish, clean, modern, and classy rooms. Choose between an on-the-square view or a quieter interior room (Sb-€60-80, Db-€140, square view-€20 extra, extra bed-€25, 15 percent discount in 2014 when you book direct by email and show this book at check-in, buffet breakfast-€8.50, air-con, elevator, free Wi-Fi, Plaza Nueva 5, tel. 958-227-536, www.maciahoteles.com, maciaplaza@maciahoteles.com).

$$ Casa del Capitel Nazarí, just off the church end of Plaza Nueva, is a restored 16th-century Renaissance palace transformed into 18 small but tastefully decorated rooms, all facing a courtyard that hosts changing art exhibits. Insomniacs have a choice of five different pillows (Sb-€80-103, Db-€109-129, extra bed-€36, apartments available, 5 percent discount in 2014 when you book direct and show this book at check-in, breakfast-€10, includes afternoon tea/coffee, air-con, free guest computer, free Wi-Fi, parking-€19.50/day, Cuesta Aceituneros 6, tel. 958-215-260, www.hotelcasacapitel.com, info@hotelcasacapitel.com).

$$ Hotel Anacapri is a bright, cool marble oasis with 49 modern rooms and a quiet lounge (Sb-€59-80, Db-€79-110, Tb-€95-125, extra bed-€22, includes breakfast with direct bookings in 2014 except with promotional rates, air-con, elevator, free guest computer, free Wi-Fi in lobby with this book, parking-€15/day, 2 blocks toward Gran Vía from Plaza Nueva at Calle Joaquín Costa 7, just a block from cathedral bus stop, tel. 958-227-477, www.hotelanacapri.com, reservas@hotelanacapri.com, helpful Kathy speaks Iowan).

$$ NH Hotel Inglaterra is a modern and peaceful chain hotel, with 36 rooms offering all the comforts (Db-€70-120, extra bed-€20-30, buffet breakfast-€13, air-con, elevator to third floor only, free Wi-Fi in lobby, parking-€16/day, Cetti Merien 6, tel. 958-221-559, www.nh-hotels.com, nhinglaterra@nh-hotels.com).

$ Oasis Hostel Granada offers 90 beds in 10 coed rooms and lots of backpacker bonding, just a block above the lively Moorish-flavored tourist drag (4-10 bunks per room, €16-21 per person; includes sheets and 2-for-1 welcome drink; free guest computer, free Wi-Fi, shared kitchen, laundry service-€7, Placeta Correo Viejo 3, tel. 958-215-848, www.hostelsoasis.com, oasisgranada@gmail.com).

Cheap Sleeps on Cuesta de Gomérez

These are inexpensive and ramshackle lodgings on this street leading from Plaza Nueva up to the Alhambra.

$$ Hotel Puerta de las Granadas has 16 rooms with a sterile business-class vibe, an inviting cafeteria courtyard, and a handy location (basic patio-view Db-€59-89, €5-10 more for street view, €15 more for cathedral view, €25 more for Alhambra view, book direct and ask for 10 percent Rick Steves discount, breakfast-€8 or included during slow times, air-con, elevator, free guest computer, free Wi-Fi, free tea and coffee in cafeteria all day, Cuesta de Gomérez 14, tel. 958-216-230, www.hotelpuertadelasgranadas.com, reservas@hotelpuertadelasgranadas.com).

$ Pensión Landazuri is run by friendly English-speaking Matilde Landazuri, her son Manolo, and daughters Margarita and Elisa. Their characteristic old house has 18 rooms—some are well-worn, while others are renovated. It boasts hardworking, helpful management and a great roof garden with an Alhambra view

Granada Hotels & Restaurants

TO
TRAIN & BUS
STATIONS

ALBAYZÍN
MOORISH QUARTER

MERCADO
SAN
AGUSTÍN

TO
SAN NICOLÁS
VIEWPOINT &
PLAZA LARGA

CATHEDRAL
& Royal Chapel

TO
SACRA-
MONTE

GRAN VÍA DE COLÓN

CALLE
DE VAL.

CALD. NUEVA
S. GREGORIO
CARCEL ALTA

AIRE

DARRO

PLAZA NUEVA

PL.
S.
ANA

PLAZA
DE BIB-
RAMBLA

OFICIOS

ERMITA
ZACATÍN

PLAZA
ISABEL
LA
CATÓLICA

CALLE REYES CATÓLICOS

PLAZA DEL
CARMEN

PAVANERAS

ÁNIMAS

CUESTA DE GOMÉREZ

HAMMAM
BAÑOS
ÁRABES

TO
ALHAMBRA

PUERTA
REAL

CALLE NAVAS

CALLE SAN MATÍAS

VIRGEN ROSARIO

PLAZA
MARIANA
PINEDA

TO

DCH

100 YARDS
100 METERS

Ⓑ BUS STOP w/#s
#30 TO ALHAMBRA
#31 & #35 TO
ALBAYZÍN

Ⓟ PARKING

① Hotel Casa 1800 Granada
② Hotel Maciá Plaza
③ Casa del Capitel Nazarí
④ Hotel Anacapri
⑤ NH Hotel Inglaterra
⑥ Oasis Hostel Granada
⑦ Hotel Puerta de las Granadas
⑧ Pensión Landazuri
⑨ Pensión Al Fin
⑩ Hostal Navarro Ramos
⑪ Pensión Austria
⑫ Hotel Los Tilos

⑬ To Hotel Reina Cristina, Hostals
Lima & Rodri; Zurita Pensión
⑭ Bodegas Castañeda
⑮ Restaurante Sevilla
⑯ La Cueva de 1900
⑰ Arrayanes Restaurante
⑱ Los Diamantes
⑲ Greens and Berries
⑳ Calle Calderería Nueva Tea Shops
㉑ To Taberna La Tana & Bar Los
Diamentes II
㉒ Café Futbol
㉓ Los Italianos Ice Cream
㉔ Mercado San Agustín
㉕ Pescadería Market Stalls

GRANADA

(S-€29, Sb-€39, D-€39, Db-€49, Tb-€69, Qb-€79, eggs-and-bacon breakfast-€3.50, free Wi-Fi, parking-€12/day, Cuesta de Gómérez 24, tel. 958-221-406, www.hostallandazuri.com, info@hostal landazuri.com). The Landazuris also run a good, cheap café.

$ Pensión Al Fin is located just up the street from Pensión Landazuri and run by the same family. Its five rooms feature antique wooden beams and marble columns with sultry, Moorish-style decor. A glass floor in the lobby lets you peer into a well from an ancient house (Db-€49, Tb-€69, some with balconies, breakfast-€3.50, Wi-Fi, parking-€12/day, reception at Pensión Landazuri, Cuesta de Gomérez 31, tel. 958-228-172, www .pensionalfin.com, info@pensionalfin.com).

$ Hostal Navarro Ramos is a little cash-only cheapie, renting seven rooms (five with private baths) facing an interior airshaft (S-€20, D-€30, Db-€37, free Wi-Fi, Cuesta de Gomérez 21, tel. 958-250-555, www.pensionnavarroramos.com, Carmen).

$ Pensión Austria, run by English-speaking Austrian Irene (ee-RAY-nay), rents 15 basic but tidy backpacker-type rooms (Sb-€25-30, Db-€35-40, Tb-€50-60, Qb-€65-75, Quint/b-€80-90, family rooms, air-con, free Wi-Fi, Cuesta de Gomérez 4, tel. 958-227-075, www.pensionaustria.com, pensionaustria@pension austria.com).

Near the Cathedral

$$ Hotel Los Tilos offers 30 comfortable, business-like rooms (some with balconies) on the charming traffic-free Plaza de Bib-Rambla behind the cathedral. Guests are welcome to use the fourth-floor terrace with views of the cathedral and the Alhambra (Sb-€45-55, Db-€55-80, Tb-€77-100, prices may be cheaper if you reserve online, free breakfast when you book direct and show the 2014 edition of this book at check-in, air-con, free Wi-Fi, parking-€26/day, Plaza de Bib-Rambla 4, tel. 958-266-712, www .hotellostilos.com, clientes@hotellostilos.com, friendly José María).

On or near Plaza de la Trinidad

The charming, park-like square called Plaza de la Trinidad is just a short walk west of the cathedral area (Pescadería and Bib-Rambla squares). It's also home to several good accommodations.

$$$ Hotel Reina Cristina has 55 quiet, elegant rooms a few steps off Plaza de la Trinidad. Check out the great Mudejar ceiling and the painting at the entrance of this house, where the famous Spanish poet Federico García Lorca hid until he was captured and executed by the Guardia Civil during the Spanish Civil War (Sb-€46-90, Db-€66-139, Tb-€81-169, includes breakfast—skip it to save €13 per person, air-con, elevator, Wi-Fi-€2/day, parking-€18/day, near Plaza de la Trinidad at Tablas 4, tel. 958-253-211, www.hotelreinacristina.com, clientes@hotelreinacristina.com).

$ Hostal Lima, run with class by Manolo and Carmen, has 25 small but well-appointed rooms in two buildings a block off the square. The public areas and rooms are decorated with flamboyant medieval flair—colorful tiles, wood-carved life-sized figures, and so on (Sb-€33, Db-€48, Tb-€67, breakfast-€7, home-cooked dinner available if booked in advance, air-con, elevator in one building only, free Wi-Fi, parking-€14/day, Laurel de las Tablas 17, tel. 958-295-029, www.hostallimagranada.com, info @hostallimagranada.eu).

$ Hostal Rodri, run by Manolo's brother José, has 10 similarly good rooms a few doors down that feel new and classy for their price range (Sb-€32, Db-€45, air-con, elevator, free cable Internet and Wi-Fi, parking-€14/day, Laurel de las Tablas 9, tel. 958-288-043, www.hostalrodri.com, info@hostalrodri.com).

$ Zurita Pensión, well-run by Francisco and Loli, faces Plaza de la Trinidad. Eight of the 14 rooms have small balconies, but even with their double-paned windows, they may come with night noise (S-€21, D-€34, Db-€42, Tb-€63, air-con, free Wi-Fi, parking-€14-16/day, Plaza de la Trinidad 7, tel. 958-275-020, www .pensionzurita.com, pensionzurita@gmail.com).

In the Albayzín

Note that some consider this area sketchy after dark (see sidebar on page 631).

$$ Hotel Santa Isabel la Real, an elegant medieval mansion, has 11 rooms ringing a noble courtyard. Each room is a bit different; basic rooms look to the patio, while various pricier rooms have better exterior views. Buried deep in the Albayzín and furnished in a way that gives you the old Moorish Granada ambience, it offers a warm welcome and rich memories (Db-€85-105 with breakfast, air-con, elevator, free guest computer, free Wi-Fi, parking-€14/day, midway between San Nicolás viewpoint and Plaza San Miguel el Bajo on Calle Santa Isabel la Real, immediately at a bus stop, tel. 958-294-658, www.hotelsantaisabellareal.com, info@hotel santaisabellareal.com).

$$ El Numero 8 "Casa de Rafa" is a traditional house in the heart of the Albayzín that's been converted into four small, funky kitchenette apartments with an eclectic, ever-evolving artistic feel. Chicago-raised, easygoing owner Rafa lives on-site. You'll share two tiny patios and a rooftop terrace with a spectacular, in-your-face view of the Alhambra. Contact Rafa in advance to set up a time to check in. He'll ease your arrival by meeting you at a taxi or bus drop-off point and walking you back to the apartment (Sb-€35-60, Db-€40-70, extra person-€10, 2-night minimum, fans but no air-con, free Wi-Fi, 5-minute walk from Plaza Nueva at tiny Plaza

GRANADA

Virgen del Carmen—see map on page 631, tel. 958-220-682, mobile 610-322-216, www.elnumero8.com, casaocho@gmail.com).

$$ Tournights Granada is run by Frederick, an American who rents 15 renovated and fully furnished duplexes and apartments in traditional Moorish houses situated in the Albayzín district, many with grand Alhambra views (Db-€80-100 plus €40 cleaning fee, prices vary with size—see photos and videos on website, 2-night minimum—longer during holidays, 20 percent deposit required to reserve online, pay the balance in cash after you arrive, air-con, free Wi-Fi, some units have private terraces and swimming pools, mobile 620-585-594, www.tournights.com, info@tournights.com).

$ Makuto Guesthouse, a hostel tucked deep in the Albayzín, feels like a hippie commune you can pay to join for a couple of days. With 42 beds in seven rooms clustered around a lush garden courtyard that feels made for hanging out—including several hammock-and-lounge-sofa "hang-out zones"—it exudes an easygoing Albayzín vibe (Db-€55-70, bunk in 4- to 6-bed room-€14-20, includes breakfast, dinners available, free guest computer, free Wi-Fi, Calle Tiña 18, tel. 958-805-876, www.makutoguesthouse.com, info@makutoguesthouse.com).

In or near the Alhambra

If you want to stay on the Alhambra grounds, you have two popular options (famous, overpriced, and generally booked up long in advance) and one practical and economic place above the parking lot. All are a half-mile up the hill from Plaza Nueva.

$$$ Parador de Granada San Francisco offers 40 designer rooms in a former Moorish palace that was later transformed into a 15th-century Franciscan monastery. It's considered Spain's premier parador...and that's saying something (standard Db-€336, breakfast-€20, air-con, free Wi-Fi, free parking, Calle Real de la Alhambra, tel. 958-221-440, www.parador.es, granada@parador.es). You must book months ahead to spend the night in this lavishly located, stodgy, and historic palace. Any peasant, however, can drop in for a coffee, drink, snack, or meal. For details about the history of the building, see sidebar on page 622.

$$ Hotel América is classy and cozy, with 17 rooms in an early-19th-century house next to the parador (Sb-€60-80, Db-€90-120, €25 more for bigger room with terrace, breakfast-€8.50, free Wi-Fi, parking-€15/day, closed Dec-Feb, Calle Real de la Alhambra 53, tel. 958-227-471, www.hotelamericagranada.com, reservas@hotelamericagranada.com, friendly Isabel).

$$ Hotel Guadalupe, big and modern with 58 sleek rooms, is quietly and conveniently located overlooking the Alhambra parking lot. While a 30-minute hike above the town, many (especially drivers) find this to be a practical option (Sb-€50-75, Db-€58-124, Tb-€75-135, "superior" rooms with Jacuzzis and balconies aren't worth the extra cost, continental breakfast-€13, breakfast buffet-€23, air-con, elevator, free Wi-Fi in lobby, parking in Alhambra lot-€14/day, Paseo de la Sabica 30, tel. 958-225-730, www.hotelguadalupe.es, info@hotelguadalupe.es).

Eating in Granada

Restaurants generally serve lunch from 13:00 to 16:00 and dinner from 20:00 until very late (remember, Spaniards don't start dinner until about 21:00). Many

of Granada's bars still serve a small tapas plate free with any beer or wine—a tradition that's dying out in most of Spain. Save on your food expenses by doing a tapas crawl (especially good along Calle Navas, right off Plaza del Carmen) and claim your "right" to a free tapa with every drink. (It helps to order your drink and wait for the free tapa before ordering food. If you order food with your drink, you likely won't get the freebie.) For more budget-eating thrills, buy picnic supplies near Plaza Nueva, and schlep them up into the Albayzín. This makes for a great cheap date at the San Nicolás viewpoint or on one of the scattered squares and lookout points.

In search of an edible memory? A local specialty, *tortilla Sacromonte*, is a spicy omelet with pig's brain and other organs. *Berenjenas fritas* (fried eggplant) and *habas con jamón* (small green fava beans cooked with cured ham) are worth seeking out. *Tinto de verano*—a red-wine spritzer with lemon and ice—is refreshing on a hot evening. For tips on eating near the Alhambra, see page 612.

In the Albayzín

Many interesting meals hide out deep in the Albayzín (Moorish quarter). To find a particular square, ask any local, or follow my directions and the full-color Granada map at the front of this book. If dining late, take the minibus or a taxi back to your hotel; Albayzín back streets can be poorly lit, confusing to follow, and plagued by pickpockets. Part of the charm of the quarter is the lazy ambience on its squares. My two favorites are Plaza Larga and Plaza San Miguel el Bajo.

Plaza Larga is extremely characteristic, with tapas bar tables spilling out onto the square, a morning market, and a much-loved pastry shop.

Plaza San Miguel el Bajo, the farthest hike into the Albayzín, boasts my favorite funky local scene—kids kicking soccer balls, old-timers warming benches, and women gossiping under the facade of a humble church. It's circled by half a dozen inviting little bars and restaurants—each very competitive with €10 lunch deals, more expensive à la carte and evening meals, and good seating right on the square. Drop by for lunch or dinner and spend a few minutes surveying your options: **El Acebuche,** run with pride by friendly María, promises "Andalusian flavor with a light dash of the Orient" (open daily). **Rincón de la Aurora** feels more comfortable and has tapas (closed Wed and Sun afternoon). **El Ají** is a sit-down restaurant with a mod vibe and a bit of Argentinian flair (closed Tue). And just down the street (beyond El Ají) is a little hole-in-the-wall **takeaway shop** selling cheap empanadas and pizza by the slice to munch out on the square (closed Tue). This square is a great spot to end your Albayzín visit, as there's a viewpoint overlooking the modern city a block away. Minibus #31 rumbles by every few minutes, ready to zip you back to Plaza Nueva. Or just walk five minutes down from the viewpoint.

Casa Torcuato is a hardworking eatery serving straightforward yet creative food in a smart upstairs dining room. They serve a good fixed-price lunch (€9.50), plates of fresh fish (€11-15), and prizewinning, thick, *salmorejo*—style gazpacho (closed Sun-Mon, 2 blocks beyond Plaza Larga at Calle Aqua 20, tel. 958-202-039).

Restaurante El Ladrillo, a tiny and humble joint with outdoor tables on a peaceful square (and no indoor seating), is *the* place for piles of fish. Their popular €12 *barco* ("boatload" of mixed fried fish) is a fishy feast that stuffs two to the gills. Even their €8.50 half-*barco* can be split (daily 12:00-17:00 & 19:00-23:00, on Placeta de Fátima, just off Calle Pagés, tel. 958-286-123).

Near the San Nicolás Viewpoint

This area is thoroughly touristy, so don't expect any local hangouts here. But these options are suitable for a good meal with a view you'll never forget.

Restaurante Estrellas de San Nicolás, in the former home of a well-loved Albayzín bigwig, immediately next to the view terrace, features dreamy Alhambra views from its two floors of indoor seating. Serving a mix of French and Spanish cuisine, this splurge keeps its mostly tourist clientele very happy (€10-22 starters, €20-29 main dishes, €31 fixed-price dinner, €20 or €27 fixed-price lunch, smart to reserve a view table, Atrazana Vieja 1, tel. 958-288-739, www.estrellasdesannicolas.es).

El Huerto de Juan Ranas Restaurante has a simple terrace bar immediately below the San Nicolás viewpoint, with amazing

Alhambra views and a simple menu at half the price of their restaurant (€9 dish of the day, €15 *raciones,* Calle de Atarazana 8, tel. 958-286-925).

Bar Kiki, a laid-back and popular bar-restaurant on an unpretentious square with no view, serves simple tapas. Try their tasty fried eggplant (random hours, closed Wed, just behind viewpoint at Plaza de San Nicolás 9, tel. 958-276-715).

Carmens in the Albayzín

For a more memorable but pricey experience, consider fine dining with Alhambra views in a *carmen,* a typical Albayzín house with a garden (buzz to get in). After the Reconquista, the Albayzín became depopulated. Wealthy families took larger tracts of land and built fortified mansions with terraced gardens within their walls. Today, rather than growing produce, the gardens of many of these *carmens* host dining tables and romantic restaurants.

Carmen Mirador de Aixa, small and elegant, has the dreamiest Alhambra views among the *carmens.* You'll pay a little more, but the food is exquisitely presented and the view makes the splurge worthwhile. Try the codfish or ox (€13-23 starters, €20-27 main dishes, 13:30-15:30 & 20:30-23:00, closed Sun dinner, all day Mon, and Tue lunch; next to Carmen de las Tomasas at Carril de San Agustín 2, tel. 958-223-616).

Carmen de las Tomasas serves gourmet traditional Andalusian cuisine with killer views in a dressy/stuffy atmosphere (expect to spend €40 with wine, Tue-Sat 13:30-16:00 & 20:15-23:30, closed Sun-Mon, reservations required, Carril de San Agustín 4, tel. 958-224-108, Joaquim and Cristina).

Carmen de Aben Humeya is the least expensive, least stuffy, and least romantic. Its outdoor-only seating lets you enjoy a meal or just a long cup of coffee while gazing at the Alhambra. This is a rare place enthusiastic about dinner salads (€10-20 starters and nicely presented main dishes, Mon-Tue and Thu-Fri 13:00-17:00 & 20:00-24:00, Sat-Sun 13:00-24:00, closed Wed, Cuesta de las Tomasas 12, tel. 958-226-665).

Near Plaza Nueva

For people-watching, consider the many restaurants on Plaza Nueva or Plaza de Bib-Rambla (south of cathedral). For a happening scene, check out the bars on and around Calle de Elvira. It's best to wander and see where the biggest crowds are.

Bodegas Castañeda, just a block off Plaza Nueva, is the best mix of lively, central, and cheap among the tapas bars I visited. When it's crowded, you need to power your way to the bar to order. When it's quiet, you can order at the bar and grab a little table (same budget prices). Consider their *tablas combinadas—*

variety plates of cheese, meat, and *ahumados* (four different varieties of smoked fish)—and tasty *croquetas* (breaded and fried mashed potatoes and ham). Order a glass of their gazpacho. Their €12 *plato Casteñeda* feeds two. The big kegs tempt you with different local vermouths, and the €1.70 glasses of wine come with a free tapa (€2-3 tapas, €6-13 half-*raciones*, €8-17 *raciones*, daily 11:30-16:30 & 19:00-24:00, Calle Almireceros 1, tel. 958-215-464). Don't be confused by the neighboring, similar "Antigua Bodega Castañeda" restaurant (run by a relative and not as good).

Restaurante Sevilla, with its tight and charming little dining room behind a high-energy tapas bar, has been a favorite of well-dressed natives for 75 years. Specialties include paella, other rice dishes (€24 for two), soups, and salads. You'll eat surrounded by old photos of local big shots who've dined here. On hot nights, tables pour out onto the little square facing the Royal Chapel. It's a local-feeling, elegant, urban scene. In the evenings, the bar displays a yummy spread of tapas—you get one free with any drink you buy, then pay €2 for each additional one (€10-15 starters, €14-20 main dishes, €11.50 fixed-price meal, daily from 12:00 and from 20:00, closed Sun; across from Royal Chapel at Calle Oficios 12, tel. 958-221-223, Danny).

La Cueva de 1900 is a fresh, family-friendly deli-like place on the main drag appreciated for its simple dishes and quality ingredients. Though it lacks character, it's reliable and low-stress. They're proud of their homemade hams, sausages, and cheeses—sold in 100-gram lots. Their fixed-price lunch is €10, but if you've had enough meat, try one of their good €5-7 salads (€3-4 *bocadillo* sandwiches, €8-17 meaty meals, open long hours daily, Calle Reyes Católicos 42, tel. 958-229-327).

Arrayanes is a good Moroccan restaurant a world apart from anything else listed here. Mostafa will help you choose among the many salads, the *briwat* (a chicken-and-cinnamon pastry appetizer), the *pastela* (a first-course version of *briwat*), the couscous, or *tajin* dishes. He treats his guests like old friends... especially the ladies (€4-10 starters, €10-16 main dishes, Wed-Mon 13:30-16:30 & 19:30-23:30, closed Tue, Cuesta Marañas 4, where Calles Calderería Nueva and Vieja meet, tel. 958-228-401, mobile 619-076-862).

Los Diamantes is a modern, high-energy local favorite for fresh seafood (free tapa with drink, only *raciones* and half-*raciones* on the menu, prices the same at outside table as at the bar, Mon-Fri 12:00-18:00 & 20:00-24:00, Sat-Sun 11:00-24:00, facing Plaza Nueva at #13, tel. 958-075-313).

Greens and Berries anchors Plaza Nueva, serving fresh salads, sandwiches, and real fruit smoothies to go (no seating). Try one of their €7 combos—such as the *queso de cabra y tomate* sandwich (goat cheese and tomato with caramelized onions) paired with a Caribbean smoothie—and enjoy it on a sunny plaza bench (€3-6 salads and sandwiches, daily 9:00-23:00, Plaza Nueva 1, tel. 633-895-086).

Hippie Options on Calle Calderería Nueva: From Plaza Nueva, walk two long blocks down Calle de Elvira and turn right onto the wonderfully hip and Arabic-feeling Calle Calderería Nueva, which leads uphill into the Albayzín. The street is lined with trendy *teterías*. These small tea shops, open all day, are good places to linger, chat, and imagine you're in Morocco. Many also offer the opportunity to rent a hookah (water pipe) to smoke some fruit-flavored tobacco with friends. Some are conservative and unmemorable, and others are achingly romantic, filled with incense, beaded cushions, live African music, and effervescent young hippies. They sell light meals such as crêpes, and a worldwide range of teas, all marinated in a candlelit snake-charmer ambience.

Placeta de San Gregorio: This tiny junction at the top of Calle Calderería Nueva has a special laid-back character. Grab a rickety seat here (at **Taverna 22** or **Bar las Cuevas**), under the classic church facade with potted plants and a commotion of tiled roofs, and enjoy the steady stream of hippies (and people who wish they were hippies) flowing by.

Paseo de los Tristes: This spot is like a stage set of outdoor bars on a terrace over the river gorge. While it lacks a serious restaurant and the food values are mediocre at best, the scene—cool, along a stream under trees, with the floodlit Alhambra high above and a happy crowd of locals enjoying a meal or drink out—is a winner. As this is at the base of the Albayzín, there's no issue of danger after dark here. It's a simple, level, five-minute walk back to Plaza Nueva.

Tapas Beyond Plaza del Carmen, Away from the Tourist Zone: Granada is a wonderland of happening little tapas bars. As the scene changes from night to night, it's best to simply wander and see what appeals. You'll be amazed at how the vibe changes when you venture just five minutes from the historic and touristic center. From Plaza del Carmen, wander down Calle Navas, consider a side-trip down Calle San Matías, and don't miss my favorite stretch, where Calle Navas becomes Calle Virgen del Rosario. On Virgen del Rosario, consider **Taberna La Tana** (for fine wine) and **Bar Los Diamentes II** (across the street, for seafood). And, remember, you can always wrap things up with a sit on the square at Café Fútbol for chocolate and *churros* (described later).

Gayle's Granada Tapas Tours: Seventeen years ago, Gayle Mackie moved from Scotland to Granada, and for the last decade or so she's brought visitors on tapas tours of her new city. For details, see "Tours in Granada," earlier.

Chocolate and Churros: **Café Fútbol** is the best place in town for the local coffee and doughnut-dunking ritual—but with thick hot chocolate and greasy, freshly made *churros* instead. While Café Alhambra on Plaza de Bib-Rambla is another favorite for *chocolate con churros,* I prefer Café Fútbol, with its great scene on a lazy square (€3.30 for hot chocolate and *churros,* Plaza Mariana Pineda 6, tel. 958-226-662).

Ice Cream: **Los Italianos,** Italian-run and teeming with locals, is popular for its ice cream, *horchata* (*chufa*-nut drink), and shakes. When Michelle Obama visited Granada in 2010, this is where she got her ice-cream fix. For something special, try their *cassata,* a slice (not scoop) of mixed flavors with frozen fruit in a cone (mid-March-mid-Oct daily 9:00-24:00, closed off-season, across the street from cathedral and Royal Chapel at Gran Vía 4, tel. 958-224-034).

Markets: Though heavy on meat, **Mercado San Agustín** also sells fruits and veggies. Throughout the EU, locals lament the loss of the authentic old market halls as they are replaced with new hygienic versions. If nothing else, it's as refreshingly cool as a meat locker (Mon-Sat 9:00-15:00, closed Sun, very quiet on Mon, a block north of cathedral and a half-block off Gran Vía on Calle Cristo San Agustín). Tucked away in the back of the market is a very cheap and colorful little eatery: **Cafetería San Agustín.** They make their own *churros* and give a small tapa free with each drink (menu on wall). If you are waiting for the cathedral or Royal Chapel to open, kill time in the market. The stalls around the market and the **Pescadería** square, downhill from the actual market and a block from Plaza de Bib-Rambla, are actually more popular with locals looking to buy produce.

Granada Connections

From Granada by Train to: Barcelona (1/day, 9.5 hours on Altaria and AVE, transfer in Madrid; also 1 night daily, 10.5 hours), **Madrid** (2/day on Altaria, 4.5 hours), **Toledo** (all service is via Madrid, with nearly hourly AVE connections to Toledo), **Algeciras** (3/day, 4.25-5 hours), **Ronda** (3/day, 2.5 hours), **Sevilla** (4/day, 3 hours), **Córdoba** (2/day, 2.5 hours), **Málaga** (6/day, 2.5 hours with 1 transfer—bus is better). Train info: toll tel. 902-320-320, www.renfe.com. Many of these connections have a more frequent (and sometimes much faster) bus option—see below.

By Bus to: Nerja (8/day, 2-2.5 hours, more with transfer in Motril), **Sevilla** (to Plaza de Armas Station: 7/day, 3 hours *directo,* 3.5-4.5 hours *ruta;* to El Prado Station: 2/day, 3-3.5 hours), **Córdoba** (9/day, 2.5-4 hours), **Madrid** (roughly hourly, 5-5.75 hours; most to Estación Sur, a few to Avenida de América, one

direct to Barajas Airport), **Málaga** (hourly, 1.5-2 hours), **Algeciras** (3/day *directo*, 4 hours; 1/day *ruta*, 5.5 hours), **La Línea de la Concepción/Gibraltar** (3/day, 6-7 hours, change in Algeciras), Jerez (1/day, 4.75 hours), **Barcelona** (4/day, 13-14.75 hours, often at odd times, only one fully daytime connection departs Granada at 10:00 and arrives Barcelona at 24:15). To reach **Ronda,** change in Málaga or Antequera; to reach **Tarifa,** change in Algeciras or Málaga. Bus info: Main bus station tel. 913-270-540; all of these routes are run by Alsa (tel. 902-422-242, www.alsa.es). If there's a long line at the ticket windows, you can use the machines (press the flag for English)—but these only sell tickets for some major routes (such as Málaga), and sometimes eat credit cards like a Spaniard eats *jamón.*

SEVILLA

Flamboyant Sevilla (seh-VEE-yah) thrums with flamenco music, sizzles in the summer heat, and pulses with the passion of Don Juan and Carmen. It's a place where bull-fighting is still politically correct and little girls still dream of growing up to become flamenco dancers. While Granada has the great Alhambra and Córdoba has the remarkable Mezquita, Sevilla has a soul. (Soul—or *duende*—is fundamental to flamenco.) It's a wonderful-to-be-alive-in kind of place.

The gateway to the New World in the 16th century, Sevilla boomed when Spain did. The explorers Amerigo Vespucci and Ferdinand Magellan sailed from its great river harbor, discovering new trade routes and abundant sources of gold, silver, cocoa, and tobacco. In the 17th century, Sevilla was Spain's largest and wealthiest city. Local artists Diego Velázquez, Bartolomé Murillo, and Francisco de Zurbarán made it a cultural center. Sevilla's Golden Age—and its New World riches—ended when the harbor silted up and the Spanish empire crumbled.

In the 19th century, Sevilla was a big stop on the Romantic "Grand Tour" of Europe. To build on this tourism and promote trade among Spanish-speaking nations, Sevilla planned a grand exposition in 1929. Bad year. The expo crashed along with the stock market. In 1992, Sevilla got a second chance at a world's fair. This expo was a success, leaving the city with impressive infrastructure: a new airport, a train station, sleek bridges, and the super AVE bullet train (making Sevilla a 2.5-hour side-trip from Madrid). In 2007, the main boulevards—once thundering with noisy traffic and mercilessly cutting the city in two—were pedestrianized, dramatically enhancing Sevilla's already substantial charm.

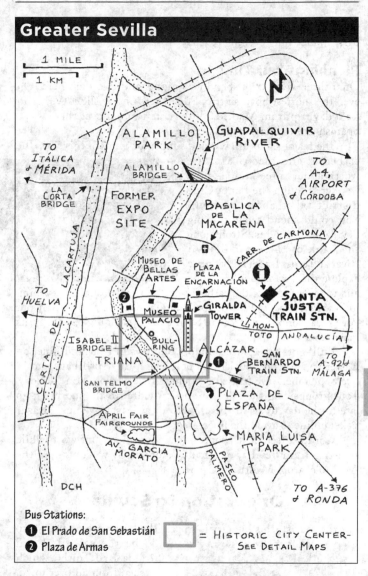

Greater Sevilla

1 MILE
1 KM

TO
ITÁLICA
& MÉRIDA

ALAMILLO
PARK

GUADALQUIVIR
RIVER

ALAMILLO
BRIDGE

TO
A-4,
AIRPORT
& CÓRDOBA

LA
CORTA
BRIDGE

FORMER
EXPO
SITE

BASÍLICA
DE LA
MACARENA

CARR. DE CARMONA

LA CARTUJA

MUSEO DE
BELLAS
ARTES

PLAZA
DE LA
ENCARNACIÓN

TO
HUELVA

❷

MUSEO
PALACIO

GIRALDA
TOWER

SANTA
JUSTA
TRAIN STN.

C. DE LA CORTA

ISABEL II
BRIDGE

TRIANA

BULL-
RING

LI MON-
TOTO   ANDALUCÍA

ALCÁZAR

SAN
BERNARDO
TRAIN STN.

TO
A-92 &
MÁLAGA

SAN TELMO
BRIDGE

PLAZA DE
ESPAÑA

APRIL FAIR
FAIRGROUNDS

MARÍA LUISA
PARK

AV. GARCIA
MORATO

PASEO PALMERO

DCH

TO A-376
& RONDA

Bus Stations:
❶ El Prado de San Sebastián
❷ Plaza de Armas

☐ = HISTORIC CITY CENTER-
SEE DETAIL MAPS

Today, Spain's fourth-largest city (pop. 704,000) is Andalucía's leading destination, buzzing with festivals, color, guitars, castanets, and street life, and enveloped in the fragrances of orange trees, jacaranda, and myrtle. James Michener wrote, "Sevilla doesn't *have* ambience, it *is* ambience." Sevilla also has its share of impressive sights. Its cathedral is Spain's largest. The Alcázar is a fantastic royal palace and garden ornamented with Mudejar (Islamic) flair. But the real magic is the city itself, with its tangled former Jewish Quarter, riveting flamenco shows, thriving bars, and teeming evening paseo.

Planning Your Time

On a three-week trip, spend two nights and two days here. On even the shortest Spanish trip, I'd zip here on the slick AVE train for a day trip from Madrid. With more time, if ever there was a Spanish city to linger in, it's Sevilla.

The major sights are few and simple for a city of this size. The cathedral and the Alcázar are worth about three hours, and a wander through the Santa Cruz district takes about an hour. You could spend a day touring Sevilla's other sights. Stroll along the bank of the Guadalquivir River and cross Isabel II Bridge to explore the Triana neighborhood and to savor views of the cathedral and Torre del Oro. An evening in Sevilla is essential for the paseo and a flamenco show. Stay out late at least once to appreciate Sevilla on a warm night—one of its major charms.

Bullfights take place on most Sundays in May and June, on Easter and Corpus Christi, daily through the April Fair, and in late September. The Museo de Bellas Artes is closed on Monday. Tour groups clog the Alcázar and cathedral in the morning; go late in the day to avoid the crowds, or at least buy your Alcázar ticket online to avoid the lines.

Córdoba (see next chapter) is a convenient and worthwhile side-trip from Sevilla, or a handy stopover if you're taking the AVE to or from Madrid or Granada.

Orientation to Sevilla

For the tourist, this big city is small. The bull's-eye on your map

should be the cathedral and its Giralda Bell Tower, which can be seen from all over town. Nearby are Sevilla's other major sights, the Alcázar (palace and gardens) and the lively Santa Cruz district. The central north-south pedestrian boulevard, Avenida de la Constitución, stretches north a few blocks to Plaza Nueva, gateway to the shopping district. A few blocks west of the cathedral are the bull-ring and the Guadalquivir River, while Plaza de España is a few blocks south. Triana, the colorful working-class area on the west bank of the Guadalquivir River, has a thriving market but lacks tourist sights. With most sights walkable, and taxis so friendly, easy, and affordable, you probably won't even bother with the bus.

Tourist Information

Sevilla has tourist offices at the **airport** (Mon-Fri 9:00-19:30, Sat-Sun 9:30-15:00, tel. 954-782-035), at **Santa Justa train station** (overlooking tracks 6-7, same hours as airport TI, tel. 954-782-003), and near the cathedral on **Plaza del Triunfo** (Mon-Fri 9:00-19:30, Sat-Sun 9:30-19:30, tel. 954-210-005).

At any TI, ask for the city map, the English-language magazine *The Tourist*, and a current listing of sights with opening times. The free monthly events guide—*El Giraldillo*, written in Spanish basic enough to be understood by travelers—covers cultural events throughout Andalucía, with a focus on Sevilla. At the TI, ask for information you might need for elsewhere in the region (for example, if heading south, pick up the free *Route of the White Towns* brochure and a Jerez map). Helpful websites are www.turismosevilla.org and www.andalucia.org.

Sightseeing Pass: The **Sevilla Card** covers admission to most of Sevilla's sights (including the cathedral, Alcázar, Flamenco Dance Museum, Basílica de la Macarena, Bullfight Museum, and more), and gives discounts at some hotels and restaurants (sold at the ICONOS shop on Avenida de la Constitución, near the Alcázar, Mon-Sat 10:00-20:00, Sun 11:00-19:00; or at the "INFHOR" stand—the train station's hotel room-finding booth, overlooking track 11). It's doubtful whether any but the busiest sightseer would save much money using the card (€33/24 hours—includes choice of 2 museums and river cruise; €53/48 hours—includes all sights and choice of river cruise or bus tour; €71/72 hours or €77/120 hours—includes all sights plus cruise and bus tour; www.sevillacard.es). If you're over 65, keep in mind that even without the Sevilla Card, you'll get into the Alcázar and the cathedral almost free.

Arrival in Sevilla

By Train: Most trains arrive at sublime Santa Justa Station, with banks, ATMs, bike rental, and a TI. Baggage storage *(cosigna)* is below track 1, next to the bike-rental office (€3-5/day depending on size of bag, security checkpoint open 6:00-24:00). The TI overlooks tracks 6-7. If you don't have a hotel room reserved, INFHOR, the room-finding booth above track 11, can help; you can also get maps and other tourist information here—a good idea

SEVILLA

if the TI line is long (Mon-Sat 9:30-14:30 & 15:30-20:00, Sun 9:30-16:30). The plush little AVE Sala Club, designed for business travelers, welcomes those with a first-class AVE ticket and reservation (across the main hall from track 1). The town center is marked by the ornate Giralda Bell Tower, peeking above the apartment flats (visible from the front of the station—with your back to the tracks, it's at 1 o'clock). To get into the center, it's a flat and boring 25-minute walk or about a €6 taxi ride. By city bus, it's a short ride on #C1 to the El Prado de San Sebastián bus station (find bus stop 100 yards in front of the train station, €1.40, pay driver), then a 10-minute walk or short tram ride (see next section).

By Bus: Sevilla's two major bus stations—El Prado de San Sebastián and Plaza de Armas—both have information offices, basic eateries, and baggage storage.

The **El Prado de San Sebastián bus station,** often called just "El Prado," covers most of Andalucía (daily 7:00-22:00, information tel. 954-417-111, generally no English spoken; baggage storage/ *consigna* at the far end of station—€1.50-3.50/day depending on size, daily 9:00-21:00). From the bus station to downtown (and Barrio Santa Cruz hotels), it's about a 10-minute walk: Exit the station to the right, and cross the busy street at the big roundabout. Turn right and keep the fenced-in gardens on your left. At the end of the fence, duck left through the Murillo Gardens and into the heart of Barrio Santa Cruz (use the color map in the front of this book to navigate). Sevilla's tram connects the El Prado station with the city center (and many of my recommended hotels): Turn left as you exit the bus station and walk to Avenida de Carlos V (€1.40, buy ticket at machine before boarding; ride it two stops to Archivo de Indias to reach the cathedral area, or three stops to Plaza Nueva).

The **Plaza de Armas bus station** (near the river, opposite the Expo '92 site) serves long-distance destinations such as Madrid, Barcelona, Lagos, and Lisbon. Ticket counters line one wall, an information kiosk is in the center, and at the end of the hall are luggage lockers (€3.50/day). Taxis to downtown cost around €5. Or, to take the bus, exit onto the main road (Calle Arjona) to find bus #C4 into the center (stop is to the left, in front of the taxi stand; €1.40, pay driver, get off at Puerta de Jerez).

By Car: To drive into Sevilla, follow *centro ciudad* (city center) signs and stay along the river. For short-term parking on the street, the riverside Paseo de Cristóbal Colón has two-hour meters and hardworking thieves. Ignore the bogus traffic wardens who direct you to an illegal spot, take a tip, and disappear later when your car gets towed. For long-term parking, hotels charge as much as a normal garage. For simplicity, I'd just park at a central garage (€15-22/day) and catch a taxi to my hotel. Try the big one under the bus station at Plaza de Armas, the Cristóbal Colón garage by the bullring and river, the Plaza Nueva garage on Albareda, or the one at Avenida Roma/Puerta de Jerez (cash only). For hotels in the Santa Cruz area, the handiest parking is the Cano y Cueto garage near the corner of Calle Santa María la Blanca and Avenida de Menéndez Pelayo (about €18/day, open 24/7, at edge of big park, unsigned and underground).

By Plane: Sevilla's San Pablo Airport (airport code: SVQ) sits about six miles east of downtown (tel. 954-449-000, www.aena-aeropuertos.es). The Especial Aeropuerto (EA) bus connects the airport with both train stations, both bus stations, and several stops in the town center (2/hour, 30-45 minutes, €4, buy ticket from driver). The two most convenient stops downtown are south of the Alcázar gardens on Avenida de Carlos V, near El Prado de San Sebastián bus station (close to my recommended Santa Cruz hotels); and on the Paseo de Cristóbal Colón, near the Torre del Oro. Look for the small *EA* sign at bus stops. If you're going from downtown Sevilla *to* the airport, verify bus stops with your hotel or the TI, as locations can change. To taxi into town, go to one of the airport's taxi stands to ensure a fixed rate (€22 by day, €24 at night and on weekends, extra for luggage, confirm price with the driver before your journey).

Getting Around Sevilla

Most visitors have a full and fun experience in Sevilla without ever riding public transportation. The city center is compact, and most of the major sights are within easy walking distance (the Basílica de la Macarena is a notable exception). On a hot day, air-conditioned buses can be a blessing.

By Taxi: Sevilla is a great taxi town. You can hail one anywhere, or find a cluster of them parked by major intersections and sights (weekdays: €1.30 drop rate, €1/kilometer, €3.60 minimum; Sat-Sun, holidays, and after hours, 21:00-7:00: €2 drop rate, €1.40/kilometer, €4.50 minimum; calling for a cab adds about €3). A quick daytime ride in town will generally fall within the €3.60 minimum. Although I'm quick to take advantage of taxis, because of one-way streets and traffic congestion it's often just as fast to hoof it between central points.

By Bus, Tram, and Metro: Thanks to ongoing construction projects in the city center, bus routes often change. It's best to check with your hotel or the TI for the latest updates.

A single trip on any form of city transit costs €1.40. For half-price trips, you can buy a Tarjeta Multiviajes card that's rechargeable and shareable (€7 for 10 trips, €1.50 deposit; buy at kiosks or at the TUSSAM transit office near the bus stop on Avenida de Carlos V, next to El Prado de San Sebastián bus station; scan it on the card reader as you board; for transit details, see www.tussam.es).

The various #C **buses,** which are handiest for tourists, make circular routes through town (note that all of them eventually wind up at Basílica de La Macarena). For all buses, buy your ticket from the driver. The #C3 stops at Murillo Gardens, Triana, then La Macarena. The #C4 goes the opposite direction, but without entering Triana. And the spunky little #C5 is a minibus that winds through the old center of town, including Plaza del Salvador, Plaza de San Francisco, the bullring, Plaza Nueva, the Museo de Bellas Artes, La Campana, and La Macarena, providing a relaxing joyride that also connects some farther-flung sights.

A new **tram** *(tramvia)* makes just a few stops in the heart of the city, but can save you a bit of walking. Buy your ticket at the machine on the platform before you board (runs about every 7 minutes until 1:45 in the morning). It makes five stops (from south to north): San Bernardo (at the San Bernardo train station), Prado San Sebastián (next to El Prado de San Sebastián bus station), Puerta Jerez (south end of Avenida de la Constitución), Archivo de Indias (next to the cathedral), and Plaza Nueva.

Sevilla also has a brand-new underground **metro,** but most tourists won't need to use it. It's designed to connect the suburbs with the center and only has one line. There are stops downtown at the San Bernardo train station, El Prado de San Sebastián bus station, and Puerto Jerez.

Helpful Hints

Festivals: Sevilla's peak season is April and May, and it has two one-week festival periods when the city is packed: Holy Week and April Fair.

While **Holy Week** (Semana Santa) is big all over Spain, it's biggest in Sevilla. It's held the week between Palm Sunday and Easter Sunday (April 13-20 in 2014). Locals start preparing for the big event up to a year in advance. What would normally be a five-minute walk can take an hour if a procession crosses your path. But even these hassles become totally worthwhile as you listen to the *saetas* (spontaneous devotional songs) and let the spirit of the festival take over.

Then, after taking enough time off to catch its communal breath, Sevilla holds its **April Fair** (April 29-May 4 in 2014). This is a celebration of all things Andalusian, with plenty of eating, drinking, singing, and merrymaking (though most of the revelry takes place in private parties at a large fairground).

Book rooms well in advance for these festival times. Prices can go sky-high, many hotels have four-night minimums, and food quality at touristy restaurants can plummet.

Rosemary Scam: In the city center, and especially near the cathedral, you may encounter women thrusting sprigs of rosemary into the hands of passersby, grunting, *"Toma! Es un regalo!"* ("Take it! It's a gift!"). The twig is free...and then they grab your hand and read your fortune for a tip. Coins are "bad luck," so the minimum payment they'll accept is €5. While they can be very aggressive, you don't need to take their demands seriously—don't make eye contact, don't accept a sprig, and say firmly but politely, *"No, gracias."*

Internet Access: Almost every hotel in town has Wi-Fi, and many also have computers for guests to use. The city itself is fairly Wi-Fi friendly. Find free Wi-Fi on the tram, at the Museo de Bellas Artes, and in Plaza de la Encarnación, among other public spaces.

Post Office: The post office is at Avenida de la Constitución 32, across from the cathedral (Mon-Fri 8:30-20:30, Sat 9:30-13:00, closed Sun).

Laundry: Lavandería Roma offers quick and economical drop-off service (€6/load wash and dry, Mon-Fri 10:00-14:00 & 17:30-20:30, Sat 10:00-14:00, closed Sun, a few blocks west of the cathedral at Calle Arfe 22, tel. 954-210-535). Near the recommended Santa Cruz hotels, **La Segunda Vera Tintorería** has two machines for self-service (€10/load wash-and-dry, €10/load drop-off service, Mon-Fri 9:30-14:00 & 17:30-20:300, Sat 10:00-13:30, closed Sun, about a block from the eastern edge of Santa Cruz at Avenida de Menéndez Pelayo 11, tel. 954-536-376).

Bike Rental: Sevilla is an extremely biker-friendly city, with designated bike lanes and a public bike-sharing program (€11 one-week subscription, first 30 minutes of each ride free, €1-2 for each subsequent hour, www.sevici.es). Ask the TI about this and other bicycle rental options. **BiciBike** rents bikes at the Santa Justa train station, and will even deliver them to your hotel at no charge (€8/3 hours, €10/6 hours, €15/24 hours, tel. 955-514-110, www.bicibike.es).

Train Tickets: For schedules and tickets, visit a RENFE Travel Center, either at the **train station** (daily 8:00-22:00, take a

Holy Week (Semana Santa) in Andalucía

Holy Week—the week between Palm Sunday and Easter—is a major holiday throughout the Christian world, but nowhere is it celebrated with as much fervor as in Andalucía, especially Sevilla. Holy Week is all about the events of the Passion of Jesus Christ: his entry into Jerusalem, his betrayal by Judas and arrest, his crucifixion, and his resurrection. In Sevilla, on each day throughout the week, 60 neighborhood groups (brotherhoods, called *hermandades* or *cofradías*) parade from their neighborhood churches to the cathedral with floats depicting some aspect of the Passion story.

As the week approaches, the anticipation grows: Visitors pour into town, grandstands are erected along the parade routes, and TV stations anxiously monitor the weather report. The floats are so delicate that rain can force the processions to be called off—a crushing disappointment.

By mid-afternoon of any day during Holy Week, thousands line the streets. The parade begins. First comes a line of "penitents" carrying a big cross, candles, and incense. The *penitentes* perform their penance publically but anonymously, their identities obscured by pointy, hooded robes. (The penitents' traditional hooded garb has been worn for centuries—long before such hoods became associated with racism in the American South.) Some processions are silent, but others are accompanied by beating drums, brass bands, or wailing singers.

A hush falls over the crowd as the floats *(los pasos)* approach. First comes a Passion float, showing Christ in some stage of the drama—being whipped, appearing before Pilate,

number and wait, tel. 902-320-320 for reservations and info) or near **Plaza Nueva** in the city center (Mon-Fri 9:30-14:00 & 17:30-20:00, Sat 10:00-13:30, closed Sun, Calle Zaragoza 29, tel. 954-211-455). You can also check schedules at www.renfe .com. Many travel agencies sell train tickets; look for a train sticker in agency windows.

Tours in Sevilla

Guided City Walks by Concepción

Concepción Delgado, an enthusiastic teacher who's a joy to listen to, takes small groups on English-only walks. Using me as her guinea pig, Concepción has designed a fine two-hour **Sevilla Cultural Show & Tell** walk. In this introduction to her home-

or carrying the cross to his execution. More penitents follow—with dozens or even hundreds of participants, a procession can stretch out over a half-mile. All this sets the stage for the finale—typically a float of the Virgin Mary, who represents the hope of resurrection.

The elaborate floats feature carved wooden religious sculptures, some embellished with gold leaf and silverwork. They can be adorned with fresh flowers, rows of candles, and even jewelry on loan from the congregation. Each float is carried by 30 to 50 men, who labor unseen (you might catch a glimpse of their shuffling feet). The bearers wear turban-like headbands to protect their heads and necks from the crushing weight (the floats can weigh as much as two tons). Two "shifts" of float carriers rotate every 20 minutes. As a sign of their faith, some men carry the float until they collapse.

As the procession nears the cathedral, it passes through the square called La Campana, south along Calle Sierpes, and through Plaza de San Francisco. (Some parades follow a parallel route a block or two east.) Grandstands and folding chairs are filled by VIPs and Sevilla's prominent families. Thousands of candles drip wax along the well-trod parade routes, forming a waxy buildup that causes car tires to squeal for days to come.

Being in Sevilla for Holy Week is both a blessing and a curse. It's a remarkable spectacle, but it's extremely crowded. Parade routes can block your sightseeing for hours. Check printed schedules if you want to avoid them. If you do find a procession blocking your way, look for a crossing point marked by a red-painted fence, or ask a guard. Even if all you care about on Easter is a chocolate-bearing bunny, the intense devotion of the Andalusian people during their Holy Week traditions is an inspiration to behold.

town, she shares important insights the average visitor misses. Her tour rounds out the rest of your Sevilla experience, brilliantly complements your independent visits to major sights, and clues you in on what's new and what's going on around town during your visit. I think it's worthwhile even if you're only in town for one day (€15/person, minimum 4 people, Feb-July and Sept-Dec Mon-Sat at 10:30; Jan and Aug on Mon, Wed, and Fri only; meet at statue in Plaza Nueva).

For those wanting to really understand the city's two most

Sevilla

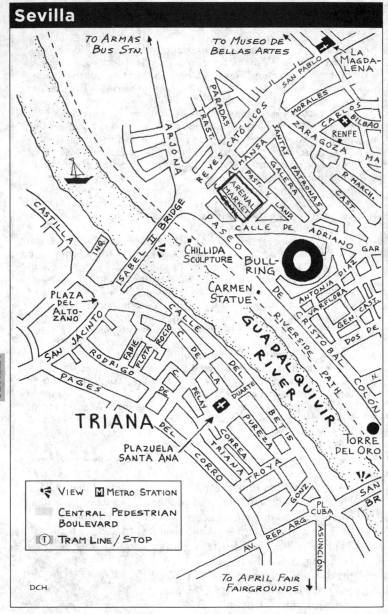

TO ARMAS BUS STN.

TO MUSEO DE BELLAS ARTES

LA MAGDALENA

SAN PABLO

MORALES

CARLOS BILBAO

RENFE

ZARAGOZA

PARADAS

TRAST.

ARJONA

REYES CATÓLICOS

SANTAS PATRONAS

GALERA

ALMANSA

PAST. Y LAND.

ARENAL MARKET

P. MARCH.

CAST.

MA

PASEO

CALLE DE ADRIANO

GAR

ISABEL II BRIDGE

INQ.

CASTILLA

CHILLIDA SCULPTURE

BULL-RING

ANTONIA DIAZ

VARFLORA

GEN. CAST.

DOS DE

PLAZA DEL ALTOZANO

CARMEN STATUE

RIVERSIDE PATH

DE CRISTOBAL

GUADALQUIVIR RIVER

N. COLÓN

SAN JACINTO

CALLE DE LA

RODRIGO

FABIE

FLOTA

ROCIO

C. DE

PAGES

PELAY

DUARTE

BETIS

DEL

TRIANA

PLAZUELA SANTA ANA

CORREA

TRIANA

PUREZA

TROYA

TORRE DEL ORO

SAN BR.

CORRO

GONZ.

PL. CUBA

REP. ARG.

AV.

ASUNCIÓN

View **M** Metro Station

Central Pedestrian Boulevard

Ⓣ Tram Line / Stop

DCH

TO APRIL FAIR FAIRGROUNDS ↓

SEVILLA

To Museo Palacio & Plaza de la Encarnación

IGLESIA DEL SALVADOR

To Casa de Pilatos

200 YARDS
200 METERS

TETUAN

CANAL

SIERPES

S. ISIDRO

PLAZA NUEVA

PL. SAN FRAN.

CITY HALL

DRID (T)

GAMAZO

JIMIOS

CIA

DE VINUESA

ARFE

MAYO

ALVAREZ QUINTERO

FERN.

COLÓN

ALEMANES

AVENIDA DE LA CONSTITUCIÓN

FRANCOS

PAJARITOS

ARGOTE DEL MOLINA

Flamenco MUSEUM

SEGOVIAS

GIRALDA

MATEOS

GAGO

XIMÉNEZ

N

BARRIO SANTA CRUZ
(SEE DETAIL MAPS)

CATHEDRAL

(i)

Archivo DE INDIAS

PLAZA D. TRIUMFO

ALM.

Post

Hospital DE LA CARIDAD

IBARRA

TEMPRADO

BAL

SANTANDER

EA Airport Bus

(B)

A. LOBO

TELMO SANJURO

IDGE

PASEO DE

DELICIAS

HOSPITAL DE LOS VENERABLES

AGUA

ALCÁZAR

M. PIARARA

PLAZA CONT.

M. PIN.

ALCÁZAR GARDENS

PUERTA DE JEREZ

(M) (T) SAN FERNANDO

MENENDEZ

EL PRADO BUS STN.

EA Airport Bus

AV. ROMA

PALOS

Hotel ALF. XIII

UNIV.

MARIA LUISA PARK

PLAZA DE ESPAÑA →

CARLOS V

(T)(B)
TO SAN BERNARDO TRAIN STN. →

(M)

PRADO SAN SEB.

PORTUGAL

SEVILLA

important sights—which are tough to fully appreciate on their own—Concepción also offers in-depth tours of the **cathedral** and the **Alcázar,** each lasting about 1.25 hours (€7 each plus entrance fees, €2 discount if you also take the Show & Tell tour; meet at 13:00 at statue in Plaza del Triunfo; minimum 4 people; cathedral tours—Mon, Wed, and Fri; Alcázar tours—Tue, Thu, and Sat; no Alcázar tours Jan and Aug).

Although you can just show up for Concepción's tours, it's smart to confirm the departure times and reserve a spot (tel. 902-158-226, mobile 616-501-100, www.sevillawalkingtours.com, info @sevillawalkingtours.com). Concepción does no tours on Sundays or holidays. Because she's a busy mom of two young kids, Concepción sometimes sends her colleague Alfonso (who's also excellent) to lead these tours.

All Sevilla Guided Tours
This group of three licensed guides (Susana, Estela, and Elena) offers good English-language private tours and day trips (€120/3 hours, €160/half-day, tel. 954-638-883, mobile 606-217-194, www .allsevillaguides.com, info@allsevillaguides.com).

Really Discover Seville
Englishman David and Sevillan Luis have teamed up to show off their city with several creatively conceived, good-value walks and bike rides—all run with small groups and a personal touch. Their **Seville Bike Tour** takes up to 10 riders on a 2.5-hour journey around the city, stopping at—but not entering—all the major sights (€25, 3-10 people per group, includes bike, daily at 10:30, meet near the cathedral by the tall white monument in Plaza del Triunfo). Each morning they also lead a two-hour **Seville Walking Tour** (€20, 3-10 per group, daily at 10:30), then give you the option to tack on a one-hour boat tour (€19 more, 10-seat electric boat with guide). Call or email to confirm before showing up, as tours may be canceled for lack of interest (tel. 955-113-912, www.reallydiscover.com, davidcox@reallydiscover.com).

BiciBike
This outfit offers several guided bike tours of Sevilla (€20/2 hours, €30/3 hours, includes bike and helmet, daily at 10:00, leaves from their office on ground floor of Santa Justa train station, best to reserve ahead, tel. 955-514-110, www.bicibike.es). They also rent bikes from the same office (see page 659).

Hop-On, Hop-Off Bus Tours
Two competing city bus tours leave from the curb near the riverside Torre del Oro. You'll see the parked buses and salespeople handing out fliers. Each tour does about an hour-long swing through the city with recorded narration. The tours, which allow hopping on and off at four stops, are heavy on Expo '29 and Expo '92 neighborhoods—both zones of little interest in 2014. While the narra-

tion does its best, Sevilla is most interesting in places buses can't go (€17, daily 10:00-21:00, green route has shorter option).

Horse and Buggy Tours

A carriage ride is a classic, popular way to survey the city and a relaxing way to enjoy María Luisa Park (€45 for a 45-minute clip-clop, much more during Holy Week and the April Fair, find a likable English-speaking driver for better narration). Look for rigs at Plaza América, Plaza del Triunfo, the Torre del Oro, Alfonso XIII Hotel, and Avenida Isabel la Católica.

Boat Cruises

Boring one-hour panoramic tours leave every 30 minutes from the dock behind the Torre de Oro. The low energy recorded narration is hard to follow, but there's little to see anyway (overpriced at €15, tel. 954-561-692).

More Tours

Visitours, a typical big-bus tour company, does €95 all-day trips to Córdoba, as well as several other locations in Andalucía (Tue, Thu, and Sat; tel. 955-999-760, mobile 686-413-413, www.visitours.es, visitours@visitours.es). For other guides, contact one of the **Guide Associations of Sevilla:** AUITS (mobile 699-494-204, www.auits.com, guias@auits.com) or APIT (tel. 954-210-044, www.apitsevilla.com, visitas@apitsevilla.com).

Self-Guided Walk

Barrio Santa Cruz

Of Sevilla's once-thriving Jewish Quarter, only the tangled street plan and a wistful Old World ambience survive. This classy maze

of lanes (too narrow for cars), small plazas, tile-covered patios, and whitewashed houses with wrought-iron latticework draped in flowers is a great refuge from the summer heat and bustle of Sevilla. The streets are narrow—some with buildings so close they're called "kissing lanes." A happy result of the narrowness is shade: Locals claim the Barrio Santa Cruz is three degrees cooler than the rest of the city.

Orange trees abound—because they never lose their leaves, they provide constant shade. But forget about eating the oranges. They're bitter and used only to make vitamins, perfume, cat food, and that marmalade you can't avoid in British B&Bs. But when they blossom (for three weeks in spring, usually in March), the aroma is heavenly.

The barrio is made for wandering. Getting lost is easy, and

Barrio Santa Cruz Self-Guided Walk

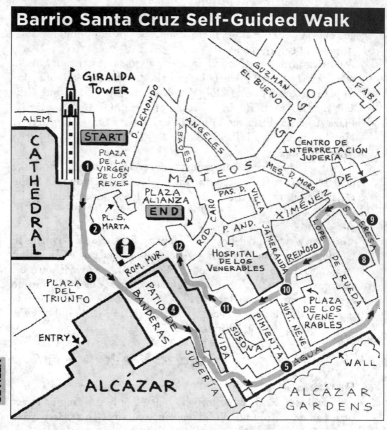

I recommend doing just that. But to get started, here's a plaza-to-plaza walk that loops you through the *corazón* (heart) of the neighborhood and back out again.

Tour groups often trample the barrio's charm in the morning. I find that early evening (around 18:00) is the ideal time to explore the quarter.

❶ **Plaza de la Virgen de los Reyes:** Start in the square in front of the cathedral, at the base of the Giralda Bell Tower. This square is dedicated to the Virgin of the Kings—see her tile on the white wall facing the cathedral. She is one of several different versions of Mary you'll see in Sevilla, each appealing to a different type of worshipper. This particular one is big here because the Spanish king reportedly carried her image with him when he retook

FARNESIO

SANTA MARIA

OLA

ENCISO

CRUCES

S. MARIA LA BLANCA

PL. S. MARIA

LA BLANCA

PLAZA SANTA CRUZ

7 PLAZA DE REFINADORES

6

PLAZA DE ALFARO

MURILLO GARDENS

50 YARDS

50 METERS

← WALKING TOUR

DCH

1 Plaza de la Virgen de los Reyes
2 Nun Goodies
3 Plaza del Triunfo
4 Patio de Banderas
5 Calle Agua
6 Plaza de la Santa Cruz
7 Plaza de Refinadores
8 Casa de Murillo
9 Monasterio de San José del Carmen
10 Plaza de los Venerables, Hospital de los Venerables & Centro Velázquez
11 Plaza de Doña Elvira
12 Plaza de la Alianza

SEVILLA

the town from the Moors in 1248. The fountain dates from 1929. The reddish Baroque building across the square is the Archbishop's Palace.

Notice the columns and chains that ring the cathedral, as if put there to establish a border between the secular and Catholic worlds. Indeed, that's exactly the purpose they served for centuries, when Sevillans running from the law merely had to cross these chains—like crossing the county line. (People in trouble didn't escape justice; they just had a bit of a choice as to who would administer it.) Many of these columns are far older than the cathedral, having originally been made for Roman and Visigothic buildings, and later recycled by medieval Catholics.

From this peaceful square, look up the street leading away from the cathedral and notice the characteristic (government-protected) 19th-century architecture. The ironwork, typical of Andalucía, is the pride of Sevilla. Equally ubiquitous is the traditional whitewash-and-goldenrod color scheme.

Another symbol you'll see throughout Sevilla is the city insignia: "NO*8*DO," the letters "NODO" with a figure-eight-like shape at their center. *Nodo* meant "knot" in the old dialect, and this symbol evokes the strong ties between the citizens of Sevilla and King Alfonso X (during a succession dispute in the 13th century, the Sevillans remained loyal to their king).

• *Keeping the cathedral on your right, walk toward the next square.*

❷ **Nun Goodies:** The white building on your left was an Augustinian convent. At #3, step inside to meet (but not see) a cloistered nun behind a *torno* (the lazy Susan the nuns spin to sell their goods while staying hidden). The sisters raise money by producing local goodies—like tasty communion wafer *tabletas* (€1—eating them is like having sin-free cookies) and lovely rosaries (€4). Consider buying something here just as a donation. The sisters, who speak only Spanish, have a sense of humor (daily 9:00-13:00 & 16:45-18:15).

• *Then step into...*

❸ **Plaza del Triunfo:** The "Plaza of Triumph" is named for the 1755 earthquake that destroyed Lisbon, but only rattled Sevilla, leaving most of this city intact. A statue thanking the Virgin for protecting the city is at the far end of the square, under a stone canopy. That Virgin faces another one (closer to you), atop a tall pillar honoring Sevillan artists, including the painter Murillo.

• *Before leaving the square, consider stopping at the TI for a map or advice. Then pass through the arched opening in the Alcázar's crenellated wall. You'll emerge into a courtyard called the...*

❹ **Patio de Banderas:** The Banderas Courtyard (as in "flags," not Antonio) was once a military parade ground for the royal guard. The barracks surrounding the square once housed the king's bodyguards. Farther back, a Moorish palace stood on this spot; archaeologists are busy excavating what remains of it. Today, the far end of this square is a favorite spot for snapping a postcard view of the Giralda Bell Tower.

• *Exit the courtyard at the far corner, through the Judería arch. Go down the long, narrow passage. Emerging into the light, you'll be walking*

Sevilla's Jews

In the summer of 1391, smoldering anti-Jewish sentiment flared up in Sevilla. On June 6, Christian mobs ransacked the city's Jewish Quarter (Judería). Around 4,000 Jews were killed, and 5,000 Jewish families were driven from their homes. Synagogues were stripped and transformed into churches. The former Judería eventually became the neighborhood of the Holy Cross-Barrio Santa Cruz. Sevilla's uprising spread through Spain (and Europe), the first of many nasty pogroms during the next century.

Before the pogrom, Jews had lived in Sevilla for centuries as the city's respected merchants, doctors, and bankers. They flourished under the Muslim Moors. After Sevilla was "liberated" by King Ferdinand III (1248), Jews were given protection by Spain's kings and allowed a measure of self-government, though they were confined to the Jewish neighborhood.

But by the 14th century, Jews were increasingly accused of everything from poisoning wells to ritually sacrificing Christian babies. Mobs killed suspected Jews, and some of Sevilla's most respected Jewish citizens had their fortunes confiscated.

After 1391, Jews faced a choice: Be persecuted (even killed), relocate, or convert to Christianity. The newly Christianized—called *conversos* (converted) or *marranos* (swine)—were always under suspicion of practicing their old faith, and thereby undermining true Christianity. Longtime Christians were threatened by this new social class of converted Jews, who now had equal status, fanning the mistrust.

To root out the perceived problem of underground Judaism, the "Catholic Monarchs," Ferdinand and Isabel, established the Inquisition in Spain (1478). Under the direction of Grand Inquisitor Tomás de Torquemada, these religious courts arrested and interrogated *conversos* suspected of practicing Judaism. Using long solitary confinement and torture, they extracted confessions.

On February 6, 1481, Sevilla hosted Spain's first auto-da-fé ("act of faith"), a public confession and punishment for heresy. Six accused *conversos* were paraded barefoot into the cathedral, made to publicly confess their sins, then burned at the stake. Over the next three decades, thousands of *conversos* were tried and killed in Spain.

In 1492, the same year the last Moors were driven from Spain, Ferdinand and Isabel decreed that all remaining Jews convert or be expelled (to Portugal and ultimately to Holland). Spain emerged as a nation unified under the banner of Christianity.

alongside the Alcázar wall. Take the first left, then right, through a small square and follow the narrow alleyway called...

❺ **Calle Agua:** As you walk along the street, look to the left, peeking through iron gates for occasional glimpses of the flower-smothered patios of exclusive private residences. The patio at #2

is a delight—ringed with columns, filled with flowers, and colored with glazed tiles. The tiles are not merely decorative; they keep buildings cooler in the summer heat. Emerging at the end of the street, turn around and look back at the openings of two old pipes built into the wall. These 12th-century Moorish pipes once carried water to the Alcázar (and today give the street its name). You're standing at an entrance into the pleasant Murillo Gardens (to the right), formerly the fruit-and-vegetable gardens for the Alcázar.

• *Don't enter the gardens now, but instead cross the square diagonally to the left, and continue 20 yards down a lane to the...*

❻ **Plaza de la Santa Cruz:** Arguably the heart of the barrio, this pleasant square, graced by orange trees and draping vines, was once the site of a synagogue (there used to be four in the barrio; now there are none), which Christians destroyed. They replaced the synagogue with a church, which the French (under Napoleon) later demolished. It's a bit of history that locals remember when they see the blue, white, and red French flag marking the French consulate, now overlooking this peaceful square. A fine 16th-century iron cross marks the center of the square and the site of the church the French destroyed. The Sevillan painter Murillo, who was buried in that church, lies somewhere below you.

At #9, you can peek into a lovely courtyard that's proudly been left open so visitors can enjoy it. The square is also home to the recommended Los Gallos flamenco bar, which puts on nightly performances (described on page 711).

• *At the far end of the square, a one-block detour along Calle Mezquita leads to nearby...*

❼ **Plaza de Refinadores:** Sevilla's most famous (if fictional) 17th-century citizen is honored here with a statue (see photo). Don Juan Tenorio—the original Don Juan—was a notorious sex addict and atheist who proudly thumbed his nose at the stifling Church-driven morals of his day.

• *Backtrack to Plaza de la Santa Cruz and turn right*

SEVILLA

(north) on Calle Santa Teresa. At #8 (on the left) is...

❽ **Casa de Murillo:** One of Sevilla's famous painters, Bartolomé Esteban Murillo (1618-1682), lived here, soaking in the ambience of street life and reproducing it in his paintings of cute beggar children (see sidebar on page 675).

• *Directly across from Casa de Murillo is the...*

❾ **Monasterio de San José del Carmen:** This is where St. Teresa stayed when she visited from her hometown of Ávila. The convent (closed to the public) keeps artifacts of the mystic nun, such as her spiritual manuscripts.

Continue north on Calle Santa Teresa, then take the first left on Calle Lope de Rueda, then left again, then right on **Calle Reinoso.** This street—so narrow that the buildings almost touch—is one of the barrio's "kissing lanes." A popular explanation suggests the buildings were built so close together to provide maximum shade. But the history is more complex than that: this labyrinthine street plan goes back to Moorish times, when this area was a tangled market. Later, this was the Jewish ghetto, where all the city's Jews were forced to live in a very small area.

• *Just to the left, the street spills onto...*

❿ **Plaza de los Venerables:** This square is another candidate for "heart of the barrio." The streets branching off it ooze local

ambience. When the Jews were expelled from Spain in 1492, this area became deserted and run-down. But in 1929, for its world's fair, Sevilla turned the plaza into a showcase of Andalusian style, adding the railings, tile work, orange trees, and other too-cute, Epcot-like adornments. A different generation of tourists enjoys the place today, likely unaware that what they're seeing in Santa Cruz is far from "authentic" (or, at least, not as old as they imagine).

The large, harmonious Baroque-style Hospital de los Venerables (1675), once a retirement home for old priests (the "venerables"), is now a cultural foundation worth visiting for its ornate church and excellent collection of paintings (see page 692).

• *Continue west on Calle de Gloria, past an interesting tile map of the Jewish Quarter (on the right). You'll soon come upon...*

Sevilla at a Glance

▲▲▲**Flamenco** Flamboyant, riveting music-and-dance performances, offered at clubs throughout town. **Hours:** Shows start as early as 19:00. See page 709.

▲▲**Cathedral and Giralda Bell Tower** The world's largest Gothic church, with Columbus' tomb, treasury, and climbable tower. **Hours:** July-Aug Mon-Sat 9:30-17:00, Sun 14:30-18:00; Sept-June Mon-Sat 11:00-17:00, Sun 14:30-18:00. See page 674.

▲▲**Alcázar** Palace built by the Moors in the 10th century, revamped in the 14th century, and still serving as royal digs. **Hours:** April-Sept daily 9:30-19:00, Oct-March daily 9:30-17:00. See page 682.

▲▲**Hospital de la Caridad** Former charity hospital (funded by the likely inspiration for Don Juan) with gorgeously decorated chapel. **Hours:** Mon-Sat 9:00-13:00 & 15:30-19:00, Sun 9:00-12:30. See page 693.

▲▲**Basílica de la Macarena** Church and museum with the much-venerated Weeping Virgin statue and two significant floats from Sevilla's Holy Week celebrations. **Hours:** Daily 9:30-14:00 & 17:00-20:30. See page 701.

▲▲**Triana** Energetic, colorful neighborhood on the west bank of the river. **Hours:** Always strollable. See page 703.

▲▲**Bullfight Museum** Guided tour of the bullring and its museum. **Hours:** Daily May-Oct 9:30-20:00, Nov-April 9:00-19:00, on fight days until 14:00. See page 706.

▲▲**Evening Paseo** Locals strolling in the cool of the evening, mainly along Avenida de la Constitución, Barrio Santa Cruz, the

⓫ Plaza de Doña Elvira: This small square—with orange trees, tile benches, and a stone fountain—sums up our barrio walk. Shops sell work by local artisans, such as ceramics, embroidery, and fans.

• *Cross the plaza and head north along Calle Rodrigo Caro into the...*

⓬ Plaza de la Alianza: Ever consider a career change? Gain inspiration at the site that once housed the painting studio of John Fulton (1932-1998; find the small plaque on the other side of the square), an American

Calle Sierpes and Tetuán shopping pedestrian zone, and the Guadalquivir River. **Hours:** Spring through fall; best paseo scene 18:00-20:00, until very late at night in summer. See page 712.

▲**Archivo de Indias** Fantastic Renaissance building (Lonja Palace) housing Spain's national archives. **Hours:** Mon-Sat 9:30-17:00, Sun 10:00-14:00. See page 691.

▲**Church of the Savior** Sevilla's second-biggest church, bristling with Baroque altarpieces. **Hours:** July-Aug Mon-Sat 9:30-17:00, Sun 14:30-18:00; Sept-June Mon-Sat 11:00-17:00, Sun 14:30-18:00. See page 695.

▲**Museo Palacio de la Condesa de Lebrija** A fascinating 18th-century aristocratic mansion. **Hours:** July-Aug Mon-Fri 9:00-15:00, Sat 10:00-14:00, closed Sun; Sept-June Mon-Fri 10:30-19:30, Sat 10:00-14:00 & 16:00-18:00, Sun 10:00-14:00. See page 697.

▲**Flamenco Dance Museum** High-tech museum explaining the history and art of Sevilla's favorite dance. **Hours:** Daily 10:00-19:00. See page 697.

▲**Museo de Bellas Artes** Andalucía's top paintings, including works by Spanish masters Murillo and Zurbarán. **Hours:** Tue-Sat 10:00-20:30, Sun 10:00-17:00, closed Mon. See page 698.

SEVILLA

▲**Bullfights** Some of Spain's best bullfighting, held at Sevilla's arena. **Hours:** Fights generally at 18:30 on most Sundays in May and June, on Easter and Corpus Christi, and daily through the April Fair and in late September. Rookies fight small bulls on Thursdays in July. See page 705.

who pursued two dreams. Though born in Philadelphia, Fulton got hooked on bullfighting. He trained in the tacky bullrings of Mexico, then in 1956 he moved to Sevilla, the world capital of the sport. His career as matador was not top-notch, and the Spaniards were slow to warm to the Yankee, but his courage and persistence earned their grudging respect. After he put down the cape, he picked up a brush, making colorful paintings in his Sevilla studio.

• *From Plaza de la Alianza, you can return to the cathedral by turning left (west) on Calle Joaquin Romero Murube (along the wall). Or, if you're ready for a bite, head northeast on Calle Rodrigo Caro, which intersects with Calle Mateos Gago, a street lined with tapas bars.*

Sights in Sevilla

▲▲Cathedral and Giralda Bell Tower

Sevilla's cathedral is the third-largest church in Europe (after St. Peter's at the Vatican and St. Paul's in London) and the largest

Gothic church anywhere. When they ripped down a mosque of brick on this site in 1401, the Reconquista Christians announced their intention to build a cathedral so huge that "anyone who sees it will take us for madmen." They built for about a hundred years. Even today, the descendants of those madmen proudly display an enlarged photocopy of their *Guinness Book of Records* letter certifying, "Santa María de la Sede in Sevilla is the cathedral with the largest area: 126.18 meters x 82.60 meters x 30.48 meters high."

Cost and Hours: €8, €3 for students and those over age 65 (must show ID), kids under age 18 free; keep your ticket, which includes free entry to the Church of the Savior—you'll save €3; July-Aug Mon-Sat 9:30-17:00, Sun 14:30-18:00; Sept-June Mon-Sat 11:00-17:00, Sun 14:30-18:00; closes 30 minutes earlier on Mondays year-round; last entry to cathedral one hour before closing, last entry to bell tower 30 minutes before closing; WC and drinking fountain just inside entrance and in courtyard near exit, tel. 954-214-971. Most of the website www.catedraldesevilla.es is in Spanish, but following the "vista virtual" links will take you to a virtual tour with an English option.

Crowd-Beating Tip: Though there's usually not much of a

line to buy tickets, you can avoid the queue altogether by buying your €8 combo-ticket at the Church of the Savior, a few blocks north (see page 695). See that church first, then come to the cathedral and waltz past the line to the turnstile.

Tours: My self-guided tour covers the basics. The €3 audioguide explains each side chapel for anyone interested in all the old paintings and dry details. For €7, you can enjoy Concepción Delgado's tour instead (see "Tours in Sevilla," earlier).

➔ Self-Guided Tour: Enter the cathedral at the south end (closest to the Alcázar, with a full-size replica of the Giralda's

Bartolomé Murillo
(1617-1682)

The son of a barber of Seville, Bartolomé Murillo got his start selling paintings meant for export to the frontier churches of

the Americas. In his 20s, he became famous after he painted a series of saints for Sevilla's Franciscan monastery. By about 1650, Murillo's sugary, simple, and accessible religious style was spreading through Spain and beyond.

Murillo painted street kids with cute smiles and grimy faces, and radiant young Marías with Ivory-soap complexions and rapturous poses (Immaculate Conceptions). His paintings view the world through a soft-focus lens, wrapping everything in warm colors and soft light, with a touch (too much, for some) of sentimentality.

Murillo became a rich, popular family man, and the toast of Sevilla's high society. In 1664, his wife died, leaving him heartbroken, but his last 20 years were his most prolific. At age 65, Murillo died after falling off a scaffold while painting. His tomb is lost somewhere under the bricks of Plaza de la Santa Cruz.

weathervane statue in the patio).

• *First, you pass through the...*

❶ Art Pavilion: Just past the turnstile, you step into a room of paintings that once hung in the church, including works by Sevilla's two 17th-century masters—Bartolomé Murillo (*St. Ferdinand*, depicting the king who freed Sevilla from the Moors) and Francisco de Zurbarán *(St. John the Baptist in the Desert)*. Find a painting showing two of Sevilla's patron saints—Santa Justa and Santa Rufina, killed in ancient Roman times for their Christian faith. Potters by trade, these two are easy to identify by their pots and palm branches (symbolic of their martyrdom), and the bell tower symbolizing the town they protect. As you tour the cathedral, keep track of how many depictions of this dynamic and saintly duo you spot. They're everywhere.

• *Walking past a rack of church maps and a WC, enter the actual church. In the center of the church, sit down in front of the...*

❷ High Altar: Look through the wrought-iron Renaissance grille at what's called the largest altarpiece *(retablo mayor)* ever made—65 feet tall, with 44 scenes from the life of Jesus and Mary carved from walnut and chestnut, blanketed by a staggering amount of gold leaf. The work took three generations to complete

Sevilla's Cathedral

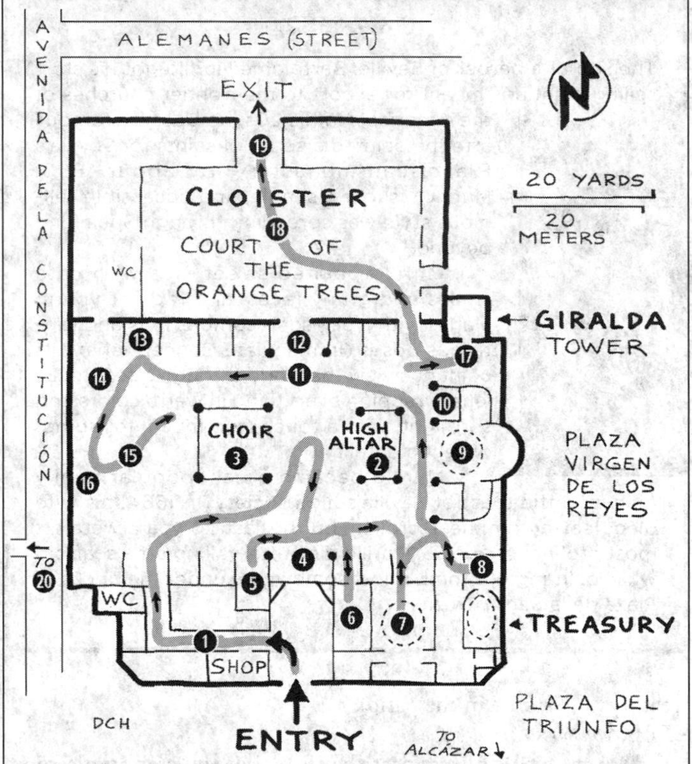

AVENIDA DE LA CONSTITUCIÓN

ALEMANES (STREET)

EXIT

N

CLOISTER

COURT OF THE ORANGE TREES

20 YARDS
20 METERS

WC

GIRALDA TOWER

⑬ ⑫ ⑰

⑭ ⑪

CHOIR
③

HIGH ALTAR
②

⑩
⑨

PLAZA VIRGEN DE LOS REYES

⑮ ⑯

TO ⑳

WC

④ ⑤

⑥ ⑦ ⑧

TREASURY

PLAZA DEL TRIUNFO

DCH

SHOP

ENTRY

TO ALCÁZAR ↓

SEVILLA

❶ Art Pavilion
❷ High Altar
❸ Choir
❹ Tomb of Columbus
❺ Virgin Antigua
❻ Sacristy
❼ Main Sacristy
❽ Treasury
❾ Royal Chapel
❿ Chapel of St. Peter

⓫ View of Plateresque Ceiling
⓬ Altar de Plata
⓭ Chapel of St. Anthony
⓮ Pennant of Ferdinand III
⓯ Back of the Nave
⓰ MURILLO – Guardian Angel
⓱ Giralda Tower Climb Entrance
⓲ Court of the Orange Trees
⓳ Moorish-Style Doorway
⓴ To Nun-Baked Goodies

(1481-1564). The story is told left to right, bottom to top. Find Baby Jesus in the manger, in the middle of the bottom row, then follow his story through the miracles, the Passion, and the Pentecost. Crane your neck to look way up to the tippy-top, where a Crucifixion adorns the dizzying summit.

• *Turn around and check out the...*

❸ **Choir:** Facing the high altar, the choir features an organ of more than 7,000 pipes (played Mon-Fri at the 10:00 Mass, Sun at the 10:00 & 13:00 Mass, not in July-Aug, free for worshippers). A choir area like this one—enclosed within the cathedral for more intimate services—is common in Spain and England, but rare in churches elsewhere. The big, spinnable book holder in the middle of the room held giant hymnals—large enough for all to chant from in a pre-Xerox age when there weren't enough books for everyone.

• *Now turn 90 degrees to the left and march to find the...*

❹ **Tomb of Columbus:** In front of the cathedral's entrance for pilgrims are four kings who carry the tomb of Christopher Columbus. His pallbearers represent the regions of Castile, Aragon, León, and Navarre (identify them by their team shirts). Notice how the cross held by Señor León has a pike end, which is piercing an orb. Look closer: It's a pomegranate, the symbol of Granada—the last Moorish-ruled city to succumb to the Reconquista (in 1492).

Columbus didn't just travel a lot while alive—he even kept it up posthumously. He was buried first in northwestern Spain (in Valladolid, where he died), then moved to a monastery here in Sevilla, then to what's now the Dominican Republic (as he'd requested), then to Cuba. Finally—when Cuba gained independence from Spain, around 1900—his remains sailed home again to Sevilla. After all that, it's fair to wonder whether the remains in the box before you are actually his. Sevillans like to think so. (Columbus died in 1506. Five hundred years later, to help celebrate the anniversary of his death, DNA samples did indeed give Sevillans some evidence to substantiate their claim.)

SEVILLA

Immaculate Conception

Throughout Sevilla—and all of Spain—you'll see paintings titled *The Immaculate Conception,* all looking quite similar (see example on page 675). Young, lovely, and beaming radiantly, these virgins look pure and untainted...you might even say "immaculate." According to Catholic doctrine, Mary, the future mother of Jesus, entered the world free from the original sin that other mortals share. When she died, her purity allowed her to be taken up directly to heaven (in the Assumption).

The doctrine of Immaculate Conception can be confusing, even to Catholics. It does not mean that the Virgin Mary herself was born of a virgin. Rather, Mary's mother and father conceived her in the natural way. But at the moment Mary's soul animated her flesh, God granted her a special exemption from original sin. The doctrine of Immaculate Conception had been popular since medieval times, though it was not codified until 1854. It was Sevilla's own Bartolomé Murillo (1617-1682) who painted the model of this goddess-like Mary, copied by so many lesser artists. In Counter-Reformation times (when Murillo lived), paintings of a fresh-faced, ecstatic Mary made abstract doctrines like the Immaculate Conception and the Assumption tangible and accessible to Catholics across Europe.

Most images of the Immaculate Conception show Mary wearing a radiant crown and with a crescent moon at her feet; she often steps on the heads of cherubs. Paintings by Murillo frequently portray Mary in a blue robe with long, wavy hair—young and innocent.

On the left is a 1584 mural of St. Christopher, patron saint of travelers. The clock above has been ticking since 1788.

• *Facing Columbus, turn right and duck into the first chapel (on your left) to find the...*

❺ **Virgin Antigua:** Within this chapel is a gilded fresco of the Virgin delicately holding a rose and the Christ Child, who's holding a bird. It's the oldest art here, even older than the cathedral itself: It was painted onto a horseshoe-shaped prayer niche of the mosque that formerly stood on this site. After Sevilla was reconquered in 1248, the mosque served as a church for about 120 years—until it was torn down to make room for this huge cathedral. The Catholic builders, who were captivated by the fresco's beauty and well aware of the Virgin Antigua's status as protector of sailors (important in this port city), decided to save the fresco.

• *Exiting the Virgin Antigua Chapel, begin your counterclockwise tour of the cathedral. As you explore, note that its many chapels are described in English, and many of the windows have their dates worked into the design.*

Just on the other side of Columbus, walk through the next small chapel and into the...

❻ Sacristy: This space is where the priests get ready each morning before Mass. The Goya painting above the altar features another portrayal of Justa and Rufina with their trademark bell tower, pots, and palm leaves.

• *Two chapels down is the entrance to the...*

❼ Main Sacristy: Marvel at the ornate, 16th-century dome of the main room, a grand souvenir from Sevilla's Golden Age.

The intricate masonry, called Plateresque, resembles lacy silverwork (*plata* means "silver"). God is way up in the cupola. The three layers of figures below him show the heavenly host; relatives in purgatory—hands folded—looking to heaven in hope of help; and the wretched in hell, including a topless sinner engulfed in flames and teased cruelly by pitchfork-wielding monsters.

Dominating the room is a nearly 1,000-pound, silver-plated monstrance (vessel for displaying the communion wafer). This is the one locals use to parade the holy host through town during Corpus Christi festivities.

• *At the far end of the main sacristy, at the left-hand corner, is a door leading to our next stop.*

❽ Treasury: The *tesoro* fills several rooms in the corner of the church. Wander deeper into the treasury to find a unique oval dome. It's in the 16th-century chapter room *(sala capitular)*, where monthly meetings take place with the bishop (he gets the throne, while the others share the bench). The paintings here are by Murillo: a fine *Immaculate Conception* (1668, high above the bishop's throne) and portraits of saints important to Sevillans.

The wood-paneled Room of Ornaments shows off gold and silver reliquaries, which hold hundreds of holy body parts, as well as Spain's most valuable crown. This jeweled crown (the Corona de la Virgen de los Reyes, by Manuel de la Torre) sparkles with thousands of tiny but precious stones, and the world's largest pearl—used as the torso of an angel. This amazing treasure was paid for by locals who donated their wealth to royally crown their Madonna.

• *Leave the treasury and cross through the church to see...*

More Church Sights: First you'll pass the closed-to-tourists ❾ **Royal Chapel,** the burial place of several of kings of Castile (open for worship only—access from outside), then the also-closed ❿ **Chapel of St. Peter,** which is filled with paintings showing scenes from the life of St. Peter. In the far corner—past the glass case displaying the *Guinness Book* certificate declaring that this is indeed the world's largest church by area—is the entry to the Giralda Bell Tower; we'll finish our visit there. But for now, continue your counterclockwise circuit. Near the high altar, in the middle, crane your neck skyward to admire the ⓫ **Plateresque tracery** on the ceiling, and take in the enormous ⓬ **Altar de Plata** rising up in a side chapel. The gleaming silver altarpiece adorned with statues looks like a big monstrance.

The ⓭ **Chapel of St. Anthony** (Capilla de San Antonio), the last chapel on the right, is used for baptisms. The Renaissance baptismal font has delightful carved angels dancing along its base. In Murillo's painting, *Vision of St. Anthony* (1656), the saint kneels in wonder as a Baby Jesus comes down surrounded by a choir of angels. Anthony, one of Iberia's most popular saints, is the patron saint of lost things—so people come here to pray for Anthony's help in finding

jobs, car keys, and life partners. Above the *Vision* is *The Baptism of Christ,* also by Murillo. You don't need to be an art historian to know that the stained glass dates from 1685. And by now you must know who the women are....

Nearby, a glass case displays the ⓮ **pennant of Ferdinand III,** which was raised over the minaret of the mosque on November 23, 1248, as Christian forces finally expelled the Moors from Sevilla. For centuries, it was paraded through the city on special days.

Continuing on, stand at the ⓯ **back of the nave** (behind the choir) and appreciate the ornate immensity of the church. Can you see the angels trumpeting on their Cuban mahogany? Any birds? The massive candlestick holder to the right of the choir dates from 1560. And before you is the gravestone of Ferdinand Columbus, Christopher's second son. Having given the cathedral his collection of 6,000 precious books, he was rewarded with this prime burial spot.

Turn around. To the left, behind an iron grille, is a niche with ⓰ **Murillo's** *Guardian Angel* pointing to the light and showing an astonished child the way.

• *Backtrack the length of the church toward the Giralda Bell Tower, and notice the back of the choir's Baroque pipe organ. The exit sign leads to the Court of the Orange Trees and the exit. But first, some exercise.*

⓱ Giralda Tower Climb: Your church admission includes entry to the bell tower. Notice the beautiful Moorish simplicity as you climb to its top, 330 feet up, for a grand city view. The spiraling ramp was designed to accommodate a donkey-riding muezzin, who clip-clopped up five times a day to give the Muslim call to prayer.

• *Back on the ground, head outside to the...*

⓲ Court of the Orange Trees: Today's cloister was once the mosque's Court of the Orange Trees (Patio de los Naranjos).

Twelfth-century Muslims stopped at the fountain in the middle to wash their hands, face, and feet before praying. The ankle-breaking lanes between the bricks were once irrigation streams—a reminder that the Moors introduced irrigation to Iberia. The mosque was made of bricks; the church is built of stone. The only large-scale remnants of the mosque today are the Court of the Orange Trees, the Giralda Bell Tower, and the site itself.

• *You'll exit the cathedral through the Court of the Orange Trees (WCs are at the far end of the courtyard, downstairs). As you leave, look back from the outside and notice the arch over the...*

⓳ Moorish-Style Doorway: As with much of the Moorish-looking art in town, this doorway is actually Christian—the two coats of arms are a giveaway. The relief above the door shows the Bible story of Jesus ridding the temple of the merchants...a reminder to contemporary merchants that there will be no retail activity in the church. The plaque on the right honors Miguel de Cervantes, the great 16th-century writer. It's one of many plaques scattered throughout town showing places mentioned in his books. (In this case, the topic was pickpockets.)

The huge green doors predate the church. They are bits of the pre-1248 mosque—wood covered with bronze. Study the fine workmanship.

Giralda Tower Exterior: Step across the street from the exit gate and look at the bell tower. Formerly a Moorish minaret from which Muslims were called to prayer, it became the cathedral's bell tower after the Reconquista. A 4,500-pound bronze statue symbolizing the Triumph of Faith (specifically, the Christian faith over the Muslim one) caps the tower and serves as a weather vane (in Spanish, *girar* means "to rotate"; a *giraldillo* is something that rotates). In 1356, the original top of the tower fell. You're looking at a 16th-century Christian-built top with a ribbon of letters proclaiming, "The strongest tower is the name of God" (you can see *Fortísima*—"strongest"—from this vantage point).

Now circle around for a close look at the corner of the tower at ground level. Needing more strength than their bricks could provide for the lowest section of the tower, the Moors used Roman-cut stones. You can actually read the Latin that was chiseled onto one of the stones 2,000 years ago. The tower offers a brief recap of the city's history: It sits on a Roman foundation, has a long Moorish section, which is capped by the current Christian age.

Today, by law, no building in the center may be higher than the statue atop the tower. (But the new Cajasol Tower, just across the river, is by far the tallest erection in the greater city—and that offends locals in this conservative town. The fact that it's the headquarters of one of Spain's major banks, which many Spaniards blame for the economic crisis, hasn't helped its popularity.)

• *Your cathedral tour is finished. If you've worked up an appetite, get out your map and make your way a few blocks for some...*

㉠ Nun-Baked Goodies: Stop by the El Torno Pastelería de Conventos, a co-op where various orders of cloistered nuns send their handicrafts (such as baptismal dresses for babies) and baked goods to be sold. You won't actually see *el torno* (a lazy Susan), since this shop is staffed by non-nuns, but this humble little hole-in-the-wall shop is worth a peek, and definitely serves the best cookies, bar nun. It's located through the passageway at 24 Avenida de la Constitución, immediately in front of the cathedral's main front door: Go through the doorway marked *Plaza del Cabildo* into the quiet courtyard (Mon-Fri 10:00-13:30 & 17:00-19:30, Sat-Sun 10:30-14:00, closed Aug, Plaza del Cabildo 2, tel. 954-219-190).

▲▲Alcázar

Originally a 10th-century palace built for the governors of the local Moorish state, this building still functions as a royal palace—the oldest in Europe that's still in use. The core of the palace features an extensive 14th-century rebuild, done by Muslim workmen for the Christian king, Pedro I (1334-1369). Pedro was nicknamed either "the Cruel" or "the Just," depending on which end of his sword you were on. Pedro's palace embraces both cultural traditions.

Today, visitors can enjoy several sections

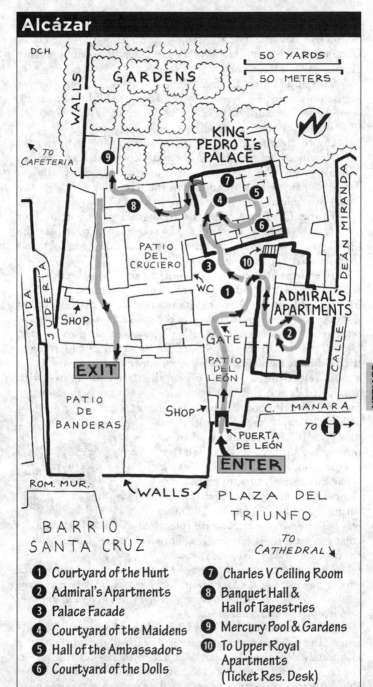

Alcázar

DCH

WALLS

GARDENS

50 YARDS
50 METERS

TO CAFETERIA

KING PEDRO I's PALACE

N

⑨

⑧

④

⑦

⑤

⑥

⑩

③

PATIO DEL CRUCIERO

WC

①

ADMIRAL'S APARTMENTS

②

DEÁN MIRANDA

VIDA

JUDERIA

SHOP

EXIT

GATE

PATIO DEL LEÓN

SHOP

PUERTA DE LEÓN

ENTER

CALLE

C. MANARA

TO ⊕→

PATIO DE BANDERAS

ROM. MUR.

WALLS

PLAZA DEL TRIUNFO

BARRIO SANTA CRUZ

TO CATHEDRAL ↘

① Courtyard of the Hunt
② Admiral's Apartments
③ Palace Facade
④ Courtyard of the Maidens
⑤ Hall of the Ambassadors
⑥ Courtyard of the Dolls

⑦ Charles V Ceiling Room
⑧ Banquet Hall & Hall of Tapestries
⑨ Mercury Pool & Gardens
⑩ To Upper Royal Apartments (Ticket Res. Desk)

SEVILLA

of the Alcázar. Spectacularly decorated halls and courtyards have distinctive Islamic-style flourishes. Exhibits call up the era of Columbus and Spain's New World dominance. The lush, sprawling gardens invite exploration.

Cost and Hours: €9 (free Mon after 15:00), €2 for students and seniors over 65—must show ID, free for children under 16, open April-Sept daily 9:30-19:00, Oct-March daily 9:30-17:00, tel. 954-502-324, www.alcazarsevilla.org.

Crowd-Beating Tips: To skip the ticket-buying line, reserve a time slot ahead online (https://oberonsaas.com/realalcazarsevilla). Mornings are the busiest with tour groups (especially on Tuesdays). It's less crowded late in the day—but note that the Royal Apartments can only be visited before 13:30.

Tours: The fast-moving, €4 audioguide gives you an hour of information as you wander. My self-guided tour hits the highlights, or you could consider Concepción Delgado's Alcázar tour (see page 660).

The **Upper Royal Apartments** can only be visited with a separate tour (€4.35, includes separate audioguide, must check bags in provided lockers). For some, it's worth the extra time and cost just to escape the mobs in the rest of the palace. If you're interested, once inside the Alcázar go directly to the desk and reserve a spot. Groups of 15 leave every half-hour from 10:00 to 13:30, listening to the 30-minute audio tour while escorted by a security guard.

➋ Self-Guided Tour: This royal palace is decorated with  a mix of Islamic and Christian elements—a style called Mudejar. It offers a thought-provoking glimpse of a graceful Al-Andalus world that might have survived its Castilian conquerors...but didn't. The floor plan is intentionally confusing, to make experiencing the place more exciting and surprising. While Granada's Alhambra was built by Moors for Moorish rulers, what you see here is essentially a Christian ruler's palace, built in the Moorish style by Moorish artisans.

• *Buy your ticket and enter through the turnstiles. Pass through the garden-like Patio of the Lions (Patio del León), with the rough stone wall of the older Moorish fortress on your left (c. 913), and through the arch into a courtyard called the . . .*

➊ Courtyard of the Hunt (Patio de la Montería): Get oriented. The palace's main entrance is directly ahead, through the elaborately decorated facade. WCs are in the far-left corner. In the far-right corner is the staircase and ticket booth for the Upper Royal Apartments—if you're interested, reserve an entry time now.

Christopher Columbus
(1451-1506)

This Italian wool-weaver ran off to sea, was shipwrecked in Portugal, married a captain's daughter, learned Portuguese and Spanish, and convinced Spain's monarchs to finance his bold scheme to trade with the East by sailing west. On August 3, 1492, Columbus set sail from Palos (near Huelva, 60 miles west of Sevilla) with 3 ships and 90 men, hoping to land in Asia, which Columbus estimated was 3,000 miles away. Ten weeks—and yes, 3,000 miles—later, with a superstitious crew ready to mutiny after they'd seen evil omens (including a falling meteor and a jittery compass), Columbus landed on an island in the Bahamas, convinced he'd reached Asia. He and his crew traded with the "Indians" and returned home to Palos harbor, where they were received as heroes.

Columbus made three more voyages to the New World and became rich with gold. But he gained a bad reputation among the colonists, was arrested, and returned to Spain in chains. Though pardoned, Columbus fell out of favor with the court. On May 20, 1506, he died in Valladolid. His son said he was felled by "gout and by grief at seeing himself fallen from his high estate," but historians speculate that diabetes or syphilis may have contributed. Columbus died thinking he'd visited Asia, unaware he'd opened up Europe to a New World.

The palace complex was built over many centuries, with rooms and decorations from the various rulers who've lived here. Moorish caliphs first built the original 10th-century palace and gardens. Then, after Sevilla was Christianized in 1248, King Pedro I built the most famous part of the complex. During Spain's Golden Age, it was home to Ferdinand and Isabel and, later, their grandson Charles V (a.k.a. Carlos I); they all left their mark. Successive monarchs added still more luxury. And today's king and queen still use the palace's upper floor as one of their royal residences.

• *Before entering the heart of the palace, start in the wing to the right of the courtyard. Step inside.*

❷ **Admiral's Apartments (Cuarto del Almirante):** When Queen Isabel debriefed Columbus here after his New World discoveries, she realized what he'd found could be big business. She created this wing in 1503 to administer Spain's New World ventures. In these halls, Columbus recounted his travels, Ferdinand

Magellan planned his around-the-world cruise, and mapmaker Amerigo Vespucci tried to come up with a catchy moniker for that newly discovered continent.

In the pink-and-red Audience Chamber (once a chapel), the **altarpiece painting** is of St. Mary of the Navigators (*Santa María de los Navegantes*, by Alejo Fernández, 1530s). The Virgin—the patron saint of sailors and a favorite of Columbus—keeps watch over the puny ships beneath her. Her cape seems to protect everyone under it—even the Native Americans in the dark background (the first time "Indians" were painted in Europe).

Standing beside the Virgin (on the right, dressed in gold, joining his hands together in prayer) is none other than Christopher Columbus. He stands on a cloud, because he's now in heaven (this was painted a few decades after his death). Notice that Columbus is blond. Columbus' son said of his dad: "In his youth his hair was blond, but when he reached 30, it all turned white." Many historians believe this to be the earliest known portrait of Columbus. If so, it's also likely to be the most accurate. The man on the left side of the painting, with the gold cape, is King Ferdinand.

Left of the painting is a **model** of Columbus' *Santa María*, his flagship and the only of his three ships not to survive the 1492

voyage. Columbus complained that the *Santa María*—a big cargo ship, different from the sleek *Niña* and *Pinta* caravels—was too slow. On Christmas Day it ran aground off present-day Haiti and tore a hole in its hull. The ship was dismantled to build the first permanent structure in America, a fort for 39 colonists. (After Columbus left, the natives burned the fort and killed the colonists.) Opposite the altarpiece (in the center of the back wall) is the family **coat of arms** of Columbus' descendants, who now live in Spain and Puerto Rico. Using Columbus' Spanish name, it reads: "To Castile and to León, Colón gave a new world."

Return to the still-used reception room, filled with big canvases. The **biggest painting** (and most melodramatic) shows a key turning point in Sevilla's history: King Ferdinand III humbly kneels before the bishop, giving thanks to God for helping him liberate the city from the Muslims (in 1248). Ferdinand promptly turned the Alcázar of the caliphs into the royal palace of Christian kings.

Pop into the room beyond the grand piano for a look at some ornate **fans** (mostly foreign and well-described in English). A long painting (designed to be gradually rolled across a screen and viewed like a primitive movie) shows 17th-century Sevilla during Holy Week. Follow the procession, which is much like today's, with traditional floats carried by teams of men and followed by a retinue of penitents.

• *Return to the Courtyard of the Hunt. Face the impressive entrance in the...*

❸ **Palace Facade:** This is the entrance to **King Pedro I's Palace** (Palacio del Rey Pedro I), the Alcázar's 14th-century nucleus. The facade's elaborate blend of Islamic tracery and Gothic Christian elements introduces us to the Mudejar style seen throughout Pedro's part of the palace.

• *Enter the palace. Pass through the vestibule (impressive, yes, but we'll see better), and continue left through the maze of rooms and passageways until you emerge into the big courtyard with a long pool in the center. This is the...*

❹ **Courtyard of the Maidens (Patio de las Doncellas):** You've reached the center of King Pedro's palace. It's an open-air

courtyard, surrounded by rooms. In the center is a long, rectangular reflecting pool. Like the Moors who preceded him, Pedro built his palace around water.

King Pedro cruelly abandoned his wife and moved into the Alcázar with his mistress, then hired Muslim workers from Granada to re-create the romance of that city's Alhambra in Sevilla's stark Alcázar. The designers created a microclimate engineered for coolness: water, sunken gardens, pottery, thick walls, and darkness. This palace is considered Spain's best example of the Mudejar style. Stucco panels with elaborate designs, colorful ceramic tiles, coffered wooden ceilings, and lobed arches atop slender columns create a refined, pleasing environment. The elegant proportions and symmetry of this courtyard are a photographer's delight.

• *Explore the rooms branching off the courtyard. Through the door at the end of the long reflecting pool is the palace's most important room, called the...*

❺ Hall of the Ambassadors (Salón de Embajadores): Here, in his throne room, Pedro received guests and caroused

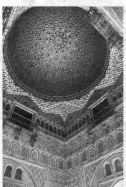

in luxury. The room is a cube topped with a half-dome, like many important Islamic buildings. In Islam, the cube represents the earth, and the dome is the starry heavens. In Pedro's world, the symbolism proclaimed that he controlled heaven and earth. Islamic horseshoe arches stand atop recycled columns with golden capitals.

The stucco on the walls is molded with interlacing plants, geometrical shapes, and Arabic writing. Here, in a Christian palace, the walls are inscribed with unapologetically Muslim sayings: "None but Allah conquers" and "Happiness and prosperity are benefits of Allah, who nourishes all creatures." The artisans added propaganda phrases, such as "Dedicated to the magnificent Sultan Pedro—thanks to God!"

The Mudejar style also includes Christian motifs. Find the row of kings, high up at the base of the dome, chronicling all of Spain's rulers from the 600s to the 1600s. Throughout the palace (as in the center of the dome above you), you'll see coats of arms—including the castle of Castile and the lion of León. There are also natural objects (such as shells and birds), which you wouldn't normally find in Islamic decor, as it traditionally avoids realistic images of nature.

Wander through adjoining rooms. Notice how it gets cooler as you go deeper into the palace. Straight ahead from the Hall of the Ambassadors, in the **Philip II Ceiling Room** (Salón del Techo de Felipe II), look above the arches to find peacocks, falcons, and

other birds amid interlacing vines. Imagine day-to-day life in the palace—with VIP guests tripping on the tiny steps.

• *Make your way to the second courtyard, nearby (in the Hall of the Ambassadors, face the Courtyard of the Maidens, then walk to the left). This smaller courtyard is the...*

❻ Courtyard of the Dolls (Patio de las Muñecas): This delicate courtyard was reserved for the king's private family life. Originally, the center of the courtyard had a pool, cooling the residents and reflecting decorative patterns that were once brightly painted on the walls. The columns—recycled from ancient Roman and Visigothic buildings—are of alternating white, black, and pink marble. (Pedro's original courtyard was a single story; the upper floors and skylight were added centuries later.) The courtyard's name comes from the tiny doll faces found at the base of one of the arches. Circle the room and try to find them. (Hint: While just a couple of inches tall, they're eight feet high.)

• *The long adjoining room with the gilded ceiling, the **Prince's Room** (Cuarto del Príncipe), was Queen Isabel's bedroom, where she gave birth to a son, Prince Juan.*

Return to the Courtyard of the Maidens. Look up and notice the second story. Isabel's grandson, Charles V, added it in the 16th century. See the difference in styles: Mudejar below (lobed arches and elaborate tracery), and Renaissance above (round arches and less decoration).

As you stand in the courtyard with your back to the Hall of the Ambassadors, the door in the middle of the right side leads to the...

❼ **Charles V Ceiling Room (Salón del Techo del Carlos V):** Emperor Charles V, who ruled Spain at its peak of New World wealth, expanded the palace. The reason? His marriage to his beloved Isabel—which took place in this room—that joined vast realms of Spain and Portugal. Devoutly Christian, Charles celebrated his wedding night with a midnight Mass, and later ordered the Mudejar ceiling in this room to be replaced with the less Islamic (but no less impressive) Renaissance one you see today.

• *We've seen the core of King Pedro's palace, with the additions by his successors. Return to the Courtyard of the Maidens, then turn right. In the corner, find the staircase built in a strikingly different style: a century older than its surroundings, it was originally Gothic, then renovated in Renaissance times. Follow the stairs up to rooms decorated with bright ceramic tiles and Gothic vaulting. Pass through the chapel and into two big, long, parallel rooms, the...*

❽ **Banquet Hall (Salón Gótico)** and **Hall of Tapestries (Salón Tapices):** The first room you enter is the big, airy banquet

hall where Charles and Isabel held their wedding reception. Tiles of yellow, blue, green, and orange line the room, some decorated with whimsical human figures with vase-like bodies. The windows open onto views of the gardens.

Next door, the walls are hung with 18th-century Spanish copies of 16th-century Belgian tapestries showing the conquests, trade, and industriousness of Charles' prosperous reign. (The highlights are described in Spanish along the top, and in Latin along the bottom.) The map tapestry of the

Mediterranean world has south pointing up. Find Genova, Italy, on the bottom; Africa on top; Lisbon *(Liboa)* on the far right; and the large city of Barcelona in between. The artist included himself holding the legend—with a scale in both leagues and miles.

Facing the map, head to the far left end of room, where the wall is filled by a dramatic portrayal of the Spanish navy. Spain ruled the waves—and thereby an empire upon which the sun never set. Its reign lasted from 1492 until the Battle of Trafalgar in 1805; after that, Britannia's navy took the helm, and it was her crown that controlled the next global empire.

• *At the far end of the Banquet Hall, head outside to the...*

❾ **Mercury Pool and Gardens:** The Mercury Pool, a reservoir fed by a 16th-century aqueduct, irrigated the palace's entire garden.

As only elites had running water, the fountain was an extravagant show of power. Check out the bronze statue of Mercury, with his cute little winged feet. The wall defining the east side of the garden was part of the original Moorish castle wall. In the early 1600s, when fortifications were no longer needed here, that end was redesigned to be a grotto-style gallery.

From the Mercury Pool, steps lead into the formal gardens. Just past the bottom of the steps, a tunnel on the right leads under the palace to the coolest spot in the city.

Finally, explore the gardens. The intimate geometric zone nearest the palace is the Moorish garden. The far-flung garden beyond that was the backyard of the Christian ruler.

Here in the gardens, as in the rest of the palace, the Christian and Islamic traditions merge. Both cultures used water and nature as essential parts of their architecture. The garden's pavilions and fountains only enhance this. Wander among palm trees, myrtle hedges, and fragrant roses. While tourists pay to be here, this is actually a public garden, and free to locals. It's been that way since 1931, when the king was exiled and Spanish citizens took ownership of royal holdings. In 1975, the Spanish people allowed the king back on the throne—but on their terms...which included keeping this garden.

• *On the other side of the east wall is an air-conditioned* **cafeteria** *with a nice terrace overlooking the gardens.*

If you've booked a spot to visit the Upper Royal Apartments (see "Tours" on page 684), return to the Courtyard of the Hunt, and head upstairs.

❿ Upper Royal Apartments (Cuarto Real Alto): This is the royal palace of today's monarchs. Fifteen public reception rooms are open to visitors: the official dining room, Audience Hall, and so on. The rooms are amply decorated with Versailles-like furniture, chandeliers, carpets, and portraits of 19th-century nobility. The highlight is the Audience Room, a Mudejar-style room overlooking the Patio de la Montería.

• *Your Alcázar tour is over. From the Moors to Pedro the Cruel to Ferdinand and Isabel, and from Charles V to King Juan Carlos and Queen Sofía, we've seen the home of a millennium of Spanish kings and queens. When you're ready to go, head out through the **Patio de Banderas**, once the entrance for guests arriving by horse carriage. Enjoy a classic Giralda Bell Tower view as you leave.*

Near the Cathedral
▲Archivo de Indias in the Lonja Palace

The Lonja Palace, across the street from the Alcázar, houses the historic archives for all of Spain. Its four miles of shelving contain the precious documents of a once-mighty empire. While little of interest is actually on show, a visit is free, easy, and gives a look at one of the finest Renaissance palaces in Spain. Designed by royal architect Juan de Herrera, the principal designer of El Escorial, the building evokes the greatness of the Spanish empire at its peak (c. 1600).

Cost and Hours: Free, Mon-Sat 9:30-17:00, Sun 10:00-14:00, Avenida de la Constitución 3, tel. 954-500-528.

Visiting the Palace: Originally this was a market for traders—an early stock market. But by the end of the 1600s, Sevilla had become a backwater (after suffering plagues and the silting up of its harbor, which allowed Cádiz to overtake Sevilla as Spain's main port of embarkation), and in 1717, the building was abandoned. In 1785, it was put to new use as the storehouse for all the documents the country was quickly amassing from its discovery and conquest of the New World.

Start you visit on the ground floor, where an interesting 15-minute intro video plays in a continuous loop. Then climb the extravagant stairs to the top floor and make a big circle to check out the temporary exhibits.

Avenida de la Constitución

Old Sevilla is bisected by this grand boulevard. Its name celebrates the country's 1978 adoption of a democratic constitution, as the Spanish people moved quickly to re-establish their government after the 1975 death of longtime dictator Francisco Franco.

The busy avenue was converted into a pedestrian boulevard in 2007. Overnight, the city's paseo route took on a new dimension.

Suddenly cafés and shops here had fresh appeal. (Two Starbucks moved in, strategically bookending the boulevard, but they're having a tough time winning over locals who prefer small €1 coffees to mammoth €4 ones.) The new tram line (infamously short, at only about a mile long) is controversial, as it violates what might have been a more purely pedestrian zone.

In Barrio Santa Cruz

For a self-guided walk through this neighborhood, see page 665.

Hospital de los Venerables

Buried in the Barrio Santa Cruz, this former charity-run old-folks' home and hospital comes with a Baroque church and an exquisite painting gallery that includes the Centro Velázquez, which displays works by one of Spain's premier artists. Everything is well-explained by the included audioguide.

Cost and Hours: €5.50, free on Sunday evenings, open daily 10:00-14:00 & 16:00-20:00, Plaza de los Venerables 8, tel. 954-562-696, www.focus.abengoa.es.

Visiting the Hospital: In the **courtyard,** with its sunken fountain, you get a sense of how this facility housed retired priests and Sevilla's needy.

The **church,** which takes you back to the year 1700, is bursting with Baroque decor, one of Spain's best pipe organs, and frescoes by Juan de Valdés Leal. The decor exalts the priesthood and Spain's role as standard-bearer of the pope.

The top-notch **painting gallery** is dedicated to one of the world's greatest painters, Diego Velázquez (1599-1660), who was born here in Sevilla, where he also worked as a young man. Velázquez's *Vista de Sevilla* helps you imagine the excitement of this thriving city in 1660 when, with 140,000 people, it was the fourth-largest in Europe. You'll recognize landmarks like the Giralda Tower, the cathedral, and the Torre del Oro. The pontoon bridge leads to Triana—where citizens of all ranks strolled the promenade together, as they still do today.

The Sevilla that shaped Velázquez was the gateway to the New World. There was lots of stimulation: Adventurers, fortune hunters, and artists passed through here, and many stayed for years. Of the few Velázquez paintings remaining in his hometown, three are in this gallery.

Centro de Interpretación Judería de Sevilla

This small, overpriced interpretive museum, standing in the heart of Barrio Santa Cruz, chronicles the history of Sevilla's Jews, who once called this neighborhood home. Bilingual placards and a few displays give visitors a glimpse of Sevilla's Sephardic heritage. However, most find the Casa de Sefarad in Córdoba (described on page 748) more interesting.

SEVILLA

Cost and Hours: €6.50, Mon-Sat 10:30-15:30 & 17:00-20:00, Sun 11:00-19:00, guided tours in English may be available on request, Calle Ximénez de Enciso 22, tel. 954-047-089, www.juderiadesevilla.es.

Between the River and the Cathedral
▲▲Hospital de la Caridad

This charity hospital, which functioned as a place of final refuge for Sevilla's poor and homeless, was founded in the 17th century by the nobleman Don Miguel Mañara. Your visit includes an evocative courtyard, his office, a church filled with powerful art, and a good audioguide that explains it all. This is still a working hospice, so when you pay your entrance fee, you're advancing the work Mañara started back in the 17th century.

Cost and Hours: €5, includes good audioguide, Mon-Sat 9:00-13:00 & 15:30-19:00, Sun 9:00-12:30, last entry 30 minutes before closing, Calle Temprado 3, tel. 954-223-232, www.santa-caridad.es.

Background: The Hospice and Hospital of the Holy Charity in Sevilla was founded by the Venerable Servant of God, Don Miguel Mañara (1626-1679). Mañara was a big-time playboy and enthusiastic sinner who, late in life, had a massive change of heart. He spent his last years dedicating his life to strict worship and taking care of the poor. In 1674, Mañara acquired some empty warehouses in Sevilla's old shipyard and built this 150-ward "place of heroic virtues."

Mañara could well have been the inspiration for Don Juan, the quasi-legendary character from a play set in 17th-century Sevilla, popularized later by Lord Byron's poetry and Mozart's opera *Don Giovanni* ("Don Juan" in Italian). While no one knows for sure, I think it makes sense...and it adds some fun to the visit.

One thing's for sure: Mañara is on the road to sainthood. His supporters request that you report any miraculous answers to prayers asking him to intercede—you need to perform miracles to become a saint.

Visiting the Hospital: The **courtyard** gives a sense of the origin of the building and its ongoing work as a hospice for the poor. The statues come from Genova, Italy, as Mañara's family were rich Genova merchants who moved to Sevilla to get in on the wealth from New World discoveries. The Dutch tiles (from Delft), depicting scenes from the Old and New Testament, are a reminder that the Netherlands was under Spanish rule in centuries past.

The **Sala de Cabildos,** a small room at the end of the courtyard, is Mañara's former office. Here you'll see his original desk, a painting of him at work (busy preaching against materialism and hedonism), a treasure box with an elaborate lock mechanism, his sword (he killed several people in his wilder days), a whip that was part of his austere style of worship, and his death mask.

The **chapel,** which Mañara had built, is the highlight. Once inside, notice the graphic painting over the door you entered that provided a vivid Mañara-style sendoff to worshippers.

Juan de Valdés Leal's *The End of the Glories of the World* shows Mañara and a bishop decaying together in a crypt, with worms and roaches munching away. Above, the hand of Christ—pierced by the nail—holds the scales of justice: sins (on the left) and good deeds (on the right).

Immediately opposite is Leal's *In the Blink of an Eye* (*In ictu oculi*). In it, the Grim Reaper extinguishes the candle of life. Filling the canvas are the ruins of worldly goods, knowledge, power, and position. It's all gone in the blink of an eye—true in the 1670s...and true today.

Sit in a pew and take it in: This is Sevillan Baroque. Seven original or replica Murillo paintings celebrate good deeds and charity: feeding the hungry, tending the sick, and so on. The altar is carved wood with gold leaf. A dozen hardworking cupids support the Burial of Christ. The duty of the order of monks here was to give a Christian burial to the executed and drowned. See the tombstone worked into the altar scene (on the right). Above are the three main Christian virtues (left to right): faith, charity, hope.

Before leaving the church, do Don Miguel Mañara a favor. Step on his **tombstone.** Located just outside the central door in the back, it's served as a welcome mat since 1679. He requested to be buried outside the church where everyone would step on him as they entered. It's marked "the worst man in the world."

Leaving the church, return to the courtyard, go straight across, and around to the left. Wander around, noticing the brick Gothic arches of the huge halls of the 13th-century shipyards, whose original floors are 15 feet below. Overlooking the courtyard, immediately behind the church's altar, were the rooms where Mañara spent his last years. Here he could be close to his charity work and his intensely penitent place of worship.

Across the street from the entry is a park. Pop in and see Don Juan—wracked with guilt—carrying a poor, sick person into his hospital.

Torre del Oro (Gold Tower) and Naval Museum

Sevilla's historic riverside Gold Tower was the starting and ending point for all shipping to the New World. It's named for the golden tiles that once covered it—not for all the New World booty that landed here. Ever since the Moors built it in the 13th century, it's been part of the city's fortifications, and long anchored a heavy chain that draped from here across the river to protect the harbor. Today it houses a dreary little naval museum. Looking past the dried fish and knot charts to find the mural showing the world-spanning journeys of Vasco da Gama, the model of Columbus' *Santa María* (the first ship to land in the New World), and an interesting mural of Sevilla in 1740. Enjoy the view from the balconies upstairs. The Guadalquivir River is now just a trickle of its former self, after canals built in the 1920s siphoned off most of its water to feed ports downstream.

Cost and Hours: €3, €2 audioguide, Mon-Fri 9:30-18:45, Sat-Sun 10:30-18:45, tel. 954-222-419.

North of the Cathedral

Plaza Nueva

This pleasant "New Square" is marked by a statue of King Ferdinand III, who liberated Sevilla from the Moors in the 13th century and was later sainted. For centuries afterward, a huge Franciscan monastery stood on this site; it was a spiritual home to many of the missionaries who colonized the California coast. (It was destroyed in 1840, following the disbanding of the monastic system under a government keen to take back power from the Church.) Today it's the end of the line for Sevilla's short tram system (which zips down Avenida de la Constitución to the San Bernardo train station).

Running along the top of the square is the relatively modern **City Hall.** For a more interesting look at this building, circle around to the other end (on the smaller square, called Plaza de San Francisco) where you can see how the structure has expanded right along with the city it governs: architectural styles evolve, from left to right, along the facade. The newest, right part of the facade is more or less undecorated—a blank canvas for future artists to leave their mark. This square has been used for executions, bullfights, and (today) big city events.

▲Church of the Savior (Iglesia del Salvador)

Sevilla's second-biggest church, built on the site of a ninth-century mosque, gleams with freshly scrubbed Baroque pride. While the larger cathedral is a jumble of styles, this church is uniformly Andalusian Baroque—the architecture, decor, and statues are all from the same time period. The church is home to some of the most beloved statues that parade through town during religious festivals.

Cost and Hours: €3, or free with €8 cathedral ticket (also sold here, with shorter lines), audioguide-€2.50, same hours as cathedral, Plaza del Salvador, tel. 954-211-679.

Visiting the Church: The church's 14 richly decorated altarpieces, many from the 18th century, are its highlight (and come with excellent English descriptions). Start at the **high altar,** with the whirling pair of angels holding lamps with red ropes. Then look high above to see frescoes that, once long forgotten, were revealed by a recent cleaning.

In the right transept stands another venerable Mary; this one is **Our Lady of the Waters,** who predates this church by about 400 years. Though permanently parked now, for centuries she was paraded through Sevilla in times of drought.

In the left transept is the chapel with one of the city's most beloved statues (visible through the bars): the gripping **Christ of the Passion,** who is carrying the cross to his death (from 1619, by Juan Martínez Montañés). The statue is so revered by pilgrims and worshippers that the chapel has its own separate entrance (access through the courtyard, free, daily 10:00-14:00 & 17:00-21:00). For centuries the faithful have come here to pray, marvel at the sadness that fills the chapel, then kiss Jesus' heel (to join them, head up the stairs behind the altar). Jesus is flanked by a red-eyed John the Evangelist and a grieving María Dolorosa, with convincing tears and a literal dagger in her heart. Under the chapel's main altar, notice the skulls of two Jesuit missionaries who were martyred in Japan. In the adjacent shop, a wall tile shows the statue in a circa-1620 procession.

In the **courtyard,** you can feel the presence of the mosque that once stood on this spot. Its minaret is now the bell tower, and the mosque's arches are now halfway underground. What's left of the structure functions today as part of the church's crypt.

Nearby: Finish your visit by enjoying **Plaza del Salvador,** a favorite local meeting point. Strolling this square, you become part of the theater of life in Sevilla.

Casa de Pilatos

This 16th-century palace offers a scaled-down version of the royal Alcázar (with a similar mix of Gothic, Moorish, and Renaissance styles) and a delightful garden. The nobleman who built it was inspired by a visit to the Holy Land, where saw the supposed mansion of Pontius Pilate. If you've seen the Alcázar, this might not be worth the time or money. Your visit comes in two parts: the stark ground floor and garden (with audioguide); and a plodding, 25-minute guided tour of the lived-in noble residence upstairs (English/Spanish spiel, about 2/hour, check schedule at entry).

Cost and Hours: €8, includes audioguide and tour, daily 10:00-19:00, 9:00-18:00 off-season, Plaza de Pilatos 1.

▲Museo Palacio de la Condesa de Lebrija

This aristocratic mansion takes you back into the 18th century like no other place in town. The Countess of Lebrija was a passionate collector of antiquities. Her home's ground floor is paved with Roman mosaics (which you can actually walk on) and lined with musty old cases of Phoenician, Greek, Roman, and Moorish artifacts—mostly pottery. To see a plush world from a time when the nobility had a private priest and their own chapel, take a quickie tour of the upstairs, which shows the palace as the countess left it when she died in 1938.

Cost and Hours: €5 for unescorted visit of ground floor, €8 includes English/Spanish tour of "lived-in" upstairs offered every 45 minutes; July-Aug Mon-Fri 9:00-15:00, Sat 10:00-14:00, closed Sun; Sept-June Mon-Fri 10:30-19:30, Sat 10:00-14:00 & 16:00-18:00, Sun 10:00-14:00; free and obligatory bag check, Calle Cuna 8, tel. 954-227-802, www.palaciodelebrija.com.

Plaza de la Encarnación

Several years ago, in an attempt to revitalize this formerly nondescript square, the city unveiled what locals call "the mush-

rooms": a gigantic, undulating canopy of five waffle-patterned, toadstool-esque, hundred-foot-tall structures. Together, this structure (officially named *Metropol Parasol*) provides shade, a gazebo for performances, and a traditional market hall. While the market is busy each morning, locals don't know what to make of the avant-garde structure, and the square is pretty lifeless in the afternoon and evening. A ramp under the canopy leads down to ancient-Roman-era street level, where a museum displays Roman ruins found during the building process. From the museum level, a €1.30 elevator takes you up top, where you can do a loop walk along the terrace to enjoy its commanding city views. It feels like walking on a roller-coaster track. Although the structure is a bit newsy, I found it not worth the time or trouble. Other views in town are free, more central, and just as good (such as from the rooftop bar of the EME Catedral Hotel, across the street from the cathedral).

▲Flamenco Dance Museum (Museo del Baile Flamenco)

Though small and pricey, this museum is worthwhile for anyone looking to understand more about the dance that embodies the spirit of southern Spain.

The main exhibition, on floor 1, takes about 45 minutes to see. It features well-produced videos, flamenco costumes, and other artifacts collected by the grande dame of flamenco, Christina

Hoyos, including a collection of posters celebrating notable flamenco artists of yore (be sure to stand directly under the "sound showers"). The top floor and basement house temporary exhibits, mostly of photography and other artwork. On the ground floor and in the basement, you can watch flamenco lessons in progress—or even take one yourself (one hour, first person-€60, €20/person after that, shoes not provided).

Cost and Hours: €10, €24 combo-ticket includes evening concert, 10 percent discount with this book, daily 10:00-19:00, pick up English booklet at front desk, about 3 blocks east of Plaza Nueva at Calle Manuel Rojas Marcos 3, tel. 954-340-311, www .flamencomuseum.com.

Performances: Live flamenco performances take place here nightly, just after the museum closes; for details, see page 710.

▲Museo de Bellas Artes

Sevilla's passion for religious art is preserved and displayed in its Museum of Fine Arts. While most Americans go for El Greco, Goya, and Velázquez (not a forte of this collection), this museum gives a fine look at other, less-appreciated Spanish masters: Zurbarán and Murillo. Rather than exhausting, the museum is pleasantly enjoyable.

Cost and Hours: €1.50, Tue-Sat 10:00-20:30, Sun 10:00-17:00, closed Mon, tel. 955-542-942, www.museosdeandalucia.es.

Getting There: The museum is at Plaza Museo 9, a 15-minute walk from the cathedral, or a short ride on bus #C5 from Plaza Nueva. If coming from the Basílica de la Macarena, take bus #C4 to the Torneo stop and walk inland four blocks. Pick up the English-language floor plan, which explains the theme of each room.

Background: Sevilla was once Spain's wealthy commercial capital (like New York City) at a time when Madrid was a newly built center of government (like Washington, DC). Spain's economic Golden Age (the 1500s) blossomed into the Golden Age of Spanish painting (the 1600s), especially in Sevilla. Several of Spain's top painters—Zurbarán, Murillo, and Velázquez—lived here in the 1600s. Like their contemporaries, they labored to make the spiritual world tangible, and forged the gritty realism that marks Spanish painting. You'll see balding saints and monks with wrinkled faces and sunburned hands. The style suited Spain's spiritual climate, as the Catholic Church used this art in its Counter-Reformation battle against the Protestant rebellion.

In the early 1800s, Spain's government, in a push to take

some power from the Church, began disbanding convents and monasteries. Secular fanatics had a heyday looting churches, but fortunately, much of Andalucía's religious art was rescued and hung safely here in this convent-turned-museum.

◑ Self-Guided Tour: The permanent collection features 20 rooms in neat chronological order. It's easy to breeze through once with my tour, then backtrack to what appeals to you.

• *Enter and follow signs to the permanent collection, which begins in Sala I (Room 1).*

Rooms 1-4: Medieval altarpieces of gold-backed saints, Virgin-and-babes, and Crucifixion scenes attest to the religiosity that nurtured Spain's early art. Spain's penchant for unflinching realism culminates in Room 2 with Pedro Torrigiano's 1525 statue of an emaciated San Jerónimo, and in Room 3 with the painted clay head of St. John the Baptist—complete with severed neck muscles, throat, and windpipe. This kind of warts-and-all naturalism would influence the great Sevillan painter Velázquez (some of whose works are often displayed in Room 4).

• *Continue through the pleasant outdoor courtyard to the former church that is now Room 5.*

Room 5: This room shows off the works of another hometown boy, **Bartolomé Murillo** (mur-EE-oh, 1617-1682). His signature subject is the Immaculate Conception, the doctrine that holds that Mary was exempt from original sin. Several *Inmaculadas* may be on display. Typically, Mary is depicted as young, dressed in white and blue, standing atop the moon (crescent or full). She clutches her breast and gazes up rapturously, surrounded by tumbling winged babies. Murillo's tiny *Madonna and Child* (*Virgen de la Servilleta*, 1665; at the end of  the room in the center, where the church's altar would have been) shows the warmth and appeal of his work.

Murillo's sweetness is quite different from the harsh realism of his fellow artists, but his work was understandably popular. For many Spaniards, Mary is their main connection to heaven. They pray directly to her, asking her to intercede on their behalf with God. Murillo's Marys are always receptive and ready to help. (For more on Murillo, see page 675.)

Besides his *Inmaculadas,* Murillo painted popular saints. They often carry sprigs of plants, and cock their heads upward, caught up in a heavenly vision of sweet Baby Jesus. Murillo is also known for his "genre" paintings—scenes of common folk and rascally street urchins—but the museum has few of these.

Also in Room 5 is *The Apotheosis of St. Thomas Aquinas (Apteosis de Santo Tomás de Aquino)* by Francisco de Zurbarán—considered to be Zurbarán's most important work. It was done at the height of his career, when stark realism was all the rage. In a believable, down-to-earth way, Zurbarán presents the pivotal moment when the great saint-theologian experiences his spiritual awakening. We'll see more of Zurbarán upstairs in Room 10.

• *Now head back outside and up the stairs to the first floor.*

Rooms 6-9: In Rooms 6 and 7, you'll see more Murillos and Murillo imitators. Room 8 is dedicated to yet another native Sevillan (and friend of Murillo), Juan de Valdés Leal (1622-1690). He adds Baroque motion and drama to religious subjects. His surreal colors and feverish, unfinished style create a mood of urgency.

Room 10: Francisco de Zurbarán (thoor-bar-AHN, 1598-1664) painted saints and monks, and the miraculous things they experienced, with an unblinking, crystal-clear, brightly lit, highly detailed realism. Monks and nuns could meditate upon Zurbarán's meticulous paintings for hours, finding God in the details.

In Zurbarán's *St. Hugo Visiting the Refectory (San Hugo en el Refectorio)*, white-robed Carthusian monks gather together for their simple meal in a communal dining hall. Above them hangs a painting of Mary, Baby Jesus, and John the Baptist. Zurbarán created paintings for monks' dining halls like this. His audience: celibate men and women who lived in isolation, as in this former convent, devoting their time to quiet meditation,  prayer, and Bible study. Zurbarán shines a harsh spotlight on many of his subjects, creating strong shadows. Zurbarán's people often stand starkly isolated against a single-color background—a dark room or the gray-white of a cloudy sky. He was the ideal painter for the austere religion of 17th-century Spain.

Find *The Virgin of the Caves (La Virgen de las Cuevas)* and study the piety and faith in the monks' weathered faces. Zurbarán's Mary is protective, with her hands placed on the heads of two monks. Note the loving detail on the cape embroidery, the brooch, and the flowers at her feet. But also note the angel babies holding the cape, with their painfully double-jointed arms. Zurbarán was no Leonardo.

The Rest of the Museum: Spain's subsequent art, from the 18th century on, generally followed the trends of the rest of Europe. Room 12 has creamy Romanticism and hazy Impressionism. You'll see typical Sevillan motifs such as matadors, cigar-factory girls, and river landscapes. Enjoy these painted slices of Sevilla, then exit to experience similar scenes today.

Far North of the Cathedral
▲▲Basílica de la Macarena

Sevilla's Holy Week celebrations are Spain's grandest. During the week leading up to Easter, the city is packed with pilgrims wit-

nessing 60 processions carrying about 100 religious floats. If you miss the actual event, you can get a sense of it by visiting the Basílica de la Macarena and its accompanying museum to see the two most impressive floats and the darling of Semana Santa, the statue of the Virgen de la Macarena. Although far from the city center, it's located on Sevilla's ring road and easy to reach. (While La Macarena is the big kahuna, for a more central look at beloved procession statues, consider stopping by the Church of the Savior, described earlier; or Tirana's Church of Santa Ana, described later.)

Cost and Hours: Church-free, treasury museum-€5, audioguide-€1, daily 9:30-14:00 & 17:00-20:30.

Getting There: Wave down a taxi and say "Basilica Macarena" (about €6 from the city center). All the #C buses go there, including bus #C3 and #C4 from Puerta de Jerez (near the Torre de Oro) or Avenida de Menéndez Pelayo (the ring road east of the cathedral), tel. 954-901-800, www.hermandaddelamacarena.es.

◑ Self-Guided Tour: Despite the long history of the Macarena statue, the Neo-Baroque church was only built in 1949 to give the oft-moved sculpture a permanent home.

• *Grab a pew and study the...*

Weeping Virgin: La Macarena is known as the "Weeping

Virgin" for the five crystal teardrops trickling down her cheeks. She's like a Baroque doll with human hair and articulated arms, and is even dressed in underclothes. Sculpted in the late 17th century (probably by Pedro Roldán), she's become Sevilla's most popular image of Mary.

Her beautiful expression—halfway between smiling and crying—is ambiguous, letting worshippers project their own emotions onto her. Her weeping can be contagious—look around you. She's also known as La Esperanza, the Virgin of Hope, and she promises better times after the sorrow.

Installed in a side chapel (on the left) is the **Christ of the Judgment** (from 1654), showing Jesus on the day he was condemned. This statue and La Macarena stand atop the two most important floats of the Holy Week parades.

• *To see the floats and learn more, visit the treasury museum (exit the church; museum entrance is on the left side of the church).*

Tesoro (Treasury Museum): This small three-floor museum tells the history of the Virgin statue and the Holy Week parades. Though rooted in medieval times, the current traditions developed around 1600, with the formation of various fraternities *(hermandades)*. During Holy Week, they demonstrate their dedication to God by parading themed floats throughout Sevilla to retell the story of the Crucifixion and Resurrection of Christ (for more, see sidebar on page 660). The museum displays ceremonial banners, scepters, and costumed mannequins; videos show the parades in action (some displays in English).

The three-ton float that carries the Christ of the Judgment is slathered in gold leaf and shows a commotion of figures acting out the sentencing of Jesus. (The statue of Christ—the one you saw in the church—is placed before this crowd for the Holy Week procession.) Pontius Pilate is about to wash his hands. Pilate's wife cries as a man reads the death sentence. During the Holy Week procession, pious Sevillan women wail in the streets while relays of 48 men carry this float on the backs of their necks—only their feet showing under the drapes—as they shuffle through the streets from midnight until 14:00 in the afternoon every Good Friday. The men rehearse for months to get their choreographed footwork in sync.

La Macarena follows the Christ of the Judgment in the procession. Mary's smaller 1.5-ton float seems all silver and candles—"strong enough to support the roof, but tender enough to quiver in the soft night breeze." Mary has a wardrobe of three huge mantles, worn in successive years; these are about 100 years old, as is her six-pound gold crown/halo. This float has a mesmerizing effect on the local crowds. They line up for hours, then clap, weep, and throw roses as it slowly sways along the streets, working its way through town. A Sevillan friend once explained, "She knows all the problems of Sevilla and its people; we've been confiding in her for centuries. To us, she is hope."

The museum collection also contains some matador paraphernalia. La Macarena is the patron saint of bullfighters, and they give thanks for her protection. Copies of her image are popular in bullring chapels. In 1912 the bullfighter José Ortega, hoping for protection, gave La Macarena the five emerald brooches she wears. It worked for eight years...until he was gored to death in the ring. For a month, La Macarena was dressed in widow's black—the only time that has happened.

Macarena Neighborhood: Outside the church, notice the best surviving bit of Sevilla's old walls. Originally Roman, what remains today was built by the Moors in the 12th century to (unsuccessfully) keep the Christians out. And yes, it's from this city that a local dance band (Los del Río) changed the world by giving us the popular 1990s song "The Macarena." He-e-y-y, Macarena!

South of the Cathedral

University

Today's university was yesterday's *fábrica de tabacos* (tobacco factory), which employed 10,000 young female *cigareras*—including the saucy femme fatale of Bizet's opera *Carmen*. In the 18th century, it was the second-largest building in Spain, after El Escorial. Wander through its halls as you walk to Plaza de España. The university's bustling café is a good place for cheap tapas, beer, wine, and conversation (Mon-Fri 8:00-21:00, Sat 9:00-13:00, closed Sun).

Plaza de España

This square, the surrounding buildings, and the nearby María Luisa Park are the remains of the 1929 international fair, where for

a year the Spanish-speaking countries of the world enjoyed a mutual-admiration fiesta. When they finish the restoration work here (it's taking years), this delightful area—the epitome of world's fair-style architecture—will once again be great for people-watching (especially during the 19:00-20:00 peak paseo hour). The park's highlight is the former Spanish Pavilion. Its tiles—a trademark of Sevilla—show historic scenes and maps from every province of Spain (arranged in alphabetical order, from Álava to Zaragoza). Climb to one of the balconies for a fine view. Beware: This is a classic haunt of thieves and con artists; many pose as lost tourists, and may come at you with a map unfolded to hide their speedy, greedy fingers. Believe no one here.

▲▲Triana, West of the River

In Sevilla—as is true in so many other European cities that grew up in the age of river traffic—what was long considered the "wrong side of the river" is now the most colorful part of town. Sevilla's Triana is a proud neighborhood, famed for its flamenco

SEVILLA

soul (characterized by the statue that greets arrivals from across the river) and its independent spirit. Locals describe crossing the bridge toward the city center as "going to Sevilla."

Visiting Tirana: From downtown Sevilla, head southwest on the busy Calle Reyes Católicos (which passes just north of the bullring), crossing the Puente de Isabel II. Just off the bridge, on the right as you cross into Triana, is the neighborhood's covered **market.** Built in 2005 in the Moorish Revival style, it sits upon the ruins of an Inquisition-era castle (the scant remains of which you can see). The market bustles in the mornings and afternoons with traditional fruit and vegetable stalls as well as colorful tapas bars and cafés.

Calle San Jacinto, straight ahead just beyond the bridge, was recently liberated from car traffic. It's the hip center of the people scene—a festival of life each evening (see my favorite eating options on page 721). Venturing down side lanes, you find classic 19th-century facades with fine ironwork and colorful tiles. Long home to several tile factories, the district's crusty and flamenco-flamboyant character was shaped by its working-class industrial heritage and a sizeable Roma (Gypsy) population. You can still see a few flowery back courtyards that were once the *corrales* (communal patios) of Roma clans who shared one kitchen, bathroom, and fountain.

The first cross-street intersecting Calle San Jacinto, Calle Pureza, cuts (left) through the historic center of Triana, passing the **Church of Santa Ana,** nicknamed "the Cathedral of Triana." It's the home of the beloved Virgin statue called Nuestra Señora de la Esperanza de Triana (Our Lady of Hope of Triana). She's a big deal here—in Sevilla, upon meeting someone, it's customary to ask not only which football team they support, but which Virgin Mary they favor. The top two in town are the Virgen de la Macarena and La Esperanza de Triana. On the Thursday of Holy Week, it's a battle royale of the Madonnas, as Sevilla's two favorite Virgins are both in processions on the streets at the same time.

As you wander, pop into bars and notice how the decor mixes bullfighting lore with Virgin worship. Keep your eyes peeled for *abacerías*, traditional neighborhood grocers who also function as neighborhood bars (such as La Antigua Abacería, at Calle Pureza 12).

Near Sevilla

Itálica

One of Spain's most impressive Roman ruins is found outside the sleepy town of Santiponce, about six miles northwest of Sevilla. Founded in 206 B.C. for wounded soldiers recuperating from the Second Punic War, Itálica became a thriving town of great agricultural and military importance. It was the birthplace of famous Roman emperors Trajan and Hadrian. Today its best-preserved ruin is its amphitheater—one of the largest in the Roman Empire—with a capacity for 30,000 spectators. Other highlights include beautiful floor mosaics, such as the one in Casa de los Pájaros (House of the Birds), with representations of more than 30 species of birds. In summer, plan your visit to avoid the midday heat—arrive either early or late in the day, and definitely bring water.

Cost and Hours: €1.50; April-May Tue-Sat 9:00-20:00, Sun 10:00-17:00; June-mid-Sept Tue-Sat 9:00-15:30, Sun 10:00-17:00, mid-Sept-March Tue-Sat 9:00-18:30, Sun 10:00-17:00; closed Mon year-round; last entry 30 minutes before closing, tel. 955-123-847, www.museosdeandalucia.es.

Getting There: You can get to Itálica on bus #M-172A (30-minute trip, frequent departures from Sevilla's Plaza de Armas station). If you're driving, head west out of Sevilla in the direction of Huelva; after you cross the second branch of the river, turn north on SE-30/A-66, and after a few miles, get off at Santiponce. Drive past pottery warehouses and through the town to the ruins at the far (west) end.

Experiences in Sevilla

Bullfighting
▲Bullfights

Some of Spain's most intense bullfighting is done in Sevilla's

14,000-seat bullring, Plaza de Toros. Fights are held (generally at 18:30) on most Sundays in May and June; on Easter and Corpus Christi; daily during the April Fair; and at the end of September (during the Feria de San Miguel). These serious fights, with adult matadors, are called *corrida de toros* and often sell out in advance. On many Thursday evenings in July, the *novillada* fights take place, with teenage novices doing the killing and smaller bulls doing the dying. *Corrida de toros* seats range from €25 for high seats looking into the sun to €150 for the first three rows in the shade under the royal box; *novillada* seats are half that—and easy to buy at the arena a few minutes before show time (ignore scalpers outside; get information at a TI, your hotel, by phone, or online; tel. 954-210-315, www.plazadetorosdelamaestranza.com).

▲▲Bullring (Plaza de Toros) and Bullfight Museum (Museo Taurino)

Follow a bilingual (Spanish and English) 40-minute guided tour through the bullring's strangely quiet and empty arena, its museum, and the chapel where the matador prays before the fight. (Thanks to readily available blood transfusions, there have been no deaths in nearly three decades.) The two most revered figures of Sevilla, the Virgen de la Macarena and the Jesús del Gran Poder (Christ of All Power), are represented in the chapel. In the museum, you'll see great classic scenes and the heads of a few bulls—awarded the bovine equivalent of an Oscar for a particularly good fight. The city was so appalled when the famous matador Manolete was killed in 1947 that even the mother of the bull that gored him was destroyed. Matadors—dressed to kill—are heartthrobs in their "suits of light." Many girls have their bedrooms wallpapered with posters of cute bullfighters. See page 924 for more on the "art" of bullfighting.

Cost and Hours: €7, entrance with escorted tour only—no free time inside, 3/hour, daily May-Oct 9:30-20:00, Nov-April 9:00-19:00, until 14:00 on fight days, when chapel and horse room are closed. The last tour departs 15 minutes before closing. While they take groups of up to 50, it's still wise to call or drop by to reserve a spot in the busy season (tel. 954-224-577, www.realmaestranza.com).

The April Fair

For a seven-day period that falls a week or two after Easter, much of Sevilla is packed into its vast fairgrounds for a grand party (April 29-May 4 in 2014). The fair, seeming to bring all that's Andalusian together, feels friendly, spontaneous, and very real. The local passion for horses, flamenco, and sherry is clear—riders are ramrod straight, colorfully clad girls ride sidesaddle, and everyone's drinking sherry spritzers. Women sport outlandish dresses that would look clownish elsewhere, but  are somehow brilliant here en masse. Horses clog the streets in an endless parade until about 20:00, when they clear out and the streets fill with exuberant locals. The party goes on literally 24 hours a day for the entire week.

Countless private party tents, called *casetas,* line the lanes. Each tent is the private party zone of a family, club, or association. You need to know someone in the group—or make friends quickly—to get in. Because of the exclusivity, it has a real family-affair feeling. In each *caseta,* everyone knows everyone. It seems like a thousand wedding parties being celebrated at the same time.

Any tourist can have a fun and memorable evening by simply crashing the party. The city's entire fleet of taxis (who'll try to charge double) and buses seems dedicated to shuttling people from downtown to the fairgrounds. Given the traffic jams and inflated prices, you may be better off hiking: From the Torre del Oro, cross the San Telmo Bridge to Plaza de Cuba and hike down Calle Asunción. You'll see the towering gate to the fairgrounds in the distance. Just follow the crowds (there's no admission charge). Arrive before 20:00 to see the horses, but stay later, as the ambience improves after the *caballos* giddy-up on out. Some of the larger tents are sponsored by the city and open to the public, but the best action is in the streets, where party-goers from the livelier *casetas* spill out. Although private tents have bouncers, everyone is so happy that it's not tough to strike up an impromptu friendship, become a "special guest," and be invited in. The drink flows freely, and the food is fun and cheap.

Shopping in Sevilla

For the best local shopping experience, follow my shopping stroll

(described next). The popular pedestrian streets Sierpes and Tetuán/Velázquez—along with the surrounding lanes near Plaza Nueva—are packed with people and shops.

Clothing and shoe stores stay open all day. Other shops generally take a siesta, closing between 13:30 and 16:00 or 17:00 on weekdays, as well as on Saturday afternoons and all day Sunday. Big stores such as El Corte Inglés stay open (and air-conditioned) right through the siesta.

El Corte Inglés also has a supermarket downstairs and a good but expensive restaurant (Mon-Sat 10:00-22:00, closed Sun). Popular souvenir items include ladies' fans, shawls, *mantillas,* other items related to flamenco (castanets, guitars, costumes), ceramics, and bullfighting posters.

Collectors' markets hop on Sunday: stamps and coins at Plaza del Cabildo (near the cathedral) and art on Plaza del Museo (by the Museo de Bellas Artes).

Mercado del Arenal, the covered fish-and-produce market, is perfect for hungry photographers (Mon-Sat 9:00-14:30, closed Sun, least lively on Mon, on Calle Pastor y Landero at Calle Arenal, just beyond bullring). For tips on dining here, see page 730.

▲▲Shopping Paseo Tour

Although many tourists never get beyond the cathedral and the Santa Cruz neighborhood, it's important to wander west into the lively pedestrian shopping center of town. The best shopping streets—Calle Tetuán, Calle Sierpes, and Calle Cuna—also happen to be part of the oldest section of Sevilla. A walk here is a chance to join one of Spain's liveliest paseos—that bustling celebration of life that takes place before dinner each evening, when everyone is out strolling, showing off their fancy shoes and checking out everyone else's. This walk, if done between 18:00 and 20:00, gives you a chance to experience the paseo scene while getting a look at the town's most popular shops. You'll pass windows displaying the best in both traditional and trendy fashion. The walk ends at a plush mansion of a local countess (open to the public).

Start on the pedestrianized **Plaza Nueva,** a 19th-century square facing the ornate city hall, which features a statue of Ferdinand III, a local favorite because he freed Sevilla from the Moors in 1248. From here wander the length of **Calle Tetuán** (notice the latest in outrageous shoes). Calle Tetuán becomes **Calle Velázquez,** and ends at La Campana (a big intersection and popular meeting point, with the super department store, El Corte Inglés, just beyond, on Plaza del Duque de la Victoria).

Turn right. At the corner of **Calle Sierpes** awaits a venerable pastry shop, Confitería La Campana, with a fine 1885 interior... and Sevilla's most tempting sweets. From here, head down Calle Sierpes, which is great for shopping and strolling. Calle Sierpes is the main street of the Holy Week processions—imagine it packed with celebrants and its balconies bulging with spectators. At the corner of Sierpes and Jovellanos/Sagasta, you're near several fine shops featuring Andalusian accessories. Drop in to see how serious local women are about their fans, shawls, *mantillas* (ornate head scarves), and *peinetas* (combs designed to secure and prop up the *mantilla*). The most valuable *mantillas* are silk, and the top-quality combs are made of tortoise shell (though most women opt for much more affordable polyester and plastic). Andalusian women have various fans to match different dresses—they're considered an accessory. The *mantilla* comes in black (worn only on Good Friday and by the mother of the groom at weddings) and white (worn at bullfights during the April Fair).

From here turn left down **Calle Sagasta.** Notice that the street has two names—the modern version and a medieval one: Antigua Calle de Gallegos ("Ancient Street of the Galicians"). With the Christian victory in 1248, the Muslims were given one month to evacuate. To consolidate Christian control during that time, settlers from Galicia, the northwest corner of Iberia, were planted here; this street was the center of their neighborhood.

Finally, you'll arrive at charming Plaza del Salvador. It's teeming with life at the foot of the Church of the Savior (described on page 695 and well worth a visit). Backtrack left along **Calle Cuna,** famous for its exuberant flamenco dresses and classic wedding dresses. Local women save up to have flamenco dresses custom-made for the April Fair: They're considered an important status symbol. If all this shopping wasn't enough to make you feel like a countess, follow Calle Cuna to the Museo Palacio de la Condesa de Lebrija. Nearby is the mod, mushroom-shaped structure that towers over Plaza de la Encarnación (both described on page 697).

Nightlife in Sevilla

▲▲▲Flamenco

This music-and-dance art form has its roots in the Roma (Gypsy) and Moorish cultures. Even at a packaged "flamenco evening,"

sparks fly. The men do most of the flamboyant machine-gun footwork. The women often concentrate on the graceful turns and smooth, shuffling step of the *soléa* version of the dance. Watch the musicians. Flamenco guitarists, with their lightning-fast finger-roll strums, are among the best in the world. The intricate rhythms are set by castanets or the hand-clapping (called *palmas*) of those who aren't dancing at the moment. In the raspy-voiced wails of the singers, you'll hear echoes of the Muslim call to prayer.

Like jazz, flamenco thrives on improvisation. Also like jazz, good flamenco is more than just technical proficiency. A singer or dancer with "soul" is said to have *duende.* Flamenco is a happening, with bystanders clapping along and egging on the dancers with whoops and shouts. Get into it.

Hotels push tourist-oriented, nightclub-style flamenco shows, but they charge a commission. Fortunately, it's easy to book a place on your own. And if you don't care to see an actual show, you can still clap your castanets at the Flamenco Dance Museum (described on page 697).

Sevilla's flamenco offerings tend to fall into one of three categories: serious concerts (usually about €18 and about an hour long), where the singing and dancing take center stage; touristy dinner-and-drinks shows with table service (generally around €35—not including food—and two hours long); and—the least touristy option—casual bars with late-night performances, where for the cost of a drink you can catch impromptu (or semi-impromptu) musicians at play. Here's the rundown for each type of performance:

Serious Flamenco Concerts

While it's hard to choose among these three nightly, one-hour flamenco concerts, I'd say enjoying one is a must during your Sevilla visit. To the novice viewer, each company offers equal quality. They cost about the same, and each venue is small, intimate, and air-conditioned. For most, they are preferable to the "shows" listed later (which are half the cost, half the length, and have half as many seats). They also take place relatively early in the evening, especially compared with the flamenco you can see for free in various bars around town (that scene doesn't ignite until very late at night).

My recommended concerts are careful to give you a good overview of the art form, covering all the flamenco bases. At each venue you can reserve by phone and pay upon arrival, or drop by early to pick up a ticket. While La Casa del Flamenco is the nicest and most central venue, the other two have exhibits that can add to the experience.

La Casa de la Memoria is a strangely wide venue (just two rows deep), where everyone gets a close-up view and room to stretch out (€16, nightly at 19:30 and 21:00, no drinks, no children under six, 80 seats, Calle Cuna 6, tel. 954-560-670, www.casadelamemoria.es, flamencomemoria@gmail.com, run by Rosanna). They also have an exhibit on one easy, well-described floor, with lots of photos and a few artifacts (€3, or free with concert ticket—but only open 10:00-18:00).

The **Flamenco Dance Museum,** while the most congested venue (with 115 tightly packed seats), has a bar and allows drinks, and you can visit the museum immediately before the show. It has festival seating—the doors open at 18:00, when you can grab the seat of your choice, then spend an hour touring the museum and enjoying a drink before the show (€20, nightly at 19:00, €24 combo-ticket includes the museum and a show, see museum listing on page 697).

La Casa del Flamenco is in a delightful arcaded courtyard right in the Barrio Santa Cruz (€18, €2 discount when booking direct with this book, nightly at 21:00 in April-Sept, at 19:30 in Oct-March, no drinks, no kids under 6, 60 spacious seats, reception at adjacent Hotel Alcántara serves as the box office, Calle Ximénez de Enciso 33, tel. 954-500-595).

Razzle-Dazzle Flamenco Shows

These packaged shows can be a bit sterile—and an audience of tourists doesn't help—but I find both Los Gallos and El Arenal entertaining and riveting. While El Arenal may have a slight edge on talent, and certainly feels slicker, Los Gallos has a cozier setting, with cushy rather than hard chairs—and it's cheaper.

Los Gallos presents nightly two-hour shows at 20:15 and 22:30 (€35 ticket includes a drink, €3/person discount with this book in 2014—but limited to two people, arrive 30 minutes early for best seats, noisy bar but no food served, Plaza de la Santa Cruz 11, tel. 954-216-981, www.tablaolosgallos.com, owners José and Blanca promise goose bumps).

Tablao El Arenal has arguably more professional performers and a classier setting for its show—but dinner customers get the preferred seating, and waiters are working throughout the performance (€38 ticket includes a drink, €60 includes tapas, €72 includes dinner, 1.5-hour shows at 20:00 and 22:00, near bullring at Calle Rodó 7, tel. 954-216-492, www.tablaoelarenal.com).

El Patio Sevillano is more of a variety show, with flamenco as well as other forms of song and dance. While hotels may recommend this, they're just working for kickbacks. I like the other two much better.

Impromptu Flamenco in Bars

Spirited flamenco singing still erupts spontaneously in bars throughout the old town after midnight—but you need to know where to look. Ask a local for the latest.

La Carbonería Bar, the sangria equivalent of a beer garden, is a few blocks north of the Barrio Santa Cruz. It's a sprawling place with a variety of rooms leading to a big, open tented area filled with young locals, casual guitar strummers, and nearly nightly flamenco music from about 22:30 to 24:00. Located just a few blocks from most of my recommended hotels, this is worth finding if you're not quite ready to end the day (no cover, €2.50 sangria, daily 20:00-3:00 in the morning; near Plaza Santa María—find Hotel Fernando III, the side alley Céspedes dead-ends at Levies, head left to Levies 18, unsigned door; tel. 954-214-460, for location, see map on page 714).

While the days of Gypsies and flamenco throbbing throughout Triana are mostly long gone, a few bars still host live dancing; **Lo Nuestro** and **Rejoneo** are favorites (at Calle Betis 31A and 31B).

▲▲Evening Paseo

Sevilla is meant for strolling. The paseo thrives every non-winter evening in these areas: along either side of the river between the San Telmo and Isabel II bridges (Paseo de Cristóbal Colón and Triana district; see "Eating in Sevilla," page 720), up Avenida de la Constitución, around Plaza Nueva, at Plaza de España, and throughout the Barrio Santa Cruz. On hot summer nights, even families with toddlers are out and about past midnight. Spend some time rafting through this river of humanity.

Nighttime Views

Savor the view of floodlit Sevilla by night from the Tirana side of the river—perhaps over dinner.

For the best late-night drink with a cathedral view, visit the trendy top floor of EME Catedral Hotel (at Calle Alemanes 27). Ride the elevator to the top, climb the labyrinthine staircases to the bar, and sit down at a tiny table with a big view.

Sleeping in Sevilla

All of my listings are centrally located, mostly within a five-minute walk of the cathedral. The first are near the charming but touristy Santa Cruz neighborhood. The last group is just as central but closer to the river, across the boulevard in a more workaday, less touristy zone.

Room rates as much as double during the two Sevilla fiestas (Holy Week and the weeklong April Fair, held a week or two after Easter). In general, the busiest and most expensive months are April, May, September, and October. Hotels put rooms on the discounted push list in July and August—when people with good sense avoid this furnace—and from November through February. A price range indicates low- to high-season prices (but I have not listed festival prices).

If you do visit in July or August, you'll find the best deals in central, business-class places. They offer summer discounts and provide a (necessary) cool, air-conditioned refuge. But be warned that Spain's air-conditioning often isn't the icebox you're used to, especially in Sevilla.

Santa Cruz Neighborhood

These places are off Calle Santa María la Blanca and Plaza Santa María. The most convenient parking lot is the underground Cano y Cueto garage (see page 657). A self-service launderette is a couple of blocks away up Avenida de Menéndez Pelayo (see "Helpful Hints" on page 658).

Sleep Code

(€1 = about $1.30, country code: 34)
S = Single, **D** = Double/Twin, **T** = Triple, **Q** = Quad, **b** = bathroom,
s = shower only. Unless otherwise noted, credit cards are
accepted, hoteliers speak enough English, and breakfast
costs extra. Some hotels include the 10 percent IVA tax in the
room price; others tack it onto your bill.

To help you easily sort through these listings, I've divided
the accommodations into three categories based on the price
for a double room with bath during high season:

$$$ **Higher Priced**—Most rooms €110 or more.
$$ **Moderately Priced**—Most rooms between €60-110.
$ **Lower Priced**—Most rooms €60 or less.

Prices can change without notice; verify the hotel's current rates online or by email. For the best prices, always book
direct.

$$$ Hotel Casa 1800, well-priced for its elegance, is worth
the extra euros. Located dead-center in the Barrio Santa Cruz
(facing a boisterous tapas bar that quiets down after midnight), its
24 rooms circle an elegant chandeliered patio lounge that hosts a
daily free afternoon tea for guests. With a rooftop terrace offering
an impressive cathedral view and elegantly appointed rooms with
high, beamed ceilings, it's a winner (standard Db-€147, superior
Db with private patio-€164, deluxe Db with terrace and outdoor
Jacuzzi-€194, "grand deluxe" Db with all of the above and
more-€320, breakfast-€9.50, air-con, elevator, guest computer,
free Wi-Fi, Calle Rodrigo Caro 6, tel. 954-561-800, www
.hotelcasa1800.com, info@hotelcasa1800.com).

$$$ Hotel Las Casas de la Judería has 178 quiet, elegant
rooms and suites, many of them tastefully decorated with hardwood
floors and a Spanish flair. The service can be stiff and stuffy, but
the rooms, which surround a series of peaceful courtyards, are a
romantic splurge. Some are rather dated, though, so request one of
the newer ones (Sb-€110-160, Db-€120-244 depending on season,
mention this book for 10 percent discount, check their website for
even better rates, expensive but great buffet breakfast-€19, air-con,
elevator, free Wi-Fi in lobby, pool in summer, valet parking-€20/
day, Plaza Santa María 5, tel. 954-415-150, www.casasypalacios
.com, juderia@casasypalacios.com).

$$$ El Rey Moro encircles its spacious, colorful patio (which
tourists routinely duck into for a peek) with 19 rooms. Colorful

Santa Cruz Hotels, Restaurants & Flamenco

and dripping with quirky Andalusian character, and thoughtful about including extras (such as free loaner bikes and private rooftop Jacuzzi time), it's a class act (Sb-€79-99, Db-€100-129, breakfast-€9—or free if you reserve on their website, check their site for other specials, air-con, elevator, guest computer, free Wi-Fi, Calle Lope de Rueda 14, tel. 954-563-468, www.elreymoro .com, hotel@elreymoro.com).

$$$ Hotel Amadeus is a little gem that music lovers will appreciate (it even has a couple of soundproof rooms with pianos— something I've never seen anywhere else in Europe). The rooms, lovingly decorated with a musical motif, are situated around small courtyards. Elevators take you to two roof terraces (one with an under-the-stars Jacuzzi). Though small, this 24-room place is classy and comfortable, with welcoming public spaces and a very charming staff. The €8.50 breakfast comes on a trolley—enjoy it in your room, in the lounge, or on a terrace (Sb-€90, Db-€105,

① Hotel Casa 1800
② Hotel Las Casas de la Judería
③ El Rey Moro
④ Hotel Amadeus, La Música de Sevilla & Pensión Córdoba
⑤ Hotel Palacio Alcázar
⑥ YH Giralda
⑦ Hotel Alcántara & La Casa del Flamenco
⑧ Hotel Murillo
⑨ Plaza Santa Cruz Hostal
⑩ To Samay Hostel & Launderette
⑪ Bodega Santa Cruz
⑫ Las Teresas Bar
⑬ Cervecería Giralda
⑭ Restaurante San Marco
⑮ Casa Roman Taberna
⑯ Taberna Poncio
⑰ Tapas Trio
⑱ Restaurante Modesto
⑲ Freiduría Puerta de la Carne
⑳ Bar Restaurante El 3 de Oro
㉑ Café Bar Carmela
㉒ Villar Ice Cream
㉓ Los Gallos (Flamenco)
㉔ To La Carbonería Bar

SEVILLA

big Db-€120, suites-€165-195, cheaper July-Aug, air-con, elevator, guest computer, free Wi-Fi—plus iPads in every room, laundry-€15, parking-€20/day, Calle Farnesio 6, tel. 954-501-443, www.hotelamadeussevilla.com, reservas@hotelamadeussevilla.com, wonderfully run by María Luisa and her staff—Zaida and Cristina). Their next-door annex is every bit as charming, and a similarly good value: **$$$ La Música de Sevilla** offers six beautifully appointed rooms—three facing the interior patio, and three streetside rooms with small balconies (patio Db-€110, exterior Db-€130, air-con, reserve through and check in at Hotel Amadeus).

$$$ Hotel Palacio Alcázar is the former home and studio of John Fulton, an American who moved here to become a bullfighter and painter. This charming boutique hotel has 12 crisp, modern rooms, and each soundproofed door is painted with a different scene of Sevilla. Triple-paned windows keep out the noise from

Sevilla Hotels

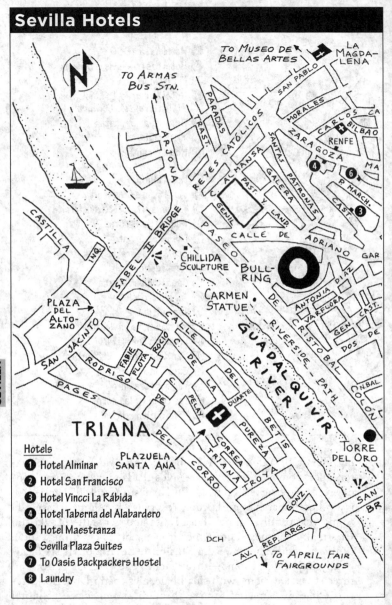

Hotels
1 Hotel Alminar
2 Hotel San Francisco
3 Hotel Vincci La Rábida
4 Hotel Taberna del Alabardero
5 Hotel Maestranza
6 Sevilla Plaza Suites
7 To Oasis Backpackers Hostel
8 Laundry

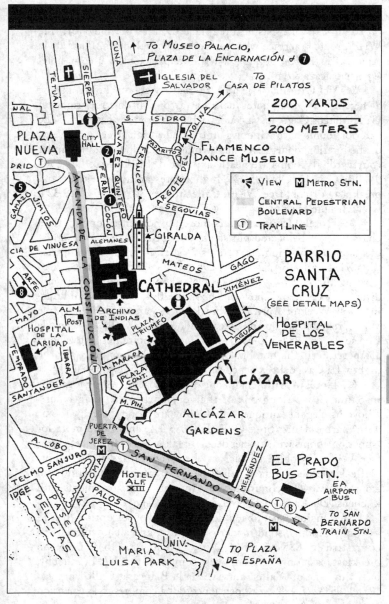

To Museo Palacio,
Plaza de la Encarnación & 7

IGLESIA DEL SALVADOR

To Casa de Pilatos

TETUAN

SIERPES

CUNA

NAL

S. ISIDRO

PLAZA NUEVA

City Hall

DRID

GAMAZO

JIMIOS

ALVAREZ QUINTERO

FERNANDEZ COLON

FRANCOS

PAJARITOS

ARGOTE DEL MOLINA

200 YARDS
200 METERS

Flamenco Dance Museum

SEGOVIAS

CIA DE VINUESA

ARFE

ALEMANES

Giralda

MATEOS

GAGO

VIEW   M Metro Stn.

Central Pedestrian Boulevard

T Tram Line

BARRIO SANTA CRUZ
(SEE DETAIL MAPS)

MAYO

Hospital de la Caridad

AVENIDA DE LA CONSTITUCIÓN

ALM.

Post

Archivo de Indias

Cathedral

XIMÉNEZ

Plaza D. Triumfo

Hospital de los Venerables

TEMPRADO

IBARRA

SANTANDER

M. MARAPA

Plaza Cont.

M. PIN.

Alcázar

AGUA

Puerta de Jerez

San Fernando

Alcázar Gardens

A. LOBO

TELMO SANJURO

IDGE

DELICIAS

PASEO

AV ROMA

PALOS

Hotel Alf XIII

SAN FERNANDO CARLOS

MENÉNDEZ

El Prado Bus Stn.

EA Airport Bus

T B

To San Bernardo Train Stn.

Univ.

Maria Luisa Park

To Plaza de España

SEVILLA

the plaza (Sb-€85-120, Db-€95-130, Tb-€130-145, prices depend on room size and season, breakfast-€9, air-con, elevator, free Wi-Fi, rooftop terrace with bar and cathedral views, Plaza de la Alianza 11, tel. 954-502-190, www.hotelpalacioalcazar.com, hotel @palacioalcazar.com).

$$ YH Giralda, once an 18th-century abbots' house, is now a charming 14-room hotel tucked away on a little street right off Calle Mateos Gago, just a couple of blocks from the cathedral. The exterior rooms have windows onto a pedestrian street, and a few of the interior rooms have small windows that look into the inner courtyard; all rooms are neatly appointed (Sb-€50-84, Db-€50-94, Tb-€75-115, Qb-€85-135, higher rates are for weekends, no breakfast, air-con, free Wi-Fi, Calle Abades 30, tel. 954-228-324, www.yh-hoteles.com, yhgiralda@yh-hoteles.com).

$$ Hotel Alcántara offers more no-nonsense comfort than character. Well-located but strangely out of place in the midst of the Santa Cruz jumble, it rents 21 slick rooms at a good price (Sb-€71, small Db-€82, bigger Db twin-€93, fancy Db-€117; 10 percent discount or a free breakfast—your choice—if you book direct, pay cash, and show this book in 2014, offer not valid during Holy Week or April Fair; breakfast-€6, air-con, elevator, free Wi-Fi, rentable laptop and bikes, outdoor patio, Calle Ximénez de Enciso 28, tel. 954-500-595, www.hotelalcantara.net, info@hotel alcantara.net). The hotel also functions as the box office for the nightly La Casa del Flamenco show, next door (see page 710).

$$ Hotel Murillo enjoys one of the most appealing locations in Santa Cruz, along one of the very narrow "kissing lanes." Above its elegant, antiques-filled lobby are 57 nondescript rooms with marble floors (Sb-€69-95, Db-€85-111, about €30 more for "superior" rooms with fancier decor, breakfast-€9, air-con, elevator, free Wi-Fi in lobby, bar across the street closes at midnight, Calle Lope de Rueda 7, tel. 954-216-095, www.hotelmurillo .com, reservas@hotelmurillo.com). They also rent apartments with kitchens (Db-€90-120, see website for details).

$$ Pensión Córdoba, a homier and cheaper option, has 12 tidy, quiet rooms, solid modern furniture, and a showpiece tiled courtyard (S-€35-45, Sb-€40-55, D-€50-65, Db-€60-75, no breakfast, cash only, air-con, guest computer, free Wi-Fi in lobby, on a tiny lane off Calle Santa María la Blanca at Calle Farnesio 12, tel. 954-227-498, www.pensioncordoba.com, reservas@pension cordoba.com, Ana and María).

$ Plaza Santa Cruz Hostal is a charming little place, with thoughtful touches that you wouldn't expect in this price range. The 17 clean, basic rooms surround a bright little courtyard that's buried deep in the Barrio Santa Cruz, just off Plaza Santa Cruz (Sb-€55, Db-€60, Qb-€75, includes breakfast, air-

con, free Wi-Fi, Calle Santa Teresa 15, tel. 954-228-808, www
.hostalplazasantacruz.com, info@hostalplazasantacruz.com).

$ Samay Hostel, on a busy street a block from the edge of
the Barrio Santa Cruz, is a youthful, well-run slumbermill with
90 beds in 23 rooms (bunk in 4- to 10-bed dorm-€15-20, Db-€50-
64, includes linens, buffet breakfast-€2.50, shared kitchen, air-
con, elevator, guest computer, free Wi-Fi, laundry service, 24-hour
reception, rooftop terrace, Avenida de Menéndez Pelayo 13, tel.
955-100-160, www.samayhostels.com, Pablo).

Near the Cathedral

$$$ Hotel Alminar, plush and elegant, rents 12 fresh, slick,
minimalist rooms (Sb-€60-95, Db-€95-125, superior Db with
terrace-€115-155, extra bed-€25, breakfast-€6, air-con, elevator,
loaner laptop-€2/hour, free Wi-Fi, just 100 yards from the cathe-
dral at Calle Álvarez Quintero 52, tel. 954-293-913, www.hotel
alminar.com, reservas@hotelalminar.com, run by well-dressed,
never-stressed Francisco).

$ Hotel San Francisco may have a classy facade, but inside
its 17 rooms are sparsely decorated, with metal doors. It's centrally
located, clean, and quiet, except for the noisy ground-floor room
next to the TV and reception (Sb-€40-55, Db-€50-68, Tb-€62-
80, no breakfast, air-con, elevator, small rooftop terrace with
cathedral view, free Wi-Fi in lobby with loaner netbook, located
on pedestrian Calle Álvarez Quintero at #38, tel. 954-501-541,
www.sanfranciscoh.com, info@sanfranciscoh.com, Carlos).

West of Avenida de la Constitución

$$$ Hotel Vincci La Rábida, part of a big, impersonal hotel
chain, offers four-star comfort with its 103 rooms, huge and invit-
ing courtyard lounge, and powerful air-conditioning. Its pricing is
dictated by a computer that has it down to a science (see website
for prices—rates can spike to €400 with high demand and dip to
€80 during slow times, when that air-con is most welcome; elevator, pay Wi-Fi, Calle Castelar 24, tel. 954-501-280, www.vincci
hoteles.com, larabida@vinccihoteles.com).

$$$ Hotel Taberna del Alabardero is unique, with only
seven rooms occupying the top floor of a poet's mansion (above
the classy recommended restaurant, Taberna del Alabardero). It's
nicely located, a great value, and the ambience is perfectly circa-
1900 (Db-€90-140, Db suite-€122-190, includes breakfast, 10
percent discount with this book in 2014, air-con, elevator, free
Wi-Fi, parking-€20/day, closed in Aug, Zaragoza 20, tel. 954-
502-721, www.tabernadelalabardero.es, rest.alabardero@esh.es).

$$ Hotel Maestranza, sparkling with loving care and charm,
has 18 simple, small, clean rooms well-located on a street just off

SEVILLA

Plaza Nueva. It feels elegant for its price. Double-paned windows help to cut down on noise from the tapas bars below (Sb-€41-53, Db-€57-87, family suite-€105-135, extra bed-€20, 5 percent cash discount, no breakfast, air-con, elevator, free Wi-Fi, Gamazo 12, tel. 954-561-070, www.hotelmaestranza.es, sevilla@hotel maestranza.es, Antonio).

$$ Sevilla Plaza Suites rents 10 self-catering apartments with kitchenettes. Just opened in 2013, it's squeaky clean, family friendly, and well-located—and comes with an Astroturf sun terrace with a cathedral view. While service is scaled down, reception is open long hours (8:00-22:00) and rooms are cleaned daily (small Db-€75, big Db-€90, Qb apartment-€85-100, 6b apartment-€100-150, no breakfast, air-con, inside rooms are quieter, best deals though their website are nonrefundable, a block off Plaza Nueva at Calle Zaragoza 52, tel. 955-038-533, www.suites sevillaplaza.com, javier@suitessevillaplaza.com, Javier).

North of Plaza Nueva, Between Plaza de la Encarnación and Plaza de la Alfalfa

$ Oasis Backpackers Hostel is a good place for cheap beds, and perhaps Sevilla's best place to connect with young backpackers. Each of the eight rooms, with up to eight double bunks, comes with a modern bathroom and individual lockers. The rooftop terrace—with lounge chairs, a small pool, and adjacent kitchen— is well-used (€15-44/bed, includes breakfast, guest computer, free Wi-Fi, just off Plaza de la Encarnación on the tiny and quiet lane behind the church at #29 1/2, tel. 954-293-777, www.hostelsoasis .com, sevilla@hostelsoasis.com). Oasis also runs popular branches in Granada, Málaga, and Lisbon.

Eating in Sevilla

Eating in Sevilla is fun and affordable. People from Madrid and Barcelona find it a wonderful value. Make a point to get out and eat well when in Sevilla.

A clear eating trend in Sevilla is the rise of gourmet tapas bars, with spiffed-up decor and creative menus, at the expense of traditional restaurants. Even in difficult economic times, when other businesses are closing down, tapas bars are popping up all over. (Locals explain that with the collapse of the construction industry here, engineers, architects, and other professionals— eager for a business opportunity—are investing in trendy tapas bars.) Old-school places survive, but they often lack energy, and it seems that their clientele is aging with them. My quandary: I like the classic *típico* places. But the lively atmosphere and the best food are in the new places. On thing's for certain: If you want a good "restaurant" experience, your best value these days is to find a trendy tapas bar that offers good table seating, and sit down to enjoy some *raciones*.

Before heading out, review my "Tapas Menu Decoder" on page 34, and drinks vocabulary on page 38.

In Triana

Crusty and colorful Triana, across the river from the city center, offers a nice range of eating options. Its covered market is home to a world of tempting lunchtime eateries—take a stroll, take in the scene, and take your pick (busiest Tue-Sat morning through afternoon). Beyond the market, the neighborhood has three main restaurant zones to consider: trendy Calle San Jacinto, the neighborhood scene behind the Church of Santa Ana, and several riverside restaurants with views of central Sevilla.

On or near Calle San Jacinto

The area's newly pedestrianized main drag is lined with tables of several easy-to-enjoy restaurants.

Taberna Miami is a reliable bet for seafood. Grab a table with a good perch right on the street (€7 half-*raciones*, €11 *raciones*, Wed-Mon 11:00-17:00 & 20:00-23:30, closed Tue, Calle San Jacinto 21, tel. 954-340-843).

Blanca Paloma Bar is an untouristy classic that's a hit with the neighborhood crowd. It offers plenty of small tables for a sit-down meal, a delightful bar, and a fine selection of good Spanish wines by the glass, listed on the blackboard (tapas at bar only, €7 half-*raciones*, €12 *raciones*, Mon-Sat 12:00-17:00 & 20:00-24:00, Sun 12:00-17:00 only, at the corner of Calle Pagés del Corro, tel. 954-333-640).

Las Golondrinas Bar ("The Little Sparrows") is the talk of the Triana tapas scene, with a wonderful list of cheap and tasty tapas. Favorites here are the pork *solomillo* (sirloin) and *champiñónes* (mushrooms). Complement your meat with a veggie plate from the *aliños* section of the menu. Though they don't post a wine list, they serve plenty of nice wines by the glass. Cling to a corner of the bar and watch the amazingly productive little kitchen jam; you'll need to be aggressive to get an order in. To make a sit-down meal of it, nab one of the tables upstairs (Tue-Sun 13:00-16:00 & 20:00-24:00, may also be open Mon; one block down Calle San Jacinto from Isobel II Bridge—take the first right onto Calle Alfarería, then the first left onto Calle Antillano Campos to #26; tel. 954-331-626). The same owners also have a modern, less atmospheric place a couple of blocks away at Calle Pagés del Corro 76.

SEVILLA

Sevilla Restaurants & Flamenco

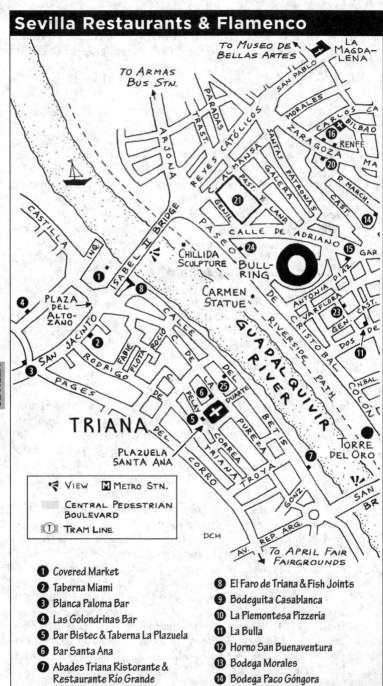

TO MUSEO DE BELLAS ARTES

LA MAGDALENA

TO ARMAS BUS STN.

CHILLIDA SCULPTURE

BULL-RING

CARMEN STATUE

PLAZA DEL ALTOZANO

GUADALQUIVIR RIVER

TRIANA

PLAZUELA SANTA ANA

TORRE DEL ORO

VIEW   M METRO STN.

CENTRAL PEDESTRIAN BOULEVARD

Ⓣ TRAM LINE

TO APRIL FAIR FAIRGROUNDS

DCH

❶ Covered Market
❷ Taberna Miami
❸ Blanca Paloma Bar
❹ Las Golondrinas Bar
❺ Bar Bistec & Taberna La Plazuela
❻ Bar Santa Ana
❼ Abades Triana Ristorante & Restaurante Río Grande

❽ El Faro de Triana & Fish Joints
❾ Bodeguita Casablanca
❿ La Piemontesa Pizzeria
⓫ La Bulla
⓬ Horno San Buenaventura
⓭ Bodega Morales
⓮ Bodega Paco Góngora

15 Bar Arenal & Freiduría

16 La Azotea Bar

17 Zelai Bar Restaurant

18 Abacería Casa Moreno

19 Restaurante Enrique Becerra

20 Taberna del Alabardero

21 Mercado del Arenal

22 La Casa de la Memoria (Flamenco)

23 Tablao El Arenal (Flamenco)

24 El Patio Sevillano (Flamenco)

25 Lo Nuestro & Rejoneo Bars

26 EME Catedral Hotel Rooftop Bar

27 El Torno Pastelería de Conventos

Behind the Church of Santa Ana

This is the best place in the area to take a break from the trendy dining scene. It offers a charming setting where you can sit down under a big tree to eat dinner along with local families.

Bar Bistec, with most of the square's tables, does grilled fish with gusto. They're enthusiastic about their cod fritters and calamari, and brag about their pigeon, quail, and snails in sauce. Before taking a seat out on the square, consider the indoor seating and the fun action at the bar (€8 half-*raciones,* €14 *raciones,* daily 11:30-16:00 & 20:00-24:00, Plazuela de Santa Ana, tel. 954-274-759). **Taberna La Plazuela,** which shares the square, is simpler, doing fried fish, grilled sardines, and *caracoles* (tree snails).

Bar Santa Ana, just a block away alongside the church, is a rustic neighborhood sports-and-bull bar with great seating on the street. Peruse the interior, draped in bullfighting and Weeping Virgin memorabilia. It's always busy with the neighborhood gang, who enjoy fun tapas like *delicia de solomillo* (tenderloin) and appreciate the bar's willingness to serve even cheap tapas at the outdoor tables. If you stand at the bar, they'll keep track of your bill by chalking it directly on the counter in front of you (facing the side of the church at Pureza 82, tel. 954-272-102).

Along the River

Abades Triana Ristorante is the new hit in town for special occasions and fancy riverfront dining. It's a dressy restaurant with formal waiters serving modern Mediterranean cuisine. You'll sit in air-conditioned comfort behind a big glass wall facing the river or on a classy outdoor terrace (€3.50 cover, €15-20 starters, €20-25 fish and meat plates, daily 13:30-16:00 & 20:00-24:00, directly across from Torre del Oro at Calle Betis 69, tel. 954-286-459, www.abadestriana.com, reservations smart but they don't reserve specific tables).

Restaurante Río Grande is your stuffy, traditional, candlelit-fancy option—a good place for a restaurant dinner, with properly attired waiters, a full menu rather than tapas, and lots of seafood. Dining on the terrace (closer to the bridge) is less expensive and more casual (€3 tapas, €10-20 starters, €18-25 main dishes, daily 13:00-16:00 & 20:00-24:00, air-con, next to the San Telmo Bridge, tel. 954-273-956).

More Riverside Dining: **El Faro de Triana** charges high prices for basic food, but its fun setting—on four levels within the old yellow bridge tower overlooking the Isabel II Bridge—might make it worthwhile (€7-9 half-*raciones,* €12-18 *raciones,* open daily, tel. 954-336-192). The little fish joints fronting the river just beyond the bridge (**La Taberna del Pescador, Betis 12 La Terraza,** and **Taberna Antigua Barberia**) charge a little extra for their scenic setting, but if you want to eat reasonably on the river, they are worth considering.

In Barrio Santa Cruz
Tapas with the Tourists

For tapas, the Barrio Santa Cruz is trendy and *romántico*. Plenty of atmospheric-but-touristy restaurants fill the neighborhood near the cathedral and along Calle Santa María la Blanca. From the cathedral, walk up Calle Mateos Gago, where several classic old bars—with the day's tapas scrawled on chalkboards—keep tourists and locals well fed and watered.

Bodega Santa Cruz (a.k.a. **Las Columnas**) is a popular, user-friendly standby with cheap, unpretentious tapas. You're not coming here for the food (which is basic), but for the bustling atmosphere, as locals and tourists alike crowd the place, inside and out, for hours on end. You can keep an eye on the busy kitchen from the bar, or hang out like a cowboy at the tiny stand-up tables out front. Separate chalkboards list €2 tapas and €2 *montaditos* (little sandwiches served on a bun).

Las Teresas is a characteristic small bar draped in fun photos. It serves good tapas from a tight little menu. Prices at the bar and outside tables (for fun tourist-watching) are the same, but they serve tapas only at the bar. The hams (with little upside-down umbrellas that catch the dripping fat) are a reminder that the Spanish are enthusiastic about their cured-meat dishes (€3-4 tapas, €8-10 half-*raciones,* €14-20 *raciones,* open daily, Calle Santa Teresa 2, tel. 954-213-069).

Cervecería Giralda is a long-established meeting place for locals. With an almost genteel tiled setting and stiff waiters, it has an exclusive air. It's famous for its fine tapas, but feels particularly touristy—confirm prices, and stick with straight items on the menu rather than expensive trick specials proposed by waiters. You can order from the same menu, and at the same prices, whether you sit outside, at an inside table, or at the bar (€3-4 tapas, €10 *raciones,* daily 9:00-24:00, Calle Mateos Gago 1, tel. 954-256-162).

Restaurante San Marco serves basic, reasonably priced Italian cuisine under the arches of what was a Moorish bath in the Middle Ages (and a disco in the 1990s). The air-conditioned atmosphere may feel rather upscale, but it's also easygoing and family-friendly, with live Spanish guitar every night (€7-9 salads, pizza, and pastas; €11-12 meat dishes, daily 13:00-16:15 & 20:00-24:00, Calle Mesón del Moro 6, tel. 954-564-390, staff speaks English, welcoming Angelo).

Casa Roman Taberna has a classic bar and tavern interior, with good tables inside and a few more on a great little square outside. When they're quiet, they may serve tapas at the tables (ask); otherwise, it's your standard *raciones* (easy menu, lots of wines by the glass, Plaza de los Venerables 1, tel. 954-228-483).

On or near Calle Santa María la Blanca

This lively street, which defines the eastern boundary of the Barrio Santa Cruz, has an inviting concentration of eateries and is only slightly less touristy.

Taberna Poncio, with a well-known chef who recently downsized from a formal restaurant to a gourmet tapas bar, offers about 30 different €5-10 plates (including desserts). It's good for restaurant-type seating, both inside or on a quiet square at the edge of the Barrio Santa Cruz (Mon-Sat 13:00-16:00 & 20:00-24:00, closed Sun, just off Plaza Santa María la Blanca at Calle Ximénez de Enciso 33, tel. 954-460-717).

Tapas Restaurants on Paseo Catalina de Ribera: Three easy and good-value places located next to each other are worth considering; they have similar prices (€3-4 tapas, €8-10 plates), fine bars, good indoor seating, and wonderful tables outside on a busy sidewalk facing the Murillo Gardens at the east end of the Barrio Santa Cruz. **Modesto Tapas** is the old-fashioned place, with standard tapas and a crowd that seems averse to trendiness. The other two are more happening and creative. **Vinería San Telmo** advertises "vino and tapas" and offers lots of wine by the glass (tel. 954-410-600). **Catalina Tapas Bar** is my favorite—like me, it's more up-to-date and creative than Modesto, but less hip than San Telmo (tel. 954-412-412).

Restaurante Modesto is a local favorite serving pricey but top-notch Andalusian fare—especially fish—with a comfortable dining room and atmospheric outdoor seating in the bright, bustling square just outside the Barrio Santa Cruz. It offers creative, fun meals—look around before ordering—and a good €20 fixed-price lunch or dinner served by energetic, occasionally pushy waiters. The €9 house salad is a meal, and the €15.50 *fritura modesto* (fried seafood plate) is popular (€7-15 starters, €12-20 main dishes, daily 12:00-17:00 & 20:00-24:00, near Santa María la Blanca at Calle Cano y Cueto 5, tel. 954-416-811).

Freiduría Puerta de la Carne and **Bar Restaurante El 3 de Oro** are a two-for-one operation. Freiduría is a fried-fish-to-go place, with great outdoor seating, while El 3 de Oro is a fancier restaurant across the street that serves fine wine or beer to the fry shop's outdoor tables. First go into the fry shop and order a cheap cone of tasty fried fish with a tomato salad. Study the photos of the various kinds of seafood available; *un quarto* (250 grams, for €5-7) serves one person. Then head out front and flag down a server to order a drink (technically from the restaurant), all while enjoying a great outdoor setting—almost dining for the cost of a picnic

(Freiduría open daily in summer 20:00-24:30, also open for lunch in off-season; Santa María la Blanca 34, tel. 954-426-820).

Breakfast and Dessert on Plaza Santa María la Blanca: Several nondescript places work to keep travelers happy at breakfast time on the sunny main square near most of my recommended hotels. I like **Café Bar Carmela.** For the cost of a continental breakfast at your hotel (€5.50-7.50), you can be out on the square, with your choice of either a smaller, local-style breakfast, or a hearty American-style meal (breakfast served 9:00-13:00, easy menus, Calle Santa María la Blanca 6, tel. 954-540-590).

Villar Ice Cream is the neighborhood favorite. *Maestro Heladero* Antonino has been making ice cream in Sevilla for the past 40 years, with a focus on fresh, natural, and inventive products. They are generous with samples and creative with their offerings, so try a few wild flavors before choosing. Antonino's friendly wife, Cecilia, speaks English and doles out samples (daily 12:00-24:00, Puerto de la Carne 3, mobile 664-608-960).

Between the Cathedral and the River

I don't like the restaurants surrounding the cathedral, but many good places are nearby, just across Avenida de la Constitución. In the area between the cathedral and the river, you can find tapas, cheap eats, and fine dining. Calle García de Vinuesa leads past several colorful and cheap tapas places to a busy corner surrounded with an impressive selection of happy eateries (where Calle de Adriano meets Calle Antonia Díaz).

Bodeguita Casablanca is famously the choice of bullfighters, and even the king. Just steps from the touristy cathedral area, this classy place seems a world apart, with elegant locals, a great menu, and a dressy interior complete with a stuffed bull's head. Sit inside for a serious meal of half-*raciones*. Be bold and experiment with your order—you can't go wrong here (€2.50 tapas, Mon-Fri 13:30-24:00, closed Sat-Sun, across from Archivo de Indias at Calle Adolfo Rodríguez Jurado 12, tel. 954-224-114).

La Piemontesa Pizzeria creates its own world, with a calm, spacious, elegant interior built upon 12th-century Moorish ruins (look through the glass floor) and under historic arches of what used to be the city's treasury. It's a good, dressy Italian alternative to the tapas commotion, with mellow lighting and music (€12 salads, pastas, and pizzas; Calle Santander 1, tel. 954-503-921).

La Bulla feels like the brainchild of a gang of local foodies who, intent upon mixing traditional dishes, create an inventive international menu that's a welcome break from the usual fare. The place is bohemian-chic, with rickety tables gathered around a busy kitchen. The day's offerings are only listed on big chalkboards; insist on a stand-up English-language tour of what's available.

While risotto is their signature dish, I prefer their other offerings. You'll enjoy gourmet presentation, a hip local crowd, easy jazz ambience, and good-looking servers. There's no bar—only table seating (and only indoors)—and the €4-10 dishes are easily splittable; three will stuff two people (daily 12:00-16:30 & 20:00-24:00, midway between cathedral and Torre del Oro at Calle 2 de Mayo 26, tel. 954-219-262, no reservations).

Horno San Buenaventura, across from the cathedral on the corner of Calle García de Vinuesa and Avenida de la Constitución, is a big, venerable bakery with tables out on the *avenida* and a quiet dining room upstairs. Its slick, chrome-filled, spacious main floor is lined with long display cases of sandwiches and desserts. The tapas bar upstairs has table service only (open daily, light meals are posted by the door, avoid the frozen paella).

Bodega Morales, farther up Calle García de Vinuesa (at #11), oozes old-Sevilla ambience. The front area is more of a drinking bar; for food, go in the back section (use the separate entrance around the corner). Here, sitting among huge adobe jugs, you can munch tiny sandwiches *(montaditos)* and tapas; both are just €2 (€6 half-*raciones,* order at the bar, good wine selection, daily 13:00-16:00 & 19:30-24:00, tel. 954-221-242).

Bodega Paco Góngora is colorful and a bit classier than most tapas bars, with a tight dining area and delightful tapas. Its sit-down meals are well presented and reasonably priced (€3-4 tapas at bar only, €8 half-*raciones,* €11 *raciones* at tables, daily 12:00-16:00 & 20:00-24:00, ask for the English menu, off Plaza Nueva at Calle Padre Marchena 1, tel. 954-214-139).

Bar Arenal is a classic bull bar with tables spilling out onto a great street-corner setting. It's good for just a drink and to hang out with a crusty crowd. While they sell cheap, old-school tapas, you can complete the experience memorably by buying a load of fried fish from **El Arenal Freiduría** next door—this is perfectly permissible (€6-7 fresh-fried portions can feed two, open evenings only, bar is at Calle Arfe 2, tel. 954-223-686).

Near Plaza Nueva

La Azotea Bar is a modern place that makes up for its lack of traditional character with gourmet tapas—made with local, seasonal ingredients—that have earned it a loyal following. It's run by Juan Antonio and his partner from San Diego, Jeanine, who've taken care to make the menu easy and accessible for English speakers. You can dine elegantly, yet cheaply, on tapas at the bar, or enjoy a sit-down meal at its tables—but you'll need to arrive early. The big, €10 half-*raciones* feed two (Mon-Sat lunch starts at 13:30, dinner at 20:30, closed Sun, Calle Zaragoza 5, tel. 954-564-316).

Zelai Bar Restaurant is completely contemporary, without a hint of a historic-Sevilla feel or touristy vibe. Their pricey gourmet tapas (€5-6) and *raciones* (€10-13) are a hit with a smart local crowd, who enjoy the fusion of Basque, Andalusian, and international flavors. They also have a dressy little restaurant in back (reservations generally required) with a €40 tasting *menu* (closed Sun-Mon, just off Plaza Nueva at Calle Albareda 22, tel. 954-229-992).

Abacería Casa Moreno is a rare, classic *abacería,* a neighborhood grocery store that doubles as a standing-room-only tapas bar. Squeeze into the back room and you're slipping back in time—and behind a tall language barrier. Help yourself to the box of pork scratchings at the bar while choosing from an enticing list of €2.50 tapas. They're proud of their top-quality *jamón serrano* and *queso manchego,* and serve hot tapas only at lunch. Rubbing elbows here with local eaters, under a bull's head, surrounded by jars of peaches and cans of sardines, you feel like you're in on a secret (Mon-Fri 8:00-15:30 & 19:30-22:30, closed Sat-Sun, 3 blocks off Plaza Nueva at Calle Gamazo 7, tel. 954-228-315).

Restaurante Enrique Becerra is a fancy little 10-table place popular with local foodies. It's well-known for its gourmet Andalusian cuisine and fine wine. Muscle past the well-dressed locals at the tapas bar for gourmet snacks and wine by the glass, or head to the quieter, more elegant upstairs dining room. While the restaurant satisfies its guests with quality food, given the tight seating and its popularity with tourists, it can feel like a trap (€3-4 tapas available at the bar and ground-floor tables, €10 half-*raciones,* €20 plates upstairs, Mon-Sat 13:00-16:30 & 20:00-24:00, closed Sun, reservations essential, Gamazo 2, tel. 954-213-049, www.enriquebecerra.com).

Taberna del Alabardero, one of Sevilla's finest restaurants, serves refined Spanish cuisine in chandeliered elegance just a couple of blocks from the cathedral. If you order à la carte, it adds up to about €45 a meal, but for €48 (or €58 with wine) you can have a fun five-course fixed-price meal with lots of little surprises from the chef. Or consider their €18/person (no sharing) starter sampler, followed by an entrée. The service in the fancy upstairs dining rooms gets mixed reviews (carefully read and understand your bill)...but the setting is stunning (daily 13:00-16:30 & 20:30-24:00, closed Aug, air-con, reservations smart, Zaragoza 20, tel. 954-502-721, www.tabernadelalabardero.es).

Taberna del Alabardero Student-Served Lunch: The ground-floor dining rooms (elegant but nothing like upstairs) are popular with local office workers for a great-value, student-chef-prepared, fixed-price lunch sampler (three delightful courses-€13 Mon-Fri, €18 Sat-Sun; €20 dinner available daily, drinks not included, open daily 13:00-16:30 & 20:00-23:30). To avoid a wait at lunch, arrive before 14:00 (no reservations possible).

At the Arenal Market Hall

Mercado del Arenal, the covered fish-and-produce market, is ideal for both snapping photos and grabbing a cheap lunch. As with most markets, you'll find characteristic little diners with prices designed to lure in savvy shoppers, not to mention a crispy fresh world of picnic goodies—and a riverside promenade with benches just a block away (Mon-Sat 9:00-14:30, closed Sun, sleepy on Mon, on Calle Pastor y Landero at Calle Arenal, just beyond bullring).

Marisquería Arenal Sevilla is a popular fish restaurant that thrives in the middle of the Arenal Market, but stays open after the market closes. In the afternoon and evening, you're surrounded by the empty Industrial Age market, with workers dragging their crates to and fro. It's a great family-friendly, finger-licking-good scene that's much appreciated by its enthusiastic local following. Fish is priced by weight, so be careful when ordering, and double-check the bill (€6-18 fish plates, Tue-Sat 13:00-17:00 & 21:00-24:00, closed Sun-Mon, reservations smart for dinner, enter on Calle Pastor y Landero 9, tel. 954-220-881).

Sevilla Connections

Note that many destinations are well served by both trains and buses.

By Train

Most trains arriving and departing Sevilla, including all high-speed AVE trains, leave from the larger, more distant **Santa Justa Station.** But many *cercanías* and inter-regional trains heading south to Granada, Jerez, Cádiz, and Málaga also stop at the smaller **San Bernardo** station a few minutes away, which is connected to downtown by tram. Hourly *cercanías* trains connect both stations (about a 3-minute trip). For tips on arrival at either station, see "Arrival in Sevilla," earlier.

From Sevilla by AVE Train to Madrid: The AVE express train is expensive but fast (2.5 hours to Madrid; hourly departures 7:00-23:00, see page 511 for more on the Sevilla-Madrid train route). Departures between 16:00 and 19:00 can book up far in advance, but surprise holidays and long weekends can totally jam up trains as well—reserve as far ahead as possible.

From Sevilla by Train to Córdoba: There are three options for this journey: slow and cheap **regional** trains (7/day, 80 minutes), fast and cheap regional high-speed **Avant** trains (9/day, 45 minutes, requires reservation), and fast and expensive **AVE** trains en route to Madrid (2-3/hour, 45 minutes, requires reservation). Unless you must be on a particular departure, there's no reason to pay more for AVE; Avant is just as quick and a third the price. (If you have a railpass, you still must buy a reservation; Avant reservations cost about half as much as ones for AVE.)

Other Trains from Sevilla to: Málaga (6/day, 2 hours on Avant; 5/day, 2.5 hours on slower regional trains), **Ronda** (5/day, 3-4 hours, transfer in Bobadilla, Antequera, or Córdoba), **Granada** (4/day, 3 hours), **Jerez** (nearly hourly, 1.25 hours), **Barcelona** (11/day, 5.5-6 hours; plus one overnight train, 13 hours), **Algeciras** (3/day, 5-6 hours, transfer at Antequera or Bobadilla—bus is better). There are no direct trains to **Lisbon,** Portugal, so you'll have to take AVE to Madrid, then overnight to Lisbon; buses to Lisbon are far better (see later). Train info: Tel. 902-320-320, www.renfe.com.

By Bus

Sevilla has two bus stations: The El Prado de San Sebastián station, just south of the Alcázar, primarily serves regional destinations; the Plaza de Armas station, farther north (near the bullring), handles most long-distance buses. Bus info: Tel. 954-908-040 but rarely answered, go to TI for latest schedule info.

From Sevilla's El Prado de San Sebastián station to Andalucía and the South Coast: Regional buses are operated by Comes (www.tgcomes.es), Los Amarillos (www.losamarillos.es), and Linesur (www.linesur.com). Connections to **Jerez** are frequent, as many southbound buses head there first (7-10/day, 1.5 hours, run by all three companies; note that train is also possible—see above). Los Amarillos runs buses to some of Andalucía's hill towns, including **Ronda** (8/day, 2-2.5 hours, some via Villamartín, fewer on weekends) and **Arcos** (1-2/day, 2 hours; many more departures possible with transfer in Jerez). For the Costa del Sol, a handy Comes bus departs Sevilla four times a day and heads for **Tarifa** (2.5-3.25 hours), **Algeciras** (3-4 hours), and **La Línea/Gibraltar** (4-4.5 hours). However, if **Algeciras** is your goal, Linesur has a much faster direct connection (8/day, fewer on weekends, 2.5-3 hours). There are also two buses a day from this station to **Granada** (2/day, 3-3.5 hours); the rest depart from the Plaza de Armas station.

From Sevilla's Plaza de Armas station to: Madrid (9/day, 6 hours, www.socibus.es, tel. 902-229-292), **Córdoba** (7/day, 1-2 hours), **Granada** (7/day, 3 hours *directo*, 3.5-4.5 hours *ruta*), **Málaga** (6/day direct, 2.5-3 hours), **Nerja** (2/day, 4-5 hours), **Barcelona** (2/day, 16.5 hours, including one overnight bus). Information: Tel. 902-450-550.

By Bus to Portugal: The best way to get to **Lisbon,** Portugal, is by bus (2/day, departures at 15:00 and 24:00, 7 hours, departs Plaza de Armas station, tel. 954-905-102, www.alsa.es). The midnight departure continues past Lisbon to **Coimbra** (arriving

10:30) and **Porto** (arriving 12:15). Sevilla also has direct bus service to **Lagos,** Portugal, on the Algarve (4/day in summer, 2/day off-season, about 4.5 hours, buy ticket a day or two in advance May-Oct, tel. 954-907-737, www.damas-sa.es). The bus departs from Sevilla's Plaza de Armas bus station and arrives at the Lagos bus station. If you'd like to visit Tavira on the way to Lagos, purchase a bus ticket to Tavira, have lunch there, then take the train to Lagos.

CÓRDOBA

Straddling a sharp bend of the Guadalquivir River, Córdoba has a glorious Roman and Moorish past, once serving as a regional capital for both empires. It's home to Europe's best Islamic sight after Granada's Alhambra: the Mezquita, a splendid and remarkably well-preserved mosque that dates from A.D. 784. When you step inside the mosque, which is magical in its grandeur, you can imagine Córdoba as the center of a thriving and sophisticated culture. During the Dark Ages, when much of Europe was barbaric and illiterate, Córdoba was a haven of enlightened thought—famous for religious tolerance, artistic expression, and dedication to philosophy and the sciences. To this day, you'll still hear the Muslim call to prayer in Córdoba.

Beyond the magnificent Mezquita, the city of Córdoba has two sides: the extremely touristy maze of streets immediately surrounding the giant main attraction, lined with trinket shops, hotels, and restaurants; and the workaday part of town (centered on Plaza de las Tendillas). While the over-commercialized vibe of the touristy area can be off-putting, a quick walk takes you to real-life Córdoba.

Planning Your Time

Ideally, Córdoba is worth two nights and a day. Don't rush the magnificent Mezquita, but also consider sticking around to experience the city's other pleasures: Wander the evocative Jewish Quarter, enjoy the tapas scene, and explore the modern part of town.

However, if you're tight on time, it's possible to do Córdoba more quickly—especially since it's conveniently located on the

AVE bullet-train line (and because, frankly, Córdoba is less interesting than the other two big Andalusian cities, Sevilla and Granada). To see Córdoba as an efficient stopover between Madrid and Sevilla (or as a side-trip from Sevilla—frequent trains, 45-minute trip), focus on the Mezquita: Taxi from the station, spend two hours there, explore the old town for an hour...and then scram.

Orientation to Córdoba

Córdoba's big draw is the mosque-turned-cathedral called the Mezquita (for pronunciation ease, think female mosquito). Most of the town's major sights are nearby, including the Alcázar, a former royal castle. And though the town seems to ignore its marshy Guadalquivir River (a prime bird-watching area), the riverbank sports a Renaissance triumphal arch next to a stout "Roman Bridge." The bridge leads to the town's old fortified gate (which now houses a museum on Moorish culture, the Museum of Al-Andalus Life). The Mezquita is buried in the characteristic medieval town. Around that stretches the Jewish Quarter, then the modern city—which feels much like any other in Spain, but with some striking Art Deco buildings at Plaza de las Tendillas and lots of Art Nouveau lining Avenida del Gran Capitán.

Tourist Information

Córdoba has helpful TIs at the train station, Alcázar, and Plaza de las Tendillas (all open daily 9:00-14:00 & 17:00-19:30, tel. 902-201-774, www.turismodecordoba.org). Another TI, near the Mezquita, is run separately and covers all of Andalucía (Mon-Fri 9:00-19:30, Sat-Sun 9:00-15:00, Torrijos 10, tel. 957-355-179).

Arrival in Córdoba

By Train or Bus: Córdoba's train station is located on Avenida de América. Built in 1991 to accommodate the high-speed AVE train line, the slick train station has ATMs, restaurants, a variety of shops, a TI booth (on the concourse above the track), an information counter, and a small lounge for first-class AVE passengers. Taxis and local buses are just outside, to the left as you come up the escalators from the platforms.

The bus station is across the street from the train station (on Avenida Vía Augusta, to the north). There's no luggage storage at the train station, but the bus station has lockers (€4, look for *consigna* sign and buy token at machine).

To get to the old town, hop a **taxi** (€7 to the Mezquita) or catch **bus #3** (buy €1.20 ticket on board, ask driver for *"mezquita,"* get off at Calle San Fernando, and take Calle del Portillo, following the

Córdoba

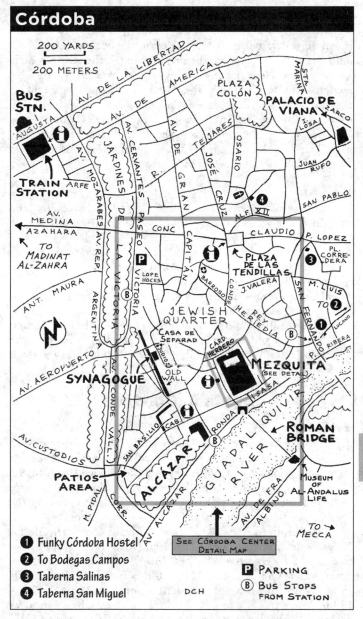

200 YARDS
200 METERS

BUS STN.

TRAIN STATION

AV. DE LA LIBERTAD

AV. DE AMERICA

PLAZA COLÓN

PALACIO DE VIANA

ARCO

STA. MARINA

AUGUSTA

ARFE

JARDINES

AV. CERVANTES

AV. DE

AV. DE GRAN CAPITÁN

TEJARES

JOSÉ CRUZ

OSARIO

JUAN RUFO

SAN PABLO

❹

ALF. XII

AV. MONÁRABES

AV. REP.

DE LA VICTORIA

AV. MEDINA AZAHARA

↖ TO MADINAT AL-ZAHRA

ANT. MAURA

AV. AEROPUERTO

PASEO VICTORIA

CONC

CLAUDIO

P. LOPEZ

P LOPE HOCES

Ⓑ

PLAZA DE LAS TENDILLAS

J. VALERA

PL. CORREDERA

M. LUIS

❸

TO

❷

LUCANO

AGUAYO

BARROSO

CONDE HEREDIA

REY HEREDIA

SAN FERNANDO

❶

Ⓑ

P. RIBERA

ARGENTINA

JEWISH QUARTER

CASA DE SEFARAD

CARD. HERRERO

MEZQUITA
(SEE DETAIL)

OLD WALL

SYNAGOGUE

ISASA

ROMAN BRIDGE

AV. CONDE VALL.

CAB.

AV. CUSTODIOS

SAN BASILIO

RONDA

Ⓑ

ALCÁZAR

GUADALQUIVIR RIVER

AV. DE FRA ALBINO

MUSEUM OF AL-ANDALUS LIFE

PATIOS AREA

M. PIDAL

CORR.

AV. ALCÁZAR

TO MECCA

SEE CÓRDOBA CENTER DETAIL MAP

❶ Funky Córdoba Hostel
❷ To Bodegas Campos
❸ Taberna Salinas
❹ Taberna San Miguel

P PARKING
Ⓑ BUS STOPS FROM STATION

DCH

CÓRDOBA

twists and turns—and occasional signs—to the Mezquita).

It's about a 25-minute **walk** from either station to the old town. To walk from the train station to the Mezquita, turn left onto Avenida de América, then right through the Jardines de la Victoria park. Near the end of the park, on the left, you'll see a section of the old city walls. The Puerta de Almodóvar gate marks the start of Calle Cairuan—follow this street downhill, with the wall still on your left, until you reach Plaza Campo de los Martires. Consider popping in to the TI on this square for a city map. Then head left, past the Alcázar, down Calle Amador de los Reyes, which leads directly to the Mezquita.

Helpful Hints

Closed Days: The synagogue, Alcázar, Madinat Al-Zahra, and Palacio de Viana are closed on Monday. The Mezquita is open daily.

Festivals: May is busy with festivals. During the first half of May, Córdoba hosts the Concurso Popular de Patios Cordobeses—a patio contest (see sidebar on page 752).

Local Guides: Isabel Martinez Richter is a charming archaeologist who loves to make the city come to life for curious Americans (€130/3 hours, mobile 669-369-645, isabmr@gmail .com). **Angel Lucena** is also a good teacher and a joy to be with (€100/3 hours, mobile 607-898-079, lucenaangel@hot mail.com).

Sights in Córdoba

▲▲▲Mezquita

This massive former mosque—now with a 16th-century church rising up from the middle—was once the center of Western Islam and the heart of a cultural capital that rivaled Baghdad and Constantinople. A wonder of the medieval world, it's remarkably well-preserved, giving today's visitors a chance to soak up the ambience of Islamic Córdoba in its 10th-century prime.

Cost and Hours: €8, ticket kiosk inside the Patio de los Naranjos, Mon-Sat free entry until 10:00 (because they don't want to charge a fee to attend the 9:30 Mass), dry €3.50 audioguide; open March-Oct Mon-Sat 8:30-19:00, Sun 8:30-11:30 & 15:00-19:00; Nov-Feb Mon-Sat 8:30-18:00, Sun 8:30-11:30 & 15:00-18:00; last entry 30 minutes before closing, Christian altar accessible only after 11:00 unless you attend Mass, try to avoid midday crowds (11:00-15:00) by coming early or late; tel. 957-470-512, www.catedraldecordoba.es. You can also enjoy the Mezquita on a sound-and-light tour on some summer evenings (described on page 753).

The Mezquita

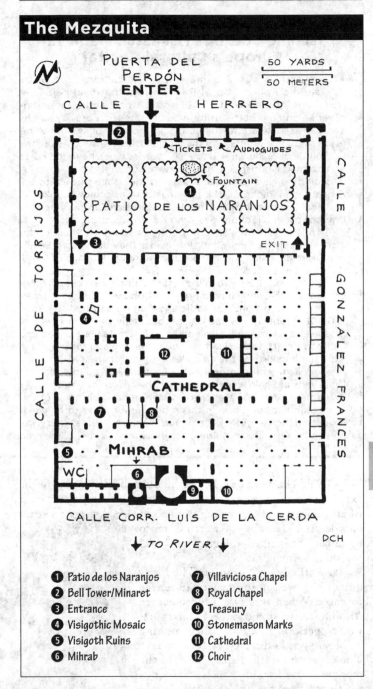

PUERTA DEL PERDÓN
ENTER

50 YARDS
50 METERS

CALLE HERRERO

CALLE DE TORRIJOS

CALLE GONZÁLEZ FRANCÉS

← TICKETS ← AUDIOGUIDES

PATIO DE LOS NARANJOS

Fountain

❶

❷

❸

EXIT

❹

CATHEDRAL

❶❷

❶❶

❼

❽

❺ MIHRAB

WC

❻

❾

❿

CALLE CORR. LUIS DE LA CERDA

↓ TO RIVER ↓

DCH

CÓRDOBA

❶ Patio de los Naranjos
❷ Bell Tower/Minaret
❸ Entrance
❹ Visigothic Mosaic
❺ Visigoth Ruins
❻ Mihrab
❼ Villaviciosa Chapel
❽ Royal Chapel
❾ Treasury
❿ Stonemason Marks
❶❶ Cathedral
❶❷ Choir

Islamic Córdoba (756-1236): Medieval Europe's Cultural Capital

After his family was slaughtered by political rivals (A.D. 750), 20-year-old Prince Abd Al-Rahman fled the royal palace at Damascus, headed west across North Africa, and went undercover among the Berber tribesmen of Morocco. For six years he avoided assassination while building a power base among his fellow Arab expatriates and the local Muslim Berbers. As an heir to the title of "caliph" (akin to an emperor-pope), he sailed north and claimed Moorish Spain as his own, confirming his power by decapitating his enemies and sending their salted heads to the rival caliph in Baghdad. This split in Islam was somewhat like the papal schism that stirred up medieval Christian Europe, when the Church split into factions over who was the rightful pope.

Thus began an Islamic flowering in southern Spain under Abd Al-Rahman's family, the Umayyads. They dominated Sevilla and Granada, ruling the independent state of "Al-Andalus," with their capital at Córdoba.

By the year 950—when the rest of Europe was mired in poverty, ignorance, and superstition—Córdoba was Europe's greatest city, rivaling Constantinople and Baghdad. It had well over 100,000 people (Paris had a third that many), with hundreds of mosques, palaces, and public baths. The streets were paved and lighted at night with oil lamps, and running water was piped in from the outskirts of the city. Medieval visitors marveled at the size and luxury of its mosque (the Mezquita), a symbol that the Umayyads of Spain were the equal of the caliphs of Baghdad.

This Golden Age was marked by a remarkable spirit of tolerance and cooperation in this region among the three great monotheistic religions: Islam, Judaism, and Christianity. As a proudly Andalusian guide once explained to me, "Umayyad

CÓRDOBA

◆ Self-Guided Tour: Before entering the patio, take in the exterior of the Mezquita. The mosque's massive footprint is clear when you survey its sprawling walls from outside. At 600 feet by 400 feet, it seems to dominate the higgledy-piggledy medieval town that surrounds it.

❶ Patio de los Naranjos: The Mezquita's big, welcoming courtyard is free to enter. When this was a mosque, the Muslim faithful would gather in this courtyard to perform ablution—ritual washing before prayer, as directed by Muslim law. The courtyard walls display many of the mosque's carved ceiling panels and beams, which date from the 10th century.

Al-Andalus was not one country with three cultures. It was one culture with three religions...its people shared the same food, dress, art, music, and language. Different religious rituals within the community were practiced in private. But clearly, Muslims ruled. No church spire could be taller than a minaret, and while the call to prayer rang out five times daily, there was no ringing of church bells."

The university rang with voices in Arabic, Hebrew, and Latin, sharing their knowledge of medicine, law, literature, and *al-jibra*. The city fell under the enlightened spell of the ancient Greeks, and Córdoba's 70 libraries bulged with translated manuscripts of Plato and Aristotle, works that would later inspire medieval Christians.

Ruling over the Golden Age were two energetic leaders—Abd Al-Rahman III (912-961) and Al-Hakam II (961-976)—who conquered territory, expanded the Mezquita, and boldly proclaimed themselves caliphs.

Córdoba's Y1K crisis brought civil wars that toppled the caliph (1031), splintering Al-Andalus into several kingdoms. Córdoba came under the control of the Almoravids (Berbers from North Africa), who were less sophisticated than the Arab-based Umayyads. Then a wave of even stricter Islam swept through Spain, bringing the Almohads to power (1147) and driving Córdoba's best and brightest into exile. The city's glory days were over, and it was replaced by Sevilla and Granada as the centers of Spanish Islam. On June 29, 1236, Christians conquered the city. That morning Muslims said their last prayers in the great mosque. That afternoon the Christians set up their portable road altar and celebrated the church's first Mass. Córdoba's days as a political and cultural superpower were over.

CÓRDOBA

❷ **Bell Tower/Minaret:** Gaze up through the trees for views of the bell tower (c. 1600), built over the remains of the original Muslim minaret. For four centuries, five times a day, a singing cleric (the muezzin) would ride a donkey up the ramp of the minaret, then call to all Muslims in earshot that it was time to face Mecca and pray.

• *Buy your ticket (and, if you wish, rent an audioguide at a separate kiosk to the right). Enter the building by passing through the keyhole gate at the far-right corner (pick up an English map-brochure as you enter).*

❸ **Entrance:** Walking into the former mosque from the patio, you pass from an orchard of orange trees into a forest of delicate columns (erected here in the eighth century). The more than 800 red-and-blue columns are topped with double arches—a round Romanesque arch above a Visigothic horseshoe arch—made from alternating red brick and white stone. The columns and capitals

(built of marble, granite, and alabaster) were recycled from ancient
Roman ruins and conquered
Visigothic churches. (Golden Age
Arabs excelled at absorbing both
the technology and the building
materials of the people they conquered—no surprise, considering
the culture's nomadic roots; cen-

turies of tentmaking didn't lend much stoneworking expertise.)
The columns seem to recede to infinity, as if reflecting the immensity and complexity of Allah's creation.

Although it's a vast room, the low ceilings and dense columns
create an intimate and worshipful atmosphere. The original mosque
was brighter, before Christians renovated the place for their use
and closed in the arched entrances from the patio and street. The
giant cathedral sits in the center of the mosque. For now, pretend it
doesn't exist. We'll visit it after exploring the mosque.

• *From the entrance, walk along the side wall five columns in and find a
glass floor over a section of mosaic floor below. Look in.*

❹ **Visigothic Mosaic:** The mosque stands on the site of the
early-Christian Church of San Vicente, built during the Visigothic
period (sixth century). Peering down, you can see a mosaic that
remains from that original church. This is important to Catholic
locals, as it proves there was a church here before the mosque—
thereby giving credence to those who see the modern-day church
on this spot as a return to the site's original purpose, rather than a
violation of the mosque.

• *Walk straight ahead to the far right corner (opposite the entrance),
where you'll find more...*

❺ **Visigothic Ruins:** On display in the corner are rare bits of
carved stone from that same sixth-century church. (Most other
stonework here had been scrubbed of its Christian symbolism
by Muslims seeking to reuse them for the mosque.) Prince Abd
Al-Rahman bought the church from his Christian subjects before
leveling it to build his mosque. From here, pan to the right to
take in the sheer vastness of the mosque. (Keep panning to find a
hidden WC and drinking fountain in the corner.)

• *Walk to your left until you come to the mosque's focal point, the...*

❻ **Mihrab:** The mosque equivalent of a church's high altar,
this was the focus of the mosque and remains a highlight of the
Mezquita today. Picture the original mosque at prayer time, with a
dirt floor covered by a patchwork of big carpets...more than 20,000
people could pray at once here. Imagine the multitude kneeling in
prayer, facing the mihrab, rocking forward to touch their heads to
the ground, and saying, *"Allahu Akbar, la illa a il Allah, Muhammad*

razul Allah"—"Allah is great, there is no god but Allah, and Muhammad is his prophet."

The mihrab, a feature in all mosques, is a decorated "niche"—in this case, more like a small room with a golden-arch entrance. During a service, the imam (prayer leader) would stand here to read scripture and give sermons. He spoke loudly into the niche, his back to the assembled crowd, and the architecture worked to amplify his voice so all could hear. Built in the mid-10th century by Al-Hakam II, the exquisite room reflects the wealth of Córdoba in its prime. Three thousand pounds of multicolored glass-and-enamel cubes panel the walls and domes in mosaics designed by Byzantine craftsmen, depicting flowers and quotes from the Quran. Gape up. Overhead rises a colorful, starry dome with skylights and interlocking lobe-shaped arches.

• *Now turn around so that you're facing away from the mihrab. Ahead of you, and a bit to the left, is a roped-off open area. Step up, and gaze into the first chapel built within the mosque after the Christian Reconquista.*

❼ Villaviciosa Chapel: In 1236, Saint-King Ferdinand III conquered the city and turned the mosque into a church. The

higher ceiling allowed for clerestory windows and more light, which were key to making it feel more church-like. Still, the locals continued to call it "la Mezquita," and left the structure virtually unchanged (70 percent of the original mosque structure survives to this day). Sixteen columns were removed and replaced by Gothic arches to make this first chapel. It feels as if the church architects appreciated the opportunity to incorporate the sublime architecture of the pre-existing mosque into their church. Notice how the floor was once almost entirely covered with the tombs of nobles and big shots eager to make this their final resting place.

• *Immediately to your right (as you face the main entrance of the Mezquita), you'll see the...*

❽ Royal Chapel: The chapel—designed for the tombs of Christian kings—is completely closed off. While it was never open to the public, the tall, well-preserved Mudejar walls and dome are easily visible. Notice the elaborate stucco work. The lavish Arabic-style decor dates from the 1370s, done by Muslim artisans after the

CÓRDOBA

Reconquista. The floor is a bit higher here to accommodate tombs buried beneath it. The fact that a Christian king chose to be buried in a tomb so clearly Moorish in design indicates the mutual respect between the cultures (before the Inquisition changed all that).

• *Return to the mihrab, then go through the big door to your immediate left, which leads into the Baroque...*

❾ **Treasury (Tesoro):** The treasury is filled with display cases of religious artifacts and the enormous monstrance that is paraded through the streets of Córdoba each Corpus Christi, 60 days after Easter (notice the handles).

The monstrance was an attempt by 16th-century Christians to create something exquisite enough to merit being the holder of the Holy Communion wafer. As they believed the wafer actually was the body of Christ, this trumped any relics. The monstrance is designed like a seven-scoop ice-cream cone, held together by gravity. While the bottom is silver-plated 18th-century Baroque, the top is late Gothic—solid silver with gold plating courtesy of 16th-century conquistadors.

The big canvas nearest the entrance shows Saint-King Ferdinand III, who conquered Córdoba in 1236, accepting the keys to the city's fortified gate from the vanquished Muslims. The victory ended a six-month siege and resulted in a negotiated settlement: The losers' lives were spared, providing they evacuated. Most went to Granada, which remained Muslim for another 250 years. The same day, the Spaniards celebrated Mass in a makeshift chapel right here in the great mosque.

Among the other Catholic treasures, don't miss the ivory crucifix (next room, body carved from one tusk, arms carefully fitted on) from 1665. Get close to study Jesus' mouth—it's incredibly realistic. The artist? No one knows.

• *Just outside the treasury exit, a glass case holds casts that show many...*

❿ **Stonemason Marks:** These stones still bear the marks and signatures left by those who cut them to build the original Visigothic church. Try to locate the actual ones on nearby columns. (I went five for six.) This part of the mosque has the best light for photography, thanks to skylights put in by 18th-century Christians.

The mosque grew over several centuries under a series of rulers. Remarkably, each ruler kept to the original vision—rows and rows of multicolored columns topped by double arches. Then came the Christians.

• *Find the towering church in the center of the mosque and step in.*

⓫ **Cathedral:** Rising up in the middle of the forest of columns is the bright and newly restored cathedral, oriented in the Christian tradition, with its altar at the east end. Gazing up at the rich decoration, it's easy to forget that you were in a former mosque

just seconds ago. While the mosque is about 30 feet high, the cathedral's space soars 130 feet up. Look at the glorious ceiling.

In 1523 Córdoba's bishop proposed building this grand church in the Mezquita's center. The town council opposed it, but Charles V (called Carlos I in Spain) ordered it done. If that seems like a travesty to you, consider what some locals will point out: Though it would have been quicker and less expensive for the Christian builders to destroy the mosque entirely, they respected its beauty and built their church into it instead.

As you take in the styles of these two great places of worship, ponder how they reflect the differences between Catholic and Islamic aesthetics and psychology: horizontal versus vertical, intimate versus powerful, fear-inspiring versus loving, dark versus bright, simple versus elaborate, feeling close to God versus feeling small before God.

The basic structure is late Gothic, with fancy Isabelline-style columns. The nave's towering Renaissance arches and dome emphasize the triumph of Christianity over Islam in Córdoba. The twin pulpits feature a marble bull, eagle, angel, and lion—symbols of the four evangelists. The modern *cátedra* (the seat of the bishop) is made of Carrara marble.

While churches and mosques normally both face east (to Jerusalem or Mecca), this space holds worship areas aimed 90 degrees from each other, since the mihrab faces south. Perhaps it's because from here you have to go south (via Gibraltar) to get to Mecca. Or maybe it's because this mosque was designed by the Umayyad branch of Islam, whose ancestral home was Damascus—from where Mecca lies to the south.

• *Facing the high altar is a big, finely decorated wooden enclosure.*

⓬ Choir: The Baroque-era choir stalls were added much later—made in 1750 of New World mahogany. While cluttering up a previously open Gothic space, the choir is considered one of the masterpieces of 18th-century Andalusian Baroque. Each of the 109 stalls (108 plus the throne of the bishop) features a scene from the Bible: Mary's life on one side facing Jesus' life on the other. The lower chairs feature carved reliefs of the 49 martyrs of Córdoba (from Roman, Visigothic, and Moorish times), each with a palm frond symbolizing martyrdom and the scene of their death in the background.

The medieval church strayed from the inclusiveness taught by Jesus: Choirs (which were standard throughout Spain) were for clerics (canons, priests, and the bishop). The pews in the nave were for nobles. And the peasants listened in from outside. (Lay people didn't understand what they were hearing anyway, as Mass was held in Latin until the 1960s.) Those days are long over. Today, a public Mass is said—in Spanish—right here most mornings (Mon-Sat at 9:30).

Near the Mezquita

All of these sights are within a few minutes' walk of the Mezquita.

On and near the River

Just downhill from the Mezquita is the Guadalquivir River, which flows on to Sevilla and eventually out to the Atlantic. While silted up today, it was once navigable from here. The town now seems to turn its back on the Guadalquivir, but the arch next to the Roman Bridge (with its ancient foundation surviving) and the fortified gate on the far bank (now housing a museum, described later) evoke a day when the river was key to the city's existence.

Triumphal Arch and Plague Monument

The unfinished Renaissance arch was designed to give King Philip II a royal welcome, but he arrived before its completion—so the job was canceled. ("Very Andalusian," according to a local friend.) The adjacent monument with the single column is an 18th-century plague monument dedicated to St. Raphael (he was in charge of protecting the region's population from its main scourges: plague, hunger, and floods).

The modern visitors center behind the arch is unlikely to be open during your visit—like so many other projects affected by Spain's economic crisis, the completion of the building's interior has been abandoned for the time being.

Roman Bridge

The bridge, which sits on its first-century-A.D. foundations and retains its 16th-century arches, was poorly restored in 2009. It feels like so much other modern work along this riverbank—done on the cheap. As it was the first bridge over this river, it established Córdoba as a strategic place. Walk across the bridge for a fine view of the city—especially the huge mosque with its cathedral busting through the center. You'll be steps away from the museum described next.

▲Museum of Al-Andalus Life

The Museo Vivo de Al-Andalus fills the fortified gate (built in the 14th century to protect the Christian city) at the far side of the

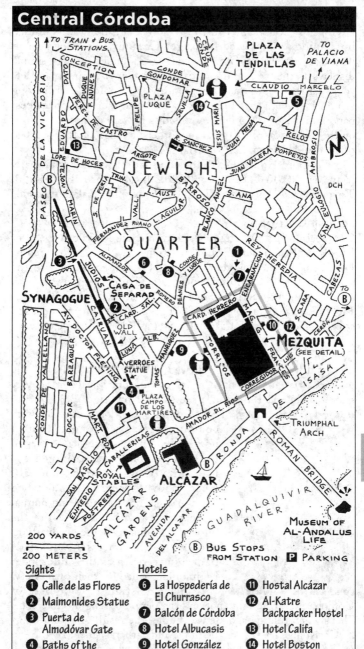

Central Córdoba

Sights
1. Calle de las Flores
2. Maimonides Statue
3. Puerta de Almodóvar Gate
4. Baths of the Caliphate Alcázar
5. Café La Gloria

Hotels
6. La Hospedería de El Churrasco
7. Balcón de Córdoba
8. Hotel Albucasis
9. Hotel González
10. Hotel Mezquita
11. Hostal Alcázar
12. Al-Katre Backpacker Hostel
13. Hotel Califa
14. Hotel Boston

CÓRDOBA

Roman Bridge. It is a velvety, philosophical, almost evangelical attempt to explain the Muslim Moorish culture, and is funded by a foundation started by Roger Garaudy, a former French politician and writer. Don a headset and wander through simple displays as the clear and engrossing (if gauzy) commentary lets you sit at the feet of the great poets and poke into Moorish living rooms. It's worth the climb up to the rooftop terrace for the best panoramic view of Córdoba. Garaudy's flowery audiotour focuses on the formation of the great monotheistic religions...the greatest of which—in his opinion—is Islam.

Cost and Hours: €4.50, includes one-hour audio tour, daily May-Sept 10:00-14:00 & 16:30-20:30, Oct-April 10:00-18:00, Torre de la Calahorra, tel. 957-293-929, www.torrecalahorra.com.

Jewish Córdoba

Córdoba's Jewish Quarter dates from the late Middle Ages, after Muslim rule and during the Christian era. Now little remains. For a sense of the neighborhood in its thriving heyday, visit the synagogue and the cultural center located a few steps away (both described in this section). For a pretty picture, find **Calle de las Flores** (a.k.a. "Blossom Lane"). This narrow flower-bedecked street frames the cathedral's bell tower as it hovers in the distance (the view is a favorite for local guidebook covers).

Synagogue (Sinagoga)

The small yet beautifully preserved synagogue was built in 1315, under Christian rule, but the Islamic decoration has roots way back to Abd Al-Rahman I (see sidebar on page 738). During

Muslim times, Córdoba's sizable Jewish community was welcomed, though its members paid substantial taxes to the city—money that enlarged the Mezquita and generated goodwill. That goodwill came in handy when Córdoba's era of prosperity and mutual respect ended with the arrival of the intolerant Almohad Berbers. Christians and Jews were repressed, and brilliant minds—such as the philosopher Maimonides—fled for their own safety.

The Christian Reconquista of Córdoba (1236) brought another brief period of religious tolerance. That's when this synagogue was built—the result of a joint effort by Christians, Jews, and Muslim (Mudejar) craftsmen. By the end of the 14th century, however, Spain's Jews were again persecuted. They were finally expelled or forced to convert in 1492; this is one of only three surviving synagogues in Spain built before that year.

Córdoba's Jewish Quarter: A Ten-Point Scavenger Hunt

Whereas most of the area around the Mezquita is commercial and touristy, the neighborhood to the east seems somehow almost untouched by tourism and the modern world (as you leave the Mezquita, turn right and exit the orange-grove patio, then wander into the lanes immediately behind Hotel Mezquita). To catch a whiff of Córdoba as it was before the onslaught of tourism and the affluence of the 21st century, explore this district. Just meander and observe. Here are a few characteristics to look for:

1. **Narrow streets.** Skinny streets make sense in hot climates, as they provide much-appreciated shade. The ones in this area are remnants from the old Moorish bazaar, crammed in to fit within the protective city walls.
2. **Thick, whitewashed walls.** Both features serve as a kind of natural air-conditioning—and the chalk ingredient in the whitewash "bugs" bugs.
3. **Colorful doors and windows.** In this famously white city, what little color there is—mostly added in modern times—helps counter the boring whitewash.
4. **Iron grilles.** Historically, these were more artistic, but modern ones are more practical. Their continued presence is a reminder of the persistent gap through the ages between rich and poor. The wooden latticework covering many windows is a holdover from days when women, held to extreme standards of modesty, wanted to be able to see out while still keeping their privacy.
5. **Stone bumpers on corners.** These protected buildings against reckless drivers. Scavenged secondhand ancient Roman pillars worked well.
6. **Scuff guards.** Made of harder materials, these guards sit at the base of the whitewashed walls—and, from the looks of it, are serving their purpose.
7. **Riverstone cobbles.** These stones were cheap and local, and provided drains down the middle of a lane. They were flanked by smooth stones that stayed dry for walking (and now aid the rolling suitcases of modern-day tourists).
8. **Pretty patios.** Cordovans are proud of their patios. Walk up to the inner iron gates of the wide-open front doors and peek in (see "Patios" sidebar, later).
9. **Remnants of old towers from minarets.** Muslim Córdoba peaked in the 10th century with an estimated 600,000 people, which meant lots of neighborhood mosques.
10. **A real neighborhood.** People really live here. There are no tacky shops, and just about the only tourist is... you.

Rich Mudejar decorations of intertwined flowers, arabesques, and Stars of David plaster the walls. What appear to be quotes from the Quran in Arabic are actually quotes from the Bible in Hebrew. On the east wall (the symbolic direction of Jerusalem), find the niche for the Ark, which held the scrolls of the Torah (the Jewish scriptures). The upstairs gallery was reserved for women. This synagogue, the only one that survives in Córdoba, was left undisturbed because it was used as a church until the 19th century (look for the cross painted into a niche).

Cost and Hours: Free, Tue-Sun 9:30-14:00 & 15:30-17:30, closed Mon, Calle de los Judíos 20, tel. 957-202-928. To learn more about the synagogue and its community, head next to the Casa de Sefarad, just 10 steps uphill.

Casa de Sefarad

Set inside a restored 14th-century home directly across from the synagogue, this interpretive museum brings to life Córdoba's rich Jewish past. Eight rooms around a central patio are themed to help you understand different aspects of daily life for Spain's former Jewish community. The rooms focus on themes such as contributions from women in the community, Jewish holidays, and musical traditions. Upstairs is an interpretive center for the synagogue, along with rooms dedicated to Maimonides, the Inquisition, and the synagogue. The Casa de Sefarad is a cultural center for Sephardic (the Hebrew word for "Spanish") Jewish heritage. Jaime and his staff stress that the center's purpose is not political or religious, but cultural. Along with running this small museum, they teach courses, offer a library, and promote an appreciation of Córdoba's Jewish heritage.

Cost and Hours: €4, Mon-Sat 11:00-18:00, Sun 11:00-14:00, 30-minute guided tours in English available by request if guide is available, next to synagogue at the corner of Calle de los Judíos and Calle Averroes, tel. 957-421-404, www.casadesefarad.es. The Casa de Sefarad hosts occasional concerts—acoustic, Sephardic, Andalusian, and flamenco—on its patio (€15, some Sat in season, usually at 19:00).

City Walls

Built upon the foundation of Córdoba's Roman walls, these fortifications date mostly from the 12th century. While the city stretched beyond the walls in Moorish times, these walls protected its political, religious, and commercial center. Of the seven original gates, the Puerta de Almodóvar (near the synagogue) is best preserved today. Just outside this gate, you'll find statues of Córdoba's great thinkers: Seneca (the Roman philosopher and adviser to Nero), Maimonides, and Averroes.

CÓRDOBA

Statues of Maimonides and Averroes

Statues honor two of Córdoba's deepest-thinking homeboys—one Jewish, one Muslim, both driven out during the wave of intolerance after the fall of the Umayyad caliphate. (Maimonides is 30 yards downhill from the synagogue; Averroes is at the end of the old wall, where Cairuán and Doctor Fleming streets meet.)

Moses Maimonides (1135-1204), "the Jewish Aquinas," was born in Córdoba and raised on both Jewish scripture and the philosophy of Aristotle. Like many tolerant Cordovans, he saw no conflict between the two. An influential Talmudic scholar, astronomer, and medical doctor, Maimonides left his biggest mark as the author of *The Guide for the Perplexed*, in which he asserted that secular knowledge and religious faith could go hand-in-hand (thereby inspiring the philosophy of St. Thomas Aquinas). In 1148, Córdoba was transformed when the fundamentalist Almohads assumed power, and young Maimonides and his family were driven out. Today tourists, Jewish scholars, and fans of Aquinas rub the statue's foot in the hope that some of Maimonides' genius and wisdom will rub off on them.

The story of **Averroes** (1126-1198) is a near match of Maimonides', except that Averroes was a Muslim lawyer, not a Jewish physician. He became the medieval world's number-one authority on Aristotle, also influencing Aquinas. Averroes' biting tract *The Incoherence of the Incoherence* attacked narrow-mindedness, asserting that secular philosophy (for the elite) and religious faith (for the masses) both led to truth. The Almohads banished him from the city and burned his books, ending four centuries of Cordovan enlightenment.

Alcázar
Alcázar de los Reyes Cristianos

Tourists line up to visit Córdoba's overrated fortress, the "Castle of the Christian Monarchs," which sits strategically next to the Guadalquivir River. (I think they confuse it with the much more worthy Alcázar in Sevilla.) Upon entering, look to the right to see a big, beautiful garden rich with flowers and fountains. To the left is a modern-feeling, unimpressive fort. While it was built along the Roman walls in Visigothic times, constant reuse and recycling has left it sparse and barren (with the exception of a few interesting Roman mosaics on the walls). Crowds squeeze up and down the congested spiral staircases of "Las Torres" for meager views. Ferdinand and Isabel donated the castle to the Inquisition in 1482, and it became central in the church's effort to discover "false converts to Christianity"—mostly Jews who had decided not to flee Spain in 1492.

Cost and Hours: €4.50, free Tue-Fri 8:30-10:30; open mid-June-mid-Sept Tue-Sun 8:30-14:30; off-season Tue-Fri 8:30-19:30, Sat 9:30-16:30, Sun 9:30-14:30; closed Mon year-round. On Fridays and Saturdays, you're likely to see people celebrating civil weddings here.

Baths of the Caliphate Alcázar (Baños Califales)

The scant but evocative remains of these 10th-century royal baths are all that's left from the caliph's palace complex. They date from a time when the city had hundreds of baths to serve a population of several hundred thousand. The exhibit teaches about Arabic baths in general and the caliph's in particular. A 10-minute video (normally in Spanish, English on request) tells the story well.

Cost and Hours: €2.50, free Tue-Fri 8:30-10:30, open same hours as Alcázar, just outside the wall—near the Alcázar.

Away from the Mezquita

Plaza de las Tendillas

While most tourists leave Córdoba having seen only the Mezquita and the cute medieval quarter that surrounds it, the modern city offers a good peek at urban Andalucía. Perhaps the best way to sample this is to browse Plaza de las Tendillas and the surrounding streets. The square, with an Art Deco charm, acts like there is no tourism in Córdoba. On the hour, a clock here chimes the guitar chords of Juan Serrano—a Cordovan classic.

Characteristic cafés and shops abound. For example, **Café La Gloria** provides an earthy Art Nouveau experience. Located just down the street from Plaza de las Tendillas, it has an unassuming entrance, but a sumptuous interior. Carved floral designs wind around the bar, mixing with *feria* posters and bullfighting memories. Pop in for a quick beer or coffee (daily from 8:00 until late, quiet after the lunch crowd clears out, Calle Claudio Marcelo 15, tel. 957-477-780).

Palacio de Viana

Decidedly off the beaten path, this former palatial estate is a 25-minute walk northeast from the cluster of sights near the Mezquita. A guided tour whisks you through each room of an exuberant 16th-century estate, while an English handout drudges through the dates and origin of each important piece. But the house is best enjoyed by ignoring the guide and gasping at the massive collection of—for lack of a better word—stuff. Decorative-art fans will have a field day. The sight is known as the "patio museum" for its 12 connecting patios, each with a different theme.

Cost and Hours: House-€8, patios only-€5, July-Aug Tue-Sun 9:00-15:00, Sept-June Tue-Sun 10:00-19:00 closed Mon year-round, last entry one hour before closing, no photos inside, Plaza Don Gome 2, tel. 957-496-741.

Near Córdoba
Madinat Al-Zahra (Medina Azahara)

Five miles northwest of Córdoba, these ruins of a once-fabulous

palace of the caliph were completely forgotten until excavations began in the early 20th century. Built in A.D. 929 as a power center to replace Córdoba, Madinat Al-Zahra was both a palace and an entirely new capital city—the "City of the Flower"—covering nearly half a square mile (only about 10 percent has been uncovered). Extensively planned with an orderly design, Madinat Al-Zahra was meant to symbolize and project a new discipline on an increasingly unstable Moorish empire in Spain. It failed. Only 75 years later, the city was looted and destroyed.

The site is underwhelming—a jigsaw puzzle waiting to be reassembled by patient archaeologists. Upper terrace excava-

tions have uncovered stables and servants' quarters. Farther downhill, the house of a high-ranking official has been partially reconstructed. At the lowest level, you'll come to the remains of the mosque—placed at a diagonal, facing true east. The highlight of the visit is an elaborate reconstruction of the caliph's throne room, capturing a moody world of horseshoe arches and delicate stucco. Legendary accounts say the palace featured waterfall walls, lions in cages, and—in the center of the throne room—a basin filled with mercury, reflecting the colorful walls. The effect likely humbled anyone fortunate enough to see the caliph.

Cost and Hours: €1.50, Tue-Sat 10:00-20:00, Sun 10:00-17:00, closed Mon, tel. 957-352-860.

Getting There: Madinat Al-Zahra is located on a back road

CÓRDOBA

Patios

In Córdoba, patios are taken very seriously, as shown by the fiercely fought contest, the Concurso Popular de Patios Cordobeses, which takes place the first half of every May to pick the city's most picturesque. Patios, a common feature of houses throughout Andalucía, have a long history here. The Romans used them to cool off, and the Moors added lush, decorative touches. The patio functioned as a quiet outdoor living

room, an oasis from the heat. Inside elaborate ironwork gates, roses, geraniums, and jasmine spill down whitewashed walls, while fountains play and caged birds sing. Some patios are owned by individuals, some are communal courtyards for several homes, and some grace public buildings like museums or convents.

Today homeowners take pride in these mini-paradises, and have no problem sharing them with tourists. Keep an eye out for square metal signs that indicate historic homes. As you wander Córdoba's back streets, pop your head into any wooden door that's open. The proud owners (who keep inner gates locked) enjoy showing off their picture-perfect patios. A concentration of patio-contest award-winners runs along Calle de San Basilio and Calle Martín Roa, just across from the Alcázar gardens. Some of these winners have banded together to keep their patios open to the public on a daily basis (€5, daily Sept-May 11:00-14:00 & 17:00-20:00, June 11:00-14:00 & 19:00-22:00, closed July-Aug, get tickets at at their office on Calle de San Basilio, tel. 957-043-325, www.patiosdelalcazarviejo.com). Many other nearby patios, however, are open and free to visit.

five miles from Córdoba. By **car,** head to Avenida de Medina Azahara (one block south of the train station), following signs for *A-431;* the site is well-signposted from the highway. Though the ruins aren't accessible by regular public transportation, the TI runs a **shuttle bus** that leaves twice a day and returns 2.5 hours later (€7, must buy ticket at any of the city TIs; runs year-round Tue-Sun at 9:30 and 10:15, no buses on Mon; informative English booklet provided). Catch the bus near the Cruz Roja Hospital at Paseo de la Victoria.

Entertainment in Córdoba

Caballerizas Reales de Córdoba

This equestrian show at the royal stables (just beyond the Alcázar) combines an artful demonstration of different riding styles with flamenco dance (€15; 1-hour shows generally Wed, Fri, and Sat at 21:00; Sun at 12:00, no shows Mon-Tue, outside in summer, inside in winter, mobile 671-949-514, tel. 957-497-843, www .caballerizasreales.com). During the day, you can tour the stables for free (Tue-Sat 11:00-13:30 & 17:00-20:00, Sun 10:00-11:30, closed Mon).

Flamenco

While flamenco is better in nearby Sevilla, you can see it in Córdoba, too. **Tablao Flamenco El Cardenal** is the city's most popular show, with 200 seats in a former archbishop's palace, just across the street from the Mezquita (€23, includes one drink, 1.5-hour shows nightly at 22:30, Calle de Torrijos 10, tel. 957-483-320).

El Alma de Córdoba

To experience "the soul of Córdoba"—or at least the Mezquita by night—you can take this pricey one-hour audiotour, joining about 80 people to be shepherded around the complex listening via headset to an obviously Christian-produced sound-and-light show (€18, at least four nights a week most of year, Fri-Sat in winter, 1-2 shows a night, book at TI or at Mezquita, www.elalmadecordoba .com).

Sleeping in Córdoba

I've listed prices for the high season; most of these are cheaper outside peak times. If it's hot and you've got a lot of luggage, don't bother with the inconvenient city buses; just hop in a taxi.

Near the Mezquita

These are all within a five-minute stroll of the Mezquita.

$$$ La Hospedería de El Churrasco is a nine-room jewel box of an inn, featuring plush furniture, tasteful traditional decor, and hardwood floors. Quiet and romantic, it's tucked in the old quarter just far enough away from the tourist storm, yet still handy for sightseeing (Sb-€135, Db-€155, superior Db-€199, €20 more per room in April-May and Oct, website shows each distinct room, no twin rooms, includes breakfast, air-con, guest computer, free Wi-Fi, parking-€21/day, midway between Puerta de Almodóvar and the Mezquita at Calle Romero 38, tel. 957-294-808, www .elchurrasco.com, hospederia@elchurrasco.com).

$$$ Balcón de Córdoba is an elegant little boutique hotel buried in the old town, just steps away from the Mezquita. With

---

Sleep Code

(€1 = about $1.30, country code: 34)
S = Single, **D** = Double/Twin, **T** = Triple, **Q** = Quad, **b** = bathroom, **s** = shower only. Unless otherwise noted, credit cards are accepted, English is spoken, and breakfast costs extra. Some hotels include the 10 percent IVA tax in the room price; others tack it onto your bill.

To help you easily sort through these listings, I've divided the accommodations into three categories based on the price for a standard double room with bath during high season:

　$$$ **Higher Priced**—Most rooms €100 or more.
　　$$ **Moderately Priced**—Most rooms between €60-100.
　　　$ **Lower Priced**—Most rooms €60 or less.

Prices can change without notice; verify the hotel's current rates online or by email. For the best prices, always book direct.

---

10 stylish rooms, generous public spaces, plenty of thoughtful touches, and a magnificent rooftop terrace, it's a lot of luxury for the price. It feels both new and steeped in tradition (Db-€140—though prices fluctuate depending on room and season, includes breakfast, check website for special promotions, Calle Encarnación 8, tel. 957-498-478, www.balcondecordoba.com, reservas@balcondecordoba.com).

$$ Hotel Albucasis, at the edge of the tourist zone, features 15 basic, clean rooms, all of which face quiet interior patios. The friendly, accommodating staff and cozy setting make you feel right at home (Sb-€55, Db-€85, breakfast-€7, air-con, elevator, free Wi-Fi in lobby, parking-€14/day but free in off-season, Buen Pastor 11, tel. 957-478-625, www.hotelalbucasis.com, hotelalbucasis @hotmail.com).

$$ Hotel González, with many of its 29 basic rooms facing its cool and peaceful patio, is sparse but sleepable. It's clean and well-run, with a good location and price (Sb-€42, Db-€75, Tb-€110, higher prices for busy times—especially weekends, breakfast-€5, air-con, elevator, free Wi-Fi in lobby, Calle de los Man ríquez 3, tel. 957-479-819, www.hotelgonzalez.com, recepcion @hotelgonzalez.com).

$$ Hotel Mezquita, just across from the main entrance of the Mezquita, rents 31 modern and comfortable rooms. The grand entrance lobby elegantly recycles an upper-class mansion (Sb-€45, Db-€89, Tb-€135, breakfast-€6, air-con, elevator, free Wi-Fi in lobby, Plaza Santa Catalina 1, tel. 957-475-585, www.hotel

mezquita.com, recepcion@hotelmezquita.com).

$ Hostal Alcázar is your best cheapie option. Run-down and budget-priced, without a real reception desk, this friendly place is just outside the old city wall on a quiet, cobbled, traffic-free street known for its prizewinning patios. Its 16 rooms are split between 2 homes on opposite sides of the lane, conveniently located 50 yards from a taxi and bus stop (Sb-€20, D-€30, small Db-€36, bigger Db-€50, Tb-€60, 2-room apartment-€60 for 3 or €80 for 4, rooms with air-con cost more, breakfast-€4, free Wi-Fi on patio, parking-€6/day, near Alcázar at Calle de San Basilio 2, tel. 957-202-561, www.hostalalcazar.com, hostalalcazar@hotmail.com, ladies' man Fernando and family, son Demitrio speaks English).

$ Al-Katre Backpacker is a fun new hostel run in a homey way by three energetic girlfriends. Its 13 rooms, with 32 beds total, gather around a cool courtyard (about €20 per person in 2-, 4-, and 6-bed rooms, D-€45-50, includes breakfast, lockers, free Wi-Fi, guest kitchen, Calle Martinez Rucker 14, tel. 957-487-539, www.alkatre.com, alkatre@alkatre.com).

In the Modern City

While still within easy walking distance of the Mezquita, these places are outside of the main tourist zone—not buried in all that tangled medieval cuteness.

$$ Hotel Califa, a modern 65-room business-class hotel belonging to the NH chain, sits on a quiet street a block off busy Paseo Victoria, on the edge of the jumbled old quarter. Still close enough to the sights, its slick modern rooms can be a great value if you get a deal (vast price range depending on demand but Db generally €80-90 during the week, €120 weekends, around €70 in heat of summer, Tb generally €20-25 more, air-con, elevator, guest computer, pay Wi-Fi in rooms, free Wi-Fi in lobby, parking-€15/day, Lope de Hoces 14, tel. 957-299-400, www.nh-hotels.com, nhcalifa@nh-hotels.com).

$$ Hotel Boston, with 39 rooms, is a decent budget bet if you want a reliable, basic hotel away from the touristy Mezquita zone. It's a taste of workaday Córdoba (Sb-€45-55, Db-€60-85, Tb-€75-110, check website for best price, breakfast-€5, air-con, elevator, pay guest computer, free Wi-Fi, parking-€12/day, Calle Málaga 2, just off Plaza de las Tendillas, tel. 957-474-176, www.hotel-boston.com, info@hotel-boston.com).

$ Funky Córdoba Hostel rents dorm beds and simple doubles in a great neighborhood (dorm beds-€13-22, Sb-€22, Db-€40-56, air-con, free Wi-Fi, terrace, kitchen, self-service laundry, lots of hostel-type info and help, right by Potro bus stop—take #3 from station—at Calle Lucano 12, tel. 957-492-966, www.funkycordoba.com, funkycordoba@funkyhostels.es).

Eating in Córdoba

Córdoba is a great dining town, with options ranging from obvious touristy bars in the old center to enticing, locals-only hangouts a few blocks away. Specialties include *salmorejo,* Córdoba's version of gazpacho. It's creamier, with more bread and olive oil and generally served with pieces of ham and hard-boiled egg. Most places serve white wines from the nearby Montilla-Moriles region; these *finos* are slightly less dry but more aromatic than the sherry produced in Jerez de la Frontera.

Near the Mezquita

Touristy options abound near the Mezquita. By walking a couple of blocks north or east of the Mezquita, you'll find plenty of cheap, accessible little places offering a better value.

Bodegas Mezquita is one of the touristy places, but it's easy and handy—a good bet for a bright, air-conditioned place a block from the mosque. They have a good *menú del día,* or you can order from their menu of €3-4 tapas, €4-10 half-*raciones,* and €8-16 *raciones* (long hours daily, one block above the Mezquita garden at Céspedes 12, tel. 957-490-004).

La Abacería is another good option on a touristy street in the old center. They have a fun and accessible menu with good €3 tapas and €8 *raciones* (open daily, Calle de los Deanes 1, tel. 957-487-050, Blanca).

Bar Santos, facing the Mezquita, supplies the *tortillas de patatas* (potato omelettes) that you see locals happily munching on the steps of the mosque. All of their food is served "to go" in disposable containers. A hearty €2 *tortilla* and a €2 beer makes for a very cheap meal; add a €3 *salmorejo* and it feels complete (daily 10:00-24:00, Calle Magistral González Francés 3, tel. 957-484-975).

Barrio San Basilio

This delightful little quarter outside the town wall, just a couple of minutes' walk west of the Mezquita and behind the royal stables, is famous for its patios. It's traffic-free, quaint as can be, and feels perfectly Cordovan without the crush of tourists around the Mezquita.

La Posada del Caballo Andaluz is a fresh, modern place with tables delightfully scattered around a courtyard. Enjoy tasty traditional Cordovan cuisine at great prices (all half-*raciones* are €5, all *raciones* €8) while sitting amid flowers and under the stars (closed Sun, Calle de San Basilio 16, tel. 957-290-374).

Mesón San Basilio, just across the street, is the longtime neighborhood favorite, with no tourists and no pretense. Although

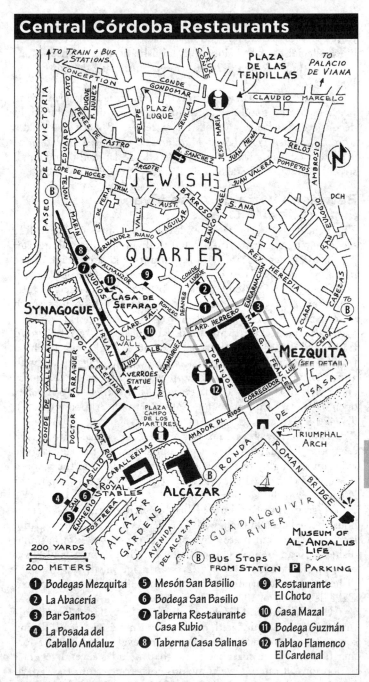

Central Córdoba Restaurants

1. Bodegas Mezquita
2. La Abacería
3. Bar Santos
4. La Posada del Caballo Andaluz
5. Mesón San Basilio
6. Bodega San Basilio
7. Taberna Restaurante Casa Rubio
8. Taberna Casa Salinas
9. Restaurante El Choto
10. Casa Mazal
11. Bodega Guzmán
12. Tablao Flamenco El Cardenal

Ⓑ Bus Stops From Station Ⓟ Parking

200 YARDS
200 METERS

CÓRDOBA

there's no outside seating, it still offers a certain patio ambience, with a view of the kitchen action (classic €16 fixed-priced meal, €9 lunch special weekdays, lots of €9-15 fish and meat dishes, Mon-Sat 13:00-16:00 & 20:00-24:00, closed Sun, Calle de San Basilio 19, tel. 957-297-007).

Bodega San Basilio, around the corner, is rougher, serving rustic tapas and good meals to workaday crowds. The bullfight decor gives the place a crusty character—and you won't find a word of English here (€5 half-*raciones,* €8 *raciones,* €9 fixed-price meal, closed Tue, on the corner of Calle de Enmedio and small street leading to Calle de San Basilio at #29, tel. 957-297-832).

Between Puerta de Almodóvar and the Jewish Quarter

The evocative Puerta de Almodóvar gate connects a park-like scene outside the wall with a delightfully jumbled Jewish quarter just inside it, where cafés and restaurants take advantage of the neighborhood's pools, shady trees, and dramatic face of the wall. The first two recommendations are immediately inside the gate; the others are on or near Calle de los Judíos, which runs south from there.

Taberna Restaurante Casa Rubio serves reliably good traditional dishes with smart service and several zones to chose from: on the sidewalk, with classic people-watching; inside, with a timeless interior; or on the rooftop, with dressy white tablecloths and a view of the old wall (€2 tapas, €4 half-*raciones,* €6 *raciones,* open daily, easy English menu, Calle Puerta de Almodóvar 5, tel. 957-420-853).

Taberna Casa Salinas is a more basic place with a fine reputation for quality food at a good price (run by the same people who run the highly recommended Taberna Salinas in the modern town, at Puerta de Almodóvar gate at Calle Puerta de Almodóvar 2, tel. 957-290-846).

Restaurante El Choto is bright, formal, and dressy steak house buried deep in the Jewish Quarter. With a small leafy patio, it's touristy yet intimate, serving well-presented international dishes with an emphasis on grilled meat. The favorite is kid goat with garlic—*choto al ajillo* (€22 fixed-price meal, €15-28 main dishes, closed Sun evening year-round and all day Mon in summer, Calle de Almanzor 10, tel. 957-760-115).

Casa Mazal, run by the nearby Casa de Sefarad Jewish cultural center, serves updated, modern Jewish cuisine. Small dining rooms sprawl around the charming medieval courtyard of a former house. With a seasonal menu that includes several vegetarian options, it offers a welcome dose of variety from the typical Spanish standards (€6-12 starters, €10-18 main dishes, daily 12:30-

CÓRDOBA

17:00 & 20:00-24:00, Calle de Tomás Conde 3, tel. 957-941-888).

Bodega Guzmán could hardly care less about attracting tourists. This rough, dark holdover from a long-gone age proudly displays the heads of brave-but-unlucky bulls, while serving cold, very basic tapas to locals who burst into song when they feel the flamenco groove. Notice how everyone seems to be on a first-name basis with the waiters. It may feel like a drinks-only place, but they do serve rustic €2-3 tapas and €6 *raciones* (ask for the list in English). Choose a table or belly up to the bar and try a €1 glass of local white wine, either dry *(blanco seco)* or sweet *(blanco dulce)*. If it's grape juice you want, ask for *mosto* (closed Thu; if entering the old town through Puerta de Almodóvar take the first right—it's 100 yards from the gate at Calle de los Judíos 7, tel. 957-290-960).

Just East of the Mezquita Zone

Bodegas Campos, my favorite place in town, is a historic and venerable house of eating, attracting so many locals it comes with its own garage. It's worth the 10-minute walk from the tourist zone. They have a stuffy and expensive formal restaurant upstairs (€12-20 starters, €17-27 main dishes), but I'd eat in the more relaxed and affordable tavern on the ground floor (€6-11 half-*raciones*). The service is great and the menu is inviting. In two visits I nearly ate my way through the offerings, a half-*ración* at a time, and enjoyed each dish. Experiment—you can't go wrong. House specialties are bull-tail stew (*rabo de toro*—rich, tasty, and a good splurge) and anything with *pisto,* the local ratatouille-like vegetable stew. Don't leave without exploring the sprawling complex, which fills 14 old houses that have been connected to create a network of dining rooms and patios, small and large. The place is a virtual town history museum: Look for the wine barrels signed by celebrities and VIPs, the old refectory from a convent, and a huge collection of classic, original *feria* posters and great photos (Mon-Sat 12:00-17:00 & 20:00-24:00, Sun 12:00-17:00 only; from river end of Mezquita walk east along Calle Cardenal González, then continue 10 minutes straight to Calle de Lineros 32; tel. 957-497-500). Its trendy annex, called **Pick and Go,** serves dishes from the same fine kitchen, but with livelier music and a hipper crowd.

In the Modern City

These are worth the 10-to-15-minute walk from the main tourist zone—walking here, you feel a world apart from the touristy scene. Combine a meal here with a paseo through the Plaza de las Tendillas area to get a good look at modern Córdoba. If Taberna Salinas is full, as is likely, there are plenty of characteristic bars nearby in the lanes around Plaza de la Corredera.

Taberna Salinas seems like a movie set designed to give you the classic Córdoba scene. Though all the seating is indoors, it's still pleasantly patio-esque, and popular with locals for its traditional cuisine and exuberant bustle. The seating fills a big courtyard and sprawls through several smaller, semi-private rooms. The fun menu features a slew of enticing €6-7 plates (spinach with chickpeas is a house specialty). Study what locals are eating before ordering. There's no drinks menu—just basic beer or inexpensive wine. If there's a line (as there often is later in the evening), leave your name and throw yourself into the adjacent tapas-bar mosh pit for a drink (Mon-Sat 12:30-16:00 & 20:00-23:30, closed Sun and Aug; from Plaza de las Tendillas walk 3 blocks to the Roman temple, then go 1 more block and turn right to Tundidores 3; tel. 957-480-135).

Taberna San Miguel is nicknamed "Casa el Pisto" for its famous vegetable stew *(pisto)*. Well-respected, it's packed with locals who appreciate regional cuisine, a good value, and a place with a long Cordovan history. There's great seating in its charming interior or on the lively square (€2-3 tapas at bar only, €6-10 half-*raciones,* €7-14 *raciones,* closed Sun and Aug, 2 blocks north of Plaza de las Tendillas at Plaza San Miguel 1, tel. 957-478-328).

Córdoba Connections

From Córdoba by Train: Córdoba is on the slick **AVE** train line (reservations required), making it an easy stopover between **Madrid** (2-3/hour, 1.75 hours) and **Sevilla** (2-3/hour, 45 minutes). The **Avant** train connects Córdoba to Sevilla just as fast for nearly half the price (9/day, 45 minutes; railpass reservations also about half-price). The slow **regional** train to Sevilla takes about twice as long, but doesn't require a reservation and is even cheaper (7/day, 80 minutes).

Other trains go to **Granada** (2/day on Altaria, 2.5 hours—bus is more frequent, cheaper, and nearly as fast), **Ronda** (2/day direct on Altaria, 1.75 hours, 1/day cheaper but much longer with transfer in Bobadilla, 3.75 hours), **Jerez** (to transfer to Arcos; 8/day, 2-2.5 hours), **Málaga** (fast and cheap Avant train, 6/day, 1 hour; fast and expensive AVE train, 10/day, 1 hour), and **Algeciras** (2/day direct, 3.25 hours, more with transfer, 5-5.5 hours). **Train info:** Toll tel. 902-320-320.

By Bus to: Granada (7/day *directo,* 2.75 hours; 2/day *ruta,* 4 hours, **Sevilla** (7/day, 1-2 hours), **Madrid** (6/day, 4.75 hours), **Málaga** (4/day, 2.5-3.5 hours *directo*), **Barcelona** (2/day, 10 hours). The efficient staff at the information desk prints bus schedules for you—or you can check all schedules at www.estacionautobuses cordoba.es. **Bus info:** Tel. 957-404-040.

ANDALUCÍA'S WHITE HILL TOWNS

*Arcos de la Frontera • Ronda • Zahara
and Grazalema • Jerez*

Just as the American image of Germany is Bavaria, the Yankee dream of Spain is Andalucía. This is the home of bullfights, flamenco, gazpacho, pristine whitewashed hill towns, and glamorous Mediterranean resorts. The big cities of Andalucía (Granada, Sevilla, and Córdoba) and the South Coast (Costa del Sol) are covered in separate chapters. This chapter explores Andalucía's hill-town highlights.

The Route of the White Hill Towns (Ruta de los Pueblos Blancos), Andalucía's charm bracelet of cute towns perched in the sierras, gives you wonderfully untouched Spanish culture. Spend a night in the romantic queen of the white towns, Arcos de la Frontera. (Towns with "de la Frontera" in their names were established on the front line of the centuries-long fight to recapture Spain from the Muslims, who were slowly pushed back into Africa.) Farther east, the larger town of Ronda stuns visitors with its breathtaking setting—straddling a gorge that thrusts deep into the Andalusian bedrock. Ronda's venerable old bullring, smattering of enjoyable sights, and thriving tapas scene round out its charms. Smaller hill towns, such as Zahara and Grazalema, offer plenty of beauty. As a whole, the hill towns—no longer strategic, no longer on any frontier—are now just passing time peacefully. Join them.

Between Sevilla and the hill towns, the city of Jerez—teeming with traffic and lacking in charm—is worth a peek for its famous Horse Symphony and a glass of sherry on a sherry bodega tour.

To study ahead, visit www.andalucia.com for information on hotels, festivals, museums, nightlife, and sports in the region.

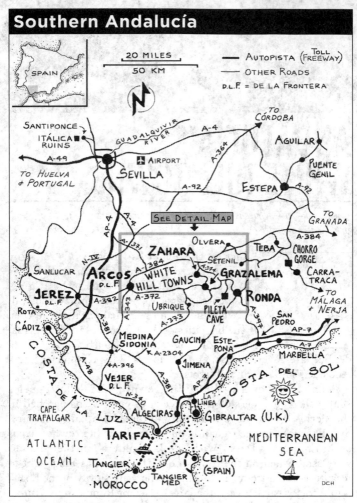

Southern Andalucía

20 MILES
50 KM

━━━ AUTOPISTA (TOLL) (FREEWAY)
─── OTHER ROADS
D.L.F. = DE LA FRONTERA

SPAIN

TO CÓRDOBA

SANTIPONCE
ITÁLICA RUINS ■
GUADALQUIVIR RIVER
A-4
A-364
AGUILAR

A-49
✈ AIRPORT
SEVILLA
PUENTE GENIL

TO HUELVA & PORTUGAL
A-92
ESTEPA
A-92

SEE DETAIL MAP

TO GRANADA

AP-4
A-4
OLVERA
TEBA
A-384
CHORRO GORGE

A-331
ZAHARA
SETENIL
A-374
GRAZALEMA
CARRA-TRACA

SANLUCAR
N-IV
ARCOS D.L.F.
A-384
WHITE HILL TOWNS
RONDA
TO MÁLAGA & NERJA

JEREZ D.L.F.
A-382
A-343
A-372
UBRIQUE
PILETA CAVE
A-373
SAN PEDRO
AP-7

ROTA
A-397

CÁDIZ
MEDINA SIDONIA
GAUCIN
ESTE-PONA
A-7
MARBELLA

A-48
A-2304
JIMENA
COSTA DEL SOL

VEJER D.L.F.
A-396
A-381

CAPE TRAFALGAR
N-340
AP-7
LA LINEA
COSTA DE LA LUZ
ALGECIRAS
GIBRALTAR (U.K.)

TARIFA
MEDITERRANEAN SEA

ATLANTIC OCEAN
TANGIER
CEUTA (SPAIN)

MOROCCO
TANGIER MED

DCH

Planning Your Time

On a three-week vacation in Spain, Andalucía's hill towns are worth two nights and up to two days sandwiched between visits to Sevilla and Tarifa. Arcos makes the best home base, as it's close to interesting smaller towns, near Jerez, and conveniently situated halfway between Sevilla and Tarifa. The towns can also be accessed from the Costa del Sol resorts via Ronda.

See Jerez on your way in or out, spend a day hopping from town to town in the more remote interior (including Grazalema and Zahara), and enjoy Arcos early and late in the day. For more details on exploring this region by car, see "Route Tips for Drivers" at the end of this chapter.

Without a car, keep things simple and focus only on Arcos and Jerez (both well-served by frequent-enough public buses from Sevilla). Ronda, however, is also easy to visit—right on a train line.

Spring and fall are high season throughout this area. In summer you'll encounter intense heat, but empty hotels, lower prices, and no crowds.

Arcos de la Frontera

Arcos smothers its long, narrow hilltop and tumbles down the back of the ridge like the train of a wedding dress. It's larger than most other Andalusian hill towns, but equally atmospheric. Arcos consists of two towns: the fairy-tale old town on top of the hill and the fun-loving lower, or new, town. The old center is a labyrinthine wonderland, a photographer's feast. Viewpoint-hop through town. Feel the wind funnel through the narrow streets as cars inch around tight corners. Join the kids' soccer game on the churchyard patio. Enjoy the moonlit view from the main square.

Though it tries, Arcos doesn't have much to offer other than its basic whitewashed self. The locally produced English guidebook on Arcos waxes poetic and at length about very little. You can arrive late and leave early and still see it all.

Orientation to Arcos

Tourist Information

The **main TI,** on the road leading up into the old town, is helpful and loaded with information, including bus schedules (Mon-Sat 9:30-14:00 & 15:00-19:30, Sun 10:00-14:00; Cuesta de Belén 5, tel. 956-702-264, www.turismoarcos.es). On the floors above the TI is a skippable local history museum called Centro de Interpretación Ciudad de Arcos (CICA), with sparse exhibits described only in Spanish.

The TI organizes a one-hour **walking tour** through the old town, covering Arcos' history, lifestyles, and Moorish influences. It includes the history museum and gives you a peek at a private courtyard patio (€4; Mon-Sat at 11:00; also at 18:00 but only if you reserve ahead, 5-person minimum—off-season at 17:00; none on Sun, meet at main TI, in Spanish and/or English; for private tours, call TI).

There's also a small **TI kiosk** at the top of Plaza de España, handy for those parking in the pay lot there (Mon-Sat 10:30-13:30 & 16:30-19:30, Sun 10:30-13:30).

WHITE HILL TOWNS

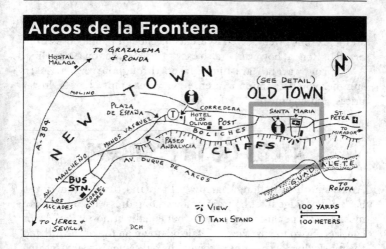

Arcos de la Frontera

(map showing NEW TOWN, OLD TOWN, CLIFFS, and key locations)

- HOSTAL MÁLAGA
- TO GRAZALEMA & RONDA
- MOLINO
- PLAZA DE ESPAÑA
- CORREDERA
- HOTEL LOS OLIVOS
- POST
- BOLICHES
- SANTA MARIA
- ST. PETER
- TO MIRADOR
- PASEO ANDALUCIA
- AV. DUQUE DE ARCOS
- GUAD. LE.T.E.
- TO RONDA
- MANCHEÑO
- MUÑOS VAZQUEZ
- BUS STN.
- AV. LOS ALCADES
- CORRE-GIDORES
- TO JEREZ & SEVILLA
- DCH

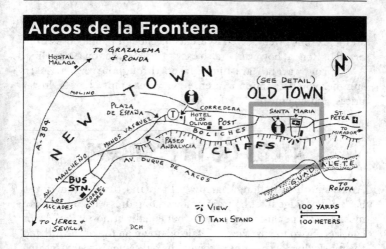

⚲ VIEW
Ⓣ TAXI STAND

100 YARDS
100 METERS

Arrival in Arcos

By Bus: The bus station is on Calle Corregidores, at the foot of the hill. To get up to the old town, catch the shuttle bus marked *Centro* from inside the station (€1, pay driver, 2/hour, runs roughly Mon-Fri 7:00-22:00, Sat 9:00-14:30, none on Sun), hop a taxi (€5 fixed rate; if there are no taxis waiting, call 956-704-640), or hike 20 uphill minutes (see map).

By Car: The old town is a tight squeeze with a one-way traffic flow from west to east (coming from the east, circle south under town). The TI and my recommended hotels are in the west. If you miss your target, you must drive out the other end, double back, and try again. Driving in Arcos is like threading needles (many drivers pull in their side-view mirrors to buy a few extra precious inches). Turns are tight, parking is frustrating, and congestion can lead to long jams.

Small cars can park in the main square of the old town at the top of the hill (Plaza del Cabildo). Buy a ticket from the machine (€0.70/hour, 2-hour maximum, only necessary Mon-Fri 9:00-14:00 & 17:00-21:00 and Sat 9:00-14:00—confirm times on machine).

It's less stressful (and better exercise) to park in the modern underground pay lot at Plaza de España in the new town (€15/day). From this lot, hike 15 minutes, or catch a taxi or the shuttle bus up to the old town (2/hour; as you're looking uphill, the bus stop is to the right of the traffic circle).

Getting Around Arcos

The old town is easily walkable, but it's fun and relaxing to take a circular **minibus** joyride. The little shuttle bus (also mentioned in "Arrival in Arcos," above) constantly circles through the town's one-way system and around the valley (€1, 2/hour, runs roughly

Mon-Fri 7:00-22:00, Sat 9:00-14:30, none on Sun). For a 30-minute tour, hop on. You can catch it just below the main church in the old town near the mystical stone circle (generally departs roughly at :20 and :50 past the hour). Sit in the front seat for the best view of the tight squeezes and the school kids hanging out in the plazas as you wind through the old town. After passing under a Moorish gate, you enter a modern residential neighborhood, circle under the eroding cliff, and return to the old town by way of the bus station and Plaza de España.

Helpful Hints

Internet Access: Most hotels have Wi-Fi for guests, and some also have guest computers. There's no real Internet café in Arcos' old town, but the TI has a terminal where you can pay to get online (€0.40 for 15 minutes, €1 for first hour, €0.20/hour after that).

Post Office: It's at the lower end of the old town at Paseo de los Boliches 24, a few doors up from Hotel Los Olivos (Mon-Fri 8:30-14:30, Sat 9:30-13:00, closed Sun).

Money: There are no ATMs in the old town. To reach one, take the main street past the Church of Santa María toward Plaza de España; you'll find several ATMs along Calle Corredera.

Viewpoint: For drivers, the best town overlook is from a tiny park just beyond the new bridge on the El Bosque road. In town, there are some fine viewpoints (for instance, from the main square), but the  church towers are no longer open to the public.

Arcos Old-Town Walk

This walk will introduce you to virtually everything worth seeing in Arcos.

• *Start at the top of the hill, in the main square dominated by the church. (Avoid this walk during the hot midday siesta.)*

Plaza del Cabildo: Stand at the viewpoint opposite the church on the town's main square. Survey the square, which in the old days doubled as a bullring. On your right is the parador, a former palace of the governor. It flies three flags: green for Andalucía, red-and-yellow for Spain, and blue-and-yellow for the European Union. On your left are City Hall, below the 11th-century Moorish castle where Ferdinand and Isabel held Reconquista strategy meetings

Arcos de la Frontera's Old Town

NOT TO SCALE –
PLAZA CABILDO TO
MARKET IS ABOUT
A 3-MINUTE WALK

SANTA
MARIA

HIG CAPOTE

TO ⑧
CORREPERA

BELÉN

DEÁN ESP.

MONJAS

BOTICAS

⑨

⑫

⑥

⑤

④ NÚÑEZ
MARKET TO ST.
PETER

BOLICHES

ⓘ

NUEVA

⑩

PLAZA
CABILDO

⑪ ② ①

MALDONADO

TO ⑦
BUS STN. &
NEW TOWN

CASTLE
(NOT OPEN)

P

① ② ③

PARADOR

C L I F F S

C L I F F S

🄽

VIEWPOINT

👁 VIEW
Ⓣ TAXI STAND

TO
BUS STN. &
NEW TOWN ←

AV. DUQUE DE ARCOS

RIO
GUADALETE

TO
RONDA

① Parador de Arcos
de la Frontera

② Hotel El Convento

③ La Casa Grande

④ Rincón de las Nieves

⑤ Hostal & Bar San Marcos

⑥ Hostal Callejón de las Monjas

⑦ To Hotel Los Olivos

⑧ To Hostal Málaga

⑨ Bar La Carcel

⑩ Alcaraván Restaurante

⑪ Plaza Boticas, Mesón Don
Fernando, Mesón Los
Murales & Cloistered Nuns

⑫ Mama Ttina

WHITE HILL TOWNS

(castle privately owned and closed to the public).

Now belly up to the railing and look down. The people of Arcos boast that only they see the backs of the birds as they fly. Ponder the parador's erosion concerns (it lost part of its lounge in the 1990s when it dropped right off), the orderly orange groves, and fine views toward Morocco. The city council considered building an underground parking lot to clear up the square, but nixed it because of the land's fragility. You're 330 feet above the Guadalete River. This is the town's suicide departure point for men (women jump from the other side).

• Looming over the square is the...

Church of Santa María: After Arcos was retaken from the Moors in the 13th century, this church was built atop a mosque. Notice the church's fine but chopped-off bell tower. The old one

fell in the earthquake of 1755 (famous for destroying Lisbon). The replacement was intended to be the tallest in Andalucía after Sevilla's—but money ran out. It looks like someone lives on an upper floor. Someone does—the church guardian resides there in a room strewn with bell-ringing ropes.

Buy a ticket (€2, Mon-Fri 10:00-13:00 & 16:00-19:00, Sat 10:00-14:00, shorter hours in winter, closed Sun and Jan-Feb), and step into the center, where you can see the beautifully carved choir. The organ was built in 1789 with that many pipes. At the very front of the church, the nice Renaissance high altar—carved in wood—covers up a Muslim prayer niche that survived from the older mosque. The altar shows God with a globe in his hand (on top), and scenes from the life of Jesus (on the right) and Mary (left). Circle the church counterclockwise and notice the elaborate chapels. Although most of the architecture is Gothic, the chapels are decorated in Baroque and Rococo styles. The ornate statues are used in Holy Week processions. Sniff out the "incorruptible body" (miraculously never rotting) of St. Felix—a third-century martyr (directly across from the entry). Felix may be nicknamed "the incorruptible," but take a close look at his knee. He's no longer skin and bones...just bones and the fine silver mesh that once covered his skin. Rome sent his body here in 1764, after recognizing this church as the most important in Arcos. In the back of the church, under a huge fresco of St. Christopher (carrying his staff and Baby Jesus), is a gnarly Easter candle from 1767.

• Back outside, examine the...

Church Exterior: Circle clockwise around the church, down four steps, to find the third-century Roman votive altar with a carving of the palm tree of life directly in front of you. Though the Romans didn't build this high in the mountains, they did have a town and temple at the foot of Arcos. This carved stone was discovered in the foundation of the original Moorish mosque, which stood here before the first church was built.

Head down a few more steps and come to the main entrance (west portal) of the church (closed for restoration). This is a good example of Plateresque Gothic—Spain's last and most ornate kind of Gothic.

In the pavement, notice the 15th-century magic circle with 12 red and 12 white stones—the white ones have various "constellations" marked (though they don't resemble any of today's star charts). When a child would come to the church to be baptized, the parents stopped here first for a good Christian

exorcism. The exorcist would stand inside the protective circle and cleanse the baby of any evil spirits. While locals no longer do this (and a modern rain drain now marks the center), many Sufi Muslims still come here in a kind of pilgrimage every November. (Down a few more steps and 10 yards to the left, you can catch the public bus for a circular minibus joyride through Arcos; see "Getting Around Arcos," earlier.)

Continuing along under the **flying buttresses,** notice the scratches of innumerable car mirrors on each wall (and be glad you're walking). The buttresses were built to shore up the church when it was damaged by an earthquake in 1699. (Thanks to these supports, the church survived the bigger earthquake of 1755.) The security grille (over the window above) protected cloistered nuns when this building was a convent. Look at the arches that prop up the houses downhill on the left; all over town, arches support earthquake-damaged structures.

• *Now make your way...*

From the Church to the Market: Completing your circle around the church (huffing back uphill), turn left under more arches built to repair earthquake damage and walk east down the bright, white Calle Escribanos. From now to the end of this walk, you'll basically follow this lane until you come to the town's second big church (St. Peter's). After a block, you hit Plaza Boticas.

On your right is the last remaining **convent** in Arcos. Notice the no-nunsense, spiky window grilles high above, with tiny peepholes in the latticework for the cloistered nuns to see through. Step into the lobby under the fine portico to find their one-way mirror and a spinning cupboard that hides the nuns from view. Push the buzzer, and one of the eight sisters (several are from Kenya and speak English well) will spin out some boxes of excellent, freshly baked cookies—made from pine nuts, peanuts, almonds, and other nuts—for you to consider buying (€6-7, open daily but not reliably 8:30-14:30 & 17:00-19:00; be careful—if you stand big and tall to block out the light, you can actually see the sister through the glass). If you ask for *magdalenas*, bags of cupcakes will swing around (€2.50). These are traditional goodies made from natural ingredients. Buy some goodies to support their church work, and give them to kids as you complete your walk.

The **covered market** *(mercado)* at the bottom of the plaza (down from the convent) resides in an unfinished church. At the entry, notice what is half of a church wall. The church was being built for the Jesuits, but construction stopped in 1767 when King Charles III, tired of the Jesuit appetite for politics, expelled the order from Spain. The market is closed on Sunday and Monday—they rest on Sunday, so there's no produce, fish, or meat ready for Monday. Poke inside. It's tiny but has everything you need. Pop into the *servicio público* (public WC)—no gender bias here.

• *As you exit the market, turn right and continue straight down Calle Botica...*

From the Market to the Church of St. Peter: As you walk, peek discreetly into private patios. These wonderful, cool-tiled courtyards filled with plants, pools, furniture, and happy family activities are typical of Arcos. Except in the mansions, these patios are generally shared by several families. Originally, each courtyard served as a catchment system, funneling rainwater to a drain in the middle, which filled the well. You can still see tiny wells in wall niches with now-decorative pulleys for the bucket.

At the next corner (Calle Platera), look back and up at the corner of the tiled rooftop on the right. The tiny stone—where the corner hits the sky—is a very eroded mask, placed here to scare evil spirits from the house. This is Arcos' last surviving mask from a tradition that lasted until the mid-19th century.

Also notice the ancient columns on each corner. All over town, these columns—many actually Roman, appropriated from their original ancient settlement at the foot of the hill—were put up to protect buildings from reckless donkey carts and tourists in rental cars.

As you continue straight, notice that the walls are scooped out on either side of the windows. These are a reminder of the days when women stayed inside but wanted the best possible view of any people action in the streets. These "window ears" also enabled boys in a more modest age to lean inconspicuously against the wall to chat up eligible young ladies.

Across from the old facade ahead, find the **Association of San Miguel.** Duck right, past a bar, into the oldest courtyards in town—you can still see the graceful Neo-Gothic lines of this noble home from 1850. The bar is a club for retired men—always busy when a bullfight's on TV or during card games. The guys are friendly, and drinks are cheap. You're welcome to flip on the light and explore the old-town photos in the back room.

Just beyond, facing the elegant front door of that noble house, is Arcos' second church, **St. Peter's** (€1 donation, Mon-Fri 9:00-14:00 & 15:30-18:30, Sat 10:00-14:00, closed Sun). You know it's St. Peter's because St. Peter, mother of God, is the centerpiece of the facade. Let me explain. It really is the second church, having had an extended battle with Santa María for papal recognition as the leading church in Arcos. When the pope finally favored Santa

María, St. Peter's parishioners changed their prayers. Rather than honoring "María," they wouldn't even say her name. They prayed "St. Peter, mother of God." Like Santa María, it's a Gothic structure, filled with Baroque decor, many Holy Week procession statues, humble English descriptions, and relic skeletons in glass caskets (two from the third century A.D.).

In the cool of the evening, the tiny square in front of the church—about the only flat piece of pavement around—serves as the old-town soccer field for neighborhood kids. Until a few years ago, this church also had a resident bellman—notice the cozy balcony halfway up. He was a basket-maker and a colorful character, famous for bringing a donkey into his quarters, which grew too big to get back out. Finally, he had no choice but to kill and eat the donkey.

Twenty yards beyond the church, step into the nice **Galería de Arte San Pedro,** featuring artisans in action and their reasonably priced paintings and pottery. Walk inside. Find the water drain and the well.

Across the street, a sign directs you to **Mirador**—a tiny square 100 yards downhill that affords a commanding view of Arcos. The reservoir you see to the east of town is used for water sports in the summertime, and forms part of a power plant that local residents protested—to no avail—based on environmental concerns.

From the Church of St. Peter, circle down and around back to the main square, wandering the tiny neighborhood lanes. Just below St. Peter's (on Calle Maldonado), is a delightful little Andalusian garden (formal Arabic style, with aromatic plants such as jasmine, rose, and lavender, and water in the center). A bit farther along on Maldonado, peek into **Belén Artístico,** a quirky, little cave-like museum, featuring miniatures of favorite Nativity scenes (free, but donations accepted). The lane called Higinio Capote, below the Church of Santa María, is particularly picturesque with its many geraniums. Peek into patios, kick a few soccer balls, and savor the views.

Nightlife in Arcos

Evening Action in the New Town

The newer part of Arcos has a modern charm. In the cool of the evening, all generations enjoy life out around Plaza de España (10-minute walk from the old town). Several good tapas bars

WHITE HILL TOWNS

border the square or are nearby.

The big park (Recinto Ferial) below Plaza de España is the late-night fun zone in the summer (June-Aug) when *carpas* (restaurant tents) fill with merrymakers, especially on weekends. The scene includes open-air tapas bars, disco music, and dancing.

Sleeping in Arcos

Hotels in Arcos consider April, May, August, September, and October to be high season. Note that some hotels double their rates during the motorbike races in nearby Jerez (usually April or May, varies yearly, call TI or ask your hotel) and during Holy Week (the week leading up to Easter); these spikes are not reflected in the prices below.

In the Old Town

For an overnight stay, avoid the parking lot on the main square, which has a two-hour daytime limit. Instead, park in the lot at Plaza de España, and catch a taxi or the shuttle bus up to the old town (see "Arrival in Arcos," earlier).

$$$ Parador de Arcos de la Frontera is royally located, with 24 elegant, recently refurbished and reasonably priced rooms (8 have balconies). If you're going to experience a parador, this is a good one (Sb-€80-137, Db-€95-171, Db with terrace-€130-206, cheaper rates are for Nov-Feb, breakfast-€16, air-con, elevator, Wi-Fi, free parking, Plaza del Cabildo, tel. 956-700-500, www.parador.es, arcos@parador.es).

$$ Hotel El Convento, deep in the old town just beyond the parador, is the best value in town. Run by a hardworking family and their wonderful staff, this cozy hotel offers 13 fine rooms—all with great views, most with balconies. In 1998 I enjoyed a big party with most of Arcos' big shots as they dedicated a fine room with a grand-view balcony to "Rick Steves, Periodista Turístico." Guess where I sleep when in Arcos...(Sb with balcony-€62, Sb with terrace-€78, Db with balcony-€82, Db with terrace-€97, extra person-€18; 10 percent discount in 2014 when you book direct, pay in cash, and show this book; usually closed Nov-Feb; Wi-Fi, Maldonado 2, tel. 956-702-333, www.hotelelconvento.es, reservas@hotelelconvento.es). Over an à la carte breakfast, bird-watch on their view terrace, with all of Andalucía spreading beyond your *café con leche.*

Sleep Code

(€1 = about $1.30, country code: 34)
S = Single, **D** = Double/Twin, **T** = Triple, **Q** = Quad, **b** = bathroom,
s = shower only. Unless otherwise noted, credit cards are
accepted, and English is spoken, but breakfast is not included.
Some hotels include the 10 percent IVA tax in the room price;
others tack it onto your bill.

To help you easily sort through these listings, I've divided
the accommodations into three categories based on the price
for a standard double room with bath during high season:

$$$ Higher Priced—Most rooms €100 or more.
$$ Moderately Priced—Most rooms between €50-100.
$ Lower Priced—Most rooms €50 or less.

Prices can change without notice; verify the hotel's current rates online or by email. For the best prices, always book
direct.

$$ La Casa Grande is a lovingly appointed *Better Homes and
Moroccan Tiles* kind of place that rents eight rooms with big-view
windows. As in a lavish yet very authentic old-style B&B, you're
free to enjoy its fine view terrace, homey library, and atrium-like
patio, where you'll be served a traditional breakfast. They also
offer guided visits and massage services (Db-€73-89; junior suites:
Db-€89-119, Tb-€109-119, Qb-€123-140; breakfast-€9, air-con,
Wi-Fi in public areas, Maldonado 10, tel. 956-703-930, www
.lacasagrande.net, info@lacasagrande.net, Elena).

$$ Rincón de las Nieves, with simple Andalusian style, has
a cool inner courtyard surrounded by three rooms and a sprawling
apartment that can accommodate up to seven people. Two of the
rooms have their own outdoor terraces with obstructed views, and
all have access to the rooftop terrace (Db-€50-65, higher for Holy
Week and Aug, apartment-€20-24/person, air-con, Boticas 10, tel.
956-701-528, mobile 656-886-256, www.rincondelasnieves.com,
info@rincondelasnieves.com).

$ Hostal San Marcos, above a neat little bar in the heart of
the old town, offers four air-conditioned rooms and a great sun
terrace with views of the reservoir (Sb-€25, Db-€35, Tb-€45, air-
con, Wi-Fi, Marqués de Torresoto 6, best to reserve by phone, tel.
956-105-429, mobile 664-118-052, sanmarcosdearcos@hotmail
.com, José speaks some English).

$ Hostal Callejón de las Monjas (a.k.a. Hostal El Patio)
offers the best cheap beds in the old town. With a tangled floor
plan and nine simple rooms, it's on a sometimes-noisy street

behind the Church of Santa María (Sb-€20, D-€27, Db-€35, Db with terrace-€45, Tb-€50, Qb apartment-€70, air-con, Wi-Fi, Calle Callejón de las Monjas 4, tel. 956-702-302, mobile 605-839-995, www.mesonelpatio.com, padua@mesonelpatio.com, staff speak no English). The bar-restaurant with bullfighting posters in the cellar serves breakfast, tapas, and several fixed-priced meals.

In the New Town

$$ Hotel Los Olivos is a bright, cool, and airy place with 19 rooms, an impressive courtyard, roof garden, generous public spaces, bar, view, friendly folks, and easy parking. The five view rooms can be a bit noisy in the afternoon, but—with double-paned windows—are usually fine at night (Sb-€46-51, Db-€72-87, Tb-€87-102, extra bed-€15, breakfast-€9; 10 percent discount when you book direct, pay in cash, and show this book; Wi-Fi, Paseo de Boliches 30, tel. 956-700-811, www.hotel-losolivos.es, reservas@hotel-losolivos.es, Raquel and Miguel Ángel).

$ Hostal Málaga is surprisingly nice, if for some reason you want to stay on the big, noisy road at the Jerez edge of town. Nestled on a quiet lane between truck stops on A-382, it offers 17 clean, attractive rooms and a breezy two-level roof garden (Sb-€20-25, Db-€35-38, Qb apartment-€50, air-con, Wi-Fi, easy parking, Ponce de León 5, tel. 956-702-010, www.hostalmalaga .com, hostalmalagaarcos@hotmail.com, Josefa speaks German and a *leetle* English).

Eating in Arcos

Restaurants generally serve lunch from 13:00 to 16:00 and dinner from 20:00 until very late (Spaniards don't start dinner until about 21:00).

View Dining

The **Parador** (described earlier, under "Sleeping in Arcos") has a restaurant with a cliff-edge setting. Its tapas and *raciones* are reasonably priced but mediocre; still, a drink and a snack on the million-dollar-view terrace at sunset is a nice experience (€2.50-4 tapas, €6-14 *raciones*, €22 three-course fixed-price meal at lunch or dinner, daily 13:30-16:00 & 20:30-23:00, shorter hours off-season, on main square).

Cheaper Eating in the Old Town

Several decent, rustic bar-restaurants are in the old town, within a block or two of the main square and church. Most serve tapas at the bar and *raciones* at their tables. Prices are fairly consistent (€2 tapas, €5 *media-raciones*, €8 *raciones*).

WHITE HILL TOWNS

Bar La Carcel ("The Prison") is run by a hardworking family that brags about its exquisite tapas and small open-faced sandwiches. I would, too. The menu is accessible; prices are the same at the bar or at the tables; and the place has a winning energy, giving the traveler a fun peek at this community (Tue-Sun 12:00-16:00 & 20:00-24:00, closed Mon; July-Aug it's open Mon and closed Sun; Calle Deán Espinosa 18, tel. 956-700-410).

Alcaraván tries to be a bit trendier yet *típico*, with a hibachi hard at work out front. A flamenco ambience fills its medieval vault in the castle's former dungeon. This place attracts French and German tourists who give it a cool vibe. Francisco and his wife cook from 13:00 and again starting at 21:00 (closed Mon, Calle Nueva 1, tel. 956-703-397).

Bar San Marcos is a tiny, homey bar with five tables, an easy-to-understand menu offering hearty, simple home cooking, and cheap €5 plates and a variety of €7 fixed-price meals (kitchen open long hours Mon-Sat, closed Sun, Marqués de Torresoto 6).

Mesón Don Fernando gives rustic a feminine twist with an inviting bar and both indoor and great outdoor seating on the square just across from the little market (Tue-Thu 13:30-16:00 & 20:15-23:00 for food, closed Wed, longer hours for drinks on the square, on Plaza Boticas).

Mesón Los Murales serves tasty, affordable tapas, *raciones,* and fixed-price meals in their rustic bar or at tables in the square outside (€2.50 tapas and *montaditos,* €6-12 *raciones,* fixed-price meals from €9, Fri-Wed 10:00-24:00, closed Thu, at Plaza Boticas 1, tel. 685-809-661).

Mama Ttina gives you an Italian break from Andalucía, with pizza and pastas to go along with the Italian pop music and international Italian/Andaluz/Moroccan/British staff (€6-12 pizzas and pastas, Thu-Mon 13:00-16:00 & 18:30-24:00, Tue-Wed 18:30-24:00 only, Deán Espinosa 10, tel. 956-703-937).

Tapas in the New Town

Plaza de España, in the lower new town, is lined with tapas bars and restaurants. For a great perch while enjoying the local family scene, consider the busy **Restaurante Bar Terraza** (€12 plates) at the end of Plaza de España.

Arcos Connections

By Bus

Leaving Arcos by bus can be frustrating (especially if you're going to Ronda)—buses generally leave late, the schedule information boards are often inaccurate, and the ticket window usually isn't open (luckily, you can buy your tickets on the bus). But local buses do give you a glimpse at *España profunda* ("deep Spain"), where everyone seems to know each other, no one's in a hurry, and despite any language barriers, people are quite helpful when approached.

Two bus companies—Los Amarillos and Comes—share the Arcos bus station. Call the Jerez offices for departure times, or ask your hotelier for help. If you want to find out about the Arcos-Jerez schedule, make it clear you're coming from Arcos (Los Amarillos tel. 902-210-317, www.losamarillos.es; Comes tel. 956-291-168, www.tgcomes.es). Also try the privately run www.movelia.es for bus schedules and routes.

From Arcos by Bus to: Jerez (hourly, 30 minutes), **Ronda** (1-2/day, 2 hours), **Cádiz** (4-5/day, 1.25 hours), **Sevilla** (2/day, 2 hours, more departures with transfer in Jerez). Buses run less frequently on weekends. The closest train station to Arcos is Jerez.

Route Tips for Drivers

The trip to **Sevilla** takes about 1.5 hours if you pay €7 for the toll road. To reach **southern Portugal,** follow the freeway to Sevilla, skirt the city by turning west on C-30 in the direction of Huelva, and it's a straight shot from there.

For more driving tips for the region, see the end of this chapter.

Ronda

With more than 35,000 people, Ronda is one of the largest white hill towns. It's also one of the most spectacular, thanks to its gorge-

straddling setting. Approaching the town from the train or bus station, it seems flat... until you reach the New Bridge and realize that it's clinging to the walls of a canyon.

While day-trippers from the touristy Costa del Sol clog Ronda's streets during the day, locals retake the town in the early evening, making nights peaceful. If you liked Toledo at night, you'll love the local feeling of evenings in Ronda. Since it's served by train and bus, Ronda makes a relaxing break for non-drivers traveling between Granada, Sevilla, and Córdoba. Drivers can use Ronda as a convenient base from which to explore many of the other *pueblos blancos*.

Ronda's main attractions are its gorge-spanning bridges, the oldest bullring in Spain, and an intriguing old town. The cliffside

WHITE HILL TOWNS

setting, dramatic today, was practical back in its day. For the Moors, it provided a tough bastion, taken by the Spaniards only in 1485, seven years before Granada fell. Spaniards know Ronda as the cradle of modern bullfighting and the romantic home of 19th-century *bandoleros*. The real joy of Ronda these days lies in exploring its back streets and taking in its beautiful balconies, exuberant flowerpots, and panoramic views. Walking the streets, you feel a strong local pride and a community where everyone seems to know everyone.

Orientation to Ronda

Ronda's breathtaking ravine divides the town's labyrinthine Moorish quarter and its new, noisier, and more sprawling Mercadillo quarter. A massive-yet-graceful 18th-century bridge connects these two neighborhoods. Most things of touristic importance (TI, post office, hotels, bullring) are clustered within a few blocks of the bridge. The paseo (early evening stroll) happens in the new town, on Ronda's major pedestrian and shopping street, Carrera Espinel.

Tourist Information

Ronda's **TI,** across the square from the bullring, covers not only the town but all of Andalucía. It gives out good, free maps of the town, Andalusia's roads, Granada, Sevilla, and the Route of the White Towns. It also sells the Bono Turístico city pass, has listings of the latest museum hours, and organizes walking tours—see details under "Tours in Ronda," later (TI open Mon-Fri 10:00-19:30, until 18:00 late-Oct-late March; Sat-Sun 10:00-14:00 & 15:00-17:00; Paseo Blas Infante, tel. 952-187-119, www.turismoderonda.es).

Sightseeing Pass: If you're an avid sightseer, consider getting the €10 **Bono Turístico** city pass, which gets you into five sights (including the Arab Baths, Museo Joaquín Peinado, and Mondragón Palace). It's valid for one week and sold at the TI and a few participating sights (including the Arab Baths and Museo Joaquín Peinado).

Arrival in Ronda

By Train: The small station has ticket windows, a train information desk, and a café, but no baggage storage (there are lockers at the nearby bus station).

From the station, it's a 15-to-20-minute **walk** to the center: Turn right out of the station on Avenida de Andalucía, and go through the roundabout (you'll see the bus station on your right). Continue straight down the street (now called San José) until you

Ronda

TO Pileta Cave, Arcos, Sevilla ④

TO Train Station & ⑩

BUS STATION

PLAZA MERCED

WC • ALAMEDA DEL TAJO

BULLRING

PARADOR

GUADALEVÍN RIVER

NEW BRIDGE

TRAIL TO PUERTA DE LOS MOLINOS

PLAZA DE MARÍA AUXILIADORA

MONDRAGÓN PALACE

SANTA MARÍA LA MAYOR

PLAZA DUQUESA DE PARCENT

CITY HALL

CALLE JEREZ

CALLE SAN JOSÉ

MADRID

ANDALUCÍA

LAURIA

MONTEREJAS

INFANTES

ALMENDRA

CRUZ VERDE

VIRGEN DE LA PAZ

POZO

GOUBIRON

Post

NARANJA

ESPINEL

NUEVA

VILLANUEVA

LOS REMEDIOS

CANTOS

REAL

PEÑAS

CORTES

M. CABRERA

PLAZA C. ABELA

PLAZA DEL SOCORRO

PLAZA DE ESPAÑA

TENORIO

ARMIÑAN

S. DOMINGO

M. SALV

ARMIÑAN

MERCADILLO QUARTER

MOORISH QUARTER

OLD BRIDGE

ARAB BRIDGE

ARAB BATHS MUSEUM

CITY WALL

BANDOLERO MUSEUM

TO ALMOCÁBAR GATE, COSTA DEL SOL & ⑫

200 YARDS
200 METERS

Ⓣ TAXI STAND
🔭 VIEW
Ⓟ PARKING

① Hotel San Gabriel
② Hotel Ronda
③ Hotel Alavera de los Baños
④ To Hotel Catalonia Reina Victoria
⑤ Hotel Enfrente Arte Ronda
⑥ Hotel Don Miguel
⑦ Hotel El Tajo
⑧ Hotel San Francisco
⑨ Hotel Royal
⑩ To Hotel Andalucía
⑪ Hostal Doña Carmen
⑫ To Hotel Bandolero
⑬ Laundry
⑭ Internet Café
⑮ House of the Moorish King & Garden
⑯ Palace of the Marquis of Salvatierra
⑰ Lara Museum
⑱ Joaquín Peinado Museum

reach Calle Jerez. Turn left and walk downhill past a church and the Alameda del Tajo park. Keep going down this street, passing the bullring, to get to the TI and the famous bridge. A **taxi** to the center costs about €6.50.

By Bus: To get to the center from the bus station, leave the station walking to the right of the roundabout, then follow the directions for train travelers (described earlier). To use the station's baggage lockers, buy a token *(ficha)* at the kiosk by the exit (€3.50).

By Car: Street parking away from the center is often free. The handiest place to park in the center of Ronda is the underground lot at Plaza del Socorro (one block from bullring, €18/24 hours).

Helpful Hints

Laundry: HigienSec has one machine for self-service. For twice the cost, they will wash, dry, and fold your clothes, and offer same-day service if you drop off early enough (€6/load wash-and-dry, €12/load drop-off service, Mon-Fri 10:00-14:00 & 17:00-20:30, Sat 10:00-14:00, closed Sun, 2 blocks east of the bullring at Calle Molino 6, tel. 952-875-249).

Internet Access: Almost every hotel in town has Wi-Fi, and many also have computers for guest use. You can get online, make international phone calls, print, and fax at **Internet Mundi@l** (€0.50/15 minutes, Mon-Sat 10:00-14:00 & 16:00-22:00, Sun 16:00-22:00, near the recommended Hotel El Tajo at Calle Cruz Verde 21, tel. 952-161-588).

Baggage Storage: Use the lockers at the bus station (see "Arrival in Ronda," earlier).

Tours in Ronda

Walking Tours

The TI offers two-hour guided walks of the city (Sat-Sun at 13:00; in summer also Thu-Sat at 20:00). Reserve and pay at the TI (€18 daytime tour includes Mondragón Palace and bullring; €15 evening tour includes Mondragón Palace and Arab Baths; sometimes in two languages). Tours can be canceled if there aren't enough sign-ups.

Local Guide

Energetic and knowledgeable **Antonio Jesús Naranjo** will take you on a two-hour walking tour of the city's sights. He showed Michelle Obama around when she was in town (from €120/day, reserve early, tel. 952-870-614, mobile 639-073-763, www.guiaoficialderonda.com, guiajesus@yahoo.es). The TI has a list of other local guides.

Sights in Ronda

Ronda's New Town

▲▲▲The Gorge and New Bridge (Puente Nuevo)

The ravine, called El Tajo—360 feet down and 200 feet wide—divides Ronda into the whitewashed old Moorish town (La Ciudad) and the new town (El Mercadillo) that was built after the Christian reconquest in 1485. The New Bridge mightily spans the gorge. A different bridge was built here in 1735, but fell after six years. This one was built from 1751 to 1793. Look down...carefully.

You can see the foundations of the original bridge (and a super view of the New Bridge) from the Jardines de Cuenca park (daily in summer 9:30-21:30, winter 9:30-18:30): From Plaza de España, walk down Calle Rosario, turn right on Calle Los Remedios, and then take another right at the sign for the park. There are also good views from the parador, which overlooks the gorge and bridge from the new-town side.

From the new-town side of the bridge, on the right, you'll see the entrance to the **New Bridge Interpretive Center,** where you can pay to climb down and enter the structure of the bridge itself (€2; Mon-Fri 10:00-19:00, late Oct-late March until 18:00; Sat-Sun 10:00-15:00 year-round; mobile 649-965-338). Inside the mostly empty-feeling hall are modest audiovisual displays about the bridge's construction and famous visitors to Ronda. But the views of the bridge and gorge from the outside are far more thrilling than anything you'll find within.

▲▲▲Bullring (Real Maestranza de Caballería de Ronda)

Ronda is the birthplace of modern bullfighting, and this was the first great Spanish bullring. Philip II initiated bullfighting as war training for knights in the 16th century. Back then, there were two kinds of bullfighting: the type with noble knights on horseback,

and the coarser, man-versus-beast entertainment for the commoners (with no rules...much like when the WWF wrestlers bring out the folding chairs). Ronda practically worships Francisco Romero, who melded the noble and chaotic kinds of bullfighting with rules to establish modern bullfighting right here in the early 1700s. He introduced the scarlet cape, held unfurled with a stick. His son Juan further developed the ritual (local aficionados would never call it a "sport"—you'll read newspaper coverage of fights not on the sports pages but in the culture section), and his grandson Pedro was one of the first great matadors (killing nearly 6,000 bulls in his career).

Ronda's bullring and museum are Spain's most interesting (even better than Sevilla's). To tour the ring, stables, chapel, and museum, buy a ticket at the back of the bullring, the farthest point from the main drag.

Cost and Hours: €6.50, daily April-Sept 10:00-20:00, March and Oct 10:00-20:00, Nov-Feb 10:00-18:00, no photography in museum, tel. 952-874-132, www.rmcr.org. The excellent €2 audioguide describes everything and is essential to fully enjoy your visit.

Bullfights: Bullfights are scheduled only for the first weekend of September during the *feria* (fair) and occur very rarely in the spring. Whereas every other *feria* in Andalucía celebrates a patron saint, the Ronda fair glorifies legendary bullfighter Pedro Romero. For September bullfights, tickets go on sale the preceding July. (As these sell out immediately, Sevilla and Madrid are more practical places for a tourist to see a bullfight.)

Visiting the Bullring: I'd visit in this order. Directly to the right as you enter is the bullfighters' **chapel.** Before going into the ring, every matador would stop here to pray to Mary for safety—and hope to see her again.

• *Just beyond the chapel are the doors to the museum exhibits: horse gear and weapons on the left, and the story of bullfighting on the right, with some English translations.*

The **horse gear and guns exhibit** makes the connection with bullfighting and the equestrian upper class. As throughout Europe, "chivalry" began as a code among the sophisticated, horse-riding gentry. (In Spanish, the word for "gentleman" is the same as the word for "horseman" or "cowboy"—*caballero*.) And, of course, nobles are into hunting and dueling, hence the fancy guns. Don't miss the well-described

dueling section with gun cases for two, as charming as a picnic basket with matching wine glasses.

Backtrack past the chapel to see Spain's best **bullfighting exhibit.** It's a shrine to bullfighting and the historic Romero family. First it traces the long history of bullfighting, going all the way back to the ancient Minoans on Crete. Historically, there were only two arenas built solely for bullfighting: in Ronda and Sevilla. Elsewhere, bullfights were held in town squares—you'll see a painting of Madrid's Plaza Mayor filled with spectators for a bullfight. (For this reason, to this day, even a purpose-built bullring is generally called *plaza de toros*—"square of bulls.") You'll also see stuffed bull heads, photos, "suits of light" worn by bullfighters, and capes (bulls are actually colorblind, but the traditional red cape was designed to disguise all the blood). One section explains some of the big "dynasties" of fighters. At the end of the hall are historic posters from Ronda's bullfights (all originals except the Picasso). Running along the left wall are various examples of artwork glorifying bullfighting, including original Goya engravings.

• *From the museum, take advantage of the opportunity to walk in the actual arena.*

Here's your chance to play *toro*, surrounded by 5,000 empty seats. The two-tiered **arena** was built in 1785—on the 300th anniversary of the defeat of the Moors in Ronda. Notice the 136 classy Tuscan columns, creating a kind of 18th-century Italian theater. Lovers of the "art" of bullfighting will explain that the event is much more than the actual killing of the bull. It celebrates the noble heritage and the Andalusian horse culture. When you leave the museum and walk out on the sand, look across to see the ornamental columns and painted doorway where the dignitaries sit (over the gate where the bull enters). On the right is the place for the band (marked *música*), which, in the case of a small town like Ronda, is most likely a high school band.

• *Just beyond the arena are more parts of the complex.*

From the arena, walk through the bulls' entry into the bullpen and the **stables.** There are six bulls per fight (plus two backups)—and three matadors. The bulls are penned up here beforehand, and ropes and pulleys safely open the right door at the right time. Climb upstairs and find the indoor arena (Picadero) and see Spanish thoroughbred horses training from the **Equestrian School** of the Real Maestranza (Mon-Fri).

Alameda del Tajo Park

One block away from the bullring, the town's main park is a great place for a picnic lunch, people-watching, a snooze in the shade, or practicing your Spanish with seniors from the old folks' home.

WHITE HILL TOWNS

Ronda's Old Town

▲Church of Santa María la Mayor (Iglesia de Santa María)

This 15th-century church with a fine Mudejar bell tower shares a park-like square with orange trees and City Hall. It was built on and around the remains of Moorish Ronda's main mosque (which was itself built on the site of a temple to Julius Caesar). With a pleasantly eclectic interior that features some art with unusually modern flair, and a good audioguide to explain it all, it's worth a visit.

Cost and Hours: €4, includes audioguide, daily April-Sept 10:00-20:00, March and Oct 10:00-19:00, Nov-Feb 10:00-18:00, closed Sun 12:30-14:00 for Mass, Plaza Duquesa de Parcent in the old town.

Visiting the Church: In the room where you purchase your ticket, look for the only surviving mosque **prayer niche** (that's a mirror; look back at the actual mihrab, which faces not Mecca, but Gibraltar—where you'd travel to get to Mecca). Partially destroyed by an earthquake, the reconstruction of the church resulted in the Moorish/Gothic/Renaissance/Baroque fusion (or confusion) you see today.

The front of the church interior is dominated by a magnificent Baroque **high altar** with the standard statue of the *Immaculate Conception* in the center. The even more ornate chapel directly to the right is a good example of Churrigueresque architecture, a kind of Spanish Rococo in which decoration obliterates the architecture—notice that you can hardly make out the souped-up columns. This chapel's fancy decor provides a frame for an artistic highlight of the town, the "Virgin of the Ultimate Sorrow." The big fresco of St. Christopher with Baby Jesus on his shoulders (on the left, where you entered) shows the patron saint both of Ronda and of travelers.

Facing the altar is an elaborately carved **choir** with a wall of modern bronze reliefs depicting scenes from the life of the Virgin Mary. Similar to the Via Crucis (Way of the Cross), this is the Via Lucis (Way of the Light), with 14 stations (such as #13— the Immaculate Conception, and #14—Mary's assumption into heaven) that serve as a worship

aid to devout Catholics. The centerpiece is Mary as the light of the world (with the moon, stars, and sun around her).

Head to the left around the choir, noticing the bright **paintings** along the wall by French artist Raymonde Pagegie, who gave sacred scenes a fresh twist—like the Last Supper attended by female servants, or the scene of Judgment Day, when the four horsemen of the apocalypse pause to adore the Lamb of God.

The **treasury** (at the far-right corner, with your back to the high altar) displays vestments that look curiously like matadors' brocaded outfits—appropriate for this bullfight-crazy town.

Mondragón Palace (Palacio de Mondragón)

This beautiful, originally Moorish building was erected in the 14th century, and is the legendary (but not actual) residence of Moorish kings. The building was restored in the 16th century (notice the late Gothic courtyard), and its facade dates only from the 18th century. At the entrance (free to view without a ticket) is a topographic model of Ronda, which helps you envision the fortified old town apart from the grid-like new one. The rest of the building houses Ronda's Municipal Museum, focusing on prehistory and geology. Wander through its many rooms to find the kid-friendly prehistory section, with exhibits on Neolithic toolmaking and early metallurgy (described in English). If you plan to visit the Pileta Cave (see page 786), find the panels that describe the cave's formation and shape. Even if you have no interest in your ancestors or speleology, the building's architecture is impressive; linger in the two small gardens, especially the shaded one.

Cost and Hours: €3; Mon-Fri 10:00-19:00, late Oct-late March until 18:00; Sat-Sun 10:00-15:00; on Plaza Mondragón in old town, tel. 952-870-818.

Nearby: Leaving the palace, wander left a few short blocks to the nearby Plaza de María Auxiliadora for more views and a look at the two rare *pinsapos* (resembling extra-large Christmas trees) in the middle of the park; this part of Andalucía is the only region in Europe where these ancient trees still grow. For an intense workout but a picture-perfect view, find the *Puerta de los Molinos* sign and head down, down, down. (Just remember you have to walk back up, up, up.) Not for the faint of heart or in the heat of the afternoon sun, this pathway leads down to the viewpoint where windmills once stood. Photographers go crazy reproducing the most famous postcard view of Ronda—the entirety of the New Bridge. Wait until just before sunset for the best light and cooler temperatures.

Lara Museum (Museo Lara)

This discombobulated collection of Ronda's history in dusty glass cases displays everything from sewing machines to fans to old movie projectors to matador outfits (with decent English explanations). The highlight for many is the basement, with juvenile displays showing torture devices from the Inquisition and local witchcraft.

Cost and Hours: €4, audioguide-€1, daily 11:00-20:00, mid-Oct-mid-March until 19:00, Calle Arminan 29, tel. 952-871-263, www.museolara.org.

Bandit Museum (Museo del Bandolero)

This tiny museum, while not as intriguing as it sounds, has an interesting assembly of *bandolero* photos, guns, clothing, knickknacks, and old documents and newspaper clippings. The Jesse Jameses and Billy el Niños of Andalucía called this remote area home. One brand of romantic bandits fought Napoleon's army—often more effectively than the regular Spanish troops. The exhibits profile specific *bandoleros* and display books (from comics to pulp fiction) that helped romanticize these heroes of Spain's "Old West." The museum feels a bit like a tourist trap (with a well-stocked gift shop), but brief but helpful English descriptions make this a fun stop. Next door is a free 22-minute movie about *bandoleros,* (only in Spanish).

Cost and Hours: €3.75, daily May-Sept 11:00-20:00, Oct-April until 18:30, across main street below Church of Santa María la Mayor at Calle Armiñan 65, tel. 952-877-785, www.museobandolero.com.

▲Joaquín Peinado Museum (Museo Joaquín Peinado)

Housed in an old palace, this fresh museum features an impressively large professional overview of the life's work of Joaquín Peinado (1898-1975), a Ronda native and pal of Picasso. Because Franco killed creativity in Spain for much of the last century, nearly all of Peinado's creative work was done in Paris. His style evolved through the big "isms" of the 20th century, ranging from Expressionist to Cubist, and even to erotic. While Peinado's works seem a bit derivative, perhaps that's understandable as he was friends with one of the art world's biggest talents. The nine-minute movie that kicks it off is only in Spanish, though there are good English explanations throughout the museum. You'll have an interesting modern-art experience here, without the crowds of Madrid's museums. It's fun to be exposed to a lesser-known but very talented artist in his hometown.

Cost and Hours: €4, Mon-Fri 10:00-17:00, Sat 10:00-15:00, closed Sun, Plaza del Gigante, tel. 952-871-585, www.museojoaquinpeinado.com.

Walk Through Old Town to Bottom of Gorge

From the New Bridge you can descend down Cuesta de Santo Domingo (crossing the bridge from the new town into the old, take the first left at the former Dominican Church, once the headquarters of the Inquisition in Ronda) into a world of whitewashed houses, tiny grilled balconies, and winding lanes—the old town.

A couple of blocks steeply downhill (on the left), you'll see the **House of the Moorish King** (Casa del Rey Moro). It was never the home of any king; it was given its fictitious name by the grandson of President McKinley, who once lived here. It offers visitors entry to the fine "Moorish-Hispanic" belle époque garden, designed in 1912 by a French landscape architect (the house interior is not open to visitors). Follow signs to the "Mine," an exhausting series of 280 slick, dark, and narrow stairs (like climbing down and then up a 20-story building) leading to the floor of the gorge. The Moors cut this zigzag staircase into the wall of the gorge in the 14th century to access water when under siege, then used Spanish slaves to haul water up to the thirsty town (€4, generally daily 10:00-20:00).

Fifty yards downhill from the garden is the **Palace of the Marquis of Salvatierra** (Palacio del Marqués de Salvatierra, closed to public). As part of the "distribution" following the Reconquista here in 1485, the Spanish king gave this grand house to the Salvatierra family (who live here to this day). The facade is rich in colonial symbolism from Spanish America—note the pre-Columbian-looking characters (four Peruvian Indians) flanking the balcony above the door and below the family coat of arms.

Just below the palace, stop to enjoy the view terrace. Look below. A series of square vats are all that remains of the old tanneries. There are two old bridges, with the Arab Baths just to the right, and at the edge of town is a rectangular horse-training area.

Twenty steps farther down, you'll pass through the Philip V gate, for centuries the main gate to the fortified city of Ronda.

Continuing downhill, you come to the **Old Bridge** (Puente Viejo), rebuilt in 1616 upon the ruins of an Arabic bridge. Enjoy the views from the bridge (but don't cross it yet), then continue down the old stairs. From the base of the staircase, look back up to glimpse some of the surviving highly fortified Moorish city walls. You've now reached the oldest bridge in Ronda, the Arab Bridge (also called the San Miguel Bridge). Sometimes given the misnomer of Puente Romano (Roman Bridge), it was more likely built long after the Romans left. For centuries, this was the main gate to the fortified city. In Moorish times, you'd purify both your body and your soul here before entering the city, so just outside the gate was a little mosque (now the ruined chapel) and the Arab Baths.

The **Arab Baths** (Baños Árabes), worth ▲, are evocative ruins that warrant a quick look. They were located half underground to

maintain the temperature and served by a horse-powered water tower. You can still see the top of the shaft (30 yards beyond the bath rooftops, near a cyprus tree, connected to the baths by an aqueduct). Water was hoisted from the river below to the aqueduct by ceramic containers that were attached to a belt powered by a horse walking in circles. Inside, two of the original eight columns scavenged from the Roman ruins still support brick vaulting. A delightful 10-minute video brings the entire complex to life—Spanish and English versions run alternately (€3, free on Mon; open Mon-Fri 10:00-19:00, Nov-April until 18:00; Sat-Sun 10:00-15:00 year-round; sometimes open later in summer, call ahead before making the trip, mobile 656-950-937).

From here, hike back to the new town along the other side of the gorge: Return to the bridge just uphill. Cross it and take the stairs immediately on the left, which lead scenically along the gorge up to the New Bridge.

Near Ronda: Pileta Cave

The Pileta Cave (Cueva de la Pileta) offers Spain's most intimate look at Neolithic and Paleolithic paintings that are up to 25,000 years old. Set in a dramatic, rocky limestone ridge at the eastern edge of Sierra de Grazalema Natural Park, Pileta Cave is 14 miles from Ronda, past the town of Benaoján, at the end of an access road. It's particularly handy if you're driving between Ronda and Grazalema.

Cost and Hours: €8, one-hour tours generally depart daily at 13:00 & 16:00, additional tours go between 10:00-13:00 and 16:00-18:00 if enough people gather (Nov-mid-April until 17:00), closing times indicate last tour, €10 guidebook, no photos, tel. 952-167-343, www.cuevadelapileta.org.

Getting There: It's possible to get here without wheels, but I wouldn't bother (you'd have to take the Ronda-Benaoján bus—2/day, departs at 8:30 and 13:00, 30 minutes—and then it's a 2-hour, 3-mile uphill hike). You can get from Ronda to the cave by taxi—it's about a half-hour drive on twisty roads—and have the driver wait (€60 round-trip). If you're driving, it's easy: Leave Ronda through the new part of town, and take A-374. After a few miles, passing Cueva del Gato, exit left toward Benaoján on MA-555. Go through Benaoján and follow the numerous signs to the cave. Leave nothing of value in your car.

Visiting the Cave: Farmer José Bullón and his family live down the hill from the cave, and because they strictly limit the number of visitors, Pileta's rare paintings are among the best-preserved in the world. Señor Bullón and his son lead up to 25 people at a time through the cave, which was discovered by Bullón's grandfather in 1905. Call the night before to see if there's a tour and space available at the time you want. Note that if you simply show up for the 13:00 tour, you'll risk not getting a spot—and it'll be another three hours before the next one starts. Bring a sweater and good shoes. You need a good sense of balance to take the tour. The 10-minute hike, from the parking lot up a trail with stone steps to the cave entrance, is moderately steep. Inside the cave, there are no handrails, and it can be difficult to keep your footing on the slippery, uneven floor while being led single-file, with only a lantern light illuminating the way.

Señor Bullón is a master at hurdling the language barrier. As you walk the cool half-mile, he'll spend an hour pointing out lots of black, ochre, and red drawings, which are five times as old as the Egyptian pyramids. Mostly it's just lines or patterns, but there are also horses, goats, cattle, and a rare giant fish, made from a mixture of clay and fat by finger-painting prehistoric *hombres*. The 200-foot main cavern is impressive, as are some weirdly recognizable natural formations such as the Michelin man and a Christmas tree.

Eating near the Cave: Nearby Montejaque has several good restaurants clustered around the central square.

Sleeping near the Cave: A good base for visiting Ronda and the Pileta Cave (as well as Grazalema) is **$$ Cortijo las Piletas.** Nestled at the edge of Sierra de Grazalema Natural Park (just a 15-minute drive from Ronda, with easy access from the main highway), this spacious family-run country estate has nine rooms and plenty of opportunities for swimming, hiking, bird-watching, and exploring the surrounding area. They can also arrange for biking and horseback riding (Sb-€71-76, Db-€86-92, extra bed-€15-18, includes breakfast but not tax, dinner offered some days—book in advance, mobile 605-080-295, www.cortijolaspiletas.com, info @cortijolaspiletas.com, Pablo and Elisenda). Another countryside option is **$$ Finca La Guzmana,** run by expat Brit Peter. Six beautifully appointed pastel rooms surround an open patio at this renovated estate house. Bird-watching, swimming, and trekking are possible (Db-€75-80, includes breakfast, mobile 600-006-305, www.laguzmana.com, info@laguzmana.com).

WHITE HILL TOWNS

Sleeping in Ronda

Ronda has plenty of reasonably priced, decent-value accommodations. It's crowded only during Holy Week (the week leading up to Easter) and the first week of September (for bullfighting season). Most of my recommendations are in the new town, a short stroll from the New Bridge and about a 10-minute walk from the train station. In the cheaper places, ask for a room with a *ventana* (window) to avoid the few interior rooms. Breakfast is usually not included.

In the Old Town

Clearly the best options in town, these hotels are worth reserving early. The first two are right in the heart of the Old Town, while the Alavera de los Baños is a steep 15-to-20-minute hike below, but still easily walkable to all the sights (if you're in good shape) and in a bucolic setting.

$$ Hotel San Gabriel has 22 pleasant rooms, a kind staff, public rooms filled with art and poetry books, a cozy wine cellar, and a fine garden terrace. It's a large 1736 townhouse, once the family's home, that's been converted to a characteristic hotel, marinated in history. If you're a cinephile, kick back in the charming TV room—with seats from Ronda's old theater and a collection of DVD classics—then head to the breakfast room to check out photos of big movie stars (and, ahem, bespectacled travel writers) who have stayed here (Sb-€66, Db-€88, bigger superior Db-€98, Db junior suite-€115, lavish honeymoon suite-€150, breakfast-€5, air-con, incognito elevator, guest computer, Wi-Fi, double-park in front and they'll direct you to a €9/day parking spot, follow signs on the main street of old town to Calle Marqués de Moctezuma 19, tel. 952-190-392, www.hotelsangabriel.com, info@hotelsangabriel.com, family-run by José Manuel and Ana).

$$ Hotel Ronda provides an interesting mix of minimalist and traditional Spanish decor in this refurbished mansion, which is both quiet and homey. Although its five rooms are without views, the small, lovely rooftop deck overlooks the town (Sb-€55, Db-€70, additional bed-€22, no breakfast, air-con, Wi-Fi, Ruedo Doña Elvira 12, tel. 952-872-232, www.hotelronda.net, laraln @telefonica.net, some English spoken).

$$ Alavera de los Baños, a delightful oasis located next to ancient Moorish baths at the bottom of the hill, has nine small rooms and big inviting public places, with appropriately Moorish decor. This hotel offers a swimming pool, a peaceful Arabic garden, and a selection of sandwiches for lunch. The artistic ambience urges, "Relax!" You're literally in the countryside, with sheep and horses outside near the garden (Sb-€60-70, Db-€85-

97, Db with terrace-€95-107, includes breakfast, Wi-Fi in some rooms and lobby, free and easy parking, closed Jan, steeply below the heart of town at Calle Molino de Alarcón, tel. 952-879-143, www.alaveradelosbanos.com, alavera@telefonica.net, well-run by personable Christian and Inma).

In the New Town

More convenient than charming (except the Hotel Enfrente Arte Ronda—in a class all its own), these hotels put you in the thriving new town.

$$$ Hotel Catalonia Reina Victoria hangs royally over the gorge at the edge of town and has a marvelous view—Hemingway loved it. Its 89 renovated rooms are sleek and modern but lack character. Rooms with a gorge view cost €15 more—and they're worth it (Sb-€97-117, Db-€115-156, breakfast-€13, air-con, elevator, Wi-Fi in lobby, pool, parking-€15/day, 10-minute walk from city center; easy to miss—look for intersection of Avenida Victoria and Calle Jerez, Jerez 25; tel. 952-871-240, www.hoteles-catalonia.com, reinavictoria@hoteles-catalonia.com).

$$ Hotel Enfrente Arte Ronda, on the edge of things a steep 10-to-15-minute walk below the heart of the new town, is relaxed, funky, and friendly. The 12 rooms are spacious and exotically decorated, but dimly lit. It features a sprawling maze of exuberantly decorated public spaces, including a peaceful bamboo garden, game and reading room, small swimming pool, sauna, and terraces with sweeping countryside views. Guests can help themselves to free drinks from the self-service bar. This one-of-a-kind place is in all the guidebooks, so reserve early—Madonna even stayed here once (Db-€80-105, extra bed-€28-40, includes buffet breakfast, air-con, elevator, Wi-Fi in lobby, Real 40, tel. 952-879-088, www .enfrentearte.com, reservations@enfrentearte.com).

$$ Hotel Don Miguel, facing the gorge just left of the bridge, has disinterested staff and all the charm of a tourgroup hotel, but it couldn't be more central. Of its 30 sparse but comfortable rooms, 20 have gorgeous views at no extra cost. Street rooms come with a little noise (Sb-€59-70, Db-€91-108, Tb-€110-135, free buffet breakfast, 10 percent discount if you book direct via email and mention this book, air-con, elevator, Wi-Fi in lobby, parking garage a block away-€12/day, Plaza de España 4, tel. 952-877-722, www.dmiguel.com, reservas@dmiguel.com).

$$ Hotel El Tajo has 33 decent, quiet rooms—once you get past the tacky faux-stone Moorish decoration in the foyer (Sb-€39, Db-€55, breakfast-€6, air-con, elevator, Wi-Fi in some rooms, parking-€10/day, Calle Cruz Verde 7, a half-block off the pedestrian street, tel. 952-874-040, www.hoteleltajo.com, reservas @hoteleltajo.com).

$$ Hotel San Francisco offers 27 small, nicely decorated rooms a block off the main pedestrian street in the town center (Sb-€35-40, Db-€50-65, Tb-€70-80, breakfast-€3.50, air-con, elevator, parking-€8.50/day, María Cabrera 20, tel. 952-873-299, hotelronda@terra.es).

$ Hotel Royal has a dreary reception and 29 clean, spacious, simple rooms—many on the main street that runs between the bullring and bridge. Thick glass keeps out most of the noise, while the tree-lined Alameda del Tajo park across the street is a treat. Some rooms and hallways are dimly lit (Sb-€30-38, Db-€40-50, Tb-€55-60, breakfast-€4, air-con, Wi-Fi, parking-€10/day, 3 blocks off Plaza de España at Calle Virgen de la Paz 42, tel. 952-871-141, www.ronda.net/usuar/hotelroyal, hroyal@ronda.net).

$ Hotel Andalucía has 12 clean, comfortable, and recently renovated rooms immediately across the street from the train station (Sb-€25, Db-€35, Tb-€50, breakfast-€2, air-con and TV in all rooms, Wi-Fi, easy street parking or €6/day in nearby garage, Martínez Astein 19, tel. 952-875-450, www.hotel-andalucia.net, info@hotel-andalucia.net).

$ Hostal Doña Carmen, a basic cheapie, rents 32 bare-bones rooms in two sections. The rooms sharing a shower down the hall, with no air-con or TV, are especially reasonable (S-€17, Sb-€25, D-€28, Db-€45, T-€40, Tb-€55, no breakfast, air-con and TV only in rooms with bath, Wi-Fi in lobby, Calle Naranja 28, tel. 952-871-994, www.hostaldonacarmen.com, mturrillo@yahoo.es).

Near Ronda, in Júzcar

The village of Júzcar is about 15 miles south of Ronda. In 2011 Júzcar's white façades were painted "Smurf blue" to promote a Smurfs movie. When it came time to restore the buildings to their normal white color, the villagers realized they weren't eager to lose the tourist traffic the stunt had brought in—and voted to leave their town blue (for the time being, at least).

$$ Hotel Bandolero is for nature lovers. Settle into the rustic rooms, go hiking and bird-watching, or take a dip in the pool (Sb-€35-49, standard Db-€59-96, superior Db-€69-106, Db suite-€80-117, higher prices are for half-board, Wi-Fi, restaurant with Cordon Bleu chef, Avenida Havaral 43, Júzcar, tel. 952-183-660, www.hotelbandolero.com, reservas@hotelbandolero.com, David).

Eating in Ronda

Plaza del Socorro, a block in front of the bullring, is an energetic scene, bustling with tourists and local families enjoying the square and its restaurants. The pedestrian-only **Calle Nueva** is lined with hardworking eateries. To enjoy a drink or a light meal with the

Ronda Restaurants

1. Confitería Daver (2)
2. Alameda Market
3. Día Supermarket
4. Tragatapas
5. Bar Lechuguita
6. Café & Bar Faustino
7. La Tradicional
8. To Bar-Restaurante Almocábar, La Cepa & Bodega San Francisco
9. Restaurante Mirador de la Espinela
10. Restaurante Pedro Romero
11. Restaurante Casa Santa Pola

best view in town, consider the terraces of Hotel Don Miguel just under the bridge. For coffee and pastries, locals like the elegant little **Confiteria Daver** (café open daily 8:00-20:30, take-away until 21:00, two locations—Calle Virgen de los Remedios 6 and Calle Padre Mariano Soubiron 8). Picnic shoppers find the **Alameda Market** (Mon-Sat 8:30-21:00, Sun 9:00-15:00, Calle Virgen de La Paz 23) conveniently located next to Alameda del Tajo park, which has benches and a WC. The **Día** supermarket, opposite Hotel El Tajo, is also very central (Mon-Sat 9:15-21:15, closed Sun, Calle Cruz Verde 18).

Tapas in the City Center

Ronda has a fine tapas scene. You won't get a free tapa with your drink as in some other Spanish towns, but these bars have accessible tapas lists, and they serve bigger plates. Each of the following places could make a fine solo destination for a meal, but they're close enough that you can easily try more than one.

Tragatapas, the accessible little brother of the acclaimed gourmet Restaurante Tragabuches, serves super-creative and always-tasty tapas in a stainless-steel minimalist bar. There's just a handful of tall tiny tables and stools inside, with patio seating on the pedestrian street, and an enticing blackboard of the day's specials. If you want to sample Andalusian gourmet (e.g., a handful of €1.70-3 tapas such as asparagus on a stick sprinkled with manchego cheese grated coconut-style) without going broke, this is the place to do it (also €6-12 larger plates, daily 12:00-17:00 & 20:00-24:00, Calle Nueva 4, tel. 952-877-209).

Bar Lechuguita, a hit with older locals early and younger ones later, serves a long and tasty list of tapas for a good price. Rip off a tapas inventory sheet and mark which ones you want (most cost €0.80; €5 plates also available). Be adventurous and don't miss the bar's namesake, *Lechuguita* (#15, a wedge of lettuce with vinegar, garlic, and a secret ingredient). The order-form routine makes it easy to communicate and get exactly what you like, plus you know the exact price (Mon-Sat 13:00-15:15 & 20:15-23:30, closed Sun, no chairs or tables, just a bar and tiny stand-up ledges, Calle Virgen de los Remedios 35).

Café & Bar Faustino is a place Brueghel would paint—a festival of eating with a fun and accessible menu that works both at the bar and at tables. The atmosphere makes you want to stay, and the selection makes you wish your appetite was even bigger (lots of €1 tapas, €3 sandwiches, €5-8 *raciones,* Tue-Sun 12:00-24:00, closed Mon, just off Plaza Carmen Abela at Santa Cecilia 4, tel. 952-190-307).

La Tradicional, run by Elias (from Casa María—described below), serves up €1.20 tapas and €4-11 *raciones* with an emphasis on meats (Thu-Tue 12:00-17:00 & 18:30-24:00, closed Wed, Las Tiendas 2, tel. 952-875-683).

Outside the Almocábar Gate

To entirely leave the quaint old town and bustling city center with all of its tourists and grand gorge views, hike 10 minutes out to the far end of the old town, past City Hall, to a big workaday square that goes about life as if the world didn't exist outside Andalucía.

Bar-Restaurante Almocábar is a favorite eatery for many Ronda locals. Its restaurant—a cozy eight-table room with Moorish tiles and a window to the kitchen—serves up tasty, creative, well-presented meals from a menu that's well-described in English (plus a handwritten list of the day's specials). Many opt for the good €8-15 salads—rare in Spain. At the busy bar up front, you can order anything from the dining room menu, or choose from the list of €1.50-2 tapas (€5-15 starters, €12-20 main dishes, closed Tue, Calle Ruedo Alameda 5, tel. 952-875-977).

La Cepa (formerly Casa María) is a small tapas bar offering typical Andalusian fare in a homey setting. In summer, their tables spill out onto the plaza (€1-3 tapas, €7-9 *raciones,* Wed-Mon 12:30-24:00, closed Tue, facing Plaza Ruedo Alameda at #27, tel. 676-126-822).

Bodega San Francisco is a rustic bar with tables upstairs and a homey restaurant across the street, offering an accessible list of €4-9 *raciones* and €1 tapas, as well as serious plates and big splittable portions (same menu in bar and restaurant). This place is understandably a neighborhood favorite (closed Thu, Ruedo de Alameda 32, tel. 952-878-162).

Dining in the City Center

Ronda is littered with upscale-seeming restaurants that toe the delicate line between a good dinner spot and a tourist trap. While (admittedly) none of the following could be called "untouristy," they each offer decent food with either a striking setting, a venerable ambience, or both. For a more authentic dining experience, do a tapas crawl through town, or head for the far more characteristic eateries just outside the Almocábar Gate (both described above).

Restaurante Mirador de la Espinela (locals often refer to it by its former name, El Escudero) serves lovingly presented Spanish food with a posh modern touch in a crystal- and cream-colored dining room or on a terrace overlooking the gorge (€12-18.50 fixed-price meals, €29 gourmet tasting meals, €7-13 starters, €16-20 main dishes, daily 12:00-22:30 except closed Sun eve in summer, behind bullring at Paseo Blas Infante 1, tel. 952-871-367).

Restaurante Pedro Romero, though touristy and overpriced, is a venerable institution in Ronda. Assuming a shrine to bullfighting draped in *el toro* memorabilia doesn't ruin your appetite, it gets good reviews. Rub elbows with the local bullfighters or dine with the likes (well, photographic likenesses) of Orson Welles, Ernest Hemingway, and Francisco Franco (€16 and 25 fixed-price meals, €7-12 starters, €16-20 main dishes, daily 12:00-16:00 & 19:30-23:00, air-con, across the street from bullring at Calle Virgen de la Paz 18, tel. 952-871-110).

Restaurante Casa Santa Pola offers gourmet versions of traditional food with friendly, professional service, with several small dining rooms and a delightful terrace perched on the side of the gorge—worth reserving ahead (€12-14 starters, €16-24 main dishes; good oxtail stew, roasted lamb, and honey-tempura eggplant; daily 12:30-16:30 & 19:00-22:30; after crossing New Bridge from the bullring, take the first left downhill and you'll see the sign, Calle Santo Domingo 3; tel. 952-879-208, www .rsantapola.com).

Ronda Connections

Note that some destinations are linked with Ronda by both bus and train. Direct bus service to other hill towns can be sparse (as few as one per day), and train service usually involves a transfer in Bobadilla. It's worth spending a few minutes in the bus or train station on arrival to plan your departure. Your options improve from major transportation hubs such as Málaga.

From Ronda by Bus to: Algeciras (1/day, 2.75 hours, Comes), **La Línea/Gibraltar** (no direct bus, transfer in Algeciras; Algeciras to Gibraltar—2/hour, 45 minutes, can buy ticket on bus), **Arcos** (1-2/day, 2 hours, Comes), **Jerez** (2/day, 2.5-3 hours, Comes), **Grazalema** (2/day, 45 minutes, Los Amarillos), **Zahara** (2/day, Mon-Fri only, 45 minutes, Comes), **Sevilla** (8/day, 2-2.5 hours, fewer on weekends, some via Villamartín, Los Amarillos; also see trains, next page), **Málaga** (*directo* 10/day Mon-Fri, 6/day Sat-Sun, 1.75-2 hours, Los Amarillos; *ruta* 2/day, 4 hours, Portillo; access other Costa del Sol points from Málaga), **Marbella** (2/day, 1.25 hours, Los Amarillos), **Fuengirola** (2/day, 1.75 hours, Los Amarillos), **Nerja** (4 hours, transfer in Málaga; can take train or bus from Ronda to Málaga, bus is better). If traveling to **Córdoba**, it's easiest to take the train since there are no direct buses (see below). **Bus info:** Los Amarillos (tel. 902-210-317, www.losamarillos.es), Portillo (tel. 902-450-550, http://portillo .avanzabus.com), and Comes (tel. 956-291-168, www.tgcomes .es). It's best to just drop by and compare schedules (at the station on Plaza Concepción García Redondo, several blocks from train station), or pick up a bus timetable from the city TI.

By Train to: Algeciras (5-6/day, 1.5-2 hours), **Bobadilla** (4/day, 1 hour), **Málaga** (1/day, 2 hours, more with transfer in Bobadilla), **Sevilla** (5/day, 3-4 hours, transfer in Bobadilla, Antequera, or Cordboa), **Granada** (3/day, 2.5 hours), **Córdoba** (2/day direct, 1.75 hours; more with transfer in Bobadilla or Antequera, 3.75 hours), **Madrid** (2/day, 4 hours). Transfers are a snap and time-coordinated in Bobadilla; with four trains arriving and departing simultaneously, double-check that you're jumping on the right one. **Train info:** tel. 902-320-320, www.renfe.com.

Zahara and Grazalema

There are plenty of interesting hill towns to explore. Public transportation is frustrating, so I'd do these towns only by car. Useful information on the area is rare. Fortunately, a good map, the tourist brochure (pick it up in Sevilla or Ronda), and a spirit of adventure work fine.

Along with Arcos, Zahara de la Sierra and Grazalema are my favorite white villages. While Grazalema is a better overnight stop, Zahara is a delight for those who want to hear only the sounds of the wind, birds, and elderly footsteps on ancient cobbles.

Zahara de la Sierra

This tiny town in a tingly setting under a Moorish castle (worth ▲ and the climb) has a spectacular view over a turquoise lake. While the big church facing the town square is considered one of the richest in the area, the smaller church has the most-loved statue. The Virgin of Dolores is Zahara's answer to Sevilla's Virgin of Macarena (and is similarly paraded through town during Holy Week).

The **TI** is located in the main plaza (Mon-Fri 9:00-14:00 & 16:00-19:00, Sat-Sun 10:00-12:30, gift shop, Plaza del Rey 3, tel. 956-123-114). It has a single computer with very slow Internet access (€1.50, one-hour limit). Upstairs from the TI are Spanish-only displays about the flora and fauna of nearby Sierra de Grazalema Natural Park.

WHITE HILL TOWNS

Drivers can park for free in the main plaza, or continue up the hill to the parking lot at the base of the castle, just past the cliffside **$$ Hotel Arco de la Villa,** the town's only real hotel (16 small modern rooms, Sb-€36, Db-€60, breakfast-€3, tel. 956-123-230,

Route of the White Hill Towns

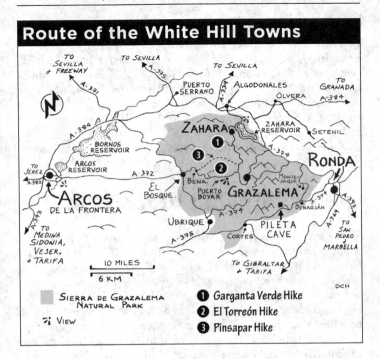

TO SEVILLA & FREEWAY
TO SEVILLA
TO SEVILLA
TO GRANADA
A-371
A-375
PUERTO SERRANO
ALGODONALES
OLVERA
A-384
A-384
ZAHARA
ZAHARA RESERVOIR
SETENIL
BORNOS RESERVOIR
ARCOS RESERVOIR
RONDA
A-384
A-372
BENA.
MONTE-JAQUE
TO JEREZ
A-382
EL BOSQUE
PUERTO BOYAR
GRAZALEMA
A-374
A-373
ARCOS DE LA FRONTERA
A-374
BENAOJÁN
TO MEDINA SIDONIA, VEJER, & TARIFA
UBRIQUE
A-375
CORTES
PILETA CAVE
A-369
TO SAN PEDRO & MARBELLA
10 MILES
6 KM
TO GIBRALTAR & TARIFA
DCH

SIERRA DE GRAZALEMA NATURAL PARK

VIEW

① Garganta Verde Hike
② El Torreón Hike
③ Pinsapar Hike

www.tugasa.com, arco-de-la-villa@tugasa.com). The street that connects both churches, Calle de San Juan, is lined with busy tapas bars and restaurants.

Sights in Zahara: During Moorish times, Zahara lay within the fortified castle walls above today's town. It was considered the gateway to Granada and a strategic stronghold for the Moors by the Christian forces of the Reconquista. Locals tell of the Spanish conquest of the Moors' castle (in 1482) as if it happened yesterday: After the Spanish failed several times to seize the castle, a clever Spanish soldier  noticed that the Moorish sentinel would check if any attackers were hiding behind a particular section of the wall by tossing a rock and setting the pigeons in flight. If they flew, the sentinel figured there was no danger. One night a Spaniard hid there with a bag of pigeons and let them fly when the sentinel tossed his rock. Upon seeing the birds, the guard assumed he was clear to enjoy a snooze. The clever Spaniard then scaled the wall and opened the door to let in his troops, who conquered the castle. Ten years later Granada fell, the Muslims were back in Africa, and the Reconquista was complete.

It's a fun climb up to the remains of the **castle** (free, tower always open). Start at the paved path across from the town's upper parking lot. It's a moderately easy 15-minute hike past some Roman ruins and along a cactus-rimmed ridge to the top, where you can enter the tower. Use your penlight or feel along the stairway to reach the roof, and enjoy spectacular views from this almost impossibly high perch far above the town. As you pretend you're defending the tower, realize that what you see is quite different from what the Moors saw: The huge lake dominating the valley is a reservoir—before 1991, the valley had only a tiny stream.

Grazalema

A beautiful postcard-pretty hill town, Grazalema offers a royal balcony for a memorable picnic, a square where you can watch old-

timers playing cards, and plenty of quiet whitewashed streets and shops to explore. Situated within Sierra de Grazalema Natural Park, Grazalema is graced with lots of scenery and greenery. Driving here from Ronda on A-372, you pass through a beautiful park-like grove of cork trees. While the park is known as the rainiest place in Spain, the clouds seem to wring themselves out before they reach the town—I've only ever had blue skies. If you want to sleep in a small Andalusian hill town, this is a good choice.

The **TI** is located at the car park at the cliffside viewpoint, Plaza de los Asomaderos. It has WCs and a small gift shop featuring locally produced products (daily 10:00-14:00 & 15:30-19:00, tel. 956-132-052, www.grazalemaguide.com). Enjoy the view, then wander into the town.

A tiny lane leads a block from the center rear of the square to Plaza de Andalucía (filled by the tables of a commotion of tapas bars). Shops sell the town's beautiful and famous handmade wool blankets and good-quality leather items from nearby Ubrique. A block farther uphill takes you to the main square with the church, Plaza de España. A coffee on the square here is a joy. Small lanes stretch from here into the rest of the town.

Popular with Spaniards, the town makes a good home base for exploring Sierra de Grazalema Natural Park—famous for its spectacularly rugged limestone landscape of cliffs, caves, and gorges (see sidebar). For outdoor gear and adventures, including hiking, caving, and canoeing, contact **Horizon** (summer

Sierra de Grazalema Natural Park

Sierra de Grazalema Natural Park is unique for its rugged mountain landscape and its relatively rainy climate, which support a wide variety of animals and plant life.

One-third of Spain's flowers bloom here, wild ibex (mountain goats) climb the steep slopes, and Europe's largest colony of griffon vultures soars high above. The park's plant poster child is the *pinsapo*, a type of fir tree left over from the last Ice Age (the park is one of the few places in Europe where these trees still grow). About a fifth of the 200-square-mile park is a special reserve area, where access is limited, largely to protect these rare trees from forest fires. Hikers need to get (free) permits for most trails in the reserve.

Zahara, Grazalema, and the Pileta Cave all fall within the park boundaries. Drivers will get an eyeful of scenery just passing through the park on their way to these sights.

If you want to more fully experience the park—by hiking, caving, canoeing, kayaking, or horseback riding—the easiest way is to take a tour from Zahara Catur (in Zahara, www.zahara catur.com) or Horizon (in Grazalema, www.horizonaventura .com). They also handle the permit procedure for you.

If you want to hike in the park on your own, you'll need a park map, a permit for most hikes within the reserve area (see hiking permit procedure), and a car to get to the trailhead. From July through September, you may have to go with a guided

Tue-Sat 9:00-14:00 & 17:00-20:00, rest of year Tue-Sat 9:00-14:00 & 16:00-19:00, closed Sun-Mon year-round, off Plaza de España at Corrales Terceros 29, tel. 956-132-363, mobile 655-934-565, www.horizonaventura.com).

Sleeping in Grazalema: **$$ La Mejorana Guesthouse** is the best bet in town—if you can manage to get one of its six rooms. You won't want to leave this beautifully perched garden villa, with its royal public rooms overlooking the valley from the upper part of town (Db-€58, includes breakfast, Wi-Fi, pool, located at top of town on tiny lane below Guardia Civil headquarters at Santa Clara 6, tel. 956-132-327, mobile 649-613-272, www.lamejorana .net, info@lamejorana.net, Ana and Andres can help with local hiking options).

$$ Hotel Peñón Grande, named for a nearby mountain, is just off the main square and rents 16 comfortable business-class rooms (Sb-€38, Db-€56, extra bed-€14, air-con, Plaza group anyway, if you want to hike in the reserve (about €13/person for a half-day hike, offered by Zahara Catur and Horizon).

Popular hikes in the reserve (all requiring permits) include:

Garganta Verde: Explore a canyon with a huge open cave near vulture breeding grounds (1.5 miles each way, initially gentle hike then very steep descent, allow 4-5 hours).

El Torreón: Climb the park's highest mountain, at 5,427 feet (1.75 miles each way, steep incline to summit, allow 4-5 hours).

Pinsapar: Hike on mountain slopes forested with *pinsapo* trees (8.5 miles each way, steep climb for first third of trail then downhill, allow 6 hours).

Information: The TIs in Grazalema and Zahara sell a Spanish-only park guide with descriptions and trail maps (€15).

Getting a Hiking Permit: A permit is free but required; a ranger will fine you if you don't have one. To get a permit, email, call, or visit the park office in the town of El Bosque, a gateway to the park. You can request a permit for a specific hike up to 30 days in advance. Pick up the permit in El Bosque, or have them fax it to the TI in Grazalema or Zahara (El Bosque park office hours generally Mon-Sat 10:00-14:00 & 17:00-19:00, Sun 9:00-14:00, Avenida de la Diputación, tel. 956-727-029 or 956-709-733, cv_elbosque@egmasa.es). Include the date, the number of people in your group, the hike you want to do, and your passport number (allow plenty of time for this process).

Hikes from Grazalema (No Permit Required): If you'd rather not hassle with getting a permit, or if you don't have a car to reach the trailheads, try one of several hikes that start from the town of Grazalema. You'll find descriptions in pamphlets available at the Grazalema TI or Horizon (€1).

Pequeña 7, tel. 956-132-434, www.hotelgrazalema.com, hotel@hotelgrazalema.com).

$ Casa de Las Piedras, just a block from the main square, has 16 comfortable rooms with private baths (Sb-€35, Db-€48); 2 other rooms that share a single bathroom and have access to a kitchen and washing machine (D-€42); and 14 super-cheap basic rooms that share 5 bathrooms (D-€28, no access to kitchen or washing machine). The beds feature the town's locally made wool blankets (10 percent discount with this book and two-night minimum stay, buffet breakfast-€6, Calle Las Piedras 32, tel. 956-132-014, mobile 627-415-047, www.casadelaspiedras.es, reservas@casadelaspiedras.net, Caty and Rafi.

Eating in Grazalema: Grazalema offers many restaurants and bars. Tiny Plaza de Andalucía has several good bars for tapas with umbrella-flecked tables spilling across the square, including **Zulema** (big salads), **La Posadilla,** and **La Cidulia.**

Grazalema

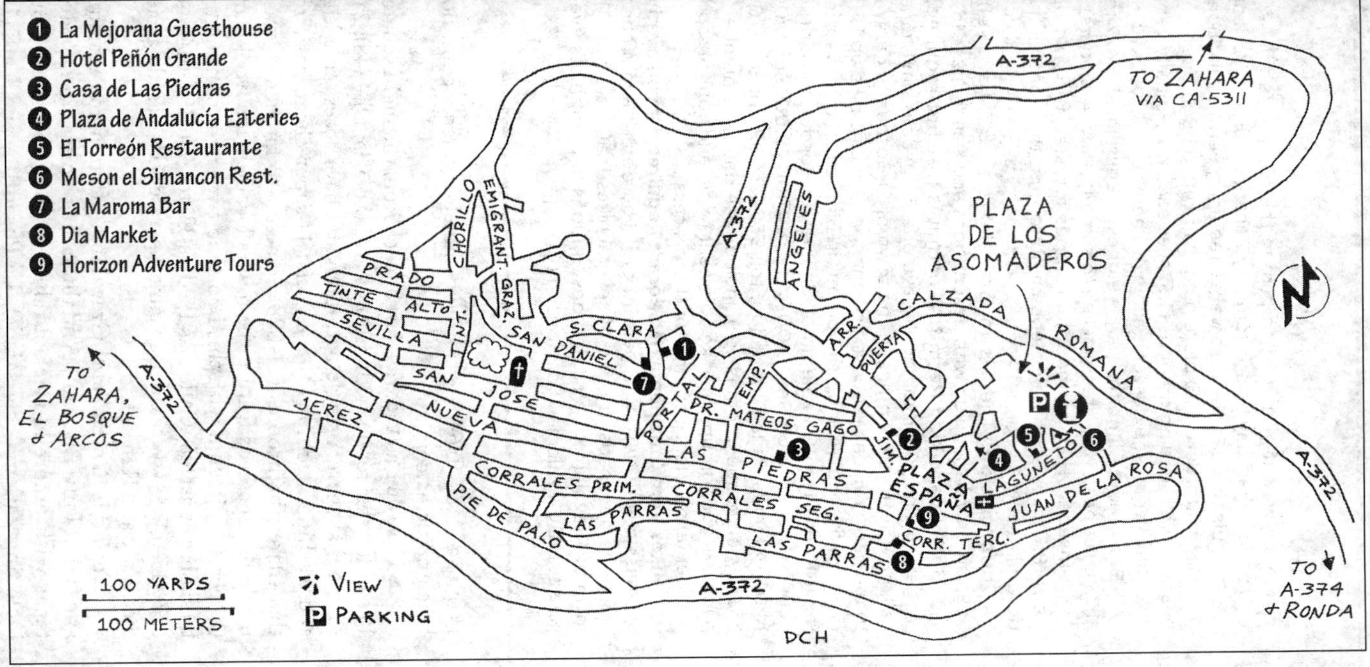

1 La Mejorana Guesthouse
2 Hotel Peñón Grande
3 Casa de Las Piedras
4 Plaza de Andalucía Eateries
5 El Torreón Restaurante
6 Meson el Simancon Rest.
7 La Maroma Bar
8 Dia Market
9 Horizon Adventure Tours
A-372
TO ZAHARA VIA CA-5311
PLAZA DE LOS ASOMADEROS
CALZADA
ROMANA
ANGELES
CHORILLO
EMIGRANT.
GRAZ.
PRADO
TINTE
ALTO
SEVILLA
TINT.
SAN DANIEL
S. CLARA
SAN
JOSE
JEREZ
NUEVA
PORTAL
EMP.
ARR.
PUERTA
DR. MATEOS GAGO
LAS PIEDRAS
JIM.
PLAZA ESPAÑA
LAGUNETO
JUAN DE LA ROSA
CORRALES PRIM.
CORRALES SEG.
CORR. TERC.
PIE DE PALO
LAS PARRAS
LAS PARRAS
TO ZAHARA, EL BOSQUE & ARCOS
TO A-374 & RONDA
100 YARDS
100 METERS
VIEW
PARKING
DCH

The recommended **Casa de Las Piedras** (earlier) has an adjacent restaurant (same name) that offers tapas, fixed-price meals, and several vegetarian options. To pick up picnic supplies, head to the **Día** supermarket (Mon-Sat 9:00-14:00 & 17:00-21:00, Sun 9:00-14:00, on Calle Corrales Terceros 3).

El Torreón specializes in local lamb and game dishes, and also has many vegetarian options (closed Wed, Calle Agua 44, tel. 956-132-313).

Meson el Simancon serves well-presented cuisine typical of the region in a romantic setting. While a bit more expensive, it's considered the best restaurant in town (closed Tue, facing Plaza de los Asomaderos and the car park, tel. 956-132-421).

La Maroma Bar serves home-cooked regional specialties, three meals a day, at affordable prices (€1.20-3 tapas, €4-8 meat and fish plates, daily 8:00 until late, Calle Santa Clara, near La Mejorana Guesthouse, tel. 617-543-756, José & María).

Grazalema Connections: **From Grazalema by Bus to: Ronda** (2/day, 45 minutes), **El Bosque** (2/day, 45 minutes). Bus service is provided by Los Amarillos (www.losamarillos.es).

Jerez

With more than 200,000 people, Jerez (officially Jerez de la Frontera) is your typical big-city mix of industry and dusty concrete suburbs, but it has a lively old center and two claims to touristic fame: horses and sherry. Jerez is ideal for a noontime visit on a weekday. See the famous horses, sip some sherry, wander through the old quarter, and swagger out.

Orientation to Jerez

Thanks to its complicated, medieval street plan, there is no easy way to feel oriented in Jerez—so ask for directions liberally.

Tourist Information

The helpful TI, on Plaza del Arenal, gives out free maps and info on the sights (June-Sept Mon-Fri 9:00-15:00 & 17:00-19:00, Sat-Sun 9:30-14:30; Oct-May Mon-Fri 8:30-15:00 & 16:00-18:30, Sat-Sun 9:00-15:00; tel. 956-338-874, www.turismojerez.com). If you're walking to see the horses, ask here for detailed directions, as the route is a bit confusing.

WHITE HILL TOWNS

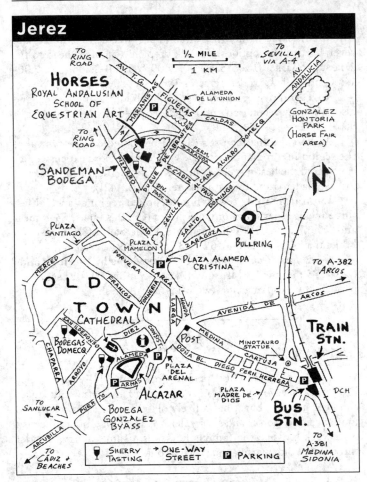

Jerez

HORSES
ROYAL ANDALUSIAN
SCHOOL OF
EQUESTRIAN ART

SANDEMAN
BODEGA

PLAZA
SANTIAGO

OLD

TOWN

CATHEDRAL

BODEGAS
DOMECQ

ALCÁZAR

BODEGA
GONZALEZ
BYASS

TO
SANLUCAR

TO
CÁDIZ +
BEACHES

TO
RING
ROAD

TO
RING
ROAD

AV. T. G.

ALAMEDA
DE LA UNION

CALDAS

PLAZA
MAMELON

PLAZA ALAMEDA
CRISTINA

PORVERA

MERCED

FRANCOS

LARGA

TORNERIA

LARGA

HONDA

AVENIDA   DE   ARCOS

MEDINA

POST

PLAZA
DEL
ARENAL

PLAZA
MADRE DE
DIOS

MINOTAURO
STATUE

CARTUJA

DIEGO FERN HERRERA

TO
A-382
ARCOS

TRAIN
STN.

BUS
STN.

DCH

TO
A-381
MEDINA
SIDONIA

BULLRING

GONZALEZ
HONTORIA
PARK
(HORSE
FAIR
AREA)

TO
SEVILLA
VIA A-4

½ MILE

1 KM

🍷 SHERRY
TASTING   → ONE-WAY
STREET   🅿 PARKING

Arrival in Jerez

By Bus or Train: The bus and train stations are located side by side, near the Plaza del Minotauro (with enormous headless statue). Unfortunately, you can't store luggage at either one. You can stow bags for free in the Royal Andalusian School's *guardaropa* (coat room) if you attend their Horse Symphony show, but only for the duration of the performance.

Cheap and easy **taxis** wait in front of the train station (€4 to TI; about €5 to the horses). It's a 20-minute **walk** from the stations to the center of town and the TI: Angle to the left across the brick plaza (in front of train station, with two black smokestacks) to find Calle Diego Fernández de Herrera. Go right, following this street faithfully for several blocks until you reach Plaza de las Angustias. Head left toward the church and continue in the same direction, straight down Calle Corredera, until you arrive at Plaza del Arenal (ringed with palm trees, with a large fountain in the center)—the TI is across the plaza on your left.

By Car from Arcos: Driving in Jerez can be frustrating. The outskirts are filled with an almost endless series of roundabouts. Continuing straight through each one will eventually bring a rail bridge into sight. Continue to follow traffic and signs to *centro ciudad*. The route may seem circuitous (it is), but it will ultimately take you into Plaza Alameda Cristina. From here, it's best to park in one of the many underground garages (at Plaza Alameda Cristina or Plaza Arenal, €1.30/hour) and catch a cab or walk. For street parking, blue-line zones require prepaid parking tickets on your dashboard (Mon-Fri 9:00-13:30 & 17:00-20:00, Sat 9:00-14:00, free on Sun and July-Aug afternoons).

Sights in Jerez

▲▲Royal Andalusian School of Equestrian Art

If you're into horses, a performance of the Royal Andalusian School of Equestrian Art (Fundación Real Escuela Andaluza del

Arte Ecuestre) is a must. Even if you're not, this is art like you've never seen.

Getting There: On foot, from the TI at Plaza del Arenal, it's about a half-hour walk down mostly pedestrianized shopping streets to the horses. Leave the plaza on Calle Lanceria, heading to the left of the rounded Tino La Ina Fundador building to Calle Larga. Turn right into Plaza Alameda Christina, which leads into Plaza Memelon. From here, follow the *Real Escuela de Arte Ecuestre* signs.

From the bus or train stations to the horses, it's about a €5 **taxi** ride. Taxis wait in Plaza Mamelon for the return trip.

One-way streets mean there is only one way to arrive by **car.** Follow signs to *Real Escuela de Arte Ecuestre.* Expect to make at least one wrong turn, so allow a little extra time. You'll find parking behind the school.

Horse Symphony Show

This is an equestrian ballet with choreography, purely Spanish music, and costumes from the 19th century. The stern riders and their talented, obedient steeds prance, jump, hop on their hind legs, and do-si-do in time to the music, all to the delight of an arena filled with mostly tourists and local horse aficionados.

The riders cue the horses with subtle dressage commands,

either verbally or with body movements. You'll see both purebred Spanish horses (of various colors, with long tails, calm personalities, and good jumping ability) and the larger mixed breeds (with short tails and a walking—not prancing—gait). The horses must be three years old before their three-year training begins, and most performing horses are male (stallions or geldings), since mixing the sexes brings problems.

The equestrian school is a university, open to all students in the EU, and with all coursework in Spanish. Although still a male-dominated activity, there have recently been a few female graduates. Tight-fitted mushroom hats are decorated with different stripes to show each rider's level. Professors often team with students and evaluate their performance during the show.

Cost and Hours: General seating-€21, "preference" seating-€27; 1.5-hour show runs Tue and Thu at 12:00 most of the year (also on Fri in Aug, Nov-Feb Thu only); no photos allowed in show, stables, or museum; tel. 956-318-008, tickets available online at www.realescuela.org. General seating is fine; some "preference" seats are too close for good overall views. The show explanations are in Spanish.

Training Sessions

The public can get a sneak preview at training sessions on non-performance days. Sessions can be exciting or dull, depending

on what the trainers are working on. Afterward, you can take a 1.5-hour guided tour of the stables, horses, multimedia and carriage museums, tack room, gardens, and horse health center. Sip sherry in the arena's bar to complete this Jerez experience.

Cost and Hours: €11; Mon, Wed, and Fri—except no Fri in Aug, also on Tue in Nov-Feb; arrive anytime between 10:00 and 14:00—they'll start the tour when they have a large-enough group. Tour groups crowd in at 11:00 and schedules may vary, so it's wise to call ahead.

▲▲Sherry Bodega Tours

Spain produces more than 10 million gallons per year of the fortified wine known as sherry. The name comes from English attempts to pronounce Jerez. Although sherry was traditionally the drink of England's aristocracy, today's producers are leaving the drawing-room vibe behind. Your tourist map of Jerez is speckled with *venencia* symbols, each representing a sherry bodega that offers tours and tasting. *Venencias* are specially designed ladles for

Sherry

Spanish sherry is not the sweet dessert wine sold in the States as sherry. In Spain, sherry is (most commonly) a chilled very dry fortified white wine, often served with appetizers such as tapas, seafood, and cured meats.

British traders invented the sherry-making process as a way of transporting wines so they wouldn't go bad on a long sea voyage. Some of the most popular brands (such as Sandeman and Osbourne) were begun by Brits, and for years it was a foreigners' drink. But today, sherry is typically Spanish.

Sherry is made by blending wines from different grapes and vintages, all aged together. Start with a strong, acidic wine (from grapes that grow well in the hot, chalky soil around Jerez). Mature it in large vats until a yeast crust *(flor)* forms on the surface, protecting the wine from the air. Then fortify it with distilled alcohol.

Next comes sherry-making's distinct *solera* process. Pour the young fortified wine into the top barrel of a unique contraption—a stack of oak barrels called a *criadera*. Every year, one-third of the oldest sherry (in the barrels on the ground level) is bottled. To replace it, one-third of the sherry in the barrel above is poured in, and so on. This continues until the top barrel is one-third empty, waiting to be filled with the new year's vintage.

Fino is the most popular type of sherry (and the most different from Americans' expectations)—white, dry, and chilled. The best-selling commercial brand of *fino* is Tío Pepe; *manzanilla* is a regional variation of *fino,* as is *montilla* from Córdoba. Darker-colored and sometimes sweeter varieties of sherry include *amontillado* and *oloroso.* And yes, Spain also produces the thick, sweet cream sherries served as dessert wines. A good raisin-y, syrupy-sweet variety is Pedro Ximénez, made from sun-dried grapes of the same name.

dipping inside the sherry barrel, breaking through the yeast layer, and getting to the good stuff.

Sandeman

Just around the corner from the horse school is the venerable Sandeman winery, founded in 1790 and the longtime choice of English royalty. This tour is the aficionado's choice for its knowledgeable guides and their quality explanations of the process. Each stage is explained in detail, with visual examples of *flor* (the yeast crust) in backlit barrels, graphs of how different blends are made,

and a quick walk-through of the bottling plant. The finale is a chance to taste three varieties. For efficiency, first see the Horse Symphony, which ends at 13:30, then walk to Sandeman's for the next English tour.

Cost and Hours: €7 for regular sherries, up to €21 for rare sherries, €7.50 adds tapas to the tasting, tour/tasting lasts 1-1.5 hours; English tours Mon, Wed, and Fri at 11:30, 12:30, and 13:30 plus April-Oct also at 14:30; Tue and Thu at 10:30, 12:00, 13:00, and 14:00; Sat by appointment only, closed Sun; reservations not required, tel. 665-655-318, mobile 675-647-177, www.sandeman.eu.

González Byass

The makers of the famous Tío Pepe offer a tourist-friendly tour, with more pretense and less actual sherry-making on display (that's done in a new, enormous plant outside town). The tourist train through fake vineyards and a video presentation are forgettable, but the grand circle of sherry casks signed by a *Who's Who* of sherry drinkers is worthwhile. Taste two sherries at the end of the 1.5-hour tour.

Cost and Hours: €12.50, light tapas lunch with tour-€17; tours run Mon-Sat at 12:00, 13:00, 14:00, and 17:00; Sun at 13:00 and 14:00; Manuel María González 12, tel. 956-357-017, www.bodegastiopepe.com.

Other Sherry Bodegas

You'll come across many other sherry bodegas in town, including **Fundador Pedro Domecq,** located near the cathedral. This bodega is the oldest in Jerez, and the birthplace of the city's brandy. Tastings here are generous (€8, April-Oct tours run Mon-Fri hourly between 10:00-13:00 & 17:00-19:00, July-Sept also Mon-Fri at 20:00; €13 tastings with tapas are offered Tue-Wed and Sat at 14:00—call to confirm times, Calle San Ildefonso 3, tel. 956-151-152, www.bodegasfundadorpedrodomecq.com).

Alcázar

This gutted castle looks tempting, but don't bother. The €5 entry fee doesn't even include the Camera Obscura (€7 combo-ticket covers both, Mon-Fri 9:00-18:00—or until 20:00 in mid-July-mid-Sept, Sat-Sun 9:00-15:00). Its underground parking is convenient for those touring González Byass (€1.30/hour).

Jerez Connections

Jerez's bus station is shared by six bus companies, each with its own schedule. The big ones serving most southern Spain destinations are Los Amarillos (tel. 902-210-317, www.losamarillos.es), Comes (tel. 956-291-168, www.tgcomes.es), and Linesur (tel. 956-341-063, www.linesur.com). Shop around for the best departure time and most direct route. While here, clarify routes for any further bus travel you may be doing in Andalucía—especially if you're going through Arcos de la Frontera, where the ticket office is often closed. Also try the privately run www.movelia.es for bus schedules and routes.

From Jerez by Bus to: Tarifa (1/day on Algeciras route, 2 hours, more frequent with transfer in Cádiz, Comes), **Algeciras** (2/day, 2.5 hours, Comes; 6/day, fewer on weekends, 1.5 hours, Linesur), **Arcos** (hourly, 30 minutes), **Ronda** (2/day, 2.5-3 hours), **La Línea/Gibraltar** (1/day, 2.5 hours), **Sevilla** (hourly, 1-1.5 hours), **Granada** (1/day, 4.75 hours).

By Train to: Sevilla (nearly hourly, 1 hour), **Madrid** (3-4/day direct, 3.75 hours; nearly hourly with change in Sevilla, 4 hours), **Barcelona** (nearly hourly, 7-9 hours, all with change in Sevilla and/or Madrid). **Train info:** tel. 902-320-320, www.renfe.com.

Near the Hill Towns

If you're driving between Arcos and Tarifa, here are several sights to explore.

Yeguada de la Cartuja

This breeding farm, which raises Hispanic Arab horses according to traditions dating back to the 15th century, offers shows on Saturday at 11:00 (€21.50 for best seats in *tribuna* section, €15.50 for seats in the stands, Finca Fuente del Suero, Carretera Medina-El Portal, km 6.5, Jerez de la Frontera, tel. 956-162-809, www.yeguadacartuja.com). From Jerez, take the road to Medina Sidonia, then turn right in the direction of El Portal—you'll see a cement factory on your right. Drive for five minutes until you see the farm. A taxi from Jerez will cost about €15 one-way.

Medina Sidonia

This town is as whitewashed as can be, surrounding its church and hill, which is topped with castle ruins. I never drive through here without a coffee break and a quick stroll. Signs to *centro urbano* route you through the middle to Plaza de España (lazy cafés, bakery, plenty of free parking just beyond the square out the gate). If it's lunchtime, consider buying a picnic, as all the necessary shops are nearby and the plaza benches afford a solid workaday view of a perfectly untouristy Andalusian town. According to its own TI, the town is "much appreciated for its vast gastronomy." Small lanes lead from the main square up to Plaza Iglesia Mayor (church and TI open daily 10:30-14:00 & 16:30-18:30, tel. 956-412-404, www.medinasidonia.com). At the church, a man will show you around for a tip. Even without giving a tip, you can climb yet another belfry for yet another vast Andalusian view. The castle ruins just aren't worth the trouble.

Vejer de la Frontera

Vejer, south of Jerez and just 30 miles north of Tarifa, will lure all but the very jaded off the highway. Vejer's strong Moorish roots give it a distinct Moroccan (or Greek Island) flavor—you know, black-clad women whitewashing their homes, and lanes that can't decide if they're roads or stairways. The town has no real sights—other than its women's faces—and very little tourism, making it a pleasant stop. The TI is at Calle de los Remedios 2 (tel. 956-451-736, www.turismovejer.es).

The coast near Vejer has a lonely feel, but its pretty, windswept beaches are popular with windsurfers and sand flies. The Battle of Trafalgar was fought just off Cabo de Trafalgar (a nondescript lighthouse today). I drove the circle so you don't have to.

Sleeping in Vejer: A newcomer on Andalucía's tourist map, the old town of Vejer has just a few hotels.

$$ Hotel Convento San Francisco is a poor man's parador in a refurbished convent with pristine, spacious rooms and elegant public lounges (Sb-€52, Db-€74, breakfast-€3.35, air-con, Wi-Fi in lobby, La Plazuela, tel. 956-451-001, www.tugasa.com, convento-san-francisco@tugasa.com).

$ Hostal La Posada's 10 clean and charming rooms, in a modern apartment flat, are cheap and funky. This family-run place has no reception (S-€20-25, Db-€35-40, higher prices are for mid-July-Aug, Calle de los Remedios 21, tel. 956-450-258, www.hostal-laposada.com, no English spoken).

Route Tips for Drivers

The road-numbering system from the coast into Sevilla was changed a few years back—don't rely on an old driving map.

Sevilla to Arcos (55 miles): The remote hill towns of Andalucía are a joy to tour by car with Michelin map 578 or any other good map. Drivers can zip south on N-IV from Sevilla along the river, following signs to *Cádiz*. Take the fast toll expressway (blue signs, E-5, A-4); the toll-free N-IV is curvy and dangerous. About halfway to Jerez, at Las Cabezas, take CA-403 to Villamartín. From there, circle scenically (and clockwise) through the thick of the Pueblos Blancos—Zahara and Grazalema—to Arcos.

It's about two hours from Sevilla to Zahara. You'll find decent but winding roads and sparse traffic. It gets worse (but very scenic) if you take the tortuous series of switchbacks over the 4,500-foot summit of Puerto de Las Palomas (Pass of the Pigeons, climb to the viewpoint) on the direct but difficult road from Zahara to Grazalema (you'll see several hiking trailheads into Sierra de Grazalema Natural Park, though most require free permits—see sidebar on page 798).

Another scenic option through the park from Grazalema to Arcos is the road that goes up over Puerto del Boyar (Pass of the Boyar), past the pretty little valley town of Benamahoma, and down to El Bosque. The road from Ronda to El Gastor, Setenil (cave houses and great olive oil), and Olvera is another picturesque alternative.

Arcos to Tarifa (80 miles): You can drive from Arcos to Jerez in about 40 minutes. If you're going to Tarifa, take the tiny C-343 road at the Jerez edge of Arcos toward Paterna and Vejer. Later, you'll pick up signs to *Medina Sidonia,* and then to *Vejer* and *Tarifa.*

Costa del Sol to Ronda and Beyond: Drivers coming up from the coast catch A-397 at San Pedro de Alcántara and climb about 20 miles into the mountains. The much longer, winding A-369 offers a scenic alternative that takes you through a series of whitewashed villages.

WHITE HILL TOWNS

COSTA DEL SOL

Nerja • Gibraltar • Tarifa

Spain's south coast—the famous Costa del Sol—is so bad, it's interesting. To northern Europeans, the sun is a drug, and this is their needle. Anything resembling a quaint fishing village has been bikini-strangled and Nivea-creamed. Oblivious to the concrete, pollution, ridiculous prices, and traffic jams, tourists lie on the beach like game hens on skewers—cooking, rolling, and sweating under the sun.

Where Europe's most popular beach isn't crowded by high-rise hotels, most of it's in a freeway choke hold. Wonderfully undeveloped beaches between Tarifa and Cádiz, and east of Almería, are ignored, while human lemmings make the scene where the coastal waters are so polluted that hotels are required to provide swimming pools. It's a fascinating study in human nature. The Costa del Sol has suffered through the recent economic crisis: Real estate, construction, and tourism had powered the economy, and the effects of its decline are still apparent. Crime and racial tension have risen, as many once-busy individuals are now without work.

Particularly in the resorts west of Málaga, most of the foreigners are British—you'll find beans on your breakfast plate and Tom Jones for Muzak. Spanish visitors complain that some restaurants have only English menus, and indeed, the typical expats here actually try *not* to integrate. I've heard locals say of the British, "If they could, they'd take the sun back home with them—but they can't, so they stay here." They enjoy English TV and radio, and many barely learn a word of Spanish. (Special school buses take British children to private English-language schools that connect with Britain's higher-education system.) For

Costa del Sol

☺ DELIGHTFUL
☺ TOLERABLE
☹ AWFUL

an insight into this British community, read the free local expat magazines.

Laugh with Ronald McDonald at the car-jammed resorts. But if you want a place to stay and play in the sun, unroll your

beach towel at Nerja, the most appealing beach-resort town on the coast. And don't forget that you're surprisingly close to jolly olde England: The land of tea and scones, fish-and-chips, pubs and bobbies awaits you—in Gibraltar. Although a British territory, Gibraltar has a unique cultural mix that makes it far more interesting than the anonymous resorts that line the coast. Beyond "The Rock," the whitewashed port of Tarifa—the least-developed piece of Spain's generally overdeveloped southern coast—is a workaday town with a historic center, broad beaches, and good hotels and restaurants. Most importantly, Tarifa is the perfect springboard for a quick trip to Tangier, Morocco (see next two chapters). These three places alone—Nerja, Gibraltar, and Tarifa—make the Costa del Sol worth a trip.

Planning Your Time

My negative opinions on the "Costa del Turismo" are valid for peak season (mid-July–mid-Sept). If you're there during a quieter time and you like the ambience of a beach resort, it can be a pleasant stop. Off-season it can be neutron-bomb quiet.

The whole 150 miles of coastline takes six hours by bus or three hours to drive with no traffic jams. You can resort-hop by bus across the entire Costa del Sol and reach Nerja for dinner. If you want to party on the beach, it can take as much time as Mazatlán.

To day-trip to Tangier, Morocco, head for Tarifa.

Nerja

While cashing in on the fun-in-the-sun culture, Nerja has actually kept much of its quiet Old World charm. It has good beaches, a fun evening paseo (strolling scene) that culminates in the proud Balcony of Europe terrace, enough pastry shops and nightlife, and locals who get more excited about their many festivals than the tourists do.

Although Nerja's population swells from about 22,000 in winter to about 90,000 in the summer, it's more of a year-round destination and a real town than many other resorts. Thanks to cheap airfares and the completion of the expressway, real estate boomed here in the last decade (property values doubled in six years). The bubble collapsed to some extent with the recent financial crisis, but Nerja has remained hardier than other parts of the Costa del Sol. New restaurants and hotels open here all the time.

Nerja is more diverse than many of the rival resorts—in addition to British accents, you'll overhear French, German, Dutch, and Scandinavian languages being spoken on the beaches. There's also a long tradition of Spanish people retiring and vacationing here. Pensioners from northern Spain move here—enjoying long life spans, thanks in part to the low blood pressure that comes from a diet of fish and wine. While they could afford to travel elsewhere, an inertia remains from Franco's day, when people generally vacationed within the country. In summer, to escape the brutal heat of inland Spain, many Spanish moms take the kids to condos on the south coast while dads stay home to work. This is a time when husbands get to "be Rodriguez" (*estar de Rodríguez*), an idiom whose meaning ranges from "temporary bachelor" to "when the cat's away, the mouse will play."

Orientation to Nerja

The tourist center of Nerja is right along the water and crowds close to its famous bluff, the "Balcony of Europe" (Balcón de Europa). Fine strings of beaches flank the bluff, stretching in either direction. The old town is just inland from the Balcony, while the more modern section slopes up and away from the water.

Tourist Information

The helpful English-speaking TI has bus schedules, tips on beaches and side-trips, and brochures for nearby destinations, such as the Caves of Nerja, Frigiliana, Málaga, and Ronda (July-Aug Mon-Sat 10:00-14:00 & 18:00-22:00, Sun 18:00-22:00; April-June and Sept-Oct Mon-Sat 10:00-14:00 & 17:00-21:00, Sun 10:00-14:00; Nov-March daily 10:00-14:00; 100 yards from the Balcony of Europe and half a block inland from the big church, tel. 952-521-531, www.nerja.org). Ask for a free city map and the *Leisure Guide*, which has a comprehensive listing of activities. Their *Hiking the Sierra of Nerja and Cliffs of Maro* booklet describes good local walks.

Arrival in Nerja

By Bus: The Nerja bus station is actually just a bus stop with an info kiosk on Avenida de Pescia (Mon-Tue and Fri 6:00-20:15, Wed-Thu and Sat-Sun 7:00-12:00 & 14:45-19:15, schedules posted, Alsa tel. 902-422-242, www.alsa.es). To travel from Nerja, buy tickets at the kiosk—don't assume they're available on the bus. Because many buses leave at the same times, arrive at least 15 minutes before departure to avoid having to elbow other tourists.

By Car: For the most central parking, follow *Balcón de Europa* signs, and then pull into the big underground parking lot beneath the Plaza de España (which deposits you 200 yards from the Balcony of Europe; €2.10/hour, €22.25/24 hours). The enormous Parking Carabeo, just east of the Balcony, is slightly cheaper (€1.80/hour, €18/24 hours). The handiest free parking is about a 10-minute walk farther out, next to the bridge over the dry riverbed (near the town bus stop, just off N-340). Street parking in Nerja is free and unlimited, but it's very tight. If you do find a space, avoid parking next to yellow lines, and read signs carefully—on certain days of the month you're required to move your car.

Helpful Hints

Internet Access: Nerja's scenically situated Internet café, **Europ@ Web,** is on a square overlooking Playa la Torrecilla, where Calle de Castilla Pérez meets Calle Málaga (€2.50/30 minutes, daily 10:00-21:00, until 24:00 in summer, tel. 952-526-147).

COSTA DEL SOL

Nerja

COSTA DEL SOL

To Nerja Caves, Cantarriján Beach & Granada

Carabeo **P**

Carabeo Beach

To Burriana Beach, Cantarriján Beach & ⑲

Sea

1. Hotel Balcón de Europa
2. Hotel Plaza Cavana
3. Hotel Carabeo & Restaurant 34
4. Hostal Marissal & Cochran's Terrace
5. Hostal Don Peque
6. Hostal Miguel
7. Pensión Mena
8. Hostal Lorca
9. Papagayo Beach Rest.
10. Nerja Museum
11. Pepe Rico & El Pulguilla Restaurante
12. Pinocchio Restaurante
13. Haveli Restaurante
14. Coach & Horses Pub
15. El Chispa/Bar Dolores
16. La Puntilla Bar Restaurante
17. Los Cuñaos
18. La Taberna de Pepe
19. To Ayo's Café
20. Bar El Molino
21. El Burro Blanco
22. Bodega Los Bilbainos
23. Black & White Bar
24. El Valenciano Helados Ice Cream
25. Mercadona Supermarket
26. Launderette
27. To Internet Café

* NOT TO SCALE -
BUS INFO KIOSK TO
BALCONY OF EUROPE
IS A 10 MIN. WALK

B BUS STOP
◀ VIEW
P PARKING

COSTA DEL SOL

Laundry: Bubbles Burbujas is a full-service launderette run by friendly Jo from England (€6/small load, same-day service if you drop off in the morning, no self-service, Mon-Fri 9:00-17:00, Sat 9:00-13:00, closed Sun; a few blocks north of Plaza de Cavana at Calle Manuel Marín 1, just off Calle Granada—look for Pasaje Granada pedestrian passage on left, just past the Irish-Nordic Properties building, tel. 665-539-256).

British Media: For a taste of the British expat scene, pick up the monthly magazines *Street Wise* or *Soltalk,* or tune in to Coastline Radio at 97.6 FM.

Local Guide: Carmen Fernandez is good, with knowledge of the entire region (€125/5-hour day, mobile 610-038-437, mfeyus @yahoo.es).

Massage: Tiny yet muscular Marie, who moved here from France, runs a massage parlor out of her apartment. She does an excellent one-hour massage for €40 (€10 more on weekends)—just give her a call (**Amarilys Masaje,** Calle de Castilla Perez 10, mobile 667-825-828).

Getting Around Nerja

You can easily **walk** anywhere you need to go.

Nerja's **taxis** are pricey—the in-town minimum is €6-7, even for a short trip. They don't use meters—instead, most journeys have a set fee (e.g., €7 to Burriana Beach, €12 to Frigiliana, tel. 952-524-519 or 952-520-537).

To clip-clop in a **horse-drawn buggy** through town, it's €35 for about 25 minutes (you'll usually find these at the Plaza de los Cangrejos above Playa la Torrecilla).

Sights in Nerja

▲▲Balcony of Europe (Balcón de Europa)

The bluff, jutting happily into the sea, is completely pedestrianized. It's the center of Nerja's paseo and a magnet for street performers.

The mimes, music, and puppets can draw bigger crowds than the Balcony itself, which overlooks the Mediterranean, miles of coastline, and little coves and caves below. A castle, and later a fort, occupied this spot from the ninth century until the earthquake of 1884. Now it's a people-friendly view terrace.

Built in the early 1800s to defend against Napoleon, the English-Spanish fort here protected the harbor with the help of seven cannons. When the 1884 earthquake destroyed the castle

Costa del Sol History

Many Costa del Sol towns come in pairs: the famous beach town with little history, and its smaller yet much more historic partner established a few miles inland—safely out of reach of the Barbary pirate raids that plagued this coastline for centuries. Nerja is a good example of this pattern. Whereas it has almost no history and was just an insignificant fishing village until tourism hit, its more historic sister, Frigiliana, hides out in the nearby hills. The Barbary pirate raids were a constant threat. In fact, the Spanish slang for "the coast is clear" is *"no hay moros en la costa"* (there are no Moors on the coast).

Nerja was overlooked by the tourism scene until about 1980, when the phenomenal Spanish TV show *Verano Azul (Blue Summer)* was set here. This post-Franco program featured the until-then off-limits topics of sexual intimacy, marital problems, adolescence, and so on in a beach-town scene (imagine combining *All in the Family*, *Baywatch*, and *The Hills*). To this day, when Spaniards hear the word "Nerja," they think of this TV hit.

Despite the fame, development didn't really hit until about 2000, when the expressway finally and conveniently connected Nerja with the rest of Spain. Thankfully, a building code prohibits any new buildings higher than three stories in the old town.

and fort, it sent the cannons into the sea. A century later, two were salvaged, cleaned up, and placed here. Study the beautifully aged metal work.

The cute statue of King Alfonso XII reminds locals of how this popular sovereign—the great-grandfather of today's King Juan Carlos—came here after the devastating earthquake (a huge number of locals had died). He mobilized the local rich to dig out the community and put things back together. Standing on this promontory amid the ruins of the earthquake-devastated castle, he marveled at the view and coined its now-famous name, Balcón de Europa.

The Nerja castle was part of a 16th-century lookout system. After the Christian Reconquista in 1492 drove Muslim Moors into exile, pirate action from Muslim countries in North Africa picked up. Lookout towers were stationed within sight of one another all along the coast. Warnings were sent whenever pirates threatened (smoke by day, flames by night). Look to the east—you can see three towers crowning bluffs in the distance.

Also to the east you can just see the tip of Burriana Beach. Spaniards love their *chiringuitos,* as local beach restaurants are called. The *chiringuito* immediately below you, Papagayo, is understandably popular.

Scan the horizon. Until recently this was a favored landing spot (just beyond the tighter security zone near Gibraltar) for illegal immigrants and drug runners coming in from Africa. Many Moroccan teens try to sneak into Europe here, as local laws prohibit turning away undocumented children (the police use DNA tests to determine the age of recent arrivals—if they're under 18, they stay). Laws also grant automatic EU citizenship to anyone born in Europe, so many pregnant women try to slip in (once the baby's born, the mother's legal, too). However, illegal immigration is down: With the help of a new high-tech satellite-scanning system, the Guardia Civil can now detect floating objects as small as makeshift rafts and intercept them before they reach land.

Walk beneath the Balcony for views of the scant remains (bricks and stones) of the ninth-century Moorish castle. Locals claim an underground passage connected the Moorish fortress with the mosque that stood where the Church of San Salvador stands today.

Church of San Salvador
Just a block inland from the Balcony, this church was likely built upon the ruins of a mosque (c. 1600). Its wooden ceiling is Mudejar—made by Moorish artisans working in Christian times. The woodworking technique is similar to that featured in the Alhambra in Granada. The modern fresco of the *Annunciation* (in the rear of the nave) is by Paco Hernandez, the top local artist of this generation. In front, on the right, is a niche featuring Jesus with San Isidoro (as a little boy). Isidoro is the patron saint of Madrid, Nerja, and farmers (sugarcane farming was the leading industry here before tourism hit). From the porch of the church, look inland to see City Hall, marked by four flags (Andalucía's is green for olive trees and white for the color of the houses in this part of Spain).

Nerja Museum (Museo de Nerja)
This mildly interesting and slightly disjointed museum is a good option on a rainy day or if you've just had too much sun. It's run in association with the Nerja Caves (see page 822), with exhibits focusing on the history of Nerja and the surrounding region, from prehistoric to modern times. Each of its four floors contains interactive exhibits and displays, including prehistoric tools, weapons, and a skeleton found within the Nerja Caves.

Cost and Hours: €4, €2 if also getting Nerja Caves ticket;

July-Aug Tue-Sun 10:00-14:00 & 18:00-22:00, Sept-June Tue-Sun 10:00-14:00 & 16:00-18:30, closed Mon year-round; Plaza de España 4, tel. 952-527-224, www.cuevadenerja.es.

Town Strolls

Nerja was essentially destroyed after the 1884 earthquake—and at the time there was little more here beyond the castle anyway—so there's not much to see in the town itself. However, a few of its main streets are worth a quick look. From the Balcony of Europe head inland. Consider first grabbing some ice cream at El Valenciano Helados, a local favorite run by a Valencia family. Try the refreshing *chufa*-nut Valencian specialty called *horchata*.

A block farther inland, the old town's three main streets come together. The oldest street, Calle Carabeo, heads off to your right (notice how buildings around here are wired on the outside). On the left, Calle Pintada heads inland. Its name means "the painted street," as it was spiffed up in 1885 for the king's visit. Today it's the town's best shopping street. And between those streets runs Calle Almirante Ferrándiz, Nerja's restaurant row, which is particularly lively in the evenings.

Beaches

The single best thing to do on a sunny day in Nerja is to hit the beach: swim, sunbathe, sip a drink, go for a hearty hike along the rocky coves...or all of the above.

Nerja's many beaches are well-equipped, with bars and restaurants, free showers, and rentable lounge chairs and umbrellas (about €4/person for chair and umbrella, same cost for 10 minutes or all day). Nearby restaurants rent umbrellas, and you're welcome to take drinks and snacks out to your spot. Spanish law requires that all beaches are open to the public (except the one in Rota, which is reserved for American soldiers). While there are some nudist beaches (such as Cantarriján, described on page 821), keep in mind that in Europe, any beach can be topless. During the summer, Spanish sun worshippers pack the beach from about 11:00 until around 13:30, when they move into the beach restaurants for relief from the brutal rays. Watch out for red flags on the beach, which indicate when the seas are too rough for safe swimming (blue = safe, orange = caution, red = swimming prohibited). Don't take valuables to the beach, as thieves have fast fingers.

Beaches lie east and west of the Balcony of Europe. For each area, I've listed beaches from nearest to farthest. Even if you're not swimming or sunbathing, walking along these beaches (and the trails that connect them, if open) is a delightful pastime.

East of the Balcony of Europe

Coastal Promenade (Paseo de los Carabineros)

One of Nerja's most appealing draws has been the walkway called the Paseo de los Carabineros, which scampers up and down cliffs, just above the pebbles and sand, to connect the enticing beaches east of the Balcony. Unfortunately, due to erosion concerns and a lack of funds (and municipal motivation), the path has been closed for the past few years. For now, only the first little bit, to Calahonda Beach (described next), is completely open. To reach the other beaches east of the Balcony of Europe, you'll have to walk through the modern town above the beaches...less fun.

To discourage people from using the Paseo de los Carabineros, city officials have erected concrete barriers in a few places along the walkway, removed guardrails (so in some cases you're walking precariously along the cliffs), and allowed the path to become overgrown with plants. While it's possible to follow this pathway at your own risk, it's quite treacherous—in a couple of places you have to actually scale a wall. (Because the path closure is well-advertised at both ends, you're completely liable if anything happens.) Gung-ho travelers still make this walk (I did...carefully), and in summer and at low tide, you can likely walk along the sand and pebbles around the giant rocks (slow going)—but it's not recommended if a pleasant stroll is what you want. The good news is that plans are afoot to restore and reopen the Paseo de los Carabineros. Ask locally, but don't be disappointed if this often-delayed project fails to materialize.

Calahonda Beach (Playa Calahonda)

Directly beneath the Balcony of Europe (to the left as you face the sea) is one of Nerja's most characteristic little patches of sun. This pebbly beach is full of fun pathways, crags, and crannies, and its humble Papagayo restaurant—one of my recommended eateries—is open all day. Antonio can be seen each morning working with his nets and sorting through his fish. His little pre-tourism beach hut—a stuccoed-and-whitewashed marshmallow bulge with blue trim burrowed into the cliff—is wonderfully photogenic. To get here from the Balcony, simply head down through the arch across from the El Valenciano Helados ice-cream stand...you'll be on the beach in seconds.

Carabeo Beach (Playa Carabeo)

Less developed than the others listed here, Carabeo is wedged into a cove between the bustling Calahonda and Burriana beaches. For many, its lack of big restaurants is a plus. If the Paseo de los Carabineros is closed, you can reach the beach by walking along

Calle Carabeo and taking the stairs down from the viewpoint at the park.

Burriana Beach (Playa de Burriana)

Nerja's leading beach is a 20-minute walk east from the Balcony of Europe. Big, bustling, crowded, and fun, it's understandably a top attraction. Burriana is fun for families, with paddleboats, play-grounds, volleyball courts, and other entertainment options. The beach is also lined with a wide range of cafés and restaurants—but the best is the recommended Ayo's, whose paella feast is a destination in itself (see listing on page 829).

Getting There: Assuming the Paseo de los Carabineros is closed, walk along Calle Carabeo. You'll pass the viewpoint park with the stairs leading down to Carabeo Beach; keep going until you're forced to jog left (up Cómpeta) into a dull modern part of town. You'll see the boxy parador on your right; circle around behind it, following the low-profile signs for *Playa Burriana* (near the parador entrance) to the right. Curl around to the right, then twist down the switchback road to the beach. Or take a taxi for €7.

Cantarriján Beach (Playa del Cantarriján)

The only beach listed here not within easy walking distance of Nerja, this is the place if you're craving a more desolate beach (and have a car). Drive about 4.5 miles (15 minutes) east (toward Herradura) to the Cerro Gordo exit, and follow *Playa Cantarriján* signs (paved road, just before the tunnel). Park at the viewpoint and hike 30 minutes down to the beach (or, in mid-June-Sept, ride the shuttle bus down). Down below, rocks and two restaurants separate two pristine beaches—one for people with bathing suits (or not); the other, more secluded, more strictly for nudists. As this beach is in a natural park and requires a long hike, it provides a fine—and rare—chance to experience the Costa del Sol in some isolation.

West of the Balcony of Europe

Unlike the walkways east of the Balcony, the promenades to the west are open for business—making this a delightful place to stroll.

Del Salón Beach (Playa del Salón)

The sandiest (and most crowded) beach in Nerja is down the walkway to the right of Cafetería Marissal, just west of the Balcony of Europe (to the right as you look out to sea). For great drinks with a view, stop by the recommended Cochran's Terrace on the way down. Continuing farther west, you'll reach another sandy beach, **Playa la Torrecilla,** at the end of Calle Málaga.

El Playazo ("Big Beach")

A short hike on a promenade west of Playa la Torrecilla, this beach is preferred by locals, as it's less developed than the more central ones, offering a couple of miles of wide-open spaces that allow for fine walks and a chance to "breathe in the beach."

Sights near Nerja

▲Nerja Caves (Cuevas de Nerja)

These caves (2.5 miles east of Nerja, exit 295), with an impressive array of stalactites and stalagmites, are a classic roadside attraction. The huge caverns, filled with backlit formations, are a big hit with cruise-ship groups and Spanish families. The visit involves a 30-minute unguided ramble deep into the mountain, up and down 400 dark stairs. At the end you reach the Hall of the Cataclysm, where you'll circle the world's largest stalactite column (certified by *Guinness Book of World Records*). Someone figured out that it took one trillion drops to make the column.

The free exhibit in the Centro de Interpretación explains the cave's history and geology (in house next to bus parking; exhibit in Spanish, but includes free English brochure).

Cost and Hours: €8.50, €6.50 if also getting Nerja Museum ticket, daily 10:00-14:00 & 16:00-18:30, July-Aug until 19:30, easy parking-€1/day, tel. 952-529-520, www.cuevadenerja.es.

Concerts: During the festival held here the third week of July, the caves provide a cool venue for hot flamenco and classical concerts (tickets sold out long in advance).

Services: The restaurant offers a view and three-course fixed-price meals for €10, and the picnic spot (behind the ticket office) offers pine trees, benches, and a kids' play area.

Getting There: To reach the caves, catch a bus across the street from Nerja's main bus stop (€1.05, 13/day, 10 minutes) or a taxi (€8 one-way).

Frigiliana

The picturesque whitewashed village of Frigiliana (free-*h*ee-lee-AH-nah), only four miles inland from Nerja, is easily reached by bus (€1, 9/day, none on Sun, 15 minutes) or taxi (€12 one-way). While it doesn't match up to the striking white hill towns listed in the preceding chapter, its proximity to Nerja makes it an enticing side-trip if this is the nearest you'll get to hill towns on your trip.

The bus stop is in the middle of town, on Plaza del Ingenio. This is also the point that separates the new town from the old town (the steep old Moorish quarter climbing the hill up ahead). The **TI** is a 100-yard walk uphill, in the new town (Mon-Fri 10:00-

17:30, Sat-Sun 10:00-14:00 & 16:00-20:00, tel. 952-534-261, www
.frigiliana.es). Pick up a map and the translations of the tile you'll
see displayed around town. The TI shares a building with the
archaeological museum, with artifacts unearthed near Frigiliana;
their prized piece is the fifth-century B.C. skull of a 10-year-old
child (free, same hours as TI).

Focus your visit on the old town. Begin by climbing up to the
terrace in front of the factory *(ingenio)*—
the blocky, un-whitewashed, double-
smokestack building that dominates the
town. Dating from the 16th century, this
still produces sugarcane honey. From
the end of the terrace, hike up the steep
street, bearing right at the fork up Calle
Hernando el Darra. At #10 (on the
right), notice the tile in the wall—the
first in a series of a dozen around town
that describe, in poetic Spanish, the
story of the 1568 Battle of Peñón. At the
next fork, bear right (uphill) on Calle
Amargura and walk steeply uphill, enjoying the flowerpot-lined
lane. Notice the distinctive traditional door-knockers, shaped like
a woman's hand. More common in Morocco, these are the "hand
of Fatima"—the daughter of the Prophet Muhammad—and are
intended to ward off evil.

After turning the corner, take the left/downhill road at the
next fork, than head right up Calle Sta. Teresa de Ávila. Then head
left down the steep, stepped Calle del Garral. You'll pop out just
below the main church. Before going there, detour a few steps to
the right, then head left to Plaza de la Fuente Vieja—home of a
17th-century fountain that's one of the town's trademarks. Then
head back up the way you came to find your way to the inviting
café-lined plaza in front of the Church of San Antonio of Padua
(with a stark interior). From here, you can follow the main drag
back to where you entered town, or enjoy exploring Frigiliana's
back lanes.

Hiking

Europeans visiting the region for a longer stay generally use Nerja
as a base from which to hike. The TI can describe a variety of
hikes. One of the most popular is a refreshing two-to-three-hour
walk up a river (at first through a dry riverbed, and later up to your
shins in water; 7.5 miles one-way). Another, more demanding
hike takes you to the 5,000-foot summit of El Cielo for the most
memorable king-of-the-mountain feeling this region offers.

Nightlife in Nerja

Bar El Molino offers live Spanish folk singing nightly in a rustic cavern that's actually an old mill—the musicians perform where the mules once tread. It's touristy but fun (starts at 22:00 but pretty dead before 23:00, no cover—just buy a drink, Calle San José 4). The local sweet white wine, *vino del terreno*—made up the hill in Frigiliana—is popular here (€3/glass).

El Burro Blanco is a touristy flamenco bar that's enjoyable and intimate, with shows nightly from 22:30. Keeping expectations pretty low, they advertise "The Best One in Nerja" (no cover—just buy a drink, live music Fri-Sat after flamenco, fewer shows off-season, on corner of Calle Pintada and Calle de la Gloria).

Bodega Los Bilbainos is a classic dreary old dive—a favorite with local men and communists (tapas and drinks, Calle Alejandro Bueno 8).

For more trendy and noisy nightlife, check out the **Black and White Bar,** with karaoke nightly, on Pintada (near El Burro Blanco at Calle Pintada 35) and the bars and dance clubs on Antonio Millón and Plaza Tutti Frutti.

Sleeping in Nerja

The entire Costa del Sol is crowded during August and Holy Week (the week leading up to Easter), when prices are at their highest. Reserve in advance for peak season—basically mid-July through mid-September—which is prime time for Spanish workers to hit the beaches. Any other time of year, you'll find that Nerja has plenty of comfy, easygoing low-rise resort-type hotels and rooms. Room rates are generally three-tiered: low season (Nov-March), middle season (April-June and Oct), and high season (July-Sept).

Compared to the pricier hotels, the better *hostales* are an excellent value. Hostal Don Peque, Hostal Miguel, and Pensión Mena are all within a few blocks of the Balcony of Europe.

Breakfast: Some hotels here overcharge for breakfast. Don't hesitate to go elsewhere, as many places serve breakfast for more reasonable prices. For a cheap breakfast with a front-row view of the promenade action on the Balcony of Europe, head to **Cafetería Marissal** (in the recommended *hostal* of the same name) and grab a wicker seat under the palm trees (€4.50-5.50 options include English breakfasts, daily from 9:00). The recommended **Papagayo** serves breakfast on the beach, just below the Balcony of Europe, to those who don't mind a little sand in their coffee (from 10:00). If you're up for a short hike before breakfast, consider the recommended **Ayo's** on Burriana Beach (daily from 9:00).

Sleep Code

(€1 = about $1.30, country code: 34)
S = Single, **D** = Double/Twin, **T** = Triple, **Q** = Quad, **b** = bathroom, **s** = shower only. Unless otherwise noted, credit cards are accepted and English is spoken, but breakfast is not included. Some hotels include the 10 percent IVA tax in the room price; others tack it onto your bill.

To help you easily sort through these listings, I've divided the accommodations into three categories based on the price for a standard double room with bath during high season:

$$$ Higher Priced—Most rooms €100 or more.
 $$ Moderately Priced—Most rooms between €60-100.
  $ Lower Priced—Most rooms €60 or less.

Prices can change without notice; verify the hotel's current rates online or by email. For the best prices, always book direct.

Close to the Balcony of Europe

$$$ Hotel Balcón de Europa is the most central place in town. It's right on the water and the square, with the prestigious address Balcón de Europa 1. It has 110 rooms with modern style, plus all the comforts—including a pool and an elevator down to the beach. It's popular with groups. All the suites have seaview balconies, and most regular rooms also come with views (Sb-€84/96/125, standard Db-€115/135/165, about €30 extra for sea view and balcony, breakfast-€13.50, air-con, elevator, Wi-Fi, parking-€12/day, tel. 952-520-800, www.hotelbalconeuropa.com, reservas@hotelbalconeuropa.com).

$$$ Hotel Plaza Cavana, with 39 rooms, overlooks a plaza lily-padded with cafés. It feels a bit institutional, but if you'd like a central location, marble floors, modern furnishings, an elevator, and a small unheated rooftop swimming pool, dive in (Sb-€35-100, Db-€50-125, bigger superior Db-€10 more, Tb-20 percent more, Qb-30 percent more; 10 percent discount for Rick Steves readers for 1-to-2-night stays, 15 percent for stays of 3 nights or more, and free breakfast for those booking direct with this guidebook in 2014; some view rooms, air-con, elevator, pay guest computer, free Wi-Fi in lobby, second small unheated pool in basement, parking-€10-15/day, 2 blocks from Balcony of Europe at Plaza de Cavana 10, tel. 952-524-000, www.hotelplazacavana.es, info@hotelplazacavana.com).

$$$ Hotel Carabeo, a boutique-hotel splurge, has seven classy rooms on the cliff east of downtown—less than a 10-minute walk away, but removed from the bustle of the Balcony of Europe (non-view Db-€85-100; seaview Db-€160-205, price range depends on type of room, air-con, free Wi-Fi in lobby, Calle Carabeo 34, tel. 952-525-444, www.hotelcarabeo.com, info@hotelcarabeo .com). This is also home to the recommended Restaurant 34.

$$ Hostal Marissal has an unbeatable location next door to the fancy Balcón de Europa hotel, and 23 modern, spacious rooms with old-fashioned furniture and clever gadgets on the doors to prevent them from slamming. Some rooms have small view balconies overlooking the Balcony of Europe action. Their cafeteria and bar, run by helpful staff, make the Marissal even more welcoming (Sb-€30/35/45, Db-€40/50-60/60-70, apartment for up to 4 people-€80-160, breakfast-€4.50-5.50, double-paned windows, air-con, elevator, Wi-Fi, Balcón de Europa 3, reception at Marissal café, tel. 952-520-199, www.hostalmarissal.com, reservas @hostalmarissal.com).

$$ Hostal Don Peque sits in a dull urban zone an easy couple of blocks' walk from the Balcony of Europe—but it compensates with 10 bright, colorful, and cheery rooms (8 with balconies—a few with sea views). Owners Roberto and Clara moved here from France and have infused the place with their personality. They rent beach equipment at reasonable prices, but their bar-terrace with rooftops-and-sea views may be more enticing (Sb-€35/55/75, Db-€40/65/85, Tb-€55/75/100, bunk-bed family room for up to 4-€15 more than Tb, breakfast-€6, air-con, thin walls, Wi-Fi, Diputación 13, tel. 952-521-318, www.hostaldonpeque.com, info @hostaldonpeque.com).

$ Hostal Miguel offers nine sunny and airy rooms in the heart of "Restaurant Row" (some street noise in front rooms). Breakfast is served on the pretty green terrace with mountain views. The owners—British expats Ian, Jane, and Hannah— are long-time Nerja devotees (Sb-€30-38, Db-€40-58, book direct for these prices, 4 percent more if paying with credit card, breakfast-€5, family suite, no air-con but fans and fridges, Wi-Fi in most rooms, laundry service-€5, beach equipment available on request, Almirante Ferrándiz 31, tel. 952-521-523, mobile 696-799-218, www.hostalmiguel.com, hostalmiguel@gmail.com).

$ Pensión Mena rents 11 nice rooms—four with seaview terraces (€7 extra and worth it)—and offers a quiet, breezy garden (Sb-€20-30, Db-€29-45, no breakfast, some street noise, Wi-Fi in lobby, El Barrio 15, tel. 952-520-541, www.hostalmena.es, info @hostalmena.es, María). The reception has limited hours (daily 9:30-13:30 & 17:00-20:30); if they're closed when you arrive to check in, report to their sister hotel, Hotel Mena Plaza, a few blocks away at Plaza de España 2.

In a Residential Neighborhood

$ Hostal Lorca is located in a quiet residential area a five-minute walk from the center, three blocks from the bus stop, and close to a small, handy grocery store. Run by a friendly young Dutch couple, Femma and Rick, this *hostal* has nine modern, comfortable rooms and an inviting compact backyard with a terrace, a palm tree, and a small pool. You can use the microwave and take drinks (on the honor system) from the well-stocked fridge. This quiet, homey place is a winner (Sb-€25-34, Db-€29-55, extra bed-€12, no air-con but fans, Wi-Fi, look for yellow house at Mendez Nuñez 20, tel. 952-523-426, www.hostallorca.com, info@hostallorca.com).

Eating in Nerja

There are three Nerjas: the private domain of the giant beachside hotels; the central zone, packed with fun-loving (and often tipsy) expats and tourists eating and drinking from trilingual menus; and the back streets, where local life goes on as if there were no tourists. The whole old town (around the Balcony of Europe) is busy with lively restaurants. Wander around and see who's eating best.

To pick up picnic supplies, head to the **Mercadona** supermarket (Mon-Sat 9:15-21:15, closed Sun, inland from Plaza Ermita on Calle San Miguel).

Near the Balcony of Europe

Papagayo, a classic *chiringuito* (beach restaurant), lounges in the sand a few steps below the Balcony of Europe. You may be paying for the location, but it's quite a location. They serve drinks and snacks to those enjoying their beach umbrellas (€2-8 breakfasts, €4-12 snacks and meals, open with demand, daily breakfast from 10:00, lunch 12:00-17:00, tel. 952-523-816, "moon beach parties" on summer evenings).

Cochran's Terrace serves mediocre meals in a wonderful seaview setting, overlooking Del Salón Beach (€7-12 main dishes, open daily all day for drinks, 12:00-15:00 & 19:00-23:00 for meals, shorter hours off-season, just behind Hostal Marissal).

Restaurant 34, in Hotel Carabeo, manages white-tablecloth elegance in a relaxed atmosphere that successfully mixes eclectic antiques with modern accents. More tables sprawl outside, along the swimming pool and toward sweeping sea views (call ahead to reserve a seaview table). They offer inexpensive *raciones*—and a free tapa if you buy a drink in the bar. The staff is friendly, and the cuisine features seasonal local produce (€9-15 starters, €17-24 main dishes, €25 three-course fixed-price meal, Tue-Sun 12:30-15:30 & 19:00-late, closed Mon, Calle Carabeo 34, tel. 952-525-444).

COSTA DEL SOL

Along Restaurant Row

Strolling up Calle Almirante Ferrándiz (which changes its name farther uphill to "Cristo"), you'll find a good variety of eateries, albeit filled with tourists. On the upside, the presence of expats means you'll find places serving food earlier in the evening than the Spanish norm.

Pepe Rico is the most romantic (in a schlocky adult-contemporary way) along this street, with a big terrace and a cozy dining room (€6-12 starters, €16-22 main dishes, €28 four-course meals, Mon-Sat 12:30-15:00 & 19:00-23:00, closed Sun, Calle Almirante Ferrándiz 28, tel. 952-520-247).

Pinocchio is the local family-friendly favorite for Italian (€7-9 pizzas and pastas, €12-18 fish and meat plates, daily 12:00-late, Calle Almirante Ferrándiz 51, tel. 952-527-248).

Haveli, run by Amit and his Swedish wife, Eva, serves good Indian food in an informal atmosphere. For more than two decades, it's been a hit with Brits, who know their Indian food (€10-18 plates, daily 19:00-24:00 in summer, closed Mon off-season, Calle Almirante Ferrándiz 42, tel. 952-524-297).

Coach and Horses is a British pub run by no-nonsense expat Catherine. Although she serves the only real Irish steaks in town, she also caters to vegetarians, with daily specials that go beyond the usual omelet (€7-17 meals, daily 10:30-15:00 & 18:30-late, closed Mon off-season, Calle Almirante Ferrándiz 19, tel. 952-520-071).

El Pulguilla is a great, high-energy place for Spanish cuisine, fish, and tapas. Its two distinct zones (tapas bar up front and more formal restaurant out back) are both jammed with enthusiastic locals and tourists. The lively no-nonsense stainless-steel tapas bar doubles as a local pick-up joint later in the evening. Drinks come with a free small plate of clams, mussels, shrimp, chorizo sausage, or seafood salad. For a sit-down meal, head back to the gigantic terrace. Though not listed on the menu, half-portions *(media-raciones)* are available for many items, allowing you to easily sample different dishes (€10-16 dinners, Tue-Sun 12:30-16:00 & 18:30-23:30, closed Mon, Calle Almirante Ferrándiz 26, tel. 952-521-384).

Tapas Bars near Herrera Oria

A 10-minute gently uphill hike from the water takes you into the residential thick of things, where the sea views come thumbtacked to the walls, prices are lower, and locals fill the tables. The first three are tapas bars within a few blocks of one another. Each is a colorful local hangout with different energy levels on different nights. Survey all three before choosing one, or have a drink and tapa at each. These places are generally open all day for tapas and drinks, and serve table-service meals during normal dining hours. If you prefer a restaurant setting to a bar, try the last listing, La Taberna de Pepe.

Remember that in Nerja, tapas are snack-size portions, generally not for sale but free with each drink. To turn them into more of a meal, ask for the menu and order a full-size *ración,* or half-size *media-ración.* The half-portions are generally bigger than you'd expect.

El Chispa (a.k.a. Bar Dolores) is big on seafood, which locals enjoy on an informal terrace. Their *tomate ajo* (garlic tomato) is tasty, and their piping-hot *berenjena* (fried and salted eggplant) is worth considering—try it topped with molasses-like sugarcane syrup. They serve huge portions—*media-raciones* are enough for two (€5-12 *raciones,* daily, San Pedro 12, tel. 952-523-697).

La Puntilla Bar Restaurante is a boisterous little place, with rickety plastic furniture spilling out onto the cobbles on hot summer nights (generous €4-6 splittable salads, €3-6 half-*raciones,* €5-13 *raciones,* show this book and get a free *digestivo,* daily 12:00-24:00, a block in front of Los Cuñaos at Calle Bolivia 1, tel. 952-528-951).

Los Cuñaos hangs the banners of the entire soccer league on the walls. Local women hang out to chat, and kids wander around like it's home. Although it has the least interesting menu, it has the most interesting business card (€6.50 meals, €16-17 two-person meals, €8 and €12 tapas plates come with a bottle of wine, closed Mon, Herrera Oria 19, tel. 678-663-997).

La Taberna de Pepe is more of a sit-down restaurant, though it does have a small bar with tapas. The tight, cozy (almost cluttered) eight-table interior is decorated with old farm tools and crammed with happy eaters choosing from a short menu of well-executed seafood. It feels classier than the rough-and-tumble tapas bars listed above, but isn't pretentious (€6-15 dishes, Fri-Wed 12:15-16:00 & 19:00-24:00, closed Thu, Herrera Oria 30, tel. 952-522-195).

Paella Feast on Burriana Beach

Ayo's is famous for its character of an owner and its €6.50 beachside all-you-can-eat paella feast at lunchtime. For 30 years, Ayo—a lovable ponytailed bohemian who promises to be here until he dies—has been feeding locals. Ayo is a very big personality—one of the five kids who discovered the Nerja Caves, formerly a well-known athlete, and now someone who makes it a point to hire hard-to-employ people as a community service. The paella fires get stoked up at about noon and continue through mid-afternoon. Grab one of a hundred tables under the canopy next to the rustic open-fire cooking zone, and enjoy the beach setting in the shade with a jug of sangria. For €6.50, you can fill your plate as many times as you like. It's a 20-minute walk from the Balcony of Europe, at the east end of Burriana Beach—look for Ayo's rooftop pyramid (daily "sun to sun," for breakfast—see below, paella served only at lunch, Playa de Burriana, tel. 952-522-289).

Breakfast at Ayo's: Consider arriving at Ayo's at 9:00. Locals order the *tostada con aceite de oliva* (toast with olive oil and salt—€0.50). Ayo also serves toasted ham-and-cheese sandwiches and good coffee.

Nerja Connections

While there are some handy direct bus connections from Nerja to major destinations, many others require a transfer in the town of **Málaga**. The closest train station to Nerja is in Málaga. Fortunately, connections between Nerja and Málaga are easy, and the train and bus stations in Málaga are right next to each other.

Nerja

Almost all buses from Nerja are operated by Alsa (tel. 902-422-242, www.alsa.es), except the local bus to Frigiliana, which is run by Autocares Nerja (tel. 952-520-984). Remember to double-check the codes on bus schedules—for example, 12:00*S* means 12:00 daily except Saturday.

From Nerja by Bus to: Málaga (1-2/hour, 1 hour *directo*, 1.5 hours *ruta*, €4.30), **Nerja Caves** (13/day, 10 minutes), **Frigiliana** (9/day, none on Sun, 15 minutes), **Granada** (8/day, 2-2.5 hours, more with transfer in Motril), **Córdoba** (2/day, 4-5.5 hours), **Sevilla** (2/day, 4-5 hours), **Algeciras** (with connections to La Línea de la Concepción/Gibraltar and Tarifa; 1/day direct, 3.5 hours, more with transfer in Málaga; there are also connections to La Línea de la Concepción/Gibraltar and Tarifa via Málaga). To reach **Ronda,** you'll transfer in Málaga.

To Málaga Airport (about 40 miles west): First catch the bus to Málaga (see above). To reach the airport from Málaga, take a local bus (about 2/hour, 30 minutes, €2, buy ticket on board) or train (2/hour, 30 minutes, €2.20; Málaga's train station is a quick 5-minute walk across the street from the bus station). If you'd rather take a taxi from Nerja to the airport, figure on paying about €65, or ask your Nerja hotelier about airport shuttle transfers (airport code: AGP, tel. 952-048-804).

Málaga

This seaside city's busy airport is the gateway to the Costa del Sol. Málaga's bus and train stations—a block apart at the western edge of Málaga's town center—both have pickpockets and lockers (the train station's lockers are more modern).

Málaga's big, airy U-shaped **bus station,** on Paseo de los Tilos, has long rows of counters for the various bus companies. In the center of the building is a helpful info desk that can print out schedules for any destination and point you to the right ticket window (daily 7:00-22:00, tel. 952-350-061, www.estabus .emtsam.es). Flanking the information desk on either side are old-fashioned lockers (buy a €3.20 token, or *ficha,* from the automated machine). The station also has several basic eateries, newsstands, and WCs. The train station is just a five-minute walk away: Exit at the far corner of the bus station, cross the street, and enter the big shopping mall labeled *Estación María Zambrano*—walk a few minutes through the mall to the train station.

The **train station** (Estación María Zambrano) is slick and modern, inside a big shopping mall (with a food court upstairs). Modern lockers are by the entrance to tracks 10-11 (€3-5 depending on size, security checkpoint), and car-rental offices are by the entrance to tracks 1-9 (Hertz, Avis, Europcar, and National/ Atesa). A **TI** kiosk is in the main hall, just before the shopping mall. To reach the bus station (5 minutes away on foot), enter the mall by the TI kiosk and follow signs to *estación de autobuses.*

From Málaga by Bus to: Nerja (1-2/hour, 1 hour *directo,* 1.5 hours *ruta,* Alsa), **Ronda** (*directo* buses by Los Amarillos: 10/day Mon-Fri, 6/day Sat-Sun, 1.75-2 hours; avoid the *ruta* buses by Portillo: 2/day, 4 hours), **Algeciras** (hourly, 2.25 hours *directo,* 3 hours *ruta*, Portillo), **La Línea de Concepción/Gibraltar** (5/day, 3 hours, Portillo), **Tarifa** (2-3/day, 2.5-4 hours, Portillo), **Sevilla** (6/day direct, 2.5-3 hours, Alsa), **Granada** (hourly, 1.5-2 hours, Alsa), **Córdoba** (4/day, 2.5-3.5 hours *directo,* Alsa), **Madrid** (5/ day, 6 hours, Daibus), **Marbella** (hourly, 55 minutes *directo,* 1.25 hours *ruta,* Portillo). **Bus info:** Alsa (tel. 902-422-242, www.alsa .es), Los Amarillos (tel. 902-210-317, www.losamarillos.es), Daibus (tel. 902-277-999, www.daibus.es), Portillo (tel. 902-450-550, http: //portillo.avanzabus.com).

From Málaga by Train to: Ronda (1/day, 2 hours, more with transfer in Bobadilla), **Algeciras** (4/day, 4 hours, transfer in Bobadilla—same as Ronda train, above), **Madrid** (12/day, 2.5-3 hours on AVE), **Córdoba** (best option: 6/day on Avant, 1 hour; more expensive but no faster on AVE: 10/day, 1 hour), **Granada** (6/ day, 2.5 hours, 1 transfer—bus is better), **Sevilla** (6/day, 2 hours on Avant; 5/day, 2.5 hours on slower regional trains), **Jerez** (3/day on AVE and Avant, 3-3.5 hours, transfer in Córdoba), **Barcelona** (2/ day direct on AVE, 5.75 hours; more with transfer). **Train info:** tel. 902-320-320, www.renfe.com.

Between Nerja and Gibraltar

Buses take five hours to make the Nerja-Gibraltar trip, including a transfer in Málaga, where you may have to change bus companies. Along the way, buses stop at each of the following towns (see map on page 811).

Fuengirola and Torremolinos

The most built-up part of the region, where those most determined to be envied settle down, is a bizarre world of Scandinavian package tours, flashing lights, pink flamenco, multilingual menus, and all-night happiness. Fuengirola is like a Spanish Mazatlán with a few older, less-pretentious budget hotels between the main drag and the beach. The water here is clean and the nightlife fun and easy. James Michener's idyllic Torremolinos has been strip-malled and parking-metered.

Marbella

This is the most polished and posh town on the Costa del Sol. High-priced boutiques, immaculate streets set with intricate pebble designs, and beautifully landscaped squares testify to Marbella's arrival on the world-class-resort scene. Have a *café con leche* on the beautiful Plaza de Naranjos in the old city's pedestrian section. Wander down to new Marbella and the high-rise beach-front apartment buildings to walk along the wide promenade lined with restaurants. Check out the beach scene. Marbella is an easy stop on the Algeciras-Málaga bus route (as you exit the bus station, take a left to reach the center of town). You can also catch a handy direct bus here from the Málaga airport (roughly every 1-2 hours, fewer off-season, 45 minutes, http://portillo.avanzabus.com).

San Pedro de Alcántara

This town's relatively undeveloped sandy beach is popular with young travelers. San Pedro's neighbor, Puerto Banús, is "where the world casts anchor." This luxurious, Monaco-esque jet-set port, complete with casino, is a strange mix of Rolls-Royces, yuppies, boutiques, rich Arabs, and budget browsers.

Gibraltar

One of the last bits of the empire upon which the sun never set, Gibraltar is a quirky mix of Anglican propriety, "God Save the  Queen" tattoos, English book-stores, military memories, and tourist shops. It's understand-ably famous for its dramatic Rock of Gibraltar, which rock-ets improbably into the air from an otherwise flat terrain, dwarf-ing everything around it. If the Rock didn't exist, some clever military tactician would have tried to build it to keep an eye on the Strait of Gibraltar.

Britain has controlled this highly strategic spit of land since they took it by force in 1704, in the War of Spanish Succession. In 1779, while Britain was preoccupied with its troublesome overseas colonies, Spain (later allied with France) declared war and tried to retake Gibraltar; a series of 14 sieges became a way of life, and the already imposing natural features of the Rock were used for defensive purposes. During World War II, the Rock was further fortified and dug through with more and more strategic tunnels. In the mid- to late-20th century, during the Franco period, tensions ran high—and Britain's grasp on the Rock was tenuous.

Strolling Gibraltar, you can see that it was designed as a modern military town (which means it's not particularly charming). But over the last 20 years the economy has gone from one dominated by the military to one based on tourism (as, it seems, happens to many empires). On summer days and weekends, the tiny colony is inundated by holiday-goers, primarily the Spanish (who come here for tax-free cigarettes and booze) and British (who want a change in weather but not in culture). As more and more glitzy high-rise resorts squeeze between the stout fortresses and ramparts—as if trying to create a mini-Monaco—there's a sense that this is a town in transition.

Though it may be hard to imagine a community of 30,000 that feels like its own nation, real Gibraltarians, as you'll learn when you visit, are a proud bunch. They were evacuated during World War II, and it's said that after their return, a national spirit was forged. If you doubt that, be here on Gibraltar's national holiday—September 10—when everyone's decked out in red and white, the national colors.

Gibraltarians have a mixed and interesting heritage. Spaniards call them Llanitos (yah-NEE-tohs), meaning "flat" in Spanish, though the residents live on a rock. The locals—a fun-loving and

Gibraltar

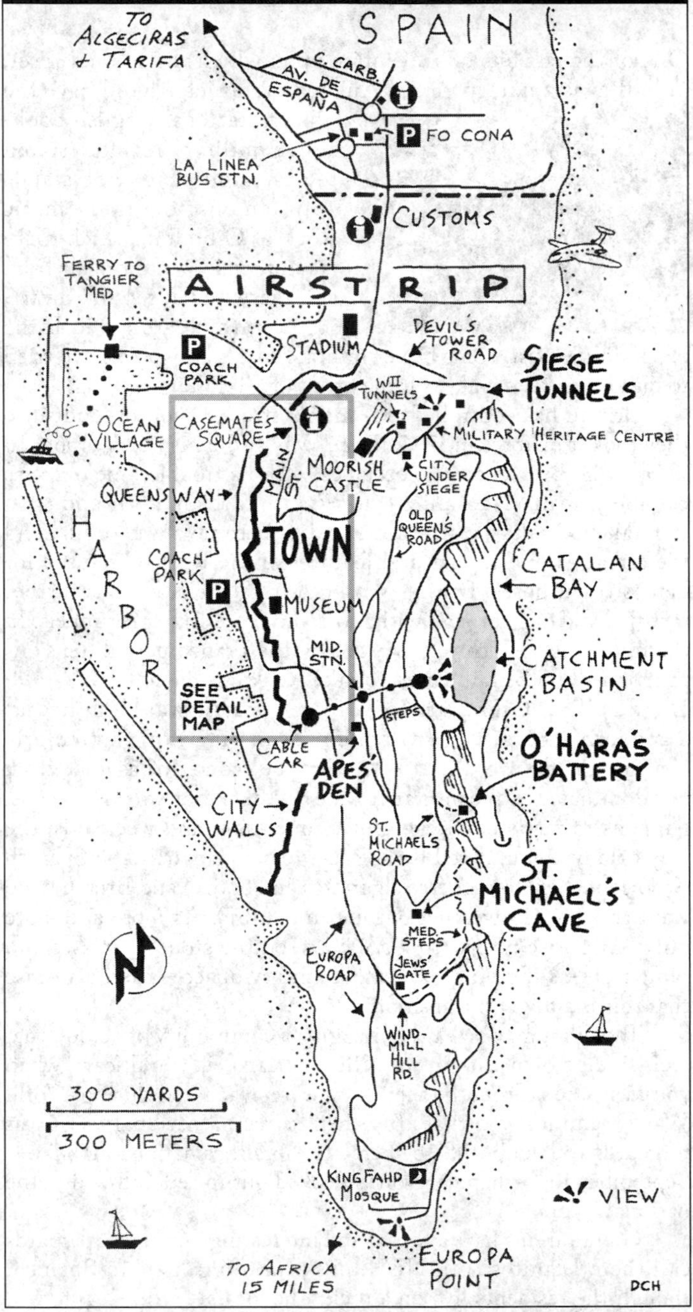

SPAIN

TO ALGECIRAS & TARIFA

C. CARB.

AV. DE ESPAÑA

🛈

P FO CONA

LA LÍNEA BUS STN.

🛈 CUSTOMS

FERRY TO TANGIER MED

A I R S T R I P

STADIUM

DEVIL'S TOWER ROAD

SIEGE TUNNELS

P COACH PARK

WII TUNNELS

MILITARY HERITAGE CENTRE

OCEAN VILLAGE

CASEMATES SQUARE

🛈

MOORISH CASTLE

CITY UNDER SIEGE

QUEENSWAY

MAIN ST.

TOWN

OLD QUEEN'S ROAD

CATALAN BAY

COACH PARK

P

MUSEUM

CATCHMENT BASIN

H A R B O R

MID. STN.

STEPS

O'HARA'S BATTERY

SEE DETAIL MAP

CABLE CAR

APES DEN

CITY WALLS

ST. MICHAEL'S ROAD

ST. MICHAEL'S CAVE

N

MED STEPS

JEWS' GATE

EUROPA ROAD

WIND-MILL HILL RD.

300 YARDS

300 METERS

KING FAHD MOSQUE

VIEW

TO AFRICA 15 MILES

EUROPA POINT

DCH

tolerant mix of British, Spanish, and Moroccan, virtually all of whom speak the Queen's English—call their place "Gib."

From a traveler's perspective, Gibraltar—with its quirky combination of Brits, monkeys, and that breathtaking Rock—is an offbeat detour that adds some variety to a Spanish itinerary. If you're heading to Gibraltar from Spain (as you almost certainly are), be aware most Spaniards still aren't thrilled with this enclave of the Commonwealth on their sunny shores. They basically ignore the place—so, for example, if you're inquiring about bus schedules, don't ask how to get to Gibraltar, but rather to La Línea de la Concepción, the neighboring Spanish town. A passport is required to cross the border.

Planning Your Time

Make Gibraltar a day trip (or just one overnight); rooms are expensive compared to Spain.

For the best day trip to Gibraltar, consider this plan: Walk across the border, catch the red bus #5, and ride it to the Market Square stop near Casemates Square. From there, catch blue bus #2 or walk through town to the cable-car station and ride to the peak for Gibraltar's ultimate top-of-the-rock view. Then, either walk down or take the cable car back into town. From the cable-car station, follow my self-guided town walk all the way back to Casemates Square. Spend your remaining free time in town before returning to Spain. Note that, with all the old walls and fortresses, Gibraltar can be tricky to navigate. Ask for directions: Locals speak English.

Tourists who stay overnight find Gibraltar a peaceful place in the evening, when the town can just be itself. No one's in a hurry. Families stroll, kids play, seniors window-shop, and everyone chats...but the food is still pretty bad.

There's no reason to take a ferry from Gibraltar to visit Morocco—for many reasons, it's a better side-trip from Tarifa (specifics covered on page 879).

Orientation to Gibraltar

Gibraltar is a narrow peninsula (three miles by one mile) jutting

into the Mediterranean. Virtually the entire peninsula is dominated by the steep-faced Rock itself. The locals live down below in the long, skinny town at the western base of the mountain (much of it on reclaimed land).

For information on all the

COSTA DEL SOL

Spain vs. Gibraltar

Spain has been annoyed about Gibraltar ever since Great Britain nabbed this prime 2.5-square-mile territory in 1704 (during the War of Spanish Succession) and was granted it through the Treaty of Utrecht in 1713. Although Spain long ago abandoned efforts to reassert its sovereignty by force, it still tries to make Gibraltarians see the error of their British ways. Over the years Spain has limited

Gibraltar's air and sea connections, choked traffic at the three-quarter-mile border, and even messed with the local phone system in efforts to convince Britain to give back the Rock. Still, given the choice—which they got in referenda in 1967 and 2002—Gibraltar's residents steadfastly remain Queen Elizabeth's loyal subjects, voting overwhelmingly (99 percent in the last election) to continue as a self-governing British dependency. Gibraltar's governor is popular for dealing force-fully and effectively with Spain on these issues.

little differences between Gibraltar and Spain—from area codes to electricity—see "Helpful Hints," later.

Tourist Information

Gibraltar's helpful TI is at Casemates Square, the grand square at the Spain end of town. Pick up a free map and—if it's windy—confirm that the cable car is running (Mon-Fri 9:00-17:30, Sat 10:00-15:00, Sun 10:00-13:00, tel. 74982, www.visitgibraltar.gi). There's also a TI window at the border in the customs building (Mon-Fri 9:00-16:30, closed Sat-Sun).

Arrival in Gibraltar

No matter how you arrive, you'll need your passport to cross the border. These directions will get you as far as the border; from there, see "Getting from the Border into Town," later.

By Bus: Spain's La Línea de la Concepción bus station is a five-minute walk from the Gibraltar border. To reach the border, exit the station and bear left toward the Rock (you can't miss it). If you need to store your bags, you can do so at the Gibraltar Airport (see "Helpful Hints," later).

By Car: Customs checks at the border create a bit of a bottleneck for drivers. But at worst there's a 15-minute wait during the morning rush hour into Gibraltar and the evening rush hour back out. Parking in town is free and easy except for weekday working hours, when it's tight and frustrating. It's simpler to park in La Línea (explained below) and just walk across the border.

Freeway signs in Spain say *Algeciras* and *La Línea*, pretending that Gibraltar doesn't exist until you're very close. After taking the La Línea-Gibraltar exit off the main Costa del Sol road, continue as the road curves left (with the Rock to your right). Enter the left-hand lane at the traffic circle before the border and you'll end up in La Línea. The Fo-Cona underground parking lot is handy (€2.40/hour, €16.50/day, on Avenida 20 de Abril, near the bus station). You'll also find blue-lined parking spots in this area (€1.25/hour from meter, 6-hour limit 9:00-20:00, free before and after that, bring coins, leave ticket on dashboard). From La Línea, it's a five-minute stroll to the border, where you can catch a bus or taxi into town (see "Getting from the Border into Town," below).

If driving into Gibraltar, drive along the sea side of the ramparts (on Queensway—but you'll see no street name). There are big parking lots here and at the cable-car terminal. Parking is generally free—if you can find a spot. By the way, while you'll still find English-style roundabouts, cars here stopped driving on the British side of the road in the 1920s.

Getting from the Border into Town

The "frontier" (as the border is called) is a chaotic hubbub of travel agencies, confused tourists, crafty pickpockets, and duty-free shops (you may see people standing in long lines, waiting to buy cheap cigarettes). The guards barely even look up as you flash your passport. Before exiting the customs building, pick up a map at the TI window on your left (Mon-Fri 9:00-16:30, closed Sat-Sun). Note that as soon as you cross the border, the currency changes from euros to pounds (see "Helpful Hints," next).

To reach downtown, you can walk (30 minutes), catch a bus, or take a taxi. To get into town by **foot,** walk straight across the runway (look left, right, and up), then head down Winston Churchill Avenue, angling right at the Shell station on Smith Dorrien Avenue.

From the border, you can ride the red **bus** #5 (regular or London-style double-decker, runs every 15 minutes) three stops to Market Square (just outside Casemates Square, with the TI), or stay on to Cathedral Square, at the center of town. From Market Square, blue Gibraltar city buses head various points on the peninsula—the most useful route for most tourists is blue bus #2, which goes to the cable-car station and Europa Point (Gibraltar's southernmost point). Tickets are the same price on the privately run red border buses and the blue city buses (€1.30/£1 one-way, €2/£1.50 for an all-day "hoppa" ticket)—although frustratingly, tickets are not transferable between the two systems.

A **taxi** from the border is pricey (€9/£6 to the cable-car station). If you plan to join a taxi tour up to the Rock (see page 843), note that you can book one right at the border.

Helpful Hints

Gibraltar Isn't Spain: Gibraltar, a British colony, uses different coins, currency (see below), stamps, and phone cards than those used in Spain. Note that British holidays such as the Queen's (official) Birthday (June 9 in 2014) and Bank Holidays (May 5, May 26, and Aug 25 in 2014) are observed, along with local holidays such as Gibraltar's National Day (Sept 10).

Use Pounds, not Euros: Gibraltar uses the British pound sterling (£1 = about $1.60). A pound is broken into 100 pence (abbreviated p). Like other parts of the UK (such as Scotland, Wales, and Northern Ireland), Gibraltar mints its own Gibraltar-specific banknotes and coins featuring local landmarks, people, and historical events—offering a colorful history lesson. Gibraltar's pounds are interchangeable with other British pounds.

Merchants in Gibraltar also accept euros...but at about a 20 percent extra cost to you. Gibraltar is expensive even at fair exchange rates. You'll save money by hitting up an ATM and taking out what you'll need. But before you leave, stop at an exchange desk and change back what you don't spend (at about a 5 percent loss), since Gibraltar currency is hard to change in Spain. (If you'll be making only a few purchases, you can try to avoid this problem by skipping the ATM and buying things with your credit card.) Be aware that if you pay for anything in euros, you may get pounds back in change.

Hours: This may be the United Kingdom, but Gibraltar follows a siesta schedule, with some businesses closing from 13:00 to 15:00 on weekdays, and shutting down at 14:00 on Saturdays until Monday morning.

Electricity: If you have electrical gadgets, note that Gibraltar uses the British three-pronged plugs (not the European two-pronged ones). Your hotel may be able to loan you an adapter.

Phoning: To telephone Gibraltar from anywhere in Europe, dial 00-350-200 and the five-digit local number. To call Gibraltar from the US or Canada, dial 011-350-200-local number.

Internet Access: The **King's Bastion Leisure Centre** has free Wi-Fi, but no terminals (see "Activities," next page). **Café Cyberworld** has several computers (£0.10/minute, £2.50/30 minutes, £4.50/hour, daily 12:00-24:00, Queensway 14, in Ocean Heights Gallery, an arcade 100 yards toward the water from Casemates Square, tel. 51416). There's also Internet access at the cultural center, listed below.

Baggage Storage: You can't store your luggage at the bus station, but there is a bag check at the Gibraltar Airport, which is right across the border (£8/day, go to airport information desk in departures hall).

John Mackintosh Cultural Centre: This is your classic British effort to provide a cozy community center. Without a hint of tourism, the upstairs library welcomes drop-ins to enjoy local newspapers and publications, and to check their email (Mon-Fri 9:30-19:30, closed Sat-Sun, 308 Main Street, tel. 75669).

Activities: The **King's Bastion Leisure Centre** fills an old fortification (the namesake bastion) with a modern entertainment complex. On the ground floor is a huge bowling alley; upstairs are an ice-skating rink and a three-screen cinema (www.leisure cinemas.com). Rounding out the complex are bars, restaurants, discos, and lounges. Many of the activities are geared for families, especially tweens and teens. It's easy to find, just outside Cathedral Square (daily 10:00-24:00, air-con, free Wi-Fi, tel. 44777).

Side-Trip to Tangier, Morocco: While a very sporadic ferry does run from Gibraltar directly to Tangier, it's designed for Moroccan workers (returning home to Tangier for the weekend) and doesn't work for a same-day round-trip. Instead, either go via Tarifa (best choice, with direct connections to downtown Tangier—see page 879) or via Algeciras (closer to Gibraltar, but ferries drop you at a port farther from downtown Tangier). Various travel agencies in town sell package tours that include a bus transfer to the boat in Algeciras.

Self-Guided Walk

Welcome to Gibraltar

Gibraltar town is long and skinny, with one main street (called Main Street). Stroll the length of it from the cable-car station to Casemates Square, following this little tour. A good British pub and a room-temperature pint of beer await you at the end.

From the cable-car terminal, turn right (as you face the sea) and head into town. Soon you'll come to the **Trafalgar cemetery,** a reminder of the colony's English military heritage. Next you come to the **Charles V wall**—a reminder of its Spanish military heritage—built in 1552 by the Spanish to defend against marauding pirates. Gibraltar was controlled by Moors (711-1462), Spain (1462-1704), and then the British (since 1704). Passing through the Southport Gates, you'll see one of the many red history plaques posted about town.

Heading into town, you pass the tax office, then the **John Mackintosh Cultural Centre,** which has Internet access and a copy of today's *Gibraltar Chronicle* upstairs in its library. The *Chronicle* comes out Monday through Friday and has covered the local news since 1801. The Methodist church sponsors the recommended **Carpenter's Arms** tearoom.

The pedestrian portion of Main Street begins near the **Governor's Residence.** The British governor of Gibraltar took over a Franciscan convent, hence the name of the local white house: The Convent. The **Convent Guard Room,** facing the Governor's Residence, is good for photos.

Gibraltar's courthouse stands behind a **small tropical garden,** where John and Yoko got married back in 1969 (as the ballad goes, they "got married in Gibraltar near Spain"). Sean Connery did, too. Actually, many Brits like to get married here because weddings are cheap, fast (only 48 hours' notice required), and legally recognized as British.

Main Street now becomes a **shopping drag.** You'll notice lots of colorful price tags advertising tax-free booze, cigarettes, and

sugar (highly taxed in Spain). Lladró porcelain, while made in Valencia, is popular here (because it's sold without the hefty Spanish VAT—Value-Added Tax). The Catholic cathedral retains a whiff of Arabia (as it was built upon the remains of a mosque), while the big **Marks & Spencer department store** helps vacationing Brits feel at home.

Continue several more blocks through the bustling heart of Gibraltar. If you enjoy British products, this is your chance to stock up on Cadbury chocolates, digestive biscuits, wine gums, and Weetabix—but you'll pay a premium, since it's all "imported" from the UK.

The town (and this walk) ends at **Casemates Square.** While a lowbrow food circus today, it originated as a barracks and place for ammunition storage. When Franco closed the border with Spain in 1969, Gibraltar suffered a labor shortage, as Spanish guest workers could no longer commute into Gibraltar. The colony countered by inviting Moroccan workers to take their place—ending a nearly 500-year Moroccan absence, which began when the Moors fled in 1462. As a result, today's Moroccan community dates only from the 1970s. Whereas the previous Spanish labor force simply commuted into work, the Moroccans needed apartments, so Gibraltar converted the Casemates barracks for that purpose. Cheap Spanish labor has crept back in, causing many locals to

Gibraltar Town

1. O'Callaghan Eliott Hotel
2. Bristol Hotel
3. Cannon Hotel
4. Emile Hostel
5. The Clipper Pub
6. The Star Bar
7. Carpenter's Arms
8. Gaucho's Steakhouse
9. All's Well Pub
10. Market Place & Produce Market
11. Marks & Spencer; Bon Bon Cash & Carry
12. To Ocean Village
13. Queensway Quay Marina & Eateries

14. Cathedral Square
15. John Mackintosh Cultural Centre
16. Governor's Residence
17. Convent Guard Room
18. John & Yoko's Wedding Site
19. Café Cyberworld
20. King's Bastion Leisure Centre

TO TANGIER MED FERRY

TO AIRSTRIP & BORDER

CASEMATES SQUARE

TO MOORISH CASTLE & SIEGE TUNNELS

QUEENSWAY

RECLAMATION RD

WALL RD

IRISH TOWN

MAIN

BELL LANE

ENGINEER LANE

CORNWALL

CASTLE RD

WILLIS'S RD

COOP. PARL.

TUCK.

COLL.

KING

LINE

SYNAGOGUE

MUSEUM

P PARKING

50 YARDS
50 METERS

CANNON STREET

LIB.

GEO.

GOV.

MAIN ST

TOWN RANGE

ST.

PRINCE EDWARD'S ROAD

FLAT BASTION RD

N

QUEENSWAY QUAY & MARINA

QUEENSWAY

CHARLES V WALL

SOUTHPORT GATES

TRAFALGAR CEMETERY

DCH

EUROPA RD

ROSIA

BOYD

BOTANICAL GARDENS

CABLE-CAR STATION

TO TOP OF THE ROCK

TO ST. MICHAEL'S CAVE

COSTA DEL SOL

resent store clerks who can't speak proper English.

At the far end of Casemates Square is a **crystal shop** that makes its own crystal right there (you can watch). They claim it's the only thing actually "made in Gibraltar." But just upstairs, on the upper floor of the barracks, you'll find a string of local crafts shops.

If you go through the triple arches at the end of the square (behind the TI), you'll reach the covered **produce market** and food stalls. Across the busy road a few minutes' walk farther is the well-marked entrance to the **Ocean Village** boardwalk and entertainment complex (described later, under "Eating in Gibraltar").

Sights in Gibraltar

In Town

▲Gibraltar Museum

Built atop a Moorish bath, this museum tells the story of a chunk of land that has been fought over for centuries. Start with the fine 15-minute video overview of the story of the Rock—a worthwhile prep for the artifacts (such as ancient Roman anchors made of lead) you'll see in the museum. Then wander through the scant remains of the 14th-century Moorish baths. Upstairs you'll see military memorabilia, a 15-foot-long model of the Rock, wonderful century-old photos of old Gibraltar, paintings by local artists, and, in a cave-like room off the art gallery, a collection of prehistoric remains and artifacts. The famous skull of a Neanderthal woman found in Forbes' Quarry is a copy (the original is in the British Museum in London). Found in Gibraltar in 1848, this was the first Neanderthal skull ever discovered. No one realized its significance until a similar skull found years later in Germany's Neanderthal Valley was correctly identified—stealing the name, claim, and fame from Gibraltar.

Cost and Hours: £2, Mon-Fri 10:00-18:00, Sat 10:00-14:00, closed Sun, last entry 30 minutes before closing, no photos, on Bomb House Lane near the cathedral.

On the Rock of Gibraltar

The actual Rock of Gibraltar is the colony's best sight. Its attractions include the stupendous view from the very top, quirky apes, a hokey cave (St. Michael's), and the impressive Siege Tunnels drilled through the rock face for military purposes. Frankly, the sights that charge admission aren't that exciting; the Rock's best attractions—enjoying views from the top and seeing the monkeys—are free. Hikers can ride the lift up and take a long, steep, scenic walk down, connecting the various sights by strolling along paved military lanes.

Cost: There's a £0.50 fee to enter the grounds of the Rock, technically called the Upper Rock Nature Reserve—that's just to walk around and enjoy the views and the monkeys. A £10 nature reserve ticket is required to visit any or all of these major sights within the reserve: St. Michael's Cave, Siege Tunnels, Moorish Castle, Military Heritage Centre, and City Under Siege exhibit (includes the £0.50 nature reserve entrance fee). If you take a taxi tour, entry to the nature reserve and sights is included; if you ride the cable car, the nature reserve grounds entry fee is included, but you'll have to buy the £10 ticket to go in the sights. (Both options are explained below.)

Hours: Daily 9:30-19:15, until 18:15 late Oct-late March, last entry 30 minutes before closing.

Additional Sights at the Rock: Two attractions at the Rock are not part of the official £10 nature reserve ticket, and have their own separate tickets and hours: O'Hara's Battery and the World War II Tunnels (both described later).

Visiting the Rock: You have two options for touring the Rock—take a taxi tour or ride the cable car. The **taxi tour** includes entry to St. Michael's Cave and the Siege Tunnels, a couple of extra stops, and running commentary from your licensed cabbie/guide. Because the cable car doesn't get you very close to the cave and tunnels (and doesn't cover cave and tunnel admission), take the taxi tour if you'll be visiting these sights and don't want to walk. On the other hand, the **cable car** takes you to the very top of the Rock (which the taxi tours don't). You can still see the sights, but you'll have to pay for an entry ticket and connect them by foot (not a bad thing—it's a pleasant walk down). Both options are explained in more detail below.

There's no reason to take a big-bus tour (advertised and sold all over town) considering how fun and easy the taxi tours are. Private cars are not allowed high on the Rock.

By Taxi Tour: Minibuses driven by cabbies trained and licensed to lead these 1.5-hour trips are standing by at the border and at various points in town (including Cathedral Square, John Mackintosh Square, Casemates Square, and Trafalgar

Cemetery near the cable-car station). They charge £22/person (4-person minimum, or £65 for only 2 people in one taxi, includes reserve sights ticket, tel. 70027). Taxi tours and big buses do the same 1.5-hour loop tour with four stops: a Mediterranean viewpoint (called the Pillar of Hercules), St.

Michael's Cave (15-minute visit), a viewpoint near the top of the Rock where you can get up close to the monkeys, and the Siege Tunnels (20-minute visit). Buddy up with other travelers and share the cost.

By Cable Car to the Summit: A ticket for just the cable car is £8.50 one-way and £10.50 round-trip. The £18.50 Nature Reserve ticket (combining a one-way cable-car ride and the £10 ticket to the sights) doesn't save any money over buying the tickets separately. You'll probably want to skip the €20.50 round-trip option, as I recommend walking downhill to the sights rather than taking the cable car down.

The cable car runs every 10-15 minutes, or continuously in busy times (daily from 9:30; April-Oct last ascent at 19:15, last descent at 19:45; Nov-March last ascent at 17:15, last descent at 17:45). Lines can be long if a cruise ship is in town. The cable car won't run if it's windy or rainy; if the weather is questionable, ask at the TI before heading to the station. The cable-car ride includes a handheld videoguide that explains what you're seeing from the spectacular viewpoints (pick it up at the well-marked booth when you disembark at the top—must leave ID as a deposit—and return it before leaving the summit). In winter (Nov-March), the cable car stops halfway down for those who want to get out, gawk at the monkeys, and take a later car down—but you'll probably see monkeys at the top anyway.

To take in all the sights, you'll want to **hike down,** rather than take the cable car back (be sure to specify that you want a one-way ticket up). Simply hiking down without visiting the sights is enjoyable, too. Approximate hiking times: from the top of the cable car to St. Michael's Cave—25 minutes; from the cave to the Apes' Den—20 minutes; from the Apes' Den to the Siege Tunnels—30 minutes; from the tunnels back into town, passing the Moorish Castle—20 minutes. Total walking time, from top to bottom: about 1.5 hours (on paved roads with almost no traffic), not including sightseeing. For hikers, I've connected the dots with directions below.

▲▲▲The Summit of the Rock

The cable car takes you to the real highlight of Gibraltar: the summit of the spectacular Rock itself. (Taxi tours don't go here; they stop on a ridge below the summit, where you enjoy a commanding view—but one that's nowhere near as good.) The limestone massif, or large rock mass, is nearly a mile long, rising 1,400 feet high with very sheer faces. According to legend, this was one of the Pillars of Hercules (paired with Djebel

Musa, another mountain across the strait in Morocco), marking the edge of the known world in ancient times. Local guides say that these pillars are the only places on the planet where you can see two seas and two continents at the same time.

In A.D. 711, the Muslim chieftain Tarik ibn Ziyad crossed over from Africa and landed on the Rock, beginning the Moorish conquest of Spain and naming the Rock after himself—Djebel-Tarik ("Rock of Tarik"), which became "Gibraltar."

At the top of the Rock (the cable-car terminal) there's a view terrace and a restaurant. From here you can explore old ramparts and drool at the 360-degree view of Morocco (including the Rif Mountains and Djebel Musa), the Strait of Gibraltar, the bay stretching west toward Algeciras, and the twinkling Costa del Sol arcing eastward. The views are especially crisp on brisk off-season days. Below you (to the east) stretches the giant catchment system that the British built to collect rainwater in the not-so-distant past, when Spain allowed neither water nor tourists to cross its disputed border. Broad sheets catch the rain, sending it through channels to reservoirs located inside the rock.

• *Up at the summit, you'll likely see some of the famed...*

▲▲Apes of Gibraltar

The Rock is home to about 200 "apes" (actually, tailless Barbary macaques—a type of monkey). Taxi tours come with great monkey

fun, but if you're on your own, you'll probably see them at the top and at various points on the walk back down (basically, the monkeys congregate anywhere that tourists do—hoping to get food). The males are bigger, females have beards, and newborns are black. They live about 15-20 years. Legend has it that as long as the monkeys remain here, so will the Brits. (According to a plausible local legend, when word came a few decades back that the ape population was waning, Winston Churchill made a point to import reinforcements.) Keep your distance from the monkeys. (Guides say that for safety reasons, "They can touch you, but you can't touch them." And while guides feed them, you shouldn't—it disrupts their diet.) Beware of the monkeys' kleptomaniac tendencies; they'll ignore the peanut in your hand and claw after the full bag in your pocket. Because the monkeys associate plastic bags with food, keep your bag close to your body: Tourists who wander by absentmindedly, loosely clutching a bag, are apt to have it stolen by a purse-snatching simian. If there's no ape action, wait for a banana-toting taxi tour to stop by and stir some up. Guides love to get the monkeys to actually climb onto the backs and shoulders of their tour members—always a crowd-pleaser.

• *If you're hiking down, you'll find that your options are clearly marked at most forks. I'll narrate the longest route down, which passes all the sights en route.*

From the top cable-car station, exit and head downhill on the well-paved path (toward Africa). You'll pass the viewpoint for taxi tours (with monkeys hanging around, waiting for tour groups to come feed them), pass under a ruined observation tower, and eventually reach a wide part of the road. Most visitors will want to continue to St. Michael's Cave (skip down to that section), but you also have an opportunity to hike (or ride a shuttle bus) steeply up to...

O'Hara's Battery

At 1,400 feet, this is the actual highest point on the Rock. A massive 9.2-inch gun sits on the summit, where a Moorish lookout post once stood. The battery was built after World War I, and the last test shot was fired in 1974. Locals are glad it's been mothballed—during test firings, they had to open their windows, which might otherwise have shattered from the pressurized air blasted from this gun. The battery was recently opened to the public; you can go inside to see not only the gun, but also the powerful engines underneath that were used to move and aim it. The iron rings you see every 30 yards or so along the military lanes around the Rock once anchored pulleys used to haul up guns like the huge one at O'Hara's Battery.

Cost and Hours: £3.50, not covered by the £10 nature reserve ticket, shuttle runs up every 20 minutes when open, Mon-Fri 10:30-17:00, closed Sat-Sun.

• *From the crossroads below O'Hara's Battery, taking the right (downhill) fork leads you down to a restaurant and shop, then the entrance to...*

▲St. Michael's Cave

Studded with stalagmites and stalactites, eerily lit, and echoing with classical music, this cave is dramatic, corny, and slippery when wet. Considered a one-star sight since Neolithic times, these caves were alluded to in ancient Greek legends—when the caves were believed to be the Gates of Hades (or the entrance of a tunnel to Africa). All taxi tours stop here (entry included in cost of taxi tour). This sight requires a long walk for cable-car riders (who must have the £10 nature reserve ticket to enter; same hours as other nature reserve sights). Walking through takes about 15 minutes; you'll pop out at the gift shop.

• *From here, most will head down to the Apes' Den (see next paragraph), but serious hikers have the opportunity to curl around to Jews' Gate at the tip of the Rock, then circle around the back of the Rock on the strenuous **Mediterranean Steps** (leading back up to O'Hara's Battery).*

To do this, turn sharply left after St. Michael's Cave and head for Jews' Gate. Since it's on the opposite side from the town, it's the closest thing in Gibraltar to "wilderness." If this challenging 1.5-to-2-hour hike sounds enjoyable, ask for details at the TI.

*The more standard route is to continue downhill. At the three-way fork, you can take either the middle fork (more level) or the left fork (hillier, but you'll see monkeys at the Apes' Den) to the Siege Tunnels. The **Apes' Den**, at the middle station for the cable car, is a scenic terrace where monkeys tend to gather, and where taxi tours stop to do some monkeying around.*

Continue on either fork (they converge), following signs for Siege Tunnels, *for about 30 more minutes. Eventually you'll reach a terrace with three flags (from highest to lowest: United Kingdom, Gibraltar, EU) and a fantastic view of Gibraltar's airport, "frontier" with Spain, and the Spanish city of La Línea de la Concepción. From here, the Military Heritage Centre is beneath your feet (described later), and it's a short but steep hike up to the...*

▲Siege Tunnels

Also called the Upper Galleries, these chilly tunnels were blasted out of the rock by the Brits during the Great Siege by Spanish

and French forces (1779-1783). The clever British, safe inside the Rock, wanted to chip and dig to a highly strategic outcrop called "The Notch," ideal for mounting a big gun. After blasting out some ventilation holes for the miners, they had an even better idea: Use gunpowder to carve out a whole network of tunnels with shafts that would be ideal for aiming artillery. Eventually they excavated St. George's Hall, a huge cavern that housed seven guns. These were the first tunnels inside the Rock; more than a century and a half later, during World War II, 30 more miles of tunnels were blasted out. Hokey but fun dioramas help recapture a time when Brits were known more for conquests than for crumpets. All taxi tours stop here (entry included in cost of taxi tour); hikers must have the £10 nature reserve ticket to enter (same hours as other nature reserve sights).

• *Hiding out in the bunker below the three flags (go down the stairs and open the heavy metal door—it's unlocked) is the...*

Military Heritage Centre

This small one-room collection features old military photographs from Gibraltar. The second room features a poignant memorial to the people who "have made the supreme sacrifice in defence of Gibraltar" (covered by nature reserve ticket—but tickets rarely checked, same hours as other nature reserve sights).

• *From here, the road switchbacks down into town. At each bend in the road you'll find one of the next three sights.*

City Under Siege

This hokey exhibit is worth a quick walk-through if you've been fascinated by all this Gibraltar military history. Displayed in some of the first British structures built on Gibraltar soil, it re-creates the days of the Great Siege, which lasted for more than three and a half years (1779-1783)—one of 14 sieges that attempted but failed to drive the Brits off the Rock. With evocative descriptions, some original "graffiti" scratched into the wall by besieged Gibraltarians, and some borderline-hokey dioramas, the exhibit explains what it was like to live on the Rock, cut off from the outside world, during those challenging times (covered by nature reserve ticket—but tickets rarely checked, same hours as other nature reserve sights).

World War II Tunnels

This privately run operation takes you on a tour through some of the tunnels carved out of the Rock during a much later conflict than the others described here. You'll emerge back up at the Military Heritage Centre.

Cost and Hours: £8, not covered by £10 nature reserve ticket, daily 10:00-16:30.

Moorish Castle

Actually more a tower than a castle, this recently restored building is basically an empty shell. (In the interest of political correctness, the tourist board recently tried to change the name to "Medieval Castle"...but it *is* Moorish, so the name didn't stick.) It was constructed on top of the original castle built in A.D. 711 by the Moor Tarik ibn Ziyad, who gave his name to Gibraltar.

• *The tower marks the end of the Upper Rock Nature Reserve. Heading downhill, you begin to enter the upper part of modern Gibraltar. While you could keep on twisting down the road, keep an eye out for staircase shortcuts into town (most direct are the well-marked Castle Steps).*

Nightlife in Gibraltar

If you're coming from the late-night bustle of Spain, where you'll see young parents out strolling with their toddlers at midnight, you'll find Gibraltar extremely quiet after-hours. Main Street is completely dead (with the exception of a few lively pubs, mostly a block or two off the main drag). Head instead to the **Ocean Village** complex, a five-minute walk from Casemates Square, where the boardwalk is lined with bars, restaurants, and a casino. Another waterfront locale—a bit more sedate—is the **Queensway Quay Marina.** (Both areas are described later, under "Eating in Gibraltar.") Kids love the **King's Bastion Leisure Centre** (described earlier, under "Helpful Hints").

Some pubs, lounges, and discos—especially on Casemates Square—offer live music (look around for signs, or ask at the TI). **O'Callaghan Eliott Hotel** hosts free live jazz on Thursday evenings.

Sleeping in and near Gibraltar

Gibraltar is not a good value for accommodations. There are only a handful of hotels and (disappointingly) no British-style B&Bs. As a general rule, the beds are either bad or overpriced. Remember, you'll pay a 20 percent premium if paying with euros—pay with pounds or by credit card. As an alternative, consider staying at one of my recommended accommodations in La Línea de la Concepción, across the border from Gibraltar in Spain, where hotels are a much better value.

In Gibraltar Town

$$$ O'Callaghan Eliott Hotel, with four stars, boasts a rooftop pool with a view, a fine restaurant, bar, terrace, inviting sit-a-bit public spaces, and 122 modern, mildly stylish business-class rooms—all with balconies (sky-high rack rates of Db-£240-270, but often around Db-£100 with online booking for non-peak days, breakfast-£15, non-smoking, air-con, elevator, pay Wi-Fi,

---

Sleep Code

(£1 = about $1.60, €1 = about $1.30, tel. code: 350-200)
S = Single, **D** = Double/Twin, **T** = Triple, **Q** = Quad, **b** = bathroom, **s** = shower only. All of these places accept credit cards, and their staffs speak English. Unless otherwise noted, breakfast is not included. Prices in Gibraltar are in pounds, while prices in La Línea de la Concepción are in euros. Some La Línea hotels include the 10 percent IVA tax in the room price; others tack it onto your bill.

To help you easily sort through these listings, I've divided the accommodations into three categories, based on the price for a standard double room with bath during high season:

$$$ **Higher Priced**—Most rooms £85/€105 or more.
$$ **Moderately Priced**—Most rooms between
£50-85/€60-105.
$ **Lower Priced**—Most rooms £50/€60 or less.

Prices can change without notice; verify the hotel's current rates online or by email. For the best prices, always book direct.

parking-£12/day, centrally located at Governor's Parade 2, up Library Street from main drag, tel. 70500, www.ocallaghanhotels .com, eliott@ocallaghanhotels.com).

$$$ Bristol Hotel offers 60 basic, slightly worn English rooms in the heart of Gibraltar (Sb-£69-74, Db-£86-93, Tb-£99-103, higher prices for exterior rooms, breakfast-£6, air-con, elevator, free Wi-Fi in lobby, swimming pool; limited free parking—first come, first served; Cathedral Square 10, tel. 76800, www.bristolhotel.gi, reservations@bristolhotel.gi).

$$ Cannon Hotel is a run-down dive. But it's also well-located and has the only cheap hotel rooms in town. Its 18 rooms (most with wobbly cots and no private bathrooms) look treacherously down on a little patio (S-£30, D-£42, Db-£53, T-£52.50, Tb-£60, includes full English breakfast, free Wi-Fi, behind cathedral at Cannon Lane 9, tel. 51711, www.cannonhotel .gi, cannon@sapphirenet.gi).

$ Emile Hostel, simple and the cheapest place in town, welcomes people of any age (42 beds, bunk in 6-bed dorm-£18, S-£25, D-£40, à la carte breakfast—full English is £3.95, cash only, free Wi-Fi, on Montagu Bastion diagonally across the street from Shell station, ramped entrance on Line Wall Road, tel. 51106, www.emilehostel.net, emilehostel@yahoo.co.uk).

Across the Border, in La Línea

Staying in Spain—in the border town of La Línea de la Concepción—offers an affordable, albeit less glamorous alternative to sleeping in Gibraltar. The streets north of the bus station are lined with inexpensive *hostales* and restaurants. These options are just a few blocks from the La Línea bus station and an easy 10-15 minute walk to the border—get directions when you book. All but Asur Campo are basic, family-run *hostales*, offering simple, no-frills rooms at a good price.

$$ Asur Campo de Gibraltar is a huge blocky building, with 227 cookie-cutter rooms spread over seven floors. It's a big, impersonal, business-class hotel, but it's the closest hotel to the border—just a 10-minute walk and easy to find if you have a car, as it's right on the main road as you drive in (Sb-€59/64/89, Db-€66/71/96, check website for deals, includes breakfast, air-con, elevator, pay Wi-Fi, pool, large patio, underground parking-€6/day, located at the intersection of Avenida Príncipe de Asturias and Avenida del Ejército, tel. 956-691-211, www.campodegibraltarhotel.com, lalinea@asurhoteles.com).

$ Hostal La Campana has 17 recently remodeled rooms at budget prices. Run by Ivan and his dad Andreas, this place is simple, clean, and friendly, but lacks indoor public areas except for its recommended restaurant (Sb-€27-42, Db-€36-48, Tb-€45-

56, Qb-€52-64, air-con, elevator, free Wi-Fi, limited free street parking, pay parking in nearby underground garage-€18/day, just off Plaza de la Constitución at Calle Carboneros 3, tel. 956-173-059, www.hostalcampana.es, info@hostalcampana.es).

$ Hostal Margarita is a bit farther from the border, but its fresh, modern rooms are a step above the other *hostales* in the area (Sb-€41-46, Db-€53-60, air-con, elevator, free Wi-Fi, parking-€6.60/day, Avenida de España 38, tel. 856-225-211, www.hostalmargarita.com, info@hostalmargarita.com).

Eating in and near Gibraltar

In Gibraltar Town

Take a break from *jamón* and sample some English pub grub: fish-and-chips, meat pies, jacket potatoes (baked potatoes with fillings),

or a good old greasy English breakfast. English-style beers include chilled lagers and room-temperature ales, bitters, and stouts. In general, the farther you venture away from Main Street, the cheaper and more local the places become. Since budget-priced English food isn't exactly high cuisine, the best plan may be to stroll the streets and look for the pub with the ambience you like best (various options: lots of chatting, sports fans riveted to a football match, noisy casino machines, or whatever). I've listed a few of my favorites below. Or venture to one of Gibraltar's more upscale recent developments at either end of the old town: Ocean Village or Queensway Quay.

Downtown, near Main Street

The Clipper pub offers filling £7 meals and Murphy's stout on tap (English breakfast-£5, Mon-Fri 9:30-22:00, Sat 9:30-16:00, Sun 10:00-22:30, on Irish Town Lane, tel. 79791).

The Star Bar, which brags that it's "Gibraltar's Oldest Bar," is on a quiet street with a pubby interior and good £6-9 plates (Mon-Sat 7:00-23:30, Sun 7:00-22:00, food served daily until 22:00, on Parliament Lane off Main Street, across from Corner House Restaurant, tel. 75924).

Carpenter's Arms is a fast, cheap-and-cheery café run by the Methodist church, serving snacks and meals starting at £3 with a missionary's smile. It's upstairs in the Methodist church on Main Street (Mon-Fri 9:30-14:00, closed Sat-Sun and Aug, volunteer-run, 100 yards past the Governor's Residence at 297 Main Street).

Gaucho's is a classy, atmospheric steakhouse actually inside the casemates, just outside Casemates Square (£5-8 starters, £16-24 steaks, daily 12:00-16:00 & 19:00-23:00, Waterport Casemates, tel. 59700).

Casemates Square Food Circus: The big square at the entrance of Gibraltar contains a variety of restaurants, ranging from fast food (fish-and-chips joint, Burger King, and Pizza Hut) to inviting pubs spilling out onto the square. The **All's Well** pub serves £8-10 meals (Moroccan *tajine*, salads, burgers, fish-and-chips, and more) and offers pleasant tables with umbrellas under leafy trees (daily 10:00-19:00, tel. 72987). Fruit stands and cheap take-out food stalls bustle just outside the entry to the square at the **Market Place** (Mon-Sat 9:00-14:00, closed Sun).

Groceries: The **Bon Bon Cash & Carry** minimarket is on the main drag, off Cathedral Square (daily 9:30-19:00, Main Street 239). Nearby, **Marks & Spencer** has a small food market on the ground floor, with pre-made meals and fresh-baked cookies (Mon-Thu 9:00-19:00, Fri 11:00-18:00, Sat 9:30-17:00, closed Sun).

Ocean Village

This development is the best place to get a look at the bold new face of Gibraltar. Formerly a dumpy port, it's been turned into a swanky marina fronted by glassy high-rise condo buildings. The boardwalk arcing around the marina is packed with shops, restaurants, and bars—Indian, Mexican, sports bar, pizza parlor, Irish pub, fast food, wine bar, and more. Anchoring everything is Gibraltar's casino. While the  whole thing can feel a bit corporate, it offers an enjoyable 21st-century contrast to the "English village" vibe of Main Street (which can be extremely sleepy after-hours).

Queensway Quay Marina

To dine in yacht-club ambience, stroll the marina and choose from a string of restaurants serving the boat-owning crowd. When the sun sets, the quay-side tables at each of these places are prime dining real estate. **Waterfront Restaurant** has a lounge-lizard interior and great marina-side tables outside (£5-8 starters, £10-16 main dishes, daily specials, Indian and classic British, daily 9:00-24:00, last orders at 22:45, tel. 45666). Other options include Indian, Italian, trendy lounges, and (oh, yeah) Spanish.

In La Línea

These places are close to my recommended accommodations in La Línea, on the Spanish side of the border.

Restaurante La Campana, attached to the recommended *hostal* of the same name, is particularly good. It's popular with locals for its traditional Spanish dishes made using quality ingredients and offered at affordable prices (€9 fixed-price lunch and dinner *menus* daily, Calle Carboneros 3).

Tahj Mahal, an Indian/Pakistani restaurant, offers a welcome relief from tapas. It serves all the standard Indian dishes, including several vegetarian options, along with a daily €5 combo-plate that's a great deal (just across from the La Línea TI on Plaza de la Constitución and Avenida del Ejército).

On Calle Real: This pedestrian street, several blocks north of the La Línea bus station, is lined with inexpensive cafeterias, restaurants, and tapas bars.

Gibraltar Connections

By Bus

The nearest bus station to Gibraltar is in La Línea de la Concepción in Spain, five minutes from the border (tel. 956-291-168 or 956-172-396). The nearest train station is at Algeciras, which is the region's main transportation hub (for Algeciras connections, see page 868).

From La Línea de la Concepción by Bus to: Algeciras (2/hour, less on weekends, 45 minutes), **Tarifa** (2/day direct, 1 hour; more possible with change in Algeciras, 1.5 hours), **Málaga** (5/day, 3 hours), **Ronda** (no direct bus, transfer in Algeciras; Algeciras to Ronda: 1/day, 2.75 hours), **Granada** (3/day, 6-7 hours, change in Algeciras), **Sevilla** (4/day, 4-4.5 hours), **Jerez** (1/day, 2.5 hours), **Córdoba** (1/day, 5.25 hours), **Madrid** (1/day, 8 hours).

By Plane

From Gibraltar, you can fly to various points in Britain: British Airways flies to London Heathrow (www.ba.com); easyJet connects to London Gatwick and Liverpool (www.easyjet.com); and Monarch Airlines goes to London Luton and Manchester (www.monarch.co.uk). The airport is easy to reach; after all, you can't enter town without crossing its runway, one way or another (airport code: GIB, www.gibraltarairport.gi).

Tarifa

Mainland Europe's southernmost town is whitewashed and Arab-feeling, with a lovely beach, an old castle, restaurants swimming in fresh seafood, inexpensive places to sleep, enough windsurfers to sink a ship, and best of all, hassle-free boats to Morocco. Though Tarifa is pleasant, the main reason to come here is to use it as a springboard to Tangier, Morocco—a remarkable city worth ▲▲.

As I stood on Tarifa's town promenade under the castle, looking out at almost-touchable Morocco across the Strait of Gibraltar, my only regret was that I didn't have this book to steer me clear of gritty Algeciras on earlier trips. Tarifa, with 35-minute boat transfers to Tangier departing about every hour, is the best jumping-off point for a Moroccan side-trip, as its ferry route goes directly to Tangier's city-center Medina Port. (The other routes, from Algeciras or Gibraltar, take you to the Tangier MED Port, 25 miles east of Tangier city.) For details on joining an easy belly-dancing-and-shopping excursion-type tour of Tangier from Tarifa, or taking the ferry on your own, see the Tangier chapter (page 878).

Tarifa has no blockbuster sights (and can be quiet off-season), but it's a town where you just feel good to be on vacation. Don't expect a snazzy Riviera-style beach resort, à la Nerja. Tarifa is a functional, dreary-in-parts port city with an atmospheric old town and a long, broad stretch of relatively undeveloped but wildly popular sandy beach. The town is a hip and breezy mecca among windsurfers, drawn here by the strong winds created by the bottleneck at the Strait of Gibraltar. Tarifa is mobbed with young German and French adventure seekers in July and August. This crowd from all over Europe (and beyond) makes Tarifa one of Spain's trendiest-feeling towns. It has far more artsy boutique hotels than most Spanish towns its size, and its restaurant offerings are atypically eclectic for normally same-Jane Spain—you'll see vegetarian and organic, Italian and Indian, gourmet burgers and tea houses, and on each corner, it seems, there's a stylish bar-lounge with techno music, mood lighting, and youthful Europeans just hanging out.

Orientation to Tarifa

The old town, surrounded by a wall, slopes gently up from the water's edge (and the port to Tangier). The modern section stretches farther inland from Tarifa's fortified gate.

Tourist Information

The TI is on Paseo de la Alameda (Mon-Fri 10:00-13:30 & 16:00-18:00, Sat-Sun 10:00-13:30; hours may be longer in summer and shorter on slow or bad-weather days, tel. 956-680-993, www.aytotarifa.com, turismo@aytotarifa.com).

Experiencia Tarifa: This organization, run by can-do Quino of the recommended Hostal Alborada, produces a good free magazine and town map featuring hotels, restaurants, and a wide array of activities (also online at www.experienciatarifa.com).

Arrival in Tarifa

By Bus: The bus station (actually a couple of portable buildings with an outdoor sitting area) is on Batalla del Salado, about a five-minute walk from the old town. (The TI also has bus schedules.) Buy tickets directly from the driver if the ticket booth is closed (Mon-Fri 7:30-12:30 & 14:15-18:00, Sat-Sun 14:00-20:00, hours vary slightly with the season, bus station tel. 956-684-038, Comes bus company tel. 956-291-168). To reach the old town, walk away from the wind turbines perched on the mountain ridge.

By Car: If you're staying in the center of town, follow signs for *Alameda* or *Puerto,* and continue along Avenida de Andalucía. Follow signs to make an obligatory loop to the port entrance, then swing right and park for free in the lot at the far end of Calle Alcalde Juan Núñez (on the harbor, at the base of the castle). During the busiest summer months (July-Aug), this parking lot can fill up, in which case you'll need to use a pay lot, such as the one to the east of the old-town wall (ask your hotelier for ideas). Or you can try finding street parking, which is most abundant in the new town just north of the old-town walls. Blue lines indicate paid parking, and yellow lines are no-parking areas.

Helpful Hints

Internet Access: Pandor@, in the heart of the old town, has 16 computers across from Café Central, near the church (€2.50/hour, generally daily in summer 10:00-23:00, in winter 10:00-14:30 & 17:00-19:00, tel. 956-680-816).

Laundry: Top Clean Tarifa will wash, dry, and fold your clothes. If you drop off your laundry early in the day, they can get it back to you on the same day (€13/load wash-and-dry, full service only, Mon-Fri 10:00-16:00, closed Sat-Sun, Avenida

Tarifa

ATLANTIC OCEAN

1. Hostal Alborada
2. Hotel La Mirada
3. La Sacristía
4. Casa Blan+co
5. Hotel Misiana
6. Dar Cilla Guesthouse & Apartments
7. La Casa Amarilla
8. Hostal La Calzada
9. Hostal Alameda
10. Hostal Africa
11. Pensión Correo
12. Hostal Villanueva
13. Restaurante Morilla
14. To El Puerto Restaurante
15. La Oca da Sergio
16. Ristorante La Trattoria
17. To Restaurante Souk & Surfing Sushi
18. Bar El Francés
19. Café Bar Los Melli & Bar El Pasillo
20. El Otro Melli
21. La Posada
22. Café Central & FIRMM
23. Casino Tarifeno
24. Mesón El Picoteo
25. Confitería La Tarifeña
26. Churrería La Palmera
27. Chilimoso Restaurante
28. Supermarket
29. Mercado (Farmers' Market)
30. Laundry
31. Internet Café
32. Girasol Adventure
33. Whale Watch Tarifa & Baelo Tour
34. FRS Ferry Office (2)
35. Tarifa Travel
36. Travelsur

COSTA DEL SOL

TO BEACH

BULLRING

BERING

CASTILLEJOS

ALMADRABA

AVENIDA   DE

AV. FUERZAS ARMADAS

PADRE FONT

HUERTA DEL REY

J.T. ARTIGAS

CRUZ ROJA

CALLE ALCALDE   JUAN NÚÑEZ

DOUBLE ARCH

TO 14, BEACH FREE P & ISLA DE LAS PALOMAS

BOAT TO TANGIER (MOROCCO)

HARBOR

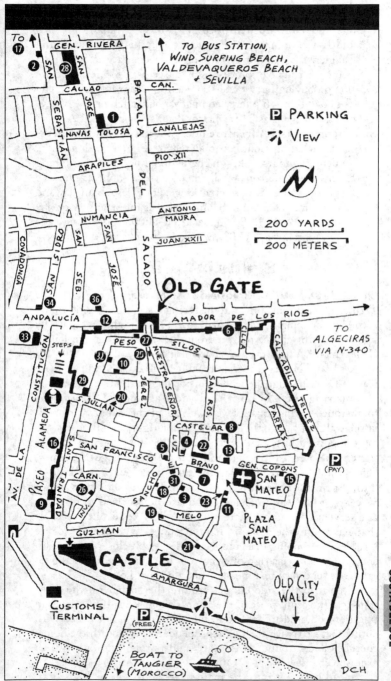

COSTA DEL SOL

de Andalucía 24, tel. 956-680-303).

Tickets and Tours to Morocco: Two ferry companies—FRS and InterShipping—make the crossing between Tarifa and Tangier. You can buy tickets for either boat at the port. FRS also has a couple of offices in town (see page 879 for information on buying ferry tickets). If taking a tour to Tangier, you can book through a ferry company, your hotel, or one of several travel agencies in Tarifa (for details, see page 881).

Excursions: Girasol Adventure offers a variety of outdoor excursions, including mountain-bike rentals (€18/day with helmet), guided bike tours, hikes in the national park, rock-climbing classes, tennis lessons, and, when you're all done...a massage (€50/hour). The various activities generally last a half-day and cost around €25-35. Ask Sabine or Chris for details (Mon-Fri 10:00-14:00 & 18:30-20:30, Sat 11:00-14:00, closed Sun, Calle Colón 12, tel. 956-627-037, www.girasol-adventure.com).

Sights in Tarifa

Church of St. Matthew (Iglesia de San Mateo)

Tarifa's most important church, facing its main drag, is richly decorated for being in such a small town. Most nights, it seems life squirts from the church out the front door and into the fun-loving Calle Sancho IV El Bravo. Wander inside.

Cost and Hours: Free, daily 9:00-13:00 & 17:30-20:30; there may be English-language leaflets inside on the right.

Visiting the Church: Find the fragment of an **ancient tombstone**—a tiny square (eye-level, about the size of this book) in the wall just before the transept on the right side. Probably the most important historical item in town, this stone fragment proves there was a functioning church here during Visigothic times, before the Moorish conquest. The tombstone reads, in a kind of Latin Spanish (try reading it), "Flaviano lived as a Christian for 50 years, a little more or less. In death he received forgiveness as a servant of God on March 30, 674. May he rest in peace." If that gets you in the mood to light a candle, switch on an electric "candle" by dropping in a coin. (It works.) A bit closer to the main entrance, you'll see a sign offering you the chance to light a digital candle by sending a text message (for a pricey €1.50).

Step into the side chapel around the corner, in the right transept. The centerpiece of the **altar** is a boy Jesus. By Andalusian tradition, he used to be naked, but these days he's clothed with outfits that vary with the Church calendar. Underneath the dome, cherubs dance around on the pink-and-purple interior above an exquisite chandelier.

Head back out into the main nave, and face the high altar.

A statue of **St. James the Moor-Slayer** (missing his sword) is on the right wall of the main central altar. Since the days of the Reconquista, James has been Spain's patron saint. For more on this important figure—and why he's fighting invaders that came to Spain centuries after his death—see page 362.

The left side of the nave harbors several **statues**—showing typically over-the-top Baroque emotion—that are paraded through town during Holy Week. The **Captive Christ** (with hands bound) evokes a time when Christians were held captive by Moors. The door on the left side of the nave is the **"door of pardons."** For a long time Tarifa was a dangerous place—on the edge of the Reconquista. To encourage people to live here, the Church offered a second helping of forgiveness to anyone who lived in Tarifa for a year. One year and one day after moving to Tarifa, they would have the privilege of passing through this special "door of pardons," and a Mass of thanksgiving would be held in that person's honor.

Castle of Guzmán el Bueno

This castle, little more than a concrete hulk in a vacant lot, is interesting only for the harbor views from its ramparts (the

interior is undergoing a lengthy restoration and will most likely be closed for several years). It was named after a 13th-century Christian general who gained fame in a sad show of courage while fighting the Moors. Holding Guzmán's son hostage, the Moors demanded he surrender the castle or they'd kill the boy. Guzmán refused, even throwing his own knife down from the ramparts. It was used on his son's throat. Ultimately, the Moors withdrew to Africa, and Guzmán was a hero. *Bueno.*

Cost and Hours: €2; May-Sept Tue-Sat 11:00-14:00 & 18:00-20:00, Sun 11:00-14:00; Oct-April Tue-Sat 11:00-14:00 & 16:00-18:00, Sun 11:00-14:00; closed Mon year-round, last entry 30 minutes before closing.

Nearby: If you skip the castle, you'll get equally good views from the plaza just left of the town hall. Follow *ayto* signs to the ceramic frog fountain in front of the Casa Consistorial and continue left.

Bullfighting

Tarifa has a third-rate bullring where novices botch fights on occasional Saturdays through the summer. Professional bullfights take place during special events in August and September. The ring is a short walk from town. You'll see posters everywhere.

▲Whale-Watching

Several companies in Tarifa offer daily whale- and dolphin-watching excursions. Over the past four decades, people in this area went from eating whales to protecting them and sharing them with 20,000 visitors a year. Talks are under way between Morocco and Spain to protect the Strait of Gibraltar by declaring it a national park.

For any of the tours, it's wise (but not always necessary) to reserve one to three days in advance. You'll get a multilingual tour and a two-hour boat trip. Sightings occur on nearly every trip: Dolphins and pilot whales frolic here any time of year (they like the food), sperm whales visit from March through July, and orcas pass through in July and August. In bad weather, trips may be canceled or boats may leave instead from Algeciras (in which case, drivers follow in a convoy, people without cars usually get rides from staff, and you'll stand a lesser chance of seeing whales).

The best company is the Swiss nonprofit **FIRMM** (Foundation for Information and Research on Marine Mammals), which gives a 30-minute educational talk before departure. To reserve, it's best to call ahead or stop by one of their two offices (€30/person, 1-5 trips/day April-Oct, sometimes also Nov, also offers intensive week-long courses that include boat trips, one office around the corner from Café Central—one door inland at Pedro Cortés 4, second office inside the ferry port, tel. 956-627-008, mobile 619-459-441, www.firmm.org, mail@firmm.org). If you don't see any whales or dolphins on your tour, you can join another trip for free.

Whale Watch Tarifa is another good option. In addition to a two-hour whale-watching trip (€30), they offer a three-hour orca trip in July and August (€45, Avenida de la Constitución 6, tel. 956-627-013, mobile 639-476-544, www.whalewatchtarifa.net, whalewatchtarifa@whalewatchtarifa.net, run by Lourdes).

Isla de las Palomas

Extending out between Tarifa's port and beaches, this island connected by a spit is the actual "southernmost point in mainland Europe." Walk along the causeway, with beaches stretching to your right and a bustling port to your left, to the tip, which was fortified in the 19th century to balance the military might of Britain's nearby Rock of Gibraltar. The actual tip, still owned by the Ministry of Defense, is closed to the public, but a sign at the gate still gives you that giddy "edge of the world" feeling.

▲▲Beach Scene

Tarifa's vast, sandy beach stretches west for about five miles. You can walk the beach from Tarifa, while those with a car can explore farther (following Cádiz Road). On windy summer days, the sea is littered with sprinting windsurfers, while kitesurfers flutter in the sky. Paddleboarding is also popular here. It's a fascinating scene: A long string of funky beach resorts is packed with vans and fun-mobiles from northern Europe under mountain ridges lined with modern energy-generating windmills. The various resorts each have a sandy access road, parking, a cabana-type hamlet with rental gear, beachwear shops, a bar, and a hip, healthy restaurant. I like

Valdevaqueros beach (five miles from Tarifa), with a wonderful thatched restaurant serving hearty salads, paella, and burgers. Camping Torre de la Peña also has some fun beach eateries.

In July and August, inexpensive buses do a circuit of nearby campgrounds, all on the waterfront (€2, departures about every 1-2 hours, confirm times with TI). Trying to get a parking spot in August can take the joy out of this experience.

Nightlife in Tarifa

You'll find plenty of enjoyable nightspots—the entire town seems designed to cater to a young, international crowd of windsurfers and other adventure travelers. Just stroll the streets of the old town and dip into whichever trendy lounge catches your eye. For something more sedate, the evening paseo fills the park-like boulevard called Paseo de la Alameda (just outside the old-town wall); the Almedina bar hosts flamenco shows every Thursday (at the south end of town, just below Plaza de Santa María); and the theater next to the TI sometimes has musical performances (ask at the TI or look for posters).

Sleeping in Tarifa

Room rates vary with the season. For many hotels, I've listed the three seasonal tiers (lowest prices—winter; medium prices—spring and fall; and highest prices—mid-June-Sept).

Outside the City Wall

These hotels are about five blocks from the old town, right off the main drag, Batalla del Salado, in the plain, modern part of town. While in a drab area, both are well-run oases that are close to the beach and the bus station, with free and easy street parking.

$$ Hostal Alborada is a squeaky-clean, family-run 37-room place with two attractive courtyards and modern conveniences.

Sleep Code

(€1 = about $1.30, country code: 34)
S = Single, **D** = Double/Twin, **T** = Triple, **Q** = Quad, **b** = bath-room, **s** = shower only. Unless otherwise noted, credit cards are accepted and English is spoken. Breakfast is not included (unless noted). Some hotels include the 10 percent IVA tax in the room price; others tack it onto your bill.

To help you easily sort through these listings, I've divided the accommodations into three categories, based on the price for a standard double room with bath during high season:

$$$ Higher Priced—Most rooms €100 or more.
$$ Moderately Priced—Most rooms between €50-100.
$ Lower Priced—Most rooms €50 or less.

Prices can change without notice; verify the hotel's cur-rent rates online or by email. For the best prices, always book direct.

Father Rafael—along with sons Quino (who speaks English and is generous with travel tips), Fali, and Carlos—are happy to help make your Morocco tour or ferry reservation, or arrange any other activities you're interested in. If they're not too busy, they'll even give you a free lift to the port (Sb-€40/60/65, Db-€50/70/90, Tb-€80/90/110, pay for first night when reserving, 10 percent discount when you book direct and show this book in 2014—not valid July-Sept, strict 15-day cancellation policy, basic breakfast-€2.50, larger breakfast with delicious tomato bread-€5, air-con, pay guest computer, free Wi-Fi, laundry-€14, Calle San José 40, tel. 956-681-140, www.hotelalborada.com, info @hotelalborada.com).

$$ Hotel La Mirada, which feels sleek and stark, has 25 mod and renovated rooms—most with sea views at no extra cost. While the place lacks personality, it's well-priced and comfortable (Sb-€45/55/60, Db-€65/75/90, breakfast-€5, elevator, free Wi-Fi, expansive sea views from large roof terrace with inviting lounge chairs, Calle San Sebastián 41, tel. 956-684-427, www.hotel-la mirada.com, reservas@hotel-lamirada.com, Antonio and Salvador).

Inside or next to the City Wall

The first three listings are funky, stylish boutique hotels in the heart of town—*muy* trendy and a bit full of themselves.

$$$ La Sacristía, formerly a Moorish stable, now houses travelers who want stylish surroundings. It offers 10 fine and uniquely decorated rooms, mingling eclectic elements of chic

Spanish and Asian style. They offer spa treatments, custom tours of the area, and occasional special events—join the party since you won't sleep (Db-€117, superior Db-€137, extra bed-€35, can be cheaper off-season, includes breakfast, air-con, massage room, sauna, small roof terrace, very central at San Donato 8, tel. 956-681-759, www.lasacristia.net, tarifa@lasacristia.net, helpful Serafín and Sandra). They also rent 10 apartments at a separate location.

$$$ Casa Blan+co, where minimalist meets Moroccan, is the newest reasonably priced designer hotel on the block. Each of its seven rooms (with double beds only—no twins) is decorated (and priced) differently. The place is decked out with practical amenities (mini-fridge and stovetop) as well as romantic touches—loft beds, walk-in showers, and subtle lighting (high-season Db-€92-133, low-season Db-€52-69, small roof terrace, free Wi-Fi in lobby, off main square at Calle Nuestra Señora de la Luz 2, tel. 956-681-515, www.casablanco.es, info@casablanco.es).

$$$ Hotel Misiana has 15 comfortable, recently remodeled, spacious rooms above a bar-lounge. Their designer gave the place a mod pastel boutique-ish ambience. To avoid noise from the lounge below (open until 3:00 in the morning), request a room on a higher floor (Sb-€50/75/115, Db-€75/110/140, fancy top-floor Db suite-€200/230/300, low- and mid-season rates are €10-20 more on weekends, includes breakfast, double-paned windows, elevator, free Wi-Fi, 100 yards directly in front of the church at Calle Sancho IV El Bravo 16, tel. 956-627-083, www.misiana.com, info@misiana.com).

$$$ Dar Cilla Guesthouse & Apartments is an old Moroccan-style *dar* (or guest house), built into the town wall and remodeled into eight chic apartments surrounding a communal courtyard. Each apartment has a kitchen and is decorated in modern Moroccan style, with earth-tone walls, tile floors, and Moroccan rugs (Sb-€50/55/65, Db-€100/110/130, superior Db-€120/130/165, Qb-€190/210/240, extra person-€25, 2-night minimum, bigger rooms have air-con, free Wi-Fi, large roof terrace with beautiful view over the old town to the sea, just east of the old-town gate at Calle Cilla 7, tel. 653-467-025, www.darcilla .com, info@darcilla.com).

$$ La Casa Amarilla ("The Yellow House") offers 10 posh apartments with tiny kitchens, plus three smaller studios with modern decor (studio Db-€52/77/105, apartment Db-€70/100/120, reserve with credit card, free Wi-Fi, across street from Café Central, Calle Sancho IV El Bravo 9, tel. 956-681-993, www .lacasaamarilla.net, info@lacasaamarilla.net).

$$ Hostal La Calzada has eight airy, well-appointed rooms right in the lively old-town thick of things, though the management is rarely around (Db-€50-105, higher in Aug, extra bed-€20, closed Dec-March, air-con, free Wi-Fi in lobby, 20 yards from church at Calle Justino Pertinez 7, tel. 956-681-492, www .hostallacalzada.com, info@hostallacalzada.com).

$$ Hostal Alameda, overlooking a square where the local children play, glistens with pristine marble floors and dark red decor. The main building has 11 bright rooms and the annex has 16 more-modern rooms; both face the same delightful square (Db-€60/70/90, extra bed-€25-35, air-con, free Wi-Fi, Paseo de la Alameda 4, tel. 956-681-181, www.hostalalameda.com, reservas @hostalalameda.com, Antonio).

$$ Hostal Africa, with 13 bright rooms and an inviting roof terrace, is buried on a very quiet street in the center of town. Its dreamy blue-and-white color scheme and stripped-down feel give it a Moorish ambience (S-€20/25/35, Sb-€25/35/50, D-€30/40/ 50, Db-€35/50/65, Tb-€50/75/100, laundry-€10, free Wi-Fi on terrace, storage for boards and bikes, Calle María Antonia Toledo 12, tel. 956-680-220, mobile 606-914-294, www. hostalafrica.com, hostal_africa@hotmail.com, Miguel and Eva keep the reception desk open only 9:00-24:00).

$$ Pensión Correo rents nine simple rooms (three sharing two bathrooms, one available with kitchen during high season) at a fair value. Room 8 has a private roof terrace, and rooms 6 and 7 have gorgeous views of the town (S-€20/30/50, D-€30/50/65, Db-€40/60/80, Tb-€50/75/90, Qb-€60/90/100, extra bed-€10, reservations more than 24 hours in advance require first night prepaid by credit card—refundable up to 3 days in advance, free Wi-Fi, roof terrace, Coronel Moscardo 8, tel. 956-680-206, www .pensioncorreo.com, welcome@pensioncorreo.com, Luca).

$ Hostal Villanueva offers 12 remodeled rooms at budget prices. It's simple, clean, and friendly. It lacks indoor public areas, but has an inviting terrace overlooking the old town on a busy street. Pepe (who speaks a smidgen of English) asks that you reconfirm your reservation by phone the day before you arrive (Sb-€25-30, Db-€35-55, free Wi-Fi, just west of the old-town gate at Avenida de Andalucía 11, access from outside the wall, tel. 956-684-149, hostalvillanueva@hotmail.com).

Eating in Tarifa

I've grouped my recommendations below into two categories: Sit down to a real restaurant meal, or enjoy a couple of the many characteristic tapas bars in the old town.

Restaurants
Seafood
Restaurante Morilla, facing the church, is on the town's prime piece of people-watching real estate. This is a real restaurant (€1.50 tapas sold only at the stand-up bar and sometimes at a few tables), with good indoor and outdoor seating. It serves tasty local-style fish, grilled or baked—your server will tell you about today's fish; it's sold by weight, so confirm the price carefully (€4-11 starters, €10-17 main dishes, daily 9:00-24:00, Calle Sancho IV El Bravo, tel. 956-681-757).

El Puerto, in a dreary and untouristy area between the port and the beach (near the causeway out to Isla de las Palomas), has a great reputation for its pricey but very fresh seafood. Locals swear that it's a notch or two above the seafood places in town (€8-14 starters, €10-22 seafood dishes and some meats, Thu-Mon 12:00-16:00 & 20:00-24:00, Tue-Wed 12:00-16:00 only, Avenida Fuerzas Armadas 13, tel. 956-681-914).

Italian
La Oca da Sergio, cozy and fun, is one of the numerous pizza-and-pasta joints supported by the large expat Italian community. Sergio prides himself on importing authentic Italian ingredients (€7-11 starters, €9-14 pastas, €7-10 pizzas, €14-16 meat and fish dishes, indoor and outdoor seating, daily 13:00-16:00 & 20:00-24:00 except closed Tue in winter; around the left side of the church and straight back, just before the Moorish-style old-folks' home at Calle General Copons 6; tel. 956-681-249, mobile 615-686-571).

Ristorante La Trattoria, on the Alameda, is another good Italian option, with cloth-napkin class, friendly staff, and ingredients from Italy. Sit inside, near the wood-fired oven, or out along the main strolling street (€7-18 starters and pastas, €6-15 pizzas, €14-25 meat dishes; daily 19:30-1:00 in the morning, July-Aug also Sat-Sun 13:00-16:00, closed Wed off-season; Paseo de la Alameda, tel. 956-682-225).

In the New Town
These two restaurants are in a residential area just above the beach, about a 15-minute walk (or easy car or taxi ride) from the old town. They're worth a detour for their great food, and for the chance to see an area away from the main tourist zone (though the sushi bar is on the beach and is no stranger to tourists). To get to either, begin by heading up Calle San Sebastián, which turns into Calle Pintor Pérez Villalta. When you see a big staircase immediately on your right, take it to reach Restaurante Souk, or turn left toward

the beach to find Surfing Sushi in the large beige Surla building.

Restaurante Souk serves a tasty fusion of Moroccan, Indian, and Thai cuisine in a dark, exotic, romantic, purely Moroccan ambience. The ground floor (where you enter) is a bar and atmospheric tea house, while the dining room is downstairs (€6-10 starters, €12-16 main dishes; July-Sept daily 20:00-3:00 in the morning; Oct-June Wed-Mon 20:00-1:00, closed Tue; good wine list, Mar Tirreno 46, tel. 956-627-065, friendly Claudia).

Surfing Sushi, part of a cool surfer bar called Surla, serves up wonderfully executed sushi using only the freshest of ingredients. Situated just a few steps above the beachfront walkway, it's at the center of a sprawling zone of après-surf hangouts. They also offer delivery (€16-21 shareable sushi platters, daily 21:00-24:00 except closed Wed off-season, possible to order delivery sushi by phone at other times, Calle Pintor Pérez Villalta 1, tel. 956-685-175).

Tapas

Bar El Francés is a thriving hole-in-the-wall where "Frenchies" (as the bar's name implies) Marcial and Alexandra serve tasty little plates of tapas. From Café Central, follow the cars 100 yards to the first corner on the left to reach this simple, untouristy standing-and-stools-only eatery. This spot is popular for its fine *raciones* (€6-10) and tapas (€1.30-1.80)—especially oxtail *(rabo del toro)*, fish in brandy sauce *(pescado in salsa al cognac)*, pork with spice *(chicharrones)*, and garlic-grilled tuna *(atún a la plancha)*. The outdoor terrace with restaurant-type tables (no tapas served here) is an understandably popular spot to enjoy a casual meal. Show this book and Marcial will be happy to bring you a free glass of sherry (open daily long hours June-Aug; closed Wed-Thu March-May and Sept-Nov; closed Dec-Feb; Calle Sancho IV El Bravo 21A, mobile 685-867-005).

Café Bar Los Melli is a local favorite for feasts on rickety tables set on cobbles. This family-friendly place, run by Ramón and Juani, offers a good chorizo sandwich and *patatas bravas*—potatoes with a hot tomato sauce served on a wooden board (€5 half-*raciones*, €8 *raciones,* Thu-Tue 20:00-24:00, Sat-Sun also 13:00-16:00, closed Wed; from Bar El Francés, cross parking lot and take Calle del Legionario Ríos Moya up one block; mobile 605-866-444). **Bar El Pasillo,** next to Los Melli, also serves tapas (closed Mon-Tue). **El Otro Melli,** run by Ramón's brother José, is a few blocks away on Plaza de San Martín.

La Posada, a local-feeling place a block beyond the main tourist zone (and just up the street from Los Melli), takes pride in its fresh ingredients. There's a small dining room, a nondescript bar with a giant stone beer tap that's a replica of the city's first communal faucet, and tables out front near the real thing (€1.50 *montaditos,* €3 *tostadas,* €4-6 half-*raciones,* €7-11 *raciones;* July-Aug daily 13:00-16:30 & 20:00-24:00; Sept-June Wed-Mon 20:00-24:00, also open Sat-Sun 13:00-16:30, closed Tue; Calle Guzman el Bueno 3A, mobile 636-929-449).

Café Central is *the* happening place nearly any time of day— it's the perch for all the cool tourists. Less authentically Spanish than the others I've listed, it has a hip, international vibe. The bustling ambience and appealing setting in front of the church are better than the food (€1.30 tapas, €5 half-*raciones*), but they do have breakfast with eggs (€2-4), good €7 salads (study the menu), and impressively therapeutic healthy fruit drinks (daily 8:30-24:00, off Plaza San Mateo, near church, tel. 956-682-877).

Casino Tarifeno is just to the sea side of the church. It's an old-boys' social club "for members only," but it offers a musty Andalusian welcome to visiting tourists, including women. Wander through. There's a low-key bar with tapas, a TV room, a card room, and a lounge. There's no menu, but prices are standard. Just point and say the size you want: tapa (€1.20), *media-ración* (€4), or *ración* (€7). A far cry from some of the trendy options around town, this is a local institution (daily 12:00-24:00).

Mesón El Picoteo is a small, characteristic bar popular with locals and tourists alike for its good tapas and *montaditos.* Eat in the casual, woody interior or at one of the barrel tables out front (€1.30 tapas & *montaditos,* €3-7 half-*raciones,* €5-14 *raciones,* €7-15 meat and fish plates, long hours daily, a few blocks west of the old town on Calle Mariano Vinuesa, tel. 956-681-128).

Pastries, Beach Bars, and Picnics

Breakfast or Dessert: **Confitería La Tarifeña** serves super pastries and flan-like *tocino de cielo* (daily 9:00-21:00, at the top of Calle Nuestra Señora de la Luz, near the main old-town gate).

Churrería La Palmera serves breakfast before most hotels and cafés have even turned on the lights—early enough for you to get your coffee fix, and/or bulk up on *churros* and chocolate, before hopping the first ferry to Tangier (daily 6:00-13:00, Calle Sanchez IV El Bravo 34).

Chilimoso, literally a small hole in the old-town wall, serves fresh and healthy vegetarian options, homemade desserts, and a variety of teas. It's a rare find in meat-loving Spain. Eat at one of the few indoor tables, or get it to go and find a bench on the nearby Paseo de la Alameda (daily 12:30-15:30 & 19:30-23:00, just west of the old town gate on Calle del Peso).

Windsurfer Bars: If you have a car, head to the string of beaches. Many have bars and fun-loving thatched restaurants that keep the wet-suited gang fed and watered (see "Beach Scene" on page 860).

Picnics: Stop by the *mercado municipal* (farmers' market, Mon-Sat 8:00-14:00, closed Sun, in old town, inside gate nearest TI), any grocery, or the **superSol supermarket** (Mon-Sat 9:30-21:30, closed Sun, has simple cafeteria, near the hotels in the new town at Callao and San José).

Tarifa Connections

Tarifa
From Tarifa by Bus to: La Línea de la Concepción/Gibraltar (2/day direct, 1 hour, starting around 12:00; more possible with transfer in Algeciras, 1.5 hours), **Algeciras** (14/day, less on weekends, 45 minutes, Comes), **Jerez** (1/day, 2 hours, more frequent with transfer in Cádiz), **Sevilla** (4/day, 2.5-3.25 hours), and **Málaga** (2-3/day, 2.5-4 hours, Portillo). **Bus info:** Comes (tel. 956-291-168, www.tgcomes.es), Portillo (tel. 902-450-550, http://portillo.avanzabus.com).

Ferries from Tarifa to Tangier, Morocco: Two boat companies make the 35-minute journey to Tangier's city-center Medina Port about every hour (see page 880 in the Tangier chapter for details).

Algeciras
Algeciras (ahl-*h*eh-THEE-rahs, with a guttural *h*) is only worth leaving. It's useful to the traveler mainly as a transportation hub, with trains and buses to destinations in southern and central Spain (it also has a ferry to Tangier, but it takes you to the Tangier MED port about 25 miles from Tangier city—going from Tarifa is much better). If you're headed for Gibraltar or Tarifa by public transport, you'll almost certainly change in Algeciras at some point.

Everything of interest is on Juan de la Cierva, which heads inland from the port. The **TI** is about a block in (Mon-Fri 9:00-20:00, Sat-Sun 9:30-15:00, tel. 956-784-131), followed by the side-by-side **train station** (opposite Hotel Octavio) and **bus station** three more blocks later.

Trains: If arriving at the train station, head out the front door: The bus station (called San Bernardo Estación de Autobuses) is ahead and on the right; the TI is another three blocks ahead (the road becomes Juan de la Cierva when the road jogs), also on the right; and the port is just beyond.

From Algeciras by Train to: Madrid (2/day, 5.5 hours, arrives at Atocha), **Ronda** (5-6/day, 1.5-2 hours), **Granada** (3/day, 4.25-5 hours), **Sevilla** (3/day, 5-6 hours, transfer at Antequera or

Bobadilla, bus is better), **Córdoba** (2/day direct on Altaria, 3.25 hours; more with transfer in Antequera or Bobadilla, 5-5.5 hours), **Málaga** (3/day, 3.5 hours, transfer in Bobadilla; bus is faster). With the exception of the route to Madrid, these are particularly scenic trips; the best (though slow) is the mountainous journey to Málaga via Bobadilla.

Buses: Algeciras is served by three different bus companies (Comes, Portillo, and Linesur), all located in the same terminal (called San Bernardo Estación de Autobuses) next to Hotel Octavio and directly across from the train station. The companies generally serve different destinations, but there is some overlap. Compare schedules and rates to find the most convenient bus for you. By the ticket counter you'll find an easy red letter board that lists departures. Lockers are near the platforms—purchase a token at the machines (€3.20).

From Algeciras by Bus: Comes (tel. 956-291-168, www .tgcomes.es) runs buses to **La Línea/Gibraltar** (2/hour, less on weekends, 45 minutes), **Tarifa** (14/day, less on weekends, 45 minutes), **Ronda** (1/day, 2.75 hours), **Sevilla** (4/day, 3-4 hours), **Jerez** (2/day 2.5 hours), and **Madrid** (5/day, 8 hours).

Portillo (tel. 956-654-304, http://portillo.avanzabus.com) offers buses to **Málaga** (hourly, 2.25 hours *directo*, 3 hours *ruta*), **Málaga Airport** (2/day, 2 hours), and **Granada** (3/day *directo*, 4 hours; 1/day *ruta*, 5.5 hours).

Linesur (tel. 956-667-649, www.linesur.com) runs the most frequent direct buses to **Sevilla** (8/day, fewer on weekends, 2.5-3 hours) and **Jerez** (6/day, fewer on weekends, 1.5 hours).

Ferries from Algeciras to Tangier, Morocco: Although it's possible to sail from Algeciras to Tangier, the ferry takes you to the Tangier MED Port, which is 25 miles east of Tangier city and a hassle. You're better off taking a ferry from Tarifa: They sail direct to the port in Tangier. If you must sail from Algeciras, buy your ticket at the port (skip the divey-looking travel agencies littering the town). Official offices of the boat companies are inside the main port building, directly behind the helpful little English-speaking info kiosk (8-22 ferries/day, port open daily 6:45-21:45, tel. 956-585-463).

Route Tips for Drivers

Tarifa to Gibraltar (45 minutes): This short drive takes you past a silvery-white forest of windmills, from peaceful Tarifa past Algeciras to La Línea (the Spanish town bordering Gibraltar). Passing Algeciras, continue in the direction of Estepona. At San Roque, take the La Línea-Gibraltar exit.

Gibraltar to Nerja (130 miles): Barring traffic problems, the trip along the Costa del Sol is smooth and easy by car—much of it on a new highway. Just follow the coastal highway east. After Málaga, follow signs to *Almería* and *Motril*.

Nerja to Granada (80 miles, 1.5 hours, 100 views): Drive along the coast to Motril, catching N-323 north for about 40 miles to Granada. While scenic side-trips may beckon, don't arrive late in Granada without a confirmed hotel reservation.

MOROCCO

MOROCCO

Al-Maghreb

A young country with an old history, Morocco is a photographer's delight and a budget traveler's dream. It's cheap, exotic, and easier and more appealing than ever. Along with a rich culture, Morocco offers plenty of contrast—from beach resorts to bustling desert markets, from jagged mountains to sleepy, mud-brick oasis towns. And there's been a distinct new energy since King Mohammed VI took the throne in 1999.

Morocco (*Marruecos* in Spanish; *Al-Maghreb* in Arabic) also provides a good dose of culture shock—both bad and good. It makes Spain seem meek and mild. You'll encounter oppressive friendliness, brutal heat, the Arabic language, the Islamic faith, ancient cities, and aggressive beggars.

While Morocco is clearly a place apart from Mediterranean Europe, it doesn't really seem like Africa either. It's a mix, reflecting its strategic position between the two continents. Situated on the Strait of Gibraltar, Morocco has been flooded by waves of invasions over the centuries. The Berbers, the native population, have had to contend with the Phoenicians, Carthaginians, Romans, Vandals, and more.

The Arabs brought Islam to Morocco in the seventh century A.D. and stuck around, battling the Berbers in various civil wars. A series of Berber and Arab dynasties rose and fell; the Berbers won out and still run the country today.

From the 15th century on, European countries carved up much of Africa. By the early 20th century, most of Morocco was under French control, and strategic Tangier was jointly ruled by multiple European powers. The country wasn't granted independence until 1956. In the late 1970s, Morocco itself became an invading country, grabbing Spain's Western Sahara territory and causing the relatively few inhabitants to clamor for independence. Western Sahara's claim

Islam 101

Islam has more than a billion adherents worldwide, and traveling in an Islamic country is an opportunity to better understand the religion. This admittedly basic and simplistic outline (written by a non-Muslim) is meant to help travelers from the Christian West understand a very rich but often misunderstood culture.

Muslims, like Christians and Jews, are monotheistic. They call God "Allah." The most important person in the Islamic faith is the prophet Muhammad, who lived in the sixth and seventh centuries A.D. The holy book of Islam is the Quran, believed by Muslims to be the word of Allah as revealed to Muhammad.

The "five pillars" of Islam are the core tenets of the faith. Followers of Islam should:

1. Say and believe, "There is only one God, and Muhammad is his prophet."

2. Pray five times a day, facing Mecca. Modern Muslims explain that it's important for this ritual to include washing, exercising, stretching, and thinking of God.

3. Give to the poor (one-fortieth of your wealth, if you are not in debt).

4. Fast during daylight hours through the month of Ramadan. Fasting is a great social equalizer and helps everyone to feel the hunger of the poor.

5. Make a pilgrimage to Mecca. Muslims who can afford it, and who are physically able, are required to travel to the sacred sites in Mecca and Medina at least once in their lifetimes.

Just as it helps to know about spires, feudalism, and the saints to comprehend European sightseeing, a few basics on Islam help make your sightseeing in Morocco more meaningful.

still has not been settled by the United Nations.

Unfortunately, most of the English-speaking Moroccans the typical tourist meets are hustlers. Many visitors develop some intestinal problems by the end of their visit. Most women are harassed on the streets by horny but generally harmless men. And in terms of efficiency, Morocco makes Spain look like Sweden.

When you cruise south across the Strait of Gibraltar, leave your busy itineraries and split-second timing behind. Morocco must be taken on its own terms. In Morocco things go smoothly

MOROCCO

Morocco

only *"Inshallah"*—if God so wills.

Politics and Safety: As throughout the Arab world, Morocco has had its share of political unrest in recent years. Widespread but mostly peaceful protests in 2011, influenced by the Arab Spring, called for greater democracy and economic reforms. A new constitution, adopted later that year, gave more power to the legislative branch and the prime minister—the ostensible head of government (although critics say King Mohammmed VI retained actual authority).

Morocco is also struggling to reconcile tensions between Islamist and secular factions within its government and in the region. Bombings attributed to Islamic fundamentalists killed 45 people in Casablanca in 2003 and 17 in Marrakech in 2011, and were met with widespread condemnation by the Moroccan people.

Americans pondering a visit may wonder how they'll be received in this Muslim nation. Al Jazeera blares from televisions in all the bars, but I've seen no angry graffiti or posters and felt no animosity toward American individuals there (even on my last visit, literally days after US forces killed Osama bin Laden). And it's culturally enriching for Westerners to experience Morocco—a Muslim monarchy with many women still in traditional dress and roles, succeeding on its own terms without embracing modern Western "norms."

If you're still concerned, check the state department's website for travel advisories: www.travel.state.gov.

Hustler Alert: Moroccans may be some of Africa's wealthiest people, but you are still incredibly rich to them. This imbalance

causes predictable problems. Wear your money belt. Assume con artists are more clever than you. Haggle when appropriate; prices skyrocket for tourists (see "Bargaining Basics," page 898). You'll attract hustlers like flies at every famous tourist site or whenever you pull out your guidebook or a map. In the worst-case scenario, they'll lie to you, get you lost, blackmail you, and pester the heck out of you. Never leave your car or baggage where you can't get back to it without someone else's "help." Anything you buy in a guide's company gets him a 20 percent commission. Normally locals, shopkeepers, and police will come to your rescue if the hustlers' heat becomes unbearable. Consider hiring a guide, since it's helpful to have a translator, and once you're "taken," the rest seem to leave you alone.

Marijuana Alert: In Morocco, marijuana *(kif)* is as illegal as it is popular, a fact that many Westerners in local jails would love to remind you of. As a general rule, just walk right by those hand-carved pipes in the marketplace. Some dealers who sell it cheap make their profit after you get arrested. Cars and buses are stopped and checked by police routinely throughout Morocco—especially in the north and in the Chefchaouen region, which is Morocco's *kif* capital.

Health: Morocco is much more hazardous to your health than Spain. Eat in clean—not cheap—places. Peel fruit, eat only cooked vegetables, and drink reliably bottled water (Sidi Ali or Sidi Harazem). When you do get diarrhea—and you should plan on it—adjust your diet (small and bland meals, no milk or grease) or fast for a day, but make sure you replenish lost fluids. Relax: Most diarrhea is not serious, just an adjustment that will run its course.

Closed Days and Ramadan: Friday is the Muslim day of rest, when most of the country (except Tangier) closes down. During the major month-long religious holiday of Ramadan (June 28-July 27 in 2014), Muslims focus on prayer and reflection. Following Islamic doctrine, they refrain during daylight hours from eating, drinking (including water), smoking, and having sex. On the final day of Ramadan, Muslims celebrate *Eid* (an all-day feast and gift-giving party, similar to Christmas), and travelers may find some less-touristy stores and restaurants closed.

Money: Euros work here (as do dollars and pounds). If you're on a five-hour tour, bring along lots of €1 and €0.50 coins for tips, small purchases, and camel rides. But if you plan to do anything independently, change some money into Moroccan dirhams upon arrival (8 dh = about $1). For more money tips, see "Helpful Hints" on page 888.

Information: Travel information, English or otherwise, is rare here. For an extended trip, bring guidebooks from home or Spain—Lonely Planet and Rough Guide both publish good ones. Buy the best map you can find locally—names are always changing, and if you need to ask someone, it's helpful to have towns, roads, and place names written in Arabic.

Language: With its unique history of having been controlled by so many different foreign and domestic rulers, Tangier is a babel of languages. Most locals speak Arabic first and French second (all Moroccans must learn it in schools); sensing that you're a foreigner, they'll most likely address you in French. Spanish ranks third, and English a distant fourth. The Arabic squiggle-script, its many difficult sounds, and the fact that French is Morocco's second language combine to make communication tricky for English-speaking travelers. A little French goes a long way, but learn a few words in Arabic. Have your first local friend help you with the pronunciation:

English	Arabic	Pronounced
Hello. ("Peace be with you")	*Salaam alaikum.*	sah-LAHM ah-LAY-koom
Hello. (response: "Peace also be with you")	*Wa alaikum salaam.*	wah ah-LAY-koom sah-LAHM
Please.	*Min fadlik.*	meen FAHD-leek
Thank you.	*Shokran.*	SHOH-kron (like "sugar on")
Excuse me.	*Ismahli.*	ees-SMAH-lee
Yes.	*Yeh.*	EE-yeh
No.	*Lah.*	lah
Give me five. (kids enjoy this...not above but straight ahead)	*Ham sah.*	hahm sah
OK.	*Wah hah.*	wah hah
Very good.	*Miz yen biz ef.*	meez EE-yehn beez ehf
Goodbye.	*Maa salama.*	mah sah-LEM-ah

Moroccans are more touchy-feely than their Spanish neighbors. Expect lots of hugs if you make an effort to communicate. When greeting someone, a handshake is customary, followed by placing your right hand over your heart. Listen carefully and write new words phonetically. Bring an Arabic phrase book. It helps to know that *souk* means a particular market (such as for leather, yarn, or metalwork), while a *kasbah* is loosely defined as a fortress (or a town within old fortress walls). In markets, I sing, "la la la la la" to my opponents. *Lah shokran* means "No, thank you."

TANGIER

Tanja

Go to Africa. As you step off the boat, you realize that the crossing (less than an hour) has taken you further culturally than did the trip from the US to Spain. Morocco needs no museums; its sights are living in the streets. For decades, its once-grand coastal city of Tangier deserved its reputation as the "Tijuana of Africa." But that has changed. King Mohammad VI is enthusiastic about Tangier, and there's a fresh can-do spirit in the air. The town is as Moroccan as ever...yet more enjoyable and less stressful.

Morocco in a Day?

Though Morocco certainly deserves more than a day, many visitors touring Spain see it in a quick side-trip. And, though such a short sprint through Tangier is only a tease, it's far more interesting than another day in Spain. A day in Tangier gives you a good introduction to Morocco, a legitimate taste of North Africa, and a nonthreatening slice of Islam. All you need is a passport (no visa or shots required) and around €60 for a tour package or the round-trip ferry crossing.

Your big decisions: where to sail from; whether to go on your own or buy a ferry/guided tour day-trip package; and whether to make it a day trip or spend the night. Of these, the most important question is:

With a Tour or on My Own?: Because the ferry company expects you to do a lot of shopping (providing them with kickbacks), it's actually about the same cost to join a one-day tour as it is to buy a round-trip ferry ticket. Do you want the safety and comfort of having Morocco handed to you on a user-friendly platter? Or do you want the independence to see what you want to see, with a more authentic experience, fewer cultural clichés, and less forced shopping? There are pros and cons to each approach, depending on your travel style.

On a package tour, visitors are met by a guide, taken on a bus tour and a walk through the old-town market, offered a couple of crass Kodak moments with snake charmers and desert dancers, and given lunch with live music and belly-dancing. Then they visit a big shop and are hustled back down to their boat where—five hours after they landed—they return to the First World thankful they don't have diarrhea.

The alternative is to simply take the ferry on your own. Things are cheap and relatively safe. Since more than 90 percent of visitors choose the comfort of a tour, independent adventurers rarely see another tourist and avoid all the kitsch. You can catch a morning boat and spend the entire day, returning that evening; extend with an overnight in Tangier; or even head deeper into Morocco (if you do that, you'll need another guidebook).

My preferred approach is sort of a hybrid: Go to Morocco "on your own," but arrange in advance to meet up with a local guide to ease your culture shock and accompany you to your choice of sights (I've listed several guides on page 889, or you can book a tour with the ferry company and pay for the "VIP" option). While this costs a bit more than joining a package tour, ultimately the cost difference (roughly €10-20 more per person) is pretty negligible, considering the dramatically increased cultural intimacy. Doing it entirely on your own (no guide at all) can be a great adventure, but potentially more stressful.

Time Difference: Morocco is on Greenwich Mean Time (like Great Britain), so it's one hour behind Spain. It typically observes Daylight Saving Time, but its summer hours last about two months less than in Europe. Morocco "springs forward" in late April (about a month after Spain) and "falls back" in late September (about a month before Spain). Therefore, during the summer months, Morocco is either one hour (if they've changed) or two hours (if they haven't changed, or have already changed back) behind Spain. In general, ferry and other schedules use the local time (if your boat leaves Tangier "at 17:00," that means 5:00 p.m. Moroccan time—not Spanish time)...be sure to change your watch when you get off the boat.

Terminology: Note that the Spanish refer to Morocco as "Marruecos" (mar-WAY-kohs) and Tangier as "Tánger" (TAHN-hair, with a guttural *h*).

Going on Your Own, by Ferry from Tarifa

While the trip to Tangier can be made from various ports, only the ferry from Tarifa takes you to Tangier's city-center port, called the Tangier Medina Port (Spaniards call it the *Puerto Viejo*, "Old Port"). Boats from Algeciras or Gibraltar dock instead at the Tangier MED Port (Spaniards call it the *Puerto Nuevo*, "New Port"), about 25 miles east of the city center. (Note: Confusingly, because the city-center port is being remodeled, some Moroccans call it the "new port"—exactly the opposite of the Spaniards.) Tangier's city-center port has been closed to cargo shipping, and is in the midst of a massive renovation and beautification project, set to be completed in 2016, which will extend the pier to accommodate large cruise ships and create a marina for yachts.

I'll describe the trip assuming you're sailing from Tarifa to Tangier's city-center Medina Port—the most logical route for the typical traveler.

Ferry Crossing: Two ferry companies make the 35-minute crossing from Tarifa, Spain to Tangier, Morocco about every hour from 8:00 to 22:00: **FRS** (tel. 956-681-830, www.frs.es) and newcomer **InterShipping** (tel. 956-684-729, info.intershipping @gmail.com). FRS ferries depart Tarifa on odd hours (9:00, 11:00,  and so on); InterShipping boats leave Tarifa on even hours (8:00, 10:00, and so on). Prices are roughly €33 one-way and €60 round-trip. Return boats from Tangier to Tarifa run from about 7:00 to 21:00.

Tickets are very easy to get: You can buy them at the port, through your hotel in Tarifa, or from a local travel agency. You can also get FRS tickets at either of their offices in Tarifa: One is just outside the old-town wall, at the corner of Avenida de Andalucía and Avenida de la Constitución (Mon-Fri 8:00-21:00, Sat 8:00-15:00, closed Sun, tel. 956-681-830, www.frs.es). The other location, with longer hours on weekends, is near the port on Calle Alcalde Juan Núñez 2 (daily 9:00-13:00 & 15:00-21:00; see map on page 856 for both locations). InterShipping has an office at the Tarifa's port, but none in town. You can almost always just buy a ticket and walk on, though in the busiest summer months (July-Aug), the popular 8:00 & 9:00 departures could be booked up with tours. Boats are most crowded in July, August, and during the month of Ramadan. A few crossings a year are canceled because of storms or wind, mostly in winter.

Procedure: The ferry from Tarifa is a fast Nordic hydrofoil that theoretically takes 35 minutes to cross. It often leaves late, but you'll still want to arrive early to give yourself time to clear customs (making the whole trip take closer to an hour). You'll go through Spanish customs at the port and Moroccan customs on the ferry. Whether taking a tour or traveling on your own, you *must* get a stamp (available on board) from the Moroccan immigration officer. After you leave Spain, find the customs desk on the boat, line up early, and get your passport and entry paper—which they keep—stamped. If you're coming back the same day and know your return time, the immigration official may also give you an exit stamp (for your return from Morocco), which prevents delays at the port at departure time. The ferry is equipped with WCs, a shop, and a snack bar. Tarifa's modern little terminal has a cafeteria and WCs.

Hiring a Guide: Even if you're visiting Morocco independently, I recommend hiring a local guide to show you around Tangier (for a list of recommended guides, see "Local Guides," on page 889).

Tangier MED Port: Ferries from Algeciras and Gibraltar arrive at the Tangier MED Port, 25 miles from downtown. While this wastes time (it's about an hour each way from the boat to downtown Tangier), the connection is simple: A free shuttle bus picks up passengers at the Tangier MED Port terminal and brings them right to the entrance of the Tangier Medina Port, in the city center.

Returning to Tarifa: It's smart to return to the port about 30 minutes before your ferry departs. If you didn't get your passport's exit stamp on the way over, you must wait in line to get it stamped at the Tangier ferry terminal before you board the boat.

Taking a Package Tour

Taking a package tour is easier but less rewarding than doing it on your own or with a private local guide. A typical day-trip tour

includes a round-trip crossing and a guide who meets your big group at a prearranged point in Tangier, then hustles you through the hustlers and onto your tour bus. Several guides await the arrival of each ferry in Tangier and assemble their groups. (Tourists wear stickers identifying which tour they're with.) All offer essentially the same five-hour Tangier experience: a city bus tour, a drive through the ritzy palace neighborhood, a walk through the Medina (old town), and an overly thorough look at a sales-starved carpet shop (where prices include a 20 percent commission for your guide and tour company; some carpet shops are actually owned by the ferry company). Longer tours may include a trip to the desolate Atlantic Coast for some rugged African scenery, and the famous ride-a-camel stop (five-minute camel ride for a couple of euros). Any tour wraps up with lunch in a palatial Moroccan setting with live music (and non-Moroccan belly dancing), topped off by a final walk back to your boat through a gauntlet of desperate merchants.

Sound cheesy? It is. But no amount of packaging can gloss over this exotic and different culture. This kind of cultural voyeurism is almost embarrassing, but it's nonstop action.

The day trip is so tightly organized that tourists have hardly any time alone in Tangier. For many people, that's just fine. But frankly, seeing a line of day-trippers clutching their bags nervously like paranoid kangaroos reminded me of a self-imposed hostage crisis. It was pathetic.

You rarely need to book a tour more than a day in advance, even during peak season. Tours generally cost about €60 (about the same as a round-trip ferry ticket alone—they make their money off commissions if you shop, and get a group rate on the ferry tickets). Prices are roughly the same no matter where you buy. While some agencies run their own tours, others simply sell tickets on excursions operated by FRS. Ultimately, it's the luck of the draw as to which guide you're assigned. Don't worry about which tour company you select. (They're all equally bad.)

Tours leave Tarifa on a variable schedule: For example, one tour may depart at 9:00 and return at 15:00, the next could run 11:00-19:00 (offering a longer experience), and the next 13:00-19:00. If you're an independent type on a one-day tour, you could stay with your group until you return to the ferry dock, and then just slip back into town on your own, thinking, "Freedom!" You're welcome to use your return ferry ticket on any later boat. (Although FRS and InterShipping both have departures generally every other hour, tickets are *not* interchangeable between the two ferry companies).

You can pay extra for various add-ons. For an extra €15 per person beyond the cost of a standard tour, they will arrange a **"VIP tour"** for up to four people—you'll get a private guide and vehicle, plus lunch. This is actually quite economical, especially if you're traveling as a foursome and would prefer a more personalized experience.

If you want a longer visit, it's cheap to book a package through the ferry company that includes staying in a Tangier hotel for one night (only €30-35 more than the regular tour, €10 extra in peak season, includes guiding and 2 lunches and 1 dinner). If you stay overnight, the first day is the same as the one-day tour, but rather than catching the boat that afternoon, you take the same boat—on your own—24 hours later. There's also a two-day option that includes no guiding or meals (€25-30 more than regular tour, €12 extra in peak season).

Booking a Package Tour: If you're taking one of these tours, you may as well book direct with the **ferry company** (see contact information earlier, under "Ferry Crossing," or visit their offices at the port in Tarifa), or through your **hotel** (you'll pay the same, but the hotel gets a commission; if you know you want to visit Morocco with a tour, ask your hotel to book it when you reserve). There's not much reason to book with a **travel agency,** but offices all over southern Spain and in Tarifa sell ferry tickets and seats on tours. In Tarifa, Luís and Antonio at Baelo Tour offer Rick Steves readers a 10 percent discount (daily in summer 7:00-21:00, across from TI at Avenida de la Constitución 5, tel. 956-681-242); other Tarifa-based agencies are Tarifa Travel and Travelsur (both on Avenida de Andalucía, above the old-town walls). For travel agency locations in Tarifa, see the map on page 856.

Tangier

Artists, writers, and musicians have always loved Tangier. Delacroix and Matisse were drawn by its evocative light. The Beat generation, led by William S. Burroughs and Jack Kerouac, sought the city's multicultural, otherworldly feel. Paul Bowles found his sheltering sky here. From the 1920s through the 1950s, Tangier was an "international city," too strategic to give to any one nation, and jointly governed by as many as nine different powers, including France, Spain, Britain, Italy, Belgium, the Netherlands...and Morocco. The city was a tax-free zone (since there was no single authority to collect taxes), which created a booming free-for-all atmosphere, attracting playboy millionaires, bon vivants, globetrotting scoundrels, con artists, and expat romantics. Tangier enjoyed a cosmopolitan golden age that, in many ways, shaped the city visitors see today.

Tangier is always defying expectations. Ruled by Spain in the 19th century and France in the 20th, it's a rare place where signs are in three languages...and English doesn't make the cut. In this Muslim city, you'll find a synagogue, Catholic and Anglican churches, and the town's largest mosque in close proximity.

Because of its "international zone" status, Morocco's previous king effectively disowned the city, denying it national funds for improvements. Over time, neglected Tangier became the armpit of Morocco. But when the new king—Mohammed VI—was

crowned in 1999, the first city he visited
was Tangier. His vision has been to
restore Tangier to its former glory.

While the city (with a population
of 700,000 and growing quickly) has a
long way to go, restorations are taking
place on a grand scale: The beach has
been painstakingly cleaned, pedestrian
promenades are popping up, and gardens
bloom with lush new greenery. A brand-
new futuristic soccer stadium opened in
2011, and the city-center port is being converted into a huge, slick
leisure-craft complex that will handle cruise megaships, yachts,
and ferries from Tarifa.

I'm uplifted by the new Tangier—it's affluent and modern
without having abandoned its roots and embraced Western values.
Many visitors are impressed by the warmth of the Moroccan
people. Notice how they touch their right hand to their heart after
shaking hands or saying, "thank you"—a kind gesture meant to
emphasize sincerity. (In Islam, the right hand is holy, while the
left hand is evil. Moroccans who eat with their hands—as many
civilized people do in this part of the world—always eat with their
right hand; the left hand is for washing.)

A visit to Morocco—so close to Europe, yet embracing the
Arabic language and script and Muslim faith—lets a Westerner
marinated in anti-Muslim propaganda see what Islam aspires to be
and can be...and realize it is not a threat.

Planning Your Time

If you're not on a package tour, pre-arrange for a guide to meet you
at the ferry dock (see "Local Guides," on page 889), hire a guide
upon arrival, or head on your own to the big square called the
Grand Socco to get oriented (you can walk or catch a Petit Taxi
from the port to the Grand Socco). Get your bearings with my
Grand Socco spin-tour, then delve into the old town (the lower
Medina, with the Petit Socco, market, and American Legation
Museum; and the upper Medina's Kasbah, with its museum and
residential lanes). With more time, take a taxi to sightsee along the
beach and then along Avenue Mohammed VI, through the urban
new town, and back to the port. You'll rarely see other tourists
outside the tour-group circuit.

After Dark: Nighttime is great in Tangier. If you're spending
the night, don't relax in a fancy hotel restaurant. Get out and about
in the old town after dark. It's an entirely different experience
and a highlight of any visit. (But remember, this isn't night-owl
Spain—things die down by around 22:00.)

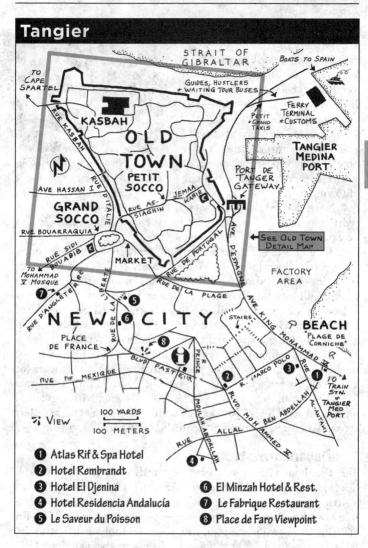

TANGIER

Map legend:

1. Atlas Rif & Spa Hotel
2. Hotel Rembrandt
3. Hotel El Djenina
4. Hotel Residencia Andalucía
5. Le Saveur du Poisson
6. El Minzah Hotel & Rest.
7. Le Fabrique Restaurant
8. Place de Faro Viewpoint

Orientation to Tangier

Like almost every city in Morocco, Tangier is split in two: old and new. From the ferry dock you'll see the old town (Medina)—encircled by its medieval wall—on your right, behind Hotel Continental. (The wall itself is being restored, with completion expected sometime in 2016.) The old town has the markets, the Kasbah (with its palace and the mosque of the Kasbah—marked by the higher of the two minarets you see), cheap hotels, characteristic guesthouses, homes both decrepit and recently renovated, and

2,000 wannabe guides. The twisty, hilly streets of the old town are caged within a wall accessible by keyhole gates. The larger minaret (on the left) belongs to the modern Mohammed V mosque—the biggest one in town.

The new town, with the TI and modern international-style hotels, sprawls past the industrial port zone to your left. The big square, Grand Socco, is the hinge between the old and new parts of town.

Note that while tourists (and this guidebook) refer to the twisty old town as "the Medina," locals consider both the old and new parts of the city center to be medinas.

Tangier is the fifth-largest city in Morocco, and many visitors assume they'll get lost here. While the city could use more street signs, it's laid out simply—although once you enter the mazelike Medina, all bets are off. Nothing listed under "Sights in Tangier" is more than a 20-minute walk from the port. Petit Taxis (described later, under "Getting Around Tangier") are a remarkably cheap godsend for the hot and tired tourist. Use them liberally.

Because so many different colonial powers have had a finger in this city, it goes by many names: In English, it's Tangier (or Tangiers); in French, Tanger (tahn-zhay); in Arabic, it's Tanja (TAHN-zhah); in Spanish, Tánger (TAHN-hair, with a guttural h); and so on. Unless you speak Arabic, French is the handiest second language, followed by Spanish and (finally) English.

Tourist Information

The TI, about a 15-minute gradual uphill walk from the Grand Socco, is not particularly helpful (English is in short supply, but a little French goes a long way). But at least you can pick up a free town brochure—in French only—with a town map (Mon-Fri 8:30-16:30, closed Sat-Sun, in new town at Boulevard Pasteur 29, tel. 0539-94-80-50). There's also a TI desk at the Tangier MED Port, and there may be one at the city-center Tangier Medina Port in the future.

The urban area around the Tangier TI has a few interesting features. The yellow building across the small street from the TI (toward the Grand Socco) is a synagogue. A block farther is the beautiful Place de Faro terrace, with its cannons and views back to Spain. (Nicknamed "Terrace of the Lazy Ones," this momentum-killing spot is usually lined with men relaxing and enjoying the views.) Beyond that, Rue de la Liberté leads directly into the Grand Socco square, the hub of old Tangier.

Arrival in Tangier
By Ferry

If you're taking a tour, just follow the leader. If you're on your own, you'll want to head for the Grand Socco to get oriented. You can

either take a taxi (cheap) or walk (about 10 gently uphill minutes through the colorful but confusing lanes of the Medina). Note that the entire port area is undergoing extensive reconstruction through 2016, so you may find some changes from the way things are described here.

TANGIER

A small blue **Petit Taxi** is your easiest way to get from the port into town (described later, under "Getting Around Tangier"); unfortunately, prices are not regulated from the port. An honest cabbie will charge you 20-30 dh (about $3) for a ride from the ferry into town; less scrupulous drivers will try to charge closer to 100 dh. Set your price before hopping in.

To **walk** into town, head out through the port entrance checkpoint (by the mosque) and bear left at the stubby wall, passing the big bus parking lot and the white Hotel Continental on your right-hand side. After a few minutes, at the end of the bus lot, look for a mosque's white minaret with green tile high on the hill, and head toward it by going up the street just beyond the long, high white wall (behind the buses). Go through the yellow gateway (Bab Dar Dbagh) marked *1921* and *1339*. Bear right/uphill at the T-intersection, then turn left/uphill on Rue de la Marine. You'll pass a school on the right, then the mosque with the green minaret on your left. Continue straight up to the café-lined Petit Socco square, then continue to the top of the street and turn left before the white gate to enter the Grand Socco. Leave mental breadcrumbs as you walk, so you can find your way back to your boat. If all else fails, head downhill.

By Plane

The Tangier Airport (Aeroport Ibn Battouta, airport code: TNG) is very new-feeling, slick, and well-organized, with ATMs, cafés, and other amenities. Iberia, Royal Air Maroc, easyJet, and Ryanair fly from here to Madrid (easyJet also has a route to Paris). Jet4you, another low-cost airline, is based in Casablanca, but offers flights from Tangier to Barcelona and Brussels (www.jet4you.com). To get into downtown Tangier, taxis should run you about 150 dh and take 30-45 minutes.

Getting Around Tangier

There are two types of taxis: Avoid the big, beige Mercedes "Grand Taxis," which are the most aggressive and don't use their meters (they're designed for longer trips outside of the city center, but have been known to take tourists for a ride in town...in more ways than one). Look instead for **Petit Taxis**—blue with a yellow stripe (they fit 2-3 people). These generally use their meters, are very cheap, and only circulate within the city. However, at the port, Petit Taxis are allowed to charge whatever you'll pay without using the meter, so it's essential to agree on a price up front.

Be aware that Tangier taxis sometimes "double up"—if you're headed somewhere, the driver may pick up someone else who's going in the same direction. However, in this case you don't get to split the fare—each of you pays full price (even though sometimes the other passenger's route takes you a bit out of your way).

Helpful Hints

Money: The exchange rate is 8 dh = about $1; 11 dh = about €1. While most businesses happily take euros or dollars, it's classier to use the local currency—and you'll save money. If you're on a tour, they'll rip you off anyway, so just stick with euros. If you're on your own, it's fun to get a pocket full of dirhams.

A few ATMs are around the Grand Socco (look for one just to the left of the archway entrance into the Medina); more are opposite the TI along Boulevard Pasteur. ATMs work as you expect them to. Banks and ATMs have uniform rates.

Exchange desks are quick, easy, and fair. (Just understand the buy-and-sell rates—they should be within 10 percent of one another with no other fee. If you change €50 into dirhams and immediately change the dirhams back, you should have about €45.) Look for the official *Bureaux de Change* offices, where you'll get better rates than at the banks. There are some on Boulevard Pasteur, and a handful between the Grand and Petit Soccos. The official change offices all offer the same rates, so there's no need to shop around.

Convert your dirhams back to euros before catching the ferry—it's cheap and easy to do here (change desks at the port keep long hours), but very difficult once you're back in Spain.

Phoning: To call Tangier from Spain, dial 00 (Europe's international access code), 212 (Morocco's country code), then the local number (dropping the initial zero). To dial Tangier from elsewhere in Morocco, dial the local number in full (keeping the initial zero).

Keeping Your Bearings: Tangier's maps and street signs are frustrating. I ask in French for the landmark: *Où est...?*

("Where is...?," pronounced oo ay, as in *"oo ay Medina?"* or *"oo ay Kasbah?"*). It can be fun to meet people this way. However, most people who offer to help you (especially those who approach you) are angling for a tip—young and old, locals see dollar signs when a traveler approaches. To avoid getting unwanted company, ask for directions only from people who can't leave what they're doing (such as the only clerk in a shop) or from women who aren't near men. There are fewer hustlers in the new (but less interesting) part of town. Be aware that most people don't know the names of the smaller streets (which don't usually have signs), and tend to navigate by landmarks. In case you get the wrong directions, ask three times and go with the consensus. If there's no consensus, it's time to hop into a Petit Taxi.

Mosques: Tangier's mosques (and virtually all of Morocco's) are closed to non-Muslim visitors.

Tours in Tangier

Package Tours

For information on guided day-trip tours including the ferry to Tangier from Tarifa, Spain, see "Taking a Package Tour" on page 881.

Local Guides

If you're on your own, you'll be to street guides what a horse's tail is to flies...all day long. Seriously—it can be exhausting to

constantly deflect come-ons from anyone who sees you open a guidebook. In order to have your own translator, and a shield from less scrupulous touts who hit up tourists constantly throughout the old town, I recommend hiring a guide. Stress your interest in the people and culture rather than

shopping. Guides, hoping to get a huge commission from your purchases, can cleverly turn your Tangier day into the Moroccan equivalent of the Shopping Channel. Truth be told, some of these guides would work for free, considering all the money they make on commissions when you buy stuff.

I've worked with a variety of guides who speak great English, are easy to get along with, will meet you at the ferry dock, and charge fixed rates. They've promised me they won't make you do any more shopping than you want to—so be very clear about your interests. If one of these guides is busy (or takes a long time

TANGIER

Women in Morocco

Most visitors to Tangier expect to see the women completely covered head-to-toe by their kaftan. In fact, only about one-quarter of Moroccan women still adhere strictly to this religious code. Some just cover their head (allowing their face to be seen), while others eliminate the head scarf altogether. Some women wear only Western-style clothing. This change in dress visibly reflects deeper, more fundamental shifts in Moroccan attitudes about women's rights.

Morocco happens to be one of the most progressive Muslim countries around. As in any border country, contact with other cultures fosters the growth of new ideas. Bombarded with Spanish television and visitors like you, change is inevitable. Another proponent of change is King Mohammed VI, who was only 35 years old when he rose to the throne in 1999. For the first time in the country's history, the king personally selected a female adviser to demonstrate his commitment to change. The king also married a commoner for...get this...*love*. And even more shocking, she's seen in public. (It's a first—locals don't even know what King Mohammed VI's mother looks like, as she is never in the public view.)

Recent times have brought even more sweeping transformations to Moroccan society. In order to raise literacy levels and understanding between the sexes, schools are now coed—something taken for granted in the West for decades. In 2004, the Mudawana, or judiciary family code, was shockingly overhauled, and Morocco became a trendsetter for women's equality in the Islamic world. The legal age for women to marry is now 18 (just like men) instead of 15. Other changes make it more difficult to have a second wife. Verbal divorce and abandonment are no longer legal—disgruntled husbands must now take their complaints to court. And for the first time, women can divorce their husbands. If children are involved, whoever takes care of the kids gets the house. Morocco took another step forward with its 2011 constitutional reforms, which now guarantee women "civic and social" equality.

responding to your email), try the others. Any of these guides will make your Tangier experience more enjoyable for a negligible cost. They can also book your ferry tickets for the same cost as booking direct: They'll give you a reference number to give at the ticket office in Tarifa, then you'll pay them for the tickets when you meet in Tangier. While each has their own specific itineraries, the two basic options are more or less the same: a half-day walking tour around the Medina and Kasbah (generally 3-5 hours); or a full-day "grand tour" that includes the walk around town as well as a minibus ride to outlying viewpoints—the Caves of Hercules and Cape Spartel (7-8 hours, generally also includes lunch at your expense in a restaurant the guide suggests). Prices are fairly standard from guide to guide. If you're very pleased with your guide, he'll appreciate a tip.

TANGIER

Aziz Begdouri, who enjoys teaching about Moroccan society and culture, has been a big help to me with my guidebook-writing and TV production in Tangier (half-day walking tour-€15/person, groups limited to 4-5 people; 8-hour grand tour-€35/person; mobile 06-6163-9332, from Spain dial 00-212-6-6163-9332, aziztour@hotmail.com).

Salah Abdi grew up in the Medina and has devoted the past 30 years to showing tourists around his hometown. He is a delight, full of historical knowledge and American sports trivia, and his tours give you an intimate insider experience (half-day walking tour-€15/person, groups limited to 4-5 people; full-day grand tour-€35/person for up to 10 people; call to book at least a day in advance, mobile 06-4943-4911, from Spain dial 00-212-6-4943-4911).

Ahmed Taoumi, who has been guiding for more than 30 years, has a professorial style (half-day walking tour-€18/person, full-day grand tour with minibus-€35/person, also offers minibus side-trips to nearby destinations and discounted ferry tickets, mobile 06-6166-5429, from Spain dial 00-212-6-6166-5429, www.visitangier.com, taoumitour@hotmail.com).

If Aziz Begdouri, Salah, or Ahmed are busy, consider one of the following youthful go-getters who are a bit lighter on information, but enjoyable to spend time with and dedicated to making visitors comfortable: **Aziz ("Africa") Benami** (half-day walking tour-€15/person; full-day minibus and walking tour-€35/person, full-day tour including round-trip ferry to/from Tarifa-€79/person, lunch in traditional kasbah home-€15/person, mobile 06-6126-3335, from the US or Canada dial toll-free 1-888-745-7305, www.tangierprivateguide.com, info@tangierprivateguide.com) and **Abdellatif ("Latif") Chebaa** (half-day walking tour-€15/person, grand tour-€35/person, mobile 06-6107-2014, from Spain dial 00-212-6-6107-2014, visittangier@gmail.com).

Other Options: If you don't want to plan too far ahead, and any guide will do, you can book a **"VIP tour"** through the ferry company in Tarifa for approximately the same prices listed above (for details, see page 882). I've also had good luck with the **private guides who meet the boat**. If you're a decent judge of character, try interviewing guides when you get off the ferry to find one you click with, then check for an official license and negotiate a good price. These hardworking, English-speaking guides offer their services for the day for €15.

Sights in Tangier

▲▲The Grand Socco

This big, bustling square is a transportation hub, market, popular meeting point, and the fulcrum between the new town and the old town (Medina). A few years ago, it was a pedestrian nightmare and a perpetual traffic jam. But now, like much of Tangier, it's on the rise. Many of the sights mentioned in this spin-tour are described in more detail later in this chapter.

⊙ Self-Guided Spin Tour: The Grand Socco is a good place to get oriented to the heart of Tangier. Stand on the square between the fountain and the mosque (the long building with arches and the tall tower). We'll do a slow clockwise spin.

Start by facing the **mosque**—newly remodeled with a long arcade of keyhole arches, and with a colorfully tiled minaret.

Morocco is a decidedly Muslim nation, though its take on Islam (see "Islam 101," page 873) is progressive, likely owing to the country's crossroads history. For example, women are relatively free to dress as they like. Five times a day, you'll hear the call to prayer echo across the rooftops of Tangier, from minarets like this one. Unlike many Muslim countries, Morocco doesn't allow non-Muslims to enter its mosques (with the exception of its biggest and most famous one, in Casablanca). This custom may have originated decades ago, when occupying French foreign legion troops spent the night in a mosque, entertaining themselves with wine and women. Following this embarrassing desecration, it was the French government—not the Moroccans—

Tangier's Old Town

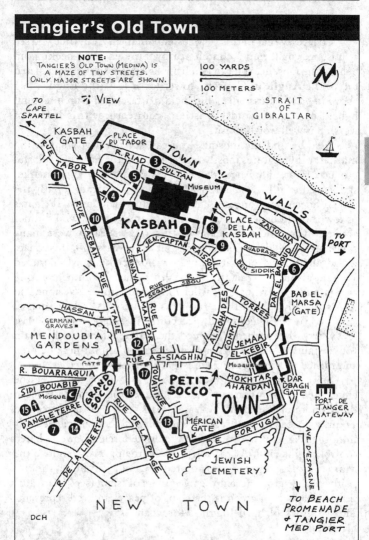

NOTE: Tangier's Old Town (Medina) is a maze of tiny streets. Only major streets are shown.

100 YARDS
100 METERS

STRAIT OF GIBRALTAR

TO CAPE SPARTEL

VIEW

KASBAH GATE

PLACE DU TABOR

RUE TABOR

R. RIAD

SULTAN

TOWN

Museum

KASBAH

WALLS

PLACE DE LA KASBAH

QUADRASS

TO PORT

GEN. CAPTAN

BEN SIDDIK

DAR EL BAROUD

RAISSOUL

R. SEGAYA

R. SBOU

OLD

BAB EL-MARSA (GATE)

RUE KASBAH

RUE D'ITALIE

GENAYA ALMANZOR

RUE ALMANZOR

ALMOHADES

TORRES

COMM.

HASSAN I

GERMAN GRAVES

MENDOUBIA GARDENS

GATE

JEMAA EL-KEBIR

Mosque

DAR DBAGH GATE

PORT DE TANGER GATEWAY

R. BOUARRAQUIA

RUE AS-SIAGHIN

TOUAHINE

PETIT SOCCO

TOWN

MOKHTAR AHARDAN

SIDI BOUABIB

Mosque

GRAND SOCCO

RUE DE LA PLAGE

MÉRICAN GATE

RUE DE PORTUGAL

AVE. D'ESPAGNE

D'ANGLETERRE

R. DE LA LIBERTÉ

JEWISH CEMETERY

NEW TOWN

TO BEACH PROMENADE & TANGIER MED PORT

DCH

1. Dar Chams Tanja
2. La Maison Blanche
3. La Tangerina
4. Dar Nour
5. Dar Sultan
6. Hotel Continental
7. Maison Communitaire des Femmes (Café)
8. Le Salon Bleu Restaurant
9. Le Nabab Restaurant
10. Hamadi Restaurant
11. Marhaba Palace Restaurant
12. Mamounia Palace Rest.
13. Tangier American Legation Mus.
14. Cinema Rif
15. Anglican Church
16. Market
17. Bureau de Change

TANGIER

who instituted the ban that persists today.

Locals say that in this very cosmopolitan city, anytime you see a mosque, you'll find a church nearby. Sure enough, peeking up behind the mosque, you can barely make out the white, crenellated top of the **Anglican Church**'s tower (or at least the English flag above it—a red cross on a white field). A fascinating architectural hybrid of Muslim and Christian architecture, this house of worship is well worth a visit.

Also behind the mosque, you can see parts of a sprawling **market.** (This features mostly modern goods; the far more colorful produce, meat, and fish market is across the square.) Those market stalls used to fill the square you're standing in; traditionally the Grand Socco was Tangier's hub for visiting merchants. The gates of town would be locked each evening, and vendors who did not arrive in time spent the night in this area. (Nearby were many caravanserai—old-fashioned inns.) But a few years ago, this square was dramatically renovated by the visionary king, Mohammed VI, and given a new name: "April 9th Square," commemorating the date in 1947 when an earlier king, Mohammed V, appealed to his French overlords to grant his country its independence. (France eventually complied, peacefully, in 1956.) In just the last few years, Mohammed VI tamed the traffic, added the fountain you're standing next to (there was never a fountain here before), and turned this into a delightfully people-friendly space.

Spin a few more degrees to the right, where you'll see the crenellated gateway marked *Tribunal de Commerce*—the entrance to the **Mendoubia Gardens,** a pleasant park with a gigantic tree and a quirky history that reflects the epic story of Tangier (particularly from the 1920s to the 1950s, when multiple foreign powers shared control of this city). At the top of the garden gateway, notice the Moroccan flag: a green five-pointed star on a red field. The five points of the star represent the five pillars of Islam (see "Islam 101" sidebar, page 873); green is the color of peace, and red represents the struggles of hard-fought Moroccan history.

Spinning farther right, you'll see the **keyhole arch** marking the entrance to the Medina. (If you need cash, notice the exchange booths and ATM just to the left of this gateway.) To reach the heart of the Medina—the Petit Socco (the café-lined little brother of the square you're on now)—go through this arch and take the first right.

In front of the arch, you'll likely see **day laborers** looking for work. Each one stands next to a symbol of the kind of work he specializes in: a bucket of paintbrushes for a painter, a coil of wiring for an electrician, and a loop of hose for a plumber.

Speaking of people looking for work, how many locals have offered to show you around ("Hey! What you looking for? I help you!") since you've been standing here, holding this guidebook? Get used to it. While irritating, it's understandable. To these very poor people, you're impossibly rich—your pocket change is at least a good day's wage. If someone pesters you, you can simply ignore them, or say *"Lah shokran"* (No, thank you). But be warned: The moment you engage them, you've just prolonged the sales pitch.

Back to our spin-tour: To the right of the main arch, and just before the row of green rooftops, is the low-profile entrance to the **market** *(souk)*. A barrage on all the senses, this is a fascinating place to explore. The row of green rooftops leads toward Rue de la Plage, with more market action.

Continue spinning another quarter-turn to the tall, white building at the top of the square labeled **Cinema Rif.** This historic movie house still plays films (in Arabic and French). The street to the left of the cinema takes you to Rue de la Liberté, which eventually leads through the modern town to the TI (about a 15-minute walk). Just to the right of the cinema, notice the yellow terrace, which offers the best view over the Grand Socco (just go up the staircase). It's also part of a café, where you can order a Moroccan tea (green tea, fresh mint, and lots of sugar), enjoy the view over the square, and plot your next move.

Near the Grand Socco

These sights are near the Grand Socco, but still outside the Medina (old town).

▲Anglican Church

St. Andrew's Anglican Church, tucked behind a showpiece mosque, embodies Tangier's mingling of Muslim and Christian

tradition. The land on which the church sits was a gift from the sultan to the British community in 1881, during Queen Victoria's era. Shortly thereafter, this church was built. Although fully Christian, the church is designed in the style of a Muslim mosque. The Lord's Prayer rings the arch in Arabic, as verses of the Quran would in a mosque. Knock on the door—Ali or his son Yassin will greet you and give you a "thank you very much" tour. The garden surrounding the church is a tranquil, park-like cemetery.

Cost and Hours: A tip of about 20

dh is appreciated; daily 9:00-18:00 except closed during Sunday services.

Mendoubia Gardens

This pleasant park, accessed through the castle-like archway off of the Grand Socco, is a favorite place for locals to hang out, and also

has a surprising history. Walk through the gateway to see the trunk of a gigantic banyan tree, which, according to local legend, dates from the 12th century. Notice how the extra supportive roots have grown from the branches down to the ground. The large building to the left—today the business courthouse (*Tribunal de Commerce*)—was built to house the representative of the Moroccan king, back in the early 20th century when Tangier was ruled as a protectorate of various European powers and needed an ambassador of sorts to keep an eye out for Moroccan interests. The smaller house on the right (behind the giant tree) is currently the marriage courthouse (used exclusively for getting married or divorced), but it was once the headquarters of the German delegation in Tangier. France originally kept Germany out of the protectorate arrangement by giving them the Congo. But in 1941, when Germany was on the rise in Europe and allied with Spain's Franco, it joined the mix of ruling powers in Tangier. Although Germans were only here for a short time (until mid-1942), they have a small cemetery in what's now the big park in front of you. Go up the stairs and around the blocky Arabic monument. At the bases of the trees beyond it, you'll find headstones of German graves...an odd footnote in the very complex history of this intriguing city.

The Medina (Old Town)

Tangier's Medina is its convoluted old town—a twisty mess of narrow stepped lanes, dead-end alleys, and lots of local life spilling out into the streets. It's divided roughly into two parts: the lower Medina, with the Petit Socco, market, American Legation, and bustling street life; and, at the top, the more tranquil Kasbah.

The Lower Medina and Petit Socco

A maze of winding lanes and tiny alleys weave through the old-town market area. Write down the name of the gate you came in, so you can enjoy being lost—temporarily.

Petit Socco

This little square, also called Souk Dahel ("Inner Market"), is the center of the lower Medina. Lined with tea shops and cafés, it has a romantic quality that has long made it a people magnet. In the 1920s, it was the meeting point for Tangier's wealthy and influential elite; by the 1950s and '60s, it drew Jack Kerouac and his counterculture buddies. Nursing a coffee or a mint tea here, it's easy to pretend you're a Beat Generation rebel, dropping out from Western society and delving deeply into an exotic, faraway culture. More recently, filmmakers have been drawn here. Scenes from both *The Bourne Ultimatum* and *Inception* were filmed on the streets between the Grand and Petit Soccos.

The Petit Socco is ideal for some casual people-watching over a drink. You can go to one of the more traditional cafés, but **Café Central**—with the modern awning—is the most accessible, and therefore the most commercialized and touristy (7-12-dh coffee drinks, 20-45-dh meals, daily 6:00-24:00).

▲▲Market (Souk)

The Medina's market, just off the Grand Socco, is a highlight. Wander past piles of fruit, veggies, and olives, countless varieties of bread, and fresh goat cheese wrapped in palm leaves. Phew! You'll find everything but pork.

Entering the market through the door from the Grand Socco, turn right to find butchers, a cornucopia of produce (almost all of it from Morocco), more butchers, piles of olives, and yet more butchers. The chickens are plucked and hung to show they have been killed according to Islamic guidelines (halal): Animals are slaughtered with a sharp knife in the name of Allah, head to Mecca, and drained of their blood. The far aisle (parallel and to the left of where you're walking) has more innards and is a little harder to stomach.

You'll see women vendors—often wearing straw hats decorated with ribbons or colorful striped skirts—scattered around the market; these are Berbers, who ride donkeys to the city from the nearby Rif Mountains, mostly on Tuesdays and Thursdays. (Before taking photos of these women, or any people you see here, it's polite to ask permission.)

Eventually you'll emerge into the large white market of fish-sellers; with the day's catch from both the Mediterranean and the Atlantic, this is like a textbook of marine life. The door at the far end of the fish market pops you out on the Rue Salah El-dine

TANGIER

Bargaining Basics

No matter what kind of merchandise you buy in Tangier, the shopping is...Moroccan. Bargain hard! The first price you're offered is simply a starting point, and it's expected that you'll try to talk the price way down. Bargaining can become an enjoyable game if you follow a few basic rules:

Determine what the item is worth to you. Before you even ask a price, decide what the item's value is to you. Consider the hassles involved in packing it or shipping it home.

Determine the merchant's lowest price. Many merchants will settle for a nickel profit rather than lose the sale entirely. Work the cost down to rock bottom, and when it seems to have fallen to a record low, walk away. That last price the seller hollers out as you turn the corner is often the best price you'll get. If the price is right, go back and buy.

Look indifferent. As soon as the merchant perceives the "I gotta have that!" in you, you'll never get the best price.

Employ a third person. Use your friend who is worried about the ever-dwindling budget or who doesn't like the price or who is bored and wants to return to the hotel. This can help to bring the price down faster.

Show the merchant your money. Physically hold out your money and offer him "all you have" to pay for whatever you are bickering over. He'll be tempted to just grab your money and say, "Oh, OK."

If the price is too much, leave. Never worry about having taken too much of the merchant's time. They are experts at making the tourist feel guilty for not buying. It's all part of the game.

Al Ayoubi; a right turn takes you back to the Grand Socco, but a left turn leads to the (figurative and literal) low end of the market—a world of very rustic market stalls under a corrugated plastic roof. While just a block from the main market, this is a world apart, and not to everyone's taste. Here you'll find cheap produce, junk shops, electronics (such as recordable CDs and old remote controls), old ladies sorting bundles of herbs from crinkled plastic bags, and far less sanitary-looking butchers than the ones inside the main market hall (if that's possible). Peer down the alley filled with a twitching poultry market, which encourages vegetarianism.

The upper part of the market (toward the Medina and Petit

Socco) has a few food stands, but more non-perishable items, such as clothing, cleaning supplies, toiletries, and prepared foods. Scattered around this part of the market are spice and herb stalls (usually marked *hérboriste*), offering a fragrant antidote to the meat stalls. In addition to cooking spices, these sell homegrown Berber cures for ailments. Pots hold a dark-green gelatinous goo—a kind of natural soap.

If you're looking for souvenirs, you won't have to find them... they'll find you, in the form of aggressive salesmen who approach you on the street and push their conga drums, T-shirts, and other trinkets in your face. Most of the market itself is more focused on locals, but the Medina streets just above the market are loaded with souvenir shops. Aside from the predictable trinkets, the big-ticket items here are tilework (such as vases) and carpets. You'll notice many shops have tiles and other, smaller souvenirs on the ground floor, and carpet salesrooms upstairs.

▲▲▲Exploring the Medina

Appealing as the market is, one of the most magical Tangier experiences is to simply lose yourself in the lanes of the Medina. A first-time visitor cannot stay oriented—so don't even try. I just wander, knowing that uphill will eventually get me to the Kasbah and downhill will eventually lead me to the port. Expect to get a little lost... going around in circles is part of the fun. Pop in to see artisans working in their shops: mosaic tile-makers, thread spinners, tailors. While shops are on the ground level, the family usually lives upstairs. Doors indicate how many families live in the homes behind them: one row of decoration for one, another parallel row for two.

Many people can't afford private ovens, phones, or running water, so there are economical communal options: phone desks (called *tele-boutiques*), baths, and bakeries. If you smell the aroma of baking bread, look for a hole-in-the-wall bakery, where locals drop off their ready-to-cook dough (as well as meat, fish, or nuts to roast). You'll also stumble upon communal taps, with water provided by the government, where people come to wash. Cubby-hole rooms are filled with kids playing video games on old TVs—they can't afford their own at home, so they come here instead.

Go on a photo safari for ornate "keyhole" doors, many of which lead to neighborhood mosques (see photo next page). Green doors are the color of Islam and symbolize peace. The ring-shaped door knockers double as a place to hitch a donkey.

As you explore, notice that some parts of the Medina seem starkly different, with fancy wrought-iron balconies. This is the approximately 20 percent of the town that was built and controlled by Spaniards and Portuguese living here (with the rest being Arabic and Berber). The two populations were separated by a wall, the remains of which you can still trace running through the Medina. It may seem at first glance that these European zones are fancier and "nicer" compared to the poorer-seeming Arabic/Berber zones. But the Arabs and Berbers take more care with the inside of their homes—if you went behind these humble walls, you'd be surprised how pleasant the interiors are. While European cultures externalize resources, Arab and Berber cultures internalize them.

Tangier American Legation Museum

Located at the bottom end of the Medina (just above the port), this unexpected museum is worth a visit. Morocco was one of the

first countries to recognize the newly formed United States as an independent country (in 1777). The original building, given to the United States by the sultan of Morocco, became the fledgling government's first foreign acquisition.

Cost and Hours: Free entry but donations appreciated, Mon-Thu 10:00-13:00 & 15:00-17:00, Fri 10:00-12:00 & 15:00-17:00, during Ramadan holiday daily 10:00-15:00, closed Sat-Sun year-round, ring bell, Rue d'Amérique 8, tel. 0539-935-317, www .talimblog.org.

Visiting the Museum: This was the US embassy (or consulate) in Morocco from 1821 to 1961, and it's still American property—our only National Historic Landmark overseas. Today this nonprofit museum and research center, housed in a 19th-century mansion, is a strangely peaceful oasis within Tangier's intense old town. It offers a warm welcome and lots of interesting artifacts—all well-described in English. The ground floor is filled with an art gallery. In the stairwell, you'll see photos of kings with presidents, and a letter with the news of Lincoln's assassination. Upstairs are more paintings, as well as model soldiers playing out two battle scenes from Moroccan history. These belonged to American industrialist Malcolm Forbes, who had a home in Tangier (his son donated these dioramas to the museum). Rounding out the upper floor are more paintings, and wonderful old maps of Tangier and Morocco. A visit here is a fun reminder of how long the US and Morocco have had good relations.

• *When you've soaked in enough old-town atmosphere, make your way to the Kasbah (see map). Within the Medina, head uphill, or exit the Medina gate and go right on Rue Kasbah, which follows the old wall uphill to Bab Kasbah (a.k.a. Porte de la Kasbah), a gateway into the Kasbah.*

TANGIER

Kasbah

Loosely translated as "fortress," a *kasbah* is an enclosed, protected residential area near a castle that you'll find in hundreds of Moroccan towns. Originally this was a place where a king or other leader could protect his tribe. Tangier's Kasbah comprises the upper quarter of the old town. A residential area with twisty lanes and some nice guesthouses, this area is a bit more sedate and less claustrophobic than parts of the Medina near the market below.

▲Kasbah Museum

On Place de la Kasbah, you'll find the Dar el-Makhzen, a former sultan's palace that now houses a history museum with a few historical artifacts. While there's not a word of English, some of the exhibits are still easy to appreciate, and the building itself is beautiful.

Cost and Hours: 10 dh, Wed-Mon 9:00-16:00, closed for prayer Fri 11:30-13:30, closed all day Tue, tel. 0539-932-097.

Visiting the Museum: Most of the exhibits surround the central, open-air courtyard; rooms proceed roughly chronologically

as you move counterclockwise, from early hunters and farmers to prehistoric civilizations, Roman times, the region's conversion to Islam, and the influence of European powers. The two-story space at the far end of the courtyard focuses on a second-century mosaic floor depicting the journey of Venus. The big 12th-century wall-size map (in Arabic) shows the Moorish view of the world: with Africa on top (Spain is at the far right). Nearby is an explanation of terra-cotta production (a local industry), and upstairs is an exhibit on funerary rituals. Near the entrance, look for signs to *jardin* and climb the stairs to reach a chirpy (if slightly overgrown) garden courtyard. While the building features some striking tilework, you just can't shake the feeling that the best Moorish sights are back in Spain.

TANGIER

Place de la Kasbah

Because the Kasbah Museum (while modest) is the city's main museum, the square in front of the palace attracts more than

its share of tourists. That means it's also a vivid gauntlet of amusements waiting to ambush parading tour groups: snake charmers, squawky dance troupes, and colorful water vendors. These colorful Kodak-moment hustlers make their living off the many tour groups passing by daily. (As you're cajoled, remember that the daily minimum wage here for men as skilled as these beggars is $10. That's what the gardeners you'll pass in your walk earn each day. In other words, a €1 tip is an hour's wage for these people.) If you draft behind a tour group, you won't be the focus of the hustlers. But if you take a photo, you must pay.

Before descending out of the Kasbah, don't miss the ocean viewpoint—as you stand in the square and face the palace, look to the right to find the hole carved through the thick city wall (Bab Dhar, "Sea Gate"). This leads out to a large natural terrace with fine views over the port, the Mediterranean, and Spain.

The lower gate of the Kasbah (as you stand in Place de la Kasbah facing the palace, it's on your left) leads to a charming

little alcove, between the gates, where you can see a particularly fine tile fountain: The top part is carved cedarwood, below that is carved plaster, and the bottom half is hand-laid tiles. In this area, poke down the tiny lane to the left of the little shop—you'll find that it leads to a surprisingly large courtyard ringed by fine homes.

Matisse Route

The artist Matisse, who traveled to Tangier in 1912, was inspired by his wanderings through this area, picking up themes that show up in much of his art. The diamond-shaped stones embedded in the street (you'll see them on the narrow lane leading up along the left side of the palace) mark a "Matisse Route" through the Kasbah, from the lower gate to the upper; those familiar with his works will recognize several scenes along this stretch.

Tangier Beach

Lined with lots of fishy eateries and entertaining nightclubs, this fine, wide, white-sand crescent beach (Plage de Corniche)

stretches eastward from the port. The locals call it by the Spanish word *playa*. It's packed with locals doing what people around the world do at the beach—with a few variations. Traditionally-clad moms let their kids run wild. Along with lazy camels, you'll see people—young and old—covered in hot sand to combat rheumatism. Early, late, and off-season, the beach becomes a popular venue for soccer teams. The palm-lined pedestrian street along the waterfront was renamed for King Mohammed VI, in appreciation for recent restorations. While the beach is cleaner than it once was, it still has more than its share of litter—great for a stroll, but maybe not for sunbathing or swimming. If you have a beach break in mind, do it on Spain's Costa del Sol.

Just past the beach on the port side (between here and the Medina) is a zone of nondescript factories where local women sew clothing for big, mostly European, companies that pay about $8 a day. Each morning and evening rush hour, the street is filled with these women commuters...on foot.

Nightlife in Tangier

Most important: Be out in the **Medina** around 21:00. In the cool of the evening, the atmospheric squares and lanes become even more alluring. Then at about 22:00 things get dark, lonely, and foreboding.

El Minzah Hotel hosts traditional music most nights for those having dinner there (see "Eating in Tangier," later; 85 Rue de la Liberté, tel. 0539-935-885).

The **Cinema Rif,** the landmark theater at the top of the Grand Socco, shows movies in French—which the younger generation is required to learn—and Arabic. The cinema is worth popping into, if only to see the Art Deco interior. As movies cost only 20 dh, consider dropping by to see a bit of whatever's on...in Arabic (closed Mon, tel. 0539-934-683).

Sleeping in Tangier

I've recommended two vastly different types of accommodations in Tangier: cozy Moroccan-style (but mostly French-run) guesthouses in the maze of lanes of the Kasbah neighborhood, at

Sleep Code

(8 dh = about $1, country code: 212, area code: 539)
S = Single, **D** = Double/Twin, **T** = Triple, **Q** = Quad, **b** = bathroom, **s** = shower only. Unless otherwise noted, credit cards are accepted, English is spoken, and breakfast is included. Most hotels charge an extra tax of 15-25 dh per person per night (typically not included in the prices I've listed here).

To help you easily sort through these listings, I've divided the accommodations into three categories, based on the price for a standard double room with bath (during high season):

$$$ Higher Priced—Most rooms 1,000 dh or more.
  $$ Moderately Priced—Most rooms between 500-1,000 dh.
    $ Lower Priced—Most rooms 500 dh or less.

Prices can change without notice; verify the hotel's current rates online or by email. For the best prices, always book direct.

the top of the Medina (old town); and big, modern international-style hotels in the urban-feeling new town, a 10-to-20-minute walk from the central sights.

Remember, if you want to call Tangier from Europe, dial 00 (Europe's international access code), 212 (Morocco's country code), then the local number (dropping the initial zero). June through mid-September is high season, when rooms may be a bit more expensive and reservations are wise.

Guesthouses in the Kasbah

In Arabic, *dar* means "guesthouse." You'll find these in the Medina, or atmospheric old quarter. While the lower part of the Medina is dominated by market stalls and tourist traps—and can feel a bit seedy after dark—the upper part (called the Kasbah, for the castle that dominates this area) is more tranquil and feels very residential. All of my recommendations are buried in a labyrinth of lanes that can be very difficult to navigate; the map on page 893 gives you a vague sense of where to go, but it's essential to ask for very clear directions when you reserve. If you're hiring a guide in Tangier, ask them to help you find your *dar*. (If you're on your own, you can try asking directions when you arrive—but many local residents take that as an invitation to tag along and hound you for tips.) All of these are in traditional old houses, with rooms surrounding a courtyard atrium, and all have rooftop terraces where you can relax and enjoy sweeping views over Tangier. Most include breakfast, unless noted; many also serve good, Moroccan dinners, which cost extra and should be arranged beforehand, typically that morning. Some also offer hammams (Turkish-style baths) with massages and spa treatments. Many lack stand-alone showers; instead, in Moroccan style, you'll find a handheld shower in a corner of the bathroom.

$$$ Dar Chams Tanja, just below the lower Kasbah gate, has seven elegant, new-feeling rooms with all the comforts surrounding a clean-white inner courtyard with lots of keyhole windows. While pricey, it's impeccably decorated, calm, and boasts incredible views from its rooftop terrace (five big Db-1,580 dh, two small Db-1,250 dh, sometimes discounts in slow times—check website, air-con, free Wi-Fi, hammam, massage service, Rue Jnan Kabtan 2, tel. 0539-332-323, www.darchamstanja.com, darchamstanja@gmail.com).

$$$ Dar Sultan rents six romantically decorated rooms on a pleasant street in the heart of the Kasbah (Db-1,210 dh, larger Db-1,224 dh, Db with terrace-1,446 dh, Jean Pierre promises a 10 percent discount if you book directly with the hotel and mention this book when you reserve, cash only, free Wi-Fi in lobby and cable Internet in rooms, Rue Touila 49, tel. 0539-336-061, www.darsultan.com, dar-sultan@menara.ma).

$$$ La Maison Blanche ("The White House"), run by tour guide Aziz Begdouri, has nine rooms in a traditional Moroccan house with modern amenities in the Kasbah (Sb-1,000 dh, Db-1,100 dh, all with bathtubs, air-con, free Wi-Fi, just inside the upper gate of the Kasbah at Rue Ahmed Ben Ajiba 2, tel. 0539-373-545, www.lamaisonblanchetanger.com, info @lamaisonblanchetanger.com).

$$ La Tangerina, run by Jürgen (who's German) and his Moroccan wife, Farida, has 10 comfortable rooms that look down into a shared atrium. At the top is a gorgeous rooftop seaview balcony (Db-600-935 dh in April and June-mid-Sept, otherwise Db-500-770; suite-1,520-1,650 dh in April and June-mid-Sept, otherwise 1,100-1,320 dh; prices depend on size, cash only, free Wi-Fi, wood-fired hammam, turn left as you enter the upper Kasbah gate and hug the town wall around to Riad Sultan 19, tel. 0539-947-731, www.latangerina.com, info@latangerina.com).

$$ Dar Nour, run with funky French style by Philippe, Jean-Olivier, and Catherine, has an "Escher-esque" floor plan that sprawls through five interconnected houses (it's "labyrinthine like the Medina," says Philippe). The 10 homey rooms feel very traditional, with lots of books and lounging areas spread throughout (Db-720 dh, junior suite Db-950 dh, suite Db-1,300 dh, cash only, free Wi-Fi in lobby, Rue Gourna 20, mobile 06-6211-2724, www.darnour.com, contactdarnour@yahoo.fr).

Modern Hotels in the Modern City

These hotels are centrally located, near the TI, and within walking distance of the Grand Socco, Medina, and market. The first two are three-star hotels and take credit cards; the others are cash-only.

$$$ Atlas Rif & Spa Hotel, recently restored to its 1970s glamour, is a worthy splurge. Offering 127 plush, modern rooms, sprawling public spaces, a garden, pool, and grand views, it feels like an oversized boutique hotel. Overlooking the harbor, the great Arabic lounge—named for Winston Churchill—compels you to relax (Sb-1,200 dh, Db-1,400 dh, 200 dh more July-Aug, 200 dh extra for sea view, see website for specials, breakfast-100 dh, air-con, elevator, free Wi-Fi in lobby, 3 restaurants, spa and sauna, Avenue Mohammed VI 152, tel. 0539-349-300, www.hotelsatlas .com, atlastanger@menara.ma).

$$ Hotel Rembrandt feels just like the 1940s, with a restaurant, a bar, and a swimming pool surrounded by a great grassy garden. Its 70 rooms are outdated and simple, but clean and comfortable, and some come with views (Sb-484-594 dh, Db-594-704 dh, higher prices are for sea view, 90-dh extra June-Aug, breakfast included, air-con, elevator, free Wi-Fi, a 5-minute walk above the beach in a busy urban zone at Boulevard Mohammed VI 1, tel. 0539-333-314, www.hotel-rembrandt.com, reservation@hotel -rembrandt.com).

$$ Hotel Continental—actually in the Medina (at the bottom of the old town, facing the port)—is the Humphrey Bogart option, a grand old place sprawling along the old town. It has lavish, atmospheric, and recently renovated public spaces, a chandeliered breakfast room, and 55 spacious bedrooms with rough hardwood floors and new bathrooms. Jimmy, who's always around and runs the shop adjacent to the lobby, says he offers everything but Viagra. When I said, "I'm from Seattle," he said, "206." Test him—he knows your area code (Sb-495 dh, Db-635 dh, Tb-765 dh, Qb-890 dh, about 100 dh more July-Sept, includes breakfast, free Wi-Fi, Dar Baroud 36, tel. 0539-931-024, www.continental -tanger.com, hcontinental@iam.net.ma). This hotel's terrace aches with nostalgia. Back during the city's glory days, a ferry connected Tangier and New York. American novelists would sit out on the terrace of Hotel Continental, never quite sure when their friends' boat would arrive from across the sea...

$ Hotel El Djenina is a local-style business-class hotel— extremely plain, reliable, safe, and well-located. Its 40 rooms are a block off the harbor, midway between the port and the TI. Request a room on the back side to escape the street noise (Sb-319-357 dh, Db-382-463 dh, higher prices are for mid-May-Sept, cash only, no breakfast, no air-con, elevator, free Wi-Fi, tel. 0539-942-244, Rue al-Antaki 8, eldjenina@menara.ma).

$ Hotel Residencia Andalucía is solid, clean, and minimal. It's buried in a totally non-touristy area in the new town, about a 20-minute walk from the Grand Socco. It has 19 rooms, a small reception, and a peaceful lobby (Sb-200-230 dh, Db-230-260 dh, higher prices are for mid-June-mid-Sept, cash only, Rue Omar Ben Abdelaziz 14, tel. 0539-941-334, Azdeen speaks a little English). Don't confuse it with the similarly named but very exclusive Hotel Andalucía Golf across town.

Eating in Tangier

Moroccan food is a joy to sample. First priority is a glass of the refreshing "Moroccan tea"—green tea that's boiled and steeped once, then combined with fresh mint leaves to boil and steep some more, before being loaded up with sugar. Tourist-oriented restaurants have a predictable menu. For starters, you'll find Moroccan vegetable soup *(harira)* or Moroccan salad (a combination of fresh and stewed vegetables). Main dishes include couscous (usually with chicken, potatoes, carrots, and other vegetables and spices); *tagine* (stewed meat served in a fancy dish with a cone-shaped top); and *briouates* (small savory pies). Everything comes with Morocco's distinctive round, flat bread. For dessert, it's pastries—typically, almond cookies.

I've mostly listed places in or near the Medina. (If you'd prefer the local equivalent of a yacht-club restaurant, survey the places along the beach.) Moroccan waiters expect about a 10 percent tip.

Le Saveur du Poisson is an excellent bet for the more adventurous, featuring one room cluttered with paintings adjoining a busy kitchen. There are no choices here. Just sit down and let owner Muhammad or his son, Hassan, take care of the rest. You get a rough hand-carved spoon and fork. Surrounded by lots of locals and unforgettable food, you'll be treated to a multicourse menu. Savor the delicious fish dishes—Tangier is one of the few spots in Morocco where seafood is a major part of the diet. The fruit punch—a mix of seasonal fruits brewed overnight in a vat— simmers in the back room. Ask for an explanation, or even a look. The desserts are full of nuts and honey. The big sink in the room is for locals who prefer to eat with their fingers (200-dh fixed-price meal, Sat-Thu 12:00-16:00 & 19:00-22:00, closed Fri and during Ramadan; walk down Rue de la Liberté roughly a block toward the Grand Socco from El Minzah Hotel, look for the stairs leading down to the market stalls and go down until you see fish on the grill; Escalier Waller 2, tel. 0539-336-326).

Maison Communitaire des Femmes, a community center for women, hides an inexpensive, hearty lunch spot that's open to everyone. A tasty three-course lunch is only 60 dh. Profits support the work of the center (Mon-Sat 12:00-16:00, last order at 15:30, also open 8:00-11:00 & 15:30-18:00 for cakes and tea, closed Sun, pleasant terrace out back, near slipper market just outside Grand Socco, Place du 9 Avril, tel. 0539-947-065).

El Minzah Hotel offers a fancier yet still authentic experience. The atmosphere is classy but low-stress. It's where unadventurous tourists and local elites dine. Dress up and choose between two dining zones: The white-tablecloth continental (French) dining area, called El Erz, is stuffy (80-150-dh starters, 140-240-dh main dishes); while in the Moroccan lounge, El Korsan, you'll be serenaded by live traditional music (music nightly 20:00-23:30, belly-dance show at 20:30 and 22:30, no extra charge for music; 70-120-dh starters, 140-240-dh main dishes). There's also a cozy wine bar here—a rarity in a Muslim country (50-120-dh starters, 130-190-dh main dishes, decorated with photos of visiting celebrities). At lunch, light meals and salads are served poolside (all dining areas open daily 13:00-16:00 & 20:00-22:30, Rue de la Liberté 85, tel. 0539-333-444, www.leroyal.com/morocco).

Le Salon Bleu has decent Moroccan food and some of the most spectacular seating in town: perched on a whitewashed terrace overlooking the square in front of the Kasbah Museum, with 360-degree views over the rooftops. Hike up the very tight spiral staircase to the top level, with the best views and lounge-a-while sofa seating. French-run (by the owners of Dar Nour guesthouse), it offers a simple menu of Moroccan fare—the 80-dh appetizer plate is a good sampler for lunch or to share for an afternoon snack. While there is some indoor seating, I'd skip this place if the weather's not ideal for lingering on the terrace (30-40-dh starters, 80-120-dh main dishes, 90-dh fixed-price meals, daily 10:00-22:00, Place de la Kasbah, mobile 06-6211-2724). You'll see it from the square in front of the Kasbah; to reach it, go through the gate to the left (as you face it), then look right for the stairs up.

Le Fabrique has nothing to do with old Morocco. But if you want a break from couscous and keyhole arches, this industrial-mod brasserie with concrete floors and exposed brick has a menu of purely French classics—a good reminder that in the 20th century, Tangier was nearly as much a French city as a Moroccan one (50-140-dh starters, 120-250-dh main dishes; Tue-Sat 12:00-14:30 & 20:00-23:00, closed Sun-Mon, in winter open for dinner only; Rue d'Angleterre 7, tel. 0539-374-057). It's a steep 10-minute walk up from the Grand Socco: Head up Rue d'Angleterre (left of Cinema Rif) and hike up the hill until the road levels out—it's on your left.

Le Nabab is geared for tourists, but offers more style and less crass commercialism than the tourist traps listed below. Squirreled away in a mostly residential neighborhood just below the lower

Kasbah gate (near the top of the Medina), Le Nabab offers a menu of predictable Moroccan favorites in a sleek concrete-and-white-tablecloths dining room with a few echoes of traditional Moroccan decor (170-dh three-course meal is a good deal to sample several items, 40-55-dh starters, 110-130-dh main dishes, Mon-Sat 19:30-23:30, closed Sun; below the lower Kasbah gate—bear left down the stairs, then right, and look for signs; Rue Al Kadiria 4, mobile 06-6144-2220).

Tourist Traps

Tangier seems to specialize in very touristy Moroccan restaurants designed to feed and entertain dozens or even hundreds of tour-group members with overpriced and predictable menus of Moroccan classics, and often live music and belly-dancing. The only locals you'll see here are the waiters. For day-trippers who just want a safe, comfortable break in the heart of town, these restaurants' predictability and Moroccan clichés are just perfect. For other travelers, these places are tour-group hell and make you thankful to be free. Each local guide has their own favorite, but these are the best-known.

Hamadi is as luxurious a restaurant as a tourist can find in Morocco, with good food at reasonable prices (25-40-dh starters, 60-80-dh main dishes, long hours daily, Rue Kasbah 2, tel. 0539-934-514).

Marhaba Palace has the most impressive interior, with huge keyhole arches ringing a grand upstairs hall slathered in colorful tilework. It also has the highest prices—hardly a good value. It's near the upper gate to the Kasbah, so it's convenient for a meal just before heading downhill through town to the Medina and market (170-240-dh fixed-price meals, Mon-Sat 10:00-23:00, closed Sun, Rue Kasbah, tel. 0539-937-927).

Mamounia Palace, considered by most the bottom of the barrel, is right on the Petit Socco and more in the middle of the action. At least it has a Hollywood connection: The Moroccan teahouse scenes from the movie *Inception* were filmed on its upstairs balcony. A meal here will cost you about 100 dh for four courses (no à la carte, daily 11:00-22:00, tel. 0539-935-099).

Tangier Connections

In Tangier, all train traffic comes and goes from the suburban Gare Tanger Ville train station, one mile from the city center and a short Petit Taxi ride away (10-20 dh). If you're traveling inland, check the information booth at the entrance of the train station for schedules (www.oncf.ma).

From Tangier by Train to: Rabat (7/day, 3.5-4 hours),

Casablanca (station also called **Casa Voyageurs,** 7/day, 5 hours; a new train line will cut the trip to about 2 hours by 2014), **Marrakech** (7/day, 8.5-9 hours, transfer in Casablanca or Sidi Kacem; 1 direct overnight train, 10.5 hours), **Fès** (4/day, 4.5 hours).

Bus information is available at the sporadically functioning CMT bus company website (www.ctm.ma, tel. 0522-541-010).

From Tangier by Bus to: Ceuta and **Tétouan** (hourly, 1 hour).

From Fès to: Casablanca (10/day, 5.5 hours), **Marrakech** (4/day, 8 hours), **Rabat** (8/day, 3.5 hours), **Meknès** (10/day, 45 minutes), **Tangier** (6/day, 7 hours).

From Rabat to: Casablanca (2/hour, 45 minutes), **Fès** (5/day, 3 hours), **Tétouan** (5 buses/day, 4.5-6 hours, 4 trains/day, 6 hours).

From Casablanca to: Marrakech (9/day, 3.5 hours).

From Marrakech to: Meknès (2/day, 7 hours), **Ouarzazate** (6/day, 4 hours).

By Plane: Flights within Morocco are convenient and reasonable (about $110 one-way from Tangier to Casablanca).

Morocco Beyond Tangier

Morocco gets much better as you go deeper into the interior. The country is incredibly rich in cultural thrills, though you'll pay a price in hassles and headaches— it's a package deal. But if adventure is your business, Morocco is a great option. Moroccan trains are quite good. Second class is cheap and comfortable. Buses connect all smaller towns very well. By car, Morocco is easy. Invest in a good Morocco guide-
book to make this trip. Here are a few tips and insights to get you started.

If you're relying on public transportation for your extended tour, sail to Tangier, blast your way through customs, ignore any hustler who tells you there's no way out until tomorrow, and hop in a Petit Taxi for the Tanger Ville train station one mile away. From there set your sights on Rabat, a dignified European-type town with fewer hustlers, and make it your get-acquainted stop in Morocco. Trains go farther south from Rabat.

If you're driving a car, crossing the border can be a bit unnerving, since you'll be forced to jump through several bureaucratic hoops. You'll go through customs at both borders, buy Moroccan insurance for your car (cheap and easy), and feel at the mercy of a bristly bunch of shady-looking people you'd rather not be at the mercy of. Don't pay anyone on the Spanish side. Consider tipping a guy on the Moroccan side if you feel he'll shepherd you through. Relax and let him grease those customs wheels. He's worth it. As soon as possible, hit the road and drive to Chefchaouen, the best first stop for those with their own wheels. Drive defensively and never rely on the oncoming driver's skill. Night driving is dangerous. Pay a guard to watch your car overnight.

TANGIER

Moroccan Towns

▲▲Chefchaouen
Just two hours by bus or car from Tétouan, this is the first pleasant town beyond the north coast. Monday and Thursday are colorful market days. Stay in the classy old Hotel Chaouen on Place el-Makhzen. The Hotel Parador (historic inn, but not the same as the Spanish government-run chain) faces the old town and offers good meals and a refuge from hustlers. Wander deep into the whitewashed old town from here.

▲▲Rabat
Morocco's capital and most European city, Rabat is the most comfortable and least stressful place to start your North African trip. You'll find a colorful market (in the old neighboring town of Salé), bits of Islamic architecture (Mausoleum of Mohammed V), the king's palace, mellow hustlers, and fine hotels.

▲▲▲Fès
More than just a funny hat that tipsy Shriners wear, Fès is Morocco's religious and artistic center, bustling with craftspeople, pilgrims, shoppers, and shops. Like most large Moroccan cities, it

has a distinct new town from the French colonial period, as well as an exotic (and stressful) old walled Arabic town (the Medina), where you'll find the market.

For 12 centuries, traders have gathered in Fès, founded on a river at the crossroads of two trade routes. Soon there was an irrigation system; a university; resident craftsmen from Spain; and a diverse population of Muslims, Christians, and Jews. When France claimed Morocco in 1912, they made their capital in Rabat, and Fès fizzled. But the Fès marketplace is still Morocco's best.

▲▲▲Marrakech
Morocco's gateway to the south, Marrakech is where the desert, mountain, and coastal regions merge. This market city is a constant

folk festival, bustling with Berber tribespeople and a colorful center. The new city has the train station, and the main boulevard (Mohammed V) is lined with banks, airline offices, a post office, a tourist office, and comfortable hotels. The old city features the maze-like market and the huge Djemaa el-Fna, a square seething with people—a 43-ring Moroccan circus.

▲▲▲Over the Atlas Mountains

Extend your Moroccan trip several days by heading south over the Atlas Mountains. Take a bus from Marrakech to Ouarzazate (short stop), and then to Tinerhir (great oasis town, comfy hotel, overnight stop). The next day, go to Er Rachidia and take the overnight bus to Fès.

By car, drive from Fès south, staying in the small mountain town of Ifrane, and then continue deep into the desert country past Er Rachidia, and on to Rissani (market days: Sun, Tue, and Thu). Explore nearby mud-brick towns still living in the Middle Ages. Hire a guide to drive you past where the road stops, and head cross-country to an oasis village (Merzouga), where you can climb a sand dune and watch the sun rise over the vastness of Africa. Only a sea of sand separates you from Timbuktu.

TANGIER

SPAIN: PAST & PRESENT

The distinctive Spanish culture has been shaped by the country's parade of rulers. Roman emperors, Muslim sultans, hard-core Christians, conquistadors, French dandies, and Fascist dictators have all left their mark on Spain's art, architecture, and customs. Start by understanding the country's long history of invasions and religious wars, and you'll better appreciate the churches, museums, and monuments you'll visit today.

History

In 1492, Columbus sailed the ocean blue—and Spain became a nation, too. The sunny weather, fertile soil, and Mediterranean ports of the Iberian Peninsula made it a popular place to call home. A mix from various migrations and invasions, the original "Iberians" crossed the Pyrenees around 800 B.C. The Phoenicians established the city of Cádiz around 1100 B.C., and Carthaginians settled around 250 B.C.

Romans (c. 200 B.C.-A.D. 400)

The future Roman Emperor Augustus finally quelled the last Iberian resistance (19 B.C.), making the province of "Hispania" an agricultural breadbasket (olives, wine) to feed the vast Roman Empire. The Romans brought the Latin language, a connection to the wider world, and (in the fourth century) Christianity. When the empire began crumbling around A.D. 400, Spain made a peaceful transition, ruled by Christian Visigoths from Germany who had strong Roman ties. Roman influence remained for centuries after, in the Latin-based Spanish language, irrigation methods, and building materials and techniques. The Romans' large farming estates would change hands over the years, passing from Roman senators to Visigoth kings to Islamic caliphs to Christian nobles. And, of course, the Romans left wine.

Moors (711-1492)

In A.D. 711, 12,000 zealous members of the world's newest religion—Islam—landed on the Rock of Gibraltar and, in three short years, conquered the Iberian Peninsula. These North African Muslims—generically called "Moors"—dominated Spain for the next 700 years. Though powerful, they were surprisingly tolerant of the people they ruled, allowing native Jews and Christians to practice their faiths, so long as the infidels paid extra taxes.

The Moors themselves were an ethnically diverse culture, including both crude Berber tribesmen from Morocco and sophisticated rulers from old Arab families. From their capital in Córdoba, various rulers of the united Islamic state of "Al-Andalus" pledged allegiance to foreign caliphs in Syria, Baghdad, or Morocco.

With cultural ties that stretched from Spain to Africa to Arabia to Persia and beyond, the Moorish culture in Spain (especially around A.D. 800-1000) was perhaps Europe's most advanced, a beacon of learning in Europe's so-called "Dark" Ages. Mathematics, astronomy, literature, and architecture flourished. Even winemaking was encouraged, though for religious reasons the Muslims didn't drink alcohol. The Moorish legacy lives on today in architecture (horseshoe arches, ceramic tiles, fountains, and gardens), language (the Spanish *el* comes from Arabic *al*)...and wine.

Reconquista (711-1492)

The Moors ruled for more than 700 years, but throughout that time they were a minority ruling a largely Christian populace. Pockets of independent Christians remained, particularly in the mountains in the peninsula's north. Local Christian kings fought against the Moors whenever they could, whittling away at the Muslim empire, "reconquering" more and more land in what's known as the Reconquista. The last Moorish stronghold, Granada, fell to the Christians in 1492.

The slow, piecemeal process of the Reconquista split the peninsula into many independent kingdoms and dukedoms, some Christian, some Moorish. The Reconquista picked up steam after A.D. 1000, when Al-Andalus splintered into smaller regional states—Granada, Sevilla, Valencia—ruled by local caliphs. Toledo fell to the

Six Dates That Changed Spain

711 Arab Muslims ("Moors") from North Africa invade and occupy Iberia.

1492 Columbus sails Spain into a century of wealth and power.

1588 Spain's Armada is routed by the British, and the country's slow decline begins.

1898 Thrashed by the US in the Spanish-American War, Spain reaches a low ebb.

1936 The Spanish Civil War begins, killing hundreds of thousands during its three-year span, and brings on more than three decades of Franco's fascist rule.

1975 Juan Carlos I is anointed king; he later leads the nation to democracy and the European Union.

Christians in 1085. By 1200 the neighboring Christian state of Portugal had the borders it does today, making it the oldest unchanged state in Europe. The rest of the peninsula was a battleground, a loosely knit collection of small kingdoms, some Christian, some Muslim. Heavy stone castles dotted the interior region of Castile, as lords and barons duked it out. Along the Mediterranean coast (from the Pyrenees to Barcelona to Valencia), three Christian states united into a sea-trading power, the kingdom of Aragon.

In 1469, Isabel of Castile married Ferdinand II of Aragon. These so-called Catholic Monarchs (Reyes Católicos) united the peninsula's two largest kingdoms, instantly making Spain a European power. In 1492, while Columbus explored the seas under Ferdinand and Isabel's flag, the Catholic Monarchs drove the Moors out of Granada and expelled the country's Jews, creating a unified, Christian, militaristic nation-state, fueled by the religious zeal of the Reconquista.

The Golden Age (1500-1600)

Spain's bold sea explorers changed the economics of Europe, opening up a New World of riches and colonies. The Spanish flag soon flew over most of South and Central America. Gold, silver, and agricultural products (grown on large estates with cheap labor) poured into Spain. In return, the stoked

Spaniards exported Christianity, converting the American natives with persistent Jesuit priests and cruel conquistadors.

Ferdinand and Isabel's daughter (Juana the Mad) wed a German prince (Philip the Fair), and their son inherited both crowns. Charles V (1500-1558, called Carlos I in Spain) was the most powerful man in the world, ruling an empire that stretched from Holland to Sicily, from Bohemia to Bolivia. The aristocracy and the clergy were swimming in money. Art and courtly life flourished during this Golden Age, with Spain hosting the painter El Greco and the writer Miguel de Cervantes.

But Charles V's Holy Roman Empire was torn by different languages and ethnic groups, and by protesting Protestants. He

spent much of the nation's energies at war with Protestants, encroaching Muslim Turks, and Europe's rising powers. When an exhausted Charles announced his abdication (1555) and retired to a monastery, his sprawling empire was divvied up among family members, with Spain and its possessions going to his son, Philip II (1527-1598).

Philip II conquered Portugal (1580, his only successful war), moved Spain's capital to Madrid, built El Escorial, and continued fighting losing battles across Europe (the Netherlands, France) that drained the treasury of its New World gold. In the summer of 1588, Spain's seemingly unbeatable royal fleet of 125 ships—the Invincible Armada—sailed off to conquer England, only to be unexpectedly routed in battle by bad weather and Sir Francis Drake's cunning. Just like that, Britannia ruled the waves, and Spain spiraled downward, becoming a debt-ridden, overextended, flabby nation.

Slow Decline (1600-1900)

The fast money from the colonies kept Spain from seeing the dangers at home. The country stopped growing its own wheat and neglected its fields. Great Britain and the Netherlands were the rising sea-trading powers in the new global economy. During the centuries when science and technology developed as never before in other European countries, Spain was preoccupied by its failed colonial politics. (Still, 1600s Spain produced the remarkable painter Diego Velázquez.)

By 1700, once-mighty Spain lay helpless while rising powers France, England, and Austria fought over the right to pick Spain's next king in the War of the Spanish Succession (1701-1714), which was fought partly on Spanish soil (Britain held out against the

French in the Siege of Gibraltar). Spanish king Charles II didn't have an heir, so he willed his kingdom to Louis XIV's grandson, Philip of Anjou, who was set to inherit both France and Spain. But the rest of Europe didn't want powerful France to become even stronger. The war ended in compromise: Philip became king of Spain (Spain lost several possessions), but he had to renounce claims to any other thrones. The French-born, French-speaking Bourbon King Philip V (1683-1746) ruled Spain for 40 years. He and his heirs made themselves at home, building the Versailles like Royal Palace in Madrid and La Granja near Segovia.

The French invaded Spain under Napoleon, who installed his brother as king in 1808. The Spaniards rose up (chronicled by Goya's paintings of the second and third of May 1808), sparking the Peninsular War—called the War of Independence by Spaniards—that finally won Spain's independence from French rule.

Nineteenth-century Spain was a backward nation, with internal wars over which noble family should rule (the Carlist Wars), liberal revolutions put down brutally, and political assassinations. Spain gradually lost its global possessions to other European powers and to South American revolutionaries. Spain hit rock bottom in 1898, when the upstart United States picked a fight and thrashed them in the Spanish-American War, taking away Spain's last major possessions: Cuba, Puerto Rico, and the Philippines.

The 20th Century

A drained and disillusioned Spain was ill-prepared for modern technology and democratic government.

The old ruling class (the monarchy, church, and landowners) fought new economic powers (cities, businessmen, labor unions) in a series of coups, strikes, and sham elections. In the 1920s, a military dictatorship under Miguel Primo de Rivera kept the old guard in power. In 1930 he was ousted and an open election brought a modern democratic Republic to power. But the right wing regrouped under the Falange (fascist) party, fomenting unrest and sparking a military coup against the Republic in 1936, supported by General Francisco Franco (1892-1975).

For three years (1936-1939), Spain fought a bloody civil war between Franco's Nationalists (also called Falangists) and the Republic (also called Loyalists). Some 500,000 Spaniards died (due to all causes), and Franco won. (For more on the Spanish Civil War, see page 527.) For nearly the next four decades, Spain was ruled by Franco, an authoritarian, church-blessed dictator who tried to modernize the backward country while shielding it from corrupting modern influences. Spain was officially neutral

Notable Spaniards

Hadrian (A.D. 76-138)—Roman emperor, one of three born in Latin-speaking Hispania (along with Trajan, reigned 98-117, and Marcus Aurelius, reigned 161-180), who ruled Rome at its peak of power.

El Cid (1040?-1099)—A real soldier-for-hire who inspired fictional stories and Spain's oldest poem, El Cid (literally, "The Lord") fought for both Christians and Muslims during the wars of the Reconquista. He's best known for liberating Valencia from the Moors.

St. Teresa of Ávila (1515-1582)—Mystic nun whose holiness and writings led to convent reform and to her sainthood. Religiously intense Spain produced other saints, too, including Dominic (1170-1221), who founded an order of wandering monks, and Ignatius of Loyola (described later).

Ferdinand (1452-1516) **and Isabel** (1451-1504)—Their marriage united most of Spain, ushering in its Golden Age. The "Catholic Monarchs" drove out Moors and Jews, and financed Columbus' lucrative voyages to the New World.

Francisco Pizarro (1476-1541)—Conquistador who vanquished the Incan Empire in the 1530s and then founded Peru's current capital, Lima. He was later assassinated by the vengeful son of a military rival.

Ponce de León (1460-1521)—Although he sailed on Columbus' second voyage to the New World, de León is primarily known for being the first European to explore Florida. His quest for the Fountain of Youth is a myth popularized by American author Washington Irving three centuries later.

Hernán Cortés (1485-1547)—A minor Spanish nobleman seeking his fortune, Cortés conquered Mexico in 1521. Along with fellow conquistadors Francisco Pizarro and Vasco Núñez de Balboa (who discovered the Pacific), Cortés and other Spaniards explored the New World and exploited its indigenous peoples.

in World War II, and the country spent much of the postwar era as a world apart. (On my first visit to Spain, in 1973, I came face-to-face with fellow teenagers—me in backpack and shorts, the Spaniards in military uniforms, brandishing automatic weapons.)

Before Franco died, he handpicked his protégé, King Juan Carlos I, to succeed him. But to everyone's surprise, the young, conservative, mild-mannered king stepped aside, settled for a figurehead title, and guided the country quickly and peacefully toward democratic elections (1977).

Spain had a lot of catching up to do. Culturally, the once-conservative nation exploded and embraced new ideas, even

Ignatius of Loyola (1491-1556)—After being wounded on a battlefield, this devout Basque founded the Society of Jesus—a.k.a. the Jesuits, a Catholic order of "intellectual warriors" and a leading force in the Counter-Reformation.

Miguel de Cervantes (1547-1616)—Author of the classic satirical romance *Don Quixote,* Cervantes was also a poet and a playwright whose works shaped Spanish literature and the language itself.

Charles V (1500-1558)—Called Carlos I in Spain, Charles was barely able to speak Spanish. The Flanders-born grandson of Ferdinand and Isabel assumed the Spanish throne in 1516 and led the Holy Roman Empire from 1519, ruling over much of Western Europe, the Far East, and the Americas. He abdicated in 1556, retiring to a monastery.

Francisco Franco (1892-1975)—The general who led the military uprising against the elected Republic, sparking Spain's Civil War (1936-1939). After victory, he ruled Spain for more than three decades as an absolute dictator, maintaining its Catholic, aristocratic heritage while slowly modernizing the country (see page 917).

Placido Domingo (b. 1941)—The son of zarzuela singers in Madrid (but raised in Mexico), this operatic tenor is just one of many classical musicians from Spain, including fellow "Three Tenors" singer José Carreras, composer Manuel de Falla, cellist Pablo Casals, and guitarist Andrés Segovia.

Spaniards in the News Today—King Juan Carlos I and his Greek-born wife, Queen Sofía; their son Felipe and his wife, Letizia; conservative Popular Party prime minister Mariano Rajoy (who swept into power in late 2011 on his pledge to lift Spain out of its debt crisis); architect Santiago Calatrava; Tour de France cyclist Alberto Contador; golfer Sergio Garcia; tennis star Rafael Nadal; pop singer Julio Iglesias (father of pop singer Enrique Iglesias); Oscar Award-winning actors Javier Bardem and Penélope Cruz; and movie directors Pedro Almodóvar and Alejandro Amenábar.

plunging to wild extremes. In the 1980s Spain flowered under left-leaning prime minister Felipe González. Spain showed the world its new modern face in 1992, hosting both a World Exhibition at Sevilla and the Summer Olympics at Barcelona.

Spain Today

From 1996 to 2004, Spain was led by prime minister José María Aznar. He adopted moderate policies to minimize the stress on the country's young democracy, fighting problems such as unemployment and foreign debt with reasonable success. However, his support of the United States' war in Iraq was extremely unpopular. In spring of 2004, the retiring Aznar supported a similarly centrist successor, Mariano Rajoy, who seemed poised to win the election. On the eve of the election, on March 11, three Madrid train stations were bombed at the height of rush hour, killing 191 people. The terrorist group claiming responsibility denounced Spain's Iraq policy, and three days later, Aznar's party lost the election. The new prime minister, left-of-center José Luis Rodríguez Zapatero, quickly began pulling Spain's troops out of Iraq, as well as enacting sweeping social changes. But Zapatero and his party were shown the door in 2011, a casualty of the economic crisis. The more-conservative Popular Party regained the majority, and Mariano Rajoy became prime minister.

Spain enjoyed a strong economy through the late 1990s and early 2000s, thanks in part to a thriving tourism industry and a boom in housing construction. But the country was hit hard by the 2009 global economic downturn, and its economy entered a recession. Spain's real-estate bubble burst, banks stopped lending, and by 2013 unemployment had soared to 27 percent. So many young Spaniards are out of work (one-fourth of those under 30, and nearly half of those under 25) that a new name was coined to describe them: *"generación ni-ni"* (the neither-nor generation). In danger of default, Spanish banks in 2012 received over $100 billion in bailout loans from the EU. Under pressure from the EU to cut its national debt, Spain's government has limited payouts to new parents, scaled back government pensions and salaries, and made cuts in education and health care. These "austerity measures" have drawn criticism from unions and the public.

Artists

El Greco (1541-1614) exemplifies the spiritual fervor of much Spanish art. Known for his ethereal paintings of "flickering" saints, the drama, surreal colors, and intentionally unnatural distortion of his compositions have the intensity of a religious vision. (For more on El Greco, see page 573.)

Diego Velázquez (1599-1660) went to the opposite extreme. His masterful royal court portraits are studies in camera-eye realism and cool detachment from his subjects. Velázquez was unmatched in using a few strokes of paint to suggest details.

Francisco de Goya (1746-1828) lacked Velázquez's detachment. He let his liberal tendencies shine through in unflattering portraits of royalty and in emotional scenes of abuse of power. He unleashed his inner passions in the eerie, nightmarish canvases of his last, "dark" stage. (For more on Goya, see page 465.)

Bartolomé Murillo (1617-1682) painted a dreamy world of religious visions. His pastel soft-focus works of cute Baby Jesuses and radiant Virgin Marys helped make Catholic doctrine palatable to the common folk at a time when many were defecting to Protestantism. (For more on Murillo, see page 675.)

In the 20th century, **Pablo Picasso, Joan Miró,** and Surrealist **Salvador Dalí** made their marks. Great museums featuring all three are in or near Barcelona. Although Picasso (1881-1973) lived most of his adult life in France, the 20th-century's greatest artist explored Spanish themes, particularly in his inspirational antiwar *Guernica* mural, which depicts civil war destruction (described on page 472). A flamboyant, waxed-mustachioed Surrealist painter, Salvador Dalí (1904-1989) and a fellow Spaniard, filmmaker Luis Buñuel, made the landmark art film *Un Chien Andalou* (see page 180).

Besides the works of its native sons, Spain's museums have plenty of foreign art. During its Golden Age, wealthy Spanish aristocrats bought wagonloads of the most popular art of the time—Italian Renaissance and Baroque works by Titian, Tintoretto, Veronese, and others. They also loaded up on paintings by Peter Paul Rubens, Hieronymus Bosch, and Pieter Brueghel from the Low Countries, which were then under Spanish rule.

Architecture

Spanish History Set in Stone

The two most fertile periods of architectural innovation in Spain were during the Moorish occupation and in the Golden Age. Otherwise, Spanish architects marched obediently behind the rest of Europe. Modern architects have finally brought Spain back to the forefront of construction and design.

Spain's history is dominated by 700 years of pushing the Muslim Moors back into Africa (711-1492). Throughout Spain, it seems every old church was built upon a mosque (Sevilla's immense cathedral, for one, and Córdoba's remarkable Mezquita, which preserved the mosque but plopped a cathedral right in the middle of it). Granada's Alhambra is the best example of the secular Moorish style. It's an *Arabian Nights* fairy tale: finely etched domes, lacy arcades, stalactite-studded ceilings, keyhole arches, and lush gardens. At its heart lies an elegantly proportioned courtyard, where the designers created an ingenious microclimate: water, plants, pottery, thick walls, and darkness...all to be cool. The stuccoed walls are ornamented with a stylized Arabic script, creating a visual chant of verses from the Quran. Meanwhile, simple Romanesque churches dotted the northern part of Spain not controlled by the Moors (such as along the Camino de Santiago and in the folds of the Picos de Europa).

As the Christians slowly reconquered Iberian turf, they

Typical Church Architecture

History comes to life when you visit a centuries-old church. Even if you don't know your apse from a hole in the ground, learning a few simple terms will enrich your experience. Note that not every church has every feature, and a "cathedral" isn't a type of church architecture, but rather a designation for a church that's a governing center for a local bishop.

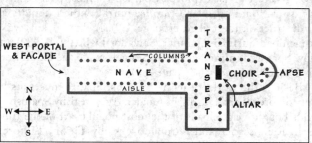

Aisles: The long, generally low-ceilinged arcades that flank the nave.

Altar: The raised area with a ceremonial table (often adorned with candles or a crucifix), where the priest prepares and serves the bread and wine for Communion.

Apse: The space beyond the altar, generally bordered with small chapels.

Barrel Vault: A continuous round-arched ceiling that resembles an extended upside-down U.

Choir: A cozy area, often screened off, located within the church nave and near the high altar, where services are sung in a more intimate setting.

Cloister: Covered hallways bordering a (usually square-shaped) open-air courtyard, traditionally where monks and nuns got fresh air.

Facade: The exterior surface of the church's main (west) entrance, viewable from outside and generally highly decorated.

Groin Vault: An arched ceiling formed where two equal barrel vaults meet at right angles. Less common usage: term for a medieval jock strap.

Narthex: The area (portico or foyer) between the main entry and the nave.

Nave: The long, central section of the church (running west to east, from the entrance to the altar) where the congregation sits or stands during the service.

Transept: In a traditional cross-shaped floor plan, the transept is one of the two parts forming the "arms" of the cross. The transepts run north-south, perpendicularly crossing the east-west nave.

West Portal: The main entry to the church (on the west end, opposite the main altar).

turned their fervor into stone, building churches in the lighter, heaven-reaching stained-glass Gothic style (Toledo and Sevilla). Gothic was a French import, trickling into conservative Spain long after it had swept through Europe.

As Christians moved in, many Muslim artists and architects stayed, giving the new society the Mudejar style—Moorish in appearance, but commissioned by Catholics. (Mudejar means "those who stayed.") In Sevilla's Alcázar, the Arabic script on the walls relates not the Quran, but New Testament verses and Christian propaganda, such as "Dedicated to the magnificent Sultan, King Pedro—thanks to God!" (In contrast, the style of Christians living under Moorish rule is called Mozarabic.)

The money reaped and raped from Spain's colonies in the Golden Age (1500-1600) spurred new construction. Churches and palaces borrowed from the Italian Renaissance and the more elaborate Baroque. Ornamentation reached unprecedented heights in Spain, culminating in the Plateresque style of stonework, so called because it resembles intricate silver *(plata)* filigree work (see, for example, the facade of the University of Salamanca).

The 1500s were also the era of religious wars. The monastery/palace of El Escorial, built in sober geometric style, symbolizes the austerity of a newly reformed Catholic Church ready to strike back. King Philip II ruled his empire and directed the Inquisition from here, surrounded by plain white walls, well scrubbed floors, and simple furnishings. El Escorial was built at a time when Catholic Spain felt threatened by Protestant heretics, and its construction dominated the Spanish economy for a generation (1563-1584). Because of this bully in the national budget, Spain has almost nothing else to show from this most powerful period of her history.

For the next three centuries (1600-1900), backward-looking Spain recycled old art styles.

As Europe leapt from the 19th into the 20th century, it celebrated a rising standard of living and nearly a hundred years without a major war. Art Nouveau architects forced hard steel and concrete into softer organic shapes. Barcelona's answer to Art Nouveau was Modernisme, and its genius was Antoni Gaudí, with his asymmetrical "cake-in-the-rain" Barcelona buildings like Casa Milà and Sagrada Família.

Much of Spain's 20th-century architecture—the minimal fascist style of the Valley of the Fallen and ugly concrete apartments—follows patterns seen elsewhere in Europe. But Spain today produces some of Europe's most interesting structures. Santiago Calatrava (from Valencia, born 1951) uses soaring arches and glass to create bridges (such as the iconic one in Sevilla, and a brand-new one in Venice), airports, and performance halls (including Valencia's Opera House). One of the world's most striking and well-known buildings in recent years—Frank Gehry's Guggenheim Museum—is in Bilbao, and similarly innovative structures are popping up everywhere.

Bullfighting

An Authentic Ritual or a Cruel Spectacle?

The Spanish bullfight is as much a ritual as it is a sport. Not to acknowledge the importance of the bullfight is to censor a venerable part of Spanish culture. But it also makes a spectacle out of the cruel killing of an animal. Should tourists boycott bullfights? I don't know.

When the day comes that bullfighting is kept alive by tourist dollars rather than by the local culture, then I'll agree with those who say it's immoral and that tourists shouldn't encourage it by buying tickets. Consider the morality of supporting this gruesome aspect of Spanish culture before buying a ticket.

While no two bullfights are the same, they unfold along a strict pattern. The punctual ceremony begins with a parade of participants across the ring. Then the trumpet sounds, the "Gate of Fear" opens, and the leading player—*el toro*—thunders in. A ton of angry animal is an awesome sight, even from the cheap seats (with the sun in your eyes).

The fight is divided into three acts. Act I is designed to size up the bull and wear him down. With help from his assistants, the matador (literally, "killer") attracts the bull with a shake of the cape, then directs the animal past his body, as close as his bravery allows. The bull sees only things in motion and (some think) in red. After a few passes, the *picadores* enter, mounted on horseback, to spear the swollen lump of muscle at the back of the bull's neck. This tests the bull, causing him to lower his head and weakening the thrust of his horns. (Until 1927, the horses had no protective pads and were often killed.)

In Act II, the matador's assistants *(banderilleros)* continue to enrage and weaken the bull. They charge the charging bull and—leaping acrobatically across its path—plunge brightly colored barbed sticks into the bull's vital neck muscle.

After a short intermission, during which the matador may, according to tradition, ask permission to kill the bull and dedicate the kill to someone in the crowd, the final and lethal Act III begins.

The matador tries to dominate and tire the bull with hypnotic cape work. A good pass is when the matador stands completely still while the bull charges past. Then the matador thrusts a sword between the animal's shoulder blades for the kill. A quick

Man vs. Bull Through History

The exact origins of bullfighting are impossible to trace, but men have battled bulls since ancient times. In ancient Crete, Minoan athletes sprang somersaults over bulls' horns (c. 1500 B.C.). In Asia and Italy, worshippers of Mithras and Artemis slaughtered bulls in ritual sacrifice (c. 500 B.C.-A.D. 500). And in ancient Rome, animal fights were popular warm-up acts for the gladiator games, performed in large arenas while thousands cheered. (In an interesting counterpoint, in many cultures—including, some would argue, Spain—bulls are respected or even revered, from those who would worship a golden calf in Moses' time, to the people of contemporary India.)

The Romans likely introduced bullfights to Spain. In the Middle Ages (historians speculate), bullfighting became a sport for knights, both Christian and Moorish, who held tournaments on feast days. They fought on horseback with lances, assisted by squires.

It was in the town of Ronda, around 1726, that the charismatic Francisco Romero transformed bullfighting from a sport of nobles on horseback to one of commoners on foot, armed only with a sword and cape. The mounted *picador* became the support player, and the matador became the star. Successive matadors thrilled crowds by allowing the bull to come ever closer.

From Spain, bullfighting spread to southern France and Latin America (where it continues today). In the 20th century, the dictator Franco made bullfighting the national pastime. Since Franco it's become increasingly unpopular. Today, only a third of Spaniards follow it at all. Calling bullfights unsuitable for children, the government has banned live broadcasts on state-run TV, though private channels continue to cover the events. Today's matadors remain the brave-but-pretty cover boys gracing tabloids. In 2010 a couple of top matadors were gored, making the sport appear even more brutal, tragic, and edgy. In 2012, bullfighting was banned in Catalunya.

kill is not always easy, and the matador may have to make several bloody thrusts before the sword stays in and the bull finally dies.

(One of the matador's assistants may go in at the end to finish the job with a dagger between the eyes.) Mules drag the dead bull out, and his meat is in the market *mañana* (barring "mad cow" concerns—and if ever there was a mad cow...). *Rabo del toro* (bull-tail stew) is a delicacy.

Throughout the fight, the crowd shows its approval or impatience. Shouts of *"¡Olé!"* or *"¡Torero!"* mean they like what they see. Whistling or rhythmic hand-clapping greets cowardice and incompetence.

You're not likely to see much human blood spilled. In 200 years of bullfighting in Sevilla, only 30 fighters have died (and only three were actually matadors). If a bull does kill a fighter, the next matador comes in to kill him. Historically, even the bull's mother is killed, since the evil qualities are assumed to have come from her.

After an exceptional fight, the crowd may wave white handkerchiefs to ask that the matador be awarded the bull's ear or tail. A brave bull, though dead, gets a victory lap from the mule team on his way to the slaughterhouse. Then the trumpet sounds, and a new bull charges in to face a fresh matador.

Fights are held on most Sundays from Easter through September (at 18:30 or 19:30). Serious fights with adult matadors are called *corrida de toros*. These are often sold out in advance. Summer fights are often *novillada*, with teenage novices doing the killing. *Corrida de toros* seats range from €20 for nose-bleed seats in the sun to €140 for front-row seats in the shade. *Novillada* seats are half that, and generally easy to get at the arena a few minutes before showtime. Many Spanish women consider bullfighting sexy. They swoon at the dashing matadors who are sure to wear tight pants (with their *partas nobles*—noble parts—in view, generally organized to one side, farthest from the bull).

A typical bullfight lasts about two hours and consists of six separate fights—three matadors (each with his own team of *picadores* and *banderilleros*) fighting two bulls each. If you're curious to see a bullfight without making an expensive and time-consuming trip to the ring, keep an eye out for televised bullfights in bars. For a closer look at bullfighting by an American aficionado, read Ernest Hemingway's classic *Death in the Afternoon*.

APPENDIX

Contents

Tourist Information

Spain's national tourist office **in the US** will fill brochure requests and answer your general travel questions by email (newyork .information@tourspain.es). Scan their website (www.spain.info) for practical information and sightseeing ideas; you can download many brochures free of charge. If you're going to Barcelona, also see www.barcelonaturisme.cat.

In Spain your best first stop in a new city is the *Turismo,* the tourist information office (abbreviated **TI** in this book). TIs are good places to get a city map and information on public transit (including bus and train schedules), walking tours, special events, and nightlife. Many TIs have information on the entire country or at least the region, so try to pick up maps for destinations you'll be visiting later in your trip. If you're arriving in town after the TI closes, call ahead or pick up a map in a neighboring town.

While TIs are eager to book you a room, use their room-finding service only as a last resort. They are unable to give hard opinions on the relative value of one place over another. The accommodations stakes are too high to go potluck through the TI. Even if there's no "fee," you'll save money by going direct with the listings in this book.

Websites for Spain: In addition to the Spanish Tourist Board site (www.spain.info), consider visiting www.mcu.es (museums and historic sites in Spain) and www.renfe.com (train info and schedules).

For Gibraltar: Try the Gibraltar Information Bureau (www.gibraltar.gov.uk, info@gibraltar.gov.uk).

For Morocco: Contact the Moroccan National Tourist Office (from the US, dial 011-212-537-278-300; www.visitmorocco.com).

Communicating

Hurdling the Language Barrier

Spain presents the English-speaking traveler with one of the most formidable language barriers in Western Europe. Many Spanish people—especially those in the tourist trade and in big cities—speak English. Still, many people don't. Locals visibly brighten when you know and use some key Spanish words (see "Spanish Survival Phrases" on page 963). Learn the key phrases. Travel with a phrase book, particularly if you want to interact with the Spanish people. You'll find that doors open more quickly and with more smiles when you can speak a few words of the language.

Telephones

Smart travelers use the telephone to reserve or reconfirm rooms, get tourist information, reserve restaurants, confirm tour times, or phone home. This section covers dialing instructions, phone cards, and types of phones (for more in-depth information, see www.ricksteves.com/phoning).

How to Dial

Calling from the US to Spain, or vice versa, is simple—once you break the code. The European calling chart later in this chapter will walk you through it.

In Spain, numbers that start with 900 are toll-free; numbers that start with 901 and 902 have per-minute fees (about €0.04-0.07/minute from a landline; more from a mobile). Note that you can't call Spain's toll-free numbers from America, nor can you count on reaching America's toll-free numbers from Spain.

Dialing Domestically Within Spain

The following instructions apply whether you're dialing from a landline (such as a pay phone or your hotel-room phone) or a Spanish mobile phone.

About half of all European countries use area codes; the other half, including Spain, use a direct-dial system without area codes.

Land lines start with 9, and mobile lines start with 6. All phone numbers in Spain are nine digits (no area codes) that can be dialed direct throughout the country. For example, the number of one of my recommended Madrid hotels is 915-212-941. That's exactly what you dial, whether you're calling the hotel from the Madrid train station or from Barcelona.

If you're dialing within Spain using your US mobile phone, you may need to dial as if it's a domestic call, or you may need to dial as if you're calling from the US (see "Dialing Internationally," next). Try it one way, and if it doesn't work, try it the other way.

Dialing Internationally to or from Spain

If you want to make an international call, follow these steps:

• Dial the international access code (00 if you're calling from Europe, 011 from the US or Canada). If you're dialing from a mobile phone, you can replace the international access code with +, which works regardless of where you're calling from. (On many mobile phones, you can insert a + by pressing and holding the 0 key.)

• Dial the country code of the country you're calling (34 for Spain, or 1 for the US or Canada).

• Dial the local number, keeping in mind that calling many countries requires dropping the initial zero of the phone number. (For specifics per country, see the European calling chart in this chapter.)

Calling from the US to Spain: Dial 011 (US access code), 34 (Spain's country code), then the nine-digit number. For example, if you're calling the Madrid hotel I mentioned above, you'd dial 011-34-915-212-941.

Calling from any European country to the US: To call my office in Edmonds, Washington, from anywhere in Europe, I dial 00 (Europe's access code), 1 (US country code), 425 (Edmonds' area code), and 771-8303.

Mobile Phones

Traveling with a mobile phone is handy and practical. There are two basic options: roaming with your own phone (expensive but easy) or buying and using SIM cards with an unlocked phone (a bit more hassle, but potentially much cheaper).

APPENDIX

European Calling Chart

Just smile and dial, using this key:
AC = Area Code, LN = Local Number.

European Country	Calling long distance within ...	Calling from the US or Canada to ...	Calling from a European country to ...
Austria	AC + LN	011 + 43 + AC (without initial zero) + LN	00 + 43 + AC (without initial zero) + LN
Belgium	LN	011 + 32 + LN (without initial zero)	00 + 32 + LN (without initial zero)
Bosnia-Herzegovina	AC + LN	011 + 387 + AC (without initial zero) + LN	00 + 387 + AC (without initial zero) + LN
Britain	AC + LN	011 + 44 + AC (without initial zero) + LN	00 + 44 + AC (without initial zero) + LN
Croatia	AC + LN	011 + 385 + AC (without initial zero) + LN	00 + 385 + AC (without initial zero) + LN
Czech Republic	LN	011 + 420 + LN	00 + 420 + LN
Denmark	LN	011 + 45 + LN	00 + 45 + LN
Estonia	LN	011 + 372 + LN	00 + 372 + LN
Finland	AC + LN	011 + 358 + AC (without initial zero) + LN	999 (or other 900 number) + 358 + AC (without initial zero) + LN
France	LN	011 + 33 + LN (without initial zero)	00 + 33 + LN (without initial zero)
Germany	AC + LN	011 + 49 + AC (without initial zero) + LN	00 + 49 + AC (without initial zero) + LN
Gibraltar	LN	011 + 350 + LN	00 + 350 + LN
Greece	LN	011 + 30 + LN	00 + 30 + LN
Hungary	06 + AC + LN	011 + 36 + AC + LN	00 + 36 + AC + LN
Ireland	AC + LN	011 + 353 + AC (without initial zero) + LN	00 + 353 + AC (without initial zero) + LN
Italy	LN	011 + 39 + LN	00 + 39 + LN

European Country	Calling long distance within ...	Calling from the US or Canada to ...	Calling from a European country to ...
Latvia	LN	011 + 371 + LN	00 + 371 + LN
Montenegro	AC + LN	011 + 382 + AC (without initial zero) + LN	00 + 382 + AC (without initial zero) + LN
Morocco	LN	011 + 212 + LN (without initial zero)	00 + 212 + LN (without initial zero)
Netherlands	AC + LN	011 + 31 + AC (without initial zero) + LN	00 + 31 + AC (without initial zero) + LN
Norway	LN	011 + 47 + LN	00 + 47 + LN
Poland	LN	011 + 48 + LN	00 + 48 + LN
Portugal	LN	011 + 351 + LN	00 + 351 + LN
Russia	8 + AC + LN	011 + 7 + AC + LN	00 + 7 + AC + LN
Slovakia	AC + LN	011 + 421 + AC (without initial zero) + LN	00 + 421 + AC (without initial zero) + LN
Slovenia	AC + LN	011 + 386 + AC (without initial zero) + LN	00 + 386 + AC (without initial zero) + LN
Spain	LN	011 + 34 + LN	00 + 34 + LN
Sweden	AC + LN	011 + 46 + AC (without initial zero) + LN	00 + 46 + AC (without initial zero) + LN
Switzerland	LN	011 + 41 + LN (without initial zero)	00 + 41 + LN (without initial zero)
Turkey	AC (if there's no initial zero, add one) + LN	011 + 90 + AC (without initial zero) + LN	00 + 90 + AC (without initial zero) + LN

APPENDIX

- The instructions above apply whether you're calling to or from a European landline or mobile phone.

- If calling from any mobile phone, you can replace the international access code with "+" (press and hold 0 to insert it).

- The international access code is 011 if you're calling from the US or Canada.

- To call the US or Canada from Europe, dial 00, then 1 (country code for US and Canada), then the area code and number. In short, 00 + 1 + AC + LN = Hi, Mom!

Smartphones and Data Roaming

I take my smartphone to Europe, using it to make phone calls (sparingly) and send texts, but also to check email, listen to audiotours, and browse the Internet. You may have heard horror stories about people running up outrageous data roaming bills on their smartphones. But if you understand the options, it's easy to avoid these fees and still stay connected. Here's how.

For voice calls and text messaging, smartphones work like any mobile phone (as described under "Roaming with Your US Mobile Phone," below). To avoid roaming charges, connect to free Wi-Fi, and use Skype, FaceTime, or other apps to make cheap or free calls (see "Calling over the Internet," later).

To get online with your phone, you have two options: Wi-Fi and mobile data. Because free Wi-Fi hotspots are generally easy to find in Europe (at most hotels, many cafés, and even some public spaces), the cheap solution is to use Wi-Fi wherever possible.

But what if you just can't get to a hotspot? Fortunately, most providers offer an affordable, basic data-roaming package for Europe: $25 or $30 buys you about 100 megabytes—enough to view 100 websites or send/receive 1,000 text emails. If you don't buy a data-roaming plan in advance, but use data in Europe anyway, you'll pay staggeringly high rates—about $20 per megabyte, or about 80 times what you'd pay with a plan.

While a data-roaming package is handy, your allotted megabytes can go quickly—especially if you stream videos or

Roaming with Your US Mobile Phone: This pricier option can be worthwhile if you won't be making or receiving many calls, don't want to bother with SIM cards, or want to stay reachable at your US number. Start by calling your mobile-phone service provider to ask whether your phone works in Europe and what the rates are (likely $1.29-1.99 per minute to make or receive calls, and 20-50 cents to send or receive text messages). Tell them to enable international calling on your account, and if you know you'll be making multiple calls, ask your carrier about any global calling deals to lower the per-minute costs. When you land in Europe, turn on your phone and—bingo!—you have service. Because you'll pay for receiving calls and texts, be sure your family knows to call only in an emergency. Note that Verizon and Sprint use a different technology than European providers, so their phones are less likely to work abroad; if yours doesn't, your provider may be able to send you a loaner phone (arrange in advance).

Buying and Using SIM Cards in Europe: If you're comfortable with mobile-phone technology, will be making lots of calls, and want to save some serious money, consider this very music. To keep a cap on usage and avoid incurring overage charges, I manually turn off data roaming on my phone whenever I'm not actively using it. (To turn off data and voice roaming, look in your phone's menu—try checking under "Cellular" or "Network," or ask your mobile-phone provider how to do it.) As I travel through Europe, I jump from hotspot to hotspot. But if I need to get online at a time when I can't easily access Wi-Fi—for example, to download driving directions when I'm on the road to my next hotel—I turn on data roaming just long enough for that task, then turn it off again. You can also limit how much data your phone uses by switching your email settings from "push" to "fetch" (you choose when to download messages rather than having them automatically "pushed" to your device). By carefully budgeting my data this way, my 100 megabytes last a long time.

If you want to use your smartphone exclusively on Wi-Fi—and not worry about either voice or data charges—simply turn off both voice and data roaming (or put your phone in "Airplane Mode" and then turn your Wi-Fi back on). If you're on a long trip, are positive you won't be using your phone for voice or data roaming, and want to save some money, ask your provider about suspending those services altogether while you're gone.

By sticking with Wi-Fi wherever possible and budgeting your use of data, you can easily and affordably stay connected while you travel.

affordable alternative: Carry an unlocked mobile phone, and use it with a European SIM card to get much cheaper rates.

Getting an **unlocked phone** may be easier than you think. You may already have an old, unused mobile phone in a drawer somewhere. When you got the phone, it was probably "locked" to work only with one company—but if your contract is now up, your provider may be willing to send you a code to unlock it. Just call and ask. Otherwise, you can simply buy an unlocked phone: Search your favorite online shopping site for an "unlocked quad-band phone" before you go, or wait until you get to Europe and buy one at a mobile-phone shop there. Either way, a basic model costs less than $50.

Once in Europe, buy a **SIM card**—the little chip that inserts into your phone (either under the battery, or in a slot on the side)—to equip the phone with a European number. (Note that smaller "micro-SIM" or "nano-SIM" cards—used in some iPhones—are less widely available.) SIM cards are sold at mobile-phone shops, department-store electronics counters, and some newsstand kiosks for $5–10, and usually include about that much prepaid calling credit (making the card itself virtually free). In most places, buying a SIM card is as easy as buying a pack of gum—and almost as cheap. (In some countries—including Spain—it can take a bit longer, because you have to show your passport and be registered.) Because SIM cards are prepaid, there's no contract and no commitment (in fact, they expire after just a few months of disuse); I buy one even if I'm in a country for only a few days.

When using a SIM card in its home country, it's free to receive calls and texts, and it's cheap to make calls—domestic calls average 20-30 cents per minute (though toll lines can be substantially more). Rates are higher if you're roaming in another country, but as long as you stay within the European Union, these fees are capped (about 30 cents per minute for making calls or 10 cents per minute for receiving calls). Texting is cheap even if roaming in another country. Particularly inexpensive SIM card brands let you call either within Europe or to the US for less than 10 cents per minute.

When purchasing a SIM card, always ask about fees for domestic and international calls, roaming charges, and how to check your credit balance and buy more time. If text or voice prompts are in another language, ask the clerk whether they can be switched to English.

It's also possible to buy an **inexpensive mobile phone in Europe** that already comes with a SIM card. While these phones are generally locked to work with just one provider (and therefore can't be reused on future trips), they may be less hassle than buying an unlocked phone and a SIM card separately.

Mobile-Phone Calling Apps: If you have a smartphone, you can use it to make free or cheap calls in Europe by using a calling app such as Skype or FaceTime when you're on Wi-Fi; for details, see the next section.

Calling over the Internet

Some things that seem too good to be true...actually are true. If you're traveling with a smartphone, tablet, or laptop, you can make free calls over the Internet to another wireless device, anywhere in the world, for free. (Or you can pay a few cents to call from your computer or smartphone to a telephone.) The major providers are Skype, Google Talk, and (on Apple devices) FaceTime. You can get online at a Wi-Fi hotspot and use these apps to make calls without ringing up expensive roaming charges (though call quality can be spotty on slow connections). You can make Internet calls even if you're traveling without your own mobile device: Many European Internet cafés have Skype, as well as microphones and webcams, on their terminals—just log on and chat away.

Landline Telephones

Just like Americans, these days most Europeans make the majority of their calls on mobile phones. But you'll still encounter landlines in hotel rooms and at pay phones.

Hotel-Room Phones: Calling from your hotel room can be great for local calls and for international calls if you have an international phone card (described later). Otherwise, hotel-room phones can be an almost criminal rip-off for long-distance or international calls. Many hotels charge a fee for local and sometimes even "toll-free" numbers—always ask for the rates before you dial.

Public Pay Phones: Coin-op phones are becoming extinct in Europe. To make calls from public phones, you'll need a prepaid phone card, described next.

Telephone Cards

There are two types of phone cards: insertable (for pay phones) and international (cheap for overseas calls and usable from any type of phone). A phone card works only in the country where you bought it, so if you have a live card at the end of your trip, give it to another traveler to use—most cards expire three to six months after the first use.

Insertable Phone Cards: These cards, called *tarjetas telefónicas*, can be used only at pay phones, for either domestic or international calls. They're sold at post offices and many newsstand kiosks. Spanish pay phones are easy to find but refuse to be rushed. After you *"inserta"* your *"tarjeta"* into the phone, wait until the digital display says *"Marque número,"* and then dial. Dial slowly and deliberately. Push the square R button to get a dial tone for a new call. The phone doesn't beep to remind you that you've left the card in, so don't forget to remove it when you're done. The cost of the call is automatically deducted from your card.

International Phone Cards: With these cards, phone calls from Spain to the US can cost less than a nickel a minute. The cards can also be used to make local calls, and they work from any type of phone, including your hotel-room phone or a mobile phone with a European SIM card. To use the card, dial a local or toll-free access number, then enter your scratch-to-reveal PIN code. Some hotels block their phones from accepting these access numbers. (Ask your hotelier about access and rates before you call.)

You can buy an international phone card, called *tarjeta telefónica con código*, at most kiosks and newsstands, but the best selection is usually at little shops catering to immigrants, who are the leading experts on calling home cheaply. You can also find them at call centers *(locutorios)*. Buy a low denomination in case the

APPENDIX

card is a dud. Some shops also sell cardless codes, printed right on the receipt.

US Calling Cards: These cards, such as the ones offered by AT&T, Verizon, and Sprint, are a rotten value, and are being phased out. Try any of the options outlined earlier.

Useful Phone Numbers
Emergency Needs
Police: Spain—tel. 091, Morocco—tel. 190
Ambulance or Any Emergency: Spain—tel. 112, Morocco—tel. 150

Embassies and Consulates
US Embassy in Madrid, Spain: Tel. 915-872-240, after-hours emergency tel. 915-872-200 (Calle Serrano 75, http://madrid.usembassy.gov)
US Consulate in Barcelona, Spain: Tel. 932-802-227, after-hours emergency tel. 915-872-200 (Passeig Reina Elisenda 23, http://barcelona.usconsulate.gov)
US Embassy in Gibraltar: Call US Embassy in Madrid
US Consulate General in Casablanca, Morocco: Tel. 0522-267-151, after-hours emergency tel. 0661-131-939 (Boulevard Moulay Youssef 8, http://morocco.usembassy.gov)
Canadian Embassy in Madrid, Spain: Tel. 913-828-400 (Torre Espacio, Paseo de la Castellana 259D, in Torre Espacio skyscraper, www.espana.gc.ca)
Canadian Embassy in Rabat, Morocco: Tel. 0537-687-400 (13 bis Rue Jaâfa-as-Sadik, www.morocco.gc.ca)

Travel Advisories
US Department of State: Tel. 888-407-4747, from outside US tel. 1-202-501-4444, www.travel.state.gov
Canadian Department of Foreign Affairs: Canadian tel. 800-387-3124, from outside Canada tel. 1-613-996-8885, www.travel.gc.ca
US Centers for Disease Control and Prevention: Tel. 800-CDC-INFO (800-232-4636), www.cdc.gov/travel

Directory Assistance
In Spain, dial 11811 (€0.40/min) or 11818 (€0.55/call from private numbers, free from phone booths).

Trains
Train (RENFE) Reservation and Information: Tel. 902-320-320, www.renfe.com

Airports

The following airports share a customer-assistance line, toll tel. 902-404-704, and a website, www.aena-aeropuertos.es.

Barcelona: El Prat de Llobregat Airport (BCN)
Madrid: Barajas Airport (MAD)
Sevilla: San Pablo Airport (SVQ)

Internet Access

It's useful to get online periodically as you travel—to confirm trip plans, check train or bus schedules, get weather forecasts, catch up on email, blog or post photos from your trip, or call folks back home (explained earlier, under "Calling over the Internet").

Your Mobile Device: The majority of accommodations in Spain offer Wi-Fi, as do many cafés, making it easy for you to get online with your laptop, tablet, or smartphone. Access is often free, but sometimes there's a fee. At hotels that charge for a certain number of hours, save money by logging in and out of your account on an as-needed basis. You should be able to stretch a two-hour Wi-Fi pass over a stay of a day or two.

Some hotel rooms and Internet cafés have high-speed Internet jacks that you can plug into with an Ethernet cable.

Public Internet Terminals: Many accommodations offer a guest computer in the lobby with Internet access. If you ask politely, smaller places may let you sit at their desk for a few minutes just to check your email. If your hotelier doesn't have access, ask to be directed to the nearest place to get online. Spanish keyboards are a little different from ours; to type an @ *(arroba)*, try pressing the "Alt Gr" and "2" keys.

Security: Whether you're accessing the Internet with your own device or at a public terminal, using a shared network or computer comes with increased security risks. If you're not convinced a connection is secure, avoid accessing sites (such as online banking) that could be vulnerable to fraud.

Mail

You can mail one package per day to yourself worth up to $200 duty-free from Europe to the US (mark it "personal purchases"). If you're sending a gift to someone, mark it "unsolicited gift." For details, visit www.cbp.gov and search for "Know Before You Go."

The Spanish postal service works fine, but for quick transatlantic delivery (in either direction), consider services such as DHL (www.dhl.com).

Transportation

By Car or Public Transportation?

If you're debating between public transportation and car rental, consider these factors: Cars are best for three or more traveling together (especially families with small kids), those packing heavy, and those scouring the countryside. Trains and buses are best for solo travelers, blitz tourists, city-to-city travelers, and those who don't want to drive in Europe. Though a car gives you more freedom, trains and buses zip you effortlessly and scenically from city to city, usually dropping you in the center, often near a TI. Cars are an expensive headache in places like Madrid or Barcelona.

Public Transportation

Public transportation in Spain is slick, modern, and efficient. The best option is to mix bus and train travel. Always verify schedules before your departure. Don't leave a station without your next day's schedule options in hand. To ask for a schedule at an information window, say, *"Horario para _____* (fill in name of city), *por favor."* (The local TI will sometimes have schedules available for you to take or copy.) To study train schedules in advance, visit Germany's excellent all-Europe website, www.bahn.com, or Spain's site, www.renfe.com. Bus schedules are more difficult to track down because routes are operated by different companies; for the names of regional carriers, check the "Connections" section of each destination chapter in this book. You can also try www.movelia.es, a third-party site listing several (but not all) bus companies.

Trains

You can buy a Spain "flexi" railpass that allows travel for a given number of days over a longer period of time, but you'll pay separately ($10-35) for seat reservations on all trains. Buying individual train tickets in advance or as you go in Spain can be less expensive, and gives you better access to seat reservations (which are limited for railpass holders). Some individual ticket prices already include seat reservations when required (for instance, for fast trains).

If your trip also includes a neighboring country, consider the France-Spain, Portugal-Spain, or Italy-Spain passes (see chart). A Eurail Select Pass lets you travel even farther. Spain also offers a rail-and-drive pass, which gives you the ease of big-city train hops and the flexibility of a car for rural areas such as the Andalusian hill towns. These passes are sold only outside Europe. For specifics, check the railpass chart, contact your travel agent, or see my *Guide to Eurail Passes* at www.ricksteves.com/rail. Even if you have a railpass, use buses when they're more convenient and direct than

Railpasses

Prices listed are for 2013 and are subject to change. For the latest prices, details, and train schedules (and easy online ordering), see my comprehensive *Guide to Eurail Passes* at www.ricksteves.com/rail.

"Saver" prices are per person for two or more people traveling together. "Youth" means under age 26. The fare for children 4–11 is half the adult individual fare or Saver fare. Kids under age 4 travel free.

SPAIN RAIL & DRIVE PASS

Any 3 rail days and 2 car days in 2 months.

Car Category	1st Class	2nd Class	Extra car day
Mini	$355	$295	$48
Compact	362	301	54
Standard	388	327	80
Intermediate auto.	425	365	118
Premium	453	392	145

Prices are per person, two traveling together. Solo travelers pay about $100 extra. Third and fourth people sharing the car buy only the railpass. Extra rail days (max 2) cost $36-$45 per day. To order Rail & Drive passes, call your travel agent or Rail Europe at 800-438-7245. *This pass is not sold by Europe Through the Back Door.*

Map key:

Approximate point-to-point one-way second-class rail fares in US dollars. First class costs 50 percent more. Add up fares for your itinerary to see whether a railpass will save you money. Dashed lines are buses and ferries (not covered by passes).

SPAIN PASS

	1st Class	2nd Class
3 days in 2 months	$299	$240
Extra rail days (max 10)	41-48	33-39

SPAIN-PORTUGAL PASS

	Individual 1st Class	Saver 1st Class
3 days in 2 months	$340	$290
Extra rail days (max 7)	45-48	38-41

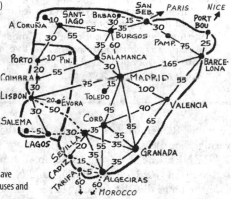

SELECTPASS

This pass covers travel in three adjacent countries, not including France. Please visit **www.ricksteves.com/rail** for four- and five-country options.

	Individual 1st Class	Saver 1st Class	Youth 2nd Class
5 days in 2 months	$486	$414	$317
6 days in 2 months	536	457	350
8 days in 2 months	634	540	413
10 days in 2 months	735	625	479

FRANCE–SPAIN PASS

	Individual 1st Class	Individual 2nd Class	Saver 1st Class	Saver 2nd Class	Youth 2nd Class
4 days in 2 months	$411	$350	$350	$299	$269
Extra rail days (max 6)	45-51	38-44	38-44	33-37	29-32

Buying Train Tickets

Trains can sell out, so it's smart to buy your tickets a day in advance, even for short rides. You have four options for buying train tickets: at the station, at a travel agency, online, or by phone. Since station ticket offices can get very crowded, most travelers will find it easiest to go to a travel agency, most of which charge only a nominal service fee.

At the Station: You will likely have to wait in a line to buy your ticket. First find the correct line—at bigger stations, there might be separate windows for short-distance, long-distance, advance, and "today" *(para hoy)* tickets. To avoid wasting time in the wrong line, read the signs carefully, and ask a local (or a clerk at an information window) which line you need. You might have to take a number—watch others and follow their lead. While clerks accept regular US credit cards, most RENFE ticket machines only take chip-and-PIN credit cards.

As another option, you could buy tickets or reservations at the RENFE offices located in more than 100 city centers. These are more central and multilingual—also less crowded and confusing—than the train station.

Travel Agency: The best choice for most travelers is to buy tickets at an English-speaking travel agency. The El Corte Inglés department stores (with locations in most Spanish cities) often have handy travel agencies inside. I've recommended these and other travel agencies throughout this book. Look for a train sticker in agency windows.

the trains. Remember to reserve ahead for the fast AVE trains and overnight journeys.

RENFE (the acronym for the Spanish national train system) used to mean "Really Exasperating, and Not For Everyone," but it has moved into the 21st century. For information and reservations, dial RENFE's national number (toll tel. 902-320-320) from anywhere in Spain, or visit www.renfe.com. For tips on buying tickets, see the sidebar.

Spain categorizes trains this way:

The high-speed train called the **AVE** (AH-vay, stands for *Alta Velocidad Española*) whisks travelers between Madrid and Toledo in 30 minutes, Madrid and Sevilla or Barcelona in three hours, and Madrid and Málaga in less than three hours. For decades, Spain's trains didn't fit on Europe's tracks, but AVE trains run on standard

Online: Although the website www.renfe.com is useful for confirming schedules and prices, you cannot dependably buy tickets online unless you have a European credit card. The website rejects nearly every attempt to use a US card, but with patience and enough Spanish language skill, you may be able to nab an online discount of up to 60 percent (available two weeks to two months ahead of travel). Another option is www.rumbo .es. This travel website (select English at the very bottom of the page) sells discounted tickets for a small service fee (about €5). Other online vendors include www.raileurope.com and www .petrabax.com (higher fees).

By Phone: You can purchase your ticket by phone (toll tel. 902-240-202), then pick it up at the station by punching your confirmation code (*localizador*) into one of the automated machines. Discounts up to 40 percent off are offered a week or more ahead by phone (and at stations).

You can also reserve tickets by phone, then buy them at the station, which you must do a few days before departure (at a ticket window, usually signed "*venta anticipada*"). You can't pay for reserved tickets at the station on your day of travel.

The Fine Print: First-class tickets cost 50 percent more than second class—often as much as a domestic flight (see "Cheap Flights" on page 950). Discounted tickets come with restrictions, such as being nonrefundable and nonchangeable. Be sure to read all the details carefully at time of purchase.

European-gauge rails. AVE trains can be priced differently according to their time of departure. Peak hours (*punta*) are most expensive, followed by *llano* and *valle* (quietest and cheapest times). AVE is almost entirely covered by the Eurail Pass (book ahead, a seat reservation fee from Madrid to Sevilla costs Eurailers about $23 in second class; $38 for first class, includes meal). If doing the recommended Sevilla-to-Córdoba day trip by AVE, it's smart to bring your passport (conductors may ask for identification, especially if you have a railpass).

A related high-speed train, the **Alvia,** runs on AVE lines but can switch to Iberian track without stopping. On the Madrid-San Sebastián route, for example, it reaches the Basque Country in five hours.

Avant trains are also high-speed—typically about as fast as AVE—but designed for shorter distances. They also tend to be cheaper than AVE, even on the same route. Railpass reservations also cost about half as much for Avant as for AVE. If you're on a tight budget, compare your options before buying.

The **Talgo** is fast, air-conditioned, and expensive, and runs

Public Transportation Routes in Iberia

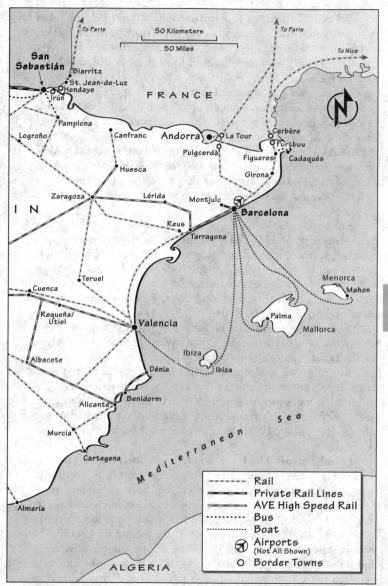

APPENDIX

on AVE rails. **Intercity** and **Electro** trains fall just behind Talgo in speed, comfort, and expense. **Rápido, Tranvía, Semidirecto,** and **Expreso** trains are generally slower. **Cercanías** are commuter trains for big-city workers and small-town tourists. **Regional** and **Correo** trains are slow, small-town milk runs. Trains get more expensive as they pick up speed, but all are cheaper per mile than their northern European counterparts. Spain loves to name trains, so you may encounter types of trains not listed here. The names Euromed, Alaris, Altaria, and Arco all indicate faster trains that require reservations. These can cost significantly less than AVE on some routes (for example, on the Córdoba-Sevilla route, AVE costs nearly double Altaria, but they take the same amount of time). Ask about the travel time for each option when buying your tickets.

Salidas means "departures," and *llegadas* is "arrivals." On train schedules, "LMXJVSD" stands for the days of the week in Spanish, starting with Monday. A train that runs "LMXJV-D" doesn't run on Saturdays. *Laborables* can mean Monday through Friday or Monday through Saturday.

Overnight Trains: For long trips, I go overnight on the train or I fly (domestic shuttle flights are generally less than $100). Overnight trains (and buses) are usually less expensive and slower than the daytime rides. Most overnight trains have berths and beds that you can rent (not included in the cost of your train ticket or railpass). A sleeping berth *(litera)* costs extra, with the price depending on the route and type of compartment. Night trains are popular, so it's smart to reserve in advance, even from home. Travelers with first-class reservations are entitled to use comfortable "Intercity" lounges in train stations in Spain's major cities.

Hotel Trains: The term Trenhotel ("Hotel Train") usually means fancy and expensive. The pricey overnight Trenhotel between Madrid and Lisbon is called the Lusitania (approximate prices: first class-$200, including a bed in a double compartment; second class-$120 in a quad; about $55 or more for a sleeper if you have a railpass, additional cost for singles or a shower in your compartment; advance-purchase deals available at stations and www.renfe.com). Unfortunately, no other rail option exists between these two capital cities. You can save money by taking a bus, or save time by taking a plane. Trenhotel prices are at least as high between other major cities, such as Barcelona-Valencia or Barcelona-Madrid.

High-priced international Trenhotels used to connect Paris with Spain but were discontinued in 2013. To travel overnight to Paris, you can take a train trip that involves a transfer near the Spanish border (at Cerbère on the eastern side). You'll connect to a normal night train with $35 sleeping berths *(literas/couchettes)* on one leg of the trip. This plan is time-consuming, and may take two days of a flexipass. Consider flying instead to save time (see "Cheap Flights," later).

Buses

Spain's bus system is confusing (www.movelia.es is a good place to begin researching schedules and carriers). There are a number of different bus companies (though usually clustered within one building), sometimes running buses to the same destinations and using the same transfer points. If you have to transfer, make sure to look for a bus with the same name/logo as the company you bought the ticket from. The larger stations have a consolidated information desk with all the schedules. In smaller stations, check the destinations and schedules posted on each office window. (If your connection requires a transfer to another company's bus in a different city, don't count on getting help from the originating clerk to figure out the onward connection.) Bus service on holidays, Saturdays, and especially Sundays can be less frequent.

If you arrive in a city by bus and plan to leave by bus, stick around the station upon your arrival to check your departure options and buy a ticket in advance if necessary (and possible). If you're downtown, need a ticket, and the bus station isn't central, save time by asking at the tourist office about travel agencies that sell bus tickets.

You can (and most likely will be required to) stow your luggage under the bus. Your ticket comes with an assigned seat; if the bus is full, you should take that seat, but if it's uncrowded, most people just sit where they like. For longer rides, give some thought to which side of the bus will get the most sun, and sit on the opposite side, even if the bus is air-conditioned and has curtains. Your ride likely will come with a soundtrack: taped Spanish pop music, radio, or sometimes videos. If you prefer silence, bring earplugs. Buses are non-smoking.

Drivers and station personnel rarely speak English. Buses generally lack WCs, but they stop every two hours or so for a break (usually 15 minutes, but can be up to 30). Drivers announce how long the stop will be, but if in doubt, ask the driver, "How many minutes here?" *("¿Cuántos minutos aquí?")* so you know if you have time to get out. Listen for the bus horn as a final call before departure. Bus stations have WCs (rarely with toilet paper) and cafés that offer quick and slightly overpriced food.

Taxis

Most taxis are reliable and cheap. Drivers generally respond kindly to the request, "How much is it to _____, more or less?"

("¿Cuánto cuesta a _____, más o menos?"). Spanish taxis have extra supplements (for luggage, night-time, Sundays, train/bus-station or airport pickup, and so on). Rounding up the fare (maximum of 10 percent) is adequate for a tip. City rides cost €4-6. Keep a map in your hand so the cabbie knows (or thinks) you know where you're going. Big cities have plenty of taxis. In many cases, couples travel by cab for little more than the cost of two bus or subway tickets.

Renting a Car

If you're renting a car in Spain, bring your driver's license. You're also required to have an International Driving Permit—an official translation of your driver's license (sold at your local AAA office for $15 plus the cost of two passport-type photos; see www.aaa .com). While that's the letter of the law, I've often rented cars in Spain without having this permit. If all goes well, you'll likely never be asked to show the permit—but it's a must if you end up dealing with the police.

Rental companies require you to be at least 21 years old and to have held your license for one year. Drivers under the age of 25 may incur a young-driver surcharge, and some rental companies do not rent to anyone 75 or older. If you're considered too young or old, look into leasing (covered later), which has less stringent age restrictions.

Research car rentals before you go. It's cheaper to arrange most car rentals from the US. Call several companies and look online to compare rates, or arrange a rental through your hometown travel agent.

Most of the major US rental agencies (including Avis, Budget, Enterprise, Hertz, and Thrifty) have offices throughout Europe. Also consider the two major Europe-based agencies, Europcar and Sixt. It can be cheaper to use a consolidator, such as Auto Europe (www.autoeurope.com) or Europe by Car (www.ebctravel.com), which compares rates at several companies to get you the best deal. However, my readers have reported problems with consolidators ranging from misinformation to unexpected fees; because you're going through a middleman, it can be more challenging to resolve disputes that might arise with the rental agency.

Regardless of the car-rental company you choose, always read the fine print carefully for add-on charges—such as one-way drop-off fees, airport surcharges, or mandatory insurance policies—that aren't included in the "total price." You may need to query rental

Spain by Car: Mileage & Time

FRANCE

Santiago de Compostela — 285M·6H — Comillas — Santillana del Mar — 80M·1.5H — Bilbao — St-Jean-de-Luz — 20M·.75H — San Sebastián

270M·4.5H — 95M 10M·.25H — Potes — 2.5H — 125M — 60M 2.5H — 55M·1.5H — Barcelona to Cerbère (French border) 110M·2h

140M·2.5H — León — 120M·2H — 50M·1.5H — 135M·1.5H — 125M·2.25H (VIA VITORIA) — Pamplona

Porto — 220M·4H — 210M·3.5H — Burgos — Segovia — 115M 2H

75M·1.25H — Salamanca — 60M 1.5H — 85M 1H — Segovia — Zaragoza — Barcelona

Coimbra — 185M·4H — Ávila — 60M 1.25H — Madrid — 205M 3.5H — 220M·3.5H

125M·2H — 320M·9H — 70M·1.5H — 45M 1H — 225M·4H — Valencia

Lisboa — 315M·5.5H — Toledo — S P A I N

Évora — 85M 1.5H — 200M·3.5H — 220M 4H — Córdoba — 330M·5.5H

Salema — 195M·3.5H — 180M·3H — Sevilla — 90M·2H — 100M·3H — 225M — Granada

55M·1.5H — 155M·3H — 3.5H

70M·2H — Arcos — 80M·2H — 120M·2H — 65M·1.25H

50M·1.25H — Tarifa — 70M·1.5H — Nerja

.5H FERRY — 60M·1.75H — Gibraltar

Tangier

m = miles
h = hours
···· = ferry

NOTE: YOUR TIMES MAY VARY BASED ON TRAFFIC, CONSTRUCTION & ROAD CONDITIONS.

APPENDIX

agents pointedly to find out your actual cost.

For the best deal, rent by the week with unlimited mileage. To save money on fuel, ask for a diesel car. I normally rent the smallest, least-expensive model with a stick shift (generally much cheaper than an automatic). Almost all rentals are manual by default, so if you need an automatic, request one in advance; be aware that these cars are usually larger models and not as maneuverable on narrow, winding roads (such as in Andalucía's hill towns).

For a one-week rental, allow roughly $250-450. Allow extra for insurance, fuel, tolls, and parking. For trips of three weeks or more, look into leasing (described later); you'll save money on insurance and taxes.

You can sometimes get a GPS unit with your rental car or leased vehicle for an additional fee (around $15/day; be sure it's set to English and has all the maps you need before you drive off). Or, if you have a portable GPS device at home, consider taking it with you to Europe (buy and upload European maps before your trip). GPS apps are also available for smartphones, but downloading maps in Europe could lead to an exorbitant data-roaming bill (for more details, see the sidebar on page 932).

Compare pickup costs (downtown can be less expensive than the airport) and explore drop-off options. Always check the hours of the location you choose: Many rental offices close from midday Saturday until Monday morning and, in smaller towns, at lunchtime.

When selecting a location, don't trust the agency's description of "downtown" or "city center." In some cases, a "downtown" branch can be on the outskirts of the city—a long, costly taxi ride from the center. Before choosing, plug the addresses into a mapping website. You may find that the "train station" location is handier. But returning a car at a big-city train station or downtown agency can be tricky; get precise details on the drop-off location and hours, and allow ample time to find it.

When you pick up the rental car, check it thoroughly and make sure any damage is noted on your rental agreement. Find out how your car's lights, turn signals, wipers, and fuel cap function, and know what kind of fuel the car takes. When you return the car, make sure the agent verifies its condition with you.

Car Insurance Options

When you rent a car, you are liable for a very high deductible, sometimes equal to the entire value of the car. Limit your financial risk with one of these three options: Buy Collision Damage Waiver (CDW) coverage from the car-rental company, get coverage through your credit card (free, if your card automatically includes zero-deductible coverage), or buy coverage through Travel Guard.

CDW includes a very high deductible (typically $1,000-1,500). Though each rental company has its own variation, basic CDW costs $15-35 a day (figure roughly 30 percent extra) and reduces your liability, but does not eliminate it. When you pick up the car, you'll be offered the chance to "buy down" the basic deductible to zero (for an additional $10-30/day; this is sometimes called "super CDW").

If you opt for **credit-card coverage,** there's a catch. You'll technically have to decline all coverage offered by the car-rental company, which means they can place a hold on your card (which can be up to the full value of the car). In case of damage, it can be time-consuming to resolve the charges with your credit-card company. Before you decide on this option, quiz your credit-card company about how it works.

Finally, you can buy collision insurance from **Travel Guard** ($9/day plus a one-time $3 service fee covers you for up to $35,000, $250 deductible, tel. 800-826-4919, www.travelguard.com). It's valid everywhere in Europe except the Republic of Ireland, and some Italian car-rental companies refuse to honor it. Note that various states differ on which products and policies are available to their residents—check with Travel Guard *before* you rent your car.

For more on car-rental insurance, see www.ricksteves.com /cdw.

Leasing

For trips of three weeks or more, consider leasing (which automatically includes zero-deductible collision and theft insurance). By technically buying and then selling back the car, you save lots of money on tax and insurance. Leasing provides you a brand-new car with unlimited mileage and a 24-hour emergency assistance program. You can lease for as little as 21 days and as long as six months. Car leases must be arranged from the US. One of many companies offering affordable lease packages is Europe by Car (US tel. 800-223-1516, www.ebctravel.com).

Driving

Driving in rural Spain is great—traffic is sparse and roads are

generally good. But a car is a pain in big cities such as Madrid. Drive defensively. If you're involved in an accident, you will be in for a monumental headache.

Good maps are available and inexpensive throughout Spain. In smaller towns, following signs to *centro ciudad* will get you to the heart of things.

Freeways and Tolls: Spain's freeways come with tolls, but save huge amounts of time. Each toll road *(autopista de peaje)* has its own pricing structure, so tolls vary (for example, Madrid-Toledo: €2.20; Málaga-Gibraltar: €13.15). Near some major cities, you must prepay for each stretch of road you drive; on other routes, you take a ticket where you enter the freeway, and pay when you exit. Payment can be made in cash or by credit or debit card (credit-card-only lanes are labeled *"vias automáticas"*).

Because road numbers can be puzzling and inconsistent, be ready to navigate by city and town names. On freeways, navigate by direction *(norte, oeste, sur, este)*. Mileage signs are in kilometers (see page 958 for conversion formula into miles).

Road Rules: Seatbelts are required by law. Children under 12 must ride in the back seat, and children up to age 3 must have a child seat. You must put on a reflective safety vest any time you get out of your car on the side of a highway or unlit road (most rental-car companies provide one, but check when you pick up the car). Those who use eyeglasses are required by law to have a spare pair in the car. It is illegal to talk on a cell phone while driving (unless using a fully hands-free system).

Drivers must turn on headlights during daylight hours if visibility is poor. Spain does not allow a right turn at a red light. For more on road rules, ask your car-rental company, or check the US State Department website (www.travel.state.gov, click on "International Travel," then specify "Spain" and "Traffic Safety and Road Conditions").

Traffic Cops: Watch for traffic radars and expect to be stopped for a routine check by the police (be sure your car-insurance form is up-to-date). Small towns come with speed traps and corruption. Tickets, especially for foreigners, are issued and paid for on the spot. Insist on a receipt *(recibo),* so the money is less likely to end up in the cop's pocket.

Fuel: Gas and diesel prices are controlled and the same everywhere—about $7 a gallon for gas, less for diesel (gas is priced by the liter in Spain). Unleaded gas *(gasolina sin plomo)* is either *normal* or *super.* Note that diesel is called *diesel* or *gasóleo*—pay attention when filling your tank.

Theft: Choose parking places carefully. Stow valuables in the trunk during the day and leave nothing worth stealing in the car overnight. While you should avoid parking lots with twinkly asphalt, thieves break car windows anywhere, even at stoplights. If your car's a hatchback, take the trunk cover off at night so thieves can look in without breaking in. Try to make your car look locally owned by hiding the "tourist-owned" rental-company decals and putting a local newspaper in your front or back window. Parking attendants all over Spain holler, *"Nada en el coche"* ("Nothing in the car"). And they mean it. Ask your hotelier for advice on parking. In cities you can park safely but expensively in guarded lots.

Cheap Flights

If you're considering a train ride that's more than five hours long, a flight may save you both time and money. When comparing your options, factor in the time it takes to get to the airport and how early you'll need to arrive to check in.

The best comparison search engine for both international and intra-European flights is www.kayak.com. For inexpensive flights within Europe, try www.skyscanner.com or www.hipmunk.com. If you're not sure who flies to your destination, check its airport's website for a list of carriers.

For flights within Spain and around Europe, try the national carriers Vueling (www.vueling.com), Air Europa (www.aireuropa.com), or Iberia (www.iberia.com). Other well-known cheapo airlines include easyJet (www.easyjet.com) and RyanAir (www.ryanair.com).

Be aware of the potential drawbacks of flying on the cheap: nonrefundable and nonchangeable tickets, minimal or nonexistent customer service, treks to airports far outside town, and stingy baggage allowances with steep overage fees. If you're traveling with lots of luggage, a cheap flight can quickly become a bad deal. To avoid unpleasant surprises, read the small print before you book.

Resources

Resources from Rick Steves

Rick Steves' Spain 2014 is one of many books in my series on European travel, which includes country guidebooks, city guide-

books (Barcelona, Rome, Florence, Paris, London, etc.), Snapshot Guides (excerpted chapters from my country guides), Pocket Guides (full-color little books on big cities), and my budget-travel skills handbook, *Rick Steves' Europe Through the Back Door*. Most of my titles are available as ebooks. My phrase books—for Spanish, Italian, French, German, and Portuguese—are practical and budget-oriented. My other books include *Europe 101* (a crash course on art and history designed for travelers); *Mediterranean Cruise Ports* and *Northern European Cruise Ports* (how to make the most of your time in port), and *Travel as a Political Act* (a travelogue sprinkled with tips for bringing home a global perspective). A more complete list of my titles appears near the end of this book.

Video: My public television series, *Rick Steves' Europe*, covers European destinations in 100 shows, with 10 episodes on Spain. To watch episodes, visit www.hulu.com; for scripts and local airtimes, see www.ricksteves.com/tv.

Audio: My weekly public radio show, *Travel with Rick Steves,* features interviews with travel experts from around the world. All of this audio content is available for free at Rick Steves Audio Europe, an extensive online library organized by destination. Choose whatever interests you, and download it via the Rick Steves Audio Europe smartphone app, www.ricksteves.com/audioeurope, iTunes, or Google Play.

Maps

The black-and-white maps in this book, designed by David Hoerlein, are concise and simple. The maps are intended to help you locate recommended places and get to TIs, where you can pick up more in-depth maps of cities or regions (usually free). Better maps are available—and cheaper than in the US—throughout Spain at newsstands, bookstores, and gas stations. Before you buy a map, look at it to be sure it has the level of detail you want. Drivers will want to pick up a good, detailed map in Europe (I'd recommend a 1:200,000- or 1:300,000-scale map).

Other Guidebooks

If you're like most travelers, this book is all you need. But if you're heading beyond my recommended destinations, $40 for extra maps and books can be money well spent. If you'll be spending a lot of time in Barcelona, consider *Rick Steves' Barcelona.*

The following books are worthwhile, though most are not updated annually; check the publication date before you buy. Lonely Planet's guide to Spain is well researched, with good maps and hotel recommendations for low- to moderate-budget travelers. The similar *Rough Guide to Spain* is hip and insightful, written by British researchers. Students and vagabonds like the highly opinionated *Let's Go: Spain & Portugal,* updated by Harvard students. *Let's Go* is best for backpackers who stay at hostels, use railpasses, and dive into the youth and nightlife scene.

The *Eyewitness* series has about a dozen editions covering Spain, including Barcelona, Madrid, and Sevilla/Andalucía. They're extremely popular for great, easy-to-grasp graphics and photos, but the written content in *Eyewitness* is relatively skimpy, and the books weigh a ton. I simply borrow them for a minute from other travelers at certain sights to make sure I'm aware of that place's highlights. *Time Out* travel guides provide good, detailed coverage of Madrid, Barcelona, and Andalucía, particularly on arts and entertainment.

The popular skinny Michelin Green Guides to Spain are

Begin Your Trip at www.ricksteves.com

At our travel website, you'll discover a wealth of free information on European destinations, including fresh monthly news and helpful tips from thousands of fellow travelers. You'll find my latest guidebook updates (www.ricksteves.com/update), a monthly travel enewsletter, my personal travel blog, and my free Rick Steves Audio Europe smartphone app (if you don't have a smartphone, you can access the same content via podcasts). You can also follow me on Facebook and Twitter.

Our **online Travel Store** offers travel bags and accessories that I've designed specifically to help you travel smarter and lighter. These include my popular bags (rolling carry-on and backpack versions), money belts, totes, toiletries kits, adapters, other accessories, and a wide selection of guidebooks, planning maps, and DVDs.

Choosing the right **railpass** for your trip—amid hundreds of options—can drive you nutty. Our website will help you find the perfect fit for your itinerary and your budget.

Want to travel with greater efficiency and less stress? We organize **tours** with more than three dozen itineraries and more than 600 departures reaching the best destinations in this book...and beyond. Our Spain tours include Barcelona and Madrid in 8 days, the Basque Country of Spain and France in 8 days, a My Way: Spain "unguided" tour in 11 days, and Spain in 14 days. You'll enjoy great guides, a fun bunch of travel partners (with small groups of generally around 24 to 28 travelers), and plenty of room to spread out in a big, comfy bus. You'll find European adventures to fit every vacation length. For all the details, and to get our Tour Catalog and a free Rick Steves Tour Experience DVD (filmed on location during an actual tour), visit www.ricksteves.com or call us at 425/608-4217.

APPENDIX

excellent, especially if you're driving. They're known for their city and sightseeing maps, dry but concise and helpful information on major sights, and good cultural and historical background. English editions, covering most of the regions you'll want to visit, are sold in Spain.

I like Cadogan guides for their well-presented background information and coverage of cultural issues. Their recommendations suit upscale travelers. Older travelers enjoy Frommer's Spain guides, even though these, like the Fodor's guides, ignore alternatives that enable travelers to save money by dirtying their fingers in the local culture. The encyclopedic Blue Guides are dry as the plains in Spain, but just right for arty and scholarly types.

If you'll be traveling to neighboring countries, consider *Rick Steves' Portugal* and *Rick Steves' France.*

Recommended Books and Movies

Spain is overwhelmingly rich in history, art, and culture. To learn more about Spain's past and present, check out a few of these books or films.

Nonfiction

Spain has undergone incredible changes since the death of Franco in 1975 and the end of his nearly four-decade dictatorship. *The New Spaniards* (Hooper) is a survey of all aspects of modern Spain, including its politics, economy, demographics, education, religion, and popular culture.

For a sympathetic cultural history of the Basque people, their language, and contributions from Roman times to the present, read *The Basque History of the World* (Kurlansky).

George Orwell traded his press pass for a uniform, fought against Franco's Fascists in the Spanish Civil War of 1936-1939, and then wrote an account of his experiences in his gripping *Homage to Catalonia*. *The Battle for Spain* (Beevor) re-creates the political climate during the civil war.

James Michener traveled to Spain for several decades, and his tribute, *Iberia*, describes how Spain's dark history created a contradictory and passionately beautiful land.

Hemingway shows his journalistic side in two books on bullfighting: *Death in the Afternoon* and *The Dangerous Summer*.

How Muslims, Jews, and Christians created a culture of tolerance in medieval Spain is vividly brought to life in *The Ornament of the World* (Menocal).

Travelers' Tales: Spain (McCauley) offers dozens of essays about Spain and its people from numerous authors.

Penelope Casas has written many popular books on the food of Spain, including tapas, paella, and regional cooking. Her *Discovering Spain: An Uncommon Guide* blends references to history, culture, and food with travel information. For deciphering menus in restaurants, foodies like *The Marling Menu-Master for Spain*.

The nature of pilgrimage is explored along the famous Camino de Santiago trail in northern Spain in *Following the Milky Way* (Aviva) and *On Pilgrimage* (Lash).

The eccentricities of village life in the mountains south of Granada are lovingly detailed in a British expat's 1920s experiences in *South from Granada* (Brenan). A contemporary family's adjustments to living in the same region are described in *Driving Over Lemons: An Optimist in Spain* (Stewart) and the author's later books.

Two cultural histories focus on the city of Barcelona and the Catalan psyche: *Homage to Barcelona* (Toibin) and *Barcelona* (Hughes).

Fiction

Fans of classic literature will want to read Cervantes' *Don Quixote*. Another classic, Irving's *Tales of the Alhambra*, weaves fact, mythical tales, and descriptions of Granada and its beautiful Moorish castle complex—the Alhambra—during the author's 19th-century visit.

Hemingway fans will enjoy *The Sun Also Rises;* this story of expats living in post-WWI France and Spain introduced many readers to bullfighting. Hemingway's *For Whom the Bell Tolls*, a tale of idealism and harsh reality, is set against the complexity of the civil war.

That ugly period of Spanish history is also the subject of *The Carpenter's Pencil* (Rivas), an unsentimental tale of an imprisoned revolutionary haunted by his past.

The brutality and intolerance of the dark years of the Spanish Inquisition are illuminated in Winstein's *The Heretic,* with Sevilla as the backdrop. *The Last Jew* (Gordon) is one man's story of survival in Inquisition-era Spain. *Stories from Spain* (Barlow and Stivers) relates well-known Spanish legends that chronicle nearly 1,000 years of Spanish history.

The 2005 best-selling thriller *The Shadow of the Wind* (Zafón) takes place in 1950s Barcelona; sequels include *The Angel's Game* and *The Prisoner of Heaven*. Robert Wilson's popular police thrillers, including *The Blind Man of Seville*, are set in Spain and Portugal.

Films

In *The Mystery of Picasso* (1956), Picasso is filmed painting from behind a transparent canvas, allowing a unique look at his creative process.

Peter O'Toole and Sophia Loren star in the musical version of Don Quixote, *Man of La Mancha* (1972).

In the first of Carlos Saura's flamenco dance trilogy, *Blood Wedding* (1981), he adapts Federico García Lorca's play about a wedding imposed on a bride in love with another man. *Carmen* (1983) shows a Spanish cast rehearsing the well-known French novel and opera. *El Amor Brujo* (1986) is a ghostly love story.

L'auberge Espagnole (2002) tells the story of the loves and lives of European students sharing an apartment in Barcelona.

In *Barcelona* (1994), two Americans in Spain try to navigate the Spanish singles scene and the ensuing culture clash.

The Spanish film *Open Your Eyes* (1997) inspired the 2001 Tom Cruise thriller *Vanilla Sky,* where a car accident sets off an intricate series of events.

Woody Allen's *Vicky Cristina Barcelona* (2008) stars Javier Bardem as a macho Spanish artist romancing two American

APPENDIX

women, when suddenly his stormy ex-wife (Penélope Cruz, in an Oscar-winning role) re-enters his life.

Pedro Almodóvar's piquant films about relationships in the post-Franco era have garnered piles of international awards. Spanish actors Bardem, Cruz, and Antonio Banderas have starred in his films. Almodóvar's best-known films include *Women on the Verge of a Nervous Breakdown* (1988), *All About My Mother* (1999), *Talk to Her* (2002), *Volver* (2006), *Broken Embraces* (2009), *The Skin I Live In* (2011), and *I'm So Excited* (2013).

Holidays and Festivals

This list includes selected festivals in Spain, plus national holidays observed throughout the country. Many sights and banks close on national holidays—keep this in mind when planning your itinerary. Before planning a trip around a festival, verify its dates by checking the festival's website or TI sites (www.spain.info).

In 2014, be prepared for big crowds during these holiday periods: Holy Week (Semana Santa) and Easter weekend, especially in Sevilla; April Fair in Sevilla; the San Isidro festival in Madrid; Labor Day; Dos de Mayo, Madrid; Ascension; Pentecost weekend; Assumption weekend; Spanish National Day; Constitution Day, followed closely by the Feast of the Immaculate Conception—both the previous and following weekends may be busy; and Christmas and New Year's. Look out  for any local holiday that falls on a Tuesday or Thursday—the Spanish will often take Monday or Friday off as well to have a four-day weekend.

Jan 1	New Year's Day
Jan 6	Epiphany
Early Feb	La Candelaria (religious festival), Madrid
Feb 28	Day of Andalucía (some closures), Andalucía
April 13-20	Holy Week
April 20	Easter
April 21	Easter Monday
April 29-May 4	Feria de Abril (April fair), Sevilla
May 1	Labor Day (closures)
May 2	Dos de Mayo, Madrid
Mid-May	Feria del Caballo (horse pageantry), Jerez

2014

JANUARY

S	M	T	W	T	F	S
			1	2	3	4
5	6	7	8	9	10	11
12	13	14	15	16	17	18
19	20	21	22	23	24	25
26	27	28	29	30	31	

FEBRUARY

S	M	T	W	T	F	S
						1
2	3	4	5	6	7	8
9	10	11	12	13	14	15
16	17	18	19	20	21	22
23	24	25	26	27	28	

MARCH

S	M	T	W	T	F	S
						1
2	3	4	5	6	7	8
9	10	11	12	13	14	15
16	17	18	19	20	21	22
23/30	24/31	25	26	27	28	29

APRIL

S	M	T	W	T	F	S
		1	2	3	4	5
6	7	8	9	10	11	12
13	14	15	16	17	18	19
20	21	22	23	24	25	26
27	28	29	30			

MAY

S	M	T	W	T	F	S
				1	2	3
4	5	6	7	8	9	10
11	12	13	14	15	16	17
18	19	20	21	22	23	24
25	26	27	28	29	30	31

JUNE

S	M	T	W	T	F	S
1	2	3	4	5	6	7
8	9	10	11	12	13	14
15	16	17	18	19	20	21
22	23	24	25	26	27	28
29	30					

JULY

S	M	T	W	T	F	S
		1	2	3	4	5
6	7	8	9	10	11	12
13	14	15	16	17	18	19
20	21	22	23	24	25	26
27	28	29	30	31		

AUGUST

S	M	T	W	T	F	S
					1	2
3	4	5	6	7	8	9
10	11	12	13	14	15	16
17	18	19	20	21	22	23
24/31	25	26	27	28	29	30

SEPTEMBER

S	M	T	W	T	F	S
	1	2	3	4	5	6
7	8	9	10	11	12	13
14	15	16	17	18	19	20
21	22	23	24	25	26	27
28	29	30				

OCTOBER

S	M	T	W	T	F	S
			1	2	3	4
5	6	7	8	9	10	11
12	13	14	15	16	17	18
19	20	21	22	23	24	25
26	27	28	29	30	31	

NOVEMBER

S	M	T	W	T	F	S
						1
2	3	4	5	6	7	8
9	10	11	12	13	14	15
16	17	18	19	20	21	22
23/30	24	25	26	27	28	29

DECEMBER

S	M	T	W	T	F	S
	1	2	3	4	5	6
7	8	9	10	11	12	13
14	15	16	17	18	19	20
21	22	23	24	25	26	27
28	29	30	31			

APPENDIX

May 15	San Isidro (religious festival); also bullfights and zarzuelas all month long), Madrid
May 29	Ascension
Late May–Early June	La Patum (religious festival), Berga (near Barcelona)
June 7-9	Pentecost weekend
June 19	Corpus Christi
June 24	Festival of St. John the Baptist (bonfires and fireworks)
June-July	International Festival of Music and Dance, Granada
July 6-14	Running of the Bulls (Fiesta de San Fermín), Pamplona
July 25	Feast Day of St. James, Santiago de Compostela

Aug	Gràcia Festival, Barcelona
Mid-Aug	Verbena de la Paloma (folk festival), Madrid
Aug 15	Assumption of Mary (religious festival)
Aug 21-27	Festival of St. Bartholomew, Sitges (major festivities on Aug 23-24)
Sept	Autumn Festival (flamenco, bullfights), Jerez
Sept 23	Festival of St. Tecla, Sitges
Late Sept	La Mercé (parade), Barcelona
Late Sept	Feria de San Miguel (bullfights), Sevilla
Late Sept (last weekend)	Little San Fermín (concerts, parades), Pamplona
Oct 12	Spanish National Day
Late Oct-Nov	International Jazz Festival, Madrid
Nov 1	All Saints' Day
Nov 9	Virgen de la Almudena, Madrid
Dec 6	Constitution Day
Dec 8	Feast of the Immaculate Conception
Dec 13	Feast of Santa Lucía
Dec 25	Christmas
Dec 31	New Year's Eve

Conversions and Climate

Numbers and Stumblers

- Europeans write a few of their numbers differently than we do. 1 = 1, 4 = 4, 7 = 7.
- In Europe, dates appear as day/month/year, so Christmas is 25/12/14.
- Commas are decimal points and decimals are commas. A dollar and a half is $1,50, and there are 5.280 feet in a mile.
- When counting with fingers, start with your thumb. If you hold up your first finger to request one item, you'll probably get two.
- What Americans call the second floor of a building is the first floor in Europe.
- On escalators and moving sidewalks, Europeans keep the left "lane" open for passing. Keep to the right.

Metric Conversions

A kilogram is 2.2 pounds, and 1 liter is about a quart, or almost four to a gallon. A kilometer is six-tenths of a mile. I figure kilometers to miles by cutting the kilometers in half and adding back 10 percent of the original (120 km: 60 + 12 = 72 miles, 300 km: 150 + 30 = 180 miles).

1 foot = 0.3 meter	1 square yard = 0.8 square meter
1 yard = 0.9 meter	1 square mile = 2.6 square kilometers
1 mile = 1.6 kilometers	1 ounce = 28 grams
1 centimeter = 0.4 inch	1 quart = 0.95 liter
1 meter = 39.4 inches	1 kilogram = 2.2 pounds
1 kilometer = 0.62 mile	32°F = 0°C

Clothing Sizes

When shopping for clothing, use these US-to-European comparisons as general guidelines (but note that no conversion is perfect).

- Women's dresses and blouses: Add 30
  (US size 10 = European size 40)
- Men's suits and jackets: Add 10
  (US size 40 regular = European size 50)
- Men's shirts: Multiply by 2 and add about 8
  (US size 15 collar = European size 38)
- Women's shoes: Add about 30
  (US size 8 = European size 38-39)
- Men's shoes: Add 32-34
  (US size 9 = European size 41; US size 11 = European size 45)

Spain's Climate

First line, average daily high; second line, average daily low; third line, average days without rain. For more detailed weather statistics for destinations in this book (as well as the rest of the world), check www.wunderground.com.

	J	F	M	A	M	J	J	A	S	O	N	D
SPAIN												
Madrid												
	47°	52°	59°	65°	70°	80°	87°	85°	77°	65°	55°	48°
	35°	36°	41°	45°	50°	58°	63°	63°	57°	49°	42°	36°
	23	21	21	21	21	25	29	28	24	23	21	21
Barcelona												
	55°	57°	60°	65°	71°	78°	82°	82°	77°	69°	62°	56°
	43°	45°	48°	52°	57°	65°	69°	69°	66°	58°	51°	46°
	26	23	23	21	23	24	27	25	23	22	24	25
Almería (Costa del Sol)												
	60°	61°	64°	68°	72°	78°	83°	84°	81°	73°	67°	62°
	46°	47°	51°	55°	59°	65°	70°	71°	68°	60°	54°	49°
	25	24	26	25	28	29	31	30	27	26	26	26
MOROCCO												
Tangier												
	61°	63°	64°	66°	72°	77°	82°	84°	81°	75°	68°	63°
	48°	48°	50°	52°	55°	61°	66°	66°	64°	61°	54°	50°
	12	19	21	21	24	27	30	29	27	22	20	19

Temperature Conversion:
Fahrenheit and Celsius

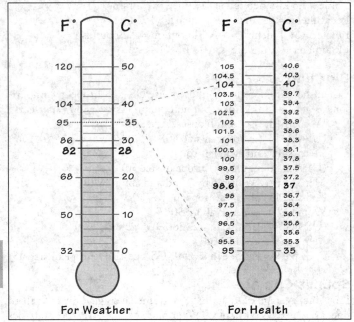

Europe takes its temperature using the Celsius scale, while we opt for Fahrenheit. For a rough conversion from Celsius to Fahrenheit, double the number and add 30. For weather, remember that 28°C is 82°F—perfect. For health, 37°C is just right.

Packing Checklist

Whether you're traveling for five days or five weeks, here's what you'll need to bring. Pack light to enjoy the sweet freedom of true mobility. Happy travels!

❏ 5 shirts: long- & short-sleeve
❏ 1 sweater or lightweight fleece
❏ 2 pairs of pants
❏ 1 pair of shorts
❏ 5 pairs of underwear & socks
❏ 1 pair of shoes
❏ 1 rainproof jacket with hood
❏ Tie or scarf
❏ Swimsuit
❏ Sleepwear
❏ Money belt
❏ Money—your mix of:
  ❏ Debit card
  ❏ Credit card(s)
  ❏ Hard cash ($20 bills)
❏ Documents plus photo-copies:
  ❏ Passport
  ❏ Printout of airline eticket
  ❏ Driver's license
  ❏ Student ID, hostel card, etc.
  ❏ Railpass/train reservations/car-rental voucher
  ❏ Insurance details
❏ Guidebooks & maps
❏ Address list (for sending emails & postcards)
❏ Notepad & pen
❏ Journal
❏ Daypack
❏ Toiletries kit:
  ❏ Toiletries
  ❏ Medicines & vitamins
  ❏ First-aid kit
  ❏ Glasses/contacts/sunglasses (with prescriptions)
❏ Small towel/washcloth
❏ Laundry supplies:
  ❏ Laundry soap
  ❏ Clothesline
❏ Sewing kit

❏ Electronics—your choice of:
  ❏ Camera (& related gear)
  ❏ Mobile phone
  ❏ Portable media player (iPod or other)
  ❏ Laptop/netbook/tablet
  ❏ Ebook reader
  ❏ Headphones or earbuds
  ❏ Chargers for each of the above
  ❏ Plug adapter(s)
❏ Alarm clock
❏ Earplugs
❏ Sealable plastic baggies
❏ Empty water bottle
❏ Postcards & photos from home

If you plan to carry on your luggage, note that all liquids must be in 3.4-ounce or smaller containers and fit within a single quart-size sealable baggie. For details, see www.tsa.gov/travelers.

Pronunciation Guide for Place Names

For Spanish names, emphasize the bolded syllable and pronounce *"h"* as a guttural sound. The few French names (from the Basque Country) have equally stressed syllables.

Spanish	Pronunciation
Algeciras	ahl-*h*eh-**thee**-rahs
Andalucía	ahn-dah-loo-**see**-ah
Arcos de la Frontera	**ar**-kohs day lah frohn-**teh**-rah
Atapuerca	ah-tah-**pwehr**-kah
Ávila	**ah**-vee-lah
Barcelona	bar-theh-**loh**-nah
Bayonne	bai-yuhn
Biarritz	bee-ah-ritz
Bilbao	bil-**bow**
Burgos	**boor**-gohs
Cadaqués	kah-dah-**kehs**
Cantabria	kahn-**tah**-bree-ah
Catalunya	kah-tah-**loon**-yah
Ciudad Rodrigo	thee-oo-**dahd** roh-**dree**-goh
Comillas	koh-**mee**-yahs
Córdoba	**kor**-doh-bah
El Escorial	ehl ehs-kor-ee-**ahl**
Figueres	feeg-**yehr**-ehs
Frigiliana	free-*h*ee-lee-**ah**-nah
Fuenterrabía	fwehn-teh-rah-**bee**-ah
Galicia	gah-**lee**-thee-ah
Gibraltar	*h*ee-**brahl**-tar
Granada	grah-**nah**-dah
Grazalema	grah-zah-**lay**-mah
Guernica	**gehr**-nee-kah
Hendaye	**hehn**-day
Hondarribia	hohn-dah-**ree**-bee-ah
Jerez	*h*eh-**reth**
La Mancha	lah **mahn**-chah
Laguardia	lah-**gwar**-dee-ah
León	lay-**ohn**
Lequeitio	leh-**kay**-tee-oh
Logroño	loh-**grohn**-yoh
Madrid	mah-**dreed**
Marbella	mar-**bay**-yah
Montserrat	mohnt-seh-**raht**
Nerja	**nehr**-*h*ah
O Cebreiro	oh theh-**bray**-roh
Orreaga	oh-ray-**ah**-gah
Pamplona	pahm-**ploh**-nah
Picos de Europa	**pee**-kohs day yoo-**roh**-pah
Potes	**poh**-tays
Rioja	ree-**oh**-*h*ah
Roncesvalles	rohn-thes-**va**-yes
Ronda	**rohn**-dah
Salamanca	sah-lah-**mahn**-kah
St. Jean-Pied-de-Port	san zhahn-pee-ay-duh-por
St. Jean-de-Luz	san zhahn-duh-looz
San Sebastián	sahn seh-bah-stee-**ahn**
Santiago de Compostela	sahn-tee-**ah**-goh day kohm-poh-**steh**-lah
Santillana del Mar	sahn-tee-**yah**-nah del mar
Segovia	seh-**goh**-vee-ah
Sevilla	seh-**vee**-yah
Sitges	**seet**-juhz
Tangier	Tánger (**tahn**-*h*air) in Spanish, Tanja (**tahn**-zhah) in Arabic
Tarifa	tah-**ree**-fah
Toledo	toh-**lay**-doh
Vejer de la Frontera	vay-**hehr** day lah frohn-**teh**-rah
Zahara	tha-**ah**-rah

Spanish Survival Phrases

Spanish has a guttural sound similar to the J in Baja California. In the phonetics, the symbol for this clearing-your-throat sound is the italicized **h**.

English	Spanish	Pronunciation
Good day.	*Buenos días.*	**bway**-nohs **dee**-ahs
Do you speak English?	*¿Habla Usted inglés?*	**ah**-blah oo-**stehd** een-**glays**
Yes. / No.	*Sí. / No.*	see / noh
I (don't) understand.	*(No) comprendo.*	(noh) kohm-**prehn**-doh
Please.	*Por favor.*	por fah-**bor**
Thank you.	*Gracias.*	**grah**-thee-ahs
I'm sorry.	*Lo siento.*	loh see-**ehn**-toh
Excuse me.	*Perdóneme.*	pehr-**doh**-nay-may
(No) problem.	*(No) problema.*	(noh) proh-**blay**-mah
Good.	*Bueno.*	**bway**-noh
Goodbye.	*Adiós.*	ah-dee-**ohs**
one / two	*uno / dos*	**oo**-noh / dohs
three / four	*tres / cuatro*	trays / **kwah**-troh
five / six	*cinco / seis*	**theen**-koh / says
seven / eight	*siete / ocho*	see-**eh**-tay / **oh**-choh
nine / ten	*nueve / diez*	**nway**-bay / dee-**ayth**
How much is it?	*¿Cuánto cuesta?*	**kwahn**-toh **kway**-stah
Write it?	*¿Me lo escribe?*	may loh ay-**skree**-bay
Is it free?	*¿Es gratis?*	ays **grah**-tees
Is it included?	*¿Está incluido?*	ay-**stah** een-kloo-**ee**-doh
Where can I buy / find ___?	*¿Dónde puedo comprar / encontrar...?*	**dohn**-day **pway**-doh kohm **prar** / ayn **kohn trar**
I'd like / We'd like...	*Quiero / Queremos...*	kee-**ehr**-oh / kehr-**ay**-mohs
...a room.	*...una habitación.*	**oo**-nah ah-bee-tah-thee-**ohn**
...a ticket to ___.	*...un billete para ___.*	oon bee-**yeh**-tay **pah**-rah ___
Is it possible?	*¿Es posible?*	ays poh-**see**-blay
Where is...?	*¿Dónde está...?*	**dohn**-day ay-**stah**
...the train station	*...la estación de trenes*	lah ay-stah-thee-**ohn** day **tray**-nays
...the bus station	*...la estación de autobuses*	lah ay-stah-thee-**ohn** day ow-toh-**boo**-says
...the tourist information office	*...la oficina de turismo*	lah oh-fee-**thee**-nah day too-**rees**-moh
Where are the toilets?	*¿Dónde están los servicios?*	**dohn**-day ay-**stahn** lohs sehr-**bee**-thee-ohs
men	*hombres, caballeros*	**ohm**-brays, kah-bah-**yay**-rohs
women	*mujeres, damas*	moo-**heh**-rays, **dah**-mahs
left / right	*izquierda / derecha*	eeth-kee-**ehr**-dah / day-**ray**-chah
straight	*derecho*	day-**ray**-choh
When do you open / close?	*¿A qué hora abren / cierran?*	ah kay **oh**-rah **ah**-brehn / thee-**ay**-rahn
At what time?	*¿A qué hora?*	ah kay **oh**-rah
Just a moment.	*Un momento.*	oon moh-**mehn**-toh
now / soon / later	*ahora / pronto / más tarde*	ah-**oh**-rah / **prohn**-toh / mahs **tar**-day
today / tomorrow	*hoy / mañana*	oy / mahn-**yah**-nah

In a Spanish Restaurant

English	Spanish	Pronunciation
I'd like / We'd like...	Quiero / Queremos...	kee-**ehr**-oh / kehr-**ay**-mohs
...to reserve...	...reservar...	ray-sehr-**bar**
...a table for one / two.	...una mesa para uno / dos.	**oo**-nah **may**-sah **pah**-rah **oo**-noh / dohs
Non-smoking.	No fumador.	noh foo-mah-**dohr**
Is this table free?	¿Está esta mesa libre?	ay-**stah** ay-stah **may**-sah **lee**-bray
The menu (in English), please.	La carta (en inglés), por favor.	lah **kar**-tah (ayn een-**glays**) por fah-**bor**
service (not) included	servicio (no) incluido	sehr-**bee**-thee-oh (noh) een-kloo-**ee**-doh
cover charge	precio de entrada	**pray**-thee-oh day ayn-**trah**-dah
to go	para llevar	**pah**-rah yay-**bar**
with / without	con / sin	kohn / seen
and / or	y / o	ee / oh
menu (of the day)	menú (del día)	may-**noo** (dayl **dee**-ah)
specialty of the house	especialidad de la casa	ay-spay-thee-ah-lee-**dahd** day lah **kah**-sah
tourist menu	menú turístico	meh-**noo** too-**ree**-stee-koh
combination plate	plato combinado	**plah**-toh kohm-bee-**nah**-doh
appetizers	tapas	**tah**-pahs
bread	pan	pahn
cheese	queso	**kay**-soh
sandwich	bocadillo	boh-kah-**dee**-yoh
soup	sopa	**soh**-pah
salad	ensalada	ayn-sah-**lah**-dah
meat	carne	**kar**-nay
poultry	aves	**ah**-bays
fish	pescado	pay-**skah**-doh
seafood	marisco	mah-**ree**-skoh
fruit	fruta	**froo**-tah
vegetables	verduras	behr-**doo**-rahs
dessert	postres	**poh**-strays
tap water	agua del grifo	**ah**-gwah dayl **gree**-foh
mineral water	agua mineral	**ah**-gwah mee-nay-**rahl**
milk	leche	**lay**-chay
(orange) juice	zumo (de naranja)	**thoo**-moh (day nah-**rahn**-hah)
coffee	café	kah-**feh**
tea	té	tay
wine	vino	**bee**-noh
red / white	tinto / blanco	**teen**-toh / **blahn**-koh
glass / bottle	vaso / botella	**bah**-soh / boh-**tay**-yah
beer	cerveza	thehr-**bay**-thah
Cheers!	¡Salud!	sah-**lood**
More. / Another.	Más. / Otro.	mahs / **oh**-troh
The same.	El mismo.	ehl **mees**-moh
The bill, please.	La cuenta, por favor.	lah **kwayn**-tah por fah-**bor**
tip	propina	proh-**pee**-nah
Delicious!	¡Delicioso!	day-lee-thee-**oh**-soh

For hundreds more pages of survival phrases for your trip to Spain, check out *Rick Steves' Spanish Phrase Book.*

INDEX

MAP INDEX

Join a Rick Steves tour

Enjoy Europe's warmest welcome... with the flexibility and friendship of a small group getting to know Rick's favorite places and people. It all starts with our free tour catalog and DVD.

Great guides, small groups, no grumps.

Start your trip at

Free information and great gear to

▶ Plan Your Trip

Browse thousands of articles and a wealth of money-saving tips for planning your dream trip. You'll find up-to-date information on Europe's best destinations, packing smart, getting around, finding rooms, staying healthy, avoiding scams and more.

▶ Eurail Passes

Find out, step-by-step, if a railpass makes sense for your trip—and how to avoid buying more than you need. Get free shipping on online orders

▶ Graffiti Wall & Travelers Helpline

Learn, ask, share—our online community of savvy travelers is a great resource for first-time travelers to Europe, as well as seasoned pros.

Rick Steves' Europe Through the Back Door, Inc.

Rick Steves®

www.ricksteves.com

Rick Steves guidebooks are published by Avalon Travel,
a member of the Perseus Books Group.

NOW AVAILABLE: eBOOKS, DVD & BLU-RAY

TRAVEL CULTURE

Europe 101
European Christmas
Postcards from Europe
Travel as a Political Act

eBOOKS

Nearly all Rick Steves guides are available as eBooks. Check with your favorite bookseller.

RICK STEVES' EUROPE DVDs

11 New Shows 2013–2014
Austria & the Alps
Eastern Europe
England & Wales
European Christmas
European Travel Skills & Specials
France
Germany, BeNeLux & More
Greece, Turkey & Portugal
Iran
Ireland & Scotland
Italy's Cities
Italy's Countryside
Scandinavia
Spain
Travel Extras

BLU-RAY

Celtic Charms
Eastern Europe Favorites
European Christmas
Italy Through the Back Door
Mediterranean Mosaic
Surprising Cities of Europe

PHRASE BOOKS & DICTIONARIES

French
French, Italian & German
German
Italian
Portuguese
Spanish

JOURNALS

Rick Steves' Pocket Travel Journal
Rick Steves' Travel Journal

PLANNING MAPS

Britain, Ireland & London
Europe
France & Paris
Germany, Austria & Switzerland
Ireland
Italy
Spain & Portugal

Credits

Researchers

To help update this book, Rick relied on...

Rich Earl

Spain has long been one of Rich's favorite travel destinations. When he's not searching for the best *café con leche*, he's exploring the rest of Europe, assisting on Rick Steves' tours, and working as a travel consultant at Rick Steves' Europe Through the Back Door.

Robert Wright

Raised in Memphis, Robert Wright eventually made his home even further south... in Argentina! But he travels to Spain and Portugal every year for a food and wine fix while exploring architecture and digging into Iberia's complex history.

Amanda Zurita

Amanda Zurita caught the travel bug at an early age and has been flying since before she could walk. When she's not tapas-hopping and hiking through hill towns, she's dreaming up her next big adventure from her home in Seattle.

Suzanne Kotz

Suzanne, an editor with Rick Steves' Europe Through the Back Door, began her travel career riding in a station wagon with her six siblings from Michigan to Florida. Since then, she's broadened her destinations to include much of Europe and parts of Asia. A librarian by training and a longtime editor of art publications, she's happiest when she has a red pen in one hand and a book in the other. She lives in Seattle with her husband and son.

Contributor

Gene Openshaw

 Gene is the co-author of 10 Rick Steves guidebooks. For this book he wrote material on art and history. When not traveling, Gene enjoys composing music, recovering from his 1973 trip to Europe with Rick, and living everyday life with his daughter.

Acknowledgments

Thanks to Cameron Hewitt for writing this book's original chapters on the Camino de Santiago, Santiago de Compostela, and Cantabria.

Chapter Images

The following list identifies the chapter-opening images and credits their photographers.

Barcelona: Barcelona's Montjuïc		David C. Hoerlein
Near Barcelona: Cadaqués		Rick Steves
Basque Region: Guggenheim Bilbao		Rick Steves
Camino de Santiago: Puente de la Reina		Cameron Hewitt
Santiago de Compostela:		
Santiago's Cathedral		Cameron Hewitt
Cantabria: Picos de Europa		Cameron Hewitt
Salamanca: Salamanca's Plaza Mayor		Rick Steves
Madrid: Madrid's Retiro Park		David C. Hoerlein
Northwest of Madrid:		
Segovia's Aqueduct		Rick Steves
Toledo: Toledo Overview		Rick Steves
Granada: The Alhambra		Robert Wright
Sevilla: Sevilla Skyline		Rick Steves
Córdoba: Córdoba's Mezquita		Robert Wright
Andalucía's White Hill Towns: Arcos		David C. Hoerlein
Costa del Sol: Nerja		Rick Steves
Morocco: Moroccan Woman, Tangier		Rick Steves
Tangier: Market Vendor		Rick Steves